D1609036

Handbook of
the Sociology of Gender

Handbooks of Sociology and Social Research

Series Editor:
Howard B. Kaplan, *Texas A&M University, College Station, Texas*

HANDBOOK OF THE SOCIOLOGY OF GENDER
Edited by Janet Saltzman Chafetz

HANDBOOK OF THE SOCIOLOGY OF MENTAL HEALTH
Edited by Carol S. Aneshensel and Jo C. Phelan

Handbook of
the Sociology of Gender

Janet Saltzman Chafetz

University of Houston
Houston, Texas

Kluwer Academic / Plenum Publishers
New York, Boston, Dordrecht, London, Moscow

ISBN 0-306-45978-7

© 1999 Kluwer Academic / Plenum Publishers
233 Spring Street, New York, N.Y. 10013

10 9 8 7 6 5 4 3 2 1

A C.I.P. record for this book is available from the Library of Congress

Printed in the United States of America

Contributors

Joan Acker, Department of Sociology, University of Oregon, Eugene, Oregon, 97403-1291

Denise D. Bielby, Department of Sociology, University of California at Santa Barbara, Santa Barbara, California, 93106

Janet Saltzman Chafetz, Department of Sociology, University of Houston, Houston, Texas, 77204-3474

Becca Cragin, Institute for Women's Studies, Emory University, Atlanta, Georgia, 30322

Cynthia Cranford, Department of Sociology, University of Southern California, Los Angeles, California, 90089

Mikaela J. Dufur, Department of Sociology, Ohio State University, Columbus, Ohio, 43210

Dana Dunn, Office of the Provost, University of Texas at Arlington, Arlington, Texas, 76019

Cynthia Fuchs Epstein, Department of Sociology, Graduate Center, City University of New York, New York, 10025

Elizabeth M. Esterchild, Department of Sociology, University of North Texas, Denton, Texas, 76203

Mary Frank Fox, School of History, Technology, and Society, Georgia Institute of Technology, Atlanta, Georgia, 30332-0345

Denise C. Herz, Department of Criminal Justice, University of Nebraska at Omaha, Omaha, Nebraska, 68182

Shirley A. Hill, Department of Sociology, University of Kansas, Lawrence, Kansas, 66045

Pierrette Hondagneu-Sotelo, Department of Sociology, University of Southern California, Los Angeles, California, 90089

Joan Huber, Department of Sociology, Ohio State University, Columbus, Ohio, 43210

Mary R. Jackman, Department of Sociology, University of California at Davis, Davis, California, 95616

Carrie James, Department of Sociology, New York University, New York, New York, 10003

Trivina Kang, Department of Sociology, New York University, New York, New York, 10003

v

Erin L. Kelly, Department of Sociology, Princeton University, Princeton, New Jersey, 08544

Diane Kobrynowicz, Department of Psychology, The College of New Jersey, Ewing, New Jersey, 08628

Jennie Jacobs Kronenfeld, School of Health Administration and Policy, Arizona State University, Tempe, Arizona, 85287-4506

Helena Znaniecka Lopata, Department of Sociology and Anthropology, Loyola University Chicago, Chicago, Illinois, 60626

Adair T. Lummis, Center for Social and Religious Research, Hartford Seminary, Hartford, Connecticut, 06105

Sara S. McLanahan, Office of Population Research, Princeton University, Princeton, New Jersey, 08544

Irene Padavic, Department of Sociology, Florida State University, Tallahassee, Florida, 32306-2011

Cynthia Fabrizio Pelak, Department of Sociology, Ohio State University, Columbus, Ohio, 43210

Caroline Hodges Persell, Department of Sociology, New York University, New York, New York, 10003

Jean L. Pyle, Department of Regional Economic and Social Development, University of Massachusetts at Lowell, Lowell, Massachusetts, 01854

Barbara F. Reskin, Department of Sociology, Harvard University, Cambridge, Massachusetts, 02138

Cecilia L. Ridgeway, Department of Sociology, Stanford University, Stanford, California, 94305

Mady Wechsler Segal, Department of Sociology, University of Maryland, College Park, Maryland, 20742

Beth Anne Shelton, Department of Sociology and Anthropology, University of Texas at Arlington, Arlington, Texas, 76019

Wendy Simonds, Department of Sociology, Georgia State University, Atlanta, Georgia, 30303

Sally S. Simpson, Department of Criminology and Criminal Justice, University of Maryland, College Park, Maryland, 20742

Sheryl Skaggs, Department of Sociology, North Carolina State University, Raleigh, North Carolina 27695

Lynn Smith-Lovin, Department of Sociology, University of Arizona, Tucson, Arizona 85721

Karrie Snyder, Department of Sociology, New York University, New York, New York, 10003

Joey Sprague, Department of Sociology, University of Kansas, Lawrence, Kansas, 66049

Jean Stockard, Department of Sociology, University of Oregon, Eugene, Oregon, 97403-1291

Verta Taylor, Department of Sociology, Ohio State University, Columbus, Ohio, 43210

Nancy Whittier, Department of Sociology, Smith College, Northampton, Massachusetts, 01063

Mary K. Zimmerman, Department of Health Policy and Management, University of Kansas, Lawrence, Kansas, 66045

Preface

During the past three decades, feminist scholars have successfully demonstrated the ubiquity and omnirelevance of gender as a sociocultural construction in virtually all human collectivities, past and present. Intrapsychic, interactional, and collective social processes are gendered, as are micro, meso, and macro social structures. Gender shapes, and is shaped, in all arenas of social life, from the most mundane practices of everyday life to those of the most powerful corporate actors. Contemporary understandings of gender emanate from a large community of primarily feminist scholars that spans the gamut of learned disciplines and also includes non-academic activist thinkers. However, while incorporating some cross-disciplinary material, this volume focuses specifically on sociological theories and research concerning gender, which are discussed across the full array of social processes, structures, and institutions.

As editor, I have explicitly tried to shape the contributions to this volume along several lines that reflect my long-standing views about sociology in general, and gender sociology in particular. First, I asked authors to include cross-national and historical material as much as possible. This request reflects my belief that understanding and evaluating the here-and-now and working realistically for a better future can only be accomplished from a comparative perspective. Too often, American sociology has been both tempero- and ethnocentric. Second, I have asked authors to be sensitive to within-gender differences along class, racial/ethnic, sexual preference, and age cohort lines. This request reflects the growing sensitivity of feminist scholars to the white, middle-class, and heterosexist biases implicit in much of our past work, which has effectively glossed over differences among women (especially) and consigned many categories of women to invisibility. Third, I have intentionally omitted a chapter on men and masculinity and asked authors to take seriously the fact that there are *two* genders that require examination and comparison. Too often, works in gender sociology are about women only or, less frequently, men only. Just as one cannot understand the experiences, constraints, and consciousness of an ethnic or racial minority without understanding its relationship to the dominant group, one cannot understand those of women apart from their relationship to men, culturally defined masculinity and male-dominated institutions. Indeed, one cannot adequately understand dominant groups without simultaneously examining their relationships to subordinate groups. Happily, the chapter authors have taken my various suggestions seriously, to the extent that available research and space in this volume permit.

Because gender permeates all aspects of sociocultural life, the breadth of our field is enormous. This is reflected in the large number of chapters (27) in this book, including discussions of virtually every social institution (the economy, the family, the polity, the legal, military and criminal justice systems, health care, education, science, sport, religion) as well as numerous social structures and processes at both the macro- and micro-levels. The purpose of this handbook is to cover the breadth of the field of gender sociology. The purpose of each chapter is to provide reasonably in-depth discussions of the various facets of the field, including an up-to-date bibliography of the major sources. The intended audiences comprise professional sociologists and graduate students who seek information about the current state of knowledge in gender sociology generally or in one or more of its specialized subdivisions, as well as feminist scholars in other disciplines who seek to incorporate into their work the knowledge developed by their sociological counterparts.

The book is divided into four sections. Part I, Basic Issues, consists of three chapters that address gender theory, feminist epistemology, and the sociology of gender differences and similarities. The seven chapters in Part II focus on macrolevel structures and processes, and deal with the topics of societal evolution, national development, migration, poverty, social movements, organizations, and culture as they relate to gender. Consisting of four chapters, Part III is devoted to microlevel structures and processes, including discussions of socialization, social roles, interaction, and violence and harassment, as they shape and are shaped by gender. The last section of the book, Part IV, concerns the relationship between gender and the social institutions listed above, and totals 13 chapters. The authors of each chapter were carefully selected for their expertise in the relevant topic, and collectively they constitute some of the best talent in gender sociology today. I am very proud to have my name as editor associated with those of these authors.

When I was first invited to edit this volume, I was reluctant to accept because I had never edited a book, but had heard often what a time-consuming and frustrating job it could be. To get a feel for what it might entail, I developed a draft table of contents and sent it to about a dozen gender sociologists whose work I respect and who are personal friends and acquaintances. I also asked each to volunteer to write a chapter and to suggest other possible chapter authors. I received excellent suggestions for additions and alterations to the table of contents, as well as for potential authors. Equally important, nearly everyone I initially contacted was enthusiastic about the importance of the project. Given these responses, I accepted the editorship.

What followed was even more exciting, for as I began to call people to ask if they would write specific chapters, their responses were overwhelmingly positive and enthusiastic. The result was that I was able to line up outstanding authors for each chapter within about a two week period. As is the case with most edited books, many chapters came in later than anticipated, and a few never materialized at all. The reasons for many of the delays and absences reflect the status of the authors, most of whom had a variety of other professional commitments and some of whom accepted new jobs and moved during the process of writing their chapters. Also reflected were the realities of life for professional women: an adopted baby and a couple of births; care for aged and infirm parents; and, unfortunately, a few cases of ill health and a house that burned down, taking with it a draft of the chapter manuscript. Nevertheless, in the end, because of the quality and dedication of the authors, the job of editing this book proved to be a most gratifying experience.

In addition to thanking all the contributors to this volume, who have worked hard to produce excellent chapters, I would like to thank Howard Kaplan of Texas A & M University, the editor of the Plenum series of sociology handbooks, who invited me to edit this one. Eliot Werner, my Plenum editor, has been a pleasure to work with and has expedited every step of the process with efficiency and good cheer. Finally, thanks to all those who provided me potential author names and suggestions for revising my original table of contents: Elizabeth Almquist (now Esterchild), Margaret Andersen, Dana Dunn, Paula England, Joan Huber, Helena Lopata, Judith Lorber, Barbara Reskin, Beth Schneider, and Ruth Wallace.

Janet Saltzman Chafetz
University of Houston,
Houston, Texas

Contents

PART I

BASIC ISSUES

CHAPTER 1

The Varieties of Gender Theory in Sociology

Janet Saltzman Chafetz

1. INTRODUCTION

As editor, I have chosen to begin this handbook where I believe all sociology should begin: with a review of the array of theoretical ideas available to, in this case, gender sociologists as they explore the social world, in the United States and elsewhere, looking at both the present and earlier times. Because they constitute the conceptual toolkit that helps gender sociologists make sense of the empirical world, many of the theories discussed in this chapter are developed further in later, substantive ones. In this chapter, I review the major gender/feminist theories in sociology, beginning with a review of what classical, nineteenth and early twentieth century theorists said about gender, but focusing most attention on theories developed since 1970, when the impact of second wave feminist activism began to be felt in our discipline. I generally confine my discussion to theories developed by sociologists, although the full corpus of feminist theory is far broader in its origins, both activist and academic. Omitted from this chapter are discussions of relatively narrow, substantive theories, which appear in subject-appropriate chapters. Also omitted is Standpoint Theory, the topic of an entire chapter (2), an approach sometimes considered virtually synonymous with the term "feminist theory." The current chapter demonstrates the many other types of contemporary feminist theory that emanate from, reflect, and significantly revise the rich variety of theoretical traditions in sociology (see Chafetz, 1988, 1997; England, 1993; Wallace, 1989, on the varieties of contemporary feminist sociological theory).

Janet Saltzman Chafetz • Department of Sociology, University of Houston, Houston, Texas, 77204-3474.
Handbook of the Sociology of Gender, edited by Janet Saltzman Chafetz. Kluwer Academic/ Plenum Publishers, New York, 1999.

All theory pertaining to gender is not feminist, although all feminist theory centers much or all of its attention on gender. Three features make a gender theory specifically feminist: (1) a (not necessarily exclusive) focus on the inequities, strains, and contradictions inherent in gender arrangements; (2) an assumption that gender relations are not immutable but rather changeable social creations; and (3) a normative commitment that societies should develop equitable gender arrangements (Alway, 1995, p. 211; Chafetz, 1988, p. 5).

2. THE CLASSICAL TRADITION

The nineteenth and early twentieth century founding *fathers* of sociology lived amidst the international protest of first wave women's movements, an intellectual, political, and social ferment that compelled most to address the "woman question" in some manner (Kandal, 1988). Regardless of their views concerning feminism, most confined their discussion of women largely to issues of family, emotion, and sexuality, embedded within broader theories that typically stressed the importance of other, male-dominated structures (e.g., social class and the economy; political, legal, and military systems; bureaucracy; religion). Moreover, women and femininity constituted the problem or issue. The effects of culturally defined masculinity on shaping the structures and processes central to their theories were largely unrecognized, males were infrequently examined in terms of gender, and male-dominated social structures/institutions were implicitly defined as if they were gender neutral. With few exceptions, the best that can be said for our classical tradition is that gender issues were peripheral; at worst, some theorists promulgated a crude biological determinism to justify gender inequities. The contemporary version of the sociological theory canon, as exemplified in all but a handful of theory texts, continues this androcentric bias, largely ignoring or short-shrifting both the topic of gender and the contributions of contemporary feminist theories, which remain substantially ghettoized (Alway, 1995; Stacey & Thorne, 1985; Ward & Grant, 1991). Moreover, many contemporary "general" theorists, such as James Coleman, Jeffrey Alexander, Peter Berger, and Anthony Giddens, ignore the topic of gender entirely (Seidman, 1994, p. 304).

2.1. The Biological Approach: Apologists for the Status Quo

Several early founders of sociology assumed that men and women are innately different and unequal in their intellectual, emotional, and moral capacities. Herbert Spencer, the founder of British sociological theory, began as a liberal feminist, as reflected in his book *Social Statics*, in which he devoted a chapter to "The Rights of Women." He argued that men and women deserve equal rights, inasmuch as there are only "trifling mental variations" between them (Kandal, 1988, p. 32). Within 4 years he had embarked on Social Darwinism and decided that biology (not culture) produced profound (no longer trivial) sex differences. Women, whose brains are smaller, are deficient in the sense of justice and reasoning ability required of all life beyond the care of husband and children. Moreover, women naturally prefer to be protected by a powerful man. Permitting women to enter public life would therefore be antithetical to human progress (Kandal, 1988, pp. 32–46). The founder of French sociology, Auguste Comte, echoed these sentiments. Because of their emotional and spiritual "superiority," women are perfectly fit for family and domestic life, but their state of "perpetual infancy" and intellectual inferiority to men render them unfit for anything else (Kandal, 1988, pp. 46–77). Similar stereotypes about the innate natures of women and men, and conclusions about the appropriate roles and status of each, were repeated by founders of German (Ferdinand Toennes) and Italian (Vilfredo Pareto) sociology (Kandal, 1988, pp. 177–182 and 193–201).

The most famous early French sociologist, Emile Durkheim, also resorted to a biological explanation of what he recognized as women's social subordination (Kandal, 1988, pp. 77–88, especially 85; Lehmann, 1990, 1994). In *Suicide*, his statistics demonstrated that marriage produces opposite effects for men, for whom it lowers the suicide rate, and women, among whom the rate is higher among the married. He concluded that marriage ought some day to be reformed but, in the interim, men must be protected from suicide through the maintenance of a form of marriage that produces more stress and disadvantage for women (Kandal, 1988, p. 88). His justification was that the increase in suicide for married women is less than that for unmarried men because women have fewer "sociability needs," are more "instinctive," have a less developed "mental life," and therefore are more easily satisfied. Men are more "complex," and their psychological balance is more precarious and in need of the constraining protections afforded by existing marital arrangements (Kandal, 1988, pp. 83–85). Feminism supported divorce and, therefore, Durkheim opposed it as rooted in "unscientific" thinking (Lehmann, 1990). Durkheim also referred to the topic of gender in *The Division of Labor in Society*, where he argued that increasing physical and cultural differentiation have evolved over time between the sexes, allowing for increasing specialization of labor between them and, therefore, "conjugal solidarity." A state of gender similarity and equality is a "primitive" one associated with unstable marital unions (Lehmann, 1990, pp. 164–165; Kandal, 1988, pp. 80–81).

2.2. Gender as Inequitable but Peripheral

Proponents of classical Marxist theory were well aware that gender arrangements are both the product of social life and inequitable. The most fully developed statement of this approach, Friedrich Engels' *The Origin of the Family, Private Property and the State*, is an evolutionary theory describing three stages, each characterized by a different form of marriage. Gender inequality originated during the third stage, when an inheritable economic surplus first arose due to technological development and the institution of private property. Men overthrew the traditional matrilineal system to ensure that their sons would inherit, and instituted all manner of controls over women to insure "proper" paternity. During this stage household work became private service, and women were excluded from social production and became legally subordinated to men (p. 104). The solution to gender inequality is the abolition of capitalism, which would eliminate concerns about inheritance and paternity and return women to "public industry" (pp. 105–106). Women's emancipation was a stated goal of most Marxist parties and thinkers in subsequent decades. However, orthodox Marxism, including its feminist proponents (e.g., Rosa Luxemburg and Clara Zetkin), juxtaposed their position to that of "bourgeoisie feminism" by claiming that gender inequities were the byproduct of social class inequality and that the replacement of capitalism with socialism would automatically resolve women's problems.

Max Weber, under the influence of his activist mother and wife, supported the liberal branch of the women's rights movement (Kandal, 1988, pp. 126–156). In *General*

Economic History, he refined Engels' theory in describing the transition from matriar-chal tribes to patriarchal agrarian societies, a process by which the gender division of labor within the family increased and the status of women declined. Reflecting his gen-eral theoretical orientation, Weber responded to the ghost of Marx by arguing that this transition was not simply a function of economic change, but also reflected alterations in the military, religion, and magic (Kandal, 1988, pp.146–147 and 149–151). He under-stood that the process of societal rationalization, a central theme in Weber's work, was a masculine phenomenon. Despite his sensitivity to the historically specific subordination of women, Weber failed to explore the conditions under which they challenge gender inequality and in his premier essay on social inequality, "Class, Status and Party," he was curiously silent about gender.

2.3. Gender as Central, but . . .

Another early German sociologist, Georg Simmel, devoted extensive attention to gender in many of his best known essays and in *The Philosophy of Money* (see Coser, 1977; Kandal, 1988, pp. 156–177; Oakes, 1984). Kandal describes Simmel as sensitive to the fact that male-dominated culture hinders women's autonomy and prevents them from contributing to the common culture. Moreover, the standards used to evaluate social achieve-ments "are formally generically human, but are in fact masculine in terms of their historical formation" (Kandal, 1988, p. 158), leaving women to be judged by criteria developed by and for men within a context where women are denied the opportunity to achieve them (p. 159). Women thereby become the object of contempt and come to evaluate themselves as means for others', specifically their families', satisfaction. In a search for recognition within a context in which they are denied other avenues, women devote themselves to personal adornment and fashion. Simmel recognized that women develop social groups to defend themselves against men. Although most often the form such protection takes is staunch defense of custom, he also examined the social conditions that prompt women to develop groups that challenge male privilege (Kandal, 1988, pp. 169–171).

Although Simmel was closer to writing feminist theory than other classical sociolo-gists, his ideas nonetheless were "ideologically contradictory" (Kandal, 1988, p.165). He recognized that gender differences and the level of gender inequality vary over time and space, but he also posited innate gender differences. Oakes (1984) argues that Simmel rejected all of the contemporary approaches to "the woman question": traditional, liberal, and Marxist. Rather, he posited an inherent difference in male and female "modes of being," which are embodied in inexorably opposed, universal, male and female cultures. Simmel's solution to "the woman question" is a "separate but equal 'female culture' expressed in the theater and in the home . . . " (Kandal, 1988, p. 177).

The most recent theorist incorporated into the classical theory canon is Talcott Par-sons. Because of his focus on normative consensus as it arises chiefly through socializa-tion, Parsons devoted considerable attention to the family and to "sex roles," including several essays and *Family, Socialization and Interaction Process*. In his description of then-contemporary, American, middle-class, family life, Parsons demonstrated sen-sitivity to the contradictions, inequities, and strains with which women lived, noting also that the occupations available to single women are considerably below those available to their male class peers. Because they are generally denied the opportunity to combine wife/mother and employment roles, and are confined to the "pseudo occupation" of "home management," wives' status becomes asymmetrical with that of their husbands. Given a society that strongly emphasizes individual achievement, yet strongly values domesticity for wives and mothers, widespread tensions and strain are inherent in the feminine role (Kandal, 1988, pp. 228–234). Parsons discussed alternatives to the drudgery of house-work (e.g., perfecting it as an "art," using domestic servants (!), doing volunteer work with children and the sick, and the "glamour pattern" of emphasizing sex appeal), but concluded that all were problematic. He also recognized that married women could as-sume the "masculine pattern" and compete with male class peers in the labor force, but suggested that this would result in "profound alterations in the structure of the family" (Kandal, 1988, pp. 230–233).

Parsons' explanation for why family structure and sex roles took the form they did reflected his general evolutionary theory that focused on increasing functional specializa-tion and integration. A more specialized type of family emerged with industrialization that, having lost its economic and political functions, became a "factory" for producing human personalities through childhood socialization and the stabilization of adult per-sonalities. Using his famous instrumental/expressive dichotomy, Parsons described the contemporary family as an institution devoted to the expressive function. As jobs became separated from the household, men came to specialize in the instrumental role of earning a living for the family. Because they bear and nurture children, women came to specialize in the expressive role, that is, the production of human personalities within the house-hold. For Parsons, as for Durkheim, this evolutionary process accentuated role complementarity (Kandal, 1988, pp. 233–234).

For 30 years, feminists have interpreted Parsons' argument as one that not only described the then-modern family and explained its evolution, but also prescribed its continuation based on functional necessity. However, Johnson (1989, 1993) argues that, although not advocating radical family change, neither did Parsons oppose it; he only (rather presciently) predicted it as an outcome if married women entered the labor force in large numbers. Moreover, although he failed to foresee the looming rebirth of feminist activism, he nonetheless was sensitive to many of the inequities and strains that helped cause it. Regardless of which interpretation one accepts, it was clearly the case in the 1950s and 1960s that Parsonian-influenced family sociologists explicitly suggested that the widespread employment of married women would endanger the "proper" socializa-tion of children and the "health" of the family as a social system (Ehrlich, 1971).

2.4. Turn-of-the-Century Feminist Social Thought: The Forgotten Tradition[1]

Few women worked as academic social scientists before the mid-twentieth century: how-ever, a number of turn-of-the-century feminist activists and social service administrators in the United States received Ph.D.s in the social sciences and produced writings that should be considered feminist theory. Fitzpatrick (1988) describes four, one of whom, Frances Kellor, received a Ph.D. in sociology. Another activist sociologist was Charlotte Perkins Gillman, whose book, *Women and Economics*, made her the leading late nine-

---

[1] After this volume went to press, an excellent book was published by Lengermann and Niebrugge-Brantley (1998) that discusses in depth the contributions of more than a dozen United States and European founding mothers of feminist social theory.

teenth century feminist intellectual (Kandall, 1990, p. 220). Yet a third feminist thinker and activist trained as a sociologist was Jane Addams, founder of Hull House, which served as the intellectual and activist center of feminist social science (Deegan, 1988). Rosenberg (1982) describes a number of additional feminist social scientists in the United States and Lengermann and Niebrugge (1996) list a myriad of European feminist women who contributed to nineteenth and early twentieth century sociological thought. Together, these founding *mothers* constitute the largely forgotten feminist tradition in classical sociology, one totally ignored in the contemporary theory canon.

It is beyond the scope of this chapter to review the accomplishments of these remarkable women (see detailed accounts in Deegan, 1988; Fitzpatrick, 1990; and Rosenberg, 1982). Several male sociologists at the University of Chicago, such as Lester Ward, W. I. Thomas, and George Herbert Mead, supported the Women's Movement and Hull House, mentored female graduate students, and wrote about the topic of gender from a liberal feminist perspective. Opinions differed concerning the primary cause(s) of and solution(s) to women's problems. Ward, Jessie Taft, and Charlotte Perkins Gilman rejected the notion that the sexes are fundamentally different and focused on the sociocultural roots of observed differences. Others, such as Jane Addams, accepted the Victorian-era belief in sex differences, especially women's moral superiority. She argued that, given changed circumstances resulting from industrialization, by which the role of the family had diminished, women sought public roles precisely to express their moral nature. Moreover, social progress depended on women achieving them. Taft and Gillman emphasized that both genders needed to change, women by assuming more of the rational, competitive, adventurous attributes of men, men by taking on the peaceful and nurturant attributes of women. However, where Gillman focused on economic restrictions and advocated economic independence for women, Taft stressed political and psychological, as well as economic issues. In general, turn-of-the-century, feminist social scientists in the United States wrestled with issues of the nature, degree, and origins of gender differences, guided by abiding commitments to gender equity and to Progressive-era social reforms. That feminist sociologists still wrestle with these same issues will be apparent throughout this volume, especially Chapter 3.

2.5. Conclusion

The theorists reviewed in Part II were motivated to address gender issues by the intellectual and political ferment arising from the first wave women's movement. Although few works today considered theory classics met the criteria specified for feminist theory, the theories discussed subsequently do. Some nonfeminist gender theory has been developed since 1970, notably sociobiology, which is briefly reviewed in Chapter 3. However, I confine my review of contemporary gender theory to its feminist varieties, which are grouped into four parts: Macrostructural, Microstructural, Interactionist, and Childhood Engenderment. Like their predecessors, contemporary gender theorists have been inspired by the broader intellectual and political ferment of an ongoing feminist movement.

3. FEMINIST MACROSTRUCTURAL THEORIES

The theories reviewed in Part III seek to explain systems of gender stratification, or patriarchy, at the societal level, primarily with reference to other societal-level structures and processes. This part of the chapter is divided into four sections: World Systems Theory, Marxist-Inspired Theory, Other Macrostructural Approaches, and Multiple Jeopardy Theory.

3.1. World Systems Theory

General World Systems Theory, which focuses on the outcomes of inequitable relationships between wealthy, core nations and poorer, semiperipheral and peripheral ones, has ignored the vital role women play in the economies of Third World countries, as described in the huge Women and Development literature (Ward, 1990, 1993). This literature, which is the subject of Chapter 5, demonstrates that capital penetration of poor by core nations usually increases the level of gender inequality. The most basic corrections required of the general theory are to cease considering women only as members of male-headed households, to cease assuming that household members have unitary interests, and to analyze women's independent economic contributions as members of the global economy, participants in the informal labor market, as household workers, and as food producers (Blumberg, 1989; Ward, 1993). Ward (1984) theorizes that the effects of Western capital penetration on women's work and status can be understood by examining preexisting patterns of "patriarchal relations," which include both ideologies of male supremacy and institutionalized forms of male dominance. In addition, gendered assumptions made by Western male capitalists in the planning and execution of their projects alter the distribution of constraints and opportunities between women and men in peripheral nations. Together, local patriarchal relations and androcentric capitalist bias usually result in new economic, educational, and political opportunities and resources being disproportionately awarded to local men. Gender inequality is exacerbated further as women's traditional subsistence agriculture, trade, and small-scale handicraft production suffer from competition with newly developing foreign trade, which is in the hands of men (Ward, 1984, p. 21). New opportunities on the global assembly line are often open to women, but they frequently are confined to the young and unmarried and are insecure, tightly supervised, and very poorly paid. The result is that the greater the peripheral nation's trade dependency on core nations, and the higher the level of foreign investment, the greater the level of gender inequality (Ward, 1984, p. 40–43).

3.2. Marxist-Inspired Theory

Although twentieth century socialist nations usually ameliorated women's problems, substantial gender inequities persisted, a point not lost when feminism reemerged in the 1960s. Contemporary Marxist-inspired feminists, who call themselves socialist feminists, propound a theory that analytically separates class and patriarchal forms of oppression and analyzes their interpenetration as a major mechanism that sustains both. They explicitly recognize that patriarchy predated capitalism, but argue that its form is very different and constantly changing under capitalism. Unlike their orthodox Marxist predecessors, socialist feminists view the demise of capitalism as a necessary but not sufficient condition to end women's oppression.

Under capitalism, women are responsible for the unpaid work of maintaining and reproducing the labor force, work that directly profits capitalists. Like men, they may also be involved in the production of surplus value through waged work. One of the major

recent transformations of capitalism has been from denying most women the opportunity
to become "social adults" through waged work (Sacks, 1974) to seeking them as a source
of cheap labor in a highly sex-segregated labor market (Eisenstein, 1979). Women are
doubly exploited by capitalism, in the household and the economy, thereby producing far
greater surplus value than do men (Shelton & Agger, 1993). The gender inequities women
experience in the labor market are linked, ideologically and practically, to their domestic
responsibilities (Shelton & Agger, 1993; Vogel, 1983). Capitalists foster an ideology of
patriarchy (male supremacy) that justifies women's nonwaged domestic and child rearing work with reference to biologically rooted reproductive differences between the sexes,
and justifies labor market inequities based on women's domestic obligations (Eisenstein,
1979). Male workers derive advantages both at home and in the labor market: their wives'
unpaid services and subservience as well as better paying jobs protected from competition
by women. In return for husbands' economic resources, wives provide subservience and
domestic labor, which in turn surpresses their wages (Hartmann, 1984). Thus "compensated" for their subordination to capitalist domination, working class men are less likely
to develop class consciousness (Shelton & Agger, 1993; Sokoloff, 1980). Moreover, because wives are economically dependent, their husbands are tied more securely to
wage-earning jobs, which they are less likely to jeopardize by rebellion against the capitalist system (Eisenstein, 1979; Hartmann, 1984; Vogel, 1983). The result is that capitalism and patriarchy buttress one another.

A variant of feminist socialism, developed by Dorothy Smith (1990, 1987), combines Marxist insights with those of Foucault on the role of knowledge in the (re)production
of the "social relations of ruling," which include both capitalism and patriarchy. Smith
analyzes how "male-created discourse" functions to oppress women. Similarly, Patricia
Hill Collins (1990) identifies white, male-produced knowledge as a major component of
a racist, classist, and sexist "matrix of domination." To the extent that women adopt male
discourse in their work as professionals in major institutions, including as scholars, they
provide "alienated labor" in the Marxist sense that they contribute to the order that op-
presses them (Smith, 1990, p. 19; also 1987, p. 3–5). Smith and Collins relate their
analyses of domination to broader epistemological discussions that comprise Standpoint
Theory, the topic of Chapter 2. The relationship between knowledge systems and gender
inequality is also explored in the chapter on science (20).

3.3. Other Macrostructural Approaches

Six categories of theoretical constructs provide the starting points for the diverse and
eclectic theories considered in this section: cultural, environmental, technological, economic, demographic, and political. Many of these theories are sufficiently complex, in
number of constructs and of linkages posited as connecting them, so as to defy brief
summary beyond the listing of central ideas. These anthropological and sociological theories share a focus on delineating the conditions that explain variation in the level of
gender stratification across time and space. Chafetz (1984, Chapter 1) defines gender
stratification as the degree to which men and women, who are otherwise social equals,
are unequal in their access to the scarce and valued resources and opportunities of their
society, suggesting 11 dimensions that may be unequally distributed and an additive approach to combining them. Blumberg (1979) conceptualizes gender inequality as comprising three forms of power: political, coercive, and, most importantly, economic, and

later (Blumberg, 1984) adds a fourth, ideological. Using a factor analytic technique to examine a grab-bag of 52 variables, Whyte (1978) inductively defines nine dimensions of gender stratification that vary independently. Clearly, much work remains to conceptualize adequately gender stratification in a manner that enables cross-national and historical comparison.

Virtually all macro-level feminist theories agree that cultural or ideological definitions of masculinity and femininity (see especially Connell, 1987, on hegemonic masculinity), and of "gender-appropriate" behaviors, responsibilities, and privileges, are fundamental components of systems of gender inequality (a topic discussed in Chapters 10 and 27). Some anthropologists make a cultural construct the most central to their explanations, and of these, Peggy Sanday's work (1981) is the most nuanced. She argues that each society develops an overarching cultural orientation rooted in the kinds of environmental conditions most important to the society's survival strategy. An "inner orientation" arises in relatively benign environments, treats nature as sacred, and emphasizes the "female creative principle," as embodied in creation myths which include females as central actors. An "outer orientation" arises in more physically harsh and/or warlike environments, where nature in defined as dangerous, men's activities as hunters and warriors are revered, and creation myths stress masculine progenitors. Each society develops a "sex role plan" based on one of these cultural orientations. The level of gender inequality reflects that plan and is highest where an "outer orientation" prevails.

Another anthropologist, Marvin Harris (1978), links environmental harshness to warfare, female infanticide, and gender inequality. He argues that population pressure and resource shortages produce warfare in technologically simple societies, which control population through female infanticide. Infanticide is made possible by the devaluation of nonwarriors, that is, females, which develops as a mechanism to encourage masculine fierceness and aggressiveness. The level of gender inequality is a function of the frequency of warfare and its location—remote (which may reduce male advantage) or proximate (which enhances it). The military as a masculine institution is explored in Chapter 25.

Sanday and Harris focus on technologically simple societies. A broader range of societies is incorporated into theories developed by Martin and Voorhies (1975), Huber (1988), Blumberg (1978), and Chafetz (1984), who employ variants of Lenski's fivefold typology (ranging from foraging to industrial societies), wherein types are defined in terms of dominant technology and related size of the economic surplus. These works describe and explain a curvilinear relationship, beginning with very low levels of gender inequality in most non-surplus-producing, technologically simple foraging societies, peaking in agrarian/pastoral societies, and tapering off gradually in advanced industrial ones. This relationship comprises the topic of Chapter 4.

Demographic variables have also been used as independent constructs. As stated previously, Harris (1978; also Chafetz, 1984) defines population density as an important impetus for gender inequality. Huber (1991) focuses on the negative impact of high fertility rates on the relative status of women. Guttentag and Secord (1983) discuss the effects of skewed sex ratios on women's opportunities to marry and to participate in the labor force, on dyadic power within heterosexual relationships, and on women's likelihood of collectively rebelling against the system.

Randall Collins (1975) links a typology of political structure to gender inequality. He distinguishes between nation–states, which monopolize the legitimate use of force, and earlier, household-based polities in which it was decentralized into the hands of (male) household heads. In the latter case, individual men have the legitimate right to physically coerce wives (and other household members), a variable that, when coupled with women's level of economic opportunity, constitutes the most important construct explaining the degree of gender inequality. Male violence against women is the topic of Chapter 14, and the relationship between gender and political life is explored in Chapter 23.

Economic power, or the extent to which women produce economic surplus, and especially control the products of, and/or income derived from their labor, constitutes a central construct in most macrostructural theories (e.g., Blumberg, 1984; Chafetz, 1984, 1990; Collins, 1975; Collins, Chafetz, Blumberg, Coltrane, & Turner, 1993). The more economic resources women produce and control, the lower is the level of gender stratification. Blumberg (1984) adds the concepts "nesting" and "discount rate." The relative economic power of women varies at different societal levels (household, community, social class, and society), with the broader levels controlling (nesting) those below. Coercive, political, and ideological forms of power, although less important than economic, tend to flow from higher social levels downward and are less accessible to women than economic power. Therefore, males tend to be more dominant at higher levels, which discounts the amount of power women receive based on their economic resources. The relationship between gender and the economy is explored in Chapters 15 and 16.

Finally, macrostructural theories often include family structure and culture as intervening constructs. Like the socialist feminists, they (e.g., Blumberg, 1978, 1984, 1988; Chafetz, 1984, 1990; Collins et al., 1993) define the domestic (i.e., reproductive and household maintenance) division of labor as important for understanding women's economic roles: the more responsible women are for domestic labor, the less their opportunity to achieve economic resources, and vice versa. Locality and lineage systems are also incorporated: women fare worst under patrilocal and patrilineal systems of marriage and family (Blumberg, 1978; Chafetz, 1984; Martin & Voorhies, 1975). Family relations and the division of domestic labor, as they are impacted by gender, constitute the focus of Chapters 18 and 19. Further, secular and religious idea systems reflect and buttress systems of gender inequality by "explaining" gender difference and justifying male privilege (e.g., Blumberg, 1978, 1984, 1988; Chafetz, 1984, 1990). This substantial array of structural constructs is woven together in complex and varying ways by the different theorists.

3.4. Multiple Jeopardy Theory

In recent years, feminist scholars have become aware of the white, middle-class biases of much of their work, as reflected in a recent emphasis on the topic called "The Intersection of Race, Class and Gender." This literature is mostly descriptive, although the work of Patricia Hill Collins (1990) provides a basic theoretical approach. Collins (1990, Chapter 11) conceptualizes "one overarching structure of domination" that includes, in addition to race, class, and gender, the dimensions of age, religion, and sexual orientation. Rejecting an additive approach to understanding how these various systems of inequality affect people, she recommends that we focus on how they interact. She uses a "both/and" (rather than an "either/or") approach to argue that people can simultaneously be oppressed and oppressor, privileged and penalized; "a matrix of domination contains few pure victims or oppressors" (p. 229). Although individuals and groups may define one form of oppression as more fundamental than others that they simultaneously experience, no one form is primary. The matrix of domination has several layers, including persons, group or community culture, and social institutions, and different systems of oppression rely on varying degrees of interpersonal versus systemic means of domination. All layers are sites of potential resistance to systems of domination, as are all forms of oppression. The next task in the development of this promising theoretical approach is to delineate the general conditions under which: (1) any specific form of oppression is likely to be perceived as more fundamental than other forms simultaneously experienced; (2) the various levels of domination constitute more or less important loci of oppression; and (3) collective resistance is likely to arise in response to particular forms of dominance. A fully developed theory of multiple jeopardy could constitute a major vehicle for moving gender (and race/ethnicity) to the center of sociological theory, where social inequality, defined narrowly as class/status, has long played a fundamental role.

4. FEMINIST MICROSTRUCTURAL THEORY

The theories included in Part IV focus on explaining the gendered behaviors and choices of individuals, and gendered interaction patterns between them, as outcomes of gender inequality at the macro-level. Four sections comprise this part of the chapter: Network Theory, Utilitarian Theories of Exchange and Rational Choice, Role Theory, and Status Expectations Theory.

4.1. Network Theory

Network Theory is concerned with the nature (structure) of linkages between actors, not with characteristics of actors. Nonetheless, Smith-Lovin and McPherson (1993) use this theory to shed light upon issues of gender difference and inequality. They argue that gender differentiation begins with what appear to be inconsequentially small differences in the network structures and ties of young boys and girls. They review a considerable body of empirical literature to show how single-sex childhood networks cumulate over the life course, resulting in substantial differences in the kinds of networks in which women and men are typically located and the nature of the ties within gender homophilous networks. In turn, different types of networks and ties have major impacts on the development of aspirations, the level and forms of opportunities people enjoy, and behavior, differences summarized by the title of their article: "You Are Who You Know." As adults, women and men are different and unequal because of the effects of their current network ties, which, although begun in childhood, are potentially changeable.

4.2. Utilitarian Theories of Exchange and Rational Choice

Contemporary theories of Rational Choice and Exchange, derived from classical Utilitarian thought, have been criticized by feminists (e.g., England, 1989; England & Kilbourne, 1990; Harstock, 1985) on the basis that they assume selfish, separative, and nonemotional actors who are presumably masculine, and ignore connective, altruistic, and emotional motivations said to be characteristically feminine. Nonetheless, both types of theories have provided the basis of feminist theorizing.

Social Exchange Theory has been used by feminist thinkers to explain inequities between spouses (e.g., Bell & Newby, 1976; Chafetz, 1980, 1990; Curtis, 1986; Parker & Parker, 1979), a topic explored in Chapters 17 and 18. They begin by noting that social structural arrangements function to allow most husbands far greater access than their wives to resources that families require and desire. The major, but not sole resource of interest is economic, with prestige, superior knowledge, and culturally based male authority constituting other important resources. The higher level of access by husbands to resources generated outside the family must be "balanced" in some fashion by wives for the relationship to continue. Wives typically provide compliance and deference (as well as domestic labor) as their part of the exchange. In a nuanced description of spousal exchanges under these conditions, Curtis distinguishes economic from social exchange, noting that the former type is based on the advance specification of what is to be traded for what. In social exchanges, gifts and favors are given with an implicit understanding that the debtor will eventually fulfill some diffuse, unspecified obligation. Because it is unspecified, the amount of debt "can be infinite in effect," inasmuch as it is unclear when it has been discharged (Curtis, 1986, p. 179). Husbands acquire considerable power over their wives because of their superior ability to provide gifts and favors. Exchange-based spousal inequality tends to handicap women in the labor force, thereby reinforcing macro-level gender inequality (Chafetz, 1990). However, as Parker and Parker (1979; also Chafetz, 1980) note, as women increase their access to resources generated outside the family, the nature of spousal exchanges alters, often resulting in either increased equality or in divorce.

Friedman and Diem (1993) review a considerable body of feminist empirical work to demonstrate the implicit Rational Choice Theory inherent in it. They argue that three central Rational Choice mechanisms are often employed to explain differences in the choices made by men and women: institutional constraints, opportunity costs, and preferences (p. 101). They demonstrate how gender-related choices made by parents (e.g., regarding investing in sons' versus daughters' educations), employers (e.g., whether to hire/promote men or women in various kinds of jobs), and individual women (e.g., whether to be a full-time homemaker) can be understood using these Rational Choice concepts. Chafetz and Hagan (1996) employ a modified version of this theory, using the concept "satisficing" (seeking a satisfactory rather than maximal level of some good) to understand how women increasingly try to balance preferences for individual achievement and for long-term romantic commitment and children. Their theory explains a set of family changes experienced by all industrial nations (increased ages at first marriage and first birth, decreased completed fertility, increased divorce and cohabitation rates) as primarily the result of changes in the rationally calculated choices women make as they confront a new set of opportunities and an old set of constraints.

4.3. Role Theory

Despite intense feminist criticism of Parsonian Theory in the 1960s and 1970s, the newly emerging field of gender sociology originally called itself by the Parsonian label, the Sociology of Sex Roles. This term, which assumes the existence of overarching, general, feminine and masculine roles, has since been discredited and abandoned, because it obscures power differences between men and women, thereby depoliticizing the study of gender (Stacey & Thorne, 1985), and because it fails to recognize situational variation in role enactment (Lopata & Thorne, 1978). However, because so many specific social roles are exclusively (e.g., mother, husband) or largely (many occupations) specific to one sex, and because women's roles have changed considerably in recent decades, Role Theory remains important to the study of gender, as demonstrated in Chapter 12.

A major theme in the literature concerning women's roles is conflict between domestic and employment roles. Coser and Rokoff (1982) theorize that role conflicts are avoided for men because normative expectations specify priority for employment over family obligations. For women, cultural definitions are the opposite, so in cases of conflict they are supposed to disrupt their work organization rather than family. Because of this, employers often restrict women's opportunities, women tend to have low career aspirations and they readily relinquish careers. Female-dominated occupations are structured to assume high rates of absenteeism and relatively low levels of commitment and are therefore under-valued and -rewarded.

A recent feminist Role Theory (Lopata,1994) examines the effects of societal modernization on the major types of roles women play (family, kinship, employment, domestic, community, student) and compares three ideal-typical kinds of women—modern, traditional, and transitional—in terms of their role-playing. While emphasizing the modern role pattern, Lopata recognizes that within a modern society such as the United States, different categories of women vary in the extent to which they enjoy the opportunity to assume modern role options. Women perform the duties of their numerous roles within a "social circle" comprising all those with whom they interact in their role enactments. Given cultural definitions of various roles, some combinations ("role clusters") are easier to negotiate and create less conflict and strain than others. Lopata also explores the relationship between role enactments and gendered personal identity, using a life course perspective to focus on transitions between various roles and the differing levels of role salience women experience during their lifetimes. The modern role-player deals with a more complex role set, a wider social circle, and greater opportunities to negotiate her role performances than a traditional one. In this way, Lopata's theory links changing, socioculturally generated definitions, constraints, and opportunities to individually negotiated role performances and identities of women.

4.4. Status Expectations Theory

Status Expectations Theory explains how gender is related to power and influence in mixed-sex, goal-oriented groups (see review essay by Ridgeway, 1993). The theory assumes that males enjoy higher social status than females. Both men and women typically enter mixed-sex groups with expectations that men will behave more competently than women in moving the group toward task achievement, that is, their "performance expectations" favor males. The theory recognizes that the salience of gender is context specific and, in some instances (e.g., when the task is traditionally feminine), performance expectations will not privilege males. Normally, however, they do and they become self-fulfilling prophecies that result in a reduction of women's self-confidence, prestige, and power in group interactions. Moreover, such expectations are usually accepted by group members as legitimate and, therefore, an individual woman's attempt to counteract them will be rejected as inappropriate by members of both sexes (Meeker & Weitzel-O'Neill, 1985). The outcomes of mixed-sex groups will typically reflect the preferences of their male members, and group processes will usually enhance male power and status (Ridgeway, 1993), reinforcing gender-based status expectations in future group settings and the wider society. This body of research and theory is explored further in Chapter 13.

4.5. Conclusion

The theories discussed in Part IV explain how gendered differences in resources, opportunities, constraints, and social definitions, generated at the macro-level, influence individuals' choices, behaviors, and interaction patterns in gender differentiated and unequal ways. In turn, micro-level responses to structured inequality feed back to buttress the macro-level system. They at least implicitly recognize that change is possible, its major source and direction flowing from the macro- to the micro-levels.

5. FEMINIST INTERACTIONIST THEORY

The theories discussed in Part V, Ethnomethodology and Symbolic Interactionism, focus on how interaction processes (re)produce gender in everyday life, a topic also explored in Chapter 13. They differ from the theories in Part IV because they focus much more attention on actors' interpretations of situations and how meanings are attached to behaviors, and because they imply greater individual agency than the more structurally focused theories discussed to this point.

5.1. Ethnomethodology

The Ethnomethodological approach views gender as an ongoing accomplishment that emerges during virtually all interactions, both within- and between-sex (Gerson, 1985). Gender is neither an individual-level trait nor a stable feature of social structure (West & Fenstermaker, 1993). Rather, people are constantly re-creating their own and their interaction partners' sense of gender as they interact, which is what West and Zimmerman (1987) label "doing gender." Gender is "omnirelevant" in that any action can be interpreted as exemplifying it (West & Fenstermaker, 1993). Specific definitions of masculinity and femininity vary (in ways and for reasons that are not theorized), but the notion that men and women are fundamentally different does not. The taken-for-granted view is that there exist two and only two sexes, and everyone is a member of one and only one (Kessler & McKenna, 1978). Using a variety of different kinds of cues, people characterize self and others by sex ("gender attribution") and then interpret all kinds of behavior through the lens of gender-normative "appropriateness." Individuals, therefore, hold themselves and others accountable for their behavior as men and as women and are legitimated or discredited accordingly (West & Fenstermaker, 1993, p. 157). Gender (as well as race and class) are conceptualized as emergent features of social situations, accomplishments whose relevance cannot be determined apart from the context in which they are accomplished (West & Fenstermaker, 1995).

5.2. Symbolic Interaction Theory

Symbolic Interactionism has influenced a number of feminist theories. Lopata's Role theory, discussed earlier, is grounded in the Symbolic Interactionist emphasis on role negotiation, rather than the more static and deterministic Parsonian concept of role. Socialization Theory, to be discussed in Part VI, employs Symbolic Interactionist insights on the development of self-identity in delineating the processes that produce gendered selves. A number of feminist sociolinguists, social psychologists, and sociologists focus on what this theory tradition defines as the key medium through which "mind, self and society" are produced: symbolic communication or language (e.g., Fishman, 1982; Mayo & Henley, 1981; West & Zimmerman, 1977). This body of work (see Bonvillain, 1995; Chapter 9, for a comprehensive review) theorizes that gender inequality is sustained because men dominate conversations (which women work hard to sustain), whereas women use verbal and body language in ways that weaken their ability to assert themselves. Moreover, most languages, including English, build gender bias into their vocabularies. Fishman (1982, p. 178) concludes: "the definition of what is appropriate conversation becomes men's choice. What part of the world [they] . . . maintain the reality of, is his choice . . . ," that is, through talk men create the definition of the situation.

Scripting and Labeling Theories are offshoots of Symbolic Interaction Theory also used by feminist theorists. Gender is reproduced because the social scripts for many tasks are specifically associated with one gender; as people go about doing those tasks, they automatically "do gender" (West & Fenstermaker, 1993). The division of domestic labor, for instance, provides gendered scripts for numerous tasks that make the household a veritable "gender factory" (Fenstermaker Berk, 1985). The gendered scripts of many female occupations include "emotional labor" (the need to fake or hide one's feelings in order to please others; Hochschild, 1983), which functions to deny women an "integrated autonomous identity" (Kasper, 1986, p. 40). Schur (1984) uses Labeling Theory to demonstrate how the devalued and stigmatized master status of femaleness results in the selective perception of women based on stereotypes, and in their objectification as things rather than persons. In turn, objectification allows others to treat women in degrading and exploitative ways that produce self-fulfilling prophecies by which women come to define themselves as inferior and to suffer from low self-esteem, in-group hostility, and identification with their male oppressors. The relationship between gender and mental (as well as physical) health is explored in Chapters 21 and 22.

The most explicit use of Symbolic Interaction Theory is provided by Ferguson (1980). She argues that men possess the power to define both specific situations and the generalized other, by which women come to define themselves "by reference to standards that brand them as inferior" (p. 155). The result is that women's self-identity is undermined and they assume self-blame for their problems. In addition, women become highly adept at taking the role of the male other, anticipating his wants and attempting to please, flatter, and acquiesce to avoid punishment by the more powerful other (pp.161–162).

Recently, Cecilia Ridgeway (1997) developed a fascinating theoretical explanation of the persistence of gender hierarchy in the labor force, rooted in an interactionist perspective but synthesizing ideas from several social psychological theories. Her starting point is that of the ethnomethodologists: the pervasive tendency in nearly all interactions to dichotomously "sex categorize." She traces the implications of this for understanding gender stereotyping, the salience level of gender in interactions, and the development of gender status beliefs, demonstrating how these in turn affect the gendered distribution of rewards and of men's and women's relative feelings of entitlement (thus making her theory more general than simply an explanation of labor market phenomena). Finally, she applies her theory to an analysis of how jobs come to be sex labeled and inequitably rewarded.

6. CHILDHOOD ENGENDERMENT THEORIES

The last two types of feminist approaches to understanding gender difference and inequality focus on childhood experiences and learning, a topic examined in Chapter 11. These are theorized as producing gendered personalities, cognitive styles, preferences, and values that are assumed to be quite stable and influential throughout life, and to be the wellspring from which macrostructural gender inequities arise and/or are maintained. The two theories of childhood engenderment are Socialization and Neo-Freudian. Both create problems for explaining change in gender arrangements to the extent that they stress the lifelong importance of early learning, and both tend to lead to an exaggerated picture of the extent of gender difference.

6.1. Socialization Theory

The Socialization Theory of childhood engenderment utilizes Symbolic Interactionism and Cognitive Development Theory to identify the basic processes by which children develop "appropriately" gendered self-identities and learn gender-normative behaviors. It assumes, at least implicitly, that such identities and behavioral repertoires shape behavior across specific roles and situations over the lifecourse because the theory is linked with the Parsonian concept gender role. The engenderment process begins at birth with sex-labeling of infants and differences in responses to them by parents/caretakers based on assigned sex (e.g., naming, how infants are handled and spoken to, nursery decor, toys, clothing). The result is that toddlers develop a stable identity as female or male that is an integral part of their developing self-identity, and then actively seek confirmation from others of that gendered identity (Cahill, 1983; Lewis & Weinraub, 1979). They also become increasingly adept at labeling others according to gender. Modeling same-sex parent, siblings, peers, media figures, etc., along with positive and negative feedback from adults and peers concerning their behavior, teach children gender-specific behavioral norms (Constantinople, 1979). Gender-specific forms of sport, play, and games are also important for teaching children gender-appropriate physical, cognitive, and interaction skills (Cahill, 1983; Lever, 1976), skills that traditionally orient females to domestic roles and close, interpersonal relationships, and males to employment roles and emotional inexpressiveness (Sattel, 1976). The relationship between gender and sport is explored in Chapter 26.

6.2. Neo-Freudian Theory

For reasons that are not clear, interest among gender sociologists in Socialization Theory waned as interest in a Neo-Freudian approach to engenderment waxed, beginning in the late 1970s, despite feminist criticism of Freud as intense as that of Parsons. The theorist who has most influenced feminist sociology in the United States is Nancy Chodorow (especially 1978; also 1974, 1989), who combines Object Relations Theory with a revision of Freudian ideas (see Kurzweil, 1989 and Williams, 1993 for reviews of feminist Freudian thought). Although hotly contested among feminist sociologists (e.g., Lorber, Coser, Rossi, & Chadorow, 1981), few feminist sociological theories have been as widely cited as hers.

Chodorow begins with the observation that infant and toddler caretaking is done overwhelmingly by women; that for young children of both sexes, their "primary love object" is female. Oedipal-stage boys must separate from their female love object in order to acquire a gendered self-identity. Similarly aged girls, however, can continue close bonds with their same-sex primary love object during the process of acquiring their gendered identity. The result is that girls grow into women whose primary concern is with interpersonal connection and nurturance, while boys mature into men who focus on individuation, deny affect, and strive to prove themselves through social achievement. Male dominance and misogyny are also posited as results of the fact that women "mother" male children. Using Chodorow's ideas, Gilligan (1982) theorizes that males and females develop different forms of moral reasoning; men emphasize abstract principles, women concrete, personal obligations as the basis of moral behavior.

Gender system change could occur from this perspective if men assumed substantially greater responsibility for the daily nurturance of infants and young children. This solution is problematic for two reasons: What would motivate the "typical" male produced by this (or, for that matter, the socialization) process to become substantially more nurturant? Also, would any feminist want to see children raised by individuating, emotionally unexpressive, misogynistic fathers? Miriam Johnson (1988) questions this solution for a different reason. In response to Chodorow, Johnson theorizes that fathers constitute the primary agents who teach young children gender difference and inequality. Children of both sexes become "human" through their interactions with (female) primary love objects, but mothers tend to minimize, while fathers actively differentiate their children along gender lines. In addition, children observe husband–wife interactions, which model gender inequality.

6.3. Conclusion

Theories of childhood engenderment provide an important basis for most feminist interactionist theories, to the extent that "doing gender" involves the ongoing search for confirmation of fundamentally gendered self-identities. In general, microstructural approaches theorize in a "downward" direction from macrostructure, whereas interactionist theories, at least in part, move "up" from personality and self-identity, both attempting to explain how people's everyday choices, behaviors, and interactions are thoroughly gendered. In addition, childhood engenderment and most interactionist approaches imply that macrostructural gender inequality is rooted in micro-level processes, while microstructural theories suggest that gendered interactions are shaped by macrostructual inequity.

7. CONCLUSION

The review of feminist sociological theories demonstrates the rich variety of approaches to understanding gender difference and inequality developed in recent years. They reflect every general theoretical approach in our discipline. Each provides a useful, albeit partial contribution to the solution of a giant puzzle: a full explanation of the mechanisms by which systems of gender inequality are produced, maintained, and changed at all levels of social life. Although some efforts at broad theoretical synthesis have been made (e.g.,

Chafetz, 1990; Collins et al., 1993, Connell, 1987; Lorber, 1994), one challenge for gender theorists in sociology is to continue the work of theoretical integration. A second challenge is to explore more fully the effects of gender on all social processes, structures, and institutions; to use gender difference and inequality more systematically as independent, rather than primarily as dependent constructs. A third challenge is only slightly less compelling than it was when first explicated over a decade ago by Stacey and Thorne (1985): to end the ghettoization of feminist theories by fully integrating their insights into the sociological theory canon, thereby incorporating gender as a fundamental feature of social life into the basic fabric of our discipline.

REFERENCES

Alway, J. (1995). The trouble with gender: Tales of the still-missing feminist revolution in sociological theory. *Sociological theory, 13,* 209–228.

Bell, C. & Newby, H. (1976). Husbands and wives: The dynamics of the deferential dialectic. In D. L. Baker & S. Allen (Eds.), *Dependence and exploitation in work and marriage* (pp. 152–168). London: Longman.

Blumberg, R. L. (1978). *Stratification: Socioeconomic and sexual inequality.* Dubuque, IA: William C. Brown.

Blumberg, R. L. (1979). A paradigm for predicting the position of women: Policy implications and problems. In J. Lipman-Blumen & J. Bernard (Eds.), *Sex roles and social policy* (pp. 113–142). Beverly Hills, CA: Sage.

Blumberg, R. L. (1984). A general theory of gender stratification. In R. Collins (Ed.), *Sociological theory, 1984* (pp. 23–101). San Francisco: Jossey-Bass.

Blumberg, R. L. (1988). Income under female versus male control: Hypotheses from a theory of gender stratification and data from the third world. *Journal of Family Issues, 9,* 51–84.

Blumberg, R. L. (1989). Toward a feminist theory of development. In R.Wallace (Ed.), *Feminism and sociological theory* (pp. 161–199). Beverly Hills, CA: Sage

Bonvillain, N. (1995). *Women and men: Cultural constructs of gender.* Englewood Cliffs, NJ: Prentice-Hall.

Cahill, S. (1983). Reexamining the acquisition of sex roles: A symbolic interactionist approach. *Sex Roles, 9,* 1–15.

Chafetz, J. S. (1980). Conflict resolution in marriage: Toward a theory of spousal strategies and marital dissolution rates. *Journal of Family Issues, 1,* 397–421.

Chafetz, J. S. (1984). *Sex and advantage: A comparative, macrostructural theory of sex stratification.* Totowa, NJ: Rowman and Allanheld.

Chafetz, J. S. (1988). *Feminist sociology: An overview of contemporary theories.* Itasca, IL: F. E. Peacock.

Chafetz, J. S. (1990). *Gender equity: A theory of stability and change.* Newbury Park, CA: Sage.

Chafetz, J. S. (1997). Feminist theory and sociology. In J. Hagan (Ed.), *Annual review of sociology, 1997.* Palo Alto, CA: Annual Reviews.

Chafetz, J. S. & J. Hagan (1996). The gender division of labor and family change in industrial societies: A theoretical accounting. *Journal of Comparative Family Studies, 27:* 187–217.

Chodorow, N. (1974). Family structure and feminine personality. In M. Z. Rosaldo & L. Lamphere (Eds.), *Women, culture and society* (pp. 43–66). Stanford, CA: Stanford University Press.

Chadorow, N. (1978). *The reproduction of mothering: Psychoanalysis and the sociology of gender.* Berkeley, CA: University of California Press.

Chadorow, N. (1989). *Feminism and psychoanalytic theory.* New Haven, CT: Yale University Press.

Collins, P. H. (1990). *Black feminist thought: Knowledge, consciousness and the politics of empowerment.* Boston: Unwin Hyman.

Collins, R. (1975). *Conflict sociology: Toward an explanatory science.* New York: Academic Press.

Collins, R., Chafetz, J. S., Blumberg, R. L., Coltrane, S., & Turner, J. (1993). Toward an integrated theory of gender stratification. *Sociological Perspective, 36,* 185–216.

Connell, R. W. (1987). *Gender and power: Society, the person and sexual politics.* Stanford, CA: Stanford University Press.

Constantinople, A. (1979). Sex-role acquisition: In search of the elephant. *Sex Roles, 5,* 121–133.

Coser, L. A. (1977). Georg Simmel's neglected contributions to the sociology of women. *Signs, 2,* 869–876.

Coser, R. L., & Rokoff, G. (1982). Women in the occupational world: Social disruption and conflict. *Social Problems, 18,* 535–554.

Curtis, R. (1986). Household and family in theory on inequality. *American Sociological Review, 51*, 168–183.

Deegan, M. J. (1988). *Jane Addams and the men of the Chicago school, 1892–1918*. New Brunswick, NJ: Transaction Books.

Ehrlich, C. (1971). The male sociologists' burden: The place of women in marriage family texts. *Journal of Marriage and the Family, 33*, 421–30.

Eisenstein, Z. (1979). Developing a theory of capitalist patriarchy and socialist feminism, and some notes on the relations of capitalist patriarchy. In Z. Eisenstein (Ed.), *Capitalist patriarchy and the case for socialist feminism* (pp. 5–55). New York: Monthly Review Press.

Engels, F. (1972). *The origin of the family, private property and the state*. New York: Penguin Books (translated by Alick West; first published 1884).

England, P. (1989). A feminist critique of rational choice theories: Implications for sociology. *The American Sociologist, 20*, 14–20.

England, P. (1993). *Theory on gender/feminism on theory*. New York: Aldine De Gruyter.

England, P., & Kilbourne, B. S. (1990). Feminist critique of the separative model of the self: Implications for rational choice theory. *Rationality and Society, 2*, 156–171.

Fenstermaker Berk, S. (1985). *The gender factory*. New York: Plenum Press.

Ferguson, K. (1980). *Self, society, and womankind*. Westport, CT: Greenwood.

Fishman, P. (1982). Interaction: The work women do. In R. Kahn-Hut, A. K. Daniels. & R.Colvard (Eds.), *Women and work* (pp. 170–180). New York: Oxford University Press.

Fitzpatrick, E. (1990). *Endless crusade: Women social scientists and progressive reform*. New York: Oxford University Press.

Friedman, D., & Diem, C. (1993). Feminism and the pro(rational) choice movement: Rational choice theory, feminist critiques, and gender inequality. In P. England (Ed.), *Theory on gender/feminism on theory* (pp. 91–114). New York: Aldine DeGruyter.

Gerson, J. M. (1985). Boundaries, negotiation, consciousness: Reconceptualizing gender relations. *Social Problems, 32*, 317–331.

Gilligan, C. (1982). *In a different voice*. Cambridge, MA: Harvard University Press.

Guttentag, M. & Secord, P. (1983). *Too many women? The sex role question*. Beverly Hills, CA: Sage.

Harris, M. (1978). *Cannibals and Kings: The origins of cultures*. London: Collins.

Harstock, N. (1985). *Money, sex and power*. Boston: Northeastern University Press

Hartmann, H. (1984). The unhappy marriage of Marxism and feminism: Towards a more progressive union. In A. Jaggar & P. Rothenberg (Eds.), *Feminist frameworks: Alternative theoretical accounts of the relations between women and men* (pp. 172–189). New York: McGraw-Hill.

Hochschild, A. (1983). *The managed heart: Commercialization of human feeling*. Berkely, CA: University of California Press.

Huber, J. (1988). A theory of family, economy, and gender. *Journal of Family Issues, 9*, 9–26.

Huber, J. (1991). Macro-micro links in gender stratification. In J. Huber (Ed.), *Macro-micro linkages in sociology* (pp. 11–25). Newbury Park, CA:Sage.

Johnson, M. M. (1988). *Strong mothers, weak wives: The search for gender equality*. Berkeley, CA: University of California Press.

Johnson, M. M. (1989). Feminism and the theories of Talcott Parsons. In R. Wallace (Ed.), *Feminism and Sociological Theory* (pp. 101–118). Newbury Park, CA: Sage.

Johnson, M. M. (1993). Functionalism and feminism: Is estrangement necessary? In P. England (Ed.), *Theory on gender/feminism on theory* (pp. 115–130). New York: Aldine DeGruyter.

Kandal, T. R. (1988). *The woman question in classical sociological theory*. Miami: Florida International University Press.

Kasper, A. (1986). Consciousness re-evaluated: Interpretive theory and feminist scholarship. *Sociological Inquiry, 56*, 30–49.

Kessler, S. & McKenna, W. (1978). *Gender: An ethnomethodological approach*. New York: John Wiley & Sons.

Kurzweil, E. (1989). Psychoanalytic feminism: Implications for sociological theory. In R. Wallace (Ed.), *Feminism and Sociological theory* (pp. 82–97). Newbury Park, CA: Sage.

Lehmann, J. M. (1990). Durkheim's response to feminism: Prescriptions for women. *Sociological Theory, 8*, 163–187.

Lehmann, J. M. (1994). *Durkheim and women*. Lincoln: University of Nebraska Press.

Lengermann, P. M. & Niebrugge, J. (1996). Contemporary feminist theory. In G. Ritzer, *Sociological theory* (pp. 436–486). New York: McGraw-Hill.

Lengermann, P. M. & Niebrugge, J. (1998). *The Women Founders: Sociology and Social Theory, 1830–1930.* Boston: McGraw-Hill.

Lever, J. (1976). Sex differences in the games children play. *Social Problems, 3–4,* 478–487.

Lewis, M. & Weinraub, M. (1979). Origins of early sex-role development. *Sex Roles, 5,* 135–153.

Lopata, H. Z. (1994). *Circles and settings: Role changes of American women.* Albany, NY: State University of New York Press.

Lopata, H. Z., & Thorne, B. (1978). On the term "sex roles". *Signs, 3,* 718–721.

Lorber, J. (1994). *Paradoxes of gender.* New Haven, CT: Yale University Press.

Lorber, J., Coser, R., Rossi, A., & Chodorow, N. (1981). On the reproduction of mothering: A methodological debate. *Signs, 6,* 482–514.

Martin, M. K., & Voorhies, B. (1975). *Female of the species.* New York: Columbia University Press.

Mayo, C., & Henley, N. (1981). Nonverbal behavior: Barrier or agent for sex roles change? In C. Mayo & N. Henley (Eds.), *Gender and nonverbal behavior* (pp. 3–13). New York: Springer-Verlag.

Meeker, B., & Weitzel-O'Neill, P. (1985). Sex roles and interpersonal behavior in task-oriented groups. In J. Berger & M. Zeldich, Jr. (Eds.), *Status, rewards and influence* (pp. 379–405). San Francisco: Jossey-Bass.

Oakes, G. (1984). *Georg Simmel: On women, sexuality, and love.* New Haven: Yale University Press.

Parker, S., & Parker, H. (1979). The myth of male superiority: Rise and demise. *American Anthropologist, 81,* 289–309.

Ridgeway, C. L. (1993). Gender, status, and the social psychology of expectations. In P. England (Ed.), *Theory on gender/feminism on theory* (pp. 175–197). New York: Aldine DeGruyter.

Ridgeway, C. L. (1997). Interaction and the conservation of gender inequality: Considering employment. *American Sociological Review, 62,* 218–235.

Rosenberg, R. (1982). *Beyond separate spheres: Intellectual roots of modern feminism.* New Haven, CT: Yale University Press.

Sacks, K. (1974). Engels revisted: Women, the organization of production, and private property. In M. Z. Rosaldo & L. Lamphere (Eds.), *Woman, culture and society* (pp. 207–222). Stanford, CA: Stanford University Press.

Sanday, P. R. (1981). *Female power and male dominance: On the origins of sexual inequality.* Cambridge: Cambridge University Press.

Sattel, J. (1976). The inexpressive male: Tragedy or sexual politics? *Social Problems, 23–4,* 469–477.

Schur, E. (1984). *Labeling women deviant: Gender, stigma, and social control.* New York: Random House.

Seidman, S. (1994). *Contested knowledge: Social theory in the postmodern era.* Cambridge, MA: Blackwell.

Shelton, B. A., & Agger, B. (1993). Shotgun wedding, unhappy marriage, no-fault divorce? Rethinking the feminism-Marxism relationship. In P. England (Ed.), *Theory on gender/feminism on theory* (pp. 25–41). New York: Aldine DeGruyter.

Smith, D. (1987). *The everyday world as problematic: A feminist sociology.* Boston: Northeastern University Press.

Smith, D. (1990). *The conceptual practices of power: A feminist sociology of knowledge.* Boston: Northeastern University Press.

Smith-Lovin, L., & Miller McPherson, J. (1993). You are who you know: A network approach to gender. In P. England (Ed.), *Theory on gender/feminism on theory* (pp. 223–251). New York: Aldine DeGruyter.

Sokoloff, N. (1980). *Between money and love: The dialectic of women's home and market work.* New York: Praeger.

Stacey, J. & Thorne, B. (1985). The missing feminist Revolution in sociology. *Social Problems, 32,* 301–316.

Vogel, L. (1983). *Marxism and the oppression of women: Toward a unitary theory.* New Brunswick, NJ: Rutgers University Press.

Wallace, R. (1989). *Feminism and sociological theory.* Newbury Park, CA: Sage.

Ward, K. (1984). *Women in the world-system: Its impact on status and fertility.* New York: Praeger.

Ward, K. (1990). *Women workers and global restructuring.* Ithaca, NY: ILR Press.

Ward, K. (1993). Reconceptualizing world system theory to include women. In P. England (Ed.), *Theory on gender/feminism on theory* (pp. 43–68). New York: Aldine DeGruyter.

Ward, K., & Grant, L. (1991). On a wavelength of their own? Women and sociological theory. *Contemporary Perspectives in Social Theory, 11,* 117–140.

West, C., & Fenstermaker, S. (1993). Power, inequality, and the accomplishment of gender: An ethnomethodological view. In P. England (Ed.), *Theory on gender/feminism on theory* (pp. 151–174). New York: Aldine DeGruyter.

West, C., & Fenstermaker, S. (1995). Doing difference. *Gender & Society, 9,* 8–37.

West, C., & Zimmerman, D. (1977). Women's place in everyday talk: Reflections on parent–child interaction. *Social Problems, 24,* 521–529.
West, C., & Zimmerman, D. (1987). Doing gender. *Gender & Society, 1,* 125–151.
Whyte, M. K. (1978). *The status of women in preindustrial societies.* Princeton, NJ: Princeton University Press.
Williams, C. (1993). Psychoanalytic theory and the sociology of gender. In P. England (Ed.), *Theory on gender/ feminism on theory* (pp. 131–149). New York: Aldine DeGruyter.

CHAPTER 2

A Feminist Epistemology

JOEY SPRAGUE
DIANE KOBRYNOWICZ

1. INTRODUCTION

The tradition of Western science is built on positivism an epistemology of the fact. For both natural and social science, the world of experience is generally believed to be an objective world, governed by underlying regularities, even natural laws. Facts are empirical observations, outcroppings of these underlying regularities. If, and only if, we systematically and dispassionately observe the data of the empirical world can we detect the patterns of which they are evidence. August Comte had such confidence in the principles of positivism that he believed it was not only possible but also desirable to build a science of society, sociology, upon them.

Positivism is the hegemonic epistemology in scientific discourse, so that its specific way of connecting beliefs about knowing with research practices appears seamless: we often fail to see any distinctions among epistemology, methodology, and method. Harding's (1987) distinctions are useful in disaggregating the issues. Epistemology, Harding says, is a theory about knowledge, about who can know what and under what circumstances. A method, Harding notes, is a technique for gathering and analyzing information, for example, forms of listening, watching, or examining records. A methodology is an argument about how these two are linked, that is, about the implications of an epistemology for the practice of research.

Every epistemology, Genova (1983) says, involves assumptions about the points of a triad: the knower, the known, and the process of knowing. He describes the history of Western philosophical debates about epistemology as focused on one or another of the

JOEY SPRAGUE • Department of Sociology, University of Kansas, Lawrence, Kansas 66049
DIANE KOBRYNOWICZ • Department of Psychology, The College of New Jersey, Ewing, New Jersey 08628

Handbook of the Sociology of Gender, edited by Janet Saltzman Chafetz. Kluwer Academic/Plenum Publishers, New York, 1999.

points on this triad. Ring (1987) identifies the same three elements, but in her representation we are drawn to their connection. Epistemologies, for Ring, are accounts of the knowing subject, the object of study, and the relationship between them. An epistemology directs us in how to approach an understanding of a phenomenon. The basic issue it resolves is the grounds for choosing one theory, or account of that phenomenon, over another (Alcoff, 1989).

At the heart of positivist epistemology is the focus on objectivity. Positivism assumes that truth comes from eliminating the role of subjective judgments and interpretations, thus sharply enforcing the dichotomy between the knower and the known (Ring, 1987). According to positivist epistemology, subjectivity is an obstacle to knowledge: the observer's personality and feelings introduce errors in observation. The practices of research are designed to minimize and hopefully erase any impact of the researcher's subjectivity from the data. Observations are made through a process of objective measurement, which circumvents the subjectivity of the observer, allows for the application of statistical analyses, and makes data collection and interpretation open to replication and testing by others.

Positivism offered some clear advantages over the epistemology that prevailed prior to it, an epistemology based on faith and revelation, an authority based on tradition (Lovibond, 1989). The reliance on evidence and clear, replicatable procedures for collecting and interpreting it, open up the production of knowledge to many more than a chosen few. The emphasis on systematic procedures presents knowledge claims in a context that is open to critique, argument, even refutation. Positivist epistemology has generated methods with democratic potential.

However, positivism has its problems, as has been shown by scholars from Mannheim (1936) to contemporary social constructionists who have argued that official knowing, as we have inherited it, is not the objective, unbiased, apolitical process it represents itself to be. Rather, scholarly paradigms, like other forms of human consciousness, are the expression of specific world views.

For example, the goal of removing subjectivities has never been met. All observations are "theory-laden;" that is, making any observation requires the acceptance of background assumptions—a system of beliefs to interpret what it is that we are seeing. Holding background assumptions thwarts the ideal of knowing pure facts outside of theory (see Bechtel, 1988). Furthermore, when testing any one hypothesis, a scientist is also testing a set of auxiliary hypotheses—all the background assumptions contributing to the world view that supports the hypothesis in the first place. If a test of the hypothesis fails to achieve the predicted results, the scientist does not necessarily reject the hypothesis but can tinker with the background assumptions, arriving at a way to make sense of the data and maintaining the original thought. This process, discussed as the Quine–Duhem thesis in the philosophy of science literature, portends negatively for a pure test of scientific ideas.

Extending this line of criticism, Longino (1989) identifies another major flaw of positivist logic: the assumption that the data directly support hypotheses. She argues that the data do not say what hypothesis they are evidence for. In fact, the same data can be used to support contradictory hypotheses and which connection gets made depends on the background assumptions being made (Longino, 1989; cf. Alcoff, 1989). Because these background assumptions are based in values, science cannot be value neutral (Alcoff, 1989). Moreover, as we will show, the values that pervade the background assumptions support the continued hegemony of privileged white men. Positivism has become the epistemology of the fathers.

The primary contender to positivist epistemology has been radical constructivism (see Jussim, 1991). If positivism is the epistemology of fact, radical constructivism is an epistemology of fiction. From this perspective, reality is created through discourse about it (Weedon, 1987). Thus, the object of knowledge, the truth, is the outcome of the process that "discovers" it (Alcoff, 1989; Foucault, 1972; Fraser, 1989; Haraway, 1988). Knowledge is a narrative, a text, even an act of faith based on cult membership (Haraway, 1988).

Postmodernists have gone so far as to argue that in contemporary Western society knowledge and social domination are the same thing. Foucault (1972) maintains that modern knowledge amounts to intensive surveillance of individuals and groups of people, creating official standards of normality, and prompting us to monitor and discipline ourselves to try to conform to those standards (see Fraser, 1989). Our subjectivity is a social construction; our values and even our sense of having a self are aspects of the way modern power works. Thus there is no basis for rationally choosing between one theory and another. In terms of the relationship between subject and object, radical constructivism dissolves the object into the subject.

Of course, it is curious that just when women and ethnic minorities have begun to demand a voice in creating knowledge, an epistemology emerges claiming there is no truth to be known. Haraway's term for this impact is "epistemological electro-shock therapy" (1988, p. 578). It is easy to imagine the effects of such a stance on struggles to overcome oppression. If uniting people across diversity requires a shared world view of mutual interests, the potential for creating bonds across people evaporates when analyses of experiences are considered mere texts or subjectivities (Fraser & Nicholson, 1988; Mascia-Lees, Sharpe, & Cohen, 1989). Thus, we might consider radical constructivism the epistemology of the sons. But these are not our only choices.

2. FEMINIST STANDPOINT THEORY

Standpoint theorists begin by rejecting positivism's pretentions of creating a view from nowhere in favor of the postulate that each subject is specific, located in a particular time and place. Thus a knower has a particular perspective on the object. At the same time, this locatedness gives access to the concrete world; knowing is not relative, as radical constructivists maintain, rather it is partial (Haraway, 1988; Hartsock, 1983). In most versions of standpoint theory there are certain social positions that allow for developing better understandings. Marxist epistemology generally privileges the standpoint of the working class because their role in process allows one to understand the social and relational character of production (Bar On, 1993; Lukacs, 1971). In feminist standpoint theory, epistemic privilege is often accorded to the standpoint of women and/or other oppressed people. We outline the arguments of Hartsock (1983, 1985), Haraway (1978, 1988, 1990, 1993), Smith (1979, 1987, 1990), and Collins (1986, 1989, 1990).

Hartsock (1983, 1985), a political scientist who pioneered the notion of standpoint, carefully distinguished a standpoint from the spontaneous subjectivity of social actors. A standpoint, she says, is "achieved rather than obvious, a mediated rather than immediate understanding" (1985, p. 132). Capitalists and workers experience the same immediate reality and may even interpret it in similar ways. The difference between their standpoints is that the workers have the potential to get beneath the surface through analysis and struggle, to get a different, deeper understanding. Hartsock uses the example of varying ways to understand power. Capitalists, she argues can know power only as a commodity. However, if workers engage in class struggle and reflect on their position, they can begin to understand power as a relationship of domination.

Hartsock builds her analysis on a critique of Marxist epistemology, which, she maintains, errs in the application of its own logic. She is convinced by the logic of historical materialism that to understand people you have to start with the circumstances under which they meet their daily needs for food, clothing, and shelter. However, in privileging the standpoint of the worker, Marxist epistemology ignores the most fundamental site of production, those places where the satisfaction of people's needs is directly produced, particularly the domestic setting. Both in wage work and in the home, women's work keeps them involved in a world of directly meeting needs "in concrete, many-qualitied, changing material processes" (1985, p. 235). This standpoint—the one of meeting human needs, the standpoint of women—is the one that Hartsock privileges. From this standpoint, she argues, we are able to understand power as potentially nonhierarchical, as a capacity.

As Hartsock faults Marxism for violating its own assumptions, Haraway (1978, 1988, 1990, 1993), an anthropologist, makes a similar critique of positivism. Haraway notes that positivism is based on the primacy of data, that is, information that is directly detectable through the senses. Positivist epistemology is, then, logically grounded in the materiality of people's bodies. Yet, positivism denies the presence of these bodies in making its claims to validity. For example, those dominating the production of knowledge in the Western tradition have, for the most part, been upper-class, white, and male, and surely their observations are shaped by their specific experience. Haraway agrees with Positivist arguments that it is through our sensory experience, our bodies, that we have access to the world, but that very grounding is both the basis of valid knowledge and a limit on it. She coined the term "embodied vision" to emphasize that our vision is located in some specific place, that our knowledge is "situated" and thus partial.

How can we compensate for the partiality of any perspective? Haraway says the best way to gain a critical perspective on one's situated view is to know how things look from a different position. Access to two ways of looking at a phenomenon reveals the limits and constructedness of each. Because each of us experiences life and our selves in multiple facets that are "stitched together imperfectly" (1988, p. 586), empathy is possible and, through it, two knowers in distinct situations can make a partial connection. By translating across distinct perspectives and connecting ever-shifting situated knowledges, we can rationally build some collective, if provisional, agreement on the whole.

Women cross boundaries between perspectives as a matter of daily life, Smith notes (1987, 1990). The sexual division of labor, both within sociology and between professional and domestic work, creates a breach between the means by which we develop our understandings of social life and the concrete work of keeping social life going. Thus, the standpoint of women in sociology offers leverage to integrate two perspectives. It gives us the opportunity to see sociology as a masculine institution that plays a role in the broader practices by which we are all organized and managed, what Smith calls "the relations of ruling."

The organization of professional work has caused men to focus on the conceptual world while ignoring their bodily existence. This has been possible only because women have been providing for their human needs and for those of their children. Similarly, at work women provide the material forms to men's conceptual work—clerical work, interviewing, taking care of patients, and so on. It is as though these men live in an ephemeral world of abstract ideas. Never does the mundane reality of physical existence impede their thoughts; their thoughts stay lofty and disconnected from reality. Women transverse the divide between this ephemeral world and the actual world of human practices, attending to these men's inevitable material needs. The better the women are at their work, the more it is invisible to men, who can thus take it for granted and have their own authority bolstered in the process.

The result is a sociology that is alienated from social life. Typical scientific practice only superficially overcomes the split between official knowledge and concrete existence. Smith's imagery is powerful: she says we reach out through our conceptual frameworks to pluck bits of the empirical world and retreat to our office to organize the data to fit our frameworks. The pictures we end up with are more likely to correspond to official organizational charts than to the daily experience of the front line actors whose practices are the stuff of social institutions. Sociological practices "convert what people experience directly in their everyday/everynight world into forms of knowledge in which people as subjects disappear and in which their perspectives on their own experience are transposed and subdued by the magisterial forms of objectifying discourse" (1990, p. 4). Sociology becomes an aspect of the relations of ruling.

Smith disagrees with those who say there is no difference between science and ideology, following Marx's argument that what is real is people's concerted action to address material imperatives. Creating knowledge is revealing the ways practical activity to meet human needs is shaped and constrained by social relations of domination, particularly those that go beyond the immediate context. Making ideology is letting concepts and abstractions dominate and obscure those material relations (1990, p. 34). We need to peer behind facts and abstractions and ask how they are the outcome of the concerted activity of specific people in concrete circumstances. For example, saying that technology is propelling us into a future outside of human control is ideology; showing how powerful elites promote specific technologies to maximize their social control is not.

Women sociologists, especially those with children, dwell in both the conceptual and the practical realms; they experience on a daily basis the concrete work of meeting human needs, coordinating with child care and schools, etc., and how these conflict with the work of sociology. The standpoint of women within sociology means we can and must work to transform its practices away from its role of supporting the relations of ruling.

Beginning from a marginalized standpoint, one that integrates the perspectives of black feminists as academic outsiders and other black women, Patricia Hill Collins (1986, 1989, 1990) develops a black feminist epistemology that exposes the systematic and particular character of hegemonic sociology at the same time it offers an alternative. Collins identifies four parameters of Black feminist epistemology (1990, pp. 203–218). First concrete experience and the wisdom developed out of everyday experience is valued in evaluating knowledge claims. Second, knowledge claims are not hierarchically imposed by an elite but rather worked out through dialogue with everyday social actors. Third, emotions such as empathy and attachment are incorporated into the notion of intellect. Finally, part of the assessment of an idea is via what is known about the character and biography of the person advancing it.

With this understanding of standpoint theory, we can turn a critical eye to sociology. One of our first observations is that mainstream sociology flows from the standpoint of privileged men. Before elaborating on the impact of this particular standpoint for sociology, we first describe the specifics of a privileged male standpoint.

3. THE STANDPOINT OF PRIVILEGED MEN

There are a variety of accounts of the ways that the experience of privileged men in the social organization of white supremacist, capitalist, patriarchal society has prompted the development of a distinct form of consciousness. The analyses of Chodorow (1978, 1991) and O'Brien (1981, 1989) operate within distinct theoretical traditions, yet display a remarkably strong degree of consensus about the parameters of hegemonic male consciousness.

Drawing on interview material from her clinical practice as a psychotherapist, Nancy Chodorow (1978, 1991) deconstructs traditional psychoanalysis to identify gendered dynamics. Chodorow argues that gender differences in structures of consciousness are the outcome of the child's development of self in gendered social arrangements: men are absent from nurturing in a culture in which gender is employed as an important organizer of social relations. Distinctions in boys' and girls' early experiences lead to development of gender differences in sense of self and relationship to others: men develop a highly individuated sense of self in opposition to others and an abstract orientation to the world; connection represents a threat of loss of identity. Women develop a connected sense of self embedded in concrete relationships.

Chodorow's analysis, like many in feminist theory, gives little attention to the dynamics of class. Her clinical data is heavily biased toward the affluent and highly educated clientele of psychoanalysis, which no doubt explains her analytic focus on the male breadwinner/female housewife nuclear family form (see Fraser & Nicholson, 1988 and Lorber, Coser, Rossi, & Chodorow, 1981, for critiques). Although the limits of her analysis imply caution should be used in extending it beyond the relatively privileged, those same biases make Chodorow's work particularly useful for identifying the consciousness of the privileged. Work in the literature on class and consciousness uses words such as individualistic and abstract to refer to the world view of capitalists, in contrast with a more collective and concrete orientation in the working class (e.g., Bulmer, 1975; Mann, 1973; Mueller, 1973; Oilman, 1972). Integrating these two perspectives, we see an argument that the consciousness of economically privileged, European–American men is more likely to be abstract and individuated than the world views of men from less privileged classes and most women.

Mary O'Brien (1981, 1989) uses a historical materialist approach to argue that differences in consciousness are the product of differences in the ways men and women have historically taken intentional action regarding the material imperative to reproduce. To assert social control over a process in which they are marginalized, men in the European traditions she is describing have historically dominated it from outside by creating and controlling the public sphere. Men's flight from involvement in the work of reproduction poses a challenge to the legitimacy of their control over the process, a challenge that is addressed by according the male role as much social significance as possible. This, O'Brien argues, is why the dominant patriarchal world view of reproduction emphasizes intercourse and male potency and overlooks the value of reproductive labor.

Having distanced themselves from the concrete community of people who do the work of caring, O'Brien says, men have created an abstract community in the state. Alienated from the concrete history of human continuity across generations, men have constructed and sanctified a history of abstractions and ideas. The culture they have reproduced encourages a consciousness that is abstract, oppositional, and discontinuous.

O'Brien's analysis resonates with the argument that the capitalistic structuring of work leads those in privileged class locations to be more individualized and have a more abstract orientation to the world (Hartsock, 1985; Lukacs, 1971).

In summary, whether looking through the lens of psychoanalysis or historical materialism, feminist scholars identify a privileged masculine consciousness that is highly abstract, individuated, oppositional, hierarchical, oriented to control rather than nurturance. These themes resonate with Hartsock's description of a masculine orientation to dominate, Haraway's critique of disembodied knowledge, Smith's account of the abstract masculine existence, and Collins' depiction of an elitist and authoritarian epistemology. They also seem to run through the kinds of criticisms feminists have raised against mainstream sociological theory and research.

4. FEMINIST CRITIQUES OF MAINSTREAM SOCIOLOGY

Although within sociology empirical research and social theory have long been operating on separate intellectual planes, there are interesting epistemological parallels between them. Empirical research is dominated by positivist epistemology with its assumption that science is independent of the social order in which it is conducted, that knowledge is neutral, and that the observer has no particular point of view but rather merely reports empirical findings (Farganis, 1986). Ring (1987) describes the epistemology guiding classic social theory as a Hegelian empiricism with similar background assumptions. Mainstream social theory constructs knowledge as a stream of ideas handed down through generations of key thinkers who, although singled out as individuals, apparently rise above their historical circumstances of gender, race, and class to identify universal rationality (Connell, 1997; Smith, 1990; Sprague, 1997). In both theory and research, then, our attention is drawn to an objective knowledge; the contribution of the knower to the shape of the knowing is invisible (Keller, 1983; Smith, 1990).

Feminists have criticized sociological theory and empirical research to varying degrees, as is true of feminist critiques of science more generally (Keller, 1982). Some merely say that research practice has been distorted by its gender biases. Critiques in this vein point to the relative lack of women scholars, the choice of questions that address the problems of men not women, designs that exclude women, and interpretations of data from a masculine point of view (American Sociological Association, 1980). The problem from this perspective is that science has not been scientific enough. Other critiques, however, dispute the very notion of science and scholarship as a distinctive social enterprise; the claim here is that science is as socially constructed as any other element of culture (Rosser, 1988). We see these critiques expressing five kinds of concerns: (1) objectivity as process and as outcome, (2) authority in the research relationship, (3) a hierarchical ordering of the social, (4) the predominance of problematic analytic categories, and (5) the role of sociology in broader relations of social domination.

4.1. The Critique of Objectivity

Many feminists challenge the degree to which social research has succeeded in being objective and some feminists go beyond challenging whether objectivity is attainable to questioning whether it is even desirable. Likewise, Longino (1989) argues that what we hold to be rational is variable but systematically so: "The only constant in Western philosophers' thinking about rationality and masculinity is their association (p. 263)." Contemporary notions of objectivity, and the approach to rationality it represents are, it is argued, the expression of masculine psychic needs to dissociate from allegedly feminine subjectivity and the need to control the threat of connection by connecting through domination (Haraway, 1978; Hartsock, 1985; Keller, 1982).

The first step in the practice of scientific objectivity is to carve up the continuity of lived experience to create objects, or facts, to investigate (Shiva, 1995; Smith, 1990). Thus, "facts" are the outcome of practices that strip phenomena of the processes that generate them, processes that are deeply social. For example, we see gender as the attribute of a person rather than as the outcome of institutionalized social practices (Lorber, 1994) or of a specific form of social organization (Acker, 1990; Sprague, 1991, 1996).

The processes that "uncover" these facts are then hidden from view (Latour & Woolgar, 1979). For example, experimental methods are held to be the best way to test a hypothesized causal relationship because of the way they control for threats to internal validity (Cook & Campbell, 1979). Yet, Fine and Gordon (1989) argue that another way to describe the practices of experimentalists makes them look irrational, obsessed with the need to purge their data of the messiness of real life, and of the contaminating details such as people's race, gender, and class. Similarly, social psychologists construct the impression of a self independent of context by posing questions such as the Twenty Statements Test's "Who Am I?" and treating the answers as facts—the self is what the test has created, not a constant in people's lived experience (Markus & Kitayama, 1991).

4.2. Authority in Social Research

Traditional research carves a sharp distinction between investigator and investigated and creates a hierarchical relationship between the two. Several feminists criticize scientific authority as the conceptual domination of researched by researcher: investigators turn subjects, the people they are trying to understand, into objects who are not capable of enlightening scholars about social phenomena (Collins, 1989, 1990). Mies (1993) sees danger in dichotomizing subject and object: objectifying what we study can lead to justifying exploitation and abuse, for example in the development of technologies that pillage the earth of its resources and in experimentation on Jews in Nazi concentration camps.

Feminist approaches have tended to replace models of control and domination with those of connection and nurturing. An early feminist assumption was that research relationships were to be constructed as collaborations (Cook & Fonow, 1986). The researcher's goal is to give voice to women who have been denied it, to express their experiences in their terms (McCall & Wittner, 1989). Feminists in this camp maintain that establishing a relationship of mutuality between researcher and subject of research through self-revelation and emotional support produces better data and richer understanding (Oakley, 1981).

More recently feminists have debated the limits of even a feminist investigator's empathic ability. Scholars of color have pointed out the degree to which our understandings of the dynamics of gender have been generalizations from the experience of economically privileged white women, evidence that investigators impose their own cultural frameworks on the data (Dill, 1983; hooks, 1981; King, 1988). As a consequence of studying the oppressed through the lens of the privileged, oppressed people are objectified, represented not as people "like us" but rather as the "other." Minh-ha (1993) is describing anthropology as an ideology of imperialism but could be talking about social science more generally when she says that what presents itself as an attempt to learn the essence of human nature is in practice "mainly a conversation of 'us' with 'us' about 'them'" (1993, p. 125).

The reaction against "othering" has led some feminists to wonder if it is legitimate to study a category over which one has privilege, for men to study women or for whites to study people of color (see Edwards, 1990; Harding, 1993). Thus, although an early theme in feminist criticism of Sociology was its failure to be sensitive to the pervasiveness of gender as a social force (Cook & Fonow, 1986), more recent critiques have been reluctant to push any abstract category, including gender, very far.

4.3. The Hierarchy of the Social

One recurrent theme in feminist critiques of sociology is that we tend to employ a pattern of selective attention that creates a systematically masculine stratification of social life: what is important is what men do (e.g., see readings in Rosaldo & Lamphere, 1974). O'Brien (1981), for example, observes that we have theories that address nearly all of the major aspects of our biological existence: providing for our physical needs (Marxism), sexuality (psychoanalysis), and death (theology and secular philosophy). The stark omission, O'Brien notes, is serious consideration of the social and philosophical issues concerning human reproduction. Social theory has placed a low priority on understanding the nurturance and development of people, and on emotions and intimate relationships in general (cf. Aptheker, 1989; Hillyer, 1993; hooks, 1990; Ruddick, 1980; Smith, 1987). Feminists criticize sociological accounts for essentially ignoring what Aptheker (1989) calls "the dailiness" of ordinary lives, the struggle to preserve quality of life for your family in the face of exploitation and oppression, to hold on to and nurture a positive sense of self in a culture that demeans and devalues you.

A pervasive, and much criticized, assumption in social theory is that the public and the private constitute distinct spheres of social life and that the public sphere, defined as the official economy, the polity, and related institutions, is more social than the private (cf. Fraser, 1989; Mies, 1986; Pateman, 1983; Sprague, 1997, 1988; Ward, 1993). Ironically and tellingly, the public sphere has then been constructed in such a way that it appears to be unpopulated. Interpersonal relationships at work and emotional aspects of work itself are excluded from view (Hochschild, 1983). Social analyses that address large-scale social institutions from the perspective of abstract structures are labeled "macro," and are understood as most important. Those that focus on individuals and the relationships among them, with an attention to process, are "micro," too often with the connotation of substantive and intellectual triviality and a suspicious drift toward psychology.

The dichotomous, hierarchical opposition of public to private represents relationships as if they did not occur within and were not constrained by social structures and makes the structures seem as if they had more reality than the regular relationships among people that constitute these structures (Smith, 1990).

4.4. Dominant Analytic Categories

Another line of feminist critique has been to challenge the analytic categories that dominate sociological discourse. The category that has drawn the most critiques from feminists is the logical dichotomy, the tendency to make sense of phenomena by opposing them to others in a construction that is represented as mutually exclusive and exhaustive (Jay, 1981). The pattern runs through the history of hegemonic Western European social thought: mind/body, city of God/city of man, capitalist/worker, nature/culture, nature/nurture, public/private, macro/micro, structure/agency (Alway, 1995; Harrison, 1985; hooks, 1994; O'Brien, 1981; Tuana, 1983).

The artificiality of these dichotomies is exposed when one tries to identify the line that demarcates them empirically. Rich (1976) notes that even a dichotomy that seems as basic as me/not-me is transcended in the experience of a pregnant woman in relationship to the fetus developing within her. The demarcating line between public and private is exposed as constructed when considering state-imposed policies such as those on sexuality, reproductive freedoms, and violence within marriage (Sprague, 1988). In fact, many of our most contentious political struggles can be seen as debates over where to draw the border between public and private in a particular domain of life (e.g., sexuality, parents' rights, school prayer, assisted suicide).

Another analytic approach common to social theory that has come under the criticism of feminists is what might be called abstract individuation. That is, individuals are seen in isolation from and unconnected with their interpersonal, historical, or physical contexts (Sprague, 1997). A prime instance of this abstract individuation is the tradition of representing people as instances of just one facet of the complex intersecting social relations through which they live their lives, for example, gender, or race, or class (Collins, 1989; Dill, 1983; hooks, 1981; King, 1988). In the process we tend to fall back to hegemonic categories: when we talk about class we see men, when we talk about race we see men, and when we talk about gender we see whites (King, 1988). Another example of a decontextualized individual is the model of rational man [sic], an actor who establishes priorities and sets out to achieve them, evaluating options along the way in terms of an abstract value system or their utility to goal attainment (e.g., Coleman, 1992). The image hides from us the degree to which most of us, especially women, find daily life an ongoing juggling of competing responsibilities emerging from the complex web of our most important relationships (England, 1989; Risman & Ferree, 1995; Smith, 1987).

We fracture people even further into abstract attributes or personality traits. The practice has been, for example, to ask whether women are more passive or use different language than men, rather than asking whether women are more often observed in relationships in which they are relatively powerless in structural terms and are responding strategically to that structural condition (Sherif, 1979). The tendency to explain problematic social behavior by resorting to syndromes (ADHD, alcoholism, chronic fatigue) and searching for biological, even genetic sources carries the fragmentation of the human being even further (Conrad, 1975, Haraway, 1993; Szasz, 1971).

Seeing the social world through logical dichotomies and abstract individuation has generated conceptual distinctions that distort the lived experience of many people. The disciplinary division of "work" and "family" hides the work of caring for a family and the nurturing aspects of many jobs (Cancian, 1985; Cancian & Oliker, 1999; Oakley, 1974). The distinction between work and leisure is not applicable to the vast majority of women who work the double shift of paid work and unpaid domestic labor (Hartmann, 1981;

Hochschild, 1989). The distinction between paid and domestic labor is not adequate to describe the lives of many women, particularly women of color, who have historically been blocked from any waged work other than paid domestic labor and child care (Collins, 1986; Glenn, 1992).

4.5. The Role of Sociology in Social Domination

What is the relationship between knowledge producers and the larger society in which they work? In ironic contrast to Marx and Weber, who were deeply engaged in the politics of their time, the intellectual projects of contemporary theorists are typically understood as individual quests to maintain, develop, and extend the stream of ideas. The role of theorist is one of detachment, only abstractly connected, if at all, to any sense of responsibility to their communities. Sociological theory has, to say the least, not been engaged in contemporary policy debates; its ranks have provided us with few public intellectuals, particularly in the United States.

Mainstream sociological research has a better record of permeating public policy debates. Still, some feminists charge that sociological research is constructed in ways that facilitate social domination. Harding has observed that "there isn't such a thing as a problem without a person (or groups of them) who have this problem: a problem is always a problem for someone or other" (1987, p. 6). She, like Smith, argues that social scientists tend to ask questions of those whose job it is to manage people, not questions of regular folks (cf. Fine, 1994). For example, we are much more likely to ask who is likely to abuse drugs than to ask what we would need to change about social organization to make drug use less likely.

Feminists have from the beginning rejected Positivism's ideal of a "value-free" science, arguing instead that the goal of research must be to help the oppressed understand and fight against their oppression (Cancian, 1992; Cook & Fonow, 1986; Harding, 1987; Mies, 1993; Smith, 1987). Cancian (1992) argues that an important feminist methodology is to engage in participatory action research (PAR), working with feminist organizations on problems they have identified in a process they control. In addition to directly supporting feminist politics, Cancian submits, involvement in PAR actually generates better data by providing localized knowledge about a subject and incorporating quasi-experimental evidence.

Asking questions in hegemonic ways can have deadly consequences, as Treichler's (1993) analysis demonstrates. As the Center for Disease Control was collecting data on early AIDS cases, the organizing framework was based on the kind of person who got AIDS, not on the kind of practices that made one vulnerable to it. The result was the "4 H's" typology of risk: homosexuals, hemophiliacs, heroin addicts, and Haitians. Further, in developing their list, some codes were "master," taken as more salient than others: gay or bisexual men who injected drugs were coded by their sexuality, not their intravenous drug use. The hegemonic view that sexual practices justify categorizing people and mark sexual minorities as deviant led to analyses that no doubt created a false sense of invulnerability to this deadly disease in those who were excluded from the typology, notably women.

An important aspect of knowledge as social domination is the prevalence of "studying down," rather than "studying up." Fine reports, for example, that when her graduate students wanted to study upper-class white women they could not find much literature on them. Fine observes that these women are not surveyed by social science agencies and there is no "scholarly discourse on their dysfunctionality" (1994, p. 73). Some have argued that the powerless are aware that official knowledge, rather than serving their interests, often works against them. This makes them appropriately suspicious of, and therefore less than authentic with, researchers (Edwards, 1990; Mies, 1993).

Another way that both theoretical and empirical sociology serves the dominant interests is by communicating in a discourse that is so opaque that colleagues cannot read one another across subspecialties, much less across disciplines (Sprague, 1997; Sprague & Zimmerman 1993). By using the passive tense and speaking in high levels of abstraction, we hide the agency both of those we study and of ourselves as researchers (Hochschild, 1983; hooks, 1994). "The author's activity is displaced in methods, which act on the data for the author" (Paget, 1990, p. 158). The scientific voice also creates emotional distance. Paget (1990) notes the scholarly norm that discredits speakers who show feelings like caring, anger, or outrage in the context of scholarly communication. The text is also severed from actual human experience, distancing the reader from caring about it, much less feeling compelled to do something about it. Hochschild (1983) draws the parallel between the emotion work of creating a dispassionate text and the steps taken in an autopsy to make sure medical students will be distanced from the humanness of the corpse so as not to be disturbed by what is being done to it. The norm of disinterested discursive style, Paget (1990) notes, conflicts with the goal of communicating about knowledge, which is to persuade.

In summary, feminist critiques of sociological practices point to a detachment, both intellectual and emotional, from the daily work of keeping life going, from the people whose lives we study, and from popular political discourse. They take issue with the way we have organized the production of knowledge, noting that it serves more to control people than to nurture them. They challenge a reliance on dichotomy and high levels of abstraction. The terms of the feminist critique roughly parallel the description of privileged masculine consciousness. As Smith (1990) says, if sociology has a subject, it is a male subject.

5. FEMINIST ALTERNATIVES

Feminists struggling with these concerns have developed some innovative and insightful strategies. Arguing that interviewing is a hierarchical form of social relationship, feminists have worked to make that relationship more democratic. They have given interviewees control over the topics to be discussed, incorporated self-disclosure on the part of the investigator, built an interviewing relationship over time, and asked interviewees for feedback on investigators' interpretations of interviews (e.g., Acker, Barry, & Esseveld, 1991; Edwards, 1990; Fine, 1994). Acker and her colleagues (1991) use these techniques of connection with research subjects in strategic alternation with more detached discussions among investigators, and report that this approach leads to more nuanced understanding of respondents' experience and particularly of how people change in response to social conditions.

Traditional notions of what is and is not data have also been reformed. It has been standard practice in interviewing, for example, to attribute the interviewee's hesitations and questions such as "Do you know what I mean?" to inarticulateness. DeVault (1990) uses them as indicators that male-dominated language does not capture women's experience. She finds these breaks in fluid speech are fruitful gateways for exploration of the distinctive experiences of women.

The concept of valid data has been expanded in other directions as well. Aptheker (1989) and Collins (1990) respond to the elite selection bias of the usual documentary evidence by expanding the field of data to include the "documents" of those who are marginalized in official discourse. They analyze the messages, for example, in the lyrics of blues songs, poetry, quilts, and gardens, as well as oral histories and kitchen table conversations. These sources organize experience in the language of daily life, making it possible to generate analytic categories that come closer to everyday categories. For example, DeVault (1991) found that women's own word for what they do for their families, "feeding," combined the notions of work and love in a way that more formal terms such as "domestic labor" or "caring" could not (cf. Yeatman, 1984).

5.1. Stereotypical Feminist Ways of Knowing

By the light of accumulated stereotypes about what makes research feminist, it would be easy to conclude that feminist research involves academic feminists using qualitative methods to reveal the insights of nonacademic women. In fact, distrust of systematic measurement practices, the desire to recognize the subjectivity of those we study, and the commitment to empowering women and other oppressed people have led many feminists to doubt that feminist research could be quantitative (Cook & Fonow, 1986; Edwards, 1990; Stacey & Thorne, 1985). Reducing complex thoughts and experiences to measurable variables, these feminists argue, sacrifices any sense of the whole, objectifies those we study, and makes it likely that the investigator's interpretations will support their continued domination. The assumption is that the only way to do feminist research is to begin with the lived experience of women and that requires the use of qualitative methods (e.g., Edwards, 1990). This reliance on qualitative methods coincides with the reluctance to make strong, broad theoretical claims, which would necessarily be generalizing from the experience of a few.

However, other feminists point out the interpersonal and political problems inherent in this stereotype of feminist research. Interpersonally, there is an inescapable power imbalance between researchers and subjects of research: researchers have choices over their vulnerability to risk, can leave the situation when they want, can choose what to report and what to disregard, and have ultimate control over the final interpretation (Risman, 1993; Sprague & Zimmerman, 1989; Stacey, 1988; Thorne, 1983).

Qualitative researchers' reliance on personal contact in long, unstructured interviews tends to draw on small, homogeneous samples and is unlikely to represent people with inflexible jobs, heavy domestic responsibility, and less verbal confidence (Canon, Higgenbotham, & Leung, 1988). Qualitative researchers have also asked the questions and reported in the categories of the hegemonic elite (Fine, 1994). Quantitative methods provide some counter to both of these sources of bias through the use of representative sampling, giving respondents control over the coding of their answers, and explicit, replicable analyses (Jayaratne & Stewart, 1991; Sprague & Zimmerman, 1989).

Perhaps the most negative consequence of an overreliance on qualitative methods is what academic feminists have failed to contribute to a broader political movement. The point of feminist scholarship is to end the oppression of women. The purpose of knowledge is empowerment, in the sense of enabling purposive action. Thus, we create knowledge about society in order to support people's ability to work together to make the lives they want and need. This has implications for what we call an adequate understanding. Social change requires a roadmap, a theory of what is and what should be (Fraser, 1989; Sprague, 1997). Democratic social change requires some degree of consensus on that roadmap, which means that scholars need to retain criteria for establishing truthfulness that do not erode "the persuasiveness of our conclusions" (Alcoff, 1989, p. 99). Reporting the numbers can be socially empowering, indicating degrees and/or pervasiveness of inequality. Telling the stories of people's experiences can be personally empowering, supporting empathy and feelings of connection. Persuasive arguments in public discourse require both.

The explanations oppressed people want and need, then, are probably not about pure truth as much as they are about how to improve their lives (Harding, 1987). To understand those lives, women and other oppressed people need to be able to see how their problems are the expression of social relations of domination (Acker et al., 1991; Mies, 1993); how the irrationalities they confront are the product of the workings of "relations of ruling" that are external to their daily experience (Smith, 1987). Also, since women are of many races and classes and vary in sexuality and in physical and mental abilities, ending the oppression of women requires working against all forms of oppression (Harding, 1991). Precisely because the social organization of knowledge has been dominated by an elite few, the explanations people need are not the ones they are likely to employ spontaneously (Sprague & Zimmerman, 1989). In other words, the goal hooks (1994) proposes for feminist pedagogy is not restricted to the classroom: to help people see the connections between their daily experience and the analytic frameworks we offer.

If we need some basis for judging among competing knowledge claims, if we know that scholars are limited by their experience and their particular interests, and if we cannot blindly trust the spontaneous consciousness of any particular group, what options are open to us? We believe that a stronger, more nuanced reading of feminist standpoint epistemology suggests a way out of the trap.

6. IMPLICATIONS OF FEMINIST STANDPOINT EPISTEMOLOGY

Feminist standpoint epistemology transforms both the subject and the object in the epistemological relation. The subject is a collective one, strategically built on diverse experience. The object is a socially constructed one: the meaningful, coordinated activity of people in daily life is what is real. The relationship between the subject and object of knowing is historically specific and dialectic. The metaphor for feminist methodology is bridging.

6.1. The Subject Is Collective

The epistemological advantage of women is that a sexist society puts them in contradictory social locations, constructing them as both subject and object. They have an "outsider within" advantage and can play on the friction created by the gap between their experience and the conceptual frameworks that are available to make sense of it (Collins, 1990; Harding, 1991; Smith, 1987, 1990). But there is no single privileged standpoint. Because women exist in a wide diversity of social locations based on class, race, ethnicity, sexuality, disability, etc., the subject of feminist knowledge is multiple and sometimes conflicting (Bar On, 1993; Bhavnani, 1993; Haraway, 1988; Herding. 1991). Further, women cannot be the only generators of feminist knowledge; men in oppressed locations need to understand themselves and contribute to our understanding of their experience from a feminist perspective (Harding, 1991).

If knowledge is grounded in experience, then we need to recognize and take into account the understandings generated by people in their daily life. However, we also need to recognize the authority that comes from the experience of having studied something, having reflected on it, and paid attention to the reflections of others. That is, those who are scholars have to take responsibility for the authority of our experience.

6.2. The Object of Knowledge Is Socially Constructed

The "thing" we are trying to know from the point of view of standpoint epistemology is more than a constructivist nuanced text but less than a positivist open book. Haraway argues that we need to see the world not as an object over which we have control but as a "coding trickster" with which we try to have conversations using the methods, or "prosthetic devices," that help us see (1988, p. 594). The world, including humanity, is socially constructed, a product of history and technology (Haraway, 1993, 1990).

To say that something is socially constructed is not to say that it is not real—merely a language game as social constructivists say—but rather that it is the product of human activity. If the grounding of knowledge is our experience in the empirical world, then practical activity, the work of supporting continued human life, is the bedrock of that knowledge. Human activity in the world is real, O'Brien (1989) submits, and so are the structures that humans devise to meet the challenges they face. If categories are used to direct human social action, those categories are real because we are making them real: race, gender, and class are real in their consequences (Thomas & Thomas, 1928).

Nonetheless, if something is socially constructed it is not the durable, detached web of lawlike operations that positivism conjures up. It is—and we are—historically specific and changeable. Rational knowledge is open ended because the world is open ended.

6.3. The Relation between Subject and Object Is Dialectical

Given these notions of subject and object, how are feminist scholars to work on producing knowledge? Feminist standpoint epistemology implies that the relation between knower and object of knowledge is, as Ring (1987) says, dialectical. Our methodology must center on "the dynamic between human experience and the material world" and assume "constant change, that is, human history" (Ring, 1987, p. 766). Truth, Ring (1987) argues, will be attained when we have finally eliminated the conflicts between subject and object, expressed as the oppositions of ideas to material reality, of consciousness to history, of thought to action. That is, truth is the outcome of our acting in the world freely, consciously, and intentionally. Since we are a diverse community, truth implies working consensus on practical activity.

To do this, we must strategically structure our discourse, both listening to and learning from the perspectives of diverse subjects and diverse scholars. This is why Haraway's notion of splitting—making a connection between two knowers in one self—is important. Mies makes a similar point in calling us to "conscious partiality," balancing empathy with distancing in a "limited identification with the subjects of research" (1993, p. 38).

Because each standpoint and what can be seen from it is limited, we need to construct our discourse as critical conversations. Longino (1989) argues that we construct a context for feminist rationality by removing the obstacles to criticism. These obstacles include repetitive and unproductive debates about background assumptions, overemphasis on novelty and originality at the expense of critical work, and restriction of our communities to those who share the same background assumptions. We have to find the courage to disagree with "correct" positions and/or persons and the commitment to engage one another to work toward consensus. We must be willing to disagree and use those disagreements as an access to better understanding.

Finally, feminist standpoint epistemology implies that academics are not individual producers of texts and courses. We are in a social relationship with the rest of the community. In the social division of labor, we are cultural workers; our product is understandings. Because the community in which we live and work is organized in relations of social domination, the work we do—the questions we pursue, the strategies we use to gather and interpret evidence, and the forms and venues in which we communicate our findings—connects us in valenced ways with either the powerful or with the oppressed. If we continue to do it as it has been done before, we will connect with the powerful, not the oppressed, whether we choose to consciously or not.

REFERENCES

Acker, J. (1990). Hierarchies, jobs, bodies: A theory of gendered organizations. *Gender & Society, 4,* 139–158.

Acker, J., Barry, K., & Esseveld, J. (1991). Objectivity and truth: Problems in doing feminist research. In M. M. Fonow & Cook, J. A. (Eds.), *Beyond methodology: Feminist scholarship as lived research* (pp. 133–153). Bloomington: University of Indiana Press.

Alcoff, L. (1989) Justifying feminist social science. In N. Tuana (Ed.), *Feminism and Science* (pp. 85–103). Bloomington: Indiana University Press.

Alway, J. (1995). The trouble with gender: Tales of the still-missing feminist revolution in sociological theory. *Sociological Theory, 13,* 209–228.

American Sociological Association Committee on the Status of Women in Sociology. (1980). *Sexist biases in sociological research: Problems and issues.* Footnotes (January). Washington, D.C.

Aptheker, B. (1989). *Tapestries of everyday life: Women's work, women's consciousness, and the meaning of daily experience.* Amherst: University of Massachusetts Press.

Bar On, B. 0. (1993). Marginality and epistemic privilege. In L. Alcoff & E. Porter (Eds.), *Feminist Epistemologies* (pp. 831–100). New York: Routledge.

Bechtel, W. (1988). *Philosophy of science: An overview for cognitive science.* Hillsdale, NJ: Lawrence Erlbaum.

Bhavnani, K. K. (1993). Tracing the contours: Feminist research and feminist objectivity. *Women's Studies International Forum, 16,* 2: 95–104.

Bulmer, M. (1975). *Working-class images of society.* London: Routledge & Kegan Paul.

Cancian, F. (1985). Gender politics: Love and power in the private and public spheres. In A. S. Rossi (Ed.) *Gender and the life course.* New York: Aldine.

Cancian, F., & Oliker, S. (1999). *Gender and care.* Thousand Oaks, CA: Pine Forge.

Cancian, F. M. (1992). Feminist science: Methodologies that challenge inequality. *Gender & Society, 6,* 623–642.

Canon, L. W., Higgenbotham, E., & Leung, M. L. A. (1988). Race and class bias in qualitative research on women. *Gender & Society, 2,* 451–462.

Chodorow, N. (1978). *The reproduction of mothering: Psychoanalysis and the sociology of gender.* Berkeley: University of California Press.

Chodorow, N. (1991). *Feminism and psychoanalytic theory.* New Haven, CT: Yale University Press.

Coleman, J. S. (1992). The rational reconstruction of society. *American Sociological Review, 58,* 1–15.

Collins, P. H. (1986). Learning from the outsider within: The sociological significance of black feminist thought. *Social Problems, 33,* 514–530.

Collins, P. H. (1989). The social construction of black feminist thought. *Signs: Journal of Women in Culture and Society. 14,* 745–773.

Collins, P. H. (1990). *Black feminist thought: Knowledge, consciousness, and the politics of empowerment.* London: HarperCollins.

Connell, R. W. (1997). Why is classical theory classical? *American Journal of Sociology, 102,* 1511–1557.

Conrad, P. (1975). The discovery of hyperkinesis: Notes on the medicalization of deviant behavior. *Social Problems, 23,* 12–21.

Cook, T. D., & Campbell, D. T. (1979). *Quasi-experimentation: Design and anaylsis for field settings.* Boston: Houghton Mifflin.

Cook, J. A., & Fonow, M. M. (1986). Knowledge and women's interests: Issues of epistemology and methodology in feminist sociological research. *Sociological Inquiry, 56,* 2–29.

DeVault, M. L. (1990). Talking and listening from women's standpoint: Feminist strategies for interviewing and analysis. *Social Problems, 37,* 96–116.

DeVault, M. L. (1991). *Feeding the family: The social organization of caring as gendered work.* Chicago: University of Chicago Press.

Dill, B. T. (1983). Race, class, and gender: Prospects for an all-inclusive sisterhood. *Feminist Studies, 9,* 131–150.

Edwards, R. (1990). Connecting method and epistemology: A white woman interviewing black women. *Women's Studies International Forum, 13,* 477–490.

England, P. (1989). A feminist critique of rational-choice theories: Implications for sociology. *The American Sociologist, 20,* 14–28.

Farganis, S. (1986). Social theory and feminist theory: The need for dialogue. *Sociological Inquiry, 56,* 50–68.

Fine, M. (1994). Working the hyphens: Reinventing self and other in qualitative research. In N. K. Denzin & Y. S. Lincoln (Eds.), *Handbook of Qualitative Research* (pp. 70–82). Thousand Oaks, CA: Sage.

Fine, M., & Gordon, S. M. (1989). Feminist transformations of/despite psychology. In M. Crawford & M. Gentry (Eds.), *Gender and thought: Psychological perspectives* (pp. 146–174). New York: Springer-Verlag.

Foucault, M. (1972). Truth and power. In C. Gordon (Ed.), *Power/knowledge: Selected interviews and other writings, 1972–1977,* edited by Colin Gordon (pp. 109–133). New York: Pantheon.

Fraser, N. (1989). *Unruly practices: Power, discourse and gender in contemporary social theory.* Minneapolis: University of Minnesota Press.

Fraser, N., & Nicholson, L. (1988). Social criticism without philosophy: An encounter between feminism and postmodernism. *Communication, 10,* 345–366.

Genova, A. C. (1983). The metaphysical turn in contemporary philosophy. *Southwest Philosophical Studies, IX,* 1–22.

Glenn, E. N. (1992). From servitude to service work: Historical continuities in the racial division of paid reproductive labor. *Signs: Journal of Women in Culture and Society, 18,* 1–43.

Harding, S. (1993). Reinventing ourselves as other: More new agents of history and knowledge. In L. Kauffman (Ed.), *American feminist thought at century's end: A reader* (140–164). Cambridge, MA & Oxford, UK: Blackwell.

Haraway, D. (1978). Animal sociology and a natural economy of the body politic, part I: A political sociology of dominance. *Signs: Journal of Women in Culture and Society, 4,* 21–36.

Haraway, D. (1988). Situated knowledges: The science question in feminism and the privilege of partial perspective. *Feminist Studies, 14,* 575–599.

Haraway, D. (1994). A manifesto for cyborgs: Science, technology, and socialist feminism in the last quarter. In L. Nicholson (Ed.), *Feminism and Postmodernism* (pp. 580–671). Durham, NC: Duke University Press.

Haraway, D. (1993). The biopolitics of postmodern bodies: Determinations of self in immune system discourse. In L. S. Kauffman (Ed.), *American feminist thought at century's end: A reader* (pp. 199–233). Cambridge, MA: Blackwell.

Harding, S. (1987). Introduction: Is there a feminist method? In S. Harding (Ed.), *Feminism and Methodology* (pp. 1–14). Bloomington: Indiana University Press.

Harding, S. (1991). *Whose science? Whose knowledge? Thinking from women's lives.* Ithaca, NY: Cornell University Press.

Harrison, B. W. (1985). The power of anger in the work of love: Christian ethics for women and other strangers. In C. S. Robb (Ed.), *Making the connections: Essays in feminist social ethics.* Boston: Beacon.

Hartmann, H. (1981). The family as the locus of gender, class, and political struggle: The example of housework. *Signs: Journal of Women in Culture and Society, 6,* 366–394.

Hartsock, N. C. M. (1983). The feminist standpoint: Developing the ground for a specifically feminist historical materialism. In S. Harding & M. Hintikka (Eds.), *Discovering reality: Feminist perspectives on epistemology, meta-physics, methodology and philosophy of science* (pp. 283–310). Dosdrect, Holland: D. Reidel.

Hartsock, N. C. (1985). *Money, sex, and power: Toward a feminist historical materialism.* Boston: Northeastern.

Hillyer, B. (1993). *Feminism & disability.* Norman, OK: University of Oklahoma Press.

Hochschild, A. R. (1983). *The managed heart: Commercialization of human feeling.* Berkeley: University of California Press.

Hochschild, A. R. (1989). *The second shift: Working parents and the revolution at home.* New York: Viking.

hooks, b. (1981). *Ain't I a woman? Black women and feminism.* Boston: South End Press.

hooks, b. (1990). *Yearning: Race, gender, and culture politics.* Boston: South End Press.

hooks, b. (1994). *Teaching to transgress: Education as the practice of freedom.* New York: Routledge.

Howard, J. A., & Hollander, J. (1997). *Gendered situations, gendered selves.* Thousand Oaks: Pine Forge.

Jay, N. (1981). Gender and dichotomy. *Feminist Studies, 7,* 38–56.

Jayaratne, T. E., & Stewart, A. J. (1991). Quantitative and qualitative methods in the social sciences. In M. M. Fonow & J. A. Cook (Eds.), *Beyond methodology: Feminist scholarship as lived research* (pp. 86–106). Bloomington: Indiana University Press.

Jussim, L. (1991). Social perception and social reality: A reflection-construction model. *Psychological Review, 98,* 54–73.

Keller, E. F. (1982). Feminism and science. *Signs: Journal of Women in Culture and Society, 14,* 42–72.

Keller, E. F. (1983). *A feeling for the organism: The life work of Barbara McClintock.* New York: Freedman.

King, D. (1988). Multiple jeopardy, multiple consciousness: The context of black feminist ideology. *Signs: Journal of Women in Culture and Society, 14,* 42–72.

Latour, B., & Woolgar, S. (1979). *Laboratory life: The social construction of scientific facts.* New York: Sage.

Longino, H. E. (1989). Feminist critiques of rationality: Critiques of science or philosophy of science? *Women's Studies International Forum, 12,* 261–269.

Lorber, J. (1994). *Paradoxes of gender.* New Haven: Yale University Press.

Lorber, J., Coser, R. L., Rossi, A., & Chodorow, N. (1981). On the reproduction of mothering: A methodological debate. *Signs: Journal of Women in Culture and Society, 6,* 482–514.

Lovibond, S. (1989). Feminism and postmodernism. *New Left Review 178* (Nov/Dec).

Lukacs, G. (1971). *History and class consciousness.* Cambridge, MA: MIT Press.

Mann, M. (1973). *Consciousness and action among the Western working class.* New York: Macmillan.

Mannheim, K. (1936). *Ideology & Utopia.* NY: Harcourt, Brace, & World.

Markus, H., & Kitayama, S. (1991). Culture and the self: Implications for cognition, emotion, and motivation. *Psychological Review, 98,* 224–253.

Mascia-Lees, F. E., Sharpe, P., & Cohen, C. B. (1989). The postmodern turn in anthropology: Cautions from a feminist perspective. *Signs: Journal of Women in Culture and Society, 15,* 7–33.

McCall, M. & Wittner, J. (1989). The good news about life histories. In H. Becker & M. McCall (Eds.), *Cultural studies and symbolic interaction.* Chicago: University of Chicago Press.

Mies, M. (1986). *Patriarchy and accumulation on a world scale: Women in the international division of labor.* Atlantic Highlands, NJ: Zed Books.

Mies, M. (1993). Feminist research: Science, violence, and responsibility. In M. Mies & V. Shiva, *Ecofeminism.* London: Zed Books.

Minh-ha, T. T. (1993). The language of nativism: Anthropology as a scientific conversation of man with man. In L. S. Kauffman (Ed.), *American feminist thought at century's end: A reader* (pp. 107–139). Cambridge, MA: Blackwell.

Mueller, C. (1973). *The politics of communication: A study in the political sociology of language, socialization, and legitimation.* New York: Oxford University Press.

Oakley, A. (1981). Interviewing women: A contradiction in terms. In H. Roberts, *Doing feminist research* (pp. 30–61). London: Routledge and Kegan Paul.

Oakley, A. (1974). *The sociology of housework.* New York: Pantheon.

O'Brien, M. (1981). *The politics of reproduction.* Boston: Routledge and Kegan Paul.

O'Brien, M. (1989). *Reproducing the world: Essays in feminist theory.* Boulder, CO: Westview.

Ollman, B. (1972). Toward class consciousness next time: Marx and the working class. *Politics & Society, 3,* 1–24.

Paget, M. A. (1990). Unlearning to not speak. *Human Studies, 13,* 147–161.

Pateman, C. (1983). Feminist critiques of the public-private dichotomy. In S. I. Benn & G. F. Gaus (Eds.), *The public and private in social life.* New York: St. Martin's.

Rich, A. (1976). *Of woman born: Motherhood as experience and institution.* New York: Norton.

Ring, J. (1987). Toward a feminist epistemology. *American Journal of Political Science, 31,* 753–772.

Risman, B. (1993). Methodological implications of feminist scholarship. *The American Sociologist, 24,* 15–25.

Risman, B., & Ferree, M. M. (1995). Making gender visible. American *Sociological Review, 60,* 775–782.

Rosaldo, M., & Lamphere, L. (Eds.) (1974). *Woman culture, and society.* Stanford: Stanford University Press.

Rosser, S. V. (1988). Good science: Can it ever be gender free? *Women's Studies International Forum, 11,* 13–19.

Ruddick, S. (1980). Maternal thinking. *Feminist Studies, 6,* 342–367.

Sherif, C. W. (1979). Bias in psychology. In J. A. Sherman & E. T. Beck (Eds.), *The prism of sex: Essays in the sociology of knowledge.* Madison: University of Wisconsin Press.

Shiva, V. (1995). Reductionism and regeneration: A crisis in science. In M. Mies & V. Shiva (Eds.), *Ecofeminism* (pp. 22–35). London: Zed Books.

Smith, D. E. (1979). A sociology for women. In J. A. Sherman & E. T. Beck (Eds.), *The prism of sex: Essays in the sociology of knowledge.* Madison: University of Wisconsin Press.

Smith, D. E. (1987). *The everyday world as problematic: A feminist sociology.* Boston: Northeastern University Press.

Smith, D. E. (1990). *The conceptual practices of power: A feminist sociology of knowledge.* Boston: Northeastern University Press.

Sprague, J. (1988). The other side of the banner: Toward a feminization of politics. In S. S. Brehm (Ed.), *Seeing female: Social roles and personal lives.* New York: Greenwood.

Sprague, J. (1991). Gender, class, and political thinking. *Research in Political Sociology, 5,* 111–139.

Sprague, J. (1996, August). Seeing gender as social structure. Paper presented at the annual meeting of the American Sociological Association, New York.

Sprague, J. (1997). Holy men and big guns: The Can[n]on in social theory. *Gender & Society, 11,* 88–107.

Sprague, J., & Zimmerman, M. K. (1989). Quantity & quality: Reconstructing feminist methodology. *The American Sociologist, 20,* 71–86.

Sprague, J., & Zimmerman, M. K. (1993). Overcoming dualisms: A feminist agenda for sociological methodology. In P. England (Ed.), *Theory on gender/feminism on theory* (pp. 255–280). New York: Aldine De Gruyter.

Stacey, J. (1988). Can there be a feminist ethnography? *Women's Studies International Forum, 11,* 21–27.

Stacey, J. & Thorne, B. (1985). The missing feminist revolution in sociology. *Social Problems, 32,* 301–316.

Szasz, T. S. (1971). The sane slave: An historical note on the use of medical diagnosis as justificatory rhetoric. *American Journal of Psychotherapy, 25,* 228–239.

Thomas, W. I., & Thomas, D. (1928). *The child in America.* New York: Knopf.

Thorne, B. (1983). Political activist as participant-observer: Conflicts of commitment in a study of the draft resistance movement of the 1960's. In R. Emerson (Ed.), *Contemporary field research: A collection of readings* (pp. 216–234). Prospect Heights, IL: Waveland Press.

Treichler, P. A. (1993). AIDS, gender, and biomedical discourse: Current contests for meaning. In L. S. Kauffman (Ed.), *American feminist thought at century's end* (pp. 281–354). Cambridge, MA: Blackwell.

Tuana, N. (1983). Re-fusing nature/nurture. *Women's Studies International Forum, 6,* 621–632.

Ward, K. B. (1993). Reconceptualizing world system theory to include women. In P. England (Ed.), *Theory on gender/feminism on theory* (pp. 43–68). New York: Aldine De Gruyter.

Weedon, C. (1987). *Feminist practice and poststructuralist theory.* Cambridge, MA: Basil Blackwell.

Yeatman, A. (1984). Gender and the differentiation of social life into public and domestic domains. *Social Analysis, 15,* 32–49.

CHAPTER 3

Similarity and Difference

The Sociology of Gender Distinctions

CYNTHIA FUCHS EPSTEIN

I. INTRODUCTION

The division of the world into female and male is found in all societies. Views that there are female and male natures, intellects, understandings, and moralities infuse religious and secular paradigms. *No less so* do views of sex differentiation pervade many scientific frameworks. Thus, from the most accepting to those whose mission it is to be critical, females and males are believed to possess distinctive innate and acquired attributes, and they are seen as demonstrating different kinds of behavior. Such attitudes and perceptions may be found in all societies and at all class levels. However, those qualities regarded as distinctly male or female may vary considerably from society to society, or group to group. In addition, invidious comparisons between those attributes regarded as female and male are common.

The creation and maintenance of boundaries defining "female" and "male" is part of a larger process whereby groups and categories of people create and perpetuate distinctions defining themselves and identifying "others." Boundaries serve to create and maintain inequalities in many spheres (Lamont & Fournier, 1992), as we see in the near universal subordination of women to men in public life. Thus, boundaries defining female and male (as well as "women" and "men," and "masculine" and "feminine") are widely accepted, although the justifications vary and are debated in religious, secular, and scholarly spheres. The underlying assumptions for the categories are to be found in the everyday experiences of individuals, in popular culture, as well as in academic scholarship.

CYNTHIA FUCHS EPSTEIN • Department of Sociology, Graduate Center, City University of New York, New York, New York 10036
Handbook of the Sociology of Gender, edited by Janet Saltzman Chafetz. Kluwer Academic/Plenum Publishers, New York, 1999.

Yet despite continuity in acceptance of the categories, today there are serious challenges to "difference" ideologies and frameworks by a substantial number of social scientists who have tested these ideas against people's actual behavior, and by individuals, many of them in social movements, who refute the basis for invidious comparison that accompanies them.

The ideas that are challenged are those that assume men and women act and feel differently with regard to a wide range of behaviors and characteristics [e.g., emotionality, intelligence, conversational style, ambition, abstract thinking, or technical skill (Epstein, 1985)]. No one disputes that males and females possess different reproductive biological organs and secondary sexual characteristics, but there is considerable debate as to whether they have different basic emotional and cognitive attributes as well. This chapter argues that inborn differences, or even early socialization, may account for differences between individuals, but not between the entire categories of male and females. Although certain qualities may cluster among groups of females and males, they are rarely seen exclusively in one or the other. Furthermore, the qualities seen as male or female in one society may be different in another, or vary in different social classes, ethnic groups, or even families. With other social scientists, I note that patterned differences may be identified for females and males, but suggest that they are socially constructed, and occur when females and males are conditioned or persuaded to act differently than each other; the patterns may persist but they could be changed through policy, law, and different opportunity structures. I refer to this as the "minimalist perspective," as juxtaposed to an "essentialist" emphasis on basic gender difference.

It is important to differentiate between *sex* differences, which refer to biological differences, and *gender* differences, which refer to the characteristics men and women (or boys and girls) exhibit (such as young women's choice of school teaching or young men's choice of business administration as occupations) that are socially constructed through socialization, persuasion, social and physical controls in the law, in the workplace, in the community, and in the family. The social construction of gender is achieved by obvious and subtle controls that assign females and males to social roles and social spheres where it is believed they should be. These rules (either set by law or traditions) are supported by values that specify such ideas as "Women's place is in the home taking care of children," or "Real men will fight to protect their family and country." In all societies many people believe that females and males come by their social roles naturally, for example, that women's personalities are very different from men's in that they are naturally nurturant and thereby desire to become mothers and to care for children, and men are naturally aggressive and thus are always anxious to get ahead in business. However, no society leaves the assignment of roles to chance. There is considerable social input into making the roles assigned to women and men seem attractive to the sex to which they apply and unattractive to the sex that is regarded as unsuited to them (Epstein, 1988).

Culture plays an important role in the choice of life options and integrates with economic explanations. Concepts such as "women's work" or "men's work" are powerful in making jobs seem suitable or unsuitable for females and males, and strongly contribute to the "sex labeling" of occupations (Oppenheimer, 1968). In this way, concepts act as symbolic boundaries. Further, structural boundaries reinforce conceptual boundaries, such as rules prohibiting men and women from doing work deemed fit only for the other.[1]

Women are certainly positioned differently than men in most societies. However, the extent of this varies considerably (Chafetz, 1984), and probably results primarily from formal and informal social controls ranging from micro-interactions to formal policies.

The sociological literature shows that there are strong disparities between men and women in access to opportunities and resources, for example, more women than men engage in low-prestige and low-paying work (Acker, 1990; Epstein, 1970; Reskin & Hartmann, 1986); women participate less in political decision-making roles (Epstein & Coser, 1981); they assume more responsibilities for the performance of family duties (Hochschild, 1989; Rossi, 1964; Shelton & Daphne, 1996) and charitable work; and women gain less recognition for their contributions to society whether they are paid or nonpaid. Social psychological studies alert us to the connection between social position and the cognitive and personality outcomes that we observe.

Cognitive differences between females and males have been largely disputed by social scientists using new statistical techniques, such as meta-analysis, as I shall show later. Personality differences are more difficult to assess. Males and females do seem to show some differences with regard to certain behaviors, such as aggressiveness, although, as I shall indicate later, such conclusions often are made on the basis of studies with limited generalizability.

Today, social scientists and the lay public are interested in the extent to which sex and gender distinctions are basic (e.g., part of their "essential" nature) because of biology or psychological processes set early in life, or result primarily from structural and cultural boundaries, and are therefore amenable to alteration through changes in law, policy, and opportunity. The essentialist belief in basic sex differences has consequences for women's position in life and has justified men's dominance and women's subordination in most spheres of social life, yet it is unsupported empirically. There are far more variations within each sex with regard to talents, interests, and intelligence than there are between each sex, although it often does not look that way. The small gender differences that show up in tests measuring certain cognitive abilities (including math and verbal skills) are perceived to be representative of the entire population of males or females, rather than the small percentages difference they are, while within-gender differences are minimized or overlooked (Baumeister, 1988; Feingold, 1988; Hyde, 1981, cited in Briton & Hall, 1995). Furthermore, men and women are often forced to display the qualities of behavior, interest, or appearance that a person of their sex is supposed to possess naturally (Goffman, 1977), which may situate them differently (or segregate them) in the family (Goode, 1964) and at work (Reskin & Hartmann, 1986). For example, women do smile and laugh more than men according to one study (Hall, 1984), but this may be because women receive positive feedback when they smile, and elicit anger when they do not.

Unlike other categories of people who are regarded as "other," such as people of color, females and males do not live in different residential communities but often cluster in separate domains within them, such as workplaces and places of recreation (Epstein, 1992; Huffman & Velasco, 1997; Bielby & Buron, 1984). Not only is gender segregation often not seen as problematic to men or women, but many people believe that a higher order, a higher morality, the good of society, or the good of each sex is served by such differentiation (e.g., advocates of single-sex schools for girls, and segregated male military schools) (Epstein, 1997; Vojdik, 1997).

Such perspectives often come from a cultural bias toward simple explanations and a bias toward consistency between ideals and behavior. Thus, most people believe there is common agreement with regard to what they mean by "man" or "woman." Yet, as with all broad categories, popular definitions and perceptions may vary considerably.

Interpretations of the "typical" male and female (as is the case with other broadly defined categories) also vary according to age, class, and the special circumstances of interaction. Assessments of what is typical and appropriate may be perceived differently in different settings. For example, in all-female groups women may act in a bawdy manner without fear of being perceived as unfeminine, although bawdiness is usually regarded as male behavior, as Westwood (1985) illustrates in her study of British hosiery company workers. Yet, in some all-male groups (e.g., in some sports and war), men often demonstrate tender and caring behavior that might be interpreted as unmanly in mixed groups. When atypical gendered behavior becomes public, however, redefinition or reinterpretation about what is "normal" for a particular category of people may occur.

Women are not only different within their gender but they may also manifest different behaviors and traits in their private lives. That is, aspects of the "selves" may include differing and even contradictory components (Crosby, 1987; Haraway, 1991; Nicholson, 1990; Spence, 1984, 1985; Thoits, 1983); or, they may show different personalities in playing different roles. Those scholars who write as if there were a single feminine self assume that women and men play out their roles with reliable consistency, as if they possessed monotone personalities. They, like many laypeople, prefer the idea of a whole person with a body and personality that match. Some believe it to be an indicator of integrity. The notion of oneness not only also fits cultural stereotypes but fits neatly into scientific categories that one can run through a computer or code on a data sheet (such as running "sex" as a variable with the underlying assumption that being male or female accounts for a behavior). Sometimes, of course, roles are consistent, or people may highlight one dimension of their "self" for political or personal purposes (e.g., Hispanic or senior citizen) to differentiate themselves from others. Thus, people may concentrate on the traits that differentiate themselves from others, not those they share, a common problem in the politics of many institutions such as the family and the workplace.

2. EXPLAINING THE ORIENTATION TOWARD DIFFERENCES

The persistent emphasis on differences between women and men with regard to their basic nature (cognitive and emotional)—whether it comes from scholars who identify themselves as feminists or nonfeminists—may be attributed to various factors: (1) inattention to the evidence that shows similarities rather than differences between the sexes; (2) incomplete and inappropriate models, such as those assuming a sex-differentiated "human nature"; (3) an ideological agenda; (4) confusion between cause and effect, such as regarding sex segregation at work as "natural" rather than the result of biases that force men and women into sex-labeled occupations; and (5) focus on sex as the primary determining variable that explains behavior. Many of these overlap (Epstein, 1991).

It was only in the last 30 years that essentialism was seriously questioned, although as far back as Plato, there have been philosophers who suggested that women might be fit to fill positions held by men (Okin, 1979). The goal of many feminist scholars who became interested in gender studies beginning in the late 1960s was to question assumptions about women's and men's attributes, to actually measure them, and to objectively report observed differences between women and men. Many also wished to uncover inequalities faced by women and men that related to their sex. Many scholars motivated by the women's movement viewed the mission as one oriented to documenting Betty Friedan's (1963) assumption that "Women were really people—no more, no less" (Johnson, 1996).

No one argued then or argues now that women and men experience the same treatment or live the same kinds of lives, although women and men are found to face many of the same privileges and restrictions of their race, ethnicity, education, and class peers.

However, the explanatory frameworks used to account for observed differences and gender inequality have evoked contentious debate. These debates have been engaged in within an historical context in which the reporting of sex differences is often biased in the direction of differences rather than similarities in characteristics and behavior between the sexes. Scholars, as well as journalists, proclaim difference (no matter how small) in ways that imply mutually exclusive qualities between women and men. Sometimes this work suggests support for the perspective that women are inferior to men because they are not capable of engaging in the activities with which men are associated (such as working as engineers and scientists), but more recently it has been used to suggest women's superiority in some attributes such as morality (see Epstein, 1988 for a discussion of this). Further, studies that report support for conventional views of women's personalities and abilities are more often reported by the press (James, 1997), but those indicating positive outcomes of women's unconventional behavior (such as superior mental health of employed women compared to homemakers) have been given short shrift by the media. The journalist and scholar Susan Faludi (1991) reports that the press failed (and continues to fail) to report paradigms and studies showing gender similarity and the positive outcomes of the changing social roles of women and men. Yet, in recent years, "difference" has been accepted by some feminist scholars and used to evaluate women as better than men on issues of "connection" or empathy (Gilligan, 1982), or to suggest that they have alternative modes of understanding (Belenky, Clinchy, Goldberger, & Tarule, 1986; Tannen 1990). I have detailed the evidence elsewhere (Epstein, 1988) for rejecting the view that women have basically different abilities than men. This view is also supported by comprehensive reviews by Aries (1996), Hyde (1990a), Feingold (1992), and by Tavris (1992), who wisely concluded in her book *The Mismeasure of Woman*, ". . . women are not the better sex, the inferior sex, or the opposite sex." Yet there has been an enormous spillover effect from the work of Gilligan (1982), who suggested that women are predisposed to an ethic of "care," into many fields, including legal studies and educational theory. The idea that women have "different way of knowing" has been developed also by social philosophers, such as(Harding 1986), and by the historian of science Keller (1978) (see also Belenky et al., 1986).

2.1. Theoretical Frameworks

The perception of gender distinctions (or gender similarities) is affected by theoretical frameworks and the assumptions inherent in them. Of course, theoretical frameworks affect all human thinking, including the very idea of gender—a theoretical construct. But analysts must be alert to the biases any framework brings to the way we see and understand behavior. Because gender analysis has been drawn from a number of theoretical camps, in the sciences and the humanities, as discussed in Chapter 1, observations of males and females and the conclusions drawn from them are often influenced by the theoretical bias of the researcher. Implicit in any of these gender are assumptions regarding how essential or minimal are gender differences in humans. Some theoretical perspectives have met serious challenge because empirical data do not support them; some are not tested or even testable; and some seem promising. To illustrate, some of the theories that shape perception of male and female differences are theories of personality (e.g., trait theory, which suggests people have particular stable personality traits); learning and development (e.g., socialization theory, which is oriented to the individual's internalization of qualities such as nurturance because of early experiences); sociobiology (e.g., biological determinism); evolutionary biology (the notion that natural selection accounts for gender differences); social construction (the model that points to the impact of social factors on an individual's behavior and attitudes); and postmodern theories (which offer a model of human nature as one of multiplicity and change). The perspective of this chapter that seems most supported by research is the social constructionist model and part of the postmodern paradigm. I outline some of the arguments below.

One of the most salient examples of the orientation toward a "difference" or "essentialist" view is the sociobiological approach. As in the case of race (Gould, 1981), social scientists have often sought to support claims to women's inferiority (Fausto-Sterling, 1985) or "otherness" with regard to cognitive and emotional factors (Sherman & Beck, 1979). For example, recently biological determinants of sex differences, particularly brain studies (see Fausto-Sterling, 1997), have been referred to for the purpose of showing the source of reported differences ranging from test scores in mathematics to "women's ways of leading." Rosener (personal communication) claims that biology is part of the explanation for the different leadership styles she argues women demonstrate (1995). Yet, as Tavris (1992) points out, citing the work of Hyde and Linn (1988) and other scientists, there are virtually no differences in the attributes that brain differences are supposed to explain, and more importantly, the brain studies themselves have been criticized for their method: some are done on rats; some are done with mentally ill or otherwise aberrant subjects; all use tiny samples; and few highlight the overlaps between the sexes (Fausto-Sterling, 1997). Furthermore, general tests of intelligence have never found differences between the sexes on measures of I.Q. (Hyde, 1990a).

Holding that women and men act differently because they use basically different reproductive strategies has many challengers among both social and physical scientists. For example, Stephen Jay Gould (1997), a paleontologist who is well known for his critique of biases within science regarding race, disputes the idea that the causes of behavior such as occupational choice may be traced to reproductive strategies of a species. Donna Haraway (1989), a philosopher of science, also offers a useful illustration of the pitfalls of these adaptions. She has shown that when feminist sociobiologists use evolutionary models to explain present-day differentiation of duties and responsibilities, as well as other behavior, they are exercising the same biases as antifeminist male anthropologists. Building on Haraway, one can identify feminist scholars whose essentialist models are derived from male scholars with biased outlooks regarding sex differentiation, such as can be found in the work of anthropologist Sandra Hrdy (1977), whose work builds on that of E. O. Wilson, the sociobiologist.

The difference or essentialist model is less prevalent among the postmodern theorists. They reject absolute categories and reject dichotomous thinking, such as that which places "male" and "female" into mutually exclusive categories. Their perspective orients the scholar to recognizing the differences between people within groups, and their multiplicity of experience and character. However, they reject the methods of science and thus confirmation or disconfirmation by the use of research. The paradigm that emphasizes the "social construction" of human behavior incorporates the benefits of the postmodern approach and allows for support or rejection of hypotheses about sex difference and similarity through observation of actual behavior in the empirical world.

2.2 Methodological Problems

Because scholarship on difference is framed by researchers and theorists in many fields and orientations, outcomes of this research are not consistent. However, "findings" are often cited across fields without attention to the methodology that produced them. Not only do some scholars use different standards of proof, but many also deny that proof is even obtainable; yet nevertheless they make claims for basic differences. For example, many scholars from the humanities look for "evidence" in support of their theories from personal experience or the narratives of individuals, and some use novels or myths as "evidence." The theories of humanists have been adopted by a number of social scientists with an essentialist orientation. Many psychologists use laboratory experiments with college students and generalize to the entire category of male or female, but their findings may not be applicable to males and females who are older or who have not gone to college. Similarly, experiments with rats may not apply at all to the human experience with its heavy overlay and interaction with culture.

Although always suggestive, for generalizability the findings of all studies should be approached with caution, especially with regard to their claims. Personal experiences may be unreliable because they may be recalled in a way that fits a normative picture. The use of objective techniques (however much they fall short of an objective ideal), such as the use of sampling with control groups, reveals much more similarity than difference between men and women.

As noted previously, similarities between the sexes with regard to cognitive and emotional qualities have been shown by analyzing clusters of studies and assessing their relative merit. Most of these (but not all; see Eagly 1996) show not only extensive between-sex overlap but that differences once found at the ends of distributions have been decreasing with time. The changes are probably due to changes in social conditions (Feingold, 1992), such as the opening of training and job opportunities for women in fields from which they were largely excluded in the past. In fact, it may be that claims of large-scale differences between females and males in the past have had the social consequence of contribution to whatever differences can still be identified through tests, observations, and other indicators because of a self-fulfilling prophecy (Merton, 1957).

2.3. Meaningful Differences

The magnitude of difference in behaviors preferences of men and women is also important to consider when establishing how meaningful a quality might be in differentiating the sexes. Usually, large differences would be the measure of meaningful sex variation. However, studies might show *statistically* significant differences when the actual differences might be quite tiny, and thus *socially* insignificant. Thus, the purpose of the inquiry ought to determine social and not merely statistical "significance." As an example, politicians are usually concerned with otherwise insignificant differences between groups because a tiny difference can determine the results of an election. From a social science point of view, it is the case that between-sex differences are far smaller than within-sex differences. For example, in the 1996 congressional race, 55% of women voted for Democrats compared to 46% of men, according to a New *York Times* poll (*New York Times*, November 7, 1996)—the notable "gender gap." The focus is on the 9% who voted differently and not the 91% who voted the same. In the 1992 Presidential race the disparity between males and females was even less—6%. As Hout and his colleagues point out (Hout, Brooks, & Manza, 1995), class differences in voting patterns are twice as large as gender difference.

Most reporting that refers to "women" and "men" as unitary collectivities does not make note of the spread of preferences or capacities found within each category and is usually based on very small percentage differences. The reporting indicates an ignorance of how to interpret a statistical distribution. It refers to categories as if they were mutually exclusive, such as "black" and "white." As in the case of sex, in defining a racial category, many of the same kinds of conceptualizations are understood to be real representations that are in fact not descriptive of individuals within a group (e.g., racial laws in some states classified individuals as black when they had one-sixteenth black "blood," and could have more easily described such an individual as "white.") Similarly, using small differences to distinguish "male" or "female" behavior (often not more than a two or three percentage point difference) or any observed characteristic is enough to convince people that a particular man or woman can be located at the end of the distribution where those small differences lie (Sherif, 1979).

The problem of the method used to assess difference is great, as can be illustrated through examination of the research in two areas, leadership and aggression.

It is widely believed that women and men have different styles of leadership (Rosener, 1995), although subordinates of women leaders (Aries, 1996. p. 67) and colleagues (Dobbins & Platz, 1986; Nieva & Gutek, 1982; Powell, 1988) indicate that they exhibit the same range of behaviors as men. However, some studies show differences whereas other studies show great similarities in the behavior of women and men. Some studies also indicate that individuals' reports on their own behavior is inconsistent with the reports of observers. For example, in one study women reported that they demonstrated less dominant and competitive behavior than men, but the researcher observed no difference (Snodgrass & Rosenthal, 1984). Other studies found no gender differences in dominance and competitive behavior (Chanin & Schneer, 1984; Rahim, 1983). In another study (Korabik, Baril, & Watson, 1993) experienced managers of both sexes failed to reveal differences in self-reported conflict management style. However, *self-reports* about preferred conflict management style are poor predictors of actual behaviors (Baril, Korabik, Watson, Grencavage, & Gutkowski, 1990; Bass, 1990; Korabik et al., 1993). It is interesting that among 374 studies of leadership styles, only 37 were observation studies and the rest were self reports (Aries, 1996).

Even when the management styles of women and men are similar, there may be a perception, and consequent evaluation of that style based on gender. For example, the study of gender differences in management style and leadership effectiveness by Korabik et al. (1993) revealed that although there were no gender differences in their management styles, male and female supervisors were evaluated differently.

Thus we see that although some men and women leaders report similar styles, others do not. Moreover, in many cases individuals report behaviors that conform to stereotypes for their sex, although observers report that they behave quite differently than their self-descriptions suggest. Because there is widespread belief in difference, many books and conferences are devoted to women's presumed different styles (see Belenky et al., 1986; Gilligan, 1982; Harding, 1986; Keller, 1978; Rosener, 1995; Smith, 1990; Tannen, 1990). Furthermore, male superiors believe women behave differently and thus offer them jobs in human resources and exclude them from staff jobs that would give them the experience to rise in a corporation (Kanter, 1977).

Aggression has been identified as a trait found to occur more in males than in females (Maccoby & Jacklin, 1974). It is important to examine this concept because aggression is supposed to account for the domination of men in the power structure of society and in their relations with women.[2] Yet the very term "aggression" refers to a loose collection of behaviors and attitudes that are often unrelated to one another [as a review by Brinkerhof and Booth (1984) points out]. Predation, initiative, competition, dominance, territorial behavior, and hostility are among the behaviors considered in studies of aggression. A comprehensive review of hundreds of experimental studies on adult female and male aggression by Frodi, Macaulay, and Thome (1977) shows that it is difficult to make a clear assessment of differences on all these dimensions. First, the studies are not all comparative and over half are studies of men only. Many studies tend to be of children or college students; however, it has been found that differences noted between boys and girls, especially preschoolers, tend to become small by adulthood (Hyde, 1990a). An overview (McKenna & Kessler, 1974) shows that of more than 80 general and theoretical discussions of aggression in books and journals, references to studies do not specify the magnitude of differences and whether they are large enough to warrant characterizing women as less aggressive than men. Using a meta-analysis, Eagly (1987), has shown that aggressive and nonaggressive behaviors are tied to social roles (see also Hyde, 1990); men are required to show aggression, when, for example, they work as soldiers or even bonds tradesmen, but women are required *not* to be aggressive as teachers or nurses. Nonetheless, men working as social workers are required to be nonaggressive and women firefighters are supposed to charge into dangerous situations. Other studies show that women are often the same or harsher than men with regard to verbal aggression or hostility (Epstein, 1988).

2.4. Choice of Indicators

"Male" and "female" or "masculine" and "feminine" are general concepts. How they are defined, however, varies in different groups and different cultures. Definitions of male and female often follow stereotypes and may not accurately reflect the actual behavior of men and women or the range of behaviors exhibited by each sex. For example, women are regarded as emotional and men as unemotional in American society, yet the opposite is true in Iran (Epstein, 1970). Probably both sexes, in all societies, manifest "emotion" publicly according to the norms that encourage or discourage such behavior and may not reflect their internal states.

"Male" and "female" are usually based on a composite of factors that seem to go together. For example, women are believed to be nurturant, self-sacrificing, and sociable. There is an underlying assumption that these are stable characteristics and consistent across situations. Many researchers assume stability when they study people at a particular point in time. This constitutes a bias in perspective that reflects the fact that individuals may vary over the course of a day, or a lifetime. It fails to recognize that individuals are complicated, and their behaviors are not necessarily consistent.

2.5. Attributes as Interactional

Most behavior identified as male and female is seen in interactional settings (Deaux & Major, 1987; Ridgeway, 1997). Individuals in interaction may put pressure on each other to conform to an expected behavior that is in line with a stereotype. For example, in my research on women in the legal profession, some women attorneys reported that male judges ordered them to smile. Of course, they had to respond to the order. This shows how the status and rank of the person with whom a female or male is interacting will cause adjustments in behavior. Females and males may therefore act quite differently when alone; with an age peer; or with a person who is older, with more power, and in a norma- tively defined role relationship. How "female" or "male" one is may very much depend on one's interactional partner. Thus, research centered on single events rarely captures the complexity created by the feedback effects of individuals in social settings.

2.6. Inattention to Variables Other than Sex

Power, age, social status, and ethnicity all structure how gender-related behaviors play out, and how they also vary in particular situations and historical periods. Therefore, researchers need to go beyond identifying the sex of a person and note the other charac- teristics that may account for his or her behavior. For, women who hold positions of authority are usually more assertive than women in powerless jobs. This is not because they become "like men," but because the positions require assertiveness and women learn to act in that manner. Similarly, men in subordinate positions are not "like women" when they defer to a boss; they are playing their role according to the rules. Characteristics thought of as "male" or "female" are also embedded in a life cycle and time framework. In any concrete situation in which maleness and femaleness are being assessed or ob- served, females and males of particular ages are being observed. Yet women and men often exhibit very different characteristics at young, middle, and older ages, women often gaining in authority, and men often demonstrating more nurturing qualities after retire- ment or during child rearing years if they take on child care responsibility (Brody, 1997).

The issue of the life course is of great interest because, as noted previously, many studies that define male and female behavior are based on studies conducted in schools or laboratory settings (using school-aged children or young adults). Yet youngsters may change their "character" either through maturity, developmental changes, socialization, or acquisition of different roles.

2.7. Impact of Social Change on Gendered Behavior

Many views about females and males are tied to particular time periods. Tastes change in popular culture and with them, men's and women's behavior. Some practices change because legal changes open women's options. Other practices change because social con- ditions permit or repress certain kinds of activity. This phenomenon is too extensive to document in this chapter, but a few examples illustrate the social construction of what are believed to be immutable sex-related behaviors.

As noted earlier, aggression is taken to be a defining characteristic of males and not females, yet its expression changes in form and incidence in different time periods. Norms regarding the appropriateness of women expressing aggression also change in societies (Zuckerman, Cole, & Bruer, 1991). Many feminist historians have documented women's assertiveness in labor union activity at certain points and places in history (Costello, 1991; Turbin, 1992; Vallas, 1993), yet traditionally public collective action was associated with men and not women.

Interest in and use of guns may be a good indicator of aggression and assertiveness. The use of firearms has been considered a natural prerogative of men, and people look to its sources in the play behavior of boys who often "turn" objects into guns and play "cops and robbers." This is used as an example of men's "natural" aggression and women's "natural" passivity. Nonetheless, girls and women now are more interested in guns than in the past. A significant number take target practice and they comprise 15% to 20% of the National Rifle Association membership (Epstein, 1995a). That organization even elected its first woman president in 1995 (*Wall Street Journal*, May 22, 1995). In Israel, women, who are conscripted into the army, commonly train with guns (unless they are religiously orthodox, in which case they are not required to join the army).

In the United States, women and men choose to go to medical and law schools in almost equal numbers (Epstein, 1993), a radical change from the time when it was believed that women did not enjoy the conflict of the courtroom (Epstein, 1993) or the challenge of the operating room (Lorber, 1984). In 1963 women constituted only 3.8% of entering classes in professional schools (Epstein, 1981) and it was believed that women had no interest in medicine or the law. Today, they constitute more than 40% of students in these professional schools.

Conversations between men and women have received much attention recently, partly because of Deborah Tannen's (1990) popular book, *You Just Don't Understand,* which was on the best seller lists for many weeks. This book implies that basic differences lead to a "two worlds" approach to gender interaction. However, studies of speech show that men's and women's voices are influenced by social expectations and social control. For example, a recent article in the *Wall Street Journal* reported that "elevator girls" in Japan who had been required to speak in a high-pitched voice deemed essentially feminine are now permitted to speak in a more natural, lower-moderated tone.

2.8. The Multiple Attributes of Men and Women

In associating various qualities with men or women, little attention is given to how much of the attribute they display. Yet people may display normative attributes for their sex in situations that demand it and not in situations in which they are not subject to controls. Furthermore, they may internalize some of the characteristics in greater or lesser amounts. It is entirely possible for a person to feel or be a little nurturant or very nurturant; one can be aggressive occasionally or very often and one may alternate such qualities in one's various social roles, or even within the same role. For example, some mothers may be loving toward their children, looking out for their interests, yet harsh and punitive in their use of corporal punishment, depending on the cultural practices of their group [as shown in the research of Waters (1994) concerning Jamaican culture].

People also exhibit certain attributes depending on the situation in which they are located and the person(s) with whom they are interacting. Organizational settings may also elicit certain traits and behaviors in people who behave differently elsewhere. In a study based on the performance evaluations of managers, researchers attempted to assess whether person-related variables or situation-related variables were related to judgments about managers (Giannantonio, Olian, & Carroll, 1995). The findings showed that although subjects' ratings were affected by the manager's communication or leadership style, they were not affected by the manager's gender.

2.9. Inappropriate "Halo Effects" of Gender Practices

Noting differences (however measured) in one sphere is used to suggest comparable differences in another, even though they may be irrelevant. Here the issue of *causality* is seriously questionable. The following illustrations point out the illogical and contradictory nature of several widely held "common sense" and scholarly assertions about the cause of gender differences in some kinds of behavior.

Many women and men explain women's low representation in the ranks of management as associated with their lack of experience in playing team sports. This comes from a romantic notion about the ennobling nature of team sports and an ideal of cooperation that is associated with them. Probably a more meaningful correlate is the fact that men in power tend to network with male friends they may have made while engaging in sports. In this example, the key variable is networking, not sports participation. Yet other scholars claim that women practice connection and are not as individualistic as men, resulting in men becoming leaders because they are more individualistic (Chodorow, 1978; Gilligan, 1982), an explanation that contradicts the supposed benefits of team sports.

Some explanations of the reason that clerical roles are overwhelmingly filled by women is that they are regarded as able to endure monotony because of the repetitious tasks they perform in the home and because of their docility. Yet their sewing ability is not regarded as useful in potential roles as surgeons, as it might well be if there were a more compelling logic to these associations.

3. TOWARD A MORE INFORMED MODEL OF GENDER

3.1. Gender Attributes as a Function of Social Roles

Position in the life course, and the social roles one assumes as a result, are probably the most important factors in determining the behavior of men and women, boys and girls, not their genes or early socialization. Most of the attributes affixed to a particular gender usually refer to attitudes and behaviors that are normatively prescribed and controlled in the context of the social roles people acquire (or have thrust upon them); they may become internalized, but even if they are, they may be activated or deactivated for the moment, or forever. For example, Arlie Hochschild (1983) and other social scientists have pointed to the "emotion work" that women are compelled to do in certain occupational roles, such as showing nurturant behavior and friendliness in their jobs as flight attendants, nurses, and waitresses. Hochschild shows that women often need to be trained to exhibit caring behavior. These behaviors are also reinforced by supervisor and peer social control.

3.2. Social Control

An overview of research on gender distinctions indicates that there has been insufficient attention to the impact of social controls on behavior in the models explaining observed sex differences. As I pointed out in *Deceptive Distinctions* (1988), when there are no controls enforcing sex-role behavior (or they are loosely applied), individuals fulfill their roles idiosyncratically, or in accordance with a variety of influences, such as their economic interests or education. This reality leads to enormous variation within each sex or gender category. However, controls on behavior—punishments for deviation—may result in patterned behavior that is then regarded as "normal," which means that individuals are unaware of how superficial and variable many attributes associated with each sex are.

4. CONCLUSION

Gender boundaries are maintained by feminists and antifeminists, scholars and laypersons alike. None of us is free from them. It is no wonder that our scholarship is oriented toward finding them. The means of boundary maintenance may appear to be mechanical and physical, but they are always conceptual and symbolic. Boundaries are reinforced in the unnoticed habits and language of everyday life, vigilantly attended to by family and friends, business associates, and colleagues. Control in the way we think is exercised at the micro-level and at the level of the group or society, through symbolic behaviors such as rituals and ceremonies. There is a vast literature in psychology and sociology on the processes by which people are oriented toward classifying themselves and others according to organizing principles such as gender, using such concepts as stereotyping schemata (Deaux & Major, 1987; Bem, 1981; Merton, [1957]) and, in current cultural sociological focus, "habitus" as defined by Bourdieu (1984) and his associates in their work on cultural reproduction. Bourdieu indicates the ways in which dominated groups contribute to their own subordination because of *habitus*, for example, class-differentiated dispositions and categories of perception shaped by conditions of existence.

Entrenched in the dominant symbolic system that contributed to its reproduction are binary oppositions. As I have pointed out previously (1970; 1988), dichotomous thinking plays an important part in the definition of women as "others," as deviants, and in their self-definitions. Although they were not the first to do so, Foucault (1977), Bourdieu (1979), and other European theorists of culture define power as the ability to impose a specific definition of reality that is disadvantageous to others. According to Chafetz (1988), the gender division of labor is the central support mechanism of gender stratification, and the means by which men acquire definitional power. It is this power, she asserts, that enables men to maintain the prevailing gender status quo.

Changing times create changes in people, although not all people are similarly adaptable to change. Over the past two decades many women have changed their destinies by going into work nontraditional for their sex; taking on leadership roles; and developing a level of confidence they never had before. Men, too, have changed, sharing a certain amount of childcare, forming more equalitarian marriages, and interacting with women coworkers more easily in their own work lives.

This demonstrates that men and women are adaptable, but their adaptability is not random. Members of some social groups or categories are permitted more diversity and change. The last few decades have provided the perfect "field experiment" to indicate how variable women and men can be. More dramatically today than at any time in history, American women (and unfortunately to a lesser extent, men) are recognized as publicly and personally complex creatures. The ambivalence that greets these changes also indicates the extent to which cultural and social controls determine the ability to change and to accept the notion of change in oneself.

Sociological studies of gender should more directly relate to this experience and we should derive our models from it, not from the armchair or the paradigmatic legacies of theorists who had a stake in the status quo. The more one goes into the field to do actual research on women's behavior, the more one finds that the concepts we call male and female—or gender—comprise multiple realities for the individual and for society. Researcher should note that "male" and "female" are concepts, not things. What they are is always in question; they are not steady states. The theory and research methodology that label gender characteristics and define them according to custom without checking them against reality cheats women and men of their right to be evaluated as individuals, with an array of human characteristics.

Acknowledgments

I would like to acknowledge the research assistance of Marie Mark, Elizabeth Wissinger and Barry Davison in the preparation of this chapter. I would also like to thank Carol Crane who helped produce this manuscript while I was in residence at the Stanford Law School, 1997–98.

ENDNOTES

[1] For example, studies conducted of "Help Wanted" ads in newspapers listed according to sex, showed that women rarely explored jobs in the "Help Wanted: Male" category and men almost never looked in the "Help Wanted: Female" category (Bem & Bem, 1973).

[2] For a fuller discussion see "It's all in the mind," Chapter 4 in Epstein (1988).

REFERENCES

Acker, J. (1990). Hierarchies, jobs, bodies: A theory of gendered organizations. *Gender & Society, 4,* 139–158

Aries, E. (1996). *Men and women in interaction: Reconsidering the differences.* New York: Oxford University Press.

Baril, G. L., Korabik, K., Watson, C., Grencavage, L. M. & Gutkowksi, J. M. (1990, June). Manager's conflict resolution behaviors as predictors of leadership effectiveness. A paper presented at the meeting of the International Association for Conflict Management, Vancouver, BC.

Bass, B. M. (1990). *Bass and Stogdill's handbook of leadership.* (3rd ed.). New York: The Free Press.

Baumeister, R. F. (1988). Should we stop studying sex differences altogether? *American Psychologist, 43,* 1092–1095.

Belenky, M. F., Clinchy, B. M., Goldberger, N. R., & Tarule, J. M. (1986). *Women's ways of knowing: The development of self, voice, and mind.* New York: Basic Books.

Bem, S. L., & Bem, D. (1973). Does sex-based job advertising aid and abet sex discrimination? *Journal of Applied Psychology 3,* 6–18.

Bielby, W. T., & Baron, J. N. (1984). A women's place is with other women: Sex segregation within organizations. In B. Reskin (Ed.), *Sex segregation in the workplace: Trends, explanations, remedies* (pp. 27–55). Washington, D.C.: National Academy Press.

Bourdieu, P. (1979). *Outline of a theory of practice.* Cambridge: Cambridge University Press.

Brinkerhof, D. B., & Booth, A. (1984). Gender dominance and stress. *Journal of Social Biological Structure, 7* (2), 159–177.

Briton, N. J., & Hall, J. A. (1995). Beliefs about female and male nonverbal communication. *Sex Roles: A Journal of Research, 32,* 79–91.

Brody, L. (1997). Gender and emotion: beyond stereotypes. *Journal of Social Issues, 53,* 369–394

Chafetz, J. S. (1984). *Sex and Advantage: A comparative macro-structural theory of sex stratification.* Totawa, NJ: Rowman & Allenheld.

Chafetz, J. S. (1988). The gender division of labor and the reproduction of female disadvantage: Toward an integrated theory. *Journal of Family Issues, 9,* 108–131.

Chanin, M. N., & Schneer, J. A. (1984). A study of the relationship between Jungian personality dimensions and conflict-handling behavior. *Human Relations, 37,* 863–879.

Chodorow, N. (1978), *The reproduction of mothering: Psychoanalysis and the sociology of gender.* Berkeley, CA: University of California Press.

Costello, C. (1991). *We're worth it!: Women and collective action in the insurance workplace.* Chicago: University of Illinois Press.

Crosby, F. (1987). *Spouse, parent, worker: On gender and multiple roles.* New Haven, CT: Yale University Press.

Deaux, K., & Major, B. (1987). Putting gender into context: An interactive model of gender-related behavior. *Psychological Review, 94,* 369–389.

Dobbins, G. H., & Platz, S. J. (1986). Sex differences in leadership: How real are they? *Academy of Management Review, 11,* 118–127.

Eagly, A. H. (1987). *Sex differences in social behavior: A social role interpretation.* Hillsdale, NJ: Erlbaum.

Epstein, C. F. (1970). *Woman's place: Options and limits in professional careers.* Berkeley, CA: University of California Press.

Epstein, C. F. (1985). Ideal roles and real roles: Or the fallacy of the misplaced dichotomy. *Research in Social Stratification and Mobility, 4,* 19–51.

Epstein, C. F. (1988). *Deceptive distinctions, sex, gender and the social order.* New Haven: Yale University Press.

Epstein, C. F. (1991). What's right and what's wrong with the research on gender. *Sociological Viewpoints, 5,* 1–14.

Epstein, C. F. (1992) Tinkerbells and pinups: The construction and reconstruction of gender boundaries at work. in M. Lamont & M. Fournier. *Cultivating differences: symbolic boundaries and the making of inequality* (pp. 232–256). Chicago, University of Chicago Press.

Epstein, C. F. (1993). *Women in law* (2nd ed.). Chicago: University of Illinois Press.

Epstein, C. F. (1995a). Pistol-packing mamas. *Dissent,* Fall, 536–537.

Epstein, C. F. (with R. Saute, B. Oglensky, & M. Gever) (1995b). Glass ceilings and open doors: The mobility of women in large corporate law firms. *Fordham Law Review, LXIV,* 291–449.

Epstein, C. F. (1997). Myths and justifications of sex segregation in higher education: VMI and the Citadel. *Duke Journal of Gender Law & Policy, 4,* 101–118.

Epstein, C. F. (1999). *The anxious American.* New York: The Free Press.

Epstein, C. F., & Coser, R. L. (1981). *Access to Power: Cross-national studies of women and elites.* London: George Allen & Unwin.

Faludi, S. (1991). *Backlash: The undeclared war against American women.* New York: Crown.

Fausto-Sterling, A. (1985). *Myths of Gender: Biological theories about women and men.* New York: Basic Books

Fausto-Sterling, A. (1997). Beyond difference: A biologist's perspective. *Journal of Social Issues, 53,* 233–258.

Feingold, A. (1988). Cognitive gender differences are disappearing. *American Psychologist, 43,* 95–103.

Feingold, A. (1992). Sex differences in variability in intellectual abilities: A new look at an old controversy. *Review of Educational Research, 62,* 61–84.

Foucault, M. (1977). *The order of things.* London: Tavistock.

Friedan, B. (1963). *The feminine mystique.* New York: Simon and Schuster.

Frodi, A., Macaulay, J., & Thome, P. R. (1977). Are women always less aggressive than men? A review of the experimental literature. *Psychological Bulletin 84,* 634–660.

Giannantonio, C. M., Olian, J. D., & Carroll, S. J. (1995). An experimental study of gender and situational effects in a performance evaluation of a manager. *Psychological Reports, 76,* 1004–1006.

Gilligan, C. (1982). *In a different voice.* Cambridge: Harvard University Press.

Goffman, E. (1977). Arrangements Between the Sexes. *Theory and Society, 4,* 301–331.

Goode, W. J. (1964). *The family* (2nd ed.). Englewood Cliffs, NJ: Prentice-Hall.

Gould, S. J. (1981). *The mismeasure of man.* New York: Norton.

Gould, S. J. (1997). Darwinian fundamentalism. *The New York Review of Books, XLIV,* June 12: 34–37.

Hall, J. A. (1984). *Nonverbal sex differences: Communication accuracy and expressive style.* Baltimore, MD: The Johns Hopkins University Press.

Haraway, D. (1991). *Simians, cyborgs, and women.* New York: Routledge.

Harding, S. (1986). *The science question in feminism.* Ithaca: Cornell University Press.

Hochschild, A. R. (1983). *The managed heart: Commercialization of human feeling.* Berkeley, CA: University of California Press.

Hochschild, A. R. (1989). *The second shift: Working parents and the revolution at home.* New York: Viking.

Hout, M., Brooks, C. & Manza, J. (1995). The democrative class struggle in the United States, 1948–1992, *American Sociological Review, 60,* 805–828.

Hrdy, S. B. (1977). *The langurs of abu: Female and male strategies of reproduction.* Cambridge: Harvard University Press.

Huffman, M. L., & Velasco, S. C. (1997) When more is less: Sex composition, organizations and earning in U.S. firms. *Work and Occupations, 24,* 214–244.

Hyde, J. S. (1981). How large are cognitive gender differences? *American Psychologist, 36,* 892–901.

Hyde, J. S. (1990a), Meta-analysis and the psychology of gender differences. *Signs, 16,* 55–73.

Hyde, J. S. (1990b). *Understanding human sexuality.* New York: McGraw Hill.

Hyde, J. S., & Linn, M. (1988). Gender differences in verbal ability: A meta–analysis. *Psychological Bulletin, 104,* 53–69.

James, J. B. (1997). What are the social issues involved in focusing on difference in the study of gender? *Journal of Social Issues, 53,* 213–232.

Johnson, D. (1996). What do women want? *The New York Review of Books,* November 28, 22–28.

Kanter, R. M. (1977). *Men and women of the corporation.* New York: Basic Books.

Keller, E. F. (1978). Gender and science. *Psychoanalysis and Contemporary Thought,* September, 409–433.

Korabik, K., Baril, G. L., & Watson, C. (1993). Managers' conflict managment style and leadership effectiveness: The moderating effects of gender. *Sex Roles: A Journal of Research, 29,* 405–421.

Lamont, M., & Fournier, M. (1992). Introduction. *Cultivating differences.* Chicago: University of Chicago Press.

Lorber, J. (1984). *Women physicians: Careers, status and power.* New York: Methuen.

Maccoby, E., & Jacklin, C. (1974). *The psychology of sex differences.* Stanford: Stanford University Press.

McKenna, W., & Kessler, S. (1974, August). *Experimental design as a source of sex bias in social psychology.* Paper presented at the meeting of the American Psychological Association, New Orleans, LA.

Merton, R. K. (1957). *Social theory and social structure.* New York: The Free Press.

New York Times, November 11, 1996, Who voted for whom in the house? B3

Nicholson, L. (1990). *Feminism/postmodernism.* New York: Routledge.

Nieva, V. F., & Gutek, B. A. (1982). *Women and work: A psychological perspective.* New York: Praeger.

Okin, S. M. (1979). *Women in Western political thought.* Princeton, NJ: Princeton University Press.

Oppenheimer, V. K. (1968). The sex labeling of jobs. *Industrial Relations, 7,* 219–234.

Powell, G. N. (1988). *Women and men in management.* Beverly Hills, CA: Sage.

Rahim, M. A. (1983). A measure of styles of handling interpersonal conflict. *Academy of Management Journal, 26,* 368–375.

Reskin, B., & Hartmann, H. (1986). *Women's work, men's work: Sex segregation on the job.* Washington, D.C.: National Academy Press.

Ridgeway, C. (1997). Interaction and the conservation of gender inequality. *American Sociological Review, 62,* 218–235.

Rosener, J. (1995). *America's competitive secret: Utilizing women as a management strategy.* New York: Oxford University Press.

Rossi, A. (1964). The equality of women: An immodest proposal. *Daedalus, 93,* 607–652.

Shelton, B. A. & Daphne. (1996). The division of household labor. *Annual Review of Sociology, 22,* 299–322.

Sherif, C. W. (1979). Bias in psychology. In J. A. Sherman & E. T. Beck (Eds.), *The prism of sex: Essays in the sociology of knowledge* (pp. 93–133). Madison: The University of Wisconsin Press.

Sherman, J., & Beck, E. (Eds.) (1979). *The prism of sex: Essays in the sociology of knowledge.* Madison: University of Wisconsin Press.

Smith, D. E. (1990). *The conceptual practices of power: A feminist sociology of knowledge.* Boston, Mass.: Northeastern University Press.

Snodgrass, S. E., & Rosenthal, R. (1984). Females in charge: Effects of sex of subordinate and romantic attachment status upon self ratings of dominance. *Journal of Personality, 52,* 355–371.

Spence, J. T. (1984). Masculinity, femininity, and gender-related traits: A conceptual analysis and critique of current research. *Progress in Experimental Personality Research, 13,* 1–97.

Spence, J. T. (1985). Gender identity and its implications for concepts of masculinity and femininity. In T. Sondregger (Ed.), *Nebraska Symposium on Motivation* (pp. 59–95). Lincoln: University of Nebraska Press.

Tannen, D. (1990). *You just don't understand: Women and men in conversation.* New York: Morrow.

Tavris, C. (1992). *The mismeasure of woman.* New York: Simon and Schuster.

Thoits, P. (1983). Multiple identities and psychological well-being: A reformulation and test of the social isolation hypothesis. *American Sociological Review, 48,* 174–87.

Turbin, C. (1992). *Working women of collar city: Gender, class, and community in Troy, New York, 1864–86.* Urbana: University of Illinois Press.

Vallas, S. (1993). *Power in the workplace: The politics of production at AT&T.* Albany, NY: State University of New York Press.

Vojdik, V. K. (1997). Girls' schools after VMI: Do they make the grade? *Duke Journal of Gender Law & Policy, 4,* 69–100.

Waters, M. (1994). Ethnic and racial identities of second-generation black immigrants in New York City. *International Migration Review, 28,* 795–820.

Westwood, S. (1985). *All day every day: Factory and family in the making of women's lives.* Champaign: University of Illinois Press.

Zuckerman, H., Cole, J., & Bruer, J. (1991). *The outer circle: Women in the scientific community.* New York: Norton.

PART II

MACROSTRUCTURES
AND PROCESSES

CHAPTER 4

Comparative Gender Stratification

Joan Huber

1. INTRODUCTION

This chapter selectively reviews more than 25 years of research in anthropology to assess the effects of premodern subsistence modes on variation in levels of sex inequality. Inasmuch as hunger is the chief determinant of human relationships (Goody, 1982, p. 15; Messer, 1984, p. 208), no society can be understood without knowing what men and women must do each day in order to eat. I also focus on two societal functions that mesh with a given subsistence technology in complex ways: reproduction and the legitimate use of force. A large interdisciplinary literature on women in development is excluded because it is reviewed elsewhere in this volume.

Most research on gender inequality has appeared since 1970, when anthropologists first began to consider women's work. Earlier, Mead (1973, p. 4) could have been speaking for all social scientists when she said that women anthropologists wanted to do the same work men did and therefore did not study the activities of women and children.

The mode of subsistence refers to the types of energy a society uses to secure food (Friedl, 1975). Subsistence modes tend to respond to population pressure on a given physical environment. The three major theorists of population dynamics—Smith, Marx, and Boserup—agree that humans, like other animal populations, inherently tend to increase toward the environment's short-term carrying capacity (Hammel & Howell, 1987; North & Thomas, 1973). Ensuing population pressure spurs technological innovation and other adaptations for the management of scarce resources (Heider, 1972, p. 211).

Influenced by earlier work in anthropology and by Duncan's (1964) powerful analysis of ecology, Lenski (1970) classified societies by the major tool used in food production to show how the interrelations of population, organization, ecology, and technology af-

JOAN HUBER • Department of Sociology, Ohio State University, Columbus, Ohio 43210

Handbook of the Sociology of Gender, edited by Janet Saltzman Chafetz. Kluwer Academic/ Plenum Publishers, New York, 1999.

fect social stratification, thus making a wide range of data from anthropology accessible to sociologists (Moseley & Wallerstein, 1978, p. 262). Earlier typologies that classified societies by the materials used to make tools (e.g., stone, iron) had been theoretically sterile, yielding no important predictions. A typology based on subsistence modes combines comprehensiveness with minimal ambiguity and maximal reliability (Lenski, 1994, p. 24).

Appearing in rough sequence by order of technological complexity, subsistence modes affected societal size and organization by limiting the number of people who lived long enough to reproduce. I focus on those preindustrial modes whose technologies developed around field and forest resources: hunting and gathering, the hoe, herding, and the plow. I regret any distortions that may result from compressing so many societal types into one chapter.

Lenski's schema went far toward explaining the emergence of caste, class, feudalism, and slavery, but said little about gender stratification. Anthropologist Ernestine Friedl (1975) was first to use a subsistence framework to explain why men tended to be more dominant than women in foraging and hoe cultures. Later, sociologists Rae Blumberg (1978, 1995), Janet Chafetz (1984, 1990), and several anthropologists (see Chafetz, 1984, p. 3) used a typology based on subsistence modes to explain societal variation in gender inequality.

The dependent variable, the level of sex inequality, is an asymmetrical concept. Like a pendulum destined to swing only to the midpoint of a trajectory, women collectively are never more advantaged than men. It is their extent of disadvantage that varies (Chafetz, 1990, p. 117) and justifies attention to causal antedecents (Sen, 1990, p. 124).

Yet the causes of cross-cultural variation in gender disadvantage remain elusive. Sociology texts have nothing to say about the topic (Ferree & Hall, 1996, p. 944). It was much studied in anthropology (under the rubric of women's status), yet reviews in the *Annual Review of Anthropology* (1977 and 1988, respectively) reported that the search for key causes had been unfruitful. What went wrong?

One possibility is that problems encountered in studies based on Murdock's (1967) cross-cultural sample (e.g., Whyte, 1978) dampened enthusiasm for macrolevel theories of women's status (Mason, 1984, p. 5; Mukhopadhyay & Higgins, 1988, p. 462; Quinn, 1977, p. 182).[1] Murdock's sampling was inadequate and the data, of uneven quality, had not been collected with the Murdock categories in mind (Fedigan, 1986, p. 47). Studies based on such data tend to yield inconclusive findings.

Another reason that causes of variation in sex inequality remain unclear is perhaps more significant. Despite their interest in political affairs, anthropologists gave little attention to a persistent question that puzzled them: men's universal monopoly on politics. They also neglected a related issue, the most puzzling in the literature: women's exclusion from institutionalized competition for prestige (Quinn, 1977, p. 222). Yet a decade later, despite the domination of gender issues in the study of small-scale societies in the 1980s (Flanagan, 1989, p. 253), the reasons for women's lack of attainment in the political or military arenas continued to receive little study (Mukhopadhyay & Higgins, 1988, p. 464; Ross, 1986, p. 844).

A third reason may stem from anthropologists' attempts to avoid nineteenth century errors entailed by grand theorizing by their tendency to concentrate on particularities, leaving theoretical issues implicit and giving little attention to the methods that com-

---

[1] For a review of studies based on cross-cultural surveys, see Burton and White (1987).

parative studies entail (Goody, 1962, p. v). Such practices make their findings hard to generalize.

Despite the problems of focusing on an area that is both underresearched and undertheorized, I proceed on the premise that the key to understanding premodern variation in sex inequality lies in the interrelations of subsistence production, the politico–military arena where rules are made, and patterns of population maintenance. I examine how subsistence modes interact with two activities overwhelmingly the province of one sex: the legitimate use of force and the bearing and rearing of children. Men fight wars. Women bear and suckle children. Are these facts related? If so, how?

2. RECONSTRUCTING HUMAN EVOLUTION

I begin by reviewing research on human social evolution for its bearing on the relationship of work, war, and population maintenance. The study of social evolution necessarily involves sociobiology, yet this area has become divisive in anthropology. Only a minority of cultural anthropologists accept the concepts of sociobiological theory, biological anthropology's basic perspective (Lieberman, 1989, p. 680). Like their counterparts in sociology,[2] feminist anthropologists have been leery of claims that biology affects gender roles, perhaps because biology had long been invoked as the sole explanation. Gender theorists contest the degree to which ecology or evolution links sex differences to the division of labor when the real problem is to assess to what extent and in what ways the differences matter (Worthman, 1995, pp. 594, 602).

It is a mistake to overlook the role of biology in gender stratification, for at least one sex difference matters. The fact that no man can bear a child makes women central to population maintenance in a way that men cannot be, and population maintenance is crucial to species survival. It would be premature to exclude biological factors when the origins of sex stratification are so imperfectly understood. Human software derives from cultural evolution; the hardware is a result of biological evolution (Leach, 1984, p. 20).

Nineteenth century evolutionists held that all human societies progress through technological and social stages to a final civilized state, as in Europe. In the twentieth century, their work was discredited for its ethnocentrism, teleology, methods, data, and conclusions in a reaction that led to the establishment of anthropology as a discipline (Orlove, 1980, p. 236). Classical anthropology then focused on topics such as kinship and symbolism, neglecting the influence of economic factors (Testart, 1988, p. 9).[3] Food production was seen as a dull topic (Netting, 1974, p. 21). The study of social evolution lay dormant until the 1960s, when interest arose on the basis of data produced by twentieth century fieldwork (Fedigan, 1986, p. 32).

Two opposing theories currently explain how the human species evolved. The older one, man the hunter, is the most popular reconstruction of early social behavior (Zihlman, 1981, p. 75). It was drawn from a literature that converged on one distinguishing human trait: the pursuit, killing, and eating of animals with the use of tools. The most influential expression of the older theory, Washburn and Lancaster (1968) argued that hunting de-

---

[2] Rossi's (1977) thesis that biology plays a part in sex-role theory was very controversial (Miller & Garrison, 1982, p. 238).

[3] For example, Marshall's (1968, p. 13) analysis of marriage in the *International Encyclopedia of the Social Sciences* defines brideprice, dowry, and polygyny without reference to women's economic contributions.

mands all those qualities of human behavior that separate man from other primates: male aggressiveness and pleasure in killing, bipedalism, elaborate toolkits, language, appreciation of beauty, the division of labor, the monogamous nuclear family, loss of female estrus, and male bonding (Fedigan, 1986, p. 32). Washburn and Lancaster (1968) argued, further, that the killing of animals with tools had so long dominated human history that it shaped the human psyche for all time (Fedigan, 1986, p. 33). Their argument was repeated in so many articles and texts that it acquired something akin to the status of a received truth.[4] Most of the authors in the two most influential compendiums of the time (Lee & DeVore, 1968; Washburn, 1961) mentioned only hunting as a way to procure food (Fedigan, 1986, p. 33).

Like Darwin himself, man-the-hunter theorists failed to apply to human females the theory of sexual selection that Darwin developed to explain secondary sex differences: men were selected for intelligence, courage, and technological ability; women, for maternal traits. This view pervades reconstructions based on the primacy of hunting (Fedigan, 1986, p. 62). Tiger and Fox (1971) saw male bonding in hunting as focal; predatory aggression was genetically wired into (male) nature (Zihlman, 1981, p. 82). Wilson (1975), despite his emphasis on parental investment and mate choice as key concepts in sociobiology, failed to apply them to female mammals or primates; nor did he use the concepts of maternal investment, female choice, and mechanisms of sexual selection to incorporate women into human evolution (Zihlman, 1981, p. 84).

Ironically, the article that championed the explanatory power of hunting (Lee & Devore, 1968) provided insights and data that led to its undoing. The data showed gathering as vital to foraging life. One of the editors, Lee (1968), even argued that hunters actually gather for a living. Lee's (1980) continuing analysis of women's contribution to subsistence was a major starting point in a reassessment of women's role in early human society (Fedigan, 1986, p. 34). Subsequent research exposed the male bias that pervaded the ethnographic studies on which the picture of man the hunter was based (Dahlberg, 1981, p. 2).

A newer view of evolution centers on woman the gatherer. Man the hunter came to be seen as a backward projection of sex stereotypes onto humans of more than a million years ago (Zihlman, 1981, p. 76), Themes of male aggression, dominance, and hunting that led to the belief that sex inequality was rooted in biological sex differences were modified to fit a growing body of data on living apes and hunter-gatherers. It is improbable that hominid mothers sat about awaiting the return of the hunters; more likely, they actively sought food while carrying infants. To postulate that early human females were sedentary denies their primate heritage (Zihlman, 1981, p. 89). There were no sedentary females in foraging societies. Available quantitative data show that women were away from camp as long as men and walk the same distances, carrying infants and heavier burdens (Fedigan, 1986, p. 49). Recent data even suggest that our hominid ancestors had no home bases (Potts, 1984), making untenable a house-bound vision of early women (Fedigan, 1986, p. 60).

Moreover, according to sociobiological theory, heavy maternal investment in offspring implies that it was females rather than males who chose mates. Burdened by dependent offspring, females must have chosen sociable males willing to share food and

[4] Lovejoy's (1981) theory, the best known, sees the central adaptation in human evolution as male provisioning of sedentary, fecund, monogamous females (Fedigan, 1986, p. 62).

protect them and their babies, turning around the older picture in which dominant males pick females who, in turn, try to remain attractive enough to secure a mate, food, protection, and offspring (Zihlman, 1981, p. 88).

Sociobiology clearly cuts more than one way with regard to theories of sex inequality. If early women were not "house-bound," waiting for their men to supply food for them and their children, how could the domestic responsibilities of women derive from nature? Although its accuracy has never been debated, the assumption that it is natural for women to be found at the hearth still undergirds most theories of human social evolution. Perhaps, as Fedigan (1986, p. 38) suggests, the only division of labor in which sex matters is the one that involves insemination, gestation, and lactation.

In the following paragraph, I discuss human adaptations based on hunting and gathering, the hoe, herding, and the plow. The analysis is based on two principles of stratification. First, a necessary condition for gender equality is that women must be economically interdependent with other producers rather than dependent on male producers (Fedigan, 1986, p. 43; Leacock, 1981). The second, Friedl's (1975) modification of the first, suggests a sufficient condition: women must not only contribute to subsistence but also exercise control over the distribution of valved goods in order to equal men in power and prestige. In sum, producers have more power and prestige than consumers and in any society those who control the distribution of valued goods beyond the family have the most power and prestige.

3. HUNTING AND GATHERING SOCIETIES

Hunting and gathering comprise a way of life that resembles the technological adapation of all *Homo sapiens* before the domestication of plants and animals about 10,000 years ago (Friedl, 1975, p. 12). Forager groups are small (about 50 persons), mobile, and nonterritorial, which constrains the accrual of a surplus and leads to an egalitarian emphasis on sharing resources (Lee & DeVore, 1968). The few peoples for whom foraging remains a major source of food today occupy land no one else wants (yet): African and South American rain forest, Arctic tundra, and Australian desert (Spielman & Eder, 1994, p. 311).

Foragers use several methods to obtain most of their food: gathering wild plants and small animals such as mice or clams; hunting large animals such as deer, caribou, whales, or seal; and fishing. Meat is always a favored food (Friedl, 1975, p. 12). Correlated with latitude, the amount in the diet ranges from 10% near the equator to 90% in the Arctic (Testart, 1978, cited in Fedigan, 1986, p. 48).

By consensus, foraging societies exhibit the least social inequality. Whether they are truly or only relatively so has been debated (Flanagan, 1989, p. 254). Feminist scholars tried to document the absence of sex inequality to prove that inequality did not derive from nature (Collier & Yanigasako, 1987); Marxists hoped to show that in the absence of private property, equality prevails (Leacock, 1981; Sacks, 1982). However, most anthropologists see social inequality as universal; all known societies use criteria of sex, age, and personal attributes in allocating power (Sahlins, 1958, p. 1).

Hunter-gatherer subsistence ensures a low level of inequality because foragers, who move when the food supply in a given area is depleted, own only what they can carry. They highly value sharing, which reduces the risks of living in groups that cannot readily buffer a variable environment (Cashden, 1980, p. 117). All foraging societies have rules that order the sharing of meat; the ones that survived were those that found ways to encourage the fulfillment of exchange obligations (Friedl, 1975, p. 20).

On average, women's contribution to foragers' food supply more or less equals men's, which leads to women's being seen as self-sufficient rather than to higher status (Schlegel & Barry, 1986; Sanday, 1973). Gathering produces only enough food for a woman and her family. Hunters earn esteem as generous hosts because hunting enables men to distribute a highly valued food to the entire band (Friedl, 1975).

Both men and women can master the needed skills, so why did women never hunt?[5] Friedl (1975, p. 16) suggests that the answer lies in a complex of interdependent conditions related to childbearing. To offset the effects of high death rates, women foragers are often pregnant or lactating. They are barred from hunting in the later stages of pregnancy by shifts in body balance; after the birth, by the burden of the child, which must remain with its mother while it is breastfed. Although food supplements are added at 1 to 6 months in all preindustrial cultures (Raphael & Davis, 1985, p. 141), lactation occupies 3 to 4 years because shorter periods tend to increase infant mortality (Cronk, 1991, p. 28). Hunting also requires distance running, which may affect ability to ovulate (Graham, 1985).

Although anthropologists traditionally have explained marriage as a male–female bond occasioned by the food needs of a female with dependents (Ember & Ember, 1983, p. 41), it is perhaps better seen as a way to recruit labor, distribute food, and provide for procreation and sexual pleasure (Friedl, 1975, p. 23). Among foragers, monogamy was the most common form. On average, a hunter typically lacked enough meat at any one time to care for more than one set of marital, paternal, and affinal obligations (Friedl, 1975, p. 26).

War is rare among foragers. Population is sparse and land is plentiful. Conflicts within bands are often settled by the departure of one party in a dispute, and women are often involved in the decision (Friedl. 1975, p. 15). Leadership roles are limited to the persuasive influence of skilled hunters, to women skillful enough to attract their married offspring to live with them as adults, and to men and women with shamanistic skills. No leader can coerce others (Friedl, 1975, p. 31). Male dominance is greatest when hunting is the sole source of food; equality is greatest where men and women together perform the major subsistence tasks.

4. HORTICULTURAL SOCIETIES

Horticulture, plant cultivation with digging stick or hoe in garden-size plots, began in Asia Minor about 10,000 years ago. It marked the beginnings of modern stratification. Boserup (1965), reversing Malthus, suggests that population pressure, driven by the need to feed more individuals, causes rather than follows intensification of cultivation, In the simple form the major subsistence tool is a digging stick. People had to move every few years to replace plots whose fertility was lost.

The advanced form of horticulture appeared about 6000 years ago with the invention of metallurgy. The hoe replaced the digging stick while metal weapons replaced sticks and stones. Because humans can be hurt more easily with metal weapons than with sticks

---

[5] Well, hardly ever. In Northern Luzon, Agta women always took part in hunting (Estioko-Griffin, 1985).

and stones, war for the first time became a profitable way to acquire food produced by someone else (Lenski, 1970). The effect on gender stratification was profound because everywhere war is men's work, associated with the devaluation of women (Hayden, 1995, p. 63).

The use of metal weapons to secure food requires a third principle of gender stratification that concerns the use of force: The more often a society engages in warfare, the more likely is social control to be vested in politico–military elites that exclude women (see Collins, 1988, p. 168–173).

Hoe societies, which exemplify the gender role diversity that provided the foundation for the relativist view of human beliefs and behaviors made popular by Boas and his students, vary in patterns of domestic exchange, postmarital residence, and household composition. The crucial variable is the control of economic resources, especially labor. The question is, which sex can command the labor of others and control the distribution of the resulting accumulation (Friedl, 1975, p. 6l)?

The gender division of labor takes three forms. Men can prepare land for cultivation (felling trees, cutting and burning underbrush) while both sexes cultivate it, a pattern common to sub-Saharan Africa. Men can clear land and women cultivate it, a pattern among Indians of the eastern United States. Men can both clear and cultivate, a rare pattern found in inland tropical south America (Friedl, 1975, p. 51).

Once the land is cleared, there is no adaptive advantage in having either men or women plant, weed, harvest, and transport crops. Lactating women can carry babies and return with loads of food as women gatherers do. The time and energy women spend on childcare are allocated under the constraints posed by their work, not the other way round. For example, early supplementary feeding of infants is more likely if women do much subsistence work (Nerlove, 1974). Norms concerning family size and systems of childcare typically conform to women's customary work requirements (Blumberg, 1978: Chafetz, 1984; Friedl, 1975; Mukhopadhyay & Higgins, 1988, p. 475; Quinn, 1977, p. 193). According to cross-cultural time allocation studies, women simply add childcare to their other tasks (Zihlman, 1997, p. 194).

In simple hoe societies the sexual division of labor consists of the male monopoly over the initial clearing of new land (Friedl, 1975, pp. 53–60). Once or twice a generation the land to be cleared lies next to land worked by other peoples, leading to warfare. A potential need for defense in the acquisition of new territory probably contributed to making the slash-and-burn process largely men's work, although land-clearing probably fails to confer the advantages that the monopoly on hunting gives forager men.

In both simple and advanced hoe societies, marriage and kinship customs tend to follow the division of labor (Friedl, 1975). Unilateral reckoning of descent is most common in hoe societies, perhaps because women sometimes produce more food than do men. Patrilineality tends to occur when both spouses cultivate. Matrilineality is found in about a quarter of hoe societies, usually when only women cultivate. Matrilineal inheritance tends to occur when women produce more than do men (Goody, 1976).

Patrilocality (postmarital residence with husband's kin) tends to occur when the male contribution to subsistence is high. It disadvantages the wife although she can compensate by bearing sons whose wives she can later dominate. Wives also can become the worms within the apple of a patrilocal domestic group (Collier, 1974, p. 92). Working together separated from kin tends to integrate them as a group and gives them a measure of power (Leis, 1974). Matrilocality typically occurs where female contribution to subsistence is high. The infrequency with which patterns of residence leave related women together and disperse related men, rather than vice versa, helps to explain why the degree of political influence exercised by Iroquois women is found in few societies (Quinn, 1977, p. 214).

The divorce rate should increase as women's share of subsistence tasks rises because couples can more easily part when it affects the food supply of neither of the spouses nor their children. Although data are sketchy, this expectation is upheld: divorce rates among hoe peoples appear high compared to U.S. rates (Friedl, 1975, p. 93).

Because warfare is common and women's subsistence contribution is also high, polygyny occurs more often in advanced hoe societies than in all other types. Warfare enhances male political control because men's service as warriors strengthens their control on rights of citizenship (Grant, 1991, p. 14). War also alters the sex ratio (Ember, 1974).[6] Under such conditions, polygyny is a way to raise productivity, as economist Ester Boserup (1970) first noted (Lesthaeghe & Surkyn, 1988) and it is widely practiced in a populist form (Huber & Spitze, 1988, p. 488). Nearly everyone marries but women marry early, men late, and a high death rate helps to even the sex ratio. Male incentives to practice polygyny lie not in the desire to collect women but in the need for children's labor (Ember & Ember, 1983, p. 13). Women's incentives likewise derive from their need for children's labor, especially for support in old age.

Warfare affects sex stratification more generally through its close ties with governance (Goldschmidt, 1959, p. 166). The requirements of waging war encourage the establishment of autocratic and hierarchical political organizations and the formation of politico–military elites in which women play no part. Among ordinary men, the presence of an outside enemy, real or imagined, stimulates solidarity and promotes the exclusion of women from political life (Rose, 1986, p. 852). In turn, exclusion from political life leads to lack of control over property. Goheen (1996, p. 137), for example, recounts how Cameroon men's earlier status as hunters and warriors led to the need for women to seek men's permission to cultivate, giving rise to the saying that men own the fields, women own the crops. By contrast, in a rare instance of women's full participation in warfare (among the Fon in Dahomey), women's political activity was also high and they could control property (Ross, 1986, p. 852; see also Collins, 1985, p. 390).

Why do women so rarely take part in organized violence? The male monopoly is often attributed to their relative strength and size within (but not across) populations and to greater aggressiveness, but such explanations pose problems. Larger, stronger males do not generally dominate shorter, weaker ones (Chafetz, 1984, p. 118); adult dominance derives from diverse social talents (flattery, deception, competence, nurturance). Interpersonal aggression may be detrimental to effective leadership (Maccoby & Jacklin, 1974, p. 274).[7]

More than 20 years ago Friedl (1975, p. 57) suggested that the male monopoly on warfare resulted from men's relative expendability in population maintenance, but scholars gave this proposal little attention either before or during the decade 1977–1987 (Mukhopadhyay & Higgins, 1988, p. 470) nor have I located research on this topic conducted after 1987. However, Friedl's conjecture makes sense. In the preindustrial reproductive cycle the most frequent states are pregnancy and lactation (Harrell, 1981). How-

---

[6] Harris (1981) sees female infanticide as the cause of frequent warfare over women but Ember and Ember (1994, p. 186) note that HRAF data fail to support his claim that this practice actually makes women scarce.

[7] Whether men's greater verbal aggressiveness is Western or pancultural has not been studied (Quinn, 1977, p. 190).

ever, pregnancy reduces combat effectiveness; depriving a suckling of nourishment reduces its chances of survival. The real costs of sending pregnant and lactating women off to war are obvious.

5. HERDING SOCIETIES

Herding and hoe societies appeared in the same time period; animals were domesticated at about the same time as plants. Pastoral economies cover the technological range of hoe and simple plow societies in areas where tillage is hard owing to mountainous terrain, short growing season, or low rainfall as in central Asia, Arabia, North Africa, parts of Europe, and sub-Saharan Africa (Lenski & Lenski, 1978, p. 235). Small-scale use of hoe or plow may occur. As explained in the section on plow societies, the herders' level of living often exceeds that of peasants (Krader, 1968, p. 458). Moreover, owing to historical accident, herding societies uniquely influenced the modern world when the gender norms of ancient Hebrew herders became embedded in law and custom across much of Eurasia and North Africa owing to the political and military victories of Christian and Muslim conquerors.

Ecology matters. Moving livestock to seasonal pastures to convert grass into human food usually requires a nomadic or seminomadic way of life. In turn, the use of spatial mobility as a survival strategy leads to competition with agrarians over territory and disputes over water and stolen animals (Beck. 1978, p. 352). Constant threat of conflict during migration stimulates growth and consolidation of political authority. Men of courage are prized as warfare becomes culturally attractive (Barfield, 1994, p. 161).

Because the open grasslands where most herders live pose few barriers to movement and political consolidation, herding societies may be huge (e.g., the empire of Ghenghis Khan) but their communities are only a little larger than foragers' because effective maintenance of herds is best done in small units and the food supply is limited (Beck, 1978, p. 352). In the ninth century BCE, Asian herders learned to ride their horses, which gave them great advantage over less mobile agrarians in ensuing waves of conquest. Herding groups repeatedly devastated Eurasian agrarian empires over a period of more than 2500 years (Lenski & Lenski, 1978, pp. 237–318.)

Generalizing about sex inequality in herding societies is risky because many of them also depend on hoe or plow (which oppositely affect women's economic productivity) and also for lack of data. A careful study of how men and women in any nomadic pastoral society influence decisions on resource allocation has yet to be made. The study of nomads was undoubtedly spurred by romantic stereotypes of fierce and independent peoples but all virtues were defined as male and the role of women was grossly neglected until after 1970 (Dyson-Hudson & Dyson-Hudson, 1980, p. 15ff).

The value placed on a politico–military elite should result in a fairly high level of inequality among men and between men and women. Herding societies are most likely to require patrilocal residence and have hereditary slavery (Lenski & Lenski, 1978, p. 237). Women are excluded from the most important subsistence tasks, a result, according to Evans-Pritchard (1965, p. 50), of their lack of experience in warfare and the diplomacy needed to settle disputes at water holes, their lesser physical strength, and herders' need to be away from home for long periods (Elam, 1973, p. 46).

The practice of polygyny in herding regimes depends on the extent to which ecological conditions permit only herding or also permit use of hoe or plow. Polygyny is rare when the environment (as in central Asia) neither offers men much chance to become rich nor women to become economically active but it may increase when an encounter with a market society gives women an opening such as carpet-making (Barfield, 1981, p. 79). If use of the hoe gives women economic opportunities, as often happens in East Africa, polygyny may be fairly common (Hakansson, 1988), appearing in the populist form common to advanced hoe societies. If the plow is used in conjunction with herding, as in North Africa, some men may become rich enough to marry more than one wife. Women then may be barred from property inheritance, although Islamic law forbids it. For example, Libyan Bedouins know it is against religious law to exclude women from inheritance but they also know that the uncontrolled alienation of property would destroy the basis of corporate life (Peters, 1978, p. 324).

6. AGRARIAN SOCIETIES

Simple agrarian societies appeared in the Middle East about 3000 BCE with the introduction of a wooden plow, probably as a result of population pressure. Techniques to smelt iron, invented about 2000 years later, provided an iron blade and marked the advent of advanced agrarian societies. Warfare became more widespread. Unlike tin and copper, iron is a common metal, which thus permits a great proliferation of weaponry.

Use of the plow spread from the Middle East until agrarian societies covered most of Asia, Europe, and North Africa.[8] Boserup's key insight was that people do not turn the earth, fodder animals, and collect manure unless they must (Netting, 1993, p. 103). With low population density and shifting tillage, women do most of the work with handheld tools; polygyny was a way to increase production. With high population density and settled agriculture, men do most of the work; women become economic liabilities, in need of a dowry as a basis for their support (Boserup, 1970, p. 35).

The most obvious effect of the plow was a vast increase in the food supply. Use of the plow made continuous cultivation possible for the first time by reducing weeds and turning soil deeply enough to restore fertility. It stimulated the domestication of draft animals. Confining them in stalls to prevent their wandering away encouraged the collection of manure to fertilize the fields. The invention of writing soon followed (the better to keep track of a surplus large enough to be stored) as did the beginnings of empire building (Lenski & Lenski, 1978, p. 177).

Eurasian stratification patterns assumed the pyramidal form common to feudalism: a political and economic elite; a sprinkling of merchants, artisans, and craft workers of lesser rank; and swarms of peasants, serfs, and slaves. The plow had a devastating effect on the lives of ordinary people. A food surplus in the countryside coupled with the availability of iron weapons tempted elites to extract as much as possible from impoverished peasants. The flatter and richer the land, the worse off were ordinary people, probably much worse off than were their forager ancestors (Lenski & Lenski, 1978, p. 206). In addition, oral health and skeletal robustness declined as a result of consumption of too many carbohydrates and reduced physical activity (Larsen, 1995).

Yet the plow depressed women's status more than men's. First, because men monopolized it, women's share of food production plummeted. With oxen, a man could plow

---

[8] The plow was rarely used in sub-Saharan Africa until the 1900s. Oxen, the best draft animals, do not thrive in Central Africa's humid tse-tse zones or in West African coastal zones (Shipton, 1994, p. 357).

in a day an area far larger than a woman could till by hoe (Childe, 1951, p. 100). The plow required the management of heavy draft animals in larger fields further from home, making it hard to arrange a schedule to suit a nursing baby (Blumberg, 1978, p. 50). The less food women produce, the more they are valued only as mothers (Goody, 1976, p. 34).

Second, plow technology makes land the chief form of wealth because a field can be tilled in perpetuity. Coupled with the huge increase in productivity and the specialization that this permits, land becomes a scarce good (Goody, 1976, p. 97). Individual land ownership gives rise to laws and customs that reflect elite men's monopoly on warfare and related political and economic institutions. Women can inherit land (see later) but typically exert little control over it (Agarwal, 1994).

The reason that land ownership so changes law and custom is that land is an impartible inheritance (unlike cattle, for example). A given piece under given technology supports only a given number of persons. Rule and custom come to ensure inheritance patterns that prevent land from being overly subdivided. The scarcer it becomes and the more intensively it is used, the greater the tendency to retain it in the nuclear family, the basic unit of production and reproduction (Goody, 1976, p. 97). Monogamy prevails lest land be dispersed among too many legal heirs, and divorce becomes difficult or impossible. The concern with women's sexual purity stems from their status as transmitters of male property. The larger her endowment, the more her behavior is controlled (Goody, 1976, p. 14). Infibulation and footbinding, for example, began as ways to ensure imperial men's exclusive access to consorts. Both practices elicited a competitive upward flow of women and downward flow of self-enforcing customs that were maintained by interdependent needs on the marriage market. Women needed resources and men needed certain knowledge of paternity (Mackie, 1996).[9]

If land is so valuable, why are women permitted to inherit it? Why does bilateral inheritance prevail in agrarian societies? The answer is that the greater volume of production that the plow affords can support an elaborate division of labor and a variety of lifestyle. If an elite male is to maintain his own and his children's style of life, he must marry a similarly endowed spouse, which is an incentive to establish a bilateral inheritance system (Goody, 1976). The political institutions that permitted elite males to control their wives' property later expand to include a broader segment of the male population.

Different strategies of heirship in sub-Saharan hoe societies and Eurasian plow societies stem from the respective value of land (Goody, 1976, p. 97). In Africa, economic differences among families are minor, land is plentiful, and there less pressure to provide an heir to an estate (Goody & Tambiah, 1973, p. 22). A daughter's marriage little affects her economic position because women, married or not, grow crops or do craft work. A daughter needs no endowment to maintain her status. In Eurasia, a man provides for his sons at his death and for his daughters by dowry at marriage lest family status decline in the social hierarchy.

Thus, women's economic contribution to subsistence declines with the introduction of the plow while powerful elites come to control a vastly increased surplus. Both women and men may inherit property but men control that of their wives. Women's sexual behavior is constrained to ensure that only her husband's children inherit his property. In effect, use of the plow puts women under guardianship of husbands or male relatives.

---

[9] With such powerful incentives as the need to ensure one's subsistence, people come to accept customs that otherwise do them much harm. Thus, Chinese women objected when footbinding was forbidden (Levy, 1966, p. 210), clitoridectomy came to play a part in Kenyan women's authority structure (Robertson, 1996), and the high-heeled shoe remains popular among women in the West.

7. THE MODERN WORLD

Urbanization began relatively late in northern Europe. In technology, Europe was then nearly a millennium behind China, which was probably the main reason why a revolutionary industrial technology could be introduced in so short a time (Boserup. 1981, p. 101),[10] altering patterns of population maintenance, subsistence work, and warfare. Infant mortality and fertility decline; by 1910 safe methods of artificial feeding end a baby's dependence on a lactating woman for survival (Huber, 1990). Education becomes universal, for the modern labor market requires workers whose qualifications are independent of ascribed characteristics (Jackson, 1984; Marwell, 1975). Warfare requires more brains, less brawn. These events spawn social movements that spur the changes in gendered behavior, belief, law, and custom (Chafetz & Dworkin, 1986) that comprise the theme of this handbook.

8. CONCLUSION

To assess the effects of subsistence technology on sex inequality, I analyze its interrelationships with patterns of population maintenance and politico–military institutions in premodern societies. Three principles of stratification guide the chapter: producers have more power than consumers, those who control the distribution of valued goods beyond the family have the most power, and the more often a society makes war, the more likely is social control to be vested in politico–military elites that include no women. The subsistence modes examined are those of foraging, hoe, herding, and plow. The basic question concerns the relationship of women's monopoly on childbearing to men's monopoly on politico-military affairs. Can women's absence from the arena where rules are made be a result of female centrality in population maintenance?

Both in hunting and gathering and simple hoe cultures, women contribute heavily to subsistence. War is rare, for weapons are inefficient, people are few, land is plentiful. The level of social and gender inequality is low.

Women's economic contribution is also high in advanced hoe cultures but warfare becomes common when the invention of metallargy improves weaponry, spurring the formation of politico–military elites that include no women because, to offset high death rates, they are so often pregnant or lactating in prime years. It is the invention of metallurgy that makes warriors and political leaders only of men.

Herding limits women's productivity while conflict over water rights and animal theft makes warfare central. Controls on women's behavior tend to moderate if the hoe is also used because women then contribute to subsistence. If the plow is the auxiliary subsistence tool, male elites can acquire many wives, secluding them at little cost for they contribute little to subsistence.

With the plow, women's economic contribution declines sharply from earlier levels while increased productivity and more effective weapons provide incentives for warfare. By making land the chief form of wealth, the plow spurs the emergence of laws and customs that benefit male elites and disadvantage women even more than ordinary men.

---

[10] Goody (1996b), unlike Marx and Weber, holds that dominant groups were similarly organized across Eurasia because they faced similar problems in managing resources. The uniqueness of the West requires no explanation. There is nothing to explain.

This chapter thus suggests (but falls short of proving) that it is the institutionalizing of warfare in advanced hoe cultures that first brings about women's absence from huts or halls of power. After the plow makes land the chief form of wealth, the institution of private property intensifies the effects of men's monopoly on warfare. Even with an ideology of sex equality, the Soviet Union's abolition of private property could not overcome the effects of militarism.

Population maintenance no longer requires serial pregnancy and lactation. Work and warfare require extensive training. Unsurprisingly, women's military participation is rising. The big increase in the number of women in U.S. services came in the 1970s when the draft ended and a volunteer force was created (Holm, 1992, pp. 246–259). The contentious issue today, first made salient by the industrial revolution, is women's service in combat (Goldman, 1982, p. 4). After the 1970s, a majority came to approve some combat roles for women (Peach, 1996, p. 186). Given the potential of biological, chemical, and nuclear warfare, barring women from combat hardly ensures their survival (Segal, 1982, p. 281). Excluding woman from combat simply limits their promotion opportunities and access to job training, education, retirement benefits, medical care, low-cost insurance, bonuses, loans, and state and federal employment preferences (Peach, 1996, p. 175).

The idea that sex inequality results from the interaction of work, war, and childbearing is based on a survey of a literature that would repay further study despite its lack of attention to women as political actors (Ross, 1986, p. 54). Such studies of relatively isolated premodern societies conducted earlier need to be integrated with the current work of anthropologists, economists, and sociologists on regions that harbor a mix of premodern subsistence and modern industrial technologies. How do the interrelations of work, war, and childbearing change when an isolated premodern society is pulled into the vortex of the world political economy? How do the findings speak to theories of sex inequality? Let the work begin.

Acknowledgments

I am grateful to Janet Chafetz for sending me down this particular path, to Cathy Rakowski for alerting me to materials that I would have overlooked, and especially to William Form for his helpful comments on every draft.

REFERENCES

Agarwal, B. (1994). *A field of one's own: Gender and land rights in Asia.* New York: Cambridge University Press.

Barfield, T. (1981). *The Central Asian Arabs in Afghanistan.* Austin: University of Texas Press.

Barfield, T. (1994). The devil's horsemen. In S. Reyna & R. Downs (Eds.), *Studying War* (pp. 157–172). Langhorne, PA: Gordon & Breach.

Beck, L. (1978). Women among Qashqa'i nomadic pastoralists in Iran. In L. Beck and N. Keddie (Eds.), *Women in the Middle East* (pp. 351–373). Cambridge: Harvard University Press.

Blumberg, R. L. (1978). *Stratification.* Dubuque, IA: Brown.

Blumberg, R. L. (1995). *Engendering wealth and well-being.* Boulder, CO: Westview.

Boserup, E. (1965). *The conditions of agricultural growth.* Chicago: Aldine.

Boserup, E. (1970). *Women's role in economic development.* London: George Allen & Unwin.

Boserup, E. (1981). *Population and technological change.* Chicago: University of Chicago Press.

Burton, M., & White, D. (1987). Cross cultural surveys today. *Annual Review of Anthropology, 16,* 143–160.

Cashden, E. (1980). Egalitarianism among hunters and gatherers. *American Anthropologist, 82,* 116–120.

Chafetz, J. S. (1984). *Sex and advantage*. Totowa, NJ: Rowman & Allanheld.

Chafetz, J. S. (1990). *Gender equity*. Newbury Park, CA: Sage.

Chafetz, J. S., & Dworkin, G. (1986). *Female revolt*. Totowa, NJ: Rowman & Allanheld.

Childe, V. G. (1951). *Man makes himself*. New York: Mentor.

Collier, J. F. (1974). Women in politics. In M. Rosaldo & L. Lamphere (Eds.), *Woman, culture and society* (pp. 89–96). Stanford: Stanford University Press.

Collier, J., & Yanigasako, S. (Eds.) (1987). *Gender and kinship*. Stanford: Stanford University Press.

Collins R. (1985). *Sociology of marriage and the family*. Chicago: Nelson-Hall.

Collins, R. (1988). *Theoretical sociology*. San Diego: Harcourt Brace Jovanovich.

Cronk, L. (1991). Human behavioral ecology. *Annual Review of Anthropology, 20,* 25–53.

Dahlberg, F. (1981). In F. Dahlberg (Ed.), *Woman the gatherer* (pp. i–xi). New Haven: Yale University Press.

Duncan, O. D. (1964). Social organization and the ecosystem. In R. Faris (Ed.), *Handbook of modern sociology* (pp. 37–82). Chicago: Rand-McNally.

Dyson-Hudson, R, & Dyson-Hudson, N. (1980). Nomadic pastoralists. *Annual Review of Anthropology, 9,* 15–61.

Elam, Y. (1973). *Social and sexual roles of Hima women*. Manchester: University of Manchester Press.

Ember, M. (1974). Warfare, sex ratio, and polygyny. *Ethnology, 13,* 197–206.

Ember, M., & Ember, D. (1983). *Marriage, Family, and Kinship*. New Haven: HRAF Press.

Ember, M., & Ember, C. (1994). Cross-cultural studies of war and peace. In S. Reyna & R. Downs (Eds.), *Studying War* (pp. 185–208). Langhorne, PA: Gordon & Breach.

Estioko-Griffin, A. (1985). Women as Hunters. In A. Estioko-Griffin & P. Griffin (Eds.), *The Agta of northeastern Luzon* (pp. 18–32). Cebu City: San Carlos.

Evans-Pritchard, E. E. (1965). *The position of women in primitive societies and other essays*. New York: Free Press.

Fedigan, L. M. (1986). The changing role of women in models human evolution. *Annual Review of Anthropology, 15,* 25–66.

Ferree, M. M., & Hall, E. (1996). Stratification from a feminist perspective. *American Sociological Review, 61,* 929–950.

Flanagan, J. (1989). Hierarchy in simple societies. *Annual Review of Anthropology, 18,* 245–266.

Friedl, E. (1975). *Women and men: An anthropologist's view*. New York: Holt, Rinehart & Winston.

Goheen, M. (1996). *Men own the land, women own the crops*. Madison: University of Wisconsin Press.

Goldman, N. L. (1982). Introduction. In N. L. Goldman (Ed.), *Female soldiers* (pp. 1–17). Westport, CT: Greenwood.

Goldschmidt, W. (1959). *Man's way*. Cleveland, OH: World.

Goody, J. (1962). *Death, property, and the ancestors*. London: Tavistock.

Goody, J. (1976). *Production and reproduction*. New York: Cambridge University Press.

Goody, J. (1982). *Cooking, cuisine, and class*. New York: Cambridge University Press.

Goody, J, (1996a). Comparative family systems in Europe and Asia. *Population and Development Review, 22,* 1–20.

Goody, J. (1996b). *The East in the West*. New York: Cambridge University Press.

Goody, J. & Tambiah, S. J. (1973). *Bridewealth and dowry*. Cambridge: Cambridge University Press.

Graham, S. (1985). Running and menstrual dysfunctions. *American Anthropologist, 87,* 878–882.

Grant, R. (1991). The sources of gender bias in international relations theory. In R. Grant & K. Newland (Eds.), *Gender and international relations* (pp. 8–26). Bloomingtom, IN: University of Indiana Press.

Hakensson, T. (1988). *Bridewealth, women, and land*. Stockholm: Almqvist and Wiksell.

Hammel, E. A., & Howell, N. (1987). Research in population and culture. *Current Anthropology, 28,* 141–160.

Harrell, B. (1981). Lactation and menstruation in cultural perspective. *American Anthropologist, 83,* 796–823.

Harris, M. (1984), A cultural and materialist theory of band and village warfare. In B. Ferguson (Ed.), *Warfare, Culture, and Environment* (pp. lll–140). Orlando, FL: Academic Press.

Hayden, B. (1995). Pathways to power. In D. Price & G. Feinman (Eds.). *Foundation of social inequality* (pp. 15–86). New York: Plenum.

Heider, K. (1972). Environment, subsistence, and society. *Annual Review of Anthropology, 1,* 207–226.

Holm, J. (1992). *Women in the military*. Novato, CA: Presidio.

Huber, J. (1990). Macro-micro links in gender stratification. *American Sociological Review, 55,* 1–10.

Huber. J., & Spitze, G. (1988). Trends in family sociology. In N. Smelser (Ed.), *Handbook of sociology* (pp. 425–448). Newbury ParK, CA: Sage.

Jackson, R. M. (1984). *The formation of craft labor markets*. Orlando, FL: Academic.

Krader, L. (1968). Pastoralism. *International Encyclopedia of the Social Sciences, 11,* 453–461.

Larsen, C. S. (1995). Biological changes in human populations with agriculture. *Annual Review of Anthropology, 24,* 185–213.

Leach, E. (1984). Glimpses of the history of British anthropology. *Annual Review of Anthropology, 13,* 1–23.

Leacock, E. (1981). *Myths of male dominance.* New York: Monthly Review Press.

Lee, R. (1968). What hunters do for a living. In R. Lee & I. Devore (Eds.), *Man the hunter* (pp. 30–48). Chicago: Aldine.

Lee, R. (1980). Lactation, ovulation, and women's work. In M. Cohen, R. Malpass, & H. Klein (Eds.), *Biosocial mechanisms of population regulation* (pp. 321–348), New Haven: Yale University Press.

Leis, N. (1974). Ijaw women's associations. In M. Rosaldo & L. Lamphere (Eds.), *Women, culture and society* (pp. 223–242). Stanford: Stanford University Press.

Lenski, G. (1970). *Human societies.* New York: McGraw-Hill.

Lenski, G. (1994). Social taxonomies. *Annual Review of Sociology, 20,* 1–26.

Lenski, G., & Lenski, J. (1978). *Human societies* (3rd ed.). New York: McGraw-Hill.

Lesthaeghe, R., & Surkyn, J. (1988). *Women in sub-Saharan demographic regimes.* Vrije Universiteit Brussel: Mimeo.

Levy, H. (1966). *Chinese footbinding.* New York: Walton Rawls.

Lieberman, L. (1989). Acceptance of human sociobiological concepts in anthropology. *Current Anthropology, 30,* 676–682.

Lovejoy, C. O. (1981). The origin of man. *Science, 211,* 341–350.

Maccoby. E., & Jacklin, C. (1974). *The psychology of sex differences.* Stanford: Stanford University Press.

Mackie, G. (1996). Ending footbinding and infibulation. *American Sociological Review, 61,* 999–1017.

Marshall, G. (1968). Marriage: Comparative analysis. *International Encyclopedia of the Social Sciences, 11,* 8–19.

Marwell, G. (1975). Why ascription? *American Sociological Review, 40,* 445–455.

Mason, K. (1984). *The status of women, fertility, and mortality.* New York: Rockefeller Foundation.

Mead, M. (1973). Changing styles of anthropological work. *Annual Review of Anthropology, 2,* 1–26.

Messer, E. (1984). Anthropological perspectives on diet. *Annual Review of Anthropology, 13,* 205–249.

Miller, J., & Garrison, H. (1982). Sex roles: The division of labor. *Annual Review of Sociology, 8,* 237–262.

Moseley, K., & Wallerstein, I. (1978). Precapitalist social structures. *Annual Review of Sociology, 4,* 259–290.

Mukhopadhyay. C., & Higgins, P. (1988). Anthropological studies of women's status revisited. *Annual Review of Anthropology, 17,* 461–495.

Murdock, G. P. (1967). Ethnographic atlas: A summary. *Ethnology, 6,* 109–236.

Nerlove, S. (1974). Women's workload and infant feeding practices. *Ethnology, 13,* 207–214.

Netting, R. (1974). Agrarian Ecology. *Annual Review of Anthropology, 3,* 21–56.

Netting, R. (1993). *Smallholders and householders.* Stanford: Stanford University Press.

North, D., & Thomas, R. P. (1973). *The rise of the Western World.* New York: Cambridge University Press.

Orlove, B. (1980). Ecological anthropology. *Annual Review of Anthropology, 9,* 235–273.

Peach, L. (1996). Gender ideology in the ethics of women in combat. In J. Stiehm (Ed.), *It's our military too* (pp. 156–194). Philadelphia: Temple University Press.

Peters, E. (1978). Women in four Middle East communities. In L. Beck & N. Keddie (Eds.), *Women in the Middle East* (pp. 311–350). Cambridge: Harvard University Press.

Potts, R. (1984). Home bases and early hominids. *American Scientist, 72,* 338–347.

Quinn, N. (1977). Anthropological studies of women's status. *Annual Review of Anthropology, 6,* 181–225.

Raphael. D., & Davis, F. (1985). *Patterns of infant feeding in traditional cultures.* Westport, CT: Greenwood.

Robertson, C. (1996). Women, genital mutilation, and collective action in Kenya, 1920–1990. *Signs, 21,* 615–642.

Ross, M. (1986), Female political participation. *American Anthropologist, 88,* 843–858.

Sacks, K. (1982). *Sisters and wives.* Westport, CT: Greenwood.

Sahlins, M. (1958). *Social stratification in Polynesia.* Seattle: University of Washington Press.

Sanday, P. (1973). Toward a theory of the status of women. *American Anthropologist, 88,* 142–150.

Schlegel, A, & Barry, H. (1986). The cultural consequences of subsistence contribution. *American Anthropologist, 88,* 142–150.

Segal, M. W. (1982). The argument for female combatants. N. L. Goldman (Ed.), *Female soldiers* (pp. 267–290). Westport, CT: Greenwood.

Sen, A. (1990). Gender and cooperative conflicts. In I. Tinker (Ed.), *Persistent inequalities* (pp. 123–149). New York: Oxford University Press.

Shipton, P. (1994). Land and culture in tropical Africa. *Annual Review of Anthropology, 23,* 347–377.

Spielman, K., & Eder, J. (1994). Hunters and farmers: Then and now. *Annual Review of Anthropology, 23,* 303–323.

Testart, A. (1978). Les societies de chasseure-cueilleurs. *Pour la Science, 16,* 99–108.

Testart, A. (1988). Some major problems in the anthropology of hunter gatherers. *Current Anthropology, 29,* 1–31.

Tiger, L. & Fox, R. (1971). *The imperial animal.* New York: Holt, Rinehart & Winston.

Washburn, S. (1961). *Social life of early man.* Chicago: Aldine.

Washburn, S., & Lancaster, C. (1968). The evolution of hunting. In R. Lee & I. Devore (Eds.), *Man the Hunter* (pp. 91–103). Chicago: Aldine.

Whyte, M. (1978). *The status of women in preindustrial societies.* Princeton, NJ: Princeton University Press.

Wilson, E. O. (1975). *Sociobiology.* Cambridge, MA: Belknap Press.

Worthman, C. (1995). Hormones, sex, and gender. *Annual Review of Anthropology, 24,* 593–616.

Yanigasako, S. J. (1979). Families and households. *Annual Review of Anthropology, 8,* 161–205.

Zihlman, A. (1981). Women as shapers of human adaptation. In F. Dahlberg (Ed.), *Woman the gatherer* (pp. 75–120). New Haven, CT: Yale University Press.

Zihlman A. (1997). Women's bodies, women's lives. In M. E. Morbeck, A. Galloway, & A. Zihlman (Eds.), *The evolving female* (pp. 185–197). Princeton, NJ: Princeton University Press.

CHAPTER 5

Third World Women
and Global Restructuring

JEAN L. PYLE

1. INTRODUCTION

This chapter surveys the status of women in Third World nations and the impact that global economic restructuring has had on their lives. It shows that there are systemic links among the forms of economic restructuring, increases in informal sector employment, rising poverty, and the continued disadvantaged economic status of women relative to men. It argues that these linkages result from characteristics of the global market system as a whole and the traditional theoretical approach (neoclassical economics) upon which the market system and much of the global restructuring is based. Understanding the overall effects and the relationships among these phenomena is critical for developing policies to enhance the well-being of women.

2. WOMEN'S STATUS IN THIRD WORLD COUNTRIES

Although women have experienced improvements in some dimensions of their lives (such as in labor force participation levels and access to education in some countries), they are at distinct economic disadvantage relative to men in almost all regards. Several publica-

Thanks to Gunseli Berik, Cathy Rakowski, Kathryn Ward, and the editor, Janet Chafetz. An earlier version was presented at American Sociological Association Annual Meetings, Toronto, Ontario, August 11, 1997.

JEAN L. PYLE • Department of Regional Economic and Social Development, University of Massachusetts at Lowell, Lowell, Massachusetts 01854

Handbook of the Sociology of Gender, edited by Janet Saltzman Chafetz. Kluwer Academic/ Plenum Publishers, New York, 1999.

tions in the last few years provide a great range of data by region of the world and by categories of information (Seager, 1997; UN 1995b; UNDP, 1995); however, in this chapter I can only briefly allude to the highlights of this wealth of information.

A disproportionate number of the poor are women. United Nations (UN) agencies estimate that 70% of the 1.3 billion poor are women (UNDP, 1995) and more than one half a billion women in rural areas, 60% of the world's rural population, live below the poverty line (UN, 1995a). It links this to unequal treatment in the labor market, their position in the family, and their treatment by the government (UNDP, 1995). Higher rates of poverty, together with the fact that women spend more hours a week working than men in almost all areas of the world, when household duties are included, reduce their quality of life (UN, 1991b, 1995b; UNDP, 1995). Much of women's work, particularly that in the home, has been undercounted and undervalued. It is estimated to be worth $11 trillion (UNDP, 1995).

From 1970 to 1990 the female share of the labor force increased in most regions except sub-Sahara Africa (UN, 1995b). However, there is considerable variation in female labor force participation among regions, ranging from 21% in North Africa to 43% in the Caribbean (UN, 1995b). Although women's share of the labor force has been increasing, it is widely documented that occupational segregation and discrimination "persist almost everywhere," a large earnings gap exists between men and women, and women "have less access to training and capital" (UN, 1991b, p. 81). Women have higher rates of unemployment in most areas of the world (UNDP, 1995). They are constrained in obtaining ownership of property in sizable areas of the world (Seager, 1997). Further, because they therefore have little collateral, it is generally very hard for women to obtain credit. Widespread labor market and societal discrimination against women have caused much of this.

According to the International Labour Organization (ILO) (1995), in many regions of the world, the informal sector labor force is growing faster than the labor force as a whole. Such employment has become the only option for many people because of stagnation or cutbacks in formal sector employment, high rates of unemployment, and the falling incomes and higher prices resulting from many structural adjustment programs. Increases are often correlated with economic crisis, but, as I will show later, as part of the trend toward more "flexible" production that gives firms more leeway to lay off workers, informal networks of production tend to grow.

The informal sector spans a wide range of small scale economic activities in agriculture, industry, and services and generally involves simple technologies, small amounts of capital, few employees if any, and little to no regulation or record keeping. In comparison to formal sector activities, informal sector activities bring lower pay, no benefits, poorer working conditions, no job security, higher prices for borrowing money and buying materials, and limited access to markets.

Women, in particular, must resort to income-generating activities in the informal sector because of economic crisis, limited access to formal sector jobs in many areas, or because informal sector jobs are easier to combine with child-care and home responsibilities. For example, as women's employment in formal sector or wage work decreased in the 1970s and 1980s in Latin America and the Caribbean, and remained very low in Africa, many women were forced to seek opportunities in the informal sector.

There was no recommended definition of the informal sector until 1993 (UN 1995b), and because of the widespread nature of the activities it encompasses and problems with data collection, data on women's participation are at best general estimates. Women's participation varies greatly between and within regions, and according to sector. To provide an example, the percentage of women in the informal sector (as approximated by self-employment) ranged from 25% in Latin America and the Caribbean to almost 60% in sub-Sahara Africa in 1985 (UN, 1991b).

In light of their disadvantaged status, women have been active in organizing, often through nongovernmental organizations (NGOs), to improve all dimensions of their lives. In addition, four major UN conferences on women have been held, in 1975, 1980, 1985, and 1995. The UN conferences assess women's progress, or lack of it, and formulate strategies to improve their status. Unfortunately, these conferences do not have the power to implement their plans but must rely on people working within their home countries to promote the goals adopted at the conferences. For example, The Nairobi Strategies, developed at the Third UN World Conference on Women in 1985, demand that governments: play key roles in ensuring that both men and women enjoy equal rights in such areas as education, training, and employment; act to remove negative stereotypes and perceptions of women; disseminate information to women about their rights and entitlements; collect timely and accurate statistics on women and monitor their situation; and encourage the sharing and support of domestic responsibilities (UN, 1991b). Two of the ten objectives for Beijing, 1995, were to address the "inequality in women's access to and participation in the definition of economic structures and policies and the productive process itself" and "the persistent and growing burden of poverty on women."

3. GLOBAL RESTRUCTURING

Global economic restructuring includes a number of different types of changes in the world economy. It may refer to any of the following:

- increased globalization of economic activities and a deliberate selection of a more market-oriented approach by many countries;
- adoption of an export-oriented development strategy;
- expanded role for multinational corporations (MNCs);
- structural adjustment programs (SAPs) advocated by the World Bank and International Monetary Fund; and
- repositioning of the relative power of major global institutions.

Given this wide scope, global restructuring includes a variety of factors that impinge on women's lives in the workplace and in the household (if the two sites differ). Global restructuring affects women in the formal sector as well as in the informal and household sectors in both rural and urban areas. The impact of global restructuring on women is a worldwide issue, affecting women in industrialized countries in many of the same ways as in developing countries. Although there have been some perceived benefits for women in industry, the overall effect has been largely negative.

Many of the types of global restructuring listed previously overlap. I will discuss each separately before exploring the linkages between them.

3.1. Globalization of Economic Activity, Increased Market Orientation of Most Economies, and Counterforces

Increasingly, many dimensions of economic activity have become global phenomena: the production and trading of goods and services, financial flows (including foreign direct investment, portfolio investment, and aid), and the movement of people in search of income-earning opportunities. This has been facilitated by rapid changes in the technologies of communication and transportation, as well as by the liberalization of trade and capital flows that have occurred.[1]

How a nation is integrated into the global economy and the way international events impact on it can have a dramatic effect on the economic roles of its women. For example, an increase in a country's trade and/or in the amount of foreign direct investment (FDI) in its consumer goods or service sectors can correspond, at least in the short term, with an increase in women's access to jobs. This occurred in some Asian countries that began industrialization in the late 1960s and early 1970s (UN, 1995a). However, it is also the case that a particular trade policy can benefit one group of women while having an adverse impact on another group of women. This happened, for example, when the terms of the North American Free Trade Agreement (NAFTA) caused some garment production done by women in the Caribbean to be shifted to women in export industries in Mexico (Joekes & Weston, 1994).

In addition to these general trends, many countries have *deliberately* chosen to become more market oriented, further augmenting international flows of goods and services, financial capital, and labor. The decision to become more market oriented or "liberalized," with a putatively reduced role for the government in their economies, may apply to internal and/or external economic activities and may be voluntary or involuntary. This renewed movement toward market orientation was begun in the early 1980s by capitalist industrialized countries, such as the United States and Great Britain, that chose to move further in the direction of market coordination of economic activities. It was followed in the early 1990s by many previously socialist countries, particularly the former USSR and the countries of Eastern Europe, that have increasingly allowed markets rather than planners to make most of their economic decisions. Formerly communist countries in Southeast Asia, such as Vietnam, have also begun this transition. Simultaneously, many Third World countries have been pressured by the International Monetary Fund (IMF) and the World Bank (WB) into more market oriented approaches as a condition for loans or as part of a structural adjustment program. The IMF and the WB argue that market orientation is the appropriate means to achieve rapid growth and development and is the way to increase revenues to pay off a country's international debt.

Although these trends toward globalization and increased market orientation offer enhanced opportunities for some women, at least in the short term, this is not the case for many women for several reasons. First, the processes of globalization have occurred very unevenly. Developing countries' share of world trade actually fell from 1980 to 1992, from 29% to 24% (Joekes & Weston, 1994). In addition, Third World countries' share of foreign direct investment has been extremely volatile, falling from 24% in 1985 to 13% in 1989, only to rise to 32% during the years 1992–94 (*Finance & Development,* 1992; Panagariya, 1995). Only a small number of developing economies are significantly involved. Two thirds of the flow of FDI to developing countries during the late 1980s went to a few countries in East Asia (China, Malaysia, and Thailand) and Latin America (Brazil, Argentina, Mexico, and Colombia) (*Finance & Development,* 1992). Integration between developed and developing countries is therefore skewed and benefits to most Third World countries are limited; many countries are left out of this type of global change and their per capita income remains at low levels. Women in these marginalized coun-

---

[1] For example, with the passage of the Uruguay Round of GATT and the establishment of the World Trade Organization, the WTO.

tries have little to no chance of participating in the economic growth and the rising standards of living that are occurring in some other countries.

Second, as a result of increased market orientation, inequalities are often widened between men and women within an economy. Increasing market orientation typically involves reduced support for social services (health or housing and food subsidies) and less regulation in hiring, wages, working conditions (health, safety, and the right to unionize), environmental conditions, and standards for products sold locally. These types of changes result in increasingly adverse conditions, particularly for women. This is the case because, almost universally, women are largely responsible for family well being and because they tend to be in jobs considered lower skilled, of lower value, and with poorer working conditions (UN, 1995b). Reduction in social services makes it much harder for women to maintain a standard of living in the household. With relaxation of regulation, any existing standards that might improve job conditions are reduced or eliminated. Such effects hold true for women in all countries moving toward increased market orientation, but particularly so for women in transitional economies. Seager (1997) points out that in 1995 women's wages in Russia were 40% of men's, whereas they had been 70%. She also states that women in Eastern Europe experienced higher unemployment rates and decreased support for child and healthcare as transition proceeded. In addition, globally, with decreased regulation there is often an increase in "flexible" forms of work–part time or outwork that entails no benefits and can be terminated almost instantaneously.

Third, because of globalization and increasing market orientation of many countries, events in some nations increasingly impact on the economies of others in ways the latter cannot control. For example, increases in the interest rate in the United States in the early 1980s (as part of the monetarist approach to macromanaging the United States economy) triggered an international debt crisis. Years of reduced or stagnating growth of output and employment ensued in much of Latin America and Africa, with particularly adverse impacts on women (ILO, 1995). Similarly, the collapse of the peso in Mexico in late 1994 and the increasing poverty and social unrest there are linked to changes in the monetary policy of the United States. Even more recently, the financial crisis affecting many countries in Asia since the summer of 1997 was triggered by devaluation of the Thai baht; the crisis in Brazil in 1998 occurred immediately after the collapse of the Russian economy in August 1998. Much social unrest has accompanied these crises. Because women are largely responsible for family welfare, the effects fall heavily on them.

In short, although these dimensions of global restructuring—increasing globalization of economic activity and the shift toward market economies by many countries—seem to draw the world together, the widening inequality within and between countries that is characteristic of more market-oriented capitalism becomes a countervailing force that is divisive.

In addition, although economic globalization has been accompanied and facilitated by the end of the Cold War and the disbanding of the major political camps into which countries were divided, there are newly arising political and religious forces that are divisive and have different economic effects by gender. On a relatively benign level, changes in the global political economy include the rise of regional trade blocks that can put countries outside the block at a competitive disadvantage, and affect the women in each accordingly. On a more violent level, political forces—increased nationalism, ethnic rivalries, and escalating conflicts often bordering on genocidal—divide countries from one another (e.g., in the Middle East), disrupt internal workings (e.g., in Sri Lanka, South Africa, Somalia, Sudan, Rwanda) or splinter countries (e.g., the former USSR and former Yugoslavia). Such political and military conflicts have had a particularly adverse impact on women's economic roles. Heyzer (1995) states that women and children are 75% of those affected or displaced in war-ravaged areas. When the Gulf War began in the early 1990s, for example, large numbers of South and East Asian women who had migrated to the Middle East for work had to return to their home countries, losing their jobs and incomes. Further, many women in war-torn countries such as Rwanda or the former Yugoslavia have been murdered. Surviving women find it extremely difficult to provide for their families during ongoing strife and its aftermath, when they must pursue their activities in devastated economies on land that is often heavily mined. In countries such as Somalia and Rwanda, they live in constant fear of being raped (Dirasse, 1995).

In addition, fundamentalism has been growing throughout much of the world in Muslim, Protestant, Catholic, Jewish, and Hindu religions and has led to more restrictions on women's legal, social, and economic roles in many areas (Seager, 1997). Christian and Muslim fundamentalism both view women's major role as being in the home. This compounds the effects of preexisting sociocultural systems that give men the more powerful positions in society, the workplace, and the household. For example, the Taliban, strict interpreters of Islam who took control in Afganistan in 1996, have prohibited women from working and closed girls' schools, severely restricting women's opportunities relative to men (Seager, 1997).

3.2 Export-Led Development Strategy

This type of global restructuring is based on the idea that high growth rates can be generated by production of manufactured goods or service activities for export. It is also referred to as the export-oriented or outward-looking strategy. In many countries it replaces an import-substitution strategy (ISI) that focused on domestic production of most producer and consumer goods needed in the country. ISI emphasized heavy industry and employed largely male workforces, whereas export-led development relies heavily on women.

Export-led development was perceived as successful in the NICs—the newly industrialized countries of Hong Kong, Taiwan, South Korea, and Singapore that adopted this strategy in the late 1960s. Because they achieved high growth rates and rising standards of living (from the late 1960s until the financial crisis in Asia in 1997) many other countries adopted this type of development approach. In addition, export-led development has been widely promoted, even pushed, by the WB and the IMF in Latin American and even in Africa.

Export-led development often involves the attraction of multinational corporations (MNCs) and sometimes includes the use of export processing zones (EPZs) to ensure high rates of production for export. Increasingly, it encompasses enlarged networks of indigenous subcontractors, varying greatly in size, and other peripheral workers in small informal workshops or engaged in home-based work. Export-led development has relied heavily on sectors such as textiles and garments, shoes, toys, athletic wear, and electronics to generate export revenues and employment.[2] It now involves service sector work,

---

[2] The establishment of an export-led development strategy requires trade liberalization, exchange rates favorable for selling exports, and incentives to attract foreign investment or MNCs (as sole owners or in joint ventures). Incentives can be in the form of lower taxes or complete tax holidays, freedom to repatriate profits, subsidies (for credit, labor training, or export), decreased (or eliminated) environmental restrictions, reduced import duties, low wages, maintaining a docile labor force (even if it means suppression of labor). Also needed are an adequate infrastructure, political stability, an adequately educated labor force, and access to markets. It is often referred to as a free-market strategy; however, as just described, it actually involves comprehensive sets of distinct policies tailored and implemented by the government in ways to benefit corporations.

such as office administration and offshore data entry and processing, word processing, and invoicing for the travel and finance industries.[3] Export-led development has been linked with the feminization of the workforce in manufacturing and in some modern service sectors (Joekes & Weston, 1994; Standing, 1989), although decreases over time in the percentage of women in the export sector workforce may modify the extent to which this can be argued.

Over the past three decades, such industries in East and Southeast Asia have been heavily based upon female labor, providing alternative types of employment for some women. Women are favored because they typically can be paid less than men and, given the level of technology, are generally considered more productive workers because of their abilities and willingness to work hard, their patience in tolerating repetitive and monotonous tasks, and their reluctance to unionize or resist (Lim, 1996). Women were lower-cost employees than men in the Asian NICs. For example, in 1982 women's earnings as a percentage of men's in manufacturing were 45% in South Korea, 63% in Singapore, and 78% in Hong Kong. In 1987, the ratios were 50% in South Korea, 58% in Singapore, and 76% in Hong Kong (Pyle & Dawson, 1990). In 1994, women still earned only 58% of men's wages in manufacturing in South Korea (Kim & Kim, 1995).

The use of women workers in export-oriented development has been most carefully examined in the case of EPZs because these are self-contained areas that are relatively easier to study than women's roles in export production in general. Broader export production includes subcontracting networks that are very fluid, with contracts initiated or terminated in rapid response to changes in demand. These networks are amorphous, hard to trace, and difficult to research. Although women comprise the larger proportion of workers in subcontracting, informal, and home-based economic activities (Joekes & Weston, 1994), comprehensive data are not available. Therefore, although EPZs hire only a small proportion of the total number of women employed worldwide, analysis of their operations sheds light on the use of women in wider export sectors.

It has been estimated that, in the early 1990s, 4 million people were employed globally in EPZs, with 70% to 80% of these women (Joekes & Weston, 1994; Lim, 1996). Although EPZs are present in over 65 countries (Seager, 1997), they are concentrated in only a few countries—Mexico, Dominican Republic, Brazil, Malaysia, Tunisia, Mauritius, Taiwan, Sri Lanka, and Guatemala (Joekes & Weston, 1994).[4] The results of studies of conditions in EPZs vary—with some suggesting that wages are somewhat better than for similar jobs locally, others finding that the pay is even worse (Joekes & Weston, 1994). The hazards to which women are exposed are typically substantial.

Two recent studies, in Sri Lanka and Malaysia, carefully document the economic and social impact of these zones on the female workers involved (Abeywardene, de Alwis, Jayasena, Jayaweera, & Sanmugam, 1994; Sivalingam, 1994). The Sri Lankan study reveals that 85% of the workers in the EPZs are women, most of them young, unmarried, and from low-income families. Women are allocated the unskilled, routine work and constitute the preponderance of production workers, whereas men hold the technical and administrative jobs. Eighty percent of the workers interviewed reported that, if possible, they would leave their jobs in EPZs because of their dissatisfaction with working conditions. The wages for women were below those for men for the same work. For example, female packers earned 1525 Sri Lankan Rupees (Rs.) a month, whereas male packers made 1800 Rs. Further, female operatives made 2000 Rs. a month while men operating

---

[3] These occur in Jamaica, Barbados, the Philippines, and China (Joekes & Weston, 1994).
[4] The sizable Special Economic Zones of China are not strictly comparable with EPZs.

the same machine earned 2500 Rs. a month. In addition, hours were often long, safety gear was rarely used, dismissals were arbitrary, and, although wages might be slightly higher than in comparable jobs outside the zones, housing accommodations were of poor quality and expensive, taking up to 50% of the monthly wage (Abeywardene et al., 1994).

The Malaysian study points out that production in EPZs is largely by foreign firms that recruit young, rural Malay women, aged 16–21, for semiskilled and unskilled production work. They don't hire women older than 23 because they fear the "older" women will demand higher wages and leave for marriage. Women comprised more than 70% of production workers in the electronics plants surveyed in 1990 and 80% of production workers in textiles/garments. However, they constituted a low percentage of the managerial and professional workers. Thus, women represented 57% of the workforce in EPZ textile/garment and electronic plants and 53% of the total workers in EPZs in 1990. Women's wages were 90% of men's in electronics and 80% in textiles/garments. Women face exposure to "excessive" (p. 43) heat and noise in textile production. In electronics, although the clean room concept makes it appear that women are working in a clean environment, they are exposed to toxic waste and hazardous chemicals. They are required to operate machines that were designed for a body larger than that of the typical woman, leading to accidents. They suffer eyestrain and deteriorating eyesight over a few years. Female electronics workers often have production standards that are excessively high, producing considerable stress. A larger percentage of the female workers are not permanent. For example, in the electronics plants, 30% of the female workforce was temporary and 20% were on probation as new employees. Turnover is high, particularly in the textile industry, because of the poor working conditions and the lack of upward job mobility (Sivalingam, 1994).

Women are also affected by export-oriented agricultural activities. However, even though large percentages of women are engaged in agriculture globally, such activities have been studied much less than those in the export manufacturing sector. Women may be included or excluded from export agricultural activities. In either case, their lives are precarious. On the one hand, women employed by agro-industry often have only seasonal work, and their income depends on the vagaries of the agricultural export markets (unpredictable supplies and varying demand). This places them in a vulnerable position. On the other hand, women may be excluded from becoming producers themselves for the export market, because, as women, they are denied access to credit, technological developments, and information. In some cases, changes in women's and men's agricultural roles are complexly related to global changes in product demand, pricing, and migratory labor. Wee and Heyzer (1995) tell how women initially replaced Malaysian men as rubber tappers but then were replaced themselves by low-wage illegal male migrants from surrounding countries that were economically more disadvantaged.

It has been widely noted that the number of women employed in industry increased during 1970–1990 in countries that adopted export-oriented development and had rapid growth in manufactured exports (Joekes & Weston, 1994; UN, 1991b, 1995a). In addition, as discussed, increasing numbers of women in some countries are being employed in export-oriented service sectors and some may be involved in agricultural endeavors. However, it should not be concluded that export orientation is necessarily the way to increase female employment. The employment effects may be rather short lived and the percentage of women in export manufacturing may decrease as the technology involved in production advances. For example, women's 53% share of Malaysian EPZ employment in 1990 cited previously was a reduction from their 70% share in 1985. Similarly, women had comprised 78% of workers in Mexico's maquiladora industries in 1975, but were only 59% in 1993 (Cardero, 1994).

In addition to the largely adverse effects on women documented previously, export-led development is a precarious strategy for maintaining or augmenting female employment for several reasons. First, this strategy involves increased competition with other countries. Not all countries can be successful in export-oriented manufacturing. Some will be more competitive than others. Although apparently successful in some areas in Southeast Asia, the strategy has been devastating in other areas, such as the Caribbean (McAfee, 1991). Its noted success in increasing female participation is limited to the eight Asian countries (Hong Kong, Indonesia, Singapore, Taiwan, China, Malaysia, Philippines, and Thailand) from which 80% of the increase in manufactured exports from developing countries came (UN, 1991b).

Second, the success of an export-oriented strategy is highly dependent on viable markets in other countries. The export-oriented country is therefore vulnerable to recessions that curtail demand in the countries to which they export. Fluctuations in demand directly impact on the female production workers involved. To illustrate, during the 1974–75 downturn, 50% of those laid off in Singapore were women, even though they were only 30% of the labor force at the time. In the 1985 recession, 60% of those laid off were women, although only 35% of the Singaporean labor force. The reason for these disparities is that 90% of the layoffs involved production workers, who were largely female (Pyle, 1994). More recently, the financial crises beginning in the summer of 1997 have reduced demand in areas ranging from Asia to Russia and Brazil, with serious effects on other nations that export to them. Many workers in the countries involved have lost their jobs. An article in *Finance & Development,* a publication of the IMF, reports that the total loss of jobs will be large (*Finance & Development,* 1998). Complete data by gender is not yet available because of the recentness of the events. Anecdotal news reports suggest that women's jobs have been heavily hit.

Last, in opening its economy to the rest of the world, the country pursuing export oriented development based largely on low-cost female labor not only exposes the women involved to the conditions (whether advantageous or disadvantageous) of this type of work, but also gives up much sovereign control. National economic outcomes now become heavily influenced by external forces, such as flows of capital, the existence of markets, or deliberate legislation passed in the importing country. The way export-oriented development operates can be for the benefit of corporations based in other countries rather than citizens of the export-oriented country. For example, Safa (1995) shows how the United States (U.S.) government shaped export-oriented development in the Caribbean in the 1980s to provide sites with low-cost labor for U.S. industry. The U.S. government established carefully tailored trade legislation that specified only assembly could occur in these areas, used U.S. Agency for International Development (USAID) financing, and heavily advertised the special zones as sites for U.S. firms to use for production. The workers involved were chiefly low-wage women. This did not lead to sustainable development in the Dominican Republic because industrial activities were limited to assembly operations performed by foreign rather than indigenous firms.

3.3 The Spread of MNCs and Their Cost-Cutting Strategies

Corporations have become much more global in terms of function, origin, and location since the early 1980s. MNCs are present internationally in sectors ranging from heavy industry (petrochemicals, automobiles) to consumer goods (shoes and clothing, electronics, toys, athletic goods) to services (hotel and airline reservations, claims processing). It is the consumer goods and some service sectors that employ large numbers of women.

MNCs now originate from increasingly diverse home countries: industrialized countries other than the United States, particularly Japan and Western Europe; the newly industrializing countries of South Korea, Taiwan, Hong Kong, and Singapore; and even other developing countries. They have expanded the areas in which they locate production to include additional tiers of developing countries (such as Bangladesh and Sri Lanka), as well as formerly socialist economies in Eastern Europe and Asia (Vietnam and China). Although FDI by multinational corporations has grown faster than world output, world trade, and domestic investment (ILO, 1995), and although flows to developing countries have increased particularly rapidly, global distribution has been skewed, affecting the economic roles of women in Third World countries accordingly. The spread of MNCs has largely been into other industrialized countries. In the developing world, just 10 countries have more than three quarters of the stock of FDI in the Third World, while the 47 least-developed nations have less than 1%.[5] Because MNCs are motivated chiefly to seek profits, among the key factors they consider in selecting a foreign location are lower-cost production opportunities (e.g., regarding wages or regulatory costs), accessibility to markets or resources, appropriately skilled (or unskilled) workers, and political stability. Competition for FDI is often very keen and many nations have little chance in the rivalry.

MNCs have a growing impact on women not only because of their increased direct presence globally but also because of the wider spheres of influence associated with their increased use of subcontracting and homework networks of production. They are the most dynamic segment of business internationally, continually increasing their geographic spread and altering their cost-cutting strategies in ways that affect growing numbers of people. In industrial sectors in which wages are a substantial portion of total costs—such as garments and textiles, electronics, toys, shoes, athletic gear—MNCs employ largely female production workers in their formal and informal networks.[6] For similar reasons, women are employed in service sector activities run by MNCs. Therefore, when these sectors expand (or contract) job opportunities are created (or diminished) for women.

It is estimated that, in 1993, MNCs directly employed 11 million people in developing countries, with a high percentage of women in the sectors just described. In addition, because the indirect networks are thought to add a multiple of between one and two, the total employment in the larger networks may be 20 to 30 million in developing countries (Joekes & Weston, 1994). MNCs provide more than 20% of manufacturing employment in Asian countries such as Singapore, Indonesia, Sri Lanka, and the Philippines. They provide more than one fifth in Latin American countries of Argentina, Mexico, Barbados, and in the African countries of Botswana and Mauritius (Joekes & Weston, 1994).

3.3.1. GENERAL EFFECTS OF MNCs.   Earlier debates over whether women benefited from or were disadvantaged by employment in MNCs have been replaced by a more complex analysis that addresses the dynamics and contradictions involved with female MNC employment. In the very short term, employment in MNCs may appear to provide

---

[5] The 10 largest host countries in the developing world in 1988–89 were Argentina, Brazil, China, Columbia, Egypt, Hong Kong, Malaysia, Mexico, Singapore, and Thailand.

[6] For the reasons cited before—because women are lower cost workers, are considered dexterous, are often willing to work long hours at very repetitive tasks, and are generally compliant.

greater material benefit to the women and their families than existing income-earning alternatives. There is also evidence that, although wages are low in MNCs relative to industrialized countries, and working conditions more adverse, MNCs in many areas offer conditions and pay that are slightly better than those of other local, domestically owned employers (Joekes & Weston, 1994; Sivalingam, 1994; Todaro, 1997). However, negative aspects are often obvious in the short term in the form of long hours, forced overtime, increased production quotas or speedups, poor working conditions or housing, stress, and harassment from management. The adverse impact is more clear in the longer term, when these women experience work-related deterioration of health, the lack of benefits, the absence of opportunities to gain skills and advance in the job hierarchy, and loss of jobs due to their health, work-related stress, or strategies of automation, retrenchment, or relocation of the MNCs (discussed later).

These general effects vary according to how long the country has been pursuing export-oriented growth and the particular corporate cost-cutting strategies adopted (discussed in the next section). Countries that utilized this strategy in earlier decades have been consciously moving from labor-intense sectors to more high-tech industries. For women employed in MNCs in the NICs, such as Singapore or Hong Kong, who have escaped loss of jobs due to strategies discussed just below, working conditions and absolute wage levels have improved somewhat over time as a result of worker resistance. Nonetheless, conditions of female employment in MNCs vary even within the NICs. For example, in Singapore there has been a dramatic increase in female employment and a narrowing of the male/female wage gap since the 1960s; in South Korea women remained a more peripheral workforce, with relatively short working lives. The difference may be due to the tighter labor market in Singapore and state support (Phongpaichit, 1988).

However, although conditions (regarding wages and perhaps health and safety standards) may have improved in some NICs, adverse conditions persist in most other developing countries. Conditions are the worst in the latest group of countries to adopt export-oriented growth—the second tier of countries to follow the NICs (Thailand, Malaysia, Indonesia, or the Philippines) or the third tier (Sri Lanka, Bangladesh, areas of China and India). As the MNCs move into the latest tier of countries that are pursuing export-led development, where local working conditions are often even worse, they adopt the same patterns regarding pay, hours, and working conditions as when they established operations in the NICs. Women often earn very low wages with no benefits and work long hours that can be increased at the will of the employer. They are often exposed to health and safety hazards (because of exposure to toxic chemicals or lint and dust and due to lack of enforcement of standards), may have limited access to sanitary facilities, and may be verbally or sexually abused.

In addition, patterns of women's participation in MNC employment networks differ by factors such as age, marital status, race/ethnicity, class, culture, and the design of state policy as well as by gender (Blumberg, Rakowski, Tinker, & Monteon, 1995; Pyle, 1998; Rakowski, 1995; Ward, 1990; Ward & Pyle, 1995). For example, age and cultural conventions interact to shape where women are employed in the greater MNC production networks. Direct employment in MNCs in labor-intensive industries in Asia typically involves young unmarried women. The subcontracting networks in Hong Kong and South Korea, however, often utilize married women who are older (Pun, 1995), as does the garment homework sector in the Philippines (Ofreneo, 1994). State policy also affects women's employment in MNCs. State policy during export-led development in Singapore was designed to bring women into the labor force and provide a workforce for MNCs; in the Republic of Ireland, another small island economy pursuing the same development strategy, state policy was explicitly designed to pursue firms that would employ larger proportions of males (Pyle, 1990, 1994).

3.3.2. EFFECTS OF COST-CUTTING STRATEGIES OF MNCs.
MNCs have used four types of global cost-cutting strategies in the past decade at an accelerated pace in both industrialized and developing countries. They are particularly intensified when competition increases. These strategies affect all industries—heavy industry that hires largely males as well as light industries that hire larger percentages of women. Although they affect both male and female workers internationally, the focus here is on the effects on the female workforces in lighter industry.

As costs have risen in specific areas in which MNCs have been producing, they have chosen one or more of the following responses: to suppress labor demands; to automate; to increase the use of homeworking or subcontracting to other businesses within the country; or to move to another tier of low-cost countries. Each of these strategies has had largely adverse effects on the women and children involved as workers in the original location.

First, although a few MNCs pay wages in some developing countries that are attractive locally, there is considerable evidence that they actively suppress workers' demands for higher wages and desires to improve other job conditions. When such refusal to negotiate leads to worker efforts to unionize, MNCs counter these activities via threats or dismissals (Safa, 1994) and some workers turn up missing, presumed dead (Ofreneo, 1994. They often quell labor unrest with the assistance of the police or the military, as recently exemplified in Indonesia, the Philippines, and South Korea. In addition, MNCs derail some management-labor conflicts via programs (such as quality circles) that appear to give workers some input into the decision-making and labor process, while not transferring effective power. Such actions harm women physically and psychologically, and tend to reinforce their subordinate status.

Second, MNCs may automate or adopt more advanced technologies. It is largely female jobs that are replaced by machines. For example, a study of the semiconductor industry in Malaysia revealed that although net employment increased between 1977 and 1984, the proportion of female workers fell. This occurred because the industry became more technical, hiring more skilled labor, technicians, and engineers, most of whom were males (Salih & Young, 1989). In addition, it is likely that as computerized processes become more viable in the garment industry, and as text and voice recognition systems are implemented in computer work, it is chiefly female employment that will drop.

Third, MNCs often relocate to lower-wage countries or areas within a country. MNCs move into a new country as direct producers, via subcontracting, or in joint ventures where a MNC and a local enterprise jointly own the business. As MNCs in labor-intensive industries relocate, women in the new location gain employment while women at the original site lose their jobs. The newly unemployed are often unable to find other employment, particularly if they gained no new marketable skills at these jobs. For example, a company closure in South Korea's Masan Free Export Zone (Mafez), where the workforce was 75% female, focused attention on what has been called an industrial ghetto for women. These women left school early to work in the MNC and had few skills transferable to more high-tech jobs when companies closed. The paradox was that, at the time, South Korea had a shortage of labor. Such misuse of female labor is inefficient, in addition to inequitable. It is widely expected to be the trend, however, throughout the labor-intensive industries in garments, footwear, and toys in South Korea and other NICs.

Fourth, under the innocuous rubric of augmenting "flexibility," corporations increasingly contract work out to subcontracting and/or homework networks throughout the industrialized and developing world. In contrast to workers in factories, workers in such networks cost MNCs substantially less because they work for significantly lower pay, can be easily terminated, have no benefits, require little to no fixed capital, and are less likely to organize or unionize. As MNCs increase the use of subcontracting and homework networks, it is often women who are employed. This type of work involves contradictions for women. On the one hand, it allows women who are married or household heads the flexibility to combine paid work with household duties. On the other hand, the women are even more vulnerable economically because they are paid less, have no benefits, and can be terminated immediately in the event of an economic downturn.

Subcontracting networks often involve informal sector jobs, illustrating how increased MNC production affects women in the informal sector as well as the formal sector. Beneria and Roldan (1987) were among the first to extend the analysis of the effect of MNCs on women beyond formal employment (paid labor in MNC factories) to the informal sector. They examined the layers of subcontracting and homework arrangements that were developed by MNCs in Mexico City and examined the blurred line between formal and informal work. This has also been studied in South Korea and the Philippines (Lee & Song, 1994; Ofreneo, 1994). Further, just as MNC networks have increasingly encompassed informal sector employment, indigenous industrial firms do so also, thereby increasing the adverse conditions for women.

Although the effects of employment in MNCs on women are somewhat contradictory, they are largely negative. This is compounded by the fact that activities in the subcontracting networks often associated with MNCs are typically more hidden from public view, providing them the opportunity to treat workers even less favorably. Additional inequities and worker abuses are rife. In spite of the visibility of a few prominent cases in recent years, these subcontracting networks are harder to influence. In addition, it is feared that MNCs originating from Asian countries (such as South Korea or Taiwan) that move production into other countries in the region will be less responsible because of their high degree of anonymity internationally. They often produce components, products that will be used to assemble other final goods, and are therefore isolated from consumer awareness; they have displayed little concern for social or environmental concerns.

3.4. Structural Adjustment Programs (SAPs)

The role of structural adjustment policies (SAPs) has been prominent and controversial for the past twenty years. In the early 1980s many developing countries encountered serious economic problems. The 1979 oil crisis, with the accompanying rapid increases in the price of oil, began a set of global recessions. Rising interest rates in the United States precipitated the international debt crisis that severely affected many countries in the developing world. With the exception of some countries in Asia, most of the developing world was engulfed in widespread stagnation or recession for the next few years. SAPs, designed to stabilize and restructure an economy, were required as a condition of borrowing from the IMF and the WB and, in turn, to obtain loans from private commercial banks in developed countries (banks required IMF backing). SAPs were established throughout Latin America and in over thirty countries in Africa during the 1980s (Haddad, Brown, Richter, & Smith, 1995). Many countries borrowed heavily from the IMF and

WB.[7] However, these programs brought hardship to people in much of the developing world, with particularly adverse impact on women (Lim, 1996; UN, 1995b). More recently, SAPs have been an integral part of financial bailout packages arranged by the IMF for many countries involved in the financial crises arising since July (for example, Thailand, Indonesia, South Korea, and Russia). The stringency of the policies required, their recessionary impact, and the way they distribute the impact of the crises on lower-income peoples have fostered considerable controversy and unrest.

SAPs are based upon traditional neoclassical economic theory—a model that is critiqued from a variety of points of view, including its failure to systematically include gender as an integral component of the analysis. SAPs have been conceptualized as having two components: one a stabilization phase (designed to stabilize key economic indicators, such as inflation rates, government budget deficits, or trade deficits), the other a restructuring or structural adjustment phase (intended to make the stabilized economy more competitive by moving toward a more market-oriented economy with less government intervention). The stabilization component was to be relatively short term and lay the foundation for enhanced economic growth, which would be encouraged over a longer term through the restructuring phase. Policies for both phases have been implemented together. Both can have unfavorable effects on women, although there is at least the possibility that the restructuring component could open up opportunities for some women.

Accomplishing these main goals involves a myriad of other deliberate economic policy changes, most of which negatively impact women. For example, according to traditional neoclassical economic theory, stabilizing prices requires contractionary fiscal policies (reducing government spending or increasing taxes) or restrictive monetary policy (higher interest rates). It can also involve wage freezes. Stabilization policies are designed to attain price stability and assist in reducing deficits; they are *not* focused on stability in employment. In addition, policies to make an economy more competitive domestically and internationally involve privatizing state-owned enterprises, devaluation of the exchange rate (to make exports more price competitive abroad), and a host of specific policies to promote export-oriented development. Opening a country to MNCs is often part of the agenda.[8]

In general, stabilization and SAPs required by the IMF and WB promote market orientation, establish policies favorable for corporations, and implicitly reinforce the lack of concern for employment, income inequality, and fair treatment for all. SAPS enacted in the 1980s and early 1990s have resulted in rising unemployment, falling incomes and standards of living, worsening income distribution, increasing poverty, deteriorating working conditions, and environmental degradation. These factors, in turn, undermine long-term growth rates, one of the goals of the SAPs in the first place (UN, 1991b).[9]

[7] The biggest borrowers from the IMF 1980–1992 were Mexico, Brazil, Venezuela, Argentina, the former Yugoslavia, the Philippines, Morocco, Ghana, Bangladesh, and Bolivia.

[8] This may involve tax holidays, free repatriation of profits, subsidies on worker training and interest rates, reduced import duties, deregulation of environmental standards and labor conditions standards regarding minimum wage, rights to form unions, and working conditions. As discussed earlier, such policies typically benefit corporations, often based in other countries.

[9] As a UN (1991b) publication states, "Although mainstream economists generally regard structural adjustment policies as necessary to lay the groundwork for steady economic growth, these policies are often criticized for failing to accomplish economic restructuring without adversely impacting long-term growth prospects and poverty and environmental sustainability concerns and for not taking account of the country-specific circumstances of economic reform" (p. 14). In the early 1990s, the IMF reevaluated to try to lessen the adverse impacts of the policies. However, because of the nature of the market system and the ideology of the prevailing orthodoxy, it is difficult to diminish the adverse effects.

It is widely concluded that the earlier rounds of SAPs have a gender bias that is unfavorable for women (Aslanbeigui, Pressman, & Summerfield, 1994; Bakker, 1994; Rakowski, 1995; Sparr, 1994; Thomas-Emeagwali, 1995; UN, 1991b, 1995a). The stabilization phase, thought to be short term, has had distinctly adverse effects on all people, but more so on women. Evaluating the effects of the restructuring phase, however, is considered more difficult because of the problems of assessing the effects of particular policy changes in a social environment where so much is changing over the medium to longer term. If women are able to benefit from changes in the incentive structure that restructuring establishes (i.e., it favors the tradable goods sectors), they can benefit from adjustment. However, women are at a distinct disadvantage because of their limited access to resources and the constraints on their ability to reallocate resources (including their own labor) in line with changes in adjustment incentives (Haddad et al., 1995).

To illustrate, government spending can be reduced in several different ways, each of which affects women adversely. It can be curtailed by cutting public sector employment (including in publicly owned industries). Because women often are employed in the public sector, this hits them disproportionately hard (UN, 1991b). Government budgets can also be reduced by curtailing spending on social services (such as health care, family planning, education, and training) and removing subsidies for basic needs, such as foodstuffs and transportation. Cuts in education and training budgets often harm women, because, in many societies, women have less access to education than men and government programs have helped to alleviate this inequity. In addition, because women are overwhelmingly responsible for family well-being, they are dramatically affected by reduction in spending on health care and family planning as well as on subsidies (UN, 1995b). They find themselves with significantly fewer resources to provide for the needs of the household. As government social services are eliminated, these formerly free goods must be paid for. Prices of needed household items also rise when subsidies on food and transportation are reduced or eliminated (UN, 1995b).

If curtailing the country's federal budget involves increases in taxes, they are typically of the type that fall regressively on the poor, of which women are a disproportionate number (UN, 1995b). In addition, contractionary fiscal policies usually result in recessions in which layoffs are widespread; as shown earlier, women's jobs are typically the most vulnerable in a recession. Restrictive monetary policies entail higher interest rates which make it even harder for women to obtain funds for entrepreneurial activity (UN, 1991b). Wage freezes unmatched by price freezes cause a decline in real purchasing power. This lowers the standard of living and increases poverty, making it harder for women to meet the needs of their families.

As women lose jobs in the formal sector and find household resources drastically squeezed by stabilization and structural adjustment policies, they are typically forced into informal sector employment, which pays less and is much more precarious (UN, 1995b). They often must work longer hours and make sacrifices in consumption and healthcare. As regulations regarding the environment and conditions at the workplace are eliminated or left unenforced, the environmental quality of worklife, as well as life in general, diminishes. As people must competitively scramble into the informal sector to eke out a living, further environmental damage occurs. Some are forced into taking part-time work (which may combine better with home duties) and others may set up an informal sector business. However, preexisting inequalities in many countries largely keep women from participating in many entrepreneurial activities. Women are typically discriminated against by formal lending agencies because they lack collateral. They must utilize informal sector money lenders, who charge much higher interest rates (UN, 1991b).

These structural adjustment programs have affected women and men throughout the world. If countries were able to recover from the contractionary stabilization policies and restructure, those who were able to move into sectors that were favored by the programs (chiefly the tradable goods sectors) could benefit (Haddad et al., 1995). The effects of these earlier rounds of SAPs on women in Asia were contradictory. It was here that women were able to achieve some benefit from structural adjustments that opened their economies to trade and possibly foreign investment. Many women gained jobs as a result of the restructuring. However, as documented earlier in the sections on export-led development and MNCs, this was not completely beneficial. Although many women had jobs that were possibly better than the alternatives they faced, we have seen how many of the conditions surrounding work (such as wages, hours, health and safety, or treatment by management) were distinctly unfavorable.

During the 1980s, many countries in Latin America, the Caribbean, and Africa initiated SAPs and opted for more market orientation and export-led development. They did so either because they were pressured by the IMF and the WB as a condition for loans or because they were suffering from recessions or stagnation and wanted to replicate the success of the NICs. SAPs particularly worsened the socioeconomic position of women in these areas. With women's wage employment falling in Latin America and unemployment rising, women were forced into the informal sector. Government cutbacks in health care were severe, as were cuts in education and training. As health deteriorates, women are less able to work; as educational opportunities decrease, women are less able to attain needed skills. In many developing countries women worked long hours to maintain even meager living standards.

Often the lower and middle income people affected by such increasing deprivation become frustrated and angry. Many demonstrations have occurred to protest the SAPs, often organized and led by women. In addition, concerns have erupted into revolt, fighting, disorder, and deaths which clearly disrupt economic and social life. SAPs contain within them seeds of their own and social destruction. Others have linked the frustrations generated by the worsening income distribution that SAPs create to the rise of "fundamentalism, fascism, and ethnic conflicts" (Sen, 1995, p. 11), which as we have seen in Section 3.1, greatly constrains women's opportunities and, in some cases, subjects them to violence ranging from beating, rape, to death.

The newest rounds of SAPs, required as conditions for IMF financial assistance designed to address the financial crises that began in 1997, appear to affect inhabitants of recipient countries in similar ways. An article in *Finance & Development* (an IMF publication) indicates that poverty will increase in Indonesia, South Korea, and Thailand through price increases and loss of jobs (*Finance & Development*, 1998). There are news reports that people in the broader group of countries affected are experiencing severe hardship and deprivation, unrest and resistance, and death. There are indications of their particularly adverse impact on women—in terms of loss of jobs and in providing for household needs. More aggregate country-wide data is now emerging in government statistics that can provide a broader basis on which to evaluate the impact of these policies by class and gender.

3.5. Institutional Restructuring

Another way to understand global restructuring is to consider changes in major institutions in the global political economy and shifts in the balance of power among them. The major institutions in the macro global economy are: MNCs and their production networks, international organizations (such as the WB, the IMF, the UN, and the ILO), national governments, and nongovernmental organizations (NGOs) or grassroots organizations concerned with gender issues. These institutions, and changes in them, shape the power structure within which women live and work.

As discussed previously, the structural changes in MNCs—their countries of origin, the areas into which they have spread, and their four-pronged cost-cutting strategies—have had a dramatic effect on women in industry. They are motivated to seek profits and increase markets, rather than by concerns for equity. They are not concerned with alleviating rising income inequality, reducing unemployment, treating women/people equally, or preserving the environment.

Among the international organizations are the IMF, and the WB, and numerous UN organizations. On the one hand, as shown previously, there is widespread documentation that the SAPs required by the WB and the IMF have hurt most women. These two institutions are motivated to loan money according to the standards of the prevailing neoclassical economic paradigm and to ensure that borrowers are able to repay loans and funds are not lost. Because they hold the pursestrings and their approval is often necessary for additional private loans, they have considerable power to enforce their view.

On the other hand, many UN organizations are motivated to improve the socioeconomic status of women, but they have limited funds and little power. The UN agencies have produced increasing amounts of information that is the basis for a better understanding of the status of women globally and their importance to development and family well-being, and for the development of strategies to improve women's lives. Among the more comprehensive recent publications in terms of data and policy recommendations are *The World's Women 1995: Trends and Statistics* (co-sponsored by 11 UN partner organizations) and the *Human Development Report 1995* of the UN Development Programme (UNDP). The latter focuses on gender disparities and, not only provides extensive data, but also develops two new measures of the development status of countries that incorporate gender: the Gender Development Index (GDI) and the Gender Empowerment Measure (GEM). The GDI considers inequalities between men and women in longevity, literacy, and standard of living whereas the GEM includes women's share of parliamentary positions, managerial and professional jobs, and income, as well as their labor force participation rates.

UNIFEM (the United Nations Development Fund for Women) had its roots in the First UN conference on Women in 1975 and is focused on promoting the economic and political empowerment of women. Its activities range from funding capacity building among women in Third World countries to reexamination of development models and formation of gender sensitive macro-models. It is designed to ensure that women and their concerns are included in mainstream development planning, to support experimental programs to benefit women and their country's overall priorities, and to be a catalyst for these concerns throughout the greater UN system (UNIFEM, 1995).

Similarly, the ILO has tried to set and increase standards in the workplace; however, it lacks enforcement powers. It published an extensive follow-up to the Fourth World Conference on Women (1995) and the World Summit for Social Development (1995) that outlines plans to implement the declarations of these two summits regarding equality of opportunity for women in employment and qualitative improvements in working conditions (see Lim, 1996, *More and Better Jobs for Women: An Action Guide, 1996*). It addresses inequalities by gender in hiring, pay, occupations, decision making, unemployment, access to training, promotions and resources, and in family responsibilities. Again, it has no authority to execute these ideas.

National governments are another set of players on the macro global scene. Most do not incorporate women into development planning. An INSTRAW study revealed that only six of 96 countries surveyed mentioned women's issues in their development plans (Vickers, 1991). National governments are interested in growth rates, price stability, and surviving financial, political, or military crises. Provision of stable levels of high employment is essentially not on their agendas. Many governments have restructured their economies, as required by the SAPs or to pursue export-led growth; many have sought to attract MNCs and FDI. There is intense international competition for FDI, and, as each country seeks to make itself an attractive location, it often further weakens any existing labor standards (regarding wages, hours, benefits, working conditions, and rights to unionize) by failing to enforce them or by deregulation. Rather than devoting substantial attention to human development or sustainable development, they take an immediate and short-run perspective that perpetuates the institutions in power. These are typically the same institutions that have resulted in past and present inequality. The effects on women have been documented throughout this chapter, particularly in the sections on export-oriented development, MNCs, and structural adjustment policies.

There are many NGOs working on gender and development issues. Chen (1995) documents the dramatic increases in women's NGOs in the past two decades and their increasing importance at the various world conferences held regarding women (1975, 1980, 1985, 1995) or the conferences on human rights (1993) and population and development (1994). These NGOs have arisen in a great number of countries; many have built large and sophisticated alliances among themselves on critical issues. They range from small grassroots organizations to coalitions that span major regions of the world, and often bridge the North–South gap that is said to exist between women and countries in general. However, it is difficult for the few international organizations that have human development as their agenda and the myriad of NGOs to stand up successfully against the corporations, the WB and IMF, national governments, and patriarchal cultural restraints. There is no major institutional grouping with the power to blunt the negative impact of the global market system on women.

4. EFFECTS OF GLOBAL RESTRUCTURING ON WOMEN IN INDUSTRY: ANALYTICAL LINKAGES

There are clear analytical linkages between the continuation of women's disadvantaged status and the various types of global restructuring—the increasing globalization and market orientation of the world's economy, export-oriented development strategies advocated by the WB and the IMF, changing corporate strategies of MNCs and their networks, and SAPs.

There are causal links, for example, between the spread of MNCs and the use of SAPs, on the one hand, and increases in women's participation in the informal sector on the other. As discussed previously, these two global phenomena have drawn increasing numbers of women into informal sector activities simply so the women could survive. When SAPs have been implemented in many countries, women have lost jobs in the formal sector and, in a variety of ways, have lost resources to provide for their families as governments cut back expenses. For both reasons women have been increasingly forced into informal sector employment. In addition, MNCs have increasingly utilized cost-cutting strategies (automation, relocation, increased subcontracting) that force many women into informal sector work. Women are often involved in informal industrial work because they can combine it with home duties. However, such employment pays much less, is very unstable, and conditions are even worse than in formal sector jobs.

Because of the characteristics of informal sector employment, poverty increases. Income is lower and women are forced to work longer hours. This trend is particularly devastating for households headed by women (up to 30% in some areas) and for immigrant women who are especially vulnerable (UN, 1991b). As poverty and inequality increase, in turn additional crises of unemployment, inflation, even famine or political upheaval result. Without some significant change, this chain of events will be perpetuated.

This dynamic and the analytic linkages between women's continued disadvantaged status and these forms of global restructuring, result from several characteristics of the global market system as a whole and the traditional neoclassical approach to economics (the prevailing orthodoxy) upon which the market system and much of the global restructuring is based: (1) gender is not a variable of analysis, resulting in a misspecified basis for policy making; (2) in addition, markets do not consider equity as a goal, which can undermine the market goals of efficiency and long-term growth; and (3) the notion that these forms of global restructuring are a move toward free markets is a myth obscuring the reality that the global economy is dominated a few powerful institutions, none of which govern or monitor it with the primary goal of human development or gender equity in mind.

First, traditional economic analysis, and the policies constructed upon its view of the socioeconomy and enacted worldwide, have not included gender as a variable of analysis. They are not, however, gender-neutral in their impact because women and men have distinctly different occupations and responsibilities in the economies of most countries. Women are largely responsible for housework (which has been invisible in national income accounts until recently) and men and women typically fill different types of jobs in the paid labor force, with women in the lower-paid jobs with less responsibility.

On the microeconomic level, according to neoclassical economic theory, the perfectly competitive economy has a large number of small actors (firms, workers, consumers), none of whom have control over prices. Forces of supply and demand interact in free markets with perfect information and therefore outcomes are fairly determined. This microeconomic approach assumes that everyone has the same opportunities. If someone is in a disadvantaged position in the labor market, for example, it is thought to be because they chose this position or because they did not acquire sufficient human capital (education, training, or experience). Any possible discrimination against particular groups (such as women) would simply be a short-term phenomenon that firms would find it profitable to eradicate (i.e., if women were paid lower wages, capitalists would make more money by hiring them, thus driving up their wages relative to those of men). Feminist economists, and others, have for years documented the fact that such variables cannot statistically account for the major proportion of the wage gap that exists between men and women.

Macroeconomic theory is even more removed from gender. It focuses on such variables as output, growth rates, prices, unemployment, interest rates, money supply, government spending, taxation, and exchange rates. People are not mentioned other than in employment/unemployment figures. Further, the focus of macroeconomic policy makers in developed countries has been on price rather than on employment variables. Traditional economics has defined work as tasks that are valued by and paid for through markets, thus making the vast amount of economic activity that women perform unpaid in households invisible. The value of these activities has been estimated at $11 trillion. To provide context for their importance, official global output is estimated at $23 trillion

(UNDP, 1995). Feminist economists have spearheaded an effort to revise systems of national accounting to incorporate women's work in the household, giving it proper visibility and respect. They have also been increasingly urging an engendering of macroeconomic policy (see for example, Bakker, 1994; Beneria, 1995; Elson, 1995; and the entire special issue of *World Development,* Nov., 1995).

The failure to include gender as a variable of analysis results in incomplete characterizations of economic life and a faulty basis for constructing policies for future growth. Omitting women from the analysis and policy prescriptions can undermine the attainment of goals, as shown directly below.

Second, in accordance with prevailing economic theory, markets are driven by concerns about efficiency and profits in the short term and are not motivated to provide equitable opportunities or outcomes, particularly by gender. This can undermine their goals for profitable growth. In most areas of the world, industries deal with issues regarding production, finance, and marketing, with little concern about fair relations with workers and income distribution in society. Workers are largely considered expendable and replaceable.[10] Others are seen as consumers at best. In many countries increased global competition leads to deteriorating labor conditions, as well as environmental and health conditions, as deregulated markets determine the quality of life. Social conditions may also deteriorate in many areas as they seek to attract corporations. I have shown above that these trends adversely affect women in particular.

Increases in inequality generated by market-oriented economies not only violate concerns of equity and fairness, but can also undermine economic growth and markets in a number of ways. In particular, inequality for women can undermine not only present growth but also future growth since women are largely in charge of providing for and raising the next generation. Women's contributions to economic development are handicapped when they have unequal access to jobs, credit, resources, markets, and the process of planning itself. In addition, when women do not have access to adequate health care and education, their capabilities as workers are impaired, as is their ability to provide an adequate standard of living for the next generation. This results in lowered productivity of future workers. Further, as inequality rises, there may be a deficiency in purchasing power to buy the goods and services produced, which undermines growth rates and can cause a contractionary cycle. In a worst case scenario, increased inequality and deprivation can cause social upheavals. As stated in a Report by the World Resources Institute in collaboration with the United Nations Environment Programme and the United Nations Development Programme (1994),

> Traditional market-oriented development policies that have failed to consider equity, the environment, human development, and women's roles in society are believed by a growing number of experts to have contributed to poverty, an increase in economic and gender inequities, and environmental degradation. Such policies, by often overlooking or even undermining women's well-being and participation in their communities, have not only hurt women but also hindered the achievement of broad sustainable development goals. (World Resources Institute, p. 57)

Neoclassical economic theory does recognize that markets can fail in a variety of ways, necessitating a role for government. For example, markets can fail to provide desired amounts of public goods, environmental protection, or education. Market-oriented systems do not provide socially optimal outcomes in these arenas of life unless they are

---

[10] It is only in some industrialized countries that organizations have been forced to recognize the dual roles of their workers (in the household as well as the workplace) and the need for policies that facilitate combining these roles.

modified by state, corporate, or NGO policies. However, what this approach does not recognize is that the failure of markets to be concerned with equity (particularly gender equity, given the importance of women in the workplace and the household) as well as short-term efficiency will eventually undermine efficiency and growth. Efficiency and growth are impaired when the health and education levels of the work force are diminished; they are also damaged by social upheavals that can erupt as a reaction to inequality.

Third, these forms of global restructuring—the move toward more market-oriented economies, export-led development, the behavior of the MNCs, and the structural adjustment policies—are all couched in the language of liberalization and free markets. This perpetuates the myth that the subsequent economic outcomes are the result of the operation of competitive markets, where everyone has similar opportunities and the role of government is minimal. However, there is a big difference between rhetoric and reality. As shown throughout Sections 3.1 to 3.4, these forms of global restructuring are based on *deliberate* interventions by government and are not "free market" strategies. All nations and all people do not have the same opportunities; overwhelming amounts of research have shown this.

The structure of the global economy is not that assumed in the traditional economic model in which most development economists receive training. The model of the perfectly competitive economy with a large number of small actors, none of whom have control over variables such as price, ignores the reality of powerful institutions. As outlined in Section 3.5, there are some major institutions acting in the global economy that have significant power. They have distinct goals and agendas that they seek to achieve using their power and resources. Gender equity is not one of them and I have shown the differential impact by gender of these forms of global restructuring, with the largely negative impact on women's lives. Although changes can occur over time (in terms of which country is preeminent, which corporations most influential), the existence of such a framework of powerful institutions creates an environment in which it is very difficult for those with less power and a different set of goals (such as governments, trade unions, or NGO groups organizing to improve women's position) to achieve any significant gains.

In spite of the myth, these countries are not purely market-oriented, efficiency-based economies. Quite the contrary, policies are often expressly tailored to the advantage of corporations or to meet conditions of large commercial banks and attract foreign corporations. The myth remains, however, in spite of evidence to the contrary such as this quote from an article in *Finance and Development* (a journal of the WB and IMF), in which Arvind Panagariya (1995) says,

> Successful export expansion, in turn, depends on the policy package, which conveys a message in no uncertain terms that the country will give priority to export-oriented activities. . . . In efficiency terms, virtually all policies—geographical targeting, preferential treatment of foreign investment in general and in export sectors in particular, and discriminatory exchange retention rights—were highly distortionary (p. 32).

In spite of the fact there are powerful actors in the global economy, there are essentially *no* effective international bodies to globally manage macroeconomic stability (which I would like to redefine broadly to include employment, gender equity as well as fairness in general, and environmental sustainability, in addition to prices and exchange rates). The G-7 (United States, United Kingdom, Germany, France, Italy, Japan, and Canada) is widely considered ineffective in influencing events—even in shaping exchange rates, which it considers its responsibility. The extremely large flows of funds from corporate financial institutions are often speculative and can easily shift, as in several Asian countries in 1997, leaving particular nations in severe economic distress. This leaves institutions such as the UN (with all its difficulties in establishing policies and affecting change), the IMF and the WB (which work on a country-by-country basis to provide funds and ensure their repayment, according to strict economic policies), and a plethora of other organizations that have been created to advance a variety of issues—women's, labor, environmental, and peace. Currently, none of them have either the power or the inclination to oversee the stability of the global economy.

Not only is there no effective international institution to stabilize the world economy, but, with globalization, national governments have reduced control over their own macroeconomic outcomes. Increasing globalization leaves countries more exposed to recessions and crises than before nations were so economically interlinked. It leads to rising vulnerability, particularly of members of society with less power, such as women. Recessions, in turn, prompt corporations to restructure further and increase their "flexibility" to relocate, automate, and retrench workers, which I have shown affects Third World women negatively. Poverty rises; inequality increases between countries; social and economic stability can be undermined.

These three characteristics of the global economy—that markets and traditional economic theory do not systematically include gender as a critical variable of analysis, nor equity as a goal, and that the language of liberalization and free markets is a myth obscuring domination of the global economy by powerful institutions—help perpetuate the dynamic wherein the effects of global restructuring on women in industry are largely negative.

5. CONCLUSIONS

The macro perspective of this chapter points out that there are several powerful global forces shaping women's roles that must be considered in analyses of the status of women and their importance to the development process and in planning for changes to improve their circumstances. They include: (1) the dynamics of the increasingly market-oriented global system; (2) the increasing adoption of export-led development strategies; (3) the spread and changing cost-cutting strategies of MNCs; (4) the effects of stabilization and structural adjustment policies (SAPs) required by the IMF and WB; and (5) inequities in the relative power of the major global institutions. The effect of these forces on women are compounded by preexisting systems of discrimination that subordinate women in the household, workplace (via lack of equal access to all jobs, and lack of resources for own businesses), political sphere, and religious institutions. This chapter has shown that there are analytical linkages between women's disadvantaged status and global restructuring. The problems that ensue for women are systemic and integral to the structure of the largely market-oriented international economy and the prevailing economic theories upon which policies for global restructuring are based. They must be addressed with this realization in mind.

REFERENCES

Abeywardene, J., de Alwis, R., Jayasena, A., Jayaweera, S., & Sanmugam, T. (1994). *Export processing zones in Sri Lanka: Economic impact and social issues.* Working Paper No. 69. Geneva: ILO.
Antrobus, P. (1995). Introduction. *Development: Journal of the Society for International Development* (Special issue prepared for the 4th UN World Conference on Women.), 5–7.

Aslanbeigui, N., Pressman, S., & Summerfield, G. (Eds.) (1994). Women and Economic Transformation. In N. Aslanbeigui, S. Pressman, & G. Summerfield (Ed.), *Women in the age of economic transformation* (pp. 1–7). London: Routledge.

Bakker, I. (Ed.) (1994). *The strategic silence: Gender and economic policy*. London: Zed.

Beneria, L. (1995). Toward a greater integration of gender in economics. *World Development, 23,* 1839–1850.

Beneria, L., & Feldman, S. (Eds.) (1992). *Unequal burden: Economic crises, persistent poverty, and women's work*. Boulder, CO: Westview Press.

Beneria, L., & Roldan, M. (1987). *The crossroads of class and gender*. Chicago: University of Chicago Press.

Bloom, D. E., & Brender, A. (1993). Labor and the emerging world economoy. *Population Bulletin, 48,* 2–39.

Blumberg, R. L., Rakowski, C. A.,; Tinker, I., & Monteon, M. (Eds.) (1995). *EnGENDERing wealth and well-being*. Boulder, CO: Westview Press.

Bose, C. E., & Acosta-Belen, E. (1995). *Women in the Latin American development process*. Philadelphia, PA: Temple University Press.

Cardero, M. E. (1994). Preface. In S. Joekes & A. Weston (Eds.), *Women and the new trade agenda*. New York: UNIFEM.

Chen, M. A. (1995). Engendering world conferences: The international women's movement and the United Nations. *Third World Quarterly, 16,* 3.

Development, Journal of the Society for International Development, Special issue prepared for the 4th UN World Conference on Women. (1995). Alternative economic frameworks from a gender perspective. 1995:1.

Dicken, P. (1992). *Global shift: The internationalization of economic activity* (2nd ed.). New York: The Guilford Press.

Dirasse, L. (1995). Gender issues and displaced populations. In N. Heyzer (Ed.), *A commitment to the world's women* (pp. 214–225). New York: UNIFEM.

Elson, D. (1995). *Male bias in the development process* (2nd ed.). Manchester, England: Manchester University Press.

Finance & Development. (1992). Recent trends in FDI for the developing world. *29,* (March), 50–51.

Finance & Development. (1998). Mitigating the social costs of the Asian Crisis. *35,* (September), 18–21.

Haddad, L., Brown, L., Richter, A., & Smith, L. (1995). The gender dimensions of economic adjustment policies: Potential interactions and evidence to date. *World Development, 23,* 881–896.

Heyzer, N. (1995). A women's development agenda for the 21st century. In N. Heyzer *(Ed.), A commitment to the world's women* (pp. 1–19). New York: UNIFEM.

ILO (International Labour Organization). (1995). *World employment 1995*. Geneva: ILO.

Joekes, S., & Weston, A. (1994). *Women and the new trade agenda*. New York: UNIFEM.

Kim, T. H., & Kim, K. H. (1995). Industrial restructuring in Korea and its consequences for women workers. In *Silk and steel: Asian women workers confront challenges of industrial restructuring* (pp. 106–155). Hong Kong: Committee for Asian Women.

Lee, S. H., & Song, H. K. (1994). The Korean garment industry: From authoritarian patriarchism to industrial paternalism. In E. Bonacich, L. Cheng, N. Chinchilla, N. Hamilton, & P. Ong (Eds.), *Global production: The apparel industry in the Pacific Rim* (pp. 147–161). Philadelphia: Temple University Press.

Lim, L. L. (1996). *More and better jobs for women: An action guide*. Geneva: International Labour Office.

McAfee, K. (1991). *Storm signals: Structural adjustment and development alternatives in the Caribbean*. Boston: South End Press.

Moser, C. (1993). *Gender planning and development: Theory, practice and training*. London: Routledge.

Ofreneo, R. P. (1994). The Philippine garment industry. In E. Bonacich, L. Cheng, N. Chinchilla, N. Hamilton, & P. Ong (Ed.), *Global production: the apparel industry in the Pacific Rim* (pp. 162–179). Philadelphia: Temple University Press.

Panagariya, A. (1995). What can we learn from China's export strategy? *Finance and Development, 32,* 32–35.

Phongpaichit, P. (1988). Two roads to the factory: Industrialisation strategies and women's employment in Southeast Asia. In B. Agarwal (Ed.) *Structures of patriarchy* (pp. 151–163). London: Zed Books.

Pun, N. (1995). Theoretical discussion on the impact of industrial iestructuring in Asia. In *Silk and steel: Asian women workers confront challenges of industrial restructuring* (pp. 18–31). Hong Kong: Committee for Asian Women.

Pyle, J. L. (1990). *The state and women in the economy: Lessons from sex discrimination in the Republic of Ireland*. Albany, NY: State University of New York Press.

Pyle, J. L. (1994). Economic restructuring in Singapore and the changing roles of women, 1957 to present. In N. Aslanbeigui, S. Pressman, & G. Summerfield (Eds.), *Women in the Age of Economic Transformation* (pp. 129–144). London: Routledge.

Pyle, J. L. (1998). Women's employment and multinational corporation networks. In N. Stromquist (Ed.), *Women in the third world: An encyclopedia of contemporary issues* (pp. 341–350). New York: Garland.

Pyle, J. L., & Dawson, L. M. (1990). The impact of technological transfer on female workforces in Asia. *Columbia Journal of World Business, 25,* 40–48.

Rakowski, C. A. (1995). Conclusion: Engendering wealth and well-being—lessons learned. In R. L. Blumberg, C. A. Rakowski, I. Tinker, & M. Monteon (Eds), *EnGENDERing wealth and well-being* (pp. 285–294). Boulder, CO: Westview Press.

Rao, A., Anderson, M. B., & Overholt, C. A. (Eds.) (1991). *Gender analysis in development planning.* West Hartford, CT: Kumarian Press.

Rowbotham, S. & Swasti M. (Eds.) (1994). *Dignity and daily bread: New forms of economic organising among poor women in the third world and the first.* London: Routledge.

Safa, H. I. (1994). Export manufacturing, state policy, and women workers in the Dominican Republic. In E. Bonacich, L. Cheng, N. Chinchilla, N. Hamilton, & P. Ong (Eds.), *In Global production: The apparel industry in the Pacific Rim* (pp. 247–256). Philadelphia: Temple University Press.

Safa, H. I. (1995). Gender implications of export-led industrialization in the Caribbean Basin. In R. L. Blumberg, C. A. Rakowski, I. Tinker, & M. Monteon (Eds.), *EnGENDERing wealth and well-being* (pp. 89–112). Boulder, CO: Westview Press.

Salih, K., & Young, M. L. (1989). Changing conditions of labour in the semiconductor industry in Malaysia. *Labor and Society, 14,* 59–80.

Seager, J. (1997). *The state of women in the world atlas* (2nd ed.). London: Penguin Reference.

Sen, G. (1995). Alternative economics from a gender perspective. *Development: Journal of the Society for International Development* (1995:1, pp. 10–13). (Special issue prepared for the 4th UN World Conference on Women.).

Sen, G., & Grown, C. (1987). *Development, crises, and alternative visions: Third world women's perspectives.* New York: Monthly Review Press.

Sivalingam, G. (1994). *The economic and social impact of export processing zones: The case of Malaysia.* Working Paper No. 66. Geneva: ILO.

Sparr, P. (Ed.) (1994). *Mortgaging women's lives: Feminist critiques of structural adjustment.* London: Zed.

Stichter, S., & Parpart, J. (Eds.) (1990). *Women, employment and the family in the international division of labour.* London: MacMillan.

Thomas-Emeagwali, G. (Ed.) (1995). *Women pay the price: Structural adjustment in Africa and the Caribbean.* Trenton, NJ: Africa World Press.

Tinker, I. (Ed.) (1990). *Persistent inequalities: Women and world development.* New York: Oxford University Press.

Todaro, M. P. (1997). *Economic development* (6th ed.). Reading, MA: Addison-Wesley.

United Nations. (1991a). *Women: Challenges to the year 2000.* New York: United Nations.

United Nations. (1991b). *The world's women 1970–1990: Trends and statistics.* New York: United Nations.

United Nations. (1994). *Participation of women in manufacturing: Patterns, determinants and future trends regional analysis, ESCAP region.* Vienna: UNIDO.

United Nations. (1995a). *Women in a changing global economy: 1994 world survey on the role of women in development.* New York: United Nations.

United Nations. (1995b). *The world's women 1995: Trends and statistics.* New York: United Nations.

United Nations Development Fund for Women (UNIFEM). (1995). *A women's development agenda for the 21st century: UNIFEM's commitment to the world's women.* New York: UNIFEM.

United Nations Development Programme (UNDP). (1995). *Human development report 1995.* New York: Oxford University Press.

Vickers, J. (1991). *Women and the world economic crisis.* London: Zed Books.

Ward, K. (Ed.) (1990). *Women workers and global restructuring.* Ithaca, NY: ILR Press.

Ward, K., & Pyle, J. L. (1995). *Gender, industrialization, transnational corporations, and development: An overview of trends.* In C. E. Bose & E. Acosta-Belen (Eds.), *Women in the Latin American Development Process* (pp. 37–64). Philadelphia, PA: Temple University Press.

Wee, V., & Heyzer, N. (1995). *Gender, poverty, and sustainable development.* Singapore: Engender.

The World Bank. (1990). *World development report 1990.* Oxford: Oxford University Press.

World Development. (1995). Special issue: Gender, adjustment and macroeconomics, *23,* 11 (November).

The World Resources Institute (in collaboration with the United Nations Environment Programme and the United Nations Development Programme). (1994). *World resources 1994-95.* New York: Oxford University Press.

CHAPTER 6

Gender and Migration

PIERRETTE HONDAGNEU-SOTELO
CYNTHIA CRANFORD

1. INTRODUCTION

A retrospective of the migration literature in various disciplines obscures women's participation in migration. In spite of all of the "women on the move" throughout the twentieth century, with few exceptions, research strategies in the same period have focused largely on men. Initial attempts to focus on women migrants in the 1970s were met at best with indifference, and at worst, with vitriolic hostility. In a 1976 article commenting on one of the first conferences on women and migration, the British urban anthropologist Anthony Leeds opined that "the category of 'women' seems to me a rhetorical one, not one which has (or can be proved to have) generic scientific utility" and he decried this focus as "individualistic, reductionist, and motivational." Leeds argued that focusing on women would deflect attention away from structural processes of capitalist exploitation. That in itself is telling, as it encodes the assumption that women do not act in economic or structural contexts, that women are somehow cloistered and sheltered from capitalist institutions. Androcentric biases, assumptions that women are "too traditional" and culture bound, or that they only migrate as family followers or "associational migrants" for family reunification, weigh heavily in the literature.

Women migrants began to receive more scholarly attention in the 1980s. The inter-

Cynthia Cranford would like to acknowledge the support of the Fred H. Bixby Fellowship for Population Research in Developing Countries. This paper was written while Pierrette Hondagneu-Sotelo was an in-resident fellow at the Getty Research Institute.

PIERRETTE HONDAGNEU-SOTELO AND CYNTHIA CRANFORD • Department of Sociology, University of Southern California, Los Angeles, Californa 90089
Handbook of the Sociology of Gender, edited by Janet Saltzman Chafetz. Kluwer Academic/ Plenum Publishers, New York, 1999.

national women's movement, and the subsequent growth of Women's Studies programs and feminist scholarship, as well as policy makers' and academics' renewed interest in migration, account for this turnabout. As one commentator observed of the burgeoning scholarship, the topic of immigration and women "has mushroomed" (Pedraza, 1991, p. 304). After decades of neglect and absence, women were "in" in the migration literature. By the early 1990s, there was enough research on the topic of women and migration to yield two substantive, review essays in prominent sociology publications in the United States (Pedraza, 1991; Tienda & Booth, 1991), as well as several edited volumes (e.g., Brettel & Simon, 1986; Buijs, 1993; Chant, 1992; Gabaccia, 1992; Phizacklea, 1983; Schenk-Sandbergen, 1995) and numerous monographs and case studies.

In spite of the focus on women and migration, gender and migration does not receive commensurate attention. Feminist scholarship shows that gender—that is, the social and cultural ideals, displays, and practices of masculinity and femininity—organizes and shapes our opportunities and life chances. The concept of gender as an organizing principle of social life, however, has encountered resistance and indifference in immigration scholarship. This is true of research efforts in various disciplines, such as economics, sociology, and even in that discipline often thought to be more hospitable to feminism, anthropology (Stacey & Thorne, 1985).

Much of the migration and immigration scholarship remains mired in an "add and stir" approach. Women are "added" as a variable to be inserted and measured, so that women's migration is examined, for example, with respect to fertility, and compared with men's employment patterns. Gender as a set of social relations that organize immigration patterns is generally ignored, and is taken into consideration only when women are the focus.

Some recent scholarship on gender and immigration has gone beyond just adding women and focuses on gender as social relations that affect and are influenced by migration (Grasmuck & Pessar, 1991; Hondagneu-Sotelo, 1994; Repak, 1995). Still, many feminist migration scholars call for a focus on women. This is understandable given that the vast majority of contemporary research on immigration and migration typically omits women, focuses exclusively on men, and operates as though men were without gender (Wright, 1995). We argue that feminist immigration scholarship would best be served by shifting the focus from women to gender. The preoccupation with writing women into migration theory stifles our theorizing of how gender relations influence migration. This tendency is most evident in the continuing use of sex role theory to explain the patterns and determinants of female migration.

In this chapter we use key insights from the burgeoning body of research on women and migration to conceptualize gender as historically situated and socially constructed, contextual power relations between women and men and we seek to show how these relations intersect with other social institutions to influence migration. We contrast different approaches to the topic, juxtaposing sex role theory with a conceptualization of gendered labor recruitment. We then review some gendered trends in women and men's migration within Africa, Latin America, and Asia and from these continents to more industrialized nations. Although, in general, men and women have different patterns of movement, we caution against formulating a universal theory of difference. Finally, we show that gender relations not only influence migration but also change with migration as they intersect with other social institutions. We end by suggesting what remains to be done in migration theory and research to adequately conceptualize gender as a set of powerful, but contested and changing, social relations.

2. FROM SEX ROLES TO GENDER RELATIONS

2.1. The Legacy of Sex Role Theory

Much of the migration literature that addresses women's migration and immigration patterns remains mired in sex role theory. Sex role theory views gender as a relatively static attribute, not as a fluid practice (Connell, 1987; Stacey & Thorne, 1985). Men's and women's activities are seen as complementary and functional, as serving the greater purpose of social cohesion. Consequently, sex role theory underemphasizes, and often ignores altogether, issues of power relations and social change. Finally, sex role theory underlines differences, rather than similarities, between women and men.

Applying this sex role framework to women and migration leads to theories emphasizing how domestic roles anchor women, while underlining how men's ties to the public sphere facilitate their movement. The general tendency for men to cross international borders more than women is also explained within this framework. Furthermore, this theoretical focus on difference, manifested in a conceptualization of stable sex roles, views important changes in women's migration patterns as an exception to a general trend. In fact, our review of some recent publications suggests that in many scholarly efforts, theorizing the determinants of female migration has not moved far beyond the formulation proposed by Thandani and Todaro's 1984 article in which they hypothesized that the extent of female migration depends upon the extent of "sex-role constraint." A recent collection, *Gender and Migration in Developing Countries* (Chant, 1992), shows that many migration scholars still look to prescribed sex roles to explain the migration of women. According to Chant (1992, p. 199), "The most prominent variations in male and female mobility in the text appear to relate most closely to men's and women's roles in generating income within household units." The editor of the volume goes on to argue that in all nations examined in the collection, including Peru, Costa Rica, Ghana, Kenya, Bangladesh, Thailand, and Indonesia, men are more likely to migrate independently than women owing to "gender-selective mobility." This type of perspective places the focus on migration *difference* between women and men, and it implies that this difference is due to seemingly inevitable, unchanging, cross-cultural sex roles.

By contrast, there is a good deal of gender and migration scholarship that defies the concept of stable sex roles. This scholarship examines gender as relations imbued with power, but also sees gender relations as a fluid and mutable system that intersects with other social institutions. In these studies, gender forms part of the social, economic, and cultural constellations that constitute migration. Using this approach, we can begin to view gender as a set of social relations that structures migration. Through this lens, we can then see familiar practices and institutions, such as labor recruitment and social networks, as components of immigration that are fundamentally gendered.

2.2. Circular Migrant Labor and Gendered Labor Recruitment

International migration opportunities are circumscribed by transnational social networks. Although the immigration literature underscores the importance of these social networks, insofar as they provide important resources and connections, most of the literature either ignores the gender-based origins and character of these networks or assumes that male-dominated immigrant networks are natural, neutral, and do not require further inquiry (e.g., Massey, Alarcon, Durand, & Gonzalez, 1987). Ironically, explanations of migration patterns based on sex role theory make similar assumptions by not asking under what circumstances gender roles are so persistent. Gendered patterns of migration derive principally from gendered labor demand and recruitment, not from immutable "sex roles." Gendered labor recruitment, in turn, influences the formation of gender-specific networks. In this way, a gendered state, economy, and social sphere intersect with women and men's traditional "roles," often leading to changes in women's and men's activities, relative power, and identities.

In various historical eras, gendered patterns of labor recruitment have been used to secure a cheap and exploitable labor force while ensuring that the development of settlement communities would not arise. This type of labor recruitment is generally circular and temporary but recurring.

Gendered recruitment patterns are also racialized. The group recruited for work is perceived as racially different and inferior, and the work is legislated along disenfranchised and sometimes coercive conditions. A classic example of a formal recruitment pattern is the United States' Bracero Program, a contract labor project designed to meet World War II labor shortages in western agriculture. The program remained in effect far beyond the end of World War II, beginning in 1942 and ending in 1964, after nearly 5 million temporary labor contracts were issued to Mexican citizens. Virtually all of the bracero contracts went to men. The history of much Asian migration to the United States occurred along these lines as well.

What has often gone without notice is the gendered aspect of circular migrant labor recruitment. Circular labor migration is characterized by the physical separation of the costs of maintaining and renewing labor (Burawoy, 1976; Glenn, 1986). Immigrant workers receive the resources necessary for daily subsistence or maintenance in the country of destination, but the workers are reproduced, or renewed, in their countries of origin. In these cases women's labor is twofold. They actively support their own family's daily reproduction and maintenance, but they also indirectly subsidize a system of labor migration that benefits primarily urban elites, many of whom are white, with access only to extremely low wages. As Bonnie Thornton Dill (1988), Evelyn Nakano Glenn (1986), and others have pointed out, contract labor systems were organized to maximize economic productivity, and offered few supports to sustain family life.

Labor recruitment has recently been seen as gendered because women are now actively recruited to work in low-wage jobs that have grown in industrialized nations since the late 1960s. One of the clearest examples is the recruitment of women from Asia and Latin America to work as nannies and housekeepers in the United States, Britain, Canada, Europe, and increasingly in the Middle East (Constable, 1997; Repak, 1995). Repak (1994) coined the term "gendered labor recruitment" to describe the initial migration of Central American women to Washington, D.C. in the 1960s and 1970s. Diplomats, who spent a term of duty in Central America, resettled in Washington, D.C. and informally recruited Central American women to work as nannies and housekeepers in D.C. Gender-specific labor recruitment can also be formally implemented, as in the cases of South Asian and Filipina migration to the Middle East (Eelens, Schampers, & Speckmann, 1992; Tyner, 1996). Gender-specific migration and recruitment does not follow from immutable sex roles. Rather, gendered patterns of migration emerge from the intersection of traditional gender relations and social, economic, and political changes. It is to these historicized patterns of migration that we now turn.

3. GENDERED PATTERNS OF MIGRATION

In this section we describe gendered patterns of migration within Africa, Asia, and Latin America as well as migration from these nations to more industrialized nations. We focus on how the social relations of gender intersect with other institutions to produce gendered recruitment and gendered networks, showing that gender is a set of fluid social relations rather than stable sex roles.

3.1. Africa

It is only fairly recently, in the late twentieth century, that women have been participating in labor migration in Africa. Men had traditionally predominated in rural–urban migration because men were vigorously recruited for work in plantations, railroads, mines, and even as domestic servants (Moodie, 1994). Under racial apartheid in South Africa, the men lived in the city of destination only while employed, and when not employed they returned to their rural or village place of origin. This system was not uncommon elsewhere in the continent.

Although African women themselves were not on the move, they played a key role in maintaining this system. The male migrant workers received the resources necessary for daily subsistence or maintenance in the city of destination, but these same workers were "renewed" in their place of origin, with the women taking on the responsibility for intensive, small-scale, subsistence farming. The women "left behind" also traded, engaged in petty commodity production, and became effective heads-of-households.

African women stayed behind not only because of their traditional "roles" in the household and in agriculture, but also because in many nations employers and government authorities deliberately kept women and children in rural hinterland areas so as to avoid the creation of permanent, black communities in white areas (Stichter, 1985; Tienda & Booth, 1991). In short, women's traditional responsibility to care for children and the home intersected with systems of racial oppression and explicit policies to ensure racial segregation.

The coercive migrant system in South Africa is a stark example of the mutability of traditional gender "roles" under certain conditions. It is rare that men are conceptualized as gendered beings, yet Moodie's (1994) historical study of the South African mines, beginning in the late nineteenth century, showed that men in the mines took on traditionally female activities such as sewing, crocheting, and making beer. Not all men did this "women's work," but the men created an alternative system of hierarchy that drew on the social relations of gender. Younger men often became the "wives" of older men who would give them gifts and money in return for domestic chores and sexual pleasure. The age hierarchy in many African cultures was central to gendered relations between the men. Older men could not be wives, although they might have served as wives in their youth. The young men eventually transitioned out of these oppressive relationships. In this manner, they did not threaten the relationship between the older man and his family back in the country. In addition, this system of relationships between men was seen as safer than relations with the few city women, who at that time were overwhelmingly prostitutes, because it prevented pregnancy.

Since the 1960s, women have increased and men have decreased their participation in rural–urban migration flows in Africa (Gugler, 1989; Stichter, 1985; Tienda & Booth,

1991). Most of these new female migrants are married women who are joining husbands in cities, but increasingly more unmarried women are also migrating (Stichter, 1985; Wilkinson, 1987). In the second half of the twentieth century, a growing number of women have migrated to West African towns and cities (Wilkinson, 1987), and one can now find settled communities around the South African mines as women's traditional farming activities are displaced by capitalist penetration into the rural hinterlands (Moodie, 1994). South African women did not merely follow their husbands to the cities, however. Their move was also structured by changes in the local political economy. For example, Pondo women now commonly migrate to escape unhappy marriages and husbands who do not support their children (Buijs, 1993; Oboo, 1980).

Although African women are now more likely to migrate to cities than before, men still predominate in international migration from African nations. Accordingly, there is not much literature on African women and international migration. Nonetheless, West African women are now recruited for paid domestic work in Italy. In Italy, however, African men, who work in construction and other public occupations, are the targets of growing anti-immigrant sentiment. Many Italians believe African immigrant men are taking their jobs, yet in contrast, African women are not in the public mind because they are "invisibly" employed in households and because they allow Italian middle-class families to run smoothly as both husband and wife are in the paid labor force. However, there is some evidence that Italians prefer lighter skinned Filipinas over West African women as paid domestic workers (Andall, 1992). In addition, upper-class Somali women, fleeing the civil war, now migrate to Britain with their families. In Britain, Somali immigrant women work as housekeepers and nannies and in the factories, while most Somali men are unemployed because it is seen as unmanly for an upper-class Somali man to do such work (Summerfield, 1993). Somali women's employment and men's unemployment in Britain are examples of how gender and class intersect to create a preference for immigrant women in the growing low-wage service and factory jobs in industrialized nations.

In this section we used the literature to show that male-dominated migration streams within Africa were gendered by the political and economic policies of nations, such as the racial apartheid system that prevailed in South Africa. Historicizing and conceptualizing male-dominated migration streams allows us to recognize the recent migration of African women as paid domestic workers to European nations, for example, as a new form of gendered migration, one that has come about with globalization.

We wish to underline that gendered migration patterns in the African continent differ from those in other developing nations. Unlike the African continent, in Asia, Latin America, and the Caribbean, most migrants to the city are women. This difference between the migration patterns of African, Latin American, and Asian women should warn against a universal theory of sex role constraint.

3.2. Asia and the Middle East

Asia's position in the global economy as a site for multinational corporations' manufacturing and assembly activities, and as a major location of U.S. military bases, has spurred migration within Asian nations (Ong, 1987; Sturdevant & Stoltzfus, 1992; Wolf, 1990). These developments are largely responsible for attracting primarily Asian women, not men, to the cities, because assembly work is low paid and because the tedious nature of assembly work is seen as more fit for women than for men.

Research conducted by Diane Wolf (1990) in Java and by Aihwa Ong (1987) in Malaysia examined the experiences of young, single women who migrated from rural areas to work in the new export processing zones. In Malaysia, the combination of declining peasant farming and the introduction of Japanese manufacturing assembly plants has induced the rural–urban migration and proletarianization of young, single women. The emergence of export-oriented textile and electronics industries in Thailand has also spurred the migration of young women to the cities (Singhanetra-Renard & Prabhudhanitisarn, 1992). In the Philippines, women from the rural provinces migrate to cities, and many of them are employed as domestic workers and prostitutes in areas around U.S. military bases. Although prostitution is illegal in the Philippines, women sell sexual labor as "hospitality women" in bars, massage parlors and night clubs. The migrant women who engage in this activity, are routinely abused economically, sexually, and physically.

Although in general, Asian women predominate in rural–urban migration, we see different patterns in the South Asian nations of India, Bangladesh, Pakistan, and Sri Lanka. In South Asia men outnumber women in the cities, owing to patterns of land tenure and agriculture (Pedraza, 1991, p. 310). The South Asian case, however, should not be seen as an exception to a general rule of female predominance in rural–urban migration in Asia. Instead, the case of South Asia indicates how the local political economy (i.e., land tenure and agriculture) intersects with gender relations to produce gender-specific migration streams, much as it did in South Africa to spur the migration of women to the cities.

International migration from South Asian nations such as India and Pakistan has been structured by past colonial relations with Britain. During the colonial period, Britain encouraged the migration of Indians and Pakistanis to become the merchants in British colonies in East Africa. Indian and Pakistani women migrated with their families to Kenya and Uganda. The first waves of Indian migration to Britain began with individual male migrant laborers, but over time women came and permanent settlement communities were formed (Clarke, Peach, & Vertovec, 1990). In addition many Indian and Pakistani women and men left East Africa for Britain, leading Bhachu (1995) to call them "twice migrants."

Today large numbers of Indians and Pakistanis have settled in Britain. Pakistani women and girls under purdah—the Islamic custom of female separation from unrelated males—work in their home sewing for local garment manufacturers. Yet these women are not isolated in their homes. Their informal networks with other Pakistani women give them some semblance of power as they discuss the going piece rate and make friendships that help buttress the hostility of white British society (Werbner, 1988). Westwood's (1988) study of Gujarati women in Britain showed that women benefited from female networks on the shop floor as well. These women garment workers were often kin, as women helped sisters and daughters get jobs. The women used their close ties to slow production to stabilize the piece rate, to challenge the white male dominated union, and to create a more hospitable environment at work with celebrations surrounding birthdays, weddings, and motherhood.

Asian women have a long history of migrating to the United States, and although Korean, Chinese, Vietnamese, and Filipina women have predominated in recent decades, only Chinese and Japanese women predominated in the past. Chinese and Japanese women began coming to the United States in the late nineteenth and early twentieth centuries, respectively, but their migration was hindered by deliberate U.S. policies of racial exclusion.

In the late nineteenth and early twentieth centuries, Chinatowns were largely "bachelor" communities, and immigrant daughters from poor, peasant families in China supplied sexual labor in cities such as San Francisco, where there were few women (Cheng, 1979). These young women were usually sold by poor families, and daughters accepted their sale and subsequent migration out of filial loyalty. Chinese patriarchal ideology forbade the migration of "decent" women, and U.S. policies also prevented the migration of all Chinese after 1882. According to Cheng, the experiences of these young migrant women were not homogeneous, as prostitution was organized in different ways. Some of the women gained autonomy and control over their lives, while others were virtual slaves.

The migration of Japanese women was distinct for each generation. In *Issei, Nisei, War Bride* (1986), Evelyn Nakano Glenn examined the migration and domestic work experiences of three generations of Japanese women in the San Francisco Bay Area. The first generation of Japanese women began arriving in the early twentieth century, rapidly transforming the ratio of Japanese men to women from 25:1 at the turn of the century, to 2:1 by 1924. Many of these women were "picture brides," and once in the United States, they worked triple shifts doing their own housework, working in family farms and businesses, and also as paid domestic workers. The 1924 Immigration Act excluded all immigration from Asian countries, effectively curtailing the growth of Asian–American communities in the United States. Although the 1952 McCarran–Walter Act established token immigration quotas, it was only the 1965 amendment to the immigration act that allowed more Asians to immigrate to the United States.

More recently Korean, Vietnamese, Filipina, and South Asian and Middle Eastern women have migrated to the United States. In recent years many educated Filipinas were recruited to the United States to fill nursing shortages in hospitals and nursing homes (Ong & Azores, 1994; Pido, 1992). Yet they were generally placed in the lowest paid nursing jobs, often in inner city county hospitals where the case loads are the highest (Ong & Azores, 1994). Iranian women came to the United States as exiles in the early 1980s, fleeing the fundamentalist revolution against the Shah, while Vietnamese women came with their families as refugees after the Vietnam War (Nacify, 1993; Ong, Bonacich, & Cheng, 1994). Korean immigration was facilitated by the presence of U.S. military bases in South Korea and women generally migrated with their families, settling primarily in Los Angeles and New York (Ong, Bonacich, & Cheng, 1994).

Recent migration streams of Filipina, Sri Lankan, and Indian women to the Middle East, where they are recruited as contracted domestic workers, offer stark examples of the mutability of traditional gender roles in changing political and economic contexts. The migration of Muslim Sri Lankan women to Saudi Arabia and other Gulf states is in sharp contrast to explanations of migration patterns based on a theory of sex roles. Until very recently, Sri Lankan women took care of the family and household chores and Sri Lankan men were the sole breadwinners. This has changed with the increasing poverty among Sri Lankan households, and rapid economic growth of Middle Eastern nations. Although there is very high unemployment among Sri Lankan men, it is the women who migrate to the Middle East owing to the gender-specific demand for domestic workers, which is activated by gendered recruitment. The demand for male migrant construction workers has slowed, with the completion of the basic physical infrastructure of these economies, but the demand for live-in housekeepers and nannies has not subsided. A tightly controlled, government-run recruitment program ensures this system of gendered migration and immigrant labor. For example, in Saudi Arabia it is more expensive for Sri Lankan men to obtain work permits than it is for Sri Lankan women (Eelens & Speckmann, 1992).

Gendered labor recruitment also funnels the migration of Filipina domestic workers to the Middle Eastern nations of Saudi Arabia and Kuwait, and to other Asian nations such as Singapore and Hong Kong (Tyner, 1996). Although most studies focus on the deployment of workers, Tyner's research focuses on the first two stages of the recruitment process, contract procurement and labor recruitment. The contract procurement stage consists of negotiations with the labor-importing nation that is seeking a low-paid labor force. The labor-importing nations have the upper hand in this current environment of labor surplus. Meanwhile, the Philippines competes with other nations, such as Indonesia and Pakistan, to represent its workers as the most docile and hardworking migrants. At this stage, gendered assumptions that women are homemakers, mistresses, or mothers are used to portray women in a range of occupations—from domestic workers to nurses to entertainment workers—that provide physical comfort. In contrast, men are portrayed in professional or construction occupations (Tyner, 1996, p. 411). The recruitment phase takes place in the Philippines as private and government recruiters try to match workers to specific contracts. In this phase, recruitment of women performing artists is often the focus because the explicitly sexualized demand is great and the payoff is larger. The selection of geographical areas from which to recruit women is also gendered and fueled by sexualized stereotypes and images that rural women are more adept at domestic skills, are more docile, and that women who frequent nightclubs are more difficult to control (Tyner, 1996, p. 413). In sum, Tyner argues that migrant women are essentially bought and sold as government and private recruiters employ these gendered representations in the labor recruitment process.

In contrast to the government-sponsored recruitment patterns that characterize the international migration of Asian women, most Latin American women's migration is facilitated by well-established networks. In Latin America and the Caribbean, as in Asia, women predominate in rural to urban migration, which increasingly corresponds to patterns of investment by multinational corporations.

3.3. Latin America and the Caribbean

Since the colonial period, young women have migrated from Latin American rural communities to cities for jobs as domestic workers in private households. In the second half of the twentieth century, Latin America urbanization accelerated and young, single women have predominated in rural–urban migration. Many of these young, single women came from poor, peasant families and they were drawn to work as domestic servants in Latin American cities. Their migration served as a "demographic safety valve" for rural communities that could not absorb the labor of these women (Tienda & Booth, 1992, p. 63). In the late twentieth century, as live-out working arrangements became more common, domestic work relations became more contractual and less personal. Alternatively, new urban jobs in retail and services also drew migrant women into the competitive sector. For poor, relatively unschooled women from the countryside, domestic work still provides one of the few means of economic survival and urban exposure, but it does not necessarily provide a stepladder to better jobs. Migrant women who are able to leave domestic service do so because they marry and become homemakers, or because they make a lateral socioeconomic move to informal sector vending (Chaney & Garcia Castro, 1989).

The general tendency for Latin American women to migrate to the cities while men migrate abroad is the result of specific historical conditions. Lourdes Arizpe (1981) made precisely this point with respect to Mexican internal migration. The pioneer stage of rural–urban migration in Mexico in the 1940s and 1950s was made up of young people with some secondary or prepatory level education who migrated to the cities to find professional jobs and a modern life (Arizpe, 1981, p. 636). Twenty years later, peasants began to migrate for survival as the proliferation of manufactured products into the rural areas encouraged greater dependency on wages. Both young men and young women migrated to the cities during this period, but women's traditional income-generating activities—weaving, sewing, pottery-making, and petty trade—declined drastically, making it nearly impossible for single women to survive in rural areas. This fueled their migration to cities.

Male migration to the United States has also accelerated women's migration and employment within Mexico. Meager remittances and the prolonged absences of migrant husbands often propelled women to migrate to cities and villages for jobs in agricultural occupations previously defined as male, in service sectors jobs, and in newly created occupations where labor is exclusively or primarily female, such as jobs in packinghouses; maquiladoras; in shoe, clothing, and textile manufacturing; and in homework assembly (Beneria & Roldan, 1987).

Since the mid-1960s, women in Mexico and the Caribbean have also been drawn to cities to work in export assembly production (Fernandez-Kelly, 1983; Nash, 1983; Tiano, 1994). As in Asian nations, particular patterns of industrialization along the United States–Mexico border and in the Caribbean have stimulated women's rural–urban migration. In 1965, in an effort to stave off rising unemployment the Mexican government instituted the Border Industrialization Program (BIP), a program designed to generate the infrastructure and legal conditions necessary to attract successfully foreign manufacturing investment along the northern border with the United States. Although the BIP was originally intended to employ male migrant workers, the plants employed predominantly young, single women because of employer preferences and the growing population of single women without the financial support of husbands or fathers. During the 1970s, women accounted for 75% to 90% of the border plant assembly workers, and many of them were young, single, childless women drawn from the interior of Mexico (Fernandez-Kelly, 1983).

Whereas in the 1960s and 1970s it was primarily single women who migrated and sought wage work in Mexico, with the economic crisis of the 1980s, financial need propelled married women with small children into the labor force. Many of these women were former migrants to the city (Escobar & Gonzalez de la Rocha, 1988; de Oliveiria, 1990). Many types of unregulated, informal sector work, for example, vending or doing assembly in the home, allow married women to still assume child-rearing and domestic responsibilities in the home. Insights into these processes led Escobar, Gonzalez de la Rocha, and Roberts (1987) to argue that women with children were more likely to migrate to Guadalajara than to the United States because they could perform outwork for pay and still care for their children. In short, the specific demand for women in the maquiladoras and the proliferation of informal sector work generated by larger political and economic changes have intersected with household gender relations to structure women's migration to the cities.

Latin American women of various nationalities, but especially Mexican, Cuban, Dominican, Salvadoran, and Guatemalan, have also migrated to the United States and many of them find work as paid domestic workers, as factory workers, and in retail. Puerto Rican women's migration to the U.S. mainland, particularly to the East Coast, is intimately tied to U.S. patterns of investment in Puerto Rico (Toro-Morn, 1995). Yet in the mainstream immigration literature the migration of women is only briefly mentioned and rarely taken as the starting point of analysis.

The tendency to minimize the size and importance of women international migrants is clear in the case of Mexican migration to the United States. Although historical studies, like Vicki Ruiz's (1987) on the California canneries, show that Mexican women and children migrated in the early decades of this century, much of the literature characterizes Mexican migration as circular, temporary, male-dominated migration. These generalizations come from a particular historical period of migration, however, namely that characterized by the Bracero Program from 1942 to 1965 and to a lesser extent by the earlier contract labor program during World War I. This gender-discriminate labor policy mandated an elastic supply of labor, one that could be synchronized with seasonal agricultural fluctuations and that would externalize labor reproduction costs to Mexico.

The Bracero Program provided the legislative foundation for the strength of men's social migrant networks. Hondagneu-Sotelo (1994) found that these male networks were not automatically extended to wives or other female kin. Instead, wives had to struggle with their husbands, and daughters with their fathers, before they could migrate. Eventually, women's migrant networks developed that allowed women to migrate to California without the approval of male kin, but with the help of an aunt or a sister already in the United States. Recent research suggests that migration networks among Puerto Ricans have also been gendered. Ellis, Conway, and Bailey (1996) found that migration decisions were made in contexts where women and men have different access to resources, such as networks and money, to pay for recruitment agencies and for the move itself.

The development of female networks facilitated the formation of permanent settlement communities (Hondagneu-Sotelo, 1994). Thus, while Mexican women with children might be more likely to migrate to Mexican cities than to the United States (Escobar et al., 1987), it is well known that Mexican women have also migrated with their children to California, Texas, and other U.S. states.

A less well-known pattern of migration involves the solo migration of women who are mothers of young children. Increasingly, many Mexican and Central American women are migrating to work in the United States while leaving their children in their countries of origin, in the care of grandmothers, other female kin, the children's fathers, or sometimes with paid caregivers. In a recent article, Hondagneu-Sotelo and Avila (1997) refer to this pattern as "Latina transnational motherhood." In some cases, the separations of time and distance are substantial; ten years may elapse before women are reunited with their children. While transnational mothering has numerous historical precursors, most of them involve the migration of men away from their children, although the separation of mothers and children during slavery, and the legacy of Caribbean and African-American women from the South leaving their children "back home" to seek work in the U.S. North are important precursors. When men come North and leave their families in Mexico, as they did during the Bracero Program and as many continue to do today, they are fulfilling familial obligations defined as breadwinning for the family. When Mexican and Central American women do so, they are embarking not only on an immigration journey, but on a more radical, gender-transformative odyssey. As they initiate separations of space and time from their communities of origin, they must cope with stigma, guilt, and criticism from others. The jobs that many of these women perform in paid domestic work are not often compatible with the daily care for one's own family. In this way, contemporary transnational motherhood continues a long legacy of people of color being incorporated into the United States through coercive systems of labor that do not recognize family rights. The job characteristics of paid domestic work, especially live-in work, virtually impose transnational motherhood for many Mexican and Central American women who have children of their own (Hondagneu-Sotelo & Avila, 1997).

A study of Central American migration to Washington, D.C. provides another example of gendered labor recruitment and gender-based social networks, in this case principally constituted by women. In this study, Terry Repak (1995) found that Central American housekeepers were initially informally recruited to Washington, D.C. during the 1960s and 1970s by diplomatic and professional families returning home after a tour of duty in Central America. In this instance, the regional structural conditions in Washington, D.C., particularly the labor demand for nannies and housekeepers, proved to be more conducive to women's than to men's migration. Occupational sex segregation in U.S. labor markets played a large part in shaping gendered patterns of labor migration. At the point of origin, the relatively low marriage rates also facilitated women's ability to migrate. While a vanguard of Central American women immigrants in the 1960s and 1970s laid the foundations of social networks, over time these networks diversified and facilitated men's migration and the emergence of permanent Central American communities in Washington, D.C.

Yet another study of Central American migrants to the United States sheds light on the gendered nature of social networks and the gendered outcomes of legalization offered by the Immigration Reform and Control Act. In a study of the Maya who have settled in Houston, Texas, sociologist Jacqueline Hagan (1994) found that the Mayan men were better able than the women to develop social networks. This is not due to traditional sex roles nor any cultural predilection on the part of the Maya. This pattern emerges, Hagan argues, due to occupational segregation by sex in the United States and specifically in Houston. In Houston, virtually all of the Mayan men worked as maintenance or stock workers for a big supermarket chain and the women as live-in domestic workers. Hagan argues that because of the men's well-developed job-finding networks, newly arrived Maya men were able to locate jobs faster than the newcomer women, who each waited to find a new, separate employer. The isolation the women encountered in their live-in jobs seemed to work against the fortification and multiplication of their own social networks.

The Houston study also shows the gendered repercussions of these networks. Hagan explains that the women, because of their less developed information networks, were less successful than the men in obtaining legalization through the Immigration Reform and Control Act. The women were also hindered, Hagan notes, by their reliance on domestic employers, who were often reluctant to sign affidavits for fear that they would be harangued by the IRS for not paying employment taxes.

Migration of political refugees is another example that defies the facile generalization that Latin American men migrate abroad while women migrate to the cities. Political refugees generally come as families and plan to settle permanently. In Chile, the 1973 military coup and overthrow of the democratically elected, socialist president, and the repressive aftermath forced many trade unionists, activists, and leftists to leave for Europe, Mexico, Canada, and the United States. Cuban women who came to Miami with their families fleeing Fidel Castro's regime derived primarily from the middle and upper classes. Familiar explanations for the Cubans' success in Miami emphasized the class privileges and human capital that they brought with them, and the politically motivated actions of the U.S. government in offering substantial resettlement assistance to those fleeing communism. Cuban women also played an important part in building Cuban economic success in the United States (Fernandez-Kelly & Garcia, 1990).

In this section we have given an overview of the general patterns of migration within Africa, Asia, and Latin America and migration from these nations to the United States and other more industrialized nations. For internal migration we have shown that, rather than immutable gender roles, local economic and political conditions interact with a traditional gender division of labor in the home to produce women's and men's migration patterns. For international migration streams we have shown the ways in which gendered recruitment patterns and the formation of gender-specific networks have led to the predominance of men in international migration during particular historical moments. Yet as changes in the economies of industrialized nations lead to demand for domestic servants, garment workers, and other gendered occupations, we see increasing female-specific recruitment and networks (Sassen-Koob, 1984). Thus, labor migration is gendered at the macro level of labor demand as well as the micro level of gendered networks. As Ellis et al., (1996) show in the case of Puerto Rican migration, restructuring incorporates women and men into industrialized economies differently, drawing on patriarchy as much as capitalism. In the next section we continue to challenge a view of gender as stable roles by showing that gender relations are not only determinants of migration but are also influenced by migration.

4. CHANGING GENDER RELATIONS WITH MIGRATION

In 1970, in her pioneering work *Women's Role in Economic Development*, Esther Boserup argued that women's status declines with industrialization and migration. Since then, scholars of migration and gender have moved beyond debating whether women benefit or lose with migration and toward understanding the contradictions in women's status that come with migration. In this section we show that with migration, women often gain status in some realms while losing it in others. Even if women's power increases and men's decreases, as is often the case with international migration where racial oppression is a factor, men generally still benefit from their status as men.

4.1. Women Who Stay Behind: Beyond a Static Portrayal

Explanations of migration patterns rarely take as a starting point the experience of the women who stay behind. Are we to assume that because they stayed behind they are inevitably tied to the singular role of housekeeping and childcare? What kinds of new activities do they take on with the departure of their husbands, fathers, and brothers? In this section we use case studies from Mexico and the Dominican Republic to conceptualize how migration influences gender relations in the sending communities.

In regions of Mexico marked by United States-bound male migration, patriarchal gender relations that structure women's work experience have shown receptiveness to change. Gail Mummert's (1988) research examined the rural villages surrounding Zamora, Michoacan, where young, single women's recent employment in commercial agriculture, in conjunction with male wage labor in the United States, has brought about rapid and significant changes in gender relations. Initially, local and regional employers' recruitment efforts obtained parental permission by assuring parents that their daughters would be properly chaperoned. Today this is no longer the case. Female employment has shifted from being a stigmatized rarity to a virtual rite of passage, an expectation for all young, single women, and an alternative to household drudgery and isolation. Today, young women are no longer cloistered in the home, but walk about with their friends, with whom they take buses outside the village to the fields and packinghouses. While the first generation of female workers turned over their entire earnings to their parents, young women now either keep all of it or contribute only part of their paychecks to their families and spend the rest as they please, usually on clothes and cosmetics. Even when working daughters compliantly turn over their salary to parents, young women have acquired more decision-making power in the domestic arena. Courting patterns are more open, and in less than two decades there has been a shift away from patrilocality to matrilocality or neolocality, as mothers and daughters pool their earnings to purchase the new couple land, and thus avoid the subordination a newly married daughter suffers when living with parents-in-law.

It would be misleading to overstate these transformations in domestic patriarchy. Although women may "take the reins" during men's long-term absences by making decisions, securing employment, and venturing beyond the domestic sphere, their behavior often remains subject to strong double standards. Sexual infidelity, for example, may be tolerated in a man, who is allowed to maintain a *casa chica* with a second woman and children, but a women left alone by her sojourning husband is often under the watchful eyes of other villagers, and any contact with an unrelated man may be cause for suspicion. Yet young women's acceptance of these double standards may be eroding. Georgina Rosado's research suggests that in the context of men's migration northward, women's beliefs about traditional double standards of sexuality are weakening. One of the young, single working women that Rosado interviewed in a rural, migratory village of Michoacan, discussed the issue of spousal sexual infidelity with her friends and her mother, and then concluded, "I don't believe as my mother does that you must put up with your husband forever if he cheats and turns outs bad" (Rosado, 1990, p. 67).

The migration of men and the remittances they send can also influence the status of women back home. Mascarenhas-Keyes' (1993) study on India showed the complex changes that can occur with men's migration. Lower caste Catholic women once provided domestic and farm labor for upper caste Catholics. With the remittances from their husbands, however, lower caste Catholic women now hire migrant Hindu women as domestics. Lower caste Catholic women have redefined themselves as no longer fit to do housework or farmwork, while Hindu migrant women have redefined themselves as marketable employees and have so gained both new independence and subordination. This is a stark example of the intersection of gender, class, and ethnicity, manifested in the severely unequal relations between two groups of women, Catholic employers and Hindu domestic workers.

Increased autonomy and power in men's absence often gives women the power to negotiate their own migration with their husbands and other male kin. This is a clear example of how gender is not made up of stable roles but of contested power relations. Recent research has looked at Mexican women who eventually migrate to the United States to join their husbands (Hondagneu-Sotelo, 1994). Although there were structural inducements to this pattern of migration, it was men's authority within families and men's access to migrant network resources that favored the husbands' initial departure. Yet their departure rearranged gender relations in the family; as women assumed new tasks and responsibilities, they learned to act more assertively and autonomously. This new sense of social power, and later, for another cohort of migrant wives, additional access to women's network resources, enabled the wives to migrate to the United States.

In many ways this study echoes the findings of Sherrie Grasmuck and Patricia Pessar (1991), who found similar dynamics among Dominican women who initially stayed behind when their husbands migrated to New York. Like the case of Mexican women, Dominican women actively negotiated their migration with their husbands. One Dominican woman convinced her husband to let her migrate by arguing that she could not survive economically back home. Yet she really wanted to migrate because a friend told her that her husband would not be able to push her around in New York. Thus a focus on gender relations also shows that migrants are not always motivated by economic gains, as is still assumed in much of the mainstream immigration literature.

These case studies show that migration of male kin can induce change in gender relations, often leading to the eventual migration of the women. More research should be done on women who stay behind, as well as on the struggles between women and men that lead to the eventual migration of women. In the next section we examine the more common question of what happens to gender relations when women move.

4.2. Women Who Migrate to the Cities

Although staying "back home" and assuming a myriad of economic and family responsibilities has been a struggle for women, it has traditionally afforded them some semblance of autonomy and independence. What happens when they migrate to cities? In a study of migrant women in Lesotho, Wilkinson (1987) found that migration did not enhance, but rather diminished women's position vis-à-vis men. As young women have acquired education, many have aspired to clerical, industrial, or technical jobs, but more often than not they do not find the jobs they seek. In the city, women work commonly as vendors, as commodity producers, and as prostitutes. In this context, migrating to the city increased women's dependence on men and intensified their subordination (Wilkinson, 1987). In the city of Maseru, Wilkinson found that women's only job opportunities were in the informal sector, while migrant men took jobs in the formal sector or the public sector. Even when migrant women have better employment opportunities and increased incomes, their relative economic position does not necessarily improve dramatically, as they often remain dependent on men to purchase their goods.

In a review of various case studies of women and migration in several African nations, Tienda and Booth (1991, p. 60) noted that the impact of migration often depends on whether a woman is married or single at the time of migration:

> For women who moved with or to join husbands, migration transferred male control over women's labour and earnings from rural to urban areas, adapting hierarchical relations to an urban setting. . . (so that) wives in poor families were unable to challenge the patriarchal relations of redistribution. . . By contrast, single women were able to improve their social position by increasing their autonomy via economic exchanges. For them the city provides the only alternative to assured subordination in the village. Because single and married women shared the economic constraints imposed by their relegation to informal activity, neither realised substantial improvements in material well-being.

Women who were married at the time of migration experienced more limited autonomy than single women in the city. Married women often lost much of the independence and control that they maintained over their own households "back home."

Ong's (1987) study of young, single, "neophyte factory women" who migrate to work in the Malaysian export processing zones showed that they did gain some autonomy because they married later than their nonmigrant peers. Moreover, although they earned low wages, they typically contributed about half of their earnings to their family of origin, thus gaining greater power in the family. These transformations, however, were not without their contradictions, as the women suffered hallucinations and "spirit attacks" on the shop floor, which Ong interpreted as a challenge to capitalist discipline and the male authority imposed on them in the factories.

In contrast, Wolf's (1990) study of Javanese migrant women suggests that it is not just earning power that brings autonomy and independence. Wolf found that the earnings of young, migrant women working in assembly factories are so low that the women workers are subsidized by their own families in rural Java. She concluded that the peasant economy is in fact subsidizing the factories. The young women contributed very little money to their families because they had to spend much of their earnings for transportation and lunch expenses. While their earnings were very modest, the young women derived satisfaction and status from their employment, and they used the modest remainders of their income to purchase cosmetics and other small consumer goods and to save for a dowry. Wolf (1990) reported that many of these women:

> exhibited an air of assertiveness compared with their peers who had never worked in a factory. Their makeup, nail polish, and in a few cases long pants were statements of modernity. ... Many stated defiantly that they, not their parents, would choose their future mate. (p. 42).

Like Indonesia and Malaysia, Mexico has opened export processing zones that prefer the labor of migrant women. Research conducted by Fernandez-Kelly (1983) and Susan Tiano (1994) in the maquiladora assembly plants revealed that the employment of migrant daughters, wives, and mothers neither eroded domestic patriarchy nor enhanced women's positions in families. Husbands and fathers, when present, still maintained family authority, and employed women still took primary responsibility for domestic household chores (Fernandez-Kelly, 1983). As in the United States, women in Mexico earned significantly less than did men, and they were subject to occupational segregation, sex discrimination and harassment. Also as in the United States, the inferior earnings of Mexican women were often justified by patriarchal assumptions that men deserve wages large enough to support their families, and that women are necessarily secondary or supplementary earners and thus deserve less pay (Tiano, 1994). One arena of control that did appear to be affected by women's employment in the maquiladoras is women's enhanced spatial mobility and concentration in new public spaces. Fernandez-Kelly reported that during their leisure hours, the young women congregated in discotheques and the all-female *cervezerias* (beer bars).

4.3. Women Who Cross International Borders

When women and men cross international borders they meet other systems of oppression based on race, nationality, and citizenship, that intersect with gender relations. According to Glenn (1986), the primary struggle for Japanese immigrant women and their daughters—and perhaps for all subordinate racial–ethnic immigrants—has not been with fighting gender subordination within the family, but rather with struggling against a racist society and an exploitative, stratified labor system. Although gender and generational conflicts within the family existed, they were overshadowed by societal oppression. In this regard, Japanese–American women used the family as a source of protection. Confronted with both racism and sexism, migrant women have been instrumental in forging a community and sustaining their culture in the new society. Black migrant women were central to the "southernization" of the Northeast and the Midwest United States (Hine, 1991). Indian immigrant women in Britain reconstructed marriage rituals and the dowry system as they moved into the paid labor force (Bhachu,1995). Similarly, Hondagneu-Sotelo's (1994) work showed that Mexican immigrant women actively consolidated settlement by participating in and forging a community. It is they who negotiated with new institutions, such as schools, hospitals, and workplaces, in the new country to carry out their continued responsibilities in the home and the family.

In industrialized economies characterized by a labor market segmented by race and citizenship, immigrant men are rarely able to be the sole breadwinner and women's income earning activities become essential to the survival of the family. This is evident by Hondagneu-Stoelo's (1994) finding that Mexican women gained power and autonomy and men lost some of their authority and privilege with migration. During spousal separations, some men learned to cook and wash dishes. In other instances, men began to concede to their wives' challenges to their authority. These behaviors were not readily discarded when the spouses reunited. This relative change in power was seen in the emergence of a more egalitarian household division of labor and by shared decision making power (Hondagneu-Sotelo, 1994). These gains and losses were reflected in the women's near unanimous preference for permanent settlement in the United States and in men's desire for return migration—a finding that echoes Patricia Pessar's (1986) data on Dominicans in New York City.

In some cases immigrant women have struck a more blatant "patriarchal bargain" (Kandiyotti, 1989) with their husbands. Nazli Kibria's (1993) research on Vietnamese immigrant families in Philadelphia explored how immigrant women used traditional gender ideology to force men to support their families. Although many of these women were working, and their income was essential to the survival of the family, they could not support the family alone. These women informally forced the men to be accountable to their wives by gossip. Furthermore, to some extent women benefited from traditional patriarchal household relations because they gave women control over their children.

Fernandez-Kelly and Garcia (1990), in an article titled "Power Surrendered, Power Restored," found a similar dynamic among Cuban immigrant women and men. Cuban women's work in building family businesses contributed much to the success of the Cuban economic enclave in Miami. For instance, when the family opened a garment factory, the women would sew until it could afford to hire other workers. While the women momentarily gained in autonomy and resources, they "surrendered" these benefits to preserve traditional, patriarchal notions of manhood and womanhood. Family economic power ultimately strengthened their allegiance to family patriarchy.

In other cases, immigrant women fare better in the new societies than men because they are better able than men to mesh their traditional responsibilities, for the home and the children, with work for pay. Yet men's gender identity is often based on being the sole breadwinner. Whether or not this was completely the case back home, it is difficult to sustain this ideology in the United States owing to men's precarious labor market position. In contrast, when immigrant women work for wages they often reason that their wage work allows them to be a better mother by providing for their children, as Eastmond (1993) found among Chilean women in central California. In contrast, the Chilean men lost much of the public status and life meaning that they had previously derived from political and trade union activities. Hitchcox (1993) also argued that Vietnamese women in Hong Kong refugee camps were better able to accommodate to the camp's ideology that refugees were dependent and docile due to their dependence on men back home, while men were severely affected by this change from their former autonomy and control.

More research must be done on how men react to the decline in power resulting from migration. Recent studies suggest that some men reassert control over women in new ways. In a study of Vietnamese in Hong Kong refugee camps, Hitchcox (1993) showed how Vietnamese men reasserted control over Vietnamese women by restricting their movement and raping them in response to their feelings of powerlessness. Palestinian men in Germany also found new ways to control Palestinian women with migration. German policies ensured that Palestinians cannot work, leading to men's presence in the home all day. Men's presence in the home did not cause them to do more household tasks but allowed them to restrict the mobility and the social life of the women and girls (Abdulrahim, 1993). Finally, Peña (1991) argued that Mexican male migrant workers in California's agricultural fields strove to make up for their class and racial oppression by objectifying women in their *charritas colorados*, or jokes focusing on sadism toward women and sodomy toward males.

The reassertion of control and masculinity with migration should not be seen as inevitable but instead due to the intersection of gender relations with new systems of racial and class oppression. Indeed, a study of a Cambodian community in California found that the men felt less depressed by their inability to be the "rice-winner" owing to the high unemployment among Cambodian men within the enclave (Ui, 1991, p. 166). These Cambodian men took on more housework and asked their wives' permission before they spent money. Furthermore, women reassert their own gender identities in the face of rapid social and economic change. Jacobs and Papma (1992) found that upon return from the Middle East, Sri Lankan women focused on spiritual purity, such as praying, rather than religious rules restricting women's mobility. In doing so, they redefined themselves as spiritually pure because they had been to the Holy Land, in an attempt to buttress the negative view of women who migrate. These two studies suggest that future research should pay close attention to reassertions of masculinities and femininities within particular contexts.

In this section we focused on how gender relations change with migration. Even if the women stay behind, they often gain autonomy in the absence of their husbands, fathers, and brothers. In some cases, this newfound power allows them to negotiate their own migration. Women who migrate from the rural areas to work in export processing zones or U.S. military bases in the cities generally gain some control over their lives, but are also met with occupational segregation, sexual harassment at work, and meager wages. Women who cross international borders meet similar constraints in labor markets now segmented by race and citizenship as well as gender. Yet immigrant women are defying the facile public–private split by incorporating wage work into their definition of a good mother. More research must be done on the contradictions immigrant men face as their status as the sole breadwinner is abruptly eroded in the new society.

5. FINAL THOUGHTS

In this chapter we used the growing literature on women and migration to argue for the use of gender, rather than women or sex roles, as an analytical focal point in our theories and empirical work on migration. Still, we wish to emphasize that the vast majority of migration and immigration research continues to exhibit androcentric biases. This is equally true for mainstream scholarship that seeks to evaluate, for instance, labor market competition between recent immigrants and native-born minorities, and for the latest, theoretical approach in migration studies, transnationalionism. Emerging from postcolonial, postmodern-inspired anthropology, and explicitly challenging the linear, bipolar model of "old country" and "new world," of "sojourner" and "settler," transnationalist proponents argue that the international circulation of people, goods, and ideas creates new transnational cultures, identities, and community spheres (Basch, Glick-Schiller, & Blanc-Szanton, 1994; Kearney, 1995; Rouse, 1991). That the transnationalist perspective should be so androcentric is striking, especially since its proponents assume radical posturing and early pioneers of the perspective include three women (Basch et al., 1994). With the exception of Mahler's work (n.d.), and a short piece calling for gendered analysis (Sutton, 1991), transnationalism, like the assimilationist models that it counters, ignores gender altogether. The androcentric bias in most immigration theory and empirical work alerts us once again to the difficulties of theorizing gender when women are not the explicit focus.

As immigration research moves into the new century and millennium, we need research strategies that do more than simply "add" women to the picture. A truly gendered understanding of migration requires that we use gender as an analytical tool equally relevant to the study of men's migration as it is to women's. In this chapter we used existing literature to begin to explore male-dominated migration streams as gendered. We argued that the Mexican contract labor program, the Bracero Program, that recruited only males but relied on the reproduction work of women back home, was gendered. We also showed that male migrants within South Africa drew on gendered power dynamics in their relations with one another (Moodie, 1994).

We do not need more theorizing and empirical research that examines sex differences in migration, but rather approaches that probe the gendered nature of immigration. Nevertheless, faced with the androcentric bias in the literature, giving space to women's migrant experiences is still a necessary first step toward a gendered analysis. There are several ways that women's experiences can be made visible even while the central unit of analysis is gender, rather than women. These include focusing on how social relations between women and men circumscribe gender-specific migration streams in some cases, and under what circumstances these gendered patterns exhibit change. Do migration patterns change with alterations in development policy in the sending nation, with transformations in labor demand, with new relations between nations resulting from globalization, or some combination of these alternatives? A gendered analysis would show how social relations between women and men intersect with other institutions, such as the state and the economy, to produce gendered migration patterns. We also call for a focus on how women's and men's statuses are rearranged with migration and to what extent unequal gender relations are reconstructed with migration. Future immigration research questions might include the following: What is the relationship between gender and the politics of immigration, xenophobia, and citizenship? How does gender help to construct new racial and ethnic identities? As immigrants pose a challenge to nationalist constructs of nation, how does gender emerge to advance or retard these new constructions of nation? The answers to these questions, and others, await the next generation of "gender and migration" research.

REFERENCES

Abdulrahim, D. (1993). Defining gender in a second exile: Palestinian women in West Berlin. In G. Buijs (Ed.), *Migrant women: Crossing boundaries and changing identities* (pp. 55–82). Oxford: Berg.

Andall, J. (1992). Women migrant workers in Italy. *Women's Studies International Forum, 15,* 41–48.

Arizpe, L. (1981). The rural exodus in Mexico and Mexican migration to the United States. *International Migration Review, 15,* 626–649.

Basch, L., Glick-Schiller, N., & Blanc-Scanton, C. (Eds.) (1994). *Nations unbound: Transnational projects, postcolonial predicaments, and deterritorialized nation states.* New York: Gordon & Breach.

Beneria, L. & Roldan, M. (1987). *The crossroads of class and gender: Industrial homework, subcontracting and household dynamics in Mexico City.* Chicago and London: University of Chicago Press.

Bhachu, P. (1995). New cultural forms and transnational South Asian women: Culture, class, and consumption among British Asian women in the diaspora. In P. Van der Veer (Ed.), *Nation and migration: The politics of space in the South Asian diaspora* (pp. 222–244). Philadelphia: University of Pennsylvania Press.

Brettel, C. B., & Simon, R. (Eds) (1986). *International migration: The female experience.* New Jersey: Rowman Publishers.

Buijs, G. (Ed.) (1993). *Migrant women: Crossing boundaries and changing identities.* Oxford: Berg.

Burawoy, M. (1976I. The functions and reproduction of migrant labor: Comparative material from Southern Africa and the United States. *American Journal of Sociology, 81,* 1050–1087.

Chaney, E. M., & Garcia Castro, M. (Eds) (1989). *Muchachas no more: Household workers in Latin America and the Caribbean.* Philadelphia: Temple University Press.

Chant, S. (Ed.) (1992). *Gender and migration in developing countries.* London: Behaven Press.

Cheng, L. (1979). Free, indentured and enslaved: Chinese prostitues in ninetheenth century America. *Signs 5,* 3–29.

Clarke, C., Peach, C., & Vertovec, S. (1990). Introduction: Themes in the study of the South Asian diaspora. In C. Clarke, C. Peach, & S. Vertovec (Ed.), *South Asians overseas: Migration and ethnicity* (pp. 1–32). Cambridge: Cambridge University Press.

Connel, R. W. (1987). *Gender and power.* Berkeley: University of California Press.

Constable, N. (1997). *Maid to order in Hong Kong: Stories of Filipina workers.* Ithaca: Cornell University Press.

Dill, B. T. (1988). Our mother's grief: Racial ethnic women and the maintenance of families. *Journal of Family History, 13,* 415–431.

Eastmond, M. (1993). Reconstructing life: Chilean refugee women and the dilemmas of exile. In G. Buijs (Ed.), *Migrant women: Crossing boundaries and changing identities* (pp. 35–54). Oxford: Berg Publishers.

Eelens, F., & Speckmann, J. D. (1992). Recruitment of labour migrants for the Middle East. In F. Eelens, T. Schampers, & J. D. Speckman (Eds.), *Labour migration to the Middle East: From Sri Lanka to the Gulf* (pp. 41–62). London: Keagan Paul.

Eelens, F., Schampers, T., & Speckmann, J. D. (Eds.). (1992). *Labour migration to the Middle East: From Sri Lanka to the Gulf.* London: Keagan Paul.

Ellis, M., Conway, D., & Bailey, A. (1996). The circular migration of Puerto Rican women: Towards a gendered explanation. *International Migration 34,* 31–64.

Escobar Latapi, A., & Gonzalez de la Rocha, M. (1988). Microindustria, Informalidad y Crisis en Guadalajara, 1982–1988. *Estudios Sociologicos, 6,* 553–581.

Escobar, A., Gonzalez de la Rocha, M., & Roberts, B. (1987). Migration, labour markets and the international economy: Jalisco, Mexico and the United States. In J. Eades (Ed.), *Migrants, workers and the social order* (pp. 42–64). London: Tavistock.

Fernandez-Kelly, M. P. (1983). *For we are sold: I and my people.* Albany: State University of New York Press.

Fernandez-Kelly, M. P., & Garcia, A. M. (1990). Power surrendered, power restored: The politics of work and family among hispanic garment workers in California and Florida. In L. A. Tilly & P, Gurin (Eds.), *Women, politics and change* (pp. 130–149). New York: Russell Sage Foundation.

Gabaccia, D. (Ed.) (1992). *Seeking common ground: Multidisciplinary studies of immigrant women in the United States.* Westport, CT.: Praeger.

Glenn, E. N. (1986). *Issei, nisei, warbride*. Philadelphia: Temple University Press.

Grasmuck, S., & Pessar, P. R. (1991). *Between two islands: Dominican international migration*. Berkeley, Los Angeles, and Oxford: University of California Press.

Gugler, J. (1989). Women stay on the farm no more: Changing patterns of rural-urban migration in sub-Sahara Africa. *Journal of Modern African Studies, 27*, 347–352.

Hagan, J. M. (1994). *Deciding to be legal: A Maya community in Houston*. Philadelphia: Temple University Press.

Hine, C. (1991). Black migration to the urban midwest: The gender dimensions, 1915–1945. In J. W. Trotter (Ed.), *The great migration in historical perspective: New dimensions of race, class and gender*. Bloomington and Indianapolis: Indiana Univeristy Press.

Hitchcox, L. (1993). Vietnamese refugees in Hong Kong: Behaviour and control. In G. Buijs (Ed.), *Migrant women: Crossing boundaries and changing identities* (pp. 145–160). Oxford: Berg Publishers.

Hondagneu-Sotelo, P. (1994). *Gendered transitions: Mexican experiences of immigration*. Berkeley, CA: University of California Press.

Hondagneu-Sotelo, P., & Avila, E. (1997). I'm here, but I'm there: The meanings of Latina transnational motherhood. *Gender & Society, 11,* 548–571.

Jacobs, E. J. J., & Papma, A. (1992). The socio-economic position and religious status of Sri Lankan Muslim women migrating to the Gulf. In F. Eelens, T. Schampers, & J. D. Speckman (Eds.), *Labour migration to the Middle East: From Sri Lanka to the Gulf* (pp. 199–214). London: Keagan Paul.

Jules-Rosette, B. (1985). The women potters of Lusaka: Urban migration and socioeconomic adjustment. In B. Lindsay (Ed.), *African migration and national development* (pp. 82–112). University Park: Pennsylvania State University Press.

Kandiyotti, D. (1988a). Bargaining with patriarchy. *Gender & Society 2*, 274–290.

Kearney, M. (1995). The effects of transnational culture, economy and migration on Mixtec identity in Oaxacalifornia. In M. Smith, & J. Feagin (Eds.), *The bubbling cauldron: Race, ethnicty and the urban crisis* (pp. 226–243). Minneapolis: Unviersity of Minnesota Press.

Kibria, N. (1993). *Family tightrope: The changing lives of Vietnamese Americans*. Princeton, NJ: Princeton University Press.

Leeds, A. (1976). Women in the migratory process: A reductionist outlook. *Anthropological Quarterly, 49*, 69–76.

Mahler, S. (n.d.). Bringing gender to a transnational focus: Theoretical and empirical ideas. (Unpublished manuscript)

Mascarenhas-Keyes, S. (1993). International and internal migration: The changing identity of Catholic and Hindu women in Goa. In G. Buijs (Ed.), *Migrant women: Crossing boundaries and changing identities* (pp. 119–144). Oxford: Berg Publishers.

Massey, D., Alarcon, R., Durand, J., & Gonzalez, H. (1987). *Return to Aztlan: The social process of international migration from Western Mexico*. Berkeley, CA: Unviersity of California Press.

Moodie, T. D. with Ndatshe, V. (1994). *Going for gold: Men, mines, and migration*. Berkeley, CA: University of California Press.

Mummert, G. (1988). Mujeres de migrantes y mujeres migrantes de Michoacan: Nuevo papeles para las que se quedan y las que se van. In T. Calvo & G. Lopez (Eds.), *Movimientos de poblacion en el occidente de Mexico* (pp. 281–295). Mexico, D.F., and Zamora, Michoacan: Centre d'Estudes Mexicanines et Centramericanies and El Colegio de Mexico.

Nacify, H. (1993). *The making of exilic cultures: Iranian television in Los Angeles*. Minneapolis: University of Minnesota Press.

Nash, J. (1983). The impact of the changing international division of labor on different sectors of the labor force. In M. Fernandez-Kelly & J. Nash (Eds.), *Women, men, and the international division of labor* (pp. 3–38). Albany: State University of New York Press.

Oboo, C. (1980). *African women: Their struggle for economic independence*. London: Zed Press.

de Oliveira, O. (1990). Empleo feminino en Mexico en tiempos de recesion economica: Tendencia recientes. In N. Aguiar (Ed.), *Mujer y crisis: Respuestas ante la recession* (pp. 31–54). Caracas, Venezuela: Editorial Nueva Sociedad.

de Oliveira, O., & Garcia, B. (1984). Urbanization, migration and the growth of large cities: Trends and implications in some developing countries. In *Proceedings of the Expert Group on Population Distribution, Migration and Development*. New York: UN Department of International Economic and Social Affairs.

Ong, A. (1987). *Capitalist development and spirits of resistance: Factory women in Malaysia*. Albany: State Unviersity of New York Press.

Ong, P., & Azores, T. (1994). The migration and incorporation of Filipino nurses. In P. Ong, E. Bonacich, & L. Cheng (Eds.), *The new Asian immigration and global restructuring*. Philadelphia: Temple University Press.

Ong, P., Bonacich, E., & Cheng, L. (Eds.) (1994). *The new Asian immigration and global restructuring*. Philadelphia: Temple University Press.

Pedraza, S. (1991). Women and migration: The social consequences of gender. *Annual Review of Sociology, 17*, 303–325.

Peña, M. (1991). Class, gender and machismo: The 'treacherous woman' folklore of Mexican male workers. *Gender & Society 5*, 30–46.

Pessar, P. (1986). The role of gender in Dominican settlement in the United States. In J. Nash & H. Safa (Eds.), *Women and Change in Latin America* (pp. 273–294). Boston, MA: Bergin & Garvey Publishers.

Phizacklea, A. (Ed.) (1983). *One way ticket: Migration and female labour*. London: Routledge and Kegan Paul.

Pido, A. J. A. (1992). *The Filipinos in America: Macro/micro dimensions of immigration and integration*. New York: Center for Migration Studies.

Repak, T. (1995). *Waiting on Washington: Central American workers in the nation's capital*. Philadelphia: Temple University Press.

Rosado, G. (1990). De campesinas inmigrantes a obreras de la Fresa en el Valle de Zamora, Michoacan. In G. Mummert (Ed.), *Poblacion y Trabajo en Contextos Regionales* (pp. 45–71). Zamora: El Colegio de Michocan.

Rouse, R. (1991). Mexican migration and the social space of postmodernism. *Diaspora 1*, 8–22.

Ruiz, V. (1987). *Cannery women, cannery lives: Mexican women, unionization and the California food Processing industry, 1930–1950*. Albuquerque: University of New Mexico Press.

Sassen-Koob, S. (1984). The new labor demand in global cities. In M. P. Smith (Ed.), *Cities in transformation*. Beverly Hills, CA: Sage.

Schenk-Sandbergen, L. (Ed.) (1995). *Women and seasonal labour migration*. New Dehli: Sage.

Singhanetra-Renard, A., & Prabhudhanitisarn, N. (1992). Changing socioeconomic roles of Thai women and their migration. In S. Chant (Ed.), *Gender and migration in developing countries* (pp. 154–196). London: Behaven Press.

Stacey, J., & Thorne, B. (1985). The missing feminist revolution in sociology. *Social Problems, 32*, 301–316.

Stichter, S. (1985). *Migrant labourers*. Cambridge: Cambridge University Press.

Sturdevant, S. P., & Stoltzfus, B. (1992). *Let the good times roll: Prostitution in the U.S. military in Asia*. New York: The New Press.

Summerfield, H. (1993). Patterns of adaptation: Somali and Bangladeshi women in Britain. In G. Buijs (Ed.), *Migrant women: Crossing boundaries and changing identities* (pp. 83–98). Oxford: Berg Publishers.

Sutton, C. R. (1991). Some thoughts on gendering and internationalizing our thinking about transnational migrations. In L. Basch, N. Glick-Schiller, & C. Blanc-Szanton (Eds.), *The transnationalization of migration: New perspectives on ethnicity and race* (pp. 241–249). New York: Gordon & Breach.

Thadani, V. N., & Todaro, M. P. (1984). Female migration: A conceptual framework. In J. T. Fawcett, S.-E. Khoo, & P. C. Smith (Eds.), *Women in the cities of Asia: Migration and urban adaptation* (pp. 36–59). Boulder, CO: Westview Press.

Tiano, S. (1994). *Patriarchy on the line: Labor, gender and ideology in the Mexican maquila industry*. Philadelphia: Temple University Press.

Tienda, M., & Booth, K. (1991). Gender, migration and social change. *International Sociology, 6*, 51–72.

Toro-Moron, M. I. (1995). Gender, class, family, and migration: Puerto Rican women in Chicago. *Gender & Society, 9*, 712–726.

Tyner, J. (1996). The gendering of Philippine international labor migration. *Professional Geographer 48*, 405–416.

Ui, S. (1991). 'Unlikely heroes': The evolution of female leadership in a Cambodian ethnic enclave. In M. Burawoy (Ed.), *Ethnography unbound: Power and resistance in the modern metropolis* (pp. 161–177). Berkeley, CA: University of California Press.

Werbner, P. (1988). Taking and giving: Working women and female bonds in a Pakistani immigrant neighborhood. In S. Westwood & P. Bhachu (Eds.), *Enterprising women: Ethnicity, economy and gender relations* (pp. 177–202). London and New York: Routledge.

Westwood, S. (1988). Workers and wives: Continuities and discontinuities in the lives of Gujarati women. In S. Westwood & P. Bhachu (Ed.), *Enterprising women: Ethnicity, economy and gender relations* (pp. 103–131). London and New York: Routledge.

Wilkinson, C. (1987). Women, migration and work in Lesotho. In J. H. Momsen & J. Townsend (Eds.), *Geography of gender in the third world*. Albany, NY: SUNY Press.

Wolf, D. L. (1990). Linking women's labor with the global economy: Factory workers and their families in rural Java. In K. Ward (Ed.), *Women workers and global restructuring*. Ithaca, NY: Cornell University Press.

Wright, C. (1995). Gender awareness in migration theory: Synthesizing actor and structure in Southern Africa. *Development and Change, 26*, 771–779.

CHAPTER 7

The Feminization of Poverty

Past and Future

SARA S. MCLANAHAN

ERIN L. KELLY

1. INTRODUCTION

In 1978, Diana Pearce, a visiting researcher at the University of Wisconsin, published a
paper noting that poverty was becoming "feminized" in the United States. According to
Pearce, almost two thirds of the poor over age 16 were women. Women's economic status
had declined from 1950 to the mid-1970s, Pearce claimed, even though more women had
entered the labor force in those years. Female-headed households in particular formed a
larger and larger percentage of the poor. Pearce blamed the feminization of poverty on the
lack of government support for divorced and single women. She argued that "for many
the price of that independence has been their pauperization and dependence on welfare"
(Pearce, 1978, p. 28).

Following on Pearce's observation, Sara McLanahan and her colleagues used data
from the U.S. Census to examine trends in men's and women's poverty rates between
1950 and 1980 (McLanahan, Sorenson, & Watson, 1989).[1] While providing empirical
support for Pearce's claim that poverty was becoming feminized, they also showed that
both men's and women's poverty rates had fallen dramatically during this period. Noting
that the feminization of poverty was due to a relative rather than an absolute decline in

---

[1] Other researchers also examined the feminization of poverty. See also Fuchs (1986) and Folbre (1987).

SARA S. MCLANAHAN • Office of Population Research, Princeton University, Princeton, New Jersey 08544
ERIN L. KELLY • Department of Sociology, Princeton University, Princeton, New Jersey, 08544

Handbook of the Sociology of Gender, edited by Janet Saltzman Chafetz. Kluwer Academic/ Plenum Publishers,
New York, 1999.

women's economic status, McLanahan and her colleagues blamed the feminization of poverty on changes in the family that had uncovered women's latent economic vulnerability. Among working age adults, the growth of single parent families was the crucial factor; among the elderly, it was declines in mortality and increases in the propensity to live alone.

Recently, Paula England (1997) noted that the feminization of poverty has stopped going up and may even be reversing among some groups. England attributes these changes to improvements in women's earnings, which have risen both absolutely and relative to men's during the 1980s and 1990s. She argues that since 1980, the gains in women's employment and earnings have been large enough to offset the changes in family structure and that these gains are beginning to close the poverty gap between men and women.

In this chapter, we examine the trends in men's and women's absolute and relative poverty rates between 1950 and 1996. We discuss and assess three explanations for the feminization of poverty, including Pearce's claims that the meager welfare benefits led to the feminization of poverty, McLanahan's argument that changing family structures were the principal culprit, and England's assertion that gains in women's earnings are beginning to close the gap. We end by reviewing cross-national evidence of the feminization of poverty. These comparisons show how family structure, earnings, and government transfer programs have allowed some countries to avoid the feminization of poverty.

1.1. Defining the Terms

Before we begin our story, we need to say something about how poverty is defined and how the feminization of poverty is measured. In the United States, poverty is defined as not having enough income to pay for basic needs, such as food, clothing, and shelter. Poverty is a family attribute. In other words, if a family is classified as poor, all the members of that family are poor.[2] To determine whether or not a family is poor, the Census Bureau sums the income of all the members of the family and divides by the "need standard" or "poverty threshhold" for a family of that size.

The "needs standard" or "poverty threshold" was developed in 1964 by Mollie Orshansky, an economist at the Social Security Administration (Ruggles, 1994). To determine a family's "basic needs," Orshansky used data from an expenditure survey conducted in the mid-1950s that showed that the typical American family spent about one third of its income on food. From this study, Orshansky reasoned that to live above the poverty line, the family's income should be about three times the cost of the "basic food basket," defined as the minimal nutritional requirements for a healthy diet. To determine the latter, Orshansky used information from the Department of Agriculture. She then estimated the cost of the food basket and multiplied by a factor of three to get the official "poverty threshold" for the average American family. Ultimately, a set of thresholds was created to take account of economies of scale associated with families of different sizes and compositions. Each year the poverty thresholds are adjusted for changes in the cost of living. Otherwise they remain very similar to the ones created by Orshansky (1965) in the early 1960s.

The official poverty line used by the U.S. government has been criticized on numer-

---

[2] For single people, only their own income is counted when determining poverty. If unrelated single adults share a household, each person counts as a separate "family" for determining poverty.

ous accounts (Citro & Michael, 1995; Ruggles, 1994). First, the poverty line is based on gross earnings, before taxes. Families may be unable to meet their basic needs with the income they bring home, but they will not be counted as poor if their before-tax income is above the poverty threshhold. In this way, the current U.S. poverty rates may underestimate poverty among the working poor.

Second, government transfers, such as the Earned Income Tax Credit (EITC), food stamps, public housing, and Medicaid, are not counted as income for the purposes of determining poverty.[3] Some people may be counted as poor because their earned income is very low, but they may be able to meet their basic needs through using other government programs. In this way, the current U.S. poverty rates may overestimate poverty among people who receive benefits from certain government programs.

Third, the poverty measure implicitly assumes that money is equally shared among members of a family. This assumption is not necessarily correct. It is certainly plausible that the person who earns the money may have more control over its use, or a man might control the money as part of his breadwinner identity, or there might be some other unequal arrangement.

A fourth criticism of the poverty line measure is that it is based on an absolute rather than a relative standard. A poor family today is much worse off, relative to the average family, than a poor family was in the 1960s (McLanahan, 1995). This is because the living standards of the median family have increased dramatically during the past 35 years, while the poverty thresholds still assume that families need only three times their basic food needs. Some scholars have suggested setting the poverty line at a given proportion of the median income, rather than having it reflect a fixed amount of money. For example, families with incomes below 50% of the median family income (adjusted for family size) would be classified as poor. With a relative measure, poverty measures economic standing in the society, rather than marking economic destitution or the inability to feed, clothe, or house one's family.

Many other countries use a relative standard for poverty (Smeeding, Higgins, & Rainwater, 1990). As we will see in the cross-national comparisons later, if the United States adopted a relative standard, poverty rates would be significantly higher than they are under the official poverty measure. The difference reflects different ideas of what poverty is—relative economic disadvantage or the inability to cover basic needs.

The term feminization of poverty focuses our attention on sex differences in poverty rates and the fact that they have grown in the last half-century. Feminization describes both the unequal state of men's and women's poverty rates and the processes by which women's risk of poverty has increasingly exceeded that of men's. In her articles, Pearce (1978, 1984) focused on the proportion of the poor who were female. Other scholars, including England and McLanahan and her colleagues, have focused on the ratio of women's poverty rates to men's rates (Casper, McLanahan, & Garfinkel, 1994; McLanahan, Casper, & Sorensen, 1995; McLanahan et al., 1989). A sex/poverty ratio greater than one means that women have a higher poverty rate than men. For example, a poverty rate of 1.50, which is close to the number today for all adults, means that women's poverty rate is about 50% higher than men's.

Sex differences in poverty rates are a function of the differences in poverty rates among single men and single women weighted by the proportion of adults who are single

---

3 Government cash transfers, such as AFDC, TANF, and Social Security payments, are counted as income when
  determining poverty.

(i.e., not married). Since poverty is measured at the family level, sex differences in poverty can exist only among unmarried men and women. If all adults were married, and if boys and girls were evenly distributed across households, the sex/poverty ratio would be 1.0. Of course, some families would still be poor, but there would be no sex differences in poverty because each poor man would be linked to a poor woman.

The sex/poverty ratio, our measure of the feminization of poverty, can change when either the percentage of single adults changes or when the poverty rates of single men and women change. As we shall see later, both these factors have changed during the past four decades.

1.2. Trends in Poverty Rates and Poverty Ratios

Figure 7-1 reports poverty rates for men and women of all ages from 1950 to 1996. Several points about Fig. 7-1 are worth noting. First, blacks have much higher poverty rates than whites, regardless of their sex; and women have much higher rates than men, regardless of their race.[4] Second, poverty rates fell dramatically between 1950 and 1970, and have leveled off since then. The trends are quite similar for whites and blacks and for men and women: large declines during the 1950s and 1960s, followed by very small changes during the 1980s and 1990s.

The leveling off in poverty rates after 1970 actually masks two quite distinct trends among young adults and the elderly. After 1970 (as shown in Figs. 7-2A and B), elderly adults continued to experience falling poverty rates, while young men and women saw their rates go up. The disparity between the two age groups is especially prominent among men. In 1950, elderly males had the next to highest poverty rate; in 1996, they had the lowest rate. Over the same period, young women went from having the next to lowest poverty rate to having the highest rate.

Table 7-1 reports the trends in the sex/poverty ratios between 1950 and 1996. The first set of numbers is taken from the McLanahan et al. article (1989) which was based on the 1950, 1960, and 1970 decennial censuses. The second set of numbers is taken directly from the Current Population Surveys. Notice that the two data sets yield different ratios for young adults in 1970. This is because a different set of age cutoffs was used in the two analyses. To examine trends between 1950 and 1970, McLanahan and her colleagues used 18 to 24 as their age cutoff. To examine trends between 1970 and 1996, we used 18 to 30. Thus, we would not expect the two sets of figures to be identical in 1970. The sex/ poverty ratios for middle-aged, elderly, and the total population also differ slightly, although the discrepancy is much smaller. In this instance, the analyses used the same age cutoffs and the difference is due to differences in the data themselves.

In presenting these numbers, our point is not to provide precise estimates of the sex/ poverty ratio for any particular group or period. Rather it is to document the trends in the data. For this purpose, we are confident that our numbers tell a consistent story.

[4] We focus on whites and blacks in this chapter. Our primary purpose is to chronicle and explain the trends in poverty rates and sex differences in poverty. Because we consider changes across time, we need to look at stable populations (or groups within those populations). Hispanics are now a large minority group within the United States, but there has been so much immigration during this period that it is difficult to compare the Hispanic poverty rates over time. Also, there are no data from these sources on Hispanics until 1980. For research on poverty among various Hispanic populations, see Aponte (1993) and Tienda (1995). For information on immigrants and economic outcomes, see Portes (1996) and Portes and Rumbault (1997).

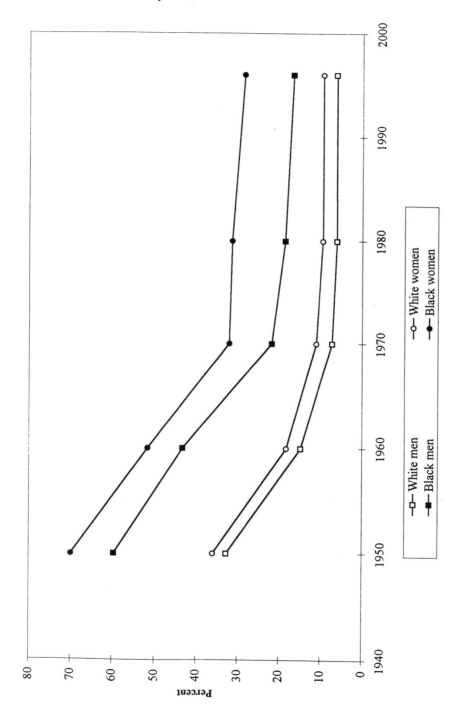

FIGURE 7-1. Poverty rates, 1950–1996.

Sara S. McLanahan AND **Erin L. Kelly**

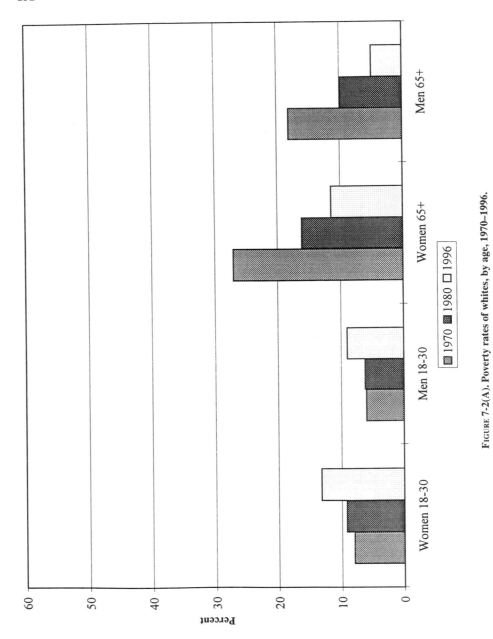

FIGURE 7-2(A). Poverty rates of whites, by age, 1970–1996.

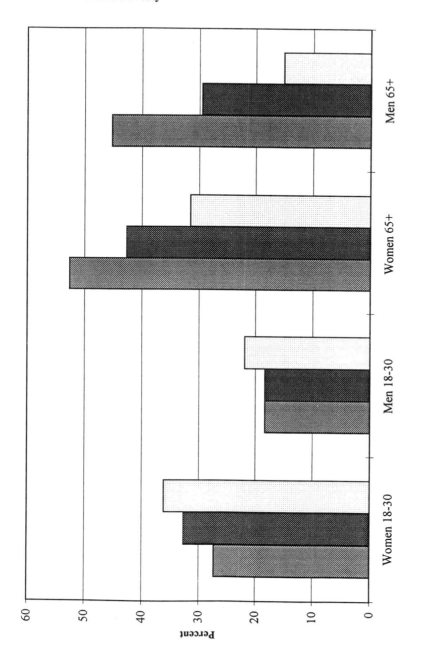

(B). Poverty rates of blacks, by age, 1970–1996.

TABLE 7-1. Poverty Ratios, 1950–1996

	1950 Census	1960 Census	1970 Census	1970 CPS	1980 CPS	1996 CPS
Whites						
Total	1.10	1.23	1.46	1.53	1.56	1.52
Young	0.83	0.99	1.00	1.33	1.48	1.47
Middle-aged	1.16	1.24	1.51	1.50	1.43	1.33
Elderly	1.13	1.24	1.45	1.49	1.64	2.33
Blacks						
Total	1.17	1.19	1.37	1.47	1.69	1.71
Young	1.05	1.11	1.11	1.49	1.78	1.65
Middle-aged	1.15	1.25	1.56	1.59	1.72	1.68
Elderly	1.05	1.05	1.14	1.16	1.44	2.09

Sources: McLanahan et al. (1989), U.S. Census for 1950, 1960, 1970, 1 in 1000 sample; Current Population Survey for 1970, 1980, 1996.
Notes: The age classifications differ by source. The Census figures use 18 to 24 for young, 25 to 64 for middle-aged, and 65+ for elderly. The CPS figures use 18 to 30 for young, 31 to 64 for middle-aged, and 65+ for elderly. The only notable effect is the difference for the young age groups, where the sex/poverty ratio is lower if only 18- to 24-year-olds are included.

To sum up briefly, a rather dramatic feminization of poverty occurred between 1950 and 1970, among all age groups and among both whites and blacks. Interestingly, it occurred at a time when poverty rates for both men and women were falling rapidly. Because men's poverty rate declined faster than women's rates, the sex/poverty ratio increased.

After 1970, the story becomes a bit more complicated. For the population as a whole, the feminization of poverty peaked in 1970 among whites and in 1980 among blacks. Then it leveled off. The latter trend masks two rather different patterns. Among the elderly, the feminization of poverty has continued to rise unabated. Between 1980 and 1996, the sex/poverty ratio grew by 69% among whites and by 65% among blacks. Whereas, in 1950, elderly women were only slightly more likely to be poor than elderly men, today they are more than twice as likely to be poor. Overall, poverty rates for elderly men and women decreased significantly, as in the earlier decades, but again, men's rates have fallen much more quickly than women's.

Among working aged adults, the feminization of poverty stopped increasing some time after 1970, and may even be reversing. Among white middle-aged adults, a "defeminization of poverty" occurred in both the 1970s and the 1980s.

2. EXPLAINING THE FEMINIZATION OF POVERTY

Why has the sex/poverty ratio grown so rapidly over the last 50 years? Why were women only slightly more likely than men to be poor in 1950, whereas today they about 50% more likely? What accounts for the leveling off, and the possible reversal, of the feminization of poverty among some age groups after 1980? In this section, we try to answer these questions. We focus on three changes that have profoundly altered the social and economic conditions of American men and women during the past 40 years: changes in the family, in the economy, and in the welfare state. As described in the following, some of these changes have clearly benefited men more than women. Others have benefited women more than men, and still others have had different effects at different times.

2.1. Changes in the Family

Starting with changes in the family, several demographic trends are important. The first of these is the delay in the age of first marriage. Throughout the 1950s, the typical young woman married when she was about 20 years old and the typical young man married when he was about 23. By 1990, however, the median age at first marriage—the age at which half of the population married for the first time—was 24 for women and 26 for men (McLanahan & Casper, 1994).

A second major change is the rise in divorce (Fig. 7-3). Whereas, in 1950, most people married and remained married until they (or their spouses) died, today more than half of all couples end their marriages voluntarily. The divorce rate—the number of divorces each year per 1000 married women—rose steadily during the first half of the twentieth century and increased dramatically after 1960. More than half of all marriages contracted in the mid-1980s were projected to end in divorce (Castro Martin & Bumpass, 1989). The divorce rate leveled off during the 1980s, but this was not necessarily a sign of greater stability. We would have expected such a leveling off, given the increase in the average age at first marriage, and given the fact that the large baby boom cohorts had reached middle age and passed through the period of their lives when they were most likely to divorce (Bumpass & Sweet, 1989).

The increase in divorce, coupled with the decline in marriage, meant that an increasing proportion of adult women were living separately from men and relying on themselves for economic support. Since women generally earn less than men for various reasons (see later), single women have a higher risk of being poor than single men. In

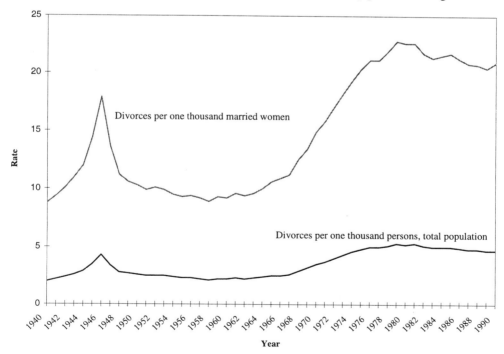

FIGURE 7-3. Divorce rates, 1940–1990. (Source: Clark, 1996, Table 1.)

short, if nothing else changes, declines in marriage will lead to increases in the sex/
poverty ratio.

We should point out that American women are more independent (socially, psychologically, and economically) today than they were in the 1950s, and more of them are
opting out of traditional family arrangements in spite of the economic costs. Since poverty measures only one aspect of well-being, we cannot say that women who live alone are
"worse off" overall than men or than women living with men. Indeed, the fact that so
many women are choosing to remain single suggests that the benefits of independence
may outweigh the costs associated with a lower standard of living.

A third trend affecting family arrangements is the increase in number of children
born outside marriage (Fig. 7-4). In 1960 about 6% of all births were to unmarried couples
whereas by 1996 more than a third fell into this category. The increase is even more
dramatic among black families—from 22% in 1960 to nearly 70% in 1996. These changes
in fertility are due to several factors, including the decline in marriage, which increases
the pool of women at risk for having an out-of-wedlock birth; the decline in the birth rate
among married couples (which was especially steep during the 1960s and early 1970s);
and the increase in the birth rate among single women (which has risen since 1980).

The net result of the changes in fertility and the increases in divorce among couples
with children has been the growth of single-mother families (Garfinkel & McLanahan,
1986). In 1960, only 8% of families were headed by a single mother; today the number is
about 27%. Blacks are much more likely than whites to fall into this category, with more
than half of all black families now consisting of a single mother and her dependent children. The trends are similar for all race and ethnic groups, however.

Single parenthood has affected women's poverty rates much more than it has men's.
Whereas in principle, responsibility for children could be evenly distributed between
mothers and fathers after a divorce or a nonmarital birth, in practice, women almost
always have custody of the child (about 90% of single parents are women). Thus, not only

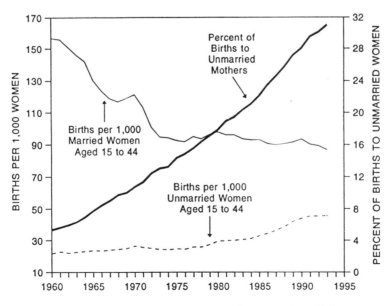

FIGURE 7-4. Fertility by marital status. (Source: Farley, 1996.)

do single women earn less money than single men, but their needs, as defined by the poverty threshold, are greater than men's because they have more dependents. Again, we should point out that most mothers, when faced with a divorce or a nonmarital birth, prefer to have custody of their child, despite the economic hardships associated with single motherhood. However, as noted previously, these women pay a high financial price for their independence.

A fourth demographic trend affecting the family life of men and women is the increase in "nonfamily" households, particularly, the increase in one-person households. In 1940, only 10% of all households were classified as "nonfamily" households, whereas in the early 1990s, more than 30% were of this type (Sweet & Bumpass, 1987). Until recently, nonfamily households were more common among blacks than among whites. Today, however, the proportions are nearly the same for both races. Hispanics, in contrast, have always had lower rates of nonfamily households.

Young adults and the elderly are especially likely to live in nonfamily households. For young people, this change is associated with the decline in marriage and the increase in cohabitation. Interestingly, couples who are cohabiting are not counted as families by the Census Bureau, even though they may be pooling their incomes and sharing expenses. Thus the poverty rates of many of these couples are likely to be overstated. Since young women are somewhat more likely to cohabit than young men, treating cohabitators as nonfamily households leads to an overestimate of women's poverty rates relative to men's (McLanahan & Casper, 1995).

The elderly are also much more likely to live independently today than they were 50 years ago (Treas, 1995). This change is generally viewed as a sign of progress, and most elderly people report that they prefer their independence. Whereas in the past, a majority of elderly people lived with their adult children once they were widowed, today, more and more widows and widowers live alone. The increase in the proportion of elderly living alone is due in part to increases in Social Security income.

A final trend affecting the sex differential in poverty rates is the increase in life expectancy. More specifically, women are likely to live longer than men and so their retirement income has to stretch over more years. The differences in men's and women's life expectancies have grown over these years. In 1940, men at age 65 had a life expectancy only 17 months shorter than that of women aged 65. In 1993, men at age 65 had a life expectancy 47 months—almost 4 years—shorter than that of women aged 65 (Advisory Council on Social Security, 1996, p. 261).

2.2. Changes in the Economy

Changes in family composition reflect changes in the needs of the family—the denominator of the poverty function. There have also been important changes in men's and women's earnings and income experiences—the numerator of the poverty function—during this period. Women's labor force participation has increased over most of the twentieth century (Blau, 1997; Spain & Bianchi, 1996). The changes have been larger in recent decades than in the early 1900s, with many American women seeking and finding employment since 1960.

The increase has been most dramatic for married women and for women with children. In the early 1950s, only about 30% of married mothers with school-aged children were working outside the home. By 1990, this number had risen to more than 73%. The figures for mothers with preschool children (under age 6) are even more dramatic. In 1960, only 19% of married mothers with preschool children were in the labor force, whereas, by 1990, 59% were employed. Women's employment increased over this entire period, but especially in the 1970s and 1980s. These years also saw some decreases in men's employment, with the reductions occurring mostly among younger and older workers (Wetzel, 1995). Young men, especially those with little education and few marketable skills, withdrew from the labor force. Older men also left work, many of them taking early retirement because their jobs were being downsized or their plants closed (Wetzel, 1995).

The increase in women's employment means that women are gaining more experience in the labor market, which, all else being equal, should increase their ability to support themselves and their families. Equally important, women are also gaining on men with respect to their hourly wages (Blau, 1997; Spain & Bianchi, 1996). From 1960 to 1980, full-time women workers averaged about 60% of full-time male workers' earnings. Since 1981, however, the ratio of women's earnings to men's earnings has increased to about 70%. During the 1980s, highly educated workers did well while those without a college education saw falling wages (Wetzel, 1995). This division was true of both men and women, but highly educated women's wages increased more than men's while less educated women's wages fell less than men's. Overall, women's earnings have increased relative to men's, raising the female-to-male wage ratio.

England's (1997) argument that women's earnings have helped reduce the sex/poverty ratio is supported by the timing of the relative wage increases and the sex/poverty ratio decreases. The declining sex gap in wages is caused by both women's increased earnings (owing to greater labor force participation and higher wage rates) and men's stagnant wages since the late 1970s. In fact, men's economic status has declined in recent years as women's earnings have improved slightly. For whites, the period in which women's relative wages began climbing corresponds to the period in which the sex/poverty ratio fell. This finding suggests that women's wages have led to the reversal in trends.

The exception to the defeminization trend also offers some support for England's argument about wage effects. If changes in women's earnings (relative to men's) are largely responsible for the reversal in the sex/poverty ratio, we would not expect to observe a reversal among the age groups who are less likely to be working, namely among retired persons. From 1970 to 1996, the sex/poverty ratio did not decline for women over 65 years. Since elderly women are less likely to be employed, and quite likely to be living without men, they did not benefit from the improvements in employment and earnings that accrued to women in the 1970s and 1980s.

2.3. Changes in Public Benefits

Besides relying on their earnings, many Americans receive income from government transfers. Government transfers serve as a buffer against the risk of poverty and economic insecurity. If a family's income from earnings does not meet its needs, transfer income may provide the extra income needed to lift the family out of poverty. However, government transfer programs differ in how generous they are, and thus how successfully they keep households out of poverty. The three main government transfer programs in the United States are Aid to Families with Dependent Children (now TANF), which is a program mostly benefiting poor single mothers and their children; Supplementary Security Income (SSI), a program benefiting disabled, blind, and poor elderly adults; and Old Age Survivors, Disability, and Unemployment Insurance, a set of programs for disabled, unemployed, and retired workers.

The first two programs, TANF and SSI, provide "income-tested" benefits which means that a family must be poor to qualify for the benefit. The income test creates a "Catch 22" with respect to poverty. If a family that qualifies for the benefit manages to increase its income (from other sources) enough to lift it above the poverty line, the family no longer qualifies for the benefit. In fact, eligibility thresholds are generally set below the poverty line, so a family can be cut off from these programs even though its income is well below the poverty line. Thus income-tested programs, by design, do not lift many families out of poverty, although they reduce the depth of their poverty. Social insurance programs, in contrast, are guaranteed to all adults who qualify, regardless of their economic status. These payments (which include most Social Security benefits) are also much larger, per person, than TANF or SSI. As a consequence, their poverty reduction effects are very large.

We should point out that several other government programs providing support to low-income families were initiated during the 1960s, 1970s, and 1980s, including food stamps, public housing and housing vouchers, Medicaid, and the Earned Income Tax Credit (EITC). The EITC, which supplements the earnings of the household head in working poor families, is one of the most generous and most effective antipoverty programs in the United States. However, since benefits are provided through the tax system, they are not counted as income in calculating the official poverty rates. Neither food stamps nor housing subsidies are counted as income, although both of these programs cover "basic needs" and are similar to cash transfers in many respects.

If government transfer programs played a large role in the feminization of poverty and the recent reversal of the trend, then changes in these programs should correspond to changes in poverty rates and sex/poverty ratios. To some extent, the trend in benefits corresponds to the trends in poverty rates. During the years in which feminization first occurred—1950 to 1970—both AFDC and Social Security were expanding rapidly, not only in terms of the number of people covered but also in terms of the value of the benefits themselves. AFDC rose during the 1950s and 1960s, as the federal government waged a "war on poverty." Similarly, Social Security pension coverage was expanded during these two decades and the value of the benefit was increased several times.

As shown in Fig. 7-1, poverty rates fell dramatically during this time. Social Security benefits undoubtedly played a role in reducing poverty among elderly men and women, and welfare did the same for single mothers. Recall that these were the years in which family structure was changing quickly, and the increased availability of AFDC probably helped to offset some of the negative consequences of these changes on women's economic status.

Many conservatives would disagree with the statement that women's poverty rates would have been higher without welfare benefits. Instead, they would argue that the growing availability of welfare benefits during this period actually increased women's risk of poverty by fueling the growth of single-mother families (Murray, 1984). While, theoretically, it makes sense to think that AFDC benefits might encourage some poor women to leave a bad marriage or to keep a child who was conceived out of wedlock, the empirical evidence on this issue indicates that the size of the effect is very small (Moffitt, 1998). This finding should not surprise anyone who is familiar with the demographic trends described earlier (delays in marriage, declines in marital fertility, increases in one-person households) since these trends have been occurring among women of all social class backgrounds, including women who have never been forced to rely on welfare. Nevertheless, the conservatives raise an important point and draw our attention to the fact that the relationships between changes in the family, the labor market, and in public transfers are probably reciprocal.

After 1970, the trends in AFDC and social insurance diverged sharply. Social Security pensions for the elderly were raised again and indexed to inflation in the early 1970s, and the value of these benefits continued to rise throughout the 1970s, 1980s, and 1990s. In contrast, welfare benefits, which were not linked to inflation, peaked in the mid-1970s and then began to fall. Initially, the decline in AFDC was due to high inflation in the second half of the 1970s. After 1980, however, declines were due to direct cuts in benefits as well as to inflation.

The decline in government transfers for women of childbearing age after the mid-1970s is consistent with the leveling off of poverty rates among women between the ages of 18 and 64 during the 1970s and 1980s. That is, poverty rates stopped declining about the time that welfare benefits stopped increasing. Similarly, the rise in Social Security benefits for retired adults after 1970 is consistent with the continuing decline in poverty rates among the elderly.

Given that Social Security has played an important role in driving down the poverty rates of the elderly, why have women's poverty rates been slower to decline than men's? The feminization of poverty among the elderly is a result of several factors. First, pensions for never married women are lower, on average, than pensions for never married men since women earn less than men while they are working. Second, retirement benefits are set when a person reaches age 65 (or retires), and despite that fact that they are indexed to inflation, the original benefit is not adjusted for increases that postdate retirement. In particular, people who retired before the early 1970s have substantially lower pensions than people who retired after 1970. Since women live longer than men, they are more likely to fall into this group than men. Finally, elderly women are more likely to live alone than elderly men, and thus they must live on one pension rather than two. For all these reasons, poverty rates among elderly women have not declined as fast as poverty rates among elderly men.

2.4. Decomposing the Trends

To try and gain a better idea of the forces behind the leveling off of the sex/poverty ratio between 1970 and 1996 and the relative importance of changes in the family and changes in labor market opportunities, we conducted a simple thought experiment. We asked, if only family structure had changed between 1970 and 1996 and everything else had stayed the same, what would the sex/poverty ratio have been? Next we asked a similar question about changes in employment and earnings. If only men's and women's personal earnings had changed between 1970 and 1996, what would the sex/poverty ratio have been? To answer these questions, we estimated multivariate regression equations that treated poverty in 1970 as a function of family characteristics, personal earnings, and a set of other variables measured in 1970. Family structure was divided into five categories: married couple (with or without children), single parent with minor children, one-person households, other households with children, and other households without children. We ran separate equations for men and women, blacks and whites, and three age groups: 18 to 30, 31 to 64, and 65+.

Next, we substituted the 1996 means for the family structure variables into the 1970 equations and obtained predicted poverty rates for men and women, holding all the other values constant. Using the predicted poverty rates, we then calculated a new set of sex/ poverty ratios for each sex, race, and age group. We repeated the process, this time substituting 1996 personal earnings for 1970 earnings and holding family structure constant. The results are reported in Table 7-2.

According to Table 7-2, if only family composition had changed between 1970 and 1996, the sex/poverty ratio for young whites would have been 1.47, which is 14 percentage points higher than the observed ratio in 1996. In contrast, if only men's and women's earnings had changed during this period, the sex/poverty ratio would have been less than 1. These simulations are only illustrative. However, they demonstrate that employment changes strongly favored women during this period and offset some of the negative effects associated with changes in family composition. The patterns for middle-aged white women and for both young and middle-aged black women are similar. If only family composition had changed between 1970 and 1996, sex/poverty ratios would have been even higher than they actually were. If only earnings had changed, the ratios would have been much closer to parity.

TABLE 7-2. Observed and Estimated Poverty Ratios for Working Age Adults

Whites, 18 to 30:	
Observed 1970 ratio	1.33
Observed 1996 ratio	1.47
Estimated 1996 ratio if only family composition had changed	1.54
Estimated 1996 ratio if only personal earnings had changed	0.73
Whites, 31 to 64:	
Observed 1970 ratio	1.50
Observed 1996 ratio	1.33
Estimated 1996 ratio if only family composition had changed	1.46
Estimated 1996 ratio if only personal earnings had changed	0.66
Blacks, 18 to 30:	
Observed 1970 ratio	1.49
Observed 1996 ratio	1.65
Estimated 1996 ratio if only family composition had changed	1.83
Estimated 1996 ratio if only personal earnings had changed	1.07
Blacks, 31 to 64:	
Observed 1970 ratio	1.59
Observed 1996 ratio	1.68
Estimated 1996 ratio if only family composition had changed	1.70
Estimated 1996 ratio if only personal earnings had changed	1.23

Sources: Current Population Surveys 1970, 1996. OLS poverty equations for 1970 with 1996 means for family composition values and then 1996 means for personal earnings substituted.

3. CROSS-NATIONAL COMPARISONS

Another approach to understanding the feminization of poverty is to ask why it does not occur in some settings. Casper et al. (1994) examined sex differences in poverty in eight countries and asked how some countries have managed to avoid the feminization of poverty (Fig. 7-5). They considered how factors related to income (i.e., age, education, and employment status) and needs (i.e., marital status, parental status) led to different poverty rates and sex/poverty ratios among these eight countries. These researchers found that large gender differentials in poverty rates have been avoided in three countries, for three different reasons. The important factors are distinctive family structures in Italy, distinctive employment patterns in Sweden, and distinctive government transfers in the Netherlands. The Netherlands findings are useful because government transfers have not played a large role in reducing poverty or preventing the feminization of poverty in the United States. This example shows that government programs can and do reduce poverty rates and close the gap between men's and women's poverty rates if they are generous enough.

Italy has very high marriage rates and so almost no difference in men's and women's likelihood of living in poverty. Because almost every adult man is paired to an adult woman, there are poor Italians but very little difference between men's and women's likelihood of living in poverty. If U.S. adults had marital patterns equal to those of Italian adults (but otherwise had the same characteristics that they actually do have), the sex/poverty ratio in the United States would be reduced by 71% (Casper et al., 1994).

In Sweden, men are actually slightly more likely than women to live in poverty. This unusual situation is explained by women's high labor force participation. Since Swedish women are very likely to be employed and there is only a small wage gap between men's and women's average earnings, women are not more likely than men to live in poverty. If U.S. women had the same labor force participation rates as Swedish women, the sex/poverty ratio would be reduced by 60%. In some other Western countries with relatively low levels of women's employment, female labor force participation rates similar to Sweden's would entirely eliminate the poverty gap (Casper et al., 1994, p. 600).

While Sweden illustrates the potential of women's earnings for reducing the sex/poverty ratio, it is important to realize that Swedish government policy facilitates women's employment and women's high relative earnings in several ways. Government policies that encourage women's employment include a tax system that taxes persons on their own earnings (rather than having a joint filing option for married couples) and a parental leave system that grants long paid leaves to mothers and fathers of infants. In addition to the leaves, government policies allow parents of young children to reduce their work hours for several years while keeping their old jobs (Kamerman & Kahn, 1991). The government also encourages wage equality between men and women through its involvement in collective bargaining agreements and the fact that the state employs a very large number of women workers itself. Therefore, earnings have aided women in Sweden, but the government has played a large role in increasing women's earnings.

The Netherlands also has a very low sex/poverty ratio, but its marriage, parenting, and employment rates are not unusual. It seems that "the low poverty rates and the low gender-poverty ratio in the Netherlands is largely due to the generous welfare system" (Casper et al., 1994, p. 602). In the Netherlands, single parenting is common and single mothers are not likely to be employed full-time. However, the Dutch have avoided sex differences in poverty rates because the government transfers to single mothers are generous enough to lift those women and their families out of poverty.

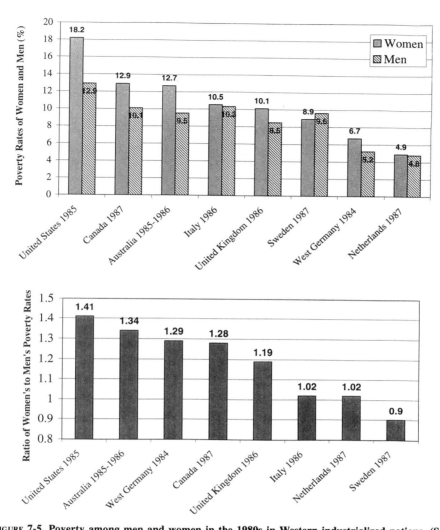

FIGURE 7-5. Poverty among men and women in the 1980s in Western industrialized nations. (Source: Luxembourg Income Study.)

The cross-national comparisons confirm the importance of family status, earnings, and transfer payments in explaining poverty rates and the feminization of poverty. This research also suggests that there may be multiple ways to reduce the disparities between men's and women's poverty rates. Americans interested in reducing the feminization of poverty could design public policies to encourage any or all three of these conditions, although these policies might increase gender inequalities in other areas.

4. CONCLUSIONS

The changes in poverty rates and sex differences in poverty have occurred in two major periods, from 1950 to 1970 and from 1970 to 1996. In the decades after World War II, poverty rates declined dramatically. This was a period of strong economic growth, including rising wages, and expansion of government benefits, such as Social Security and welfare programs. Both of these forces lowered poverty rates. As poverty rates declined, the sex/poverty ratio increased for all groups. The growing inequality in men's and women's poverty rates was caused by several factors. First, the wage growth that lowered poverty rates benefited men more than women because they were more closely attached to the labor market. Second, changes in family structure hurt women more than men, mainly because women bore more responsibility for children in the growing number of unmarried households.

After 1970, poverty rates stopped declining. During the 1970s, the economy stagnated and when it recovered in the 1980s, the main beneficiaries were college graduates rather than less educated workers living near the poverty line. The sex/poverty ratio continued to increase among the elderly, but stopped increasing among working age adults. The sex/poverty ratio may be reversing as the gap between women's and men's poverty rates closes somewhat. The sex/poverty ratio is increasing among the elderly partly because older women are living longer than men, and these older women often rely on a single Social Security benefit for many years. The sex/poverty ratio has stopped climbing for working aged adults, even though families have continued to change in ways that leave women with a large economic burden. The stagnant economy apparently has hurt men more than it has hurt women. Women's wages have slowly gained on men's over the last 15 years, stopping the increased feminization of poverty. It is important to note, however, that women are still much more likely—about 50% more likely overall—than men to live in poverty.

Cross-national comparisons show us that the feminization of poverty is avoidable. The Netherlands keeps the sex/poverty ratio low by establishing a high income floor; the welfare state does not allow anyone to be poor, regardless of family status or employment situation. Sweden keeps the sex/poverty ratio low by subsidizing employment and by keeping wages high through union agreements. Since women's labor force participation is very high, this ensures that few women are poor. Unlike the Netherlands or Sweden, Italy has fairly high levels of poverty but the high marriage rates keep sex differences in poverty very low.

REFERENCES

Advisory Council on Social Security. (1996). *Report of the 1994–95 Advisory Council on Social Security,* Vol. II. Washington, D.C.: U.S. Government Printing Office.

Aponte, R. (1993). Hispanic families in poverty. *Families in Society, 74,* 527–537.

Blau, F. D. (1997). Trends in the well-being of American women, 1970–1995. *Journal of Economic Literature, 36,* 112–165.

Bumpass, L. L., & Sweet, J. (1989). Children's experience in single-parent families: Implications of cohabitation and marital transitions. *Family Planning Perspectives, 21,* 256–260.

Casper, L. M., McLanahan, S. S., & Garfinkel, I. (19940. The gender-poverty gap: What we can learn from other countries. *American Sociological Review, 59,* 594–605.

Castro Martin, T., & Bumpass, L. L. (1989). Recent trends in marital disruption. *Demography, 26,* 37–51.

Citro, C., & Michael, R. (Eds.) (1995). *Measuring poverty: A new approach.* Washington, D.C.: National Academy Press.

Clarke, S. C. (1995). Advanced report of the final divorce statistics, 1989–1990. *Monthly Vital Statistics, 43,* 8(Suppl.).

England, P. (1997). Gender and access to money: What do trends in earnings and household poverty tell us? Paper presented at the Eighth International Meeting of the Comparative Project on Class Structure and Class Consciousness, Canberra, Australia.

Farley, R. (1996). *The new American reality.* New York: Russell Sage Foundation.

Folbre, N. (1987). The pauperization of mothers: Patriarchy and public policy in the US. In N. Gerstel & H. Gross, *Families and work: toward reconceptualization (pp. 491–511).* New York: Temple University Press.

Fuchs, V. (1986). The feminization of poverty? National Bureau of Economic Research, Working Paper no. 1934.

Garfinkel, I., & McLanahan, S. S. (1986). *Single mothers and their children.* Washington, D.C.: Urban Institute.

Kamerman, S. B., & Kahn, A. J. (Eds.) (1991). *Child care, parental leave, and the under three's: Policy innovation in Europe.* New York: Auburn House.

McLanahan, S. S. (1995). Poverty. In D. Levinson, *Encyclopedia of marriage and the family, Vol. 2* (pp. 549–556). New York: Macmillan.

McLanahan, S. S., & Casper, L. (1995). Growing diversity and inequality in the American family. In R. Farley (Ed.), *State of the Union: America in the 1990s, Vol. 2* (pp. 1–46). New York: Russell Sage Foundation.

McLanahan, S. S., Sorensen, A., & Watson, D. (1989). Sex differences in poverty, 1950–1980. *Signs, 15,* 102–122.

McLanahan, S. S., Casper, L., & Sorensen, A. (1995). Women's roles and women's poverty in eight industrialized countries. In K. O. Mason & A. M. Jensen (Eds.), *Gender and family change in industrialized countries* (pp. 258–278). Oxford: IUSSP/Oxford University Press.

Moffitt, R. (1998). The effect of welfare on marriage and fertility: What do we know and what do we need to know. In R. Moffitt (Ed.), *Welfare, the family, and reproductive behavior: Research perspectives.* Washington, D.C.: National Academy of Sciences Press.

Murray, C. (1984). *Losing ground: American social policy, 1950–1980.* New York: Basic Books.

Orshansky, M. (1965). Counting the poor: Another look at the poverty profile. *Social Security Bulletin, 28,* 3–29.

Pearce, D. (1978). The feminization of poverty: Women, work and welfare. *Urban and Social Change Review, 11,* 28–36.

Pearce, D. (1984). Farewell to alms: Women's fare under welfare. In J. Freeman (Ed.), *Women, a feminist perspective* (3rd ed., pp. 493–506). Palo Alto, CA: Mayfield.

Portes, A. (1996). *The economic sociology of immigration.* New York: Russell Sage Foundation.

Portes, A., & Rumbault, R. G. (1997). *Immigrant America: A portrait* (2nd ed.). Berkeley, CA: University of California Press.

Ruggles, P. (1994). *Drawing the line.* Washington, D.C.: Urban Institute.

Smeeding, T. M., Higgins, M. O., & Rainwater, L. (1990). *Poverty, inequality, and income distribution in comparative perspective.* New York: Harvester Wheatsheaf.

Spain, D., & Bianchi, S. M. (1996). *Balancing act: Motherhood, marriage, and employment among American women.* New York: Russell Sage Foundation.

Sweet, J., & Bumpass, L. L. (1987). *Families and households in America.* New York: Russell Sage Foundation.

Tienda, M. (1995). Latinos and the American pie: Can Latinos achieve economic parity. *Hispanic Journal of Behavioral Sciences, 17,* 403–429.

Treas, J. (1995). Older Americans in the 1990s and beyond. *Population Bulletin,* May.

Wetzel, J. R. (1995). Labor force, unemployment, and earnings. In R. Farley (Ed.), *State of the union: American in the 1990s,* Vol. 1 (pp. 56–106). New York: Russell Sage Foundation.

CHAPTER 8

Gender Movements

Cynthia Fabrizio Pelak
Verta Taylor
Nancy Whittier

1. INTRODUCTION

Although the feminist project in sociology during the last 30 years has varied theoretically, methodologically, and substantively, much of the scholarship on gender has focused on the maintenance of gender stratification and the resilience of gender inequality. Only recently have gender scholars turned to exploring and theorizing the historicity of gender and processes of gender resistance, challenge, and change. Given the persistence of gender inequality and the universality of gender oppression, it is not surprising that researchers have concentrated so heavily on documenting the extent, forms, and causes of gender stratification. We do know, however, that the dynamics of gender and the extent of gender inequality vary over time and place. Such historical and contextual variability raises important theoretical and empirical questions for sociologists interested in processes of gender change.

One area of research that has begun to examine gender transformation is the scholarship on social movements, particularly the emerging literature on feminist movements in the United States (Buechler, 1990; Ferree & Hess, 1994; Ferree & Martin, 1995; Freeman 1975; Giele, 1995; Katzenstein & Mueller, 1987; Rupp & Taylor, 1987; Ryan, 1992; Staggenborg, 1991; Whittier 1995). This literature focuses largely on the mobilization, ideologies, organizations, leadership patterns, strategies, and tactics of women's move-

Cynthia Fabrizio Pelak and Verta Taylor • Department of Sociology, Ohio State University, Columbus, Ohio 43210
Nancy Whittier • Department of Sociology, Smith College, Northampton, Massachusetts 01063

Handbook of the Sociology of Gender, edited by Janet Saltzman Chafetz. Kluwer Academic/ Plenum Publishers, New York, 1999.

147

ments. Although this body of research has illustrated the critical role that women's collective action has played in altering gender relations in the United States, scholarship on the gender effects of social movements nevertheless remains fairly descriptive. This is because social movement researchers, in general, have concentrated more on the mobilization of social movements than on their consequences. Recently, however, some movement scholars have begun to explore the gendered nature of social movements (Barnett, 1993; Brown & Ferguson, 1995; Gamson, 1997; McAdam, 1992; Naples, 1992a; Neuhouser, 1995; Reger, Whittier, & Taylor, 1995; Robnett, 1996; Taylor, 1999; West & Blumberg, 1990) and to trace the effects of social movements on gender relations (Staggenborg, 1997; Taylor, 1996; Taylor & Van Willigen, 1996). We believe that developing analytical frameworks that integrate the literatures on gender and social movements offers sociologists an excellent opportunity to understand the dynamic nature of gender and the significance of human agents in the making and remaking of femininity, masculinity, and the existing gender order (see, e.g., Taylor, 1996; Taylor & Van Willigen, 1996).

This chapter seeks to emphasize the role of social movements in gender change by examining the diverse, multiple, and often contradictory social movement activities organized around gender in the United States. Specifically, we focus on the various and sometimes paradoxical ideologies and organizational structures of the modern women's movement. Given this goal, it is useful at the outset to outline a framework for analyzing the outcomes of social movements that makes it possible to link theoretical approaches to gender with existing theory in social movements. We then trace the larger macrostructural preconditions that underlie the emergence of feminist movements in most Western societies. After a brief examination of feminist mobilization in an international context, we turn to our central purpose in this chapter, which is to examine the continuity and transformation of the contemporary feminist movement in the United States and the multiple and shifting strategies collective actors have used in the struggle for equality between women and men. We conclude by exploring two other strands of activism, men's movements and antifeminist countermovements, which also are engaged in the social construction and reconstruction of gender in the United States.

2. GENDER AND SOCIAL MOVEMENT THEORIES

If there is a single point on which gender scholars agree, it is that notions of femininity and masculinity; the gender division of labor in private and public spheres; and numerous institutions, practices, and structures that reinforce male dominance—even the very idea of gender itself—are not expressions of natural differences between women and men. Rather, gender and the gender order are socially constructed. Although there is a fairly universal adoption of social constructionist perspectives in understanding gender, there is considerable variation in the epistemologies, contexts, and levels of analyses of the theories that have been developed to explain gender stratification. Feminist explanations not only focus on different aspects of the gender system, but they also operate at various levels of analyses (for reviews, see Chafetz, 1988; England, 1993; Lorber, 1994). Those theories that explicitly address the change process have tended to be macrostructural and have stressed the relationship between societal level structural and cultural processes and the level of gender inequality in a society (Blumberg, 1984; Chafetz, 1990; Dunn, Almquist, & Chafetz, 1993; Hartmann, 1984; Huber, 1991; Smith 1990). As useful as these perspectives might be for explaining variations in gender inequality across social systems, macrostructural theories are unable to explain the shifts in gender consciousness and increases in resources and organization that social movements scholars have found to be essential for mobilization of collective action oriented toward gender system change (Buechler, 1990; Chafetz & Dworkin, 1986; Costain, 1992; Katzenstein & Mueller, 1987; Klein, 1984). We believe that theoretical frameworks that combine the insights of interactionist, network and organizational, and macrostructural gender theorists by highlighting the centrality of gender at all levels of analysis (see, e.g., Collins, 1990; Connell, 1987; Lorber, 1994; Scott, 1986) are likely to provide the most useful set of concepts for assessing the role of social movement actors in the social construction of gender.

Multilevel frameworks suggest three analytical tools for understanding the effects of social movements on the gender order. First, they view gender at the *interactional level,* calling our attention to the way women and men learn societal expectations of gender-appropriate behavior and practice them in daily interactions in the performance of femininity and masculinity (Butler, 1990; Thorne, 1994; West & Fenstermaker, 1995; West & Zimmerman, 1987). Second, they delineate the way gender operates at the *structural level,* so that gender distinctions become a basis for ranking men above women of the same race and class (Acker, 1990; Reskin, 1988). It is in this sense that Scott (1988) refers to gender as "signifying power relations" (p. 42). As a structure, gender divides work in the home and in the wider economy, legitimates existing hierarchies of authority, organizes sexual expression and emotions, and structures every aspect of social life because of its embeddedness in the family, the workplace, and the state (Connell, 1987; Lorber, 1994). Finally, at the *cultural level,* gender distinctions and hierarchy are expressed in ideology and cultural practices, such as sexuality and language, as well as in art, religion, medicine, law, and the mass media (Butler, 1990; Smith, 1990). Treating the gender system as simultaneously supported and constructed at each of these levels allows us to recognize the myriad of ways that social movements are engaged in claims-making to challenge or affirm the gender code.

Even if multilevel theories are more sensitive to the complexities of gender change, they do not offer insight into the actual processes of change. Our analysis draws upon social movement theory to demonstrate the link between social movement activism and the social construction of gender relations at these various levels. Theorists have developed complementary and competing frameworks to explain the emergence and dynamics of social movements. Our approach to social movements combines the insights of classical collective behavior theory, resource mobilization theory, and new social movements perspectives by highlighting the way grievances, ideology, and collective identity combine with organization, resources, and political context to explain the emergence, nature, and course of movements (McAdam, 1992; McCarthy & Zald, 1977; Melucci, 1989; Morris, 1984; Tarrow, 1994; Turner & Killian, 1987). Although scholars generally agree on the factors that promote feminist collective action, there is debate on the relative importance of grievances, consciousness, and collective identity, on the one hand, and resources, political opportunity, and organizations, on the other (Buechler, 1990).

Feminist researchers have placed considerable emphasis on the importance of feminist consciousness—or the belief that women are subordinated as a group on the basis of sex—in explaining the rise of women's movements. Nevertheless, diverse versions of feminism have existed and even coexisted in the same movements throughout history. To capture the diversity of feminism, historians have suggested that one fundamental debate that appears throughout the history of feminism focuses on women's "sameness" versus their "difference" from men (Black, 1989; Chafe, 1991; Cott, 1987; Offen, 1988; Tong, 1989). Feminists advocating an "equal rights" position have emphasized the similarities between women and men and pursued policies and strategies that treat women and men identically. In contrast, those who argue women's "difference" hold that, either as a result of biology or socialization, women are essentially different from men in their capacity for caring and compassion. These feminists have seen the need for female-specific political strategies that address women's maternal role.

Although the discussion of gender ideology in feminism is fruitful, we think that a concentration solely on ideas ignores the fact that feminists are social movements actors situated within an organizational and movement context. Feminism is more than gender ideology: it is a collective identity. Collective identity is the shared definition of a group that derives from members' common interests, experiences, and solidarity (Taylor, 1989; Taylor & Whittier, 1992). A collective identity approach allows us to understand feminist identity as a movement characteristic that is constructed, activated, and sustained through interaction in a wider social movement.

Even if feminist consciousness is an important ingredient of women's movements, a social movement perspective insists that we recognize that the emergence of feminist movements depends on the political opportunities for women to organize on their own behalf, the resources available to them, as well as their collective identities and interpretation of their grievances. Besides these constitutive elements, social movement scholars recognize that there are some basic structural preconditions underlying the emergence of women's collective mobilization.

3. STRUCTURAL PRECONDITIONS OF WESTERN FEMINIST MOVEMENTS

From a movement perspective, women have always had sufficient grievances to create the context for feminist activity. Indeed, instances of collective action on the part of women abound in history, especially if one includes female reform societies, women's church groups, alternative religious societies, and women's clubs. However, collective activity on the part of women directed specifically toward improving their own status has flourished primarily during periods of generalized social upheaval, when sensitivity to moral injustice, discrimination, and social inequality has been widespread in the society as a whole (Chafe, 1977; Staggenborg, 1998). The first wave of feminism in the United States grew out of the abolitionist struggle of the 1830s and peaked during an era of social reform in the 1890s, and the contemporary movement emerged out of the general social discontent of the 1960s. Although the women's movement did not die between these periods of heightened activism, it declined sharply in the 1930s, 1940s, and 1950s after the passage of the Nineteenth Amendment to the Constitution guaranteeing women the right to vote as a response to the changing social, political, and economic context (Rupp & Taylor, 1987). During this period, women who had played important roles in obtaining women's suffrage managed to keep the flames of feminism alive by launching a campaign to pass an Equal Rights Amendment (ERA) to the Constitution.

Researchers identify crucial structural conditions that underlie the emergence of feminist protest (Chafetz & Dworkin, 1986; Huber & Spitze, 1983; Oppenheimer, 1973). Broad societal changes in the patterns of women's participation in the paid labor force, increases in women's formal educational attainment, and shifts in women's fertility rates and reproductive roles disrupt traditional social arrangements and set the stage for women's movements. Chafetz and Dworkin (1986) propose that as industrialization and urbanization bring greater education for women, expanding public responsibilities create role and status conflicts for middle-class women, who then develop the discontent and gender consciousness necessary for political action. Specifically, when women, especially married middle-class women, enter the paid labor force their gender consciousness increases because they are more likely to use men as a reference group when assessing their access to societal rewards. Similarly, women often experience strains and discrepancies in their lives as their gender consciousness is raised through formal education (Klein, 1984).

Scholars also identify other important structural preconditions that set the stage for feminist mobilization, including changes in family relationships, marriage, fertility, and sexual mores (Ferree & Hess, 1994). Declines in women's childbearing rates and increasing age of women at first marriage can positively influence women's educational attainment and participation in the paid labor force which, in turn, raises women's gender consciousness (Klein, 1984). Moreover, changes in the traditional relationships between women and men in marriage and in sexual mores, such as the shift from authoritarian marriages to romantic or companionate marriages at the turn of the century in the United States and the "sexual revolution" of the 1960s, can politize gender relations and create the motivations for feminist mobilization (Ferree & Hess, 1994).

Structural preconditions underlying the genesis of feminist collective mobilizations vary with historical and geographical context. Not only the political context but also the structural preconditions underlying feminist mobilizations in the United States are different from those in Third World countries. Moreover, variable structural conditions influence the ideologies, organizations, and strategies adopted by feminist movements in different times and places. Nonetheless, scholars recognize some important commonalties between women's movements around the world.

4. FEMINIST MOVEMENTS IN AN INTERNATIONAL CONTEXT

While this chapter focuses on the women's movement in the United States, it is nonetheless important to acknowledge the multiple forms of feminist resistance around the world and to underscore the importance of the historical and geographical specificity of feminist activism. Throughout modern history, women in all regions of the world have organized collectively against the injustice and oppression in their lives and communities (Basu, 1995). Such mobilizations in diverse political, cultural, and historical contexts have varied widely in their organizations, strategies, ideologies, and structures. Gender oppression for some Third World feminists cannot be divorced from issues and histories of colonization, immigration, racism, or imperialism, and thus feminist activism in some Third World contexts may be organized around a constellation of oppressions rather than specifically around gender oppression (Jayawardena, 1986; Mohanty, Russo, & Torres, 1991). In some instances, however, ideological, organizational, and strategic differences in women's movements cannot be said to lie in the lived experiences of women but in fundamental differences in the political culture of a region (Ray, 1999). In Calcutta, India, for example, which is dominated by the Communist Party and a strong and traditional left culture, the women's movement functions more as a political party and uses strategies to address issues such as work and domestic violence that do not directly threaten the gender status quo. The women's movement in Bombay, on the other hand, which exists in a more open, contested political field and culture, is characterized by more autonomous forms of organizing and has been influenced by American feminists' analyses of domestic violence and British socialist feminist analyses of class. Although differences exist, researchers nevertheless have identified important commonalties that link women's movements over time and place (Chafetz & Dworkin, 1986; Giele, 1995; Katzenstein & Mueller, 1987; Miles, 1996).

Some scholars recognize that women's movements, particularly those in industrialized countries, generally have emerged in two waves of heightened activism. In their cross-cultural, historical analysis of 48 countries, Chafetz and Dworkin (1986) found that the mass-scale, independent women's movements of the first wave, such as those in European societies and the United States, occurred in the closing decades of the nineteenth century and the first decades of the twentieth century, while the second wave women's movements emerged since the 1960s. Major goals of the first wave of activism included women's suffrage, educational opportunities for women, basic legal reforms, inheritance and property rights, and employment opportunities for women. Chafetz and Dworkin (1986) maintain that women's demands during this first wave often were framed around middle-class women's roles as wives and mothers and reinforced gender difference by valorizing women's special virtues and moral superiority over men. Smaller scale movements during the first wave were more likely to challenge basic role differentiation between women and men and to resist doctrines and images of femininity in the culture. To the extent that the large-scale changes brought on by urbanization and industrialization in Western countries created dramatic changes in the workplace, the family, and in the lives of women and men, it is not surprising there was considerable ideological debate and diversity among first wave feminists. In the United States, for example, some factions of the nineteenth-century women's movement, which merged in 1890 to form the National American Woman Suffrage Association, were grounded in essentialist views of sex differences and were more interested in nonfeminist social reforms for which the vote was only a prerequisite (Buechler, 1990; Giele, 1995). Other branches of the nineteenth-century women's movement rejected essentialist notions of gender and, by pursuing more radical changes such as sexual freedom and the expansion of women's roles in the workplace and politics, sought to transform the gender order in more fundamental ways (Cott, 1987).

Women's movements of the second wave in Western countries, blossoming since the 1960s, have mobilized around an even broader range of issues, such as reproductive rights, sexual and economic exploitation, and violence against women (Chafetz & Dworkin, 1986; Ferree & Hess, 1994). Modern feminist movements often have developed out of women's commonalties; however, feminist scholars increasingly emphasize that differences of race, class, ethnicity, and nationality are also expressed in the collective identities deployed by feminists (Mohanty et al., 1991; Moraga & Anzaldúa, 1981). Collins (1990) maintains that African-American women have organized around interlocking structures of oppression that affect women in different ways depending on, for instance, their race, class, or sexual identities. For example, African-American and Latina women from low-income urban neighborhoods have struggled for quality education, affordable and safe housing, and expanded childcare services for their families and communities (Naples, 1992b). Naples characterizes these mobilizations as instances of "activist mothering," and she demonstrates that women's collective identities derive from the multiple and interlocking systems of race and class and are justified by the belief that "good mothering" includes nurturing practices, political activism, and community work.

Although there is debate about the definition of feminism around the world, it is difficult to deny that since the late 1960s there has been an enormous growth of feminist activity all over the globe. Some scholars argue that large independent women's movements during this period occurred primarily in Western industrial societies and that feminist movement activity was limited, in part, by the large number of repressive political regimes around the world that efficiently suppressed feminist activity (Chafetz & Dworkin, 1986). Other scholars use a broader definition of what constitutes a women's movement and conclude that feminist resistance during this period was and still is extremely widespread (Basu, 1995; Jayawardena, 1986; Miles, 1996; Mohanty et al., 1991).

Since the 1970s, there has been a phenomenal growth of regional, interregional, and international networking between feminist groups (Miles, 1996), although the origins of international women's organizations date back to the closing decades of the nineteenth century (Rupp, 1997). The United Nations' International Women's Year (1975) and Decade for Women (1975–1985) helped foster global feminist dialogues and stimulated independent, locally based feminist activities in all parts of the world. Since the beginning of the U.N. Decade for Women there have been four "official" U.N. conferences of government representatives devoted to women's issues. Four "unofficial" forums of women's groups and feminists from around the world have occurred simultaneously with these "official" conferences. Since the first forum in Mexico City in 1975, participation by women in the "unofficial" forums has increased sharply, challenging the notion that feminism has died in recent years. Although these conferences and forums have been sites of considerable debate and conflict over the meaning of "women's issues" and the definition of feminism, the events have sparked multiple forms and foci of feminist resistance and a global awareness of women's oppression that reaches beyond women's groups.

Other examples of international feminist networks, events, and organizations include the International Tribunal of Crimes against Women held in Brussels in 1976; Development Alternative with Women for a New Era (DAWN), an international organization of Third World feminist-activist researchers formed in 1984; the Women's International Tribunal and Meeting on Reproductive Rights in 1984 in Amsterdam; and the Network on Women's Rights Are Human Rights founded in 1991 (Miles, 1996). Through these and other countless networks and organizations, feminists are forging global relations around a diverse set of issues, including "health, housing, education, law reform, population, human rights, reproductive and genetic engineering, female sexual slavery and trafficking in women, violence against women, spirituality, peace and militarism, external debt, fundamentalism, environment, development, media, alternative technology, film, art and literature, publishing, and women's studies" (Miles, 1996, p. 142). Scholars of international feminism, such as Raca Ray (1999), contend that, despite variation in women's movements around the world, through international conferences the ideology and practice of radical feminism in the United States has left its mark on feminism globally.

Accompanying the burgeoning of international feminist networks, there has been a growing global awareness among feminist movements around the world since the 1970s. Scholars of international feminism, such as Agnes Miles (1996), go so far as to suggest that within the context of broad globalization processes, women's groups in all regions are more often acting locally while thinking globally. Without ignoring the tensions among feminists from different parts of the world, such as those between the North and the South, and conflicts among feminists from the same region, such as disputes between white women and women of color in the United States (Leidner, 1993) and between East and West German women in postunification Germany (Ferree, 1997), Miles contends that there is an emerging feminist global vision in which diversity and specificity are embraced rather than seen as essentially contradictory. Within this emerging global vision, some feminists are working to build theory and practice that understands the oppression in women's lives as deeply connected with other forms, structures, and manifestations of oppression. As such, feminist concerns about reproductive freedoms are not divorced from ecological issues or from the historical processes of colonization. Although much of the feminist scholarship on women's movements is focused on the development of women's movements in the United States or European societies, the feminist literature on women's movements in non-Western societies and the global feminist movement is expanding rapidly (see Miles, 1996 and Mohanty et al., 1991 for detailed bibliographies). The trajectory of the U.S. women's movement can be understood only in this global context.

5. THE CONTEMPORARY FEMINIST MOVEMENT: CONTINUITY AND CHANGE

Of all the manifestations of social activism in the 1960s in the United States, feminism is one of the few that continued to flourish in the 1970s and 1980s and remains active in the 1990s. Although feminism has changed form in the late 1980s and 1990s, neither the movement nor the injustices that produced it have vanished. We trace here the interrelationships among the ideologies, organizational structures, changing political context, and strategies of the most recent wave of the U.S. women's movement.

Most scholarly analyses of the women's movement of the late 1960s—what scholars call the "new feminist movement"—divide it into two wings, with origins in the grievances and preexisting organizations of two groups of women: older professional women who created bureaucratic organizations with a liberal ideology and adopted legal reform strategies, and younger women from the civil rights and New Left movements who formed small collective organizations with radical ideology and employed "personal as political" strategies such as consciousness-raising groups (Buechler, 1990; Cassell, 1977; Ferree & Hess, 1985; Freeman, 1975).

The ideologies, organizations, and strategies developed by these two factions have not, however, remained separate and distinct since the 1970s. The contemporary wave of feminist activism can be divided into three stages: resurgence (1966–1971), the feminist heyday (1972–1982), and abeyance (1983 to the present). Scholars generally date the feminist resurgence to the founding of the National Organization for Women (NOW) in 1966 (Buechler, 1990; Ryan, 1992). During the resurgence period, the movement established itself, forming organizations and ideologies and moving into the public eye. By 1971, major segments of feminism had crystallized: liberal feminism, embodied in the formation of groups such as NOW, the Women's Equity Action League (WEAL) in 1967, and the National Women's Political Caucus (NWPC) in 1971; radical feminism and socialist feminism, emerging from consciousness raising groups, theory groups, and small action groups such as Redstockings and the Feminists in 1969; and lesbian feminism, organized in such groups as Radicalesbians in 1970 and the Furies (initially called "Those Women") in 1971 (Echols, 1989).

The year 1972 was pivotal both for the movement's success and for its opposition. The Equal Rights Amendment (ERA) passed in Congress, and Phyllis Schafly launched her first attacks, signifying the transition to a second phase of feminist activism that lasted until the defeat of the ERA in 1982 (Mansbridge, 1986). While some authors argue that this period saw a decline in the women's movement and a retreat from radicalism (Echols 1989), we think it should be considered the movement's heyday because the feminist revolution seemed to be on the move. The campaign to ratify the ERA in the states brought mass mobilization, fostering female solidarity and enlisting women into feminism, women's studies programs proliferated on college campuses, the number and variety of feminist organizations increased phenomenally, and the movement entered the political arena and encountered active opposition (Matthews & DeHart, 1990; Ryan, 1992). Not only did feminism flourish in the ratification campaign, it spread into the political mainstream while radical and lesbian feminist organizing heightened outside it.

Following the ERA's defeat in 1982, the women's movement entered a period of the doldrums, in which it has developed new structural forms to survive a shrinking membership and an increasingly nonreceptive environment. The 1980s saw a turning away from the values of equality, human rights, and social justice and even a deliberate backlash against the feminist momentum of the 1970s. Rights won by feminists in the 1960s and 1970s—from affirmative action to legal abortion—have been under siege throughout the 1980s and 1990s. Yet the 1980s and 1990s are not the first hostile period in which feminism has endured. In the period following World War II, when strict gender roles and social and political conservatism flourished, the women's movement adopted a tightknit structure that enabled it to survive (Rupp & Taylor, 1987; Taylor, 1989). The so-called "postfeminist" era of the 1980s and 1990s no more marks the death of the women's movement than did the 1950s.

5.1. Feminist Ideology

Although ideas do not necessarily cause social movements, social movement theorists identify ideology as a central component of any social movement (Morris & Mueller, 1992). The new feminist movement, like most social movements, is not ideologically monolithic. Feminist ideology encompasses numerous ideological strands that differ in the scope of change sought; the extent to which gender inequality is linked to other systems of domination, especially class, race/ethnicity, and sexuality; and the significance attributed to gender differences. We focus here on the evolution of the dominant ideologies that have motivated participants in the two major branches of the new feminist movement from its inception, liberal feminism and radical feminism.

The first wave of the women's movement in the nineteenth century was, by and large, a liberal feminist reform movement. It sought equality within the existing social structure and, indeed, in many ways functioned like other reform movements to reaffirm existing values within the society (Ferree & Hess, 1985). Nineteenth-century feminists believed that if they obtained the right to an education, the right to own property, the right to vote, employment rights—in other words, equal civil rights under the law—they would attain equality with men. Scholars have labeled this thinking "individualist" or "equity" feminism, linking the goal of equal rights to gender assumptions about women's basic sameness with men (Black, 1989; Offen, 1988).

The basic ideas identified with contemporary liberal or "mainstream" feminism have changed little since their formulation in the nineteenth century when they seemed progressive, even radical (Eisenstein, 1981). Contemporary liberal feminist ideology holds that women lack power simply because women as a group are not allowed equal opportunity to compete and succeed in the male-dominated economic and political arenas but, instead, are relegated to the subordinate world of home, domestic labor, motherhood, and family. The major strategy for change is to gain legal and economic equalities and to obtain access to elite positions in the workplace and in politics. Thus, liberal feminists tend to place as much emphasis on changing individual women as they do on changing society. For instance, teaching women managerial skills or instructing rape victims in "survival" strategies strikes a blow at gender social definitions that channel women into traditionally feminine occupations and passive behaviors that make them easy targets of aggression by men. As several scholars have noted, liberal feminism ironically provided ideological support through the 1970s and 1980s for the massive transformation in work and family life that was occurring as the United States underwent the transition to a postindustrial order (Mitchell, 1986; Stacey, 1987). Some writers even contend that by urging women to enter the workplace and adopt a male orientation, the equal opportunity approach to feminism unwittingly contributed to a host of problems that further disadvantaged women, especially working-class women and women of color, including the rise in divorce rates, the "feminization" of working-class occupations, and the devaluation of motherhood and traditional female characteristics (Gordon, 1991).

Radical feminist ideology dates to Simone de Beauvoir's early 1950s theory of "sex class," which was developed further in the late 1960s among small groups of radical women who fought the subordination of women's liberation within the New Left (Beauvoir, 1952; Daly, 1978; Firestone, 1970; Griffin, 1978; MacKinnon, 1982, 1983; Millett, 1971; Rich, 1976, 1980). The radical approach recognizes women's identity and subordination as a "sex class," emphasizes women's fundamental difference from men, views gender as the primary contradiction and foundation for the unequal distribution of a society's rewards and privileges, and recasts relations between women and men in political terms (Echols, 1989). Defining women as a "sex class" means no longer treating patriarchy in individual terms but acknowledging the social and structural nature of women's subordination. Radical feminists hold that in all societies, institutions, and social patterns are structured to maintain and perpetuate gender inequality and that female disadvantage permeates virtually all aspects of sociocultural and personal life. Further, through the gender division of labor, social institutions are linked so that male superiority depends upon female subordination (Hartmann, 1981). In the United States, as in most industrialized societies, power, prestige, and wealth accrue to those who control the distribution of resources outside the home in the economic and political spheres. The sexual division of labor that assigns childcare and domestic responsibilities to women not only ensures gender inequality in the dominant family system but perpetuates male advantage in political and economic institutions as well.

To unravel the complex structure on which gender inequality rests requires, from a radical feminist perspective, a fundamental transformation of all institutions in society. To meet this challenge, radical feminists formulated influential critiques of the family, marriage, love, motherhood, heterosexuality, sexual violence, capitalism, reproductive policies, the media, science, language and culture, the beauty industry, sports, politics and the law, and technology. Radical feminism's ultimate vision is revolutionary in scope: a fundamentally new social order that eliminates the sex-class system and replaces it with new ways—based on women's difference—of defining and structuring experience. Central to the development of radical feminist ideology was the strategy of forming small groups for the purpose of "consciousness-raising." Pioneered initially among New Left women, consciousness-raising can be understood as a kind of conversion in which women come to view experiences previously thought of as personal and individual, such as sexual exploitation or employment discrimination, as social problems that are the result of gender inequality.

By the late 1970s, the distinction between liberal and radical feminism was becoming less clear (Carden, 1978; Whittier, 1995). Ideological shifts took place at both the individual and organizational levels. Participation in liberal feminist reform and service organizations working on such issues as rape, battering, abortion, legal and employment discrimination, and women's health problems raised women's consciousness, increased their feminist activism, and contributed to their radicalization as they came to see connections between these issues and the larger system of gender inequality (Schlesinger & Bart, 1983; Whittier, 1995). Women were also radicalized by working through their own personal experiences of sexual harassment, divorce, rape, abortion, and incest (Huber, 1973; Klein, 1984).

Radicalization has also occurred at the group level. By the end of the 1970s, liberal feminist organizations, such as NOW, the Women's Legal Defense Fund, and the National Abortion Rights Action League (NARAL), which had been pursuing equality within the law, began to adopt strategies and goals consistent with a more radical stance. NOW included in its 1979 objectives not only such legal strategies as the ERA and reproductive choice, but also broader issues such as the threat of nuclear energy to the survival of the species, lesbian and gay rights, homemakers' rights, the exploitation of women in the home, and sex-segregation in the workplace (Eisenstein, 1981). Even the ERA, which sought equality for women within the existing legal and economic structure, was based on the fact that women are discriminated against as a "sex class" (Mansbridge, 1986).

Beginning in the mid-1980s, with the defeat of the unifying issue of the ERA and the growing diversification of the movement, feminist ideology deemphasized the question of women's sameness or difference from men in favor of "deconstructing" the term "woman." Women of color, Jewish women, lesbians, and working-class women challenged radical feminists' idea of a "sex class" that implied a distinctive and essential female condition. Since women are distributed throughout all social classes, racial and ethnic groupings, sexual communities, cultures, and religions, disadvantage for women varies and is multidimensional (Spelman, 1988). The recognition that the circumstances of women's oppression differ has given way to a new feminist paradigm that views race, class, gender, ethnicity, and sexuality as interlocking systems of oppression, forming what Patricia Hill Collins (1990) refers to as a "matrix of domination."

Some scholars have charged that focusing on women's differences from one another has resulted in a retreat to "identity politics" and the demise of the women's movement. Alice Echols (1989) links disputes over difference and a focus on identity to a concentration on building an alternative women's culture rather than confronting and changing social institutions. In a similar vein, Barbara Ryan (1989) argues that internal debates over the correctness of competing feminist theories and the political implications of personal choices—what she terms "ideological purity"—tore the women's movement apart. But other scholars see the sometimes vehement arguments over women's differences from one another as a sign of life (Taylor & Rupp, 1993). Feminists organizing around diverse identities sometimes seek out new arenas of challenge that differ from traditional definitions of political activism and thus extend the reach of feminism. Self-help movements focused on the self and the body—for example, drug and alcohol abuse, incest, postpartum depression, battering, breast cancer—offer a complex challenge to traditional notions of femininity, motherhood, and sexuality and carry the potential to mobilize new constituencies (Gagné, 1998; Taylor & Van Willigen, 1996).

In any case, ideas alone are an incomplete explanation of either the direction or the consequences of a social movement (Marx & Wood, 1975; McCarthy & Zald, 1977). Much depends on a movement's structures and strategies, as well as on the larger political context.

5.2. Feminist Organizational Structures

Social movements do not generally have a single, central organization or unified direction. Rather, the structure of any general and broad-based social movement is more diffuse in that it is composed of a number of relatively independent organizations that differ in ideology, structure, goals, and tactics, is characterized by decentralized leadership; and is loosely connected by multiple and overlapping memberships, friendship networks, and cooperation in working toward common goals (Gerlach & Hine, 1970). The organizational structure of the new feminist movement has conformed to this model from its beginnings (Cassell, 1977; Ferree & Martin, 1995; Freeman, 1975). While the movement as a whole is characterized by a decentralized structure, the various organizations that comprise it vary widely in structure. The diversity of feminist organizational forms reflects both ideological differences and, as Freeman (1979) points out, the movement's diverse membership base.

There have been two main types of organizational structure in the new feminist movement since its resurgence, reflecting the two sources of feminist organizing in the late 1960s: bureaucratically structured movement organizations with hierarchical leadership and democratic decision-making procedures, such as NOW; and smaller, collectively structured groups that formed a more diffuse social movement community held together by a feminist political culture. The smaller groups must be understood as what Joan Acker (1990) has termed "gendered" organizations. Collectively organized groups, at least in theory, strove to exemplify a better way of structuring society by constructing a distinctive women's culture that valorized egalitarianism, the expression of emotion, and the sharing of personal experience. It is important to recognize, however, that while the two strands of the women's movement emerged separately, they have not remained distinct and opposed to each other, and in any case most organizations were mixed in form from the outset. The two structures have increasingly converged as bureaucratic organizations adopted some of the innovations of collectivism and feminist collectives became more formally structured (Ferree & Martin, 1995; Martin, 1990; Ryan, 1992; Staggenborg, 1988, 1989; Whittier, 1995). In addition, many individual activists are involved in a variety of organizations with differing structures.

The bureaucratically structured and professionalized movement organizations initially adopted by liberal groups such as NOW were well suited to work within the similarly structured political arena and to members' previous experience in professional organizations. The structures that radical feminist groups initially adopted, on the other hand, built on their prior involvement experiences in the New Left (Evans, 1979). Collectivist organizations grew from radical feminists' attempt to structure relations among members, processes of decision making, and group leadership in a way that reflected or prefigured the values and goals of the movement (Breines, 1982; Rothschild-Whitt, 1979). Feminist collectivist organizations made decisions by consensus, rotated leadership and other tasks among members, and shared skills to avoid hierarchy and specialization. As Jo Freeman (1972/1973) and others have noted, such groups often failed to meet their ideals and did, in fact, spawn unacknowledged hierarchies. Nevertheless, the conscious effort to build a feminist collective structure has had a lasting impact on the women's movement and has led to the growth of what Steven Buechler (1990) calls a social movement community.

Buechler proposes that movements consist not only of formal organizations, but that they also include more informally organized communities, made up of networks of people who share the movement's political goals and outlook and work toward common aims. The collectivist branch of the women's movement initially sparked the growth of a feminist social movement community in which alternative structures guided by a distinctively feminist women's culture flourished—including bookstores, theater groups, music collectives, poetry groups, art collectives, publishing and recording companies, spirituality groups, vacation resorts, self-help groups, and a variety of feminist-run businesses. This "women's culture," although it includes feminists of diverse political persuasions, has been largely maintained by lesbian feminists in the 1980s and 1990s. It nurtures a feminist collective identity that is important to the survival of the women's movement as a whole (Taylor & Rupp, 1993; Taylor & Whittier, 1992).

Both bureaucratic organizations working within mainstream politics and the alternative feminist culture have expanded and converged since the movement's emergence in the 1960s. Organizations such as NOW and the NARAL incorporated some of the innovations of collectivism, including consciousness-raising groups, modified consensus decision-making, and the use of direct action tactics and civil disobedience. A host of structural variations emerged, including formally structured groups that use consensus decision-making, organizations with deliberately democratic structures, and groups that officially operate by majority-rule democracy but in practice make most decisions by consensus (Martin, 1990; Ryan, 1992; Staggenborg, 1988, 1989; Taylor, 1996). At the same time, feminist collectives shifted their focus from consciousness-raising and radical feminist critique to the development of feminist self-help and service organizations, such as rape crisis centers, shelters for battered women, job training programs for displaced homemakers, and lesbian peer counseling groups. Moreover, many feminist collectives revised their structure to depend less on consensus decision-making and to permit specialization of skills. Feminist anti-rape groups received financial support from government agencies and private foundations to provide rape prevention and treatment services in public schools and universities (Matthews, 1994). The widespread acceptance of the feminist analysis of rape as an act of violence and power rather than a strictly sexual act attest to the impact of the feminist anti-rape movement. The distinction between "working outside the system" and "working within the system," so important in the late 1960s, no longer had the same significance.

In conjunction with the ideological shift from a universal to a differentiated category of "woman," the structures of the women's movement diversified as well. Although individual women of color and working-class women had participated in the founding of NOW and in the early protests against sexism in the civil rights movement, the women's movement attracted primarily white middle-class women. Not that women of color and working-class or poor women experienced no oppression as women or opposed feminist goals. A 1989 *New York Times*/CBS News poll revealed that, whereas only 64% of white women saw a need for a women's movement, 85% of African-American women and 76% of Hispanic women thought the women's movement was needed (Sapiro, 1991). Yet the feminist movement remained predominantly white both because of the continuation of its tradition of defining its goals with an eye to the concerns of white middle-class women and because many black women and other women of color place a priority on working with men of their own communities to advance their collective interests. Independent organizing by women of color did occur during the 1970s, and when African-American activists in the women's movement formed the National Black Feminist Organization in 1973 it grew to a membership of 1000 within its first year (Deckard, 1983). In the 1980s and 1990s independent feminist organizations and networks of women of color, such as the National Black Women's Health Project and the National Coalition of 100 Black Women, emerged. Women of color also formed active caucuses within predominantly white feminist organizations, such as the National Women's Studies Association, to work against racism within the women's movement (Leidner, 1993). Likewise, Jewish women, who had historically played important roles within the women's movement, began to organize their own groups in the 1980s and speak out against anti-Semitism within the movement (Beck, 1980; Bulkin, Pratt, & Smith, 1984).

Union women played a significant role in the formation of NOW in 1966 by providing office space and clerical services, until NOW's endorsement of the ERA in 1967 forced the women of the United Auto Workers, an organization that at the time opposed the ERA, to withdraw such support. Women committed to both feminism and the union movement, like women of color, formed their own organization, the Coalition of Labor Union Women (CLUW), in 1974 (Balser, 1987). CLUW claimed 16,000 members by 1982 and had made progress in its fight to win AFL–CIO support for feminist issues. Union women also participated in deeply gendered ways in labor movement activity such as the 1985 Wheeling–Pittsburgh Steel strike, both affirming and challenging gender (Fonow, 1998). The basic class and race composition of the movement may have changed little throughout the 1970s and 1980s, but as Buechler (1990, p. 158) put it, "A movement that began as unconsciously class-bound and race-bound has now become consciously class-bound and race-bound."

Collective action by the women's movement has both created new institutions and moved into almost every major institution of our society. However, in direct proportion to the successes of the women's movement, a countermovement, as we shall see, successfully reversed some feminist gains, stalled progress on others, and changed the face of the women's movement.

5.3. The Antifeminist Political Context

The early 1980s saw a rapid decrease in the number of feminist organizations and a transformation in the form and activities of the women's movement. In part, this was a response to the successes of the New Right: so powerful were antifeminist sentiments and forces that members of the Republican party were elected in 1980 on a platform developed explicitly to "put women back in their place." After 40 years of faithful support of the ERA, the Republican party dropped it from its platform, called for a constitutional amendment to ban abortion, and aligned itself with the economic and social policies of the New Right. After the election of the conservative Reagan administration in 1980, federal funds and grants were rarely available to feminist service organizations, and because other social service organizations were also hard hit by budget cuts, competition increased for relatively scarce money from private foundations. As a result, many feminist programs, such as rape crisis centers, shelters for battered women, abortion clinics, and job training programs were forced to end or limit their services.

The failure of the ERA in 1982 seemed to reflect the changed political climate, setting the stage for other setbacks throughout the 1980s. Abortion rights, won in 1973 with the Supreme Court's decision in Roe v. Wade, were curtailed in 1989 by the Supreme Court's decision in Webster v. Reproductive Services permitting states to enact restrictions on abortion (Staggenborg, 1991, pp. 137–138). Following the Webster decision, state governments set increasingly tight restrictions on abortion, ranging from "informed consent" laws that required a waiting period before women could have abortions, to parental consent laws for underage women, to outright bans on abortion unless the woman's life was in danger. In 1991, the Supreme Court further limited abortion rights by ruling that federally funded family planning clinics could be barred from providing information on abortion. The anti-abortion movement also escalated and hardened its tactics in the late 1980s: it bombed abortion clinics, picketed doctors who performed abortions, and attempted to dissuade women entering clinics from having abortions (Simonds, 1996; Staggenborg, 1991). Further, Women's Studies programs in colleges and universities, which had been established in the 1970s in response to feminist agitation, came under attack by conservatives in the late 1980s and early 1990s. A backlash against "multiculturalism" and "political correctness" in academia sought to restore the traditional academic focus on the "great thinkers" of Western European history, and thus to maintain the primacy of white male perspectives and experiences. Joining the attack, feminists such as Camille Paglia, Katie Roiphe, and Elizabeth Fox-Genovese drew media attention by holding radical and lesbian feminists responsible for alienating mainstream women and men from the women's movement.

The women's movement suffered not only from such attacks, but also from its apparent success. Overt opposition to the feminist movement had been muted in the mid- to late 1970s. Elites in politics, education, and industry gave the appearance of supporting feminist aims through largely ineffectual affirmative action programs and the appointment of a few token women to high positions in their respective areas. Meanwhile, the popular image of feminism advanced by the mass media suggested that the women's movement had won its goals, making feminism an anachronism. Despite the real-life difficulties women encountered trying to balance paid employment and a "second shift" of housework and childcare (Hochschild, 1989), the image of the working woman became the feminine ideal. The public discourse implied that since women had already achieved equality with men, they no longer needed a protest movement, unless they happened to be lesbians and man haters. Both popular and scholarly writers, in short, declared the 1980s and 1990s a "post-feminist" era.

But the women's movement did not die. Rather, it went into abeyance in order to survive in a hostile political climate. Movements in abeyance are in a holding pattern, during which activists from an earlier period maintain the ideology and structural base of the movement, but few new recruits join (Taylor, 1989). A movement in abeyance is primarily oriented toward maintaining itself rather than confronting the established order directly. Focusing on building an alternative culture, for example, is a means of surviving when external resources are not available and the political structure is not amenable to challenge. The structure and strategies of the women's movement have changed, then, as mass mobilization has declined and opposition to feminism has swelled. Nevertheless, feminist resistance continues in different forms.

5.4. Multiple Strategies and the Challenge to Gender

Patricia Hill Collins suggests that gender resistance, challenge, and change can occur at three levels: the individual level of consciousness and interactions, the social structural level, and the cultural level (1990, p. 227). This conceptualization allows us to recognize that movements adopt many strategies and to acknowledge the important role of women's movements in the reconstruction of gender.

5.4.1. RESISTING GENDER PRACTICES.   It is well established that the dominant gender order is created and maintained, in part, through the everyday practices of individuals who give gender meaning through the constant and contentious process of engendering behavior as separate and unequal (Butler, 1990; Chodorow, 1995; West & Zimmerman, 1987). At the level of consciousness and social interactions, individual women can and do resist norms and expectations of the dominant gender system (Thorne, 1995). It is, however, social movements or collectivities rather than isolated individuals, who perform the critical role of refashioning the gender code and calling institutions to account for gender inequality (Chafetz, 1990; Connell, 1987; Huber, 1976). One of the primary goals of the new feminist movement has been to change the unequal power relations between women and men. A general strategy used by feminists to achieve this goal has been to resist and challenge sexist practices within a diverse set of social contexts, ranging from heterosexual marriage to the gender division of labor in rearing and nurturing children to the workplace and medical establishment.

The formation of consciousness-raising groups facilitated the process of resisting and challenging gender practices and politicizing everyday life. Because consciousness-raising enables women to view the "personal as political," for most women it is an identity-altering experience. Becoming a feminist can transform a woman's entire self-concept and way of life: her biography, appearance, beliefs, behavior, and relationships (Cassell, 1977; Esterberg, 1997). As women's consciousness changes through personalized political strategies such as consciousness-raising, women individually and collectively defy normative role expectations for women and, in so doing, reconstruct interpersonal relationships between women and men.

Women active in the feminist movement of the 1960s and 1970s continue to shape their lives in the 1980s and 1990s around their feminist beliefs, even when they are not involved in organized feminist activity. Many hold jobs in government, social service organizations, or Women's Studies and other academic programs that allow them to incorporate their political goals into their work, and they continue to choose leisure activities, significant relationships, and dress and presentation of self that are consistent with feminist ideology (Whittier, 1995). Even the consciousness and lives of women who do not identify as feminist have been altered by the women's movement. In a study of gender and family life in the Silicon Valley of California, Judith Stacey (1987) argues that in the 1980s some women have incorporated portions of feminism into traditional family and work structures by combining a feminist emphasis on developing satisfying careers, sharing household work with husbands, and increasing men's emotional expressiveness through fundamentalist Christianity and its focus on the importance of the family. Such women critique men's absence from families and lack of emotional expression, reflecting both feminism and traditional religion. The effects of the women's movement stretch far beyond policies and practices that are explicitly labeled feminist.

Another example of women resisting gender practices at the interactional level is found among African American women involved in little sister fraternity programs on college campuses. In their study of such programs, Stombler and Padavic (1997) discovered that African-American women embrace a collective identity built on notions of sisterhood and womanly strength to challenge the sexist practices of fraternities. Further, these women use the fraternity little sister program to satisfy their own agendas of community service and self-enhancement. Even within the most traditional male-dominated organizations, then, gender relations are not immutable and women are employing diverse strategies to resist gender inequality.

5.4.2. CHALLENGING THE STRUCTURE OF GENDER INEQUALITY.   The challenge to gender inequality and the dominant gender order is also waged at the social structural level. As we have seen, the liberal bureaucratic strand of the new feminist movement has employed legal reform strategies and engaged in street protests to counter sex discrimination in the economic, educational, political, and domestic spheres. The legislative campaigns for equal pay for work of comparable worth and for maternity policy in the workplace illustrate challenges to institutions that essentialize differences between women and men and rank "masculine" values and attributes above those identified as feminine (Vogel, 1993). The women's movement has created a feminist policy network of elected officials, lobbying organizations, social movement organizations, and individuals who have mobilized to address policy issues ranging from abortion rights, domestic violence, and pregnancy discrimination to day care (Ferree & Hess, 1994; Gagné, 1998; Staggenborg, 1996).

As part of its legislative or legal strategies, the new feminist movement has engaged in street protests, such as picketing, mass demonstrations, and civil disobedience. Even within the conservative political climate of the 1980s, the feminist movement sparked some of the largest feminist demonstrations and actions in years. In April 1989, NOW and abortion rights groups organized a national demonstration in Washington, D.C., that drew between 300,000 and 600,000 women and men to protest restrictions on abortion. Additional national and local demonstrations followed, and pro-choice activists organized electoral lobbying, defense of abortion clinics, and conferences, and attempted to form coalitions across racial and ethnic lines and among women of different ages (Ryan, 1992; Staggenborg, 1991). The NARAL experienced a growth in membership from 200,000 in 1989 to 400,000 in 1990 (Staggenborg, 1991, p. 138), and membership in NOW also continued to grow in the late 1980s and 1990s after a decline in the early 1980s, with a membership of 250,000 in 1989. In addition, a wide variety of feminist organizations continue to pursue social change at state and local levels (Ferree & Martin, 1995).

Beyond street politics, feminist activism in the 1980s and 1990s moved into diverse institutional settings. As an indication of the success and influence of feminist mobilization in earlier years, women found niches from which to challenge and transform institutional policies and structures, from pay equity to sexual harassment to occupational sex segregation (Blum, 1991). Katzenstein (1997) questions the notion that social movements are antithetical to institutions and that unobstrusive mobilization within institutional boundaries signifies the deradicalization of feminism. In her study of women's activism in the military and the Catholic Church, she found that women in the military have formed pressure groups, such as Women Military Aviators, that fought for the opening up of combat aviation positions for women. In the Catholic Church, radical religious orders have become protected spaces for women who challenge hierarchy within the institutional church. Although the form and location of feminist protest has changed in the 1980s and 1990s, this does not necessarily denote a post-feminist era or even the deradicalization of the women's movement. The transformative potential of feminist activism within institutional settings may in some contexts be greater than pressure from outside.

5.4.3. RECONSTRUCTING THE CULTURE OF GENDER. At the cultural level, the feminist social movement community has challenged cultural values, beliefs, and norms around gender and the gender order through building alternative social and cultural institutions for women outside mainstream institutions. The strategy of creating autonomous institutions is rooted in radical feminist ideology, which emphasizes that women need to have places and events away from patriarchal society where they can develop strength and pride as women. Since the early years of the women's movement, an extensive network of institutions has emerged within which a feminist culture flourishes (Taylor & Whittier, 1992). The development of feminist communities contributes to the reconstruction of the culture of gender by challenging the devaluation of the feminine and undermining androcentric values and beliefs, at the same time that they rearticulate alternative femininities and woman-centered values and beliefs (Taylor & Rupp, 1993).

Into the 1990s, the feminist cultural community has continued to thrive, with groups such as the Lesbian Avengers, and with such events as an "annual multicultural multiracial conference on aging" for lesbians (*Off Our Backs,* 1991, p. 12), feminist cruises, several annual women's music and comedy festivals in different parts of the country. Gatherings and conferences in 1990 included groups such as Jewish lesbian daughters of holocaust survivors, women motorcyclists, "fat dykes," practitioners of Diannic Wicca, Asian lesbians, practitioners of herbal medicine, and survivors of incest. Newsletters and publications exist for groups including women recovering from addictions, women's music professionals and fans, lesbian separatists, disabled lesbians, lesbian mothers, feminists interested in sadomasochism, feminists opposed to pornography, and a multitude of others. The growth of the feminist community underscores the flowering of lesbian feminism in the late 1980s and 1990s (Esterberg, 1997; Stein, 1997). A wide variety of lesbian and lesbian feminist books and anthologies have been published on topics ranging from lesbian feminist ethics, to separatism, to sexuality, to commitment ceremonies for lesbian couples (see, e.g., Butler, 1991; Hoagland, 1988; Hoagland & Penelope, 1988; Loulan, 1990), reflecting diverse perspectives that have been hotly debated in the pages of lesbian publications and at conferences and festivals. For example, a series of letters to the editor in a national lesbian newsletter argued over the correct lesbian feminist response to lesbians serving in the armed forces in the Persian Gulf War: some readers held that the war was a manifestation of patriarchy and that lesbians in the military should be criticized; others argued that lesbian soldiers should be supported because they are lesbians in a homophobic institution, regardless of support or opposition to the war; still others argued that the Gulf War was justified and that lesbian servicewomen should be celebrated for their patriotic service (*Lesbian Connection,* 1991). Clearly, the task of building a community based on the identity "lesbian" has proven complex, if not impossible. Nevertheless, the institutional structure of the social movement community has continued to expand, and within the community feminists construct and reinforce a collective identity based on opposition to dominant conceptions of women and lesbians (Taylor & Whittier, 1992).

Another example of resistance on the cultural level is the emergence of women's self-help groups in the 1980s and 1990s that sprang directly out of the early women's health movement and continue to model feminist consciousness-raising groups (Rapping, 1996; Simonds, 1996). Some feminist writers contend that women's self-help diverts the feminist agenda away from social and political change and directs women, instead, to change themselves (Kaminer, 1992). Others argue that self-help movements, such as the postpartum depression and breast cancer movements, are contributing to the reconstruction of gender through the collective redefinition of womanhood and the cultural articulation of alternative femininities (Taylor, 1996; Taylor & Van Willigen, 1996). Rather than depoliticized and purely individually focused, self-help movements, Taylor (1996) contends, perform a critical role in calling institutions to account for gender inequality and refashioning the dominant gender code.

All of these diverse strategies, operating at different levels, challenge gender. From the individual to the social structural to the cultural plane, we can see the continuous impact of the women's movement.

5.5. Movement Continuity and Change Into the Twentieth Century

Social movement scholars understand that social movements affect one another. The abolitionist movement in the mid-nineteenth century influenced the first wave of the women's movement in the United States, and the civil rights and New Left movements of the 1960s shaped the course of the second wave of the women movement (Buechler, 1990). In turn, the women's movement has also had a substantial impact on other social movements. Meyer and Whittier (1994) argue that "the ideas, tactics, style, participants, and organizations of one movement often *spill over* its boundaries to affect other social movements" (p. 277, emphasis in the original). The gay and lesbian movement, transgender, AIDS, recovery from addictions, New Age, and animal rights movements have been profoundly influenced by feminist values and ideology, including the emphasis on collective structure and consensus, the notion of the personal as political, and the critique of patriarchy extended to the mistreatment of animals and ecological resources (Jasper & Poulsen, 1995). The women's movement also trained a large number of feminist activists in the 1970s, particularly lesbians, who have participated in new social movements and integrated feminism into them (Cavin, 1990; Whittier, 1995). The gay and lesbian movement, for example, has expanded its health concerns to include breast cancer as well as AIDS and has used strategies of the feminist anti-rape movement to confront violence against gays and lesbians. In addition, feminists have renewed coalitions with the peace, environmental, socialist, anti-U.S. intervention in Latin America, and anti-apartheid movements, transforming these movements both by creating separate feminist organizations that address these issues and by moving into mixed-sex organizations (Whittier, 1995). In a sense the women's movement has come full circle, rejoining the 1990s versions of the movements that composed the New Left in the 1960s when feminists split off to form a separate autonomous women's movement.

Although the women's movement has changed form and location in the 1980s and 1990s, the level of mass mobilization and confrontation of the social structural system clearly declined following 1982. Because feminism in the late 1980s and 1990s is focused more on consciousness and culture and has established roots in other social movements of the period, feminist protest is less visible than it was during the heyday of the women's movement. Notably, in keeping with the patterns that characterize movements in abeyance (Taylor, 1989), the most active feminists in the late 1980s and 1990s have been women who became involved with the movement during the late 1960s and 1970s, were transformed by their involvement, and formed a lasting commitment to feminist goals (Whittier, 1995). According to some recent studies (Dill, unpublished; Schneider, 1988), despite support for feminist goals, many young women do not identify themselves as feminists, apparently because the identity of feminist is stigmatized. A feminist is seen as someone who deviates from gender norms by being unattractive, aggressive, hostile to men, opposed to marriage and motherhood, lesbian, and imitative of men. Despite the gains made by women in some areas, gender norms are still so rigid and deeply internalized that they successfully deter many women, who otherwise support the feminist agenda, from participating in the movement.

Yet some younger women have joined the women's movement in the late 1980s and 1990s despite the risks entailed in identifying with a stigmatized and unpopular cause. In a study of young feminist activists in the 1990s, Kim Dill (unpublished) has found that a new generation of women has been recruited to feminism primarily through Women's Studies courses and through the transmission of feminism from mothers to daughters. The institutionalized gains of the heyday of feminist activism in the 1970s are enabling the women's movement to survive and to disseminate its ideas to new recruits. What direction the self-proclaimed "third wave" (Kamen, 1991; Walker, 1992, 1995) will take is not at all clear, but the history of the women's movement suggests that a new constituency will revise feminist ideology, renovate existing structures, respond to a changing political climate, and further develop feminist strategies.

6. ANTIFEMINIST COUNTERMOVEMENTS

The emergence of organized opposition is one indication of the successes of feminist movements. In general, it is when social movements pose a serious threat to the status quo that countermovements appear (Chafetz & Dworkin, 1987). Antifeminist resistance movements mobilized in response to first and second wave feminist movements in the United States when feminists began to gain political legitimacy and influence. For example, as the first wave of the women's movement was building support for suffrage in the late nineteenth century, an organized anti-suffrage movement began to coalesce (Marshall, 1997). Likewise, when the feminist movement of the 1970s was gaining political ground on the ratification of the Equal Rights Amendment, an anti-ERA movement blossomed (Marshall, 1984).

Antifeminist countermovements, like feminist movements, are not monolithic but vary over time and place by ideology, strategy, and organization (Blee 1991; Buechler 1990; Marshall 1985). Chafetz and Dworkin (1987) contend that antifeminist countermovements are composed of two constituencies: vested-interest groups which are typically male-dominated and oppose feminist change movements on the basis of class interests and voluntary grassroots associations made up of women who are reacting to the threat to their status as privileged traditional women.

Compared to the scholarship on movements, countermovements have been understudied and undertheorized (Meyer & Staggenborg, 1996). Moreover, research on organized opposition to feminism by women is also limited (Klatch, 1990; Marshall, 1997). Women's participation in antifeminist countermovements challenges the radical feminist notion that women are a "sex class" with clearly defined gender interests. Differences among women, particularly class status, are brought to light when we consider women's involvement in antifeminist mobilizations (Luker, 1984). Scholars often characterize antifeminist women as victims of false consciousness or as women who are passively expressing their husbands' interests. Marshall (1997) argues that these are overly simplistic interpretations and that an appreciation for the ways in which anti-suffragist leaders used their wealth, social networks, and political power to build an oppositional identity in the anti-suffrage movement suggests "a conceptual shift of the locus of conflict over suffrage from culture to politics" (p. 13). In this light, antifeminist women should be viewed as political actors who take up gendered class interests independent of their husbands (Marshall, 1997).

The interaction between opposing movements is a prominent feature of contemporary American society. Any social movement analysis is incomplete without considering the interdependence of movements and countermovements. For example, the tactics, strategies, organizational forms, and feminist identities characteristic of the feminist movement during the 1980s and 1990s cannot be fully understood without considering the effects of the anti-abortion mobilization and the rise of the New Right. The relationship between movements and countermovements are variously described by social movement scholars as loosely coupled conflict (Zald & Useem, 1987); movement conflux created by dialectical interaction (Mottle, 1980); and an ebb and flow of opposing movements (Meyer & Staggenborg, 1996; Zald & Useem, 1987).

The contemporary women's movement in the United States has been opposed by a variety of conservative antifeminist groups. In the early 1970s the Stop ERA campaign, initiated by Phyllis Schlafly, fought to block the passage of the ERA by state legislatures. Through the 1970s, the New Right grew larger and more influential, linking conservative issues, including opposition to busing, abortion, gay rights, the ERA, and governmental regulation of business through affirmative action and health and safety programs (Klatch, 1990). With the election of Ronald Reagan to the presidency in 1980, the New Right gained state support for its agenda. The antifeminist movement in the late 1980s and 1990s has spent considerable energy opposing abortion, and its successes in that area have been impressive in terms of judicial and legislative gains and disruptive demonstrations at abortion clinics (Simonds, 1996; Staggenborg, 1991). Over the years, a number of aggressive splinter groups, such as Operation Rescue, have developed out of the mainstream National Right to Life Committee, which originated within the Catholic Church. The murders of Drs. David Gunn in Pensacola, Florida, and Barnett and Slepian in Buffalo, New York, are a potent example of the radical tactics advocated by some antifeminist groups. The prevalence of antifeminist resistance throughout history highlights the significance of the family, sexuality, and reproduction for the maintenance of the dominant social order. The growth of antifeminism, however, does not imply that the women's movement has failed or run its course. On the contrary, it attests to feminism's successful challenge to the status quo.

7. MEN'S RESPONSES TO FEMINIST MOBILIZATION

Men clearly have been affected by changes in the gender system in the United States. Researchers recently have begun to examine men's organized responses to feminism and shifts in gender and family relations (Kimmel, 1987; Messner, 1997; Schwalbe, 1996). Like women's movements, organized men's responses vary broadly both ideologically and structurally. Moreover, along with feminist movements and countermovements, men's gender-based movements are becoming major players in the process of reconstituting gender and family relations.

Kimmel (1987) contends that, at the turn of the century men's responses to changes in the gender system took three forms: masculinist, antifeminist, and profeminist. The masculinist response, characterized by homosocial institutions, was an indirect reaction to the purported feminization of American manhood associated with industrialization, the separation of work from the home, and the necessity for men to prove themselves in the marketplace. The antifeminist and profeminist responses were more direct reactions to the women's movement during the period (Kimmel, 1987). Antifeminist responses, such as opposition to women's suffrage and women's participation in the public sphere, were based on the belief that the traditional patriarchal family is the God-given natural social arrangement. Profeminist responses, although variable, generally embraced feminists' demands for an expansion of women's public participation and an end to the gender division of labor in family life and were based on both a sense of justice and the belief that gender changes would also benefit men (Kimmel, 1987).

Although Kimmel's typology was developed to explain men's responses to the first wave of feminism in the United States, there are some parallels to men's oppositional movements during the second wave. Messner (1997) maps out some of the major mobilizations, which include the men's liberation movement, men's rights groups, the progressive profeminist movement, the Promise Keepers, the Million Man March, the mythopoetic movement, and racial and sexual identity movements.

Aligned with the liberal branch of the women's movement, the men's liberation movement emerged in the mid-1970s (Messner, 1997). Men's liberation took up the discourse of sex roles and organized around the belief that the dominant sex/gender system oppressed both women and men. In particular, men's liberationists stressed the costs of masculinity for men. By the late 1970s, the men's liberation movement had transformed itself into two divergent branches. The antifeminist men's rights branch, which includes organizations such as Men's Rights, Inc. formed in 1977 and The Coalition of Free Men formed in 1980, espouses the view that men are the real victims of rigid sex roles, prostitution, pornography, divorce settlements, false rape and sexual harassment accusations, and even domestic violence. Men's rights groups also claim that the feminist movement is an attempt to cover up the fact that women, as a group, possess the "real" power (Messner, 1997).

On the other end of the political spectrum, the collective identity of the progressive profeminist men's branch embraces the discourse and politics of gender hierarchy in which women are viewed as institutionally oppressed and men are believed to enjoy structurally based power and privilege over women. There are two major ideological and political positions within the profeminist men's wing. Radical profeminist men's groups focus on male sexuality and sexual violence as a major cause of women's oppression, whereas socialist profeminist men rely on Marxist feminism to incorporate the interaction of class relations and gender relations in their analyses of women's oppression. Regardless of their differences, profeminist men's organizations, such as the National Organization for Men Against Sexism (NOMAS), position themselves in opposition to the men's rights movement (Messner, 1997). Although men active in the profeminist men's movement are dedicated to improving women's status relative to men's, the size of profeminist men's mobilizations has decreased sharply from the 1970s to the present.

The political conservatism and antifeminism of the 1980s gave rise to new forms of mass mobilization by men, including the mythopoetic movement. Schwalbe (1996) describes the mythopoetic movement as a spiritual, anti-intellectual movement in which men together construct positive male identities by rediscovering and reclaiming their inherent masculinity. Robert Bly, whose national best-seller *Iron John* helped popularize the mythopoetic movement in the United States, asserts that men in postindustrial society lack masculinity rituals to connect to their deep masculine natures, which are neither feminine nor hypermasculine (Bly, 1990). Mythopoetic weekend retreats into the woods, attended by thousands of men in the 1990s, serve as such masculinizing rituals. Schwalbe (1996) argues that the mythopoetic men's movement's gender politics and strategic anti-intellectualism allow participants to deny the structural basis of gender, which creates fundamental differences in the foundations of women's and men's problems. Other scholars contend that the mythopoetic movement is essentialist, unjustly dismisses feminism, and overlooks differences of race, class, and sexuality among men (Kimmel, 1995).

Another all-male movement grounded in overt gender politics is the Promise Keepers, an evangelical Christian men's movement that emerged in the 1990s. Mobilizing through traditionally masculine organizational forms, the highly centralized Promise Keepers has orchestrated numerous mass rallies that have drawn over 2½ million men to 61 weekend conferences in football stadiums around the country. Messner (1997) contends that similar to the muscular Christianity movement at the turn of the century, which gave rise to organizations such as the Young Men's Christian Association (YMCA), the Promise Keepers, who are mostly white, middle-class, and heterosexual, represent a reassertion of essentialist views of women's and men's roles in the family and a reaction to the perceived national crisis of the feminization of the American male. However, Messner (1997) also recognizes that there are multiple contradictions embodied in the Promise Keepers movement. He maintains that the Promise Keepers can be understood, simultaneously, as Christian masculinity therapy in a confusing and anxiety-producing era, as an organized and highly politicized antifeminist, anti-gay backlash, and as a bargain struck with women to become responsible breadwinners, fathers, and husbands within the traditional family structure (Messner, 1997, p . 35).

The 1995 Million Man March, which attracted an estimated 800,000, mostly African-American men, to Washington, D.C. is another contemporary example of men's mobilization. Messner (1997) asserts that, like the Promise Keepers, the Million Man March contains contradictions and tensions that demonstrate, on the one hand, a positive and meaningful mobilization of men of African heritage to stand up for justice, and, on the other hand, a reassertion of a conservative essentialist view of the gender order. In all men's organized responses to shifting gender relations—and more broadly to larger social and economic changes—there are dimensions of the organizations, ideologies, identities, and strategies of the mobilizations that simultaneously challenge and reaffirm the dominant gender order.

8. CONCLUSION

There is a growing realization among scholars that theories of gender have tended to emphasize the maintenance and reproduction of gender inequality and to neglect, as Thorne puts it, "the countervailing processes of resistance, challenge, conflict, and change" (1995, p. 498). Over the past two centuries there have been significant changes in the lives of American women and men brought on, in part, by large-scale social and economic transformations. Although we recognize the significance of broad structural processes in creating gender change, we also believe that it is important to understand the role of human agents who promote changes in gender relations in response to the opportunities created by structural conditions (see Staggenborg, 1998 for a similar argument). Gender movements, including feminist movements, countermovements, men's movements, and even other social movements not specifically focused on gender, have played an important role in increasing women's participation in the workplace, politics, and education, as well as in pushing for men's greater participation in family life. Indeed, if one looks at the significance of gender to the collective identities of the social movements of the late 1990s—including the gay and lesbian movement, women's self-help, and the variety of men's movements—it is difficult to deny the centrality of gender for contemporary collective action. We cannot, however, fully understand the way gender figures into the dynamics of social movements, nor can we assess the contributions social movement actors make to shifts in gender relations, without a set of concepts that allows us to examine the interplay between gender and movements.

In tracing the role of social movements in the transformation of gender, we have sketched a framework that is useful for assessing the gender outcomes of collective action at multiple levels. Gender is constructed and reconstructed on various planes and our examination of social movements should be attentive to this multistory process. Multilevel theories of gender suggest that to understand the impact that a given social movement has on the gender order, we must look for evidence of changes in gender at the interactional, the structural, and the cultural levels (Connell, 1987; West & Zimmerman, 1987). This approach allows us to recognize that gender can change in a myriad of ways that do not necessarily subvert the institutional basis of gender. These theories also allow us to analyze the role of gender in social movement processes, specifically the way the clash of interests constituted within gender relations exerts influence on the opportunity structures, collective identities and ideologies, structures, and strategies that are the ingredients of collective challenges. Viewing social movements as engaged in the social construction of gender helps explain the contradictory elements displayed in many gender movements. For example, modern women's self-help movements challenge the hierarchy and practices of male-dominated medicine, but at the same time adopt mobilizing structures and strategies that assume that women's modes of relating are fundamentally different than men's, thereby reinforcing traditional notions of gender difference. It also allows us to recognize how support for changing gender relations, ironically, can come from antifeminist women's and men's movements.

Finally, we must also recognize that gender interacts with other systems of stratification, such as class, race, ethnicity, and sexuality, that mediate the collective identities, strategies, and structures of gender movements. Women's movements, as we have seen, have taken multiple forms throughout history, and women who have organized under the banner of feminism have often disagreed about the nature of gender discrimination and the best ways to meet women's needs and interests. Both outside and within dominant social institutions, feminists have challenged male dominance and connected gender inequality to a myriad of problems in their lives. Although there is a multiplicity of feminist mobilizations around the world, and even in the United States, there are also unifying ideas and common themes that have persisted within women's movements. By and large, most feminist movements are focused on challenging structurally based gender stratification and gender oppression at various levels and spheres of interaction. Feminist identity, then, is one way that women express their common interests. Connecting feminist identity to movement organizations and the larger political and historical context offers insight into the changing meaning of feminism. We believe that fuller integration of the theoretical literatures on gender and social movements will advance our understanding of gender change processes by making explicit the role of social movements in challenging and affirming the dominant gender order.

REFERENCES

Acker, J. (1990). Hierarchies, jobs, and bodies: A theory of gendered organizations. *Gender & Society, 4*, 139–158.

Balser, D. (1987). *Sisterhood and solidarity: Feminism and labor in modern times.* Boston: South End Press.

Barnett, B. McN. (1993). Invisible southern black women leaders in the civil rights movement: The triple constraints of gender, race, and class. *Gender & Society, 7*, 162–182.

Basu, A. (Ed.) (1995). *The challenge of local feminisms: Women's movements in global perspective.* Boulder, CO: Westview Press.

Beauvoir, S. de. (1952). *The second sex.* New York: Bantam.

Beck, E. T. (1980). *Nice Jewish girls: A lesbian anthology.* Watertown, MA: Persephone.

Black, N. (1989). *Social feminism.* Ithaca, NY: Cornell University Press.

Blee, K. M. (1991). *Women of the klan: Racism and gender in the 1920s.* Berkeley, CA: University of California Press.

Blum, L. M. (1991). *Between feminism and labor: The significance of the comparable worth movement.* Berkeley, CA: University of California Press.

Blumberg, R. L. (1984). A general theory of gender stratification. *Sociological Theory, 2*, 23–101.

Bly, R. (1990). *Iron John: A book about men.* Reading, MA: Addison-Wesley.

Breines, W. (1982). *Community and organization in the New Left, 1962–68.* New York: Praeger.

Brown, P., & Ferguson, F. I. T. (1995). 'Making a big stink': Women's work, women's relationships, and toxic waste activism. *Gender & Society, 9*, 145–172.

Buechler, S. M. (1990). *Women's movements in the United States.* New Brunswick, NJ: Rutgers.

Bulkin, E., Pratt, M. B., & Smith, B. (1984). *Yours in struggle: Three feminist perspectives on anti-Semitism and racism.* New York: Long Haul Press.

Butler, B. (1991). *Ceremonies of the heart: Celebrating lesbian unions.* Seattle, WA: The Seal Press.

Butler, J. (1990). *Gender trouble: Feminism and the subversion of identity.* New York and London: Routledge.

Carden, M. (1978). The proliferation of a social movement. In L. Kriesberg (Ed.), *Research in social movements, conflict, and change,* Vol. 1, (pp. 179–196). Greenwich, CT: JAI Press.

Cassell, J. (1977). *A group called women: Sisterhood and symbolism in the feminist movement.* New York: David McKay.

Cavin, S. (1990). The invisible army of women: Lesbian social protests, 1969–88. In G. West & R. Blumberg (Eds.), *Women and social protest* (pp. 321–332). New York: Oxford University Press.

Chafe, W. H. (1977). *Women and equality: Changing patterns in American culture.* New York: Oxford University Press.

Chafe, W. H. (1991). *The paradox of change: American women in the 20th century.* New York: Oxford University Press.

Chafetz, J. (1988). *Feminist sociology: An overview of contemporary theories.* Itasca, IL: F.E. Peacock.

Chafetz, J. (1990). *Gender equity: An integrated theory of stability and change.* Newbury Park, CA: Sage.

Chafetz, J., & Dworkin, G. (1986). *Female revolt.* Totowa, NJ: Rowman and Allenheld.

Chafetz, J., & Dworkin, G. (1987). In the face of threat: Organized antifeminism in comparative perspective. *Gender & Society, 1*, 33–60.

Chodorow, N. (1995). Gender as a personal and cultural construction. *Signs: Journal of Women in Culture and Society, 20*, 516–544.

Collins, P. H. (1990). *Black feminist thought.* New York: Routledge.

Connell, R. W. (1987). *Gender and power.* Stanford, CA: Stanford University Press.

Costain, A. (1992). *Inviting women's rebellion: A political process interpretation of the women's movement.* Baltimore: John Hopkins University Press.

Cott, N. (1987). *The grounding of modern feminism.* New Haven, CT: Yale University Press.

Daly, M. (1978). *Gyn/ecology.* Boston: Beacon.

Deckard, B. S. (1983). *The women's movement.* New York: Harper & Row.

Dill, K. Unpublished. Feminism in the nineties: The influence of collective identity and community on young feminist activists. Master's thesis, The Ohio State University, 1991.

Dunn, D., Almquist, E. M., & Chafetz, J. S. (1993). Macrostructural perspectives on gender inequality. In P. England (Eds.), *Theory on gender/feminism on theory* (pp. 69–90). New York: Walter de Gruyter.

Echols, A. (1989). *Daring to be bad: Radical feminism in America 1967–1975.* Minneapolis: University of Minnesota Press.

Eisenstein, Z. (1981). *The radical future of liberal feminism.* New York: Longman.

England, P, (Ed.). (1993). *Theory on gender/feminism on theory.* New York: Walter de Gruyter.

Esterberg, K. G. (1997). *Lesbian and bisexual identities: Constructing communities, constructing selves.* Philadelphia: Temple University Press.

Evans, S. (1979). *Personal politics.* New York: Knopf.

Ferree, M. M. (1997). Patriarchies and feminisms: The two women's movements of post-unification Germany. In L. Richardson, V. Taylor, & N. Whittier (Eds.), *Feminist frontiers IV* (pp. 526–536). New York: McGraw-Hill.

Ferree, M. M., & Hess, B. B. [1985] (1994). *Controversy and coalition: The new feminist movement.* Boston: Twayne.

Ferree, M. M., & Martin, P. Y. (1995). *Feminist organizations: Harvest of the new women's movement.* Philadelphia: Temple University Press.

Firestone, S. (1970). *The dialectic of sex.* New York: William Morrow.

Fonow, M. M. (1998). Protest engendered: The participation of women steel workers in the Wheeling-Pittsburgh steel strike of 1985. *Gender & Society, 12,* 710–728.

Freeman, J. (1972/3). The tyranny of structurelessness. *Berkeley Journal of Sociology, 17,* 151–164.

Freeman, J. (1975). *The politics of women's liberation.* New York: David McKay.

Freeman, J. (1979). Resource mobilization and strategy: A model for analyzing social movement organization actions. In M. N. Zald & J. D. McCarthy (Eds.), *The dynamics of social movements* (pp. 167–89). Cambridge, MA: Winthrop.

Gagné, P. (1998). *Battered women's justice: The movement for democracy and the politics of self-defense.* New York: Twayne.

Gamson, J. (1997). Message of exclusion: Gender, movement, and symbolic boundaries. *Gender and Society, 11,* 178–199.

Gerlach, L. P., & Hine, V. H. (1970). *People, power, change: Movements of social transformation.* Indianapolis: Bobbs-Merrill.

Giele, J. Z. (1995). *Two paths to women's equality: Temperance, suffrage, and the origins of modern feminism.* New York: Twayne.

Gordon, S. (1991). *Prisoners of men's dreams.* New York: Little, Brown.

Griffin, S. (1978). *Women and nature.* New York: Harper & Row.

Hartmann, H. (1981). The family as the locus of gender, class, and political struggle: The example of housework. *Signs, 6,* 366–394.

Hartmann, H. (1984). Unhappy marriage of Marxism and feminism toward a more progressive union. In A. M. Jaggar & P. S. Rothenberg (Eds.), *Feminist frameworks: Alternative theoretical accounts between women and men* (pp. 172–189). New York: McGraw-Hill.

Hoagland, S. L. (1988). *Lesbian ethics: Toward new value.* Palo Alto, CA: Institute of Lesbian Studies.

Hoagland, S. L., & Penelope, J. (Eds.) (1988). *For lesbians only.* London: Onlywomen Press.

Hochschild, A. (1989). *The second shift.* New York: Avon.

Huber, J. (1973). From sugar and spice to professor. In A. S. Rossi & A. Calderwood, *Academic women on the move.* New York: Russell Sage Foundation.

Huber, J. (1976). Toward a sociotechnological theory of the women's movement. *Social Problems, 23,* 371–388.

Huber, J. (Ed.). (1991). *Macro-micro linkages in sociology.* Newbury Park, CA: Sage Publications.

Huber, J., & Spitze, G. (1983). *Sex stratification: Children, housework, and jobs.* New York: Academic Press.

Jasper, J. M. & Poulsen, J. D. (1995). Recruiting strangers and friends: Moral shocks and social networks in animal rights and anti-nuclear protests. *Social Problems, 42,* 493–512.

Jayawardena, K. (1986). *Feminism and nationalism in the third world.* London: Zed Books.

Kamen, P. (1991). *Feminist fatale: Voices from the "twentysomething" generation explore the future of the women's movement.* New York: Donald I. Fine.

Kaminer, W. (1992). *I'm dysfunctional, you're dysfunctional: The recovery movement and other self-help fashions.* Reading, MA: Addison-Wesley.

Katzenstein, M. F. (1997). Stepsisters: Feminist movement activism in different institutional spaces. In D. Meyer & S. Tarrow (Eds.), *A movement society? Contentious politics for a new century.* Boulder, CO: Rowland and Littlefield.

Katzenstein, M. F., & Mueller, C. M. (1987). *The women's movements of the United States and Western Europe.* Philadelphia: Temple University Press.

Kimmel, M. S. (1987). Men's responses to feminism at the turn of the century. *Gender and Society, 1*, 261–283.

Kimmel, M. S. (Ed.). (1995). *The politics of manhood: Profeminist men respond to the mythopoetic men's movement (and the mythopoetic leaders answer)*. Philadelphia: Temple University Press.

Klatch, R. (1990). The two worlds of women of the new right. In L A. Tilly & P. Gurin (Eds.), *Women, politics and change*. New York: Russell Sage Foundation.

Klein, E. (1984). *Gender politics*. Cambridge, MA: Harvard University Press.

Leidner, R. (1993). Constituency, accountability, and deliberation: Reshaping democracy in the National Women's Studies Association. *NWSA Journal, 5*, 4–27.

Lesbian Connection (1991). Vols. 13 & 14. Lansing, MI: Ambitious Amazons.

Lorber, J. (1994). *Paradoxes of gender*. New Haven, CT: Yale University Press.

Loulan, J. (1990). *The lesbian erotic dance*. San Francisco: Spinsters Book Company.

Luker, K. (1984). *Abortion and the politics of motherhood*. Berkeley, CA: University of California Press.

MacKinnon, C. A. (1982). Feminism, Marxism, method, and the state: An agenda for theory. *Signs, 7*, 515–544.

MacKinnon, C. A. (1983). Feminism, Marxism, method, and the state: Toward feminist jurisprudence. *Signs, 8*, 635–658.

Mansbridge, J. (1986). *Why we lost the ERA*. Chicago: University of Chicago Press.

Marshall, S. E. (1984). Keep us on the pedestal: Women against feminism in twentieth-century America. In J. Freeman (Ed.), *Women: A feminist perspective* (pp. 568–581). Palo Alto, CA: Mayfield.

Marshall, S. E. (1985). Ladies against women: Mobilization dilemmas of antifeminist movements. *Social Problems, 32*, 348–362.

Marshall, S. E. (1997). *Splintered sisterhood: Gender and class in the campaign against woman suffrage*. Madison, WI: The University of Wisconsin Press.

Martin, P. Y. (1990). Rethinking feminist organizations. *Gender & Society, 4*, 182–206.

Marx, G. T., & Wood, J. L. (1975). Strands of theory and research in collective behavior. *Annual Review of Sociology, 1*, 363–428.

Matthews, N. (1994). *Confronting rape: The feminist anti-rape movement and the state*. London: Routledge.

Matthews, D. G., & DeHart, J. S. (1990). *Sex, gender and the politics of ERA: A state and the nation*. New York: Oxford.

McAdam, D. (1992). Gender as a mediator of the activist experience: The case of freedom summer. *American Journal of Sociology, 97*, 1211–1249.

McCarthy, J. D., & Zald, M. N. (1977). Resource mobilization and social movements: A partial theory. *American Journal of Sociology, 82*, 1212–1239.

Melucci, A. (1989). *Nomads of the present: Social movements and individual needs in contemporary society*. Philadelphia: Temple University Press.

Messner, M. A. (1997). *Politics of masculinities: Men in movements*. Thousand Oaks, CA: Sage.

Meyer, D. S. & Staggenborg, S. (1996). Movements, countermovements, and the structure of political opportunity. *American Journal of Sociology, 101*, 1628–1660.

Meyer, D. S., & Whittier, N. (1994). Social movement spillover. *Social Problems, 41*, 277–298.

Miles, A. (1996). *Integrative feminisms: Building global visions, 1960s–1990s*. New York: Routledge.

Millett, K. (1971). *Sexual politics*. New York: Avon.

Mitchell, J. (1986). Reflections on twenty years of feminism. In J. Mitchell & A. Oakley (Eds.), *What is feminism?* (pp. 34–48). Oxford: Basil Blackwell.

Mohanty, C. T., Russo, A., & Torres, L. (Eds.) (1991). *Third world women and the politics of feminism*. Bloomington, IN: Indiana University Press.

Moraga, C., & Anzaldúa, G. (1981). *This bridge called my back: Writings by radical women of color*. Watertown, MA: Persephone.

Morris, A. D. (1984). *The origins of the civil rights movement: Black communities organizing for change*. New York: The Free Press.

Morris, A. D., & Mueller, C. M. (Eds.) (1992). *Frontiers in social movement theory*. New Haven, CT: Yale University Press.

Mottle, T. L. (1980). The analysis of countermovements. *Social Problems, 27*, 620–635.

Naples, N. A. (1992a). 'Just what needed to be done': The political practice of women community workers in low-income neighborhoods. *Gender & Society, 5*, 478–494.

Naples, N. A. (1992b). Activist mothering: Cross-generational continuity in the community work of women from low-income neighborhoods. *Gender & Society, 6*, 441–463.

Neuhouser, K. (1995). 'Worse than men': Gendered mobilization in an urban Brazilian Squatter Settlement. *Gender & Society, 9*, 38–59.

Off Our Backs (1991). Passages 7-Beyond the barriers. *21*, 12.

Offen, K. (1988). Defining feminism: A comparative historical approach. *Signs, 14,* 119–157.

Oppenheimer, V. K. (1973). Demographic influence on female employment and the status of women. In Joan Huber (Ed.), *Changing women in a changing society* (pp. 184–199). Chicago: University of Chicago Press.

Rapping, E. (1996). *The culture of recovery: Making sense of the recovery movement in women's lives.* Boston: Beacon Press.

Ray, R. (1999). *Fields of protest: Women's movements in India.* Minneapolis: University of Minnesota Press.

Reger, J., Whittier, N., & Taylor, V. (1995). Gendering social movement theory. Paper presented at the Annual Meetings of the American Sociological Association, Washington, DC.

Reskin, B. (1988). Bringing the men back in: Sex differentiation and the devaluation of women's work. *Gender & Society, 2,* 58–81.

Rich, A. (1976). *Of woman born.* New York: Norton.

Rich, A. (1980). Compulsory heterosexuality and lesbian existence. *Signs, 5,* 631–660.

Robnett, B. (1996). African-American women in the civil rights movement, 1954–1965: Gender, leadership, and micromobilization. *American Journal of Sociology, 101,* 1661–1693.

Rothschild-Whitt, J. (1979). The collectivist organization: An alternative to rational-bureaucratic models. *American Sociological Review, 44,* 509–527.

Rupp, L. J. (1997). *Worlds of women: The making of an international women's movement.* Princeton, NJ: Princeton University Press.

Rupp, L. J., & Taylor, V. (1987). *Survival in the doldrums: The American women's rights movement, 1945 to 1960s.* New York: Oxford University Press.

Ryan, B. (1989). Ideological purity and feminism: The U.S. women's movement from 1966 to 1975. *Gender & Society, 3,* 239–257.

Ryan, B. (1992). *Feminism and the women's movement.* New York: Routledge.

Sapiro, V. (1991). In Janet Boles (Ed.), *The annals of the American Academy of Political and Social Science,* May, 515.

Schlesinger, M. B., & Bart, P. (1983). Collective work and self-identity: The effect of working in a feminist illegal abortion collective. In L. Richardson & V. Taylor (Eds.), *Feminist frontiers.* Reading, MA: Addison-Wesley.

Schneider, B. (1988). Political generations in the contemporary women's movement. *Sociological Inquiry, 58,* 4–21.

Schwalbe, M. (1996). *Unlocking the iron cage: The men's movement, gender politics, and American culture.* Oxford, UK: Oxford University Press.

Scott, J. (1986). Gender: A useful category of historical analysis. *American Historical Review, 91,* 1053–1075.

Scott, J. (1988). *Gender and the politics of history.* New York: Columbia University Press.

Simonds, W. (1996). *Abortion at work: Ideology and practice in a feminist clinic.* New Brunswick, NJ: Rutgers University Press.

Smith, B. (1990). *Texts, facts, and femininity: Exploring the relations of ruling.* New York: Routledge.

Spelman, E. (1988). *Inessential woman: Problems of exclusion in feminist thought.* Boston: Beacon Press.

Stacey, J. (1987). Sexism by a subtler name? Postindustrial conditions and postfeminist consciousness. *Socialist Review, 17,* 7–28.

Staggenborg, S. (1988). The consequences of professionalization and formalization in the pro-choice movement. *American Sociological Review, 53,* 585–606.

Staggenborg, S. (1989). Stability and innovation in the women's movement: A comparison of two movement organizations. *Social Problems, 36,* 75–92.

Staggenborg, S. (1991). *The pro-choice movement.* New York: Oxford University Press.

Staggenborg, S. (1996). The survival of the women's movement: Turnover and continuity in Bloomington, Indiana. *Mobilization, 1,* 143–158.

Staggenborg, S. (1998). *Gender, family, and social movements.* Thousand Oaks, CA: Pine Forge Press.

Stein, A. (1997). *Sex and sensibility: Stories of a lesbian generation.* Berkeley, CA: University of California Press.

Stombler, M., & Padavic, I. (1997). Sister acts: Resisting men's domination in black and white fraternity little sister programs. *Social Problems, 44,* 257–275.

Tarrow, S. (1994). *Power in movement: Social movements, collective action, and mass politics in the modern state.* New York: Cambridge University Press.

Taylor, V. (1989). Social movement continuity: The women's movement in abeyance. *American Sociological Review, 54,* 761–775.

Taylor, V. (1996). *Rock-a-by baby: Feminism, self-help, and postpartum depression.* New York: Routledge.

Taylor, V. (1999). Gender and social movements: Gender processes and women's self-help movements. *Gender and Society, 13,* 8–33.

Taylor, V. & Rupp, L. (1993). Women's culture and lesbian feminist activism: A reconsideration of cultural feminism. *Signs, 19*, 32–61.

Taylor, V., & Van Willigen, M. (1996). Women's self-help and the reconstruction of gender: The postpartum support and breast cancer movements. *Mobilization: An International Journal I,* 123–142.

Taylor, V., & Whittier, N. (1992). Collective identity in social movement communities: Lesbian feminist mobilization. In A. Morris & C. Mueller (Eds.), *Frontiers of social movement theory.* New Haven, CT: Yale University Press.

Thorne, B. (1994). *Gender play: Girls and boys in school.* New Brunswick, NJ: Rutgers University Press.

Thorne, B. (1995). Symposium on West and Fenstermaker's 'Doing Difference.' *Gender & Society, 9,* 498–499.

Tong, R. (1989). *Feminist thought: A comprehensive introduction.* Boulder, CO: Westview Press.

Turner, R., & Killian, L. (1987). *Collective behavior* (3rd ed.). Englewood Cliffs, NJ: Prentice-Hall.

Vogel, L. (1993). *Mothers on the job: Maternity policy in the U.S. workplace.* New Brunswick, NJ: Rutgers University Press.

Walker, R. (1992). Becoming the third wave. *Ms. 2,* 39–41.

Walker, R. (1995). *To be red: Telling the truth and changing the face of feminism.* New York: Anchor.

West, G., & Blumberg, R. L. (1990). *Women and social protest.* New York: Oxford University Press.

West, C., & Fenstermaker, S. (1995). Doing difference. *Gender & Society, 9,* 8–37.

West, C., & Zimmerman, D. (1987). Doing gender. *Gender & Society, 1,* 125–151.

Whittier, N. E. (1995). *Feminist generations: The persistence of the radical women's movement.* Philadelphia: Temple University Press.

Zald, M. N., & Useem, B. (1987). Movement and countermovement interaction: Mobilization, tactics, and state involvement. In M. N. Zald & J. D. McCarthy (Eds.), *Social movements in an organizational society* (pp. 247–272).

CHAPTER 9

Gender and Organizations

Joan Acker

As the new women's movement took shape in the 1960s, feminists criticized organizational hierarchies and bureaucratic practices as masculine, undemocratic, and oppressive, and also argued that men monopolized leading positions, even in radical organizations, excluding women from positions of power and influence. Consequently, critiques of organized male power and the organizational forms in which it was expressed were integral to feminism, and feminists attempted early on to organize in nonhierarchical, nonbureaucratic ways (Ferree & Martin, 1995; Freeman, 1972–1973). Despite this early concern about organizations and male power, gender and organizations as a field of scholarly study developed considerably later than other "gender specializations." In this chapter, I review the history of the field and examine its contents, focussing on organizational structures of gender inequality, organizations as gendered processes, masculinity and sexuality in organizations, gender and organizational change, and potential contributions of this approach to understanding contemporary societal problems.

1. A HISTORY OF THE FIELD OF GENDER AND ORGANIZATIONS

Scholarly interest in women and/or sex roles and organizations began slowly in the early 1970s with criticisms of organizational theory and research for its inattention to the presence of women in work organizations and the resulting misinterpretations of research results (Acker & Van Houten, 1974). Rosabeth Moss Kanter (1975) pointed to the male dominance of almost all complex organizations and argued that the classical rational model of organization saw organizations as sex-neutral machines while, at the same time, supporting a "masculine ethic" of rationality and reason that obscured organizational

JOAN ACKER • Department of Sociology, University of Oregon, Eugene, Oregon 97403-1291

Handbook of the Sociology of Gender, edited by Janet Saltzman Chafetz. Kluwer Academic/ Plenum Publishers, New York, 1999.

reality and supported managerial authority. Kanter's (1977) *Men and Women of the Corporation* was a case study of (male) management and (female) clerical workers that still stands, in spite of many changes in the ensuing 20 years, as a definitive statement, valid for many different countries, about the sex structuring of organizations and the consequences for women. Kanter's central thesis was that women's organizational experiences are best explained by women's structural locations, not by their personalities and socialization. Women are, in the vast majority, confined to low-level jobs at the bottom of organizational hierarchies, where they are frustrated and alienated by lack of opportunities. The few women who reach upper organizational levels are tokens who are stereotyped and exposed to criticisms not inflicted on men, who are seen as the "natural" occupants of higher positions.

In the period following Kanter's book, feminists conducted a substantial amount of research on women in management (Powell, 1988; Terborg, 1977), but engaged in little theorizing (Martin, 1981). The primary exception was Kathy Ferguson's (1984) *The Feminist Case Against Bureaucracy*, a radical feminist critique of bureaucracy as a construction of male domination, mystified through a discourse on rationality and rules. Although this was a brilliant and scathing critique, for Ferguson all organizational participants are rendered powerless by bureaucracy; thus the specificity of gender and the dominance of certain men disappears (Acker, 1990). By the early 1980s, a flood of research on women and work began to appear, vastly increasing knowledge in this area. Some of this research began to illuminate the importance of the organizational context for understanding the connections between gender and work. Cynthia Cockburn (1981, 1985) described how, in struggles over technology, skill, and power in the workplace, both class and gender relations are created (see also Hacker, 1981). Arlie Hochschild (1983) showed how the management of emotions is often an aspect of work, particularly in women's jobs in certain service organizations. Ann Game and Rosemary Pringle (1983) also showed how changing technologies, along with changing organization of production and services, were accomplished partly through changing gender relations.

Such research and conceptualization contributed to the emergence of a new understanding of gender as a fundamental aspect of social processes and structures, going far beyond the earlier ideas of gender as social role, personality component, or individual attribute (Acker, 1992a). This understanding of gender was fundamental to arguments that organizations are "gendered" social constructions and that theories of gender neutral organizations are ideological formulations that obscure organizational realities, including the pervasiveness of male power. These ideas stimulated a rapid development of work on gender and organizations in the second half of the 1980s and into the 1990s. Gender and organizations as a distinct area of study can be dated from that time. Marking the emergence of this new area in sociology was a session titled "A Feminist Critique of Bureaucracy," organized by Patricia Martin at the 1987 American Sociological Association meetings. Research and theory building has progressed primarily in the English-speaking countries, although Scandinavian (Billing, 1994; Billing & Alvesson, 1994; Czarniawska-Joerges, 1994; Kvande & Rassmussen, 1974) and Italian (Gherardi, 1995) scholars have also participated. Two anthologies, *Gendering Organizational Analysis* (1992), edited by Albert Mills and Peta Tancred, and *Gender and Bureaucracy* (1992), edited by Mike Savage and Sue Witz, brought together examples of this work. A journal, *Gender, Work, and Organization*, was founded in 1994, and the most recent *Handbook of Organization Studies* (Clegg, Hardy, & Nord, 1996) has an entry on "Feminist Approaches to Organization Studies" (Calás & Smircich, 1996). This is an interdisciplinary field that includes, in addition to sociologists, organizational theorists in schools of management and business, psychologists, political scientists, anthropologists, scholars in education, and economists. Scholars use a variety of theoretical approaches, ranging from quantitative analyses of sex roles to postmodern interpretations, but all with critical views of existing gender-neutral organizational analyses. In the 1990s, recognition that sexuality is implicated in the shaping of gendered work demands (Adkins, 1995) and gendered hierarchies (Witz, Halford, & Savage, 1996), together with the understanding that organizations are embodied processes (Acker, 1990, 1992b), have deepened the challenges to notions of organizations as abstract, gender-neutral structures.

2. ORGANIZATIONAL STRUCTURES OF GENDER INEQUALITY

Scholars began to study gender and organizations to understand better the dimensions of and reasons for continuing inequality between women and men in the workplace and the economy. Most research on gender structures has been done in public and private employing organizations, but researchers have also examined voluntary organizations such as religious groups, charity organizations, and sports associations. Although gender patterns in organizations vary between the public and private sectors and between different sectors of the private economy, as well as between different societies, enough similarity exists to be able to make general statements about these patterns for organizations in the rich Northern nations. Work organizations are obviously stratified by sex both vertically and horizontally. Managerial positions, especially those at or near the top, are still disproportionately filled by white men (Rubin, 1997). Career mobility for women and minority men is limited by a "glass ceiling"and a "sticky floor." Jobs and occupations are sex typed and often sex segregated within employing organizations as well as in the labor market as a whole (Bielby & Baron, 1984; Burchell, 1996). Women still fill the vast majority of clerical positions; men still dominate engineering and skilled blue collar occupations. As occupational tasks and demands change, the sex typing and composition of an occupation may change (Reskin & Roos, 1990), but sex typing and sex segregation often persist (Buswell & Jenkins, 1994). The wage gap between women and men is related to the sex segregation of occupations: the relative wage disadvantage for both women and men in an occupation increases as the proportion of women in the occupation increases (England, 1992). Studies of comparable worth efforts have shown how gender wage differences are built into organizational structures (e.g., Acker, 1989; Blum, 1991). Although sex typing of occupations, horizontal sex segregation, and gender differentiated wage setting have most often been studied as aggregate phenomena at regional or national levels, organizations are the actual locations within which these patterns are created and re-created. Consequently, to understand the reproduction of these sorts of inequalities, it is necessary to look at organizations and their internal processes.

Although the original impetus for the study of gender and organizations was to improve our understanding of sex inequality and women's subordination, a gender perspective may also increase our abilities to answer other questions about organizations, including questions about organizational culture, about varieties of power and control, and about emerging changes in the global organization of economic and political power characteristic of the contemporary world.

3. ORGANIZATIONS AS GENDERED PROCESSES

One of the answers to questions about how women's subordination or secondary status in working life is perpetuated is that gender is embedded in ordinary organizational processes and that inequalities are reproduced as the mundane work of the "gendered" organization is carried out. Understanding organizations as gendered entails a shift in perspective from the conventional view of organizations as rational bounded systems to organizing as processes and practices, a perspective with a long history that informs other critical approaches to organizations (Czarniawska-Joerges, 1996). The ongoing flow of activities and interactions that constitute the living processes of organizing can be accessed from different points of entry (Acker 1990, 1992b) to discover if and how gender is part of these processes. These "points of entry" are ways of analytically managing complex processes and do not represent "analytic levels."

3.1. Procedures, activities, divisions

The first point of entry or set of processes consists of things people do to keep organizations going, including hiring; promotion; performance evaluation, allocation of work, setting salaries and wages; the actual work process; inventing and enforcing rules about hours, breaks, workplace behavior, and time off; designing and introducing new technology; and reorganizing or relocating work. As these ordinary activities are carried out, they result in organizational gender divisions, such as a gendered hierarchy, gender segregation of jobs and positions, a gendered wage gap, and practices that separate the workplace from the rest of life along gender lines. Class, race, and ethnic divisions may be created in the same processes. These activities often involve routine decisions made by employees as well as managers, who may be completely unaware that they are helping to create gender divisions. An example comes from a study I (Acker, 1989) did of state employment in Oregon: the state routinely classified 7000 women workers into four job classes, although these 7000 jobs varied greatly in task complexity and degree of responsibility. The jobs were described, again routinely, at the lowest common denominator as demanding little skill and knowledge and deserving to be in the lower pay grades. Job classifications for male-predominant jobs were much more detailed and differentiated; these jobs were assigned to a broader range of pay scales. Thus, the routine classification process contributed to low wages for the majority of women, while men were spread more evenly across the wage structure. No one doing the work of classification intended to maintain the gender wage gap. Such routine decisions may, however, be consciously made along lines of gender. For example, some Swedish banks in the 1980s established a "housewive's shift", expressly to recruit women for late afternoon hours when husbands would be at home to care for the children. This policy was a conscious creation of a gender-segregated labor force (Acker, 1994a). A great deal of research has made visible the ways in which organizational practices and routine decisions reproduce gender divisions, and these practices have often been the target of efforts to increase gender equality, such as comparable worth plans and Affirmative Action programs.

Managers in specific organizations may alter their procedures in response to outside pressures, such as Affirmative Action requirements, laws on parental leave, or—to a minimal degree in the United States—labor union demands. Barbara Reskin and Patricia Roos (1990) document the complex processes, including Affirmative Action, that have caused the changed sex composition of certain occupations. Although their analysis is occupationally based, it is revealing about organizational processes and pressures in maintaining and changing gender divisions. Thus, evidence for specific organizations and occupations suggests that sometimes conscious equality efforts do result in positive changes for some women. At the same time, such efforts often fail because men in the organization oppose them (Cockburn, 1991). In addition, the formulation of equal opportunity policies and procedures may allow men to claim, against the evidence, that inequalities no longer exist (Buswell & Jenkins, 1994; Calvert & Ramsey, 1996) and that it is up to women to compete in terms of skill and commitment of time to the organization (Buswell & Jenkins, 1994). Thus, the issue of structural inequality becomes an an issue of individual effort.

Managers often use textual tools, such as screening tests, evaluation criteria, job design and evaluation protocols, job classification schemes, or various wage-setting procedures in making routine decisions. The use of such tools tends to objectify the processes, making them appear inevitable and disembodied. Job evaluation, as used in the Oregon study (Acker, 1989), is a very good example of the ways in which such tools can embed assumptions about gender (see also Steinberg, 1992). In this job evaluation scheme, the caring skills required in many female-typed jobs, such as nurse or daycare worker, were given few evaluated "points," while the material–technical skills required in many male-typed jobs, such as engineer or electrician, received more "points." Another feature of this scheme was that the demands of managerial jobs were assessed several times, resulting in "overcounting" of the value of these jobs. Because most managerial jobs, especially those at high levels in the hierarchy, were filled by men, this "doublecounting" added to gender wage differences. Job evaluation documents and rules are elements of what Dorothy Smith (1987) has called the abstract, intellectual, textually mediated relations of ruling. These texts and instructions in their proper use, often developed and sold by management consultants, encode social relations that are then reproduced as the same in many different sites.

Struggles for power and control are often struggles over bureaucratic tools. For example, in the state of Oregon, management and trade unions had their major conflicts over the classification system and the definition and use of the salary scales (Acker, 1989). Ordinary Oregon employees were quite sophisticated about these systems and often pursued individual wage increases through reclassification into higher wage grades for their own jobs, much to the distress of their managers. Knowledge of bureaucratic details is a resource in these struggles. Where there are trade unions, it has historically been union men who have that knowledge because, as in Sweden for example, men are the wage negotiators and union activists. Feminists have found in many cases (e.g., Acker, 1991) that challenging the male monopoly over knowledge and control of negotiations is necessary to promote the interests of women employees. Such challenges have been difficult for women to win partly because wage negotiations are an arena that men protect as their own. Women also have difficulty challenging male control because they have been prevented from gaining sufficient union experience by union organizational practices built around the time patterns of men. Meetings that occur after work when many women need to be at home cooking and caring for children, expectations that union activists will be available to go to weekend workshops far from home, and negotiation sessions that last long into the night are all problematic practices for women with families. Such practices keep women from gaining experience dealing with the bureaucratic systems of the organization, and thus often exclude them from leadership in union work.

Routine requirements of workplaces may, on the other hand, structure gender relations outside the work organization, at home and in the wider community. Work schedules, rules about time off and telephone use, and expectations that employees put the job first before the rest of life all can affect women in different ways than men (e.g., Bailyn, 1993; Hochschild, 1989, 1997). Such expectations may be impossible to meet for women, and occasionally men, with family obligations. A result has been that many women either move out of the job market or work part-time. Either solution involves the re-creation of patterns of male dominance within families and in the workplace. Women with the sole responsibility for children may be doubly disadvantaged in trying to adapt rigid workplace patterns to unpredictable family demands. Employing organizations vary widely in the degree to which their policies accommodate extraorganizational obligations of employees. When family friendly policies do exist, they can remain unimplemented when the company culture expects and rewards long working hours and few vacation days (Hochschild, 1997). Even in countries in which the state requires certain organizational accommodations to family life, the Scandinavian countries, for example, the person who uses the programs (usually a woman) is likely to have fewer career opportunities than the person who does not (usually a man) (Acker, 1994c).

In sum, wide variations exist in the clarity and pervasiveness of gender divisions and in the procedures and practices that create and change them. But the complete absence of divisions is rare. I find it striking how often similar patterns are repeated in widely separated locations, and how universally the power of men and the masculine is confirmed, in spite of the obvious improvement of the work situations of many women in industrial countries during the last 25 years.

3.2. Images, Symbols, Forms of Consciousness

People in organizations create images, symbols, and forms of consciousness that justify, legitimate, and even glamorize the persistent gender divisions. This is a second point of entry for examining gendered processes. Images and understandings are integral to the practices, described previously, that create an organization and its divisions. Images, symbols, and forms of consciousness function ideologically to help to naturalize relations of power. For example, organizational consultants I observed in my study of comparable worth (Acker, 1989) often appealed to "common sense" and "what everyone knows" to create a sense that hierarchy is natural. Beliefs that certain knowledge and skills are innate to women, while real skill, that which men have, comes through long training; that typical women's skills require only a basic education; that skilled, technology-based work is masculine and unskilled, routine and caring work is feminine, all naturalize male advantage. (See, e.g., Acker, 1989; Cockburn, 1983, 1985; Game & Pringle, 1983; Phillips & Taylor, 1980). Such beliefs influence hiring, promotion, and wage- setting, as do beliefs that women are suited only to particular kinds of jobs because of their competing home responsibilities (Jones & Causer, 1995).

The image of the organization as a gender-neutral, abstract hierarchy of jobs and positions, articulated in organization theory and in management thinking, plays an ideological role in both obscuring gender and in embedding an image of a male worker or manager in assumptions about how organizations should be put together (Acker, 1990, 1992b). Beginning with Weber's analysis of bureaucracy, a job or position has been seen as a space defined by tasks, responsibilities, and authority, but devoid of any human body and any ties or obligations to anything or anyone outside the organization. This image still exists in social theory and in employers' assumptions that managers and workers will place work obligations before other demands, and will spend employer-defined periods of time at work during which they will keep their attention focused on work. Taking care of physical needs, for example, eating, or social needs, for example, those created by a child's illness, are viewed as taking time from work. The "perfect worker" implied by the concept of the empty slot would not have to do any of these things. Men who have the support services of wives or secretaries can approximate this model. Women, almost by definition, cannot. It can be argued, then, that the gender-neutral model of the organization assumes a male worker and manager as well as a gendered division of labor in which women do the tasks of life maintenance and renewal, usually in a private sector removed from the organization. This image of the organization as an abstract, gender-neutral entity with its legitimate demands that supersede other demands undergirds organizational rules and practices that then help to confirm and perpetuate the image. In the process, women's disadvantages are also confirmed.

Intentional symbolic production of gender is the business of many complex organizations, particularly media organizations. But explicit gender images, in addition to the implicit images I discussed previously, are created within and infuse organizational structures of all kinds, including religious, military, political, and social movement organizations. These images usually contain implications of masculinity and male sexuality (Collinson & Hearn, 1994). Metaphors of a stereotypical hegemonic masculinity (Connell, 1987) are often ways of defining the competent, successful organization (Kanter, 1975, 1977). The lean, mean, efficient, aggressive, competitive organization is the one that will survive and prosper in today's mean and competitive economy. Feminine images, such as empathy and caring, are rarely called upon to describe a well-functioning organization, except for certain service organizations such as hospitals, food banks, and daycare centers. The content of images and metaphors changes historically, but not their gendered nature. Thus, the resurgence of the corporation as the good father and the manager as the kindly overseer is a possiblity as large business organizations contend with distrust and suspicion by their workers and the general public. On the other hand, in the course of my study of Swedish banks (Acker 1991, 1994a), I observed a change in the opposite direction. Bank employees had seen their top management and the banks themselves as benevolent, paternal, steady, and responsible. In light of a scandal involving the CEO of the largest bank; the promotion of competitive values over community and customer service; and the influx of young, aggressive, entrepeneurial male managers, the employees we interviewed were disillusioned, relinquishing their old images, but filled with apprehension about the image of the manager.

3.3. Interactions Between Individuals and Groups

The work of organizing goes on through interactions between people, women and men, women and women, men and men, supervisors and subordinates, co-workers, and between employees and customers, clients, consultants, or others from the outside. While doing the work of organizing, people are also "doing gender" (West & Fenstermaker, 1995). These interactions are the everyday contexts within which people experience and create dominance and submission, create alliances and exclusions, put together and implement policies that divide and differentiate between women and men, and produce and confirm gender images. Contexts and forms of interaction vary and they may be formally structured or informally, even subversively created. Gender is integral to many organizing practices and activities, rather than an external element that can be easily excised.

Gender is deeply embedded, for example, in the interactions between bosses and secretaries, or clerical workers and managers. The boss–secretary relationship, as well as the divisions of status and tasks between them, is rooted in a gender division in which the boss was a man and the secretary was a woman. Personal service from the secretary and paternal protection from the boss marked this relationship. It was no accident that secretaries were often called "office wives," as Rosabeth Moss Kanter (1977) pointed out. Although today there are many women managers, at least at the lower and middle levels, few men are secretaries or clerical workers. When men are in such positions, they are usually called something else, such as a research assistant (Pringle, 1989), and they are not expected to perform the supportive personal services expected from women (Pierce, 1995). Receptionists, airline stewardesses, nurses, and other service workers are also in subordinate female-typed jobs in which they are expected to interact with superiors and customers in appropriately feminine and respectful ways. Sexuality, both overt and hidden, may be a component of these interactions, supporting the dominance of certain men, solidifying relations between men, and establishing the subordination of women (Adkins, 1995; Pringle, 1989).

Situations undoubtedly exist in which gender is not present in interactions. However, the research on gender and organizations is full of descriptions of ways in which gender is produced even in ordinary encounters between equals in the workplace (Pierce, 1995). For example, Kanter (1977) documented the interactions between male managers and the few, or token, women who had achieved managerial status at that time. These interactions, shaped by the men in stereotypical terms, reaffirmed the stereotypes by defining the women managers as "mothers," "seductresses," "pets," or "iron maidens," confirming their conditional status as outsiders. In a more recent analysis of gendered interactions, Patricia Martin (1996) suggests that men enact masculinities in certain situations, conflating such enactments with their work activities and, in the process, relegating women to the situation of outsider. Martin identifies several gendered interactional styles in which men "enact masculinity" in evaluating job candidates and others' work in a university setting. Men, in her study, promoted the needs, talents, and accomplishments of themselves and other men over the talents and accomplishments of women. They asked for help from other men in pursuing their careers, while women did not seem to expect such aid. They made open criticisms of women, but not of men, and they collectively "ganged up" on women to denigrate their capacities. As Martin observes, "In exploring *interactional dynamics*, we gain insights into *how* men 'erect' barriers . . . " (1996, p 206).

3.4. Internal Mental Work

The fourth point of entry to understanding gendered organizing processes is through the internal mental work of individuals as they come to understand the organization's gendered expectations and opportunities, including the appropriate gendered behaviors and attitudes (Cockburn, 1991; Hochschild, 1983; Pierce, 1995; Pringle, 1989). Here, too, race and class are implicated and constructed. In *White Collar*, C. Wright Mills (1956) was one of the first to point to "personality markets," and the ways in which employees were expected to construct themselves as charming and sincere. Although Mills did not recognize gender as part of this process, one can easily read masculinity and femininity into his analysis. Gendered expectations may be ambiguous and contradictory, thus requiring considerable interior mental work to get it right. All workers must first recognize what is appropriate and then try to control and shape their actions and feelings in those directions. Swedish bank workers, for example, are supposed to be friendly and calm; calmness, in particular we were told, may require extreme efforts at controlling one's outer behavior in the face of long lines of waiting customers, ringing telephones, and new technology that has not been sufficiently explained. Women bank employees believed that women were much better able to handle such emotional/mental work than were men. Inappropriate behavior, for example, by a woman refusing to be a good sport about men's sexual joking, can result in ostracism and dangerous isolation (Enarson, 1984). Women then have to cope emotionally with such humiliations and transform such feelings by convincing themselves that all this was just a joke. Women who are subjected to sexual harassment often go through painful decisions about whether to complain because complaint can violate the tacit understanding of appropriate female behavior, leading to job loss. The decision about whether to tolerate or complain can mean painful inner processes involving dealing with fear and identity.

Jennifer L. Pierce's (1995) study of two law firms, *Gender Trials*, exemplifies the various processes outlined previously. She describes the history and present structure of law firms as gendered bureaucracies. On the basis of her ethnographic work, she analyzes the emotional labor construed as masculine that marks the job of the litigator and the practice of law, and contrasts the "rambo litigator" with the paralegal whose job requires deference and caregiving as emotional labor. The caregiving and deference, both feminized practices, confirm the status of the lawyers and help to reproduce the gendered hierarchy of the law firms. Some female paralegals are uncomfortable with the gendered persona required by their work, but even their resistance tends to reinforce the gender structure. Women litigators, few in number, face a double bind: if they behave as aggressively as the men, they are considered too aggressive; if they do not, they are not tough enough. Men who are paralegals, on the other hand, are not held to the same supportive behaviors as the women, functioning more as junior colleagues to the attorneys. Thus, the ordinary work of these firms assumes gendered hierarchies. These hierarchies and the ongoing work depend upon and reproduce highly gendered images of the organizations and their central members. Gender is daily reproduced in the interactions that constitute the work, and individuals must learn and cope with the gender identities appropriate to the work.

4. MASCULINITY AND ORGANIZATION

Masculinity and organization has become a major focus in the study of gender and organizing (e.g., Collinson & Hearn, 1994, 1996). As I have indicated previously, masculinity enters in various ways in the playing out of organizing practices and policies that constitute the mundane, everyday processes of organizations and in the images, identities, and interactions involved. Here I want to extend that discussion to look in more detail at some issues about masculinity and organization.

Masculinity is defined by Deborah Kerfoot and David Knights (1996) as " . . . the socially generated consensus of what it means to be a man, to be 'manly' or to display such behaviour at any one time" (p. 86). Thus, masculinity is clearly distinguished from actual men, who may differ in their practice of masculinity from this consensus. However, David Collinson and Jeff Hearn (1994) argue that masculinity is vaguely defined. "Does it refer to behaviours, identities, relationships, experiences, appearances, discourses or practices? . . . Are masculinities irreducibly related to men or are they discourses in which women can also invest" (p. 9)? Those writing on the topic do seem to agree that multiple masculinities exist in any society at any particular time, and that masculinities shift historically, as do femininities. Connell (1987, 1995) developed the concept "hegemonic masculinity" to stand for the dominant form that characterizes masculinity in positions of societal power. Hegemonic masculinity "embodies the currently accepted answer to the problem of the legitimacy of patriarchy, which guarantees (or is taken to guarantee) the dominant position of men and the subordination of women." (Connell, 1995, p. 77.) "Subordinated masculinities" are then defined in contrast to and dominated by hegemonic masculinity.

Hegemonic masculinity is the form most often linked to the management of large organizations, a form that changes over time as the organization of production changes, although at any particular moment several different masculinities may exist. Beverly Burris (1996) identifies different forms of organizational and managerial patriarchy that represent different hegemonic masculinities, including entrepreneurial patriarchy, technical patriarchy, bureaucratic patriarchy, professional patriarchy, and technocratic patriarchy (the form found in the new, information-based enterprises) (Burris, 1996, p. 68). Managerial masculinities exhibit substantial differences, for example, in the degree to which risk-taking is a significant component. However, there are similarities in the focus on rationality and the "control (of) others in pursuit of the instrumental goals of production, productivity and profit" (Kerfoot & Knights, 1996, p. 88). Kerfoot and Knights (1996, p. 83) suggest that technologies of strategic management and control are congruent with "those contemporary forms of masculinity that turn everything into an object of conquest."

Hegemonic masculinities are not only defined in the management of business, but also in other organizations such as those devoted to sports (Messner, 1992), in police departments, and in the military. Alternative hegemonic masculinities characterize religious denominations and sects, while the worlds of university professors, medical doctors, and political pundits produce their own versions of dominant masculinity. Today, as the values of the competitive market sector spread through industrial societies, a convergence among these various masculinities toward a focus on rationality and the control of others in the pursuit of instrumental goals may be occurring.

Subordinated organizational masculinities have also been studied, most obviously in research focussed on working class jobs. Cynthia Cockburn (1983, 1985) showed how working class masculinity is, or was, organized around notions of physical strength, physical skill, and toughness, including the ability to withstand dangerous and dirty working conditions. Male solidarity based on the affirmation of these attributes valorized them in contrast to women who lacked them. In his study of working class boys, Paul Willis (1977) chronicled how this sort of masculinity was produced within the peer group, guaranteeing that these boys would never be other than shop floor workers, thus reproducing class as well as gender structures. Many other studies of working class jobs are also implicitly about gender, although usually this element remained implicit. David Morgan (1992) makes this point in a provocative rereading of some sociological classics about men and their work.

For both male managers and workers, masculinity is (was) formed and defended through patterns of homosociality, men forming solidary groups that exclude women. Rosabeth Moss Kanter (1977) recognized this in *Men and Women of the Corporation* (see also Lipman-Blumen, 1976). Jennifer Pierce (1995) shows how these exclusions based on masculinity operate in law firms. Cynthia Cockburn (1985) shows how men come together in affirmations of skill and technological competence that exclude women. Male enclaves in organizations are also usually defined by heterosexuality, and solidarity may be confirmed by talk that objectifies and denigrates women while, at the same time, excluding and denigrating homosexuals. Thus gays constitute another excluded or subordinate masculinity in most work organizations. Masculinity and femininity in organizational life are thus linked to sexuality in multiple ways, as I discuss in the next section.

5. SEXUALITY AND BODIES

Sexuality and bodies were absent in prefeminist organization theory, although real organizational participants, of course, have bodies and sexes. The absence of bodies and sexuality, components of the vision of organizations as gender-neutral, rational machines, contributed to masking the underlying assumption that the prototypical organization man was indeed a man (Acker, 1990). Bodies and sexuality are now recognized by some sociologists and organizational theorists as essential aspects of organizations and work processes (Adkins & Lury, 1996; Witz et al., 1996). In a study of tourist service organizations, Adkins (1995) argues and documents that, at least in this industry, gendering of the relations of production is accomplished partly through sexualization (see also Hochschild, 1983). Women workers were routinely expected to participate in sexual banter and to accept sexual innuendoes from male customers, managers, and co-workers. Such sexualized work was part of the job: women were required to be attractive and to dress to emphasize their attractions. Failure to use the proper makeup and dress or refusal to accept the sexualization of their work relations could result in dismissal. Such requirements did not exist for men hired into the same jobs. One implication of this is, as she points out, further support for the argument that the economy is not gender neutral.

Sexuality and bodies function in many cases as resources for control by male managers and workers. For example, managers who sexualize their relationships with female subordinates are clearly using sexuality as a form of control. At the same time, gender, sexuality, and bodies can constitute problems for management. The control and management of bodies is everywhere a management task, and that control is often done on the basis of gender. Women and men may have to be separated, never allowed proximity, or separated at certain times. This was a more pressing issue in the past than it is today, at least in rich industrial countries. For example, in the late nineteenth and early twentieth centuries as women were entering the newly expanding white collar jobs, they were usually placed in women-only offices, physically segregated from men (see, e.g., Cohn, 1985). However, spatial segregation by gender continues. For example, in the United States and elsewhere, women and men must use different toilets, a symbolically important way of emphasizing gender difference. Management almost always controls breaks for eating, but often also controls toilet breaks and physical movement in the workplace in the interests of productivity; women are often controlled more rigidly than men. A widespread belief seems to exist that women's bodies—and psyches—tolerate physical confinement, repetitive tasks, and rapid movements better than do those of men. Women, therefore, are often perceived as ideal employees for jobs with these requirements. Women workers have been confined to production lines sorting beans, packing herring, or assembling small objects, while men have repaired the machines, lifted the boxes, and moved about the workplace. Explaining such divisions of labor, an electronics firm manager in the Mexican Border Industrial Zone said:

> We hire mostly women because they are more reliable than men; they have finer fingers, smaller muscles and unsurpassed manual dexterity. Also, women don't get tired of repeating the same operations nine-hundred times a day. (Fernández Kelly, 1979, quoted in Green, 1983)

Managers and co-workers often target sexuality and reproduction as objects of control, but in different ways for women and men. Women are often excluded on grounds of reproduction and objectified on grounds of sexuality, while male sexuality pervades many organizations and reinforces men's organizational power (Collinson & Collinson, 1989). Male talk about sexuality and their sense of sexual superiority can also be a source of cohesion that reinforces organizational stability. On the other hand, sexuality may be disruptive, and, according to Burrell (1984, p. 98), organizations institute mechanisms for control of sexuality early in their development. Women's challenges to exploitative male sexuality may result in management intervention, but only if the challenges are protected by law and thus become disruptive for the organization. The saga of the emergence of sexual harassment as an organizational problem is an example. Sexual harassment is an historically new concept, a product of the women's movement (MacKinnon, 1979). Although the behavior has always existed, it was not named until 1976 when two U.S. surveys on its prevalence were done (Stanko, 1985, p. 61). Some women took legal action against employers; eventually the courts, first in the United States and later in some other countries, ruled that sexual harassment is a form of sex discrimination. Sensational and sometimes expensive cases continue to occur. Thus, a dirty secret, attesting to the ubiquitous sexualization of work relations, has been transformed into a major organizational problem, but one that persists and is probably more widespread than most studies indicate (e.g., Collinson & Collinson, 1996; Thomas & Kitzinger, 1994).

These are just a few examples of the complex ways that gender, bodies, and sexuality may be both problematic for organizational managers and resources for control and management (see also Hearn & Parkin, 1987). Consideration of bodies and sexuality has stimulated renewed interest in emotions in work processes and in the constitution of gendered hierarchies (Adkins, 1995; Fineman, 1993; Pierce, 1995). Descriptions of particular organizations will reveal different ways that gender differences in bodies, emotionality, and sexuality are accommodated, expressed, and employed in ongoing organizational processes.

6. GENDER AND ORGANIZATIONAL CHANGE

Historically, the gendering processes of organizing and the gendered structures of organizations have changed with changing organization of production, changing economic conditions, increasing demands by women for equity and, on occasion, equality. However, as I argued earlier, there has also been a certain stability in the overall configuration of gendered practices and persona. In the last 10 to 15 years, organizational change and restructuring seem to have increased in pace and pervasiveness, stimulating questions about the possible consequences for women, gender inequality, men, and masculinities.

By framing the issue in this way, I am not suggesting that restructuring consists of abstract processes that then have impacts on gender, for organizational restructuring should be thought of as gendered processes (Halford & Savage, 1995).

Worldwide restructuring of capital and production, facilitated by new technologies, has included on the organizational level flattening of hierarchies, reductions in the numbers of middle managers, redistribution and reorganization of tasks and responsibilities, the development of team work, and various methods to increase flexibility (Jenson, 1989; Smith, 1993). The ideology justifying these changes is that they will increase productivity, efficiency, and profit. In addition, it has been argued, these changes require a new kind of management, one that is more humane and focussed on developing employees' capacities for creative engagement in their work (Calás & Smircich, 1993). Such changes, often recommended by management consultants, are occurring in the public as well as the private sectors. These efforts at transformation might seem to offer possibilities for reductions in gender segregation and the assignment of women to subordinate jobs and for increasing demand for women's caring and relational capacities in management positions. Contemporary change processes are complex and various. Moreover, research on the gendered outcomes and the ways in which gender enters these processes is sparse. Therefore, conclusions about what is actually happening must be tentative (Acker, 1994).

The most consistently reported changes are reductions in hierarchy, which means, of course, downsizing. Some evidence exists that women fare better in flat organizations than in hierarchical bureaucracies (e.g., Kvande & Rasmussen, 1994). However, more evidence indicates that reducing hierarchy as it is usually done, through downsizing middle management jobs and reorganizing tasks and responsibilities, has detrimental effects on both the quality of work and possibilities for advancement for women. Vicki Smith (1990) records how reducing the ranks of bank middle management was accompanied by an intensification of work for remaining employees and a centralization of control in the hands of higher management. Although she does not draw out the implications for women, women have increasingly filled middle management slots in most banks. Reporting on a study of organizational restructuring in a public sector utility, a multinational pharmaceutical company and a large insurance company, Jean Woodall, Christine Edwards, and Rosemary Welchman (1997) conclude that for women managers "the experience of organizational restructuring is akin to participation in a lottery in which they are occasionally winners, but usually losers" (p. 2). Restructuring led to "job losses in functions where women are concentrated," restricted access for women to organizational networks that provide opportunities for career development, and undermined formal equal opportunity programs. In contrast, Susan Halford and Mike Savage (1995), examining restructuring in banking and local government offices, suggest that these changes undermined traditional managerial masculinities and opened new possibilities for women. At the same time, new and more competitive managerial masculinities could be identified, while women managers often were "in posts which are not part of the mainstream departmental hierarchy" (p. 116).

Greater work loads and task variety accompanies reorganization to reduce middle management and "empower" lower level workers, Maile (1995) found in a study of a local government in Britain. I (Acker, 1994a) also found these patterns in a study of women's jobs in Swedish banks. Although at that time middle management was not being reduced, work was being reorganized on a team basis, requiring that all employees have a wide repertoire of skills and knowledge so that they could function interchangeably on the team. Their tasks were much more demanding and stressful, but, at the same time, they found their jobs more satisfying, although not more rewarding in monetary terms. Elin Kvande (1997) describes restructuring in a program providing care for the elderly in Norway in which a "new managerialism" emphasizing budgets and efficiency characterised new management positions filled by men. Nursing and caretaking were separated from budget management, and those providing care, disproportionately women, had to make the stressful decisions about who would receive the increasingly scarce care resources.

Reorganization or restructuring may also include a search for flexibility through management-initiated changes in the labor force from primarily full-time, permanent employees to a partly contingent workforce. Contingent work takes many forms, but temporary and part-time work are the primary types. These workers are primarily women (Callaghan & Hartmann, 1991). The regular use of such workers constitutes a form of horizontal segregation in organizations. While it is a change that employers welcome, it tends to create a class of workers who have no opportunities for advancement and, usually, lower pay and fewer benefits than full-time workers.

Gender may be a resource for managers in organizational restructuring (Acker, 1994b). A dramatic example was the downsizing of AT&T in the 1970s reported by Sally Hacker (1979). AT&T was planning to reduce its labor force because of new technology at about the same time that it lost a large sex discrimination suit. The company met the requirements of the legal settlement that it integrate women into male jobs by moving many women into jobs that had already been scheduled for elimination with the introduction of the new technology. The numbers of women declined as these formerly male jobs, as well some traditionally female jobs, were eliminated.

Women may be preferred for certain reconstituted management jobs that involve less autonomy but also require more difficult decisions made with fewer resources (Kvande, 1997; Maile, 1995). As overall control and strategic decision-making are centralized, hierarchies are flattened, and career channels become constricted as a result, top managers may believe that women more readily than men accept the limitations on mobility possibilities, and may therefore define women as preferred employees. In the process, gender may be used consciously as a segregating device. For example, Reskin and Roos (1990, p. 51) suggested that "employers gerrymandered the sex labels of jobs that were feminizing for other reasons, selectively invoking sex stereotypes after they decided to hire more women."

7. CONCLUSION

This review of the developments in scholarship on gender and organizations necessarily skims over an increasingly rich field of study. In conclusion, I briefly identify some implications of this perspective for issues usually falling outside the study of organizations. First, gendering organizational studies reveal some of the ways in which gender is implicated in the economy, for the actual practices that constitute the "economy" are, on the whole, organizing practices. Although economic activities exist outside formal organizations, in families for example, most production of goods and services is accomplished in organizations. Markets, including financial markets, are constructed through intra- and interorganizational processes. Distribution through wages, profits, interest, or taxes actually occurs through organizational practices. People acting in organizations do the things that we talk about as economic; gender both shapes and is created in these processes.

Most academic conceptualizations of "the economy" are abstract, gender-absent models of market processes, choices, or value creation. Feminist economists have pointed to the gendered nature of economic analysis and the male bias in economic theory (Ferber & Nelson, 1993; Kuiper & Sap, 1995; Nelson, 1996) and have argued that "the economy" is "gendered." One way to explore the gendered nature of the economy, and to redefine what is meant by "economy," is through the concrete study of gendered organizing practices.

Second, gendered organizing is a critical site in which to study the intertwined processes of class, race, and gender, as Kathy Ferguson (1994) argues. Feminists, including feminist social scientists, recognize that gender cannot be torn from its social contexts without risking distortions, including privileging gender over other components of social relations and identities and denying their importance in creating inequality and domination. These other components include, at a minimum, class and race. Work organizations, in particular, are the locations in which class relations are produced; class relations are infused with gender relations, and often with race relations, which are also reproduced in material and ideological forms as organizational activities are undertaken. Looking at actual practices and experiences of organizing can illuminate the melding of what analysis has torn apart.

Third, the dangers and possibilities in the present processes of societal and global change cannot be fully understood without looking at transformations/nontransformations in gender relations in organizing. For example, the "feminization" of the world labor force has been a major factor in the global relocation of many industrial processes from high-wage countries to low-wage countries with large potential female labor forces. Particular patterns of women's subordination in the low-wage countries may become a resource for managers in high-wage countries, as work is subcontracted to patriarchically controlled family businesses or to factories employing women desperate for work at any wage. Changing employment patterns may have an impact on gender relations and gendered identities within and outside work organizations. For example, the old working class masculinity forged in industrial production seems in decline as production organizations change. At the same time, new or reemerging entrepeneurial masculinities seem to be factors in the contemporary ascendancy of profit, efficiency, and competitive success as major values. These contrasting developments may be both positive and negative for both women and men, marking the weakening of one sort of dominating masculinity and the strengthening of another. I think that a major question to be answered in understanding global economic developments is how the mobilization of various masculinities may be implicated.

Finally, bringing bodies and sexuality, as well as gender, into analyses of processes that have always been seen as disembodied and gender neutral could change our understanding of social structures and processes. Part of the feminist project in the social sciences has been to develop alternatives to abstract, gender neutral theorizing by locating the starting point for investigation outside those theories, in the concrete, ordinary experiences of women (and men) (Smith, 1987). Experiences, including experiences in organizations, are always located in material, concrete bodies, mediated, of course, by meanings and ideologies. Organizing activities and practices are always those of actual embodied people, including those engaged in creating abstract systems. Making bodies and sexuality, in all their concreteness, one of the places to begin our investigations is part of the effort to see social relations as actively produced linkages within and between many different and dispersed local places rather than as abstract macrostructures and processes imposed from above and outside.

REFERENCES

Acker, J. (1989). *Doing Comparable Worth*. Philadelphia: Temple University Press.

Acker, J. (1990). Hierarchies, jobs, bodies: A theory of gendered organizations, *Gender & Society, 4,* 139–58.

Acker, J. (1991). Thinking about wages: The gendered wage gap in Swedish banks. *Gender & Society 5,* 390–407.

Acker, J. (1992a). From sex roles to gendered institutions. *Contemporary Sociology, 21,* 565–569.

Acker, J. (1992b). Gendering organizational theory. In A. J. Mills & P. Tancred (Eds.), *Gendering organizational analysis* (pp. 248–260). Newbury Park, CA: Sage.

Acker, J. (1994a). The gender regime of Swedish banks. *Scandinavian Journal of Management, 10,* 117–130.

Acker, J. (1994b). Power, participation, and productivity: Possibilities for workplace change in the 21st century. In J. Glass (Ed.), *Working in the 21st century: Gender and beyond* (pp. 1–28). Los Angeles: Institute of Industrial Relations, University of California.

Acker, J. (1994c). Women, families, and public policy in Sweden. In E. N. Chow & C. W. Berheide (Eds.), *Women, the family, and policy: A global perspective* (pp. 33–50). Albany: State University of New York Press.

Acker, J., & Van Houten, D. (1974). Differential recruitment and control: The sex structuring of organizations. *Administrative Science Quarterly, 19,* 152–163.

Adkins, L. (1995). *Gendered work: Sexuality, family and the labour market.* Buckingham: Open University Press.

Adkins, L., & Lury, C. (1996). The cultural, the sexual, and the gendering of the labour market. In L. Adkins & V. Merchant (Eds.), *Sexualizing the social: Power and the organization of sexuality* (pp. 204–223). London: Macmillan.

Bailyn, L. (1993). *Breaking the mold: Women, men, and time in the new corporate world.* New York: The Free Press.

Bielby, W. T., & Baron, J. N. (1984). A woman's place is with other women: sex segregation within organizations. In B. F. Reskin (Ed.), *Sex segregation in the workplace: Trends, explanations, remedies* (pp. 27–55). Washington, D.C.: National Academy Press.

Billing, Y. D. (1994). Gender and bureaucracies—A critique of Ferguson's 'The feminist case against bureaucracy.' *Gender, Work and Organization 1,* 179–193.

Billing, Y. D., & Alvesson, M. (1994). *Gender, managers, organizations.* Berlin: de Gruyter.

Blum, L. M. (1991). *Between feminism and labor.* Berkeley, CA: University of California Press.

Burchell, B. (1996). Gender segregation, size of workplace and the public sector. *Gender, Work and Organization 3,* 227–235.

Burrell, G. (1984). Sex and organizational analysis. *Organization Studies, 5,* 97–118.

Burris, B. H. (1996). Technocracy, patriarchy and management. In D. L. Collinson & J. Hearn (Eds.), *Men as managers, managers as men.* London: Sage.

Buswell, C., & Jenkins, S. (1994). Equal opportunities policies, employment and patriarchy. *Gender, Work and Organization, 1,* 83–93.

Calás, M. B., & Smircich, L. (1993). Dangerous liaisons: The 'Feminine-in-management' meets globalization. *Business Horizons,* March/April, 71–81.

Calás, M. B., & Smircich, L. (1996). From "the women's" point of view: Feminist approaches to organization studies. In S. Clegg, C. Hardy, & W. Nord (Eds.), *Handbook of Organization Studies.* London: Sage.

Callaghan, P., & Hartmann, H. (1991). *Contingent work: A chart book on part-time and temporary employment.* Washington, D.C.: Economic Policy Institute/Institute for Women's Policy Research.

Calvert, L. M., & Ramsey, V. J. (1996). Speaking as female and white: A nondominant/dominant group standpoint. *Organization, 3,* 468–485.

Clegg, S., Hardy, C., & Nord, W. (Eds.) (1996). *Handbook of organization studies.* London: Sage.

Cockburn, C. (1983). *Brothers.* London: Pluto Press

Cockburn, C. (1985). *Machinery of dominance.* London: Pluto Press.

Cockburn, C. (1991). *In the Way of Women.* Ithaca, NY: ILR Press.

Cohn, S. (1985). *The feminization of clerical labor in Great Britain.* Philadelphia: Temple University Press.

Collinson, D., & Collinson, M. (1989). Sexuality in the workplace: The domination of men's sexuality. In J. Hearn, D. L. Sheppard, P. Tancred-Sheriff, & G. Burrell (Eds.), *The sexuality of organizations* (pp. 91–109). London: Sage.

Collinson, D., & Collinson, M. (1996). 'It's only dick': The sexual harassment of women managers in insurance sales. *Work, Employment & Society, 10,* 29–56.

Collinson, D., & Hearn, J. (1994). Naming men as men: Implications for work, organization and management. *Gender, Work and Organization, 1,* 2–22.

Collinson, D., & Hearn, J. (Eds.) (1996). *Men as managers, managers as men: Critical perspectives on men, masculinities and managements*. London: Sage.

Connell, R.W. (1987). *Gender and power: Society, the person and sexual politics*. Stanford, CA: Stanford University Press.

Connell, R. W. (1995). *Masculinities*. Berkeley, CA: University of California Press.

Czarniawska-Joerges, B. (1994). Editorial: Modern organizations and Pandora's box. *Scandinavian Journal of Management*, Special Issue: The Construction of Gender in Organizations, 10, 95-98.

Czarniawska-Joerges, B. (1996). Organizing, process of. In M. Warner (Ed.), *International encyclopedia of business and management*. London: Routledge.

Enarson, E. P. (1984). *Woods-working women: Sexual integration in the U.S. Forest Service*. Tuscaloosa, AL: The University of Alabama Press.

England, P. (1992). *Comparable worth: Theories and evidence*. New York: Aldine De Gruyter.

Ferber, M. A., & Nelson, J. A. (Eds.) (1993). *Beyond economic man: Feminist theory and economics*. Chicago: University of Chicago Press.

Ferguson, K. E. (1984). *The feminist case against bureaucracy*. Philadelphia: Temple University Press.

Ferguson, K. E. (1994). On bringing more theory, more voices and more politics to the study of organization. *Organization, 1*, 81–99.

Ferree, M. M., & Martin, P. Y. (1995). *Feminist organizations*. Philadelphia: Temple University Press.

Fineman, S. (Ed.) (1993). *Emotion in organizations*. London: Sage.

Freeman, J. (1972–1973). The tyranny of structurelessness, *Berkeley Journal of Sociology, 17*, 151–64.

Game, A., & Pringle, R. (1983). *Gender at work*. London: Pluto.

Gherardi, S. (1995). *Gender, symbolism and organizational cultures*. London: Sage.

Green, S. S. (1983). Silicon Valley's women workers: A theoretical analysis of sex-segregation in the electronics industry labor market. In J. Nash & M. P. Fernández-Kelly (Eds.), *Women, men, and the international division of labor*. Albany: State University of New York Press.

Hacker, S. L. (1979). Sex stratification, technology and organizational change: A longitudinal case study of AT&T. *Social Problems, 26*, 539–557.

Hacker, S. L. (1981). The culture of engineering: Woman, workplace and machine. *Women's Studies International Quarterly, 4*, 341–353.

Halford, S., & Savage, M. (1995). Restructuring organisations, changing people: Gender and restructuring in banking and local government. *Work, Employment & Society, 9*, 97–122.

Hearn, J., & Parkin, W. (1987). *'Sex' at 'work'*. Brighton: Harvester-Wheatsheaf.

Hochschild, A. (1983). *The managed heart*. Berkeley, CA: University of California Press.

Hochschild, A. (with A. Machung) (1989). *The second shift: Working parents and the revolution at home*. New York: Viking.

Hochschild, A. (1997). *The time bind: When work becomes home and home becomes work*. New York: Metropolitan Books.

Jenson, J. (1989). The talents of women, the skills of men: Flexible specialization and women. In S. Wood (Ed.), *The transformation of work?* London: Unwin Hyman.

Jones, C., & Causer, G. (1995). 'Men don't have families': Equality and motherhood in technical employment. *Gender, Work and Organization, 2*, 51–62.

Lipman-Blumen, J. (1976). Toward a homosocial theory of sex roles: An explanation of the sex segregation of social institutions. *Signs, 1,3*, part 2:15–31.

Kanter, R. M. (1975). Women and the structure of organizations: Explorations in theory and behavior. In M. Millman & R. M. Kanter (Eds.), *Another voice*. Garden City, NY: Anchor Books.

Kanter, R. M. (1977), *Men and women of the corporation*. New York: Basic Books.

Kerfoot, D., & Knights, D. 1996. 'The best is yet to come?': The quest for embodiment in managerial work. In D. L. Collinson & J. Hearn (Eds.), *Men as managers, managers as men*. London: Sage.

Kuiper, E., & Sap, J. (1995). *Out of the margin: feminist perspectives on economics*. London: Routledge.

Kvande, E. (1997). Doing masculinities in female dominated work organizations. Unpublished manuscript. University of Trondheim.

Kvande, E., & Rasmussen, B. (1994). Men in male-dominated organizations and their encounter with women intruders. *Scandinavian Journal of Management, 10*, 163–174.

MacKinnon, C. (1979). *Sexual harassment of working women*. New Haven, CT: Yale University Press.

Maile, S. (1995). The gendered nature of managerial discourse. *Gender, Work and Organization, 2*, 76–87.

Martin, P. Y. (1981). Women, labour markets and employing organizations: A critical analysis. In D. Dunkerley & G. Salaman (Eds.), *The International Yearbook of Organization Studies*. London: Routledge and Kegan Paul.

Martin, P. Y. (1996). Gendering and evaluating dynamics: Men, masculinities and managements. In D. L. Collinson & J. Hearn (Eds.), *Men as managers, managers as men*. London: Sage.

Messner, M. A. (1992). *Power at play: Sports and the problem of masclinity*. Boston: Beacon Press.

Mills, A. J., & Tancred, P. (1992). *Gendering organizational analysis*. Newbury Park, CA: Sage.

Mills, C. W. (1956). *White collar*. New York: Oxford University Press.

Morgan, D. H. J. (1992). *Discovering men*. London: Routledge.

Nelson, J. A. (1996). *Feminism, objectivity and economics*. London: Routledge.

Phillips, A., & Taylor, B. (1980). Sex and skill: Notes toward a feminist economics, *Feminist Review, 6*, 79–88.

Pierce, J. L. (1995). *Gender trials: Emotional lives in contemporary law firms*. Berkeley, CA: University of California Press.

Powell, G. N. (1988). *Women and men in management*. Newbury Park, CA: Sage.

Pringle, R. (1989). *Secretaries talk*. London: Verso.

Reskin, B. F., & Roos, P. A. (1990). *Job queues, gender queues*. Philadelphia: Temple University Press.

Rubin, J. (1997). Gender, equality and the culture of organizational assessment. *Gender, work and organization, 4*, 24–34.

Savage, M., & Witz, A. (1992). *Gender and bureaucracy*. Oxford: Blackwell.

Smith, D. (1987). *The everyday world as problematic*. Boston: Northeastern University Press.

Smith, V. (1990). *Managing in the corporate interest*. Berkeley, CA: University of California Press.

Smith, V. (1993). Flexibility in work and employment: The impact on women. *Research in the Sociology of Organizations, 11*, 195–216.

Stanko, E. A. (1985). *Intimate instrusions*. London: Routledge & Kegan Paul.

Steinberg, R. J. (1992). Gendered instructions: Cultural lag and gender bias in the Hay system of job evaluation. *Work and Occupations, 19*,4, 387–423.

Terborg, J. (1977). Women in management: A research review. *Journal of Applied Psychology, 62*, 647–64.

Thomas, A. M., & Kitzinger, C. (1994). 'It's just something that happens': The invisibility of sexual harassment in the workplace. *Gender, Work and Organization, 1*, 151–161.

West, C., & Fenstermaker, S. (1995). Doing difference. *Gender & Society, 9*, 8–37.

Willis, P. (1977). *Learning to labour*. Farnborough, England: Saxon House.

Witz, A., Halford, S., & Savage, M. (1996). Organized bodies: Gender, sexuality and embodiment in contemporary organizations. In L. Adkins & V. Merchant (Eds.), *Sexualizing the social: Power and the organization of sexuality*. London: Macmillan.

Woodall, J., Edwards, C., & Welchman, R. (1997). Organizational restructuring and the achievement of an equal opportunity culture. *Gender, Work and Organization, 4*, 2–12.

CHAPTER 10

The Study of Gender in Culture

Feminist Studies/Cultural Studies

Becca Cragin

Wendy Simonds

1. INTRODUCTION

In this chapter we seek to outline the general ways in which feminist work on gender and cultural studies have influenced each other, and how they might be brought together fruitfully within a sociological framework. These areas—gender studies, feminist studies, and cultural studies—are often contested and multiplicitous, and each is both disparaged and championed, both within and outside of academia. It would be impossible to represent fully the range of ideas about the overlap between these amorphous and broad categories, or to summarize adequately the extent of theoretical or empirical work done in any one of them. Our goal is to familiarize readers with some of the primary debates within cultural studies, in order to explain how the feminist study of gender has shaped, and in turn been shaped by them.

While critical of some of its excesses, we feel that cultural studies scholarship has a significant contribution to make to the study of gender within all branches of feminist studies, especially sociology. Feminists have always been contributors to cultural studies, although like most mainstream disciplines and leftist academic trends, cultural studies began with a typically masculinist bent. We need to make some artificial distinctions in order to distinguish some of the dominant trends of cultural studies to which feminists within that area have had to respond.

Becca Cragin • Institute for Women's Studies, Emory University, Atlanta, Georgia 30322
Wendy Simonds • Department of Sociology, Georgia State University, Atlanta, Georgia 30303

Handbook of the Sociology of Gender, edited by Janet Saltzman Chafetz. Kluwer Academic/ Plenum Publishers, New York, 1999.

What do feminist studies and cultural studies have in common? Within mainstream academia, especially sociology, both are considered trendy fringe areas, lacking methodological rigor. For those sociologists for whom sociology is or ought to be a science, these fields are dismissed for their subjectivity and overt politicization. Even more than feminism, cultural studies is seen as suspect, perhaps because of its presumed link with postmodern theory, which denies positivism and argues for a decentered relativism that many mainstream sociologists reject.

Indeed, the association of cultural studies with postmodern theory creates a clash between some feminist theorists and cultural studies scholars, because some feminist theorists decry postmodernism for its presumed denial of lived experience and the influence of broad societal structures (e.g., Bordo, 1990; Hartsock, 1990, 1996). Yet, feminist studies and cultural studies have much more in common than not, and each could benefit from knowledge of the other. Within both fields, the relationship with postmodernism and poststructuralism is deeply contested. Both are concerned with the negotiation of power, with agency and systems of social control. Both share a theoretical grounding that is at least vaguely Marxist; scholars in both fields tend to agree that various forms of social inequality should be researched, and that such research can lead to political change. It is this politicization that makes cultural studies so attractive for feminism.

2. DEFINING CULTURAL STUDIES

Cultural studies expands the notion of a proper area of cultural research and redefines the criteria for cultural evaluation. As Douglas Kellner writes:

> Cultural studies insists that culture must be studied within the social relations and systems through which culture is produced and consumed and that the study of culture is therefore intimately bound up with the study of society, politics and economies. . . . It also subverts distinctions between "high" and "low" culture by considering a wide continuum of cultural artifacts . . . and by refusing to erect any specific cultural hierarchies or canons [it] allows us to examine and critically scrutinize the whole range of culture without prior prejudices toward one or another sort of cultural text, institution or practice. It also opens the way toward more differentiated political, rather than aesthetic, valuations . . . in which one attempts to distinguish critical and oppositional from conformist and conservative moments in a cultural artifact. (1995, pp. 6–7)

Traditional aesthetic and sociological studies of culture have not always been fully adequate for the political project of feminism. Traditional aesthetic studies often fail to analyze cultural products within their social contexts, and they also often fail to recognize that aesthetic evaluations are always necessarily political. Traditional sociological studies of culture, on the other hand, tend to emphasize social context over content, by looking at culture only in structural or organizational terms. Cultural studies can provide the feminist study of gender with a framework for analyzing in detail the content of cultural production, while leaving it anchored to the social system from which it originates.

It is difficult to define cultural studies in absolute terms, because the determination of whether a work belongs within the field often depends upon whether someone says it does. Scholars conduct interdisciplinary work on "culture" under a variety of academic rubrics—Women's Studies, Media Studies, Ethnic Studies—yet there seems to be a lack of consensus about when this work constitutes "cultural studies." Lawrence Grossberg notes that publishers' financial considerations are sometimes the motivation for virtually any work that could be considered cultural studies being represented as such (1996b, p.

135). As is also the case with other relatively new fields, such as queer studies, cultural studies seems to represent a publishing phenomenon far more than an institutional development, as most scholars produce cultural studies work from within traditional disciplines (p. 135). Is cultural studies therefore simply whatever one says it is? Todd Gitlin (1997) adopts this very position:

> The interminable examination of what exactly constitutes cultural studies—or its subject, 'culture'—is itself part of the problem I seek to diagnose. Rather, I hope to slip (if not cut) the Gordian knot with the simple statement that cultural studies is the activity practiced by people who say they are doing cultural studies. (p. 25)

As Gitlin suggests, articulating a solid definition leads one into murky waters—just as feminist scholars do not share a unanimous view of what constitutes feminism.

Another method of defining cultural studies (in contrast with Gitlin's voluntaristic strategy) is an historical approach, in which only the scholarship that derives from the work of the Centre for Contemporary Cultural Studies (founded in the early 1960s in Birmingham, England) is considered bona fide "cultural studies." This sort of scholarship tends to focus on working-class subcultures, popular culture, and the media, from a variously defined Marxist framework. From our perspective, the voluntaristic membership approach is too ambiguous and the Birmingham-derivative criterion too rigid. We define cultural studies as work that shares the following characteristics: interdisciplinarity, particularity, textuality, and antipositivism.

2.1. Interdisciplinarity

Many academic "studies" programs (such as women's studies) are multidisciplinary, in the sense that scholars from different disciplines contribute to the field, yet often, at the level of individual projects, the work resides within only one discipline (Gordon, 1995, p. 364). Most cultural studies scholarship, by contrast, draws on the methods and insights of several disciplines simultaneously. The work begins with a social problem, and the method emanates from its particulars. At times the analysis might even be called adisciplinary, following a self-generated method that corresponds to no specific disciplinary vocabulary or debate. Indeed, many critique cultural studies scholars for their pastiche of methods, or their presumed ignorance of disciplinary accomplishments (Ferguson & Golding, 1997).

We believe that much can be gained from cultural studies' lack of proper disciplinarity. The freedom to operate outside disciplines may allow critics to study culture more creatively, by focusing on a subject as it presents itself socially, rather than separating out those aspects of the problem that correspond to disciplinary demands. As with feminist scholarship, we feel that the best cultural studies work is rigorously self-reflexive about the appropriateness of its method and resulting analysis.

2.2. Particularity

Most cultural studies scholarship is highly particular in its focus as well as its claims. Unlike other social analysts who attempt to uncover broad structural connections, cultural studies scholars often take as their subject the rich details and minute patterns of a social context, in "a microsociology of everyday life" (Inglis, 1993, p. 84). As a legacy of its origins in Marxist historical materialism, cultural studies is founded upon conjunctural analysis, an approach that is "embedded, descriptive, and historically and contextually specific" (Grossberg, Nelson, & Treichler, 1992, p. 8).

2.3. Textuality

A closely related characteristic is the attention in cultural studies to texts. Reflecting the enormous influence in the past few decades of structuralism throughout the humanities, the dissemination of semiotics and discourse theory led to the expansion of the term "text" to include a wide variety of literary and visual representations. A textual analysis shifts the question from "What?" to "How?" through an examination of the grammar of a given representation. A central tenet of cultural studies, like many other fields that have been influenced by postmodernism and poststructuralism, is that subjects cannot be studied without considering the meaning-making (signification) process through which they are constituted and interpreted.

Cultural studies takes this tenet one step further, however, by expanding the notion of the means by which a grammar or language can be represented, including even behaviors and events as kinds of texts that can be read for their social (grammatical) meaning. Parallel to the movements within anthropology and sociology that utilize ethnographic methods of "thick description" to capture particular instances of "local knowledge" or ethnomethodological quests for "common-sense knowledge" (Clifford & Marcus, 1986; Garfinkel, 1967; Geertz, 1973; West & Zimmerman, 1987), cultural studies scholars analyze texts as social artifacts and social events as texts. Perhaps owing to the openness of the term "culture"—which can mean ideas, practices, or products—cultural studies scholars examine a wide range of seemingly disparate texts, such as the logic of a football game, the self-fashioning of young Madonna fans, or the semiotics of suntan lotion advertising (Bourdieu, 1993; Lewis, 1990; Williamson, 1986b).

2.4. Antipositivism

Cultural studies is largely based on a hermeneutic rather than a positivist mode of analysis. Rather than claiming to reveal the universal meaning of interactions, cultural studies scholars interpret the processes through which people create culture, and culture creates meaning, and hence, identity. In this way, cultural studies can be seen as rooted in symbolic interactionism (Blumer, 1969; Goffman 1959, 1961, 1971; Mead, 1934). Because the work tends to focus more frequently on the content of a cultural discourse than on the political economy and effects of its circulation, cultural studies scholarship is not always immediately and directly useful to those looking for cause and effect analyses, or for a means of changing society.

3. THE MISOGYNY OF REPRESENTATION

From its beginning as an academic practice in the 1960s, cultural studies has proven itself highly amenable to the feminist study of gender, owing to its leftist orientation and focus on culture as a significant arena of ideological struggle. One of the earliest projects of second wave feminism of the 1970s was the analysis of the myriad ways in which patriarchy is embedded in ordinary culture. As Meaghan Morris describes it, feminism is "a movement of discontent with 'the everyday'" (1988c, p. 197). This engagement with the politics of daily life is exemplified by the classic feminist slogan, "The personal is political." The expression suggests not only that women's individual problems are often symptoms of broader social inequality, but also that the most mundane and normalized aspects of personal/cultural life perpetuate this inequality.

Both activist and academic feminists analyzed the breadth and depth of gender inequality throughout culture, in the tyranny of "common-sense" ideas about gender and in the representation of those ideas. Across a wide array of cultural genres, feminists began the initial task of naming their oppression by highlighting the ways in which everyday culture worked against women's best interests. This early work emphasizes uncovering the misogyny within representation. While some of the first studies focus on literature and art (Millett, 1970; Nochlin, 1971), much of it analyzes the mass media.

Many feminists believe that one of the primary causes of gender-based inequality is the misrepresentation of women in media images. In the early 1970s, radical feminists staged protests against the direct sources of that imagery, from *Ladies Home Journal* to the Miss America pageant (Echols, 1989, pp. 92–96, 195–197). One of the earliest radical feminist anthologies, *Sisterhood is Powerful* (Morgan, 1970), contained attacks on a variety of media, from news broadcasts to deodorant commercials. The activism and advocacy of liberal feminists reflect a similar concern with media images, as exemplified by Betty Friedan's discussion of women's magazines in *The Feminine Mystique* (1963).

Radical and liberal feminists shared a set of assumptions about the media that shaped the direction of their analyses. In most cases, feminist critics presumed that the media not only reflect social values but also play a major role in their dissemination. Based on traditional sociological media studies that use the "hypodermic," or two-step flow models of media effects (Adorno, 1991; Adorno & Horkheimer, 1944; Katz & Lazarsfeld, 1955), most of the early studies take for granted the notion that the media have a one-directional influence on viewers. These feminist critics also assumed that the media could and should reflect reality, rather than reify harmful stereotypes. This emphasis on stereotypes is central to the dominant, "images of women" approach. Drawing on the content analysis research of the Cultural Indicators Project of the Annenberg School, feminists counted and catalogued media images. Feminist cultural critics concluded that women were both negatively represented (often this meant sexually, or in traditional, nonprofessional roles such as housewives) and substantially underrepresented. Gaye Tuchman went so far as to name this lack of representation "The Symbolic Annihilation of Women" (1978).

Feminist critics believed that improved and increased media representation of women would lead to social change (Walters, 1995, p. 36). The images-of-women approach developed according to the disciplinary demands of traditional communications research, but it met the needs of the developing political movement as well. By documenting the sexism in media images, feminists could do their own consciousness-raising, raise the larger culture's awareness of inequality, and pressure the media to change (Walters, p. 37). This was an important step, because the idea that sexism was rampant in popular culture—and even that sexism was wrong—was still a position that had to be argued. However, despite the early consensus that cultural studies were legitimate and vital projects for feminism, disagreements quickly surfaced about the proper direction for analysis to take.

4. POSTSTRUCTURAL FEMINIST ANALYSES

It was not long after the images-of-women research began to be disseminated that criticisms of this approach surfaced. Film studies was already well into the process of transforming itself from an aesthetic discipline concerned with issues of form and auteurism to a highly politicized bastion of psychoanalysis and semiotics. For many feminist film scholars, cataloging images of women proved an unsatisfactory strategy for examining misogyny, because it failed to examine the very deep structures embedded in the process of visual signification. By focusing simply on the basic outline of an image (whether or not it is female, whether or not the female is nontraditional, etc.), scholars using the images-of-women approach seemed to be missing the deeper significance of how images operate.

Critics of the images-of-women approach wanted to move away from the question of how well women were represented because they felt that what constitutes a "positive" or "negative" image was never self evident, and that images could never transparently reflect reality. Instead of assuming they knew the reality of what women were and could judge the accuracy of their representation, these feminists began to evaluate the construction and circulation of "Woman" through the processes of signification. Drawing on the poststructuralist methods of what came to be known as "Screen Theory" (because of its association with the film journal *Screen*), critics of the images-of-women approach suggested a theoretical concept to explain the status of women's representation under patriarchy: the male gaze. The feminist version of Screen Theory was expressed most succinctly and famously in Laura Mulvey's "Visual Pleasure and Narrative Cinema" (1975). This article provides a poststructuralist reading of the psychological processes that take place in "the classic realist text," in this case the mainstream Hollywood drama. Mulvey presented the provocative thesis that all film viewing is male, in the sense that the classic realist film text evokes a psychological response in viewers that is structured around a patriarchal male psyche.

To understand how Mulvey came to this conclusion, one must trace the development of feminist film theory from structuralism and psychoanalysis. Following the work of linguist Ferdinand de Saussure (1966), structuralism analyzes culture by determining the grammar of a given text. Structuralism asserts that, "Rather than reflecting an already existing reality, the function of language is to organise and construct our access to reality" (Storey, 1993, p. 55). Therefore, a structuralist study of culture would be inextricable from a study of its grammar, both linguistic and logical. Structuralism posits grammar as engaging in a series of binary oppositions, such as nature/culture, male/female, etc., out of which meaning is constructed. According to the structuralist view, meaning is always relational and contextual, and yet structuralist readings tend to be very absolute, presuming that there is one, fixed meaning of a text which can be perfectly outlined by the critic (Seiter, 1992, p. 63).

Poststructuralism, on the other hand, focuses not on the certainty and fixity of meaning but on its fluidity, ruptures, and excesses. In combining structuralism and psychoanalysis, the work of Jacques Lacan (1977a, 1977b) has been particularly important for film studies. Lacan reinterprets Freud's stages of psychological development in linguistic terms, explaining how identity formation itself is a product and process of language. For example, Lacan links the Oedipal phase of psychological development (in which the child learns to differentiate itself from the mother) to the acquisition of language (I am me, not you). In the pre-Oedipal phase, the child has no clear sense of where her own boundaries end and her mother's begin. The loss of that close bond with the original source of pleasure represents a profound lack, which is also reflected in the assumption of language (since saying one thing always involves repressing some aspect of its opposite). From this perspective, identity is a necessary fiction, a narrative position that is continually asserted to establish an ever-fragile, fictive whole. Yet the lack (the loss of the mother, the subconscious elided in the assertion of ego, the inability of language to translate a reality) is always present.

According to Lacan, the cores of our identities are not individual, private essences but social, linguistic structures. Just as structuralists described the construction of culture according to linguistic logic, poststructuralists describe the construction of self according to that same cultural logic. Because they believe that the very contours of our psyches are embedded within language, which is embedded within culture, poststructuralist critics trace the connections between psychological, textual, and cultural structures. It is within this theoretical framework that Mulvey could claim that "the gaze is male." Mulvey believes that the cinema is structured around men's psychological needs (owing to the male domination of the film industry), in a way that is harmful to women. Building on the Lacanian idea that cultural formations reflect and answer psychological formations, Mulvey states that all viewing positions have been masculinized, so that anyone viewing a film becomes caught up in "the male gaze." This masculinization occurs through film's invocation of two distinct types of visual pleasure: scopophilia and fetishism.

Scopophilia, or voyeurism, is enhanced by the nature of the viewing experience. The brightness of the screen and the darkness of the theater position the spectator as if he is spying on the characters. In this analysis, the ability to look is associated with cultural power, and the fact that the film's characters do not know they are being watched (since they almost never address the camera directly) enhances the spectatorial sense of power. Films also offer the pleasure of fetishism, the spectator's enchantment with the focus on women's bodies. Women's bodies serve in the film as sexual objects, there to receive the gaze of the camera, the male characters, and the spectator.

Mulvey sees these pleasures as distinctly related to the needs of the male psyche. The gaze of the camera addresses a male viewer, as the film is created for and from his point of view. In Western culture, according to Mulvey and sociologist John Berger (1972), the act of looking conveys and consolidates male power. Men are defined as men by their ability to look at women, and women, in turn, are defined as subordinates in part by their inability to look, their objectification. Since fetishization and voyeurism serve primarily as mechanisms for assuaging castration anxiety, the spectator the film constructs is presumed to be male. Whether through the voyeurism of film noir's investigation of female sexuality, or through the fetishism of the display of women's bodies as spectacle, in the psychology of film Woman can only represent lack.

Men, of course, also experience this lack (the inadequacies of language and loss of the mother mentioned earlier), but they project it onto women, who come to represent both the loss of the phallus (castration) as well as the phallus itself (fetishization). All that film offers to women, according to Mulvey, is the masochism of accepting the male gaze (by identifying with the female characters). The men in the film, the men behind the camera, and the men in the audience embody looking, and demonstrate the male gaze, while the women in the film, and in the audience, simply embody "to-be-looked-at-ness" (p. 19).

This understanding of the gendered nature of film pleasure has been highly useful for feminists. Mulvey's use of psychoanalysis helps explain not only why cinema is so compelling, but more importantly, why men objectify women (Smelik, 1995, p. 69). Rather than viewing women as a natural group that is inaccurately represented in film, poststructuralist feminists see women as a group that is constituted and defined by representation. Poststructuralist feminists conceive of womanhood not as biological difference from men but as a psychological effect of male domination. Drawing on the psychoanalytic analysis found in Teresa de Lauretis's *Alice Doesn't: Feminism, Semiotics, Cinema* (1984), Ann Smelik explains why signification is so important for an understanding of women's subordination:

> Telling stories is one of the ways of reproducing subjectivity in any given culture. Each story derives its structure from the subject's desire ("the hero"). Narrative structures are defined by an Oedipal desire: the desire to know origin and end. Sexual desire is intimately bound up with the desire for knowledge, that is, the quest for truth. The desire to solve riddles is a male desire *par excellence*, because the female subject is herself the riddle. "Woman" is the question ("what does woman want?") and can hence not ask the question nor make her desire intelligible (1995, pp. 73–74).

The problem for women is not just that men objectify women and that this objectification is then represented in cultural texts, but also that the psychological imperatives that initially give rise to these texts are solidified and then replicated by them. Our deepest subconscious desires become structured in patriarchal ways, so that what we want and who we understand ourselves to be, as men and women, are shaped in ways that are extremely harmful to women.

Psychoanalytic, poststructuralist criticism dominated feminist film studies of the 1970s and much of the 1980s. It provided a vocabulary feminists could use to explore the psychological structures through which cultural texts and misogyny operate, and it paid more attention to the detail of texts than the images-of-women approach. From the beginning of feminist media studies, feminists were deeply divided over not just how they would study images of women, but also what "images" and "women" were, and what the purpose of feminist cultural criticism should be. Caught between positivist social science and structuralism, Screen theory and the images-of-women approach were irreconcilable strategies for the study of gender, and the debates across the divide were strenuous.

5. THE BIRMINGHAM SCHOOL

Within cultural studies, divisive debates surrounding gender and structuralism[1] were taking place as well. As feminists became involved in cultural studies, they brought with them a strong commitment to study women's experiences. For example, in the early 1970s feminists affiliated with the Birmingham Centre for Contemporary Cultural Studies (CCCS), such as Angela McRobbie, Charlotte Brunsdon, Rosalind Coward, and Dorothy Hobson, insisted that the Center scholars make gender an integral part of their analyses (see Brunsdon, 1996). This push was so emphatic and transformative that Hall labels it an "interruption" in which feminists literally "broke into cultural studies" (1992, pp. 282–283). This desire to document the previously ignored or devalued realm of women's cultural experience, as well as the perceived excesses of the Mulvian "male gaze," had

---

[1] Owing to space limitations, we have omitted discussion of the shift within British cultural studies of the 1970s from culturalism to poststructuralism. Just as within feminist film studies there was a move from studying women as a social group to studying the representation of women, within cultural studies there was a shift from studying subcultures as communities to studying semiotic practices within subcultures. For information on this topic, see Hall (1980a), Grossberg, (1996a), and Sparks (1996).

important consequences for feminist cultural studies scholars. A new branch of feminist cultural studies formed, in rebellion against the idea that women are not actively involved in cultural reception.

Until this point, the field had been dominated by studies of male subcultures. The exclusion of women was due, in part, to a certain ambivalence toward femininity that has surfaced repeatedly throughout the history of cultural studies, as popular culture itself has been envisioned as "feminine" (Joyrich, 1996, p. 30; Modleski, 1986). The dearth of studies on girls and women could also be explained by the Marxist legacy of cultural studies. Scholars made class central (to the exclusion of other variables such as race, gender, and sexual identity), and focused on "public modes of resistance," which typically involve male actors (Joyrich, 1996, p. 13). Women and girls have long been seen by social science researchers as inheriting class from men (fathers or husbands). For the most part, men doing Marxist cultural studies view men as purely classed and ungendered, and women as indirectly classed and tainted by gender. In addition to ignoring women's subculture, McRobbie notes that male scholars often interpret the subcultures they did study in ways that were troublesome. Lacking any kind of analysis of gender inequality, and overidentifying with their subjects, they often valorize rather than critique the oppressive aspects of masculinity (such as alcohol abuse and violence) (1981, p. 114). In a criticism of the work of Dick Hebdige and Paul Willis, McRobbie offers the reminder that male subcultures which oppress women cannot accurately be called resistant of the values of the dominant culture.

6. AUDIENCE STUDIES

In the 1980s, feminist audience studies developed within and parallel to a growing trend among cultural studies scholars to examine the reception of culture. Cultural studies as a whole moved away from the strict interpretations of meaning required by structuralism toward a more fluid understanding of the impact of ideology on culture. Two crucial concepts underpinning this theoretical shift are Antonio Gramsci's "hegemony" and Ernesto Laclau's "articulation." Gramsci's (1971) concept of hegemony explains why the masses (workers) do not rise up and challenge their economic exploitation. This approach states that elite classes rule not by imposing ideology on the masses, but by wooing them. As the working classes come to accept cultural messages which are framed according to the interests of their oppressors, they are less likely to rebel. The theory of hegemony also entails moving away from the Marxist notion of base/superstructure, as not all aspects of a culture perfectly reflect the needs of the economic structure from which they emanate. Some ideas oppose structure, and some ideas don't do anything, at least not in the service of capitalism. Culture is fluid, contradictory, and a site for struggle.

Laclau (1977) develops the concept of articulation, initially presented by Gramsci and Althusser, to explain both how cultural and economic formations are relatively autonomous, and how elites use culture to maintain their hegemony. Laclau's concept of articulation depicts ideology not as a misrepresentation of reality, but rather as a link between people's experience of reality and their interpretation of it. The ruling classes win hegemony not by imposing a single worldview, but by articulating a relationship between socioeconomic conditions and ruling-class philosophy. In essence, elites define what the "problem" of society currently is, in a way that smoothes over contradictions and appeals to working class "common sense" (Slack, 1996, p. 121). This theory relates cultural values to political–economic structures, but not in a predetermined way. Ideology and experience are constantly in contradiction—both internally and with each other. They must be continually rearticulated for the ruling classes to dominate (Hall, 1996, p. 43–44).

Cultural studies scholars draw on Gramsci and Laclau to argue that cultural meaning is not a static "given" embedded in economic structures or in texts, but a process. They study how people use texts, arguing that the act of reception produces meaning. In an important early audience study, David Morley (1980) attempts to test Hall's "encoding/decoding" model of media reception on television viewers. Based on a model of articulation (Slack, 1996, p. 123–124), Hall argues that meaning resides in the production, distribution, and reception of texts (1980b). Morley's audience study was built on a previous textual analysis (Brunsdon & Morley, 1978) of the British newsmagazine program *Nationwide,* which showed how hegemonic or preferred readings were encoded in the show through its use of "the everyday" and common sense to support the dominant ideology. Morley was less successful in his own study at analyzing the decoding of the text, however. As he frankly admits, viewers' interpretations of the show did not always correspond as strongly to their class positions as he had predicted they would. In fact, he finds that viewers shifted many times between "preferred," "negotiated," and "resistant" readings, often transgressing supposed class boundaries. Morley concluded that a more detailed model of decoding was necessary to explain the viewing process, and that variables such as race and gender needed to be taken more fully into account; someone who is socially subordinate in one regard (e.g., in terms of his or her class position), and therefore somewhat more likely to express a resistant or counterhegemonic reading, may in other regards be socially dominant (by virtue of race or gender) (1992, p. 135).

While his *Nationwide* study was less conclusive than Morley had initially hoped, it nonetheless signals a fundamental shift away from structuralism into a more fluid and reader-based understanding of culture. Instead of searching for the meaning of the text, cultural studies scholars queried: What do audiences do with texts? How does reception matter in terms of culture at large? A series of related debates were taking place at the same time within feminism, focused on women viewers/cultural consumers. In response to what many perceived as the rigidity and essentialism of gaze theory, which left no conceptual space for any consideration of what a female gaze might look like, some feminists abandoned the quest to extricate or explicate the Woman trapped in the Text, to study actual women viewers/readers/interpreters of culture.

Janice Radway's *Reading the Romance: Women, Patriarchy, and Popular Literature* (1984) is perhaps the most influential feminist study of reception of the 1980s. Based on her observations of interactions among a community of romance novel readers, in addition to her analysis of the novels themselves, Radway concludes that what the women gain from the novels is fairly complex. On the one hand, the content is frequently misogynist, reaffirming conventional gender relations and encouraging women to interpret men's callousness, and even violence, as desperate cries for yet more patience and love. On the other hand, the act of reading itself functions as more than regressive escape. It ultimately serves as a protest against the gender inequities readers face in their daily lives, because they commit time and resources to nurturing themselves instead of catering only to the needs of their families. While Radway acknowledges that their reading did not lead the women to engage in active collective resistance to their oppression, it does represent a recognition, however unconscious, that they deserve more attention and respect from men. Studying their use of romance novels led Radway to quite different conclusions than she might have drawn had she only given her own readings of the texts.

Radway's ambivalent interpretation of the ultimate political meaning of romance reading for women reflected a growing tension among feminist cultural scholars (and among cultural studies scholars in general). Once they began studying audiences, they witnessed a great deal of viewing pleasure generated from the reception of politically regressive texts. How, then, should one interpret this phenomenon? What were the politics of pleasure? Reception studies reignited or reframed a feminist debate regarding pornography that had been circulating for some time, about the twin poles of pleasure and danger (Snitow, Stansell, & Thompson, 1983; Vance, 1984). As postmodernism swept over the Academy and postfeminism flooded the airwaves, feminist ethnographers began asking themselves how they should interpret the guilty pleasures of mass cultural consumption.

7. POSTMODERNISM, PLEASURE, AND RESISTANCE

Just as there were deep anxieties in political movements of the 1980s about the meaning of postfeminism and post-Marxism, in the academy postmodernism was a phenomenon that had to be responded to in some fashion. Whether it was an historical condition, an architectural style, or a media creation depended upon one's point of view; nevertheless, many academic disciplines were grappling (and still grapple) with the same questions about the usefulness or threat of postmodern theory. Within cultural studies, scholars disagree about the implications of postmodernism for their interpretations of culture, Postmodern theory exacerbates a tension that had long existed between critics who expressed varying degrees of pessimism about capitalist culture. Some scholars, such as Frederic Jameson (1984), bitterly critique postmodernism as a decadent development of late capitalism, in which most aspects of life have become hopelessly commodified. Most scholars writing about postmodernism, however, tend to be, if not celebratory, then at least markedly neutral about the subject.

The most significant aspects of a postmodern era, according to postmodern theorists, relate to the overwhelming presence of media in daily life, the breakdown of Enlightenment rationality, and the focus on particularity. Jean-François Lyotard heralds the death of the metanarrative, the end of any pretensions of universalism (1984). Baudrillard contributes the idea of the simulacra, the notion that all culture now simply recirculates existing ideas: with originality defunct, everything is simply simulation (1983). Michel Foucault incorporates his concept of power/knowledge into the term "discourse," expanding on the interrelationship between materiality and language, and proposing a more diffuse model of power than the traditional Marxist notion of bourgeois domination of the masses (1990). All of these theoretical developments fueled a growing tendency among cultural studies scholars in the 1980s to focus on the aesthetics of style over the politicized interpretation of ideology, and on the fluid nature of power and meaning. It became difficult for scholars to continue to produce macrolevel, political analyses at all, for fear of erecting their own metanarratives.

Some critics note that cultural studies does in fact have much in common with postmodernism (Chen, 1996; Hebdige, 1996). For example, Laclau's theory of articulation, and his later work with Chantal Mouffe deconstructing the stability/notion of class (1985), while originally linking materiality and textuality, paves the way for cultural critics who believe there is little if any relationship between the structure of texts and the structure of society (Slack, 1996, p. 121; Sparks, 1996, p. 89).

While some feminists speak out about what they see as the excesses of postmodern theory (Bordo, 1990; Hartsock, 1990, 1996), others welcome the new kinds of analyses that postmodernism offers (Barrett & Phillips, 1992; Butler, 1990; Flax, 1990). Feminism had already been moving in the direction of breaking down grand narratives of identity (such as the notion that women constitute a natural group whose members share similar interests) to focus on the specificity of race, class, and sexual identity.[2] For some feminists, then, postmodernism's emphasis on fragmentation and social construction allows a way to theorize this specificity without reifying differences of identity into naturalized categories.

Perhaps because Mulvey's notion of the gaze completely dismissed the possibility of women's pleasure, many among the next generation of feminist scholars responded by searching out pleasure. One of the most common textual strategies is reading against the grain, in which critics search for moments of excess and contradiction within traditional texts, such as melodramatic films and those by Hitchcock (Byars, 1991; Modleski, 1988). This approach represents quite a departure from Mulvey's assumption that only experimental feminist films that radically broke with film conventions could be nonoppressive. From this perspective, even mainstream, sexist films contain the seeds of their own undoing or deconstruction.

Just as Radway found that reading romance novels was not a masochistic activity for women, however misogynist the texts might be, other feminist ethnographers also discovered that the relationship between texts and viewers' values was complex. For example, Ien Ang (1985) has written about Dutch fans of *Dallas,* and the uses they made of this 1980s American nighttime soap opera. Ang analyzes letters viewers wrote to her in response to a newspaper ad she placed. She identifies three groups of viewers, all of whom have differing relationships to the "ideology of mass culture," the value system that dismisses shows such as *Dallas* as trash. *Dallas*-lovers, *Dallas*-haters, and ironists (those who liked mocking it) all express some form of negativity toward the show, yet all of them enjoy watching it.

Ang gives a very nuanced reading of the ways in which ideology (viewers' negativity toward popular culture) can operate independently from behavior (their viewing of it), as well as the possibility that pleasure can operate relatively independently of polities. Cora Kaplan (1986) explores the pleasure of watching a miniseries such as *The Thornbirds,* where the breaking of taboos and transgression of "reality" allows women viewers to experience temporary freedom from oppressive social norms. Viewers can enjoy texts without necessarily subscribing to their implicit values, because of the roles that irony and fantasy play in our reception and enjoyment of texts.

Dorothy Hobson's influential study of the producers and viewers of the British soap opera, *Crossroads* (1982), deals with another aspect of women's viewing pleasure for which they are often disparaged—their supposed confusion of soap opera characters with real people. Rather than reflecting an inability to distinguish reality from fantasy, she argues that viewers' interest in the characters reflects an intentional suspension of reality in order to engage with the text on the level of fantasy. The identification with the soap opera fantasy is not an all-or-nothing process, where one either believes (correctly) that the stories are fabrications, or believes (quite naively) that they are real. The viewers are well aware that they are not watching a documentary, yet soap operas can still engage

[2] Some feminist scholars have argued that feminist studies are postmodern studies, and that postmoderism has appropriated much feminist work without acknowledging this debt (Morris, 1988b; Skeggs, 1995, p. 193).

their interest and even their emotions. The emotions they express are not in response to the made-up situations in the characters' lives, but to situations in the viewers' own lives that soap operas evoke.

This insight is an important corrective, not only to the idea that soap opera viewers (or female viewers in general) lack intelligence and judgment, but also to the idea that audiences passively receive the "message" of a text. In talking with viewers of *Personal Best* and *The Color Purple,* Elizabeth Ellsworth (1986) and Jacqueline Bobo (1988), respectively, observe that viewers actively and idealistically revise the films to create for themselves pleasurable viewing.

Both authors draw a connection between this revision and the viewers' marginal status in mainstream U.S. culture as African-American and lesbian women. Viewers ignore those aspects of the film which they feel are racist and homophobic, and in the case of the *Personal Best* viewers, even rewrite (that is, read against the grain) the plots to create a more satisfying ending. Marginalized both as members of society and as film viewers (since they rarely see gratifying representations of themselves in film), they create for themselves the kinds of films they want to see. Recent scholarship on fan clubs explores the extent to which viewers take an active role in cultural consumption, forming fan communities as well as creating their own texts (Lewis, 1990; Penley, 1992).

Many feminist cultural studies scholars are relieved to have more theoretical space in which to consider the effects of cultural texts, instead of having the answer preordained by theoretical or political commitments. Some of the same feminists who focus on the pleasures of reception are also some of the strongest critics of work that is perceived as too uncritical or too optimistic about the joys of viewing (Joyrich, 1996; Modleski, 1991; Morris, 1988a; Williamson, 1986a). While still divided about the extent to which viewers can resist ideology, or the extent to which our pleasure is implicated by our politics, most feminist cultural critics nevertheless know that there is always, for women, some danger mixed with the pleasure. In the late 1980s a whole host of reception-oriented studies emerged, focusing on historical and cultural context, and "women's genres," such as soap operas, melodramas, and self-help books (Brown, 1990; Byars, 1991; Gamman & Marshment, 1988; Gledhill, 1987; Press, 1991; Pribram, 1988; Simonds, 1992, 1996; Spigel, 1992; Spigel, & Mann, 1992; Stacey, 1994).

8. CULTURAL STUDIES, FEMINIST STUDIES, AND SOCIOLOGY

One of the main contributions feminism has made to the study of culture has been the understanding that *everything* is gendered; gender is not merely one layer of meaning, but is central to the construction and organization of all meaning. Rather than simply adding women to studies of culture, feminists consider the ways in which culture is fundamentally gendered.

Empirical cultural studies have much in common, methodologically, with feminist studies. Traditional sociological method presumes a distanced observer, and casts research participants ("subjects") as untrustworthy obstacles in the quest for truth. Feminist scholars ask: Can we forge nonexploitive relationships with those we study? What do we do with the interpretations of their own lives that people offer us? How might we craft the research process to preserve the integrity of what people tell us? What do we do about the Marxist notion of false consciousness, which resonates (ironically) with the conventional sociological researcher's view of subjects? (See Acker, Barry, & Esseveld, 1996;

Fonow & Cook, 1991; Gorelick, 1996; Harding & Hintikka, 1983; Krieger, 1991; Oakley, 1981; Reinharz, 1992; Roberts, 1981; Smith, 1996; Stacey, 1988). Many feminist scholars draw on notions of grounded theory and the social construction of knowledge (Berger & Luckmann, 1966; Glaser & Strauss, 1973) to justify flexible research agendas and personalized relationships with those we research. Feminist scholars, like cultural studies scholars, are concerned with negotiating the nuanced interstices of complicity and resistance. Similarly, feminist scholars ruminate upon ways to link theory and practice, and to make accounts of both less exclusionary to nonacademics (see, e.g., essays in Gottfried, 1996). These quests are quintessentially sociological.

Cultural studies are, in fact, enmeshed in sociology, a polyglot descendant of Marxism, Weberian theory, the Frankfurt school, symbolic interaction, ethnomethodology, communications research, and critical media studies. From conceptualizations of art as cultural production (Becker, 1982; Griswold, 1986; Wolff, 1981) to examinations of the social construction of identity (Blumer, 1969; Goffman, 1959, 1961; Grodin & Lindlof, 1996), from macro-level theory about base and superstructure (Williams, 1958) to micro-level deconstruction of individual and group behavior (Garfinkel, 1967) to conversation analysis (Fisher, 1993; Mishler, 1986; Moerman, 1988; Riessman, 1990)—cultural studies may be seen as having sociological roots that run deep.

Cultural studies, like feminist gender studies, may also be seen as contesting mainstream or positivistic sociology, from rational choice theory (which posits that individuals utilize cost–benefit analyses in all decision-making) to uses and gratifications research (which seeks to articulate media effects on users). Sonia Livingstone suggests that the quantitative/qualitative split within sociological media studies may be overcome now that cultural studies scholars (or critical media studies) have refocused on reception, and now that positivists—former uses-and-gratifications proponents—have begun to reconsider cause–effect claims (1990). Drawing on Katz (1980), she describes media studies as having always "oscillat[ed] between conceptions of powerful media and powerful viewers" (p. 8). However, the way the media operate cannot be reduced to this simple dichotomy. Agency and social control, political economy, and textual detail all are important, and all must be taken into account. Wendy Griswold's concept of the cultural diamond provides a clear model for thinking about culture. At its corners are the four elements necessary for a complete understanding of culture: social world, creator, receiver, and cultural object, with each corner connected to each of the others (1987, p. 1994).

In our view, the most useful cultural studies scholarship socially grounds cultural phenomena, and draws on a variety of critical approaches, from historiography to psychoanalysis to ethnography, integrating many variables—from race, class, and gender to nationality, age, and sexual identity. While the rigor, interdisciplinarity, and high quality of much feminist cultural studies work is inspiring, it raises the question of how well we mere mortals can juggle so many scholarly demands. While this kind of grounded work is difficult to do, however, it is vital, in order for our analyses to be productive interrogations of the politics of daily life, rather than merely entertaining readings of "resistance."

REFERENCES

Acker, J., Barry, K., & Esseveld, J. (1996). Objectivity and truth: Problems in doing feminist research. In H. Gottfried (Ed.), *Feminism and social change: Bridging theory and practice.* Urbana, IL: University of Illinois Press.
Adorno, T. (1991). *The culture industry: Selected essays on mass culture.* New York: Routledge.
Adorno, T., & Horkheimer, M. (1944). *The dialectic of enlightenment.* New York: Continuum.

Ang, I. (1985). *Watching Dallas: Soap opera and the melodramatic imagination.* London: Metheun.

Barrett, M., & Phillips, A. (Eds.) (1992). *Destabilizing theory: Contemporary feminist debates.* Stanford: Stanford University Press.

Baudrillard, J. (1983). *Simulations.* New York: Semiotext(e).

Becker, H. S. (1982). *Art worlds.* Berkeley, CA: University of California Press.

Berger, J. (1972). *Ways of seeing.* New York: Penguin.

Berger, P., & Luckmann, T. (1966). *The social construction of reality: A treatise in the sociology of knowledge.* Garden City, NY: Doubleday.

Blumer, H. (1969). *Symbolic interactionism.* Englewood Cliffs, NJ: Prentice-Hall.

Bobo, J. (1988). *The Color Purple*: Black women as cultural readers. In E. D. Pribram (Ed.), *Female spectators: Looking at film and television.* New York: Verso.

Bordo, S. (1990). Feminism, postmodernism, and gender-scepticism. In L. Nicholson (Ed.), *Feminism/ Postmodernism.* New York: Routledge.

Bourdieu. P. (1993). How can one be a sports fan? In S. During (Ed.), *The Cultural Studies Reader.* New York: Routledge.

Brown, M. E. (Ed.) (1990), *Television and women's culture: The politics of the popular.* London: Sage.

Brunsdon, C. (1996). A thief in the night: Stories of feminism in the 1970s at CCCS. In D. Morley & K. Chen (Eds.) *Stuart Hall: Critical dialogues in cultural studies.* New York: Routledge.

Brunsdon, C., & Morley, D. (1978). *Everyday television: Nationwide.* London: British Film Institute.

Butler, J. (1990). Gender trouble: Feminist theory, and psychoanalytic discourse. In L. Nicholson (Ed.), *Feminism/ Postmodernism.* New York: Routledge.

Byars, J. (1991). *All that Hollywood allows: Re-reading gender in 1950s melodrama.* Chapell Hill: University of North Carolina Press.

Chen, R. (1996). Post-Marxism: Between/beyond critical postmodernism and cultural studies. In D. Morley & K. Chen. (Eds.), *Stuart Hall: Critical dialogues in cultural studies.* New York: Routledge.

Clifford, J., & Marcus, G. (Eds.) (1986). *Writing culture: The poetics and politics of ethnography.* Berkeley, CA: University of California Press.

Echols, A. (1989). *Daring to be bad: Radical feminism in America, 1967–1975.* Minneapolis: University of Minnesota Press.

Ellsworth, E. (1986). Illicit pleasures: Feminist spectators and *Personal Best. Wide Angle, 8,* 2.

Ferguson, M., & Golding, P. (Eds.) (1997). *Cultural studies in question.* Thousand Oaks, CA: Sage.

Fisher, S. (1993). Gender, power, resistance: Is care the remedy? In S. Fisher & K. Davis (Eds.), *Negotiating at the margins: The gendered discourses of power and resistance.* New Brunswick, NJ: Rutgers University Press.

Flax, J. (1990). Postmoderism and gender relations in feminist theory. In L. Nicholson (Ed.), *Feminism/ postmodernism.* New York: Routledge.

Fonow, M. M., & Cook, J. A. (Eds.) (1991). *Beyond methodology: Feminist scholarship as lived research.* Bloomington: University of Indiana Press.

Foucault, M. (1990). *The history of Sexuality, Vol. I.* New York: Vintage.

Friedan, B. (1963). *The feminine mystique.* New York: Dell.

Gamman, L., & Marshment, M. (Eds.) (1988) *The female gaze: Women as viewers of popular culture.* London: Women's Press.

Garfinkel, H. (1967). *Studies in ethnomethodology.* Englewood Cliffs, NJ: Prentice-Hall.

Geertz, C. (1973). *The interpretation of cultures.* New York: Basic Books.

Gitlin, T. (1997). The anti-political populism of cultural studies, In M. Ferguson & P. Golding (Eds.), *Cultural studies in question.* Thousand Oaks, CA: Sage.

Glaser, B, G., & Strauss, A. (1973). *The discovery of grounded theory: Strategies for qualitative research.* Chicago: Aldine.

Gledhill, C. (Ed.) (1987). *Home is where the heart is: Studies in melodrama and the woman's film.* London: British Film Institute.

Goffman, E, (1959). *The presentation of self in everyday life.* Garden City, NY: Doubleday.

Goffman, E. (1961). *Asylums: Essays on the social situation of mental patients and other inmates.* Garden City, NY: Doubleday.

Goffman, E. (1971). *Relations in public.* New York: Basic Books.

Gordon, D. (1995). Feminism and cultural studies. *Feminist Studies 21,* 363–377.

Gorelick, S. (1996). Contradictions of feminist methodology. In H. Gottfried (Ed.), *Feminism and social change: Bridging theory and practice.* Urbana, IL: University of Illinois Press.

Gottfried, H. (Ed.) (1996). *Feminism and social change: Bridging theory and practice.* Urbana, IL: University of Illinois Press.

Gramsci, A. (1971). *Selections from the prison notebooks*. New York: International Publishers.

Griswold, W. (1986). *Renaissance revivals: City comedy and revenge tragedy in the London theatre, 1576–1980*. Chicago: University of Chicago Press.

Griswold, W. (1987). A methodological framework for the sociology of culture. *Sociological Methodology, 17,* 1–35.

Griswold, W. (1994). *Culture and societies in a changing world*. Thousand Oaks, CA: Pine Forge.

Grodin, D., & Lindlof, T. (1996). *Constructing the self in a mediated world*. Thousand Oaks, CA: Sage.

Grossberg, L. (1996a). History, politics and postmodernism. In D. Morley & K. Chen. (Eds.), *Stuart Hall: Critical dialogues in cultural studies*. New York: Routledge.

Grossberg, L. (1996b). Toward a geneology of the state of cultural studies. In C. Nelson & D. Gaonkar (Eds.), *Disciplinarity and dissent in cultural studies*. New York: Routledge.

Grossberg, L., Nelson, C, & Treichler, P. (Eds.) (1992). *Cultural studies*. New York: Routledge.

Hall, S. (1980). Cultural studies: Two paradigms. *Media, Culture, and Society, 2,* 57–72.

Hall, S. (1980b). Encoding/decoding. In S. Hall, D. Hobson, A. Love, & P. Willis (Eds.), *Culture, media, language: Working papers in cultural studies, 1972–79*. Birmingham: Centre for Contemporary Cultural Studies, University of Birmingham.

Hall, S. (1992). Cultural studies and its theoretical legacies. In L. Grossberg, C. Nelson, & P. Treicher (Eds.), *Cultural studies*. New York: Routledge.

Hall, S. (1996). The problem of ideology: Marxism without guarantees. In D. Moreley & K. Chen (Eds.), *Stuart Hall: Critical dialogues in cultural studies*. New York: Routledge.

Harding, S., & Hintikka, M. B. (Eds.) (1983). *Dis-covering reality: Feminist perspectives on epistemology, methodology, and philosophy of science*. Boston: Reidel.

Hartsock, N. (1990). Foucault on power: A theory for women? In L. Nicholson (Ed.), *Feminism/postmodernism*. New York: Routledge.

Hartsock, N. (1996). Theoretical bases for coalition building: An assessment of postmodernism. In H. Gottfried (Ed.), *Feminism and social change: Bridging theory and practice*. Urbana, IL: University of Illinois Press.

Hebdige, D. (1996). Postmodernism and 'the other side'. In D. Morley & K. Chen. (Eds.), *Stuart Hall: Critical dialogues in cultural studies*. New York: Routledge.

Hobson, D. (1982). *Crossroads: The drama of a soap opera*. London: Metheun.

Inglis, F. (1993). *Cultural studies*. Cambridge, MA: Blackwell.

Jameson. F. (1984). Postmodernism: The logic of late capitalism. *New Left Review, 146,* 53–92.

Joyrich, L. (1996). *Re-viewing reception: Television, gender, and postmodern culture*. Bloomington, IN: Indiana University Press.

Kaplan, C. (1986). *Sea changes: Culture and feminism*. London: Verso.

Katz, E. (1980). On conceptualizing media effects. *Studies in Communication, 1,* 119–141.

Katz, E., & Lazarsfeld, P. F. (1955). *Personal influence*. Glencoe, IL: Free Press.

Kellner, D. (1995). Cultural studies, multiculturalism and media culture. In G. Dines & J. M. Humez (Eds.), *Gender, race and class in media: A text reader*. Thousand Oaks, CA: Sage.

Krieger, S. (1991). *Social science & the self: Personal essays on an art form*. New Brunswick, NJ: Rutgers University Press.

Lacan, J. (1977a). *Ecrits: A selection*. New York: Norton.

Lacan, J. (1977b). *The four fundamentals of psychoanalysis*. London: Hogarth.

Laclau, E. (1977). *Politics and ideology in Marxist theory*. London: New Left Books.

Laclau, E., & Mouffe, C. (1985). *Hegemony and socialist strategy: Towards a radical democratic politics*. London: Verso.

de Lauretis, T. (1984). *Alice doesn't: Feminism, semiotics, cinema*. Bloomington, IN: University of Indiana Press.

Lewis, L. (1990). *Gender politics and MTV: Voicing the difference*. Philadelphia: Temple University Press.

Livingstone, S. (1990). *Making, sense of television: The psychology of audience interpretation*. Oxford: Pergamon.

Lyotard, J. (1984). *The postmodern condition: A Report on knowledge*. Minneapolis: University of Minnesota Press.

McRobbie, A. (1981). Settling accounts with subcultures: A feminist critique. In T. Bennett, G. Martin, C. Mercer, & J. Wooldacott (Eds.), *Culture, ideology and social process: A reader*. London: Open University.

Mead, G. H. (1934). *Mind, self, & society from the standpoint of a social behaviorist*. Chicago: University of Chicago Press.

Millett, K. (1970). *Sexual politics*. Garden City, NY: Doubleday.

Mishler, E. G. (1986). *Research interviewing: Context and narrative*. Cambridge: Harvard University Press.

Modleski, T. (1986). Femininity as mas(s)querade: A feminist approach to mass culture. In C. MacCabe (Ed.), *High theory/low culture: Analyzing popular television and film*. New York: St. Martin's Press.

Modleski, T. (1988). *The women who knew too much: Hitchcock and feminist theory.* New York: Routledge.

Modleski, T. (1991). *Feminism without women: Culture and criticism in a "postfeminist" age.* New York: Routledge.

Moerman, M. (1988). *Talking culture: Ethnography and conversation analysis.* Philadelphia: University of Pennsylvania Press.

Morgan, R. (Ed.) (1970). *Sisterhood is powerful.* New York: Vintage.

Morley, D. (1980). *The* Nationwide *audience.* London: British Film Institute.

Morley, D. (1992). *Television, audience, and cultural studies.* New York: Routledge.

Morris, M. (1988a). Banality in cultural studies. In P. Mellencamp (Ed.), *Logics of television.* Bloomington, IN: Indiana University Press.

Morris, M. (1988b). Introduction: Feminism, reading, postmodernism. In M. Morris (Ed.), *The pirate's fiancee: Feminism, reading, postmodernism.* London: Verso.

Morris, M. (1988c). Things to do with shopping centres. In S. Sheridan (Ed.), *Grafts: Feminist cultural criticism.* London: Verso.

Mulvey, L. (1975). Visual pleasure and narrative cinema. *Screen, 16,* 6–8.

Nochlin, L. (1971). Why have there been no great women artists? In T. Hess & E. Baker (Eds.), *Art and sexual politics: Women's liberation, women artists, and art history* (pp. 1–39). London: Collier Books.

Oakley, A. (1981). Interviewing women: A contradiction in terms. In H. Roberts (Ed.), *Doing feminist research* (pp. 30–61). London: Routledge and Kegan Paul.

Penley. C. (1992). Feminism, psychoanalysis, and the study of popular culture. In L. Grossberg, C. Nelson, & P. Treichler (Eds.), *Cultural studies.* New York: Routledge.

Press, A. (1991). *Women watching television: Gender, class, and generation in the American television experience.* Philadelphia: University of Pennsylvania Press.

Pribram, E. D. (Ed.) (1988). *Female spectators: Looking at film and television.* New York: Verso.

Radway, J. (1984). *Reading the romance: Women, patriarchy, and popular literature.* Chapel Hill, NC: University of North Carolina Press.

Reinharz, S. (Ed.) (1992). *Feminist methods in social research.* New York: Oxford University Press.

Riessman, C. K. (1990). *Divorce talk: Women and men make sense of personal relationships.* New Brunswick, NJ: Rutgers University Press.

Roberts, H. (Ed,) (1981). *Doing feminist research.* London: Routledge and Kegan Paul.

de Saussure, F. (1966). *Course in general linguistics.* New York: McGraw-Hill.

Seiter, E. (1992). Semiotics, structuralism, and television. In R. C. Allen (Ed.), *Channels of discourse, reassembled: Television and contemporary criticism* (2nd ed.). Chapel Hill, NC: University of North Carolina Press.

Simonds, W. (1992). *Women and self-help culture: Reading between the lines.* New Brunswick, NJ: Rutgers University Press.

Simonds, W. (1996). All consuming selves: Self-help literature and women's identities. In D. Grodin & T. Lindlof (Eds,), *Constructing the self in a mediated world.* Thousand Oaks, CA: Sage.

Skeggs, B. (1995). Theorising, ethics and representation in feminist ethnography. In B. Skeggs (Ed.), *Feminist cultural theory: Process and production.* Manchester: Manchester University Press.

Slack, J. (1996). The theory and method of articulation in cultural studies. In D. Morley & K. Chen (Eds.), *Stuart Hall: Critical dialogues in cultural studies.* New York: Routledge.

Smelik, A. (1995). What meets the eye: Feminist film studies. In R. Buikema & A. Smelik (Eds.), *Women's studies and culture.* London: Zed Books.

Smith, D. (1996). Contradictions for feminist social scientists. In H. Gottfried (Ed.), *Feminism and social change: Bridging theory and practice.* Urbana, IL: University of Illinois Press.

Snitow, A., Stansell, C., & Thompson, S. (Eds.) (1983). *Powers of desire: The politics of sexuality.* New York: Monthly Review Press.

Sparks, C. (1996). Stuart Hall, cultural studies, and Marxism. In D. Morley & K. Chen. (Eds.), *Stuart Hall: Critical dialogues in cultural studies.* New York: Routledge.

Spigel, L. (1992). *Make room for TV: Television and the family ideal in postwar America.* Chicago: University of Chicago Press.

Spigel, L., & Mann, D. (Eds.) (1992). *Private screenings: Television and the female consumer.* Minnesota: University of Minneapolis Press.

Stacey, J. (1988). Can there be a feminist ethnography? *Women's Studies International Forum, 11,* 21–27.

Stacey, J. (1994). *Star gazing: Hollywood and female spectatorship.* London: Routledge.

Storey, J. (1993). *Cultural theory and popular culture.* Athens, GA: University of Georgia Press.

Tuchman, G. (1978). The symbolic annihilation of women. In G. Tuchman, A. K. Daniels, & J. Benet (Eds.), *Hearth and home: Images of women in the mass media.* New York: Oxford University Press.

Vance, C. (Ed.) (1984). *Pleasure and danger: Exploring female sexuality.* New York: Routledge.

Walters, S. (1995). *Material girls: Making sense of feminist cultural theory.* Berkeley, CA: University of California Press.

West, C., & Zimmerman, D. (1987). Doing gender. *Gender & Society, 1,* 125–151.

Williams, R. (1958). *Culture and society, 1780–1950.* Garden City, NY: Doubleday.

Williamson, J. (1986a). *Consuming passions: The dynamics of popular culture.* New York: Marion Boyars.

Williamson, J. (1986b). Woman is an island: Femininity and colonization. In T. Modleski (Ed.), *Studies in entertainment: Critical approaches to mass culture.* Indianapolis, IN: Indiana University Press.

Wolff, J. (1981). *The social production of art.* New York: St. Martin's Press.

PART III

MICROSTRUCTURES AND PROCESSES

CHAPTER 11

Gender Socialization

JEAN STOCKARD

As children grow up they form a general sense of self and the ability to relate to others and play a part in society. In this process they also develop beliefs about the roles and expectations that are associated with each sex group (gender roles) and a self-identity as a member of one sex group or the other (gender identity). This chapter describes theories and research that are related to this general process of gender socialization.

The notion of socialization is very broad. For instance, scholars may discuss occupational socialization, religious socialization, political socialization, or socialization to school. Yet, gender socialization appears to be one of the most basic aspects of this large and complex process. In part this reflects the fact that children's realization that they are male or female tends to come at a fairly young age. Long before children understand the nature of religious groups, occupations, or schooling, they realize that there are two sex groups and that they belong to one of these groups. The centrality of gender socialization also reflects the fact that our society, and all societies known to social scientists, are gendered. People throughout the world recognize that there are different sex groups and they assign different roles and responsibilities to members of these groups, as well as different rewards and values.

The theories used to analyze gender socialization were primarily developed to deal with socialization in general. That is, theories that can explain how we develop a general sense of self or how we learn roles and expectations associated with school or work are also used to account for the development of gender identity and gender role expectations. Theory and research regarding socialization is also multidisciplinary, reflecting work in academic psychology and psychoanalysis, as well as sociology. Because gender identity and views of gender roles first begin to appear at very young ages, much of this work has focused on children.

JEAN STOCKARD • Department of Sociology, University of Oregon, Eugene, Oregon 97403-1291
Handbook of the Sociology of Gender, edited by Janet Saltzman Chafetz. Kluwer Academic/ Plenum Publishers, New York, 1999.

As in all areas of research, analyses of socialization have developed and changed over the years. As empirical findings have accumulated some theories have tended to fall by the wayside and new theories have appeared (Maccoby, 1992). My discussion of gender socialization will follow a rough chronological order, describing the early tradition of social learning theory, the rise of cognitive developmental theory, and the more recent appearance of gender schema theory. I will then describe work that focuses on childhood cultures and the role of peer groups and, finally, examine psychoanalytic explanations of the role of parents in gender socialization. Before reviewing each of these approaches, I briefly discuss the influence of biological factors on gender development.

1. BIOLOGY AND GENDER SOCIALIZATION

In recent years sociologists and other scientists have become increasingly cognizant of the complex relationships between biological, psychological, environmental, and social factors in individuals' lives and development. This work suggests that infants are not a *tabula rasa* on which "society" simply writes a message. Instead, children appear to enter the world genetically prepared to interact with others and predisposed to exhibit certain behavioral tendencies. For instance, a growing body of literature reports data on identical twins, some of whom have been raised together and some apart. These studies document the very large role of genetic background in explaining individuals' personality traits, health, history of mental illness, and even social and political attitudes (Rowe, 1994, pp. 57–93; Udry, 1995). Humans also appear to be biologically "programmed" to respond to others in a social manner—to learn language and to interact with others in their environment (Schore, 1994).

At the same time, research increasingly documents the ways in which social experiences influence biological characteristics and capabilities. For instance, without proper stimulation children's intellectual and social development can be sharply curtailed (Schore, 1994). Similarly, excessive exposure to danger or stress can alter neural pathways in the brain and the ways that we respond to social situations (Massey, 1996, p. 408). Socialization, the way that individuals come to develop an idea of their roles within a society, necessarily involves an interplay between biological and social factors.

It is logical to expect that biological factors are involved, to at least some extent, in gender socialization. Males and females experience different exposure to hormones prenatally, again at adolescence, and during adulthood. Although evidence is far from complete, data from studies based on both animal and human populations indicate that variations in brain structure resulting from these different hormonal dosages can account for some behavioral differences between males and females, such as average levels of aggressiveness and nurturance (Rowe, 1994, pp. 174–179; Stockard & Johnson, 1992, pp. 126–130). One explanation for these differences comes from the developing field of evolutionary psychology. This perspective takes a very long view of human history and suggests that human behaviors and traits reflect adaptations that allowed us to survive in the often dangerous and unsure environments in which humans evolved. To the extent that there are innate differences between the sex groups, these reflect the different adaptive problems that faced men and women (Buss, 1994, 1995a, b; Buss & Malamuth, 1996; Kenrick & Trost, 1993; Rowe, 1994, pp. 179–188).

Even with such biological influences, many, if not most, aspects of gendered behavior probably result from social influences. This can be seen most clearly in the ways in which gender roles vary from one society to another. Although gender differences in a few social roles and behavioral tendencies (most notably those related to child rearing and aggression) tend to be found in all societies that have been studied (Whiting & Edwards, 1988), there appears to be a great deal of variation in the gendered nature of other social roles and behaviors from one society to another (e.g., Best & Williams, 1993; Stockard & Johnson, 1992, pp. 74–95). In addition, individuals vary in the extent to which they adhere to gender roles and exhibit gender typed behaviors, and the nature of these roles and behaviors have changed over time and can vary from one setting to another.

The extent to which physiological factors influence differences between the sex groups is an active and contentious issue and will probably not be resolved any time soon (e.g., Eagly, 1995a, b; Hyde & Plant, 1995; Jacklin, 1989; Maracek, 1995; Sternberg, 1993). While acknowledging the possibility that gender identity and gender roles may be influenced by biological factors, I focus in this chapter on theory and research that have addressed the social influences on gender-related behaviors and self-image. This work examines not just differences between average characteristics of males and females, but also variations within sex groups—why some males and some females are more likely than others to adhere strongly to traditional gender norms.

2. SOCIAL LEARNING THEORY

The broad area of social learning theory developed from the tradition of stimulus–response theory or behaviorism. For many years work in this area focused on reinforcements, suggesting that children develop sex-typed behaviors because other people reinforce activities that conform to expectations for their sex group and do not reinforce those that do not conform. Because children spend so much of their early years within the family, much of the research in this area focused on parent–child interactions. This work has produced relatively little support for the notion that differential reinforcement can account for children's gender-typed behavior (Fagot, 1985; Huston, 1983, pp. 441–442; Serbin, Tonick, & Sternglanz, 1977; Serbin, Connor, & Citron, 1978). Studies of parental behaviors show that parents tend to reinforce some gender differences in the toys children play with (Block, 1984; Fagot & Hagan, 1985; Fagot & Leinbach, 1987; Fagot, Hagan, Leinbach, & Kronsberg, 1985; Huston, 1983). However, in other areas, such as encouragement of achievement or dependency, warmth of interactions, restrictiveness, and disciplinary practices, parents tend to treat boys and girls similarly (Lytton & Romney, 1991).

By the 1960s, the social learning tradition had broadened to include the notion of modeling, suggesting that children develop sex-typed behaviors because they choose to model or copy behaviors of other males or females (Maccoby, 1992, pp. 1007–1011; Stockard & Johnson, 1992, pp. 165–167). Note that while the notion of reinforcement focuses on how agents of socialization, such as parents, influence children's behaviors, the idea of modeling tends to focus on the active role of the targets of socialization and their ability to imitate the actions of specific agents. Tests of this theory have generally involved settings where a series of models have been presented to young children. As with the idea of reinforcement, relatively little support has been found for the importance of modeling in the development of gender identity or adherence to gender roles. For instance, parents who exhibit traits that are highly stereotypically associated with one sex group or the other are not more likely than other parents to have children who exhibit such strongly stereotyped behavior (Angrilli, 1960; Hetherington, 1965; Maccoby and Jacklin, 1974; Mussen & Rutherford, 1963). In addition, when researchers have tried to specifically alter gender-related models (or reinforcements) that children receive, changes in behavior have been only temporary (Maccoby, 1992, pp. 1008, 1011; Stockard & Johnson, 1992, pp. 163–167).

3. COGNITIVE DEVELOPMENTAL THEORY

As empirical research failed to provide strong support for social learning theory, scholars began to develop other explanations of socialization in general and gender socialization in particular. The most important approach has no doubt been cognitive developmental theory, which builds on the research of Jean Piaget and his finding that children gradually develop more complex ways of interacting with others and understanding the world around them. Lawrence Kohlberg extended Piaget's notions by applying them to gender socialization, suggesting that children's views of appropriate gender roles also change as they grow older, reflecting their changing cognitive development. Kohlberg and others working within this paradigm have documented an increasing flexibility and complexity of children's views of gender roles with age (Kohlberg, 1966; Ullian, 1976). According to this perspective, the fact that very young children have much more rigid, stereotyped views of appropriate behaviors for males and females than do older children or adults can be explained by the greater cognitive flexibility and capability for complex thought that develops with age.

Cognitive developmental theory can be seen as providing two important theoretical advances over social learning theory. First, it seriously incorporates an understanding of the active role of the child and the importance of cognitive processing and understanding in the socialization process. Second, it includes an understanding of developmental changes in the process of gender socialization and specifically describes how children's interpretations and understandings of gender alter and change as their cognitive capabilities become more developed and complex.

Certain technical elements of cognitive developmental theory, however, have not withstood empirical test. Specifically, Kohlberg hypothesized that the child's active involvement in and desire to develop gender-typed behaviors becomes most important once a child has developed a strong notion of gender constancy, the understanding that one is either a boy or a girl and that this categorization will not change. Research indicates that children acquire this gender constancy by about 6 years of age (e.g., Slaby & Frey, 1975, cited by Luecke-Aleksa, Anderson, Collins, & Schmitt, 1995). Interestingly enough, however, a number of gender differences—specifically differences in choices of toys and playmates—appear long before the age at which cognitive developmental theory would expect. Fairly consistently, by the age of 2 or 3, boys and girls choose to play with different toys and in different activities, prefer to play with like-sex playmates, and exhibit differences in aggressive behaviors (Huston, 1985, 1985, p. 11; Leinbach & Fagot, 1986, p. 665; Lobel & Menashri, 1993; Martin, 1993; Stockard & Johnson, 1992, p. 169). In recent years some scholars have turned to trying to understand these very early aspects of gender socialization.

4. GENDER SCHEMAS AND COGNITIVE LEARNING THEORIES

Recent approaches to understanding gender socialization have often incorporated the notion of schemas, cognitive structures or frameworks that people use to organize and process information to which they are exposed. Schemas provide an efficient way to organize new knowledge and information and help individuals maintain consistency and predictability in new situations. Gender schemas are cognitive schemas that are used to organize information on the basis of gender categories. Theorists who use this approach suggest that children develop increasingly more elaborate gender schemas as they develop their gender identity and their understanding of gender roles. As children come across information or new situations that pertain to gender they tend to use their gender schemas as a guide for interpreting this information, a way to simplify information and decisions.

Carol Lynn Martin and Charles Halvorsen (1981, 1987) have suggested that there are two types of gender schemas based on an "in-group/out-group" model. Children categorize information based on whether it involves their own sex group (the in-group) or the other (the out-group) and then use this categorization to help choose toys and behaviors and decide whether to attend to new information. For instance, when faced with new toys or potential playmates, children use this gender schema to determine their actions (Bem, 1981; Markus, Crane, Bernstein, & Saladi, 1982; Martin, 1993; Martin & Halvorson, 1981, 1987). Research indicates that rudimentary gender schema—the ability to discriminate males and females and link characteristics such as hair and clothing styles to these differences—can appear by one year of age (Fagot & Leinbach, 1993; Leinbach & Fagot, 1993).

It is important to realize that gender schemas are both complex and multidimensional. This has been demonstrated both through an older body of research in the tradition of "masculinity–femininity" tests (Constaninople, 1973; Lewis, 1968, pp. 69–71; Stockard & Johnson, 1992, p. 153) and in newer studies of children's gender-typed behavior and personalities and developing gender schemas (Hort, Leinbach, & Fagot, 1991; Sears, Rau, & Alpert, 1965; Turner & Gervai, 1995). One carefully designed study used longitudinal data collected on children beginning at the age of 18 months and continuing until the age of 4. At various times over this period different aspects of children's cognitive understandings of gender (all of which are believed to be part of a gender schema) were assessed, including their ability to label correctly pictures of people as male or female, their knowledge of gender-typed activities and objects, their memory of gender-typed stimuli, and the salience of gender in their assessments of stimuli. The researchers found that there was very little association between each of these cognitive aspects of gender and suggested that "children fit together the puzzle pieces of gender acquisition in a variety of loosely organized, idiosyncratic ways" (Hort et al., 1991, p. 206).

In short, studies of both children and adults suggest that gender schemas are very complex and multidimensional and that children acquire gender schemas in a variety of ways (see also Huston, 1983; Levy & Fivush, 1993; Signorella, Bigler, & Liben, 1993). Data are beginning to suggest that these various components of gender schema may involve not just cognitive knowledge and stereotypes, but also affective and evaluative components, and even metaphoric qualities, such as strength, danger, or gentleness (Fagot & Leinbach, 1993, p. 220; see also Martin, 1993; Martin, Wood, & Little, 1990).

The notion of gender schemas does not refute other theories of gender socialization, but can potentially help us understand more about the influence of reinforcement, modeling, and cognitive development. For instance, there is some evidence that children who learn to correctly apply gender labels earlier than other children have parents who endorse more traditional attitudes toward women and also more often reinforce sex-typed play (Fagot & Leinbach, 1989, 1993, p. 218; Fagot, Leinbach, & O'Boyle, 1992). In addition, reinforcement may or may not change children's behavior depending upon their cognitive understandings and ways of processing information related to gender (Jacklin, 1989, p. 130). The notion of gender schemas can also explain why children may or may not choose to model certain behaviors. When children (or adults) encounter models that are contrary to their gender schema, they may either not attend to those behaviors or try to interpret them in a way that corresponds to their existing gender schemas. Similarly, when children encounter models that they believe conform to their gender schema they may be especially likely to model those behaviors. Similarly, in support of ideas from the cognitive developmental view, children's choices of who and what gender roles to model appear to be related to their cognitive understandings of gender and what they believe is relevant to their own self definitions (Maccoby, 1992, p. 1011).

As noted previously, one of the earliest manifestations of gender typed behavior is the tendency for boys and girls to prefer different toys and playmates of the same sex. By the age of three, and in some situations even earlier, boys choose to play with other boys and girls choose to play with other girls. Both psychologists and sociologists have studied the culture of peer groups to understand more about why boys and girls prefer to associate with others of the same sex and how these associations influence gender socialization.

5. PEER GROUP INTERACTIONS AND THE CULTURE OF CHILDHOOD

When examining peer groups, scholars have found that gender can be seen in social behaviors in ways that are not apparent when individuals and their traits and behaviors are looked at alone. In particular, boys and girls tend to behave differently depending upon whether they are with other boys, other girls, a mixed-sex peer group, or with adults. In short, children, like all people, act in different ways, depending upon the situation in which they find themselves. Many studies have demonstrated that children clearly prefer to play with others of the same sex. These preferences appear spontaneously, when children are not under pressure to make choices, and they are especially strong in situations that are not monitored by adults. While situations can be structured in which boys and girls interact comfortably together, the general preference for gender-segregated interactions appears very difficult to change. It appears as early as 3 years of age and increases in strength over time, maintaining a high level until at least age 11. The preferences appear to be very difficult to change and do not seem to be related to individual level measures of various aspects of masculinity and femininity. Children do maintain cross-sex friendships, but they tend to occur within their homes or neighborhoods and are often hidden from the larger peer group (Fagot, 1994; Maccoby, 1990, p. 514).

In general, children's activities may be seen as involving a "culture of childhood," a pattern of games, activities, roles, norms, and even jokes and folklore that are passed on from generation to generation of children with little, if any, active involvement by adults. Most important for our purposes, this culture is highly gendered. Cultural elements, such as norms, values, and the material elements such as toys and playthings, are strongly gender typed. In addition, there are strong subcultures that are highly gender segregated. The gendered nature of the culture of childhood is markedly different in many ways from that of adults—with, as a cognitive developmental perspective would suggest, much more rigid distinctions between roles for males and females and more extensive and apparent sanctions for violating these roles (Maccoby, 1991a, p. 538; Powlishta, 1995).

In examining children's interactions, scholars have tried to determine what distinguishes the interactions of groups of boys and groups of girls and have found differences in both games and activities as well as interactional styles. Boys tend to play in larger groups, in rougher activities, and to take up more space when they play. Their interactions tend to be focused more on their mutual interest in activities and more often tend to involve displays of dominance, with the use of interruptions, commands, threats, and boasts. Girls tend to form close, more intimate friendships with one or two other girls and are more likely to express agreements with others, allow others to have a turn in speaking, and to acknowledge points made by others. Both boys and girls successfully influence others in their interactions; they simply tend to do so through different styles (Maccoby, 1990, p. 516).

The developmental psychologist Eleanor Maccoby points to two factors that seem to underlie the development of gender segregated play groups in the preschool years. First, girls seem to find boys' more rough and tumble play styles and orientation toward competition and dominance aversive, and thus try to avoid it. Second, given their different interactive styles, girls find it difficult to influence boys, for their characteristic style of polite suggestion does not match the style of direct commands more often adopted by boys. A basic element of group process is the notion of exchange, or mutual influence. Maccoby hypothesizes that because boys and girls find it difficult to find interaction patterns that allow such mutual influence, they tend to avoid forming groups that include children of both sex groups (Maccoby, 1988, 1990, p. 515; see also Fabes, 1994).

Ethnographic studies of peer groups among children and adolescents have documented the nature of gender-segregated peer groups as children grow older. Extensive observations have revealed the importance of interactions with others of the same sex in helping children develop their gender identity and definitions of appropriate gender roles, as children actively discuss and develop definitions of masculinity and femininity. These discussions involve not just areas of toy choice or games, but also the nature of sexuality and sexual relationships (Eder, 1995; Fine, 1987; Holland & Eisenhart, 1990; Jordan & Cowan, 1995; Thorne, 1993; Voss, 1997).

It is again important to note that other theories used to understand gender socialization can be used to account for processes within peer groups. Observations of peer groups indicate that children clearly reinforce each other for behaviors that are deemed either appropriate or inappropriate in terms of gender (Fagot, 1994). Children also tend to model other children as they try to develop behaviors that they believe are appropriate. Cognitive processes, which are linked to developmental changes, are clearly involved as children decide whether or not to enter a play group and the extent to which gender segregation should be maintained. Although the processes involved in gender socialization within peer groups are not yet fully understood, most scholars in this area believe that diverse theoretical and methodological approaches will be needed to develop a full understanding (Maccoby, 1994; Martin, 1994; Serbin, Moller, Gulko, Powlishta, & Colburne, 1994).

Research is also needed to understand fully the long-term implications of childhood gender segregation for gender segregation and inequalities in adult life. Boys' peer groups seem far less amenable to direction and supervision by adults than do girls' peer groups, leading researchers to speculate about connections between peer group interactions and boys' later difficulties in school, such as lower grades and greater behavior problems (e.g., Fagot, 1994, pp. 62–63; Jordan & Cowan, 1995). Others have noted possible difficulties in children developing competencies, such as interpersonal interaction styles, that are more typical of the other sex, thus enabling more effective cross-sex interaction (e.g., Leaper, 1994). Still others have speculated about the relationship between childhood gender segregation and adult patterns of interaction, both within the family and within the world of work (e.g., Maccoby, 1991b, 1995).

Although both boys and girls prefer interactions in gender-segregated groups, data indicate that boys are far more concerned with gender segregation than are girls. Girls receive less punishment from their peers for cross-sex behaviors than do boys. In addition girls are far more likely to interact with adults than are boys, while boys are resistant to interactions with either girls or adults (Fagot, 1994, p. 60; Maccoby, 1990, p. 516; 1994, p. 88). While girls' aversion to boys' interactive and play styles can explain why girls tend to avoid boys, it cannot as easily explain why boys tend to avoid girls. Psychoanalytic theory directly addresses this issue.

6. PSYCHOANALYTIC THEORY

Psychoanalysis was founded by Sigmund Freud in the late nineteenth and early twentieth centuries. From the very early years of the discipline Freud and his students and followers debated the nature of gender socialization—how childhood experiences influence boys' and girls' ideas about themselves, their gender, and sexuality. Two general perspectives developed. One, based on Freud's own writing, emphasized the centrality of the Oedipus complex and its resolution to differences in male and female development. According to Freud, girls, unlike boys, could never fully resolve the Oedipus complex and were fated to have a weaker superego, Freud's term for the conscience. Even in Freud's lifetime this view was sharply attacked and many of Freud's students developed an alternative perspective, which has come to be one that most contemporary psychoanalysts, based on their clinical experience, accept today.

Writers in this second perspective emphasize the importance of the fact that the mother is the first person to whom all children, both boys and girls, relate. During their early years children develop strong relationships with their mother (or other female caretaker). Because this very strong early tie is almost always with a woman, children's first identification is feminine, rather than masculine. As children become older and more independent they need to lessen the very strong ties that they had with the mother figure during infancy. They also learn what it means to be a male or a female. For a girl, this is relatively easy because the mother was the first person with whom she identified. However, psychoanalytic theorists suggest, achieving gender identity is harder for a boy because in the process he must reject his first identity as feminine. In addition, because fathers and other men often are not such a central part of young boys' lives as are mothers and other women, it may be hard to develop a strong idea of just what masculinity involves.

Because the boy knows most intimately what is feminine, he comes to define masculinity as being "not-feminine." In his behaviors and relationships with others he devalues what is feminine and denies his attachment to the feminine world. To use psychoanalytic terms, he represses the feminine identification developed in his early relationship with the mother. As a result, boys' gender identity tends to be somewhat more tenuous than girls' gender identity (see especially Chodorow, 1974, 1978, 1989; Deutsch, 1944–1945; Dinnerstein, 1976; Fairbairn, 1952; Horney, 1967a, b; Klein, 1960; Mead, 1949).

The sociologist Talcott Parsons (1955, 1970) suggested that the process that psychoanalytic theorists describe as "identification" could actually be seen as learning to play a social role with another person in complementary, reciprocal role interactions. In these terms, children first learn to play the role of child, which is complementary to the role of mother. This role is not gender typed, as both boy and girl infants learn to feel loved and nurtured as well as to nurture others. As children grow older, their role relationships expand and they gradually develop more independence, loosening this first tie with the mother. At the same time, they become more aware of their identity as a boy or a girl and begin to learn roles associated with this gender identity. Miriam Johnson has noted the special role of the father in helping both boys and girls develop these understandings, as the father tends to become more involved with children as they become older and more aware of gender differences. (See Johnson, 1988; Lerman, 1986; Stockard & Johnson, 1979, 1992 for a complete discussion of these traditions.)

Both the traditional psychoanalytic view and the more sociological role-oriented version of this perspective suggest that the motives underlying boys' strong preferences for gender-segregated play groups and their avoidance of female-typed activities can be traced to these early experiences in the family and, especially, the virtually universal early relationship between infants and a mother or other female caretaker. Building on this premise, these theorists suggest that when fathers are more involved in early child rearing boys would be less likely to exhibit signs of "compulsive masculinity" and, in adulthood, would be less likely to promote strong patterns of gender stratification (e.g., Chodorow, 1974, 1978, 1989; Johnson, 1988). Support for these speculations comes from clinical evidence from the psychoanalytic tradition, ethnographic field studies of adults, and analyses of cross-cultural data on societies in which fathers take a wide range of different roles in child rearing (e.g., Coltrane, 1988, 1992; Williams, 1989).

7. SUMMARY AND CONCLUSION

Understandings of gender socialization have advanced a great deal over the last few decades. Contemporary theories emphasize the importance of the child's role in developing a gender identity and understanding of gender roles. Central to these approaches are notions of changing cognitive awareness and understandings of the world, the development of cognitive schemas, and interactions in peer groups. Psychoanalytic theory can help fill in gaps left by other approaches by explaining motives underlying boys' relatively intense support of gender-segregated activities. It also describes the central role of family relationships in the development of gender identity.

Contemporary understandings of gender socialization also highlight the ways in which gender development is complex and multidimensional. This complexity suggests that we would be well served by both theory and research that attempt to understand the common ground and linkages between the various theoretical perspectives and research traditions used in this field. Researchers in the cognitive tradition have often drawn on insights of social learning theorists. Less common has been work that attempts to integrate psychoanalytic theory, understandings from biology, and psychological and sociological theories. Some preliminary work indicates that such efforts could be fruitful (e.g., Fast, 1984, 1993; Schore, 1994), but clearly, much more remains to be done. In addition, the majority of contemporary research and theorizing has focused on the United States and Western Europe (but see Berndt, Cheung, Lau, Kit-Tai Hau, & Lew, 1993 and Turner and Gervai, 1995 for exceptions) with surprisingly little systematic comparisons across racial-ethnic and social class groups even there. Much more extensive comparative and cross-cultural work is clearly needed.

Finally, much of the writing that links gender socialization to gender stratification in the adult world (with the notable exception of the psychoanalytic tradition) is highly speculative. In the 1970s sociologists tended to shift their framework of analysis from socialization to a broader view of the lifecourse (see Elder, 1994, p. 8). Yet, there has been very little research that provides the lifecourse perspective to gender socialization and encompasses the span from early childhood to adult life. If analyses of gender socialization are to ultimately help us develop more gender equitable societies such analyses will need to become much more common.

REFERENCES

Angrilli, A. F. (1960). The psychosexual identification of pre-school boys. *Journal of Genetic Psychology, 97,* 329–340.

Bem, S. L. (1981). Gender schema theory: A cognitive account of sex typing. *Psychological Review, 88,* 354–364.

Berndt, T. J., Cheung, P. C., Lau, S., Kit-Tai Hau, K., & Lew, W. J. F. (1993). Perceptions of parenting in mainland China, Taiwan, and Hong Kong: Sex differences and societal differences. *Developmental Psychology, 29,* 156–164.

Best, D. L., & Williams, J. E. (1993). A cross-cultural viewpoint. In A. E. Beall & R. J. Sternberg (Eds.) *The psychology of gender.* (pp. 215–248). New York: Guilford Press.

Block, J. H. (1984). *Sex role identity and ego development.* San Francisco: Jossey-Bass.

Buss, D. M. (1994). *The evolution of desire: Strategies of human mating.* New York: Basic Books.

Buss, D. M. (1995a). Evolutionary psychology: A new paradigm for psychological science. *Psychological Inquiry, 6,* 1–30.

Buss, D. M. (1995b). Psychological sex differences: Origins through sexual selection. *American Psychologist, 50,* 164–168.

Buss, D. M., & Malamuth, N. (Eds.) (1996). *Sex, power, conflict: Feminist and evolutionary perspectives.* New York: Oxford University Press.

Chodorow, N. J. (1974). Family structure and feminine personality. In M.Z. Rosaldo and L. Lamphere (Eds.) *Women, culture and society* (pp. 43–66). Stanford, California: Stanford University Press.

Chodorow, N. J. (1978). *The reproduction of mothering.* Berkeley, CA: University of California Press.

Chodorow, N. J. (1989). *Feminism and psychoanalytic theory.* New Haven, CT: Yale University Press.

Coltrane, S. (1988). Father-child relationships and the status of women: A cross-cultural study. *American Journal of Sociology, 93,* 1060–1095.

Coltrane, S. (1992). The micropolitics of gender in nonindustrial societies. *Gender & Society, 6,* 86–107.

Constaninople, A. (1973). Masculinity-femininity: An exception to a famous dictum. *Psychological Bulletin, 80,* 389–407.

Deutsch, H. (1944–1945). *The psychology of women: A psychoanalytic interpretation,* Vol. 1: *Girlhood,* Vol. 2: *Motherhood.* New York: Bantam.

Dinnerstein, D. (1976). *The mermaid and the minotaur: Sexual arrangements and human malaise.* New York: Harper & Row.

Eagly, A. H. (1995a). Reflections on the commenters' views. *American Psychologist, 50,* 169–171.

Eagly, A. H. (1995b). The science and politics of comparing women and men. *American Psychologist, 50,* 145–158.

Eder, D., with Evans, C. C., & Parker, S. (1995). *School talk: Gender and adolescent culture.* New Brunswick, NJ: Rutgers University Press.

Elder, G. H. (1994). Time, human agency, and social change: Perspectives on the life course. *Social Psychology Quarterly, 57,* 4–15.

Fabes, R. (1994). Physiological, emotional, and behavioral correlates of gender segregation. In C. Leaper (Ed.), *Childhood gender segregation: Causes and consequences* (pp. 19–34). San Francisco: Jossey-Bass.

Fairbairn, R. (1952). *An object-relations theory of the personality.* New York: Basic Books.

Fagot, B. I. (1985). Beyond the reinforcement principle: Another step toward understanding sex role development. *Developmental Psychology, 21,* 1097–1104.

Fagot, B. I. (1994). Peer relations and the development of competence in boys and girls. In C. Leaper (Ed.), *Childhood gender segregation: Causes and consequences* (pp. 53–66). San Francisco: Jossey-Bass.

Fagot, B. I., & Hagan, R. (1985). Aggression in toddlers: Responses to the assertive acts of boys and girls. *Aggression, 12,* 341–351.

Fagot, B. I., & Leinbach, M. D. (1987). Socialization of sex roles within the family. In D. B. Carter (Ed.), *Current conceptions of sex roles and sex typing: Theory and research* (pp. 89–100). New York: Praeger.

Fagot, B. I., & Leinbach, M. D. (1989). The young child's gender schema: Environmental input, internal organization. *Child Development, 60,* 663–672.

Fagot, B. I., & Leinbach, M.D. (1993). Gender-role development in young children: From discrimination to labeling. *Developmental Review, 13,* 205–224.

Fagot, B. I., Hagan, R., Leinbach, M. D., & Kronsberg, S. (1985). Differential reactions to assertive and communicative acts of toddler boys and girls. *Child Development, 56,* 1499–1505.

Fagot, B. I., Leinbach, M. D., & O'Boyle, C. (1992). Gender labeling, gender stereotyping, and parenting behaviors. *Developmental Psychology, 28,* 225–230.

Fast, I. (1984). *Gender identity: A differentiation model.* Hillsdale, NJ: Erlbaum.

Fast, I. (1993). Aspects of early gender development: A psychodynamic perspective. In A. E. Beall, & R. J. Sternberg (Eds.), *The psychology of gender* (pp. 173–193). New York: Guilford.

Fine, G. A. (1987). *With the boys: Little league baseball and preadolescent culture.* Chicago: University of Chicago Press.

Hetherington, E. M. (1965). A developmental study of the effects of sex of the dominant parent on sex-role preference, identification, and imitation in children. *Journal of Personality and Social Psychology, 2,* 188–194.

Holland, D. C., & Eisenhart, M. A. (1990). *Educated in romance: Women, achievement, and college culture.* Chicago: University of Chicago Press.

Horney, K. (1967a). The dread of women: Observations on a specific difference in the dread felt by men and by women respectively for the opposite sex. In H. Kelman (Ed.), *Feminine psychology* (pp. 133–146). New York: Norton (originally published 1932).

Horney, K. (1967b). The flight from womanhood: The masculinity complex in women as viewed by men and by women. In H. Kelman (Ed.), *Feminine psychology* (pp. 54–70). New York: Norton (originally published 1926).

Hort, B. E., Leinbach, M. D., & Fagot, B. I. (1991). Is there coherence among the cognitive components of gender acquisition? *Sex Roles, 24,* 195–207.

Huston, A. C. (1983). Sex typing. In E. M. Hetherington (Ed.), *Handbook of Child Psychology* (4th ed., Vol. 4, pp. 387-467) New York: John Wiley & Sons.

Huston, A. C. (1985). The development of sex typing: Themes from recent research. *Developmental Review, 5,* 1–17.

Hyde, J. S., & Plant, E. A. (1995). Magnitude of psychological gender differences. *American Psychologist, 50,* 159–161.

Jacklin, C. N. (1989). Female and male: Issues of gender. *American Psychologist, 44,* 127–133.

Johnson, M. M. (1988). *Strong mothers, weak wives.* Berkeley, CA: University of California Press.

Jordan, E., & Cowan, A. (1995). Warrior narratives in the kindergarten classroom: Renegotiating the social contract? *Gender & Society, 9,* 727–743.

Kenrick, D. T., & Trost, M. R. (1993). The evolutionary perspective. In A. E. Beall & R. J. Sternberg (Eds.), *The psychology of gender* (pp. 148–172). New York: Guilford Press.

Klein, M. (1960). *The psychoanalysis of children.* New York: Grove Press (originally published 1932).

Kohlberg, L. (1966). A cognitive-developmental analysis of children's sex-role concepts and attitudes. In E. E. Maccoby (Ed.), *The development of sex differences.* Stanford, CA: Stanford University Press.

Leaper, C. (1994). Exploring the consequences of gender segregation on social relationships. In C. Leaper (Ed.), *Childhood gender segregation: Causes and consequences* (pp. 67–86). San Francisco: Jossey-Bass.

Leinbach, M. D., & Fagot, B. I. (1986). Acquisition of gender labels: A test for toddlers. *Sex Roles, 15,* 655–666.

Leinbach, M. D., & Fagot, B. I. (1993). Categorical habituation to male and female faces: Gender schematic processing in infancy. *Infant Behavior and Development, 16,* 317–332.

Lerman, H. (1986). *A mote in Freud's eye: From psychoanalysis to the psychology of women.* New York: Springer.

Lewis, E. C. (1968). *Developing women's potential.* Ames: Iowa State University Press.

Levy, G. D., & Fivush, R. (1993). Scripts and gender: A new approach for examining gender-role development. *Developmental Review, 13,* 126–146.

Lobel, T. E., & Menashri, J. (1993). Relations of conceptions of gender-role transgressions and gender constancy to gender-typed toy preferences. *Developmental Psychology, 29,* 150–155.

Luecke-Aleksa, D., Anderson, D. R., Collins, P. A., & Schmitt, K. L. (1995). Gender constancy and television viewing. *Developmental Psychology, 31,* 773–780.

Lytton, H., & Romney, D. M. (1991). Parents' differential socialization of boys and girls: A meta-analysis. *Psychological Bulletin, 109,* 267–296.

Maccoby, E. E. (1988). Gender as a social category. *Developmental Psychology, 26,* 755–765.

Maccoby, E. E. (1990). Gender and relationships: A developmental account. *American Psychologist. 45,* 513–520.

Maccoby, E. E. (1991a). Gender and relationships: A reprise. *American Psychologist, 46,* 538–539.

Maccoby, E. E. (1991b). Gender segregation in the workplace: Continuities and discontinuities from childhood to adulthood. In M. Frankenhaeuser, U. Lundberg, & M. Chesney (Eds.), *Women, work, and health: Stress and opportunities* (pp. 3–16). New York: Plenum Press.

Maccoby, E. E. (1992). The role of parents in the socialization of children: An historical overview. *Developmental Psychology, 28,* 1006–1017.

Maccoby, E. E. (1994). Commentary: Gender segregation in childhood. In C. Leaper (Ed.), *Childhood gender degregation: Causes and consequences* (pp. 87–97). San Francisco: Jossey-Bass.

Maccoby, E. E. (1995). The two sexes and their social systems. In P. Moen, G. H. Elder, & K. Luscher (Eds.), *Examining Lives in Context: Perspectives on the Ecology of Human Development* (pp. 347–364). Washington, D.C., American Psychological Association.

Maccoby, E. E., & Jacklin, C. N. (1974). *The psychology of sex differences.* Stanford, CA: Stanford University Press.

Maracek, J. (1995). Gender, politics, and psychology's ways of knowing. *American Psychologist, 50,* 162–163.

Markus, H., Crane, M., Bernstein, S., & Saladi, M. (1982). Self-schemas and gender. *Journal of Personality and Social Psychology, 42,* 38–50.

Martin, C. L. (1993). New directions for investigating children's gender knowledge. *Developmental Review, 13,* 184–204.

Martin, C. L. (1994). Cognitive influences on the development and maintenance of gender segregation. In C. Leaper (Ed.), *Childhood Gender Segregation: Causes and Consequences* (pp. 35–51). San Francisco: Jossey-Bass.

Martin, C. L., & Halvorson, C. F., Jr. (1981). A schematic processing model of sex typing and stereotyping in children. *Child Development, 52,* 1119–1134.

Martin, C. L., & Halvorson, C. F., Jr. (1987). The roles of cognition in sex role acquisition. In D. B. Carter (Ed.), *Current conceptions of sex roles and sex typing: Theory and research* (pp. 123–137). New York: Praeger.

Martin, C. L., Wood, C. H., & Little, J. K. (1990). The development of gender stereotype components. *Child Development, 61,* 1891–1904.

Massey, D. S. (1996). The age of extremes: Concentrated affluence and poverty in the twenty-first century. *Demography, 33,* 395–412.

Mead, M. (1949). *Male and female: A study of the sexes in a changing world.* New York: Dell.

Mussen, P., & Rutherford, E. (1963). Parent-child relations and parental personality in relation to young children's sex-role preferences. *Child Development, 34,* 589–607.

Parsons, T. (1955). Family structure and the socialization of the child. In T. Parsons & R. F. Bales. *Family socialization and interaction process* (pp. 35–131). Glencoe, IL: The Free Press.

Parsons, T. (1970). *Social structure and personality.* New York: The Free Press.

Powlishta, K. K. (1995). Intergroup processes in childhood: Social categorization and sex role development. *Developmental Psychology, 31,* 781–788.

Rowe, D. C. (1994). *The limits of family influence: Genes, experience, and behavior.* New York: Guilford.

Schore, A. N. (1994). *Affect regulation and the origin of the self: The neurobiology of emotional development.* Hillsdale, New Jersey: Lawrence Erlbaum.

Sears, R. R., Rau, L., & Alpert, R. (1965). *Identification and child rearing.* Stanford, CA.: Stanford University Press.

Serbin, L. A., Tonick, I. J., & Sternglanz, S. H. (1977). Shaping cooperative cross-sex play. *Child Development, 48,* 924–929.

Serbin, L. A., Connor, J. M., & Citron, C. C. (1978). Environmental control of independent and dependent behaviors in preschool girls and boys: A model for early independence training. *Sex Roles, 4,* 867–875.

Serbin, L. A., Moller, L. C., Gulko, J., Powlishta, K. K., & Colburne, K. A. (1994). The emergence of gender segregation in toddler playgroups. In C. Leaper (Ed.), *Childhood gender segregation: causes and consequences* (pp. 7–17). San Francisco: Jossey-Bass.

Signorella, M. L., Bigler, R. S., & Liben, L. S. (1993). Developmental differences in children's gender schemata about others: A meta-analytic review. *Developmental Review, 13,* 147–183.

Slaby, R. G., & Frey, K. (1975). Development of gender constancy and selective attention to same-sex models. *Child Development, 46,* 849–856.

Sternberg, R. J. (1993). What is the relation of gender to biology and environment? An evolutionary model of how what you answer depends on what you ask. In A. E. Beall & R. J. Sternberg (Eds.), *The psychology of gender* (pp. 1–6). New York: Guilford Press.

Stockard, J., & Johnson, M. M. (1979). The social origins of male dominance. *Sex Roles, 5,* 199–218.

Stockard, J., & Johnson, M. M. (1992). *Sex and gender in society* (2nd ed.). Englewood Cliffs, NJ: Prentice Hall.

Thorne, B. (1993). *Gender play: Girls and boys in school.* New Brunswick, NJ: Rutgers University Press.

Turner, P. J., & Gervai, J. (1995). A multidimensional study of gender typing in preschool children and their parents: Personality, attitudes, preferences, behavior, and cultural differences. *Developmental Psychology, 31,* 759–772.

Udry, J. R. (1995). Sociology and biology: What biology do sociologists need to know? *Social Forces, 73,* 1267–1278.

Ullian, D. Z. (1976). The development of conceptions of masculinity and femininity. In B. Lloyd & J. Archer (Eds.), *Exploring sex differences* (pp. 25–48). New York: Academic Press.

Voss, L. S. (1997). Teasing, disputing, and playing: Cross-gender interactions and space utilization among first and third graders. *Gender & Society, 11,* 238–256.

Whiting, B. B., & Edwards, C. P. (1988). *Children of different worlds: The formation of social behavior.* Cambridge, MA: Harvard University Press.

Williams, C. L. (1989). *Gender differences at work: Women and men in nontraditional occupations.* Berkeley, CA: University of California Press.

CHAPTER 12

Gender and Social Roles

Helena Znaniecka Lopata

1. INTRODUCTION

I begin by presenting and stressing my definition of social role, because it varies from one still being used by many sociologists, which limits the social role to a set of expectations and focuses only on the social person holding the role title. This does not make sense for two reasons. First, social life could not exist if everyone merely expected behavior and interaction; complex subidentifiers are needed to determine what actually occurs. In their major book on role theory Biddle and Thomas (1966) do not make that mistake; they define social role behaviorally. However, even their definition of an individual role refers to "all behavior of an individual" (p. 30) in terms of a "person-behavior matrix" (p. 45). This is simply too broad for analyses of specific roles, and it retains the second problem— a focus on only one individual. In real life no social role can exist without a social circle toward whom the behavior of the social person is directed and from whom corresponding action is received, the combination forming sets of social relationships. Even when using the analogy to a role in a play, as do Biddle and Thomas (1966), one must be cognizant of the fact that a theatrical role involves a circle of other actors, as well as the writer of the script, producers, audience, and a large group of workers building the set, advertising the play, and so forth.

I find a symbolic interactionist modification of Znaniecki's concept of social role most satisfactory for analysis of any particular social role or as a foundation for related concepts, such as role cluster, role strain, or role conflict. Thus, I am using the following definition in this chapter:

I wish to thank Janet Chafetz and Judith Wittner for help in idea expression and format.

Helena Znaniecka Lopata • Department of Sociology and Anthropology, Loyola University Chicago, Chicago, Illinois 60626
Handbook of the Sociology of Gender, edited by Janet Saltzman Chafetz. Kluwer Academic/ Plenum Publishers, New York, 1999.

A Social Role is a set of patterned, mutually interdependent, social relations between a social person and a social circle involving negotiated duties and obligations, rights and privileges. (Lopata, 1994b, p. 4; see also 1966, 1969, 1971, 1991b; Znaniecki, 1965)

This definition shifts the focus from the person to the set of relations necessary for the social role to be carried forth. "The social person is that 'package' of characteristics with which an individual enters a specific role" (Lopata, 1994, p. 4). These are assumed to be necessary for the performance of the role-related duties and the receipt of the role-related rights. For example, to enter the role of mother in American society a woman must give birth, adopt, or in some other way acquire a child, whom she declares to society she will mother. Official recognition of motherhood is legally established. Generally speaking, a woman entering the role of mother must have the physical and mental characteristics that ensure care of the child in ways approved of by society. She must be able to bring together, if it is not provided for her, a whole social circle with whom to rear the child. The mother must also have the ability to socialize the child so that she or he can fit into societal life. Special consideration is given to mothers who do not see, hear, speak, or have the physical ability needed to carry, feed, and protect the child, but society gives itself the right to take the child away if it considers the care to be inadequate or if the child is endangered.

In other words, the society, community, and any preexisting social circle have the right to determine the necessary qualifications of a social person entering the role of mother, physician, plumber, or any other role over which these groups have jurisdictions. A person wishing to "make" or create a social role must pull together a circle of members willing to cooperate with her or him to meet the agreed upon purpose (Lopata, 1991b; Turner, 1962). Various tests have been created to establish whether an individual has the characteristics of the social person or social circle member of a specific social role.

The social circle consists of all those persons and other social units to whom the person at the center of the social role has duties and obligations and from whom she or he receives the rights needed to perform these duties. All these are negotiated with more or less freedom on either side and can vary considerably by setting, the society, community, and specific role. The social circle usually contains beneficiaries, such as "clients," students, or children, toward whom major obligations are directed, and assistants, colleagues, persons in similar roles, and suppliers. A role requires at least the person and two others, the beneficiary and assistant or supplier of resources. By this definition, a dyad is a social relationship but it takes at least three persons to create a social role (Znaniecki, 1965).

Circle members have obligations and rights not only in relation to the social person, but often to each other as well. Thus, this concept of social circle avoids some of the problems entailed in Merton's (1957a, 1957b) concept of role set, in that it recognizes that circle members may have relations with each other based on the central role. For example, although some patients of a physician may not know each other and never interact, each relates not only to the physician, but also to her or his receptionist, nurse, and those patients who are in the waiting room together. The nurses relate with all these in their contribution to the doctor's role.

The reason people can enter social roles, as social person or circle members, is due to cultural models that define, more or less specifically, what qualifications all participants should possess, and the rights and duties on all sides. This view of social roles makes evident the possibility of role strain when different segments of the social circle make simultaneous demands, all considering their needs to be primary in importance (see Goode, 1960). Role overload, conflicting demands from different segments of the circle or from the same segment, can be prevented only if the social person has the power to establish, or can negotiate, priorities. One method of decreasing demands is by simplifying the social circle, although that solution has its own problems. Major sources of role strain result from the failure of the circle to provide adequate resources for approved action in the role. Finally, person-role strain can develop if the person does not have adequate qualifications and personal resources to meet the demands of a role or if such demands run contrary to her or his value system or personal preferences.

All persons are involved in more than one role, even if it is only as the social person of one and a circle member of another. Role clusters can contain roles within the same institution, such as the family, or in several different institutions, such as the family and occupation. The former role cluster can be identified as flat, regardless of the richness of multiple roles within it, the latter as multidimensional. Conflicts among roles are frequent, as I shall examine in relation to gender. They arise from too many or conflicting demands made on an individual by people in different roles, or from the lack of resources, such as time or money, with which to balance such demands. One way an individual may avoid some conflict is by withdrawing from a role. Organizations may also try to prevent role conflict, as in the case of the refusal in recent centuries of the Catholic Church to allow its priests to marry and have families.

Although cultures contain models of major social roles, such as mother or father, each role is carried forth by a social person in negotiated relations with circle members. This complexity results in relational problems, as each person entering a role may have very different perceptions of its obligations and rights. An employer may wish an employee to bring her or his own clothing, while the employee may assume that uniforms are provided. The matter of cost involved in these two arrangements may be a source of serious irritation. The cultural model may assume the presence of a specific circle member, such as a father in the case of the role of mother, while many American mothers must parent without a father. The title "doctor" is used by both M.D.s and Ph.D.s, but members of the society may assume it refers only to physicians (and, in not too distant a past, white male physicians). The title of the role and of the central person serves as a significant symbol for the organization of behavior by people wishing to interact with her or him. Some roles are rigidly defined, with little flexibility, as in the military. Some settings in a single society may treat same-gender partnerships the same way as traditional marriages, whereas others may forbid and even punish such relationships. The more complex the society in its composition and subcultures, the more variation there is on any social role, regardless of any assumed homogeneity. Yet, people socialized into certain symbols for social roles, such as titles, tend to take for granted an entire set of assumptions, providing constant opportunity for conflict, especially in rapidly changing settings.

I have one final comment on role theory. According to these definitions, there are no gender or race roles, only pervasive identities of social persons and circle members that enter, more or less significantly, into social roles. It is possible, and some thinkers believe this to be the case, that there are social roles of woman and man in modern society whose function is to distinguish between the genders in all social relationships. Caste roles were distinctly of such nature. However, Barrie Thorne and I (1978; see also Stacey & Thorne, 1985) have concluded that such a conceptualization of gender is meaningless, especially since it aggregates all men and all women with no internal differentiation within each category. It thus assumes that all men relate to all women in the same way, that is, according to the rules of such sex or gender roles. It appears to be more logical and realistic to visualize the situation in terms of the following processes: Sexual identification at birth, or at a time of sexual change, seems universal. This becomes a gender identification and identity into which people are socialized and remain involved as they enter different social relations and roles throughout the life course. This pervasive identity becomes an important characteristic in some roles, (e.g., mother or father), but less so in other roles (e.g., physician or store clerk). It enters more in relationship with some members of the same or the other gender, less so in other interactions. It is part of the "package" that we carry with us in our social interactions, as are racial, religious, and ethnic identities, but is more important than, for instance, red hair before voluntary hair color changes, or extremes in height.

2. GENDER AND FAMILY ROLES

I now turn to an analysis of gendered roles, mainly in the complex American society, using the above definition of social role and related concepts. This will be an historical view of the changing cultural models in family and community social roles of men and women, recognizing that none of these exist except in the relation between a social person and a social circle. The subject is complex, and many social scientists have worked hard at making sense of it in terms of its social class, racial, and ethnic variations. The shortage of space for this analysis makes some omissions unavoidable.

Major problems with understanding social roles in this society are the rapidity of social change and the enormity of social diversity. Various aspects of the cultural models of major roles are constantly changing, first as deviations from prior ones, then as more accepted guidelines, and finally as old models to be gradually replaced. An example of this are same-gender variations on sexual partnership and parenthood roles. As Gusfield (1967) pointed out many years ago, social change cannot be conceptualized bipolarly, as into traditionalism and modernity. Various aspects of social roles can change at different rates. A perfect example of such variations in the rate of social change is in the case of family roles.

In brief, contemporary family roles have been deeply influenced by past changes in the economic structures of most societies, especially American. The processes of industrialization and urbanization, of the organization of most work into jobs within economically motivated organizations, and of the development of nation–states and of a series of accompanying cultural changes split the conceptualized world in many ways, including into two spheres, private and public (Lopata, 1993a, 1994b). Much of the work pulled into occupational roles became defined as masculine, with some clearly gendered exceptions (e.g., nursing and teaching). The private sphere became the province of the home and family, extended to those aspects of community life that were defined as associated with these. This province became the domain of women, whose role cluster was reconstructed from that of member of a cooperating family integrated with the community in all institutions, to that of homemaker, wife, and mother in a privatized home. In the meantime, the men's sphere was separated from this territory and simultaneously expanded to all institutions of public life: economic, political, religious, and higher educational. The enormous consequences of this division are still visible in the images of the ideal man and woman and in the relations between the genders. The images had to be reconstructed to fit this two-sphere world, in spite of the fact that neither gender could possibly exist in only one sphere. Women had to become defined and socialized into motherly, caregiving, empathetic, "expressive," and cooperative persons, while men became defined and socialized as rational, efficient, strong, and competitive, as summarized by Parsons (1943/1954), who found such an arrangement systemically functional (see Chafetz, *this volume*). In addition, the two-sphere world visualized interaction between men and women as highly restricted, since it assumed that all they had in common was sex.[1]

Serious attempts have been made by cultural, religious, educational, and other leaders to ensure that such a dichotomized world is supported in every possible way. Such an ideal-typical world construct was never completely possible, however, and it has become increasingly apparent that it is "dysfunctional" to the system, not to mention to the lives of both men and women. Various social movements have drawn the society's and its individual members' attention to the problems of such a world. In social role terms, the attempt to create a two-sphere world and related gendered personalities resulted in tremendous problems for most social roles because it flattened the lifespace of social persons and changed the composition and characteristics of members of their social circles. This is illustrated by strains in the social roles of wife and husband, mother and father, and those in organized public life.

2.1. Wife and Husband Roles

The role of wife in pre- or even early-industrial times, especially in patriarchal, patrilineal, and patrilocal societies, involved the woman in cooperation with not only her husband, but also his family of orientation and often extended family, as well as his village (Thomas & Znaniecki, 1918–1920). It did not include her family of birth, since by marriage she joined the husband's family, often at a considerable distance from her own. Her position as a wife depended mainly upon the husband's position in his family, although her personal characteristics and her contributions to that family economically, socially, and in terms of the status she brought with her or developed were usually acknowledged. Her duties to her husband were often defined and supervised by her in-laws (Lopata, 1999). His family, in turn, granted her rights making possible the performance of these duties. For example, according to anthropologist Paul Bohannan (1963), men universally acquired certain rights over their wives upon marriage, including the right to share a domicile, sexual access, "*in genetricem* rights" of filiation of the children to the husband's line, and economic rights of various strength.[2] In return, the wife gained the right to a shared domicile; the results of sexual access (usually meaning children), shared responsibility over, and care of, the children; and economic cooperation and interdependent support. What happened to the role of wife after the death of the husband depended upon the status she held in the family and community and the status of widows. Family systems concerned with biological fatherhood usually forbade the widow to remarry, or even have sexual relations outside of the family line. They sometimes ensured that she continued having children and that these remained with the family through a levirate system, by which a male agnate of the deceased continued to impregnate her, although the resulting children were considered the offspring of the deceased (Bohannan, 1963; see also Lopata, 1987a, 1987b).[3]

---

[1] This is evident in the strong conservative objection to men and women serving alongside in the military (see Lopata, 1992).

[2] Obviously, Bohannan based this conclusion on studies of patriarchal families.

[3] Numerous studies of widowhood convinced me that the situation of widows is highly indicative of the role of wife and of the situation of women in a society and its communities (see Lopata, 1996).

In heavily patriarchal societies the role of the husband was also embedded in his other family roles. Family members helped him provide the rights and resources for his wife in her role and received rights from her because she was his wife. Thus, both marital roles were submerged in the intertwining of complex, multiple family roles. In such family systems a widower could remarry without any problems, since the lineage of the wife did not count and since the family needed the work done by a wife.

The gradual processes of expansion of societal complexity decreased considerably the power of the patriarchal line over its youths to the extent that they could obtain an education and occupational preparation away from home, take a job, marry, and even move a distance away. This changed both marital roles by decreasing obligations to the male's family. For example, the wife could now set up her own household and run it with much less interference from the husband's family. The husband gradually lost the responsibility for his aged or widowed parents, so that he could concentrate upon his family of procreation. This, however, created problems for his family of orientation, which had lived in the anticipation of support from sons in old age. It did benefit the new unit. Such a shift has been documented, for example, in the recent case of Turkish sons who emigrated to Germany. The widowed mothers left behind gradually received fewer economic benefits, as the sons shifted their allegiance with Westernization (Heisel, 1987).

While the in-law segment of the wife's social circle diminished in importance in terms of her duties toward it, this also diminished the supports she had received from it in her role of wife, so that the main responsibility for the "care" of the husband fell on her shoulders with the help of whomever she could pull into the circle. The relative absence, or at least infrequency of contact, with the male line removed a possible source of abuse from that circle, but at the same time it also removed a possible source of protection from abuse from the husband, especially in the weakening of community support as the demand for personal privacy increased. The alleged right of relational partners to safety was often neglected; in fact, wife abuse sometimes received community approval, especially in subcultures characterized by strong patriarchal power.

Thus, the wife's duties toward the husband, along with the composition of her circle, changed dramatically as his job became increasingly important in economically focused societies. Her social circle often included his work associates toward whom she had definite duties of entertainment, communication, and other forms of interaction. According to Papanek (1973, 1979), the wife became the behind-the-scenes partner in a "two-person single career" in which she performed numerous instrumental and expressive duties that enabled her husband to succeed in his job, of which he was the official center. Papanek (1973, 1979), Finch (1983), Daniels (1988), Lopata (1971, 1993a, 1994b) and many other social scientists outlined these duties as including "stroking," to decrease the stress caused by his other relationships on the job; keeping all problems of the home and family from disturbing him, which means handling them herself; fulfilling her role as homemaker or manager of the home with little help from the househusband; child-rearing; and meeting the obligations of both parents to prevent his career from being interrupted.[4] Papanek (1979) pointed to the importance of status-maintaining work in their residential and his occupational communities and with the employing organization. The required

---

[4] Interestingly enough, there is no equivalent role for a man that matches the "housewife" or more recently "homemaker" role of a woman. The label "househusband" usually refers to a husband who stays home to care for the children. It usually means that there is a wife and that she is the "breadwinner." I have not seen this concept applied to single-parent fathers, who do not automatically become homemakers.

behavior, including proper self-demeanor as well as that of properly educated and married offspring, necessitated refraining from involvement in competing social roles, such as employment. Ostrander (1984) and Daniels (1988) found that status work varied by whether the status of the family, reflected in the status of the husband, simply needed maintenance, or was also oriented toward upward mobility. The whole life of the wife became dependent upon the husband's job, its location, rhythm, costs, and benefits. The situation of Hillary Clinton is illuminating. Although she is known to be a highly successful and intelligent career woman, Americans see her not as a partner in the presidency, but only as the rather devalued "First Lady," who should model herself on the way prior "First Ladies" behaved. She was totally rebuked as the sponsor of a major presidential initiative.[5] Thus, her role is seen in two-person, single career terms.

During the height of the two-person career trend, which reached its peak in the post-World War II decades, the main function of the husband was that of being a "good provider" (Bernard, 1983), as evidenced by the home and family he supported financially. Being a good provider meant that his wife did not "need" to be employed, and that all her economic contributions to his and the rest of the family's welfare were devalued as being those of "only a housewife." When I (Lopata, 1971) asked full-time homemakers and employed suburbanites and urbanites in the 1950s and 1960s what were the most important roles of men, they most frequently listed "breadwinner," and most saw their own main, almost exclusive, roles as care of the family and motherhood. Roles outside of the family were placed last on a list of possible roles of women. Only a few of the respondents, married to business executive or professional men, felt that they had some influence on their husband' careers, thus underevaluating their contributions. Betty Friedan (1963) labeled this whole ideology *The Feminine Mystique* and started a revolutionary reconstruction of reality and roles.

Actually, when *The Feminine Mystique* was published, the behavior of women was already changing, although not yet in ideology and self-concepts, as wives began, or continued, moving into the occupational world. In the years of my *Occupation: Housewife* (1971) studies, a woman's justification for employment was that her paycheck would be used for "special projects" that did not detract from the husband's good provider role. Bird (1979) studied ways in which marital couples tried to incorporate the wife's paycheck, usually as "pin money" too insignificant to threaten the breadwinner. Although Bernard (1983) recorded the "fall" of the good provider role in the early 1980s, the wife's paycheck remains a problem in many families, especially if it is larger than that of her husband.

In the meantime, the occupational sphere, organized around the assumptions and expectations of the two-person career in which the major person is the man, has not changed much even to this day, with some exceptions on the part of some organizations that became aware of the economic advantages of flexibility in the scheduling of work. Coser (1974) called much of the occupational world "greedy" institutions. Most employing organizations still make the same demands of time, energy, and responsibility of their workers, and if they do provide, for example, paternity leaves, few male employees actually take advantage of them. The dramatic movement of wives and mothers into the labor

---

[5] She certainly has an enormous social circle in her role of wife with whose members she must interact at various levels. She is doing so differently than from the wives of most other presidents, accentuating my point concerning the complexity of the society and variations in the ways role models are negotiated and modified by the contact and characteristics of social persons and social circles.

force has not been accompanied by major changes in occupational and related institutions or in the work patterns of husbands. This places a heavy burden on the wife as she struggles to continue meeting some of the traditional obligations to her career-minded husband in spite of the demands of her own often "greedy" occupation and "greedy" family (Coser, 1974; Coser & Coser, 1974). Hochschild (1989) found wives spending considerably more time than husbands in maintaining their home, even in the absence of children, but especially in their presence. She labeled the work employed women do, in their roles of wife, mother, and homemaker *The Second Shift*. Attempts to negotiate a decrease of obligations and an increase of rights from circle members, especially husbands, have proven difficult in the presence of traditional role models and in the absence of anyone in their social circle in the role of wife who is willing to take over some of their duties. Numerous studies indicate that role conflict on the part of women is not solved in any significant way by a shift of men's priorities. A partial exception to women's second shift occurs in cases in which the wife and husband start out together focused on the public sphere. Even then, the birth of children tends to unbalance whatever symmetry of work and household responsibility the couple developed before, or during, marriage. In contrast, Blumstein and Schwartz (1983) found lesbian and gay partnerships less concerned about the division of work, money, sexuality, and emotional support than married or cohabiting heterosexual couples.

2.2. Mother and Father Roles

British Common Law, which became the foundation of the American legal system, gave "absolute right to the custody of their minor children to the father" (Lindgren & Taub, 1988; see Lopata, 1994b, p. 65). The legal system has shifted to such an extent that the mother is now seen as the main parent, responsible not only for what she does, but also for what the father does and for the behavior of the children, seen as a result of such parenting. In the event of divorce, it is mainly the mother who is now given custody. The modern stress on the economic institution released the man from many family obligations, first to his family of orientation and then even to his family of procreation (as long as he supported this unit economically) so that he could devote all his time, energy, and emotion to competition on the job and to his career. This trend, in conjunction with the removal of the husband's family from control over the role of wife, has had repercussions upon other roles in the family institution, especially those of mother and of father. The circle of the mother no longer contains an important segment of grandparents, aunts and uncles, and relatives by marriage. On the other hand, the woman's birth family has been able to increase its participation in her role of mother, since she no longer has to leave it upon marriage and no longer has major obligations to her in-laws. Chodorow's (1978) and Sokoloff's (1980) influential thesis of the inevitable bond between mother and daughter ignores much of human history. It also ignores some contemporary societies in which the birth of a daughter is not welcome because she will have to be fed and cared for until an age in which she could be helpful, and then she will cost the family an expensive dowry and be gone. She cannot even perform the duties of ancestor worship. Thus, she is a burden, rather than a joy, as numerous accounts of the lot of girls in India (Gurjal, 1987), China (Barnes, 1987); see also Lopata, 1987a, 1996), and other countries have repeatedly stressed. Even recently, human rights commissions reports in the mass media document that girl children have been allowed to die or were even sold as concubines or wives, as beggars, or prostitutes (de Mause, 1974).

The transformation of the family system has changed the relationship of the mother to her own parents, especially to her mother, who has now entered the social circle of her daughter's role of mother (Lopata, 1991b). A young woman's mother can maintain contact with her daughter over the lifecourse, and the bond becomes even closer as the daughter becomes a mother herself (Fischer, 1986). Mothers-in-law generally have few rights and provide minimal support (Lopata, 1979). Maternal assistance is today important, in the relative absence of in-laws, the complete absence of servants in all but wealthy families, and of frequent absence of fathers in daily life (Hochschild, 1989). However, the mother's contribution to her daughter's role as mother rarely includes protection against harm to her or her family, usually from the father or his substitute, because of the older woman's lack of power.

An even more recent change in the role of young mother has been the decrease of the contributions of even her mother to her social circle, because women old enough to be grandmothers are likely to be in the labor force, with little time to actively help with the children. In addition, many of the widows I (Lopata, 1973, 1979) studied in the Chicago area are unwilling to become full-time participants in their daughters' roles of mothers, having already worked in that role themselves. Moreover, many have become economically self sufficient, and they do not have to exchange childcare work for their grown children for housing and maintenance. Those who wish and need to can do childcare for pay, controlling the conditions better than if working for their own families. Societal assistants and suppliers have not yet caught up with the need to help mothers in the care of the children. Individualism and an ideology of concern with one's own children alone have permeated American culture (see Grubb & Lazerson, 1982). Yet, there is an interesting social class difference in attitudes. Americans continue to believe that middle- and upper-class women should stay home to care for their homes, but insist that poor women take jobs away from their home. In all of the discussion of "selfish mothers" or "welfare mothers" there is little acknowledgement that there are more people than just mothers who need children and future generations of contributive adults. The feeling that fathers have responsibilities that are not met has not been strong enough to push societal action toward solutions of their parental problems. Throughout the mass media and even the social science literature, people other than the mother, including the father, are seen as merely "helping;" they are not defined as responsible members of parenting circles. There is a great deal of speculation as to when the society and its communities and organizations will seriously understand that "It takes a whole village to raise a child."

As a result of changes in parental roles, the rights of parents and the obligations of children have been strongly modified. In past centuries, and even today despite the redefinition of morality in the Western world, children have been valued mainly as contributors to the economic subsistence of the family (Sommerville, 1982). They were sent to work early on family lands or businesses, to factories, or to other people's homes as servants, with the obligation to turn over to the parents the products, profits, or wages from their labor. At one time, parents even took out insurance on their children in case they died, depriving the families of their labor. It is only recently that the image of children changed from them as expendable or economically productive to being "priceless" (Zelizer, 1987) members of families in the recent "century of the child" (Ehrenreich & English, 1979). Thus, the current view of children's obligations to their mothers is mostly that they "turn out OK," preferably bringing their mothers pride as they receive honors, a good marriage, and grandchildren for occasional visits. Fathers generally have the same expectations, besides possibly being "pals" with their sons and walking down the aisle with the daughters at their wedding. Newer generations of fathers have begun to take an active, if still asymmetrical, part in parenting (Hochschild, 1989), although mothers still see themselves and are seen by the fathers as the ones most responsible for the children.

3. RACIAL, ETHNIC, AND CLASS INTERTWINING IN FAMILY ROLES

Racial, ethnic, religious, and social class variations exist in the roles of wife and husband, mother and father, but are complicated by the intertwining of these aspects and by change over time. Most American families, with a few exceptions such as among some native American tribes, have a patriarchal background in which marital and parental roles were clearly defined as to the characteristics of the social person and of the circle, as well as to the duties and rights of each role. Obedience by the wife to her husband and by children to parents was officially approved and strictly enforced by those in power, encouraged by Puritans and by other family systems. Numerous studies (de Mause, 1974; Pleck, 1983) have documented both the abuse that followed and the various means by which the dominated family members attempted to empower themselves. Rules were most strictly followed by the lower-working-class and by the status protecting upper-class, but the flavor of the relationships varied considerably and has changed considerably in recent times.

3.1. The Poor and the Working Class

Stack (1975), Liebow (1967), and others found fathers among the poor, sometimes called the underclass, less involved in parenting in the culturally defined manner than the "ideal-typical" image of the father in the middle and upper classes, primarily for socioeconomic reasons. The social circle of the role of mother may include men other than the biological father; her own family of orientation, especially mother and grandmother; friends; and neighbors. Fictive relatives appear in several roles, assisting mothers, intervening in marital relationships, and combining friendship with duties usually undertaken by socially defined kinship roles (Stack, 1975). The community of residence of the very poor, however, lacks the employment opportunities and the support of major institutions that were available to many immigrant families at the turn of the century (Wilson, 1987). Those people in the worst poverty conditions form segments of African-American, American Indian, Hispanic, and white, often of rural background, American communities, for whom a vicious circle of factors, including discrimination, lack of resources, and internal interdependence, make out-movement difficult (Stack, 1975). Female-headed households in this part of America's population are often dependent not only on Aid to Families with Dependent Children, but also on a variety of different resources that contribute small sums of money, products, or services (Edin & Lein, 1997). In the case of American Indians, the whole history of relations with the United States government involved dislocation, cultural disintegration, and social segregation, leading to numerous problems in all social roles. Wilkinson (1987) concludes that the history of family relations among native Americans has prevented movement of nuclear families away from their elderly and other kinship relations:

> Though variable, kinship bonding and obligations to relatives remain essential in familial interaction. . . ; They include residential propinquity, obligatory mutual aid, active participation in life

cycle events, and central figures around whom family ceremonies revolve. . . . Women play fundamental roles in these extended systems. . . . In many Indian tribes, the descent of children and the
ownership of property are traced through the mother's line. (pp. 191–192).

Thus, the role of mother in such families is central to women and includes numerous
relatives in the circle. The reservation housing of native Americans is very different from
the communities of Puerto Ricans, whose underclass members tend to live in internally
segregated areas of inner cities. Puerto Rican culture is very patriarchal, although "traditional norms of obedience and respect for adults, rules pertaining to endogamy, and those
governing male–female behavior have been modified" (Wilkinson, 1987, p. 192). There
remains a great deal of gender separation, women helping each other in their various
roles, with men being more distant as husbands and fathers. A similar pattern exists
among immigrant Mexican-Americans.

Asians have a different history in America, with different family results. In early
years of American development, anti-Chinese discriminatory laws created "split household families," the men coming from China for work, and returning only occasionally to
father children. The mothers remained in China with the children, because of laws for-
bidding Chinese women from entering the United States. They also took care of the elderly in-laws for whom the son was technically responsible. The prejudice against daughters continued as families became united in America, being seen as expensive "temporary
members" and reputedly sold by families to become prostitutes in the new land (Dill,
1995, pp. 247–248). The abolition of the 1880s Exclusion Act in 1943 enabled the reunification of families, assisted by community associations. Community cooperation and the
use of the American educational system have helped upward mobility of Asian families
that started at the bottom of the social class ladder in the wider society.

The employed, not-extremely poor part of the working-class, blue-collar couples
and parents usually came from immigrant backgrounds, from Europe and now from varied countries on other continents. Those who settled in urban areas built "Polonias,"
"Little Italies," or "Chinatowns" with institutional complexity and an interweaving of
relationships (Lopata, 1994b). Parents generally retained patriarchal roles, with tight
discipline unless the street life of the children engrossed them in its own code of behavior
(Kohn, 1977; Langman, 1987). Kinship members appeared often in the circle of mothers
and in-laws in the circle of wives. Husbands and wives worked hard, the men in unre-
warding jobs, the women taking in boarders and contributing elsewhere in the informal
labor market. Rubin (1976) describes the roles of wife and mother, husband and father of
such families in *Worlds of Pain*. Ethnic families gradually moved out of the ethnic ghettos to the outskirts of cities and, by the third generation, to the suburbs. Such mobility,
however, makes difficult kinship contacts, so that relatives are less apt to be involved in
each other's social circles than in the past. As they move away from ethnic backgrounds,
working-class families adopt middle-class values, adding to this large band of American
social structure.

The combination of Jewish religious and American democratic middle-class values
among even lower-class Jewish immigrants led to great sacrifices for the education of the
young in the American educational system, in addition to traditional Hebrew schools.
Such an emphasis paid off in upward mobility, as the offspring moved up the occupational ladder into professions and out of the ghettos into those suburbs that did not have
discriminatory practices (Lopata, 1994a, p. 83). The same value system and strict learning schedules enforced by families have also helped Asians move out of socioeconomic
areas of initial geographical and social settlement. Of course, some immigrants, such as

early Cubans or families from modern Hong Kong, came with language and occupational abilities and financial resources that put them immediately into the middle class. In fact, immigration into United States has often been a multiclass phenomenon, with the ability to reproduce social status in the home country in America highly dependent upon knowledge of English and the transferability of occupations, as evidenced by new waves of Poles coming to this country (Lopata, 1994a). In general, however, traditional norms of family behavior, including a strong division of labor and responsibility within the roles of wife and husband, mother and father, remain among upwardly mobile ethnic individuals who form the main part of the working class in this society.

Stacey (1992) found great complexities in the interweaving of race, class, and gender among postmodern families in the Silicon Valley, especially as blue-collar jobs declined and two-earner couples expanded when women entered the labor force.

3.2. The Middle Class

Upward mobility has been experienced by most Americans, with the exception of those in the current underclass. Mobility was accomplished through education and occupational achievement and was accompanied by geographical movement into "nicer" neighborhoods and suburbs. The successful movers were primarily white, but some African-Americans began moving out, often meeting serious problems with neighbors or finding only segregated areas in suburbia. It is within such families that the two-person career thrived for decades and that the greatest amount of change has been occurring recently. The couples that moved away from the old neighborhoods after World War II created a whole new life, dissimilar from that of their more ethnically and racially identified families (Lopata, 1971). Having mastered the new home, community, and way of mothering, with the help of Dr. Spock's baby books, women started moving out into occupational roles, as mentioned previously, creating role strain in their role of wife and conflicts within the role cluster. Recent migration waves of Asians and various groups of Hispanics are now moving to suburbia at a more rapid rate. Among these new members of the middle class, roles are becoming much more flexible, with some protest by privilege-losing husbands and fathers and some ideational coverups camouflaging continued asymmetry of responsibilities, as mentioned previously. I will discuss some of the role conflicts in a later section.

3.3. The Upper Class

Although some of the women of the upper class are converting the skills they developed in volunteer work and tasks of status development and maintenance into paid occupations, many are still restricted in several ways within the world of organized jobs. In the first place, the whole structure of this class is built upon their unpaid work in the community, the husband's career and child socialization. The servants that they pull into their various social circles must be hired, trained, and supervised, which are time- and energy-consuming tasks. The activities of associates of the offspring also need organization, transportation, and supervision. The home and how it is used are symbols of the husband's success and of the wife's ability to maintain social status. Volunteer work beautifying and making smooth the functioning of the community in which they live is still needed, although some adjustments in time of day and rhythm are made in cases of occupational involvement. Such involvement is, however, seriously discouraged because of the needs of the roles required of the women. Daniels (1988) and Ostrander (1984) describe in great detail not only the work, but also the feelings of class and community obligations, shared by the wives and mothers in the upper class of America, and descriptions of the duties of women of this class in other countries abound. The husbands remain in jobs or moneymaking ventures that are inflexible and demanding of their time and attention.

4.GENDER AND PUBLIC ROLES

When the constructed reality distinguished sharply between two spheres, women's involvement in the public sphere, aside from that which was required of them in the roles of wife, mother, or homemaker, was simply ignored. Women were earning money, products, or services in a variety of ways and performed politically or religiously significant work without carrying official titles. Unmarried women were employed, in fact, in many types of jobs besides farming and, when these developed into occupations, in nursing and teaching. However, most of the high-status occupations, especially in the professions and organizational management, were closed to women, or employed only a few as tokens (Kanter, 1977). Women also participated in the activities of all the other public institutions, but often in subsidiary roles with much resistance to their gain of higher positions, as evidenced in many struggles in religious organizations. This section is devoted to the complexities of women's entrance into a variety of occupations and levels of authority in the world of organized, paid, work.

A major obstacle to women's entry into male-dominated occupations has been the assumed lack of match between the necessary characteristics of the social person in a particular occupation and the personality characteristics inevitably connected with each gender. American culture contains stereotypes of occupations—what kind of person is most suited to perform surgical operations (rational and scientific) or teach little children (caring)—as well as gender-specific temperamental and physical characteristics. These stereotypes grew out of the two-sphere world ideology—women are caring, men are scientific and rational. One of the commonly held images, used as justification for not hiring women into high-level positions, has been that women do not like complexity in their jobs. A major study of Chicago area women aged 25 to 54 (Lopata, Miller, & Barnewolt, 1984) found this not to be true (see also Lopata, Barnewolt, & Miller, 1985). Women who expressed satisfaction with their jobs also perceived them to be "more complex than the average job" along several dimensions, such as work complexity, opportunity for self-development, independence, and creativity. An interesting aspect of the women's perceptions of job complexity is that they considered not only tasks but also social relations. Thus, even jobs that the United States Department of Labor's (1965) *Dictionary of Occupational Titles: Vol. 1, Defintion of Title* considered low in complexity such as nurse's aide or beautician, received high-complexity scores on some dimensions by more than half of the Chicago employees. The aides accepted the medical ideology of helping people get well, the beauticians the cultural ideology that they make people look good and increase their self-respect. Sales clerks did not see their jobs as complex and had low scores on our scales, but sales agents scored high, especially on independence and responsibility. Women who managed single-parent households considered their job to be less complex than did the managers of adults-only households, several comments leading us to conclude that the absence of a husband/father simplified rather than complicated life.

Our study questioned another assumption concerning women: their commitment to their occupation (see Lopata, 1993b; Schrimsher, 1996, 1998). American society assumes that women, regardless of family roles, will not be as strongly committed to their occupations and employing organizations as will men. We found many of the Chicago women, particularly the younger ones, investing serious "side bets" into their general commitment to the role of career/worker. This included occupational preparation in the past and planned future in an appropriate school or training center, selection of a job that would meet their career needs, marriage to a man who supported these decisions, self-image in terms of that occupational title, and congruence of constructed reality. However, some of these side bets were difficult to maintain, especially after entrance into the role of mother. Schrimsher (1998) used the same side bet theory and found that women graduates of Case Western Reserve University Law School in 1981 were less successful in 1991 in their career progress than were the men. The men were less apt to marry persons in demanding occupations and more apt to receive practical support from partners than were the women. Initial investment in the career throughout law school and early job search and willingness to commit time and energy heavily in the occupation did not pay off as well for the women as for the men, not because of their lack of commitment to their career, but due to the strength of the occupational-gender system, built during the two-sphere world times, that favors men and expects women to allow priority to husbands' jobs.

One of the problems with current attempts to use stereotypes of occupation and of gender in analyses of the influence of gender on the world of paid work is their focus on the characteristics of only the social person. The assumption is made, or implied, not only that all women (or all men, for that matter) are alike, but also that all jobs with the same title are alike. This ignores the fact that all social roles are negotiated sets of relations of a social person with all the members of the role's social circle. Obviously, therefore, each social role builds uniquely as the relations develop. This chapter's social role theory thus points to the illogicality of occupational stereotyping and can help illuminate the diversity of gender identities depending on job and setting. Assumption of a single pervasive identity of "woman" or "man" ignores the many nuances in a variety of settings of social persons in different jobs. Waitresses act and are related to as different persons than waiters, but also as different from women teachers. The recent expansion of women into a variety of occupations shows an even greater variety of ways in which a woman's pervasive identity varies by, for example, whether she is a truck driver or professor, manager or artist. In studying settings of employed women, I (Lopata, 1994) kept noticing how different were these roles depending also on the composition of the social circle. Teachers of small children, for example, behave differently than teachers of college students. The latter do not have to deal with the parents of their pupils. Kanter (1977) introduced the concept of token, pointing out that a token woman in a man's occupation in an industrial organization has very different relationships with others than does a woman in the same occupation when a significant number of workers have the same identity. A physician often relates to men patients differently from women patients and those relations are influenced by which assistants, such as nurses, receptionists, or technicians, are in his/her circle. A manager interacts with employees differently if they are relatives in a family business than if they are simply occupiers of a job. A surgeon in a MASH unit must function in innovative ways not necessary if she or he has all the personal or technological resources of a hospital.

5. GENDER ASPECTS OF ROLE CONFLICT

As mentioned previously, role conflict is usually referred to in terms of the role cluster of any one individual. Typically in recent American history, such conflict has been perceived in the role cluster of women, especially when they began to officially enter the world of greedy and prestigeful occupations. However, conflict between various aspects of work in the home and in family roles had been (and often still is) taken for granted as normal. Work in the informal market, such as taking care of boarders or taking in laundry, even employment in lower-status jobs, such as domestic, has also been neglected as a source of role conflict. It has long been acceptable for single women to hold jobs, regardless of their other roles. It is when women began to enter the world of prestigeful occupations, originally monopolized by men and organized with the rights and privileges of the male sphere, that American media and male family scientists began loud warnings. First, they warned women that such behavior was inappropriate because it conflicted with their obligations in the role of wife—hurting the husband's career by neglecting duties owed him. Next came the warning that the children were being hurt because jobs make impossible 24-hour presence in and around the home, as preached in the "fantasy of the perfect mother" (Chodorow & Contratto, 1982); although it was all right for her to be absent for volunteer work, which was needed by the community, as Daniels (1988) discovered in her research. The whole argument about the need for constant mothering ignores the centuries during which children were taken care of mainly by servants or sent to other people's homes as servants to be properly socialized into society (Aries, 1965). The latest argument has been that occupational involvement is bad for the woman herself, because it causes serious anxiety, a harried and pulled apart life, and guilt. This is a good example of constructed person-role cluster strain, in which there is an assumed conflict between what a person is and what the roles demand. Although this set of arguments about the inevitability of role conflict in the lives of women is still directed mainly toward those with small children, it often is extended to all women, regardless of marital or parental roles. People seem less concerned with role conflict in lesbian partnerships, possibly because these have been relatively invisible and only recently are recognized as possibly also involving children.

6. CONCLUSIONS

The social roles of men, but especially of women, have changed considerably in recent decades in America and other developed nations, moving away at least partially from the restrictions of the two-sphere world. Even before these dramatic changes, the two-sphere world existed mainly as a constructed ideology that ignored much of what went on in human life in America and Europe. Its strength lay in that it formed a consistent base of childhood socialization by forcing gender differentiation and social role segregation. However, as with all ideologies, it narrowed and constricted humans. It has taken a great deal of consciousness raising and innovative behavior to understand its detrimental effects and to open up new opportunities for role changes. This chapter is an attempt to analyze some of the revolutionary changes in pervasive gendered identities of both social persons at the center of social roles and of members of their social circles that provide resources and rights, and receive these from the person. Social roles have changed considerably, not only in the characteristics of social persons, but also in the composition of

social circles. This is apparent in the few social roles we have examined here, those of
wife and husband, mother and father. and those in the public sphere of labor force workers.

Although each culture contains models of various social roles, the role itself is carried forth in negotiated cooperation between the social person and circle members. The
more complex and internally diversified the society and heterogeneous the culture, the
greater the possibility of role strain and role conflict as people get together to carry forth
social roles. What is surprising about social life in American society is not that such
problems arise, but that people can actually carry forth their roles together. Social change
is not even; it affects members of a society, and therefore social persons and circle members, at different rates and in different ways. Recently, wives and mothers have been
changing their role definitions at a more rapid rate and in different ways than husbands
and fathers, the composition and behavior of their social circles often differing from that
of the social persons. The complexity of the interweaving of social roles can be illustrated
by problems in attempts to introduce occupational changes in complex organizations
based on a Weberian logical and rational model. These efforts often, if not usually, neglect to take into account the social roles of their employees as interdependent sets of
relations. Gerald Handel (1967) and associates have repeatedly warned family practitioners that the psychological interior of the family must be recognized when attempts are
made to change the behavior of one member. Changes in the behavior of one individual
have repercussions on the members of each of the social circles in which she or he is
involved (see also Lopata, 1990). It is no wonder that sociologists have a difficult time
analyzing any social role or role cluster.

REFERENCES

Aries, P. (1965). *Centuries of childhood*. New York: Random House.
Barnes, D. (1987). Wives and widows in China. In H. Z. Lopata (Ed.), *Widows: The Middle East, Asia and the Pacific* (pp. 195–216). Durham, NC: Duke University Press.
Bernard, J. (1983). The good provider role: Its rise and fall. In A. S. & J. H. Skolnick (Eds.), *Family in transition* (pp. 155–175). Boston: Little, Brown.
Biddle, J., & Thomas, E. J. (Eds) (1966). *Role theory: Concepts and research*. New York: John Wiley & Sons.
Bird, C. (1979). *The two-paycheck marriage*. New York: New American Library/Mentor.
Blumstein, P., & Schwartz, P. (1983). *American couples: Money, work and sex*. New York: Free Press.
Bohannan, P. (1963). *Social anthropology*. New York: Holt, Rinehart & Winston.
Brandeis, L. B., & Goldmark, J. ([1907]1969). *Women in industry*. New York: Arno and *the New York Times*.
British Parliamentary Papers. ([1842]1968). *Children's Employment Commission, first report of the commissioners, mines: Vol. 6, Industrial revolution, children's employment*. Shannon, Ireland: Irish University Press.
Chodorow, N. (1978). *The reproduction of mothering: Psychoanalysis and the sociology of gender*. Berkeley, CA: University of California Press.
Chodorow, N., & Contratto, S. (1982). The fantasy of the perfect mother. In B. Thorne with M. Yalom.(Eds.), *Rethinking the family: Some feminist questions* (pp. 1–25). New York: Longman.
Coser, L. (1974). *Greedy institutions*. New York: The Free Press.
Coser, L., & Coser, R. L. (1974). The housewife and her greedy family. In L. Coser (Ed.), *Greedy institutions* (pp. 88–100). New York: Free Press.
Daniels, A. K. (1988). *Invisible careers: Women community leaders in the volunteer world*. Chicago: University of Chicago Press.
Dill, B. T. (1995). Our mother's grief: Racial ethnic women and the maintenance of families. In M. L. Andersen & P. H. Collins (Eds.), *Race, class and gender* (2nd ed., pp. 237–260) Belmont, CA: Wadsworth.
Edin, K., & Lein, L. (1997). *Making ends meet: How single mothers survive welfare and low-wage work*. New York: Russell Sage Foundation.
Ehrenreich, B., & English, D. (1979). *For her own good*. Garden City, NY: Anchor Books.

Finch, J. (1983). *Married to the job: Wives' incorporation in men's work*. Boston: Allen & Unwin.

Fischer, L. R. (1983). Mothers and mothers-in-law. *Journal of Marriage and the Family, 45,* 187–192.

Fischer, L. R. (1986). *Linked lives: Adult daughters and their mothers*. New York: Harper & Row.

Friedan, B. (1963). *The feminine mystique*. New York: Norton.

Goode, W. (1960). A theory of role strain. *American Sociological Review, 25,* 483–496.

Gujral, J. S. (1987). Widowhood in India. In H. Z. Lopata *Widows: The Middle East, Asia and the Pacific* (pp. 43–55). Durham, NC: Duke University Press.

Grubb, N. W., & Lazerson, M. (1982). *Broken promises: How Americans fail their children*. New York: Basic Books.

Gusfield, J. R. (1967). Tradition and modernity: Misplaced polarities in the study of social change. *American Journal of Sociology, 82,* 443–448.

Handel, G. (Ed.) (1967). *The psychosocial interior of the family*. Chicago: Aldine.

Heisel, M. (1987). Women and widows in Turkey: Support systems. In H. Z, Lopata, (Ed.), *Widows: The Middle East, Asia and the Pacific* (pp. 79–105). Durham, NC: Duke University Press.

Hochschild, A. (1989). *The second shift: Working parents and the revolution at home*. New York: Viking Press.

Kanter, R. M. (1977). *Men and women of the corporation*. New York: Basic Books.

Kohn, M. (1977). *Class and conformity: A study of values*. (2nd ed.). Chicago: University of Chicago Press.

Langman, L. (1987). Social stratification. In M. Sussman & S. Stenmetz, (Eds.), *Handbook of marriage and the family* (pp. 211–249). New York: Plenum Press.

Liebow, E. (1967). *Tally's corner*. Boston: Little, Brown.

Lindgren, R. J. & Taub, N. (1988). *The law of sex discrimination*. New York: West.

Lopata, H. Z. (1966). The life cycle of the social role of housewife. *Sociology and Social Research, 51,* 5–22.

Lopata, H. Z. (1969). Social psychological aspects of role involvement. *Sociology and Social Research, 53,* 285–298.

Lopata, H. Z. (1971). *Occupation: Housewife*. New York: Oxford University Press.

Lopata, H. Z. (1973). *Widowhood in an American city*. Cambridge, MA: Schenkman.

Lopata, H. Z. (1979). *Women as widows: Support systems*. New York: Elsevier-North Holland.

Lopata, H. Z. (1987a). *Widows: The Middle East, Asia and the Pacific*, Vol. 1 and *Widows: North America*, Vol. 2. Durham, NC: Duke University Press.

Lopata, H. Z. (1987b). Widowhood: World perspectives on support systems. In H. Z, Lopata (Ed.), *Widows: The Middle East, Asia and the Pacific* (pp. 1–23). Durham, NC: Duke University Press.

Lopata, H. Z. (1990). Sociological research strategies in the study of family support systems. In S. Quah (Ed.), *The family as an asset* (pp. 63–76). Singapore: Times Academic Press.

Lopata, H. Z. (1991a.) Which child? Consequences of social development on the support systems of widows. In B. Hess & E. Markson (Eds.), *Growing old in America* (pp. 39–49). New Brunswick: Transaction.

Lopata, H. Z. (1991b). Role theory. In J. R. Blau & N. Goodman (Eds.), *Social roles and social institutions: Essays in honor of Rose Laub Coser* (pp. 1–11). Boulder Colo. Westview.

Lopata, H. Z. (1992). Testimony to the Presidential Commission on the Assignment of Women in the Armed Forces. Northwestern University, Evanston, Illinois, July 15.

Lopata, H. Z. (1993a). The interweave of public and private: Women's challenge to American society. *Journal of Marriage and the Family, 55,* 176–90.

Lopata, H. Z. (1993b). Career commitments of American women: The issue of side bets. *Sociological Quarterly, 34,* 257–277.

Lopata, H. Z. (1994a). *Polish Americans* (2nd ed.). New Brunswick, NJ: Transaction.

Lopata, H. Z. (1994b). *Circles and settings: Role changes of American Women*. Albany, NY: SUNY University Press.

Lopata, H. Z. (1996). *Current widowhood: Myths and realities*. Newbury, CA: Sage.

Lopata, H. Z. (1999). In-laws and the concept of family. In B. Settles, M. Sussman, & I. Levin (Eds.), *Concepts and definitions of family: Dialogue between theory and practice*. Binington, NY: Hayward Press.

Lopata, H. Z., & Thorne, B. (1978). On the term 'sex roles.' *Signs, 3,* 718–721.

Lopata, H. Z., Barnewolt, D., & Miller, C. A. (1985). *City women: Work, jobs, careers*, Vol. 2: *Chicago*. New York: Praeger.

Lopata, H. Z., Miller, C. A., & Barnewolt, D. (1984). *City women: Work, jobs, occupations, careers*, Vol. 1: *America*. New York: Praeger.

Lopata, H. Z., Norr, K. F., Bernewolt, D., & Miller, C. A. (1985). Job complexity as perceived by workers and experts. *Sociology of Work and Occupations, 12,* 395–415.

de Mause, L. (Ed.) (1974). *The history of childhood*. New York: The Psychohistory Press.

Merton, R. (1957a). *Social theory and social structure*. New York: Free Press.

Merton, R. (1957b). The role set. *British Journal of Sociology, 8,* 106–120.

Millett, K. (1970). *Sexual politics.* New York: Doubleday.

Ostrander, S. A. (1984). *Women of the upper class.* Philadelphia: Temple University Press.

Papanek, H. (1973). Men, women and work: Reflections on a two-person career. *American Journal of Sociology, 78,* 852–872.

Papanek, H. (1979). Family status production: The 'work' and 'nonwork' of women. *Signs, 4,* 775–781.

Parsons, T. (1943/1954). The kinship system in contemporary United States. In T. Parsons, (Ed.), *Essays in sociological theory* (pp. 177–196). Glencoe, IL: The Free Press.

Pleck, E. (1983). The old world, new rights, and the limited rebellion: Challenges to traditional authority in immigrant families. In H. L. Lopata & J. H. Pleck (Eds.), *Research in the interweave of social roles: Families and jobs* (pp. 91–112). Greenwich, CT: JAI Press.

Rubin, L. B. (1976). *Worlds of pain: Life in the working-class family.* New York: Basic Books.

Schrimsher, K. P. (1996). *Professional socialization, career patterns & commitments: A gender analysis of law school graduates.* Ann Arbor, MI: UMI Dissertation Services.

Schrimsher, K. P. (1998). Career commitments: Women and men law school graduates. In H. Z. Lopata, (Ed.), *Current research on occupations and professions,* Vol. 10: *Settings* (pp. 193–215). Greenwich, CT: JAI Press.

Sokoloff, N. J. (1980). *Between money and love: The dialectic of women's home and market work.* New York: Praeger.

Sommerville, J. (1982). *The rise and fall of childhood.* Beverly Hills, CA: Sage.

Spock, B. (1957). *Baby and child care.* New York: Cardinal/Pocket.

Stacey, J. (1992). Backward toward the postmodern family: Reflections on gender, kinshuip and class in the Silicon Valley. In B. Thorne (Ed.), *Rethinking the family: Some feminist questions* (pp. 91-118). Boston: Northeastern University Press. Revised edition.

Stacey, J., & B. Thorne. (1985). The missing feminist revolution in sociology. *Social Problems, 32,* 301–316.

Stack, C. B. (1975). *All our kin.* New York: Harper & Row.

Thomas, W. I., &. Znaniecki, F. Z. (1918–1920). *The Polish peasant in Europe and America.* Boston: Richard G. Badger.

Turner, R. (1962). Role-taking: Process versus conformity. In A. Rose (Ed.), *Human behavior and social process* (pp. 20–40). Boston: Houghton Mifflin.

United States Department of Labor. (1965). *Dictionary of occupation titles, Vol. 1: Definition of titles.* Washington, D.C.: U. S. Government Printing Office.

Wilkinson, D. (1987). Ethnicity. In M. B. Sussman & S. K. Steinmetz. (Eds.), *Handbook of marriage and the family* (pp. 183–210). New York: Plenum Press.

Wilson, W. J. (1987). *The truly disadvantaged,* Chicago: University of Chicago Press.

World Health Organization. (1996). *Female genital mutilation: Information pack.* World Health Organization Internet Home-page.

Zelizer, V. (1987). *Pricing the priceless child.* New York: Basic Books

Znaniecki, F. W. (1965). *Social relations and social roles.* San Francisco: Chandler.

CHAPTER 13

Gender and Interaction

CECILIA L. RIDGEWAY
LYNN SMITH-LOVIN

Gender is a system of social practices within society that constitutes people as different in socially significant ways and organizes relations of inequality on the basis of the difference. Like other systems of difference and inequality, such as race or class, gender involves widely shared cultural beliefs and institutions at the macro-level of analysis, behaviors and expectations at the interactional level, and self-conceptions and attitudes at the individual level of analysis. Although each component is important, events at the interactional level may be especially important for the maintenance or change of the gender system. Compared to people on opposite sides of class and racial divides, men and women in the United States interact with one another frequently, often on familiar, even intimate terms.

1. THE GENDER SYSTEM AND INTERACTION

Unlike most social differences, gender divides people into two groups of roughly equal size. Since whom you interact with is partly determined by who is available, two equal sized groups creates the maximum structural likelihood that people in both groups will have ample contact with the other group (Blau & Schwartz, 1984). The relevance of one's sex category for sexual behavior and reproduction also increases the rate of interaction between most men and women. Finally, unlike race or class, gender almost always cross-cuts kinship. Most people have opposite sex family members with whom they interact, be

CECILIA L. RIDGEWAY • Department of Sociology, Stanford University, Stanford, California 94305
LYNN SMITH-LOVIN • Department of Sociology, University of Arizona, Tucson, Arizona 85721
Handbook of the Sociology of Gender, edited by Janet Saltzman Chafetz. Kluwer Academic/ Plenum Publishers, New York, 1999.

they spouses, parents, children, or siblings. Given all the forces that keep men and women interacting with one another, the gender system of difference and inequality would be impossible to sustain if interactional events were not organized to support it.

Not only does the high rate of interaction between the sexes make the interactional level important for the gender system as a whole, but it also has significant consequences for the way gender shapes behavior in interaction. Gender appears to be deeply entwined with the basic cultural rules people use to organize their interaction with others (Ridgeway, 1997; West & Zimmerman, 1997). Coordinating interaction requires at least a minimal cultural definition of "who" self and other are. Perhaps because it is a simple, quick, habitually used cultural dichotomy, evidence suggests that people employ gender this way even when other definitions are available (e.g., employer–employee). Social cognition research has shown that people automatically sex categorize (i.e., label as male or female) any other with whom they interact (Brewer & Lui, 1989). Sex category is one of only two or three "primary" social categories that our culture has constituted as necessary to make sufficient sense out of another in relation to self so that interaction can proceed. When self and other are categorized on other social dimensions as well (e.g., occupation) those conceptions are nested within the prior understanding of self and other as male or female, often with subsequent consequences for expectations and behavior (Brewer & Lui, 1989).

Sex categorization may seem a "natural" process but ethnomethodologists have shown it to be substantially socially constructed (Kessler & McKenna, 1978; West & Zimmerman, 1987). In everyday interaction people sex categorize each other based on appearance and other cues that are culturally presumed to stand for physical sex differences. Automatic, taken-for-granted sex categorization of actors seems to be a fundamental part of organizing interaction.

The high rate of interaction between men and women has other consequences for the way gender shapes behavior. The continued, everyday acceptance of the gender system requires that men and women be understood as sufficiently different in ways that justify men's greater power and privilege. The problem of accomplishing this despite constant contact and opportunities for mutual influence probably contributes to the unusually prescriptive nature of the gender stereotypes that shape people's behavior in interaction, compared to race or class stereotypes (Fiske & Stevens, 1993; Jackman, 1994). People feel freer to criticize and otherwise sanction perceived violations of gender expectations than they do violations of race or class expectations (Fiske & Stevens, 1993).

The deep involvement of gender in the organization of interaction raises complex issues for studying its impact on behavior. In interaction, people are always many things in addition to their sex. Simple, dichotomous sex categories may make easy starting places, but, by the same token, they are too diffuse to adequately frame behavior in most contexts. People virtually always classify self and other in additional and more specific ways such as age, ethnicity, and institutional role. As a result, the interactional conduct of gender is always *enmeshed* in other identities and activities. It cannot be observed in a pure, unentangled form.

This complexity is a challenge for theories of gender and interaction. It also raises significant methodological issues for empirical studies. In drawing conclusions about gender differences in interaction, for instance, we must be careful not to attribute to gender behavioral effects that are caused by actors' other social positions and differences. Given the widespread division of labor and authority by sex in our society, male and female interactants are frequently unequal in important ways besides gender. As a consequence, commonly observed gender differences in interaction are often deceptive and misleading. Close attention to the context in which interaction occurs is necessary when interpreting the evidence for gender effects.

We begin by reviewing five current theoretical approaches that seek to explain how gender shapes behavior in interaction and how, in turn, the recurring patterns or structures of interaction that emerge from this behavior sustain (and potentially could undermine) the gender system. Absent from our survey is the familiar approach that attributes gendered behavior in interaction to stable differences in men's and women's personalities or traits (e.g., dominance or nuturance) that they have acquired through socialization (e.g., Parsons & Bales, 1955). In recent years, evidence has accumulated that men's and women's gender-related behavior varies substantially with changes in the situational context. A woman who is a tough taskmaster at work may be deferential and passive with her husband. As a result, researchers have increasingly turned away from a simple, socialized-trait approach (see, e.g., Aries, 1996; Deaux & Major, 1987; Eagly, 1987; Meeker & Weitzel-O'Neill, 1977; Ridgeway, 1992 for reviews). It is not that gendered selves, attitudes, or beliefs do not develop through socialization or that they have no impact on interaction. Rather, conceptualizing gendered selves as stable traits or dispositions that exert a constant effect on behavior across situations does not appear to be an adequate way to account for the impact of gendered selves on interaction. After surveying current theoretical approaches to gender and interaction we will turn to the empirical evidence for gender's effects on patterns of interaction.

2. THEORETICAL APPROACHES TO GENDER AND INTERACTION

2.1. The Two-Cultures Approach

Drawing an analogy from studies of interethnic communication, Maltz and Borker (1982) propose that men and women learn different cultural rules for engaging in interaction and interpreting their own and others' behavior. They argue that people acquire rules for interacting with peers (i.e., those who are not formal superiors or subordinates) from childhood peer groups. Because children's peer groups tend to be gender segregated and because children accentuate stereotypic gender differences in the process of learning gender roles, these peer groups develop different gender-typed cultures. As a result, boys and girls learn different cultural rules for interaction. Boys learn to use speech to compete for attention in the group and assert positions of dominance. Girls learn to use speech to maintain close, equal relations, to criticize in nonchallenging ways, and to interpret accurately other's intentions (Maccoby, 1990; Maltz & Borker, 1982). These taken-for-granted rules of interaction carry into adulthood, shaping men's and women's interaction.

In mixed-sex interaction, the result can be miscommunication because men and women have learned to attribute different meanings to the same behavior (Maltz & Borker, 1982). However, the effort to accommodate each other's different interactional goals in conversation modifies men's and women's behavior slightly, reducing gender differences. In same-sex interaction, on the other hand, gendered styles of interaction are reinforced. Thus the two cultures approach predicts that gender differences in behavior will be greater between men and women in same-sex contexts than in mixed-sex contexts.

The two cultures argument has gained wide attention thanks to popular presentations, such as Tannen's (1990) *You Just Don't Understand: Women and Men in Conversa-*

tion. However, criticism of this work among researchers has grown. Aries (1996), who earlier found the approach persuasive, concludes from her recent review of the evidence that it is seriously flawed. Some problems are logical. Since adult men and women (in contrast to members of different ethnic groups) interact daily, and mixed-sex interaction moderates gender differences, why don't men's and women's different cultural rules eventually break down, especially since they cause misunderstandings and problems in interaction? Also, since many children interact closely with opposite sex siblings in addition to same-sex friends, could separate cultures really develop at all?

Other problems are empirical. There is no consistent pattern of greater gender differences between same-sex groups than within mixed-sex groups—the results are contradictory depending on the behavior and context (Aries, 1996). Also, there is little reliable evidence that men and women consistently misunderstand one another or that they cannot understand each other quite well in long-term relationships. Thorne's (1993) studies of children's play groups suggests as well that they are more diverse in their rules of interaction than is represented in the two cultures approach.

2.2. Doing Gender

"Doing gender" is an ethnomethodological perspective that claims that gender itself is an interactional accomplishment, something that must be continually achieved in local interactional contexts to persist as a social phenomenon (West & Fenstermaker, 1993; West & Zimmerman, 1987). Institutionalized cultural norms dictate that there are two and only two sexes, each with certain "inherent" natures that imply and justify male dominance. However, the maintenance of these norms requires that people present themselves in interaction in culturally defined ways that allow others to sex categorize them unequivocally as male or female and hold them accountable for behaving in ways that are normatively appropriate to their sex category.

Gender, as opposed to sex (cultural rules for sex assignment, usually at birth) or sex categorization (labeling as male or female in everyday interaction), is the local management of conduct in relation to normative conceptions of appropriate behavior and attitudes for one's sex category (West & Zimmerman, 1987). Thus gender is an adverb rather than a noun in this perspective, something one "does" rather than "is." It is a quality (i.e., "womanly" or "manly") with which a person carries out any behavior during interaction. To be effective, this quality must be recognized as a culturally competent gender performance by others present. Sex category is "omnirelevant" in interaction, so that one can be held accountable for engaging in any activity in a gender-appropriate way, even in situations that are not institutionally gendered: a woman may be a physician and acknowledged as such in the situation, but she can still be held accountable for being womanly in her conduct as a physician.

The concept of gender as something one *does* has been very influential, as has the recognition that sex categorization in interaction is a distinct and important aspect of the gender process. However, the "doing gender" approach has been more important as an orienting perspective than as a predictive theory of gender's impact on behavior in interaction (but see Brines, 1994 for a predictive application to the household division of labor). Perhaps this is because the "doing gender" approach offers no explicit guidelines for the circumstances under which the salience of gender (i.e., the situated pressures for gender accountability) will vary, producing stronger or weaker gender differences in behavior.

2.3. Eagly's Social Role Theory

Eagly (1987; Eagly & Wood, 1991) has proposed a broad theory of gender differences that locates their source in the situational roles that men and women play. In our society, homemaker roles are assigned almost exclusively to women while powerful, higher-status work roles are occupied disproportionately by men. People form their gender role expectations from observing men and women around them. They see men, because of the requirements of their more powerful work roles, engaging in more *agentic* (instrumental, assertive) behaviors than women and women, owing to their homemaker roles, enacting more *communal* (friendly, concerned with others, emotionally expressive) behaviors. Besides creating stereotypic gender role expectations, society's gender division of labor creates gender-typed skills and beliefs by providing men and women with different experiences.

Behavior in general is determined by the social roles that are most salient in a given situation. Thus when a male physician and a female nurse interact in a hospital, their behavior is shaped by the power, status, and norms of their work roles rather than by gender, *per se*. In the same formal role (e.g., CEO), the theory predicts that men and women will act similarly. Evidence supports this in the case of leadership behavior in management roles (Eagly & Johnson, 1990; Johnson, 1994).

Gender role expectations shape behavior directly only when other roles are ambiguous. Eagly (1987) argues that this is the case in most laboratory research settings and accounts for the gender differences observed in many laboratory studies. Anything that makes gender roles more salient in a situation (e.g., a mixed-sex setting, a culturally gendered context) increases their impact and thus the likelihood that men's and women's behavior will differ in stereotypic fashion (Eagly & Wood, 1991). However, gender can also indirectly affect how men and women enact other roles by shaping the skills and beliefs individuals have acquired over their lives. Thus when an interactional task requires communal skills, women will generally perform better than men and be more influential in that setting (Wood, 1987). When the task is heavily agentic, both men and women will act more agentically, but men's past experiences will give them the advantage.

Thus social role theory predicts that if we look around us we will often see men acting more agentically in interaction than women and women acting more communally than men. In most settings, however, these differences will be due to differences in the situational roles that men and women are playing rather than to gender. Only in situations where gender is highly salient or the task draws on sex-typed skills will such differences be attributable to gender itself. Furthermore, when women are in agentic situational roles (e.g., boss), or when men are in communal roles (e.g., flight attendant) each will act in a counter-gender manner in accord with the requirements of his or her role. Because of its generality and sensitivity to situational variation and context, Eagly's role theory is widely cited in the research literature.

2.4. Status Characteristics and Expectation States

Another widely cited and well documented theory is expectation states theory. It argues that many, although not all, of the effects of gender on interaction are attributable to the greater status value attached to being male rather than female in western culture (Berger, Fisek, Norman, & Zelditch, 1977; Carli, 1991; Ridgeway, 1993; Wagner & Berger, 1997). Gender stereotypes not only associate men and women with different specific skills (e.g., child care or mechanics) they also attach greater status worthiness and general competence to men than women, making gender a status characteristic (Broverman, Vogel, Broverman, Clarkson, & Rosenkrantz, 1972).

Expectation states is not a theory of gender, *per se*, but a theory of the way characteristics of people that carry status value in the surrounding society shape the power and prestige hierarchies that emerge when they interact. It addresses interactions in which actors are oriented toward the accomplishment of a shared goal and seeks to explain behaviors, such as influence, participation, evaluation and allocation of rewards, that are related to inequalities in power and prestige in the situation. It acknowledges socioemotional behaviors, but considers them outside the pervue of the theory. Influence and power in interpersonal relations, particularly in goal-oriented situations, have important consequences for the social positions of wealth and power that individuals attain. Consequently, this theory claims to explain a range of gender differences in interaction that are especially important for understanding gender inequality.

When people are focused on a collective goal, they look for ways to anticipate the likely usefulness of their own suggestions, compared to those of others, in order to decide whether to speak up, whom to listen to, and with whose choices to agree. They form implicit *performance expectations* for each actor in the situation compared with the others. When gender stereotypes and the status beliefs they entail are *salient,* because they provide a basis for distinguishing the actors (i.e., a mixed-sex context, see Cota & Dion, 1986), or are *relevant* to the situation because they are linked by cultural beliefs to skill at the shared goal (e.g., a gender-typed task), they affect the actors' expectations for each other's performance in that situation. Performance expectations, in turn, shape behavior and others' reactions in a *self-fulfilling* manner. When gender status is salient, both a man and a woman will implicitly assume that he is a little more competent and has a little more to offer than she. Lower performance expectations for her compared to him make her less likely to offer task suggestions and more likely to ask for his ideas, to evaluate his ideas positively and her's negatively, and to accept his influence in task decisions, creating a behavioral power and prestige order that advantages him over her.

Because of the effects of gender status beliefs, the theory predicts that in mixed-sex interactions between men and women who are otherwise equals, men will, on average, be more influential, tend to offer more task suggestions, act more confidently and assertively, be evaluated as more competent for the equivalent performance, and expect and receive greater rewards than the women. Evidence supports this (Carli, 1991; Dovidio, Brown, Heltman, Ellyson, & Keating, 1988; Pugh & Wahrman, 1983; Wagner & Berger, 1997; Wood & Karten, 1986). Men's advantage over women will be increased further if the task is stereotypically masculine (Carli, 1991; Dovidio et al., 1988). When the task is stereotypically feminine, *women* should have a performance expectation advantage over men and be more influential and assertive than them, as Dovidio et al. (1988) and Wagner, Ford, and Ford (1986) have shown.

The theory predicts that in same-sex interaction, gender will shape performance expectations only when the task is gender typed in the culture. A "feminine" task will encourage women's assertive, task-related behavior and discourage men's in same-sex groups, while a "masculine" task will produce the opposite effects. When the task is gender neutral, men and women in same sex groups should not differ in their absolute rates of task behavior, as evidence indicates (Johnson, Clay-Warner, & Funk, 1996; Wagner & Berger, 1997).

One of the strengths of this theory is that it explicitly attends to other status-related attributes of actors (e.g., race, occupation, education, expertise) that may be salient in the situation besides gender. It argues that actors combine the positive and negative implications of all salient status information, weighted by the relevance of each to the situational task, to form aggregated performance expectations for self and others, which in turn shape each person's task behaviors, power, and prestige. As a result, the effects of gender on actors' influence and standing in the situation may be overwhelmed (or exacerbated) by countervailing factors (Wagner et al., 1986). Thus gender is not a master status in this approach. Its effects are situationally variable, but predictably so, advantaging men not over all women but over women who are otherwise their equals in most situations.

In addition to creating differences in the likelihood of becoming influential, expectation states theory argues that gender status beliefs, when salient, can affect the extent to which men and women are perceived to have a *right,* based on cultural expectations, to hold a position of influence and respect in the setting. Gender status beliefs can cause actors to assume implicitly that men are more legitimate candidates for high standing in the situation than equivalent women (Ridgeway, Johnson & Diekema, 1994). Such *legitimacy* effects add a prescriptive element to gender-based performance expectations. In trying to overcome others' low expectations for her by acting assertively in regard to the task, a woman may elicit a negative reaction unless she compensates by emphasizing her cooperative interest in helping the group (Carli, 1990; Carli, LaFleur, & Loeber, 1995; Ridgeway, 1982). A woman who attains leadership by virtue of her expertise may meet more resistance than a similar man if she tries to go beyond persuasion to exercise directive power in the group (Butler & Geis, 1990; Eagly, Makhijani & Klonsky, 1992).

Recently, expectation states theorists have also shown that the enactment of positions of higher or lower power and prestige in ongoing interactional situations causes the participants to attribute more dominant, instrumental traits to those in the high-ranking positions and more submissive, emotionally expressive traits to those in lower-ranking ones (Gerber, 1996; Wagner & Berger, 1997). This occurs regardless of whether the participants are men or women. The effect of gender status beliefs on interaction, however, results in men more frequently achieving high power and prestige positions than women. As a consequence of this interactional power and prestige advantage, men should more frequently be perceived as dominant and instrumental and women as expressive and submissive, contributing to gender stereotypes (Wagner & Berger, 1997).

Expectation states theory, then, argues that if we look around, we will usually see men acting more assertively, being more influential, and being perceived as more competent than women. However, these differences are not basic to men and women. They result from the self-fulfilling effects on interaction of cultural stereotypes that ascribe greater status and competence to men. When salient in the situation, these status beliefs create gender differences in behavior and leadership. But when they are not salient or are overwhelmed by other information in the situation, men and women will be similarly assertive, competent, and influential.

Note that expectation states theory and social role theory make many similar predictions. Expectation states theory is more precise and accurate in predicting how gender affects influence and task-related behaviors, particularly in combination with actors' other differences such as race or occupation. Role theory makes more specific predictions about gender's impact on communal, socioemotional behaviors.

2.5. Identity Theories

Perhaps the closest modern analogue to older gender role socialization approaches are the identity theories developed within the structural symbolic interactionist perspective. These theories argue that people learn a set of meanings that serve as an *idenity standard,* guiding behavior in situations where that identity is evoked. In the case of gender identities, conceptions of masculinity and femininity are based on cultural meanings associated with being a man or woman in society (Burke, 1991). Researchers in this tradition often see gender as a "master identity," a set of meanings that applies to the self across situations rather than as evoked only by specific institutional contexts (Stets & Burke, 1996). Given that some variants of identity theory posit a contrastive definition of masculinity and femininity (Burke, 1991)—being masculine as being not feminine—the idea that men and women act out master gender identities across situations seems quite close to the more traditional socialization theories.

The crucial difference is the new conceptualization of identity-driven behavior as a control system (Burke, 1991; Burke & Reitzes, 1981; Heise, 1979; Smith-Lovin & Heise, 1988). Rather than conceiving of identity as either something that is fluid and constructed anew in each situation (as in the doing gender perspective) or as stable across situations (as in the traditional socialization approaches), identity theories now posit a control process that leads to both stability and change in identity-driven behavior. Gender meanings are learned from societal definitions, and function as a standard of reference for interpreting the implications of interaction. In their interactions with others, people modify their behavior to control the perceptions of self-relevant meanings. Therefore, if the interaction is making one seem more feminine than one's fundamentally held gender identity standard, then masculine, assertive behavior might result (even if the identity standard were quite feminine). On the other hand, a situation such as a work setting that produced behavior that was too masculine in relation to that same identity standard, would produce behavior that re-affirmed the identity standard by emphasizing traditional femininity. In other words, the gendered behavior varies depending on how the meanings generated by the interaction relate to the fundamentally held identity standard; people produce a wide variety of gendered behavior to maintain their identity meanings.

Smith-Lovin and Robinson (1992) use affect control theory (Heise, 1979; Smith-Lovin & Heise, 1988), one of the identity control theories, to look at how gender identities are maintained in group conversations. They argue that both socialization and peer-group interaction lead boys and girls to develop gender identities with rather different values on evaluation (niceness), potency (powerfulness), and activity (expressiveness). These identities then affect cross-sex interaction and modify other social positions that males or females come to occupy (such as male student and female student). Using the meanings of these identities and of common conversational behaviors such as "interrupt" and "talk to," they modeled the participation and interruption structure of interaction in six-person groups.

Burke and Stets (1996), using Burke's version of identity theory (Burke, 1991a, 1991b; Burke & Reitzes, 1981) analyze positive and negative behavior among married couples who are trying to resolve a disagreement. They predict and find that those with a more masculine identity will be more likely to use negative behavior in interaction, while those with a more feminine identity will be more likely to use positive behavior. Interestingly, the results of being masculine/feminine are different from the results of being male/female. They argue that the status effects of being male or female are separate and different in direction from the meanings of masculinity and femininity. This point is supported by Stets (1997), who shows that other low-status positions—age, education, and occupational status—operate in the same way.

Within this tradition, Burke and Cast (1997) have also explored the ways in which people's "reference standard" for gender identity meanings can be shaped by major life events. They study the gender identities of newly first-married couples over a 3-year period, focusing on the birth of a new child. They find that parental status alters gender identity meanings to increase the differences between masculinity and femininity, but that role-taking processes lead to convergence of gender roles.

The strength of the control-system formulations of identity theory is that they combine two insights about gendered behavior in interaction: interactions are based on what we learn about societies' definitions of maleness and femaleness, but these behaviors are also situated and flexible; gender is displayed and maintained in different ways in different situations. The theory also allows specification of the conditions under which gender meanings are likely to change, as a result of life events or societal change. Therefore, these perspectives bring a much needed dynamic, processual element to the older gender socialization ideas.

In differing ways, each of the theoretical approaches we have discussed emphasizes the importance of societal beliefs or stereotypes of men and women for expectations and behavior in interaction. We must keep in mind, however, that although there is a culturally hegemonic form of these stereotypes, based on the experiences of white middle-class Americans, there are also differences in gender stereotypes by class and race (Connell, 1995 Filardo, 1996; Messner, 1992; West & Fenstermaker, 1995). Although we have enough evidence to recognize that subcultural differences in gender conceptions exist and probably affect interaction, there are few detailed studies based on any but white middle-class participants. This must be kept in mind in considering the research findings we discuss next.

3. RESEARCH FINDINGS

There is a voluminous body of research on gender and interaction within the disciplines of sociology, psychology, and communications. Since we cannot be encyclopedic, we focus on well-established topics and findings and key studies that illustrate them.

3.1. Women's and Men's Interactional Networks

We begin with studies of the frequency and types of interactions among men and women. The facts that men and women are roughly equal sized groups and have necessary contact through kin and romantic ties ensure high rates of interaction. However, the network literature makes clear that this interaction is patterned in ways that are significant for the character and content of gender relationships, maintaining difference and inequality. We review the life course differentiation, organizational contexts, and status configurations in which interactions between men and women occur.

3.1.1. NETWORKS IN CHILDHOOD. By the time children enter school, they have learned that sex is a permanent personal characteristic. At about the same developmental stage, researchers first observe homophily (the choice of similar companions) in play patterns and tendency for girls to play in smaller groups than boys (Block, 1979; Lever, 1978). Hallinan studied young children's peer relationships, focusing on transitivity in sentiment relations and how intransitive relations get resolved. An intransitive sentiment relation is one in which, for any three people in a group, A likes B and B likes C, but A does not like C (Hallinan, 1974). Although all children show less tolerance for intransitivity as they get older (Hallinan, 1974; Leinhardt, 1973), there are gender differences in how intransitivity is usually resolved. Eder and Hallinan (1978) found that girls are more likely to resolve intransitivity by deleting friendship choices, while boys are more likely to add them. For example, if A likes B and B likes C, a young boy would be more likely to form an A–C relation to resolve the intransitivity, while a young girl would be more likely to drop B as a friend. Furthermore, youths are more likely to delete a friendship choice than to resolve the intransitivity by adding a cross-sex friend (Hallinan & Kubitschek, 1990).

Hallinan's results have important implications for the emergence of cliques and larger peer group interactions. Youths tend to have friends who are popular peers of the same sex; this tie is likely to be reciprocated if both youths are popular. This stable dyad is most likely to expand to a stable, transitive triad if the third person is also of the same sex, is popular, and reciprocates the choice. These transitive triads are likely to continue adding people (creating more triads) to create cliques of the "popular crowd" of same sex people (Hallinan & Kubitschek, 1988, p. 91). Since each new member of a clique creates an intransitive structure that must be resolved by adding ties if the clique is to grow, girls are less likely to join larger cliques; they tend to resolve intransitivity by dropping, rather than adding, friendships. Thus, girls are less likely to extend or receive friendship. Simple, small tendencies toward homophily and differences in resolving problems in the structure of their relationships mean that boys and girls will move toward very different kinds of peer social circles. Their worlds become gender segregated, with boys in larger, more heterogeneous cliques.

Networks and knowledge coevolve, with the connections between individuals creating shared knowledge which, in turn, shifts interaction propensities (Carley, 1986a, b). Over time, knowledge overlap increases between interaction partners and decreases between people not connected in the network. As peer interactions become more organized around gender, strong perceptions of gender differences are likely to be created from in-group/out-group phenomena and from the different stores of information that these relatively isolated cliques develop. Except for siblings, cross-sex contacts will be embedded in more formal authority relations (e.g., teachers, parents), where youth occupy low-status positions within the interactions. Interactions among status equals in youth (excepting those who are thought of in romantic, sexual terms) are almost entirely same-sex interactions.

3.1.2. Personal Networks in the Adult Years.   In adult life men and women usually have networks of similar size (Fischer, 1982; Marsden 1987), but women have fewer ties to non-kin (Fischer & Oliker, 1983; Marsden, 1987; Wellman, 1985). Networks in adulthood show strong sex homophily as well as homophily in race, ethnicity, religion, age, and education (Marsden, 1988). Women typically interact more with kin and neighborhood contacts, which tends to increase the age and sex heterogeneity of their interactions while reducing racial, ethnic and religious diversity. Men, on the other hand, have more ties to co-workers and voluntary group members, which decreases age and sex diversity in their ties (Marsden, 1992).

Fischer and Oliker (1983) found that life course factors are particularly important in the development of gender differentiated networks (see also Marsden, 1987, footnote 15). Young, unmarried women and men have similar patterns of interaction. Gender differences accumulate, however, as young adults move into marriage and childbearing years. Married women, especially those with children, have fewer people that they can count on for support such as personal advice, help with odd jobs, or lending money. The exclusivity with which infant care is delegated to women may be a fundamental factor; by the time men become involved with childrearing of older children, women's networks may be fundamentally altered (Smith-Lovin & McPherson, 1992). Wellman (1985) found that having children significantly reduced cross-sex contacts for women, moving them into a female world of play groups and PTAs. Munch, McPherson, and Smith-Lovin (1997) showed that having a young child in the family restricts women's interactions with others, but also increases men's embeddedness in female, kin-oriented interactions. A study by Lynne Zucker (reported in Aldrich 1989, p. 24) using the "small world" technique showed that female networks were more densely interconnected, while men's are more extensive and less tightly linked. Interconnectedness has important implications for the usefulness of networks; Burt (1992) argued that nonredundancy of ties is more important than tie strength in promoting occupational success and other functional benefits of networks.

Fischer and Oliker (1983) found that women are much more likely to know people through their husband's co-worker networks than men are to know their wives' work friends. On the one hand, this finding implies that women benefit more from their spouses' network position than do men by using their husbands' work contacts to extend their own ties. On the other hand, Aldrich (1989) suggests that the pattern may indicate that women are more supportive of their husbands' networks than vice versa. Contacts that women make through their husbands may be less useful to women in work-related spheres, and supportive only of their roles as wives.

In a study of recent job changers in four white-collar occupations, Campbell (1988) reinforced the view that women are less tied to work peers and more affected by life course factors and geographic mobility than men. She found that women interact with people in fewer occupations than men; in particular, their networks have a "floor" that eliminates lower status occupations. Women's occupational networks are negatively affected by their having children under 6 years of age and by changing jobs in response to their spouses' mobility. When the women in Campbell's study moved with their husbands, their networks reached fewer high-status and fewer low-status occupations.

3.1.3. Organizations and the Interactions Embedded in Them.   McPherson and Smith-Lovin (1982) argued that voluntary group activities create an opportunity structure for social interaction and tie formation. Earlier research has shown that members who become acquainted through organizational activities influence one another's behavior (Whiting, 1980) and provide information about matters outside their immediate environments (Jones & Crawford, 1980).

Women belong to fewer organizations than men (Booth, 1972). Perhaps more importantly, however, they belong to much smaller groups and to groups that are organized around social and religious activities rather than work-related activities (McPherson & Smith-Lovin, 1982). The peer interactions created by voluntary organization memberships are, if anything, more gender segregated than the world of work. Nearly one half of the organizations in a study of 10 communities were exclusively female, while one fifth were all male (McPherson & Smith-Lovin, 1986). From the point of view of the individual, the typical female membership in a voluntary organization generates face-to-face interaction with about 29 other members, fewer than four of whom are men. Male memberships, on the other hand, produce contact with over 37 other members (because their organizations are larger), eight of whom are women. Men's contacts are both more numerous and more heterogeneous. Business-related and political groups (where men are likely to occupy higher status positions than women) are more likely to be gender integrated than social, child-centered, or religious groups. Far from integrating men and women, interactions within the voluntary sector tend to lower the diversity of contacts (Marsden, 1992; McPherson & Smith-Lovin; 1987). McPherson and Smith-Lovin (1987) show that choice of friends within the groups is a relatively unimportant factor; it is the opportunity structure created by the groups' composition that leads to most gender segregation.

3.1.4. NETWORKS WITHIN WORK ORGANIZATIONS.   Although not as segregated as voluntary organizations, work settings also create an opportunity structure for interaction that differentiates men and women. Women and men historically have worked in different occupations; sex segregation is even stronger at the firm level where workers actually interact (Baron & Bielby, 1984). Women are found in positions with shorter career ladders, less authority, and less discretionary power (Kanter, 1977; Miller, 1975; South, Bonjean, Corder, & Markham, 1982). While they may interact with men in other occupations (e.g., nurses with doctors or with orderlies, secretaries with managers or with janitors), cross-sex contacts are unlikely to be peer, status-equal interactions. In addition to these gender differences in the interaction opportunities created by formal position, women are usually less central in informal communication, advice, friendship, and influence networks at work (Ibarra, 1989, 1990; Lincoln & Miller, 1979; Miller, Labovitz, & Fry, 1975). This finding is understandable since women are underrepresented at upper ranks in businesses, and rank is correlated with centrality in informal interaction. There is substantial evidence, however, that even controlling for rank, women are less well connected in the informal structure.

Women in high ranks are more likely to be in a distinct minority and their token position puts them under special interactional pressures (Kanter, 1977). Brass (1985) argued that, if high-status women are usually gender minorities, they may be less central in informal networks simply because they are different. In fact, Brass (1985) found that men and women were equally central in informal networks in an organization where women were fairly equally represented. These informal networks were quite gender segregated, however, so that the women were central in networks of other women.

Ibarra and Smith-Lovin (1997) pointed out the importance of these gender interaction patterns for role modeling and identity maintenance. Women are unlikely to have good models of how people like them cope with work challenges, especially at levels above their own. They have to reach outside their own work groups to find homophilous contacts with other women, while mentor relationships with higher status co-workers are likely to be opposite sex. Women are less likely than men to have multiplex, close ties with same-sex co-workers or to have gender homophilous relationships with successful role models. All of these findings support the general image developed by Kanter (1977) and Miller (1986) that women and men find very different interactional environments within work organizations, even when they have the same rank or title.

To summarize, we find that at all life stages women and men are most likely to have status-equal, peer interactions with same-sex others. Cross-sex interactions are most likely to be embedded in formal, institutional role relationships (such as kinship or work relationships), which are often also status differentiated. Furthermore, women are more likely to occupy the low-status position in these interactions. With this understanding of women's and men's networks in hand, we turn to behavior within interactions and within friendship ties.

3.2. Bales' Task and Socioemotional Behavior

Some of the earliest systematic studies of gender and interaction developed from Bales' effort to analyze group dynamics in terms of an instrumental task dimension, consisting of behaviors directed toward achieving group goals, and a socioemotional dimension, composed of behaviors concerned with solidary relations among the actors (Parsons & Bales, 1955; Strodtbeck & Mann, 1956). Perhaps because of this, coding interaction according to Bales' (1950, 1970) interaction process analysis (IPA) continues to be a common way to examine gender differences in behavior. Each speech act is coded in terms of who said it, to whom it was directed, and whether it was task oriented (task suggestions, information, opinions, and questions asking for these) or socioemotionally oriented (agreeing/disagreeing, friendly/unfriendly, jokes or dramatizes).

While a usefully broad coding scheme, IPA has two problematic characteristics that should be kept in mind in interpreting gender differences based on it. First, acts are classified as socioemotional if they contain any socioemotional elements. Thus if a woman (or man) accompanies a task suggestion with a smile and laugh, that will be coded as a socioemotional, not a task act. Second, results are represented in terms of the proportion of a person's acts that are task or socioemotionally oriented which can be misleading. If a person speaks up only twice, but each time with a task suggestion, his or her behavior will be classified as 100% task oriented. Another, who speaks up ten times, six times with a task idea and four times to agree, disagree, or joke, will be classified as only 60% task oriented, despite having made three times the task contributions of the first person.

IPA studies of task-oriented discussion groups generally show men to have slightly (6% to 9%) higher percentages of task behavior and women to have somewhat (5% to 8%) higher proportions of socioemotional behavior and that these differences are about 3% larger between men and women in same-sex groups than between men and women in mixed-sex groups (Anderson & Blanchard, 1982; Carli, 1989, 1991; Piliavin & Martin, 1978). These findings are often cited in support of basic gender differences in interactional style, such as those predicted by the two-cultures approach. However, as several have pointed out, it is misleading to interpret them this way (Aries, 1996; Carli, 1991; Wheelan & Verdi, 1992; Wood & Rhodes, 1992). The problem is that studies examining total numbers of task behaviors, instead of relative proportions, find no differences between men and women in same sex groups (Johnson et al., 1996; Wagner & Berger, 1997), contrary to the two-cultures prediction. In these task-oriented settings, women as well as men are mostly task oriented rather than socioemotional in behavior. When Carli (1989) appointed women to the role of persuading others, their percentage of IPA behaviors resembled men's, suggesting that their interactional styles are situationally variable.

Given that IPA codes an act as socioemotional if it contains *any* socioemotional element, it seems likely that the pattern of gender differences found in IPA studies is due to women's greater display of socioemotional cues rather than their lesser propensity to engage in task behaviors (Carli, 1990; Carli et al., 1995: Dovidio et al., 1988; Hall, 1984; Wood & Rhodes, 1992). Johnson et al. (1996) found no gender differences in task behaviors in same-sex groups but some differences in expressions of social agreement versus counterarguing. Carli (1990) reports greater gender differences in mixed-sex than same-sex groups for task-oriented aspects of language but larger gender differences in same than mixed-sex groups for verbal reinforcers and intensifiers (socioemotional behaviors). Gender stereotypic expectations for greater communality and efforts to overcome the legitimacy problems created by their lower gender status (when it is salient) are among the explanations offered for women's higher rates of socioemotional behavior in mixed-sex task groups. Socioemotional behavior has been neither theorized nor studied with the care that task behavior has. We need a better understanding of the way it is affected by situational context.

3.3. Speech and Gesture Behavior in Interaction

While work within the Bales paradigm continued, a new tradition of conversational analysis began exploring the structures of women's and men's speech. In summarizing this literature, we rely heavily on two excellent reviews, by James and Clarke (1988) and by Aries (1996).

The conversational analysis literature draws heavily on the "two-cultures" perspective, taking as its point of departure an assumption that, because of their socialization in sex-separate peer groups, females and males come to have different conversational goals and styles. Much of this literature also has incorporated assumptions about the higher status and power of males relative to females, using ideas from the expectation states and doing gender perspectives.

3.3.1. SUPPORTIVE SPEECH AND BACKCHANNELING.   Whether in task groups or in everyday conversation, women seem to encourage communication and disclosure on the part of others. Conversational analysts have concentrated on variables that constitute verbal stroking of conversation partners. They found that women are more likely than men to express agreement or ask for another's opinion (Eakins & Eakins, 1978; see also the Bales literature reviewed previously), to acknowledge points made by the other speaker at the beginning of a turn, to provide backchannel support for other speakers by inserting small injections such as "mm-hum" to pause to give another the floor, and to use other conversational devices that serve to draw out one's conversational partner (McLaughlin et al., 1981). Men are more likely to use a delayed minimal response after an interaction partner ends an utterance (Zimmerman & West, 1975), which is often interpreted as lack of support for the speaker. Other studies showed that cooperative conversations have more backchannels and fewer minimal responses than competitive ones, confirming researchers' assumptions about the functions of these speech forms. They also found that gender interacted with dominance and power: men showed more backchanneling when they were in a subordinate position, while women's supportive speech patterns were less affected by their power position (Aries, 1996, pp. 123–126).

Other scholars working in this sociolinguistic tradition have highlighted the inequality implied by the patterns of men's and women's speech styles. They emphasized that women's talk is not only supportive of others, but also unassertive. Robin Lakoff

(1975), for example, reported that the communication style of women was characterized by tentative, unsure, and deferential patterns of speech, while men's conversational style was stronger and more direct. Researchers investigating these gender differences in linguistic features found that women are more likely to use questions (especially tag questions) (Brouwer, Gerritsern, & De Haan, 1979; Crosby & Nyquist, 1977; Eakins & Eakins, 1978; McMillan, Clifton, McGrath, & Gale, 1977), hedges, qualifiers, disclaimers, and other linguistic forms conveying uncertainty (Bradley, 1981; Carli, 1990; Crosby & Nyquist, 1977; Eakins & Eakins, 1978). Women also more frequently use hypercorrect grammar, including "superpolite" forms, lengthened requests, and modal constructions (Crosby & Nyquist, 1977; Lakoff, 1975; McMillan et al., 1977). Tannen (1990) argued that such gendered conversational patterns represent fundamental understandings about social interaction that may evoke emotional responses in spite of our intellectual awareness of different conversational codes. Men may respond to women's supportive conversational styles by talking more and dominating the floor; women may respond to men's lack of that style by lower participation. (The literature on participation task-oriented discussions is reviewed in the section on influence. Time talking in personal conversations has not been studied as extensively; the fact that men talk more in these non-task conversations is implied, however, in the studies of topic control, also reviewed later.)

3.3.2. INTERRUPTIONS: FREQUENCY AND FUNCTIONS. A classic paper on turn-taking in conversation by Sacks, Schegloff, and Jefferson (1974) led Zimmerman and West (1975) to concentrate on gender differences in interruptions, places where the smooth transfer of speakers was disrupted by an apparent violation of turn-taking norms. Zimmerman and West (1975) found few interruptions in same-sex conversations, but a high proportion of men interrupting women in mixed-sex conversations, leading them to make strong statements about the male dominance of male-female conversation. Other conversational analytic studies using small numbers of relatively short conversations often confirmed the Zimmerman and West finding, but later studies with larger samples of speech and more conversations have found few gender effects (see Aries, 1996, pp. 79-101 and James & Clark, 1988 for reviews of specific studies). These findings led researchers to reexamine the functions of interruptions and the conditions under which they occur.

Several patterns emerge from the large body of literature that has developed. First, all simultaneous speech is not interruption and not all interruptions are negative. Backchannels, as discussed above, represent support for, rather than intrusion into another person's speech. Overlaps at the end of a turn show weaker patterns than breaks into the middle of another speaker's utterance and probably represent timing errors rather than a true attempt to take the floor. Even structural interruptions (i.e., speech that intrudes into another's utterance and prevents him or her from completing it) need not always be unsupportive. Many interruptions express agreement, signal a need for more information or otherwise express active listenership (Kennedy & Camden, 1983; Murray, 1985; Sayers & Sherblom, 1987; Smith-Lovin & Brody, 1989; Tannen, 1983). All-female groups and supportive, lively conversations can sometimes show high levels of interruption without being negative.

Second, power or dominance typically leads to higher rates of interruptions, especially successful, negative intrusions into another's speech (Drass, 1986; Kollock, Blumstein, & Schwartz; Roger & Nesshoever, 1987; Roger & Schumaker, 1983). Such interruptions are more common in conflictual, task-oriented talk and seem to be less common in personal, intimate conversations (Trimboli & Walker, 1984). To the extent that men have positions of higher status and power in society, power/dominance effects are often interpreted as gender effects. Furthermore, there seems to be a tendency for men to respond more strongly to power position than women; here, as in the backchanneling research, dominance does not seem to be as closely related to interruption among women (Aries, 1982).

Third, if there is a gender (as opposed to status/power) effect in interruptions research, it does not seem to be in the frequency with which men and women interrupt, but rather in the gender of the person interrupted. Smith-Lovin and Brody (1989) found that men discriminated in their interruptions, interrupting women more often than other men, while women interrupted men and women at the same rate. Women were also more likely to yield the floor to an interrupter than men (see also Smith-Lovin & Robinson, 1992; but note that Kennedy and Camden found no gender differences in yielding). Jose, Crosby, and Wong-McCarthy (1980) found that women were more likely to be interrupted than men in cooperative mixed-sex conversations. In general, men seem to respond more to gender of the speaker with whom they are speaking than do women.

3.3.3. Topic Transitions in Conversations. Several researchers have shifted their attention from interruptions to control of conversational topic. Fishman (1978, 1983) coded successful and unsuccessful topic changes among three heterosexual couples over 12.5 hours of talk. She discovered that men and women raised similar numbers of topics, but that men's topics succeeded 96% of the time, while women's succeeded only 36% of the time. West and Garcia (1988) and Ainsworth-Vaughn (1992) differentiated between collaborative and unilateral/sudden topic shifts, and found that women were particularly disadvantaged in losing topics through sudden or unilateral topic changes. However, here as in other work on interruptions, there are indications that studies using larger samples of speech and more systematic, blind coding methods will find fewer gender effects. Okamoto and Smith-Lovin (1996) found no gender effects on the rate of topic introduction or loss, but a complex pattern of status and group composition effects.

3.3.4. Gestures and Gaze. In addition to speech structures, several researchers have looked at gestures and other nonverbal patterns in interaction. Dovidio et al. (1988), Balkwell and Berger (1996), and others have found that dominance displays such as gazing while talking, gazing while listening, and frequency of gesturing are structured by sex category in a way that indicates a gender status effect. Other gestures such as chin thrusts, smiling, and laughing seem to be gendered behaviors that appear across a variety of situations, even those that are not linked to status.

To summarize, it appears that many of the speech patterns that researchers thought were gendered through cultural or socialization processes are actually indicators of status or power positions within conversations. Since men are usually higher status than women in cross-sex interactions, these status/power structures have often been labeled as gender effects. Some patterns, such as backchanneling, smiling, and laughing, however, seem to be part of a consistent female interaction pattern that occurs across conversations with differing status structures and sex compositions. It also appears that men are somewhat more sensitive to their status/power position and to the gender composition of their conversation than are women, acting more supportive of other speakers when they are in a low-status position but in a more dominant manner when they are in a high-status position or interacting with a woman.

3.4. Influence, Leadership, and Dominance

Whether your thoughts and opinions are taken seriously by those with whom you interact, whether you are influential in the decisions of groups to which you belong, whether you are perceived or accepted as a leader in those groups, and how you act and are reacted to in positions of authority are important parts of the way power and inequality in society are enacted and sustained across a wide range of social contexts, from work organizations to the home. Given the high rate of interaction between men and women, influence and inequality in the interactional arena is likely to be a central site for the production and maintenance of gender difference and inequality. Not surprisingly, then, a great deal of research on gender and interaction has focused on influence, leadership, and dominance. In examining this literature, it is important to distinguish between emergent leadership, in which people form their own influence hierarchy (e.g., in a committee or among co-workers), and formal leadership, in which people have been assigned to formally hierarchical roles in an organization (e.g., manager and employee).

3.4.1. INFLUENCE AND EMERGENT LEADERSHIP. Emergent leadership has been studied in terms of a complex of behaviors that tend to be highly correlated. Most central are influence over group decisions and opinions and being perceived as a leader. These behaviors are usually also associated with how much a person participates in the interaction.

Studies clearly show that, other things equal, men in mixed-sex groups talk more (Dovido et al., 1988; James & Drakich, 1993), are more influential (Lockheed, 1985; Wagner et al., 1986; Pugh & Wahrman, 1983), and are more likely to be selected as leader than are women (Fleischer & Chertkoff, 1986; Nyquist & Spence, 1986; Wentworth & Anderson, 1984). In contrast, in same-sex groups there are no differences between men and women in rates of participation and task contributions (Carli, 1991; Johnson et al., 1996; Wagner & Berger, 1997) or in willingness to accept influence from others (Pugh & Wahrman, 1983).

In a meta-analysis of 58 studies of leadership emergence in mixed-sex interaction (measured by participation or ratings of leadership, but not influence), Eagly and Karau (1991) found that men were more likely to emerge as leaders when task leadership was assessed (effect size $d=.41$) and when general or unspecified leadership was measured ($d=.32$ and .29). These are considered moderate effect sizes. In the small percentage of studies that assessed leadership in maintaining solidary relationships, women were more likely to emerge as social leaders than men ($d=-.18$, a small effect size). Eagly and Karau interpret these results as supporting the predictions of both social role theory and expectation states theory.

As both these theories also predict, Eagly and Karau (1991) found that the gender typing of the task affected leadership emergence, as did the length of time participants interacted. Men are more likely to emerge as leader on masculine tasks ($d=.79$, a large effect size) than neutral ($d=.58$) or feminine tasks $d=.26$). The longer the period of interaction, the smaller the effect sizes favoring men. Several studies have found that gender differences in leadership emergence disappear or favor women in mixed-sex groups when the h task shifts to one that culturally favors the interests, knowledge, and expected competence of women (Dovidio et al., 1988; Wentworth & Anderson, 1984: Yamada, Tjosvold & Draguns, 1983).

What causes gender differences in leadership emergence? Among people who are otherwise equals, the mere knowledge of another's sex, independent of the other's behavior, has been shown to affect willingness to accept influence from that person, demonstrating the impact of gender status beliefs. Men increase their resistance to the other's influence when that other is a woman rather than another man. Women decrease their resistance to influence when the other is a man rather than a woman (Pugh & Wahrman, 1983).

However, the knowledge of the other's sex in goal-oriented interaction usually also affects the verbal and nonverbal confidence and assertiveness of people's behavior, which in turn affects how competent and knowledgeable they appear in the setting, as expectation states theory predicts. Carli (1990), for instance, found that when men and women interacted with a same-sex other, there were no gender differences in their use of hedges, disclaimers, and other types of tentative language. When men and women interacted with an opposite sex other, however, women used significantly more tentative language than did men. In a review of eye contact research, Ellyson, Dovidio, and Brown (1992) concluded that men show more visual dominance (which is associated with perceived competence and influence in interaction) than women in mixed-sex interaction, other factors equal. In same-sex interaction, however, there are few gender differences in visual dominance, with both men and women displaying similarly higher visual dominance when in a high- rather than low-status position in the interaction.

Wood and Karten (1986) showed that assumptions about competence mediate men's tendency to speak more and engage in more active task behaviors in mixed-sex discussion groups, as expectation states theory argues. Absent more specific information, both men and women assumed that the men were more competent, reflecting gender status beliefs. When men and women were assigned similar scores on a pretest of task aptitude, however, there were no gender differences in participation or task behavior. Instead, high scorers spoke more and were more task active than low scorers, regardless of sex. Thus assertive task behavior not only gives the impression of competence in interaction, but it is itself shaped by prior assumptions about who is more competent in the situation, assumptions that are affected by cultural beliefs about men and women that are salient in mixed-sex settings.

Studies have shown that counteracting competence information can moderate or reverse gender differences in influence in mixed-sex interaction (Pugh & Wahrman, 1983; Wagner, et al., 1986). The effect of cultural assumptions that men are more competent than women does not just go away, however, it seems to combine with the additional competence information in the situation. Thus women must be shown to be more competent than men to be equally influential with them (Pugh & Wahrman, 1983) and a given performance is seen as more indicative of ability in men than women (Foschi, 1996).

These studies of influence and emergent leadership demonstrate the impact of hegemonic cultural stereotypes that paint men as diffusely more competent, status worthy, and agentic than women. The participants in these studies are virtually all white and largely middle class, so it is not surprising that these are the gender beliefs that would affect their behavior. How does gender affect emergent leadership for social groups who may have slightly different stereotypic beliefs about men and women? There are few systematic studies, but a recent one comparing mixed-sex interaction among African-American and white adolescents suggests some general principles.

Filardo (1996) reasons that since African-American women have historically engaged in paid work as well as homemaker roles in greater numbers than white women, gender stereotypes should be less differentiated among African-Americans than among whites. On this basis, Filardo predicts, following social role and expectation states theory, that there will be greater gender equality of participation and influence in African-American mixed-sex interaction than in such interaction among whites, other factors equal. She matched African-American and white eighth graders on socioeconomic status and academic achievement and assigned them to same race groups of two boys and two girls. Among whites, Filardo observed a typical pattern of boys talking more and engaging in more influence attempts than girls while girls offered more expressions of agreement with others' comments. In African-American adolescent groups, however, there were no gender differences in participation or expressions of agreement, and differences in influence attempts were weaker. These racial differences in interactional equality resulted from white girls' lesser participation and more tentative style and African-American girls' more active, assertive behavior rather than from differences in the boys' behavior. Filardo concludes that white and African-American adolescents may bring to interaction differing cultural expectations about the competence of males and females and their respective rights to be assertive and influential.

3.4.2. DOMINANCE AND EMERGENT LEADERSHIP.

In addition to cultural stereotypes, a common assumption is that gender differences in emergent leadership may be due to men having personality traits of higher dominance or interest in control over others. Given men's higher status and more authoritative roles in society, one might argue that men are more likely than women to acquire a personality trait of dominance. A series of studies has demonstrated, however, that differences in dispositional dominance do not account for men's leadership emergence in mixed-sex interaction (Davis & Gilbert, 1989; Fleischer & Chertoff, 1986; Megargee, 1969; Nyquist & Spence, 1986). In same-sex interaction, both women and men who are high in dominance are more likely to emerge as leaders than low-dominance individuals. However, in mixed-sex interaction, men are usually chosen as leaders even when they are low in dominance and the women are high. High-dominance women often suggested to their low-dominance partner that he take the lead, showing the impact of cultural beliefs about who is a more legitimate or competent candidate for leadership. Only in the most recent of these studies (Davis & Gilbert, 1989), in which subjects had a period of interaction to get to know one another before turning to the task, did high-dominance women assume leadership over low-dominance men. They still deferred to high-dominance men, however.

Even if individual dominance differences do not determine leadership in mixed-sex contexts, some argue that they do result in men showing more concern than women for hierarchy and power relations in same-sex interaction (see Aries, 1996, pp. 55–60 for a review). Others argue that "doing masculinity" in our culture is doing power, especially with other men, although exactly how one does power/masculinity varies by race and class (Connell, 1995; Messner, 1992). The evidence that men put greater emphasis than women on displaying dominance in same-sex interaction is provocative but based on small samples or case studies. More systematic studies would be useful.

In this light, it is important to note that in task-oriented interaction the display of dominance behavior, defined as behavior that conveys control through threat (e.g., commands, a dismissive or aggressive tone, intrusive gestures) is not a good way to become influential. It is no more successful in this regard than is submissive behavior, whether the participants are all male, all female, or of both sexes (Carli et al., 1995; Ridgeway & Diekema, 1989).

3.4.3. LEGITIMACY, GENDER, AND INFLUENCE. For men in same-sex interaction and for women in same-sex interaction, a confident, active, task-oriented style that conveys competence gains influence and leadership. Yet this same style can elicit resistance when a woman uses it to gain influence over men in mixed-sex task-oriented interaction (Carli, 1990; Carli et al., 1995; Meeker & Weitzel-O'Neill, 1977; Ridgeway, 1982). Carli et al. (1995) found that a woman with a confident, assertive nonverbal style was seen as less likeable and was less influential with men than with women or than a man with that style was with either men or women. Carli (1990) also found that women who used tentative language were actually more influential with a male partner than were women who spoke more assertively. These researchers argue, following expectation states theory, that a display of assertive, high-status behavior by women is perceived by men in the situation as illegitimate unless the women also signal that they have no desire to usurp male status. Here we see the prescriptive consequences of gender status beliefs. When women accompany their confident, active bids for influence among men with statements of their cooperative intent or a friendly nonverbal style they can overcome male resistance and become highly influential (Carli et al., 1995; Ridgeway, 1982). Such added "niceness" is not required of men to be influential with either men or women (although it does not detract from influence) or of women to be influential with women.

3.4.4. FORMAL OR ESTABLISHED LEADERSHIP. The evidence clearly indicates that when men or women are placed in positions of similar formal authority, there are very few differences in the way they interact with either same or opposite sex subordinates (Eagly & Johnson, 1990; Johnson 1994). In a meta-analysis of 162 studies, Eagly and Johnson (1990) found no differences in how task-oriented male and female leaders are and very slight differences in how interpersonally oriented they are (effect size $d=.04$). The only appreciable gender difference was a small tendency ($d=.22$) for women leaders to be more democratic and participatory than men leaders. A subsequent meta-analysis of the evaluation of men and women leaders showed only a very slight overall tendency for women leaders to be evaluated less favorably ($d=.05$) but a moderate tendency ($d=.30$) for women leaders to be evaluated unfavorably when using a directive, autocratic style compared to men using this style (Eagly et al., 1992). This suggests again that the prescriptive aspects of gender stereotypes create legitimacy problems for women leaders who try to wield power in a directive manner. Eagly et al. (1992) suggest that an effort to avoid such negative reactions encourages women leaders to be somewhat more democratic in leadership style.

3.4.5. CONCLUSIONS. Men are more likely to be influential and emerge as leaders in mixed-sex interaction (at least among whites), especially when the task is a stereotypically masculine one. When the task is stereotypically feminine men's advantage declines and may be reversed with women emerging as leaders. Supporting expectation states and social role theories, these gender differences appear to be caused by cultural stereotypes that ascribe greater general competence, status worthiness, and agency to men than to women rather than basic gender differences in dominance or interaction style. Among subgroups who hold less differentiated gender stereotypes, there is greater gender equality in mixed-sex task-oriented interaction. When gender stereotypes are not salient, as in same-sex interaction in which the task is not gender typed, men and women are similar in participation and openness to influence. In general, both men and women gain influence and emerge as leaders with a confident, active style that conveys competence without being domineering. There is a revealing exception, however. To be highly influential with men, women must combine this competent, confident style with signals of friendliness and cooperation that assuage the apparent status illegitimacy of their efforts to claim leadership. In positions of established or formal leadership, men and women behave similarly.

3.5. Friendship Patterns

Unlike the family, which is based on cross-sex relationships, or work-oriented interaction, which involves a mix of same-and mixed-sex interaction, friendships in the contemporary United States are primarily same-sex ties. Yet friendship interaction, too, is shaped by and works to maintain cultural stereotypes of who men and women are and how they differ and are unequal. As the gender system and the cultural beliefs associated with it have changed over time, so have the nature of men's and women's friendships (Allen, 1989; Nardi, 1992; O'Connor, 1992).

Like all other gendered relations, friendships are situated within and affected by people's other identities, ties, and social positions. They change over the life course and differ by class and race, creating larger differences within than between genders (Nardi, 1992; O'Connor, 1992). Unfortunately, many detailed studies of interaction in friendships focus on small samples or on restricted populations, such as college students, warranting caution in generalizing from them.

Studies of contemporary same-sex friendships conclude that men's are "side-by-side" in that they focus on shared activities, while women's friendships are "face-to-face" in that they center on talking and sharing feelings (Aries & Johnson, 1983; Caldwell & Peplau, 1982; Oliker, 1989; Sherrod, 1987; Swain, 1989; Williams, 1985; Wright, 1982). Researchers often comment on the way these differences enact currently dominant gender beliefs that cast intimacy and feeling as feminine while masculinity requires power, self-sufficiency, and action. Oliker (1989) describes how women "best friends" conduct their relationships through talk and disclosure of feelings. Messner (1992) describes how men form friendship bonds through sports that unite them in displaying and validating their performances of culturally valued images of masculinity while simultaneously supporting their superiority over women and less culturally "ideal" men. This process manages uneasiness over feelings of closeness that could be seen as threats to masculinity.

Several researchers, however, caution against exaggerating the differences between the way men and women interact in same-sex friendships, noting that the differences are often smaller than assumed (O'Connor, 1992; Walker, 1994; Wright, 1988). Self-disclosure is often seen as a central difference between men's and women's friendships. Yet Dindia and Allen (1992), in a meta-analysis of more than 200 studies, found that overall gender differences in self-disclosure are small (effect size $d=.18$). Gender differences in self disclosure in same-sex interaction, however, are of moderate size ($d=.31$) while they are quite small in mixed-sex relations ($d=.08$). The situational variability of self-disclosure suggests that it is not a product of stable personality differences between men and women but a reaction to the social context of interaction. Both men and women disclose more to women.

O'Connor (1992) points out that women's lesser power and control over resources compared to men may be partly responsible for differences in their friendships. Without money and control over one's time, friendship cannot be conducted by going out and doing things together. Such friends are left with conversation, often conducted in a home environment that encourages a focus on more personal topics. Supporting this argument,

Walker (1994) reports that the working-class men she interviewed, who, also lacking resources, socialized with friends in their homes, tended primarily to talk with their friends, often discussing personal relationships. On the other hand, middle-class women who worked in male-dominated professions tended to report a lack of intimacy in their friendships similar to that often described in men's friendships.

Walker (1994) argues that conceptions of women's friendships as shared feelings and men's friendships as shared activities are more accurately viewed as gender ideologies than as observable differences in actual behavior. Most studies ask people global questions about what friendship is or what men's and women's friendship are like (e.g., Caldwell & Peplau, 1982). They also tend to focus on best friends (Oliker, 1989). Walker asked people to name a set of specific friends and describe what they did with each. She found that in response to global questions about friendship, her respondents gave gender-stereotypic answers. But when asked for details about specific relationships, gender differences were few. For instance, a man who listed shared sports events as the basis of a given friendship described most interaction with his friend as telephone discussions of personal problems and sports outings as only occasional events. A woman who described talk and shared feelings as central said that she and her friend regularly went to aerobics classes together and that was their occasion to confide. Following a "doing gender" approach, Walker argues that people interpret their behavior in friendships to conform to gender stereotypes when that behavior is in fact considerably more diverse and less gender differentiated. It would be useful to examine the argument Walker develops from in-depth interviews with data from larger and more representative samples.

4. CONCLUSION

Interactional events are an important link in the intricate web of social forces that constitutes the gender system. Given the necessarily high rate of interaction between men and women, gender difference and inequality would be impossible to maintain if interaction were not organized to reinforce it. Several findings from the literature on gender and interaction show how this organization occurs.

Sex/gender seems to be a fundamental dimension around which interaction is organized in that people automatically sex categorize others to render them as culturally meaningful interactants. Yet while this makes sex/gender stubbornly available as a basis of differentiation in interaction, the direction and size of differences in women's and men's behavior in interaction vary dramatically by situational context.

No one theory yet provides a complete account of these complex effects. Nonetheless, it is clear that widely shared societal stereotypes of (or cultural meanings associated with) men and women, which include gender status beliefs, play a central role in shaping behavior in interaction. There is a culturally hegemonic version of societal gender beliefs, but when people hold subcultural variations on these beliefs, their behavior in interaction is also different.

Societal gender beliefs appear to shape interactional behavior in at least two potentially independent ways. They act as an identity standard that the individual seeks to maintain and they shape others' expectations (and the individual's anticipation of what others expect) about the individual's comparative competence, status worthiness, and agentic or communal qualities in a manner that has self-fulfilling effects on behavior. The impact of societal gender beliefs on behavior through either process depends on the salience of gender in the situation compared to other social factors and concerns. Gender tends to be most salient and, thus, to produce the most differentiation in men's and women's behavior in mixed-sex contexts or same-sex contexts that are culturally typed in gendered terms, but it can be triggered by events and made salient in almost any situation. When salient, the unusually prescriptive aspect of gender stereotypes can result in actors being called to account by others for acting in gender-appropriate ways.

We may think of these processes as true interactional gender processes. Evidence indicates that they are sufficient in themselves to produce many common forms of gender difference and inequality. They advantage men in influence, leadership, and the appearance of competence in goal-oriented, mixed-sex interaction: they shape same-sex friendships in stereotypical ways; and so on. But these interactional gender processes usually take place within the context of institutional and organizational arrangements that further reinforce and shape them. In that sense, the maintenance of gender difference and inequality in interaction is overdetermined.

The evidence clearly indicates that, although women and men in the United States interact frequently, it is almost never as equals and, in most cases, it is men who enjoy the status/power advantage. This is a joint result of two processes. First, women's and men's networks, which are embedded in the social structures of work and voluntary organizations, usually bring men and women together on formally unequal terms. Second, interactional gender status and identity processes create difference and inequality among those men and women who are formal equals in work groups, family, and elsewhere.

This heavily structured pattern of interaction between men and women creates the daily appearance of men as essentially more agentic and women as essentially more communal in nature. Yet a closer look at the research reveals what a social construction this is. Women and men have diverse repertoires of interactional behavior and are highly reactive to situational constraints. Not only are the actual behavioral differences between men and women relatively modest, even in gender-salient situations, but when men and women are cast in roles with similar constraints, whether it be men who mother or women who manage, they behave in remarkably similar ways.

We have a good, if imperfect, understanding of the way certain differences in interactional style, often attributed to essential gender differences, in fact result from the organization of power and status in interactions. As a result of these processes, men and women differ in task-oriented, agentic behavior primarily in mixed-sex interactions rather than in same-sex ones. Revealingly, the organization of the communal, socioemotional aspect of interaction, culturally linked with women, is less well theorized and studied. The evidence available, however, suggests that both men and women act more communally when in a lower-status position. However, women do appear to engage in a somewhat more supportive, warmer speech style in same as well as mixed-sex contexts, suggesting that engaging or failing to engage in such a style is also part of the process of marking gender identity in interaction rather than just the enactment of inequality. Perhaps the clearest lesson from the study of gender and interaction, however, is that difference and inequality co-determine each other in the gender system.

REFERENCES

Ainsworth-Vaughn, N. (1992). Topic transitions in physician-patient interviews: Power, gender and discourse change. *Language in Society, 21,* 409–426.

Aldrich, H. (1989). Networking among women entrepreneurs. In O. Hagan, C. Rivchun, & D. Sexton (Eds.), *Women-owned businesses.* New York: Praeger.

Allen, G. (1989). *Friendship: Developing a sociological perspective.* Boulder, CO: Westview.

Anderson, L. R., & Blanchard, P. N, (1982). Sex differences in task and social-emotional behavior. *Basic and Applied Social Psychology, 3,* 10–139.

Aries, E. (1982). Verbal and non-verbal behavior in single-sex and mixed-sex groups: Are traditional sex roles changing? *Psychological Reports, 51,* 127–134.

Aries, E. (1996). *Men and women in interaction: Reconsidering the differences.* New York: Oxford.

Aries, E., & Johnson, F. (1983). Close friendship in adulthood: Conversational content between same-sex friends. *Sex Roles, 9,* 1183–1196.

Bales, R. F. (1950). *Interaction process analysis: A method for the study of small groups.* Reading, MA: Addison-Wesley.

Bales, R. F. (1970). *Personality and interpersonal behavior.* New York: Holt, Rinehart, and Winston.

Balkwell, J. W., & Berger, J. (1994). Gender, status and behavior in task situations. *Social Psychology Quarterly, 59,* 273–283.

Baron, J. N., & Bielby, V. T. (1984). A woman's place is with other women: Sex segregation in the workplace. In B. Reskin (Ed.), *Sex segregation in the workplace: Trends, explanations, remedies.* Washington, DC: National Academy Press.

Berger, J., Fisek, H., Norman, R., & Zelditch, M., (1977). *Status characteristics and social interaction.* New York: Elsevier.

Blau, P. & Schwartz, J., (1984). *Crosscutting social circles: Testing a macrostructural theory of intergroup relations.* New York: Academic Press.

Block, J. H. (1979). Socialization influences on personality development in males and females. In M.M. Parks (Ed.), *APA Master lecture series on issues of sex and gender in psychology.* Washington, D.C.: American Psychological Association.

Booth, A. (1972). Sex and social participation. *American Sociological Review 37,* 183–191.

Bradley, P. H. (1981). The folk-linguistics of women's speech: An empirical examination. *Communications Monographs 48,* 73–90.

Brass, D. J. (1985). Men's and women's networks: A study of interaction patterns and influence in an organization. *Academy of Management Journal, 28,* 327–343.

Brewer, M. & Lui, L. (1989). The primacy of age and sex in the structure of person categories. *Social Cognition, 7,* 262–274.

Brines, J. (1994). Economic dependency, gender, and the division of labor at home. *American Journal of Sociology, 100,* 652–688.

Brouwer, D., Gerritsern, M. M., & De Haan, D. (1979). Speech differences between men and women: On the wrong track? *Language in Society, 8,* 33–50.

Broverman, I., Vogel, S., Broverman, D., Clarkson, N, F., & Rosenkrantz, P. (1972). Sex-role stereotypes: A reappraisal. *Journal of Social Issues, 28,* 59–78.

Burke, P. J., (1991). Identity processes and social stress. American *Sociological Review 56,* 836–849.

Burke, P. J., & Cast, A. (1997). Parental status and gender identity. *Social Psychology Quarterly, 60.*

Burke, P. J., & Reitzes, D. C. (1981). The link between identity and role performance. *Social Psychology Quarterly, 44,* 83–92.

Burt, R. S, (1992). *Structural Holes.* Cambridge, MA: Harvard University Press.

Butler, D., & Geis, F. L. (1990). Nonverbal affect responses to male and female leaders: Implications for leadership evaluations. *Journal of Personality and Social Psychology, 58,* 48–59.

Caldwell, M. A., & Peplau, L. A. (1982). Sex differences in same-sex friendships. *Sex Roles, 8,* 721–732.

Campbell, K. E. (1988). Gender differences in job-related networks. *Work and Occupations, 15,* 179–200.

Carley, K. M. (1986a). An approach for relating social structure to cognitive structure. *Journal of Mathematical Sociology 12,* 137–189.

Carley, K. M. (1986b). Knowledge acquisition as a social phenomenon. *Instructional Science, 14,* 381–438.

Carli, L. L. (1989). Gender differences in interaction style and influence. *Journal of Personality and Social Psychology, 56,* 565–576.

Carli, L. (1990). Gender, language and influence. *Journal of Personality and Social Psychology, 59,* 941–951.

Carli, L. L. (1991). Gender, status, and influence. In E. J. Lawler, B. Markovsky, C. L. Ridgeway, & H. Walker (Eds.), *Advances in group processes,* Vol. 8, (pp. 89–113). Greenwich, CT: JAI Press.

Carli, L. L., LaFleur, S. J., & Loeber, C. C. (1995). Nonverbal behavior, gender, and influence. *Journal of Personality and Social Psychology, 68,* 1030–1041.

Connell, R. W. (1995). *Masculinities.* Berkeley, CA: University of California Press.

Cota, A., & Dion, K. (1986). Salience of gender and sex composition of ad hoc groups: An experimental test of distinctiveness theory. *Journal of Personality and Social Psychology, 50,* 770–776.

Crosby, F., & Nyquist, L. (1977). The female register: An empirical study of Lakoffs hypotheses. *Language in Society, 6,* 313–322.

Davis, B. M., & Gilbert, L. A. (1989). Effect of dispositional and situational influences on women's dominance expression in mixed-sex dyads. *Journal of Personality and Social Psychology, 57,* 294–300.

Deaux, K., & Major, B. (1987). Putting gender into context: An interactive model of gender-related behavior. *Psychological Review, 94,* 369–389.

Dindia, K., & Allen, M. (1992). Sex differences in self-disclosure: A meta-analysis. *Psychological Bulletin, 112,* 106–124.

Dovidio, J. F., Brown, C. E., Heltman, K. Ellyson, S. L., & Keating, C. F. (1988). Power displays between women and men in discussions of gender linked tasks: A multichannel study. *Journal of Personality and Social Psychology, 55,* 580–587.

Drass, K. A. (1986). The effect of gender identity on conversation. *Social Psychology Quarterly, 49,* 294–301.

Eagly, A. H. (1987). *Sex differences in social behavior: A social-role interpretation.* Hillsdale, NJ: Earlbaum.

Eagly, A. H., & Johnson, B. T. (1990). Gender and the emergence of leaders: A meta-analysis. *Psychological Bulletin, 108,* 233–256.

Eagly, A. H., & Karau, S. J. (1991). Gender and leadership style: A meta-analysis. *Journal of Personality and Social Psychology, 60,* 685–710.

Eagly, A. H., & Wood, W. (1991). Explaining sex differences in social behavior: A meta-analytic perspective. *Personality and Social Psychology Bulletin, 17,* 306–315.

Eagly, A. H., & Makhijani, M. G., & Klonsky, B. G. (1992). Gender and the evaluation of leaders: A meta-analysis. *Psychological Bulletin, 111,* 543–588.

Eakins, B., & Eakins, R. G. (1978). Verbal turn-taking and exchanges in faculty dialogue. In B. L. Dubois & I. Crouch (Eds.), *Proceedings of the Conference on the Sociology of Languages of American Women* (pp. 53–62). San Antonio, TX: Trinity University Press.

Eder, D., & Hallinan, M. T. (1978). Sex differences in children's friendships. *American Sociological Review, 43,* 237–256.

Ellyson, S. L., Dovidi, J. F., & Brown, C. E. (1992). The look of power: Gender differences and similarities. In C. Ridgeway (Ed.), *Gender, interaction, and inequality,* (pp. 50–80). New York: Springer-Verlag.

Filardo, E. K. (1996). Gender patterns in African American and white adolescents' social interactions in same-race, mixed-sex groups. *Journal of Personality and Social Psychology, 71,* 71–82.

Fischer, C. (1982). *To dwell among friends.* Chicago: University of Chicago.

Fischer, C. S., & Oliker, S. J. (1983). A research note on friendship, gender, and the life cycle. *Social Forces, 62,* 124–133.

Fishman, P. M. (1978). Interaction: The work women do. *Social Problems 25,* 397–406.

Fishman, P. M. (1983). Interaction: The work women do. In B. Thorne, C. Kramaraea, & N. Henley (Eds.), *Language: Social psychological perpsectives* (pp. 89–101). Oxford: Pergamon.

Fiske, S. T., & Stevens, L. E. (1993). What's so special about sex? Gender stereotyping and discrimination. In S. Oskamp & M. Costanzo (Eds.), *Gender issues in contemporary society* (pp. 173–196). Newbury Park, CA: Sage.

Fleischer, R. A., & Chertkoff, J. M. (1986). Effects of dominance and sex on leader selection in dyadic work groups. *Journal of Personality and Social Psychology, 50,* 94–99.

Foschi, M. (1996). Double standards in the evaluation of men and women. *Social Psychology Quarterly, 59,* 237–254.

Gerber, G. L. (1996). Status in same-gender and mixed-gender police dyads: Effects on personality attributions. *Social Psychology Quarterly, 59,* 350–363.

Hall, J. (1984). *Nonverbal sex differences: Communication accuracy and expressive style.* Baltimore: Johns Hopkins University Press.

Hallinan, M. T. (1974). *The structure of positive sentiment.* New York: American Elsevier.

Hallinan, M. T., & Kubitschek, W. N. (1988). The effects of individual and structural characteristics on intransitivity in social networks. *Social Psychology Quarterly, 51,* 81–92.

Hallinan, M. T., & Kubitschek, W. N. (1990). The formation of intransitive friendships. *Social Forces, 62,* 124–133.

Heise, D. R. (1979). *Understanding Events.* New York: Cambridge University Press.

Ibarra, H. (1989). Centrality and innovativeness: Effects of social network position on innovation involvement. Unpublished dissertation, Yale University.

Ibarra, H. (1990). Women's access to informal networks at work: An intergroup perspective. Paper presented at Academy of Management meetings, San Francisco.

Ibarra, H., & Smith-Lovin, L. (1997). New directions in social network research in gender and organizational careers. In S. Jackson & C. Cooper (Eds.), *Creating tomorrow's organizations: A handbook for future research in organizational behavior.* New York: Wiley.

Jackman, M. R. (1994). *The velvet glove: Paternalism and conflict in gender, class, and race relations.* Berkeley, CA: University of California Press.

James, D. & Clarke, S. (1988). Women, men and interruptions: A critical review. In D. Tannen (Ed.), *Gender and conversational interaction* (pp. 231–280). New York: Oxford University Press.

James, D., & Drakich, J. (1993). Understanding gender differences in amount of talk: A critical review of research. In D. Tannen (Ed.), *Gender and conversational interaction* (pp. 281–312). New York: Oxford.

Johnson, C. (1994). Gender, legitimate authority, and leader-subordinate conversations. *American Sociological Review, 59,* 122–135.

Johnson, C., Clay-Warner, J., & Funk, S. J. (1996). Effects of authority structures and gender on interaction in same-sex task groups. *Social Psychology Quarterly, 59,* 221–236.

Jones, J., & Crawford, G. (1980). Work and network: The relationship of the social circle to the economic action of poor men. Paper presented at the American Sociological Association meetings, New York, August 1980.

Jose, P. E., Crosby, F, & Wong-McCarthy, W. J. (1980). Androgyny, dyadic compatibility and conversational behavior. In H. Giles, W. P. Robinson, & P. M. Smith (Eds.), *Language: Social psychological perspectives* (pp. 115–119). Oxford: Pergamon Press.

Kanter, R. M. (1977). *Men and women of the corporation.* New York: Basic Books.

Kennedy, C. W., & Camden, C. T. (1983). A new look at interruptions. *Western Journal of Speech Communications 47,* 45–58.

Kessler, S., & McKenna, W. (1978). *Gender: An ethnomethodological approach.* New York: John Wiley & Sons.

Kollock, P., Blumstein, P., & Schwartz, P, (1985). Sex and power in interaction: Conversational privileges and duties. *American Sociological Review, 50,* 34–46.

Lakoff, R. (1975). Language and women's place. *Language in Society, 2,* 45–79

Leinhardt, S. (1973). The development of transitive structure in children's interpersonal relations. *Behavioral Science 12,* 260–271.

Lever, J. (1978). Sex differences in the complexity of children's play and games. *American Sociological Review, 43,* 471–483.

Lincoln, J. R., & Miller, J. (1979). Work and friendship ties in organizations: A comparative analysis of relational networks. *Administrative Science Quarterly, 24,* 181–199.

Lockheed, M. E. (1985). Sex and social influence: A meta-analysis guided by theory. In J. Berger & M. Zeldtich (Eds.), *Status, rewards, and influence* (pp. 406–429). San Francisco: Jossey-Bass.

Maccoby, E. E. (1990). Gender and relationships: A developmental account. *American Psychologist, 45,* 513–520.

Maltz, D. N., & Borker, R. A. (1982). A cultural approach to male-female miscommunication. In J. J. Gumperz (Ed.), *Language and social identity* (pp. 196–216). Cambridge: Cambridge University Press.

Marsden, P. V. (1987). Core discussion networks of Americans. *American Sociological Review, 52,* 122–131.

Marsden, P. V. (1988). Homogeneity in confiding relations. *Social Networks, 10,* 57–76.

Marsden, P. V. (1992). Network diversity, substructures and opportunities for contact. In C. Calhoun, M. Meyer, & W. R. Scott (Eds.), *Structures of power and constraint: Papers in honor of Peter M. Blau.* New York: Cambridge University Press.

McMillan, J. R., Clifton, A. K., McGrath, D. & Gale, W. S. (1977). Women's language: Uncertainty or interpersonal sensitivity and emotionality? *Sex Roles 3,* 545–559.

McPherson, J. M., & Smith-Lovin, L. (1982). Women and weak ties: Differences by sex in the size of voluntary organizations. *American Journal of Sociology, 87,* 883–904.

McPherson, J. M., & Smith-Lovin, L. (1986). Sex segregation in voluntary associations. *American Sociological Review, 51,* 61–79.

McPherson, J. M., & Smith-Lovin, L. (1987). Homophily in voluntary organizations: Status distance and the composition of face-to-face groups. *American Sociological Review, 52,* 370–379.

Megargee, E. I. (1969). Influence of sex roles on the manifestation of leadership. *Journal of Applied Psychology, 53,* 377–382.

Meeker, B. F., & Weitzel-O'Neil, P. A.. (1977). Sex roles and interpersonal behavior in task oriented groups. *American Sociological Review, 42,* 92–105.

Messner, M. A. (1992). *Power at play.* Boston: Beacon.

Miller, J. (1986). *Pathways in the workplace.* Cambridge: Cambridge University Press.

Miller, J. (1975). Isolation in organizations: Alienation from authority, control and expressive relations. *Administrative Science Quarterly 20,* 260–271.

Miller, J., Labovitz, S., & Fry, L. (1975). Inequities in the organizational experiences of women and men: Resources, vested interests and discrimination. *Social Forces, 54,* 365–381.

Munch, A. R., McPherson, J. M., & Smith-Lovin, L. (1997). Gender, children and social contact: The effects of childrearing for men and women. *American Sociological Review, 63,* 505–520.

Murray, S. O. (1985). Toward a model of members' methods for recognizing interruptions. *Language in Society, 14,* 31–40.

Nardi, P. M. (1992). *Men's friendships.* Newbury Park, CA: Sage.

Nyquist, L., & Spence, J. T. (1986). Effects of dispositional dominance and sex role expectations on leadership behaviors. *Journal of Personality and Social Psychology, 50,* 87–93.

O'Connor, P. (1992). *Friendships between women: A critical review.* New York: Guilford.

Okamoto, D., & Smith-Lovin, L. (1996). Don't change the subject: Gender and topic transitions in task-oriented groups. Paper presented to the American Sociological Association.

Oliker, S. (1989). *Best friends and marriage.* Berkeley, CA: University of California Press.

Parsons, T. & Bales, R. F. (1955). *Family socialization, and interaction process.* Glencoe, IL: The Free Press.

Piliavin, J. A., & Martin, R. R. (1978). The effects of the sex composition of groups on style of social interaction. *Sex Roles, 4,* 281–296.

Pugh, M., & Wahrman, R. (l983). Neutralizing sexism in mixed-sex groups: Do women have to be better than men? *American Journal of Sociology, 88,* 746–762.

Ridgeway, C. L. (1982). Status in groups: The importance of motivation. *American Sociological Review, 47,* 76–88.

Ridgeway, C. L. (1992). *Gender, interaction and inequality.* New York: Springer-Verlag.

Ridgeway, C. L. (1993). Gender, status, and the social psychology of expectations. In P. England (Ed.), *Theory on gender/feminism on theory* (pp. 175–198). New York: Aldine.

Ridgeway, C. L. (1997). Interaction and the conservation of gender inequality: Considering employment. *American Sociological Review, 62,* 218–235.

Ridgeway, C. L., & Diekema, D. (1989). Dominance and collective hierarchy formation in male and female task groups. *American Sociological Review, 54,* 79–93.

Ridgeway, C. L., Johnson, C., & Diekema, D. (1994). External status, legitimacy, and compliance in male and female groups. *Social Forces, 72,* 1051–1077.

Roger, D., & Nesshoever, W. (1987). Individual differences in dyadic conversational strategies: A further study. *British Journal of Social Psychology 26,* 247–255.

Roger, D., & Schumaker, A. (1983). Effects of individual differences on dyadic conversational strategies. *Journal of Personality and Social Psychology, 45,* 700–705.

Sacks, H., Schegloff, E. A., & Jefferson, G. (1974). A simplest systematics for the organization of turn-taking for conversation. *Language, 50,* 696–735.

Sayers, F., & Sherblom J. (1987). Qualification in male language as influenced by age and gender of conversational partner. *Communication Reports, 4,* 88–92.

Sherrod, D. (1987). The bonds of men: Problems and possibilities in close male relationships. In H. Bred (Ed.), *The making of masculinities: The new men's studies* (pp. 213–239). Boston: Allen and Unwin.

Smith-Lovin, L., & Brody, C. (1989). Interruptions in group discussion: The effects of gender and group composition. *American Sociological Review 54,* 424-435.

Smith-Lovin, L., & Heise, D. R. (1988). Analyzing *social interaction: Research advances in affect control theory.* New York: Gordon & Breach.

Smith-Lovin, L., & McPherson, M. (1992). You are who you know: A network perspective on gender. In P. England (Ed.), *Theory an gender/feminism on theory* (pp. 223–254). New York: Aldine.

Smith-Lovin, L., & Robinson, D. (1992). Gender and conversational dynamics. In C. Ridgeway (Ed.), *Gender, interaction, and inequality.* New York: Springer-Verlag.

South, S. J., Bonjean, C. M., Corder, J., & Markham, W. T. (1982). Sex and power in the federal bureaucracy: A comparative analysis of male and female supervisors. *Work and Occupations, 9,* 233–254.

Stets, J. (1997). Status and marital Interaction. *Social Psychology Quarterly, 60,* 185–217.

Stets, J. E., & Burke, P. J. (1996). Gender, control and interaction. *Social Psychology Quarterly 59,* 193–220.

Strodtbeck, F. L., & Mann, R. D. (1956). Sex role differentiation in jury deliberations. *Sociometry, 19,* 468–473.

Swain, S. (1989). Covert intimacy: Closeness in men's friendships. In B. J. Risman & P. Schwartz (Eds.), *Gender in intimate relationships: A microstructural approach (*pp. 71–86). Belmont, CA: Wadsworth.

Tannen, D. (1983). When is an overlap not an interruption? One component of conversational style. In R. Di Pietro, W. Frawley, & A. Wedel (Eds.), *The First Delaware Symposium on Language Studies* (pp. 119–129). Newark, NJ: University of Delaware Press.

Tannen, D. (1990). *You just don t understand: Women and men in conversation.* New York: William Morrow.

Thorne, B. (1993). *Gender play: Girls and boys in school.* New Brunswick, NJ: Rutgers University Press.

Trimboli, C., & Walker, M. B. (1984). Switching pauses in cooperative and competitive conversations. *Journal of Experimental Social Psychology, 20,* 297–311.

Wagner, D. G., & Berger, J. (1997). Gender and interpersonal task behaviors: Status expectation accounts. *Sociological Perspectives, 40,* 1–32.

Wagner, D. G., Ford, R. S., & Ford, T. W. (1986). Can gender inequalities be reduced? *American Sociological Review, 51,* 47–61.

Walker, K. (1994). Men, women, and friendship: What they say, what they do. *Gender and Society, 8,* 246–265.

Wellman, B. (1985). Domestic work, paid work and net work. In S. Duck & D. Perlman (Ed.), *Understanding personal relationships* (pp. 159–191). London: Sage.

Wentworth, D. K., & Anderson, L. R. (1984). Emergent leadership as a function of sex and task type. *Sex Roles, 11,* 513–524.

West, C., & Fenstermaker, S. (1993). Power, inequality, and the accomplishment of gender: An ethnomethodological approach. In P. England (Ed.), *Theory on gender/feminism on theory* (pp. 151–174). New York: Aldine.

West, C., & Fenstermaker, S. (1995). Doing difference. *Gender & Society, 9,* 8–37.

West, C., & Garcia, A. (1988). Conversational shift work: A study of topical transitions between men and women. *Social Problems, 35,* 551–575.

West, C., & Zimmerman, D. (1987. Doing gender. *Gender & Society, 1,* 125–151.

Wheelan, S. A., & Verdi, A. F. (1992). Differences in male and female patterns of communication in groups: A methodological artifact? *Sex Roles, 27,* 1–15

Whiting, B. (1980). Culture and social behavior: A model for the development of social behavior. *Ethos, 8,* 95–116.

Williams, D. G. (1985), Gender, masculinity-femininity, and emotional intimacy in same-sex friendships. *Sex Roles, 12,* 587–600.

Wood, W., & Karten, S. J. (1987). A meta-analytic review of sex differences in group performance. *Psychological Bulletin, 102,* 53–71.

Wood, W., & Karten, S. J. (1986). Sex differences in interaction style as a product of perceived sex differences in competence. *Journal of Personality and Social Psychology, 50,* 341–347.

Wood, W., & Rhodes, N. (1992). Sex differences in interaction style in task groups. In C. L. Ridgeway (Ed.), *Gender, interaction, and inequality* (pp. 97–121). New York: Springer-Verlag.

Wright, P. H. (1982). Men's friendships, women's friendships, and the alleged inferiority of the latter. *Sex Roles, 8,* 1–20.

Wright, P. H. (1988). Interpreting research on gender differences in friendship: A case for moderation and a plea for caution. *Journal of Social and Personal Relationships, 5,* 367–373.

Yamada, E. M., Tjosvold, D., & Draguns, J. G. (1983). Effects of sex-linked situations and sex composition on cooperation and style of interaction. *Sex Roles, 9,* 541–553.

Zimmerman, D. H., West, C. (1975). Sex roles, interruptions and silences in conversation. In B. Thorne & N. Henley (Eds.), *Language and sex: Difference and dominance* (pp. 105–129). Rowley, MA: Newbury House.

CHAPTER 14

Gender, Violence, and Harassment

MARY R. JACKMAN

Shame, aversion, and denial suffused the subject of gender and violence and sealed it into a long and almost unbroken silence over most of the twentieth century. As late as 1969, a major compendium of research on violence prepared for the National Commission on the Causes and Prevention of Violence (Graham & Gurr, 1969) made no mention of gender and violence: indeed, the only mention of the term "domestic violence" was in a chapter title to identify within-nation (as opposed to international) conflict. However, at least since the publication of John Stuart Mill's essay on "The Subjection of Women" in 1869, there have been sporadic attempts to break the silence, and by the 1970s interest in the topic began to intensify; since then an explosion of research and public interest has unfurled. The primary contributors to research have been sociologists and psychologists of gender, but it has also attracted scholars from criminology, family relations, clinical psychology, public health and medicine, political science, and anthropology.

Research on gender and violence has been driven by political imperatives emanating from both feminists and the conservative right. Paternalistic concern about the proprietary protection and control of women's bodies has long goaded conservatives to regard illegitimate physical and sexual attacks on women as particularly heinous crimes. Since the 1960s, feminists have refueled public concern about physical and sexual assaults on women, but their stance rests on women's right to autonomous control over their bodies. These seemingly incompatible political agendas have jointly fixed on the woman's body as the object of concern, spawning voluminous research on violence against women. Broader questions have usually been bypassed about the ways in which gender has conditioned the practice of violence by and against women and men.

MARY R. JACKMAN • Department of Sociology, University of California at Davis, Davis, California 95616

Handbook of the Sociology of Gender, edited by Janet Saltzman Chafetz. Kluwer Academic/ Plenum Publishers, New York, 1999.

Analysts have focused on specific acts of violence against women that have fallen under the policy spotlight. Large, specialized bodies of research have developed on domestic violence against women and on rape and sexual abuse. In the wake of women's reentry to the workplace, a growing literature on the sexual harassment of women has also emerged. More recently, some scholars have focused attention on a new concept called femicide, "the misogynist killing of women by men" (Radford & Russell, 1992, p. 3), and a literature has begun to develop on the selective abortion of female fetuses, infanticide of female babies, and neglect of female children and women in many cultures. There has also been a growing concern among journalists, activists, and scholars with female genital mutilation, practiced primarily in some African cultures. With the partial exception of work on femicide, which sometimes draws on research on other types of violence against women, research has evolved in discrete bundles of inquiry largely disconnected from each other, let alone violence against men. The result is a patchwork of information about specific forms of violence against women, with no overarching conceptual framework within which to interpret those acts, link them to each other, or situate them in a broader array of gendered behaviors that produce differential experiences of violence among women and men.

The balkanized, social-problems orientation of research on gender and violence has been endemic to research on other types of violence as well. Spurred by a sense of social urgency and the electricity of the subject matter, analysts of violence have generally short-circuited conceptual issues and proceeded directly to the analysis of specific forms of violence that have caught their attention. Thus, the wider literature on violence has been unable to provide a conceptual toolkit that could be applied to the unfurling concern with the relationship between gender and violence. In the absence of a clear, explicit conception of violence, implicit assumptions about the nature of the phenomenon have shaped the research agenda, working like a hidden hand to constrain research on gender and violence. Perhaps the two most prevalent assumptions are that violent behaviors are motivated by a hostile intent to harm the victim and that such behaviors lie outside the bounds of normal social intercourse, that is, that violence is malevolently motivated and socially, morally, or legally deviant from the mainstream. It is also commonly assumed that violence involves the use of force, that is, that the victim is an unwilling recipient of injuries. These three assumptions are so intrinsic to most conceptions of violence that they are rarely stated explicitly. In addition, most analysts focus on interpersonal violence, bypassing both self-inflicted violence and violence in which either the agents or the victims are corporate. Finally, most scholars have granted primacy to physical behaviors and injuries (or the threat thereof), with less significance generally attached to injurious behaviors that are verbal or written or to injuries that are psychological, social, or material.

The types of gender violence that have been the main object of inquiry are in accord with these assumptions. First, analysts of gender and violence have focused almost exclusively on interpersonal violence, while corporate behaviors have been only slightly examined to ascertain violent outcomes by gender. Second, the primary focus has been on the infliction or threat of physical injuries, although there has been increasing recognition of the psychological injuries suffered by victims of domestic violence, rape and sexual assault, sexual harassment, and genital mutilation. Third, analysts have attended primarily to physical behaviors, although some have argued that verbal abuse, verbal harassment, and pornographic materials contribute significantly to patterns of violence against women. Fourth, like other scholars of violence, analysts of gender violence assume that violence is motivated by ill will and the intent to harm. This assumption, combined with the almost exclusive focus on violence against women, has fostered the argument that social relations are fundamentally misogynist and that women live in a hostile and assaultive world. Fifth, driven by the assumption that violence involves the use of force on unwilling victims, analysts have taken an intense interest in the issue of victim complicity in domestic and sexual violence. Finally, the overriding assumption that violence represents a deviant course of behavior has encouraged students of gender violence to conclude that gender relations are uniquely violent, further encouraging the view that misogyny is the key to understanding gender relations and gender violence.

In sum, research on gender and violence has focused overwhelmingly on interpersonal, physical behaviors in which men inflict physical and psychological injuries on women. The extent to which women share complicity in the violence that they endure is a contentious issue to which much significance is attached. The exclusive focus of most analysts on violence against women, combined with underlying preconceptions about the nature of violence, has fostered the view that gender relations are driven by misogyny. This is reflected in the appearance of popular books with titles such as *The War Against Women* (French, 1992) and *Femicide: The Politics of Woman Killing* (Radford & Russell, 1992). The overwhelming image that emerges is of men as the hostile and abusive dominant class and women as the beleaguered and victimized subordinates.

My purpose in this chapter is to make a broad assessment of the relationship between gender and violence. In keeping with the nucleus of research, I focus primarily on violence against women, but I expand the scope to include violence against men. Detailed reviews are available elsewhere of specific forms of violence against women (e.g., Marshall, Laws, & Barbaree, 1990; Ohlin & Tonry, 1989; Reiss & Roth, 1993, 1994; Ruback & Weiner, 1995). I begin by appraising the daunting problems of observation and measurement that plague research and the main sources of available data. Second, I survey research on the broad variety of violent behaviors found in social life, to assess the prevalence and severity of various forms of violence against women as well as men. What are the main forms of violence to which women and men are vulnerable, and to what extent does each gender participate in the practice of violence? Third, I discuss the issue of cultural and legal support for violence against women and men. Does society distinctively encourage men to assault and abuse women, as some analysts have alleged? Fourth, I examine the contentious issue of victim compliance in incidents of gender violence: are women liable for their own victimization? Finally, I address the theoretical explanation of the relationship between gender and violence. After briefly discussing the leading explanations of violence against women, I propose an alternative approach based on a wider scan of violence in both women's and men's lives.

My discussion throughout is guided by a broad definition of violence as **physical, verbal, or written actions that inflict, threaten, or cause bodily, psychological, social, or material injury** (Jackman, in preparation). Note that this definition includes all injurious actions, regardless of their legality or their popular ideological construction. Violent actions may be committed against either others or oneself; be endured unwillingly or willingly; involve individual or corporate agents and/or victims; be intentional or negligent; be motivated by hostility, benevolence, masochism, or indifference for the victim; or be committed as an end in themselves or in the service of other objectives. What analysts have not acknowledged is that humans appear to have a capacity for violence— as perpetrators, victims, and observers—that is remarkably elastic. People do not have to be filled with hatred or anger to commit violence against others or with despair to inflict it on themselves. The motivations for and the social sanctioning of injurious actions vary widely.

Because the material and social injuries associated with gender relations are the subject of several other chapters in this volume, this chapter is restricted to those actions that produce bodily or psychological injuries. But even with this restriction, my definition of violence brings a broad array of injurious behaviors within view. In addition to those forms of gender violence that have been the subject of intense research (rape, domestic violence, and sexual harassment), it also includes a variety of behaviors that have usually been kept discrete from discussions of gender violence: painful or hazardous beauty practices, sexual mutilation, suicide, infanticide and progenicide, the use of demeaning or coercive images in pornographic materials, the infliction of working conditions that are hazardous or debilitating, the marketing of consumer products that put people at risk, the dispatch of young adults (usually males) into the jaws of death and mutilation in the military defense of their country, and other state-mandated violence in the form of punishments for behaviors defined as crimes. All of these actions involve the infliction of significant bodily and/or psychological harm, although they vary on many of the dimensions outlined previously. My purpose is to explore how gender affects involvement (both as victims and perpetrators) in the many faces of violence. The pertinent question for this chapter is not how and why there is violence against women, but instead, how the social organization of gender shapes the practice of violence against women and men.

1. PROBLEMS OF OBSERVATION AND MEASUREMENT

Because the social organization of gender routinely places women in institutional settings that are shielded from public view, direct observation of gender violence is difficult, if not impossible. Intimate contact between men and women has been privatized within the institution of the family, while sexual relations and sexuality range from privatized to taboo. Even as women have entered the more public sphere of the workplace, they continue to be thrown into one-on-one contacts with their male superiors or co-workers that are shielded from public view. Further, complex social norms that both stigmatize and deny incidents of rape, domestic violence, and sexual harassment make the disclosure of victimization personally costly, thus further reducing the accessibility of information about these forms of violence. When lower-status victims (and women are lower status by virtue of their gender and often according to other status positions as well) report on incidents that are unwitnessed by others, they frequently find they are granted less credibility than the higher-status perpetrator, with the result that the incident may be either denied or reinterpreted by others to place the blame on the victim herself. Even if they could be sure of successful prosecution, victims of rape, sexual assault, domestic violence, and sexual harassment may feel sufficiently defiled or shamed by the event to shrink from disclosure. In addition, sexual practices that are harmful to women, such as female genital mutilation, are enshrouded in taboos that obstruct their direct observation. In the face of such pronounced difficulties in accessing information, debates (often emotionally charged) have persisted on the incidence and seriousness of violence against women (see, e.g., Satel, 1997).

Most research on violence against women has been conducted in the United States, Canada, or Great Britain, with relatively little work in other countries and even less cross-national or cross-cultural research. The primary sources of data on domestic and sexual violence against women have been criminal justice statistics, victimization and self-report surveys, studies based on specialized samples of students, clinical or social-service clients, and medical records. In the United States, the most widely cited data sources are: (1) the FBI's Uniform Crime Reports (UCR), compiled annually from official police reports of eight index crimes; (2) the National Crime Survey (NCS), a national, probability, victimization survey administered every 6 months by the Bureau of the Census and the Department of Justice; and (3) the National Family Violence Surveys (NFVS) (Gelles & Straus, 1988; Straus & Gelles, 1990a; Straus, Gelles, & Steinmetz, 1980), which contain personal interviews with a national probability sample of 2143 individuals from intact families in 1975, and telephone interviews with a national probability sample of 6002 individual family members (including single-parent families) in 1985. Cross-national and cross-cultural data sources include the United Nations, INTERPOL, and the World Health Organization data sets, compiled from the official crime or mortality statistics of many nations; an International Crime Survey (ICS), modeled on the NCS, fielded in 1989 in 14 countries; the Conflict Tactics Scale developed in the NFVS, fielded in a number of countries; some multination surveys of perceptions of deviance or violence; and the Human Relations Area Files (HRAF). Excellent overviews of the features and problems of cross-national and cross-cultural data on violence can be found in Daly and Wilson (1988), Ember and Ember (1995), and Gartner (1995). Studies of sexual harassment have relied primarily on victimization surveys of workers or students. Perhaps the most complete data are from large, probability, mail surveys of United States Federal workers conducted by the U.S. Merit Systems Protection Board (U.S. MSPB), by mandate of the Civil Service Reform Act of 1978: these surveys were conducted in 1980, 1987, and 1994 (U.S. MSPB, 1981, 1995); sample sizes range from almost 20,000 in 1980 to about 8000 in 1987. Studies of feminine beauty practices and female genital mutilation have been primarily ethnographic (based on direct observation and informant reports), sometimes supplemented by small surveys.

These highly varied data sources have been associated with different kinds of problems. Criminal justice data underrepresent all crimes, but assaults and rapes are especially likely to be underreported, and this bias becomes stronger when victims and offenders know each other (Weis, 1989)—precisely the kinds of violence in which women are most likely to be victims. In addition, official records (such as the UCR) contain only minimal information about victim and offender characteristics: for example, the UCR reports detailed information on the relationship between the victim and the offender for homicides only, making it impossible to use these data to examine spousal assaults, and the UCR contains no information on the socioeconomic standing, education, or income of the victim or the offender for any index crime. These problems are compounded in cross-national analyses or trend studies that depend on direct comparison of criminal justice data that have been recorded according to varying rules and biases and that employ varying definitions of nonlethal violence. For these reasons, use of official statistics to analyze cross-national variance in violence is widely regarded as untenable except for some limited analyses of homicide (Gartner, 1995). The HRAF, compiled from ethnographic accounts of diverse cultures, are even more subject to inconsistencies in recording rules across ethnographers and cultures for various forms of violence.

Data from national probability surveys of victimization or self-reported violent behaviors (such as the NCS or the NFVS) provide higher estimates of violence against women than official crime statistics, since they do not depend on incidents finding their way into the criminal justice system. They also permit more ambitious analyses because they include more information about victims and offenders. However, these data are also subject to underreporting, owing to the sensitivity of the topic and the stigma attached to both perpetrator and victim in family and sexual violence. The impersonal, shotgun approach of survey interviews is ill suited to elicit the disclosure of such sensitive material, and, to make matters worse, in some cases the victim may be answering questions in the presence of either the perpetrator or children. All these factors are exacerbated in telephone interviews, which were used in the second NFVS in 1985. The NFVS probably offers the best source of systematic, detailed data on family violence, but this study has been severely criticized by some for gathering information on violent behaviors for the Conflict Tactics Scale without placing those behaviors in their social context (see, e.g., Brush, 1993; Dobash & Dobash, 1979, 1983; Kurz, 1993; Straus & Gelles, 1990a). The reality is that violence between intimates is usually made up of complex, interactive events that are lodged in ongoing interpersonal relationships that are emotionally saturated: it is a tall order to observe and measure such events with an instrument as blunt and superficial as a public-opinion survey, and yet there is no other way to gain systematic information for a cross-section of the population.

Other measurement issues plague the analysis of violence against women. Analysts have disagreed about how important it is to develop measures that are consistent with legal definitions of violent behaviors. The overriding interest in informing public policy has driven researchers to attend to the specific legal definition of crimes, but such definitions are often overly restrictive and have themselves changed over time. These problems have been especially salient in the analysis of rape and sexual assault. The traditional legal definition of forcible rape in the United States excluded many forms of coercive sex, such as forced sex in which there is a male victim, nonvaginal sex, and marital rape (Koss, 1992; Russell, 1982; Von, Kilpatrick, Burgess, & Hartman, 1991); rape statutes have been reformed in a number of states to broaden definitions along various dimensions, but jurors (and victims themselves) often have difficulty recognizing coercive sex between marital partners or other intimates or friends or become confused in trying to codify some sexually coercive behaviors. Scholars have responded to these inherent difficulties in a variety of ways, ranging from staying within legal definitions (e.g., Russell, 1982) to developing measures that depict coercion as a continuum that extends in a series of gradations from consensual sex to forcible rape (Bart & O'Brien, 1985; Kelly, 1987). Again, cross-national data sets of self-report surveys compound these problems by the introduction of noncomparability across nations in cultural and legal definitions of violence, question wording, and samples (Gartner, 1995).

The main alternatives to systematic data sets have been observational studies or in-depth interviews relying on small, nonrepresentative, purposive, or convenience samples of official offenders, social-service clients, or patients in health facilities (e.g., Dobash & Dobash, 1979; Stark, Flitcraft, & Frazier, 1979; Walker, 1979). These studies often permit greater analytic depth and sensitivity, and investigators may find subjects more willing to disclose and discuss incidents of violence in their lives because, either through their own actions or someone else's, some kind of public acknowledgment of the violence has already taken place. However, such data may also be highly misleading: sampling on the dependent variable creates serious selection bias, resulting in overestimates of the incidence of violence and possibly atypical observations of the associated causal factors (Hirschi & Selvin, 1967; Weis, 1989). A number of studies have also made use of student samples: although often convenient, these are susceptible to overestimates of the incidence of and normative support for gender-related violence because the young are both more sexually active and more violence prone (Daly & Wilson, 1988; Laumann, Gagnon, Michael, & Michaels, 1994, pp. 98, 336–337; Reiss & Roth, 1993, pp. 72–74; Wolfgang, 1967a, b).

Research on other forms of gender-related violence, such as corporate violence against women and ethnic customs or fashion dictates that result in female bodily alteration, have not usually been studied systematically. There have been some case studies of specific instances of corporate violence against women (e.g., see Finley, 1996, on the marketing of the Dalkon Shield IUD despite evidence that it was hazardous), and ethnographic observations of culturally mandated beauty practices, supplemented by interviews with medical practitioners or other knowledgeable informants (e.g., El Dareer, 1982; Lightfoot-Klein, 1989). Ethnographic research has been invaluable in exposing female genital mutilation, but it requires a major personal investment for analysts to obtain sufficient access to gain reliable and valid information about the extent of the practice and normative support for it (Lightfoot-Klein, 1989). Further, the focus in both case-study and ethnographic research on gender and violence has been overwhelmingly on female victimization, providing no information on the violence victimization of women relative to men in corporate and cultural settings.

2. GENDER AND THE PRACTICE OF VIOLENCE

The exact incidence of violence between males and females is unknown, but there is widespread agreement that in such interactions it is women who are more likely to suffer injuries. However, when one casts a broader net across all social relations, the relative victimization of women recedes and it is men who appear more vulnerable. Overall, men are both the main perpetrators and the main victims of physical violence, but women appear to be more at risk of victimization in relations involving intimate, private, or sexual interactions with men. Clearly, the woman's body is contested terrain, with many parties having a strong interest in controlling it. On this pivots both the protection of women from some forms of violence and their disproportionate victimization from others. In addition, women themselves do not abstain entirely from committing violence. In this section, I review men's and women's relative involvement in various forms of physical violence.

2.1. Homicide

Because data for homicide are more complete and accurate than for assault, some scholars have chosen to analyze spousal homicide as a way of addressing the issue of intimate, gender-related violence (e.g., Daly & Wilson, 1988; Mercy & Saltzman, 1989; Wilson & Daly, 1992a, b; Wilson, Daly, & Scheib, 1997; Wilson, Daly, & Wright, 1993; Wilson, Johnson, & Daly, 1995). Spousal homicides are rare, relative to the incidence of spousal assault, but because they are often associated with a prior history of spousal assault, their etiology is assumed to be parallel (Wilson, Daly, & Wright, 1993). Overwhelmingly, women are the victims of spousal homicide: scattered data from Australia, Canada, Denmark, England and Wales, Scotland, Africa, and India suggest that for every 100 spousal homicides perpetrated by husbands, only between 0 (India) and 40 (Scotland) are perpetrated by wives (Wilson & Daly, 1992b). In the United States, there is a sharp (and unexplained) distinction between whites and African-Americans in the relative victimization of wives and husbands from spousal homicides. For the years 1976–1985, among white Americans, wives' rate of spousal homicide victimization was 1.3 per 100,000 while for husbands it was 0.7; among African-Americans, the victimization rate was 7.1 for wives and 9.7 for husbands (Mercy & Saltzman, 1989). These rates for African-Americans are not only dramatically higher than for whites, but they also follow an entirely different pattern than for American whites, other minorities, or blacks in other nations, with African American wives showing a uniquely high rate of husband murder (Bohannan, 1967; Kruttschnitt, 1995; Mushanga, 1978; Wilson & Daly, 1992b). Since wives who murder their spouses are much more likely than their male counterparts to have been provoked to murder after suffering abuse and assault from their eventual victims (Browne, 1987; Daly & Wilson, 1988; Fagan & Browne, 1994; Jones, 1980; Langan & Dawson, 1995; Pleck, 1987, pp. 222–223; Totman, 1978; Wolfgang, 1967b, c), it would be useful to compare patterns and dynamics of domestic violence among black and white couples as well as the availability of police and social welfare interventions for battered wives in black and white communities.

Data for the United States over the past two decades (1977–1995) indicate that the rate of spousal homicide victimization has dropped precipitously for husbands (from 1.5 to 0.5 per 100,000) but has only inched down for wives (from 1.6 to 1.3) (Craven, 1996). Although the causes of this are unknown, it is possible that the increase in police and welfare interventions over this period have given battered wives more avenues of escape, thus saving men's lives, even if not women's. Systematic evidence from earlier historical periods is not available, but several factors have encouraged some scholars to presume that wife assault and murder were more frequent in the past: the existence of legal statutes permitting wife beating or murder under designated circumstances, the greatly diminished legal status of wives relative to husbands until relatively recent times (Dobash & Dobash, 1979; Fagan & Browne, 1994; French, 1992; May, 1978), and the generally higher rates of physical violence in earlier historical periods (Daly & Wilson, 1988, p. 291; Gurr, 1981; Manchester, 1992; Stone, 1983). However, Stone's (1983) analysis of fragmentary homicide data for England from 1200 to the present suggests that, although the overall homicide rate declined dramatically, the percentage of homicides involving family members has increased steadily, from about 8% in the fourteenth century to about 50% in present-day England. Pleck (1987, pp. 217–225) suggests that the family homicide rate in medieval England was fairly similar to recent rates in England and America, with a somewhat lower rate in the early modern period, and that the percentage of family homicides involving spouses generally decreased from medieval to Elizabethan times and then began to increase again in the Victorian era to the present-day level of about one half of all family murders. This suggests that wives' risk of being murdered by their husbands was fairly similar in the medieval era to what it is today in England and the United States, although women enjoyed somewhat lower risk during the Elizabethan era. Relative constancy in women's rates of homicide victimization is also suggested by analyses of homicide data for varying time periods from the 1870s to the 1980s for 16 nations in different parts of the globe, with rates for men both higher and more prone to fluctuation over time (Daly & Wilson, 1988, pp. 284–286; Verrko, 1967).

In earlier historical periods in which women lacked legal rights, a number of social constraints probably worked informally to limit the amount of physical abuse and murder that husbands could perpetrate against their wives: the lack of privacy from extended family members and other villagers in close-knit, densely housed village communities, the restricted geographic mobility of most common people (so that your reputation stuck to you), the wife's economic value as a contributing member of the household economy, and the difficulty an abusive husband might have in replacing a murdered wife in a community where everyone knows everything about you. These kinds of factors have not been discussed by feminist scholars addressing the history of wife abuse, who have instead stressed evidence suggesting the legal legitimacy of wife beating in times past.

In the past decade in the United States, spousal homicides have constituted somewhat over one half of homicides involving nuclear-family members, but only about 5% to 8% of all homicides (FBI Uniform Crime Reports, 1986–1995). Once one goes beyond intimate partner relations, it is men who are at greater risk of homicide victimization, even within the family (Reiss & Roth, 1993, p. 234). Thus, for 1995 in the United States, women were the victims in almost three quarters of the spousal homicides, but men were the victims in about 60% of the nonspousal nuclear-family homicides (those between parents and children or between siblings) (FBI UCR, 1995). Outside the family, men are overwhelmingly the victims (and the perpetrators) of homicide: in nonfamily homicides in the United States in 1988, men constituted 82% of the victims and 93% of the perpetrators (Dawson & Langan, 1994; see also Kruttschnitt, 1995). Thus, women are more at risk of being murdered by their spouses, while men are more at risk of being murdered by other family members and even more so by friends, associates, and strangers. Women are much less likely to perpetrate homicide than men, committing only about 10% of all homicides in the United States, Canada, the British Isles, and Australia (Dawson & Langan, 1994; Kruttschnitt, 1995), but most female-perpetrated homicides take place within the family, primarily with spouses or children as the victims. In the United States in 1988, women perpetrated about one third of family homicides and over one half of the murders of offspring (Dawson & Langan, 1994; see also Reiss & Roth, 1994, p. 234). Since spousal and other family homicides constitute only a small minority of all homicides in the United States, homicide is primarily a male affair, but the institution of the family puts women at risk of victimization and also provokes some women to murderous behaviors that they do not exhibit outside the family.

2.2. Suicide

Relatively little research has been done on the relationship between gender and suicide, but it is the ninth leading cause of death in the Unites States, exceeding the number of homicides every year since 1981 (Kachur, Potter, James, & Powell, 1995). More than 30,000 Americans took their own lives in 1992 (Kachur et al., 1995), compared with about 22,500 homicides (FBI UCR, 1993). As with violence directed at others, males are the main perpetrators. The age-adjusted suicide rate for white males in the United States in 1992 was 19.4 per 100,000, about four times higher than the rate of 4.6 for white females. African–American males have a lower suicide rate than white males (12.3 per 100,000), but still six times higher than the suicide rate of 2.0 for African-American females (Kachur et al., 1995). These differences in suicide rates by gender and race in the United States have been remarkably stable over the course of the twentieth century (Holinger, 1987).

2.3. Assault

Because of the daunting difficulties that beset the observation and measurement of domestic violence and the unknown degree of reporting bias for various forms of assault, researchers have yet to generate confident estimates of the relative incidence of domestic assault for men and women. Estimates of the relative perpetration by and victimization of men and women vary widely, according to the methods of observation and measurement, type of sample, and political agenda of the analyst. Most analyses of gender and assault focus on only one element of the problem, most often wife abuse and assault, making it difficult to address broader issues about the way in which gender conditions the likelihood of committing or suffering assault over the gamut of life situations.

Overall, as with homicide, men are the main perpetrators and victims of assault (Reiss & Roth, 1993, pp. 69, 74), but women's victimization increases sharply in family and sexual relationships (Bachman & Saltzman, 1995; Browne, 1993; Fagan & Browne, 1994; Kruttschnitt, 1994; Reiss & Roth, 1993, 1994). Data from the NCS for 1992–1993 indicate that assaults by intimates (that is, spouses, ex-spouses, or ex- or current boy/girlfriends) account for only a tiny fraction of all male victimizations from simple and aggravated assault (3% and 5%, respectively), whereas almost one third of the female victims of both kinds of assault have been assaulted by intimates (Bachman & Saltzman, 1995). Men are about three times more likely than women to become victims of simple or aggravated assault from a stranger, but victimization by intimates is over seven times more likely for women for simple assault and about three times more likely for aggravated assault (Bachman & Saltzman, 1995). Further, women's intimate victimizations are more likely to be repeated and to become chronic (Browne, 1993; Frieze & Browne, 1989; Langan & Innes, 1986).

The injuries experienced by battered wives have been the subject of considerable research. A recent study of patients visiting 24-hour emergency rooms at a nationwide, American sample of 31 hospitals estimates that in 1994 at least 200,000 women required emergency medical attention for injuries inflicted by intimates, compared with about 39,000 men (Rand & Strom, 1997, p. 5; Satel, 1997). Female victims are most likely to sustain injuries in the face or breasts, unless they are pregnant, in which case they are more likely to be struck in the abdomen (Schroedel & Peretz, 1994, p. 344). Pregnant victims not only sustain physical injuries to themselves but also have higher rates of miscarriage, stillbirths, and low birthweight babies, and there has been some documentation of direct injuries to the baby *in utero* (Schroedel & Peretz, 1994, pp. 345–346). Analysts of partner assaults have also taken the lead in highlighting the often chronic psychological injuries that affect victims: anxiety, depression, attempted suicide, alcoholism, low self-esteem, sense of violation, and the inability to function independently (see, e.g., Browne, 1993; Dobash & Dobash, 1979; Frieze & Browne, 1989; Reiss & Roth, 1993, pp. 237–239; Stark & Flitcraft, 1988, 1991; Tolman, 1989; Walker, 1979). The medicalized concept, Post-Traumatic Stress Disorder (or PTSD), which was originally developed to denote a range of negative psychological symptoms resulting from traumatic events such as wars, concentration camps, and airplane hijackings, has now been applied to the victims of partner abuse (see, e.g., Astin, Lawrence, & Foy, 1993; Browne, 1993; Frieze & Browne, 1989, p. 196).

Exact estimates of spousal assault in the United States vary dramatically, depending on the type of sample and methodology employed. The most commonly cited estimate comes from the National Family Violence Surveys from the 1970s and 1980s: responses to items in the Conflict Tactics Scale suggest that at least 1.8 million women (or 34 out of every 1000 wives) are assaulted by male partners each year in the United States (Browne, 1993; Frieze & Browne, 1989; Straus & Gelles, 1990b; Straus, Gelles, & Steinmetz, 1980). This estimate is substantially higher than those obtained from the NCS, but it is nonetheless widely assumed that it is still an underestimate. Quite apart from the probable underreporting of spousal assaults, the NFVS samples did not include divorced couples or nonfamilial intimate relationships such as boy/girlfriends, and women in both of these categories are known to experience higher assault victimization from their ex- or current partners than do married women who cohabit with their husbands (Daly & Wilson, 1988, p. 219; Fagan & Browne, 1994, p. 155–156; Stark, Flitcraft, & Frazier, 1979). If one could correct for these factors, the incidence of partner assault of women could be twice as high (Browne, 1993). As with other forms of interpersonal, physical violence, spousal assault is inversely related to age (see, e.g., Straus & Gelles, 1990a). Data from the NFVS also indicate that wife battering is two or three times as common among African-Americans as among white Americans (Stark & Flitcraft, 1991; Straus et al., 1980), but as with racial differences in spousal homicide, this difference has not been explained; studies consistently show only a small inverse relation between income and spousal assault (Stark & Flitcraft, 1991).

A more controversial claim from the NFVS has been that women use physically violent behaviors against their spouses at least as much as do men (Steinmetz, 1977–1978; Straus & Gelles, 1990b). This claim has sparked substantial criticism, and a number of studies have pointed to factors that appear to undermine its veracity, most notably, that men's assaultive behaviors are more frequent and severe and result in more serious injuries (see, e.g., Berk, Berk, Loseke, & Rauma, 1983; Browne, 1993; Brush, 1993; Dobash & Dobash, 1979, 1983; Fagan & Browne, 1994, pp. 169–171; Kurz, 1993; Stark & Flitcraft, 1991). Similar male–female patterns of violence (that is, reciprocity of violence but male dominance in severe violence) have been reported for dating couples (Sugarman & Hotaling, 1989, pp. 8–11). In-depth interviews with chronically abused women in Scottish shelters (Dobash & Dobash, 1979) indicated that such women had learned not to attempt resistance when their husbands were assaultive as that only resulted in more serious injuries (see also Pagelow, 1984, pp. 316–319). However, in the general population (which would include many relatively minor incidents), there may be a higher incidence of mutual combat between marital partners, even though women (usually the weaker of the two parties) are more likely to come out the losers from such encounters. There is also some evidence that women are strategic in their use of marital violence. Jones (1980, pp. 286–295) reports that in many cases of lethal retaliation against chronically abusive husbands, women wait until their husbands have temporarily disarmed themselves through heavy intoxication or sleep (see also Pagelow, 1984, p. 317). Detailed data from the items comprising the Conflict Tactics Scale in the NFVS show that men and women tend to employ different kinds of violent behaviors: for example, wives are about twice as likely to "throw something" at their spouses (a more efficacious strategy if your opponent is stronger or bigger than you) while husbands are about twice as likely to "beat up" their spouses (Gelles & Straus, 1988, pp. 250–251). Some have also argued that wives' assaultive behaviors are more likely to be in self-defense, but Straus and Gelles (1990b, pp. 104–105) reported that there was no difference between husbands and wives in the likelihood of initiating physically assaultive encounters. Another controversial finding from the NFVS is that women are at least as likely as men to abuse their children (Gelles, 1979): critics have charged that since mothers spend more time with children and are saddled with more responsibility for them, uncorrected comparisons of mothers' and fathers' use of violence toward children are invalid (Kruttschnitt, 1994, p. 311; Pagelow, 1984, pp. 184–198). The NFVS data also suggest that fathers' use of violence against children is more likely to be severe (Gelles, 1979), but recall that children are murdered by their mothers somewhat more frequently than by their fathers.

Unlike homicide, assaults by other (nonspousal) family members also appear to be directed disproportionately at female victims, at least for simple assaults, but data may suffer from reporting bias. Data from the NCS indicate that both men and women report victimization by other family members at a rate of 0.4 per 1000 for aggravated assault, but women's victimization rate for simple assault by other family members is 2.2 compared with 0.7 for men (Bachman & Saltzman, 1995). There is some evidence, however, that men's assault victimization by family members is more frequent than these data would indicate (Kruttschnitt, 1994, pp. 307–308). American men are only about half as likely as women to report simple assaults to police, and their self-reports in surveys may also be lower because they are less likely to recognize male-to-male family incidents as assault victimizations unless they sustain a serious injury. Several factors may contribute to the lower recognition of male-to-male family incidents as assaults: such incidents may seem less counternormative than those between males and females; they may involve more mutuality of both combat and injury infliction, especially for less serious assaults; and men may have more of a problem in depicting themselves as the losers/victims in physical encounters with brothers, sons, and fathers. If one could correct for these factors, the observed gender differences in assault victimization by parents, children, and siblings may well diminish, disappear, or reverse themselves—in which case the incidence of family assaults for men and women would be more consistent with the pattern for family homicides. Data from the National Incidence Studies of Child Abuse and Neglect indicate that male and female children suffer very similar rates of physical abuse in the United States (Sedlack & Broadhurst, 1996; U.S. Department of Health and Human Services, 1988), although male children may be somewhat more likely to be seriously injured (Sedlack & Broadhurst, 1996).

Data from the NCS indicate that relationships with friends and other associates pose a significant source of assault risk for both men and women: this risk is somewhat higher for men than for women, but it is still the highest source of assaults on women, with women being somewhat more likely to be assaulted by a friend or associate than by an intimate (Bachman & Saltzman, 1995, p. 3). The relative significance of friends and associates may be overstated because of greater underreporting bias with intimate assaults, but friends and associates do appear to be a significant source of physical violence in women's lives that has not been given analytic attention. For men, the primary risk of assault comes from friends or associates and from strangers, and their risk of assault exceeds women's in both of those categories but especially the latter (Bachman & Saltzman, 1995).

2.4. Rape, Sexual Assault, and Coercive Sex

This category of violent crime is the only one in which women are the prime victims: all but a minuscule proportion of rapes and sexual assaults have male offenders and female victims (Bachman & Saltzman, 1995, p. 3; Greenfeld, 1996, p. 10). In addition, female children are about three to four times more likely than male children to be sexually abused (Reiss & Roth, 1993, p. 69; Sedlack & Broadhurst, 1996; U.S. Department of Health and Human Services, 1988). The widespread incidence of rape was publicized by Brownmiller in her important book (1975). Brownmiller argued compellingly that the then-common portrayal of rape as a rare and anomalous crime was inaccurate: whenever women become a subject population through war, slavery, riots, pogroms, revolutions, imprisonment, police custody or other circumstances, rape and other forms of sexual exploitation are a routine accompaniment. Since the 1970s, scholars have struggled to develop precise estimates of the incidence of rape, a goal made elusive by both chronic underreporting and widespread confusion about what constitutes a rape. Estimates of the number of women in the United States who have been raped at least once in their lifetimes range from 3,750,000 to 16,500,000 (Von et al., 1991, p. 97). Forcible rapes, defined restrictively as "the carnal knowledge of a female forcibly and against her will," that is, forced vaginal penetration (FBI, 1989, p. 15; Greenfeld, 1997, p. 31), have comprised about 6% to 7% of all violent crimes reported to law enforcement agencies in the United States in recent years (Greenfeld, 1997; Koss, 1992, p. 63; Von et al., 1991, p. 100).

The Uniform Crime Reports (FBI, 1977–1996) for the years 1976–1995 report an annual victimization rate in the United States of about 52 forcible rapes per 100,000 females in 1976, rising steadily to a rate of about 84 in 1992 (a total of 109,060 forcible rapes), and then dropping slightly in each of the subsequent years to a rate of about 72 in 1995 (Greenfeld, 1997). Whatever the meaning of the variation in the rate of forcible rape over the past 20 years (that is, the extent to which it results from changes in willingness to report rape victimization to police or changes in the actual incidence of rape), it is widely acknowledged that rape is "one of the most underreported of all index crimes" (FBI, 1982, p. 14; Koss, 1992; Von et al., 1991). Government estimates indicate that for every rape reported to police, three to ten rapes remain unreported, and some estimates place the percentage unreported even higher (Von et al., 1991, p. 101). Data from the NCS for 1992–1993 suggest annual victimization rates for rape or sexual assault of about 400 per 100,000 for women and 50 for men, about five times the rates reported by law enforcement agencies (Bachman & Saltzman, 1995, p. 3). The NCS figures are themselves considered an underestimate by many scholars, because of the extreme sensitivity of the questions, the lack of confidentiality of the household interview, the failure to match many interviewers to respondents by gender and ethnicity, the framing of the questionnaire in terms of crime victimization (many respondents may not recognize their victimization as a crime, especially if it was committed by an acquaintance, boyfriend, or spouse), popular confusion about what constitutes a rape or sexual assault, and the exclusion of series victimizations from the calculation of rates (Koss, 1992). A national survey on sexuality conducted by the General Social Survey in 1992 employed a broader definition of forced sex: those data indicate that about 23% of women and 4% of men have been victims of forced sex at least once in their lives, and virtually all the women's cases but only one half of the men's involved a perpetrator of the opposite sex (Laumann et al., 1994, pp. 335–336; see Russell, 1984, p. 35, for similar figures for women from an earlier probability sample of women in San Francisco).

As with wife battering, the injuries sustained by rape victims are not only bodily but also psychological: analysts have emphasized that coerced sex is a traumatic event with long-term psychological consequences such as fear, anxiety, loss of control, betrayal of trust, self-blame, low self-esteem, embarrassment, humiliation, shame, depression, alcoholism, and attempted suicide (Darke, 1990; Finkelhor & Yllo, 1983; Laumann et al., 1994, pp. 338–339; Russell, 1982; Stanko, 1985, pp. 70–82; Von et al., 1991). There is also evidence that a significant proportion of rapes (about one quarter) include acts that appear to be specifically intended to humiliate the victim, such as victim stimulation of the offender, offender masturbation, or oral or anal penetration (Darke, 1990, pp. 62–65). Unfortunately, victims who avoid physically resisting their sexual assailant to minimize physical injuries may become more vulnerable to psychological injuries such as loss of control, self-blame, and low self-esteem.

Data from both victimization surveys (the NCS) and convicted, imprisoned rapists indicate that the probability of being raped or sexually assaulted is highest for women who are younger (ages 16 to 24), from low-income households, and city dwellers (Greenfeld, 1997; Perkins & Klaus, 1996; Taylor, 1997; Von et al., 1991, p. 101). As with assaults and homicides, African-American women have a higher rate of victimization than white women (Katz & Mazur, 1979, pp. 39–40; Perkins & Klaus, 1996; Reiss and Roth, 1994, pp. 69–70; Von et al., 1991, p. 101), although the racial difference may have declined in recent years, and data from the 1995 NCS show no racial difference (Taylor, 1997).

One of the most important—and provocative—facts to surface about the incidence of rape in the past 20 years is the high proportion of rapes and sexual assaults in which the offender is someone known to the victim. Only about 30% of the victims of rape offenders in State prisons were strangers: 1.5% were spouses or ex-spouses, 9% were girlfriends, 14% were children or stepchildren, 5% were other relatives, and 41% were acquaintances (Greenfeld, 1997, p. 24). Russell's landmark study of marital rape (1982) reported that in her probability sample of San Francisco women, 14% of women who had ever been married said they had been raped by a husband or ex-husband (see Finkelhor & Yllo, 1983, for similar results from a survey in Boston): Russell considers this figure an underestimate, because of underdisclosure by her respondents, confusion of many respondents about the concept of forced sex within marriage, and the conservative definition of rape used in the study (1982, pp. 58–59). Several scholars also report that marital rape often co-occurs with other forms of marital violence (see, e.g., Fagan & Browne, 1994, pp. 164–166; Frieze, 1983; Frieze & Browne, 1989, pp. 186–190; Pagelow, 1984; Walker, 1979). Of the forced sex victimizations reported by a nationally representative sample of adults, only about 4% were perpetrated by a stranger, whereas 55% were perpetrated by a spouse or someone with whom the respondent had a romantic relationship, 22% by someone else the respondent knew well, and 19% by an acquaintance (Laumann et al., 1994, p. 338).

Analysis of the prevalence of rape cross-culturally is a difficult venture, since measurement problems are exacerbated when one factors in different constructions of sexual behaviors across cultures and observers. However, Sanday (1981) conducted a careful analysis of the prevalence of rape in a sample of 156 cultures representing the six major regions of the world, dating from 1750 B.C. (Babylonians) to the late 1960s. Her coding of data from the HRAF and other ethnographic sources counted all forms of rape, including rape of enemy women, rape as a ceremonial act, and use of rape as a threat. She found wide variation in the prevalence of rape across cultures: about 18% were classified as "rape prone" (indicating rape was an accepted practice), another 35% as having a moderate propensity for rape, and in 47% of the cultures rape was reported as rare or absent. Higher rape prevalence was found in societies with high base rates of interpersonal and intergroup violence, pronounced male dominance, and sex-segregated structures or places.

2.5. Sexual Harassment

Until 1976 there was not a precise, shared social definition of sexual harassment (MacKinnon, 1979). Since then, there has been increasing awareness about unwanted physical and verbal behaviors of a sexual nature that interfere with the conduct of professional or work relations, and the inception of research on the incidence of sexual harassment. That research suggests that sexual harassment primarily, but not exclusively, involves female victims. Mail surveys of large, probability samples of American Federal workers conducted by the U.S. Merit Systems Protection Board (U.S. MSPB) in 1980, 1987, and 1994 found that more than 40% of female employees and 15% to 19% of male employees reported at least one form of sexual harassment victimization during the previous 2 years; younger women were especially likely to have been harassed (U.S. MSPB, 1995). Respondents were asked specifically about victimizations by fellow workers involving actual or attempted rape or assault; pressure for sexual favors; deliberate touching, leaning over, cornering, or pinching; sexual looks or gestures, letters, telephone calls, or materials of a sexual nature; pressure for dates; sexual teasing, jokes, remarks, or questions; and, in the 1994 survey only, unwanted following or intrusion into the respondent's personal life. Milder forms of sexual harassment were mentioned much more frequently, with 37% of the women and 14% of the men mentioning sexual teasing, jokes or remarks, and 4% of the women and 2% of the men mentioning actual or attempted rape or assault (see also Schneider, 1993, for comparable results from a cross-sectional sample drawn from street and telephone directories). In 1994, a co-worker was named as the perpetrator by almost 80% of both male and female victims of sexual harassment, but female victims were about twice as likely as male victims to have been harassed by a supervisor (28% vs. 14%), whereas male victims were more likely to have been harassed by a subordinate (11% vs. 3%) (some victims were harassed from more than one source). These gender differences probably reflect the disproportionate representation of males in supervisory positions. Sexual harassment is also a pervasive feature of student life. Victimization surveys of university students suggest that anywhere from 17% to 30% of female and about 2% of male students report having been sexually harassed by their teachers (Benson & Thomson, 1982; McCormack, 1985). Again, the disproportionate representation of males on college faculties in itself puts female students at greater risk of sexual harassment from their teachers.

Sexual harassment profoundly affects the quality of the victim's work or school life. Several studies indicate that about one in ten women leave their jobs as a result of sexual harassment, and university students who have been harassed may drop courses or change majors: all of these effects may derail careers or lower earnings (Gutek & Koss, 1997, pp. 153–154). Harassment can also cause a deterioration in interpersonal relationships at work or school, feelings of loss of control, and decreases in job satisfaction, self-esteem, feelings of competence, and work productivity (Gutek & Koss, 1997, pp. 153–154; Stanko, 1985; U.S. MSPB, 1995, pp. 26–27).

The media have been giving increasing attention to the issue of sexual harassment in the military, and it seems plausible that an organization that relies so heavily on physical harassment as an intrinsic part of the training of all recruits might be especially prone to sexual harassment. Comparative data for civilian employees in various U.S. government agencies, including the Air Force, Army, and Navy, suggest that, among civilian employees, the armed forces are at the high end of the range in levels of sexual harassment but not exceptional (U.S. MSPB, 1995, p. 15). A probability survey of enlisted personnel and officers in the Navy conducted in 1989 reported that more than 60% of the women and over 30% of the men said sexual harassment is a problem in the Navy (Culbertson, Rosenfeld, Booth-Kewley, & Magnusson, 1992, cited in Gutek & Koss, 1997). A study of 30,000 personnel in the U.S. Army reported that about 22% of the women and

7% of the men had experienced some kind of sexual harassment within the past year: the report concluded that "soldiers seem to accept such behaviors as a normal part of Army life" (Priest, 1997).

Across the gamut of public settings, the lower status of women and the pervasive, proprietary interest in their bodies has made them more vulnerable than men to a variety of forms of sexual harassment. Studies based on ethnographic, experimental, and survey data have documented the many forms of intrusive harassment to which women are disproportionately vulnerable on the street and in other public places. Catcalls, wolf whistles, staring, touching, pinching, body-grabbing, suggestive or evaluative personal comments, and verbal slurs are commonly reported (Gardner, 1995; Henley, 1977; Henley & Freeman, 1979; Henley & Harmon, 1985). The ready availability and public display of pornographic materials reinforces the sense of sexual vulnerability of women in general, as well as highlighting their self-conscious awareness of cultural demands about their personal appearance and sexual commodification (Dworkin, 1981; Flowers, 1994, pp. 179–185; MacKinnon, 1993; O'Toole & Schiffman, 1997, pp. 365–423; Reiss & Roth, 1993, pp. 111–112). Some forms of harassment, such as obscene phone calls or e-mail messages and stalking, pursue women when they retreat into their homes (Flowers, 1994, pp. 186–192; Sheffield, 1993; Smith & Morra, 1997; Spitzberg & Cupach, 1996). Criminal justice authorities have become increasingly aware of the potential for physically violent and even lethal outcomes from stalking. Data from a telephone survey of a national probability sample of 8000 women and 8000 men indicate that 8% of adult women have been stalked at some time in their lives (compared with 2% of adult men), that most stalking victims are young, and that almost one half of stalking victims are overtly threatened by their assailant (Tjaden & Thoennes, 1997). When women are stalked by former intimate partners (the majority of cases), about one third of the victims are eventually sexually assaulted by the stalker and over 80% are physically assaulted (Tjaden & Thoennes, 1997).

2.6. Bodily modifications

Women's bodies have been especially vulnerable to physical modification through a variety of invasive, painful, and often debilitating "beauty practices" and genital mutilations (Brownmiller, 1984; Wolf, 1992). These widespread practices are usually depicted as symptoms of misogyny, aimed at maiming, crippling, and weakening women. However, it is also possible that the high value placed on women's sexual and reproductive attributes is a powerful motivator to both men and women to commodify and package women's bodies in ways that exaggerate their biological distinctiveness and highlight women's contract with men to exchange exclusive sexual access rights for longterm economic support of women and their offspring (Engels, [1884] 1972).

Throughout history, women have subscribed to a variety of facial and bodily alterations that have adversely affected their physical and psychological functioning. The injuries sustained by women in the pursuit of beauty range from minor to severe: restriction of physical mobility, endurance of physical pain or discomfort, relentless lifetime effort, and constant self-criticism and sometimes humiliation before an unattainable beauty standard. Perhaps the most infamous beauty practice on record is the Chinese custom of footbinding, which survived for about 1000 years (until the early years of the twentieth century) as a rudimentary beauty standard and requirement for marriageability. Young girls (usually beginning at about 5 to 8 years of age), under their mothers' coercive super-vision, had their feet bound increasingly tightly, with a 3-inch foot being the ideal (Blake, 1994; Dworkin, 1994; Levy, [1966] 1992; Mackie, 1996; Mann, Sledzik, Owsley, & Droulette, 1990). As with many beauty ideals, few women attained it, but upper-class women (or aspirants) were held to the most rigorous standard, and thus the physically dysfunctional, crippled woman became the emblem of upper-class membership (Dworkin, 1994; Levy, [1966] 1992). The practice achieved an irreversible alteration to the girl's feet that drastically reduced her physical mobility; upper-class women could not walk unassisted and were able only to hobble over short distances. Their feet were in constant pain for at least the first 6 to 10 years of formative treatment, and complications included ulceration, paralysis, gangrene, and mortification of the lower limbs; it is estimated that footbinding injuries caused the deaths of perhaps 10% of girls (Mackie, 1996). The femi-nine struggle for small feet has not been exclusive to footbinding: women in the industri-alized nations continue to force their feet into shoes that are too small and that have high heels, thus restricting their mobility and causing a variety of foot injuries over the life span to which men are not subject (Jackson, 1990).

Several Western beauty practices have been the focus of research because of their injurious outcomes. The common use of tight corsets to produce an exaggerated hour-glass torso in the nineteenth century and earlier restricted breathing, induced fainting, broke ribs, and sometimes caused prolapse of the uterus (Brownmiller, 1984; Wolf, 1992). When women threw away their corsets in the twentieth century, "dieting" became a wide-spread female practice, whereby girls and women rely on restricted calorie intake rather than mechanical devices to decrease their body sizes. Most women in the industrialized nations impair their physical and psychological well-being through constant or sporadic dieting regimens and relentless self-criticism, and, in extreme cases, women succumb to life-threatening eating disorders such as bulimia and anorexia (new diseases undocu-mented before the demise of the corset) (Brownell & Rodin, 1994; Brownmiller, 1984; Rodin, Silberstein, & Striegel-Moore, 1985; Wolf, 1992). The recent advent of advanced surgical techniques has also encouraged an unknown number of women to submit to painful and sometimes hazardous surgeries such as face lifts, breast implants, liposuction, and laser removal of wrinkles (Siebert, 1996). An increasing number of young women in the industrialized nations resort to painful body modifications, such as body piercing (including nipple and genital piercing) and tattooing, which were formerly associated with premodern cultures. Men have not been entirely immune from the painful pursuit of modifications in physical appearance. Men in premodern societies and working-class men in industrial societies have long subjected themselves to tattoos on their arms, torsos, or faces as a way of displaying group identification as well as their ability to endure pain. In the contemporary United States, increasing numbers of men are modifying their per-sonal appearance with hair transplants and other types of cosmetic surgery (Siebert, 1996).

The urge to commodify and control women's sexual capacity perhaps finds its most explicit expression in female genital mutilation, which has been receiving increasing publicity in recent years. It is practiced in about two dozen African countries, where it is a requirement for marriageability and ethnic identification, affecting the health and well-being of an estimated 132 million women (World Health Organization, 1996). The prac-tice ranges from the relatively mild clitoridectomy (removal of the clitoris) to genital infibulation (removal of the entire outer portion of the genitals and the stitching up of what is left with just a pencil-sized aperture left for urination and menstruation). The majority of people who practice some form of female genital mutilation are poor and have no access to sterile instruments or anesthetic. Girls between early childhood and adolescence (the age varies across cultures) are subjected by their older female relatives to this excruciatingly painful operation. There are a wide range of adverse medical outcomes, both immediate and permanent, such as pain, hemorrhage, shock, psychological trauma, acute urinary retention, urinary infection, blood poisoning, fever, tetanus, or death after the procedure, and subsequently diminished sexual responsiveness (with the least invasive forms of mutilation), painful intercourse (with infibulation), infertility, hazardous childbirth, difficulty urinating and menstruating, and recurrent infections (Dorkenoo & Elworthy, 1992; El Dareer, 1982; *Harvard Law Review*, 1993; Inhorn & Buss, 1993; Lightfoot-Klein, 1989; Mackie, 1996).

The desire to control sexuality, to use sexuality as a fundamental ethnic marker, and to restrict who has sexual access to privileged women, have led primarily to a concentration of effort on the female body, but they have also impelled numerous examples of male genital mutilation. The emblem of Jewish male identity is the circumcised penis, and many premodern cultures include circumcision (without anesthetic) as part of adolescent initiation ceremonies. Several Aboriginal tribes in central Australia subject their adolescent men to genital subincision during initiation, in which an incision of about 1 inch length is cut on the underside of the penis, and the wound is ceremonially reopened at periodic intervals throughout the man's life (Berndt & Berndt, 1964; Montagu, [1937] 1974). Castration was a requirement for male employment as a household servant in the imperial courts in the Ming dynasty in China, and thousands of young men underwent this dangerous, painful, and humiliating operation in the hope of gaining such employment (Tong, 1988, p. 113). Indeed, until the late nineteenth to early twentieth century, the eunuch occupied a venerable place in the administration of secular and religious rule in a wide range of locations, including Rome, China, Byzantium, Egypt, and (until 1878) the Papal Choir of the Sistine Chapel (Tannahill, 1992, pp. 248–254). Eunuchs were viewed as sexually nonthreatening guards for harems and upper-class women and as incorruptible administrators because of their inability to father offspring. Castration was also employed as a punishment throughout history and across cultures until the early twentieth century. In the United States, it was part of the repertoire of punishment used against slaves and it was sometimes (with increasing rarity in the twentieth century) inflicted on black men who were lynched or institutionalized (Elkins, 1968; Hall, 1983; Kolchin, 1993; Stampp, [1956] 1989; Wright, 1994; Wyatt-Brown, 1982).

The reproductive ability of both men and women has been recurrently subject to attack in the cause of class or racial domination or eugenics. With the advent of more advanced surgical techniques in the late nineteenth century, women's reproductive ability became more vulnerable to control. For example, recent revelations indicate that more than 70,000 women and a much smaller number of men were sterilized in Scandanavia between 1929 and 1976 for a variety of reasons relating to their presumed reproductive fitness (*The Economist*, 1997). Some policymakers continue to view poor welfare mothers in the United States as a target for sterilization policy.

2.7. Infanticide, progenicide, femicide

In resource-poor societies, especially preindustrial ones, there is evidence that infanticide is widely practiced as a makeshift means of birth control. Minturn and Shashak (1982, cited in Ember & Ember, 1995, p. 28) report that infanticide occurs in 53% of their mostly preindustrial sample societies. It appears to be used primarily to eliminate illegitimate children with no male to support them or to achieve a spacing of children that will not strain material or social resources (see also Daly & Wilson, 1988; Skinner, 1993). Such infanticide appears to be motivated by pragmatic concerns about resource allocation in societies that do not have access to safe birth control or abortion, and it almost always occurs before the ceremony that socially marks or announces a birth (Minturn & Shashak, 1982). Scheper-Hughes' ethnographic study of poverty-stricken mothers in urban Brazil (1992) reveals that they sometimes choose to abandon or neglect weaker or sickly children in order to reallocate their meager resources to stronger children with better survival odds. Such infanticide and progenicide appears to be gender neutral in terms of its victims, but it is women—by virtue of their biological link to the child—who are generally saddled with the perpetration of the destructive behavior.

It has also come to light in recent years that in a number of economically less developed societies, female children and women are being systematically neglected, abandoned, or murdered (or female fetuses selectively aborted where technology permits), so that the ratio of females to males in the population is artificially low. There have been scattered reports of selective infanticide of female newborns, and consistent and systematic observations of the selective withholding of food and medical support from female children and women in India, China, Pakistan, and Bangladesh (Coale, 1991; Sen, 1990, 1992; Venkatramani, 1992). Symptomatic of the problem are the widespread reports of "accidental" sari burnings in many parts of India, in which young brides are allegedly burned to death or driven to suicide by their in-laws after they have procured their dowries (Kelkar, 1992). Serious shortfalls have been estimated in the proportion female in the populations of India, China, Pakistan, Bangladesh, Nepal, West Asia, Egypt, and some other North African countries (Coale, 1991; Sen, 1990, 1992). Sen (1990) originally estimated that more than 100 million women are missing worldwide (half of them in China), using the ratio of females to males in Europe, the United States, and Japan as the benchmark to evaluate the relative shortfall of women in selected Asian and African countries. However, this estimate was inflated, primarily because of the artificially low proportion of *males* in the "benchmark" countries caused by battle deaths in World Wars I and II (see *War Casualties* below), and also because it did not make appropriate adjustments for the fertility and mortality rates and population age structure of the affected countries. Coale's reanalysis yields a "rough approximation" of the number of "missing females" worldwide as about 60 million, still an enormous number. The two most populous nations in the world contribute disproportionately to this number, with 29 million missing females in China and 23 million missing in India (Coale, 1991, pp. 521–522). When expressed as a percentage of a nation's female population, it is Pakistan that is the worst offender, with just under 8% of its females missing. The comparable figure for China is 5.3%; for India 5.6%; and for Bangladesh, Nepal, West Asia, and Egypt about 2% to 4% (Coale, 1991, p. 522).

Sen argues convincingly that this rudimentary discrimination against women is explained primarily as a resource-management strategy of families in systems in which inheritance rules favor sons and make daughters costly. Whereas sons are the parents' ticket to economic security in their old age, daughters are an economic liability for the household, and thus their welfare is sacrificed to the economic interests of the remaining family members (Sen, 1990). "Surplus" daughters are especially problematic. One study in Khanna, India, found that the death rate before age 5 for daughters with no older sisters was little different from the male death rate, but for females with an older sister it was about 50% higher than for males (Das Gupta, 1987, cited in Coale, 1991, p. 521). In China, the introduction of the one-child-per-family rule in 1979 made even firstborn daughters a threat to the long-term economic prospects of the parents: that, combined with changes in economic policy that dismantled the commune system and made families more economically self-reliant, resulted in a deterioration in the relative life expectancy of women and a dramatic increase in the rate of female infant mortality from 37.7 per 1000 in 1978 to 67.2 in 1984 (Sen, 1990, p. 65). Sen insists that the selective neglect or abandonment of females in some cultures cannot be explained satisfactorily in terms of prejudice against women, but is instead explicable in terms of sons' versus daughters' economic value to the family, along with the lack of governmentally ensured old-age benefits. He suggests that in those poorer countries in which women have increased their labor force participation (even in menial jobs), women's risk of selective neglect has declined because of their enhanced economic value to their families. There is also some evidence that provision of communal social security and health programs diminishes the material bias against girls and women (Sen, 1990).

2.8. War casualties

Nations have long expected their young men to be ready to sacrifice their lives as soldiers for the security of the remaining citizenry or to protect the "national interest." The number of men whose lives have thus been squandered in international and civil wars (including only those wars with at least 1000 battle deaths) is estimated to have totalled about 5,000,000 between 1816 and 1900, while the twentieth century had, by 1980, swallowed up the lives of about 36,000,000 men in battle deaths (Small & Singer, 1982, pp. 78–99, 221–233). World War I alone took the lives of 9,000,000 soldiers in battle, and another 15,000,000 soldiers were killed in World War II. Germany sacrificed about 5% of its male population in WWI and then another 10% a few years later in WWII. By the time the USSR pulled out of WWI in December 1917, it had already lost about 2% of its males in battle, and in WWII the USSR sacrificed about another 9% of its males (Small & Singer 1982, pp. 89, 91). The most devastating recorded battle casualties were sustained by Paraguay in the Lopez War (1864–1870), in which an estimated 90% of Paraguay's male population was killed in battle (Small & Singer, 1982, p. 84). Further, for every soldier killed in action, approximately four or five soldiers are wounded in action, and at least half of those wounded suffer casualties that leave them physically or emotionally debilitated for the rest of their lives (Dunnigan, 1993). Men who have given their lives in war are typically glorified with public monuments and displays of reverence such as public holidays, speeches, and parades—but the objects of veneration are of course dead. War veterans often do not meet with the same veneration from the government or citizenry on whose behalf they fought.

The embroilment of civilians in war had been steadily declining since the 17th century, but beginning with WWII, civilian casualties have become an increasing component of war (Wright, 1965): these casualties affect noncombatant men, women, and children indiscriminately. In recent history, women have also begun to join men in the ranks as soldiers or assistants in warmaking (although women are still barred from the infantry, artillery, and armor in the U.S. Army (Richter, 1997) and most other armed services). Both of these factors have increased women's share of wartime casualties, but it is overwhelmingly males who have been selected as the cannon fodder of nations. Indeed, the proportion of many postwar nations' males that is "missing" because of battlefield deaths is roughly equivalent to the proportion of females that is missing in some less developed nations in the 1990s because of institutionally induced selective neglect or murder. The common incidence of wartime rape of women and girls (Brownmiller, 1975) should be placed in context: the men committing those rapes (usually in their most sexually active years) have themselves been transformed into a dehumanized status by the nations that deploy them in battle.

2.9. Lynching

Little work has been done on the effect of gender on participation in and victimization from mob violence, but studies of lynching in the United States are revealing. Between 1882 and the early 1950s, it is estimated that 5000 to 6000 persons were killed by lynch mobs, 82% of them in the South (Hair, 1989; White, [1929]1969). The chivalrous protection and control of white women's sexuality appears to have been a central motivating sentiment behind the violence of the Ku Klux Klan, and in that spirit, most of the victims of lynching were black men. Indeed, men constituted an even higher proportion of lynching victims (more than 95% both nationally and regionally) than did African-Americans (who were 72% of lynching victims nationally and 84% of Southern lynchings) (Hair, 1989). The sexual protection of white women was the most frequently cited justification offered in defence of lynch law, and rape or alleged rape of a white woman was the second leading cause of lynchings (closely behind murder), accounting for about one third of the lynchings of both black and white victims (Hair, 1989; see also Brundage, 1993, pp. 263–264).

Women apparently did not leave their protection entirely in the hands of their menfolk. The participants in lynch mobs appear to have been primarily—but not exclusively—male. In those lynchings carried out by mass mobs, women and even children participated prominently, by "inciting the crowd with cheers, providing fuel for the execution pyre and scavenging for souvenirs after the lynchings" (Brundage, 1993, pp. 37–38: see also Cameron, 1982). Women also provided auxiliary support through their participation in the Women of the Ku Klux Klan when the Klan went through its revival in the 1920s, and Blee argues that "the idea of 'white womanhood' was a crucial rallying point for postbellum Klan violence" (Blee, 1991, p. 13).

2.10. Workplace injuries, diseases, and fatalities

The cruel exploitation of women and children in the industrializing nations during the nineteenth century is well known. The shocking engravings in British parliamentary reports depicting the inhuman working conditions of women and children in the mines in the early 1840s (British Parliamentary Papers, [1842] 1968) graphically illustrate the raw fact that women and children were not exempted from the terrible suffering of the working class in the early days of industrial development. At the same time, reformist governmental agents chose to highlight the plight of women and children workers because their misery was more offensive and shocking to public morality than the suffering of male workers (Perot, 1990, pp. 85–87; Brandeis & Goldmark, [1907] 1969). Working conditions have steadily improved in industrialized nations in the past 150 years, and there has been a consequent decline in the incidence of work-related injuries and deaths.

For example, the number of work-related deaths in the United States (excluding work place homicides) has dropped from about 16,000 annually in the 1930s and 1940s to about 5000 annually in the 1990s (National Safety Council, 1995). Women's exposure to work hazards has been especially reduced.

Even with improvements in working conditions, serious hazards still confront many workers, especially blue-collar workers, and the issue remains sharply contested in labor–management relations (McGarity & Shapiro, 1993). The 5000 people killed by work-related injuries in the United States in 1995 do not include the 1262 workplace homicides or the estimated 47,000 to 100,000 who die annually of occupationally induced diseases (Bureau of Labor Statistics [BLS], 1996; National Safe Workplace Institute, 1990; Office of Technology Assessment, 1985; Pollack & Keimig, 1987). About three quarters of the 5000 enumerated deaths from work-related injuries in 1995 were in blue-collar jobs, and only about 5% were women (BLS, 1996). Thus, one benefit for women of sex-role segregation in the labor force has been to shield them from many of the highest risk, blue-collar occupations. Almost one half of the women killed at work are victims of homicide; even if one includes work place homicides, however, only about 9% of workplace deaths involve female victims (BLS, 1996; see also U.S. Department of Labor, 1994). There is one female-typed occupation that is very hazardous—prostitution—but its illegitimate status leaves it outside the net of BLS statistics. Prostitutes have always been vulnerable to physical assault, sexually transmitted diseases, and murder: a recent study by the Centers for Disease Control indicates that prostitutes have a much higher prevalence of AIDS than the general population, and a study of street prostitutes in Miami found 41% of those tested were HIV-positive (Flowers, 1994, p. 178).

Women's general protection from nonfatal work injuries and illnesses in the United States is not as pronounced, but still substantial. Men account for about two thirds of the 2.3 million annual work injuries and illnesses (well in excess of their 55% share of all private wage and salary workers) (BLS, 1994, p. 3). Women injured on the job usually work for health care providers, food stores, restaurants, lodging places, or other service-producing industries (BLS, 1994, p. 3). The one type of work-related injury (other than workplace assaults) from which women suffer more than men is repetitive-motion injuries and illnesses (most commonly carpal tunnel syndrome): women account for about two thirds of the 90,000 cases annually (BLS, 1994, p. 6; see also BLS, 1995).

The gradual improvement in working conditions that has marked the more highly industrialized nations is not shared by the newly industrializing countries of the world today. There is some evidence that women workers of these countries are subjected to especially gruelling work conditions and exploitative wages (Bradshaw & Wallace, 1996, pp. 4–5, 104–106). Unfortunately for such women, the same jobs whose income helps to protect them from the worst excesses of family abuse and neglect (Sen, 1990) also expose them to new work-based hazards. A number of developing countries also employ an uncounted number of women in sexually exploitative jobs (such as the thriving sex tourism industries in the Philippines and Thailand) that expose these women (and their children and subsequent sex partners) to sexually transmitted diseases such as AIDS.

2.11. Deaths and Injuries from Hazardous Consumer Products

There are no systematic data on the total injuries and fatalities that are attributable to the marketing of hazardous consumer products, and thus the overall relative risk borne by women and men in the consumer marketplace is unknown. Women's interest in controlling their fertility has made them prey to hazardous birth control products, such as the Dalkon Shield (Finley, 1996; Szockyi & Frank, 1996), and their culturally mandated preoccupation with personal appearance has led many women to use questionable or hazardous beauty products ranging from hair dyes and weight-loss products to breast implants (Claybrook, 1996; Szockyi & Frank, 1996). The female-targeted marketing of hazardous reproductive and beauty products has received sporadic publicity in the media and has been the subject of some research on corporate violence against women. However, the two most hazardous consumer products in the United States are guns and cigarettes (although the Consumer Product Safety Commission does not classify guns as consumer products; Combs & Donoghue, 1994): these two lethally dangerous products have done more damage to males' than to females' health and life expectancy.

The United States leads the industrialized world in the incidence of deaths from firearms, and the ready availability of firearms in the American consumer marketplace is more responsible than any other single factor for the unusually high homicide rate in the United States (Lynch, 1995). In the past decade in the United States, about 32,000 to 38,000 people have been killed annually by firearm injuries, which includes both homicides (60% to 70% of which are committed with firearms annually) and accidents (FBI, 1981–1995; U.S. National Center for Health Statistics, 1993, p. 101). Guns are the playthings of men more than of women, and about 85% of the victims of firearm deaths are male (U.S. National Center for Health Statistics, 1993, p. 101). African-American males have an especially high death rate from firearms—more than 64 per 100,000 (age-adjusted rate), compared with about 20 for white males, 8 for black females, and 4 for white females (U.S. National Center for Health Statistics, 1993, p. 101). This gender difference in the incidence of deaths from firearm injuries begins to appear in the 5 to 9 year-old age bracket (especially among blacks) and becomes particularly pronounced in the violence-prone teen and young-adult years (U.S. National Center for Health Statistics, 1993, p. 100).

The leading cause of premature death in industrialized nations is tobacco, and men are again disproportionately the victims. In industrialized countries in the 1990s, smoking accounts for an estimated 39% of all deaths in men between 35 and 69 years of age, compared with 15% of all deaths in women in that age bracket; over age 69, 23% of all male deaths and 8% of all female deaths are attributable to smoking (Peto, Lopez, Boreham, Thun, & Heath, 1992). In the United States alone, the total number of deaths caused by tobacco is conservatively estimated to be 390,000 to 400,000 annually (Peto et al., 1992). The prevalence of smoking in the United States has decreased from 40% of adults in 1965 to 29% in 1987, but women's use of tobacco has declined at a substantially slower rate than men's; in addition, the age of initiation to smoking has fallen over time, especially among females (U.S. Department of Health and Human Services, 1989, p. 11). As gender differences in cigarette use have been declining in the United States, the gender gap in deaths from smoking has been steadily narrowing from the 1960s to the 1990s (Peto et al., 1992).

2.12. State-Mandated Punishments

Women are less likely than men to commit crimes, especially violent crimes, but there is fairly consistent evidence that convicted female criminals receive more lenient sentences than their male counterparts (Nagel & Hagen, 1983). The relationship between gender and the criminal justice system is discussed more fully in Chapter 26 of this volume. Here, I confine myself to two crimes that have been highlighted by some scholars as exemplifying the legal harassment or control of women: spousal murder and witchcraft.

Some analysts have claimed that our legal system, whether from misogyny or male-biased myopia, has shown sympathy for husbands who murder their adulterous wives or wives' lovers, while being unsympathetic to the plight of battered wives who desperately kill their husbands after suffering years of escalating abuse (e.g., Fagan & Browne, 1994). Daly and Wilson (1988, pp. 193–196) review legal statutes cross-culturally and over time and argue that most legal systems have shown at least some degree of leniency to cuckolded husbands who turn murderous. Other scholars have emphasized that any comparable sympathy for wives is lacking. They have argued that wives are only rarely motivated by sexual jealousy to murder their husbands, but when battered wives murder their husbands at strategic moments when they are temporarily incapacitated (asleep or heavily intoxicated), their actions are not construed as self-defense in the narrow legal sense, and they are therefore subject to imprisonment for murder. Even in some cases of victim-precipitated murder of husbands (that is, in which the victim is the first to show a weapon or strike a blow), defendants may be unsympathetically imprisoned for manslaughter (Browne, 1987; Campbell, 1992; Fagan & Browne, 1994; Jones, 1980; Totman, 1978). However, a recent study of 540 spousal murder cases in the 75 largest counties of the United States (Langan & Dawson, 1995) offers no support for these arguments. The study found that wives charged with killing their husbands (41% of the cases) were somewhat less likely to be convicted than husband defendants (70% vs. 87%), more likely to be acquitted (31% vs. 6%), if convicted were slightly less likely to receive prison sentences (81% vs. 94%), and if sentenced to prison received sentences on average about 10 years shorter (6 years vs. 16.5 years). Of course, substantially more wife defendants (44%) than husband defendants (10%) had been assaulted by their spouse at or around the time of the murder. The element of victim provocation appears to explain the gender difference in conviction rates, but not in the length of prison sentences (unprovoked defendants' average prison sentences were 7 years for wives and 17 years for husbands). This study thus suggests, at a minimum, that the contemporary legal system in the United States generally is sympathetic to the mitigating circumstances that more often provoke wives to turn murderous, and there is also some evidence that wife defendants are punished more leniently, regardless of mitigating circumstances. These results are consistent with those found for other crimes and with the chivalry/paternalism thesis long entertained by criminologists (Nagel & Hagen, 1983; Wilson & Herrnstein, 1985, pp. 112–115).

The gruesome torture and punishments inflicted by state and ecclesiastical authorities on an estimated 200,000 accused witches in early modern Europe and America are well known (Barstow, 1995; Hester, 1992; Levack, 1995; Russell, 1972). Some feminist scholars have argued that the witchcraze was a classic example of femicide, in which unconventional women were targeted for severe punishment and death as a means of terrorizing and controlling all women (Barstow, 1995; Hester, 1992). That impression is certainly encouraged by a singular focus on the sadistic and often sexually oriented punishments and the bizarre, superstitious beliefs that surrounded accused witches. However, it is important to situate the witch hunts appropriately. First, they were part of a general preoccupation in the European states throughout this period with maintaining the primacy of received Christian dogma, and freedom of speech was still a long way from being invented as a human-rights principle (Levack, 1995; Manchester, 1992; Peters, 1988). Witchcraft was a popular heretical tradition that stood as a challenge to the authority of the Church (Russell, 1972), and suspected witches received treatment comparable to other accused heretics. Second, witchcraft was practiced predominantly by women, and thus it is hardly surprising that it was primarily women who fell under suspicion during state attempts to suppress it. Women constituted about 75% of accused witches in most localities in Europe and New England between 1509 and 1777, although the percentage female ranged fairly widely from lows of 32% in Russia, 42% in Estonia, and about 50% in the Scandinavian countries, to 90% or more in Basel, Belgium, and England (Levack, 1995, p. 133–134). Third, the sadistic and superstitious rules of evidence for determining witchhood were quite normal for their historical context (Manchester, 1992; Peters, 1988; Russell, 1972). Recall that the Inquisition and other state-authorized religious persecutions throughout Europe during this period had equally brutal methods for dealing with suspected religious nonconformists, and both sorcerers and scientists suffered for their wayward thoughts, as did religious practitioners who strayed from received Christian dogma (Manchester, 1992; Peters, 1988; Russell, 1972). In short, state authorities threw their suspicious and punishing gaze not only on women but on all citizens.

2.13. Summary

Perhaps because violence against women, especially that taking place in intimate relationships, was overlooked by scholars for so long, much of the literature on gender and violence in the past 20 years has focused exclusively on violence against women: wife battering, rape, and sexual harassment (e.g., Brownmiller, 1975; Dobash & Dobash, 1979; Dutton, 1988, 1995; Flowers, 1994; Stanko, 1985; Walker, 1979). This work has performed an invaluable service in identifying and highlighting an important—and previously hidden—social issue, but the singularity of focus has also fostered the perspective that women are the special targets of male violence. This, in turn, has nourished the inference that it is misogyny that drives violence against women. What has disappeared from view are two important patterns that mark the overall relationship between gender and physical violence. First, men's greater proclivity for physical violence is more likely to be directed at other men, except in the context of intimate or sexual relationships. Second, women apparently do not shrink from committing violence themselves in those circumstances where their deficits in height, weight, and muscle mass are suspended or mitigated. Within the context of male–female interactions, women have been the victims of violence more often than men, but in those contexts where their physical deficits do not make them vulnerable (as in violence against young offspring and in mob violence against overpowered victims), women have not shown a disavowal of violence. Indeed, a meta-analysis of research on gender and aggression concluded that differences between males and females are small and variable across contexts (Eagly & Steffen, 1986; see also Bjorkqvist & Niemela, 1992; Kruttschnitt, 1994, p. 328); the main systematic difference is for women to have a greater proclivity for verbal aggression and men for physical aggression.

The relationship between gender and violence thus appears to be molded by two primary factors: widespread social preoccupation with the proprietary protection and control of women's sexuality, and the respective physical strength of men and women. Men are the main perpetrators and victims of nonsexual, interpersonal violence (homicides and assaults), lethal violence against oneself (suicide), and various forms of nonsexual, corporate violence (in war, the workplace, the consumer marketplace, mob violence, and state-mandated punishments). It is only sexual violence that men direct primarily at women. Sexual access to women is generally regulated by institutional arrangements without the use of physical force, and concern with controlling sexual access to women on the basis of class or group membership has sometimes prompted surgical assaults on men's bodies (e.g., castration, circumcision, subincision). However, women are the primary victims of rape and sexual assault, and their bodies have been chronically subjected to intense proprietary control, inducing rigorous beauty standards that can be painful or hazardous, a variety of surgical assaults, persistent and invasive public evaluation of women's physical appearance, and disproportionate sexual harassment of women. By the same token, women have been kept relatively secluded from interpersonal violence emanating from non-sexual relations, as well as from the hazards of the battlefield, workplace, consumer marketplace, mob violence, and state-mandated punishments.

3. CULTURAL SUPPORTS FOR VIOLENCE

A repeated refrain has been that violence against women is condoned, justified, or excused by an infrastructure of cultural beliefs and legal statutes that are misogynist. Analysts point to a long history of laws that curtail women's rights relative to their husbands and to popular beliefs that encourage or excuse physical and sexual violence against women. I reserve until the next section a separate discussion of the issue of victim blame, which has played such a prominent role in excusing violence against women. In this section, I begin by briefly reviewing the legal record of intervention in acts of violence against women. I then address the cultural values surrounding wife beating, rape, and sexual harassment, and the belief systems that mandate painful or harmful beauty practices, as well as the values surrounding male-targeted violence. In the light of this evidence, it is difficult to sustain the view that violence against women is unequivocally or uniquely endorsed. Further, scholars have confounded violence with malice and the desire to control women with a hatred for women.

To illustrate the misogynous underpinnings of our society, a number of analysts have referred to the infamous "rule of thumb" by which English and American law as recently as the eighteenth and nineteenth centuries reputedly upheld the right of a man to beat his wife with a rod, provided it was no thicker than his thumb. However, closer examination of the legal trajectory of the rule of thumb does not support the misogyny interpretation. The rule was originally asserted in England by Judge Buller in 1783—but English legal authorities challenged him and writers and cartoonists lampooned him (May, 1978; Pleck, 1989). Some scholars have asserted that the rule of thumb became incorporated into American law as established precedent, and a ruling by the State Supreme Court of North Carolina in 1868 is a critical case cited to support this assertion (e.g., Fagan & Browne 1994, p. 123; Jones, 1980, p. 284). However, closer inspection of that ruling reveals that the North Carolina State Supreme Court repudiated both the right of a husband to beat his wife and specifically the rule of thumb, even ridiculing the latter:

> It is not true . . . that a husband has the right to whip his wife. And if he had, it is not easily seen how *the thumb* is the standard of size for the instrument which he may use, as some of the old authorities have said. . . . The standard is the *effect produced*, and not the manner of producing it, or the instrument used. (State v. Rhodes, 61 N.C. 459 [1868])

Although the North Carolina Supreme Court did uphold the lower court's ruling that the husband who had struck his wife with "three licks" from a "switch about the size of one of his fingers" had not violated the law, the judges emphasized that "The ground upon which we have put this decision is not that the husband has the *right* to whip his wife much or little; but that we will not interfere with family government in trifling cases" (State v. Rhodes, 61 N.C. 459 [1868]). The unusually long ruling (more than four pages) displays a cognizance of the sensitivity and contentiousness of the issue and a view of gender relations that is steeped, not in misogyny, but in paternalism. The wording betrays a complex set of values that includes an exalted respect for the stability and privacy of the nuclear family unit and the authority of its male head, denial of the seriousness of the specific incident, and the earnest belief that spousal love both permits and heals "impulsive violence." The language also reveals a disgust for the male defendant, albeit offset by a reticence to undermine his paternal authority. Note, too, that the case was originally brought by the State on behalf of the aggrieved wife, and was appealed to the State Supreme Court when the lower court ruled in favor of the husband—hardly evidence of callous neglect of the wife's grievances by State authorities.

Pleck's careful analysis of the historical record of legal intervention in domestic abuse cases in the United States indicates a conflicted legal approach that reflects the paternalistic impetus both to protect and control women (Pleck, 1987; 1989). Thus, the legal system has reverted back and forth between a prevailing reticence about interfering in family relations and sporadic attempts to stop wife abuse. The Puritans of New England passed the first laws against domestic violence in the 1640s, and scattered legislative acts, court rulings, and police interventions in the nineteenth century affirmed the right of battered wives to the full protection of the law and punished abusive husbands with beatings, public floggings, fines, or imprisonment (Pleck, 1987, 1989). In recent history, the criminal justice system has taken more initiative in the protection of battered women, from more vigorous prosecution of cases to the provision of temporary restraining order (TRO) workshops for women who are being harassed by assaultive partners or ex-partners (Ferraro, 1993; Pleck, 1987, 1989). Moreover, although some analysts have argued that the criminal justice system is lenient toward wife batterers, careful comparison of the legal treatment of intimate and nonintimate violent offenses found no systematic differences between them (Ferraro, 1993). Without painting too rosy a picture of the level of commitment or the efficacy of legal interventions on behalf of battered women, the recurrence of such attempts contradicts the argument that the driving force has been callous misogyny.

Popular attitudes about violence toward women betray the same ambivalent admixture as has been found in the criminal justice system. It is not difficult to find evidence of popular moral repudiation of wife beaters: May (1978, p. 141) reports that in nineteenth century England, such customs as "noisy music," the "badger's band," and "riding the stang" were employed by villagers to publicly humiliate and ridicule wife beaters; Blee (1991, pp. 80–84) reports that in the Ku Klux Klan's revival in the 1920s in Indiana, wife beaters and husbands who deserted their wives and families were included among the long list of moral reprobates who required corrective action; countless magazine articles in our contemporary era decry the moral blight of wife beating; and survey data indicate strong, widespread disapproval of husbands hitting wives, and more so than wives hitting husbands (Greenblat, 1983). Similarly, rape has long been popularly viewed as one of the most heinous of crimes. In a large, probability survey of Americans, rape was rated one of the most serious of all crimes; indeed, rape requiring hospitalization was ranked as somewhat more serious than a woman stabbing her husband to death (and both were rated as less serious than a man stabbing his wife to death) (Warr, 1994, pp. 38–45). At the same time, victims of spousal abuse, rape, and sexual harassment often meet with disbelief when they attempt to disclose their victimization, especially if the perpetrators are respected or well liked in the community; alternatively, they find that the shame is heaped upon them as well. A number of studies have documented the vulgar sexual values and aggressive sexual depictions of women that permeate fraternities and military settings (e.g., Burke, 1992; Martin & Hummer, 1993) (although these young male subcultures are marked by high base rates of male-to-male physical violence and abuse, and age has a strong inverse relationship to rape offending, Reiss & Roth, 1993, p. 73). Studies of male college students have found that 30% to 35% indicate *some* likelihood (and about 20% a somewhat stronger likelihood) that they would rape if they were assured of not getting caught (Malamuth, 1981; Stermac, Segal, & Gillis, 1990). Public-opinion studies have documented a variety of myths about rape that excuse or deny it (e.g., Burt, 1980; Malamuth, 1981). In addition, popular attitudes about sexual harassment indicate considerable confusion about appropriate norms of social and sexual interaction between men and women, with a large "gray area" in which many sexually aggressive behaviors are not readily recognized as transgressions (U.S. MSPB, 1981, 1995). Clearly, sexual access to women is highly prized and continually contested, even as societal norms try to specify the terms of such access.

Beauty practices and genital modifications that confine or mutilate women's bodies are supported by widespread belief systems to which both men and women subscribe. Despite the injurious effects of such practices, their symbolic representation in popular culture betrays no animosity toward women. Footbinding was revered as a sensual art form by both men and women in China (Levy [1966] 1992): little girls may have cried when they began the painful treatments that crippled them, but they no doubt learned to thank their mothers when their tiny feet earned them social admiration and desirable marriages. Genital mutilation in many African countries today is viewed by men and women alike as a rite of passage to womanhood that marks a woman's ethnic identity and enhances her physical appearance, sexual attractiveness, and reproductive ability (Dorkenoo & Elworthy, 1992; Lightfoot-Klein, 1989). It is a basic maxim that "you have to suffer to be beautiful," and countless generations of women have accepted that maxim as a guiding principle in their lives as they have contorted and mutilated their bodies in the quest to become more desirable social and sexual objects. The ideology is so internalized that women as well as men admire those women who excel in meeting the beauty standards of their day, thus adding further to the social and economic benefits that accrue to these behaviors. These beauty practices work to control women's behavior and sexuality, but the individuals who endorse such practices are not generally driven by misogyny: indeed, it is the value placed on women's bodies that impels men to seek control of them.

When we take a broader view of violence, it becomes apparent that women are not alone in enduring violence that is sustained by popular belief systems. Men in some Aboriginal cultures in Australia have been goaded to undergo painful genital subincision in the belief that it will enhance their sexual performance, purify their bodies, and give them a clear ethnic marker. Many cultures have circumcised their sons in the belief that it is in their long-term social and health interests. Countless young men have marched off to war at their communities' behest amid high fanfare and incitements to glory, bravery, honor, and courage. Violence does not require hostility toward its victims to propel it, and the human record indicates an elastic capacity for violence that expands and contracts according to the instrumental goals of the relevant actors (Jackman, in preparation). The intricate networks of beliefs that bolster or repudiate specific forms of violence are shaped by the political efforts of the contending parties, with stronger parties having a disproportionate impact.

The potency of such belief systems preempts the need for control through more overt means. Although some men do hate women, they are relatively rare: more commonly, as in other intergroup relations, dominant group members try to keep hostility out of their relations with subordinates in the interests of the long-term stability of the unequal exchange relations from which they benefit (Jackman, 1994). The goal of controlling subordinates is neither facilitated by, nor does it promote, hostility toward them. The infamous case of Francine Hughes, who in 1977 burned her abusive husband to death when he lay sleeping in his bed (Jones, 1980, p. 281), demonstrates the bedrock principle that dominant groups have either respected or learned the hard way: if you choose to rule by force, violence, and intimidation, you had better stay awake and alert at all times. As men have sought to control women's bodies and especially their sexuality, the coercive properties of conditional love have made paternalism the weapon of choice, not misogyny (Jackman, 1994).

4. VICTIM COMPLICITY

The issue of victim complicity has been troubling and contentious in the analysis of violence against women. It has come up at two different levels. First, at the individual level, to what extent are women responsible for precipitating interpersonal violence against themselves in the form of partner assaults and homicides, rapes, and sexual harassment? For example, why do many, if not most, battered wives stay with their abusive husbands? To what extent do they engage in behaviors that precipitate the violence against them? Do some women invite rape or sexual harassment by their behaviors? Second, at a group level, why do women participate actively in the perpetuation of customs that mutilate women's bodies (either their own or their daughters') and accede to self-destructive beauty ideals?

Like other scholars of violence, analysts of violence against women have assumed that for injurious behaviors to qualify as violence, the victims must be noncompliant. Concern about this issue has been exacerbated by the inaccessibility of direct observation of most forms of violence against women, making inferences about the victim's resistance or compliance especially susceptible to interpretation as people are reduced to a "he said, she said" scenario. A full treatment of this complex and booby-trapped issue is beyond the scope of this chapter, but I briefly outline some of the generic problems involved in the assessment of victim compliance and review the main ways that these problems apply to research on violence against women.

The issue of victim compliance is confounded on two counts (Jackman, in preparation). To begin, as the extensive literature on power has amply demonstrated, the compliance/noncompliance distinction is inherently ambiguous because people rarely act as free agents, but instead usually must make choices from a constrained set that has been predetermined by organizational or situational factors beyond their control (Bachrach & Baratz, 1970; Genovese, 1974, pp. 597–598; M. Jackman, 1994; R. Jackman, 1993; Lukes, 1974). Given a constrained set of choices, the victim's alternatives to compliance may be risky or futile. Depending on the agent's and victim's relative control over resources, compliance may be the victim's best survival strategy. Of course, individuals vary in how they respond to constraints, and situations vary in the extent to which they constrict individuals' options. However, we do not need to deny the existence of individual agency to recognize that free choices are rarer than hen's teeth.

To compound this conceptual difficulty, the compliance/noncompliance distinction is also difficult to observe empirically. People's revealed behaviors do not always reflect their preferences, especially when they are in threatening situations. Added to this, people's observation and recollection of events, especially volatile ones, are highly subject to bias and confusion. The perpetrator has self-interested reasons for portraying the victim as an instigator or confederate. The victim may lack either the self-confidence or the social credibility to counter the agent's claims effectively or she may be too shaken or humiliated by the event to formulate allegations with fortitude. Even outside witnesses are rarely unbiased, in the sense of having no personal stake in the interpretation of the event. An especially common bias among both bystanders and participants (including victims themselves) is the tendency to "blame the victim" (Bulman & Wortman, 1977; Lerner & Simmons, 1966; Miller & Porter, 1983; Stark & Flitcraft, 1988). In their interpretation of specific events, people tend to take structural risk factors as a given. Organizational arrangements are a longstanding, integral part of their social environment, and they are not subject to individual alteration. People focus instead on individual strategies for negotiating around the risk factors that have become a normal and unquestioned part of their environment. For those individuals who are themselves at risk, this has the psychological benefit of making them feel more in control of their fate, while for others it has the benefit of deflecting social responsibility on to the victim.

The intricate compounding of individual agency and situational constraints is poignantly captured in the recollections of a foot-bound woman, recorded in China in the 1930s (Levy [1966] 1992, pp. 237–238):

> When I was just six years old, mother started my footbinding. . . . By eleven, my feet were 4.5 inches long, and bowed. On grandmother's birthday, I went with mother to visit her. My cousins had tiny feet, and my uncle laughed at me for having such big and fat feet by comparison, saying "Who would be willing to be your match-maker?" Everyone who heard this remark laughed, making me so ashamed that I determined to bind my feet to the utmost in order to wipe out the disgrace. That night, when everyone was asleep, I rebound so tightly that I had to clench my teeth because of the pain.
>
> My sleep that night was filled with dreams of tiny three-inch feet. The next morning, though the pain had lessened, I had to cling to the walls for walking support. After ten days of treatment my feet measured only 3.8 inches. . . . Three or five days later, my toes became swollen and filled with pus. After one month, they had become nine-tenths of an inch smaller, or 2.9 inches. My feet had become the best of the surrounding villages!

When confronted with a choice between the threat of stigmatization and material impoverishment, on the one hand, and the promise of social admiration and economic security on the other, most women sought the latter, even though it entailed the endurance of physical pain and functional impairment. In the early years of the twentieth century, the Nationalist government introduced a brutal reversal of incentives by fining families who bound their daughters' feet and by organizing antifootbinding societies in which parents pledged to forbid their sons to marry footbound women: a striking change was achieved in women's behaviors (Levy, [1966] 1992; Mackie, 1996). Equally compelling constraints apply to the practice of female genital mutilation: in many cultures, it is not only a requirement for marriageability but also an essential component of ethnic identity, making the social and economic price of nonparticipation exorbitant (Dorkenoo & Elworthy, 1992; El Dareer, 1982; *Harvard Law Review,* 1993; Lightfoot-Klein, 1989; Mackie, 1996). The threat of economic hardship alone was sufficiently compelling for thousands of Chinese men in the Ming dynasty to have themselves castrated in the hope of gaining employment in the imperial courts (Tong, 1988), even though this involved a searing physical impairment and drastic loss of social status.

For women, there has been unremitting pressure to participate in the packaging and commodification of their physical and sexual identity. In a male-dominated institutional nexus in which control over women's bodies and reproductive capacity is a highly valued goal, these are the precious resources within a woman's sphere of action that can make the difference between social success or failure. Thus, women are driven to subject their bodies to various forms and degrees of abuse in an attempt to excel in the beauty standards of their day and enhance their life prospects. Interestingly, in the United States, men have begun to get sucked into the beauty vortex themselves, with an increasing number of men undergoing the rigors of hair transplants and other types of cosmetic surgery in an attempt to promote an image of virility and success (Siebert, 1996).

The apparent complicity of women in their own victimization from forms of violence that are not culturally mandated is equally deceptive. In discussion of sexual harassment cases, the victims are sometimes accused of "playing the game" ("an A for a lay," Taylor, 1981), or at least of failing to express noncompliance by filing a grievance or quitting their jobs. Rape victims are frequently accused by both perpetrators and third parties of precipitating the act through their social behaviors or physical appearance or of actively inviting the behavior (Burt, 1980; LaFree, Reskin, & Visher, 1985; Scully, 1990; Von et al., 1991). Battered wives are sometimes dismissed as having a pathological desire for abuse or of being insufficiently resolute in pressing charges against or leaving their abusive husbands (Browne, 1993; Jones, 1980, pp. 295–296). All of these allegations about the victim's responsibility for her fate fail to recognize the constraints that sharply curtail her options.

Workers who continue to work in settings where they are subject to sexual harassment do so because they are either unaware of alternative employment opportunities or they fear substantial economic or career losses if they move to a new job. Once they decide that their best course of action is to stay on the job, they may well surmise that their best survival strategy is to tolerate the harassment rather than to file a grievance: the same factors that make the victim vulnerable to sexual harassment (her lower institutional status and the lack of witnesses) also make it difficult for her to press charges effectively, making this a risky strategy. A few enterprising women may indeed exploit their sexual assets to promote their careers in an organizational setting that offers few other avenues of recognition. The compliance dilemma is revealed especially sharply in rape victimization. Police advise women that if they are sexually assaulted, their best survival strategy is to offer no resistance, since resistance may result in more serious injuries—but if the woman offers no evidence of physical resistance, she instantly undermines her claim to victimhood.

The options facing battered wives are also tightly constrained. They learn that attempts to resist assaults by their husbands only result in worse injuries (Dobash & Dobash, 1979), but their ensuing behavioral passivity is likely to be misinterpreted as compliance. Battered wives who fail to leave their husbands may have little reason to believe that "leaving" their husbands will actually free them from physical threat. A woman with a possessive, bullying husband may calculate (if her husband does not spell it out himself) that any attempt to leave him will only incite him to further violence, and given that she can neither physically disappear nor go into protective custody, her choices become sharply foreshortened (Browne, 1987; Fagan & Browne, 1994). Indeed, data indicate that women who have attempted to leave their partners are especially at risk of spousal homicide victimization (Campbell, 1992; Daly & Wilson, 1988, p. 219; Wilson & Daly, 1992a, b, 1993). Within the institution of marriage, the privacy that it affords (and the consequent lack of credible outside witnesses) makes it difficult to press convincing claims of victimhood. The victim is then confronted with the frustrating inconsistency of a society that expresses moral outrage about the category of behaviors but skepticism about her particular case. The battered wife's choices are constricted further by institutionalized practices that give her lower earning potential than her husband, thus reinforcing her economic dependence on him (Ferraro, 1993; Pleck, 1989). Women's vulnerability to harassment in public settings, such as the street and the workplace (Gardner, 1995; U.S. MSPB, 1995), reinforces their wariness of the outside world and drives them to settle for a partner-bodyguard, even if he poses a known physical risk himself (Jackman, 1994). In all but the most extreme cases of wife abuse, wives are also caught in the love trap that envelops paternalistic gender relations. This condones violent outbursts within intimate love relations and mandates forgiveness as the appropriate feminine response: with women's access to love and protection channelled through the institution of marriage, the social and emotional costs of exiting the marriage are escalated (Jackman, 1994, pp. 82–84). Finally, women are trapped in a general "Catch-22," in which they are exhorted to commodify their sexual attributes and to meet a feminine behavioral ideal of deference and compliance, but they are then faulted when their efforts are judged to be responsible for luring men into sexual aggression or inviting physical assault.

In short, the apparent compliance of victims is a booby-trap. Women's lack of resistance to violence against them is no more mysterious than the decision of countless armies of young men to march off to war, with reluctance or enthusiasm, on behalf of causes they may barely understand, or the recurrent decision of workers to submit to hazardous working conditions to support themselves and their families. Tobacco companies may depict cigarette smoking as a matter of individual choice, but it is hardly surprising that the unrestricted marketing of an addictive drug results in immense populations who are unable to quit, despite its known hazards. With any kind of violence, compliance and resistance are difficult to isolate conceptually and are not easily susceptible to empirical observation or measurement. The place of individual agency in submitting to violence is variable, complex, and subject to bias or confusion in its observation.

5. EXPLANATION OF THE RELATIONSHIP BETWEEN GENDER AND VIOLENCE

Theoretical explanations of the relationship between gender and violence have fallen into two fairly discrete sets, either focusing singly on violence against women, or on gender differences in the perpetration of violence. There has been little attempt to develop a broad theoretical account of how gender influences both victimization from and the perpetration of various violent actions. It is beyond the scope of this chapter to appraise fully the theoretical accounts that have been offered, but I briefly outline and comment on them. I then sketch out an explanatory approach that addresses the broad range of violent behaviors that are practiced and endured by men and women.

Explanations of the marked gender difference in the propensity to commit violent crimes have centered on whether the difference is due to biological or social factors. Early work suggested that men may be biologically predisposed to aggressive behaviors (Maccoby

& Jacklin, 1974, 1980), but this thesis has since been discredited, on the grounds both that aggression is not linked clearly to hormones and that aggressive behaviors do not differ systematically by gender (Bjorkqvist & Niemela, 1992; Eagly & Steffen, 1986; Kruttschnitt, 1994). Since men and women differ in their rates of physically violent behaviors more than in aggression *per se*, analysts have turned to socialization factors that are gender specific, citing gender differences in closeness of parental supervision and reinforcement of physically aggressive behaviors (Kruttschnitt, 1994). As with other areas of intense debate over nature versus nurture (e.g., the IQ debate), analysts have come increasingly to recognize the point that geneticists have long emphasized—that nature and nurture are not mutually exclusive choices but instead work interactively. Biological proclivities allow a broad range of behavioral expressions, depending on the presence of nourishing or inhibiting environmental factors (e.g., Hirsch, 1973).

Most analysts who have focused on the explanation of violence against women have pursued one or more of the following avenues: (1) *individual-level factors*, relating to the offender and/or the victim, such as childhood socialization into violence, substance abuse, or emotional/psychiatric disturbances that produce either anomalous tendencies toward the commission of violent behaviors, or an attraction toward violent men on the part of battered wives and victims of rape or sexual harassment (e.g., Amir, 1971; Overholser & Beck, 1986; Rada, 1978; Segal & Marshall, 1985; Straus et al., 1980; Taylor, 1981); (2) *social-interaction issues*, relating to strains, tensions, and opportunities for violence inherent in family life or in male–female interaction patterns, or ambiguities in courtship or sexual norms (e.g., Gelles, 1983; Gelles & Straus, 1988; Gillen & Muncer, 1995; Lundberg-Love & Geffner, 1989; Muehlenhard, 1989; Straus et al., 1980); and (3) *gender-politics issues*, such as patriarchal social arrangements and male dominance, whereby men use physical and sexual violence to control and intimidate women (e.g., Brownmiller, 1975; Dobash & Dobash, 1979; Ferraro, 1993; Millett, 1970; Scully, 1990; Scully & Marolla, 1993; Stark & Flitcraft, 1988). All of these theoretical approaches are discussed in more detail elsewhere (e.g., Browne, 1993; Fagan & Browne, 1994; Stark & Flitcraft, 1991; Von et al., 1991): I limit myself here to two brief comments. First, these approaches differ in their expectations about the generality of male-to-female intimate violence: the first treats it as aberrant, while the second and third approaches assume (either implicitly or explicitly) that violence is a normal part of male–female relations. Perhaps for this reason, the first line of explanation has been steadily losing ground to the second and especially the third: the view that social relations are driven by misogyny favors the depiction of violence against women as normal rather than aberrant, and the gender-politics approach is especially consistent with this view. Second, the narrow focus on male-to-female violence of all these explanatory approaches has sharply limited their power. For example, if male violence against women is explained in terms of patriarchal social arrangements or special problems inherent in the institution of the family or in male–female interaction patterns, we are left with no explanation for the more prevalent male-to-male violence.

A more general theoretical explanation of violence against women has been offered by evolutionary psychologists, namely that evolutionary selection has favored a human male with strong sexual proprietariness toward women. Because the successful reproduction of humans requires a major investment from both parents, and because paternity is intrinsically less presumptive than maternity, the human male has evolved with a strong tendency toward sexual jealousy, as men wish to ensure that their parental investment is not squandered on someone else's offspring. This theory posits that most incidents of male-to-female violence involve some element of sexual jealousy (such as suspected sexual philandering by one's partner, fear of loss of control of or loss of loyalty by one's partner, or presence of stepchildren). This theory has been expounded elegantly and rigorously in a voluminous stream of research (e.g., Burgess & Draper, 1989; Daly & Wilson, 1982, 1988; Wilson & Daly, 1992a, b, 1993; Wilson, Daly, & Daniele, 1995; Wilson et al., 1993, 1995, 1997; Wilson & Mesnick, 1997), although few review essays on violence against women include this theory, presumably on grounds of intellectual taste. Many social researchers find it repugnant to address theories of human behavior that have a biological component: they erroneously believe that the introduction of biological factors rules out the influence of culture and the possibility of socially induced variation around genetic proclivities. This theory is alone among theories of violence against women in its ability to incorporate male-to-male violence as well: Daly and Wilson hold that such violence is spawned by men's rivalrous competition for the economic and status resources that will assist them in gaining control of women and enhancing their reproductive fitness.

Despite its explanatory breadth and power, this theory has two shortcomings. First, in the attempt to subjugate all forms of violence to the drive for reproductive fitness, the latter is elevated to a motivational preeminence that at times seems stretched, especially when trying to address some of the violent behaviors manifested by women (e.g., maternal infanticide). Second, the theory cannot account satisfactorily for the relative lack of violence perpetration among women. Women have every reason to be as jealous as men (and empirical observation confirms this), since evolution should have favored a woman who works to prevent her partner from diverting his resources to other women. However, women's jealousy is less likely to be expressed in violence toward their partners.

A much simpler explanation of the relationship between gender and violence is possible. Violent actions represent one type of behavioral strategy as people negotiate their way through life, attempting to maximize their control over the social, economic, and political resources that will enable them to make the most of their lot and provide for their offspring. People's use of physically violent actions depends on the presumed efficacy of such actions in delivering those resources: when conditions are auspicious, most people apparently do not shrink from employing violent strategies. That, in turn, depends on the attributes of the perpetrator and the victim (their relative size and strength, and their relative ability to protect themselves with social, economic, or political resources), as well as on a number of other facilitating or obstructing factors, such as the presence or absence of sanctions or credible witnesses. Men, on average, commit more physical violence than women because their greater size and strength and their superior command over societal resources makes this a more opportune strategy for them. Most of their violence, however, is directed toward other men: since it is men who disproportionately control societal resources, most contests over resources precipitate encounters with other men, and violence-prone men incite each other into combat. Women—who constitute one of the resources over which men struggle—are less likely to rely on physical violence because they generaly lack the physical or institutional means to employ it successfully. However, women do employ violence strategically when it is physically or institutionally opportune: in the confinement or mutilation of their own bodies for social or economic purposes, and in their dealings with those physically or institutionally weaker than themselves (e.g., young children, lower status adults, and men who are weaker or temporarily incapacitated).

The longstanding unequal relationship between men and women has at its core the contested issue of who shall control sexual access and sexual reproduction. In this contest, men have the biological advantage of greater size and strength, but that initial advantage has long since been converted into the establishment of social, economic, and political institutions that favor men (Jackman, 1994). Those institutions make the constant use of physical force unnecessary to secure male control over women's bodies, and, indeed, stable rule is served better by less clumsy methods as men seek the amicable cooperation of women in their continued subordination (Jackman, 1994). Theorists who attribute violence against women to either patriarchal institutions or the male drive for reproductive fitness erroneously assume that the desire to control women drives men to use violent methods. On the contrary, the quest to control women's bodies has led to the evolution of paternalistic relations between men and women, by which men secure women's subordination through a system of coercive love: women are praised and rewarded for compliant behaviors and stigmatized for noncooperation (Jackman, 1994). Most of the time, this system achieves control without resorting to physical force, although some men do occasionally or habitually use violence to assert their authority. According to this approach, habitual reliance on physical violence is, indeed, an anomaly deriving from counternormative socialization or personality deficiencies, rather than being the central tendency. There is individual variability in the proclivity for physical violence, and some men are sadists, misogynists, psychologically disturbed, or unable to cope with the demands of family life or interpersonal relationships. Other men may employ physical violence on a trial-and-error basis, testing its efficacy against alternative methods of control. Younger men's greater reliance on physical violence may reflect their superior physical strength or their lesser experience with or command of institutionalized gender arrangements.

The high value placed on the resource that lies within women's bodies—sexual access and sexual reproduction—has encouraged the proprietary protection and control of women more than the physical assault of women. Men assume the role of paternalistic bodyguards to their women, and women are exhorted to become the submissive objects of that protection. Thus, most men eschew physical violence in their ongoing interactions with women, and women are generally sheltered from the worst rigors of the battlefield, workplace, consumer marketplace, mob violence, and state-mandated punishments. By the same token, women are socially rewarded for pursuing physical weakness and emotional compliance as their feminine ideals, and stigmatized for deviating from those ideals. In response to these pressures, most women develop deferential behavior patterns in their relations with men of the same class and ethnic status as themselves (but not with children, other women or lower status men), and they are moved, as necessary, to subject their bodies to physical confinement or mutilation to gain acceptance or, better yet, win social admiration. Individual men who use physical violence against women violate the basic operating principles of this system of social control, and are thus a source of profound political embarrassment, triggering both moral condemnation and denial of their actions as other men scramble to distance themselves from these occurrences, minimize them, or cover them up.

According to the routine activities theory of crime (Cohen & Felson, 1979; Cohen, Kluegel, & Land, 1981), our everyday activities prime us to become either accessible or inaccessible as victims of specific criminal or violent behaviors. If we apply this logic, it might seem that the social organization of gender relations throws women in harm's way, since their routine activities bring them into daily, intimate contact with men, who are known to be more prone to physical violence. Gender relations throw women into lifelong, intimate contact with men in an institutional setting that is emotionally saturated and legally sanctioned as an autonomous economic unit screened from public view. When one considers, further, that men generally have greater size and strength than women, it would seem that both physical and institutional factors prime women to become the perfect targets for interpersonal violence. On this basis, we should expect a high incidence of physical violence by men against women. Some men do indeed exploit the opportunities for violence against women that are thus provided them, but, in general, men are more likely to inflict violence on other men than on women. The answer to this apparent enigma lies precisely in men's long-standing concern with maintaining control over women's bodies. Although skirmishes and violent outbursts remain a part of the overall pattern of domination and subjugation, stable control is generally served more effectively by institutional means than by raw physical force. Thus, most men, most of the time, direct their physical violence toward male rivals, rather than toward female subordinates.

REFERENCES

Amir, M. (1971). *Patterns in forcible rape*. Chicago: University of Chicago Press.

Astin, M. C., Lawrence, K. J., & Foy, D. W. (1993). Posttraumatic stress disorder among battered women: Risk and resiliency factors. *Violence and Victims, 8,* 17–32.

Bachman, R., & Saltzman, L. E. (1995). *Violence against women: Estimates from the redesigned survey: Bureau of Justice Statistics special report*. Washington, D.C.: U.S. Department of Justice, Bureau of Justice Statistics, NCJ-154348.

Bachrach, P., & Baratz, M. S. (1970). *Power and poverty: Theory and practice*. New York: Oxford University Press.

Barstow, A. L. (1995). *Witchcraze: A new history of the European witch hunts*. San Francisco: Harper Collins.

Bart, P., & O'Brien, P. (1985). *Stopping rape: Successful survival strategies*. New York: Pergamon.

Benson, D. J., & Thomson, G. E. (1982). Sexual harassment on a college campus: The confluence of authority relations, sexual interest and gender stratification. *Social Problems, 29,* 236–251.

Berk, R. A., Berk, S. F., Loseke, D. R., & Rauma, D. (1983). Mutual combat and other family violence myths. In D. Finkelhor, R. J. Gelles, G. T. Hotaling, & M. A. Straus (Eds.), *The dark side of families: Current family violence research* (pp. 197–212). Beverly Hills: Sage.

Berndt, R. M., & Berndt, C. H. (1964). *The world of the first Australians: An introduction to the traditional life of the Australian Aborigines*. Sydney: Ure Smith.

Bjorkqvist, K., & Niemela, P. (Eds.) (1992). *Of mice and women: Aspects of female aggression*. San Diego: Academic Press.

Blake, C. F. (1994). Foot-binding in neo-Confucian China and the appropriation of female labor. *Signs, 19,* 676–712.

Blee, K. M. (1991). *Women of the Klan: Racism and gender in the 1920's*. Berkeley & Los Angeles, CA: University of California Press.

Bohannan, P. (1967). Patterns of homicide among tribal societies in Africa. In M. Wolfgang (Ed.), *Studies in homicide* (pp. 211–237). New York: Harper and Row.

Bradshaw, Y. W., & Wallace, M. (1996). *Global inequalities*. Thousand Oaks, CA: Pine Forge Press.

Brandeis, L. B., & Goldmark, J. ([1907]1969). *Women in industry*. New York: Arno and *the New York Times*.

British Parliamentary Papers. ([1842]1968). *Children's Employment Commission, first report of the commissioners, mines: Vol. 6, Industrial revolution, children's employment*. Shannon, Ireland: Irish University Press.

Browne, A. (1987). *When battered women kill*. New York: Macmillan/The Free Press.

Browne, A. (1993). Violence against women by male partners: Prevalence, outcomes, and policy implications. *American Psychologist, 48,* 1077–1087.

Brownell, K. D., & Rodin, J. (1994). The dieting maelstrom: Is it possible and advisable to lose weight? *American Psychologist, 49,* 781–791.

Brownmiller, S. (1975). *Against our will: Men, women, and rape*. New York: Simon & Schuster.

Brownmiller, S. (1984). *Femininity*. New York: Fawcett Columbine.

Brundage, W. F. (1993). *Lynching in the new South: Georgia and Virginia, 1880–1930*. Urbana: University of Illinois Press.

Brush, L. D. (1993). Violent acts and injurious outcomes in married couples: Methodological issues in the National Survey of Families and Households. In P. B. Bart & E. G. Moran (Eds.), *Violence against women: The bloody footprints* (pp. 240–251). Newbury Park, CA: Sage.

Bulman, R. J., & Wortman, C. B. (1977). Attributions of blame and coping in the "real world": Severe accident victims react to their lot. *Journal of Personality and Social Psychology, 35,* 351–363.

Bureau of Labor Statistics. (1994). *Work injuries and illnesses by selected characteristics, 1992.* Washington, D.C.: U.S. Department of Labor.

Bureau of Labor Statistics. (1995). *Work injuries and illnesses by selected characterisitcs, 1993.* Washington, D.C.: U.S. Department of Labor.

Bureau of Labor Statistics. (1996). *National census of fatal occupational injuries, 1995.* Washington, D.C.: U.S. Department of Labor.

Burgess, R. L., & Draper, P. (1989). The explanation of family violence: The role of biological, behavioral, and cultural selection. In L. Ohlin & M. Tonry (Eds.), *Family violence: Crime and justice, a review of research,* Vol. 11 (pp. 19–57). Chicago: University of Chicago Press.

Burke, C. (1992). The trail to Tailhook. *San Francisco Chronicle Review,* August 16.

Burt, M. R. (1980). Cultural myths and supports for rape. *Journal of Personality and Social Psychology, 38,* 217–230.

Cameron, J. (1982). *A time of terror: A survivor's story.* Baltimore: Black Classic Press.

Campbell, J. C. (1992). "If I can't have you, no one can": Power and control in homicide of female partners. In J. Radford & D. E. H. Russell (Eds.), *Femicide* (pp. 99–113). New York: Twayne.

Claybrook, J. (1996). Women in the marketplace. In E. Szockyj & J. G. Fox (Eds.), *Corporate victimization of women* (pp. 111–142). Boston: Northeastern University Press.

Coale, A. J. (1991). Excess female mortality and the balance of the sexes in the population: An estimate of the number of "missing females." *Population and Development Review, 17,* 517–523.

Cohen, L. E., & Felson, M. (1979). Social change and crime rate trends: A routine activity approach. *American Sociological Review, 44,* 588–608.

Cohen, L. E., Kluegel, J. R., & Land, K. (1981). Social inequality and criminal victimization. *American Sociological Review, 46,* 505–524.

Combs, D. L., & Donoghue, E. R. (1994). Child deaths from consumer products and guns. *The Lancet, 343* (June 25), 1642.

Craven, D. (1996). *Female victims of violent crime: Bureau of Justice Statistics selected findings.* Washington, D.C.: U.S. Department of Justice, Bureau of Justice Statistics, NCJ-162602.

Culbertson, A. L., Rosenfeld, P., Booth-Kewley, S., & Magnusson, P. (1992). *Assessment of sexual harassment in the Navy: Results of the 1989 Navy-wide survey, TR-92-11.* San Diego: Navy Personnel Research and Development Center.

Daly, M., & Wilson, M. I. (1982). Homicide and kinship. *American Anthropologist, 84,* 372–378.

Daly, M., & Wilson, M. I. (1988). *Homicide.* New York: Aldine de Gruyter.

Darke, J. L. (1990). Sexual aggression: Achieving power through humiliation. In W. L. Marshall, D. R. Laws, & H. E. Barbaree (Eds.), *Handbook of sexual assault: Issues, theories, and treatment of the offender* (pp. 55–72). New York: Plenum Press.

Das Gupta, M. 1987. "Selective discrimination against female children in rural Punjab, India." *Population and Development Review, 13,* 77–100.

Dawson, J. M., & Langan, P. A. (1994). *Murder in families: Bureau of Justice Statistics special report.* Washington, D.C.: U.S. Department of Justice, Bureau of Justice Statistics.

Dobash, R. E., & Dobash, R. (1979). *Violence against wives: A case against the patriarchy.* New York: The Free Press.

Dobash, R. E., & Dobash, R. (1983). The context-specific approach. In D. Finkelhor, R. J. Gelles, G. T. Hotaling, & M. A. Straus (Eds.), *The dark side of families: Current family violence research* (pp. 261–276). Beverly Hills: Sage.

Dorkenoo, E., & Elworthy, S. (1992). *Female genital mutilation: proposals for change.* London: Minority Rights Group.

Dunnigan, J. F. (1993). *How to make war: A comprehensive guide to modern warfare for the post-cold war era* (2nd ed.). New York: William Morrow.

Dutton, D. G. (1988). *The domestic assault of women: Psychological and criminal justice perspectives.* Boston: Allyn & Bacon.

Dutton, D. G. (1995). *The domestic assault of women: Psychological and criminal justice perspectives* (revised and expanded edition). Vancouver: University of British Columbia Press.

Dworkin, A. (1981). *Pornography: Men possessing women.* London: Women's Press.

Dworkin, A. (1994). Gynocide: Chinese footbinding. In A. M. Jaggar (Ed.), *Living with contradictions: Controversies in feminist social ethics* (pp. 213–219). Boulder, CO: Westview.

Eagly, A. H., & Steffen, V. J. (1986). Gender and aggressive behavior: A meta-analytic review of the social psychological literature. *Psychological Bulletin, 100,* 309–330.

The Economist. (1997). Nordic eugenics: Here, of all places. August 30, 36–37.

El Dareer, A. (1982). *Woman, why do you weep?: Circumcision and its consequences.* London: Zed Press.

Elkins, S. M. (1968). *Slavery: A problem in American institutional and intellectual life* (2nd ed.). Chicago: University of Chicago Press.

Ember, C. R., & Ember, M. (1995). Issues in cross-cultural studies of interpersonal violence. In R. B. Ruback & N. A. Weiner (Eds.), *Interpersonal violent behaviors: Social and cultural aspects* (pp. 25–43). New York: Springer.

Engels, F. ([1884] 1972). *The origin of the family, private property and the state.* New York: International Publishers.

Fagan, J., & Browne, A. (1994). Violence between spouses and intimates: Physical aggression between women and men in intimate relationships. In A. J. Reiss, Jr., & J. A. Roth (Eds.), *Understanding and preventing violence,* Vol. 3: *Social influences* (pp. 115–292). Washington, D.C.: National Academy Press.

Federal Bureau of Investigation. (1981–1995). *Uniform Crime Reports: Crime in the United States* (annual). Washington, D.C.: U.S. Department of Justice.

Ferraro, K. (1993). Cops, courts, and woman battering. In P. B. Bart & E. G. Moran (Eds.), *Violence against women: The bloody footprints,* (pp. 165–176). Newbury Park, CA: Sage.

Finkelhor, D., & Yllo, K. (1983). Rape in marriage: A sociological view. In D. Finkelhor, R. J. Gelles, G. T. Hotaling, & M. A. Straus (Eds.), *The dark side of families: Current family violence research* (pp. 119–130). Beverly Hills, CA: Sage.

Finley, L. M. (1996). The pharmaceutical industry and women's reproductive health. In E. Szockyj & J. G. Fox (Eds.), *Corporate victimization of women* (pp. 59–111). Boston: Northeastern University Press.

Flowers, R. B. (1994). *The victimization and exploitation of women and children: A study of physical, mental and sexual maltreatment in the United States.* Jefferson, NC: McFarland & Co.

French, M. (1992). *The war against women.* New York: Ballantine Books.

Frieze, I. H. (1983). Investigating the causes and consequences of marital rape. *Signs, 8,* 532–553.

Frieze, I. H., & Browne, A. (1989). Violence in marriage. In L. Ohlin & M. Tonry (Eds.), *Family violence: Crime and justice, a review of research,* Vol. 11 (pp. 163–218). Chicago: University of Chicago Press.

Gardner, C. B. (1995). *Passing by: Gender and public harassment.* Berkeley & Los Angeles, CA: University of California Press.

Gartner, R. (1995). Methodological issues in cross-cultural large-survey research on violence. In R. B. Ruback & N. A. Weiner (Eds.), *Interpersonal violent behaviors: Social and cultural aspects* (pp. 7–24). New York: Springer.

Gelles, R. J. (1979). *Family violence.* Beverly Hills: Sage.

Gelles, R. J. (1983). An exchange/social control theory. In D. Finkelhor, R. J. Gelles, G. T. Hotaling, & M. A. Straus (Eds.), *The dark side of families: Current family violence research* (pp.151–165). Beverly Hills: Sage.

Gelles, R. J., & Straus, M. A. (1988). *Intimate violence: The causes and consequences of abuse in the American family.* New York: Simon & Schuster.

Genovese, E. (1974). *Roll, Jordan, roll: The world the slaves made.* New York: Random House.

Gillen, K., & Muncer, S. J. (1995). Sex differences in the perceived causal structure of date rape: A preliminary report. *Aggressive Behavior, 21,* 101–112.

Graham, H. D., & Gurr, T. R. (Eds.) (1969). *Violence in America: Historical and comparative perspectives. A report to the National Commission on the Causes and Prevention of Violence,* Vols. I and II. Washington, D.C.: U.S. Government Printing Office.

Greenblat, C. S. (1983). A hit is a hit is a hit...Or is it? In D. Finkelhor, R. J. Gelles, G. T. Hotaling,, & M. A. Straus (Eds.), *The dark side of families: Current family violence research* (pp.235–260). Beverly Hills, CA: Sage.

Greenfeld, L. A. (1997). *Sex offenses and offenders: An analysis of data on rape and sexual assault.* Washington, D.C.: U.S. Department of Justice, Bureau of Justice Statistics, NCJ-163392.

Gurr, T. R. (1981). Historical trends in violent crime: A critical review of the evidence. In M. Tonry & N. Morris (Eds.), *Crime and Justice: An Annual Review of Research,* Vol. 3 (pp. 295–353). Chicago: University of Chicago Press.

Gutek, B. A., & Koss, M. P. (1997). Changed women and changed organizations: Consequences of and coping with sexual harassment. In L. L. O'Toole & J. R. Schiffman (Eds.), *Gender violence: Interdisciplinary perspectives* (pp. 151–164). New York: New York University Press.

Hair, W. I. (1989). "Lynching." In C. R. Wilson & W. Ferris (Eds.), *Encyclopedia of Southern culture*, Vol. 1 (pp. 294–297). New York: Anchor.

Hall, J. D. (1983). "The mind that burns in each body": Women, rape, and racial violence. In A. Snitow, C. Stansell, & S. Thompson (Eds.), *Powers of desire: The politics of sexuality* (pp. 328–349). New York: Monthly Review Press.

Harvard Law Review (no author attributed). (1993). Note: What's culture got to do with it? Excising the harmful tradition of female circumcision. *Harvard Law Review, 106*, 1944–1962.

Henley, N. M. (1977). *Body politics: Power, sex, and nonverbal communication*. Engelwood Cliffs, NJ: Prentice-Hall.

Henley, N. M., & Freeman, J. (1979). The sexual politics of interpersonal behavior. In J. Freeman (Ed.), *Women: A feminist perspective* (2nd ed.). (pp. 474–486). Palo Alto, CA: Mayfield.

Henley, N. M., & Harmon, S. (1985). The nonverbal semantics of power and gender: A perceptual study. In S. L. Ellyson & J. F. Dovidio (Eds.), *Power, dominance, and nonverbal behavior* (pp. 151–164). New York: Springer-Verlag.

Hester, M. (1992). The witch-craze in sixteenth- and seventeenth-century England as social control of women. In J. Radford & D. E. H. Russell (Eds.), *Femicide* (pp. 27–39). New York: Twayne.

Hirsch, J. (1973). Behavior-genetic analysis and its biosocial consequences. In K. S. Miller & R. M. Dreger (Ed.), *Comparative studies of blacks and whites in the United States* (pp. 34–51). New York: Academic Press.

Hirschi, T., & Selvin, H. C. (1967). *Delinquency research: An appraisal of analytic methods*. New York: The Free Press.

Holinger, P. C. (1987). *Violent deaths in the United States: An epidemiologic study of suicide, homicide, and accidents*. New York: Guilford Press.

Inhorn, M C., & Buss, K. A. (1993). Infertility, infection, and iatrogenesis in Egypt: The anthropological epidemiology of blocked tubes. *Medical Anthropology: Cross-Cultural Studies in Health and Illness, 15*, 217–244.

Jackman, M. R. (1994). *The velvet glove: Paternalism and conflict in gender, class, and race relations*. Berkeley & Los Angeles, CA: University of California Press.

Jackman, M. R. (in preparation). *The social capacity for violence*. Berkeley & Los Angeles, CA: University of California Press.

Jackman, R. W. (1993). *Power without force: The political capacity of nation-states*. Ann Arbor: University of Michigan Press.

Jackson, R. (1990). The Chinese foot-binding syndrome: Observations on the history and sequelae of wearing ill-fitting shoes. *International Journal of Dermatology, 29*, 322–328.

Jones, A. (1980). *Women who kill*. New York: Holt, Rinehart, & Winston.

Kachur, S. P., Potter, L. B., James, S. P., & Powell, K. E. (1995). *Suicide in the United States 1980–1992*. Atlanta: Centers for Disease Control and Prevention, National Center for Injury Prevention and Control.

Katz, S., and Mazur, M. A. (1979). *Understanding the rape victim: A synthesis of research findings*. New York: Wiley-Interscience.

Kelly, L. (1987). The continuum of sexual violence. In J. Hanmer & M Maynard (Eds.), *Women, violence and social control* (pp. 46–60). London: Macmillan.

Kelkar, G. (1992). Women and structural violence in India. In J. Radford & D. E. H. Russell (Eds.), *Femicide* (pp. 117–122). New York: Twayne.

Kolchin, P. (1993). *American slavery 1619–1877*. New York: Hill & Wang.

Koss, M. P. (1992). The underdetection of rape: Methodological choices influence incidence estimates. *Journal of Social Issues, 48*, 61–75.

Kruttschnitt, C. (1994). Gender and interpersonal violence. In A. J. Reiss, Jr., & J. A. Roth (Eds.), *Understanding and preventing violence*, Vol. 3: *Social influences* (pp. 293–376). Washington, D.C.: National Academy Press.

Kruttschnitt, C. (1995). Violence by and against women: A comparative and cross-national analysis. In R. B. Ruback & N. A. Weiner (Eds.), *Interpersonal violent behaviors: Social and cultural aspects* (pp. 89–108). New York: Springer.

Kurz, D. (1993). Social science perspectives on wife abuse: current debates and future directions. In P. B. Bart & E. G. Moran (Eds.), *Violence against women: The bloody footprints* (pp. 252–269). Newbury Park, CA: Sage.

LaFree, G. D., Reskin, B. F., & Visher, C. A. (1985). Jurors' responses to victims' behavior and legal issues in sexual assault trials. *Social Problems, 32*, 389–407.

Langan, P. A., & Dawson, J. M. (1995). *Spouse murder defendants in large urban counties*. Washington, D.C.: U.S. Department of Justice, Bureau of Justice Statistics, NCJ-153256.

Langan, P. A., & Innes, C. A. (1986). *Preventing domestic violence against women*. Washington, D.C.: U.S. Department of Justice, Bureau of Justice Statistics.

Laumann, E. O., Gagnon, J. H., Michael, R. T., & Michaels, S. (1994). *The social organization of sexuality: Sexual practices in the United States*. Chicago: University of Chicago Press.

Lerner, M. J., & Simmons, C. H. (1966). Observer's reaction to the "innocent victim": Compassion or rejection? *Journal of Personality and Social Psychology, 4,* 203–210.

Levack, Brian P. 1995. *The witch-hunt in early modern Europe* (2nd. ed.). London: Longman.

Levy, H. S. ([1966] 1992). *The lotus lovers: The complete history of the curious erotic custom of footbinding in China*. Buffalo, NY: Prometheus Books.

Lightfoot-Klein, H. (1989). *Prisoners of ritual: An odyssey into female genital circumcision in Africa*. New York: Haworth Press.

Lukes, S. (1974). *Power: A radical view*. London: Macmillan.

Lundberg-Love, P., & Geffner, R. (1989). Date-rape: prevalence, risk factors, and a proposed model. In M. A. Pirog-Good & J. E. Stets, *Violence in dating relationships: Emerging social issues* (pp. 169–184). New York: Praeger.

Lynch, J. (1995). Crime in international perspective. In J. Q. Wilson and J. Petersilia (Eds.), *Crime* (pp. 11–38, 511–517). San Francisco: ICS Press.

Maccoby, E. E., & Jacklin, C. N. (1974). *The psychology of sex differences*. Stanford, CA: Stanford University Press.

Maccoby, E. E., & Jacklin, C. N. (1980). Sex differences in aggression: A rejoinder and reprise. *Child Development, 51,* 964–980.

Mackie, G. (1996). Ending footbinding and infibulation: A convention account. *American Sociological Review, 61,* 999–1017.

MacKinnon, C. (1979). *Sexual harassment of working women*. New Haven, CT: Yale University Press.

MacKinnon, C. (1993). *Only words*. Cambridge, MA: Harvard University Press.

Malamuth, N. M. (1981). Rape proclivity among males. *Journal of Social Issues, 37,* 138-157.

Manchester, W. (1992). *A world lit only by fire: The medieval mind and the Renaissance*. Boston: Little, Brown.

Mann, R. W., Sledzik, P. S., Owsley, D. W., & Droulette, M. R. (1990). Radiographic examination of Chinese foot binding. *Journal of the American Podiatric Medical Association, 80,* 405–409.

Marshall, W. L., Laws, D. R., & Barbaree, H. E. (1990). *Handbook of sexual assault*. New York: Plenum.

Martin, P. Y., & Hummer, R. A. (1993). Fraternities and rape on campus. In P. B. Bart & E. G. Moran (Eds.), *Violence against women: The bloody footprints* (pp. 114–131). Newbury Park, CA: Sage.

May, M. (1978). Violence in the family: An historical perspective. In J. P. Martin (Ed.), *Violence and the family* (pp. 135–167). New York: Wiley.

McCormack, A. (1985). The sexual harassment of students by teachers: The case of students in science. *Sex Roles, 13,* 21–32.

McGarity, T. O., & Shapiro, S. A. (1993). *Workers at risk: The failed promise of the Occupational Safety and Health Administration*. Westport, CT: Praeger.

Mercy, J. A., & Saltzman, L. E. (1989). Fatal violence among spouses in the United States, 1976–1985. *American Journal of Public Health, 79,* 595-599.

Mill, J. S. ([1869] 1970). The subjection of women. In A. S. Rossi (Ed.), *Essays on sex equality: John Stuart Mill and Harriet Taylor Mill* (pp. 123–242). Chicago: University of Chicago Press.

Miller, D. T., & Porter, C. A. (1983). Self-blame in victims of violence. *Journal of Social Issues, 39,* 139–152.

Millet, K. (1970). *Sexual politics*. New York: Doubleday.

Minturn, L., & J. Shashak. (1982). Infanticide as a terminal abortion procedure. *Behavior Science Research, 17,* 70–90.

Montagu, A. ([1937] 1974). *Coming into being among the Aborigines: A study of the procreative beliefs of the native tribes of Australia* (revised edition). London: Routledge & Kegan Paul.

Muehlenhard, C. L. (1989). Misinterpreted dating behaviors and the risk of date rape. In M. A. Pirog-Good & J. E. Stets, *Violence in dating relationships: Emerging social issues* (pp. 241–156). New York: Praeger.

Mushanga, T. (1978). Wife victimization in East and Central Africa. *Victimology, 2,* 479–485.

Nagel, I. H., & Hagen, J. (1983). Gender and crime: Offense patterns and criminal court sanctions. In M. Tonry & N. Morris (Eds.), *Crime and justice: An annual review of research*, Vol. 4 (pp. 91–144). Chicago: University of Chicago Press.

National Safe Workplace Institute. (1990). *Beyond neglect: The problem of occupational disease in the United States—Labor Day '90 report*. Chicago: The Institute.

National Safety Council. (1995). *Accident facts*. Chicago: National Safety Council.

Office of Technology Assessment. (1985). *Preventing Illness and Injury in the Workplace*, OTA-H-256. 99th Congress. Washington, D.C.: U.S. Government Printing Office.

Ohlin, L., & Tonry, M. (Eds.) (1989). *Family violence: Crime and justice, a review of research*, Vol. 11. Chicago: University of Chicago Press.

O'Toole, L. L., & Schiffman, J. R. (Eds.) (1997). *Gender violence: Interdisciplinary perspectives*. New York: New York University Press.

Overholser, J. C., & Beck, S. (1986). Multi-method assessment of rapists, child molesters, and three control groups in behavioral and psychological measures. *Journal of Consulting and Clinical Psychology, 54,* 682-687.

Pagelow, M. D. (1984). *Family violence*. New York: Praeger.

Perkins, C., & Klaus, P. (1996). *Bureau of Justice Statistics Bulletin, National Crime Victimization Survey: Criminal victimization 1994*. Washington, D.C.: U.S. Department of Justice, Bureau of Justice Statistics, NCJ-158022.

Perrot, M. (1990). *A history of private life: From the fires of revolution to the Great War*. Cambridge, MA: The Belknap Press of Harvard University Press.

Peters, E. (1988). *Inquisition*. Berkeley & Los Angeles, CA: University of California Press.

Peto, R., Lopez, A. D., Boreham, J., Thun, M, & Heath, Jr., C. (1992). Mortality from tobacco in developed countries: Indirect estimation from national vital statistics. *The Lancet, 339,* 1268–1278.

Pleck, E. (1987). *Domestic tyranny: The making of American social policy against family violence from colonial times to the present*. New York: Oxford University Press.

Pleck, E. (1989). Criminal approaches to family violence, 1640–1980. In L. Ohlin & M. Tonry (Eds.), *Family violence: Crime and justice, a review of research*, Vol. 11 (pp. 19–57). Chicago: University of Chicago Press.

Pollack, E. S., & Keimig, D. G. (Eds.). (1987). *Counting injuries and illnesses in the workplace: proposals for a better system*. Washington, D.C.: National Academy Press.

Priest, D. (1997). Sex harassment rampant, Army reports. *Sacramento Bee,* Friday, September 12.

Rada, R. T. (1978). *Clinical aspects of rape*. New York: Grune & Stratton.

Radford, J., & Russell, D. E. H. (Eds.). (1992). *Femicide: The politics of woman killing*. New York: Twayne.

Rand, M. R., & Strom, K. (1997). *Violence-related injuries treated in hospital emergency departments*. Washington, D.C.: U.S. Department of Justice, Bureau of Justice Statistics, NCJ-156921.

Reiss, A. J., & Roth, J. A. (Eds.). (1993). *Understanding and preventing violence,* Vol. 1. Washington, D C.: National Academy Press.

Reiss, A. J., & Roth, J. A. (Eds.) (1994) *Understanding and preventing violence,* Vol. 3: *Social influences.* Washington, D.C.: National Academy Press.

Richter, P. (1997). Army seeks sweat equity in wake of sexual harassment. *Los Angeles Times,* Sunday, September 14.

Rodin, J., Silberstein, L., & Striegel-Moore. (1985). Women and weight: A normative discontent. In T. B. Sonderegger (Ed.), *Nebraska symposium on motivation 1984: Psychology and gender*, Vol. 32 (pp. 267–307). Lincoln: University of Nebraska Press.

Ruback, R. B., & Weiner, N. A. (Eds.) (1995). *Interpersonal violent behaviors: Social and cultural aspects*. New York: Springer.

Russell, J. B. (1972). *Witchcraft in the Middle Ages*. Ithica, NY: Cornell University Press.

Russell, D. E. H. (1982). *Rape in marriage*. New York: Macmillan.

Russell, D. E. H. (1984). *Sexual exploitation: Rape, child sexual abuse, and workplace harassment*. Beverly Hills, CA: Sage.

Sanday, P. R. (1981). The socio-cultural context of rape: A cross-cultural study. *Journal of Social Issues, 37,* 5–27.

Satel, S. L. (1997). Feminist numbers game. *The New York Times, Op-Ed,* September 11.

Scheper-Hughes, Nancy. (1992). *Death without weeping: The violence of everyday life in Brazil*. Berkeley & Los Angeles, CA: University of California Press.

Schneider, B. E. (1993). Put up and shut up: Workplace sexual assaults. In P. B. Bart & E. G. Moran (Eds.), *Violence against women: The bloody footprints* (pp. 57–72). Newbury Park, CA: Sage.

Schroedel, J. R., & Peretz, P. (1994). A gender analysis of policy formation: The case of fetal abuse. *Journal of Health Politics, Policy and Law, 19,* 335–360.

Scully, D. (1990). *Understanding sexual violence: A study of convicted rapists*. New York: Routledge.

Scully, D., & Marolla, J. (1993). "Riding the bull at Gilley's:" Convicted rapists describe the rewards of rape. In P. B. Bart & E. G. Moran (Eds.), *Violence against women: The bloody footprints* (pp. 26–46). Newbury Park, CA: Sage.

Sedlack, A., & Broadhurst, D. D. (1996). *Third National Incidence Study of Child Abuse and Neglect: Final report.* Washington, D.C.: U.S. Department of Health and Human Services.

Segal, Z. V., & Marshall, W. L. (1985). Heterosexual social skills in a population of rapists and child molesters. *Journal of Consulting and Clinical Psychology, 53,* 55–63.

Sen, A. (1990). More than 100 million women are missing. *New York Review of Books*, December 20, 61–65.

Sen, A. (1992). Missing women: Social inequality outweighs women's survival advantage in Asia and North Africa. *British Medical Journal, 304*, 587–588.

Sheffield, C. J. (1993). The invisible intruder: Women's experiences of obscene phone calls. In P. B. Bart & E. G. Moran (Eds.), *Violence against women: The bloody footprints* (pp. 73–78). Newbury Park, CA: Sage.

Siebert, C. (1996). The cuts that go deeper. *The New York Times Magazine*, July 7, 20–45.

Skinner, G. W. (1993). Conjugal power in Tokugawa Japanese families: A matter of life or death. In B. D. Miller (Ed.), *Sex and gender hierarchies* (pp. 236–270). New York: Cambridge University Press.

Small, M., & Singer, J. D. (1982). *Resort to arms: International and civil wars, 1816–1980*. Beverly Hills, CA: Sage.

Smith, M. D., & Morra, N. N. (1997). Obscene and threatening telephone calls to women: Data from a Canadian national survey. In L. L. O'Toole & J. R. Schiffman (Eds.), *Gender violence: Interdisciplinary persepctives* (pp. 139–145). New York: New York University Press.

Spitzberg, B. H., & Cupach, W. R. (1996). Obsessive relational intrusion: Victimization and coping. Paper presented at the International Society for the Study of Personal Relationships, Banff, Canada, August 4–8.

Stampp, K. M. ([1956] 1989). *The peculiar institution: Slavery in the ante-bellum South*. New York: Vintage.

Stanko, E. A. (1985). *Intimate intrusions: Women's experience of male violence*. London: Routledge & Kegan Paul.

Stark, E., & Flitcraft, A. H. (1988). Personal power and institutional victimization: Treating the dual trauma of woman battering. In F. M. Ochberg (Ed.), *Post-traumatic therapy and victims of violence* (pp. 115–151). New York: Brunner/Mazel.

Stark, E., & Flitcraft, A. H. (1991). Spouse abuse. In M. L. Rosenberg & M. A. Fenley (Eds.), *Violence in America: A public health approach* (pp. 123–158). New York: Oxford University Press.

Stark, E., Flitcraft, A. H., & Frazier, W. (1979). Medicine and patriarchal violence: The social construction of a "private" event. *International Journal of Health Services, 9*, 461–493.

State v. A. B. Rhodes. (1868). In *North Carolina reports*, Vol. 61: *Cases at law argued and determined in the Supreme Court of North Carolina June term, 1866 to January term, 1868 inclusive* (pp. 349–354).

Steinmetz, S. K. (1977–1978). The battered husband syndrome. *Victimology, 2*, 499–509.

Stermac, L. E., Segal, Z. V., & Gillis, R. (1990). Social and cultural factors in sexual assault. In W. L. Marshall, D. R. Laws, & H. E. Barbaree (Eds.), *Handbook of sexual assault: Issues, theories, and treatment of the offender* (pp. 143–159). New York: Plenum Press.

Stone, L. (1983). Interpersonal violence in English society, 1300–1980. *Past and Present, 101*, 122–133.

Straus, M. A., & Gelles, R. J. (Eds.) (1990a). *Physical violence in American families: Risk factors and adaptions to violence in 8,145 families*. New Brunswick, NJ: Transaction Books.

Straus, M. A., & Gelles, R. J. (Eds.) (1990b). How violent are American families? Estimates from the National Family Violence Resurvey and other studies. In M. A. Straus & R. J. Gelles (Eds.), *Physical violence in American families: Risk factors and adaptions to violence in 8,145 families* (pp. 95–112). New Brunswick, NJ: Transaction Books.

Straus, M. A., Gelles, R. J., & Steinmetz, S. (1980). *Behind closed doors: Violence in the American family*. Garden City, NJ: Anchor.

Sugarman, D. B., & Hotaling, G. T. (1989). Dating violence: Prevalence, context, and risk markers. In M. A. Pirog-Good & J. E. Stets (Eds.), *Violence in dating relationships: Emerging social issues* (pp. 3–32). New York: Praeger.

Szockyi, E., & Frank, N. (1996). Introduction. In E. Szockyj & J. G. Fox (Eds.), *Corporate victimization of women* (pp. 3–32). Boston: Northeastern University Press.

Tannahill, R. (1992). *Sex in history* (revised and updated edition). New York: Scarborough House.

Taylor, B. M. (1997). *Bureau of Justice Statistics National Crime Victimization Survey: Changes in criminal victimization, 1994–95*. Washington, D.C.: U.S. Department of Justice, Bureau of Justice Statistics, NCJ-162032.

Taylor, R. (1981). Within the halls of ivy—The sexual revolution comes of age. *Change, 13*, 22–29.

Tjaden, P., & Thoennes, N. (1997). Stalking in America: Findings from the National Violence against Women Survey. In *NIJ research in progress seminar*. Washington, D.C.: Department of Justice, National Institute of Justice.

Tolman, R. M. 1989. The development of a measure of the psychological maltreatment of women by their male partners. *Violence and Victims 4*, 159–178.

Tong, J. (1988). Rational outlaws: Rebels and bandits in the Ming Dynasty, 1368–1644. In M. Taylor (Ed.), *Rationality and Revolution* (pp. 98–128). New York: Cambridge University Press.

Totman, J. (1978). *The murderess: A psychosocial study of criminal homicide*. San Francisco: R. E. Research Associates.

U.S. Department of Health and Human Services. (1988). *Study findings: Study of National Incidence and Prevalence of Child Abuse and Neglect: 1988*. Washington, D.C.: Westat, Inc.

U.S. Department of Health and Human Services. (1989). *Reducing the health consequences of smoking: 25 years of progress. A report of the Surgeon General*. Washington, D.C.: DHHS Publication No. (CDC) 89-8411.

U.S. Department of Labor. (1994). *1993 Handbook on women workers: Trends and issues*. Washington, D.C.: U.S. Department of Labor.

U.S. Merit Systems Protection Board. (1981). *Sexual harassment in the federal workplace: Is it a problem?* Washington, D.C.: U.S. Government Printing Office.

U.S. Merit Systems Protection Board. (1995). *Sexual harassment in the federal workplace: Trends, progress, continuing challenges*. Washington, D.C.: U.S. Government Printing Office.

U.S. National Center for Health Statistics. (1993). *Vital statistics of the the United States, annual*. Washington, D.C.: U.S. National Center for Health Statistics.

Venkatramani, S. H. (1992). Female infanticide: Born to die. In J. Radford & D. E. H. Russell (Eds.), *Femicide* (pp. 1125–1132). New York: Twayne.

Verrko, V. (1967). Static and dynamic "laws" of sex and homicide. In M. E. Wolfgang (Ed.), Studies in homicide (pp. 36–44). New York: Harper & Row.

Von, J. M., Kilpatrick, D. G., Burgess, A. W., & Hartman, C. R. (1991). Rape and sexual assault. In M. L. Rosenberg & M. A. Fenley (Eds.), *Violence in America: A public health approch* (pp. 95–122). New York: Oxford University Press.

Walker, L. E. (1979). *The battered woman*. New York: Harper & Row.

Warr, M. (1994). Public perceptions and reactions to violent offending and victimization. In A. J. Reiss & J. A. Roth (Eds.), *Understanding and preventing violence,* Vol. 4: *Consequences and control,* (pp. 1–66). Washington, D.C.: National Academy Press.

Weis, J. G. (1989). Family violence research methodology and design. In L. Ohlin & M. Tonry (Eds.), *Family violence* (pp. 117–162). Chicago: University of Chicago Press.

White, W. ([1929] 1969). *Rope and faggot*. New York: Amo Press.

Wilson, J. Q., & Herrnstein, R. J. (1985). *Crime and human nature*. New York: Simon & Schuster.

Wilson, M. I., & Daly, M. (1992a). 'Til death us do part. In J. Radford & D. E. H. Russell (Eds.), *Femicide* (pp. 83–98). New York: Twayne.

Wilson, M. I., & Daly, M. (1992b). Who kills whom in spouse killings? On the exceptional sex ratio of spousal homicides in the United States. *Criminology, 30,* 189–215.

Wilson, M. I., & Daly, M. (1993). Spousal homicide risk and estrangement. *Violence and Victims, 8,* 3–16.

Wilson, M. I., & Mesnick, S. L. (1997). An empirical test of the bodyguard hypothesis. In P. A. Gowaty (Ed.), *Feminism and evolutionary biology: Boundaries, intersections, and frontiers* (pp. 431–465). New York: Chapman & Hall.

Wilson, M., Daly, M., & Wright, C. (1993). Uxoricide in Canada: Demographic risk patterns. *Canadian Journal of Criminology, 35,* 263–291.

Wilson, M. I., Daly, M., & Daniele, A. (1995). Familicide: The killing of spouse and children. *Aggressive Behavior, 21,* 275-291.

Wilson, M., Daly, M., & Scheib, J. E. (1997). Femicide: An evolutionary psychological perspective. In P. A. Gowaty (Ed.), *Feminism and evolutionary biology: Boundaries, intersections, and frontiers* (pp. 431–465). New York: Chapman & Hall.

Wilson, M. I., Johnson, H., & Daly, M. (1995). Lethal and non-lethal violence against wives. *Canadian Journal of Criminology, 37,* 331–361.

Wolf, N. (1992). *The beauty myth: How images of beauty are used against women*. New York: Anchor.

Wolfgang, M. E. (1967a). Criminal homicide and the subculture of violence. In M. E. Wolfgang (Ed.), *Studies in homicide* (pp. 3–14). New York: Harper & Row.

Wolfgang, M. E. (1967b). A sociological analysis of criminal homicide. In M. E. Wolfgang (Ed.), *Studies in homicide* (pp. 15–28). New York: Harper & Row.

Wolfgang, M. E. (1967c). Victim-precipitated criminal homicide. In M. E. Wolfgang (Ed.), *Studies in homicide* (pp. 72–87). New York: Harper & Row.

World Health Organization. (1996). *Female genital mutilation: Information pack*. World Health Organization Internet Home-page.

Wright, G. L. (1994). Deaf black man, 96, free after 68 years in asylum. *The Sacramento Bee,* Saturday, February 5.

Wright, Q. (1965). *A study of war* (2nd ed.). Chicago: University of Chicago Press.

Wyatt-Brown, B. (1982). *Southern honor: Ethics and behavior in the old South*. New York: Oxford University Press.

PART IV

INSTITUTIONS

CHAPTER 15

Gender and Paid Work in Industrial Nations

DANA DUNN

SHERYL SKAGGS

1. INTRODUCTION

Gender shapes the work opportunities, experiences, and rewards of women and men in industrial societies. Many sociologists agree that women's and men's participation in paid work, and the nature and social valuation of the work they perform, are key determinants of their overall status in society. In fact, women's labor force participation rates have been used widely in cross-national research as a measure of women's status (Clark, Ramsbey, & Adler, 1991; Ward, 1984; Young, Fort, & Danner, 1996). When women are judged to be performing valued work, especially work for pay outside the home on a comparable basis with men, then gender inequality is minimized (Chafetz, 1984; Nielsen, 1990). Given this, it is not surprising that gender is the most prevalent single subtopic in the recent sociology of work and occupations literature (Abbott, 1993; Hall, 1983). Abbott (1993) finds that about 20% of all work and occupations articles published in 1990 and 1991 focus on gender issues.

The rapid influx of women into the paid labor market during this century is a dramatic social change warranting much attention from sociologists. Women working for pay is no longer the exception to the rule. In most advanced industrial nations today, the average worker is as likely to be female as male (Bakker, 1996). While women have

DANA DUNN • Office of the Provost, University of Texas at Arlington, Arlington, Texas 76019
SHERYL SKAGGS • Department of Sociology, North Carolina State University, Raleigh, North Carolina 27695

Handbook of the Sociology of Gender, edited by Janet Saltzman Chafetz. Kluwer Academic/ Plenum Publishers, New York, 1999.

always worked, the division of labor in many early industrial societies was such that married women often performed uncompensated work in or around the home to support family members. With industrialization, some groups of women, namely racial/ethnic minority women and working-class women, began to work outside the home for pay in highly gender-segregated occupations. Over the course of the century, other groups of women joined the ranks of paid workers, causing women's labor force participation rates to increase rather steadily in industrial nations. In the United States, for example, women accounted for 46% of the labor force in 1994 (Herz & Wootton, 1996), up from 18% at the turn of the century (Kemp, 1994).

Traditionally, the study of work addressed primarily male workers (Acker, 1989). With women now representing almost one half of the labor force in industrial nations, sociologists have recognized the importance of supplying missing information about employed women. Attention has turned to issues such as: (1) What motivates women to be productive workers (Bielby & Bielby, 1984; Lorence, 1987b; Mannheim, 1983, 1993; Mortimer & Lorence, 1979; Neil & Snizek, 1987; Rowe & Snizek, 1995)? (2) What causes women to be satisfied with their work (Hodson, 1989; Loscocco, 1990; Loscocco & Spitze, 1991; Martin & Shehan, 1989; Neil & Snizek, 1989)? (3) Do women's work and management styles differ from those of men, and if so, how (Colwill, 1993; Johnson, 1976; Maile, 1995)?

Another reason sociologists have begun to focus attention on employed women is related to the increasingly important role they play as economic providers for families/households. Whereas the majority of women who work for pay today do so out of perceived economic need (Baca Zinn & Eitzen, 1993), only a few decades ago discussion of women's labor force participation presented women's employment as secondary and supplemental to men's—an expendable means of improving the family's standard of living (Dubeck & Borman, 1996). As Acker (1992, p. 54) states, "the family wage sufficient for a single worker to support dependents is fast disappearing; women's paid work is becoming necessary for family survival." The high incidence of single adult, mostly female households in modern society also points to the importance of women's paid work. The fact that, on average, women earn less than men for the work they perform contributes to disproportionately high rates of poverty in female-headed households, a serious social problem that has come to be known as the feminization of poverty (Dunn & Waller, 1996).

The emphasis in sociology on women's increased involvement in paid work is also due to the fact that women's employment has broad social consequences that extend well beyond the economy. Families, in particular, are affected by increases in women's labor force participation. Traditionally, women have borne the primary responsibility for domestic work. As they begin to spend significant numbers of hours working outside the home for pay, their ability to perform domestic work, and potentially, the quality of life of their families is affected. Families need to adapt to women's changing work roles by making other provisions for the performance of domestic work (Chafetz, 1997). Research suggests that this adaptation is slow in coming, in that many women today work a "double shift"—they still perform a disproportionate share of domestic tasks in addition to their paid work (Berk, 1985; Ferree, 1991; Hochschild, 1989; Schor, 1991; Steil, 1995). The United Nations (1995b) estimates that two thirds to three quarters of the household work in industrial countries is still performed by women. This inequity has resulted in much sociological attention to what has come to be referred to as work/family conflict (Abbott,

1993). Schools and the nonprofit sector of the economy provide other examples of social institutions/organizations profoundly affected by increases in women's labor force participation in that women today seldom have time to perform volunteer work in these settings. More research is needed to better understand the far-reaching impact of increases in women's employment.

The extensive sociological study of gender and employment results from both the importance of paid work in modern society and the dramatic changes in gendered patterns of work participation. Because women are disproportionately affected by these changes, this chapter will reflect the emphasis on employed women (as opposed to men) found in the sociological literature. The vast literature that has emerged over the last two decades on gender and work makes it impossible to provide an in-depth review of all relevant subtopics. For this reason, we provide an overview of several major topical areas in this literature, highlighting representative research and significant findings in the following areas: patterns and rates of labor force participation, worker inputs, and worker outcomes.

Before turning attention to an examination of gender and participation in the labor force, it is important to distinguish between two distinct approaches to examining issues of gender and employment. An important characteristic that differentiates among sociological theories and the empirical studies they generate is whether women's and men's labor force experiences and opportunities are viewed as affected primarily by characteristics of individual workers or by structural features of society (Coverman, 1988; Kemp, 1994). Functionalism and neoclassical economics are the best examples of the former types of theories; Marxism, Marxist feminism, and other materialist theories provide examples of the latter (Kemp, 1994; Nielsen, 1990). Because much sociological research is devoted to sorting out these two influences on gendered work patterns and experiences, the individualist versus structural theme is a recurring one in this chapter.

2. LABOR FORCE PARTICIPATION AND GENDERED PATTERNS IN THE WORKPLACE

From 1960 to 1990, women's share of the labor force increased significantly in all industrialized nations. Recent estimates show that women now constitute an average of at least 40% of their labor forces (United Nations Development Programme, 1992, 1995; World Bank, 1996). Increases in female labor force participation have been particularly marked in the Netherlands and New Zealand. Steep increases have also occurred in Australia, Canada, Greece, Norway, and the United States. A few countries, for example, France, Ireland, and Portugal, have experienced more moderate increases (OECD, 1994). The rise in women's labor force activity has been accompanied by a decrease in men's rates of labor force participation (OECD; 1985, Kemp, 1994). For this reason, gender differentials in some countries are diminishing while in others they remain pronounced. In 1991, for example, the gap between male and female rates in Sweden had been reduced to 4.2 percentage points, while in Ireland it was still 42 percentage points (OECD, 1994). Table 15-1 provides an overview of changes in women's share of the labor force in 20 industrial nations from 1980 to 1994.

The following sections provide a brief sketch of changes in women's employment over two time periods—the 1960s through the 1970s, and the 1980s to the present.

TABLE 15-1. Women's Share of the Labor force in 20
Advanced Industrial Nations, 1980 and 1994

Country	Women's Share of the Labor Force	
	1980	1994
Australia	36	42
Austria	40	40
Belgium	34	40
Canada	40	44
Denmark	44	46
Finland	46	47
France	40	44
Germany	40	41
Hong Knong	34	36
Ireland	28	33
Israel	34	38
Italy	33	37
Neatherlands	31	39
New Zealand	34	44
Norway	40	45
Japan	38	40
Portugal	39	43
Sweden	44	47
Switzerland	37	40
United Kingdom	39	43
United States	42	45

Source: Adapted from the World Bank. *World Development Report 1996*. New York: Oxford University Press.

2.1. Labor Force Participation Rates and Patterns in the 1960s and 1970s

The influx of women, especially married women, into paid employment in industrial nations accelerated in the 1960s and 1970s. Structural changes in the economy that led to a disproportionate rate of job growth in the service sector and an increased demand for part-time labor had a strong impact on women's rates of employment (Janjic, 1985; OECD, 1993c). In the United States, for example, 79% of the new jobs created between 1973 and 1987 were in the service sector (Acker, 1992). Chaftetz (1990) argues that demand factors resulting from economic expansion are a far more important determinant of women's employment than labor supply factors. This view is supported by comparative research that shows a strong relationship between economic growth and increases in women's labor force participation (Clark et al., 1991; Semyonov, 1980).

While demand factors may be most important in determining women's rates of labor force participation, numerous factors affecting the supply of women workers have also contributed to increases in their share of the labor force. In the United States and some other Western European nations, increasing divorce rates and rising numbers of impoverished displaced homemakers began to cause full-time homemakers to consider the risks of complete economic dependence on a male provider (Amott & Matthaei, 1982; Dunn, 1997). In many countries, the women's movement also played a role in making paid work appear more desirable to married women (Herz & Wootton, 1996). In addition, women's educational attainment was becoming more similar to men's and this opened doors to more interesting and lucrative employment (OECD, 1985; United Nations, 1995a). Increased employment opportunities led to a decline in the birth rate, which meant that women spent less of their adult years with preschool-aged children, and thus had more years available to spend in paid employment (Herz & Wootton, 1996; Semyonov, 1980).

Changes in occupational opportunity occurring in the 1960s and 1970s had a differential impact across groups of women (Almquist, 1995; Andersen, 1988). Age and race/ethnicity, in particular, patterned the new employment opportunities available to women in industrial nations (OECD, 1985; Ortiz, 1994). Younger women were more likely to remain out of the labor force in order to extend their education and older women were less likely to possess the skills and educational credentials required for emerging employment opportunities (United Nations, 1985). Economic discrimination resulted in limited access to new jobs for minority women in many nations, but economic disadvantage made paid work a necessity. Table 15-2 provides labor force participation rates for women in the United States by race/ethnicity for 1960 and 1970. Among the groups listed, only Mexican, Puerto Rican, and American Indian women had lower rates of labor force participation than white women. African-Americans, Chinese, Japanese, and Filipino women were all employed at higher rates than white women; however, they worked primarily in lower tier, personal service occupations (e.g., domestic, seamstress) and as factory operatives (Ortiz, 1994). More recently, improved educational opportunities for women of color, combined with legal changes, have created new job opportunities for African-American women in the United States, especially in female-dominated, semiprofessional occupations (Higginbotham, 1994; Sokoloff, 1987).

2.2. Labor Force Participation Rates and Patterns in the 1980s and 1990s

Women's labor force participation rates in industrial nations began to level off by the late 1980s and early 1990s. By 1992, female labor force participation rates ranged from a low of 46% in Italy to a high of 79% in Sweden (Baden, 1993). Economic recession in the early 1990s resulted in job loss in heavily male-dominated manufacturing and construction industries, causing men's labor force participation rates to decline. Concentrated in service sector jobs, women remained rather insulated from this recession. In most advanced industrial nations today, at least 70% of all employed women work in the service sector (United Nations Development Programme, 1992).

The high growth phenomenon of part-time employment also fueled demand for women

TABLE 15-2. Labor Force Participation Rates for Women in the United States by Selected Racial/Ethnic Groups, 1960 and 1970

	1960	1970
White	33.6	40.6
African-American	42.2	47.5
Mexican	28.8	36.4
Puerto Rican	36.3	32.3
Chinese	44.2	49.5
Japanese	44.1	49.4
Filipino	36.2	55.2
American Indian	25.5	35.3

Source: Adapted from V. Ortiz (1994), Women of color: A demographic overview. In M. Baca Zinn & B. Thornton Dill (Eds.), Women of color in U.S. society. Philadelphia: Temple University Press.

laborers in industrial nations while men's employment rates were declining (Bakker, 1996). It is important to note, however, that part-time workers in many nations earn lower hourly wages than full-time workers, receive fewer fringe benefits, and have fewer chances for career progression (OECD, 1994). Nordic countries are an exception to this pattern; part-time employment in these nations is fully regulated, resulting in higher compensation and increased access to fringe benefits. Baden (1993) reports that an increasing amount of part-time work is involuntary in that the women who perform it would prefer full-time jobs but are unable to find them. Table 15-3 presents information on the size and gender composition of the part-time labor force for 21 industrial nations. These data show that while women make up the vast majority of part-time workers in all industrial nations, the proportion employed part-time varies considerably from country to country (OECD, 1994).

A sizable share of part-time jobs are temporary. Women's share of temporary employment is greater than men's in all industrial nations except Greece, Spain, Portugal, and Turkey, where higher levels of agricultural activity create many seasonal jobs for men (Baden, 1993). In most industrial nations, the proportion of men in temporary employment has fallen since the early 1980s while that of women has increased in all countries except the Netherlands and Germany (OECD, 1993a, b). Evidence suggests that much temporary employment, like part-time work, is involuntary—the majority of temporary workers indicate they could not find permanent jobs (Baden, 1993). The disadvantages of part-time work appear to extend to temporary workers. Not only do they typically earn less and have fewer benefits, Rogers (1995) finds that temporary workers in the United States have higher levels of workplace alienation than permanent workers.

Women's participation in paid work continues to be affected by variations in age,

TABLE 15-3. Part-time Employment of a Proportion of Employment, 1991

Country	% Men	% Women	Proportion of Total Employment	Women's Share of Part-Time Employment
Australia	9.2	40.9	22.5	76.3
Austria	1.5	20.1	8.9	89.7
Belgium	2.1	27.4	11.8	89.3
Canada	8.8	25.5	16.4	70.5
Denmark	10.5	37.8	23.1	75.5
Finland	5.1	10.2	7.6	65.2
France	3.4	23.5	12.0	84.0
Germany	2.7	34.3	15.5	89.6
Greece	2.2	7.2	3.9	62.9
Ireland	3.6	17.8	8.4	71.6
Italy	2.9	10.4	5.5	65.4
Japan	10.1	34.3	20.0	69.9
Luxemburg	1.9	17.9	7.5	83.3
Netherlands	16.7	62.2	34.3	70.1
New Zealand	9.7	35.7	21.1	74.2
Norway	9.1	47.6	26.7	81.4
Portugal	4.0	10.5	6.8	66.7
Spain	1.5	11.2	4.6	78.0
Sweden	7.6	41.0	23.7	83.4
United Kingdom	5.5	43.7	22.2	86.1
United States	10.5	25.6	17.4	67.2

Source: Adapted from the *OECD Employment Outlook,* July 1993. Paris: OECD.

race/ethnicity, marital status, the presence of children, and educational level (Bakker, 1996; OECD, 1985, 1993b). These characteristics affect women's participation in the labor force for two primary reasons. First, they are related to domestic/family demands on women's time that detract from the opportunity to work (marital status and the presence of children). Second, they are related to employment and earnings opportunity and to the opportunity costs of not working (age, race/ethnicity, and education level). Table 15-4 presents selected population characteristics that illustrate their effects on labor force participation rates among women in the United States in 1994. Today, women in their late 30s and early 40s have the highest participation level, with more than 77% in the labor force (Herz & Wootton, 1996). This represents a change from the earlier part of the century when rates were highest for young, unmarried women (England & Farkas, 1986).

TABLE 15-4. Selected Population and Labor Force
Characteristics of Women in the United States,
1994 (numbers in thousands)

Characteristic	Percentage of the Population in the Labor Force
Total, females 16 years and over	58.8
Total, males 16 years and over	75.1
Women:	
Age	
16 to 19 years	51.3
20 to 24 years	71.0
25 to 54 years	75.3
25 to 34 years	74.0
35 to 44 years	77.1
45 to 54 years	74.6
55 to 64 years	48.9
65 years and over	9.2
Race and Hispanic origin*	
White	58.9
African-American	58.7
Hispanic origin	52.9
Marital status	
Never married	65.1
Married, spouse present	60.6
Widowed	17.6
Divorced	73.9
Married, spouse absent	62.9
Presence and age of children	
Without children under 18	53.1
With children under 18	68.4
6 to 17 years, none younger	76.0
Under 6 years	60.3
Under 3 years	57.1
Under 1 year	54.6

*Hispanics are included in both the white and black population groups.
Source: Adapted from Table 1.1 (p. 49) in D. E. Herz & B. H. Wootton (1996). Women in the workforce: An Overview. In C. Costello & B. K. Krimgold (Eds.), *The American woman: Where we stand.* New York: Norton.

Through the middle part of the century, women exited the labor force in significant numbers upon marriage and especially upon the birth of children, causing a dip in labor force participation rates for those under the age of 35. As these women reentered the labor force when their children reached school age, rates climbed once again, although not to the level for young unmarried women. Women today are far more likely to work continuously (Rexroat, 1992), causing their labor force participation rates to appear similar to men's; increasing through the middle years, leveling off, and then declining around retirement (Herz & Wootton, 1996). The most dramatic increases in women's labor force participation in the United States in recent decades have occurred for married women with preschool age children.

The general patterns described for the United States and presented in Table 15-4 are also found in most other advanced industrial nations. One key exception is Scandanavian countries, Sweden in particular, whose labor market policies are highly facilitative of women's employment (Rosenfeld & Kalleberg, 1990; Ruggie, 1984). Swedish labor market policies provide daycare and other forms of assistance to the mothers of young children, making it easier for them to be employed continuously. Italy and Belgium also fail to show a downturn in women's employment in the early childbearing years (Baden, 1993). Increases in women's level of education relative to men have also spurred more continuous participation in the paid labor force. Today, in most industrial nations, women receive nearly the same overall level of education as men, and the most educated groups of women are those with the highest labor force participation rates (United Nations, 1995a).

In recent years, variation in women's labor force participation by race/ethnicity has also diminished in some industrial nations. For example, increases in white women's levels of employment in the United States have served to close the gap between white and African-American women (Ortiz, 1994). Rates of participation for Hispanic women in the United States represent marked increases over previous decades, but are still about 6 percentage points lower than those for African-American and white women. The lower labor force participation rates of Hispanic women have often been attributed to cultural patterns that emphasize traditional roles in the family for women. The rapid increases in participation in paid work for women in this group suggest that such traditions are eroding, or perhaps that increased employment opportunities and economic need compel women to deviate from tradition (Ortiz, 1994; Zavella, 1987). It is important to note that while labor force participation rates vary little across racial/ethnic groups, unemployment rates are about two times higher for racial/ethnic minority women compared to white women in the United States (except Asian/Pacific Islanders) (U.S. Bureau of the Census, 1990).

2.3. Employment Concentration and Segregation by Sex

Despite dramatic increases in women's labor force activity this century, women continue to be employed in a far more narrow range of occupations and industries than their male counterparts (Roos, 1985). For example, in the Netherlands, 66.8% of women are employed in 8 of the 99 professional categories, in contrast to men who are spread across 76 professional employment categories (OECD, 1993c). In G-7 countries, 60% to 75% of all women workers are concentrated in service sector industries (Bakker, 1996). Table 15-5 presents women's share of four broad occupational categories for 13 industrial nations. Variation across nations is marked, but in general women are most likely to be employed as clerical, sales, and service workers. While women's rates of employment in the more

TABLE 15-5. Women's Share of Four Broad Occupational
Categories for 13 Industrial Nations, 1990

	Occupation			
Country	Administrative and Managerial Workers (& Women) 1990	Professional, Technical and Related Workers (% Women) 1990	Clerical Sales Workers (% Women) 1990	Service Workers (& Women) 1990
Australia	41.4	23.8	19.3	77.2
Austria	16.4	47.9	64.1	70.8
Canada	40.7	56.0	67.6	57.1
Denmark	14.7	62.9	60.9	72.5
Finland	24.1	61.4	67.4	71.4
Ireland	15.1	46.7	51.6	51.5
Japan	7.9	42.0	50.3	54.2
Netherlands	13.5	42.5	52.2	70.4
New Zealand	32.3	47.8	76.4	67.4
Norway	25.4	56.5	65.9	75.1
Spain	9.5	47.0	47.4	58.6
Seden	38.9	63.3	77.0	76.9
USA	40.1	50.8	66.7	60.1

Source: Adapted from the United Nations Human Development Report 1995. New York: Oxford Unversity Press.

lucrative administrative, managerial and professional, and technical job categories are lower, in most countries there has been an upward trend in the last decade or so in their representation in these job categories (Bakker, 1996).

Women are also heavily concentrated in public sector employment in most industrial nations (OECD, 1994). The public sector has expanded dramatically in many OECD countries during the last few decades, resulting in an increased demand for women workers. Sweden has experienced the greatest increase in public sector employment, with almost one third of all workers now employed in the public sector (Nermo, 1996). In contrast, the government's share of total employment in the United States has held constant in recent decades, suggesting that the bulk of new jobs created for women have been in the private sector. Women in the public sector in Sweden are advantaged relative to those in the private sector in terms of both wages and access to higher tier occupations. The reverse is true in the United States, where many black women are concentrated in lower tier positions in the public sector (Higginbotham, 1994; OECD, 1994).

Most studies of occupational sex segregation, the concentration of workers in predominantly same sex occupations, have been conducted at the national level and limited research exists on patterns of cross-national variation (Charles, 1992; Jacobs & Lim, 1992; Nermo, 1996). Interestingly, levels of segregation are generally lower in some relatively traditional countries, such as Japan and Italy, and higher in the more progressive Scandanavian countries. Charles (1992) argues that this pattern results primarily from the large service sector in modern economies that is associated with higher rates of female labor force participation but greater female concentration in the highly gender segregated clerical, sales, and service occupations. Other studies (Jacobs & Lim, 1992; Lorence, 1992; Nermo, 1996; OECD, 1994) shed doubt on this relationship in recent decades because they show that sex segregation has decreased somewhat in many industrial countries with large service sectors, especially the United States, Canada, and the United Kingdom.

Occupational integration occurs for differing reasons across industrial nations. Haavio-Mannila (1989), for example, found that in Eastern Europe occupational integration results primarily from women's work in traditional men's occupations in industry whereas in Southern Europe it results from men's work in traditional women's occupations of sales and private service work. Jacobs and Lim (1992) argue that it is more common for occupational integration to occur by men gaining access to women's occupations than vice versa. They found that during the period 1960–1980, with the exceptions of Austria and Greece, men experienced an increased chance of sharing an occupation with women in industrial countries, while women were more likely to experience a decline in the chances of sharing an occupation with men in all industrial nations but Greece.

In the United States, segregated employment patterns are of interest to sociologists primarily due to their association with the gender gap in wages. Studies examining the segregation–wage gap relationship across countries, however, often fail to provide support for the relationship. Rosenfeld and Kalleberg (1990) find no relationship in their study of four countries and Blau and Ferber (1986) find only a weak negative effect of segregation on the gender gap in wages in their study of 10 countries. Nermo (1992) also finds no straightforward relationship between segregation and the male–female wage gap in a study of Sweden.

2.4. Unemployment

The gap between the unemployment rates of women and men is a commonly used indicator of gender inequality in the labor market (OECD, 1994). It is important to note, however, that variations in unemployment data may in some cases reflect varying national policies that create incentives or disincentives for women to register as unemployed (Evers & Wintersberger, 1990; Grahl & Teague, 1989). Differential rates of long-term unemployment also make the interpretation of unemployment data across nations problematic, in that some nations have larger pools of discouraged workers who no longer seek work and are thus not counted in official unemployment statistics.

While there is considerable variation among countries in both levels of unemployment and relative levels of male and female unemployment (Baden, 1993), most nations experienced increases in unemployment for both sexes over the period 1979 to 1989 (OECD, 1994). Unemployment data from the 1970s and 1980s suggest that female unemployment is less sensitive to economic cycles than male unemployment, particularly in European nations (OECD, 1984). This is due largely to the sectoral distribution of employment by gender, specifically to women's concentration in service sector, public sector, and part-time employment. These forms of employment are less responsive to business fluctuations than other employment categories dominated by men (De Boer & Seeborg, 1989; OECD, 1984).

Women in the following countries had higher rates of unemployment than men in 1990–1991: Austria, Belgium, Denmark, France, Germany, Greece, Italy, the Netherlands, and Spain. The largest unemployment gaps favoring men were in Mediterranean countries—Spain (11.5%), Italy (9.8%), and Greece (7.4%). In all other industrial nations where women have higher rates of unemployment than men, the gap is around five percentage points or smaller (ILO, 1992). A gender difference exists in the distribution of the unemployed between the categories, "job search after non- participation" and "job search after loss of employment." Women are overrepresented in the first category and underrepresented in the second (OECD, 1994), suggesting that women have difficulty reentering the labor force in many nations after taking time out for family responsibilities.

3. GENDER AND WORK INPUTS

A major theme in the literature on gender and employment involves the comparison of women and men in terms of worker inputs—for example, education, hours worked, absenteeism, work values, and commitment (Abbott, 1993). This focus reflects the influence of the neoclassical economic paradigm and related human capital perspectives, which link work outcomes (e.g., earnings, occupational attainment) to the productivity-related characteristics of individual workers (Acker, 1992). These theories deemphasize the role of structural factors, such as characteristics of firms and markets, in the determination of work outcomes. However, the empirical literature assessing the importance of gender patterning in worker inputs explains a relatively small amount, and never more than 50%, of the variation in earnings and occupational attainment (see, e.g., Corcoran, Duncan, & Ponza, 1984; Polachek, 1981). Finding limited support for the importance of productivity-related differences between the sexes, these studies commonly attribute the unexplained variation to structural variables, including characteristics of firms and markets, and to discriminatory forces (Coverman, 1988).

Because empirical evidence suggests the somewhat limited importance of gender differences in quantifiable worker inputs for determining work outcomes, recent attention has turned to the examination of hypothesized gender differences in worker inputs that are less quantifiable, such as differences in work values and commitment (Agassi, 1982; Elizur, 1993; Lorence, 1987a; Mannheim, 1993; Rowe & Snizek, 1995; Siegfried, MacFarlane, Graham, Moore, & Young, 1981); work styles including communication (Booth, 1991; Fairhurst, 1985; Lakoff, 1975; Noble, 1995; Reardon, 1997; Tannen, 1995); and leadership/management styles (Colwill, 1993; Court, 1997; Dobbins & Platz, 1986; Rosener, 1990). This change in focus is also due to the fact that the sexes have begun to converge with respect to a number of more quanitifiable productivity-related characteristics. Education provides one example in that women's overall educational attainment equals or surpasses men's in many industrial nations today (OECD, 1994). Patterned differences, however, still do exist between men and women workers in terms of type of education, and empirical evidence suggests that these differences impact work outcomes. For example, sex differences in college major have been shown to have a significant impact on earnings and occupational attainment (Eide, 1994; Fuller & Schoenberger, 1991; Gerhart, 1990; Jacobs, 1996). The following sections provide a brief overview of recent literature addressing gender differences in worker inputs in the two areas listed previously.

3.1. Gender, Work Commitment, and Work Values

Two distinct sources of gender differences in both work commitment and work values are posited in the literature. The gender socialization approach suggests that women are less

332   Dana Dunn AND Sheryl Skaggs

committed than men to paid work and that they bring different values to the workplace because of their earlier gender training (Giele, 1988). This perspective also often emphasizes women's needs to allocate time and energy to both job and family roles, and the impact of gender roles on such choices (Moen & Smith, 1986). The second perspective views women's and men's differential status in the job market as responsible for commitment and value differences. Sex differences in opportunities for mobility and rewards, in particular, are seen as fostering differing values and levels of commitment for women and men (Lincoln & Kalleberg, 1990; Marsden, Kalleberg, & Cook, 1993). Empirical evidence suggests that both gender socialization and job characteristics contribute to gender differences in work values and commitment (Mannheim, 1993), but that characteristics of work may be more important in that women are less likely than men to hold jobs with commitment-enhancing features (e.g., opportunities for advancement and higher levels of other rewards) (Kanter, 1977; Lorence, 1987b; Loscocco, 1990; Marsden et al., 1993).

Research on gender differences in work values typically distinguishes between intrinsic and extrinsic aspects of jobs. This distinction involves valuing work in terms of its interest level and the opportunities it provides for growth and actualization versus valuing it because of material rewards, security, social relationships, or recognition. Studies show that women value the former aspects of work more than men, and that the sexes value different aspects of the latter—men emphasize material rewards and recognition and women emphasize interpersonal factors (Lueptow, 1980; Neil & Snizek, 1987). Recent studies show some convergence between the sexes in work values, but the differences that do emerge are still consistent with this pattern (Betz & O'Connell, 1989; Lueptow, 1996; Neil & Snizek, 1987).

The majority of studies addressing gender differences in work values and commitment are conducted with data from only one nation, the United States. One exception, a study by Elizur (1993), compares gender differences in work values for Hungary, Israel, and the Netherlands. Some values were ranked higher by men in one sample and by women in another. Personal growth, for example was ranked higher by Hungarian men than women, and higher by Dutch and Israeli women than men. Findings also indicated that gender differences in values among workers within a given nation were relatively small compared to differences across nations, suggesting that work values are culturally bound. Gender variation in work values and commitment across nations may be due to either differential gender socialization across nations or to differing work experiences and opportunities for women and men across nations. In a study of workers in Israel, Mannheim (1993) finds support for the socialization model, in that country of origin affected women worker's levels of work commitment.

3.2. Gender Differences in Management and Communication Styles

In the late 1980s and 1990s, sociologists joined in the debate over the existence of gender differences in "styles" of managing and communicating (Noble, 1995). Two popular books, *The Female Advantage* by Helgesen (1990) and *Talking 9 to 5* by Tannen (1995), spurred sociological inquiry into the existence, causes, and consequences of possible gender differences. As is the case with research on gender differences in work commitment and values, both individualistic and structural explanations have been offered for sex-linked differences in workplace communication and leadership. Individualistic explanations focus on the role of gender socialization in creating differences between women and men (e.g., men are taught to be assertive; women are taught to be conciliatory); structural explanations claim that the structure of work organizations and the location of the sexes within them (e.g., the proportion of women in the work position, hierarchical management structures) result in different work "styles" for women and men (Dunn, 1997).

Structural explanations receive the most attention from sociologists, following the influential work of Kanter (1977), who focused attention on the impact of organizational structure on women's work experiences. According to the structural perspective, the fact that women managers are disproportionately located in lower level positions lacking in authority causes them to rely on more cooperative approaches to leadership. Put simply, women with limited organizational resources to back up their power cannot successfully issue directives and orders (what some call a male-oriented management style); instead, they must enlist the cooperation and support of subordinates in order to gain their compliance (Colwill, 1993).

The primary gender difference in management style posited by those scholars who advocate difference involves women's emphasis on collaboration, teamwork, and participation (Marshall, 1984; Shakeshaft, 1989). Rosenser's (1990) study of 456 women executives, for example, found that women preferred to manage interactively, sharing power and information and empowering subordinates. Some scholars (Epstein, 1991; Powell, 1990; Sonnenfeld, 1991) caution that a range of leadership styles exist for both sexes, and suggest that within-group variation may be as great as between-group variation. These two distinct views are captured in the equity and complementary contribution models of women in management (Adler & Israeli, 1988). The former model, most pervasive in the United States, assumes similarity between the sexes and views difference as problematic; the latter, more visible in Europe and Scandanavia, assumes and values difference. The two models measure women's progress in management in quite different ways. The equity model focuses on quantitative measures of women's movement into management, arguing that as women's numerical representation increases, any structurally induced differences between the sexes in management styles will erode. The complementary contribution model views progress in terms of qualitative assessments of organizations' acceptance of female styles of managing, suggesting a need for changes in organizational culture and values (Adler & Israeli, 1988).

Somewhat less visible than the literature on gender differences in management, the literature on workplace communication differences between the sexes is less divided about the existence of difference. Conversational analyses provide much evidence of gendered patterns, including men interrupting women more often, the greater use by women of tag questions and other linguistic conventions conveying reluctance to make assertions, and more attempts by women to involve the listener (Reardon, 1997; Tannen, 1995). Studies exploring these gendered patterns often acknowledge that male-female interaction in the workplace negatively impacts women by causing them to be ignored, excluded, and/or patronized (Reardon, 1997).

In our opinion, while a range of work styles, including those characterized as both masculine and feminine, have the potential to enrich work organizations, the values that currently infuse the cultures of organizations do not often tolerate, much less value the female styles. Changing those values and the associated structures of opportunity is a difficult task. Similar issues are present in the literature on sex-based earnings differences and the value of jobs disproportionately held by women. These issues are addressed in the discussion of the wage gap and comparable worth.

4. GENDER AND WORK OUTCOMES

Sociological theory and research has addressed the relationship between gender and a number of work outcomes, including earnings (Marini, 1989; Rosenfeld & Kalleberg, 1990; Treiman & Roos, 1983), prestige (Tyree & Hicks, 1988; Xu & Leffler, 1992), authority (Mcguire & Reskin, 1993; Reskin and Ross 1992; Wright, Baxter, and Birkelund 1995), work satisfaction (Martin & Sheehan, 1989; Neil & Snizek, 1988), and mental and physical health (Stellman, 1977; Roxburgh, 1996). Of these workplace correlates of gender, earnings have received the most attention (Abbott, 1993). This emphasis reflects the ideas of early social theorists, such as Karl Marx (1967), who acknowledged the translatability of earnings into other valuable social rewards such as prestige and power. Space limitations prohibit thorough coverage in this chapter of all relevant gender-linked work outcomes. Because earnings differences between the sexes are also addressed in a later chapter, they receive only brief attention here.

4.1. Gender and Earnings

Women's nonagricultural wages in industrialized nations range between 63% and 89& of men's (see Table 15-6). Earnings ratios closer to equality are found in Nordic countries, nations classified by Rosenfeld and Kalleberg (1990) as "corporatist" because they have institutionalized centralized bargaining between the government, employers and labor. The gender gap in wages narrowed somewhat in many nations during the 1960s and 1970s, although rates of change were variable between countries. In the 1980s, progress toward the equalization of earnings slowed in most countries, and actually re-

Table 15-6. Women's Nonagricultural Wage as a Percentage of Men's*

Country	
Austria	78.0
Belgium	74.5
Canada	63.0
Denmark	82.6
Finland	77.0
France	81.0
Germany	75.8
Greece	78.0
Italy 80.0	
Luxemburg	65.2
Neatherlands	76.7
New Zealand	80.6
Japan	86.0
Spain	70.0
Sweden	89.0
Switzerland	67.6
United Kingdom	69.7
United States	75.0

*All data are post 1990 and for the latest available year.
Source: Adapted from the World Bank, *World Development Report 1996*. New York: Oxford University Press.

versed in a few cases. Out of 15 industrial nations, the wage gap narrowed during the 1980s in 5, increased in 9, and remained constant in 1 (ILO, 1994). In some countries the decline in women's earnings relative to men's resulted from changes in governmental wage policies, including wage hike ceilings, the decentralization of wage determination, and the privatization of state-owned companies (Bakker, 1996).

Until recent years, most research on the male–female wage gap was restricted to the United States, making it difficult to assess the impact on the wage gap of culturally distinct means of organizing work, family, and the state, and of coordinating these institutions. Several explanations for the earnings gap have been posited in the sociological literature focused on the United States, including a human capital explanation (women do not compare favorably to men in terms of productivity-related characteristics such as education and experience); an explanation centered on women's coordination of work and family roles which suggests they tailor their work behavior to meet their family obligations; and an explanation focused on occupational segregation and the concentration of women in low-level and/or undervalued occupations (for a thorough review of these explanations and empirical tests of each see Marini, 1989). Each of these explanations receives some support in the empirical literature on gender disparity in wages in the United States. Cross-national studies, however, find only limited support for these explanations (Rosenfeld & Kalleberg, 1990; Treiman & Roos, 1983), pointing to the need for more comparative research.

One subtopic in the literature on gender and wages has received disproportionate attention in the United States: comparable worth (Abbott, 1993). Arguing that wage hierarchies are not objectively determined on the basis of skill level, experience, and other relevant factors, but rather that the gender of the average incumbent of an occupation affects wages, writers on comparable worth both document this phenomenon and prescribe remedies (England & Dunn, 1988). Numerous studies show that a wage penalty exists for workers in female-dominated occupations, even after controlling for human capital and structural variables (Anderson & Thomaskovic-Devey, 1995; England, 1992; Figart & Lapidus, 1996; Reskin, 1993; Sorensen, 1994). Other studies examine systems of job evaluation and assess their effectiveness for eliminating the systematic undervaluing of female-dominated jobs (Steinberg, 1990, 1992; Wajcman, 1991). Several book-length case studies assess the intricacies of implementing pay equity policies designed to remedy gender-biased wage structures, exploring the political dynamics of various groups involved in the process—comparable worth advocates, employers, and unions (Acker, 1989; Blum, 1991, Evans & Nelson, 1989).

4.2. Gender, Occupational Prestige, and Workplace Authority

Occupational prestige and workplace authority are worker outcomes also shown to be related to the gender composition of jobs. Occupational prestige, a subjective assessment of the "status" of an occupation, is rather constant across nations (Treiman, 1977), yet most studies linking prestige to gender are focused on the United States. One exception is the work of Roos (1985), which examines the effects of gender, family background, education, and marital status on occupational mobility in 12 industrial nations, using occupational prestige as one of four measures of occupational attainment. She finds that education is a particularly important determinant of occupational prestige for women; in 7 of 12 countries examined it is the only significant influence for women whereas age, social origins, and marital status are also important in determining occupational prestige levels for men. Studies focused on the United States typically consider the effects of both gender and race on the prestige of occupations, and find that while female-dominated occupations receive less prestige than male-dominated occupations, race has a more powerful impact than gender on occupational prestige (Bose & Rossi, 1983; Tyree & Hicks, 1988; Xu & Leffler, 1992).

Wright et al. (1995) document considerable variability in the gender gap in authority across seven nations, with English-speaking nations exhibiting a smaller gap, Scandanavian countries a larger one, and Japan the largest. The researchers control for compositional differences among women and men workers, and find that a gender gap in authority still remains in all seven nations; thus, they attribute a significant proportion of the gender differences in authority to direct discrimination. Studies focused on the United (1992), for example, found that net of human capital variables, type of employer, and organizational level, women have less workplace authority than men.

4.3. Gender and Worker Satisfaction

Despite the inferior work conditions women experience (e.g., lower pay, prestige, and authority), they often report greater levels of job satisfaction than men (Hodson, 1989, Murray & Atkinson, 1981). This counterintuitive finding is thought to result primarily from women's lower expectations about work rewards and the reference groups to which they compare themselves (Hodson, 1989). Gender socialization and a lowering of expectations based on knowledge of gender inequity in work rewards may explain why women have lower expectations than men about the rewards they derive from work. Classic theories of job satisfaction suggest that it is the matching of a workers' expectations to what the job offers that determines levels of job satisfaction (Gruneberg, 1979); thus, women's lower expectations make it easier for them to be satisfied with their work.

Expectations are also derived from comparisons with reference groups. To the extent that workers are more likely to conduct same than other-sex comparisons when appraising their jobs, gender inequities that might otherwise compel women to be dissatisfied are obscured. Andrisani (1978) suggests that one result of women's movement activity may be to encourage cross-sex comparisons between workers, which will likely generate lower overall levels of job satisfaction for women. Gender socialization has also been posited as inhibiting women workers' expression of discontent, suggesting that actual levels of dissatisfaction for employed women may be higher than survey findings indicate (Glenn & Feldberg, 1977).

4.4. Gender, Work and Health

The early literature on women, work, and health focused primarily on pregnancy and reproductive hazards for women in the workplace and generally neglected the broader health concerns of women workers (Stellman, 1977). More recent sociological examination of the topic has emphasized gender differences in distress among paid workers, acknowledging the linkage between stress and mental and physical health. A number of studies show higher rates of distress for women workers than men (Menaghan, 1989;

Roxburgh, 1996), despite findings that employed women enjoy better mental health than nonemployed women (Cleary & Mechanic, 1983).

Two competing explanations for gender differences in distress have emerged—the differential vulnerability model and the differential exposure model (Roxburgh, 1996). The former model suggests that gender socialization causes women to experience the same workplace events as more stressful than do men. The latter argues that women are exposed to more stress producing circumstances in the workplace (e.g., a combination of high responsibility and low authority) (Karasek & Theorell, 1990), and that these stressors may be exacerbated by conflicts between work and family roles (Ulbrich, 1989). Empirical research provides mixed support for both models. For example, Turner, Wheaton, and Lloyd (1995) find that while gender differences in exposure to stress account for a considerable proportion of the variance in men's and women's distress levels, vulnerability differences account for more than 50% of the differences. One factor complicating research on gender differences in distress is the fact that women who are vulnerable to job stressors are more likely than men to select themselves out of the labor market or out of full-time employment (Roxburgh, 1996).

5. CONCLUSION

This chapter provides an overview of the major sociological literature on gender and work in industrial nations for three broad topical areas: patterns and rates of labor force participation, worker inputs, and worker outcomes. The recent proliferation of scholarship on these and other topics related to gender and work made it necessary to circumscribe coverage; thus, many relevant topics are not addressed. For example, a sizable literature on gender and particular occupations exists, both comparing women and men in the same occupations and examining differences among women in specific jobs. The range of studies is as broad as the spectrum of occupations, running the gamut from high-status professions such as medicine and law to clerical and lower-tier service sector occupations. Employing a mix of both qualitative and quantitative research methods, these studies both enrich our understanding of particular occupations and provide insight into the variable impact of gender on work experiences. Other topics also not addressed in this chapter include gender and technology in the workplace; gender, unions, and labor relations; and workplace harassment.

Despite the breadth of topics and the extensive scholarship on gender and work, comparative research on many topics is still quite limited. Recent years have seen an increase in cross-national research on gender and work, but more scholarship is needed to reconcile the varied findings of country-specific studies. Many characteristics of nations influence the relationship between gender and work—governmental structures, laws, social policies, cultural belief systems, location in the global economy, and history. Comparative research is required to understand better their role in shaping women's and men's work experiences and opportunities. Data comparability problems have traditionally limited researchers' ability to generate cross-national studies; fortunately, coordinated data collection efforts across nations and improvements in data collection and reporting techniques are occurring. This, combined with increased attention by sociologists to comparative research, bodes well for the future development of this important scholarship.

Ongoing global economic restructuring is affecting women and men workers in industrial nations, fueling the need for continued research on gender and work (Acker, 1992). As increased international competition slows economic growth, economic reform is undertaken to enhance private sector profitability and competitiveness. These reforms include policies focused on lowering inflation, increasing labor market flexibility, deregulation, and industrial restructuring. These trends need to be assessed and continually monitored to determine whether women and men workers are differentially affected by them. For example, there has been little research examining whether women have been more negatively affected than men by privatization and the contracting out of public sector services in many industrial nations (United Nations, 1995a).

In conclusion, the proliferating scholarship on gender and work is justified for the many reasons described in the beginning of this chapter and should continue into the future. Much has been learned about gender and work over the last several decades; much remains to be learned. Documenting gendered patterns in the workplace and exploring the causes of gender inequities are necessary steps toward providing remedies.

REFERENCES

Abbott, A. (1993). The sociology of work and occupations. *Annual Review of Sociology, 19,* 187–209.

Acker, J. (1989). *Doing comparable worth.* Philadelphia: Temple University Press.

Acker, J. (1992). The future of women and work: Ending the twentieth century. *Sociological Perspectives, 35,* 53–68.

Adler, W. J., & Izraeli, D. N. (1988). Women in management worldwide. In N. J. Adler & D. N. Izraeli (Eds.), *Women in management worldwide* (pp. 3-16). Armonk, NY: M. E. Sharpe.

Agassi, J. B. (1982). *Comparing the work attitudes of women and men.* Lexington, MA: D. C. Heath.

Almquist, E. M. (1995). The experiences of minority women in the United States: Intersections of race, gender, and class. In J. Freeman (Ed.), *Women: A feminist perspective* (pp. 573–606). Mountain View, CA: Mayfield.

Amott, T. L., & Matthaei, J. A. (1997). Race, class, gender, and women's work: A conceptual framework. In D. Dunn (Ed.), *Workplace/women's place: An anthology.* Los Angeles, CA: Roxbury.

Anderson, C. D., & Tomaskovic-Devey, D. (1995). Patriarchal pressures: An exploration of organizational processes that exacerbate and erode gender earnings inequality. *Work and Occupations, 22,* 328–356.

Anderson, M. L. (1988). *Thinking about women: Sociological perspectives on sex and gender.* New York: Macmillan.

Andrisani, P. J. (1978). Job satisfaction among working women. *Signs, 3,* 3.

Baca Zinn, M., & Eitzen, D. S. (1993). *Diversity in families.* New York: HarperCollins.

Baden, S. (1993). *The impact of recession and structural adjustment on women's work in developing and developed countries.* Working paper, Equality for women in employment, December. Geneva: ILO.

Bakker, I. (1996). Women's labor-force participation in advanced industrial countries. In P. J. Dubeck & K. Borman (Eds.), *Women and work: A handbook* (pp. 431–434). New York: Garland.

Berk, S. F. (1985). *The gender factory: The apportionment of work in American households.* New York: Plenum Press.

Betz, M., & O'Connell, L. (1989). Work orientations of males and females: Exploring the gender socialization approach. *Sociological Inquiry, 59,* 318–330.

Bielby, D. D., & Bielby, W. T. (1984). Work commitment, sex-role attitudes, and women's employment. *American Sociological Review, 49,* 234–247.

Blau, F. D., & Ferber, M. A. (1986). *The economics of women, men, and work.* Englewood Cliffs, NJ: Prentice Hall.

Blum, L. M. (1991). *Between feminism and labor.* Berkley, CA: University of California Press.

Booth, R. (1991). Power talk: Perceptions of women's and men's career potential in organizations. Unpublished doctoral dissertation. University of Kentucky, Lexington.

Bose, C. E., & Rossi, P. H. (1983). Gender and jobs: Prestige standings of occupations as affected by gender. *American Sociological Review, 48,* 316–330.

Chafetz, J. S. (1984). *Sex and advantage: A comparative macro-structural theory of sex stratification.* Totawa, NJ: Rowman & Allanheld.

Chafetz, J. S. (1990). *Gender equity: An integrated theory of stability and change.* Newbury Park, CA: Sage.

Chafetz, J. S. (1997). I need a (traditional) wife!: Employment-family conflicts. In D. Dunn & D. V. Waller (Eds.), *Analyzing social problems* (pp. 6–15). Englewood Cliffs, NJ: Prentice Hall.

Charles, M. (1992). Cross-national variation in occupational sex segregation. *American Sociological Review, 57,* 483–502.

Clark, R., Ramsbey, T. W., & Adler, E. S. (1991). Culture, gender, and labor force participation: A cross-national study. *Gender & Society, 5,* 47–66.

Cleary, P. D., & Mechanic, D. (1983). Sex differences in psychological distress among married persons. *Journal of Health and Social Behavior, 24,* 111–121.

Colwill, N. L. (1993). Women in management: Power and powerlessness. In B. C. Long & S. E. Kahn (Eds.), *Women, work, and coping* (pp. 73–89). Montreal: McGill-Queen's University Press.

Corcoran, M., Duncan, G. J., & Ponza, M. (1984). Work experience, job segregation, and wages. In B. F. Reskin (Ed.), *Sex segregation in the workplace: Trends, explanations and remedies* (pp. 171–191). Washington, D.C.: National Academy Press.

Court, M. (1997). Removing macho management: Lessons from the field of education. In D. Dunn (Ed.), *Workplace/women's place* (pp. 198–219). Los Angeles, CA: Roxbury.

Coverman, S. (1988). Sociological explanations of the male-female wage gap: Individualist and structuralist theories. In A. H. Stromberg & S. Harkess (Eds.), *Women working: Theories and facts in perspective* (pp. 101–115). Mountain View, CA: Mayfield.

De Boer, L. & Seeborg, M. C. (1989). The unemployment rates of men and women. *Industrial and Labor Relations Review, 42,* 404–414.

Dobbins, G. H., & Platz, S. J. (1986). Sex differences in leadership: How real are they? *Academy of Management Review, 11,* 118–127.

Dubeck, P. J., & Borman, K. (1996). *Women and work: A handbook.* In Introduction. New York: Garland.

Dunn, D. (1997). *Workplace/women's place: An anthology.* Los Angeles, CA: Roxbury.

Dunn, D., & Waller, D. V. (1996). The feminization of poverty. In D. Dunn & D. V. Waller (Eds.), *Analyzing social problems* (pp. 125–127). Englewood Cliffs, NJ: Prentice Hall.

Eide, E. (1994). College major and changes in the gender wage gap. *Contemporary Economic Policy, 12,* 55–64.

Elizur, D. (1993). Gender and work values: a comparative analysis. *The Journal of Social Psychology, 134,* 201–212.

England, P. (1992). *Comparable worth: Theories and evidence.* New York: Aldine de Gruyter.

England, P. & Dunn, D. (1988). Evaluating work and comparable worth. *Annual Review of Sociology, 14,* 227–248.

England, P., & Farkas, G. (1986). *Households, employment and gender: A social, economic and demographic view.* New York: Aldine.

Epstein, C. (1991). Debate: Ways men and women lead. *Harvard Business Review,* Jan–Feb, 150–152.

Evans, S. M., & Nelson, B. J. (1989). *Wage justice.* Chicago: University of Chicago Press.

Evers, A., & Wintersberger, H. (1990). *Shifts in the welfare mix.* Boulder, CO: Westview.

Fairhurst, G. T. (1985). Male-female communication on the job: Literature review and commentary. In R. N. Bostrom (Ed.), *Communication research,* Vol. 9 (pp. 83–116). Newbury Park, CA: Sage.

Ferree, M. M. (1991). The gender division of labor in two-earner marriages. *Journal of Family Issues, 12,* 158–80.

Figart, D. M., & Lapidus, J. (1996). The impact of comparable worth on earnings inequality. *Work and Occupations, 23,* 297–318.

Fuller, R., & Schoenberger, R. (1991). The gender salary gap: Do academic achievement, internship experience, and college major make a difference? *Social Science Quarterly, 72,* 715–726.

Gerhart, B. (1990). Gender differences in current and starting salaries: The role of performance, college major and job title. *Industrial Labor Relations Review, 43,* 418–433.

Giele, J. Z. (1988). Gender and sex roles. In N. J. Smelser (Ed.), *Handbook of sociology* (pp. 291–323). Newbury Park, CA: Sage.

Glenn, E. N., & Feldberg, R. L. (1977). Degraded and deskilled: The proletarianization of clerical work. *Social Problems, 25,* 52–64.

Grahl, J., & Teague, P. (1989). Labor market flexibility in West Germany, Britain and France. *West European Politics, 12,* 91–111.

Gruneberg, M. M. (1979). *Understanding job satisfaction.* New York: John Wiley & Sons.

Haavio-Mannila, E. (1989). Gender segregation in paid and unpaid work. In R. Jallinoja (Ed.), *Changing patterns of European family life: A comparative analysis of 14 countries* (pp. 123–140). New York: Routledge.

Hall, R. (1983). Theoretical trends in the sociology of occupations. *Sociological Quarterly, 24,* 5–23.

Helgesen, S. (1990). *Women's ways of leading.* New York: Basic Books

Herz, D. E., & Wootton, B. H. (1996). Women in the workforce: An overview. In C. Costello & B. K. Krimgold (Eds.), *The American woman: 1996–97 women and work* (pp. 44–78). New York: W. W. Norton.

Higginbotham, E. (1994). Black professional women: Job ceilings and employment sectors. In M. Baca Zinn & B. T. Dill (Eds.), *Women of color in U.S. society* (pp. 113–131). Philadelphia: Temple University Press.

Hodson, R. (1989). Gender differences in job satisfaction. Why aren't women workers more dissatisfied? *Sociological Quarterly, 30,* 385–399.

Hoschschild, A. (1989). *The second shift.* New York: Viking.

International Labour Organization. (1992). *Yearbook of labor statistics.* Geneva: ILO.

International Labour Organization. (1994). *Equality for women in employment: An interdepartmental project.* Geneva: ILO.

Jacobs, J. A. (1996). Gender inequality and higher education. *Annual Review of Sociology, 22,* 153–185.

Jacobs, J. A. & Lim, S. T. (1992). Trends in occupational and industrial sex segregation in 56 countries, 1960–1980. *Work and Occupations, 19,* 450–486.

Janjic, M. (1985). Women's work in industrialized countries: An overview from the perspective of the international labor organization. In J. Farley (Ed.), *Women workers in fifteen countries* (pp. 1–12). Ithaca, NY: ILR Press.

Johnson, P. (1976). Women and power: Toward a theory of effectiveness. *Journal of Social Issues, 32,* 99–110.

Kanter, R. (1977). *Men and women of the corporation.* New York: Basic Books.

Karasek, R. A., & Theorell, T. (1990). *Healthy work: Stress, productivity, and the reconstruction of working life.* New York: Basic Books.

Kemp, A. A. (1994). *Women's work: Degraded and devalued.* Englewood Cliffs, NJ: Prentice Hall.

Lakoff, R. (1975). *Language and women's place.* New York: Harper & Row.

Lincoln, J. R., & Kalleberg, A. L. (1990). *Culture, control, and commitment: A study of work organization and work attitudes in the United States and Japan.* New York: Cambridge University Press.

Lorence, J. (1987a). A test of the "gender" and "job" models of sex differences in job involvement. *Social Forces, 66,* 121–142.

Lorence, J. (1987b). Subjective labor force commitment of U.S. men and women. *Social Science Quarterly, 68,* 45–60.

Lorence, J. (1992). Service sector growth and metropolitan occupational sex segregation. *Work and Occupations, 19,* 128–156.

Loscocco, K. A. (1990). Reactions to blue collar work. *Work and Occupations, 17,* 152–177.

Loscocco, K. A., & Spitze, G. (1991). The organizational context of women's and men's pay satisfaction. *Social Science Quarterly, 72,* 3–19.

Lueptow, L. B. (1980). Social change and sex role change in adolescent orientations toward life, work and achievement: 1964–1975. *Social Psychology Quarterly, 43,* 48–59.

Lueptow, L. B. (1996). Gender and orientation toward work. In P. Dubeck & K. Borman (Eds.), *Women and work: A handbook.* New York: Garland.

Maile, S. (1995). The gendered nature of managerial discourse: The case of a local authority. *Gender, Work and Organization, 2,* 76–87.

Mannheim, B. (1983). Male and female industrial workers: Job-satisfaction, work role centrality, and work place preference. *Work and Occupations, 10,* 413–436.

Mannheim, B. (1993). Gender and the effects of demographics, status, and work values on work centrality. *Work and Occupations, 20,* 35–22.

Marini, M. M. (1989). Sex differences in earnings in the United States. *Annual Review of Sociology, 15,* 343–380.

Marsden, P. V., Kalleberg, A. L., & Cook, C. R. (1993). Gender differences in organizational commitment. *Work and Occupations, 20,* 368–390.

Martin, J. K., & Shehan, C. L. (1989). Education and job satisfaction: The influences of gender, wage-earning status, and job values. *Work and Occupations, 16,* 184–199.

Marx, K. (1967). *Capital: A critique of political economy.* New York: International Publishing.

Marshall, J. (1984). *Women managers: Travellers in a male world.* Chichester: Wiley.

McGuire, G. M., & Reskin, B. F. (1993). Authority hierarchies at work: The impacts of race and sex. *Gender & Society, 7,* 487–506.

Menaghan, E. G. (1989). Role changes and psychological well-being: Variations in effects by gender and role repertoire. *Social Forces, 67,* 693–714.

Moen, P., & Smith, M. (1986). Women at work: Commitment and behavior over the life course. *Sociological Forum, 1,* 24-38.

Mortimer, J., & Lorence, J. (1979). Work experience and occupational value socialization: A longitudinal survey. *American Journal of Sociology, 84,* 1361–1385.

Murray, M. A., & Atkinson, T. (1981). Gender differences in correlations of job satisfaction. *Canadian Journal of Behavioral Sciences, 13*, 1.

Neil, C., & Snizek, W. E. (1987). Work values, job characteristics and gender. *Social Perspectives, 30*, 245–265.

Neil, C. C., & Snizek, W. E. (1988). Gender as a moderator of job satisfaction: A multivariate assessment. *Work and Occupations, 15*, 201–219.

Nermo, M. (1996). Occupational sex segregation in Sweden, 1968–1991. *Work and Occupations, 23*, 319–332.

Nielsen, J. M. (1990). *Sex and gender in society: Perspectives on stratification.* Prospect Heights, IL: Waveland Press.

Noble, B. P. (1995). The debate over labor difference. In A. G. Dorenkemp, J. F. McClymer, M. M. Moymihan, & A. C. Vadern (Eds.), *Images of women in American popular culture* (2nd ed.) (pp. 322–333). Orlando, FL: Harcourt Brace.

OECD. (1984). *The employment and unemployment of women in OECD countries.* Paris: OECD.

OECD. (1985). *The integration of women into the economy.* Paris: OECD.

OECD. (1988). *Employment outlook.* Paris: OECD.

OECD. (1993a). *A mirror to the future.* Papers presented at a follow-up conference to shaping structural change: The role of women. Paris: OECD

OECD. (1993b). *Employment outlook.* Paris: OECD.

OECD. (1993c). *Women and structural change in the 1990s.* Report by Gunther Schmid. Paris: OECD.

OECD. (1994). *Women and structural change: New perspectives.* Paris: OECD.

Ortiz, V. (1994). Women of color: A demographic overview. In M. Baca Zinn & B. T. Dill (Eds.), *Women of color in U.S. society* (pp. 13–40). Philadelphia: Temple University Press.

Polachek, S. (1981). Occupational self-selection: A human capital approach to sex differences in occupational structures. *Review of Economics and Statistics, 63*, 60–69.

Powell, G. (1990). One more time: Do female and male managers differ? *Academy of Management Executive, 4*, 3.

Reardon, K. K. (1997). Dysfunctional communication patterns in the workplace: Closing the gap between women and men. In D. Dunn (Ed.), *Workplace/women's place* (pp. 165–180). Los Angeles, CA: Roxbury.

Reskin, B. (1993). Sex segregation in the workplace. *Annual Review of Sociology, 19*, 241–270.

Reskin, B. F., & Ross, C. E. (1992). Jobs, authority, and earnings among managers: The continuing significance of sex. *Work and Occupations, 19*, 342–265.

Rexroat, C. (1992). Changes in the employment continuity of succeeding cohorts of young women. *Work and Occupations, 19*, 18–34.

Rogers, J. K. (1995). Just a temp: Experience and structure of alienation in temporary clerical employment. *Work and Occupations, 22*, 137–166.

Roos, P. A. (1985). *Gender & work: A comparative analysis of industrial societies.* Albany, NY: State University of New York Press.

Rosener, J. B. (1990). Ways women lead. *Harvard Business Review, 68*, 6.

Rosenfeld, R. A., & Kalleberg, A. L. (1990). A Cross-national comparison of the gender gap in income. *American Journal of Sociology, 96*, 69–106.

Rowe, R., & Snizek, W. E. (1995). Gender differences in work values: perpetuating the myth. *Work and Occupations, 22*, 215–229.

Roxburgh, S. (1996). Gender differences in work and well-being: Effects of exposure and vulnerability. *Journal of Health and Social Behavior, 37*, 265–277.

Ruggie, M. (1984). *The state and working women: A comparative study of Britain and Sweden.* Princeton, NJ: Princeton University Press.

Schor, J. B. (1991). *The overworked American: The unexpected decline of leisure.* New York: Basic Books.

Semyonov, M. (1980). The social context of women's labor force participation: A comparative analysis. *American Journal of Sociology, 86*, 534–550.

Shakeshaft, C. (1989). *Women in educational administration.* London: Sage.

Siegfried, W. D., MacFarlane, I., Graham, D. B., Moore, N. A., & Young, P. L. (1981). A re-examination of sex differences in job preferences. *Journal of Vocational Behavior, 18*, 30–42.

Sokoloff, N. (1987). What's happening to women's employment: Issues for women's labor struggles in the 1980s–1990s. In C. Bose, R. Feldberg, & N. Sokoloff (Eds.), *Hidden aspects of women's work* (pp. 95–115). New York: Praeger.

Sonnenfeld, J. A. (1991). Debate: Ways men and women lead. *Harvard Business Review,* Jan–Feb, 159–160.

Sorensen, E. (1994). *Comparable worth: Is it a worthy policy?* Princeton, NJ: Princeton University Press.

Steil, J. M. (1995). Supermoms and second shifts: Marital inequality in the 1990s. In J. Freeman (Ed.), *Women: A feminist perspective* (pp. 149–161). Mountain View, CA: Mayfield.

Steinberg, R. J. (1990). Social construction of skill: gender, power, and comparable worth. *Work and Occupations, 17,* 449–482.

Steinberg, R. J. (1992). Gendered instructions. *Work and Occupations, 19,* 387–423.

Stellman, J. M. (1977). *Women's work, women's health: Myths and realities.* New York: Pantheon.

Tannen, D. (1995). Talking from 9 to 5: Women and men in the workplace: Language, sex and power. New York: Avon.

Treiman, D. J. (1977). *Occupational prestige in comparative perspective.* New York: Academic.

Treiman, D. J., & Roos, P. A. (1983). Sex and earnings in industrial society: A nine-nation comparison. *American Journal of Sociology, 89,* 612–650.

Turner, R. J., Wheaton, B., & Lloyd, D. A. (1995). The epidemiology of social stress. *American Sociological Review, 60,* 104–125.

Tyree, A., & Hicks, R. (1988). Sex and second moment of occupational distributions. *Social Forces, 66,* 1028–1037.

Ulbrich, P. M. (1989). The determinants of depression in two-income marriages. *Journal of Marriage and Family, 50,* 121–131.

United Nations. (1985). *The economic role of women in the ECE region.* New York: United Nations.

United Nations. (1995a). *Women in a changing global economy: 1994 world survey on the role of women in development.* New York: United Nations.

United Nations. (1995b). *The world's women 1995: Trends and statistics.* New York: United Nations.

United Nations Development Programme (1992). *Human development report.* New York: Oxford University Press.

United Nations Development Programme (1995). *Human development report.* New York: Oxford University Press.

U.S. Bureau of the Census. (1990). Census of the population: CP-S-1, supplementary reports, detailed occupation and other characteristics from the EEO file for the states.

Wajcman, J. (1991). Patriarchy, technology, and conceptions of skill. *Work and Occupations, 18,* 29–45.

Ward, K. (1984). *Women in the world system: Its impact on status and fertility.* New York: Praeger.

World Bank. (1996). *World development report 1996: From plan to market.* New York: Oxford University Press.

Wright, E. O., Baxter, J., & Birkelund, G. E. (1995). The gender gap in workplace authority: A cross-national study. *American Sociological Review, 60,* 407–435.

Xu, W., & Leffler, A. (1992). Gender and race effects on occupational prestige, segregation, and earnings. *Gender & Society, 6,* 376–392.

Young, G., Fort, L., & Danner, M. (1996). Gender inequality in labor-force participation across nations. In P. J. Dubeck & K. Borman. *Women and work: A handbook* (pp. 434–439). New York: Garland Publishing.

Zavella, P. (1987). *Women's work and Chicano families: Cannery workers of the Santa Clara Valley.* Ithaca, NY: Cornell University Press.

CHAPTER 16

Sex, Race, and Ethnic Inequality in United States Workplaces

Barbara F. Reskin
Irene Padavic

The last third of twentieth century witnessed revolutionary reductions in sex and race inequality in the workplace. At the beginning of the 1960s, employers legally could refuse to hire people, assign them to jobs, and set their pay on the basis of their sex and race. The first signs of change were already present: married women had begun to catch up with their single sisters in their participation in the labor force, and African-Americans with their migration North were also pursuing different kinds of work from when they were in the South, especially women who were abandoning domestic work as other opportunities opened to them. But it took the Civil Rights Movement of the early 1960s, the Women's Liberation Movement of the late 1960s, and a series of federal and state laws to challenge the race and sex discrimination that were customary in the United States.

As we will see in this chapter, sex, race, and ethnic inequality persist in the kinds of paid work that people do, their advancement opportunities, and their earnings. We shall also see, however, indications of the erosion of these forms of inequality since 1970. We focus on two forms of employment inequality: the differential distribution of workers across occupations and jobs based on their sex, race, and ethnicity, and pay disparities associated with these characteristics. In a departure from most research, we consider three important bases of inequality: sex, race, and ethnicity. Although workers' sex, race, and ethnicity jointly affect their work experiences, few quantitative studies have simultaneously considered both sex and race, and only a handful of studies have examined the

BARBARA F. RESKIN • Department of Sociology, Harvard, University, Cambridge, Massachusetts 02138
IRENE PADAVIC • Department of Sociology, Florida State University, Tallahassee, Florida 32306-2011

Handbook of the Sociology of Gender, edited by Janet Saltzman Chafetz. Kluwer Academic/ Plenum Publishers, New York, 1999.

joint effects of sex, race, and ethnicity (see Reskin & Charles, 1997).[1] Within the constraints of the available research, we discuss the extent and causes of sex, race, and ethnic inequality in the workplace.

1. JOB SEGREGATION BY SEX, RACE, AND ETHNICITY

Workers are not distributed across jobs based solely on their qualifications and interests; their sex, race, and ethnicity exert strong effects on the industries and occupations in which they work and thus the jobs they hold.[2] Job segregation is the linchpin in workplace inequality because the relegation of different groups to different kinds of work both facilitates and legitimates unequal treatment. Segregation facilitates unequal treatment in part because the jobs to which women and people of color are assigned are inherently less desirable than those open to white Anglo men. In addition, jobs that are filled predominantly by women and perhaps by minorities are devalued because society devalues women and minorities. Segregation legitimates unequal treatment because both U.S. values and the law permit unequal pay for different work. For these reasons, segregation generates pay and status disparities between persons of different sexes and races.

At the beginning of the twentieth century, Asians, African-Americans, and white women were confined to a limited number of occupations. A straightforward indicator of the degree to which workers are segregated based on some characteristic is the index of segregation (Duncan & Duncan, 1955). The value of this index, which ranges from 0 to 100, indicates the proportion of one of two groups that would have to change to an occupation in which that group is underrepresented for the two groups to be identically distributed across occupations. As Fig. 16-1 shows, between 1900 and 1970, the index of occupational segregation hovered around 70 for women and men (Gross, 1968). In fact, the sexes and races were so segregated that until 1940 the U.S. Census Bureau treated census returns with atypical worker–occupation combinations, such as female train engineer, as errors (Conk, 1981, p. 69).[3] Sex and race discrimination gave white men a semimonopoly over most technical, managerial, and professional jobs until the middle 1960s.[4] Race discrimination confined most blacks to menial agricultural and service jobs, and custom and law closed all but a handful of occupations to women.[5]

After 1940, however, the occupational race segregation index declined among both sexes, from 44 to 24 for men and from 65 to 22 for women. Race segregation began declining at this time because the labor shortage brought on by World War II forced factories to hire blacks. The effect of these new opportunities was revolutionary for black

---

[1] Space limitations and limitations in available research preclude our considering other factors that influence workplace outcomes, such as social class, sexual orientation, or disability.

[2] An occupation is a collection of jobs involving similar activities within or across establishments (Bielby & Baron, 1986, p. 764). The 1990 census distinguished 503 detailed occupations. In contrast, a job is a specified position in an establishment in which workers perform particular activities (Bielby & Baron, 1986, p. 764). *The Dictionary of Occupational Titles* (U.S. Department of Labor, 1977) distinguishes more than 20,000 jobs.

[3] The Census Bureau instructed its coders in 1930, for example, to "look up any occupations which involve responsibility and high standing in the community, if the person is colored, Chinese, Japanese, or other" (quoted in Conk, 1981, p. 68).

[4] Exceptions were teaching, nursing, and social work for white women, and professsional jobs serving black clientele for blacks.

[5] Among the occupations that some state laws closed to women were bartending and street car conductor.

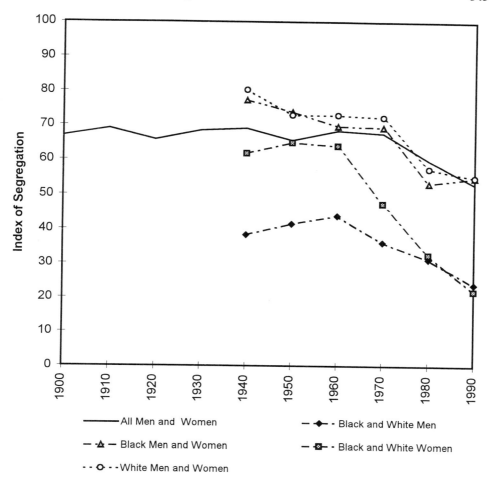

FIGURE 16-1. **Indicies of occupational sex and race segregation, 1900 to 1990.** (*Sources*: **Data from Gross, 1968, Table 2; Jacobs, 1989a, Table 2; Jacobsen, 1997; King, 1992, Chart 1; Reskin & Cassierer, 1996**).

women who formerly had few options apart from working in white people's homes.[6] In the 1970s, sex segregation also began declining. About one quarter of the drop in the segregation index was due to the shrinking proportion of the labor force working in occupations that were heavily sex segregated, such as heavy manufacturing, and the increasing proportion in occupations that were moderately integrated; the other three quarters resulted as women began integrating customarily male occupations, such as manager (Spain & Bianchi, 1996, Table 4.6). As a result, between 1970 and 1990 the index of occupational sex segregation fell from 67 to 53 (50.5 for blacks, 53.6 for whites, and 52.7 for Hispanics; Jacobs, 1989a; Reskin, 1994; additional computations from U.S. Bureau of the Census, 1992a). In 1990, to fully sex-integrate occupations would have required that 53% of all female workers—more than 32 million persons—shift to mostly male occupa-

---

[6] Despite the existence of better opportunities, some southern white women were able to hold on to their black cleaning women through the passage of local Work or Fight ordinances (Rollins, 1995, p. 163).

tions. Eliminating segregation among whites would have required that 25% of Asians (29% of men and 21% of women), 26.5% of African-Americans (28% of men and 25% of women), and 27% of Hispanics (29% of men and 24% of women) change occupations (Reskin, 1994; additional computations from U.S. Bureau of the Census, 1992a). To eliminate both sex and race segregation across occupations in 1990 would have required 60% of black women, 58% of Hispanic women, 53% of white women, and 30% of black and Hispanic men to shift to occupations in which white men predominated. Asians tend to be less segregated from same-sex whites than are blacks (Reskin, 1994).

Interpreting segregation indices as the proportion of members of a sex/race group that would have to change occupations is a convenient way of summarizing the extent of occupational segregation, but in reality such shifts would take generations under the best of conditions. In 1990, for example, almost 14 million black and white women—about one fifth of these women—held administrative-support occupations (in other words, they did clerical work) compared to 8% of black men and 5% of white men, while almost 19% of white men and 14% of black men held skilled blue-collar jobs, compared to 2% of both white and black women (U.S. Bureau of Labor Statistics, 1997, Table 10). To bring women's representation in administrative-support and skilled blue-collar occupations in line with that of white men would have meant the transfer of more than 10 million female clerical workers to skilled blue-collar occupations.

Regardless of their race, most women work in predominantly female occupations. Of the 57 million women in the labor force in 1990, one third worked in just 10 of the 503 detailed occupations (U.S. Bureau of Labor Statistics, 1996a),[7] and only one woman in nine pursued an occupation that was at least 75% male (Kraut & Luna, 1992, p. 3). Men likewise remain concentrated in predominately male occupations: one quarter of the 69 million men in the labor force worked in just 10 occupations in 1990. Only two occupations appeared on both sex's top 10 list: "manager or administrator, not elsewhere classified" and "sales supervisor or proprietor" (U.S. Bureau of Labor Statistics, 1996a), and these two heterogeneous categories conceal substantial job-level sex segregation. The large number of women working as managers, administrators, sales supervisors, and proprietors are disproportionately white. Neither manager or administrator (not elsewhere classified), nor sales supervisor or proprietor was among the five largest occupations for black women or Latinas (or Latinos) in 1995 (see Table 16-1). Except for black female nurses, none of the occupations that employed large numbers of Hispanic or black women or men were professional or managerial.[8] Black women were overrepresented in just a few professional occupations—dietitian, educational or vocational counselor, and social worker in 1995 (computed from U.S. Bureau of Labor Statistics, 1996a). Hispanic men and women were underrepresented in all professions (U.S. Bureau of the Census, 1996b, Table 637). Most of the top five occupations for black and Hispanic women and men involved cleaning or personal service (maid, private household servant, janitor, cook, gardener, nursing aide); a few involved unskilled labor (farm worker, laborer; see Table 16-1).

Ethnicity also affects workers' occupational outcomes. For example, Filipina, Ameri-

[7] The most common lines of work for women in 1990 are all but identical to those that employed the most women in 1940. The only recent addition to women's top 10 occupations is the census category "miscellaneous salaried managers."

[8] African-American female professionals were concentrated in two customarily female professions—nursing and elementary school teaching (computed from U.S. Bureau of Labor Statistics, 1995), Asian-American women were concentrated in only one profession—accounting.

TABLE 16-1. Top Occupations for Black, Hispanic, and White Women and Men, 1995

White Women	Number	%	White Men	Number	%
Secretary	2942	6.1	Manager, n.e.c*	4503	7.7
Manager, n.e.c.*	1741	3.6	Sales, supervisor, proprietor	2483	4.3
Cashier	1709	3.5	Truck driver	2301	4.0
Registered nurse	1600	3.3	Engineer	1593	2.7
Sales, supervisor, proprietor	1566	3.2	Vehicle mechanic	1516	2.6
Total labor force	48344	100.0	Total labor force	58146	100.0

Black Women	Number	%	Black Men	Number	%
Nursing aide, orderly	482	7.0	Truck driver	352	5.5
Cashier	349	5.1	Janitor	267	4.2
Cook	166	2.4	Manager, n.e.c.*	198	3.1
Maid	151	2.2	Cook	187	2.9
Registered nurse	150	2.2	Laborer, except construction	159	2.5
Total labor force	6857	100.0	Total labor force	6422	100.0

Hispanic Women	Number	%	Hispanic Men	Number	%
Secretary	210	4.8	Truck driver	285	4.2
Cashier	205	4.7	Farm worker	279	4.1
Private household servent	130	3.0	Janitor	267	4.0
Janitor	128	2.9	Cook	263	3.9
Nursing aid, orderly	126	2.9	Gardener	196	2.9
Total labor force	4403	100.0	Total labor force	6725	100.0

Note: Blacks and whites include people of Hispanic origin.
*The abbreviation "n.e.c." refers to occupations that are not elsewhere classified.
Source: Unpublished tabulations of 1995 Current Population Survey data by the U.S. Bureau of Labor Statistics (1997).

can Indian, and Puerto Rican women resembled black women in that nursing aide was among their top three occupations in 1995. Among the top three occupations for Central American, Chinese, Cuban, Korean, and Southeast Asian women was textile operative. The top three occupations for Mexican and Central American women and for Puerto Rican, Mexican, and Southeast Asian men included janitor (the second largest occupation for black men). Cook was among the top three occupations for Japanese, Chinese, Filipino, Southeast Asian, and Central American men, as it was for black women (computed from the U.S. Bureau of Labor Statistics, 1996a).[9] All recent data on race and sex workplace segregation are for occupations—a category that combines jobs involving similar activities in the same and in different establishments (Bielby & Baron, 1986, p. 764). Thus, most nominally sex or racially integrated occupations include predominantly female and male specialties (Bielby & Baron, 1984). For example, although the occupation of real estate sales has become sex integrated, women are concentrated in residential sales, while men dominate the more lucrative commercial sales (Reskin & Roos, 1990). Occupational specialties may be differentiated as well by workers' race and ethnicity. For example, black workers tend to hold jobs in which they are more intensely supervised than are white workers in the same occupation (Tomaskovic-Devey, 1993, p. 148). Often members of different race/sex groups perform the same occupation in different establish-

[9] It was the fourth largest occupation for black and Hispanic men.

ments or even different parts of the country (Reskin, 1997c). Although declining occupational sex and race segregation signals some job-level integration, the extent of job segregation far exceeds measured levels of occupational segregation (Peterson & Morgan, 1995). In general, women and people of color—regardless of their sex—are underrepresented in desirable and lucrative jobs and disproportionately concentrated in low-status, low-paying service jobs.

1.1. Hierarchical Segregation

Because the desirability of the jobs in which group members are concentrated is positively correlated with the social status of the race/sex group, job segregation is often expressed hierarchically, with women and people of color concentrated in the lower ranks within occupations and organizations and white men dominating the top positions. Hierarchical segregation—by which we mean the segregation of workers across different ranks in the same job (e.g., assistant manager versus manager)—consigns members of favored groups to jobs that are higher in occupational or organizational hierarchies and hence confer more status, authority, and pay. Thus, hierarchical segregation further exacerbates the earnings and authority gaps (McGuire & Reskin, 1993; Reskin & Ross, 1992).[10] Hierarchical segregation—as expressed in the differential distribution of the races and sexes across vertical levels within organizations or occupations—includes both "glass ceilings" that exclude minorities and women from the top jobs in organizations and "sticky floors" that confine women and minorities—especially women of color—to low-ranking jobs (Berheide, 1992). A mere handful of minorities and women have reached the top of corporate hierarchies. In 1990, only five of the 1000 CEOs listed in the *Business Week* 1000 were nonwhite, and only 2.6% of senior managers in nine Fortune 500 companies that the U.S. Department of Labor studied were not white (Bell & Nkomo, 1994). In 1995, only 57 (2.4%) of the 2430 top officers in Fortune 500 companies were women (Catalyst, 1996). Other work settings show variations on this theme. In 1990, one in 11 partners in large law firms was female, compared to one in three associates (Epstein, 1993). Although corporate sales offer a fast track to management, only one in seven saleswomen get beyond the level of district manager (Catalyst, 1996). While women held half of all federal government jobs in 1992, only one quarter of supervisors and only 10% of senior executives were women, and fewer than 2% of senior executives were minority women (U.S. Merit Systems Protection Board, 1992, p. 33). Even in traditionally female occupations such as librarian or social worker, men advance more rapidly than women (Williams, 1995).

Minorities' and women's representation in managerial jobs offers a summary indicator of hierarchical segregation. Women and people of color remain underrepresented in management compared to white men, although the disparities have been shrinking since 1970. In 1990, almost 13.1% of non-Hispanic white workers held managerial jobs (14.1% of men, 11.8% of women), compared to 12.3 percent of Asians and Pacific Islanders (13.4% of men, 11.1% of women), 7.9% of Native American groups (7.2% of men, 8.7%

[10] Even women in high-level positions seldom have as much authority as men at the same level (Reskin & Ross, 1992). For example, McGuire and Reskin (1993) found that if black and female workers had received the same authority returns to their experience and other credentials as white men, the authority gap with white men would have shrunk by 62% for white women, 71% for black women, and 93% for black men.

of women), 7.3% of African-American workers (6.6% of men, 7.4% of women), and 6.5% of Hispanics (6.2% of men, 7.0% of women; U.S. Bureau of the Census, 1992b, Table 2). Although the representation of African Americans has been increasing, as Fig. 16-2 shows, African-American men's progress stalled during the 1980s, and by 1990 African-American women were more likely to work in managerial occupations than African-American men.

While the trends depicted in Fig. 16-2 show marked progress, we must remember that women and minorities tend to be low- rather than high-level managers. It is white male managers who usually have the final say in important decisions such as hiring, firing, promotions, raises, and issues that affect other units. A study comparing the sexes' roles in decision-making found that female mangers' input was more often to provide information or make recommendations while male managers more often made final decisions (Reskin & Ross, 1992). Indeed, other evidence indicates that women and minorities are ghettoized into less desirable managerial jobs that white men eschew (Collins, 1989, p. 329; Reskin & McBrier, 1998). In addition, these and other findings suggest that some of women's and minorities' gains in managerial occupations represent "job-title inflation"—managerial titles without managerial authority—in response to increased federal scrutiny (Smith & Welch, 1984).

The patterns by sex and race in Fig. 16.2 depart from the tendency for the effect of sex to exceed that of race that holds for occupational segregation and therefore for earnings. This departure probably reflects employers' practice of selecting managers of the same or a more highly esteemed sex and race than the workers who will be their subordinates.

Group differences in promotion rates also indicate hierarchical segregation. In the early 1990s, whites were twice as likely as blacks to have been promoted and men were almost twice as likely as women to have been promoted, after taking into account education, training, experience, and type of firm (Baldi & McBrier,1997; see also Kalleberg & Reskin, 1995). In eight New York law firms, male associates were three times as likely as female associates to be promoted to partner (American Bar Association, 1996). In 1995, minority women were less likely to be promoted than white women with equivalent experience, although minority men in the federal government were promoted at the same rate as white men (U.S. Merit Systems Protection Board, 1996).

1.2. Explaining Sex and Race Segregation

Workers' sex and race are linked to the kinds of jobs they do because of employers' and workers' characteristics, preferences, and actions. However, some explanations for the relationship between workers' ascriptive characteristics and their jobs differ for race and sex. Explanations for segregation in general, and hierarchical segregation in particular, emphasize workers' characteristics and preferences—"supply-side" explanations—by assuming a two-step process: (1) people decide the kind of work they want to do, and (2) they obtain the necessary credentials. These explanations treat getting a job in one's preferred line of work as nonproblematic. Supply-side explanations for sex segregation tend to stress the first step in this process—work preferences, whereas supply-side explanations for race segregation emphasize the second step—obtaining qualifications. We review supply-side explanations first for sex segregation and then for race segregation. We then review explanations that emphasize employers' characteristics, preferences, and actions.

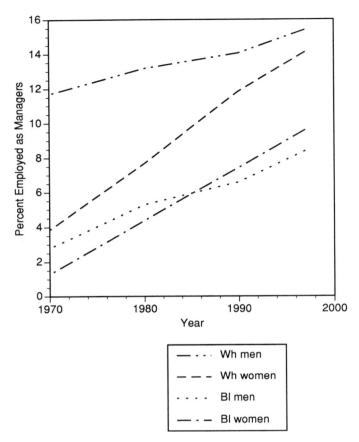

FIGURE 16-2. Percent in managerial employment, by sex and race, 1970 to 1997. (*Sources*: Data from U.S. Bureau of the Census, 1972, Table 2; 1982; U.S. Bureau of Labor Statistics, 1998.)

1.2.1. WORKERS' CHARACTERISTICS AND PREFERENCES.   The sexes are concentrated in different kinds of work, according to supply-side approaches, because women and men prefer different kinds of jobs. Social scientists have proposed two reasons the sexes' preferences differ. According to a socialization perspective, men and women pursue different kinds of jobs because gender-role socialization induces in them different life goals; instills in them different values regarding the importance of occupational success, autonomy, or high earnings; teaches them different skills; fosters different personality traits; and induces a distaste for sex-atypical activities and for working with members of the other sex (Marini & Brinton, 1984; see Chafetz, Chapter 1, *this volume*). To the extent that gender-role socialization has these effects, the kinds of jobs that attract men should disinterest women and vice versa.

Although gender-role socialization may incline young people toward jobs that society labels as appropriate for their sex (Subich, Barrett, Doverspike, & Alexander, 1989), young people's occupational aspirations are both quite unstable and unrelated to the occupations they hold as adults (Jacobs,1989b). Moreover, adults—especially women—move between predominantly female and predominantly male occupations (Jacobs, 1989b).

Despite gender-role socialization—and readers must bear in mind that no systematic data compare the socialization of contemporary women and men—the sexes tend to value the same job rewards: good pay, autonomy, and prestige (Jencks, Perman, & Rainwater, 1988; Marini, Fan, Finley, & Beutel, 1996). With respect to vertical segregation, women are as likely as men to value promotions (Markham, Harlan, & Hackett, 1987, p. 227). These and other findings suggest that early gender-role socialization is not an important cause of job segregation. Far more influential are the opportunities, social pressures, and social rewards workers face as adults (Reskin & Hartmann, 1986).

The neoclassical economic perspective, another supply-side approach, assumes that occupational preferences are sex differentiated as a result of women's and men's conscious decisions to maximize household well-being. Hypothetically, in response to their different roles in the sexual division of labor, men and women pursue different employment strategies. Men's role as primary breadwinner induces them to maximize their earnings by pursuing jobs that pay well and reward experience and by maximizing the amount of time they spend doing paid work. Women's primary responsibility for homemaking and child-rearing and their recognition that their husbands will earn enough to adequately support the family hypothetically lead women to select jobs that are compatible with domestic duties, both in scheduling and ease of reentry after time out of the labor force (see, e.g., Polachek, 1981). If women can rely on economic support by their husbands, they can eschew lucrative jobs that require overtime, continuous labor force participation, and the exertion of considerable effort, thereby reducing conflict between paid and family work. In anticipation of their differential involvement in labor-market and family work, this approach also assumes that men invest in more education and training than women, making them more qualified for jobs that require skills.

Most research evidence is inconsistent with the neoclassical explanation of sex segregation. First, researchers have found that single women are as likely as married women to work in predominantly female occupations (Reskin & Hartmann, 1986, p.71–72). In any event, women who plan to leave the labor force to have children earn more in customarily male than female jobs. Second, predominantly male and female occupations require similar levels of education and skills (England, Chassie, & McCormack, 1982), and most workers acquire their skills on the job. Contrary to the neoclassical theory, women are more likely than men to obtain training before employment (Amirault, 1992). Thus, there is little evidence that men's and women's concentration in different jobs results from their responses to their anticipated or actual family roles. The human-capital account of occupational sex segregation is problematic on other counts as well. If women place family responsibilities ahead of their careers, they should evidence less job commitment than men; yet women's commitment does not differ from men's (Marsden, Kalleberg, & Cook, 1993). Women also expend as much energy on their jobs as men do (in fact, net of family responsibilities, women expend more effort on the job than men; Bielby & Bielby, 1988). Both sexes aspire to advance at work and will work hard for a promotion (Markham et al., 1987; Reskin & Cassirer, 1996). Compared to 74% of male federal employees, 78% of women (and 86% of minority women) were willing to devote as much time as necessary to advance in their career (U.S. Merit Systems Protection Board, 1992).[11] Finally, the characteristics of predominantly female jobs are not especially compatible with stereotypical female domestic roles: jobs in predominantly female occupations are no more flexible, easier, or cleaner than those in predominantly male occupations (Glass, 1990, p.

---

[11] The publication did not report the proportion of minority men who were willing to work hard for a promotion.

791; Jacobs & Steinberg, 1990). Two types of evidence are consistent with the neoclassical explanation of sex segregation. First, women are more likely than men to work part-time (in 1990, 22.4% of women and 7.6% of men worked part-time; computed from U.S. Bureau of the Census, 1992a), and part-time employment is associated with higher levels of occupational sex segregation. Second, sex differences in college majors are consistent with the neoclassical explanation (Jacobs, 1995). For example, women earned 47% of the bachelor's degrees in business administration in 1992, but only 34% of the master's degrees. Also, the greater workers' education, the less segregated the sexes are. In 1990, the index of sex segregation was considerably lower for college graduates than for high school graduates: 16.5 points lower for blacks and 18.5 points lower for whites (computed from U.S. Bureau of the Census, 1992a; see also Jacobsen, 1997, p. 235). Nonetheless, we must be careful not to overstate the effect of education on sex segregation. Even among college graduates, the sex segregation index is 38 for blacks and 44 for whites.

The occupational preferences of men and women might differ for a reason unrelated to their domestic roles: people pursue jobs that they believe are available to them (Reskin & Hartmann, 1986; Schultz, 1991, p. 141). Prospective workers do not apply for jobs unless they have reason to expect that they might be hired. Just as the sex-segregated help-wanted ads, common before the enactment of Title VII of the 1964 Civil Rights Act, steered workers into sex-typical lines of work, the sex and race composition of jobs signal would-be employees whether they have a reasonable chance of being hired and being accepted by co-workers. Minorities and women who are pioneers in occupations typically reserved for white men often encounter resistance—heckling, sabotage, and worse—by supervisors, co-workers, or customers (Bergmann & Darity, 1981, Padavic, 1991a; Schroedel, 1985; Swerdlow, 1989; U.S. Department of Labor, 1996), contributing to the "revolving door" that returns women to sex-typical occupations (Jacobs, 1989b). When employers make customarily male jobs genuinely accessible to women and mostly white occupations accessible to minorities, the attractiveness of these jobs draws plenty of women and minorities (Reskin & Hartmann, 1986; Reskin & Roos, 1990).

The neoclassical approach to race segregation emphasizes workers' qualifications rather than their preferences. Blacks and Latinos/as have less education and job experience than whites (England, Christopher, & Reid, 1997; Kilbourne, England, & Beron, 1994a, Table 1). Increasing parity in educational quality and quantity appear to have contributed to the occupational integration of black and white women between 1940 and 1990 (King, 1992). For example, in 1990 the segregation index for black and white women was 10 points lower for college graduates than for high school graduates (King, 1992; additional computations from U.S. Bureau of the Census, 1992a). However, men's educational attainment had little effect on the extent of race segregation—the index of race segregation for male high school graduates was 28.2; for college graduates it was 25.4 (computed from U.S. Bureau of the Census, 1992a). Also, 1990 census data indicate that race and ethnic differences in educational attainment—as well as nativity and English fluency—played only minor roles in occupational segregation by race and ethnicity (Reskin, 1997a).

In sum, the neoclassical approach is consistent with white males' concentration in customarily male occupations and their underrepresentation in predominantly female occupations: white men—whose options are not limited by discrimination—pursue the most desirable jobs and eschew predominantly female jobs because they pay less and offer fewer opportunities for advancement. However, the value of neoclassical approach for explaining women's and minorities' concentration in some occupations and underrepresentation in others is limited and largely inconsistent with our understanding of how workers get jobs.[12]

1.2.2. EMPLOYERS' PREFERENCES AND PRACTICES.

A major reason women and minorities are concentrated in different jobs than white men is because employers prefer persons of different sexes and races for different jobs. They do so because of their stereotypes and biases and out of deference to their customers' or employees' biases. Employers also segregate workers as a result of superficially neutral employment practices.

One reason employers consider sex and race in filling jobs is out of loyalty to their own group—usually white men. Although little research has focused explicitly on the segregative effects of in-group preference, several studies suggest its importance for the degree of segregation in organizations. First, the sex and race of decision-makers affect their responses to members of their own group and other groups. For example, having a female agency head was associated with progress toward sex integration in California state agencies (Baron, Mittman, & Newman, 1991). In addition, a review of more than 70 studies found that evaluators rated same-race persons higher than other-race persons (Kraiger & Ford, 1985). Second, the nepotism characteristic of small firms and some industries such as construction is, of course, for one's own group (Waldinger & Bailey, 1991), and its effect is segregative. Third, a shortage of white male workers is a major reason firms employ female and minority workers in customarily white-male occupations (Padavic & Reskin, 1990; Reskin & Roos, 1990). Fourth, by restricting cronyism—that is, in-group favoritism—formalized personnel practices appear to have reduced job segregation (Dobbin, Sutton, Meyer, & Scott, 1993).

According to several recent studies, race and sex stereotyping and bias contribute to sex segregation. For example, comparisons of the job-search outcomes of white-minority pairs in "audit" studies in four cities revealed that white men were substantially more likely to receive job offers than their minority matches (Fix & Struyk, 1992).[13] Qualitative studies in several cities reveal the reasons for the patterns from the audit studies. Employers, most of whom are white men, frankly admit their reluctance to hire black workers based on their stereotypes of blacks as lazy, unintelligent, insubordinate, and prone to criminal acts (Bobo, 1996; Holzer, 1996; Kasinitz & Rosenberg, 1996; Moss & Tilly, 1996; Neckerman & Kirschenman, 1991; Smith, 1990; Wilson, 1996, Chapter 5). The refusal of some employers to hire minorities or their willingness to hire them for only menial jobs inevitably segregates the races. Stereotypes also restrict women's employment opportunities. Stereotyped as unable to do physically demanding jobs, lacking career commitment, and disinterested in advancement (Bielby & Baron, 1986; Fiske, Bersoff, Bogida, Deaux, & Heilman, 1991; Reskin & Padavic, 1988; Segura, 1992, p. 173; Williams & Best, 1986), women are excluded from rewarding white-collar and blue-collar jobs.

Sex and race stereotypes affect hiring and promotion decisions through statistical discrimination, a process in which employers impute to individuals stereotyped or actual attributes of the group to which the individual belongs to avoid the cost of screening applicants' qualifications (Bielby & Baron, 1986; Braddock & McPartland, 1987; Holzer,

---

[12] Few job seekers have their choice of jobs; most receive only one or two offers and accept the first offer that meets their minimum acceptable pay (Gera & Hasan, 1982; Kahn, 1978).

[13] An audit of sex discrimination found that more expensive restaurants favored males as server, whereas cheaper ones favored women (Newmark, Bank, & Van Nort, 1995).

1996, pp. 83, 103; Messick & Mackie, 1989; Williams & Best, 1986). Employers' and supervisors' stereotypes also bias their evaluations of women and minorities, thus reducing their chances for promotion (Baron & Bielby, 1985, p. 243; Eagly, Makhijani, & Klonsky, 1992, p. 14; Fiske et al., 1991, p. 1050). Evaluation bias leads supervisors to evaluate whites and men more positively than equally qualified blacks and women (Greenhaus & Parasuraman, 1993; Greenhaus, Parasuraman, & Wormley, 1990, Table 1; Pulakos, White, Oppler, & Borman, 1989; Sackett, Dubois, & Noe, 1991, p. 265;), in part because they hold the latter groups to higher standards (Cox & Nkomo, 1986).[14] Hiring and promotion practices that rely on informal networks are highly subjective, and the more subjective the evaluation, the greater the risk of bias (Braddock & McPartland, 1987, p. 22; Deaux, 1984; Deaux, 1985; Eagly & Wood, 1982; Pettigrew & Martin 1987, pp. 55–58). Queuing models provide a theoretical approach to the effect of employers' race and sex preferences for workers—as expressed in their ordering of the labor queue (Lieberson, 1980, p. 296; Reskin & Roos, 1990; Thurow, 1969, p. 48). According to a queuing approach to occupational segregation, the higher workers stand in labor queues, the greater their access to jobs near the top of job queues. As low-ranked groups, women and minorities obtain access to jobs usually filled with white men when those jobs become less attractive to white men compared to their alternatives. This approach makes sense of the different distributions of the sexes and races across different industries and occupations. For example, white men are overrepresented in the private sector, the highest-paying sector, leaving public-sector and government jobs for women and minorities (historically the only place outside the black community where African-Americans could find work as managers and professionals; Higginbotham, 1987; U.S. Merit Systems Protection Board, 1996).

Regardless of their source—in-group preference, out-group antipathy, stereotypes, or biases—race and sex discrimination significantly restrict workers' options. The large number of formal complaints to antidiscrimination agencies, in combination with employers' candid reports of their stereotypes, suggest that discrimination is widespread: The federal government received more than 91,000 such complaints in 1994 (Leonard, 1994, p. 24; U.S. Department of Labor, 1996).[15] When enforced, antidiscrimination laws, such as Title VII of the 1964 Civil Rights Act (which banned employment discrimination based on race, national origin, or sex) and affirmative action requirements for federal contractors, opened thousands of semiskilled and skilled blue- and white-collar jobs to black men and women (Burstein, 1979, 1985; Donohue & Heckman, 1991; Heckman & Payner, 1989; for a review, see Badgett & Hartmann, 1995). Federal scrutiny helps to reduce sex and race segregation. The requirement by the Equal Employment Opportunity Commission (EEOC; the agency charged with enforcing Title VII) that firms with at least 50 employees annually report employees' distribution across broad occupational categories by race and sex has been an incentive for employers to place more women and minorities in managerial and administrative jobs. Thus, in 1960, 2% of black women, 4% of black men, and 5.5% of white women worked in the broad occupation of managers; by 1996, 9.6% of black women, 8.3% of black men, and 14% of white women were managers (U.S. Bureau of Labor Statistics, 1961, 1997, Table 10).

Recent history shows that when the government enforces antidiscrimination and

[14] Employers in the suburbs, who hire mostly white workers, have lower standards than those in the central city, who draw more heavily on minorities (Holzer, 1996).
[15] Approximately 3% charged "reverse discrimination" (Bendick, 1996; Blumrosen, 1995).

affirmative-action regulations, minorities' and women's representation in sex- and race-atypical occupations increases (Ashenfelter & Heckman, 1976; Leonard, 1984a, b). More generally, sanctioning discriminating employers reduces job segregation (Badgett & Hartmann, 1995; Martin, 1991; Leonard, 1994, p. 21; Reskin & Roos, 1990). The uneven enforcement of the affirmative action required of federal contractors by Presidential Executive Order 11246 (11374) provided a natural experiment. During the 1980s, when there was no presidential mandate to enforce the executive order, minorities were more poorly represented at federal contractors than at noncontractors (Leonard, 1994), suggesting that federal contractors had reverted to the discriminatory practices that had prompted President Nixon to issue the executive order in the first place. Without the threat of governmental intervention, most employers do business as usual, which means making hiring and promotion decisions that are influenced by sex and race biases (Kern, 1996; Leonard, 1994).

1.2.3. STRUCTURAL DISCRIMINATION.   Employers' personnel practices—even those that seem to be race and gender neutral—nonetheless affect race and sex segregation in firms. The clearest example is filling jobs through referrals by current workers. This common recruiting practice perpetuates segregation because workers' social networks tend to be sex and race segregated (Marsden, 1994, p. 983). In contrast, open-recruitment techniques, such as posting all job openings, can reduce segregation by allowing everyone to learn of sex- and race-atypical jobs.

Requiring credentials that are more common among white men than women and minorities also contributes to segregation. Sometimes segregation itself prevents women and minorities from acquiring qualifications. For example, the military's past exclusion of women from combat positions has blocked their advancement in military careers (Williams, 1989, p. 51). Analogously, blacks' exclusion from apprenticeship programs has kept them out of well-paying unionized craft jobs. Required credentials also can disproportionately affect women and minorities because employers more frequently exempt white men than others from formal requirements (Baron & Bielby, 1985, p. 243).

Pervasive sex segregation has prompted employers to organize work schedules and the labor process on the assumption that men will do some jobs and women will do others. The result can be barriers to women performing some customarily male jobs. For example, most machinery is designed to accommodate white, Anglo men. As a result, people who are shorter than the average white, Anglo man—including many women and some Latino and Asian men—cannot operate it safely or efficiently. Some companies design plant jobs so that workers rotate across different shifts—day, evening, and graveyard—which can discourage women from these jobs by making childcare arrangements difficult (Padavic, 1991b).

Segregated entry-level jobs maintain hierarchical segregation by disproportionately concentrating women and minorities in jobs with limited opportunity for mobility because they are on short ladders, restrict workers' opportunity to acquire skills, and lack visibility (Marsden, 1994, p. 983).[16] Firms tend to employ female and minority managers in staff positions, such as personnel or public relations, while male managers are concen-

---

[16] Many employers adhere to what Bermann (1986, pp. 114–116) called an "informal segregation code" that prohibits women from supervising men and reserves the training slots leading to higher-level jobs for men. Men rule over women and junior men, women rule over women, but women rarely if ever rule over men. This code applies to minorities as well: minorities may give orders to other minorities, but not to whites.

trated in organizationally central line positions, such as sales, finance, and production, from which senior managers are selected. Employers often assign African-Americans to positions that deal with other minorities, such as community relations or affirmative action, regardless of their areas of expertise (Collins, 1989, p. 329, 1997). While staff positions provide few opportunities for workers to display their abilities, complex and challenging line jobs give incumbents a chance to develop and display their skills, such as exercising authority, supervising subordinates, or dealing with difficult situations (Bell & Nkomo, 1994, p. 39; Tomaskovic-Devey, 1994). Thus the segregation of minorities and women into nonchallenging jobs reduces their chances of being promoted by restricting their chances to acquire or demonstrate skills (Erdreich, Slavet, & Amador, 1996, p. xiii).

Minorities' and women's relegation to dead-end or short-ladder jobs is critical for hierarchical segregation (Bell & Nkomo, 1994, pp. 32, 39; Collins, 1989, 1997). To improve advancement opportunities for clerical and service workers, some companies have created "bridge" positions that help workers to switch job ladders—for example, move from a clerical job ladder to a production or administrative one—without risk or penalty (Kanter, 1976; Northrup & Larson, 1979; Roos & Reskin, 1984). Seniority systems can also affect the amount of hierarchical segregation in an organization (Kelley, 1984). For instance, USX (formerly U.S. Steel) helped to integrate customarily male production jobs by altering its seniority rules to allow workers to transfer to plant jobs without losing their seniority (Reskin & Hartmann, 1986, p. 93; Ullman & Deaux, 1981). Other case studies also demonstrate that organizations can eliminate structural barriers that exclude women and minorities from jobs (Badgett, 1995; Deaux & Ullman, 1983; DiTomaso, 1993; Northrup & Larson, 1979).

The segregation of women and men into different kinds of establishments also contributes to hierarchical segregation. The sheer size of large organizations lets them create more opportunities to promote workers, and they are more likely to have job ladders (Kalleberg, Marsden, Knoke, & Spaeth, 1996). Therefore, women's concentration in small, entrepreneurial firms and nonprofit organizations and men's concentration in large corporations and for-profit companies reduce women's odds of promotion relative to men (Kalleberg & Reskin, 1995). Some industries are better than others in promoting women. In female-intensive industries such as apparel, banking, retail trade, and insurance, women are more likely to be high-level managers (Shaeffer & Lynton, 1979). For instance, in 1990 women were only 2.2% of the officers in the chemicals industry, but 10% of the officers in the apparel industry. Although only five percent of the directors in the electronics industry were women in the late 1980s, almost 17% of the directors in the cosmetics and soap industries were (Von Glinow, 1988). Why do women have greater access to high-level jobs in female-dominated industries? Jobs in female-intensive industries pay less and are thus less desirable to men. Furthermore, firms' experience with female workers makes them less likely to stereotype women.

In sum, workplace segregation is largely due to employers' use of workers' sex, race, and ethnicity in assigning workers to jobs because of stereotypes and outright bias. Pressure from regulatory agencies, internal constituencies, and the public has prompted some employers to reduce stereotyping and bias by replacing informal personnel practices, such as word-of-mouth hiring, with formal ones, such as advertising and posting all openings, reassessing the qualifications jobs require, and using objective criteria for hiring and promotion (Roos & Reskin 1984; Szafran, 1982).

2. SEX, RACE, AND EARNINGS

White men outearn men of color and women from all racial and ethnic groups. In 1995, for example, Hispanic women employed full-time year round earned just 53% of what white men earned, Hispanic men earned 61%, black women earned 63%, white women earned 72%, and black men earned 74%. These disparities translate into a $14,994 pay gap with white men for the average Hispanic woman and a $7,744 gap for the average black man (Institute for Women's Policy Research [IWPR], 1996, Table 3). In general, the disparities between the earnings of white men and those of other groups have closed since 1970, as Fig. 16-3 shows. Black women show the most progress relative to white men. However, some reversals of some slopes from positive to negative indicate that gains are not necessarily permanent. Closest to earnings parity with white men were

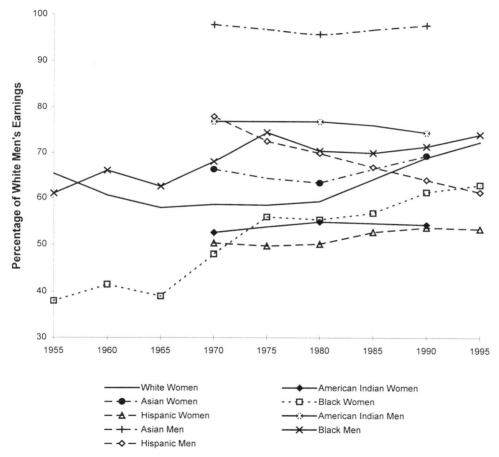

FIGURE 16-3. Median earnings of Asian, American Indian, black, and Hispanic men and women and white women as a percentage of white men's earnings for full-time, year-round employed workers, 1955 to 1995. (*Sources*: Data from Farley, 1984, Fig. 3.2; U.S. Bureau of the Census, 1981, Table 6; U.S. Bureau of the Census, 1983, Tables 37 and 39; U.S. Bureau of the Census, 1988, Tables 27 and 29; U.S. Bureau of the Census, 1991, Table 24; U.S. Bureau of the Census, 1995, Table 7; data for American Indians, Asians, and 1970 data for Hispanics from Harrison & Bennett, 1995, Table 4A.1.)

Asian men employed full-time year round; their median earnings were almost 98% of
white men's in 1970 and 1990 (computed from Harrison & Bennett, 1995, Table 4A.1).
No other group achieved even three quarters of white men's 1990 earnings.

The trends in racial differences in earnings summarized above are disconcerting.
Although the black–white earnings gap shrank between 1965 and 1975, black men's
earnings relative to white men deteriorated between 1975 and the late 1980s (Bound &
Freeman, 1992), and by 1995 black men still had not regained their 1975 earnings relative to whites (see Fig. 16-3). Figure 16-3 also displays the substantial shortfall of female
and male Hispanics' earnings relative to white men. The pay difference between Hispanic
and white men widened by 15 percentage points between 1970 and 1995. Young black
women's position relative to white women has been deteriorating since the early 1970s,
especially among college graduates (Bound & Dresser, 1997, Fig. 1). Although Hispanic
women narrowed the gap with white men between 1975 and 1990, they have not continued to do so at the same rate. American Indian women, who earned a little more than half
of what men made in 1990, have closed their earnings gap with white men by less than
one percentage point per decade since 1970, and American Indian men, who earned three
quarters of what white men made in 1990, were relatively worse off in 1990 than in 1970.

Sex differences dominate earnings inequality. In every racial group, men outearn
women. The pay gap between women and men who worked full-time, year round did not
start to close until 1975 when women earned 58.8% of what men made, the largest disparity since 1920. Although the gap in the median earnings of men and women who
worked full-time year round narrowed by more than 11 percentage points between 1975
and 1995, in 1995 men who worked full-time year round still earned $1.40 for every
dollar a woman earned (computed from IWPR, 1996, Table 1). Within broad race categories, the sex difference in annual earnings is greatest for whites ($9261) and Asians
($8740; computation based on median income from Table 4A.1 in Harrison & Bennett,
1995), reflecting white and Asian men's high median earnings, and smallest for Hispanics ($3201) and blacks ($3763), reflecting the low average earnings of Hispanic and
black men (computed from U.S. Bureau of the Census, 1996a). American Indian women's
shortfall relative to same-ethnicity men was intermediate: $5400 (computation based on
median income from Table 4A.1 in Harrison & Bennett, 1995).

2.1. Explaining Sex and Race Differences in Earnings

Explanations for sex and race disparities in earnings emphasize group differences in
workers' education, experience, and jobs, as well as the earnings payoff for these factors.
They include differences in (1) group characteristics that hypothetically affect workers'
productivity; (2) group rewards for productivity-enhancing characteristics; (3) group distributions across occupations, industries, firms, and jobs; and (4) group payoffs for the
same kind of work. A fifth explanation attributes part of the sex gap to sex differences in
orientations toward monetary versus nonmonetary rewards. In the following sections we
review the evidence for each of these explanations.

2.1.1. Productivity Differences.   To the extent that employers reward productivity,
differences by race and sex in productivity will give rise to pay differences across groups.
The difficulty of measuring productivity has led researchers to use as proxies for produc-

tivity the amount of time and effort workers spend at work and characteristics that hypothetically increase workers' productivity, such as education and experience.

In general, men are employed more hours per year than women, because they work more hours per week and more weeks per year.[17] Even among workers employed full-time year round, men averaged 3 hours more per week than women in the same broad racial group (computed from U.S. Bureau of the Census, 1992a). Whites tend to work more hours per week than people of color, although this does not hold for Asian compared to white women and is a reversal from the past for African-American compared to white women (Farley, 1984, Table A.2).[18] Whites work more weeks per year than same-sex Asians, Hispanics, or African-Americans (computed from U.S. Bureau of the Census, 1992a).[19] Although the proportion of women employed full-time year round has been increasing since 1970 (Spain & Bianchi, 1996, Table 84) and has helped to reduce the pay gap between the sexes, men's greater average number of hours of paid work per week explains a little of the sex gap in pay: the sexes' earnings ratio tends to be 2 to 4 percentage points closer to equity for hourly earnings than weekly earnings (Bianchi, 1995, p. 129; IWPR, 1996, Table 1; Mishel & Bernstein, 1994, p. 125). As Fig. 16-4 shows, in 1995 the sex gap among full-time workers was smallest for hourly pay, slightly larger for weekly earnings, and slightly larger for annual earnings. The pattern in Fig. 16-4 for all workers varies by race. Although the sex gap in median earnings in 1995 was 12.6% larger for annual earnings than weekly earnings, the difference in weekly and annual earnings explained just 2.4% of the gap between Hispanic women and white men and 9% of the gap between white women and men. Black women's, black men's, and Hispanic men's gaps in weekly pay compared to white men are larger than their annual earnings gaps because white men average more hours (IWPR, 1996, Table 3; U.S. Bureau of Labor Statistics,1996b, Table 37).

Differences in the extent of employment across groups are not solely a consequence of workers' preferences. Although some people deliberately limit their paid work in response to other demands on their time, such as education and family, others cannot obtain as many hours of paid work as they want or need (Carnoy, 1994, p. 82). In 1995, for example, one in five part-timers (17.5% of women and 27.7% of men) could not find a full-time job (computed from U.S. Bureau of Labor Statistics, 1996a). Thus, variation in the earnings gaps explained by group differences in extent of employment may not reflect group differences in preference for paid work time.

[17] In 1990, all employed men averaged 6 hours more per week than all women (42.3 compared to 36.3 hours), and they worked, on average, 2 more week per year (46.4 compared to 44.5), according to unpublished analyses of the 1990 census data (U.S. Bureau of the Census, 1992a). The sex differences in hours was smallest among African-Americans (2.8 hours per week) and largest among whites (6.6 hours). Hispanic and Asian men averaged 3.5 to 4 more hours per week than did same-race women. In terms of weeks per year, black men worked only .4 more weeks than black women, Hispanic and Asian men worked about 1.5 weeks more than same-race women, and white men averaged 2.1 more weeks than white women.

[18] According to unpublished analyses of the 1990 census data (U.S. Bureau of the Census, 1992a), white men employed in 1990 worked an average of 42.7 hours per week, compared to 41.6 hours for Asian men, 41.3 hours for Hispanic men, 39.9 hours for black men, 37.9 hours for Asian women, 37.1 hours for black women, 37.0 hours for Hispanic women, and 36.1 hours for white women.

[19] Employed white men averaged 46.9 weeks per year, compared to 45.7 for Asian men, 44.8 for white women, 44.2 for Asian women, 44.1 for Hispanic men, 43.9 for black men, 43.5 for black women, and 42.5 for Hispanic women.

[20] The hourly pay of minority women—except for American Indians—slightly exceeded that of white women in 1989, when education region, occupation, and industry were controlled (Harrison & Bennett, 1995, Table 4.5).

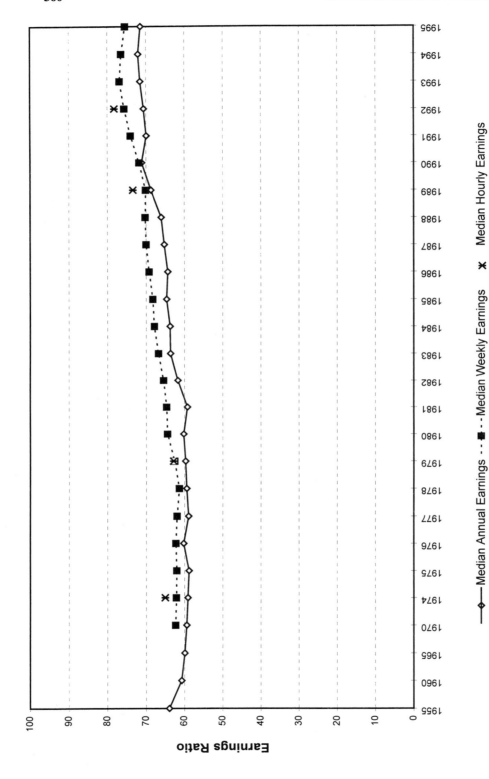

FIGURE 16-4. Women's median annual, weekly, and hourly earnings as a percentage of men's earnings, 1955 to 1995. (*Sources:* Data from Institute for Women's Policy Research, 1996, Table 1; Mishel & Bernstein, 1994, Table 3.9.)

Note: Annual and weekly data are for full-time workers.

Although group differences in effort could give rise to unequal pay, there is no evidence that differences in work effort explain white men's higher pay. In fact, the few studies that compared the sexes suggest that women work at least as hard as do men (Bielby & Bielby, 1988; Major, McFarlin, & Gagnon, 1984); we found no similar studies by race.

Neoclassical economists assume that workers' education, training, and experience affect—and are thus proxies for—their productivity. If so, then sex and race differences in education or experience could explain part of the earnings gaps. Overall, women workers have one month less schooling than men, although the difference varies by race, with whites averaging the same number of years of schooling (13.3), Asian men averaging about a half a year more than Asian women (14.0 compared to 13.4), and African-American and Hispanic women averaging slightly more years schooling than their male counterparts (black women average 12.7 years, black men 12.2, Hispanic women 11.3, and Hispanic men 10.5). On average, men are less likely than women to have completed high school and more likely than women to have postgraduate education (Bianchi, 1995). The sexes and races also tend to major in different subjects, but over the past 20 years, college majors have become more similar across sex and race categories (Jacobs, 1995), and women have been catching up with men in the likelihood of postgraduate education. According to O'Neill and Polachek (1993, p. 221), 17% of the declining sex gap in pay between 1976 and 1989 resulted from the convergence in women's and men's years of schooling. However, by 1990, educational differences played a minor role at most in the earnings gap between young-to-middle-aged women and men (England, Reid, & Kilbourne, 1996: England et al., 1997, Table 7).

Race differences in education contribute to racial disparities in earnings, because blacks and Hispanics average less schooling than whites (Mare, 1995, p.158).[21] During the 1980s, whites pulled further ahead of blacks, Hispanics, and American Indians in college graduation (Harrison & Bennett, 1995, Fig. 4.5). This difference—a consequence of past discrimination and an indicator of ongoing residential and economic disadvantages of people of color—may contribute to whites' higher earnings, either by making whites more productive or because employers require degree completion for well-paying jobs. One way to assess the importance of race and sex differences in education on the earnings gap is to compare how much minorities' earnings would increase if they averaged the same amount of education as white men. (Equalizing education with white men would not reduce the gap between white women and men because white females workers had as many years of education as white males in 1989.) Having white men's years of schooling would have raised black females' 1989 earnings by 7 percentage points, black males' by 9 points, Latinas' by 13 points, and Latinos' by 19 points (Carnoy, 1994, Table 4.6). Among workers who were 28 to 35 years old in 1993, schooling differences explained about one sixth of the race gap between black and white men, one eighth to one fifth of the gap between black and white women, three eighths to two thirds of the gap between white men and Latinos, and four fifths to 100% of the gap between white women and Latinas (England et al., 1997, Table 3).

Because college graduation strongly affects earnings, the growing black–white disparity in college completion works against reducing race differences in earnings. Discrimination in apprenticeship programs further inhibits minorities' representation in high-

---

[21] In 1990, blacks averaged 12.5 years of education and Hispanics averaged 10.8 years, compared to 13.3 years for whites and 13.7 years for Asians (unpublished analysis, U.S. Bureau of the Census, 1992a).

paying jobs (Waldinger & Bailey, 1991). Minorities also tend to be underrepresented in occupations that allow them to acquire skills on the job. For example, people of color in contingent work are disproportionately concentrated in occupations that involve tasks that are less complex than those in which white men work; such jobs are less likely to provide the opportunity to acquire job skills that could lead to regular jobs (Reskin, 1997b).

Men average more job experience than women, although the difference has been declining. This convergence has contributed to the narrowing of the sex gap in pay (Mishel & Bernstein, 1994, p. 119; O'Neill & Polachek, 1993). The declining sex difference in work experience produces a positive association between workers' age and the size of the pay gap. In 1995, for example, the median weekly earnings of 25- to 29-year-old women employed full time was 80% of what same-age men earned, while 40- to 44-year-old women earned just 62% of male age peers' wages (IWPR, 1996, Table 6; see also O'Neill & Polachek, 1993, Table 2).[22] Among mature workers surveyed between 1966 and 1988, experience accounted for one fourth to one third of the sex gap in earnings among African-Americans and one third to one half of the sex gap for whites (Kilbourne et al., 1994a). In contrast, among workers who were ages 14 to 22 in 1979, sex differences in experience explained just 1% of the gap among whites and 9% among blacks (England et al., 1996; see also England et al., 1997, Table 4 for race-specific results).

Race differences in experience—although small (Farley, 1984, Table A2)—contribute to the earnings gap among men. Among mature workers, race differences in experience explained two fifths of the gap between black and white men (England et al., 1996, Table 1). In the past, black women had more job experience, on average, than white women, but young white women are now more experienced than young black women (England et al., 1996, Table 1). Black women's declining years of experience relative to white women contributed to the increasing earnings gap with white women during the 1980s (Blau & Beller, 1992). Experience differences explain 6% to 30% of the pay gap between young Latinas and white women, and 13% to 17% of the gap between young Latinos and white men (England et al., 1997, Table 7). Experience explains between 7% and 20% of the pay gap between black and white women and men (Anderson & Shapiro 1996, p. 277; England et al., 1997, Table 7; Kilbourne et al., 1994a).

In sum, race and sex groups have become more similar in their education and experience (with the exception of black men's falling rates of college participation in the early 1990s), and these changes have contributed to shrinking earnings disparities between groups. Importantly, the extent to which these differences affect workers' productivity depends in part on employers' decisions regarding the organization of work and the use of technology, as well as race and sex segregation in job assignments. The disappearance of educational and experience differences across groups cannot produce earnings equality unless employers assign workers to jobs without regard to their race and sex and compensate workers at the same rate for their education and experience. In the following section, we assess the importance of the last factor for race- and sex-based earnings disparities.

2.1.2. Unequal Rates of Return to Education and Experience.

Pay disparities between groups stem partly from employers rewarding workers from different race-sex groups unequally for the same credentials. Schooling, for example, has a smaller payoff for women than men and for nonwhites than whites (Farley, 1984, p. 68). In 1995, white

---

[22] The low pay that young workers of both sexes command necessarily restricts the size of the pay gap among younger workers. The larger gap among older workers also reflects the positive association between the extent of sex segregation and workers' age and men's greater returns to experience (reported below).

female college graduates who worked full-time year round earned $500 less, on average, than white male high school graduates who worked full-time year round, and white male college graduates outearned white women with postgraduate degrees by almost $12,000 (computed from IWPR, 1996, Table 4). Black and Hispanic women with high school and college diplomas earned 70% to 75% of what same-race men with the same education earned, and Hispanic and black women with postgraduate degrees earned around 85% of what similar men earned (IWPR, 1996, Table 4).

Blacks have been falling behind whites in returns to education—especially for college graduates—offsetting their increasing parity in schooling. The earnings of young blacks have been lagging behind whites with the same amount of education (Carnoy, 1994, pp. 121, 123). For example, in 1985, young black male college graduates earned 89% of the earnings of white male college graduates, but by 1991 the ratio had fallen to 76%. Young black female college graduates slightly outearned white female graduates in 1976, but earned 13% less in 1991. During this period, Latinos/as also lost ground relative to Anglos with equal years of schooling, although the amount varies across Hispanic groups (Carnoy & Rothstein, 1996; Corcoran, Heflin, & Reyes, 1997).

Young Asians with at least some college were the only racial group who enjoyed higher returns to education than comparably educated, same-sex whites (Mare, 1995). At the other extreme are American Indian women, who were furthest from parity, followed by African-American and Hispanic women. American Indian college graduates who were 16 to 34 years old, for example, earned 86% of the earnings similar white women, black women earned 92%, Hispanic women earned 99%, and Asian American women earned 105% (see Carnoy, 1994, Table 6.2). Among men, blacks received the lowest rewards for their education relative to whites, followed by American Indians, and then Hispanics (Mare, 1995, p. 207; see also Harrison & Bennett, 1995, pp. 174–176). In 1995, men of color earned two thirds to three quarters of what white men with the same degrees earned, while women of color earned between 90% and 100% of what white women earned (computed from IWPR, 1996, Table 4). White male high school graduates without any additional schooling were particularly overrewarded for their schooling compared to minority men (Harrison & Bennett, 1995, pp. 174–175). The same patterns hold after controlling for experience and region: in 1973 blacks at all educational levels earned 10.3% less than whites with the same education, experience, and region, compared to 16% less in 1989 (Mishel & Bernstein, 1994, Table 3.9). These trends mean that additional education will not be sufficient for minorities to catch up with whites in earnings (Harrison & Bennett, 1995, p. 175).

Group differences in payoff for hours worked and years of work experience also contribute to the pay disparities that we have been examining. Net of other factors that affect earnings, men received higher returns to both hours and weeks worked in 1990 than did women (Harrison & Bennett, 1995, Table 4.5), and a year's experience was worth considerably more to men than women (Farley, 1984, Table A.3). Men's greater returns to experience mean that the sex-linked pay disparity increases as workers age. Workers' payoff for experience also differs by race. Although this difference shrank during the 1960s and 1970s—contributing to the declining earnings gap between blacks and whites—in 1980 whites still received about twice the payoff to experience that blacks did (Farley, 1984, pp. 68, 78, Table A.3), and this difference held for young to middle-aged workers (England et al., 1996, Table 2).

These race and sex differences in how employers reward workers' education and experience almost certainly result partly from discrimination. Of course, unequal rewards for the same levels of schooling or experience may reflect unmeasured differences in the quality of education or experience, but sex differences in the returns to experience probably derive largely from job segregation. Whether discrimination stems from segregated jobs that do not provide incumbents with equally valuable experience or from employers' failure to reward education and experience equally for persons regardless of their race or sex, actions by employers perpetuate earnings disparities.

2.1.3. JOB SEGREGATION BY SEX AND RACE. The sex and race composition of jobs is associated with incumbents' average pay for two reasons. First, segregation disproportionately relegates women and minorities to the kinds of jobs that employers compensate poorly. Second, employers devalue workers' achievements in jobs filled primarily by women and minorities. Although each of these mechanisms reduces the pay of women and minorities relative to white men, each affects the earnings of white men as well.

Employers' allocation of workers into higher- and lower-paying jobs based on their sex or race guarantees unequal pay across sex/race groups (England, 1992; Hirsch & Schumacher, 1992; Sorensen, 1989).[23] For example, if a retail store employs minority women as janitors, minority men as stock clerks, white women as cashiers, and white men as managers, white men will outearn the other three groups and minority women will earn the least. The relationship between the proportion of women in an occupation and its earnings particularly disadvantages women for two reasons. First, women are more likely than men to work in heavily female occupations, and second, the penalty for holding a mostly female job is stronger for women—especially women of color—than for men (England et al., 1996, Table 3; Kilbourne et al., 1994a). If young women had been distributed across more and less female occupations in the same way as young men in the 1980s, the disparity in the sexes' starting pay on a job would have been at least one fifth smaller among both blacks and whites (England et al., 1996, p. 519).

Comparing the median weekly earnings of female and male workers employed full time all year in the same occupations illustrates the more negative effect of a female-dominated job on women than men. For example, in the mid-1990s, the median weekly pay of female sewing-machine operators was about 86% of men's earnings of $280, and female cashiers averaged 87% of men's $265 (computed from U.S. Bureau of Labor Statistics 1995, 1996b, 1997, Table 39). The larger penalty of working in a female occupation for women than men can have two sources: (1) employers pay men more than women who do identical tasks, and (2) employers segregate men and women in the same occupation into different jobs. The first alternative is illegal under the 1963 Equal Pay Act. In the second instance, although taking into account sex and race in assigning jobs is illegal under Title VII of the 1964 Civil Rights Act, it is legal under the Equal Pay Act, and high levels of segregation are common.The more workers earn, the larger the sex pay gap tends to be. According to a 1993 survey of corporate executives, women at the vice presidential level and higher earned 70% of what their male counterparts earned (Brooks, 1993). Women who sold securities and financial services, for example, earned 55% of men's $951, and female financial managers averaged two thirds of men's earnings of $937 (computed from U.S. Bureau of Labor Statistics, 1995, 1996b, 1997, Table 39).

Women's concentration in low-paying service jobs has insulated them from the big pay cuts that some men experienced as the United States lost well-paying manufacturing

---

[23] Although neoclassical economists and sociologists disagree regarding the causes of occupational sex segregation, they agree that it is an important mechanism in the pay gap between the sexes.

jobs. Almost three fourths of the decline in the wage gap between the sexes between 1979 and 1993 resulted from the decline in men's wages stemming from the loss of traditionally male blue-collar jobs and from falling pay in surviving male blue-collar jobs (Mishel & Bernstein, 1994, pp. 124–125). In response, many men entered service work that was overwhelmingly female. Therefore, although women's likelihood of employment in a job with poverty-level wages is 10 percentage points higher than men's, their likelihood of holding such a job has been declining since 1973, while men's likelihood has been growing since 1979 (Mishel & Bernstein, 1994, p. 127).

Racial segregation increases racial differences in earnings: the more black workers in a job, the lower the pay for black and white women and men. Given the size of estimated effects, working in all-black jobs would lower the pay of white women by 15%, that of black women by 24%, that of black men by 39%, and that of white men by 52% (Hirsch & Schumacher, 1992). Moreover, the narrowing of the earnings gap between black and white women between 1940 and 1980 was due largely to declining race segregation by occupation and industry (Cunningham & Zalokar, 1992, p. 548). Minority workers' concentration in unskilled labor and service occupations and in low-paying specialties within more skilled occupations lowers their pay. For example, more than half of black, American Indian, and Hispanic male college-educated professionals worked as elementary or secondary teachers, social or religious workers, writers, artists, or entertainers—all low-paying professions (Harrison & Bennett, 1995, p. 181). Blacks'—and presumably Hispanics'—concentration in low-paying, nonunionized industries and in occupations and cities with low wage growth has exacerbated the black–white wage disparity (Mishel & Bernstein, 1994, pp. 188–189). The loss of manufacturing jobs that reduced men's average earnings in the late 1980s and early 1990s also adversely affected women of color, who were disproportionately concentrated in these industries (Bound & Dresser, 1997; Mishel & Bernstein, 1994, pp. 124–125).

2.1.4. THE DEVALUATION OF FEMALE- AND MINORITY-DOMINATED JOBS.

Given the societal devaluation of women and minorities, employers may devalue and hence underpay jobs that are performed primarily by women or minorities. Sociologists have argued that predominantly female jobs are underpaid relative to the skills and responsibilities they involve because the devaluation of women leads to the undervaluation of stereotypically female work (Acker, 1989, 1990; England, 1992; Reskin, 1988). Although the same logic holds for people of color, their small numbers may prevent occupations from being labeled minority and hence devalued. In sum, although all workers in a devalued job earn less than their job warrants as reflected in its qualifications and duties, the predominance of women or minority men in devalued jobs means that the effect of any devaluation will fall disproportionately on women and minorities and hence contribute to earnings disparities. This tendency to underpay jobs solely because of their sex or race composition has been termed "comparable-worth discrimination."

Comparable-worth discrimination is apparent when an occupation's sex composition affects incumbents' pay, net of measures of workers' education, experience, and job complexity (England, 1992; England et al., 1996; Kilbourne et al., 1994a; Kilbourne, England, Farkas, Beron, & Weir, 1994b; Treiman & Hartmann, 1981). For example, among middle-aged workers, performing nurturing tasks customarily sex-typed as female—such as nursing or childcare—is associated with pay losses for all workers, but especially women (Kilbourne et al., 1994b). In other segments of the population, occupations' sex composition explains up to 30% of the pay gap between the sexes (England,

1992, p. 181; Sorensen, 1989). Among workers in their late 20s and early 30s in 1993, sex composition explained between 10% and 42 percent of the sex difference in hourly wages among whites, 45% to 73% among blacks, and 3% to 21% among Latinas/os (England et al., 1997, Table 6).[24] Whether the race composition of occupations or jobs contributes to the racial gap in earnings because predominantly minority jobs are devalued has not been established, because the few studies of the earnings effect of race composition have not controlled for occupational skills. Controlled studies have found no effect of minority composition on earnings, net of job characteristics (England, 1992), presumably because minorities make up too small a proportion of the labor force to comprise a majority in any occupation. (Even in occupations in which minorities are concentrated, such as nursing aide, janitor, or cook, the majority of workers are white.) According to appellate and Supreme Court decisions, the 1963 Equal Pay Act does not prohibit employers from paying workers in predominantly female jobs less than workers in equally demanding but different jobs dominated by men. For instance, the U.S. Court of Appeals allowed the city of Denver to pay nurses, 97% of whom were female, less than tree trimmers and sign painters, male-dominated jobs (Lemons v. City and County of Denver, 1978). These rulings have led to pressure for laws that require employers to provide equal pay to workers in different jobs that involve similar amounts of skill, effort, and responsibility. Such laws could reduce the pay gap between the sexes by one third (IWPR, 1993, p. 1). Indeed, a Minnesota pay-equity law for state workers reduced a 28-point pay gap to 18% in 4 years (IWPR, 1993). However, bureaucratic inertia and political resistance have set limits on the effectiveness of pay equity as a widespread solution to the pay gap (Bridges & Nelson, 1989; Steinberg, 1987).

2.1.5. COMPENSATING DIFFERENTIALS. Some neoclassical economists suggest that the pay gap between the sexes may stem partly from different job values held by male and female workers. They argue that men seek jobs that will maximize their earnings, even when they involve physically difficult, dirty, or dangerous work; women, in contrast, trade off pay for job characteristics that facilitate combining work and family or for desirable working conditions. There is almost no support for this explanation of the pay gap, however (but see Filer, 1989). Researchers have found that female occupations pay less, net of working conditions (England et al., 1996; Glass & Camarigg, 1992), and that undesirable working conditions are associated with lower, not higher wages (Jacobs & Steinberg, 1990).

3. CONCLUSIONS

Workplace inequality by sex, race, and ethnicity is linked to inequality in all social institutions because people's jobs distribute so many social and economic rewards. Jobs are mechanisms that govern workers' access to earnings, authority, status, and mobility opportunities as well as their exposure to pleasant or unpleasant working conditions. Job segregation is a key mechanism in workplace inequality. Although few data exist on the extent of job segregation, occupations—which aggregate similar jobs—are substantially segregated by workers' sex and somewhat less so by their race and ethnicity. A variety of

---

[24] The racial disparities in earnings in this sample did not stem from comparable-worth discrimination (England et al., 1997, Table 5).

factors affect the extent of segregation. Workers' education and experience play a limited role in sex segregation and a slightly larger one in race/ethnic segregation. Although workers' preferences matter, most workers "choose" between options that are constrained by employers' preferences and employment practices. Indeed, employers' personnel practices shape workers' preferences (Schultz, 1991, p. 141), as do antidiscrimination and affirmative action regulations that open sex- and race-atypical jobs to minorities and women.

The importance of segregation is seen in its effect on earnings disparities between sex, race, and ethnic groups. The concentration of men and women of different races in different occupations, industries, and jobs is the foremost cause of the earnings gap between the sexes and races. Race segregation contributes to the earnings gap between whites and minorities by disproportionately relegating people of color to lower-paying jobs that prevent incumbents from acquiring and using skills that employers compensate. Sex segregation contributes to the pay gap between the sexes both by concentrating women in jobs that do not reward or enhance their productive capacity and because of the devaluation of predominantly female jobs. Anything that fosters job integration helps to reduce the pay gap between the sexes and races. Thus, the enforcement of antidiscrimination and affirmative action regulations has induced employers to integrate jobs, thereby making a dent in the pay gaps between sex/race groups. Eliminating all of the barriers to women's and minorities' employment in the full range of jobs would go far toward reducing the pay gap. However, job segregation by sex is still the rule, and race segregation—while less extensive—is prevalent. Job segregation means that equalizing human capital will not remedy the earnings disparities across race/sex groups. Pay-equity laws that cover public employees in some states have had a modest effect in reducing the sex gap in earnings.

Sex and race differences in productivity play a minor role in the pay disparities across race/sex groups. Although white men outperform other groups on one or another measure of productivity, the differences are small and have minor effects on earnings differences. However, women and minority men receive lower payoffs than white men for some of the factors that researchers treat as proxies for productivity, and these differences contribute to earnings disparities.

Discrimination is an important source of the earnings disparities between race-sex groups (Anderson & Shapiro, 1996, p. 286; Cunningham & Zalokar, 1992, p. 554; Farley, 1984, p. 68; Gill, 1994; Mishel & Bernstein, 1994, p. 189). First, some group differences in indicators of productivity, such as job experience, result from earlier discrimination by employers, and their contribution to earnings disparities between groups must be chalked up to discrimination. Discrimination also occurs when women and minorities are compensated at a lower rate than white men for the same inputs.[25] Sex and race segregated job assignments also contribute to pay discrimination by denying female and minority workers access to well-paying jobs or jobs in which they can acquire skills that will enhance their future earnings. These discriminatory effects are seen in the association between occupations' sex and race composition and incumbents' pay. When the sex composition of a job is associated with incumbents' pay, net of job demands, discrimination results from the devaluation of female-dominated tasks. Legal prohibitions against most of these forms of discrimination have contributed to the declining rate of wage inequality, but the

---

[25] To the extent that different returns to productivity reflect unmeasured differences in productivity, treating these differences as indicative of discrimination will overestimate the amount of discrimination.

effectiveness of laws depends on good faith efforts by enforcing agencies and the ability of victims to detect their discriminatory treatment (which is impaired by social psychological processes; Clayton & Crosby, 1992, pp. 72–79) and to challenge it.

In the 35 years since the 1963 Equal Pay Act outlawed unequal pay for equal work, women have been catching up with men in earnings at a rate of one third of a percent a year, and the pay gap between the sexes has declined by about 13 cents on the dollar. If this rate of progress continues (and it appears to have slowed in the early 1990s), the sexes would not achieve earnings parity until almost the end of the twenty-first century. Achieving earnings equality more quickly will require women to accumulate work experience more in line with that of men, employers to integrate customarily male jobs, and the spread of pay-equity principles that compensate workers for the worth of their job and not the sex of their co-workers. Racial disparities in earnings also declined in the 1970s and early 1980s. Although minorities are closer to earnings parity with same-sex whites than women are to same-race men, the trend toward declining inequality changed direction in the late 1980s, making it impossible to predict when racial equality in earnings might cease to exist.

Finally, we believe that progress depends in part on the evidence that researchers bring to bear on the extent of inequality in work opportunities and rewards by sex, race, and ethnicity. As we noted at the outset, little research examines the joint effects of race, sex, and ethnicity. Race is typically treated as black/white or minority/white. Available data indicate that the economic situation of groups that are neither white nor black differs from the situations of both blacks and whites. Variation exists, too, among different Asian and different Latin national groups. We encourage researchers to compare the situations of as many groups as their data allow. Such comparisons are essential for identifying the greatest needs for policy intervention and for recommending policies that can reduce workplace inequality.

Acknowledgments

We are grateful to Kathryn A. Barry for her help with the references, Naomi R. Cassirer for her help with data analysis, and Debra B. McBrier for preparing the table and figures.

REFERENCES

Acker, J. (1989). *Doing comparable worth: Gender, class, and pay equity.* Philadelphia: Temple University Press.

Acker, J. (1990). Hierarchies, jobs, and bodies: A theory of gendered organizations. *Gender & Society, 4,* 139–158.

American Bar Association Commission on Opportunities for Women in the Profession. (1996). *Unfinished business.* Chicago: The American Bar Association.

Amirault, T. (1992). Training to qualify for jobs and improve skills, 1991. *Monthly Labor Review, 115,* 31–36.

Anderson, D., & Shapiro, D. (1996). Racial differences in access to high-paying jobs and the wage gap between black and white women. *Industrial and Labor Relations Review, 49,* 273–286.

Ashenfelter, O., & Heckman, J. (1976). Measuring the effect of an anti-discrimination program. In O. Ashenfelter & J. Blum (Eds.), *Evaluating the labor market effects of social programs* (pp. 46–84). Princeton, NJ: Princeton University Press.

Badgett, M. V. L. (1995). Affirmative action in a changing legal and economic environment. *Industrial Labor Relations, 34,* 489–506.

Badgett, M. V. L., & Hartmann, H. I. (1995). The effectiveness of equal employment opportunity policies. In M. C. Simms (Ed.), *Economic perspectives on affirmative action* (pp. 55–97). Washington: Joint Center for Political and Economic Studies.

Baldi, S., & McBrier, D. B. (1997). Do the determinants of promotion differ for blacks and whites? Evidence from the U.S. labor market. *Work and Occupations, 24,* 470–497.

Baron, J. N., & Bielby, W. T. (1985). Organizational barriers to gender equality: Sex segregation of jobs and opportunities. In A. S. Rossi (Ed.), *Gender and the life course* (pp. 233–251). New York: Aldine.

Baron, J. N., Mittman, B. S., & Newman, A. E. (1991). Targets of opportunity: Organizational and environmental determinants of gender integration within the California Civil Service, 1979–1985. *American Journal of Sociology, 96,* 1362–1401.

Bell, E. L. J., & Nkomo, S. (1994). Barriers to workplace advancement experienced by African-Americans. *Report to the Glass Ceiling Commission.* U.S. Department of Labor, April.

Bendick, M., Jr. (1996). *Declaration.* (Brief challenging California Civil Rights Initiative.) Submitted to the California State Court of Appeals.

Bergmann, B. R. (1986). *The economic emergence of women.* New York: Basic Books.

Bergmann, B. R., & Darity, W., Jr. (1981). Social relations, productivity, and employer discrimination. *Monthly Labor Review, 104,* 47–49.

Berheide, C. W. (1992). Women still 'stuck' in low-level jobs. *Women in public services: A bulletin for the Center for Women in Government* 3 (Fall).

Bianchi, S. (1995). Changing economic roles of women and men. In R. Farley (Ed.), *State of the union: America in the 1990s.* Vol. 1: *Economic trends* (pp. 107–155). New York: Russell Sage Foundation.

Bielby, W. T., & Baron, J. N. (1984). A woman's place is with other women: Sex segregation within organizations. In B. F. Reskin (Ed.), *Sex segregation in the workplace* (pp. 27–55). Washington, D.C.: National Academy Press.

Bielby, W. T., & Baron, J. N. (1986). Men and women at work: Sex segregation and statistical discrimination. *American Journal of Sociology, 91,* 759–799.

Bielby, D. D., & Bielby, W. T. (1988). She works hard for the money: Household responsibilities and the allocation of work effort. *American Journal of Sociology, 93,* 1031–1059.

Blau, F., & Beller, A. (1992). Black-white earnings over the 1970s and 1980s: Gender differences in trends. *Review of Economics and Statistics, 74,* 276–286.

Blumrosen, A. W. (1995). Draft report on reverse discrimination, commissioned by U.S. Department of Labor: How courts are handling reverse discrimination cases. *Daily Labor Report,* March 23. Washington, D.C.: The Bureau of National Affairs.

Bobo, L. (1996). *Declaration.* Submitted to the California State Court of Appeals. November 1.

Bound, J., & Dresser, L. (1997). The erosion of the relative earnings of young African American women during the 1980s. In I. Browne (Ed.), *Race, gender, and economic inequality: African American and Latina women in the labor market.* New York: Russell Sage Foundation.

Bound, J., & Freeman, R. B. (1992). What went wrong? The erosion of relative earnings among young black men in the 1980s. *Quarterly Journal of Economics, 107,* 201–232.

Braddock, J. H., & McPartland, J. M. (1987). How minorities continue to be excluded from equal employment opportunities: Research on labor market and institutional barriers. *Journal of Social Issues, 43,* 5–39.

Bridges, W. P., & Nelson, R. L. (1989). Markets in hierarchies: Organizational and market influences on gender inequality in a state pay system. *American Journal of Sociology, 95,* 616–658.

Brooks, N. R. (1993). Gender pay gap found among top executives. *Los Angeles Times,* June 30, D1, D3.

Burstein, P. (1979). Equal employment opportunity legislation and the income of women and nonwhites. *American Sociological Review, 44,* 367–391.

Burstein, P. (1985). *Discrimination, politics, and jobs.* Chicago: University of Chicago Press.

Carnoy, M. (1994). *Faded dreams: The politics and economics of race in America.* New York: Cambridge University Press.

Carnoy, M., & Rothstein, R. (1996). *Hard lessons.* Washington, D.C.: Economic Policy Institute.

Catalyst. (1996). *Women in corporate leadership.* New York: Catalyst.

Clayton, S. D., & Crosby, F. J. (1992). *Justice, gender, and affirmative action.* Ann Arbor, MI: University of Michigan Press.

Collins, S. M. (1989). The marginalization of black executives. *Social Problems, 36,* 317–331.

Collins, S. M. (1997). *Black corporate executives: The making and breaking of a black middle class.* Philadelphia: Temple University Press.

Conk, M. (1981). Accuracy, efficiency and bias: The interpretation of women's work in the U.S. Census of Occupations, 1890–1940. *Historical Methods, 14,* 65–72.

Corcoran, M., Heflin, C. M., & Reyes, B. I. (1997). Latina women in the U.S.: The economic progress of Mexican and Puerto Rican women. In I. Browne (Ed.), *Race, gender, and economic inequality: African American and Latina women in the labor market.* New York: Russell Sage Foundation.

Cox, T. H., & Nkomo, S. M. (1986). Differential performance appraisal criteria: A field study of black and white managers. *Group & Organization Studies, 11,* 101–119.

Cunningham, J. S., & Zalokar, N. (1992). The economic progress of black women, 1940–1980: Occupational distribution and relative wages. *Industrial and Labor Relations Review, 45,* 540–555.

Deaux, K. (1984). From individual differences to social categories: Analysis of a decade's research on gender. *American Psychologist, 39,* 105–115.

Deaux, K. (1985). Sex and gender. *Annual Review of Psychology, 36,* 49–81.

Deaux, K., & Ullman, J. P. (1983). *Women of steel: Female blue-collar workers in the basic steel industry.* New York: Praeger.

DiTomaso, N. (1993). *Notes on Xerox case: Balanced work force at Xerox.* Unpublished.

Dobbin, F., Sutton, J., Meyer J., & Scott, W. R. (1993). Equal opportunity law and the construction of internal labor markets. *American Journal of Sociology, 99,* 396–427.

Donohue, J. J., & Heckman, J. (1991). Re-evaluating federal civil rights policy. *Georgetown Law Review, 79,* 1713–1735.

Duncan, O.D., & Duncan, B. (1955). A methodological analysis of segregation indices. *American Sociological Review, 20,* 200–217.

Eagly, A. H., & Wood, W. (1982). Inferred sex differences in status as a determinant of gender stereotypes about social influence. *Journal of Personality and Social Psychology, 43,* 915–928.

Eagly, A. H., Makhijani, M. G., & Klonsky, B. G. (1992). Gender and the evaluation of leaders: A meta-analysis. *Psychological Bulletin, 111,* 3–22.

England, P. (1992). *Comparable worth: Theories and evidence.* New York: Aldine de Gruyter.

England, P., Chassie, M., & McCormack, L. (1982). Skill demands and earnings in female and male occupations. *Sociology and Social Research, 66,* 47–68.

England, P., Reid, L. L., & Kilbourne, B. S. (1996). The effect of sex composition on the starting wages in an organization: Findings from the NLSY. *Demography, 33,* 511–522.

England, P., Christopher, K., & Reid, L. L. (1997). How do intersections of race-ethnicity and gender affect pay among young cohorts of African Americans, European Americans, and Latinos/as? In I. Browne (Ed.), *Race, gender, and economic inequality: African American and Latina women in the labor market.* New York.: Russell Sage.

Epstein, C. F. (1993). *Women in law.* Urbana: University of Illinois Press.

Erdreich, B., Slavet, B., & Amador, A. (1996). *Fair and equitable treatment: A progress report on minority employment in the federal government.* Washington, D.C.: U.S. Merit Systems Protection Board.

Farley, R. (1984). *Blacks and whites: Narrowing the gap.* Cambridge, MA. Harvard University Press.

Filer, R. (1989). Occupational segregation, compensating differentials, and comparable worth. In R. T. Michael, H. I. Hartmann, & B. O'Farrell (Eds.), *Pay equity: Empirical inquiries* (pp.153–171). Washington, D.C.: National Academy Press.

Fiske, S. T., Bersoff, D. N., Borgida, E., Deaux, K., & Heilman, M. E. (1991). Social science research on trial: Use of sex stereotyping research in Price Waterhouse v. Hopkins. *American Psychologist, 46,* 1049–1060.

Fix, M., & Struyk, R. J. (Eds.). (1992). *Clear and convincing evidence. Measurement of discrimination in America.* Washington, D.C.: The Urban Institute.

Gera, S., & Hasan, A. (1982). More on returns to job search: A test of two models. *Review of Economics and Statistics, 64,* 151–156.

Gill, A. (1994). Incorporating the causes of occupational differences in studies of racial wage differentials. *Journal of Human Resources, 29,* 20–41.

Glass, J. (1990). The impact of occupational segregation on working conditions. *Social Forces, 68,* 779–796.

Glass, J., & Camarigg, V. (1992). Gender, parenthood, and job-family compatibility. *American Journal of Sociology, 98,* 131–151.

Greenhaus, J. H., & Parasuraman, S. (1993). Job performance attributions and career advancement prospects: An examination of gender and race effects. *Organizational Behavior and Human Decision Processes, 55,* 273–297.

Greenhaus, J. H., Parasuraman, S., & Wormley, W. M. (1990). Effects of race on organizational experiences, job performance evaluations, and career outcomes. *Academy of Management Journal, 33,* 64–86.

Gross, E. (1968). Plus ca change: The sexual segregation of occupations over time. *Social Problems, 16,* 198–208.

Harrison, R. J., & Bennett, C. (1995). Racial and ethnic diversity. In R. Farley (Ed.), *State of the union: America in the 1990s.* Vol. 2: *Social trends* (pp. 141–210). New York: Russell Sage Foundation.

Heckman, J. J., & Payner, B. S. (1989). Determining the impact of anti-discrimination policy on the economic status of blacks: A study of South Carolina. *American Economic Review, 79,* 138–177.

Higginbotham, E. (1987). Employment for professional black women in the twentieth century. In C. Bose & G. Spitze (Eds.), *Ingredients for women's employment policy* (pp. 73–99). Albany, NY: SUNY Press.

Hirsch, B. T., & Schumacher, E. J. (1992). Labor earnings, discrimination, and the racial composition of jobs. *Journal of Human Resources, 27,* 602–628.

Holzer, H. J. (1996). *What employers want.* New York: Russell Sage Foundation.

Institute for Women's Policy Research. (1993). State pay equity programs raise women's wages. *News release,* May 20. Washington, D.C.: Institute for Women's Policy Research.

Institute for Women's Policy Research. (1996). *The wage gap: Women and men's earnings.* Washington, D.C.: Institute for Women's Policy Research.

Jacobs, J. A. (1989a). Long-term trends in occupational segregation by sex. *American Journal of Sociology, 95,* 160–173.

Jacobs, J. A. (1989b). *Revolving doors.* Stanford, CA: Stanford University Press.

Jacobs, J. A. (1995). Gender and academic specialties: Trends among degree recipients during the 1980s. *Sociology of Education, 68,* 81–98.

Jacobs, J. A., & Steinberg, R. J. (1990). Compensating differentials and the male-female wage gap: Evidence from the New York State Comparable Worth Study. *Social Forces, 69,* 439–468.

Jacobsen, J. P. (1997). Trends in workforce segregation: 1980 and 1990 Census figures. *Social Science Quarterly, 78,* 234–235.

Jencks, C., Perman, L., & Rainwater, L. (1988). What is a good job? A new measure of labor-market success. *American Journal of Sociology, 93,* 1322–1357.

Kahn, L. M. (1978). The returns to job search: A test of two models. *Review of Economics and Statistics, 15,* 496–503.

Kalleberg, A. & Reskin, B. F. (1995). Gender differences in promotion in the U.S. and Norway. *Research in Social Stratification and Mobility, 13,* 237–264.

Kalleberg, A., Marsden, P. V., Knoke, D., & Spaeth, J. L. (1996). Formalizing the employment relationship: Internal labor markets and dispute resolution procedures. In A. L. Kalleberg, D. Knoke, P. V. Marsden, & J. L. Spaeth (Eds), *Organizations in America* (pp. 87–112). Newbury Park, CA: Sage.

Kanter, R. M. (1976). The policy issues: Presentation VI. In M. Blaxall & B. Reagan (Eds.), *Women and the workplace* (pp. 282–291). Chicago: University of Chicago Press.

Kasinitz, P., & Rosenberg, J. (1996). Missing the connection: Social isolation and employment on the Brooklyn waterfront. *Social Problems, 43,* 180–196.

Kelley, M. R. (1984). Commentary: The need to study the transformation of job structures. In B. F. Reskin (Ed.*)*, *Sex segregation in the workplace: Trends, explanations, remedies (*pp. 261–264). Washington, D.C.: National Academy Press.

Kern, L. (1996). Hiring and seniority: Issues in policing in the post-judicial intervention period. Unpublished paper. Columbus, OH: Ohio State University.

Kilbourne, B., England, P., & Beron, K. (1994a). Effects of individual, occupational, and industrial characteristics on earnings: Intersections of race and gender. *Social Forces, 72,* 1149–1176.

Kilbourne, B., England, P., Farkas, G., Beron, K., & Weir, D. (1994b). Returns to skill, compensating differentials, and gender bias: Effects of occupational characteristics on the wages of white women and men. *American Journal of Sociology, 100,* 689–719.

King, M. C. (1992). Occupational segregation by race and sex, 1940–88. *Monthly Labor Review, 115,* 30–36.

Kraiger, K., & Ford, J. K. (1985). A meta-analysis of ratee race effects in performance ratings. *Journal of Applied Psychology, 70,* 56–65.

Kraut, K., & Luna, M. (1992*). Work and wages: Facts on women and people of color in the workforce.* Washington, D.C.: National Committee on Pay Equity.

Lemons v. City and County of Denver, 17 FEP cases 906 (D. Col. 1978), 620 F. 2d 228 (10th Cir.) 1978.

Leonard, J. S. (1984a). The impact of affirmative action on employment. *Journal of Labor Economics, 2,* 439–463.

Leonard, J. S. (1984b). Employment and occupational advance under affirmative action. *The Review of Economics and Statistics, 66,* 377–385.

Leonard, J. S. (1994). Use of enforcement techniques in eliminating glass ceiling barriers. Report to the Glass Ceiling Commission, U.S. Department of Labor, April.

Lieberson, S. (1980). *A piece of the pie.* Berkeley, CA: University of California Press.

Major, B., McFarlin, D. B., & Gagnon, D. (1984). Overworked and underpaid: On the nature of gender differences in personal entitlement. *Journal of Personality and Social Psychology, 47,* 1399–1412.

Mare, R. D. (1995). Changes in educational attainment and school enrollment. In R. Farley (Ed.), *State of the Union: America in the 1990s.* Vol. 1: *Economic Trends* (pp.155–214). New York: Russell Sage Foundation.

Marini, M. M., & Brinton, M. C. (1984). Sex typing in occupational socialization. In B. F. Reskin (Ed.), *Sex segregation in the workplace: Trends, explanations, remedies* (pp.192–232). Washington, D.C.: National Academy Press.

Marini, M. M., Fan, P., Finley, E., & Beutel, A. (1996). Gender and job values. *Sociology of Education, 69,* 49–65.

Markham, W. T., Harlan, S., & Hackett, E .J. (1987). Promotion opportunity in organizations. *Research in Personnel and Human Resource Management, 5,* 223–287.

Marsden, P. V. (1994). The hiring process: recruitment methods. *American Behavioral Scientist, 7,* 979–991.

Marsden, P. V., Kalleberg, A. L., & Cook, C. R. (1993). Gender differences in organizational commitment: Influences of work positions and family roles. *Work and Occupations, 20,* 368–390.

Martin, S. E. (1991). The effectiveness of affirmative action: The case of women in policing. *Justice Quarterly, 8,* 489–504.

McGuire, G. M., & Reskin, B. F. (1993). Authority hierarchies at work: The impact of race and sex. *Gender & Society, 7,* 487–506.

Messick, D. M., & Mackie, D. (1989). Intergroup relations. *Annual Review of Psychology, 40,* 45–81.

Mishel, L., & Bernstein, J. (1994). *The state of working America,* 1994–95. Armonk, NY: M. E. Sharpe.

Moss, P., & Tilly, C. (1996). 'Soft' skills and race. *Work and Occupations, 23,* 252–276.

Neckerman, K. M., & Kirschenman, J. (1991). Hiring strategies, racial bias, and inner-city workers: An investigation of employers' hiring decisions. *Social Problems, 38,* 433–447.

Neumark, D., Bank, R., & Van Nort, K. (1995). Sex discrimination in the restaurant industry: An audit study. Working Paper No. 5024. Washington, D.C.: National Bureau of Economic Research.

Northrup, H. R., & Larson, J. A. (1979). The impact of the AT&T-EEO consent decrees. *Labor Relations and Public Policy Series,* No. 20. Philadelphia: Industrial Research Unit, University of Pennsylvania.

O'Neill, J., & Polachek, S. (1993). Why the gender gap in wages narrowed in the 1980s. *Journal of Labor Economics, 11,* 205–228.

Padavic, I. (1991a). The re-creation of gender in a male workplace. *Symbolic Interaction, 14,* 279–294.

Padavic, I. (1991b). Attractions of male blue-collar jobs for black and white women: Economic need, exposure, and attitudes. *Social Science Quarterly, 72,* 33–49.

Padavic, I., & Reskin, B. F. (1990). Men's behavior and women's interest in blue-collar jobs. *Social Problems, 37,* 613–628.

Peterson, T. & Morgan, L. (1995). Separate and unequal: Occupation-establishment sex segregation and the gender wage gap. *American Journal of Sociology, 101,* 329–365.

Pettigrew, T., & Martin, J. (1987). Shaping the organizational context for black American inclusion. *Journal of Social Issues, 43,* 41–78.

Polachek, S. (1981). A supply side approach to occupational segregation. Presented at the American Sociological Association meeting, Toronto.

Pulakos, E. D., White, L. A., Oppler, S. L., & Borman, W. C. (1989). Examination of race and sex effects on performance ratings. *Journal of Applied Social Psychology, 74,* 770–780.

Reskin, B. F. (1988). Bringing the men back in: Sex differentiation and the devaluation of women's work. *Gender & Society, 2,* 58–81.

Reskin, B. F. (1994). Segregating workers: Occupational differences by ethnicity, race, and sex. *Annual Proceedings of the Industrial Relations Research Association, 46,* 247–255.

Reskin, B. F. (1997a). Dimensions of segregation: An MDS analysis of occupational segregation by race, ethnicity, and sex. Paper presented at the University of Pennsylvania, March.

Reskin, B. F. (1997b). Gender, race, and economic vulnerability in nonstandard working arrangements. Paper presented at Northwestern University Institute for Policy Research, February 24.

Reskin, B. F. (1997c). Occupational segregation by race and ethnicity among female workers. In I. Browne (Ed.), *Race, gender, and economic inequality: African American and Latina women in the labor market.* New York: Russell Sage Foundation.

Reskin, B. F., & Cassirer, N. (1996). The effect of organizational arrangements on men's and women's promotion expectations and experiences. Unpublished manuscript. Columbus: Ohio State University.

Reskin, B. F., & Charles, C. Z. (1997). Now you see 'em, now you don't: Theoretical approaches to race and gender in labor markets. In I. Browne (Ed.), *Race, gender, and economic inequality: African American and Latina women in the labor market.* New York: Russell Sage Foundation.

Reskin, B. F., & Hartmann, H. I. (1986). *Women's work, men's work: Sex segregation on the job.* Washington, D.C.: National Academy Press.

Reskin, B. F., & McBrier, D. B. (1998). Organizational determinants of the sexual division of managerial labor. Unpublished manuscript.

Reskin, B. F., & Padavic, I. (1988). Supervisors as gatekeepers: Male supervisors' response to women's integration in plant jobs. *Social Problems, 35,* 401–415.

Reskin, B. F., & Roos, P. (1990). *Job queues, gender queues.* Philadelphia: Temple University Press.

Reskin, B. F., & Ross, C. E. (1992). Jobs, authority, and earnings among managers: The continuing significance of sex. *Work and Occupations, 19,* 342–365.

Rollins, J. (1995). *All is never said: The narrative of Odette Harper Hines.* Philadelphia: Temple University Press.

Roos, P. A., & Reskin, B. F. (1984). Institutionalized barriers to sex integration in the workplace. In B. F. Reskin (Ed.), *Sex segregation in the workplace* (pp. 235–60). Washington, D.C.: National Academy Press.

Sackett, P. R., DuBois, C. L., & Noe, A. W. (1991). Tokenism in performance evaluations: The effect of work group representation on male-female and white-black differences in performance ratings. *Journal of Applied Psychology, 76,* 263–267.

Schroedel, J. (1985). *Alone in a crowd.* Philadelphia: Temple University Press.

Schultz, V. (1991). Telling stories about women and work: judicial interpretation of sex segregation in the work-place in Title VII cases raising the lack of interest argument. In K. Bartlett & R. Kennedy (Eds.), *Feminist legal theory* (pp. 124–43). Boulder, CO: Westview.

Segura, D. (1992). Chicanas in white-collar jobs: "You have to prove yourself." *Sociological Perspectives, 35,* 163–182.

Shaeffer, R. G., & Lynton, E. F. (1979). Corporate experience in improving women's job opportunities. Report no. 755. New York: The Conference Board.

Smith, J. P., & Welch, F. (1984). Affirmative action and labor markets. *Journal of Labor Economics, 2,* 269–301.

Smith, T. W. (1990). Ethnic images. *General Social Survey Report.* Chicago: National Opinion Research Center.

Sorensen, E. (1989). Measuring the effect of occupational sex and race composition on earnings. In R. T. Michael, H. I. Hartmann, & B. O'Farrell (Eds.), *Pay equity: Empirical inquiries* (pp. 49–69). Washington, D.C.: National Academy Press.

Spain, D., & Bianchi, S. M. (1996). *Balancing act: Motherhood, marriage, and employment among American women.* New York: Russell Sage Foundation.

Steinberg, R. (1987). Radical challenges in a liberal world: The mixed success of comparable worth. *Gender & Society, 1,* 466–475.

Subich, L. M., Barrett, G. V., Doverspike, D., & Alexander, R. A. (1989). The effects of sex-role related factors on occupational choice and salary. In R. T. Michael, H. I. Hartmann, & B. O'Farrell (Eds.), *Pay equity: Empirical inquiries* (pp. 91–104). Washington, D.C.: National Academy Press.

Swerdlow, M. (1989). Men's accommodations to women entering a nontraditional occupation: A case of rapid transit operatives. *Gender & Society, 3,* 373–387.

Szafran, R. F. (1982). What kinds of firms hire and promote women and blacks? A review of the literature. *Sociological Quarterly, 23,* 171–190.

Thurow, L. (1969). *Poverty and discrimination.* Washington, D.C.: The Brookings Institute.

Tomaskovic-Devey, D. (1993). *Gender and racial inequality at work The sources and consequences of job segregation.* Ithaca, NY: ILR Press.

Tomaskovic-Devey, D. (1994). Race, ethnicity, and gender earnings inequality: The sources and consequences of employment segregation. Report to the Glass Ceiling Commission, U.S.   Department of Labor.

Treiman, D. J., & Hartmann, H. I. (1981). *Women, work, and wages.* Washington, D.C.: National Academy Press.

Ullman, J. P., & Deaux, K. (1981). Recent efforts to increase female participation in apprenticeship in the basic steel industry in the Midwest. In V. M. Briggs, Jr. & F. Foltman (Eds.), *Apprenticeship research: Emerging findings and future trends (*pp. 133–149*).* Ithaca: N.Y. State School of Industrial and Labor Relations, Cornell University.

U.S. Bureau of the Census. (1972). *U.S. census of the population, 1970. Subject Reports, 7C, Occupational characteristics.* Washington, D.C.: Census Bureau.

U.S. Bureau of the Census. (1982). *Census of population and housing, 1980: Public use microdata samples U.S.* [machine-readable data files, prepared by the Bureau of the Census]. Washington, D.C.: Census Bureau.

U.S. Bureau of the Census. (1992a*). Census of population and housing, 1990: public use microdata samples U.S.* [machine-readable data files, prepared by the Bureau of the Census]. Washington, D.C.: Census Bureau.

U. S. Bureau of the Census. (1992b). *Detailed occupation and other characteristics from the EEO file for the United States. 1990 CP-S-1-1.* Washington, D.C.: U.S. Department of Commerce.

U.S. Bureau of the Census. (1996a). Money income in the U.S., 1995. *Current Population Reports,* Series P-60. Washington, D.C.: Census Bureau.

U.S. Bureau of the Census. (1996b). *Statistical abstract of the United States: 1996.* 116th edition. Washington, D.C.: Census Bureau.

U.S. Bureau of Labor Statistics. (1961). *Employment and earnings 8 (January)*. Washington, D.C.: U. S. Government Printing Office.

U.S. Bureau of Labor Statistics. (1995). *Employment and earnings 42 (January)*. Washington, D.C.: U.S. Government Printing Office.

U.S. Bureau of Labor Statistics. (1996a). *Current population survey, February 1995: Contingent work supplement* [machine-readable data file]. Conducted by the Bureau of the Census for the Bureau of Labor Statistics. Washington, D.C.: Bureau of the Census [producer and distributor].

U.S. Bureau of Labor Statistics. (1996b). *Employment and earnings 43 (January)*. Washington, D.C.: U. S. Government Printing Office.

U.S. Bureau of Labor Statistics. (1997). *Employment and earnings 44 (January)*. Washington, D.C.: U.S. Government Printing Office.

U.S. Bureau of Labor Statistics. (1998). Web page. www.bls.gov

U.S. Department of Labor. (1977). *Dictionary of occupational titles* (4th ed.). Washington, D.C.: U. S. Government Printing Office.

U.S. Department of Labor. (1996). Employment standards administration, Office for Federal Contract Compliance Programs. OFCCP egregious discrimination cases. Nov. 19. Washington, D.C.: U.S. Department of Labor.

U.S. Merit Systems Protection Board. (1992). *A question of equity: Women and the glass ceiling in the federal government*. A Report to the President and Congress by the U.S. Merit Systems Protection Board. Washington, D.C.: U.S. Merit Systems Protection Board.

U.S. Merit Systems Protection Board. (1996). *Fair and equitable treatment A progress report on minority employment in the federal government*. Washington, D.C.: U.S. Merit Systems Protection Board.

Von Glinow, M. A. (1988). Women in corporate America: A caste of thousands. *New Management, 6*, 36–42.

Waldinger, R. & Bailey, T. (1991). The continuing significance of race: Racial conflict and racial discrimination in construction. *Politics and Society, 19*, 291–323.

Williams, C. L. (1989*). Gender differences at work: Women and men in nontraditional occupations*. Berekely, CA: University of California Press.

Williams, C. L. (1995). *Still a man's world: Men who do "women's work."* Berkeley, CA: University of California Press.

Williams, J. B., & Best, D. (1986). Sex stereotypes and intergroup relations. In S. Worchel & W. G. Austin (Eds.), *Psychology of intergroup relations* (pp. 244–259). Chicago: Nelson-Hall.

Wilson, W. J. (1996). *When work disappears: The world of the new urban poor*. New York: Knopf.

CHAPTER 17

Gender and Unpaid Work

Beth Anne Shelton

Most commonly, research on gender and unpaid work focuses on housework, although there are at least two other types of unpaid labor that warrant attention. In this chapter I consider not only housework time, but also childcare time and time spent doing volunteer work. I consider housework and childcare separately because some aspects of child care are not included in most estimates of housework, but nonetheless constitute significant investments of time. For example, while a measure of housework normally would include estimates of time spent preparing meals for children (under a general estimate of time spent preparing meals), it would not necessarily include time spent working with children on homework or helping children get dressed for school. These latter activities are time consuming and involve work, and gender is associated with how much time individuals spend doing them (Coverman & Sheley, 1986). Thus, I evaluate research on gendered patterns of child care time separately from a consideration of housework time.

In addition, the summary of research on gender and unpaid work includes a review of the research on volunteer work. Since the 1970s sociologists have recognized that the activities of maintaining a home and children constitute work, even when unwaged, but we have been slower to incorporate measures of volunteer time into our analyses of gendered patterns of unpaid work time. Indeed, in measures of women's and men's total "work" time, volunteer work time is not included (Marini & Shelton, 1993), although much of the work associated with children, for example, is volunteer work that would be unmeasured in either housework or child care measures (e.g., PTO activities, soccer coach). Thus, the gender "equity" in total work time noted by some authors is based on an accounting that excludes an important category of unpaid work (Ferree, 1991). In addition

BETH ANNE SHELTON • Department of Sociology and Anthropology, University of Texas at Arlington, Arlington, Texas 76019

Handbook of the Sociology of Gender, edited by Janet Saltzman Chafetz. Kluwer Academic/ Plenum Publishers, New York, 1999.

to summarizing gendered patterns of unpaid work, I review explanations of these patterns and assess their success in accounting for gender differences in unpaid work.

1. HOUSEWORK TIME

There are a variety of ways that housework time and the division of household labor have been measured. The highest quality estimates are based on time diaries typically completed for a 24-hour period (Marini & Shelton, 1993). This method results in the most detail, as well as in the most accurate estimates. Nevertheless, studies comparing the variety of ways that housework time has been measured indicate that direct questions about typical time expenditures result in some overestimation, but that measures of women's and men's shares of housework are similar no matter what the measurement method. This is especially true when the measures ask individuals to estimate their time spent on a variety of housework tasks (e.g., doing dishes, preparing meals, doing laundry, cleaning house) rather than on a generic category called "housework." Since time diary estimates are expensive, most studies rely on some sort of direct question.

No matter how housework time is measured, it is clear that gender is related to the distribution of housework. Women continue to spend significantly more time on housework than do men and this pattern is true whether or not women are employed (Berardo, Shehan, Leslie, 1987; Marini & Shelton, 1993; Presser, 1994). In the United States, most estimates are that women do between 65% and 80% of household labor (Greenstein, 1996). Studies done in other countries also consistently show that women do the majority of household labor, although the magnitude of the gender gap varies (Gershuny & Robinson, 1988).

Most of the studies of housework are based on samples of married women and men, a restriction that obscures the impact of marital status on the gender gap in housework time. In comparisons of married, single, and unmarried cohabiting women and men, researchers report that the gap between women's and men's housework time is greater among married couples than among either single women and men or cohabiting couples (McAllister, 1990; Stafford, Backman, & Dibona, 1977). Most the differences in the gender gap in housework time by marital status are due to variation in women's housework Time (Shelton & John. 1993a; South & Spitze, 1994). Married women spend more time on housework than either cohabiting or single women.

Interestingly, remarried men appear to spend more time on housework than men in first marriages, although the reverse is true for women (Demo & Acock. 1993; Ishii-Kuntz & Coltrane, 1992). This pattern suggests that there may be some reevaluation of family roles for both women and men after divorce and that the result is a slightly more equal division of housework in second than in first marriages.

Recent time diary estimates of women's and men's housework time indicate that women spend 19.5 hours per week on housework compared to 9.8 hours per week for men (see Table 17-1). Estimates based on direct questions about housework time are higher than time diary estimates for both women and men but the pattern is similar. Data from the *National Survey of Families and Households* indicate that women spend approximately 37 hours per week on housework while men spend 18 hours per week (Greenstein, 1996; see also Kamo, 1991; Marini & Shelton, 1993).

Measures of task segregation indicate that household tasks are highly segregated as well (Blair & Lichter, 1991). Thus, in addition to men spending less time on housework

TABLE 17-1. U. S. Housework Time
by Year and Gender

Year	Hours Per Week	
	Men	Women
1965	4.6	27.0
1975	7.0	21.7
1985	9.8	19.5

Source: Robinson, J. P. (1988). Who's doing the housework?
American Demographics, 10, 24–63.

than women, they spend their time on different household tasks than women (Berk, 1985). Berk and Berk (1979) find, in addition, that men are less likely than women to do more than one task at a time and that men's tasks are more likely to be discretionary than are women's (see also Meissner, Humphries, Meis, & Scheu, 1975). That is, men are more likely to spend time on tasks that can be scheduled for convenience than are women (e.g., yard care versus meal preparation). One reflection of the gender differences in household tasks may be the greater proportion of men who view their housework tasks as leisure or semileisure (Horna & Lupri, 1987). A final difference in housework time is related to the simultaneity of tasks. With respect to doing more than one task at a time, women are more likely than men to prepare a meal, make lunches for school and do laundry more or less at the same time (Berk & Berk, 1979). Moreover, a greater proportion of men's housework tasks are done with someone else, whereas women are more likely to do tasks alone (Horna & Lupri, 1987; Sullivan, 1996).

1.1. Housework in Other Countries

Possibly because of Sweden's reputation for governmental encouragement of gender equity at home, there are a relatively large number of studies of the gender division of unpaid labor in Sweden. Swedish women spend significantly less time cooking and grocery shopping than U.S. women and Swedish men spend more time cooking and cleaning house than their American counterparts, although there are no significant gaps in Swedish and American women's and men's time spent washing dishes or doing laundry (Calasanti & Bailey, 1991). Moreover, there is still a gap between Swedish women's and men's total housework time (Juster & Stafford, 1991; Wright, Shire, Hwang, Dolan, & Baxter, 1992). Gustafsson and Kjulin (1994) report that Swedish men do approximately 35% of the housework and childcare and their time estimates are similar to figures for the United States (see also Juster & Stafford, 1991).

While Swedish couples have been studied to determine the impact of state efforts to encourage gender equity at home, Japanese couples often are of interest because of their supposed traditionalism (Moringa, Sakata, & Koshi, 1992). In fact, studies of Japanese couples help illustrate the relatively minor differences among industrialized countries. Researchers' reports of Japanese men's and women's housework time vary widely. Kamo (1994) finds that Japanese men do about 25% of the housework, whereas Juster and Stafford (1991) report that Japanese men spend only 10% as much time as women on housework. Moreover, Juster and Stafford's (1991) estimates of Japanese men's time are significantly lower than estimates for men in other industrialized countries. They report that Japanese men spend only 3.5 hours per week on housework compared to almost 14 hours for men in the United States and more than 18 hours per week for men in Sweden.

Interestingly, they report less variation in women's housework time across industrialized countries than in men's.

Sanchez (1994a) has studied men's participation in household labor in Java, Sudanese Indonesia, the Philippines, Taiwan, South Korea, and the United States. Although she does not have time estimates, she does find differences in the percentage of men who regularly participate in household labor (as reported by their wives). The range is from 60% for Korea to 17% for Sudanese Indonesia. It is not, however, clear that all wives are referring to the same type of "help." Juster and Stafford (1991), using time estimates, report that women in rural Botswana and Nepal spend significantly more time and men less time on housework than in industrialized countries.

There is quite a bit of variation in women's and men's housework time across societies, but in no instance do men and women spend an equal or near equal amount of time on housework. Moreover, variations in the amount of time spent on housework do not vary systematically with the availability of labor saving household technology, suggesting that it does not always operate to reduce household demands (Robinson, 1980).

1.2. Historical Trends in Housework Time

There are a number of studies documenting the impact of technological innovations on both the character of housework and how it is divided. Some emphasize the labor saving aspects of new technologies (Bose, 1979; Bose, Bereano, & Malloy, 1984; Day, 1992; Jackson, 1992), while others focus on the way innovations affect women's and men's housework differently (Cowan, 1983). Cowan (1983), in particular, details how new household technologies not only made some tasks easier, but created new tasks. An example she provides is the invention of the stove, which raised expectations regarding an appropriate meal and involved additional work to clean and maintain the stove. She recognizes that the stove improved the standard of living for most households, but also that it increased the workload for women. In addition, she details how the stove decreased the need for large quantities of wood, and thereby reduced some of men's housework.

As technological innovations made housework easier, they also justified reducing middle-class women's reliance on servants. This trend not only left work for middle-class women to do, it also led to a greater homogenization of the standard of living. As poor women were not hired as domestic servants they were able to work to maintain their households at a middle-class standard, thereby reducing class differences in the quality of home life (Jackson, 1992; Strasser, 1982). Bose (1979) argues that as women were drawn into paid labor they were increasingly able to maintain their housework standards because of technological innovations that made housework less time consuming and less physically demanding (see also Bose et al., 1984; Day, 1992).

Oakley (1974) focuses on the extent to which industrialization and men's movement into the paid labor force made "housework" increasingly invisible (see also Cowan, 1983). Men's absence from the home during the day and their participation in paid work encouraged housework activities to be viewed as something other than work. In addition, the work of maintaining a household was visible only to those who were home during the day—women and young children.

That housework was invisible to many members of the family does not mean that it was not time consuming. New technologies that encouraged higher standards of living (e.g., better and/or more complicated meals because of the stove, cleaner bathrooms because of indoor plumbing) meant that although housework became somewhat easier during the nineteenth and the first half of twentieth centuries, women did not spend significantly less time on it (Cowan, 1983; Robinson, 1985). Oakley (1974) reports that women in the United States were spending more time on housework in 1945 than in 1929. Later studies indicating that women's household labor has decreased over time also show that their total work time (including paid work time) has not declined (Robinson, 1985).

More recent investigations of the impact of technology on household labor time suggest that even modern conveniences, such as the microwave oven, do not significantly reduce women's housework time. Robinson and Milkie (1997) report that women who own microwave ovens spend only 4 minutes less per day cooking than women without microwave ovens and those with automatic dishwashers spend only 1 minute less per day cleaning up after meals than those without dishwashers. Thus, "labor-saving" devices save less than is commonly assumed. This may reflect the higher standards associated with owning labor-saving appliances (e.g., washing clothes more often if you own a washing machine), or simply inefficiencies of the appliances (e.g., rinsing dishes before loading them in the dishwasher).

A number of studies evaluate relatively recent shifts in men's housework time or in their proportional share of housework time. Researchers vary in the extent to which they report significant change in the division of housework. Some argue that the division of household labor has become more equal over time (Robinson, 1988), while others report little shift in the division of household labor (Goldscheider & Waite, 1991). Much of the disagreement reflects differences in how shifts in housework time are interpreted. Those studies that document men's increased responsibility for housework often measure men's relative share, obscuring the fact that men's share most often increases because of a decrease in women's housework time, rather than an increase in men's (Coltrane & Ishii-Kuntz, 1992b; Goldscheider & Waite, 1991; Hiller & Philliber, 1986; Spitze, 1986). Coverman and Sheley (1986) report that men's housework time was stable from 1965 to 1975, although they estimate that their relative share went from 28% to 34% during the same period because women reduced their housework time by almost an hour per day.

One explanation for how households are maintained, given women's decreased housework time and men's modest increases, suggests that couples are relying more on purchased services, such as lawn care, dry cleaning, and grocery delivery (Brines, 1993). However, operationalizing such rates of "commodity substitution" has proven difficult (for an attempt see Brines, 1993).

Gershuny and Robinson (1988) report that from the 1960s to the 1980s, women's housework time decreased, even after paid work time and number of children were taken into account (see also Coverman & Sheley, 1986; Robinson, 1988). Women in the 1960s spent about 8 more hours per week cooking meals, cleaning up after meals, cleaning house, and doing laundry than women in the 1980s, whereas men spent about 2 hours more on these tasks in the 1980s than in the 1960s (Robinson, 1988). In spite of the convergence, a large gap between women's and men's housework time remains (see Table 17.1).

Trends in men's and women's housework time in a variety of other countries generally are similar to U.S. trends (Gershuny & Robinson, 1988). From the 1970s to the 1980s, when men's proportional share of housework in the United States increased modestly, men's share of housework in the United Kingdom, Canada, and Norway also increased, although there was no shift in Holland (Gershuny & Robinson, 1988) (see Table 17.2). Nonetheless, in every nation women do at least 80% of the housework.

TABLE 17.2. Cross-cultural Comparisons of Minutes Spent per Day on Housework and Proportional Share of Housework Time by Country, Year, and Gender

Year	United States		Canada		United Kingdom		Holland		Norway	
	Women	Men	Women	Men	Women	Men	Women	Men	Women	Men
1970s (Minutes)	175	20	203	29	202	17	211	28	259	25
1970s (Proportion)	89.7	10.3	87.5	12.5	92.2	7.8	88.3	11.7	91.2	8.8
1980s (Minutes)	156	38	158	40	188	37	210	27	195	35
1980s (Proportion)	80.4	19.6	79.8	20.2	83.6	16.4	88.6	11.4	84.8	15.2

Source: Gershuny, J., & Robinson, J. (1988). Historical changes in the household division of labor. *Demography, 24*, 550.

1.3. Race and Housework Time

The gendered pattern of housework time varies somewhat by race as well, although the studies are not completely consistent. Researchers either report that black couples divide housework similarly to white couples (Broman, 1988, 1991; Cronkite, 1977; Hossain & Roopnarine, 1993; Wilson, Tolson, Hinton & Kiernan, 1990) or that the division of housework among black couples is more equal than among white couples (Beckett & Smith, 1981; Ross, 1987; Shelton & John, 1993b). In spite of the inconsistency in research findings, it is clear that although black women and men are more likely than their white counterparts to think that housework is women's responsibility (Cronkite, 1977), they do not divide it less equally. One of the more interesting patterns with respect to race is the relationship between men's paid work time and their housework time. Among black men, the more time they spend on paid work the more time they spend on housework, while the reverse is true for white men (Shelton & John, 1993b). This patterns suggests that the way black men interpret family responsibilities may be different than the way white men interpret them.

The gender gap in housework time differs between Mexican-Americans and Anglos, although most research suggests that the image of the patriarchal Mexican-American family is exaggerated. Golding (1990) reports that although Mexican-American men do less housework than Anglo men, the difference is due to differences in educational level. Similarly, Shelton and John (1993b) find that there is no difference in the housework time of Mexican-American and Anglo men once sociodemographic characteristics are taken into account.

2. CHILD CARE

Most research suggests that men have increased their time spent on childcare more than is the case for housework (Darling-Fisher & Tiedje, 1990; Pleck, 1985; Presser, 1988). This, however, usually means interaction with children rather than care of infants and toddlers (Goldscheider & Waite, 1991; Pleck, 1985). Similarly, men are more likely to be childcare "helpers," leaving women responsible for the care of children (Ehrensaft, 1987; Brannen & Moss, 1987). Researchers consistently report that women, in general, continue to spend more time on childcare than men (Barnett & Baruch, 1987; Deutsch, Lussier, & Servis, 1993; Wilson, Tolson, Hinton, & Kiernan, 1990). Leslie, Anderson, and Branson (1991) report than among employed women and men, men spend an average of 36 minutes per day caring for their children compared to 1 hour and 12 minutes for women. Coverman and Sheley's (1986) examination of the changes in men's childcare time from 1965 to 1975 found that despite wives' increasing labor force participation, men's childcare contributions did not change significantly.

In other research, Barnett and Baruch (1987) show that the gap between the amount of time parents and children are home together and awake and the amount time spent in solo interaction with children is greater for men than for women. Men are at home and awake when their children are there an average of 29.4 hours per week compared to 44.45 hours for women; men spend only 5.48 hours per week in solo interaction with their children compared to 19.56 hours per week far women, regardless of the wife's employment status. This significantly larger gap between time available and time spent in solo interaction is consistent with other researchers' reports that women are more likely to be *responsible* for the care of children than men (Gerson, 1993).

Research on Sweden reveals that child care patterns are similar to those in the United States, although men do proportionally more in Sweden than in the United States. Gustafsson and Kjulin (1994) report that men spend approximately 5.0 hours per week on "active child care" compared to 9.7 hours for women (see also Lamb, Hwang, Broberg, Bookstein, Hult, & Frodi, 1988). These estimates are similar to those for the United States (see Leslie, Anderson & Branson, 1991). As is the case for the United States, Lamb et al. (1988) find that men spend more time playing with children than caring for them. In other words, more of men's childcare time is discretionary than is the case for women, and men spend more time on relatively pleasurable aspects of childcare than do women (e.g., playing with children versus changing diapers). Unlike other researchers, Hannah and Quarter (1992) report that Canadian men and women spend similar amounts of time on childcare but that women spend significantly more time on housework than do men, although they do not report on the nature of men's and women's childcare activities. This is in contrast to Homa and Lupri's (1987) findings that although Canadian fathers have a relatively high degree of participation in childcare, mothers still are responsible for the greatest proportion of childcare tasks.

3. UNDERSTANDING THE DISTRIBUTION OF HOUSEWORK AND CHILDCARE

The variety of perspectives that have been developed to account for the division of household labor can, in most cases, be applied to understanding childcare time as well. In the majority of cases, however, childcare is considered only to the extent that care of children is measured in housework items (e.g., meal preparation, indoor cleaning), rather than in a separate measure of childcare.

There is a large body of literature that focuses on accounting for the division of household labor. At least three dominant explanations for the division of household labor have emerged from this research tradition, although none of them alone or in combination can fully account for the pattern of the division of housework. The most common explanations for the division of household labor identify time constraints, ideology, and relative resources as possibly accounting for it (Ross, 1987; Shelton, 1992).

The time constraints approach, also known as the demand/response capability (Coverman, 1985) or situational view (England & Farkas, 1986), conceptualizes the division of household labor as a consequence of other demands on individuals' time. This explanation identifies women's greater household labor time as a consequence of their fewer hours spent in paid labor and number and ages of children (Greenstein, 1996; Silver & Goldscheider, 1994).

The majority of studies evaluating the impact of women's and men's paid work time on their housework time find that the more time individuals spend in paid labor the less time they spend on housework (Acock & Demo, 1994; Brines, 1993; Demo & Acock, 1993) and childcare (Coverman & Sheley, 1986; McHale & Huston, 1984). However, most studies also note that the association is stronger for women than it is for men (McHale & Huston, 1984) and that women continue to do more housework and childcare than men no matter how much time they spend in paid labor (Beckett & Smith, 1981; Kamo, 1991; Newell, 1993). Thus, although, paid work time is associated with housework time, it cannot account for all of the gender gap in housework time.

A number of studies investigate the relationship between women's paid work time and their husbands' housework time. These studies report inconsistent findings, with some indicating that husband's housework time is responsive to their wives' paid work time (Blair & Lichter, 1991; Brines, 1993; Nickels & Metzen, 1982), although many report a weak or nonexistent association (Levant, Slattery, & Loiselle, 1987). Particularly problematic are studies that evaluate the effect of wives' paid work time on men's relative share of housework (Coltrane & Ishii-Kuntz, 1992a; Kamo, 1988; Ross, 1987). Measuring relative share of housework makes it impossible to identify the source of any variation in men's share. It may be due to shifts in women's and/or men's actual housework time. Since it is clear that women reduce their housework time in response to paid work demands, at least some portion of the association between women's paid work time and men's relative share of housework will be due to changes in wives' housework time.

Among those who have evaluated the impact of wives' paid work time on husbands' housework and childcare time, some find a weak association (Blair & Lichter, 1991) and some find no statistically significant relationship at all (Brayfield, 1992). Beckett and Smith (1981) report that paid labor time affects white women's child care time more than it affects their husbands' time and Tuttle (1994) finds that wives' work hours are negatively associated with husbands' childcare participation (see also Barnett & Baruch, 1987; John, 1996). Similarly, Leslie et al. (1991) find that women's paid work time is associated with the amount of time they are responsible for their children, but that it has no effect on the time husbands are responsible.

Men's housework *tasks* also may be affected by their wives' or their own paid work time. Atkinson and Huston (1984) report that men do more female-typed tasks in response to their wives' greater paid work time while Blair and Lichter (1991) find that household tasks are more segregated the more time men spend in paid labor. These studies point to an important aspect of the division of household labor—the gendered nature of the housework tasks that women and men undertake.

Rather than simply evaluating husbands' and wives' paid work time, Kingston and Nock (1985) examined the impact of work schedule on the division of household labor (see also Blair & Lichter, 1991; Brayfield, 1995; Presser, 1994; Wharton, 1994), while Presser (1988) evaluated the impact of shift work on child care time. These studies find that off-scheduling (husbands and wives working somewhat different hours) is associated with men spending more time on housework (Kingston & Nock, 1985) and childcare (Presser, 1988). That is, when men have time at home when their wives are at work they do more housework than when they work the same hours as their wives. A few studies also have documented a similar positive effect of off-scheduling on women's housework time (Pleck & Staines, 1985).

Although a wife's paid work time is not clearly associated with her husband's housework time, her employment may be associated with it. That is, it may be wife's employment *per se*, rather than hours spent in paid labor that affects husband's household labor time. In addition, employment may be even more strongly associated with housework time than paid work time for women. Studies comparing dual-earner and single-earner households indicate that women do most of the housework no matter what their employment status (Berardo et al., 1987; Bergmann, 1986; Mederer, 1993; Pleck & Staines, 1985), but that women in dual-earner households share more of the responsibility for household tasks than women in single-earner households (Maret & Finlay, 1984). The sex typing of household tasks is similar in single-earner and dual-earner households (Coltrane, 1990; Mederer, 1993).

Just as paid work time has a greater effect on women's than on men's household labor, children also affect women's housework time more than men's (Gershuny & Robinson, 1988; Shelton, 1992). Berk (1985) found that the presence of a single infant increased the total monthly household tasks by more than 400 hours, adding more than 105 minutes to each household work day. Studies using representative samples report that the more children and the younger the children in a household the more time women, and to a much smaller extent, men, spend on housework (Brines. 1993; Presser, 1994).

The greater effect of both children and paid work on women's than on men's housework poses some problems for the time constraints explanation of the division of household labor. The perspective provides no rationale for the different effects of time constraints (e.g., paid work and children) on women's and men's housework time. In addition, it is difficult to determine the extent to which there is a simple, unidirectional effect of paid work time on housework, or whether there are reciprocal effects (but see Kalleberg & Rosenfeld, 1990). Thus, both the nature of the empirical association between paid work time and housework time and the explanation itself have serious limitations with respect to helping us understand the gendered division of household labor.

A second approach to explaining the division of household labor focuses on ideology or gender role attitudes to account for women's greater housework time (Huber & Spitze, 1983; Spitze, 1988). According to this explanation, women's greater household labor time can be explained by reference to their own and their husband's attitudes about who should do the housework. Thus, the hypothesis is that the more egalitarian women's and men's sex role attitudes, the less housework women will do and the more housework men will do. In general, studies support this explanation, although the strength of the association varies by gender and men's attitudes have more impact on their wives' household labor than wives' attitudes have on their husbands' housework time.

The majority of studies indicate that the more egalitarian men's gender role attitudes, the more equal the division of household labor (Coltrane & Ishii-Kuntz, 1992b; Kamo, 1988; Ross, 1987), although some report that this effect is due mostly to the impact of men's attitudes on women's housework time, rather than to the effect of men's attitudes on their own housework time (Presser, 1994; Sanchez, 1994b). This pattern is consistent with a number of qualitative studies that illustrate the extent to which women's housework time is a function of their husbands' expectations (DeVault, 1991). Wives' responsiveness to their husbands is also supported by studies indicating that women's gender role attitudes are less strongly associated with their housework time than are their husbands' gender role attitudes (Presser, 1994), although Greenstein (1996) reports an interaction effect between wives' and husbands' gender role ideologies.

With the exception of a few studies that have poor measures of either gender role attitudes (Brayfield, 1992) or housework time (Ross, 1987), the findings regarding the impact of gender role attitudes on housework time are consistent. Nevertheless, when considering the entire gender gap in housework time, gender role attitudes can account for only a small part of it. In addition, although attitudes are associated with housework time, the variation is around a very unequal base, so that, in general, even those couples with egalitarian attitudes have an unequal division of household labor, one that is only somewhat less unequal than other couples'. Men with traditional gender role attitudes are not any less likely to participate in childcare than men with more egalitarian attitudes (Barnett & Baruch, 1987; McHale & Huston, 1984) and some find that men with more traditional childcare attitudes spend more time on child care (Tuttle, 1994).

One of the oldest approaches to understanding the division of household labor is based on Blood and Wolfe's (1960) study of relative resources and their impact on decision-making. This approach is based on the view that individuals will seek to minimize their time spent on housework (because it is unpleasant) and that they will use any resource advantage to do so. Thus, the spouse with the most resources will use them to negotiate his or her way out of housework (Brines, 1993) or childcare (Coverman & Sheley, 1986; Deutsch et al., 1993; John, 1996). Resources most often are conceptualized and measured as education, occupational prestige, and earnings.

An alternative explanation for the expected relationship between relative resources and housework time is offered by neoclassical economists who argue that relative resources will be associated with household labor time because of *households'* attempts to most efficiently allocate effort (Becker, 1981, 1985). According to the neoclassical model, the person with the most resources will maximize utilities for the household by concentrating his or her effort in paid labor while household utilities will be similarly maximized if the individual with fewer resources devotes him- or herself to household labor. The important distinction between the relative resource and neoclassical models involves the conceptualization of the family. In the relative resource model individuals seek to maximize utilities whereas in the neoclassical model families seek to maximize utilities. Since women's earnings are generally lower than men's, both models are consistent with women doing more housework than men, although for different reasons.

With important exceptions, the empirical evaluations of the relative resource model support it. The smaller the earnings gap between husbands and wives the more equal the division of household labor (Blair & Lichter, 1991; Presser, 1994) and child care (Deutsch et al., 1993). However, Leslie et al., (1991) find no significant effect of the mother's relative earnings on the division of childcare work. In addition, although the greater the woman's earnings relative to her husband's the less time she spends on housework, the size of the effect is small (Goldscheider & Waite, 1991). Moreover, the fact that the majority of wives earn less than their husbands creates problems for interpreting the effect. The relative resource model predicts that not only should an individual's relative earnings be associated with the division of household labor when the wife earns less than the husband (as is true in the majority of households), but that this association should hold for those households where the wife earns more than the husband. Somewhat problematically for the relative resource explanation, Brines (1994) reports that men who are economically dependent on their wives compensate by not increasing their housework time, a pattern that she interprets as supporting a "gender display" interpretation for the division of household labor. Whether the gender display interpretation works or not, the unequal association between women's and men's earnings and housework time, as well as the pattern for couples where the wife earns more than the husband, pose problems for the relative resource/neoclassical explanation for the division of household labor.

Educational attainment is often used as a supplemental measure of resources, but is more problematic than earnings because education is associated with gender role ideology, thus making interpretation of any association between education and housework difficult. In fact, men's level of education is typically positively associated with their own and negatively associated with their wives' housework time, suggesting that education may be a better measure of ideology than of resources (Haddad, 1994; Presser, 1994; South & Spitze, 1994). Women's educational level is negatively associated with their housework time (Bergen, 1991; Brines, 1993; South & Spitze, 1994), supporting both the relative resource and ideology explanations. Women with more education have more resources and may be able to negotiate or buy their way out of housework, but those with more education also typically have more egalitarian attitudes and may spend less time on housework in response to attitudes rather than resources (Huber & Spitze, 1983).

Studies investigating the impact of occupational prestige on household labor are even less consistent. Some find that men's occupational prestige is negatively associated with their housework time (McAllister, 1990), while others find that it is positively associated with housework time (Berk & Berk, 1978; Deutsch et al., 1993). It is not clear that it is the resources associated with occupational prestige that account for the association. Aytac (1990) finds that the husbands of wives who are decision-makers on the job spend more time on housework than men whose wives are not decision-makers. Men's decision-making authority on the job also may account for some of the association between occupational prestige and housework time. Further undermining the usefulness of the relative resource explanation is the finding that women's occupational prestige is not associated with their housework time (McAllister, 1990).

As a consequence of the failure of the time constraint, ideology, and relative resource explanations to adequately account for the gender gap in housework time or for variables measuring time constraints, ideology, or resources to be associated in expected ways with housework time, some researchers have proposed a social construction of gender (Berk, 1985; Potuchek, 1992; West & Zimmerman, 1987) or gender display (Brines, 1993, 1994) explanation for the gendered division of household labor (DeVault, 1991). A basic premise of the gender display explanation is a reconceptualization of housework; within this approach, housework may be a resource for the production of gender or a way to display gender, rather than simply something that women and men seek to minimize (Berk, 1985; West & Fenstermaker, 1993). As such, this approach potentially may account for economically dependent men's low involvement in housework (Brines, 1994), economically successful women's involvement in housework (Silberstein, 1992), as well as for the anomalous findings with respect to measures of time constraints, ideology and resources.

For example, the gender differences in the way paid work time and children are associated with housework time may be partially accounted for by the gender display model. Women may respond to children differently than men because, through their response, they attend not only to the needs of children but also produce themselves appropriately as women. In addition, the meaning attached to employment may be different for men and women. For men, employment may help them construct themselves as men, thus freeing them to participate in housework, whereas men who are not able to construct themselves as men through employment may resort to other forms of "gender display" (Brines, 1994). Silberstein (1992) argues that a similar dynamic may account for economically successful women's participation in some forms of housework; through their employment they fail to construct themselves as women, so they too resort to other forms of gender display (in this case participation in household labor) that may appear irrational if housework is conceptualized only as a means of producing a meal or a clean house rather than also gender itself.

4. VOLUNTEER WORK

An important but often neglected type of unpaid work is volunteer work. Those studies that consider it generally seek to understand women's and men's participation in volunteer activities and only incidentally make a connection between household work and volunteer activities. The best known studies of women's volunteer work focus on its status production (Daniels, 1988) or class maintenance (Ostrander, 1984) effects. Mueller (1975) argues that women also may participate in volunteer work because it enhances their human capital (see also Schram & Dunsing, 1981), although there is no indication that volunteer work enhances human capital in a way that translates into employment (Blau, 1976).

Blau (1976) asserts that women participate in volunteer work because of the constraints placed on them by their families, especially children. That is, they volunteer because time constraints make paid work impossible. An alternative interpretation is that participating in volunteer activities is an extension of childcare and housework responsibilities. McPherson and Smith-Lovin (1982) and Booth (1972) document women's greater participation in "domestic" or "expressive" voluntary associations compared to men's greater participation in job-related volunteer associations. Domestic associations include youth and neighborhood associations, both of which involve activities closely related to what is typically defined as housework and childcare. In spite of this, research on women's unpaid work has focused almost exclusively on housework and childcare done in the home (Daniels, 1988 is an exception).

Hayghe (1991) reported that 18.8% of women performed unpaid volunteer work for school or other educational institutions, compared to 10.5% of men. In addition, women were more likely to participate in religious organizations. Of those who did volunteer work, women typically worked more weeks per year than men, although their hours spent per week on volunteer activities were similar. The majority of both women and men spent less than 5 hours per week on volunteer activities, around 20% spent from 5 to 9 hours, and the remainder spent 10 hours or more per week on volunteer activities.

If women's participation includes parent-teacher organizations, organizing children's recreational activities, or other activities related to children it can be counted as additional childcare. Their neighborhood and community activities are an extension of the status production aspects of their housework (Daniels 1988; Ostrander, 1984) and some of these activities may be communal versions of housework (neighborhood cleanup campaigns).

5. CONCLUSIONS

Gender remains strongly associated with women's and men's patterns of unpaid work. The amount of time invested in unpaid work as opposed to paid work, the distribution of unpaid work time among specific tasks, and the patterns of care and responsibility are all determined to a large degree by one's gender. Women continue to spend more time than men on housework, whether they are employed or not; they continue to do more of the work involved in caring for children and to take more responsibility for that work; and finally, women's volunteer activities are more likely to be related to family than are men's.

There have been numerous attempts to explain the gendered patterns of time spent on housework and childcare and, although there is support for each of them, none can fully account for the gendered patterns of unpaid work time. The gender display approach offers some hope for better understanding the relationship between gender and unpaid work time, but efforts to evaluate its usefulness are necessarily indirect. That is, there is no simple way to determine the extent to which unpaid work time is an expression of gender; we can only determine whether a particular pattern is consistent with the gender display model.

It remains clear that the nature of women's and men's participation in housework, childcare and volunteer work are different and that changes in women's labor force participation are not sufficient to eliminate gender differences in unpaid work activities.

Acknowledgments

This research was supported, in part, with funds from the Department of Sociology and Anthropology, The University of Texas at Arlington and Oberlin College. Joseph Nehrenberg, Sheryl Skaggs, Sarah Wyatt, and Jessica Christensen provided research assistance. Daphne John provided helpful comments.

REFERENCES

Acock, A., & Demo, D. H. (1994). *Family diversity and well being.* Thousand Oaks, CA: Sage.

Atkinson, J. & Huston, T. L. (1984). Sex role orientation and division of labor early in marriage. *Journal of Personality and Social Psychology, 46,* 330–345.

Aytac, I. (1990). Sharing household tasks in the United States and Sweden: A reassessment of Kohn's theory. *Sociological Spectrum, 10,* 357–371.

Barnett, R. C., & Baruch, G. K. (1987). Determinants of fathers' participation in family work. *Journal of Marriage and the family, 49,* 29–40.

Becker, G. S. (1985). Human capital, effort, and the sexual division of labor. *Journal Labor Economics, 3,* S33–S58.

Becker, G. (1981). *A treatise on the family.* Cambridge, MA: Harvard University Press.

Beckett, J. O., & Smith, A. D. (1981). Work and family roles: Egalitarian marriage in black and white families. *Social Service Review, 55,* 314–326.

Berardo, D. H., Shehan, C. L., Leslie, G. P. (1987). A residue of tradition: Jobs, careers, and spouses' time in housework. *Journal of Marriage and the Family, 49,* 381–390.

Bergen, E. (1991). The economic context of labor allocation. *Journal of Family Issues, 12,* 140–157.

Bergmann, B. R. (1986). *The economic emergence of women.* New York: Basic Books.

Berk, R. A., & Berk, S. F. (1978). A simultaneous equation model for the division of household labor. *Sociological Methods and Research, 6,* 431–468.

Berk, R. A., & Berk, S. F. (1979). *Labor and leisure at home: Content organization of the household day.* Beverly Hills, CA: Sage.

Berk S. (1985). *The gender factory: The apportionment of work in American households.* New York: Plenum Press.

Blair, S. L., & Lichter, D. T. (1991). Measuring the division of household labor: Gender segregation of housework among American couples. *Journal of Family Issues, 12,* 91–113.

Blau, F. D. (1976). Comment on Mueller's "Economic determinants of volunteer work by women" *Signs: Journal of Women in Culture and Society, 2,* 251–254.

Blood, R. O., & Wolfe, D. M. (1960). *Husbands and wives.* Glencoe, IL: The Free Press.

Booth, A. (1972). Sex and social participation. *American Sociological Review, 37,* 183–192.

Bose, C. (1979). Technology and changes in the division of labor in the American home. *Women's Studies International Quarterly, 2,* 295–304.

Bose, C. E., Bereano, P. L., & Malloy, M. (1984). Household technology and the social construction of housework. *Technology and Culture, 25,* 53–82.

Brannen, J., & Moss, P. (1987). Fathers in dual-earner households through mothers' eyes. In C. Lewis & M. O'Brien (Eds.), *Reassessing Fatherhood* (pp. 203–232). Beverly Hills, CA: Sage.

Brayfield, A. (1992). Employment resources and housework in Canada. *Journal of Marriage and the Family, 54,* 9–30.

Brayfield, A. (1995). Juggling jobs and kids: The impact of employment schedules on fathers' caring for children. *Journal of Marriage and Family, 57,* 321–332.

Brines, J. (1993). The exchange value of housework. *Rationality and Society, 5,* 302–340.

Brines, J. (1994). Economic dependency, gender, and the division of labor at home. *American Journal of Sociology, 100,* 652–688.

Broman, C. L. (1988). Household work and family life satisfaction of blacks. *Journal of Marriage and the Family, 50,* 743–748.

Broman, C. L. (1991). Gender, work-family roles, and psychological well-being of blacks. *Journal of Marriage and the Family, 53,* 504–520.

Calasanti, T. M., & Bailey, C. A. (1991). Gender inequality and the division of household labor in the United States and Sweden: A socialist-feminist approach. *Social Problems, 38,* 34–52.

Coltrane, S. (1990). Birth timing and the division of labor in dual-earner families: exploratory findings and suggestions for future issues. *Journal of Family Issues, 11,* 157–181.

Coltrane, S., & Ishii-Kuntz, M. (1992a). Predicting the sharing of household labor: Are parenting and household labor distinct? *Sociological Perspectives, 35,* 629–647.

Coltrane, S., & Ishii-Kuntz, M. (1992b). Men's housework: A lifecourse perspective. *Journal of Marriage and the Family, 54,* 43–57.

Coverman, S. (1985). Explaining husbands' participation in domestic labor. *The Sociological Quarterly, 26,* 81–97.

Coverman, S., & Sheley, J. F. (1986). Change in men's housework and child-care time. *Journal of Marriage and the Family, 48,* 413–422.

Cowan, R. S. (1983) *More work for mother: The ironies of household technology from the open hearth to the microwave.* New York: Basic Books.

Cronkite R. C. (1977). The determinants of spouses' normative preferences for family roles. *Journal of Marriage and the Family, 39,* 575–585.

Daniels, A. (1988). *Invisible Careers: Women civic leaders from the volunteer world.* Chicago: University of Chicago Press.

Darling-Fisher, L. S., & Tiedje, L. B. (1990). The impact of maternal employment characteristics on father's participation in child care. *Family Relations, 39,* 20–26.

Day, T. (1992). Capital-labor substitutions in the home. *Technology and Culture, 32,* 302–327.

Demo, D. H., & Acock, A. C. (1993). Family diversity and the division of domestic labor: How much have things really changed? *Family Relations, 42,* 323–331.

Deutsch, F. M., Lussier, J. B., & Servis, L. J. (1993) Husbands at home: Predictors of paternal participation in childcare and housework. *Journal Personality and Social Psychology, 65,* 1054–1066.

DeVault, M. L. (1991). *Feeding the family: The social organization of caring as gendered work.* Chicago: University of Chicago Press.

Ehrensaft, D. (1987). *Parenting together: Men and women sharing the care of their children.* Urbana, IL: University of Illinois Press.

England, P., & Farkas, G. (1986). *Households, employment and gender: A social, economic and demographic view.* New York: Aldine de Gruyter.

Ferree, M. M. (1991). The gender division of labor in two-earner marriages. *Journal of Family Issues, 12,* 158–180.

Gershuny, J., & Robinson, J. P. (1988). Historical changes in the household division of labor. *Demography, 25,* 537–552.

Gerson, K. (1993). *No man's land: Men's changing commitments to family and work.* New York: Basis Books.

Golding, J. M. (1990). Division of household labor, strain, and depressive symptoms among Mexican Americans and non-Hispanic Whites. *Psychology of Women Quarterly, 14,* 103–117.

Goldscheider, F. K., & Waite, L. J. (1991). *New families, no families? The transformation of the American home.* Berkeley/Los Angeles/Oxford: University of California Press.

Greenstein, T. N. (1996) Husbands' participation in domestic labor: Interactive effects of wives' and husbands' gender ideologies. *Journal of Marriage and the Family, 58,* 585–595.

Gustafsson, B., & Kjulin, U. (1997). Time use in child care and housework and the total cost of children, *Population Economics, Spring, 287–306.*

Haddad, T. (1994). Men's contribution to family work: A reexamination of "time availability." *International Journal of Sociology of the Family, 24,* 87–111.

Hannah, J., & Quarter, J. (1992). Sharing household labour: "Could you do the bedtime story while I do the dishes?" *Canadian Journal of Community Mental Health, 11,* 147–162.

Hayghe, H. V. (1991). Volunteers in the U.S.: Who donates the time? *Monthly Labor Review,* February: 17–23.

Hiller, D. V., & Philliber, W. W. (1986). The division of labor in contemporary marriage. Expectations, perceptions, and performance. *Social Problems, 33,* 191–201.

Horna, J., & Lupri, E. (1987). Father's participation in work, family, life and leisure: A Canadian experience. In C. Lewis & M. O'Brien (Eds), *Reassessing fatherhood* (pp. 54–73). Beverly Hills, CA: Sage.

Hossain, Z., & Roopnarine, J. L. (1993). Division of household labor and child care in dual-earner African-American families with infants. *Sex Roles, 29,* 571–583.

Huber, J., & Spitze, G. (1983). *Sex stratification: Children, housework, and jobs.* New York: Academic Press.

Ishii-Kuntz, M., & Coltrane, S. (1992). Remarriage, step parenting and household labor. *Journal of Family Issues, 13,* 215–233.

Jackson, S. (1992). Towards a historical sociology of housework: A materialist feminist analysis. *Women's Studies International Forum, 15,* 153–172.

John, D. (1996). Women's reports of men's childcare participation: an examination of African-American and white families. *The Journal of Men's Studies, 5,* 13–30.

Juster, F. T., & Stafford, F. P. (1991). The allocation of time: Empirical findings, behavioral models, and problems of measurement. *Journal of Economic Literature, 28,* 471–522.

Kalleberg, A. L., & Rosenfeld, R. A. (1990). Work in the family and in the labor market: A cross-national, reciprocal analysis. *Journal of Marriage and the Family, 52,* 331–346.

Kamo, Y. (1988). Determinants of household division of labor: Resources, power, and ideology. *Journal of Family Issues, 9,* 177–200.

Kamo, Y. (1991). A nonlinear effect of the number of children on the division of household labor. *Sociological Perspectives, 34,* 205–218.

Kamo, Y. (1994). Division of household work in the United States and Japan. *Journal of Family Issues, 15,* 348–378.

Kingston, P. W., & Nock, S. L. (1985). Consequences of the family work day. *Journal of Marriage and the Family, 47,* 619–630.

Lamb, M. E., Hwang, L., Broberg, A., Bookstein, F. L., Hult, G., & Frodi, M. (1988). The determinants of parental involvement in primiparous Swedish families. *International Journal of Behavioral Development, 11,* 433–449.

Leslie, L. A., Anderson, E. A., & Branson, M. P. (1991). Responsibility for children: The role of gender and employment. *Journal of Family Issues, 12,* 197–210.

Levant, R. F., Slattery S. C., & Loiselle J. E. (1987). Father's involvement in housework and child care with school-aged daughters. *Family Relations, 36,* 152–157.

Maret, E., & Finlay, B. (1984). The distribution of household labor among women in dual-earner families. *Journal of Marriage and the Family, 46,* 357–364.

Marini, M. M., & Shelton, B. A. (1993). Measuring household work: Recent experience in the United States. *Social Science Research, 22,* 361–382.

McAllister, I. (1990). Gender and the division of labor: Employment and earnings variation in Australia. *Work and Occupations, 17,* 79–99.

McHale, S., & Huston, T. (1984). Men and women as parents: Sex role orientation, employment, and parental roles with infants. *Child Development, 55,* 1349–1361.

McPherson. J. M., & Smith-Lovin, L. (1982). Women and weak ties: Differences by sex in the size of voluntary organizations. *American Journal of Sociology, 87,* 883–904.

Mederer, H. J. (1993). Division of labor in two-earner homes: Task accomplishment versus household management as critical variables in perceptions about family work. *Journal of Marriage and the Family, 55,* 133–145.

Meissner, M., Humphries E. W., Meis, S. M., & Scheu, W. J. (1975). No exit for wives: Sexual division of labor and the cumulation of household demands. *Canadian Review of Sociology and Anthropology, 12,* 424–439.

Morinaga, Y., Sakata, K., & Koshi, R. (1992). Marital satisfaction and division of family-related tasks among Japanese married couples. *Psychological Reports, 70,* 163–168.

Mueller, M. (1975). Economic determinants of volunteer work by women. *Signs: Journal of Women in Culture and Society, 1,* 325–338.

Newell, S. (1993). The Superwoman syndrome: Gender difference in attitudes towards equal opportunities at work and towards domestic responsibilities at home. *Work Employment and Society, 7,* 275–289.

Nickols, S. Y., & Metzen, E. J. (1982). Impact of wife's employment upon husband's housework. *Journal of Family Issues, 3,* 199–216.

Ostrander. S. A. (1984). *Women of the upper class.* Philadelphia: Temple University Press.

Pleck, J. H., & Staines, G. L. (1985). Work schedules and family life in two earner couples. *Journal of Family Issues, 6,* 61–82.

Potuchek, J. L. (1992). Employed wives' orientations to breadwinning: A gender theory analysis. *Journal of Marriage and the Family, 54,* 548–558.

Presser, H. (1988). Shift work and child care among young dual-earner American parents. *Journal of Marriage and the Family, 50,* 133–148.

Presser, H. B. (1994). Employment schedules among dual-earner spouses and the division of household labor by gender. *American Sociological review, 59,* 348–364.

Robinson, J. P. (1980). Housework technology and household work. In S. F. Berk (Ed.), *Women and household labor.* Beverly Hills, CA: Sage.

Robinson, J. P. (1985). The validity and reliability of diaries versus alternative time use measures. In F. T. Juster & F. P. Stafford (Eds.), *Time, goods, and well-being* (pp. 33–62). Ann Arbor, MI: Survey Research Center, University of Michigan.

Robinson J. P. (1988). Who's doing the housework? *American Demographics, 10,* 24–63.

Robinson, J. P., & Milkie, M. (1997). Dances with dust bunnies: Housecleaning in America. *American Demographics, 19,* 36–40.

Ross, C. E. (1987) The division of labor at home. *Social Forces, 65,* 816–833.

Sanchez, L. (1994a). Material resources, family structure resources, and husbands' housework participation: A cross-sectional comparison. *Journal of Family Issues, 15,* 379–402.

Sanchez, L. (1994b). Gender, labor allocations, and the psychology of entitlement within the home. *Social Forces, 73,* 533–553.

Schram, V., & Dunsing, M. (1981). Influences on married women's volunteer work participation. *Journal of Consumer Research, 7,* 372–379.

Shelton, B. A. (1992). *Women, men, and time: Gender differences in paid work, housework, and leisure.* Westport, CT: Greenwood.

Shelton, B. A., & John, D. (1993a). Does marital status make a difference? *Journal of Family Issues, 14,* 401–420.

Shelton, B. A., & John. D. (1993b). Ethnicity, race and difference: A comparison of white, black and hispanic men's household labor time. In J. C. Hood (Ed.), *Men, work and family* (pp. 131–150). Newbury Park, CA: Sage.

Silberstein, L. R. (1992). *Dual-career marriage: A system in transition.* Hillsdale, NJ: Lawrence Erlbaum.

Silver, H., & Goldscheider, F. (1994). Flexible work and housework: Constraints on women's domestic labor. *72,* 1103–1119.

South, S. J., & Spitze, G. (1994). Housework in marital and nonmarital households. *American Sociological Review, 59,* 327–347.

Spitze, G. (1986). The division of task responsibility in U.S. households: Longitudinal adjustments to change. *Social Forces, 64,* 689–701.

Stafford, R., Backman E., & Dibona, P. (197;). The division of labor among cohabiting and married couples. *Journal of Marriage and the Family, 50,* 595–618.

Strasser, S. (1982). *Never done: A history of American housework.* New York: Pantheon.

Sullivan, 0. (1996). Time co-ordination, the domestic division of labour and affective relations: Time use and the enjoyment of activities within couples. *Sociology, 30,* 70–100.

Tuttle, R. L. (1994). Determinants of father's participation in child care. *International Journal of Sociology of the Family, 24,* 113–125.

West, C., & Fenstermaker, S. (1993). Power, inequality and the accomplishment of gender: An ethnomethodological view. In P. England (Ed.), *Theory on gender/feminism on theory* (pp. 151–174). New York: Aldine De Gruyter.

West, C., & Zimmerman, D. H. (1987). Doing gender. *Gender & Society, 1,* 125–151.

Wharton, C. S. (1994). Finding time for the "second shift": The impact of flexible work schedules on women's double days. *Gender and Society, 8,* 189–205.

Wilson, M. N., Tolson, T. F. J., Hinton, I. D., & Kiernan, M. (1990). Flexibility and sharing of childcare duties in black families: *Sex Roles, 22,* 409–425.

Wright, E. O., Shire, K., Hwang, S. L., Dolan, M., & Baxter, J. (1992). The non-effects of class on the gender division of labor in the home. *Gender & Society, 6,* 252–282.

CHAPTER 18

Gender and Family Relations

Denise D. Bielby*

1. INTRODUCTION

Among the institutional transformations witnessed by industrial societies over the past century, one of the most profound is the emergence of the private, nuclear family. According to historians, the nuclear family has been around since the seventeenth century (see Cherlin, 1983), but the existence of the *private* nuclear family, organized around the husband as breadwinner and wife as homemaker, was not ascendant until the 1920s. With industrialization, production moved out of the household, the family became the primary locus for emotional satisfaction, and the private nuclear form took on normative expectations that were institutionalized and idealized by the 1950s as the "traditional" family. Families "are the places of sexuality, eating, sleeping, and of the thick and close forms of relatedness imaged by biological ('blood') ties of kinship" (Thorne, 1992, p. 10), although the social arrangements that constitute them are both numerous and variable. However, as feminists and others have observed for more than a decade, the monolithic notion of the traditional, nuclear family is difficult to dispel because it seems to be the most natural and biological, the most timeless and unchanging of all social institutions.

Although the family is a central, enduring, and taken-for-granted social institution, it is also one of the most variable, contested, debated, and analyzed by scholars, policymakers, special interest groups, and family members alike. Feminist scholars argue that the family is an ideological concept as much as it is an institution, and that even its

*With the assistance of Carmen Ochoa.

Denise D. Bielby • Department of Sociology, University of California at Santa Barbara, Santa Barbara, California 93106
Handbook of the Sociology of Gender, edited by Janet Saltzman Chafetz. Kluwer Academic/ Plenum Publishers, New York, 1999.

boundedness as a private institution unto itself that can be wholly separated from the public sphere needs reconsideration (Ferree, 1990; Osmond, 1987). Embodied in cultural assumptions and gender relations are the practical, material, and ideological notions that construct the family. According to Coontz and Parson (1997, p. 446), the emerging notion of the private nuclear family was "an emotional and ethical substitute for more political and social ways of conceptualizing interpersonal and intergenerational obligations. The new ideology also reframed socioeconomic and racial inequalities as differences in family organization and maternal roles, paving the way for today's debate over 'family values.' " It is within this context of variation, transformation, and debate that I review theory and research on gender and family relations, and in particular, the ways in which their intersection constitutes what is defined as "family." While the focus of this chapter is to examine gender and family relations, I also address gender *in* family relations as a pivotal issue.

Neo-institutional theory is used to organize my analysis of gender and family relations. According to the neo-institutionalist perspective, "institutions do not merely reflect the preferences and power of the units constituting them; the institutions themselves shape those preferences" (DiMaggio & Powell, 1991, p. 7). Institutionalization itself is seen as a process by which certain social relationships and actions gradually come to be taken for granted. In addition, institutions such as the family are built upon shared cognitions that define "what has meaning and what actions are possible" (DiMaggio & Powell, 1991, p. 9). Thus, the notion of the private, nuclear family has become entrenched as "monolithic," and is itself a resource that can be appropriated by politicians and others concerned with delineating the moral boundaries of society.

Institutional theory tends to deemphasize actors' deliberate construction of social arrangements to achieve desired outcomes. However, individuals do act purposively, demonstrating agency based upon understandings, shared or otherwise, of their social context as the basis for action (Sewell, 1992). Thus, individual agency, manifested as choices and preferences, must be considered in cultural and historical contexts. Choices and preferences themselves are not universal and unchanging, although once a set of social practices are "institutionalized" they become self sustaining. This occurs because "institutions do not just constrain options: they establish the very criteria by which people discover their preferences" (DiMaggio & Powell, 1991, p. 11). Thus, people choose actions because they offer socially constructed and legitimate paths for solving certain social and individual needs. For example, same-sex couples might participate in a "commitment ceremony" to demonstrate their dedication to a relationship that is not legally sanctioned by the state. By doing so, they are drawing upon and transforming institutionalized scripts about marriage and family. Institutionalization constrains choices, but the sources of constraint come from unspoken understandings shared among actors (DiMaggio & Powell, 1991, p. 12).

Institutional analysis draws attention to the ideological and symbolic significance of gendered social arrangements within the family as they relate to the organization and enactment of familial relationships themselves. Members' social scripts and cognitive schemas are guides to action within family relationships. Consequently, attributions (such as assumptions about fathers as providers), habit (such as division of labor in household tasks or in caretaking of kin), and practical action (such as who organizes family dinners or holiday events) are central to ongoing participation within the family and inform this analysis.

In this chapter, I first address gender and emotion work, focusing on how emotion labor genders the social scripts of caring relations within the family. Then I review research on parenting, attending to variability in the gendered enactment of mothering and fathering. The summary of research on kinship focuses on intergenerational caregiving and women's pivotal role in the allocation of care to others. I then go on to address how gender interacts with waged labor to affect power in domestic relationships. I conclude with a discussion of conceptualizations of the family and the gendered nature of the range of practices that can be subsumed under the concept of family.

2. GENDER AND EMOTION WORK

Theories and research on family structure that were influential in the 1950s and 1960s have been reevaluated by feminist scholars who have emphasized the genderedness of family relations (see, e.g., Beneria & Stimpson, 1987; Thorne & Yalom, 1992). Evelyn Nakano Glenn (1987) provided a comprehensive discussion of the paradigm shift that occurred within family sociology in the 1980s, including the inadequacies of then-prevailing structural–functionalist, exchange, and interactionist theoretical approaches, and the then-emerging "feminist rethinking" about family life. Glenn gave special emphasis to three emerging issues of central importance to a gendered understanding of the family: motherhood and mothering, power and inequality, and households and the political economy. In particular, Glenn's analysis deconstructed the family, addressed the importance of separating mothering from motherhood as a social construction, explained how exposing hierarchical divisions within the family illuminates conflicting interests among family members, and invited a more adequate understanding of the family's complex relationship to the economy and the state, including how that relationship varies by race and class.

The social constructs of masculinity and femininity are integral to every aspect of the social organization of biological sex, and the symbolic display of gender in domestic settings is one of the most deep-seated of cultural expectations (Goffman, 1977). In a study of households comprised of married couples, Brines (1993) found that economically dependent husbands contribute less to household labor than do husbands with better labor market prospects. She reasoned that economic insecurity causes men to become more concerned with their roles as "providers," which would be threatened by taking on a greater share of household responsibilities. Thus, gender does more than organize the labor associated with sleeping, child-raising, eating, and other basic human activities. The enactment of gender, both symbolically and practically, also defines the extent to which individuals are considered to be fulfilling their sex- and gender-linked rights, responsibilities, duties, and obligations within the family (see also Kane, 1994).

Emotion work occurs in both work and household settings. In each, women are expected to assume the tasks of attending carefully to how a setting affects others in it, creating comfortable ambiance through expressions of gaiety, warmth, and sympathy; conveying cheerful, affectionate concern for and interest in others; and attending to the behavior of group members so that no one is left out or ill at ease (Hochschild, 1983; Luxton, 1980). Women are the primary providers of emotional support in families, just as they are of the physical activities of running a household, but that emotional labor is largely unrecognized. As Erickson notes, "The invisibility of emotion work persists despite clear indications that providing emotional support is as much embedded within women's daily family routine as is the performance of housework and childcare duties" (1993, p. 890). Emotion work is invisible in two ways. First, it is unacknowledged and undervalued, as are many of the skills and contributions women bring to paid work. Second, it is literally invisible; others are not even aware of the effort, time, and energy that goes into such activities, and women themselves often see this work as "natural" and simply part of getting things done (see also Daniels, 1987). Thus, the family division of labor in emotion work and its management is another manifestation of the symbolic significance of the most basic activities that take place in the household. In sum, gender defines the normative expectations for and of those who comprise the domestic unit and the activities within it, and emotion labor, including its type, degree, and management, are central to the gendered social construction and enactment of the family.

2.1. Emotion Work and the Gendered Division of Labor

Wharton and Erickson's (1993) analysis of emotion management at home and on the job identified three categories of emotions that are particularly relevant to family: those that integrate, such as love, loyalty, and pride, which bind groups together; ones that differentiate, such as fear, anger, and contempt, causing groups to splinter; and those that mask affect, which encompass displays of neutrality and restraint. Although each of these categories has received attention by scholars, feminist research has tended to focus upon the integrative ones, such as nurturance and caregiving, because they entail the gendered labor that binds members together along culturally prescribed notions of what a "family" ought to be. Wharton and Erickson (1993) observed that the effort associated with this labor involves not only creating the substance or content of emotions, but also their management, including their allocation and coordination. "Family roles are thus characterized by an 'emotional division of labor,' whereby women and men are expected to perform different kinds and amounts of emotion management" (1993, p. 471).

The emotion work that is done in family contexts has a unique relationship to responsibility and obligation. Heimer (1996) observed that this connection is especially strong when responsibilities are "fates," such as responsibilities for children or relatives, where there is little to no opportunity to undo the relationship, rather than "opportunities," such as workplace assignments or educational decisions, where an individual's decision to "take responsibility" involves more personal choice. Conformity to normative expectations that obligate women to become invested in the familial realm leads to further gender specialization. Over time, "the gender differences in distributions of caring work encumber women with responsibilities that are far less easily shifted to others, leaving men freer to invest in responsibilities that are both more likely to lead to rewards and easier to escape should they become burdensome" (Heimer, 1996, p. 243).

Not only is caring work less easily shifted to others, as England and Kilbourne (1990) noted, but it also requires one to invest in developing skills that are not easily transferred to other intimate relationships. Examples they provide include forming attachments with in-laws, learning a partner's sexual preferences, or learning how to resolve disagreements with a partner. Thus, not only is emotion work typically an obligation rather than a choice, but upon dissolution of a relationship the partner who has specialized in such tasks has made investments that have little value in a new relationship. In contrast, the payoff for skills that have value in the paid labor market is unchanged by dissolution of a relationship. Thus, as England and Kilbourne pointed out, a traditional household division of labor doubly disadvantages women. First, compared to their partners, they have less invested in skills that are valued in the market for paid labor. Second, while their partner's labor market skills retain their value regardless of whether the intimate relationship is dissolved, the woman's investment in the unique, relationship-specific skills required to manage the emotional requirements of a relationship are of little or no value in a new relationship. The consequences of this asymmetry for power in relationships are discussed in the following paragraphs.

In Western culture, dyadic love relationships between adults create the basis for family units. In such relationships, the provision of care and caregiving is a central component of intimacy and commitment (Cancian, 1987). Caregiving is the activity of attending and responding to another's suffering, desires, and needs, and of striving to prevent harm and protect and promote another's welfare (Thompson, 1993). Gilligan's (1982) study of gender differences in relationships found that the nonhierarchical ordering that tends to characterize women's relationships with others, regardless of status or position, fosters a belief in the ethic of care and caregiving. This ethic defines the self and other as interdependent, thus forming the basis for the "ideal of responsibility" and "equality of rights" in intimate relationships (1982, pp. 74, 149, 166). These gendered differences are, in turn, associated with differences in how men and women conduct themselves within domestic relationships. For example, women, on average, are more likely than men to define the anticipation of another's needs as care (Dressel & Clark, 1990).

The impact of gender and gender ideology on the domestic distribution and enactment of emotion work is not limited to the study of heterosexual couples. Burgeoning research on gay and lesbian partners shows how same-sex couples are also affected by the normative ideologies of both gender and the family. Blumstein and Schwartz's pioneering 1983 study of the domestic practices of same-sex and heterosexual couples found that household responsibilities, including emotion work, are more equally shared among gays and lesbians, regardless of employment status. However, compared to lesbians, gays tend to have a more traditional division of labor in the household (McWhirter & Mattison, 1984; Peplau & Cochran, 1990). In a study of lesbian coparents, Sullivan (1996) found that in many couples, partners allocated their paid work and family responsibilities so that neither parent assumed an unequal share of the labor, and so that neither partner was economically dependent on the other. However, achieving such equity required a conscious and deliberate effort to countervene social scripts that otherwise prescribe role relationships.

2.2. Parenting, Mothering, and Fathering

With the emergence of the private, nuclear family, family relations shifted from those marked by patriarchal authority, distance, and deference to ones fostering individual autonomy, more intense affective bonds, and the pursuit of personal happiness (Laslett, 1973; Stone, 1977). Chodorow's (1978) analysis of the reproduction of mothering captures the consequences of this shift for parenting in the private, nuclear family. In particular, her work reveals the unique way in which mothering is reproduced by heterosexual couples who engage in a traditional division of household labor, and how that reproduction assures that women remain primarily responsible for the affective aspects of parenting, especially caretaking and nurturance. Chodorow's psychoanalytic analysis also uncovers how parental roles become affectively charged. As a result of the relatively diffuse boundaries of women's identity, itself the product of both a woman's mothering and a daughter's resolution of her own psychosocial development within the nuclear family, women are predisposed to mothering practices that reproduce this pattern. As Chodorow describes, "Women's mothering, then, produces psychological self-definition and capacities appropriate to mothering in women, and curtails and inhibits these capacities and this self-definition in men" (1978, p. 208). In addition, a gender ideology that obligates women to maternal roles reinforces and sustains the identity processes described by Chodorow (Glenn, 1987).

Men are not subject to comparable cultural scripts or identity processes regarding parenthood (Belsky & Volling, 1987; Cowan & Cowan, 1987, 1988; Cowan et al., 1985). While the concept of "paternity" defines a father's position relative to child and mother, it does not prescribe the activities that constitute "fathering." Fathering as caretaking and caregiving is far less scripted than mothering as ideology or action (Amato, 1989; Phares, 1993, 1996; Ruddick, 1989; Silverstein, 1996). In a relatively early study of men's self-definitions of the fathering role, Heath (1976) found that both men and women report being invested in expressive involvement (e.g., demonstrating love, affection, and enjoyment of one's children, and spending time with them), but fewer men than women feel the need to fulfill their responsibility to their children's socialization in this way. Similarly, fathers and mothers have different involvements in activities that facilitate children's growth; fathers are less inclined to see sharing in child-rearing decisions and activities, possessing knowledge of children and child-rearing techniques, or developing specific character traits in their children as essential for competent fathering (see also Simons & Beaman, 1996). Other research finds that the strength of this role specialization is stronger among married men who are more ideologically traditional; men who believe that their primary role in the family is one of provider define their subjective distribution of commitments to work and family accordingly (Bielby & Bielby, 1989, 1992). While gender ideology shapes men's orientation toward parenting, even egalitarian couples who self-consciously share the parenting role still divide involvements with childcare along fairly traditional lines (Coltrane, 1996).

If belief in the provider role prescribes how married men contribute to parenting, divorce has little effect in expanding their notions of fathering (Furstenberg & Nord, 1985). Although it is presumed that children of divorced parents are less likely to experience emotional and behavioral problems when nonresidential fathers remain involved in their children's upbringing, research by psychologists who measured child adjustment following marital disruption found limited support for this hypothesis (Amato, 1993). Instead, rather than seeing expanded possibilities as caregivers, divorced fathers tended to define their responsibilities around notions of entertainment and play, interacting with their children as if they were adult friends or relatives (Arendell, 1986; Furstenberg & Nord, 1985). In contrast, some research suggests that men who remarry and form blended families tend to assume greater responsibility for household labor, including stereotypical "feminine" chores. It is uncertain how remarriage affects men's contributions to fathering, but the challenges posed by blended families may broaden both expectations and practices. As Coltrane (1996, pp. 171–172) observed, blended families "lack normative prescriptions for role performance, institutionalized procedures to handle problems, and easily accessible social support." Thus, remarriage has the potential to liberate men and women from traditional expectations about household roles, allowing more opportunities for experimentation and change in gendered familial responsibilities.

Scholarship on gender ideology, and parenting has been criticized for its portrayals of homogeneous cultural prescriptions and uniform parenting practices (Baber & Allen, 1992; Joseph & Lewis, 1981; Lorber, 1981; Thorne & Yalom, 1992). For example, the analysis of working class Chicana/o parenting by Segura and Pierce (1993) demonstrates how the identity processes described by Chodorow take on a very different form in a community with strong norms about familism and collective responsibility for the task of mothering. However, while practices such as multiple female caretakers demonstrate the stability of alternatives to the "traditional" nuclear family in different social contexts, the research by Segura and Pierce also shows how those alternatives are similarly shaped and gender inequality is sustained by patriarchal institutions.

In an analysis of African American mothering, Hill Collins (1992) showed that parenting accomplished through women's reliance upon networks of female kith and kin provides a physical and psychic base for their children and creates strong and devoted, although less demonstratively affectionate, mother–daughter bonds. A daughter's "growing up means developing a better understanding that even though she may desire more affection and greater freedom, her mother's physical care and protection are acts of maternal love" (Hill Collins, 1992, p. 228). Hill Collins suggests that daughters' eventual recognition of the differences between traditional, popular notions of maternal love and acceptance of the reasons for stern female disciplinarians in their lives was essential to the development of their own identity as women and their capacity to mother. In a community where mothers are both providers and caregivers, and patriarchal norms are secondary, daughters ultimately understand that mothering brings rewards, but at a high personal cost. This complexity makes mothering a contradictory institution for some African-American women, one that overtly includes ambivalence in its reproduction.

Research on parenting by gays and lesbians also provides an important comparative context for studying the intersection of gender ideology and practice (Patterson, 1995). For example, recent research explored whether deliberate efforts to avoid patriarchically based gender inequality in lesbian households makes a difference in the instrumental and affective division of labor in lesbian co-parenting practices. Sullivan (1996) found that when partners explicitly and self-consciously commit to gender-equitable parenting, neither parent assumed a disproportionate share of household tasks relative to the primary wage earner of the couple. However, when lesbian couples decided to adhere to a traditionally gendered breadwinner/primary caregiver arrangement, the stay-at-home partner was rendered economically vulnerable by foregoing ties to paid employment. In particular, this arrangement resulted in a noticeable decline in the stay-at-home partner's capacity to influence family decisions and negotiate for her own needs associated with childcare and other domestic practices. The intrusion of economic dependency reaffirms, once again, the importance of gender and income for power and other aspects of family relations.

3. KINSHIP AND THE FAMILY UNIT

Family units are organized around marital unions or other partnering arrangements, sibling relationships, and intergenerational bonds, all of which exist on the basis of blood, legal, or fictive ties. These ties can extend beyond the immediate household to encompass the community and beyond as kith. Taking anthropological evidence of the family's variability across cultures and social groups as a point of departure (e.g., Morgan, 1870; Stack, 1974; Weston, 1991), some of the earliest work by sociologists focused on the boundaries of the family, particularly along intergenerational lines (Bengtson & Black, 1973; Hagestad, 1981; Shanas, Townsend, Wedderburn, Friis, Milhoj, & Stehouwer, 1968), for example, by exploring the extendedness of the middle class nuclear family (Litwak,

1960). Research on the normative and affective bases of family solidarity (Aldous & Hill, 1965; Atkinson, Kivett, & Campbell, 1986; Cicirelli, 1983; Di Leonardo, 1992; Roberts, Richards, & Bengtson, 1991) clarified the unique role of women in the kin matrix. Rossi and Rossi's comprehensive *Of Human Bonding* (1990) emphasized how the mother-daughter relationship contributed "to the structure of the ties that hold families together in a socially embedded way" (Rossi, 1995, p. 275).

Women play a distinctive role across a range of kinship ties (Waite & Harrison, 1992), with much of the research focusing on intergenerational relations. Declining mortality and fertility increase the length of time individuals spend in multigenerational kinship networks (Farkas & Hogan, 1995). In an analysis of cross-national data collected in Australia, West Germany, Great Britain, Italy, Austria, Hungary, and the United States in the late 1980s, Farkas and Hogan affirm earlier work (Shanas et al., 1968) showing that residents of the United States have more frequent contact with kin after controlling for proximity. They also find that in *all* of the countries studied, women contact kin more frequently than men. This tendency persists after statistically controlling for availability of adult kin, lineage position, generational structure, and age. Farkas and Hogan also found that women expect to solicit help from kin more frequently than do men, regardless of marital status and generational composition, and that Americans expect to rely on kin assistance less frequently than do their counterparts in other countries.

Families are the primary providers of caregiving to elderly parents, and the responsibility is gendered in its provision, type, and management (Abel, 1991). Controlling for the composition of the family network, sons and daughters are not interchangeable resources for parent care (Coward & Dwyer, 1990; Spitze & Logan, 1990), and it is daughters, particularly unmarried daughters, who have a substantially higher probability of fulfilling the primary caregiver role (Abel, 1991; Dwyer & Coward, 1991; Soldo, Wolf, & Agree, 1990; Wolfe, Freedman, & Soldo, 1997). Analysis of data from a 1982 government survey reveals that women represent more than 70% of all caregivers to the elderly and over three quarters of all adult children providing care (Stone, Cafferata, & Sangl, 1987). Moreover, adult daughters constitute almost one-third of caregivers to frail elderly, the most demanding type of responsibility for care to older persons because of its intensively emotional and physical labor (Stone et al., 1987). According to research cited by Abel (1991, p. 5; also see Pavalko & Artis, 1997), the strategies for incorporating caregiving for elders into other work and family responsibilities is gendered (that is, daughters relinquish paid employment, rearrange their schedules, and take time off without pay, while sons reduced the number of hours devoted to parental care), and daughters who provide support to elders receive less assistance themselves from other family members than sons who assist elderly parents. Because of increased life expectancy, contemporary women can expect to spend more years caring for elderly parents than they do rearing children (Watkins, Menken, & Bongaarts, 1987).

Family assistance norms and their implementation vary depending on the type of family ethos organizing kin networks. Pyke and Bengtson (1996) place family belief systems on a continuum ranging from individualistic to collectivistic. "Individualistic" families view caregiving as burdensome labor, and are more likely to rely on formal institutional supports. "Collectivistic" families are more likely to view caregiving as a joint familial responsibility and avoid formal sources of assistance. Although not voluminous, some studies address the degree to which caregiving strategies are gendered and the extent to which they differ by race, ethnicity, and social class. For example, a small body of research on support resources in African-American families shows that adult daughters, in particular, are most often selected as an informal helper to older parents (see e.g., Chatters & Jayakody, 1995; Chatters, Taylor, & Jackson, 1986), but little is known about how these practices are affected by socioeconomic status, or the occupational mobility of African-American daughters (Wharton & Thorne, 1997). The often-assumed dysfunctionality of embedded family ties that characterize Hispanic families has been challenged by Tienda, who has shown how the presence of extended kin encourages creative income strategies to cope with economic hardship. In particular, extended kin facilitate the labor force participation of women by assuming caregiving responsibilities and relieving other domestic burdens (Tienda & Angel, 1982; Tienda & Glass, 1985; see also Hurtado, 1995). The norm of patrilineally organized filial piety underlying families of Asian origin and descent is well documented (Sung, 1990), but there is evidence that daughters are the preferred caregivers, even in the face of strong patrilineal family ideals (Rindfuss, Liao, & Tsuya, 1994).

These findings affirm Rossi's claim that as child-rearers, caregivers, and kin keepers, "women are the unsung heroines of social integration" (Rossi, 1995, p. 275). They also illustrate the bind in which women find themselves as, on the one hand, they perform the duties and obligations that provide for, protect, and maintain the dignity of vulnerable family members, while on the other hand, they encumber themselves in ways many find stressful (Brody, 1981) or oppressive (Aronson, 1992). The matter of care for family elders is just one component of an emerging feminist debate about the sharing of rights and responsibility of care between men and women (see Aronson, 1992).

4. GENDER, POWER, AND FAMILY RELATIONS

In any domestic relationship, an unequal division of labor in household and paid work shapes the relative power each partner has to pursue her or his interests. Social exchange theory (Emerson, 1976), applied to couples' decision-making (Blood & Wolfe, 1960) and marital conflict (Scanzoni, 1970), reveals how financial resources provide leverage in bargaining between spouses; the partner with the greater earning capacity is consistently better able to pursue his or her self-interest (Blumstein & Schwartz, 1983; Duncan & Duncan, 1978).

Exchange theory is gender neutral in its treatment of power in domestic relationships. Gender differences in the distribution of resources and in alternative opportunities are exogenous; whichever partner happens to have greater resources and better alternatives brings more power to the relationship. Research motivated by feminist concerns shows how gender ideology and gendered institutions shape exchange within domestic relationships (Pyke, 1996). For example, as noted previously, England suggested that women are more likely to invest in relationship-specific skills, placing them at a disadvantage relative to partners whose skills and resources are unaffected by the dissolution of an intimate relationship (England & Kilbourne, 1990). England also emphasized the effects of a cultural ideology that devalues traditionally female work and encourages women to altruistically pursue joint familial interests rather than personal self-interest [what Heimer (1996) refers to more appropriately as a normatively prescribed *obligation* rather than altruism].

Similarly, Bielby and Bielby (1992) showed that gender ideology introduces asymmetry in husbands' and wives' decisions about relocating for a better job. That research tested the neoclassical economic model of family migration decisions among dual-earner couples (Mincer, 1978). The neoclassical model is also gender neutral: both husbands and wives should be unwilling to relocate if doing so disrupts a spouse's career and fails to improve the economic well-being of the family. Accordingly, the model predicts that all else constant, one's willingness to move for a better job will be negatively related to the spouse's current income. In fact, contrary to the predictions of the neoclassical model, willingness to relocate for a better job was highly contingent on both gender and gender-role beliefs. Women behaved as predicted by the model: the higher their husband's earnings, the less willing they were to relocate for a better job for themselves. In contrast, traditional males—those who believed in the primacy of a husband's role as provider and who disapproved of employed mothers—were not influenced at all by their wives' earnings. Instead, they gave primacy to their own careers or overall family well-being. However, not all placed their own career interests ahead of those of other family members. Men who rejected traditional gender-role ideology were deterred from relocating if their spouses were in well-paid jobs, although even these men were less sensitive to disruption of their spouses' careers than were employed wives under comparable circumstances. These findings suggest the extent to which the household division of labor is negotiated around symbols of masculinity and femininity (see Brines, 1993; Goffman, 1977) and is contingent on the degree to which spouses hold themselves accountable to cultural definitions of gender (see also Blumstein & Schwartz, 1983; Bolak, 1997; Pyke & Coltrane, 1996; Thompson, 1991).

One promising way of disentangling the effect of gendered institutions and, specifically, notions of masculinity, upon family relations is to compare decision-making and power among heterosexual, lesbian, and gay couples (Kurdek, 1993). Blumstein and Schwartz (1983) find that the relationship between earnings capacity and power was greatest among gay couples and lowest among lesbians, suggesting that culturally defined notions of masculinity shape power dynamics. Sullivan (1996) finds some circumstances under which lesbian couples have a seemingly traditional division of labor, but she claims these arrangements are truly the result of rational calculations, uncontaminated by gender ideology or cultural notions of provider roles. While the findings of these different studies are not fully consistent with one another, they offer insights about gendered institutions not found in studies limited to heterosexual relationships.

Gender, relative power, and perceived inequity are central to the duration of marriage and other domestic partnerships. In an analysis of heterosexual marriage, England and Farkas (1986) conceptualize marriage as an implicit contract. Exogenous social, cultural, and economic factors, including gender role socialization and labor market discrimination, create a domestic division of labor in which men have greater bargaining power relative to women. Specifically, men's tendency to avoid relationship-specific investments not only frees them to accumulate resources, primarily in the form of earning power, that they may transfer to another partner, it also buys them greater bargaining power regarding their own interests within the relationship itself. Women's dependent ties on men explain their greater acceptance of gender inequality, especially in the home. Men's gendered interests, and privilege, and the relative power that assures them dominance, encourages them to accept domestic inequality.

However, the power imbalance within marriage has changed for two reasons. First, men's bargaining advantage decreases with women's earnings capacity outside the home.

Second, if the emphasis on love and emotion in marriage is increasing, then women's bargaining power is enhanced precisely because women are seen as uniquely qualified to bring those qualities to a marriage (England & Farkas, 1986). If the balance of power within marriage is becoming less unequal, then women should be becoming better positioned both to leave relationships that are not fully satisfying and to voice their concerns about inequities within marital relationships. In short, the dynamics of family life have been altered by women's increased standing in the labor force, creating options for women that have always existed for men: "exit" (i.e., divorce), and "voice" (i.e., bargaining or demands for change in the marital relationship), in addition to "loyalty" to traditional domestic arrangements (England & Kilbourne, 1990).

The relationship between women's labor force participation, earnings, and marital dissolution is well documented (Martin & Bumpass, 1989; Goldscheider & Waite, 1991). Recent research also suggests that women's increased power within marriage has indeed contributed to a greater tendency to voice concerns about inequities within relationships. For example, research shows that perceived equity in the division of household labor and childcare, particularly among dual-earner couples, is an important determinant of marital satisfaction (White, 1983; Yogev & Brett, 1985), and disagreements on these issues lead to dissatisfaction and marital instability (Booth, Johnson, White, & Edwards, 1984). In addition, the more housework the husband does, the lower the chances are that the wife has considered divorce (Huber & Spitze, 1983). Goldscheider and Waite (1991) found that husbands use their earnings to "buy" out of sharing household tasks, while wives use their earnings to "buy" increased participation by their husbands.[1] Gender-linked solutions such as these are so deep seated that when domestic confrontations occur over inequities, spouses even disagree on the extent of their disagreements (Benis & Agostinelli, 1988). Criticism of perceived gender inequality at home and at work is higher, on average, among women than among men, but at the same time, consistent with England's analysis, married women are less critical than single women of men's propensity not to share more equally in household responsibilities (Kane & Sanchez, 1994; see also Kane, 1994). Thus, from an institutionalist perspective, cultural scripts about marriage appear to be in a state of flux (Barich & Bielby, 1996), and both discourse and practice are shaping new understandings about marriage and domestic relationships.

5. AGENCY, GENDER IDEOLOGY, AND FAMILY RELATIONS

To this point, my analysis of gender and family relations has emphasized the ways in which practices within the social institution of the family are shaped by gender norms and ideologies. I observed how those practices, centered on the provision of care and caregiving, are affected by prevailing beliefs about masculinity and femininity and by other exogenous factors such as waged labor, and how they vary by differences in cultural contexts. An institutionalist lens has allowed consideration of how both prevailing social scripts that prescribe family life, and symbolic displays and enactments of gender, socially construct the family (Barich & Bielby, 1996).

In particular, institutionalist analysis focuses attention on the taken-for-granted na-

---

[1] Goldscheider and Waite (1991, p. 277) clarify that absolute levels of earnings, as well as education, have a greater effect on the division of household labor than do relative earnings.

ture of gender as an organizing feature of family relations. Taken-for-grantedness is the practical knowledge comprising shared understandings of social reality (Zucker, 1991), and taken-for-granted notions of action within the family fundamentally organize the gendered enactment of roles, behaviors, and expectations of household members. The practical knowledge that systematizes individuals' shared understandings of men's and women's place within the family also organizes expectations of what constitutes the family and how it is accomplished. One of the most fundamental notions of domestic arrangements is that they must be gendered to be enacted; many analyses go no further than considering how they are gendered.

Institutionalist analysis also recognizes the reality of members' agency. Causality does not operate in just one direction; practices and institutions are reciprocally related. Family members' practices modify the institutionalized scripts of gendered domestic life, sometimes by default, when there are no "legitimate" scripts for unconventional lifestyle choices. However, scholars are just beginning to appreciate the importance of developing theory and research to examine how agency operates as a causal force in institutional change. From its inception, feminist scholarship on the family has made note of the reality of multiple discourses and varied practices, but has lacked a conceptual framework for specifying how this diversity modifies family as an institution and ideology (see Glenn, 1987). We know that although constrained by dominant institutions and ideologies, family members experiment with and invent new strategies for dealing with the everyday challenges of domestic life. In doing so, they open up a space for new discourse about what constitutes legitimate practice within families, and even what constitutes a family. One recent treatment of this issue includes Weston's (1991) study of how lesbian and gay domestic arrangements redefine kinship networks. This work challenges the "opposite gender model" of parenthood and kinship relations, which views kinship relations as determined solely on the basis of blood (consanguinity) or marriage (affinity).

Another is Gubrium and Holstein's (1990, 1993; Holstein & Gubrium, 1995) analysis of the family that responds to scholars who decry the "disappearance" of the family (Popenoe, 1993; Smelser, 1980). In conceptualizing "family," they shift emphasis away from defining it as a specific set of social relationships that take place only within households. They argue that it should also include relationships that take place in settings where family activity routinely extends, such as nursing homes, daycare centers, and residential treatment facilities.[2] On the one hand, Gubrium and Holstein acknowledge the power of the notion of "family" as it relates to the sentiments associated with the private space of house and home. On the other hand, they place in the foreground members' sentiments, in particular feelings, values, and commitments, as well as their activities and the meanings those actions create (Gubrium & Holstein, 1990). The enactment of family *relations* as a set of practices becomes the primary focus.

While this expanded conceptualization allows a more diverse range of practices to be subsumed under the concepts of "family" and "family relations," it is important to recognize that gender is still enacted, even in domestic arrangements that depart from the traditional heterosexual nuclear family. Gender ideologies still legitimate relations of power and the division of emotional and physical labor, however differently those relations are configured.

---

[2] Going a step further, Hochschild (1997) has suggested that family-like relationships and bonds extend into the workplace and may indeed supplant those that take place in domestic units.

Acknowledgments

I thank William Bielby, Susan Dalton, Krista Paulson, Lisa Torres, Britta Wheeler, Raymond Wong, and my other colleagues in the Comparative Institutions Proseminar, Department of Sociology, University of Calfornia, Santa Barbara, for their helpful comments and criticisms.

REFERENCES

Abel, E. K. (1991). *Who cares for the elderly? Public policy and the experiences of adult daughters.* Philadelphia: Temple University Press.

Aldous, J., & Hill, R. (1965). Social cohesion, lineage type and intergenerational transmission. *Social Forces, 43,* 471–482.

Amato, P. R. (1989). Who cares for children in public places? Naturalistic observation of male and female caretakers. *Journal of Marriage and the Family, 51,* 981–990.

Amato, P. R. (1993). Children's adjustment to divorce: Theories, hypotheses, and empirical support. *Journal of Marriage and the Family, 55,* 23–38.

Arendell, T. (1986). *Mothers and divorce.* Berkeley, CA: University of California Press.

Aronson, J. (1992). Women's sense of responsibility for the care of old people: "But who else is going to do it?" *Gender & Society, 6,* 8–29.

Atkinson, M. P., V. R. Kivett, & Campbell, R. T. (1986). Intergenerational solidarity: An examination of a theoretical model. *Journal of Gerontology, 41,* 408–416.

Baber, K. M., & Allen, K. R. (1992). *Women and families: Feminist reconstructions.* New York: Guildford.

Barich, R., & Bielby, D. (1996). Rethinking marriage: Change and stability in expectations, 1967–1994. *Journal of Family Issues, 17,* 139–169.

Belsky, J., & Volling, B. (1987). Mothering, fathering, and marital interaction in the family triad during infancy. In P. Berman & F. Pederson (Eds.), *Men's transitions to parenthood* (pp. 37–63). Hilldale, NJ: Lawrence Erlbaum.

Beneria, L., & Stimpson, C. (1987). *Women, households, and the economy.* New Brunswick, NJ: Rutgers University Press.

Bengtson, V., & Black, K. D. (1973). Intergenerational relations and continuities in socialization. In P. Baltes & K. W. Schaie (Eds.), *Life-span developmental psychology: Personality and socialization* (pp. 207–234). New York: Academic Press.

Benis, M. H., & Agostinelli, J. (1988). Husbands and wives' satisfaction with the division of labor. *Journal of Marriage and the Family, 50,* 349–361.

Bielby, W., & Bielby, D. (1989). Family ties: Balancing commitments to work and family in dual earner households. *American Sociological Review, 54,* 76–89.

Bielby, W., & Bielby, D. (1992). I will follow him: Family ties, gender-role beliefs, and reluctance to relocate for a better job. *American Journal of Sociology, 97,* 1241–1267.

Blood, R. O. Jr., &. Wolfe, D. M. (1960). *Husbands and wives: The dynamics of married living.* Glencoe, : The Free Press.

Blumstein, P., & Schwartz, P. (1983). *American couples.* New York: William Morrow.

Bolak, H. C. (1997). When wives are major providers: Culture, gender, and family work. *Gender & Society, 11,* 409–433.

Booth, A., Johnson, D. R., White, L., & Edwards, J. N. (1984). Women, outside employment and marital instability. *American Journal of Sociology, 90,* 567–583.

Brines, J. (1993). The exchange value of housework. *Rationality and Society, 5,* 367–374.

Brody, E. M. (1981). 'Women in the middle' and family help to older people. *The Gerontologist, 21,* 471–480.

Cancian, F. (1987). *Love in America.* New York: Cambridge University Press.

Chatters, L. M., & Jayakody, R. (1995). Commentary: Intergenerational support within African-American families: Concepts and methods. In V. L. Bengtson, K. W. Schaie, & L. M. Burton (Eds.), *Adult intergenerational relations: Effects of societal change* (pp. 97–117). New York: Springer.

Chatters, L. M., Taylor, R. J., & Jackson, J. S. 1986. Size and composition of the informal helper networks of elderly blacks. *Journal of Gerontology: Social Sciences, 41,* S94–S100.

Cherlin, A. (1983). Changing family and household: Contemporary lessons from historical research. *Annual Review of Sociology, 9,* 51-66.

Chodorow, N. (1978). *The reproduction of mothering*. Berkeley, CA: University of California Press.

Cicirelli, V. G. (1983). Adult children's attachment and helping behavior to elderly parents: A path model. *Journal of Marriage and the Family, 45*, 815–823.

Collins, P. H. (1992). Black women and motherhood. In B. Thorne & M. Yalom (Eds.), *Rethinking the family* (pp. 215–245). Boston: Northeastern University Press.

Coltrane, S. (1996). *Family man*. New York: Oxford University Press.

Coontz, S., & Parson, M. (1997). Complicating the contested terrain of work/family intersections. *Signs, 22*, 440–452.

Cowan, C., & Cowan, P. (1987). Men's involvement in parenthood: Identifying the antecedents and understanding the barriers. In P. Berman & F. Pederson (Eds.), *Men's transitions to parenthood* (pp. 145–174). Hilldale, NJ: Lawrence Erlbaum.

Cowan, C., & Cowan, P. (1988). Who does what when partners become parents: Implications for men, women, and marriage. *Marriage and Family Review, 3/4*, 105–131.

Cowan, C., Cowan, P., Heming, G., Garrett, E., Coysh, W., Curtis-Boles, H., & Boles, A. (1985). Transitions to parenthood: His, hers, and theirs. *Journal of Family Issues, 6*, 451–481.

Coward, R. T., & Dwyer, J. W. (1990). The association of gender, sibling network composition, and patterns of parent care by adult children. *Research on Aging, 12*, 158–181.

Daniels, A. K. (1987). Invisible work. *Social Problems, 34*, 403–415.

Di Leonardo, M. (1992). The female world of cards and holidays: Women, families, and the work of kinship. In B. Thorne & M. Yalom (Eds.), *Rethinking the family* (pp 246–261). Boston: Northeastern University Press.

DiMaggio, P., & Powell, W. (1991). Introduction. In W. Powell & P. DiMaggio (Eds.), *The new institutionalism in organizational analysis* (pp. 1–38). Chicago: University of Chicago Press.

Dressel, P. L., & Clark, A. (1990). A critical look at family care. *Journal of Marriage and the Family, 52*, 769–782.

Duncan, B., & Duncan, O. D. (1978). *Sex typing and social roles: A research report*. New York: Academic Press.

Dwyer, J. W., & Coward, R. T. (1991). A multivariate comparison of the involvement of adult sons versus daughters in the care of impaired adults. *Journal of Gerontology: Social Sciences, 46*, S259–S269.

Emerson, R. (1976). Social exchange theory. *Annual Review of Sociology, 2*, 335–362.

England, P., & Farkas, G. (1986). *Households, employment, and gender*. New York: Aldine.

England, P., & Kilbourne, B. (1990). Markets, marriages, and other mates: The problem of power. In R. Friedland & A. F. Robertson (Eds.), *Beyond the marketplace: Society and economy*. New York: Aldine.

Erickson, R. (1993). Reconceptualizing family work: The effect of emotion work on perceptions of marital quality. *Journal of Marriage and the Family, 55*, 888–900.

Farkas, J. I., & Hogan, D. P. (1995). The demography of changing intergenerational relationships. In V. L. Bengtson, K. W. Schaie, & L. M. Burton (Eds.), *Adult intergenerational relations: Effects of societal change* (pp. 1–29). New York: Springer.

Ferree, M. M.. (1990). Beyond separate spheres. *Journal of Marriage and the Family, 52*, 866–884.

Furstenberg, F., & Nord, C. W. (1985). Parenting apart: patterns of child-rearing after marital disruption. *Journal of Marriage and the Family, 47*, 893–904.

Gilligan, C. (1982). *In a different voice*. Cambridge, MA: Harvard University Press.

Glenn, E. N. (1987). In B. Hess & M. M. Ferree (Eds.), *Analyzing gender* (pp. 348–380). Newbury Park, CA: Sage.

Goffman, E. (1977). The arrangement between the sexes. *Theory and Society, 4*, 301–331.

Goldscheider, F., & Waite, L. (1991). *New families, no families?* Berkeley, CA: University of California Press.

Gubrium, J., & Holstein, J. (1990). *What is family?* Mountain View, CA: Mayfield.

Gubrium, J., & Holstein, J. (1993). Family discourse, organization embeddedness, and local enactment. *Journal of Family Issues, 14*, 66–81.

Hagestad, G. O. (1981). Problems and promises in the social psychology of intergenerational relations. In R. W. Fogel, E. Hatfield, S. B. Kielser, & E. Shanas (Eds.), *Aging: Stability and change in the family* (pp. 11–47). New York: Academic Press.

Heath, D. C. (1976). Competent fathers: Their personalities and marriages. *Human Development, 19*, 26–39.

Heimer, C. (1996). Gender inequalities in the distribution of responsibility. In J. Baron, D. Grusky, & D. Treiman, *Social Differentiation and Social Inequality* (pp. 241–273). Boulder, CO: Westview Press.

Hess, B., & Ferree, M. M. (1987). *Analyzing gender*. Newbury Park, CA: Sage.

Hochschild, A. (1983). *The managed heart*. Berkeley, CA: University of California Press.

Hochschild, A. (1997). *The time bind*. New York: Metropolitan Books.

Holstein, J., & Gubrium, J. (1995). Deprivatization and the construction of domestic life. *Journal of Marriage and the Family, 57*, 894–908.

Huber, J., & Spitze, G. (1983). *Sex stratification: Children, housework, and jobs*. New York: Academic Press.

Hurtado, A. (1995). Variations, combinations, and evolutions: Latino families in the United States. In R. E. Zambrana (Ed.), *Understanding Latino families: Scholarship, policy, and practice,* Vol. 2 (pp. 40–61) Thousand Oaks, CA: Sage.

Joseph, G. I., & Lewis, J. (1981). *Common differences: Conflicts in black and white feminist perspectives.* Garden City, NY: Anchor/Doubleday.

Kane, E. (1994). Gender, labor allocations, and the psychology of entitlement withing the home. *Social Forces, 73,* 533–553.

Kane, E., & Sanchez, L. (1994). Family status and criticism of gender inequality at home and at work. *Social Forces, 72,* 1079–1102.

Kurdek, L. (1993). The allocation of household labor in gay, lesbian, and heterosexual married couples. *Journal of Social Issues, 49,* 127–39.

Laslett, B. (1973). The family as a public and private institution. An historical perspective. *Journal of Marriage and the Family, 35,* 480–492.

Litwak, E. (1960). Occupational mobility and extended family cohesion. *American Sociological Review, 25,* 9–20.

Lorber, J. (1981). On *The reproduction of mothering*: A methodological debate. *Signs, 6,* 482–513.

Luxton, M. (1980). *More than a labor of love: Three generations of women's work in the home.* Toronto: Women's Press.

Martin, P. C., & Bumpass, L. L. (1989). Recent trends in marital disruption. *Demography, 26,* 37–51.

McWhirter, D. P., & Mattison, A. M. (1984). *The male couple: How relationships develop.* Englewood Cliffs, NJ: Prentice-Hall.

Mincer, J. (1978). Family migration decisions. *Journal of Political Economy, 86,* 749–75.

Morgan, L. H. (1870). *Systems of consanguinity and affinity of the human family,* Vol, 17 (pp. 1–590). Washington, D.C.: Smithsonian Institution.

Osmond, M. (1987). Feminist theories: The social construction of gender in families and society. In P. Boss, (Ed.), *Sourcebook of family theories and methods.* New York: Plenum Press.

Patterson, C. (1995). Families of the lesbian baby boom: Parents' division of labor and children's adjustment. *Developmental Psychology, 31,* 115–123.

Pavalko, E., & Artis, J. (1997). Women's caregiving and paid work: Causal relationships in late life. *Journal of Gerontology, 52B,* S170–S179.

Peplau, L. A., & Cochran, S. D. (1990). A relational perspective on homosexuality. In D. P. McWhirter, S. A. Sanders, & J. M. Reinisch (Eds.), *Homosexuality/heterosexuality: Concepts of sexual orientation* (pp. 321–349). New York: Oxford University Press.

Phares, V. (1993). Perceptions of mothers' and fathers' responsibility for children's behavior. *Sex Roles, 29,* 839–851.

Phares, V. (1996). Conducting nonsexist research, prevention, and treatment with fathers and mothers: A call for change. *Psychology of Women Quarterly, 20,* 55–77.

Popenoe, D. (1993). American family decline, 1960–1990: A review and appraisal. *Journal of Marriage and the Family, 55,* 527–555.

Pyke, K. (1996). Class-based masculinities: The interdependence of gender, class, and interpersonal power. *Gender and Society, 10,* 527–549.

Pyke, K., & Bengtson, V. (1996). Caring more or less: Individualistic and collectivist systems of family eldercare. *Journal of Marriage and the Family, 58,* 379–392.

Pyke, K., & Coltrane, S. (1996). Entitlement, obligation, and gratitude in family work. *Journal of Family Issues, 17,* 60–82.

Rindfuss, R., Liao, T. F., & Tsuya, N. O. (1994). In L.-J. Cho & M. Yada (Eds.), *Tradition and change in the Asian family.* Honolulu: East West Center and the University of Hawaii Press.

Roberts, E. L., Richards, L. N., & Bengtson, V. L. (1991). Intergenerational solidarity in families: Untangling the ties that bind. *Marriage and Family Review, 16,* 11–46.

Rossi, A. (1995). Commentary: Wanted: Alternative theory and analysis models. In V. L. Bengtson, K. W. Schaie, & L. M. Burton (Eds.), *Adult intergenerational relations: Effects of societal change* (pp. 264–276). New York: Springer.

Rossi, A., & Rossi, P. (1990). *Of human bonding.* New York: Aldine De Gruyter.

Ruddick, S. (1989). *Maternal thinking.* Boston: Beacon Press.

Scanzoni, J. (1970). *Opportunity and the family.* New York: Macmillan.

Segura, D., & Pierce, J. (1993). Chicana/o family structure and gender personality: Chodorow, familism, and psychoanalytic sociology revisited. *Signs, 19,* 63–91.

Sewall, W. H. Jr. (1992). A theory of structure: Duality, agency, and transformation. *American Journal of Sociology, 98,* 1–29.

Shanas, E., Townsend, P., Wedderburn, D., Friis, H., Milhoj, P., & Stehouwer, J. (1968). *Old people in three industrial societies*. New York: Atherton Press.

Silverstein, L. B. (1996). Fathering as a feminist issue. *Psychology of Women Quarterly, 20,* 3–37.

Simons, R. L., & Beaman, J. (1996). Father's parenting. In R. L. Simons & Associates (Eds.), *Understanding differences between divorced and intact families* (pp. 94-103). Thousand Oaks, CA: Sage.

Smelser, N. (1980). Vicissitudes of work and love in Anglo-American society. In N. Smelser & E. Erikson (Eds.), *Themes of work and love in adulthood* (pp. 105–119). Cambridge, MA: Harvard University Press.

Soldo, B. J., Wolf, D. A., & Agree, E. M. (1990). Family, households, and care arrangements of frail older women: A structural analysis. *Journal of Gerontology: Social Sciences, 45,* S238–S249.

Spitze, G., & Logan, J. (1990). Sons, daughters, and intergenerational social support. *Journal of Marriage and the Family 52,* 420–430.

Stack, C. (1974). *All our kin.* New York: Harper & Row.

Stone, L. 1977. *The past and the present.* Boston: Routledge and Kegan Paul.

Stone, R. I., Cafferata, L., & Sangl, J. (1987). Caregivers of the frail elderly: A national profile. *The Gerontologist, 27,* 616–626.

Sullivan, M. (1996). Rozzie and Harriet? Gender and family patterns of lesbian coparent. *Gender & Society, 10,* 747–767.

Sung, K. (1990). A new look at filial piety: Ideals and practices of family-centered parent care in Korea. *Gerontologist 30,* 610–617.

Thompson, L. (1991). Family work: Women's sense of fairness. *Journal of Family Issues, 12,* 181–196.

Thompson, L. (1993). Conceptualizing gender in marriage: The case of marital care. *Journal of Marriage and the Family, 55,* 557–569.

Thorne, B. (1992). Feminism and the Family: Two decades of thought. In B. Thorne & M. Yalom (Eds.), *Rethinking the family* (pp. 3–30). Boston: Northeastern University Press.

Thorne, B., & Yalom, M. (1992). *Rethinking the family.* Boston: Northeastern University Press.

Tienda, M., & Angel, R. (1982). Headship and household composition among blacks, Hispanics, and other whites. *Social Forces, 61,* 508–531.

Tienda, M., & Glass, J. (1985). Household structure and labor force participation of black, Hispanic, and white mothers. *Demography, 22,* 381–394.

Waite, L., & Harrison, S. (1992). Keeping in touch: How women in mid-life allocate social contacts among kith and kin. *Social Forces, 70,* 637–655.

Watkins, S. C., Menken, J. A., & Bongaarts, J. (1987). Demographic foundations of family change. *American Sociological Review, 52,* 346–358.

Weston, K. (1991). *Families we choose.* New York: Columbia University Press.

Wharton, A., & Erickson, R. (1993). Managing emotions on the job and at home: Understanding the consequences of multiple emotional roles. *Academy of Management Review, 18,* 457–486.

Wharton, A., & Thorne, D. K. (1997). When mothers matter: The effects of social class and family arrangements on African American and white women's perceived relations with their mothers. *Gender & Society, 11,* 656–681.

White, L. K. (1983). Determinants of spousal interaction: Marital structure or marital happiness. *Journal of Marriage and the Family, 45,* 511–519.

Wolf, D. A., Freedman, V., & Soldo, B. (1997). The division of family Labor: care for elderly parents. *Journal of Gerontology: Social Sciences,* Series B, *52B* (Special Issue), 102–109.

Yogev, S., & Brett, J. (1985). Perceptions of the division of housework and child care and marital satisfaction. *Journal of Marriage and the Family, 47,* 609–618.

Zucker, L. (1991). The role of institutionalization in cultural persistence. In W. Powell & P. DiMaggio (Eds.), *The new institutionalism in organizational analysis* (pp. 83–107). Chicago: University of Chicago Press.

CHAPTER 19

Gender and Education
in Global Perspective

CAROLINE HODGES PERSELL
CARRIE JAMES
TRIVINA KANG
KARRIE SNYDER

Education is a key institution for understanding gender in society because it mirrors social relationships in societies as well as being a fulcrum for struggles and changes occurring within them. Is education a source of liberation, empowerment, and advancement for women, as liberal feminists tend to assume, or does education tend to reproduce gender inequalities in society, as some gender-centered theorists argue? Our thesis is that education *both* empowers women and reproduces gender inequalities. The question is, In what ways and in what situations is education liberating and when is it more likely to reproduce unequal power relations between men and women? This more general concern with gender and education raises two distinct but interrelated questions: (1) What is the relationship between gender and educational access, experiences, achievement, and attainment? and (2) Does education affect gender equity in society, and if so, how? We address the first question in Sections 1 and 2 of this chapter, and the third in Section 3.

Historically, women's limited social roles were reflected in their highly restricted access to education. As societies changed and as women and cross-national influences shaped conceptions of the state and citizenship, the education of women began to change

CAROLINE HODGES PERSELL, CARRIE JAMES, TRIVINA KANG, AND KARRIE SNYDER • Department of Sociology, New York University, New York, New York 10003

Handbook of the Sociology of Gender, edited by Janet Saltzman Chafetz. Kluwer Academic/ Plenum Publishers, New York, 1999.

as well. Early efforts focused on gaining literacy and access to education, issues that remain alive in many countries. Universal access to education, at least through primary schooling, is an official goal of most states in the world today, and the vast majority of educational institutions are state supported and run. Thus, education represents the one universal experience of official political and social philosophy for large numbers of citizens. As a vehicle of intentional public policy, it reflects the state of gender relations in a society as well as providing a potential pressure point for change.

It may not be surprising that the relationship between education and gender is complex, paradoxical, and interacts with other factors. Perhaps more than any other social institution, education operates simultaneously to privilege and constrain individuals in a society by both producing and maintaining, as well as challenging and changing gender inequality at all levels of social life (see, e.g., Collins, 1990). Education does not operate the same way for all individuals in a society, but depends on their social locations in the matrix of gender, class, ethnic, and other axes of stratification in a society, as well as on the global location of a particular society with respect to economic, political, and military power and resources. Education offers opportunities for exposure to new knowledge and resources and the possibility of obtaining passkeys to new statuses, but it may also reproduce gender (and other) stratified values, attitudes, and behaviors.

In reviewing the research on gender and education we have been struck by several points. First, much of the early research on education ignored gender both in the United States (Grant, Horan, & Watts-Warren, 1994) and in Great Britain (Acker & David, 1994; Delamont, 1996). Second, where gender is included, it is often simply as another variable, rather than as a central theoretical focus, although publications by Mickelson (1989) and Wrigley (1992) are important exceptions to this statement. Differences in the way gender is conceptualized are reflected in the theoretical perspectives that guide research, as we explicate in each section.

1. GENDER PARITY IN EDUCATIONAL ACCESS AND ATTAINMENT

In the United States, studies of educational access and attainment have tended to be framed by human capital, status attainment, or class reproduction approaches. The human capital perspective begins with the microeconomic assumption that social and economic events result from the individual decisions of rational actors (Becker, 1964, 1967). Individual decisions, such as obtaining more education, are the key shapers of labor market positions and pay and hence of social and economic inequality. While demographic factors such as gender, race, and urban/rural location are acknowledged as affecting rates of return to education, they are seen as outside the social processes of interest rather than as central features. Yet even recent research suggests that the higher the college wage premium, the more likely men are to attend college, while women's decisions are less affected by higher wage premiums (Averett & Burton, 1996). Human capital theory fails to consider that the "rational choices" of parents and students are heavily constrained by the social fields in which they are embedded, and that gender is a defining element of those situations.

Human capital theory has been incorporated sociologically in functionalist technocratic–meritocratic theories of status attainment, which model how individuals attain occupations of different status (Sewell & Hauser, 1975). Many early studies in this tradition excluded women from analysis. Later studies that included women (e.g., Alexander

& Eckland, 1974 and Marini, 1980) found that the model had less predictive power for women and African-Americans than it did for men or whites. Like human capital theory, the status attainment model assumes that differential outcomes are due to deficits on the part of individuals or members of certain groups, rather than to any systemic deficits. Moreover, this model overlooks the ways that societal and family differences affect the types and levels of education people attain. The assumption is that men and women have similar experiences in schools, and the perspective fails to consider that gender inequalities may produce educational inequalities.

Among feminist theories, liberal feminism bears some resemblance to the human capital and status attainment perspectives. Liberal feminism tends to assume a just social system, with deviations from equality due to incorrect socialization, lack of information, and/or the absence of corrective legislation. The state is considered a benevolent institution that can design and implement legislation to ensure gender equity. Like functionalists, liberal feminists find it difficult to explain the source of discrimination toward women and their unequal socialization, except to say that discrimination is a residue of an earlier era that has not yet been overcome by the state. Much of the research on access to education has been conducted within a liberal feminist framework, for example, quantitative studies of literacy, educational access, enrollment and graduation rates, programs of study, and achievement. The liberal feminist framework has been criticized by Stromquist (1989), who suggests that a "symbiotic relationship may emerge between family and state to preserve the unequal social and educational chances of women" (1989, p. 171). For example, historically colonial educational authorities in Africa cooperated with conservative and patriarchal indigenous leaders in Senegal (Barthel, 1985), Congo (Yates, 1982), and Kenya (Kay, 1979).

A common question shared by all perspectives is whether gender is a barrier to equal educational access. Historically, the ideal of equal access to education for men and women is relatively new. In the United States, for example, as recently as the 1830s, women's education was severely restricted and vastly inferior to that of men (Curti, 1935/1968, p. 53). Oberlin College was founded in 1833 and was the first institution of higher education to admit both men and women. However, women studied in the "Ladies Course," a subcollege program, under close supervision, and they were segregated from men (Sadker & Sadker, 1994, p. 21). U.S. women comprised 21% of undergraduates in 1870, 40% in 1910, and 47% in 1920, before their numbers declined in the 1950s (Graham, 1978).

Worldwide there is currently a trend toward increasing numerical gender parity in educational access at all levels of education, from basic literacy to higher education, with only a few notable exceptions. Despite this trend, however, women have achieved numerical parity in only a few regions of the world. Women today face a different educational reality than their mothers and grandmothers, but in many parts of the world even numerical gender parity in educational access has not been fully achieved. While access is measured different ways, here we use literacy and enrollment rates in secondary and higher education.

1.1. Literacy

In every region of the world, a smaller percentage of women compared to men are literate. Nearly three quarters of women aged 25 and older in sub-Saharan Africa are illiterate, nearly 60% in the Middle East, 37% in Asia, 21% in South America and the Carribean, 7% in Europe, and 3% in the United States (Fig. 19-1).[1] Although male illiteracy is similarly distributed in these regions, illiteracy among women is consistently higher (Fig. 19-1). The gender gap in literacy has been shrinking over time, however, and is smaller among younger cohorts (those aged 15 to 24) than among those 25 and over. Among women aged 15 to 24, illiteracy drops to 46% in sub-Saharan Africa, 24% in the Middle East, 21% in Asia, 8% in South America and the Carribean (about the same as men's), and about 1% in Europe and the United States (Fig. 19-1). Thus, literacy rates are rising for both men and women and the gender gap in literacy is declining, but gender parity even in basic literacy has not yet been achieved.

1.2. Secondary Education

In some regions and countries, namely sub-Saharan Africa, the Middle East, Asia, Europe, Australia, Canada, and New Zealand, women are underrepresented in secondary education compared to men (Fig. 19-2, darker bar). In South America, the Carribean, and the United States, however, the proportions of women are equal to or greater than those of men in secondary education.

1.3. Higher (Tertiary) Education

In sub-Saharan Africa, the Middle East, and Asia women are underrepresented in higher education compared to men (Fig. 19-2, lighter bar). However, in South America, the Carribean, Europe, the United States, Australia, New Zealand, and Canada the proportions of women are equal to or greater than those of men in higher education. The United States has the highest female–male enrollment ratio in higher education (115), although Latin America and the Caribbean are a close second at 112 (Fig. 19-2). What these generalized ratios hide is that some individual countries in Latin America and the Caribbean have substantially higher ratios, some of which are among the highest in the world; for example, Bahamas (216), Jamaica (149), and St. Vincent (209). Several countries in the Middle East, for example, Saudi Arabia, also have high female-to-male ratios in higher education. Consistent with illiteracy rates and secondary female–male enrollment ratios, sub-Saharan Africa has the lowest ratio (36).

A possible explanation for the extremely high ratios in the Caribbean is that very different job opportunities exist for men and women. Men can earn relatively high wages in jobs not needing secondary education, including cab driving, construction, or other blue-collar work. Women need more education to enter somewhat higher paying office and governmental jobs, the main alternative to low-paying female jobs such as housekeeping. [For more on the school adaptations of West Indian young men and women see Gibson on St. Croix (1991), Foner (1973) on Jamaica, and Brown (1978, cited in Gibson, 1991) on the Bahamas.] In the Middle East, possible explanations may be that males are sent abroad for schooling or are likely to inherit the family business and thus do not need higher education, while education is socially acceptable for women until they marry. In

---

[1] These results should be interpreted with caution. All data come from United Nations sources. Behrman and Rosenzweig find that studies using time series of cross-country data to look at the impact of education, "make little or no effort to evaluate the quality of the data" (1994, p. 148). Information provided by individual countries is subject to many intertemporal and inter-country comparability problems. Data quality concerns come from many sources, including countries using different definitions and data collecting instruments, estimating instead of actually calculating figures, and using flawed instruments to collect data. In addition, gaps in data are not handled in consistent ways by countries. For a complete discussion, see Behrman and Rosenzweig (1994).

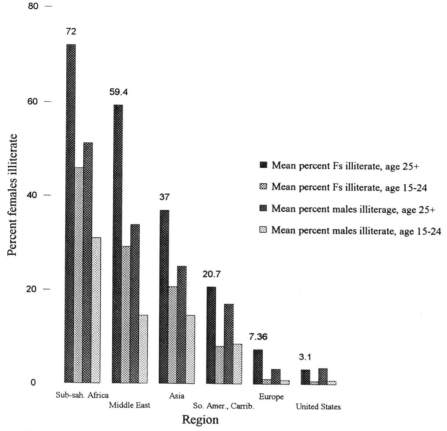

FIGURE 19-1. **Percentage of males and females illiterate by region, 1990. (Data source: United Nations, 1995a.)**

Saudi Arabia, oil wealth has been used to expand female education, but within very traditional and segregated boundaries (El-Sanabary, 1994).

1.4. Explanations for the Gender Gap and Trends in Educational Access

Can we explain why gender disparities in educational access are greater in some countries compared to others, why they favor women in a few countries, why gender differences are declining almost everywhere, and where and why they are increasing? Both structural and cultural factors are important. Structurally, the percentage of a population in agriculture is the single biggest factor correlated with gender disparities in access. This is highly related to the resources a country possesses and can spend on education, to urbanization, and to the availability of labor markets requiring educational credentials. Structural factors are related (although not perfectly) to cultural conditions as well. Receptivity to Western cultural ideals of citizenship and individualism and openness to so-called modern rather than traditional values and norms seems to foster greater gender equity in educational access, which may explain the shrinking gender gap in educational access even in some agricultural countries. Islam and other patriarchal ideologies and practices such as female genital mutilation may be related to low rates of educational

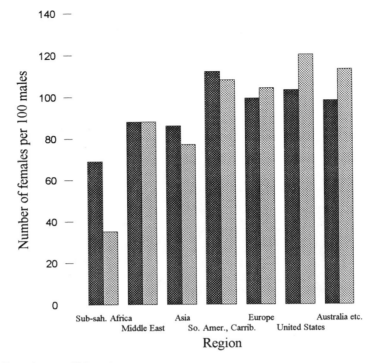

■ Females per 100 males, secondary level

▨ Females per 100 males, tertiary level

FIGURE 19-2. Number of females per 100 males at secondary and tertiary levels by region, 1990. (*Data source*: United Nations, 1995a.)

parity, although it is difficult to obtain systematic data on such practices. The one country where gender inequities in access are increasing is Afghanistan, where a tenuous revolutionary fundamentalist Islamic government has decreed that women should not work or attend school outside the home.

The few countries where women's rates of educational access exceed those of men suggest two different explanations. In the United States and some Caribbean and Latin American countries, growing opportunities in the labor market for women appear to be related to their avid pursuit of education. There is also little resistance in those countries to Western ideologies. Those Middle Eastern countries where women outnumber men in secondary or higher education suggest the anomalous possibility that while access may be equal, the content or consequences of education are not necessarily equal. While such countries have expanded access, they have done so by developing gender-segregated schooling and courses of study. They have rejected many Western ideologies and forms, while reaffirming traditional, heavily patriarchal ideologies and practices.

These broad structural and cultural conditions interact with features of educational design that may also affect numerical gender parity. For instance, is there universal, compulsory, and free education? If so, through what ages? How stringently is attendance enforced? World agencies such as UNESCO acknowledge that reliance on literacy and enrollment rates ignores potentially pertinent issues such as rates of absenteeism and dropout (United Nations, 1995a). Stromquist (1989) and Finn, Dulberg, and Reis (1979) review studies suggesting that women worldwide are often more likely than men to be absent from and drop out of school.

In the absence of strong state support for universal attendance, families may press girls into household work (Kelly, 1987). For lower-income families especially, sending girls to school is likely to be seen as an economic strain, especially when education is not free. Families may sacrifice to send boys to school but may succumb to cultural norms about a woman's place in society and the limited economic opportunities for women after completing formal education. The sexual division of labor in many countries may lead to girls being kept at home disproportionately for housekeeping, child-minding, and even income-earning activities (Kelly, 1987).

In 1990 in all countries, the percentage of the population in agriculture is strongly and positively related to the percent of younger females (ages 15 to 24) who are illiterate (Table 19-1, column 1). This finding is consistent with reports that girls living in urban areas are more likely to attend school and be literate than girls living in rural areas. Urban young women are two to three times more likely to be literate than young women in rural areas, and sometimes more (United Nations, 1995a). Stromquist suggests that one reason for this may be the "social norms controlling the sexuality of women" (1989, p. 160). Throughout the world women's sexuality is repressed and channeled toward motherhood (Stromquist, 1992). The desire to control women's sexuality is clearly evident in the practice of female genital mutilation, which is more likely in rural areas. Negative attitudes toward the education of women suggest that their education may be perceived as a threat to male dominance. In rural areas, schools are also likely to be further from children's homes than in urban areas, thus increasing the chances that girls will be out of range of parental supervision. Research in Bangladesh, Cameroon, India, Sierra Leone, Vanuatu, and Jamaica found that rural location was associated with negative attitudes about females going to school (Cammish, 1993). Niles (1989) found that rural parents in Nigeria also have unfavorable attitudes toward female education and the long distance girls have to travel to school was a deterrent in Ethiopia, Gambia, Guinea, Kenya, Mali, Sierra Leone, Tanzania, and Zimbabwe (Brock & Cammish, 1997; Ilon, 1992; Kane, 1995; and Odaga & Ward, 1995).

Among women over 25, the percentage of women in the labor force is also negatively and significantly related to illiteracy rates (Table 19-1, column 2), suggesting that countries where women experience greater opportunity to participate in the paid labor force provide reasons for them to become literate.

The percentage of the population in agriculture is the largest and only significant variable related to the ratio of women to men in both secondary and higher education (Table 19-1, columns 3 and 4). A case study of women who achieved higher education in Malawi, one of the 25 least-developed countries in the Third World, revealed that a strong motivating factor was the women's desire to obtain professional wage-earning careers (Powers, 1995). Another factor was the important role of single-sex secondary schools in fostering the academic achievement and educational attainment of the women (Powers, 1995).

Bradley and Ramirez (1996) analyzed the social correlates of the expansion of women's share of higher education from 1965 to 1985. In a multivariate analysis of 90 nations, they found several factors that are significantly related to gains in women's share, including the size of the gender gap in 1965. Countries with bigger gender gaps in 1965 made larger gains by 1985, perhaps, they suggest, because of the increasing prevalence of a strong, transnational norm of relative gender parity. They also found that countries with

TABLE 19-1. Estimated Coefficients of Factors Affecting Educational Access of Women in All Countries in 1990

Variables	Female illiteracy 15 to24 years of age[b]	Female illiteracy above 25 years[b]	Ratio of females to males in secondary education[b]	Ratio of females to males in tertiary education[b]
Percentage of population in agriculture[a]	0.8643**	0.9400***	-1.1600***	-0.8864**
Percentage of females in labor force[a]	-0.1746	-0.3264*	0.1163	-0.0392
Per capita energy consumption[a]	-0.1137	-0.1543	0.1291	-0.0774
Percentage of women in parliament 1987[b]	0.0145	0.0085	0.0280	0.0160
Percentage of women as subministers 1985[b]	0.0120	0.0090	0.0162	0.0195
Percentage of population living in urban areas[a]	0.1846	0.2652	-0.2584	-0.3011
Education expenditures 1985[c]	0.0192	0.0563	0.1215	-0.0563
GNP per capita[a] (logged)	0.5095	0.5680	0.5041	0.4087
R^2	0.5095	0.5680	0.5041	0.4087

* $p < 0.05$.
** $p < 0.01$.
*** $p < 0.001$.
Pairwise deletion of variables was used.
Data sources: [a] World Bank (1996); [b] United Nations (1995a); [c] United Nations (1995b).

systems of higher education founded since 1965 had greater increases in women's share of higher education than countries with older systems. Level of economic development in 1965 had a strong positive effect on growth in women's share of higher education in economically developing countries, but not in more developed countries. The authority of the state had positive and significant effects on the growth in women's share of higher education in economically developing countries, but not in more developed ones. Finally, having a population that was 80% or more Islamic was negatively related to increasing women's share of higher education in economically developing countries. Their models explain more than half the variance in developing countries and just under half the variance in more economically developed countries.

The negative effect of large Islamic populations is consistent with some feminist theories that suggest that women's subordination arises from unequal power relations based on different reproductive roles, around which an ideological system of patriarchy is constructed that infuses the family and education. The state is a "key agent" in perpetuating women's subordination, by defending mothers and families, while relegating them to a private sphere separate from the public sphere. Schools also transmit patriarchal ideologies in the way they construct and control sexuality. In countries where the state is unwilling to challenge the tradition of female genital mutilation, the state institution of education may be less willing to challenge women's subordinate position in society more generally. The traditional Islamic country, Saudi Arabia, has a dual system of male and female education and gender-segregated schools and colleges with gender-specific curricula emphasizing women's domestic functions (El-Sanabary, 1994).

1.5. Summary

In terms of literacy and numerical enrollment, gender parity has not yet been achieved in all areas of the world, but there is a general tendency toward greater numerical parity, particularly among younger women.

A notable feature of cross-national research on gender and education is that it shifts the unit of analysis from individuals to countries, thus breaking somewhat from the individualistic focus of human capital and status attainment approaches. Some efforts, notably that by Bradley and Ramirez (1996), have begun to analyze how political, economic, and cultural features of societies are related to increasing gender parity in access to higher education.

The focus on equal access assumes that education is a gender-neutral institution, a condition that seems unlikely in gender-stratified societies. Numerical parity alone is an incomplete measure of gender equity because numerical presence is only a threshold condition in the complicated mosaic of potential opportunities and constraints. The next question is, What happens inside the schoolroom door? This question goes beyond the point of numerical parity, into what might be called experiential gender equity in education. Therefore, we need to consider whether and how educational systems may reflect or resist the inequalities in society and/or participate in the construction of gender norms, thereby helping to create and reproduce gender inequalities or to reduce them.

2. GENDER AND EXPERIENCES WITHIN EDUCATIONAL SYSTEMS

The experiences that girls and boys have in schools are seen as important by various theorists, although for somewhat different reasons. Liberal feminists, with their focus on the individual level of analysis and action, see gender as one of many statuses that individuals occupy, but by no means their master status. Hence, they seek to know whether women receive equal treatment within schools, just as they may consider similar questions with regard to race and social class. They ask whether boys and girls receive equal encouragement from peers and teachers and whether they participate equally in all school and extracurricular activities, such as class discussions, sports, school governance, and curriculum. They also focus attention on the availability of male and female role models, equal representation in educational materials, equal access to educational resources, equal social relationships, classroom practices, and equal protection from sexual harassment. The assumption within the liberal feminist paradigm is that educational institutions have the potential to be gender-neutral institutions, if only they can function fairly. Research in this tradition tends to rely most heavily on survey or other forms of quantitative research, which depict the large contours of the educational landscape and the distributions of young men and women within it.

In contrast, more gender-centered theories begin with the assumption that all social institutions are organized around gender relations (Acker, 1992; Grant et al., 1994) and hence it is unlikely that schools will operate in a gender-neutral way. Such theories not only conceive of gender as a master, or dominant, status but they go beyond an individualistic, trait-like conception of gender, to focus on gender as a *system* of deeply rooted and unequal social relations that affects all aspects of social life. At least two versions of gender-centered theories can be identified (Anderson, 1993; Grant et al., 1994), namely gender difference theories, called cultural feminism by Hansot (1993), and gender process theories. Concerning education, Grant et al. note, "Gender difference theorists sometimes argue that educational institutions—and the content and form of knowledge itself—is masculine, with women having at best marginal status in universities and the knowledge-production enterprise. To achieve success within such domains, women have to distort their 'feminine' approaches to conform to masculine curriculums, pedagogical forms, substantive interests, and interaction styles" (1994, p. 91). Research conducted within this framework relies primarily on critical ethnographies, narratives, and other tools that seek to analyze women's lives on their own terms (see, e.g., Reinharz, 1992).

From this perspective, the liberal feminist ideal of equal educational opportunities with men would not meet the needs of women. Cultural feminists argue that women's distinctive gender attributes should be encouraged by appropriately different educational experiences. For them, equitable gender relations in education might require periods of single-sex education, different curricular content, and other gender-specific experiences.

Like gender difference theorists, gender process theorists also put gender at the center of sociological analysis but they see gender as more mutable and variable in different contexts and for members of different classes, races, and ages. They direct attention to educational institutions as arenas within which gender is constructed, and stress that much of this engendering activity occurs within peer relations and activities that lie largely beyond the control of school authorities. Drawing on resistance theory in educational research more broadly, this approach focuses on cultural creation by young people, sometimes in opposition to formal school ideologies.

Social reproduction and resistance theories do not accept gender and other social categories as "given," but rather seek to explain how such statuses and inequalities are produced and reproduced over time (Holland & Eisenhart, 1990). In so doing, they bridge the gap between macro-level theories of gendered social systems and gender process theory that highlights the agency of individual actors. In Holland and Eisenhart's *Educated in Romance* (1990), social reproduction and resistance theories are used to explain the ways women in universities participate in the construction of gender norms.

Gender theorists agree widely that education is an important socializing institution and a key gate-keeping or credentialing institution. Hence they agree that it is worth examining what happens within schools and how gender interacts with educational experiences. Here we consider seven features of the within-school experience, namely: peer interactions, teacher–student interactions, staffing patterns, curricula, Women's Studies programs, single-sex and coeducational schooling, and achievement. Cross-national research on educational experiences within schools is much more difficult to find than research within the United States. Therefore, we refer to research conducted in other countries when we have found it, while noting the difficulty of achieving a truly global perspective on these issues.

2.1. Informal and Peer Interactions

Peer interactions are important sites where gender roles are constructed and reinforced. Even among 4- and 5-year-olds, research suggests that boys bring different styles of play and different mythic elements into schools than do girls. Jordan and Cowan (1995) find that Australian kindergarten boys learn about masculinity from warrior narratives about knights, superheros, and other "good guys" who can use violence legitimately when involved in a struggle between good and evil. The authors trace the struggle enacted in peer play between the warrior narrative and the school's conception of masculinity as rationality, responsibility, and commitment to civil society and the social contract. Given this conflict, the warrior narrative must be disguised, go underground, or get expressed within the realm of sports, since violence, shouting, and running are banned within the classroom. Girls, on the other hand, face no such conflict between the conceptions of femininity with which they enter and what is acceptable within the school. The authors suggest that the conflict between larger societal narratives and school rules compels boys to transform their warrior urges, with social dominance over girls being one possible compensation. Studies such as this illustrate how social reproduction theory sees schools and their students as active negotiators of gender identities that prevail in the larger society.

Other studies underscore how gender may become more sharply differentiated in peer-mediated play than in classrooms, although adults may contribute to the formation of gender relationships, for example, with the forms of address they use ("boys and girls") and in their sorting of children for various activities (Thorne, 1993). Studying 9- to 11-year-old children in the United States, Thorne and Luria (1986) analyze how gender relationships form. Sex-segregated arrangements in middle childhood play time serve as contexts for learning gender roles and boundaries. Boys interact in larger and more visible groups, play outside more, and use more space. They show more aggressive behavior and develop more hierarchical and competitive relations. Girls play in smaller groups or pairs, and stress cooperation. Boys are more likely than girls to challenge school rules, for example, regarding the use of dirty words. Partly because they play in larger groups, teachers are less likely to interrupt such rule violations. Thorne and Luria suggest that these activities result in the solidification of distinctive male and female subcultures that intensify as adolescence approaches (1986, p. 55).

In extracurricular activities, Murtaugh (1988) found that boys in the United States were significantly more likely than girls to be involved in extracurricular activities (80% compared to 50%). For average academic achievers outside activities provide an important alternative source of achievement and self-esteem (Murtaugh, 1988). This may be why extracurricular activities have been found by other researchers, such as McNeal (1995), to be related to school retention. If girls are less likely to participate in school activities, they are less likely to receive the benefits of such participation.

Eder and Parker (1987) examined the effect of athletic activities on the peer-group culture of students at a predominantly working-class middle school in the United States. They found that popular activities, such as male athletic contests, construct messages about socially sanctioned gender roles, and they note, "Since male athletic events are the main social events of the school, both male athletes and female cheerleaders have considerable visibility and are likely to be members of the elite group. . . . Male athletes are encouraged to be achievement oriented and competitive, and cheerleaders are reminded of the importance of appearance and emotion management" (1987, p. 200). Others have analyzed sports as arenas for learning conceptions of masculinity and femininity (e.g., Bryson, 1987; Curry, 1991; Fine, 1987; Graydon, 1983; Hargreaves, 1986; Kidd, 1987; Kimmel, 1990; Messner, 1989, 1990; Sabo & Panepinto, 1990; Theberge, 1981). Through competitive sports, boys learn to equate masculinity with aggressiveness and they carry aggression into their relationships with girls through insults, sexual comments, and the objectification of girls (Eder, 1997). In addition, schools generally provide a hostile environment for gay or lesbian students who are given little official protection against harassment from peers. In San Francisco and Los Angeles, for example, a disproportionate number of school dropouts are gay or lesbian (Dennis & Harlow, 1986, cited in Grayson, 1992). Homophobia discourages both men and women from deviating from traditional male and female roles out of fear of being labeled gay (Grayson, 1992).

Higher education is another arena in which gender roles are constructed, particularly in informal interactions. For example, the U.S. report, *Out of the Classroom: A Chilly Campus Climate for Women?* discusses unequal participation and recognition for men and women in athletics and student government and notes how a "male locker room atmosphere" in co-ed dorms may create hostile environments for women, as may fraternity activities such as wet T-shirt contests (Hall & Sandler, 1987). There are also problems reported of sexual harassment and assault on campuses. Martin and Hummer (1996), for instance, analyze the social norms and rituals of male fraternities that contribute to violence against women, including gang rapes, on many college campuses.

Since the 1980s awareness of sexual harassment has been elevated in the college environment, as a result of the establishment of policies and procedures for filing complaints, as well as the development of preventative programs, conferences, and symposia focusing on the issue (Riggs et al., 1993). However, as Riggs, Murrell, and Cutting (1993, p. 1) note, the number of reported sexual harassment complaints at college and university campuses has increased, which may or may not be attributed to awareness programs. Dziech and Weiner (1984) report that 20% to 30% of undergraduate female students experience some form of sexual harassment from at least one professor and Boyer (1990) notes that more than 60% of college presidents indicated sexual harassment is a problem. When young women complained of acts of harassment, one study found that no action was taken in 45% of the cases (Stein, Marshall, & Troop, 1993, cited in Bailey, 1993).

Holland and Eisenhart (1990) studied U.S. college women at a predominantly white and an historically black college in the South and found that for women the peer culture elevated the culture of romance and popularity above the value of educational attainment, while men could obtain status through popularity, governance activities, or sports. Applying social reproduction theory, the authors examine the active role that women play in constructing gender identity, frequently reinforcing mainstream roles, but sometimes resisting such conceptions. Gender construction is continually occurring in formal and informal educational situations. Whether such construction reproduces gender inequities or reduces them depends on the nature of the work being done.

2.2. Classroom Interactions

Considerable gender reproduction appears to occur in the informal social relationships occurring outside educational classrooms. What happens within formal educational settings? In terms of teacher attention, one frequent finding at all educational levels in the United States is that boys receive more attention than girls (Kelly, 1988; Krupnick, 1985, cited in Bailey; Long, Sadker, & Sadker, 1986; Sadker & Sadker, 1994; Swann & Graddol, 1988). This attention is both positive (Hamilton, Blumfeld, Akoh, & Miura, 1991) as well as negative or disciplinary in nature (e.g., Eccles & Blumenfeld, 1985).

In their observations of British youth, Hendry, Shucksmith, Love, and Glendinning (1993) suggested that teachers perceive boys to be more rebellious and hence pay them more attention to avert academic failure. However, as a Scottish study (MacIntosh, 1990) indicates, the content of the attention matters less than the fact that teachers spend more time with their male students. Students of both sexes perceive this extra attention as an indication that boys and their activities are more worthwhile.

Although many studies report more teacher attention to boys than to girls, some do not. Studies done in American, Japanese, and Chinese elementary schools (Lee, Ichikawa, & Stevenson, 1987; Stevenson, Lee, & Stilger, 1986) find little evidence that teachers communicate differently with boys and girls. Merrett and Wheldall's (1992) research in Britain also finds virtually no difference in teachers' use of praise and reprimand with elementary school boys and girls, although they do observe that both male and female teachers pay more attention to boys in their secondary school sample. Evidence from Cameroon, Sierra Leone, Malawi, Guinea, and Rwanda indicates that both male and female teachers believe boys are academically superior to girls (Anderson-Levitt, Bloch, & Soumare, 1994; Brock & Cammish, 1997). These mixed results highlight some of the problems noted by Foster, Gomm, and Hammersly (1996), such as overgeneralized anecdotal accounts, failure to show that examples are representative, absence of probability samples, lack of explicit evaluative standards, decontextualized reporting of interactions, and the failure to consider alternative explanations.

Differential teacher attention seems to be more common above elementary school, and more evident in certain subjects, such as science (Baker, 1986; Dart, & Clarke, 1988; Jones & Wheatley, 1990; Lee, Marks, & Knowles, 1991). Morse and Handley (1985) suggest that student behavior may in part account for differential teacher attention. During their 2-year study, they found a striking change in the behavior of girls in science class from the seventh to the eighth grades. Girls became less assertive in class while boys became more vocal and involved in class affairs. Increased male initiation of interactions swung teacher attention in their direction. Teaching teachers to give equal attention to boys and girls may be necessary if schools are to avoid contributing to gender inequities.

In higher education, differential treatment varies in extent, as the Association of American Colleges report illustrates (Hall & Sandler, 1982). Examples include overt sexism, such as faculty making disparaging comments about women as a group, showing slides of women in bikinis, sexual overtures by professors toward women students, and more subtle forms, such as offering to help women in a way that stresses their incompetence (for example, "I know women have trouble with spatial concepts, but I'll be happy to give you extra help."). Faculty also often encouraged female invisibility in class discussions by ignoring women and recognizing men students even when women clearly volunteered to participate in class, interrupting women students more than men, responding more extensively to men's than to women's comments, and crediting men's comments to their "author" but not giving authorship to women's comments (Hall & Sandler, 1982, p. 8–9). While the report raised a number of important issues, it is not always clear when its conclusions are based on research, anecdotal evidence, or conjecture. Subsequent research suggests variability in the nature, extent, and sources of bias in college classrooms (Brady & Eisler, 1995; Constantinople, Cornelius, & Gray, 1988) and has introduced additional variables, such as class size (Crawford & MacLeod, 1990) or gender composition of the classroom. Brady and Eisler call for more empirical research on this subject (1995).

Although it is likely that male and female students may frequently obtain different treatment from their teachers in one form or another, it is less clear what the effects of such behavior are on the students and their learning. For example, Eccles and Blumenfeld's

(1985) study of attitudes toward math among 275 students in fifth to ninth grades found that teacher's behavior mattered less than the student's self-perception of ability.

In graduate school in the social sciences, however, students are "negatively affected when they experience or witness unfair gender behavior in the classroom" and women are more negatively affected than men (Myers & Dugan, 1996, p. 339). Being affected does not have a significant effect on student grades or participation levels, but sexist behaviors by professors are related to lower student perceptions of professors' expertness, attractiveness, and trustworthiness (Myers & Dugan, 1996).

2.3. Staffing Patterns

As an institution, education is not gender neutral in its staffing patterns. In the United States, women comprise the vast majority of elementary teachers, a majority of secondary school teachers (72% of all classroom teachers are women in the United States), a minority (20%) of college and university teachers, and a very small minority of school principals (28%) and superintendents (5%) (American Association of School Administrators, cited in Bailey, 1993). Women are underrepresented in administrative positions, and when they earn them they are more likely to be in undesirable schools (either large urban or small rural schools) where funding and resources are problems (Tallerico, 1997). A national study of nearly 9000 U.S. teachers found that female high school teachers feel empowered when they have women principals but male teachers feel less powerful in such a situation, suggesting one reason for the persistent underrepresentation of women as school principals (Lee, Smith, & Cioci, 1993). There are gender patterns by subject as well, with men more likely to teach math, science, and shop courses, women more likely to teach English, other languages, social studies, history, typing, and home economics courses.

In higher education, those women who teach in colleges and universities are more likely to teach in 2-year or 4-year colleges and less likely to teach in research universities. Moreover, 42% of women faculty are employed as part-time adjunct instructors compared to 29% of men (National Education Association, 1995). In a study of all coeducational 4-year institutions offering baccalaureate degrees in 1985 in the United States, Tolbert and Oberfield (1991) found that women comprised 20% of the faculty overall. The percentage of women students in a college was positively related to the percentage of women faculty, but the percentage of research expenditures was not. Institutions with higher levels of slack resources had smaller proportions of women faculty. They theorize that schools with more resources have greater means to discriminate in hiring practices and are more able to hire more sought after, higher-priced faculty who are often male. Women are also considerably less likely than men to be department chairs, deans, vice presidents, or presidents of institutions of higher education, especially coeducational ones. The boards of directors of institutions of higher learning are also disproportionately comprised of men.

In developing nations, most teachers at all levels are men. In Mexico, women have gained increased access to educational careers since the 1960s, but they have not received equal pay and they work primarily in the lower levels of education (Cortina, 1995). As secondary and higher education expand, men move up to better-paid positions of greater prestige at secondary and higher levels. While women predominate in many teaching areas, the overwhelming majority of professors at the highest level in all fields are still men, even when the majority of their students are women (United Nations, 1995a, pp. 94–95).

These gendered patterns of staffing in educational institutions may create and preserve patterns of gender inequality in society in several ways. The presence of women teachers and educational leaders provides role models for women students. This has been frequently mentioned as one of the benefits of single-sex education (see later). Visible career opportunities at all levels of education motivate some young people to pursue further learning. If men and women are unequally placed in education by level, field, prestige, and pay, the message conveyed is that certain fields are gendered and thus "appropriate" only for members of that gender. Finally, there is growing awareness that curricula are not gender neutral.

2.4. Curricula

Curricula have both socializing and gatekeeping implications. This requires that we focus, as do liberal feminists, on whether men and women are studying the same subjects and obtaining the same knowledge, but also pay attention, as gender-focused theories do, to the gendered nature of curricula.

2.4.1. MATH AND SCIENCE.   The answer to the liberal feminists' concerns varies, depending on what aspect of the curriculum is scrutinized. For example, in the United States, gender differences in math course enrollments are small. The National Science Board of the National Science Foundation reported that from 1982 to 1987 the average number of math credits that male high school students received increased from 2.61 to 3.04, while for females the average number of math credits increased from 2.46 to 2.93. About the same percentages of boys and girls took math courses up to calculus, which was taken by 7.6% of the boys but only 4.7% of the girls (AAUW, 1992, p. 26). In 1982 and 1987, males received .12 more science credits than did females (AAUW, 1992, p. 27).

2.4.2. TRACKING.   If the focus is on tracking, however, we find that in the United States, high school girls are more likely to be tracked into clerical and domestic vocational courses, while boys are more likely to be tracked into industrial and technical courses (Gaskell, 1985; Simpson, 1974). This sex-segregated trend has not changed in the past decade (Wirt, Murasicin, Goodwin, & Meyer, 1989, cited in AAUW, 1992, p. 42 and Tuma & Burns, 1996). This finding is supported by Burge and Stenstrom's (1995) comparison of Finnish and U.S. secondary vocational students, which found that in both countries females are more likely to enter programs in service/caring while males are more likely to enter production/industry-related areas of study.

2.4.3. COLLEGE MAJORS.   At the tertiary level in the United States, even though more women than men have earned college degrees since 1982, they continue to study different subjects. However, there have been variations in this trend. From the late 1960s to the early 1980s, the segregation of men and women in fields of study dropped precipitously. For example, in 1964, 51.4% of women college students would have had to change majors to match men's distribution, but by 1984 this figure had dropped to 31% (Jacobs, 1995, p. 81). However, the late 1980s witnessed a dramatic slowdown in the trend toward gender integration which Jacobs suggests is explained by a decline in support for new opportunities for women and the absence of societal support for men entering predominantly female fields. To the degree that college major is related to occupational placement, significant gender differences in what is studied may affect the availability of particular careers. For example, in computer science, only 4% of full professors are women (Feigenbaum, Hargittai, & O'Rourke, 1994).

2.4.4. TEXTBOOKS AND READERS. Early research by U.S. social scientists documented the unequal representation and treatment of girls and women in reading textbooks (Frasher & Walker, 1972; Women on Words and Images, 1972), elementary school textbooks (Weitzman & Rizzo, 1976), high school history textbooks (Treckler, 1973), and testing (Saario, Jacklin, & Tittle, 1973). The assumption underlying such research is that the language and images of a dominant group can affect the self-images and belief systems of members of another group, and that equitable language and imagery can contribute to gender equity (O'Rourke, 1995).

There is recent evidence that the frequency of depicting males and females has become more evenly distributed in children's picture books. However, girls continue to be shown as passive and dependent as was the case earlier (Kortenhaus & Demarest, 1993). Gonzalez-Suarez and Ekstrom (1989) found in their content analysis of seven representative elementary school textbooks that males represent 64% of the text examples and 61% of the illustrations. Males were likely to be presented in occupational roles or as historical figures whereas females were shown in ways that emphasized their personality characteristics. They did, however, indicate that when compared with a study done a decade before, they found some evidence of efforts to reduce sex bias.

Several international studies of gender bias in textbooks in the Caribbean and Britain (Whiteley, 1996), Australia (Connell, 1989), and Singapore (Sunderland, 1992) have found imbalances in the representation of women in physics texts, general textbooks, and English texts, suggesting that unequal gender representation is not confined to the United States. In his study on Kenya, Obura (1991) points out that in book-scarce nations textbooks are crucial in shaping self perception. The fact that women are largely absent in textbooks, even in agricultural countries where they contribute most of the productive labor, is extremely telling.

In college-level sex-education textbooks, sexual dimorphism and heterosexuality are assumed to be normal, and women's sexuality is defined in terms of male pleasure (Myerson, 1992).

2.4.5. COMPUTER USAGE. In the United States, numerous studies have documented that girls gain less access than boys to personal computers in school (e.g., Collis, 1985; Lockheed, 1985; Miura & Hess, 1983; Sanders & Stone, 1986), even at elite preparatory schools (Persell & Cookson, 1987). Similar results were reported in Australia (Kinnear, 1995). In many schools, the computer room is perceived as boys' space, and girls feel they don't belong. "But when parents and teachers make special efforts to involve female students, they find converts. 'Subtlety does not work,' says Jo Sanders, coauthor of *The Neuter Computer*. 'You have to transmit the message loud and clear that girls and computers belong together.'" (cited in Sadker & Sadker, 1994, p. 123).

Several studies have begun to document ways of achieving greater gender equity in computer usage. For example, Linn (1985) and Lockheed and Frakt (1984) suggest that when girls have more opportunities to use computers, their attitudes toward using them improve and their usage increases (Fish, Gross, & Sanders, 1986). Kramer and Lehman (1990) stress the importance of taking into consideration the variety of contexts and contents of computing, as well as the cultural norms and values that surround it.

Given the extensive incorporation of computers into many workplaces and the fact that one of the fastest growing areas of well-paid jobs lies in the broad field of computers, the incomplete inclusion of girls in this field has potentially significant negative consequences for their futures. It may also affect the majors they select in college. The two most evident challenges to existing educational practices appear in the curricular development of Women's Studies programs and in single-sex schooling, although neither are monolithic with respect to where they stand on the issue of equal access to "mainstream" knowledge compared to the creation and transmission of alternative knowledges.

2.5. Women's Studies Programs

The first Women's Studies program was approved in 1970 at San Diego State University. Today, more than 621 Women's Studies programs and departments exist throughout the country and more than 1 million students annually take more than 30,000 Women's Studies courses (Antler, 1995; Chamberlain, 1988; Musil, 1992). In 1990 the National Women's Studies Association (NWSA) reported there were 102 graduate level programs (Musil, 1992, p. 2).

Women's Studies programs affect the individuals involved, the school environment, and the larger society. Curricula outside the Women's Studies offerings on campuses have been influenced by the interdisciplinary nature of Women's Studies. Women's Studies draws on the faculty and resources of other departments and is thereby integrated into other, more traditional departments, such as sociology, biology, economics, history, and English. While this may lead to tensions, such as faculty having primary allegiances to more powerful, established departments (Butler & Schmitz, 1992) or Women's Studies programs not having the prestige of a full-fledged department, the Women's Studies interdisciplinary approach has been able to influence the curricular offerings throughout colleges. Other attempts to transform curricula include mainstreaming, that is, "efforts to integrate the subject of women and the substance of Women's Studies into curriculum" (Stimpson & Cobb, 1986).

Students within these classes are touched as well. After conducting in-depth case studies of seven Women's Studies programs, Musil (1992) concluded that most notably the female students of these programs often found self-empowerment and their own voice. According to Musil, Women's Studies classes are more inclusive and participatory. Women who felt stifled and invisible in male-dominated class discussions find a place where they can express their thoughts concerning course material that is deeply connected to their own lives. Through finding their own voice students feel empowered not only personally, but this empowerment translates into social responsibility. Luebke and Reilly's somewhat broader study (1995) of 89 graduates from 43 programs across the United States notes outcomes similar to Musil's. They found that graduates who majored in Women's Studies report feelings of "being empowered; developing self-confidence; learning to think critically; understanding differences; discovering the intersections among . . . [various] forms of oppression; and experiencing community" (1995, p. 199).

Women's Studies flourished in a time of political activism. Although critics of such programs charge they are too political, advocates see examining the experiences of women as no less political than excluding the voices of diverse groups. The increased social responsibility and empowerment of students, as described by Musil (1992), and the dedication of politically minded faculty offer a picture of women's scholarship as closely and actively linked to social change. Stimpson and Cobb, however, caution that the influence of Women's Studies may impact academic scholarship more than its institutional setting, "Scholars outside women's studies are far more likely to include an article on the history of child care in their research than to support a child-care center at their colleges. A professional association would rather endorse women's studies than affirmative action or paid parental leave" (1986, p. 18).

Women's Studies programs and classes exist throughout the world, in both industrial and developing nations, including Sweden, Australia, Canada, Bangladesh, Japan, Mexico, and Brazil (Chamberlain, 1988; Kelly, 1989; Stimpson & Cobb, 1986), although the degree of institutionalization varies widely (Jacobs, 1996; Kelly, 1989). Just as Musil (1992) concludes that U.S. programs reflect their unique environments, Women's Studies programs internationally reflect their particular social and political contexts (Stimpson & Cobb, 1986). For example, developing countries may have more need to be concerned with literacy issues than do developed nations. Women's Studies programs internationally sometimes suffer from censorship, limited funding opportunities, politics that divide potential women allies, and criticisms that they are a Western fad (Stimpson & Cobb, 1986). Women's Studies programs in other countries tend to be peripheral to mainstream higher education, with programs located in special training programs or within research institutes (Fiol-Matta & Chamberlain, 1994).

2.6. Single-Sex versus Coeducational Schools

In U.S. higher education, the relative benefits of single-sex versus coeducational colleges have been much discussed. Originally founded because women were denied admission to most institutions of higher education, there remained about 300 women-only colleges in the United States as recently as the 1960s. By 1992, the figure had dropped, however, to about 71 four-year colleges and 13 junior colleges, or about 6.5% of all U.S. colleges and universities (Kim & Alverez, 1995; Riordan, 1994). In an extensive literature review, Canada and Pringle (1995) suggest that compared to women who attend mixed-sex colleges, women who attend women's colleges have greater self-esteem at graduation (Astin, 1977; Miller-Bernal, 1993; Riordan, 1990; Smith, 1990), have career aspirations that are less gender stereotypical (Bressler & Wendell, 1980; Carnegie Commission, 1973), become more engaged in college activities (Miller-Bernal, 1993; Smith, 1990), are more likely to enter traditionally male professions such as medicine and the natural sciences (Tidball, 1985, 1986; Tidball & Kistiakowsky, 1976), are likely to earn higher salaries (Conaty, Alsalam, James, & To, 1989; Riordan, 1994), and likely to reach higher levels of career achievement (Oates & Williamson, 1978; Rice & Hemmings, 1988; Tidball, 1973, p. 1980). In addition, Smith (1990) reported that students in women's colleges evaluated their academic programs as stronger than did their mixed-sex college counterparts; Rice and Hemmings (1988) found that women in women's colleges have lower dropout rates than women in mixed-sex colleges; and Ledman, Miller, and Brown (1995) suggest that graduate education may be a factor intervening in the career success of women's college graduates.

Internationally, the effects of single-sex education appear to vary. In England, one team of researchers found evidence for less gender stereotyping of school subjects in single sex schools among pupils aged 11 to 12, but not among older students (Colley, Comber, & Hargreaves, 1994). In Australia, private single-sex schools were better for girls' achievement (Jones, 1990), although no advantages for participation or attainment in science were found in single-sex schools in Northern Ireland (Daly, 1995). In Kenya, girls in an all-girls school found it easier to use scarce science resources, such as microscopes and lab equipment, than did girls in coeducational schools who deferred to the boys (Ndunda & Munby, 1991), although social class may have been a confounding factor there. In Islamic countries single-sex education is prescribed by religion and custom (purdah) and seems designed to keep women in their proper roles in society (Abul-Husn, 1995; El-Sanabary, 1994; King & Al-Musalam, 1989).

The problem with much of the research in the United States is that the women who attend single-sex and mixed-sex colleges are not comparable in terms of their social backgrounds and possibly other factors as well. Studies that try to control statistically for preexisting differences have reported more mixed results or the absence of positive effects for single-sex education (e.g., Lee & Bryk, 1986, 1989; Marsh, 1989a, b; Marsh, Owens, Meyers, & Smith, 1989; Riordan, 1992, 1994; Stoecker & Pascarella, 1991). As a result, some authors remain skeptical about various alleged advantages (e.g., Giele, 1987; Kim & Alverez, 1995; Oates & Williamson, 1981).

Several studies use national samples with extensive statistical controls on background characteristics (e.g., Kim & Alvarez, 1995; Riordan, 1990, 1994; Stoecker & Pascarella, 1991). Stoecker and Pascarella (1991) found that after controlling for students' background characteristics, institutional selectivity, achievement in college, and subsequent educational attainment, attending women-only colleges had only a trivial net impact on graduates' early career earnings. Riordan (1994) used the National Longitudinal Study of the High School Class of 1972 and found that women's college attendance was not related to educational attainment but was related to occupational attainment and indirectly related to personal income via occupation, when controlling for parental socioeconomic status, SAT scores, marital status, work hours, geographic region, and years attending a women's college (Riordan, 1994). He explains these results by theorizing that women-only colleges provide more social capital for women students, meaning that they provide more encouragement, attention, security, comfort, trust, and sense of identity, although this interpretation needs to be tested empirically in future research. In a similar vein, the greater social and academic integration of students within their institutions has been used to explain the higher rates of college persistence in women's and historically black colleges (Baker & Velez, 1996). These conclusions are consistent with Tidball's finding (1989) that the critical mass of role models, valuation of women, and unparalleled opportunities for women contribute to all-women's colleges' ability to confer advantages on their students.

Canada and Pringle (1995) caution that it is difficult to assess, once and for all, which is better: single-sex or mixed-sex education because such comparisons inevitably rely on central tendencies, which not only obscure variability within categories but overlook the possibilities for change. Thus, single-sex schools may sometimes be as sexist, or even more so, as mixed-sex schools, as Lee, Marks, and Byrd (1994) found, perhaps because many variables besides sex composition affect the kinds and frequency of sexism in classrooms, including the gender mix and the institution's policy stance. They studied all-girls, all-boys, and coed private secondary schools and found forms of sexism in all three types, although both the form and severity varied. "The most problematic forms of sexism in single-sex environments—explicit sexuality in boys' schools and encourage-ment of dependence in girls' schools—were rarer in mixed-sex classrooms. Sexism in coeducational schools commonly took the form of either gender domination or active discrimination and was most common in one curricular area (chemistry)" (Lee et al., 1994, p. 114). Three factors were strongly related to sexism: subject matter (chemistry), balanced numbers (compounded with chemistry), and school policies.

Given evidence that sexism ocurs in both mixed-sex and single-sex schools, many educational researchers seeking ways to ensure gender equity have turned their attention to policies. Lee et al. argue that "...sexism in the classroom is not inevitable. In fact, schools and classrooms are exactly the locations from which change should spring. Aware of continuing societal sexism, the school community should recognize its responsibility to set a proactive tone on gender issues" (Lee et al., 1994, pp. 115–116). School policy can foster positive engenderment, that is, consciously strive "to provide equitable educa-tion for both sexes, including attempts to counter sexism and its residual effects" (Lee et al., 1994, p. 98).

2.7. Achievement

In the United States, girls get somewhat higher grades than boys throughout their school careers and national test score differences between boys and girls have been shrinking in recent years. A national study of eighth-grade U.S. students showed females did not lag their male classmates in science achievement tests, grades, and course enrollments, al-though they had less positive attitudes toward science, participated in fewer relevant extracurricular activities, and aspired less often to science careers than did males (Catsambis, 1995).

International data on gender and educational achievement reveal mixed results. Among students in grades 8 and 9 in Botswana, math achievement scores were roughly equal, and girls scored higher than boys in literacy and reading skills (Fuller, Hua, & Snyder, 1994). In France, among students ages 11 to 12, girls surpass boys in school achievement (Felouzis, 1993). However, in Nigeria (Badejo, 1990), Bangladesh (Mohsin, Nath, & Chowdhury, 1996), Pakistan (Warwick & Jatoi, 1994), and Malawi (Davison & Kanyuka, 1992) boys achieve at higher levels than girls, because of active sex discrimina-tion in Nigeria and lower educational expectations for females in Malawi. In Pakistan, many students live in rural areas, but rural areas are inhospitable to good female teachers. Female students, especially, do better in math when taught by female teachers with uni-versity degrees. Therefore, the gender gap in math achievement appears to be due to the interaction of teacher gender and rural education (Warwick & Jatoi, 1994).

Using comparative international data on 19 countries concerning gender differ-ences in math achievement, Baker and Jones (1993) found that girls perform better in math than boys in some countries (French-speaking Belgium, Finland, Hungary, and Thailand), the same in some countries (British Columbia, England-Wales, Hong Kong, Japan, Nigeria, Scotland, Sweden, and the United States), and not as well in others (France, Israel, Luxembourg, Netherlands, New Zealand, Ontario, Canada, and Swaziland). Overall gender differences in math achievement appear to be decreasing over time. Gender differ-ences in achievement appear to be related to differences in women's labor market oppor-tunities in various countries, since where females have more access to advanced training and to the workplace, sex differences in mathematical performance decrease (Baker &

Jones, 1993, p. 96). In countries where opportunities are less gender stratified, boys and girls are more likely to study the same mathematics curricula and parents are more likely to encourage them equally to learn mathematics (Baker & Jones, 1993, p. 99).

2.8. Summary

Liberal feminist concerns highlight gender inequities in educational experiences, while gender-focused and especially gender-difference perspectives offer a fundamental critique of "schools, curricula, pedagogical styles, academic disciplines, methodological conventions, and predominant theoretical frames as constructed more in accordance with men's than women's ways of knowing, with the result that women are disadvantaged both as learners and as producers of knowledge" (Grant et al., 1994, p. 93). Gender-difference theorists are concerned less with seeing that women achieve equal treatment and exposure within existing structures and more with constructing alternative educational structures that respect and foster women's presumably unique ways of knowing. Patricia Hill Collins and Dorothy Smith "believe that all sociological theory is written from a 'standpoint' " which affects what one studies, the methods used, and the interpretations one makes, suggest Grant et al. (1994, pp. 88–89). Hence the question of whose knowledge is being developed, recognized, taught, established, and whose voices are being heard requires consideration.

Within educational institutions there is evidence that informal social relations sometimes reproduce gendered identities and inequalities. At the same time, there is trend evidence suggesting that the formal curricula of schools is moving toward challenging and changing traditional gender identities and inequities, although counterexamples continue to exist. There is evidence for decreasing gender differences in educational achievement in the United States and other countries. There are also numerous examples of curricula and programs that are challenging the content and processes of conventional education, in Women's Studies programs and all-women's schools and colleges. These suggest some of the complex ways that education may operate to reproduce but also to challenge existing gender stratification. Whether the emphasis on the distinctiveness of feminine experience and knowledge will reinforce dimorphism and gender distinctions in society and thereby increase the chances that invidious gender distinctions will persist is an interesting potential paradox to consider.

Mary Wollstoncraft (1759–1799) argued in the eighteenth century for educational parity between men and women so that both genders could develop their full human potential. However, as Tong (1989, p. 17) notes, "unless society also provides the equally educated woman with the same civil liberties and economic opportunities a man has, she will be able to exercise her hard won autonomy only within the private, or domestic, realm." Thus it becomes essential to consider not only issues of access to education and equity within education, but also the question of whether men and women enjoy the same consequences of education.

3. INDIVIDUAL AND SOCIAL CONSEQUENCES OF EDUCATION

The major theoretical perspectives tend to focus on different consequences of education and offer varied explanations for those different outcomes. Not surprisingly, liberal feminists tend to stress the occupational and income effects of education, to see if education pays off equally for individual men and women, while gender-focused perspectives may consider how education affects health, fertility, economic development, and social attitudes. When faced with the unequal benefits of education for women compared to men, liberal feminists tend to hope that antidiscriminatory policies by the state will level the playing field. Gender-focused theorists help to highlight other formal and informal structural conditions necessary for relatively equal benefits to occur. In this section we consider briefly the effects of education on health and fertility, economic development, political participation and social attitudes, and occupational status and income.

3.1. Health and Fertility

In the United States, higher levels of education are related to greater knowledge of nutrition and health (Hyman, Wright, & Reed, 1975), to better health for both men and women (Ross & Wu, 1995), and to increasing life expectancy for both men and women (Elo & Preston, 1996), although educational differentials in mortality appear to have narrowed for white women since 1960 (Preston and Elo, 1995). Major cross-national research on 26 developing countries shows conclusively that more educated women have considerably lower fertility rates than uneducated women in all the societies studied (Martin, 1995, p. 189). For example, in North Africa more educated women have between two and three fewer children on average than less educated women, and the negative effect of education on fertility is relatively linear. Education is also related to age at marriage in all 26 countries, to women's family-size preferences, and to contraceptive use, especially modern forms of contraception (Martin, 1995, pp. 193–195). Others find that more educated women are more likely to use contraceptives effectively (Rosenzweig, 1996), and to have lower rates of discontinuation and failure, at least in the United States (Grady, Hirsch, Keen, & Vaughn, 1981). In Egypt, El Saadawi (1980, cited in Taylor et al., 1985) found that more educated families were somewhat less likely than less educated families to practice some form of female genital mutilation (66% compared to 98% of uneducated families), a practice that may cause extreme pain, infection, and sometimes death. The education of the families was not, however, related to the girls' lack of knowledge about the physical, psychological, and sexual effects of the procedure. The girls interviewed by El Saadawi were equally ignorant often not knowing what had been done to them, regardless of their own educational level or that of their families.

3.2. Economic Development

Cross-national data on 96 countries from 1960 to 1985 "found clear evidence that in less-developed countries, especially some of the poorest, educational expansion among school-age girls at the primary level has a stronger effect on long-term economic prosperity than does educational expansion among school-age boys" (Benavot, 1989, p. 25). Moreover, the primary education of females has a strong effect on economic growth, "even after the rates of fertility and participation in the labor force are controlled" (Benavot, 1989, p. 41). Secondary and tertiary education of both males and females has a relatively weak impact on economic growth in less developed countries, perhaps because the graduates work in management positions for foreign enterprises or in the public sector and because they may be more oriented to the centers of world culture and may even emigrate there (Benavot, 1989, p. 42). In heavily agricultural countries, literate farmers obtain higher crop yields than do illiterate farmers (Lockheed, Jamison, & Lau, 1980; Rosenzweig, 1996, pp. 27, 28), another way education contributes to productivity.

Because the education of women contributes significantly to the economic development of developing countries, major world agencies, such as the United Nations and the World Bank, strongly support educational equity for females. However, such support is not universally applauded in all societies. There has been resistance to the goal of gender equity in education, especially in heavily Islamic nations. For example, in Afganistan, the fundamentalist Taliban has at least temporarily barred most women from working outside the home or going to school (Crossette, 1996). The Secretary General of the United Nations warned the new Islamic rulers that the United Nations objects to the extreme discrimination they practice against women and warned of "serious repercussions" for the foreign aid program there (Crossette, 1996, p. A1). The results of such conflict between international cultural norms and local Islamic mores is yet to be seen.

3.3. Political Participation and Social Attitudes

Educational attainment is related to the act of voting in the United States (Hyman, Wright, & Reed, 1975; Persell, Green, Gurevich, & Seidel, 1997). Even as early as the 1960s, education increased the politization of U.S. women (Lansing, 1972). The education of women in the United States may be related to the growing gender gap in voting, with educated women more likely to vote Democratic than similarly educated men, although ideology may be an intervening factor (Gotsch & Campbell, 1987). Education is related to greater political participation among men and women in Norway (Petterson & Rose, 1996), the Netherlands (Smeenk, 1994), and Greece (Dobratz, 1992). In the United States, post-secondary education enhances participation in political activities of all kinds (voting, political discussions, campaign activity), community activities (volunteer work, social action, and neighborhood groups, youth organizations, church-related activities), and espousal of civic life goals (working for social justice, being a leader in the community) (Lindsay, Knox, & Kolb, 1991). Moreover, in the United States educated women were at the forefront of both waves of the feminist movement (Ferree & Hess, 1985) and colleges and universities continue to be fertile sites for the development of feminist activism (Tyack & Hansot, 1992).

However, Stromquist (1997) found that other factors interfered with the emancipatory potential of education. In her study of women's participation in a literacy program in Brazil, she found that length of previous schooling, family support for literacy, distance to class, domestic work, responsibility for children, health problems, and poverty all affected the capacity of education to increase political participation and change women's daily lives. Thus the material conditions of women's lives seem to interact with education and affect its outcomes.

At least in the United States, higher levels of education are related to more egalitarian attitudes toward gender roles and to greater espoused racial and gay tolerance (Persell et al., 1997). Among Muslim men in India, however, more educated men are no more likely than less educated men to favor advancing women's status, in education, employment, politics, or the family (Indukumari, 1978). In Matlab, Bangladesh, a poor, traditional society with low status for women, schooling alone is not enough to motivate women to abandon their strong preference for sons (Chowdhury, 1994). These results suggest that the effects of education are contingent upon cultural factors as well as upon material conditions.

3.4. Occupational Advancement and Earnings

In developed countries, women are entering the labor market in increasing numbers. As more occupations professionalize, they require ever more advanced educational credentials, at least in societies in which some significant proportion of the population works in occupations other than agriculture (Collins,1979; Ishida, Muller, & Ridge, 1995). Worldwide, higher levels of educational attainment are related to the performance of higher status occupations (Treiman, 1977). In Japan, however, more educated women are more likely to leave the labor force when they marry than are less educated women (Hirao, 1996), a pattern that was more prevalent in the United States in the 1950s than it is today.

To obtain occupational equity it is necessary for women to enter the full range of male occupations, which they have not yet done (Reskin & Roos, 1992). "To do this, we need sex equity in educational institutions and job training programs to ensure that women are well represented in the labor queues for nontraditional jobs" (Reskin & Roos, 1992, p. 318). The process is somewhat circular, since women are less likely to major in fields, such as engineering, where women are greatly underrepresented which in turn makes them less likely to enter such fields. Occupational gender stratification was noted in the 25 industrial countries studied by Charles (1992), although the extent varied by size of the service sector, fertility rates, gender ideologies, and forms of political decision-making. Bradley (1997) reflects on how educational structures may be linked to occupational gender stratification cross-nationally. Reskin and Roos point out that even when women enter historically male fields, including high-status professional occupations, they are likely to be ghettoized within those fields into a few specialties which are often lower paid (Reskin & Roos, 1992, p. 318). Thus women and men still do not receive equal occupational outcomes from their education even in the United States. Within certain sectors, however, such as the U.S. federal civil service, gender integration of occupations proceeded more rapidly and steadily from 1976 to 1992 than in the general economy (Lewis, 1996).

For individual women in the United States, employed women with more education earn more than those with less education, even though they do not, on average, earn as much as men with comparable educational backgrounds (Reskin & Padavic, 1994). The gender gap in wages at first job is bigger among those with only a high school education (20%) than for those with more education (13%) (Marini & Fan, 1996). In Turkey, educational level is related to both participation in the labor force and returns to education, but the returns to women are somewhat smaller compared to those for men (Tansel, 1994). In Brazil, education had a powerful effect on income for both men and women, even though men earned more than women on average (Haller & Saraiva, 1992). Reporting on returns to education in 78 nations, Psacharopoulos (1994) notes that at the societal level, the highest rates of return to education accrue to investments in the secondary schooling of females.

3.5. Summary

The various effects of education on gender equity interact with economic, political, and cultural conditions, and the nature of that interaction shapes how education can affect gender equity. Education has various kinds of value, including use value, exchange value, social value, and symbolic value. Its use value includes the value of literacy and numeracy for gaining some measure of knowledge and control over many environments, the stimulation of cognitive development, the gains in actual knowledge obtained, competence in gaining further information about an issue, reasoning ability, rational planning, and increasing awareness of alternative possibilities. Exposure to new ideas and lifestyles may increase a person's tendency to question traditional norms and practices. Schools also serve as important agents of socialization, shaping attitudes, opinions, and values. The use value of education may have been what prompted the nineteenth century Scotch-American feminist, Frances Wright, to advocate the educational emancipation of women in the broadest sense of the word. She believed that uneducated women were at the mercy of all who would prey on their ignorance and credulity (Curti, 1935/1968, p. 180). To some degree, the use value of education for women operates independently of their social, political, and economic power in society, although it may be limited in scope. For individuals and societies, education can enhance economic productivity, health, fertility, life expectancy, as well as their children's health, life expectancy, and educational success (Adetunji, 1995; Chowdhury, 1994; Hill & King, 1995; Kalmijn, 1994; Mwamwenda, 1994).

The exchange value of education in an economic market depends on the existence of labor market opportunities for women (Carnoy & Gong, 1996; King, 1996). Similarly, education cannot provide political gains for women in the absence of opportunities for political participation. Moreover, education is unlikely to alter gender and power relations in a society if education is structured so as to reproduce gender divisions and inequalities, for example as El-Sanabary (1994) suggests is the case in Saudi Arabia.

The social value of education includes the forging of networks of relationships with others who have knowledge, who control key resources, and with whom one can productively interact as a relative social equal. Thus, for individuals education may provide important mentors and role models for women seeking entrance into graduate school and certain occupations and for a society education contains the potential for transnational communication.

Finally, education has symbolic value in that higher levels of education are assumed to confer certain cultural and social status. As such, education is a resource for individual women that may offset the expectations for superior performance by males in goal-oriented groups (Webster, 1996). Countries seeking respect in the wider world increasingly see the importance of education for their citizens, both male and female.

4. SUMMARY AND CONCLUSIONS

Gender equity in access to education is not yet fully achieved worldwide, nor is equal treatment fully available in schools. There is, however, evidence for progress toward greater gender equity in access and experience, as well as a continuing need to push for full equality. Governments can be antithetical to gender equity, as in Afghanistan and Saudi Arabia, or supportive, as in countries where the state mandates and pays for equal education for males and females. The presence of transnational organizations, such as the United Nations and World Bank, which challenge blatantly sexist practices and have resources they can threaten to withhold may provide some support for gender equity, at least with respect to educational access. The strong presence of national and transnational commitments to gender equity may help women in negotiating with educational institutions, as liberal feminists suggest. However, when there are state-sanctioned differences in the education provided to men and women, education is more likely to contribute to the reproduction of gender inequalities in society, as critical feminists suggest.

Even when there is equal access, educational institutions can be sexist, neutral, or proactive in fostering gender equity. Education is an important arena within which distinctively gendered identities are constructed. As such, as long as gender is a salient distinction in society, education contributes to the potential for inequities based on that distinction. Within the institution of education, Women's Studies programs, gay and lesbian studies programs, and all-women's colleges may challenge existing structures, practices, and knowledge by providing an independent power base and support for the development of new knowledge. Paradoxically, such programs also risk intellectual ghettoization and intensified dimorphism. Coeducational as well as single-sex schools can sustain positive engenderment policies. In these and other ways, education may provide pressure points for change. Paradoxically, education can also reproduce gendered identities and inequalities, for example in informal social relations within schools or in Saudi Arabia today. Informal peer cultures emerge as a central site for constructing the gendered identities and ideologies of the larger society. While sometimes constrained by the gender equity ideologies of a school, such identities and beliefs may survive underground or on the fringes of official school culture.

Even the development of separate but unequal educational systems, while clearly not preferable, may provide a pressure point for future change. This was certainly the case historically in the United States. Single-sex schools appear to promote gender equity under some conditions while undermining it in others.

The benefits of education, while not fully available to women compared to men, are becoming increasingly accessible. Education can empower individual women by improving their health, fertility control, and life expectancy, and in the public sphere of politics and economics. These gains for individual women also benefit their societies, perhaps making it harder for individual men to oppose the education of women. Some of education's benefits for individual women depend upon economic options, legal rights, and political opportunities within a society. The exchange value of education is contingent upon the level of economic and technical development in a society that influences the degree to which occupations and positions rely upon educational credentials rather than characteristics of an individual's family background, land ownership, gender, race, religion, and so forth. Education appears to encourage people to be more involved politically in many countries, although such effects seem contingent upon other conditions as well. Education appears to be liberating for women when it takes a proactive stance toward gender equity and when it operates in a society that provides economic, political, legal, and social opportunities for women. Even within substantially inequitable societies, however, education can begin to provide some personal and societal benefits, such as gains in fertility control, health, and economic development. It may also provide resources for women as they seek to push for greater gender equity in the political and economic realms. In short, in various ways education can empower women even while it may also construct gender inequalities.

Acknowledgments

We would like to thank all the members of the Gender and Inequality Workshop at New York University, and Adam Green, in particular, for their constructive criticisms of an earlier draft of this paper. We are also very grateful to Janet S. Chafetz, Edith W. King, Francisco O. Ramirez, and members of the audience at a presentation at Cleveland State University, May 15, 1997, for their comments and questions on a previous draft.

We acknowledge with thanks the permission of the United Nations to use their data in Table 19-1 and Figures 19-1 and 19-2. The sources consulted were: United Nations (1995a), *The World's Women 1995: Trends and Statistics. Social Statistics and Indicators* Series K: No. 12. New York: United Nations. 95 XVII 2. United Nations (1995b). *Statistical yearbook 1993.* New York: United Nations. Sales No. E/F.95.XVII.1.

We also acknowledge with thanks the permission of the World Bank to use their data from *Social indicators of development 1996* (data on diskette). Washington, D.C.: The World Bank, in the analysis performed in Table 19-1.

REFERENCES

Abul-Husn, R. (1995). Does education empower women? *Al-Raida, 11,* 9.

Acker, J. (1992). Gendered institutions: From sex roles to gendered institutions. *Contemporary Sociology, 21,* 565–569.

Acker, S., & David, M. E. (1994). *Gendered education: Sociological reflections on women, teaching, and feminism.* Buckingham: Open University Press.

Adetunji, J. A. (1995). Infant mortality and mother's education in Ondo State, Nigeria. *Social Science and Medicine, 40,* 253–263.

Alexander, K. L., & Eckland, B. K. (1974). Sex differences in the educational attainment process. *American Sociological Review, 39,* 668–682.

American Association of University Women. (1992). *The AAUW report: How schools shortchange girls: A study of major findings on girls and education.* Washington, D.C.: AAUW/The Wellesley College Center for Research on Women.

Anderson, M. (1993). *Thinking about women: Sociological and feminist perspectives* (3d ed.). New York: Macmillan.

Anderson-Levitt, K., Bloch, K. M., & Soumare, A. (1994). *Inside classrooms in Guinea: Girls' experiences.* Washington, D.C.: The World Bank.

Antler, J. (1995). Whither women's studies: A women's studies university? *Academe,* July–August, 36–38.

Astin, A. (1977). *Four critical years.* San Francisco: Jossey-Bass.

Averett, S. L., & Burton, M. L. (1996). College attendance and the college wage premium: Differences by gender. *Economics of Education Review, 15,* 37–49.

Badejo, O. O. (1990). Sex-based teacher classroom-behavior in sub-Saharan Africa: A case study of Borno secondary schools (Nigeria). *Afrikanistische Arbeitspapiere, 21,* 123–137.

Bailey, S. M. (1993). The current status of gender equity research in American schools. *Educational Psychologist, 28,* 321–339.

Baker, D. (1986). Sex differences in classroom interaction in secondary science. *Journal of Classroom Interaction, 22,* 212–218.

Baker, D. P., & Jones, D. P. (1993). Creating gender equality: Cross-national gender stratification and mathematical performance. *Sociology of Education, 66,* 91–103.

Baker, T. L., & Velez, W. (1996). Access to and opportunity in postsecondary education in the United States: A review. *Sociology of Education, 69,* 82–101.

Barthel, D. (1985). Women's educational experience under colonialism: Toward a diachronic model. *Signs 11,* 137–154.

Becker, G. S. (1964). *Human capital: A theoretical and empirical analysis with special reference to education.* New York: National Bureau of Economic Research.

Becker, G. S. (1967). *Human capital and the personal distribution of income: An analytical approach.* Ann Arbor, MI: Institute of Public Administration.

Behrman, J. R., & Rosenzweig, M. R. (1994). Caveat emptor: Cross-country data on education and the labor force. *Journal of Development Economics, 44,* 131–146.

Benavot, A. S. (1989). Education, gender, and economic development: A cross-national study. *Sociology of Education, 62,* 14–32.

Boyer, E. L. (1990). *A special report. Campus life: In search of community.* Princeton, NJ: The Carnegie Foundation for the Advancement of Teaching.

Bradley, K. 1997. Gender differences and gender parity: Cross-national trends in the expansion of systems of higher education. Paper presented at the American Sociological Association annual meeting, Toronto, Canada.

Bradley, K., & Ramirez, F. O. (1996). World polity and gender parity: Women's share of higher education, 1965–85. In A. Pallas (Ed.), *Research in sociology of education and socialization 11* (pp. 63–91). Greenwich, CT: JAI Press.

Brady, K. L., & Eisler, R. M. (1995). Gender bias in the college classroom: A critical review of the literature and implications for future research. *Journal of Research and Development in Education, 29,* 9–19.

Bressler, M., & Wendell, P. (1980). The sex composition of selective college and gender differences in career aspirations. *Journal of Higher Education, 51,* 650–63.

Brock, C., & Cammish, N. K. (1994). *Factors affecting female participation in education in seven developing countries.* London: ODA.

Brown, R. (1978). Problems in educational development in the Bahamas. In N. A. Niles & T. Gardner (Eds.), *Perspectives in West Indian education.* East Lansing, MI: West Indian Association, Michigan State University.

Bryson, L. (1987). Sport and the maintenance of masculine hegemony. *Women's Studies International Forum, 10,* 349–360.

Burge, P. L., & Stenstrom, M. L. (1995). Comparison of American and Finnish gender-linked vocational program choices. *International Journal of Vocational Education and Training, 3,* 7–24.

Butler, J., & Schmitz, B. (1992). Ethnic studies, women's studies and multiculturalism. *Change, 24,* 36–41.

Cammish, N. K. (1993). Sons and daughters: Attitudes and issues affecting girls' education in developing countries. *Oxford Studies in Comparative Education, 3,* 87–107.

Canada, K., & Pringle, R. (1995). The role of gender in college classroom interactions: A social context approach. *Sociology of Education, 68,* 161–186.

Carnegie Commission on Higher Education. (1973). *Opportunities for women in higher education.* New York: McGraw-Hill.

Carnoy, M., & Gong, W. (1996). Women and minority gains in a rapidly changing local labor market: The San Francisco Bay area in the 1980s. *Economics of Education Review, 15,* 273–287.

Catsambis, S. (1995). Gender, race, ethnicity, and science education in the middle grades. *Journal of Research in Science Teaching, 32,* 243–257.

Chamberlain, M. K. (1988). *Women in academe: Progress and prospects.* New York: Russell Sage Foundation.

Charles, M. (1992). Cross-national variation in occupational sex segregation. *American Sociological Review, 57,* 483–502.

Chowdhury, M. K. (1994). Mother's education and effect of son preference on fertility in Matlab, Bangladesh. *Population Research and Policy Review, 13,* 257–273.

Colley, A., Comber, C., & Hargreaves, D. J. (1994). School subject preferences of pupils in single sex and co-educational secondary schools. *Educational Studies, 20,* 379–385.

Collins, P. H. (1990). *Black feminist thought: Knowledge, consciousness, and the politics of empowerment.* New York: Unwin Hyman.

Collins, R. (1979). *The credential society.* New York: Academic Press.

Collis, B. (1985). Sex differences in secondary school students' attitudes toward computers. *Computing Teacher, 12,* 33–36.

Conaty, J. C., Alsalam, N., James, E., & To, D . L. (1989). College quality and future earnings: Where should you send your sons and daughters to college? Paper presented at the American Sociological Association annual meeting, San Francisco.

Connell, R. W. (1989). Cool guys, swots and wimps: The interplay of masculinity and education. *Oxford Review of Education, 15,* 291–303.

Constantinople, A., Cornelius, R., & Gray, J. (1988). The chilly climate: Fact or artifact? *Journal of Higher Education, 59,* 527–550.

Cortina, R. (1995). Women's education in Latin America: The profession of teaching in Mexico. *Estudios-Sociologicos, 13,* 595–611.

Crawford, M., & MacLeod, M. (1990). Gender in the college classroom: An assessment of the "chilly climate" for women. *Sex Roles, 23,* 101–122.

Crossette, B. (1996). Afghans draw U.N. warning over sex bias. *The New York Times,* October 8, A1, A8.

Curti, M. ([1935] 1968). *The social ideas of American educators.* Totowa, NJ: Littlefield, Adams & Co.

Curry, T. J. (1991). Fraternal bonding in the locker room: A profeminist analysis of talk about competition and women. *Sociology of Sport Journal, 8,* 119–135.

Daly, P. (1995). Science course participation and science achievement in single sex and co-educational schools. *Evaluation and Research in Education, 9*, 91–98.

Dart, B. C., & Clarke, J. A. (1988). Sexism in schools : A new look. *Educational Review, 40*, 41–49.

Davison, J., & Kanyuka, M. (1992). Girls' participation in basic education in southern Malawi. *Comparative Education Review, 36*, 446–466.

Delamont, S. (1996). *A woman's place in education: Historical and sociological perspectives on gender and education.* Avebury: Aldershot.

Dennis, D. I., & Harlow, R. E. (1986). Gay youth and the right to education. *Yale Law and Policy Review, 4*, 446–478.

Dobratz, B. A. (1992). The political involvement and participation patterns of Greek men and women. Paper presented at the American Sociological Association annual meeting.

Dziech, B. W., & Weiner, L. (1984). *The lecherous professor: Sexual harassment on campus.* Boston: Beacon Press.

Eccles, J. S., & Blumenfield, P. (1985). Classroom experiences and student gender: Are there differences and do they matter? In C. Wilkinson & C. B. Marrett (Eds.), *Gender influences in classroom interaction* (pp. 79–114). New York: Academic Press.

Eder, D. (1997). Sexual aggression within the school culture. In J. Bank & P. Hall (Eds.), *Gender, equity, and schooling: Policy and practice* (pp. 92–112). New York: Garland.

Eder, D., & Parker, S. (1987). The cultural production and reproduction of gender: The effect of extracurricular activities on peer-group culture. *Sociology of Education, 60*, 200–213.

Elo, I. T., & Preston, S. H. (1996). Educational differentials in mortality: United States, 1976–85. *Social Science and Medicine, 42*, 47–57.

El Saadawi, N. (1980). *The hidden face of eve: Women in the Arab world* (pp. 34–35). London: Zed Books Ltd. Translated by Dr. Sherif Hetata.

El-Sanabary, N. (1994). Female education in Saudi Arabia and the reproduction of gender division. *Gender and Education, 6*, 141–150.

Feigenbaum, J., Hargittai, E., & O'Rourke, J. (1994). Expanding the pipeline, CRAW database aids academic recruiters. *Computing Research News*, September, 1.

Felouzis, G. (1993). Class interactions and success at school: An analysis comparing boys and girls. *Revue francaise de Sociologie, 34*, 199–222.

Ferree, M. M., & Hess, B. B. (1985). *Controversy and coalition: The new feminist movement.* Boston: Twayne.

Fine, G. (1987). *With the boys: Little league baseball and preadolescent culture.* Chicago: University of Chicago Press.

Finn, J. D., Dulberg, L., & Reis, J. (1979). Sex differences in educational attainment: A cross-national perspective. *Harvard Educational Review, 49*, 477–503.

Fiol-Matta, L., & Chamberlain, M. K. (1994). *Women of color and the multicultural curriculum.* New York: Feminist Press.

Fish, M. C., Gross, A. L., & Sanders, J. S. (1986). The effect of equity strategies on girls' computer usage in schools. *Computers in Human Behavior, 2*, 127–134.

Foner, N. (1973). *Status and power in rural Jamaica: A study of educational and political change.* New York: Teachers College Press.

Foster, P., Gomm, R., & Hammersly, M. (1996). *Constructing educational inequality: An assessment of research on school processes.* London: Falmer Press.

Frasher, R., & Walker, A. (1972). Sex roles in early reading textbooks. *The Reading Teacher, 25*, 41–49.

Fuller, B., Hua, H. Y., & Snyder, C. W., Jr. (1994). When girls learn more than boys: The influence of time in school and pedagogy in Botswana. *Comparative Education Review, 38*, 347–376.

Gaskell, J. (1985). Course enrollment in the high school: The perspective of working-class females. *Sociology of Education, 58*, 48–57.

Gibson, M. A. (1991). Ethnicity, gender and social class: The school adaptation patterns of West Indian youths. In M. A. Gibson & J. U. Ogbu (Eds.), *Minority status and schooling: A comparative study of immigrant and involuntary minorities* (pp. 169–203). New York: Garland.

Giele, J. Z. (1987). Coeducation or women's education: A comparison of alumnae from two colleges: 1934–79. In C. Lasser (Ed.), *Educating men and women together* (pp. 91–109). Urbana: University of Illinois Press.

Gonzalez-Suarez, M., & Ekstrom, R. B. (1989). Are U.S. elementary school reading textbooks sex stereotyped? Paper presented at the American Educational Research Association annual meeting.

Gotsch, S. T., & Campbell, T. S. (1987). Perceptions of social problems and gender differences in behavior: The 1984 presidential election. Paper presented at the Society for the Study of Social Problems annual meeting.

Grady, W. R., Hirsch, M. B., Keen, N., & Vaughn, B. (1981). *Differentials in contraceptive use failure among married women aged 15–44 years: United States 1970–76.* Washington, D.C.: National Center for Health Statistics.

Graham, P. A. (1978). Expansion and exclusion: A history of women in American higher education. *Signs, 3,* 759–773.

Grant, L., Horan, P. M., & Watts-Warren, B. (1994). Theoretical diversity in the analysis of gender and education. In A. Pallas (Ed.), *Research in sociology of education and socialization* (pp. 71–109). Greenwich, CT: JAI Press.

Graydon, J. (1983). But it's more than a game. It's an institution: Feminist perspectives on sport. *Feminist Review, 13,* 5–16.

Grayson, D. (1992). Emerging equity issues related to homosexuality in education. In S. Klein (Ed.), *Sex equity and sexuality in education* (pp. 171–189). Albany: State University of New York Press.

Hall, R. M., & Sandler, B. R. (1982). *The classroom climate: A chilly one for women?* Washington, D.C.: Association of American Colleges.

Hall, R. M., & Sandler, B. R. (1987). *Out of the classroom: A chilly campus climate for women?* Washington, D.C.: Association of American Colleges.

Haller, A. O., & Saraiva, H. U. (1992). The income effects of education in a developing country: Brazil 1973 and 1982. In R. Althauser & M. Wallace (Eds.), *Research in social stratification and mobility* (pp. 295–336). Greenwich, CT: JAI Press.

Hamilton, V. L., Blumenfeld, P. C, Hiroshi, A., & Miura, K. (1991). Group and gender in Japanese and American elementary classrooms. *Journal of Cross-cultural Psychology, 22,* 317–346.

Hansot, E. (1993). Historical and contemporary views of gender and education. In S. K. Biklen & D. Pollard (Eds.), *Gender and education. Ninety-second yearbook of the National Society for the Study of Education, Part I* (pp. 12–24). Chicago: University of Chicago Press.

Hargreaves, J. A. (1986). Where's the virtue? Where's the grace? A discussion of the social production of gender relations in and through sport. *Theory, Culture, & Society, 3,* 109–21.

Hendry, L. B., Shucksmith, J., Love, J., & Glendinning, A. (1993). *Young people's leisure and lifestyle.* London: Routledge.

Hill, A. M., & King, E. M. (1995). Women's education and economic well-being. *Feminist Economics, 1,* 21–46.

Hirao, K. (1996). The effect of education on the rate of labor force exit for married Japanese women. Paper presented at the American Sociological Association annual meeting, New York.

Holland, D. & Eisenhart, M. (1990). *Educated in romance: Women, achievement, and college culture.* Chicago: University of Chicago Press.

Hyman, H. H., Wright, C. R., & Reed, J. S. (1975). *The enduring effects of education.* Chicago: University of Chicago Press.

Ilon, L. (1992). Fitting girls schooling into the existing economic paradigms: Confronting the complexities. *International Journal of Education Development, 12,* 147–159.

Indukumari, M. (1978). Attitude and practice of Muslim men: A major determinant of Muslim women's status. Paper presented at the International Sociological Association annual meeting.

Ishida, H., Muller, W., & Ridge, J. M. (1995). Class origin, class destination, and education: A cross-national study of ten industrial nations. *American Journal of Sociology, 101,* 145–193.

Jacobs, J. A. (1995). Gender and academic specialties: Trends among recipients of college degrees in the 1980's. *Sociology of Education, 68,* 81–98.

Jacobs, J. A. (1996). Gender inequality and higher education. *Annual Review of Sociology, 22,* 153–185.

Jones, J. (1990). Outcomes of girls' schooling: Unraveling some social differences. *Australian Journal of Education, 24,* 153–167.

Jones, M. G., & Wheatley, J. (1990). Gender differences in teacher-student interaction in science classrooms. *Journal of Research in Science Teaching, 27,* 861–874.

Jordan, E., & Cowan, A. (1995). Warrior narratives in the kindergarten classroom: Renegotiating the social contract? *Gender & Society, 9,* 727–743.

Kalmijn, M. (1994). Mother's occupational status and children's schooling. *American Sociological Review, 59,* 257–275.

Kane, E. (1995). *Seeing for yourself: Research handbook for girls' education in Africa.* Washington, D.C.: Economic Development Institute, World Bank.

Kay, S. (1979). Early educational development in East Africa: A case study. *Comparative Education Review 23,* 66–81.

Kelly, A. (1988). Gender differences in teacher–pupil interactions: A meta-analytic review. *Research in Education, 39,* 1–23.

Kelly, G. P. (1987). Setting state policy on women's education in the third world. *Comparative Education, 23,* 95–102.

Kelly, G. P. (1989). *International handbook of women's education.* New York: Greenwood.

Kidd, B. (1987). Sports and masculinity. In Michael Kaufman (Ed.), *Beyond patriarchy: Essays by men on pleasure, power, and change* (pp. 250–265). Toronto, Canada: Oxford University Press.

Kim, M., & Alvarez, R. (1995). Women's only colleges: Some unanticipated consequences. *Journal of Higher Education, 66,* 641–668.

Kimmel, M. (1990). Baseball and the reconstitution of American masculinity, 1880–1920. In M. A. Messner & D. F. Sabo (Eds.), *Sport, men, and the gender order: Critical feminist perspectives* (pp. 55–65). Champaign, IL: Human Kinetics.

King, E. M. (1996). Education, work and earnings of Peruvian women. *Economics of Education Review, 15,* 213–230.

King, E. W. (1997). Human rights and the American teacher: The growing concern over female genital mutilation in the U.S. Paper presented at the American Sociological Association annual meeting, Toronto, Canada.

King, E. W., & Al-Musalam, M. (1989). The credit-hour curriculum of girls' secondary schools in Kuwait. Paper presented at the American Sociological Association annual meeting.

Kinnear, A. (1995). Introduction of microcomputers: A case study of use and children's perceptions. *Journal of Educational Computing Research, 13,* 27–40.

Kortenhaus, C. M., & Demarest, J. (1993). Gender role stereotyping in children's literature: An update. *Sex Roles, 28,* 219–232.

Kramer, P. A., & Lehman, S. (1990). Mismeasuring women: A critique of research on computer ability and avoidance. *Signs: Journal of Women in Culture and Society, 16,* 158–172.

Krupnick, D. (1985). Women and men in the classroom: Inequality and its remedies. *On Teaching and Learning: Journal of the Harvard Danforth Center, 1,* 18–25.

Lansing, M. (1972). Sex differences in voting and activism. *Michigan Academician, 5,* 171–175.

Ledman, R. E., Miller, M., & Brown, D. R. (1995). Successful women and women's colleges: Is there an intervening variable in the reported relationship? *Sex Roles, 33,* 489–497.

Lee, S., Ichikawa, V., & Stevenson, H. S. (1987). Beliefs and achievement in mathematics and reading : A cross-national study of Chinese, Japanese and American children and their mothers. In M. Meagher (Ed.), *Advances in motivation* (pp.149–179). Greenwich, CT: JAI Press.

Lee, V., Marks, H., & Knowles, T. (1991). Sexism in single-sex and co-educational secondary school classrooms. Paper presented at American Sociological Association annual meeting.

Lee, V. E., & Byrk, A. S. (1989). Effects of single-sex secondary schools on student achievement and attitudes. *Journal of Educational Psychology, 78,* 381–395.

Lee, V. E., Smith, J. B., & Cioci, M. (1993). Teachers and principals: Gender-related perceptions of leadership and power in secondary schools. *Educational Evaluation and Policy Analysis, 15,* 153–180.

Lee, V. E., Marks, H. M., & Byrd, T. (1994). Sexism in single-sex and coeducational independent secondary school classrooms. *Sociology of Education, 67,* 92–120.

Lewis, G. B. (1996). Gender integration of occupations in the federal civil service: Extent and effects on male-female earnings. *Industrial and Labor Relations Review, 49,* 472–83.

Lindsay, P., Knox, W. E., & Kolb, M. N. (1991). Lasting effects of higher education on civic commitment: A longitudinal study. Paper presented at the American Sociological Association annual meeting.

Linn, M. (1985). Gender equity in computer learning environments. *Computers and the Social Sciences, 1,* 19–27.

Lockheed, M. E. (1985). Women, girls, and computers: A first look at the evidence. *Sex Roles, 13,* 115–122.

Lockheed, M., & Frakt, S. (1984). Sex equity: Increasing girls' use of computers. *Computing Teacher, 11,* 16–18.

Lockheed, M., Jamison, D., & Lau, L. (1980). Farmer education and farmer efficiency. In T. King (Ed.), *Education and income* (pp. 111–152). Washington, D.C.: World Bank.

Long, J. E., Sadker, D., & Sadker, M. (1986). The effects of teacher sex equity and effectiveness training on classroom interaction at the university level. Paper presented at the American Educational Research Association annual meeting, San Francisco.

Luebke, B. F., & Reilly, M. E. (1995). *Women's studies graduates: The first generation.* New York: Teachers College Press.

MacIntosh, M. (1990). Caught between the two: Gender and race in a Scottish school. In F. Paterson & J. Fewell (Eds.), *Girls in their prime: Scottish education revisited* (pp. 54–70). Edinburgh: Scottish Academic Press.

Marini, M. M. (1980). Sex differences in the process of occupational attainment: A closer look. *Social Science Research, 9,* 307–361.

Marini, M. M., & Fan, P. L. (1996). Education and the gender gap in earnings at career entry. Paper presented at the American Sociological Association annual meeting, New York.

Marsh, H. W. (1989a). Effects of attending single-sex and coeducational high schools on achievement, attitudes, behaviors, and sex differences. *Journal of Educational Psychology, 81,* 70–85.

Marsh, H. W. (1989b). Effects of single-sex and coeducational schools: A response to Lee and Bryk. *Journal of Educational Psychology, 81,* 651–653.

Marsh, H. W., Owens, L., Meyers, M. R., & Smith, I. D. (1989). The transition from single-sex to co-educational high schools: Effects on multiple dimensions of self-concept and on academic achievement. *American Educational Research Journal, 25*, 237–269.

Martin, P., & Hummer, R. A. (1996). Fraternities and rape on campus. *Gender & Society, 3*, 457–473.

Martin, T. C. (1995). Women's education and fertility: Results from 26 demographic and health surveys. *Studies in Family Planning, 26*, 187–202.

McNeal, R. B., Jr. (1995). Extracurricular activities and high school dropouts. *Sociology of Education, 68*, 62–80.

Merrett, F., & Wheldall, K. (1992). Teacher's use of praise and reprimands to boys and girls. *Educational Review, 44*, 73–79.

Messner, M. A. (1989). Masculinities and athletic careers. *Gender & Society, 3*, 71–88.

Messner, M. A. (1990). Boyhood, organized sports, and the construction of masculinities. *Journal of Contemporary Ethnography, 18*, 416–444.

Mickelson, R. (1989). Why does Jane read and write so well? The anomaly of women's achievement. *Sociology of Education, 62*, 47–63.

Miller-Bernal, L. (1993). Single-sex versus coeducational environments: A comparison of women students' experiences at four colleges. *American Journal of Education, 102*, 23–54.

Miura, I., & Hess, R. D. (1983). Sex differences in computer access, interest and usage. Paper presented at the American Psychological Association Annual Meeting, Anaheim, CA.

Mohsin, M., Nath, S. R., & Chowdhury, A. M. R. (1996). The influence of socioeconomic factors on basic competencies of children in Bangladesh. *Journal of Biosocial Science, 28*, 15–24.

Morse, L., & Handley, H. (1985). Listening to adolescents : Gender differences in science classroom interactions. In C. Wilkinson & C. B. Marrett (Eds.), *Gender influences in classroom interaction* (pp. 37–56). New York: Academic Press.

Murtaugh, M. (1988). Achievement outside the classroom: The role of nonacademic activities in the lives of high school students. *Anthropology and Education Quarterly, 19*, 382–395.

Musil, C. M. (Ed.) (1992). *The courage to question: Women's studies and student learning.* Washington, D.C.: National Women's Studies Association.

Mwamwenda, T. S. (1994). Women and education in Africa. *South African Journal of Sociology, 25*, 143–147.

Myers, D. J., & Dugan, K. B. (1996). Sexism in graduate school classrooms: Consequences for students and faculty. *Gender & Society, 10*, 330–350.

Myerson, M. (1992). Sex equity and sexuality in college-level texts. In S. Klein (Ed.), *Sex equity and sexuality in education* (pp. 149-170). Albany, NY: SUNY Press.

National Education Association Higher Education Research Center. (1995). Part-time Faculty Members. *Update 1.*

Ndunda, M., & Munby, H. (1991). "Because I am a woman": A study of culture, school, and futures in science. *Science Education, 75*, 683–699.

Niles, F. S. (1989). Parental attitudes toward female education in northern Nigeria. *Journal of Social Psychology, 129*, 13–20.

Oates, M. J., & Williamson, S. (1978). Women's colleges and women achievers. *Signs: Journal of Women in Culture and Society, 3*, 795–806.

Oates, M. J., & Williamson, S. (1981). Comments on Tidball's 'Women's colleges and women achievers revisited.' *Signs: Journal of Women in Culture and Society, 6*, 342–345.

Obura, A. (1991). *Changing images—portrayal of girls and women in Kenyan textbooks.* Nairobi: ACTS Press.

Odaga, A., & Ward, H. (1995). *Girls and schools in sub-saharan Africa.* Washington, D.C.: The World Bank.

O'Rourke, L. (1995). Male dominated language and its relationship to adolescent assumptions about gender (Doctoral dissertation, Claremont graduate school, 1994). *Dissertation Abstracts International, 55*, 3174.

Persell, C. H., & Cookson, P. W., Jr. (1987). Microcomputers and elite boarding schools: Educational innovation and social reproduction. *Sociology of Education, 60*, 123–134.

Persell, C. H., Green, A., Gurevich, L., & Seidel, K. (1997). The interdependence of economic conditions, civil society, and social tolerance. Unpublished manuscript, New York University.

Pettersen, P. A., & Rose, L. E. (1996). Participation in local politics in Norway: Some do, some don't; some will, some won't. *Political Behavior, 18*, 51–97.

Powers, M. H. (1995). Factors that influence the educational attainment levels of women students at the University of Malawi, Africa. (Doctoral dissertation, Indiana University, 1994). *Dissertation Abstracts International, 56*, 474.

Preston, S. H., & Elo, I. T. (1995). Are educational differentials in adult mortality increasing in the United States? *Journal of Aging and Health, 7*, 476–496.

Psacharopoulos, G. (1994). Returns to investment in education: A global update. *World Development, 22*, 1325–1343.

Reinharz, S. (1992). *Feminist methods in social research*. New York: Oxford University Press.

Reskin, B., & Padavic, I. (1994). *Women and men at work*. Thousand Oaks, CA: Pine Forge Press.

Reskin, B. F., & Roos, P. A. (1992). *Job queues, gender queues: Explaining women's inroads into male occupations*. Philadelphia: Temple University Press.

Rice, J. K., & Hemmings, A. (1988). Women's colleges and women achievers: An update. *Signs: Journal of Women in Culture and Society, 13*, 546–59.

Riggs, R., Murrell, P., & Cutting, J. (1993). Sexual harassment in higher education from conflict to community. *ERIC Digest*. Published on the World Wide Web at http://136.242.172.58/db/riecije/ed364134.htm. ERIC Document Reproduction Service No. ED364134.

Riordan, C. (1990). *Girls and boys in school: Together or separate?* New York: Teachers College Press.

Riordan, C. (1992). The case for single-sex schools. In D. K. Holliger & R. Adamson (Eds.), *Single sex schools: Proponents speak out* (pp. 47–54). Washington, D.C.: U.S. Department of Education.

Riordan, C. (1994). The value of attending a women's college: Education, occupation, and income benefits. *Journal of Higher Education, 62*, 394–406.

Rosenzweig, M. R. (1996). When investing in education matters and when it does not. *Challenge: The Magazine of Economic Affairs*, March–April, 22–29.

Ross, C. E., & Wu, C. (1995). The links between education and health. *American Sociological Review, 60*, 719–745.

Saario, T., Jacklin, C., & Tittle, C. (1973). Sex role stereotyping in the public schools. *Harvard Educational Review, 43*, 386–416.

Sabo, D. F., & Panepinto, J. (1990). Football ritual and the social reproduction of masculinity. In M. A. Messner & D. F. Sabo (Eds.), *Sport, men, and the gender order: Critical feminist perspectives* (pp. 115–126). Champaign, IL: Human Kinetics.

Sadker, M., & Sadker, D. (1994). *Failing at fairness: How America's schools cheat girls*. New York: Maxwell Macmillian.

Sanders, J. S., & Stone, A. (1986). *The neuter computer: Computers for girls and boys*. New York: Neal-Schuman.

Sewell, W. H., & Hauser, R. M. (1975). *Education, occupation, and earnings*. New York: Academic Press.

Simpson, R. L. (1974). Sex stereotypes of secondary school teaching subjects. *Sociology of Education, 47*, 388–398.

Smeenk, W. H. (1994). Non-voting in the Netherlands and the United States. Paper presented at the American Sociological Association annual meeting.

Smith, D. G. (1990). Women's colleges and coed colleges: Is there a difference for women? *Journal of Higher Education, 61*, 181–95.

Stevenson, H. W., Lee, S. Y., & Stilger, J. W. (1986). Mathematics achievement of Chinese, Japanese and American children. *Science, 231*, 693–699.

Stimpson, C. R., & Cobb, N. K. (1986). *Women's studies in the United States*. New York: The Ford Foundation.

Stoecker, J. L., & Pascarella, E. T. (1991). Women's colleges and women's career attainments revisited. *Journal of Higher Education, 62*, 394–409.

Stromquist, N. P. (1989). Determinants of educational participation and achievement of women in the third world: A review of evidence and a theoretical critique. *Review of Educational Research, 59*, 143–83.

Stromquist, N. P. (1992). Global perspectives on sexuality and equity in education. In S. Klein (Ed.), *Sex equity and sexuality in education* (pp. 55–82). Albany, NY: SUNY Press.

Stromquist, N. P. (1997). *Literacy for citizenship: Gender and grassroots dynamics in Brazil*. Albany, NY: SUNY Press.

Sunderland, J. (1992). Gender in the EFL classroom. *ELT Journal, 46*, 81–91.

Swann, J., & Graddol, D. (1988). Gender inequalities in classroom talk. *English in Education, 22*, 48–65.

Tallerico, M. (1997). Gender and school administration. In J. Bank & P. Hall (Eds.), *Gender, equity, and schooling: Policy and practice* (pp. 182–210). New York: Garland.

Tansel, A. (1994). Wage employment, earnings and returns to schooling for men and women in Turkey. *Economics of Education Review, 13*, 305–320.

Taylor, D., Brekke, T., Davis, A.,. Emecheta, B., French, M., Greer, G., Poniatowska, E., el Saadawi, N., Sirazi, M., & Tweedie, J. (1985). *Women: A world report*. Oxford: Oxford University Press.

Theberge, N. (1981). A critique of critiques: Radical and feminist writings on sport. *Social Forces, 60*, 341–353.

Thorne, B. (1993). Boys and girls together...but mostly apart. In L. Richardson & V. Taylor (Eds.), *Feminist Frontiers III* (pp. 115–125). New York: McGraw-Hill.

Thorne, B., & Luria, Z. (1986). Sexuality and gender in children's daily worlds. *Social Problems, 33*, 176–190.

Tidball, M. E. (1973). Perspective on academic women and affirmative action. *Educational Record, 54*, 130–135.

Tidball, M. E. (1980). Women's colleges and women achievers revisited. *Signs: Journal of Women in Culture and Society, 5*, 504–517.

Tidball, M. E. (1985). Baccalaureate origins of entrants into American medical schools. *Journal of Higher Education, 56*, 385–402.

Tidball, M. E. (1986). Baccalaureate origins of recent natural science doctorates. *Journal of Higher Education, 57*, 606–620.

Tidball, M. E. (1989). Women's colleges: Exceptional conditions, not exceptional talent, produce high achievers. In C. S. Pearson, D. L. Shavlik, & J. G. Touchton (Eds.), *Educating the majority: Women challenge tradition in higher education* (pp. 157–172). New York: Collier Macmillan.

Tidball, M. E., & Kistiakowsky, V. (1976). Baccalaureate origins of American scientists and scholars. *Science, 193*, 646–652.

Tolbert, P. S., & Oberfield, A. A. (1991). Sources of organizational demography: Faculty sex ratios in colleges and universities. *Sociology of Education, 64*, 305–315.

Tong, R. (1989). *Feminist thought: A comprehensive introduction.* Boulder, CO: Westview Press.

Treckler, J. L. (1973). Women in U.S. history high school textbooks. *International Review of Education, 19*, 133–139.

Treiman, D. J. (1977). *Occupational prestige in comparative perspective.* New York: Academic Press.

Tuma, J., & Burns, S. K. (1996). Trends in participation in secondary vocational education: 1982–1992. Statistical Analysis Report. ERIC Document Reproduction Service No. ED 392973 http://136.242.172.58db/riecije/ed392973.htm.

Tyack, D., & Hansot, E. (1992). *Learning together: A history of coeducation in American schools.* New Haven: Yale University Press.

United Nations (1995a). The world's women 1995: Trends and statistics. *Social Statistics and Indicators* Series K: No.12. New York: United Nations.

United Nations (1995b). *Statistical yearbook 1995.* New York: United Nations.

Warwick, D. P., & Jatoi, H. (1994). Teacher gender and student achievement in Pakistan. *Comparative Education Review, 38*, 377–399.

Webster, M. (1996). Experimental methods to study status. Talk at the Research Methods Workshop, Department of Sociology, New York University, November 7.

Weitzman, L., & Rizzo, D. (1976). *Biased textbooks: Images of males and females in elementary school textbooks.* Washington, D.C.: Center on Sex Roles in Education.

Whiteley, P. (1996). The gender balance of physics textbooks: Caribbean and British books, 1985–91. *Physics Education, 31*, 169–174.

Women on Words and Images. (1972). *Dick and Jane as victims: Sex stereotyping in children's readers.* Princeton, NJ: Carolingian Press.

World Bank. (1996). *Social indicators of development 1996* (data on diskette). Washington, D.C.: The World Bank.

Wrigley, J. (Ed.) (1992). *Education and gender inequality.* Washington, D.C.: Falmer Press.

Yates, B. A. (1982). Church, state, and education in Belgian Africa: Implications for contemporary third world women. In G. P. Kelly & C. M. Elliott (Eds.), *Women's education in the third world: Comparative perspectives* (pp. 127–151). Albany: SUNY Press.

CHAPTER 20

Gender, Hierarchy, and Science

MARY FRANK FOX

1. INTRODUCTION

In the study of gender and society, science is a strategic analytical research site—because of the hierarchical character of gendered relations, generally, and of science, particularly. Gendered relations are hierarchical inasmuch as women and men are not simply social groups neutrally distinguished from each other, but rather, are differentially ranked and evaluated according to a standard of masculine norms and behavior. Science, in turn, is fundamentally hierarchical. It is an institutional medium of power, marked by immense inequality in status and rewards, with the valued attributes of science being those more ascribed to men compared to women.

In the classifications of the National Research Council and National Science Foundation, the eight science fields are physical, mathematical, computer, environmental, life sciences, and engineering, as well as psychology and social sciences. In this chapter, science refers primarily to these fields, excluding psychology and social sciences—except in the national data or specific samples on career-attainments, where data are both aggregated across and disaggregated by the eight fields and are specified as such.

My aims are to analyze the hierarchical gendered relations—or stratification by gender—operating in: (1) attainments within and constraints upon participation, performance, and rewards in scientific careers; and (2) arguments about the construction of scientific knowledge. We shall see that science both exemplifies and expands gender stratification within society.

MARY FRANK FOX • School of History, Technology, and Society, Georgia Institute of Technology, Atlanta, Georgia 30332-0345

Handbook of the Sociology of Gender, edited by Janet Saltzman Chafetz. Kluwer Academic/ Plenum Publishers, New York, 1999.

1.1. Science as a Focal Case

What warrants the focus upon science? In the sociology of gender, science is a focal case because science is an agent of power, with consequences for the present and future human condition (see also Cockburn, 1985; Wajcman, 1991). Grounded in abstract and systematic theory and rationality, science is a prototype of professional claim to "authoritative knowledge" (Fox & Braxton, 1994, p. 374). Science defines what is "taken for granted" in daily lives and activities by literally billions of people (Cozzens & Woodhouse, 1995, p. 551). To be in control of science is to be involved in directing the future, and this is highly valued (Wajcman, 1991, p. 144). Tellingly, other occupations (from law to librarianship) have tried to mimic scientific authority and practice in their strategies for professional dominance and control (Derber, Schwartz, & Magress, 1990, p. 33).

1.1.1. SCIENCE, POWER, AND SOCIAL INSTITUTIONS. As a agent of power, science reflects and connects with central social institutions, especially education and the state. Mathematics and its integral relationship to science operate as critical filter subjects in progression through educational levels. In higher education, science has been central to the development of the modern, complex university. Further, science and the political order sustain each other—with the "scientific ethos" of merit and equity operating as part of the belief system that underlies public support of science. The institutional connections between science, education, and the state, and the belief systems underlying them, point to the importance of science as an agent of power, and as a critical case in the study of gender and society. In understanding the relationship between gender and science, we need to apprehend the connections between science, power, and social institutions, addressed in the following sections.

1.1.1.1. Science and Education. When the church controlled education, Latin was the "filter," the foundational subject that needed to be mastered, and that operated as a sieve in successive filtering of students through educational levels. By the eighteenth century, the church had lost its dominance over education. The rising bourgeoisie gained influence, and Latin began to give way, initially to philosophy and logic, and then to science and mathematics as prominent subjects. Science and mathematics began to function as "proofs of competence" and a means of upward social and occupational mobility, based upon meritocratic performance (see Artz, 1966, pp. 66–67; Hacker, 1989, pp. 60–66; Noble, 1977, pp. 20–32; Schneider, 1981). In the process, mathematics tests came to serve as determinants of educational success or failure (Hacker, 1990, p. 141). Proficiency in math and science came to be used as indicators—both cultural and technical—of rationality (Hodgkin, 1981), and of self-discipline and "habits of industry" (Cardwell, 1957).

The ascendance of math and science as prominent features and filters in the educational system has gendered significance. Technical, particularly engineering, education in the United States became situated, directly and indirectly, within a masculine, military model. In direct modeling, engineering education was founded in the United States at the Military Academy at West Point (1821), patterned on the French Ecole Polytechnic.[1]

---

[1] The term "engineering" had its origins in the fifteenth century, and denoted the design of devices for warfare. In 1747, the first formal school of engineering, the Ecole Nationale des Fonts et Chausses (National School of Bridges and Roads), was established in France. At the end of the eighteenth century, engineering began to acquire standing as a discipline, and the qualifier "civil" engineering was applied to indicate its extramilitary applications (for an overview of "the birth of engineering," see Ambrose, Dunkle, Lazarus, Nair, & Harkus, 1997, pp. 13–14).

Indirectly, the military institutions constructed technical "competition, merit, and especially discipline and control [that] defined both masculinity and success" (Hacker, 1989, p. 66). More currently, engineering faculty interviewed about the importance of calculus and other forms of mathematics in the curriculum believed that it had "little relevance for job performance," but stressed it as important "to show that you can do it" and "to develop a proper frame of mind" (Hacker, 1990, p. 149).

Science also structured higher education more broadly. In the United States, science and higher education have evolved, in fact, as "reciprocal developments" (see Fox, 1996, pp. 266–268). First, from the nineteenth century onward, science acted to break up the generalist curriculum that trained graduates for ministry, law, or government service. Science helped introduce to the curriculum lectures, seminars, and independent work that largely replaced classical pedagogy emphasizing drill and recitation. Second, science paved the way for graduate education across fields, and in like manner, led the way in securing federal support for research and training. Third, with specialization, federal support for research, and winning of autonomy in research—forces largely related to developments in science—the university became decentralized. Power in making appointments and in controlling research funds moved from central administration to academic departments. Such decentralization has come to define the complex university, which continues to dominate higher education in the United States. Within academia—and for the public support and funding essential to it—science became a model (albeit frequently faltering) of research expertise and a standard for research training and apprenticeship.

1.1.1.2. Science and the State.   As with education, a strong institutional connection between science and the state points to science as an operant of power—and grasping this connection is important to understanding science as a focal case in the sociology of gender.

The connection between science and the larger political order is such that science and the larger political order are created and re-created, reciprocally—so that they sustain each other (see Cozzens & Woodhouse, 1995; Jasanoff et al., 1995, pp. 527–531). The root is this: science costs, and the government finances. The state, in turn, has a strong stake in science.

Science is supported largely through public funds, distributed through federal agencies. In 1989, 20 U.S. federal agencies each spent more than 50 million dollars on research, with six agencies—National Institutes of Health, Department of Defense, National Aeronautics and Space Administration, Department of Energy, National Science Foundation, and Department of Agriculture–accounting for 90% of all federal support for research (Morin, 1993, Table 4-1).

Under the "social contract for science"–an arrangement originally outlined by Vannevar Bush (1945/1990)—the federal government provides funds for basic research and scientific training, and agrees not to interfere with scientific decision-making, in exchange for unspecified benefits to the public good expected to result ultimately from science. In practice, however, scientific research and resulting knowledge are infused with the assumptions and interests of both scientists and their federal sponsors (Cozzens & Woodhouse, 1995). The shaping of scientific research by sponsors and their public and congressional constituencies is manifest in areas such as oceanography, funded by the Office of Naval Research, "the war on cancer," and research attention to AIDS and to Alzheimer's disease, funded by National Institutes of Health. Scientific products and attainments have been taken as gauges of national resourcefulness, power, and prestige.

1.1.1.3. The Ethos of Science. Underlying the public support of science is an ethos that helps justify the federal investment and also makes science a strategic case for analysis of gendered hierarchies. As articulated over 50 years ago by Robert Merton (1942/1973), the normative structure of science has an ethos of "universalism," which prescribes that social relations be governed by "uniform terms." This is contrasted with "particularism," relations governed by "particular properties" of people. Universalism entails two connected requirements: (1) When a scientist offers a contribution to scientific knowledge, the scientific community's assessment of the validity of that claim should not be influenced by the scientist's personal or social attributes (such as race or gender). (2) Relatedly, a scientist should be rewarded for contributions, with "careers open to talent" and with characteristics such as race and gender irrelevant for making claims and gaining rewards.[2]

Science has been characterized both as a universalistic institution and as one in which universalistic standards fall short (see Cole, 1992, pp. 157–176; Mitroff, 1974; and Mulkay, 1976 for a review of this debate). At the same time, however, it is well established that science is an institution with immense inequality in career attainments and rewards (Zuckerman, 1988, pp. 526–527). Whether the inequality is "equitable" or "inequitable" depends upon the extent to which it can be explained by normatively justifiable—largely merit or achievement-based—criteria (see, e.g., Fox, 1981). For the purposes here, the "scientific ethos," with its belief-system of race-, gender-, and ethnic-neutrality, heightens the strategic value of science as a focal case for analysis of gender stratification in career attainments, and in arguments about the construction of scientific knowledge.

2. GENDER, HIERARCHY, AND CAREER ATTAINMENTS IN SCIENCE[3]

Gender shapes participation, location, rank, performance, and rewards in science. Women have long been "in science," but not central to science, in significant or influential roles (see accounts in Rossiter, 1982; Zuckerman, Cole, & Bruer, 1991). Before World War II, in the United States, women with doctoral degrees[4] in science were often unemployed, and if employed, had prospects limited to either working in a dependent position as a research associate in a laboratory controlled by the principal investigator, or teaching in a women's college where human and material resources for research were modest to negligible (Rossiter, 1982).

2.1. Participation

Over the century, levels of women's and men's participation in science are difficult to track precisely, because data on employment levels by gender are not available systematically over time. However, data on doctoral degrees awarded are, and they indicate the proportions of women compared to men who were professionally trained, and thus qualified for participation.

These proportions do not represent a simple, linear trend of increasing improvement

---

[2] See Long and Fox (1995) for a current assessment of the meaning, measurement, conditions for, and problems of "universalism and particularism" in scientific careers.

[3] Data and discussion on gender and career attainments draw from Fox (1995, 1996) and Long and Fox (1995).

[4] This chapter focuses upon doctoral-level scientists, because it is for this group that issues of research and research productivity and impact are most pertinent.

in degrees attained by women. The proportions of doctoral degrees awarded to women compared to men in the United States[5] in the 1920s (12.3%) and the 1930s (11%) are higher than the proportions in the 1940s (8.9%), the 1950s (6.7%), or even the 1960s (7.9%).[6] It was the 1970s before the proportions of doctoral degrees awarded to women (14.9%) equaled or surpassed the pre-1940 proportions. Continuing gains were made in the 1980s, and for the period 1980–1988, women earned 26% of all doctoral degrees in science (Fox, 1995, p. 206).

In 1993, women were 20% of the employed doctoral level scientists in the United States compared with 14% a decade earlier (CPST, 1997, Table 4-16). Employment of women is disproportionately low in the scientific workforce of most industrialized nations. Although less is known about participation by gender in developing countries of Africa, Latin America, and Asia, the trends show women's proportional participation to be as low or lower than in industrialized nations (Rathgeber, 1995).

With the exception of Asians, participation of U.S. ethnic and racial minorities is disproportionately low in science. In 1993, 2.1% of doctoral level scientists and engineers were African-American, 11% were Asian, 0.37% were Native American, and 2% were Hispanic (CPST, 1997, Table 4-16). Beyond their low rates of participation, relatively little is known about the conditions and experiences of racial/ethnic minorities in science. Racial and ethnic minorities have been regarded by researchers as a "statistical rarity" (Bechtel, 1989), groups for whom detailed, reliable data have been difficult to obtain and for whom inferences have been difficult to make (Cole & Cole, 1973, pp. 152–153). Few studies include racially comparative groups, and much remains to be known about the status and attainments of racial and ethnic groups in science. What we know about women as an aggregate, which of course, includes both white and nonwhite women, is much broader (Long & Fox, 1995, pp. 48–49).

As to why so few women "choose" science compared to other areas such as arts, humanities, and social services, the answer lies in a complex set of factors that are difficult to untangle. Given limitations of space and focus, these factors can only be briefly addressed. They include: (1) social constructions of what is regarded as appropriate work for women, and thus issues of social and gender identity; (2) an educational "pipeline" for science fields that starts early in life and forms a tracked and ordered sequence of study; (3) perceived barriers for women in science compared to other fields; and (4) inequitable resources and opportunities offered to women compared to men in both education for, and professional attainment in, science (Evetts, 1996; Hanson, 1996).

Beyond their rates of participation, women and men employed in science are differentiated in the fields they occupy, the places they work, and the ranks they hold, as well as their levels of research productivity, addressed in the following sections.

2.2. Fields

Between fields, the distributions of women and men are highly uneven (Table 20-1). In 1993, the vast majority (82%) of women were in three fields—life sciences, psychology,

---

[5] National data on scientific personnel are compiled by the National Research Council (Survey of Earned Doctorates, and Survey of Doctoral Recipients) and National Science Foundation (Survey of Graduate Students and Postdoctorates in Science and Engineering). In this chapter, data referred to are for U.S. scientists, unless otherwise indicated.

[6] Although the number of degrees awarded to women increased in post-1920 decades, the point is that the women's *proportion* of total degrees awarded *decreased*.

TABLE 20-1. **Employed Doctoral Scientists and Engineers,**
by Field of Doctorate and Gender, 1993

Field	% Female	N	Men	Women
Physical science	10.0	98,530	24.0%	10.5%
Computer science	12.1	27,940	6.7	3.6
Environmental science	.7	3,850	1.0	0.4
Life science	26.3	120,730	24.1	33.9
Psychology	40.6	71,020	11.4	30.9
Social science	24.9	65,660	13.4	17.4
Engineering	4.3	75, 120	19.5	3.4
Total employed*	20.0	462,870	100.0%	100.0%

*Entries may not add to totals due to rounding.
Source: Commission on Professionals in Science and Technology. (1997). *Professional women and minorities: A total resource data compendium* (12th ed.). Washington, D. C., calculated from Table 4-11.

and social sciences. In contrast, only half of men were employed in these fields. Men were twice as likely as women to be in physical, computer, and environmental sciences, and six times more likely to be in engineering.

These distributions of women and men by field suggest nonuniform processes of selection by field (both self-selection and selection by institutions). However, the factors governing employment by field, particularly the higher proportions of women in life sciences and men in physical sciences, are not well understood (Zuckerman, 1987, p. 128). Even less is known about gender distributions by research subfield, such as new compared to established, high-growth compared to low-growth, and more theoretical (basic) compared to less theoretical (applied) areas, and the consequences of such distributions for resources acquired and impact made in science (Fox, 1995, p. 209).

2.3. Locations

Within science, women and men are employed in different sectors. As of 1993, doctoral-level women in science were more likely than men to be located in educational institutions (52% vs. 47%), and less likely to be in industry (21% vs. 33%). The higher proportion of women compared to men in educational institutions and the lower proportion in industry reflect the disparate proportions of doctoral level women and men in engineering, in particular. Compared to other fields, engineering is more likely to be practiced in the industrial sector.

Education is the predominate sector for doctoral—level scientists—and the vast preponderance (over 90%) of those in education are in higher education. Stratification in science is linked to stratification in higher education. Key here is that the activities and resources of science departments—their research projects, graduate training programs, and external funding—contribute heavily to the prestige-, revenue-, and ranking-levels of academic institutions. Universities with active research programs, strong graduate education, and external funding have the highest ranking. Those with undergraduate only programs have lower ranking, although these vary with the selectivity of admissions and credentials of the faculty. Comprehensive colleges, which evolved from teacher's colleges, have vaguer identity and lower distinction (Clark, 1987).

The data on women's and men's location within types of academic institutions are for broad classifications: universities, 4-year colleges, medical schools, and 2-year colleges. The university category, for example, is aggregated across type of institutions, except medical schools. What the data show (Table 20-2) is that in 1987 (the most recent year for which these data are available), 70% of the men were concentrated in universities (excluding medical colleges); in contrast, 57% of the women worked in these locations. Women were more apt than men to be in medical schools—21% of the women compared to 13% of the men were employed in these settings. This may reflect the concentration of women in life sciences and the fact that microbiology programs are often located in medical schools; it may also reflect the large number of low-ranking, off-track positions (instructorships, lectureships) in those settings. Few scientists were in precollege settings, but women were three times more likely than men (4% vs. 1.3%) to work in these lower-prestige institutions (Fox, 1996, pp. 269–270).

The difference in the proportion of women and men scientists working in universities, which must be considered in combination with their ranks within them, is notable because it is in universities that time, equipment, and facilities for research, and graduate students' involvement in research projects, are concentrated. These resources provide the ways and means for research performance, to be discussed subsequently.

2.4. Rank

In academia, ranks are clearly, and in most cases uniformly, specified as professorial levels and thus revealing of career attainments by gender. Because of the variable, nonuniform titles for scientists across nonacademic locations, it is difficult to determine patterns of gender and rank for these locations.

In considering academic rank, we need to look at distributions of women and men by rank—that is, the proportion of women and of men who hold levels of professorial positions in science. It is also important to consider women as a proportion of faculty at each rank. This proportion reflects women's participation or nonparticipation relative to men by rank, and the availability of women at higher ranks for matters of influence in teaching and research. Thus, while a given department may have three women, and the distribution is one woman at each rank, what is equally, or more, important as an indicator of status by gender is the proportion of faculty that women represent at each rank.

Considering first the distributions of women and men by rank, we find gender inequalities at the upper and lower ranks. Most notably, in 1993, 44% of the men compared

TABLE 20-2. Doctoral Scientists and Engineers Employed in Academe, by Type of Institution and Gender, 1987

Type of Academic Institution	% Female	N	Men	Women
Pre-college	41	4,019	1.3%	4.0%
Two-year college	23	5,226	2.2	2.9
Four-year college	20	31,693	13.7	15.5
Medical school	27	31,711	12.5	20.7
Other university	16	153,154	70.3	57.0
Total academe*	19	225,803	100.0%	100.0%

*Percents may not add to 100 due to rounding.
Source: National Research Council. (1991). *Women in science and engineering: Increasing their numbers in the 1990s.* Washington, D.C.: National Academy Press, Table 6.

to 17% of the women were full professors; 35% of the women were at the level of assistant professor or lower, compared to 15% of the men (CPST, 1997: calculated from Table 5-1).

Second, examining the proportion of women compared to men at each rank, the pattern is one of marked disparity by gender (Table 20-3). Across science and engineering fields, the higher the rank, the lower the proportion of women. As of 1993, women were 32% of the assistant professors, 22% of the associate professors, and 10% of the full professors. While this pattern prevails across fields, certain fields have stronger gender disparity by rank. Just as women are concentrated in three fields—life science, psychology, and social science—so correspondingly, in these fields we find higher proportions of women at each rank. In life sciences, psychology, and social sciences, women were 38%, 47%, and 32%, respectively, of assistant professors; and 28%, 33%, and 26%, respectively, of the associate professors.

However, for each field except psychology, the proportions of women at the rank of full professor are meager. In half of the field-categories—that is, in physical, mathematical, and environmental sciences and engineering—women are 6% or fewer of full professors. Only in psychology are women more than 13% of the full professors.

Despite the number of women with doctorates earned in the 1970s and 1980s and the passage of years for these women to have matured in professional terms, the proportion of women who are full professors has not kept pace with the growth of women with doctorates. In 1973, women were 4% of the full professors in science and engineering

TABLE 20-3. **Doctoral Scientists and Engineers in Academic Institutions, by Field and Rank, 1993**

Field	Total*	Full Professor	Associate Professor	Assistant Professor
Physical sciences	30,030	12,690	5,690	4,670
% Women		3.5	10.2	20.6
Mathematical sciences	13,832	5,827	4,407	2,328
% Women	8.6	4.6	10.2	14.8
Computer specialties	2,453	362	807	1,064
% Women	13.3	8.0	11.4	15.7
Environmental sciences	5,370	1,890	1,395	728
% Women	11.8	5.6	6.8	23.4
Life sciences	62,100	19,780	13,860	13,040
% Women	27.8	12.6	28.4	35.9
Psychology	21,395	7,695	5,200	3,987
% Women	35.8	20.5	33.4	46.5
Social sciences	41,859	16,368	12,298	8,478
% Women	23.4	11.2	26.3	32.1
Engineering	20,900	9,240	4,960	4,180
% Women	4.3	1.5	3.2	11.7
Total, all fields	190,640	72,020	45,160	38,380
% Women	21.7	9.8	21.9	32.3

*Total includes instructor/lecturer, other faculty, "does not apply," and "no report."
Source: Commission on Professionals in Science and Technology. (1997). *Professional Women and Minorities: A Total Human Resource Data Compendium* (12th ed.). Washington, D.C.: Table 5-1.

fields, in 1987, that proportion was 7%, and in 1993, still just 10%; and these figures are inflated by the numbers of women in psychology (also see Gibbons, 1992).

Even allowing up to 15 years from doctorate to full professor, women's degrees are not translating into expected rank over time. Such discrepancies are documented in chemistry, in mathematics, indeed across fields in higher education (American Statistical Association, 1993, p. 4; University of Wisconsin, 1991, p. ix; Vetter, 1992, pp. 37–38). In chemistry, for example, at doctoral-granting institutions between 1985 and 1990, women went from 11% to 18% of assistant professors; from 9% to 13% of associate professors; but only from 3% to 4% of full professors (Roscher, 1990, pp. 72–73). These proportions are to be considered against the growth in women's share of doctoral degrees awarded in chemistry: 7.7% in 1970, 11% in 1975, 17% in 1980, 20% in 1985, and 25% in 1990 (National Center for Education Statistics, 1993, Table 240; Roscher, 1990, Table 11)— and the maturation of the cohorts over the period.

These data on gender and rank and those on discrepancy between the availability of women with doctorates and rank over time do not control for research productivity. Studies that do, however, indicate that academic rank may be the area of greatest gender disparity in scientific career attainments. Accordingly, Cole (1979) found that for scientists at each productivity level considered, men had higher average rank than women. This held for scientists in institutions at varying levels of prestige. Further, with a sample of biochemists who received Ph.D.s between 1956 and 1967, Long, Allison, and McGinnis (1993) found that rates of promotion from assistant to associate to full professor were lower and slower for women than for men. Being in a prestigious department delays promotion for both genders, but the effect is stronger for women. In addition, in their study of recipients of prestigious postdoctoral fellowships between 1955 and 1986, Sonnert and Holton (1995a) found that women's lower rank cannot be explained by their lower productivity, because women's rank is lower at each level of productivity. The disadvantage in rank for women was concentrated in fields outside of biology, that is, in physical sciences, mathematics, and engineering. This highlights again the issue of gender patterns by field in science.

2.5. Research Productivity

Research productivity refers to actual *outcomes* of research—in basic science—publications. Publication productivity is not strictly equivalent to research productivity, but the one (publication) is an indicator of the other (research). No guarantee exists that a big producer of publications makes a significant contribution or that a given nonpublisher makes no contribution. However, in the aggregate, the correlation is high between quantity of publications and impact, assessed through awards and recognition in science (see Blume & Sinclair, 1973; Cole & Cole, 1973; Gaston, 1978).

In the analysis of gender and career attainments in science, publication productivity is important for three reasons. First, publication is an important social process of science, because it is through publication that research findings are communicated and verified, and that priority of work is established (see Fox, 1983). Second, and accordingly, until we understand productivity differences, we cannot adequately assess other gender differences in location, rank, and rewards, because they are related to—although not wholly explained by—productivity (Fox, 1991). Third, as discussed in the Introduction, the "ethos of science" is that "merit governs rewards in science," and that factors such as gender and race are illegitimate determinants. Because publication is a indicator of merit in and contributions to science, it is important in assessing whether science abides by or abrogates its manifest value-system. The extent to which science is "universalistic," with contributions to knowledge governing rewards, or "particularistic," with personal factors, such as race and gender, accounting for rewards, has probably been the most widely debated issue in the sociology of science (Cole, 1992: Long & Fox, 1995; Zuckerman, 1988).

What do we know about the publication productivity of women and men? First, as described in Fox (1995), numbers of studies indicate that women publish less than men. Across fields, women publish about half as much as men in a given period. Over a 12-year period, across the fields of chemistry, biology, psychology, and sociology, Cole (1979) reports that the median number of papers published was eight for men and three for women. In a sample of women and men scientists matched by field and year of Ph.D., as well as doctoral department, Cole and Zuckerman (1984) found that women published 6.4 papers, compared to 11.2 for men. Although particular levels of gender difference vary by field, women are found to publish significantly fewer papers than men in chemistry (Reskin, 1978), biochemistry (Long et al., 1993), ecology (Primack & O'Leary, 1989), and psychology (Helmreich, Spence, Beane, Lucker, & Matthews, 1980), as well as four social science fields (Fox, 1995). For biological and social sciences, the gap between women's and men's number of publications has been narrowing more recently (Sonnert & Holton, 1995a; Ward & Grant, 1995).

Second, while women and men publish at different rates, the distribution for both is strongly skewed: low, even null, performance is most frequent, and high, or even moderate, performance is rare (Fox, 1995). To put it differently, the distribution of productivity is such that most work is produced by a few, while the majority publish little (Cole & Zuckerman, 1984). This pattern of highly variable and strongly skewed productivity, documented nearly 75 years ago in Lotka's (1926) analysis of physics journals, is characteristic of both men and women in science.

Publication productivity is both cause *and* effect of gender disparity in career attainments. That is, it both reflects women's depressed rank and prestige of institutional locations, and it partially accounts for that status (Fox, 1991). "Partially" is the key term: holding constant levels of publication productivity, women's attainments in science, especially rank, remain lower than men's, as discussed previously. Although understanding is incomplete of the processes leading to gender disparity in career attainments, the evidence is that "universalism falters in science" and that "women are less able to translate their productivity into resources and recognition" (Long & Fox, 1995, p. 68).

3. GENDER, HIERARCHY, AND KNOWLEDGE IN SCIENCE

In positivist[7] tradition, the scientist is depicted as a "model of impartiality, a passive observer, collector and collator of natural facts, someone whose activities [are] unsullied by personal bias or emotion, unscarred by political and religious standing, or by cultural values . . . " (Benjamin, 1991, p. 6). In such representations, science is "other-worldly"—disembodied, extrasocial, culturally neutral, governed by it own internal logic and coherence.

[7] The essence of positivism is its tenet that the content of science is determined by "reality" or "facts."

In the 1970s, a sociology of scientific knowledge, developed in Europe, countered the positivist view that science merely reveals nature, with scientists acting as neutral agents or mediators. The work of Barnes (1974), Bloor (1976), and Mulkay (1979), for example, emphasizes ways in which social, political, and economic interests of particular groups construct scientific findings and generalizations. Sociologists of scientific knowledge have been slower to point to ways in which science and technology reflect and reinforce the interests of—and systems based upon dominance by—gender (Harding, 1983).

A feminist analysis, which asserts that "evidence is a question of interpretation, and theories are accounts of and for specific kinds of lives," including those of women and of men (Harraway, 1989, p. 8), has *popular* roots in the women's health movement of the late 1960s and early 1970s, and classic volumes associated with it (Boston Women's Health Collective, 1971/1976; Ehrenreich & English, 1973). The women's health movement has challenged scientific medical knowledge, as produced by men and applied to women; knowledge that has been thought to define women in ways that supported female subordination and inferiority. More specifically, the movement has challenged a "sexual politics of sickness and health," that constructed women as "weak, dependent, and diseased," female functions of menstruation, pregnancy, and childbirth as "pathologies," and menopause as "terminal illness," "the death of the woman in the woman" (Ehrenreich & English, 1978, pp. 92–100). Parallel critiques have posed correspondence between women's subordination and the domination of "nature," that is, land and earth as feminine entities, subject to exploitation and control by men (Kolodny, 1975; Merchant, 1980; Ortner, 1972).

With this feminist analysis of medicine in particular, critical "floodgates" opened:

> If medical knowledge—as one form of scientific knowledge—was patriarchal, then what about the rest of science, in which men were similarly dominant? What about other forms of systemic knowledge? Was the whole intellectual realm gender-biased? Was there more than one kind of rationality? Was there a 'male' and a 'female' rationality? Or was 'rationality' itself a tainted concept denoting a blinkered and limited approach to understanding the human condition? (McNeil, 1987, pp. 29–30)

The critique of medicine has encouraged resistance to other knowledge and expertise as power relations between men and women. This has included challenge to dogmas of psychiatry: theories and concepts such as "female masochism," female achievement as "castrating" and "unwomanly drives to power," and of periodic maternal absence as "deprivation of children." Further, speculation has arisen about the ways in which gender may shape the meaning of scientific knowledge more broadly—the ways in which scientific questions are framed, data interpreted, and applications made.

These considerations of mind, nature, and masculinity (Fox, 1986) are represented especially in the work of Evelyn Fox Keller (1985, 1995, and elsewhere), who maintains that science is inherently masculine in character, not just male dominated in numbers. The consequence, Keller argues, is not simply an exclusion of women, but a schism between masculine and feminine, subjective and objective, understanding and control. She argues, for example, that the tension between scientific explanations that stress hierarchies and unidirectional causal paths and those that stress multiple interactions and multidirectional pathways stem from different and gendered views of nature, domination, and control (Keller, 1985).

Analyses of gender and scientific knowledge have flourished at a philosophical level (although not at an empirical level), and have been the basis for theorizing about the possibility of a more diverse—including a feminist—science. What might such science look like, and how would it be practiced? Would a different agenda of problems or methods be pursued? What values might prevail?

Keller's (1983) biography of geneticist, Barbara McClintock, portrays a struggle between ideology and practice in the production and interpretation of science. In doing so, it depicts the science of a woman who was a theoretical and methodological maverick in genetics. McClintock challenged the "master molecule theory" of genetic control within a hierarchical organization. She integrated (rather than divided) subject and self in scientific investigation, and respected "difference" in the organism (maize) rather than aiming for a cosmic unity of control. McClintock offered a different view of nature, a view of subject and object that were outside the mainstream and, Keller argues, outside of gender-defined definitions and boundaries. After being largely underappreciated, McClintock was awarded a Nobel Prize in her 80s for work she had began 40 years earlier.

In interviews with women and men scientists, few report that they believe a "male" or "female" scientific method or orientation operates (as in profiles in Sonnert & Holton, 1995b and Zuckerman et al., 1991). However, in systematic case studies, a pattern of gendered *behavioral practice* is perceived by the scientists interviewed and observed by the investigators, Sonnert and Holton (1995b): "women are more cautious and careful in their methods and pay more attention to detail" (p. 152). This tendency is a response to the conditions experienced, with women reporting the need to "prove themselves," "avoid failure and criticism," "be meticulous," "do more comprehensive work" (pp. 152–153). This suggests that women have—and take—less latitude with error or mistakes in their work. Such practices are consistent with women's lower rate of publication productivity, and also with women's citation rates, which, *per article*, are as high or higher than men's (Sonnert & Holton, 1995b; p. 153; see also Long, 1992). Compared to men, the pattern for women may be "lower quantity and higher quality."

Critiques of medicine and biology have maintained that in studying certain subjects, particularly bodies, health, and sickness, male scientists reveal themselves as much as "men" as "scientists" (McNeil, 1987, p. 31). Meanings of gender and gender hierarchies are reflected in this knowledge, and in turn, the scientific knowledge reifies patterns of male superordination and female subordination. It is less clear how such meanings may operate outside of life sciences, in areas of chemistry and physics, for example. Further, although speculation has flourished about the possibilities of diverse, including feminist, science, the inquiry has been at a philosophical level, and empirical studies have been few. Case studies, such as Sonnert's and Holton's, are useful is disclosing how gender influences modes of scientific behavior. As to whether gender influences theories of the natural and physical world and patterns and approaches of inquiry remains an ongoing question.

4. SUMMARY AND CONCLUSION

Science is an institutional medium of power that connects with central social institutions, particularly education and the state, and is marked by immense inequality in status and rewards. It is a fundamentally hierarchical institution, and its valued attributes of rationality and control have been more ascribed to men than to women. Science represents a strategic site for study of gender in hierarchical context—and in summary, it reflects and supports gender stratification in these ways:

1. Science is disproportionately done by men, and moreover, controlled by men. Compared to women, men are more likely to be located in universities than in four year colleges; to be in more powerful fields—physical, mathematical, environmental, and computer sciences and engineering[8]; to hold high rank; and to experience higher levels of research productivity, as both cause and effect of their status. Thus, gender shapes participation, location, rank, and performance in science.

2. Because science is a source of power and is characterized by such gender divisions and hierarchies in participation, location, rank, and productivity, it *exemplifies* gendered relations. Owing to its powerful domains, science not only reflects, but also serves to *expand* gender stratification in society.

3. Historically, in areas of medicine and biology, especially, science has defined women in ways that have supported female subordination and inferiority and male superordination—and has done so from a position of "authoritative knowledge." In this way, science has been an agent in constructing and supporting hierarchical definitions of gender.

4. The extent to which gender shapes the content and methods of science, including the ways in which questions are framed, approaches are taken, and interpretations are formed, remains open to inquiry. If the authority of a dominant scientific culture defines the cognitive content of science, and if that authority is gender-specific, then the connection between gender and science will prove to be yet more profound than analyzed here.

In conclusion, it is notable that research, policy, and practice on issues of women and men in science have focused frequently upon "increasing the numbers of women in science" (Fox, 1998). Gender disparity in participation is a complex issue, and a justifiable concern for reasons of utilization of underrepresented groups as human resources, and for social equity. However, increasing numbers of women will not necessarily change patterns of gender and hierarchy in science.

Women have long been present in science, although not in valued, highly rewarded, or even visible roles. Accounts have documented how the contributions of both outstanding and little-known women scientists have been marginalized, misunderstood, or miscredited to others (see, particularly, Rossiter, 1982; Sayre, 1975). Further and relatedly, for science as for other professions, the relationship between gender, education, and status is complex—not a simple matter of increasing education and increasing social and economic status. We have seen that the proportion of women who are full professors has not kept pace with the growth in the number of women with doctorates in science, and that women's educational attainments do not translate into career attainments, especially advancement in rank, on a par with men's. The idea of education, by itself, as emblematic of progress for women in science is questionable (Fox, 1996, p. 278).

In addition, to the extent that increasing numbers of women are present in science but hide their "difference," gender neutrality, and, in turn, a hidden "male norm," are likely to prevail (Cockburn & Furst-Dilic, 1994). For example, if women attempt to conceal, obscure, and "overcome" certain observed (Sonnert & Holton, 1995b) behavioral styles, such as tendencies to confirm and integrate research findings before releasing

---

[8] However, women are disproportionately located in life sciences, fields that have flourished in the past three decades.

them for publication, the pattern of proliferation of fragmented pieces of published work may continue to constitute an unchallenged standard for scientific productivity.[9] It is not the mere "difference" in any style that is critical, or that men and women in science differ widely in their practices. Rather, what is important is the power to determine and maintain what is a valued standard and what is not, and the adherence of groups to such designated standards.

In science, as in any other institution, some groups benefit from existing arrangements, and others do not. Men in science have been more likely than women to benefit in institutional locations, rank, promotion, and access to human and material resources, as well as a culture and climate that reflects their understandings and interests. Because there are beneficiaries, strong incentives exist to preserve current arrangements. These include arrangements such as autonomy of the advisor in relationships with students; relatively nonsystematic criteria in hiring, promotion, and allocation of rewards; and limited accountability in evaluation of students and faculty (see Fox, 1998). Such organizational arrangements have advantages for the institution: they enable flexible and rapid response to problems by individual groups, for example (Harrison, 1994). However, the same factors (individual autonomy, nonsystematic processes, limited accountability) have also been found to activate "particularistic considerations"—bias in the allocation of rewards on the basis of "social similarity" (including race and gender) to those who currently dominate[10] (see Fox, 1991; Long & Fox, 1995, pp. 62–64).

The prevailing focus and attention upon "increasing numbers of women in science" are understandable. Increasing the presence of women, and other underrepresented groups such as African-Americans and Hispanics, can occur without changing the conditions of work or the current distribution of power in science. The challenge ahead is not simply an attempt to increase the flow of women through the proverbial "scientific pipeline" and fit them to existing structures. Rather, it is to better understand—and possibly be so bold as to modify—gendered hierarchy, practices, and processes, and their consequences for scientific organizations, occupations, and institutions.

Acknowledgments

I thank Janet S. Chafetz and Donna Hughes for their reading of, and comments on, this chapter.

REFERENCES

Ambrose, S., Dunkle, K., Lazarus, B., Nair, I., & Harkus, D. (1997). *Journeys of women in science and engineering*. Philadelphia: Temple University Press.
American Statistical Association (1993). Women Ph.D.s continue to face hurdles in employment in doctoral-granting institutions. *Amstat News, 204*, 4.

[9] It should be noted that federal funding agencies have taken steps to discourage over-proliferation of fragmented work by limiting, in grant proposals, the listing of principal investigators' publications to their most relevant papers.

[10] Particularistic considerations are more likely to operate in fields with low, compared to high, consensus about research issues, methods, and course curricula. Consensus is lower in social—compared to natural, physical, biological, mathematical, and engineering—sciences. In turn, particularistic variables account more for outcomes in careers (Hargens & Hagstrom, 1982), in editorial policies and practices (Beyer, 1978; Yoels, 1974), and allocation of grants (Pfeffer, Salanick, & Leblebici, 1976) in social sciences. These (cited) studies of consensus and outcomes, however, have not focused upon particularistic factors of race and gender, but rather upon those of personal ties and networks.

Artz, F. (1966). *The development of technical education in France: 1500–1800*. Cambridge: MIT Press.

Barnes, B. (1974). *Interests and the growth of knowledge*. London: Routledge & Kegan Paul.

Bechtel, H. K. (1989). Introduction. In W. Pearson & H. K. Bechtel (Eds.), *Blacks, scientists, and American education* (pp. 1–20). New Brunswick, NJ: Rutgers University Press.

Benjamin, M. (1991). Introduction. In M. Benjamin (Ed.), *Science and sensibility: Gender and scientific inquiry, 1750–1984* (pp. 1–23). Cambridge, MA: Basil Blackwell.

Beyer, J. M. (1978). Editorial policies and practices among leading journals in four scientific disciplines. *Sociological Quarterly, 19*, 68–88.

Bloor, D. (1976). *Knowledge and social imagery*. London: Routledge & Kegan Paul.

Blume, S. S., & Sinclair, R. (1973). Chemists in British Universities. *American Sociological Review, 38*, 126–138.

Boston Women's Health Collective (1971/1976). *Our bodies, ourselves* (revised and expanded second edition). New York: Simon & Schuster [first edition published by New England Free Press, 1971].

Bush, V. (1945/1990). *The endless frontier*. Washington, D.C.: National Science Foundation.

Cardwell, D. S. L. (1957). *The organization of science in England*. London: Heinemann.

Clark, B. (1987). *The academic life: Small worlds, different worlds*. Princeton, NJ: Princeton University Press.

Cockburn, C. (1985). *Machinery of dominance: Women, men, and technical knowhow*. London: Pluto Press.

Cockburn, C., & Furst-Dilic, R. (1994). Introduction: Looking for the gender/technology relation. In C. Cockburn & R. Furst-Dilic (Eds.), *Bringing technology home: Gender and technology in a changing Europe* (pp. 1–21. Buckingham, England: Open University Press.

Cole, J. (1979). *Fair science: Women in the scientific community*. New York: The Free Press.

Cole, J. & Cole, S. (1973). *Social stratification in science*. Chicago: University of Chicago Press.

Cole, J., & Zuckerman, H. (1984). The productivity puzzle: Persistence and change in patterns of publication among women and men scientists. In P. Maehr & M. W. Steinkamp (Eds.), *Women in science* (pp. 217–256). Greenwich, CT: JAI Press.

Cole, S. (1992). *Making science: Between nature and society*. Cambridge, MA: Harvard University Press.

Commission on Professionals in Science and Technology (CPST) (1997). *Professional women and minorities: A total human resources data compendium* (12th ed.). Washington, D.C.: CPST.

Cozzens, S., & Woodhouse, E. (1995). Science, government, and the politics of knowledge. In S. Jasanoff, G. Markle, J. Petersen, & T. Pinch (Eds.), *Handbook of science and technology studies* (pp. 533–553). Thousand Oaks, CA: Sage.

Derber, C. W., Schwartz, W., & Magress, Y. (1990). *Power in the highest degree; Professionals and the rise of a new Mandarin order*. New York: Oxford University Press.

Ehrenreich, B., & English, D. (1973). *Complaints and disorders: The sexual politics of sickness*. Old Westbury, NY: The Feminist Press.

Ehrenreich, B., & English, D. (1978). *For her own good: 150 years of the experts' advice to women*. Garden City: NY: Anchor/Doubleday.

Evetts, J. (1996). *Gender and career in science and engineering*. London: Taylor & Francis.

Fox, M. F. (1981). Sex, salary, and achievement: Reward-dualism in academia. *Sociology of Education, 54*, 71–84.

Fox, M. F. (1983). Publication productivity among scientists. *Social Studies of Science, 13*, 285–305.

Fox, M. F. (1986). Mind, nature, and masculinity. *Contemporary Sociology, 15*, 197–199.

Fox, M. F. (1991). Gender, environmental milieu, and productivity in science. In H. Zuckerman, J. Cole, & J. Bruer (Eds.), *The outer circle: Women in the scientific community* (pp. 188–204). New York: Norton.

Fox, M. F. (1995). Women and scientific careers. In S. Jasanoff, G. Markle, J. Petersen, & T. Pinch (Eds.), *Handbook of science and technology studies* (pp. 205–223). Thousand Oaks, CA: Sage.

Fox, M. F. (1996). Women, academia, and careers in science and engineering. In C. Davis, A. Ginorio, C. Hollenshead, B. Lazarus, & P. Rayman (Eds.), *The equity equation: Fostering the advancement of women in the sciences, mathematics, and engineering* (pp. 265–289). San Francisco: Jossey-Bass.

Fox, M. F. (1998). Women in science and engineering: Theory, practice, and policy in programs. *Signs: Journal of Women in Culture and Society, 24*, 201–223.

Fox, M. F., & Braxton, J. M. (1994). Misconduct and social control in science. *The Journal of Higher Education, 65*, 373–383.

Gaston, J. (1978). *The reward system in British and American science*. New York: John Wiley & Sons.

Gibbons, A. (1992). Key issue: Tenure. *Science, 255*, 1386.

Hacker, S. (1989). *Pleasure, power, and technology*. Boston: Unwin Hyman.

Hacker, S. (1990). *"Doing it the hard way": Investigations of gender and technology*. Boston: Unwin Hyman.

Hanson, S. (1996). *Lost talent: Women in the sciences*. Philadelphia: Temple University Press.

Harding, S. (1983). Why has the sex gender system become visible only now? In S. Harding & M. B. Hintikka (Eds.), *Discovering reality* (pp. 311–324). Dordrecht: D. Reidel .

Hargens, L. & Hagstrom, W. (1982). Consensus and status attainment patterns in scientific disciplines. *Sociology of Education, 55,* 183–196.

Harraway, D. (1989). *Primate visions: Gender, race, and nature in the world of modern science.* New York: Routledge & Kegan Paul.

Harrison, M. I. (1994). *Diagnosing organizations: Methods, models, and processes.* Thousand Oaks, CA: Sage.

Helmreich, R., Spence, J., Beane, W., Lucker, W., & Matthews, K. (1980). Making it in academic psychology: Demographic and personality correlates of attainment. *Journal of Personality and Social Psychology, 39,* 896–908.

Hodgkin, L. (1981). Mathematics and revolution from Lacroix to Cauchy. In H. Mehrtens, H. Bos, & I. Schneider (Eds.), *Social history of nineteenth century mathematics* (pp. 50–71). Boston: Birkhauser.

Jasanoff, S., Markle, G. Petersen, J., & Pinch, T. (1995). *Handbook of science and technology studies.* Thousand Oaks, CA: Sage.

Keller, E. F. (1983). *A feeling for the organism: The life and work of Barbara McClintock.* New York: W. H. Freeman.

Keller, E. F. (1985). *Reflections on gender and science.* New Haven, CT: Yale University Press.

Keller, E. F. (1995). The origin, history, and politics of the subject called 'gender and science'. In S. Jasanoff, G. Markle, J. Petersen, & T. Pinch (Eds.), *Handbook of science and technology studies* (pp. 80-94). Thousand Oaks, CA: Sage.

Kolodny, A. (1975). *The lay of the land: Metaphor as experience and history in American life and letters.* Chapel Hill, NC: University of North Carolina Press.

Long, J. S. (1992). Measures of sex differences in scientific productivity. *Social Forces, 71,* 159–178.

Long, J. S., Allison, P., McGinnis, R. (1993). Rank-advancement in Academic careers: Sex differences and the effects of productivity. *American Sociological Review,* 58, 703–722.

Long, J. S., & Fox, M. F. (1995). Scientific careers: Universalism and particularism. *Annual Review of Sociology, 21,* 45–71.

Lotka, A. J. (1926). The frequency distribution of scientific productivity. *Journal of the Washington Academy of Sciences, 26,* 317.

McNeil, M. (1987). Being reasonable feminists. In M. McNeil (Ed.), *Gender and expertise* (pp. 13–61). London: Free Association Press.

Merchant, C. (1980). *The death of nature: Women, ecology, and the scientific revolution.* New York: Harper & Row.

Merton, R. K. (1942/1973). The normative structure of science. In N. Storer (Ed.), *The sociology of science* (pp. 267–278). Chicago: University of Chicago Press.

Mitroff, I. (1974). Norms and counternorms in a select group of Apollo moon scientists. *American Sociological Review, 39,* 379–395.

Morin, A. J. (1993). *Science policy and politics.* Englewood Cliffs, NJ: Prentice-Hall.

Mulkay, M. (1976). Norms and ideology in science. *Social Science Information, 15,* 627–636.

Mulkay, M. (1979). *Science and the sociology of knowledge.* London: Allen and Unwin.

National Center for Education Statistics (1993). *Digest of education statistics.* Washington, D.C.: U.S. Department of Education.

Noble, D. (1977). *America by design.* New York: Knopf .

Ortner, S. (1972). Is female to male as nature is to culture? *Feminist Studies, 1,* 5–31.

Pfeffer, J., Salanick, G. R., & Leblebici, H. (1996) The effect of uncertainty on the use of social influence in organizational decision making. *Administrative Science Quarterly, 21,* 227–245.

Primack, R. B., & O'Leary, V. E. (1989). Research productivity of men and women ecologists. *Bulletin of the Ecological Association of America, 70,* 7–12.

Rathgeber, E. M. (1995). Schooling for what? In United Nations Commission on Science and Technology for Development (Ed.), *Missing links: Gender equity in science and technology for development* (pp. 181–200). New York: International Development Research Centre.

Reskin, B. (1978). Scientific productivity, sex, and location in the institution of science. *American Journal of Sociology, 83,* 1235–1243.

Roscher, N. M. (1990). *Women chemists,* 1990. Washington, D.C.: American Chemical Society.

Rossiter, M. (1982). *Women scientists in America: Struggles and strategies to 1940.* Baltimore: Johns Hopkins University Press.

Sayre, A. (1975). *Rosalind Franklin and DNA.* New York: Norton.

Schneider, I. (1981). Introduction. In H. Mehrtens, H. Bos, & I. Schneider (Eds.), *Social history of nineteenth century mathematics* (pp. 75–88). Boston: Birkhauser

Sonnert, G., & Holton, G. (1995a). *Gender differences in science careers.* New Brunswick, NJ: Rutgers University Press.

Sonnert, G. & Holton, G. (1995b). *Who succeeds in science? The gender dimension.* New Brunswick, NJ: Rutgers University Press.

University of Wisconsin (1991). *Retaining and promoting women and minority faculty: Problems and possibilities.* Madison, WI: Office of Equal Opportunity and Policy Studies.

Vetter, B. (1992). Ferment: Yes, progress: Maybe, change: Slow. *Mosaic, 23,* 34–41.

Wajcman, J. (1991). *Feminism confronts technology.* University Park, PA: Pennsylvania State University Press.

Ward, K., & Grant, L. (1995). Gender and academic publishing. In J. Smart (Ed.), *Higher education: Handbook of theory and research, Vol. 11* (pp. 175–215). New York: Agathon.

Yoels, W. C. (1974). The structure of scientific fields and the allocation of editorships on scientific journals: Some observations on the politics of knowledge. *Sociological Quarterly, 15,* 264–276.

Zuckerman, H. (1987). Persistence and change in careers of men and women scientists and engineers. In L. Dix (Ed.), *Women: Their underrepresentation and career differentials in science and engineering* (pp. 123–156). Washington, D.C.: National Academy Press.

Zuckerman, H. (1988). The sociology of science. In N. J. Smelser (Ed.), *Handbook of sociology* (pp. 511–574). Newbury Park, CA: Sage.

Zuckerman, H., Cole, J., & Bruer, J. (1991). *The Outer circle: Women in the scientific community.* New York: Norton.

CHAPTER 21

Gender and Health Status

JENNIE JACOBS KRONENFELD

1. INTRODUCTION

Compared to other areas of gender sociology, health is one in which issues of gender as a social construct and sex as a physiological construct intersect to the largest extent. Clearly, physiological differences between men and women play a role in health status. Moreover, some of the major life events that also relate to health have a physiological basis (child-bearing, menstruation, menopause). Thus, variation in health status between men and women, and in the importance of various types of diseases and health problems, is a complex mixture of both gender as a sociocultural factor and physiological variations between men and women, as well as individual-level variation among men and women. The last 20 years have seen an increased importance placed on genetics and genetic factors in health status, resulting in heightened emphasis on biology and physiology in explaining variation in health status. In fact, genetics as an explanatory factor for differences in health status is now viewed by epidemiologists as more important than at any other time in the history of medicine.

In an era of growing emphasis on genetics and heredity in health status, the role of social factors must still be addressed. The importance of gender (as one among several major social factors) in health care use and in variation in how people respond to illness continues to receive a great deal of attention by social scientists and growing interest within the health services research community as well. This topic is addressed in the next chapter, however, in terms of the topic of this chapter, health status and gender, current research has focused less attention on social factors. Nonetheless, one important debate in recent studies concerns the role of factors such as income and racial/ethnic classifica-

JENNIE JACOBS KRONENFELD • School of Health Administration and Policy, Arizona State University, Tempe, Arizona 85287-4506

Handbook of the Sociology of Gender, edited by Janet Saltzman Chafetz. Kluwer Academic/ Plenum Publishers, New York, 1999.

tion as social categories rather than as physiologically based comparisons (Cooper & David, 1986; Krieger & Fee, 1994a). Some of these studies focus on gender and sexism as well as race/ethnicity and racism as interactional processes and their implications for health status (Krieger, 1990; Krieger, Rowley, Herman, Avery, & Phillips, 1993). When gender constitutes the specific focus, one issue is often the interplay between social assumptions about men and women and physiological and genetic differences.

Psychosocial factors are likely to affect the health of men and women differentially because they often engage in social roles that differ in quality if not in quantity. At present in U.S. society, as well as in most others, differences in role expectations; role burdens related to domains of paid work and family; and imbalances in power, equality, and control are all factors likely to create differentiation in health status between men and women (Rodin & Ickovics, 1990). These psychosocial factors go far beyond genetics, although genetic differences will underlie health status variations.

A recent book on women's health has argued that models of women's health need to be reconceptualized (Ruzek, Olesen, & Clarke, 1997). The editors argue that models of health need to emerge that reflect the social, not just the biological, dimensions of health and illness. For the most complete models, psychological and spiritual dimensions could also be added. In addition, they suggest that if women's health is conceptualized as embedded in communities, not just in women's individual bodies, this would help to expand the definition of health away from a more narrow disease-focused model and into a social model.

Interest in women's health in the United States by governmental agencies has increased in recent years. In 1986, a National Conference on Women's Health Status jointly sponsored by the Food and Drug Administration and the Public Health Service Coordinating Committee on Women's Health was held in Bethesda, Maryland (Proceedings of the National Conference on Women's Health, 1987). The New York Academy of Sciences and its section on Women in Science (the newest section in that organization) held a special symposium entitled "Forging A Women's Health Research Agenda" in October, 1992 (Sechzer, Griffin, & Pfafflin, 1994). One of the goals of this conference was to frame an agenda for future research on women's health. Based on these and other efforts, the National Institutes of Health have clarified policies concerning the inclusion of women as research subjects within almost all funded research and have funded a special Women's Health Study to examine issues of breast cancer, use of estrogen supplements after menopause, and other health problems specific to women. Given the growing interest in the overall topic of women's health, no one chapter can include all the material. This chapter focuses most heavily on physical health status, but also includes a discussion of mental health issues. I also focus most heavily on gender and health status within the United States, although some international comparisons are briefly discussed. In the first section, I discuss views of women held by the medical profession in an historical context, including placing the increasing attention to women's health within the context of the women's movement generally and the women's health movement specifically. The second section deals with physical health concerns, examining overall mortality and morbidity rates. The third section focuses on life cycle concerns specific to women. The last section before the conclusion deals with mental health issues. Some material is presented in several sections about specific diseases and important health behaviors, because there are important linkages between these topics and health status and gender, although health behavior and health care are addressed in more detail in Chapter 22.

2. HISTORICAL VIEWS HELD BY THE MEDICAL PROFESSION OF WOMEN AS PATIENTS

2.1. Views of Women Held by the Medical Profession in the Past

The history of medicine and the manner in which the field has dealt with women and health status has not incorporated complicated views of gender, or even complicated views of biological factors and health status. The introductory chapter of this volume discussed the biological approach used by several founders of sociology to the study of men and women and their assumption that males and females are innately different and unequal in their intellectual, emotional, and moral capacities. This negative view of women found in much early sociological theory is also found in medical models of women and health status from the 1800s. Feminist writers have amply documented how early beliefs and practices concerning women by the medical profession viewed many of their everyday physiological functions as abnormal and as the reason for viewing all women as "sick" most of the time (Ehrenreich & English, 1972, 1973). Women were expected to be "indisposed" by monthly periods and pregnancy; to rest in bed and limit their social roles, which thus condemned women to a public image as sickly and weak. In the early writings of physicians in the United States, females were portrayed as weak, hypochondriacal, hysterical, and chronic invalids. While the worst of these stereotypes are now totally discredited, some of the damage remains, as in controversies about premenstrual syndrome (PMS) and whether this disqualifies women from certain important positions in society. Medical training emphasizes a distrust of natural processes and a focus on pathology, so that even natural events such as pregnancy and menopause become viewed as situations requiring medical intervention (Klass, 1987). Given the focus on specific symptoms and signs in medical training, if a woman has no other pathology and does not demonstrate emotional problems thought common in women, reproductive functions still may become the foci of the greatest concern by physicians (Klass, 1987; Wilkinson & Kitzinger, 1994).

2.2. The Women's Movement and Its Impact on Views and Studies of Gender and Health

The gender bias of biomedicine discussed in the preceding section continued until the 1970s. Up to that point, women were omitted from much medical research on conditions such as heart disease, diabetes, and cancer, unless the cancer affected specifically female organs. Moreover, the care for women's reproductive organs was relegated to one subfield of medicine, obstetrics–gynecology (Martin, 1987; Turshen, 1993). The resurgence of the women's movement in the 1960s and 1970s led to the development of a new epistemology in academia that eventually influenced medicine also. One well-publicized merging of these concerns was the publication of *Our Bodies, Ourselves: A Book by and for Women* by the Boston Women's Health Collective (1973). The growth of a separate women's health movement has helped increase public awareness of special problems concerning gender and health (Geary, 1995; Ruzek, 1978). This effort to include more women in health-related research has been led by the National Women's Health Network (Narragan,

Zones, Worcester, & Grad, 1997). Over time, health problems for women began to be viewed more inclusively, and the medical community grew more respectful of treating women as mature adults, not childlike creatures who needed extra help.

Some of these trends were national and others had an international dimension as well. The 1980s saw the growth of the woman's movement beyond the United States and developed countries and the emergence of nongovernmental women's organizations. Some of these organizations in other countries focused on the fact that the only access many women had to biomedicine was through contraceptive services (Muecke, 1996). The 1994 International Conference on Populations and Development in Cairo, Egypt, helped to shift the focus away from population control to a broader focus on reproductive health and the empowerment of women (Crane & Issacs, 1995).

In the United States, one initiative, which has a long-term potential to improve the health of women, is the effort to include women more extensively in medical research as subjects. The establishment of the Office of Women's Health in the National Institutes of Health in 1990 helped to lead to policies requiring that women be included as subjects in medical research (LaRosa, 1997; Mastroianni, Faden, & Federman, 1994). This broadened focus is now also part of official U.N. pronouncements that stress gender equity in health and provide worldwide standards that governments can implement (Muecke, 1996). The Women's Health Initiative of NIH is one example of a major, federally funded study with this broadened focus. This study is examining many issues of health status specific to women, including the effects for menopause, the consequences of hormone replacement therapy, dietary modifications and nutritional supplements on menopause, and breast cancer, among other problems (Cotton, 1992; Pinn, 1992b). Improved knowledge about health conditions specific to women, as well as greater inclusion of women in studies of major diseases that affect both men and women, have the long-term potential to improve the health status of women. Despite some large, new studies that focus on women as research subjects, a recent review of AIDS studies found that of the 14,799 participants enrolled in such trials as of January, 1992, only 1151 were women (Stapleton, 1997). Because of such low numbers of women in studies, the Food and Drug Administration proposed a rule in September, 1997 that would no longer allow researchers to exclude women from potentially life-saving clinical trials purely on the grounds of reproductive toxicity concerns. The women's movement in general, as well as the women's health movement, have been important in leading the medical research establishment to recognize previous systematic biases in the exclusion of women from much biomedical research (Clancy & Massion, 1992).

3. LIFE EXPECTANCY AND MORTALITY DIFFERENCES BETWEEN MEN AND WOMEN

Gender differences in life expectancy and mortality are very different in the United States and most other nations today than they were in past centuries or even at the beginning of the twentieth century. Until the post-Civil War period in the United States, and this century in much of the world, women had a shorter life span than men, resulting mostly from complications of childbirth as well as from problems of chronic malnutrition in many regions of the world (Pinn, 1992a). Chronic malnutrition has often been worse for women in many societies, because men may be fed first and take more of the available calories, and because in situations of limited food availability, women often will limit their own intake to provide for their children. Overall, progress in improving life expectancy for both sexes is one of the important achievements in U.S. health status in the twentieth century, with almost a 30-year improvement in life expectancy from the beginning of the twentieth century to the present (National Center for Health Statistics, 1992). Although women were already outliving men in this country by 1900, the difference then was less than 2 years (Phillips, Sexton, & Blackman, 1997). Between 1940 and 1970, the differences in life expectancy at birth between men and women increased from 4.4 years in 1940 to 7.6 years in 1970. The gap remained stable throughout the 1970s and then began to shift slightly, as male life expectancy began improving from better management of major chronic diseases. One important aspect of the improvement in female life expectancy from 1950 to 1989 was a 90% decline in maternal mortality during that time period. By 1993, life expectancy at birth was 6.6 years longer for women than for men, or 78.8 years for women versus 72.2 for men (NCHS, 1996). Projections indicate that life expectancies will continue to increase for both sexes (Phillips, Sexton, & Blackman, 1997). The advantages in health status of women are true at every life stage (Strickland, 1988). More male fetuses are conceived (125 male for every 100 female fetuses) but 27% more boys than girls die in the first year of life. By the time people reach 100, only one man is alive for every five women (Rodin & Ickovics, 1990). In every age category, more men than women die.

Gender and race are both important as factors in life expectancy, although gender is more important than race in predicting life expectancy. Both white and African-American women have a longer life expectancy than men and, despite the racial gap in life expectancy, African-American women born in 1989 are expected to outlive white men by 0.8 years (NCHS, 1992). While life expectancy consistently has been lower among African-American women than among white women in the United States, trends have shifted back and forth over the past 30 years. Between 1970 and 1984, the difference in life expectancy between African-American and white women narrowed from 7.3 to 5.1 years because increases in African-American women's life expectancy were outpacing those of white women. During the mid-1980s, however, life expectancy for African-American women declined somewhat and resulted in an increase in the differential (NCHS, 1996). The life expectancy gap between African-American and white women narrows after age 65 to only 2 years.

While causes of death vary some by gender, changes in causes of death are occurring, especially for women. Heart disease continues to be the leading cause of death among all women, as it is among men (NCHS, 1996). If the figures are looked at separately by age groups, there are some differences. Heart disease is the second leading cause of death among women 45 to 74 years of age, following cancer. The types of cancer that are most important as causes of death for women are also changing. While breast cancer is still a very important cause of death for women, and indeed one of the causes of death most feared by women, lung cancer has now surpassed breast cancer as the leading cause of cancer death among women (Strickland, 1988). For women 75 and over, heart disease is the leading cause of death. For men, heart disease is the leading cause of death for all those 45 and over, with cancer in second place. Other leading causes of death for women 45 to 74 years of age are chronic obstructive pulmonary disease, stroke, and diabetes. Taken together, heart disease, cancer, and stroke account for 67% of American women's deaths (WHO, 1992). Some racial differences occur among women. Heart disease has been overtaken by cancer as the leading cause of death for white women, but remains the leading cause of death for African-American women. Stroke and diabetes are also more common causes of death for African-American women; their rates of mortality from diabetes are twice as high as those of white women and nearly twice as high for stroke (Collins, Rowland, Salganicoff, & Chait, 1994).

Even though the United States has seen great improvements in life expectancy, it is not the world leader in this statistic. For women, life expectancy at birth for women is highest in Japan (82.5 years for those born in 1990), followed by France with 81.5, Canada with 80.6, and Sweden with 80.1 years. American and British women have a similar life expectancy of 78.6 and 78.7, respectively (WHO, 1992). One thing that is true throughout most of the world (with the possible exception of South Asia) is that women live longer than men, even in developing countries in which the average life expectancy is low (Kane, 1991).

An easy, but incorrect, conclusion to draw from the data presented so far is that because women live longer than men they enjoy a higher quality of life in terms of health status or that they are healthier in general than men. Why women now live longer than men is still a matter of debate and research, but many experts believe that females may have more biological protection than males in some respects, although both are at risk for many of the same health problems. While many of the gains in the past century in life expectancy for women came from reductions in maternal mortality, this area is unlikely to lead to further improvements in life expectancies for women except in South Asia. Most of the recent gains have come from reductions in mortality for people 45 years and older. Men have benefitted from this less than women. Men often die from a health problem while women live on but with a serious disability, so that it is much less clear that women achieve a higher quality of life as regards overall health status than it is that they live more years than do men (Collins et al., 1994). Whether this is a biological difference alone or a biological difference aided by social considerations (such as that women may monitor their health more closely than men and be more willing to visit a health provider quickly at signs of health problems) is not yet clear (Collins et al., 1994; Kane, 1991).

While data on specific diseases and issues for women are discussed in more detail in the next section as part of a discussion of changes across the life cycle, some differences in morbidity (sickness) need to be reviewed before considering some of the explanations for gender variations in health. Although men are at higher risk than women for many fatal diseases, women have a higher risk of incurring many nonfatal chronic conditions, such as some mental health problems discussed in a later section of the chapter, as well as such physical health problems as arthritis and osteoporosis. Arthritis is the most common condition for women over 45 and affected one half of all women over 65 years of age in 1993–1994. Hypertension is less common for women under 50 than for men in the same age group. By age 70 to 79, however, the prevalence of hypertension is 12% higher among women than men (NCHS, 1996). Because so many of the conditions that are more prevalent among women are disabling, women tend to have higher rates of activity limitation and disability than do men. For example, the proportion of women 45 to 64 years of age with activity limitation due to arthritis was 2.7 times that of men. In 1991, the proportion of middle-aged and older persons reporting difficulty performing home management activities and/or physical care activities was more than 75% higher among women than men (NCHS, 1996).

Differences between men and women are also noted for acute diseases and conditions. Women over the age of 45 have higher rates than men of infective/parasitic diseases, respiratory conditions, digestive system conditions, and injuries. Health statistics are better at capturing serious health problems than minor ones. Many experts believe that health problems that women experience more often than men, such as the bothersome symptoms of nonfatal chronic conditions and acute conditions, are less well captured by the major national and international data sets that have provided most of the statistics discussed so far in this chapter (Macintyre, Hunt, & Sweeting, 1996; Verbrugge, 1985). The issue of better collection of data for serious problems as compared to more minor problems has often been conceptualized as the "iceberg of morbidity," in which only a small part of total morbidity is visible through most available health statistics. Even though only a small part of the total "iceberg of morbidity" may be visible in health statistics, the gender hue of the iceberg probably varies from deeply feminine at the bottom, to gradually fading, to more heavily masculine at the top, but the bulk of the iceberg is probably a feminine shade (Verbrugge, 1985).

One recent British review of gender differences in health concluded that the pattern of sex differences in morbidity is more complicated than conventional wisdom would assume (MacIntyre et al., 1996). This article reviewed two recent British data sets and argued that the direction and magnitude of sex differences in health vary according to the particular symptom or condition and according to the life cycle phase. They found that only six of seventeen conditions (depression or nervous disorder, varicose veins, high blood pressure, migraine, piles or hemorrhoids and cancer) show a female preponderance at all or most ages and the differences are significant mostly for cancer. Another six conditions (bronchitis, other chest problems, diabetes, liver problems, epilepsy, and stroke) show no significant sex differences for any age group.

Two different types of explanations are discussed in the literature to account for the mortality and morbidity differences between men and women. One is biological and the second is social (Gove & Hughes, 1979; Krieger & Fee, 1994a; Rodin & Ickovics, 1990; Strickland, 1988; Verbrugge, 1983, 1985, 1989; Wingard, 1982). The most important social explanation concerns variation by gender in patterns of health services use, explanations linked to health reporting behavior and prior use of health care (mostly topics of the next chapter in this book). In this chapter, I focus on the contrast between biological explanations and social defined primarily as acquired risks. The biological explanation argues that women have more biological protections against early death than men. Genetics are one part of a biological explanation, focusing partially on the idea that redundant genetic material in the second X chromosome of females is protective. Another part of the biological explanation focuses upon hormonal differences between men and women, especially across the life cycle. The best known of these is hormonal protection from cardiovascular disease prior to menopause (Rodin & Ickovics, 1990). Data indicate that estrogen may serve to keep the levels of high-density lipoproteins elevated and those of low-density lipoproteins lower and thus decrease the risk for heart disease (Bush et al., 1987). Some contradictory evidence, however, is that estrogen from oral contraceptives appears to increase the risk of coronary heart disease in women who smoke (Mathews, 1989).

While the biological factors are important, the social factors should not be discounted. The leading causes of death in the United States today are linked to dysfunctional lifestyles and behavior. It is estimated that as much as 50% of mortality from the leading causes of death overall in the population can be traced to such aspects of lifestyle as cigarette smoking, excessive consumption of alcoholic beverages, use of illicit drugs, harmful dietary practices, reckless driving, nonadherence to medication regimens, and maladaptive responses to social pressures (Rodin & Ickovics, 1990). Moreover, some of these factors are interactive with each other and perhaps also with biological factors. For example, women (especially African-American women) are more likely than men to live in poverty and may experience greater stress due to this difficult situation, which in turn may increase the rates of many health problems. This may be one reason for the finding in some studies of a declining sex mortality ratio for people over 45. Social roles for women are undergoing major changes in many countries, and two important lifestyle changes are women's increased substance use and much higher rates of labor-force participation (Rodin & Ickovics, 1990; Verbrugge, 1989). The impact of these types of social changes on aggregate health statistics will become much clearer in the next few decades.

4. SPECIAL LIFE CYCLE CONCERNS

As the previous section pointed out, many patterns of health status vary depending on age. Primary health concerns of women of reproductive age often differ from those of postmenopausal women. This section discusses first the special health concerns of younger women and then those of older women, especially postmenopausal women who are generally 50 years of age or older. The first section for each stage of the life cycle focuses on reproductive-related concerns that are mostly unique to women. The other sections examine major diseases or health conditions that occur at the specific stage of life.

4.1. Health Concerns of Younger Women

Some of the special health concerns of younger women are linked with sexuality and reproductive roles. These include sexually transmitted diseases, AIDS, and pelvic inflammatory disease. Other problems are related to mental health concerns such as eating disorders which often start from a psychological concern, but become one of the more serious mortality risks for young women. Finally, autoimmune diseases will be discussed.

4.1.1. REPRODUCTIVE HEALTH.   One special focus for women compared to men, especially younger women, is the link between health status and reproductive functions. Certainly fertility control is not a concern only for women nor should it be a responsibility only for women, even though it is usually seen as such because women usually bear the major burden of the consequences of the lack of fertility control. An interesting trend in the United States is that the ratio of abortions to live births has been decreasing in the past decade, while the proportion of births resulting from unintended pregnancies has remained fairly stable (NCHS, 1996). Young women (under 20) have both higher abortion rates and higher proportions of unintended pregnancies. In 1992, the abortion rate for women 15 to 19 years of age was 52% higher than for women 25 to 34 years of age. During the late 1980s, 72% of all live births to women 15 to 19 resulted from unintended pregnancies, a figure 136% higher than among women in the 25 to 34 year age group. Thus, unintended pregnancies are an important concern for a segment of very young women. They are especially likely to lead to live births for poor women who have less access to abortion and may be members of a racial/ethnic or religious group (such as in some Latina populations) that discourages abortion as a solution to unintended pregnancy.

These statistics should not lead to the conclusion that fertility is increasing among U.S. women. Fertility rates have declined from those of the 1950s and 1960s. There were about 69 births per 1000 women aged 15 to 44 years in 1992 compared to 123 in 1957.

Overall fertility rates were stable during the 1980s. Between 1990 and 1993, the fertility rate in the United States declined by 5%. The rate of decline for African-American women was nearly twice that for white women. Even for teenagers 15 to 17 and 18 to 19 years of age, the ages that have received the most public attention and condemnation for child-bearing, birth rates have declined on average about 1% per year since 1991 (although increases did occur from 1986 to 1991) (NCHS, 1996). Levels of childbearing are closely related to social and economic factors. During times of economic and social distress such as the Great Depression in the 1930s and World War II in the 1940s, one in five women remained childless (Taeuber, 1996). This dropped in the 1950s, but changing social roles for women that have increased their opportunities for careers and to engage in many activities outside of the home (perhaps along with higher divorce rates) are leading to more women remaining childless in the United States. Currently, based on what childless women in their 30s report as their expectations, as well as current first-childbearing patterns, some 15% to 20% of women will remain childless throughout their lifetimes. Many other women are delaying childbearing in the United States and other industrialized nations. In 1993, 44% of women 25 to 29 had not had one live birth, compared with only 20% in 1960 (NCHS, 1996). The interaction of class, gender, and ethnicity plays an important role in these types of statistics within the Unted States.

Issues of fertility rates and reproductive health, while important in the United States, are even more important elsewhere in the world, especially in developing countries, which traditionally have much higher fertility rates. Increasingly in the policy arena, shifts are underway to switch from discussions of fertility control to reproductive health (Lane, 1994), reflecting experts' frustration with the fragmentation of issues that touch on women's health into disparate programs, such as family planning, sexually transmitted diseases (STDs), maternal mortality, and child survival. The linkages between reproductive health and the topic of STDs and AIDS are quite close. A recent United Nations Conference, the decennial International Conference on Population and Development (ICPD), concluded that the UN needs to focus on six of the most pressing reproductive health concerns: gender inequalities, access to contraceptive services, sexually transmitted diseases (including HIV infection), maternal mortality, unsafe abortion, and adolescent pregnancy (Miller & Rosenfeld, 1996). Several recent articles review these topics in greater detail than possible in this chapter, but it is important to recognize the strong links between health status and reproductive health, especially for younger women (Lane, 1994; Miller & Rosenfeld, 1996).

4.1.2. STDs, AIDS.   A range of serious health problems for women occur as the result of sexually transmitted diseases. The incidence of the traditional STDs of chlamydia, gonorrhea, and syphilis has been increasing, as has that of pelvic inflammatory disease (PID), although none of these is life threatening. AIDS is the opposite, a disease that at this point is incurable with high death rates. One complication in prevention and treatment of sexually transmitted diseases (STDs), as well as AIDS, is moral judgments about those who suffer from these diseases, and this has been true throughout the nineteenth and twentieth centuries (Brandt, 1985). Past campaigns against STDs, and even some current ones, often contain the notion that STDs are a problem only for women of "loose" morals, and that "good" women need protection from the taint of these diseases (Leonardo & Chrisler, 1992). As with AIDS today, stigmatization of the person with the disease often occurs, and reporting by physicians may be less than accurate, especially for private, upper-class patients.

The United States has been experiencing a resurgence of STDs, partially because of the growth of penicillin-resistant strains of the bacterium that causes gonorrhea as well as some increases in the rates of teenage sexual activity. Infection rates are higher among adolescent girls than boys, perhaps because of contact between adolescent girls and older men (Leonardo & Chrisler, 1992). Among African-American women, the incidence of gonorrhea is four to five times the national rate (Collins et al., 1994). Also, STDs are more easily transferred from males to females than the reverse, and infection in women is often asymptomatic and less likely to be identified and treated early. This places women at greater risk than men of long-term consequences for these problems. Untreated, STDs can impair reproductive capacity. Most seriously in this decade, a person with a history of STDs is at greater risk of contracting AIDS through skin irritated by infection (Collins et al., 1994). PID is an acute infection of a woman's upper reproductive tract. This infection can be transmitted sexually or may result from an overgrowth of normal bacteria. The risk of PID is highest for young women, and is sometimes first detected by the presence of an ectopic pregnancy (a pregnancy growing outside of the uterus) which is life threatening if not treated promptly (Althaus, 1991).

The most serious sexually transmitted disease today is AIDS (acquired immunodeficiency syndrome). While AIDS is a potential threat to all women, large racial and ethnic differences occur at present in the United States. In the 12 months ending June 1995, non-Hispanic African-American women had nearly 17 times the rate of AIDS as non-Hispanic white women. Rates were also higher for Hispanic women and American Indian women (NCHS, 1996).

Despite the general sense in the media that AIDS is a more heavily male problem (especially for gay males and those using injected drugs), the gender differential in the prevalence of AIDS is decreasing. In 1985, the incidence of AIDS was 13 times higher in men than in women, but by the second half of 1994, the number for men was just under five times that for women (NCHS, 1996). AIDS now represents the fourth leading cause of death for women ages 25 to 44. Younger women (ages 15 to 24) account for most (84%) of the cases, with three fourths of the cases occurring among Hispanic and African-American women (Update, 1995). The most common suspected modes of transmission of the disease for women are use of injected drugs and heterosexual contact with an infected partner. For women, heterosexual contact is the most rapidly increasing transmission category (Update, 1995).

As with other STDs, the stigmatization of those with AIDS is high, both in the United States and in developing countries in which AIDS is becoming a more serious problem. Many women experience shame and isolation, and this is even truer for those in the sex industry where rates of infection are quite high (Abercrombie, 1996). In Third World countries, rates of infection are very high in the sex industries and are a major health problem for this group of women in countries such as Thailand. In many countries in Africa, AIDS is as frequent in women as in men, and has had a major, population level impact so that many children are now being raised by grandparents because the parents have died from AIDS. In contrast in the United States, AIDS, while a major health problem, is still more concentrated in certain subgroups of the population. Women with AIDS in the United States often face the triple burden of racism, classism, and sexism as AIDS is so much more common among poorer and minority women. Many of the preventive techniques have not focused on women, and many experts argue that preventive interventions targeted toward women need to become a public health priority (Wingood & DiClemente, 1996).

4.1.3. EATING DISORDERS.

The eating disorders of anorexia nervosa and bulimia nervosa are disproportionately problems of women, and especially of young women. Females are at a 10 times greater risk than males, and most at risk are young, white adolescents. A distorted body image may lead an adolescent to believe she is seriously overweight when she is not. These problems are complicated, and while their origins are behavioral and often linked to difficulties in adolescent adjustment, they are exacerbated by the extreme emphasis American society places on thinness in women. While the outward manifestations may seem to be only a more extreme version of the focus on weight control and dieting found among many American women, about 9% of anorexic individuals actually die from the problem, either from suicide or starvation (Horton, 1992).

Bulimia (binge eating followed by vomiting) is more common than anorexia. It often occurs in late adolescence and a national survey of students estimates that as many as 4% of eighth and tenth graders are bulimic (Horton, 1992). Physical complications that occur include constant sore throat and problems with the stomach and teeth. Even women athletes may be bulimic, believing that lowering body fat will increase their athletic performance, especially in sports such as figure skating and gymnastics with more subjective judging, in which a slim appearance is an asset (Jacobs, 1994). Fortunately, bulimia has a better recovery rate than does anorexia. Both these health problems arise from a confluence of concern over gender roles and social pressures of adolescence and the desire to be popular (and thin), but can cause long-lasting and serious health consequences.

4.1.4. AUTOIMMUNE DISEASES.

Autoimmune diseases are much more common among women than men. These health problems are conditions in which the body makes antibodies against some of its own parts. Systematic lupus erythematosus (SLE) and rheumatoid arthritis (RA) are two of the better known examples of these kinds of diseases. Women are nine times more likely to develop lupus, and three times more likely to develop RA (Horton, 1992). SLE is mostly a disease of younger women, developing often in the 20s although sometimes as late as the sixth decade of life. In SLE, parts of the body become inflamed, including skin, joints, kidneys, and nervous system. In contrast, RA generally develops at a later age, between 35 and 45, and affects joints, especially those of the hand (Collins et al., 1994).

One serious complication of SLE occurs if a woman is pregnant. The condition can be transferred to the fetus, and miscarriage is more common. Often symptoms are exacerbated in late pregnancy or after delivery. Treatment of the pregnant woman is also more difficult, and this problem is a major source of disability among young women. While the multiple roles of a young woman may exacerbate the disease (such as being pregnant and trying to work and raise a family), its origins are probably genetic, perhaps exacerbated by hormonal factors, which may account for the increased severity following pregnancy.

4.2. Health Concerns of Older Women

Some of the health concerns of older woman are linked with biological differences between men and women and reproductive concerns. This is certainly true for menopause, a biological event with different levels of significance depending upon sociocultural factors. The other portions of this section focus upon specific diseases (which menopause is not), many of which are chronic conditions associated with aging and how it differentially impacts women. The diseases and conditions reviewed are: heart disease and cardiovascular disease (CVD), cancer of various types, diabetes, osteoporosis, and Alzheimer's disease.

4.2.1. MENOPAUSE. Menopause is one of the more controversial subjects in the area of gender and health today. Until this century in the United States, and later in countries with worse health status statistics, menopause was not a major concern because most women did not spend much of their life postmenopausal. Not until after 1900 did U.S. women's life expectancy exceed 50 (Clarke, 1990). To the extent that physicians paid much attention to menopause before 1950, it was viewed as a physiological crisis but received little specific attention. Negative images of women as they aged existed in the general culture as well as among health care professionals.

From 1960 forward, the availability of estrogen replacement therapy (ERT), also called hormone replacement therapy (HRT), has led to fierce debate over its necessity (Col et al., 1997; McCrae, 1983). Some feminist researchers employed a medicalization framework to argue that, especially within the United States, menopause has been socially constructed by the medical care community as a deficiency disease that can be "cured" by medication (McCrae, 1983; McCrae, & Markle, 1984). Medical researchers have argued that HRT may increase life expectancy for nearly all postmenopausal women and improve the comfort of the transition to menopause for many women (Col et al., 1997).

During the last 10 years, the debate within the medical literature has continued. For example, a recent meta-analysis of 31 observational studies found a 50% reduction in coronary heart disease risk among current users of estrogen replacement therapy (Stampfer & Colditz, 1991), while other studies have reported less clear benefits. Similarly, controversy abounds over the protective effects of estrogen against osteoporosis and the role of ERT in increasing the risk of breast cancer, especially for women who already possess several other risk factors (Harlow & Ephross, 1995). A 20-year review of the effect of estrogen therapy on health status concludes that it decreases risk for coronary artery disease and hip fracture, but that long-term therapy increases the risk for endometrial cancer and might be associated with a small increase in the risk for breast cancer (Grady et al., 1992). A recent article presented a series of decision trees that women and their physicians could employ to help make the decision about ERT (Col et al, 1997). This article, using a modeling approach that includes incidence rates for diseases such as breast cancer, endometrial cancer, heart disease, and hip fracture; as well as assumptions about risk factors such as smoking, relatives with diseases, and blood pressure and cholesterol, argues that hormone replacement therapy should increase the life expectancy of most postmenopausal women, except those at the greatest risk for breast cancer (Col et al., 1977). Clear answers await the completion of ongoing clinical trials, and part of the recent debate about the need to include women in more medical studies and to conduct studies focusing on special health problems of women have arisen because of the debate over ERT.

4.2.2. HEART DISEASE AND CARDIOVASCULAR DISEASE. This section discusses both coronary heart disease (angina or intermittent heart pains, and heart failure), which accounts for more than 30% of female deaths, and cerebrovascular disease or CVD (stoke, multiinfarct dementia), which accounts for about 9% of deaths among women. Heart disease in women is largely a postmenopausal phenomenon, with women typically developing symptoms 10 or more years later than men do. Illness and death rates from heart disease rise rapidly in women after the age of 55 (Lerner & Kannel, 1986). Risk factors are similar for men and women, but the first sign of coronary heart disease for men is generally a heart attack, whereas for women it is often angina. Women are also more likely to die from heart attacks when they do occur (Hendel, 1990). One important issue in the literature concerns the fact that women do not appear to respond as well to many of the current therapies (Clyne, 1990). Since most of these therapies were initially tested on men alone, this finding may be less than surprising. Moreover, there is increasing evidence that women undergo intensive or invasive evaluations and treatments for heart disease less frequently than do men with symptoms of similar or lesser severity (Wenger, Speroff, & Packard, 1993).

Mortality for women from CVD is lower than for men; however important racial differences exist. The rate of CVD for African-American women is 80% higher than the rate for white women (NCHS, 1996). In addition to being a major cause of death, CVD is a major cause of physical and mental disability for women. CVD is very much a disease of the old, with almost 90% of the deaths and three quarters of the hospitalizations occurring for those 65 and over.

Growing numbers of studies indicate that psychosocial stress and psychosocial factors are important in coronary heart disease for women. Low social class, low educational attainment, the double loads of work and family that women often carry, and lack of social support all emerge as risk factors for women in recent reviews (Brezinka & Kittel, 1995; Elliott, 1995). Psychosocial adjustment in women after a heart attack appears to be worse than in men, and return to work rates are also lower. Overall rehabilitation outcomes are not as good for women, making heart disease quite important in lowering the health status of older women.

4.2.3. CANCER.   Cancer is a name for cells that divide inappropriately, and can occur in many different parts of the body. The risk factors for the disease and the complications vary by site. Breast cancer and lung cancer are the most commonly occurring cancers in women, together responsible for almost half of all cancer deaths in women. Another major category of cancers for women are the gynecological ones (cancer of the cervix, uterus, and ovaries). Breast cancer is the most common cancer in women, accounting for 32% of all newly diagnosed cases (Kelsey & Bernstein, 1996). Cancer was the leading cause of death for women 45 to 64 years of age in 1993 (NCHS, 1996).

Lung cancer has been growing in importance as a cause of death for women. Although twice as many men still die of lung cancer as do women, the death rate for men is stabilizing, while the death rate for women continues to climb (American Cancer Society, 1992). Between the early 1970s and the early 1990s, the age-adjusted incidence rate for lung cancer for women more than doubled and the age-adjusted death rate rose 182%. These increases substantially exceeded those for men in the same time period (NCHS, 1996). Beginning in 1987, more women died from lung cancer than from breast cancer. Proportionate to their numbers in the population, African-American women are more likely to have lung cancer. However, because they are even more likely to have breast cancer, lung cancer is now the leading cause of cancer death among white women but second among African-American women.

The major explanation for the trend of increasing lung cancer deaths among women and the time period in which it is now beginning to show up is the length of time it takes for lung cancers to develop and the time period during which women began smoking in large numbers. Cigarette smoking is the major risk factor for lung cancer, accounting for about 85% of all cases (CDC, 1990). Between 1965 and 1990, cigarette smoking decreased more among men. In 1965, the age-adjusted prevalence of cigarette smoking for people 18 years of age and over was 52% for men and 34% for women. By 1990, the comparable figures were 28% for men and 23% for women (NCHS, 1996). Smoking is now one of the major preventable health risks of women (Kendrick & Merritt, 1996).

Breast cancer rates have been increasing in recent decades, leading to growing fears and concern about the disease. It has long been one of the more feared cancers among women because of the disfigurement entailed by treatment and the association of breasts with sexuality, especially in American culture. In publicity about the disease, the American Cancer Society has used figures of aggregate risk, and these statements of risk have increased from 1 in 12 in the 1980s to 1 in 9 women currently who can expect to be diagnosed with cancer during their lifetimes (American Cancer Society, 1992). Close to 50,000 U.S. women now die of breast cancer each year.

Risk factors include having relatives with the disease, increasing age, never having been married, high socioeconomic status, and, for breast cancer diagnosed after age 45, being white (Kelsey & Bernstein, 1996; Wooster, Neuhausen, Mangion, et al., 1994). The pattern of breast cancer incidence and mortality differs by race. Between 1973 and 1991, the number of new cases (incidence) was between 15% and 25% higher for white women than for African-American women. Beginning in the 1970s, the age-adjusted death rate from breast cancer for African-American women began to exceed that for white women and the gap is continuing to widen. Breast cancer mortality was 28% higher for African-American women in 1993 than it was for white women (NCHS, 1996). The major explanation for this is that earlier detection at a more curable stage is more common for white women, who have better access to healthcare. In addition, there is some evidence that African-American women develop the disease at an earlier age, and many experts believe that the disease in younger women is of a different nature and more difficult to treat successfully (Kelsey & Bernstein, 1996).

One important controversy is about the use of mammography as an early detection method for breast cancer. A related debate is about the usefulness of preventive techniques, such as dietary change and medication. Evidence from randomized trials indicates that screening for breast cancer by mammography reduces mortality in women over 50. What is much less clear is its usefulness for women under 50. Because of this, the National Cancer Institute (NCI) has not recommended screening for women 40 to 49, although other organizations, such as the American College of Radiology and the American Cancer Society, have (Kelsey & Bernstein, 1996). Because of the growing public concern over conflicting recommendations, the NCI changed its recommendations in 1997, primarily in response to political concerns rather than new scientific evidence.

Two large randomized trials are now underway concerning breast cancer, partially as a response to the criticism by feminists and the resurgent women's health movement that research into diseases that predominantly affect women have been underfunded. The Women's Health Initiative is designed to test strategies to reduce the risk for cardiovascular disease, breast cancer, colorectal cancer, and osteoporotic fractures. It is very large, including 63,000 women in one of its studies, mainly because of the large sample needed to test the hypothesis that dietary modifications can reduce the incidence of breast cancer. The trial of this hypothesis has received criticism, since the evidence is fairly weak that a diet high in fat increases the risk for breast cancer (Institute of Medicine, 1993; Kelsey & Bernstein, 1996). The Breast Cancer Prevention Trial tests whether tamoxifen, a synthetic, nonsteroidal antiestrogen to breast tissue, is effective in the prevention of breast cancer. One controversy surrounding this trial is whether large numbers of healthy women should be treated with a potentially toxic drug to prevent a relatively rare event (Kelsey & Bernstein, 1996). Results from these two trials will not be available for some while, leaving women with difficult decisions to reach about whether to undertake lifestyle changes that might have a minor effect on breast cancer risk as well as at what age to undergo regular mammography.

Of the gynecological cancers, cervical cancer is one of the most detectable and treatable, with 5-year survival rates as high as 90% to 100% if the cancer is detected early (American Cancer Society, 1992). Because of the advent of the Pap smear test to detect cervical cancer, mortality rates have steadily declined in the past 40 years. The number of new cases of cervical cancer is still higher for African-American women by one third, and the mortality rate is three times as high, owing primarily to problems of obtaining adequate healthcare, including regular Pap smears. In contrast, ovarian cancer is more common among white women. Ovarian cancer is much harder to detect, and therefore is diagnosed at a later stage. Survival rates for this disease are the lowest among the gynecologic cancers, with fewer than 40% surviving 5 years after diagnosis (American Cancer Society, 1992). Risk factors are poorly understood, although some evidence suggests that oral contraceptives that suppress ovulation may help protect against ovarian cancer (Hankinson, Vital-Herne, & Goldstein, 1992). Rates for endometrial cancer (cancer of the uterus) have remained stable over the past decade. This disease generally occurs in women over 50, with a relatively positive prognosis of 85% survival 5 years after diagnosis (American Cancer Society, 1992). Besides age, a history of infertility, failure to ovulate, obesity, and use of estrogen therapy are the best known risk factors for endometrial cancer.

4.2.4. DIABETES. Diabetes is a serious disease that often leads to disability and can even lead to death if not treated or if poorly managed. It is a major cause of death for women, ranking seventh recently for white women and fourth for African-American women (McBarnette, 1996). The rates are also higher for Mexican-American and American Indian women than for white women. Sixty percent of new cases of diabetes are diagnosed in women (Tinker, 1994).

Although some forms of diabetes begin at a younger age, especially gestational diabetes linked with pregnancy, diabetes disproportionately affects older age groups, and death is four times more likely for women 65 to 74 than for women 45 to 64 (NCHS, 1991). It is associated with increased risk for many other chronic health problems and complicates the management of many diseases. Diabetes can contribute to kidney disease, eye disease leading eventually to blindness, peripheral vascular disease that can lead to amputation of limbs, and increased risk of death from coronary heart disease and stroke (Lerner & Kannel, 1986). Diabetes contributes to the mortality of more than 80,000 women in the United States, either directly (as an underlying cause of death) or indirectly (contributing to another cause of death), a number nearly twice as high as the number of women who die from breast cancer even though that disease has received more public and media attention recently (Tinker, 1994).

A complication for women in successful management of this problem is that lifestyle changes are generally required, especially dietary changes. In some cultural groups, women may place their own health behind, keeping the family content by continuing to cook ethnically accepted foods even if they are not those recommended for control of diabetes (Anderson, Blue, & Lau, 1991). Thus gender roles may interact with successful control of diabetes, leading to the high rates of deaths from the disease and its complications.

4.2.5. OSTEOPOROSIS.   Osteoporosis has already been discussed briefly as part of the debate about whether women should take ERT after menopause. One of the clearest findings of the studies of ERT and menopause is that ERT does help hinder the development of osteoporosis, but to do this it must be taken for a long period of time, with recent evidence that maximum protection does not occur until after 10 years of therapy (Col et al., 1997; Kiel, Felson, Anderson, Wilson, & Moskowitz, 1987). Osteoporosis is a condition in which the bone density is reduced. If serious enough, fractures can result from minor accidents or even normal physical activity in the most severe cases. Osteoporosis is more common in women than in men because women are smaller, on average, and have less bone mass to begin with. In addition, the loss of bone is accelerated in women by menopause and the decline in estrogen levels linked to that event (Collins et al., 1994). Some decline in bone mass occurs in much of the population. Current estimates are that more than 50% of women over age 45 and 90% of women over 70 have some osteoporosis, making it one of the most common health problems of women as they age.

Fractures of the hip, wrist, and vertebrae are among the most common clinical manifestations of osteoporosis, but hip fractures are more important for overall health status because of their linkage to severe impairment and death (Col et al., 1997; Horton, 1992). In one study, 25% of hip fractures required institutionalization and 20% resulted in death (Resnick & Greenspan, 1989). From 75% to 80% of hip fractures occur to women. Less severe in their overall consequences are vertebral fractures, which often lead to spinal deformity, chronic back pain, and the loss of height often noted in elderly women.

Risk factors for osteoporosis include being white, being thin, a history of smoking, past family history of the disease, and having experienced amenorrhea. More recent studies support the role of continued physical activity in limiting the impact of osteoporosis (Lappe, 1993; Marcus et al., 1992). Some sociocultural factors may exacerbate osteoporosis in women, making the gender differences appear larger than they are due to genetics alone. Women are more likely to diet to keep weight down to low levels throughout their lives and to limit intake of foods rich in calcium as a means of weight control. For the current generation of elderly women, exercise was often viewed as unimportant. One debate about osteoporosis is whether future generations of women will be at as high a risk as their grandmothers, given their greater involvement in sports and exercise both at a younger age and throughout their lifetimes, and whether the heightened risk of breast cancer and other health problems outweighs the protective effects of ERT for women. Another challenge to the medical approach to osteoporosis is raised by some feminists who question whether lifelong drug regimens for healthy women are appropriate (Ray, 1996).

4.2.6. ALZHEIMER'S DISEASE.   A health problem of aging women that is less open to debate in terms of medicalization and the need for a feminist and critical examination is Alzheimer's disease (AD). This is an illness characterized by a gradual loss of memory and cognitive abilities. By the most advanced stages of the disease, people do not even recognize their own relatives and are unable to live safely by themselves without constant attention. AD has become one of the common reasons why people, especially women, are sent to nursing homes and long-term care facilities.

AD increases rapidly in both men and women after the age of 70, but since women live longer than men, many more women develop it. Some studies argue that women have a higher incidence, even taking into account the higher proportion of females among the aged (Schoenberg, Anderson, & Haerer, 1985; Schoenberg, Kokman, & Okazaki, 1987), although whether women are at greater risk is not yet resolved. Why people develop AD is also not yet clearly known, and therefore attempts at preventive measures to control risk factors are not available. History of head trauma, association with heart attacks and stroke, and family history are among the risk factors currently discussed by researchers (Advisory Panel on Alzheimer's Disease, 1991; Aronson, Ooi, & Morganstern, 1990).

5. MENTAL HEALTH STATUS

The research on mental health and gender encompasses a huge literature that is quite difficult to review in a brief space. This section therefore focuses on only a few issues linked to gender and mental health, specifically, variation in rates of mental illness and a more detailed examination of depression, one of the most important categories of mental illness, especially for women.

5.1. RATES OF MENTAL ILLNESS.   Important gender differences have been noted in the rates of specific mental disorders. Disorders that are predominant in women include clinical depression, seasonal affective disorder, the depressed phase of bipolar disorder, eating disorders (as already discussed previously under life cycle concerns of younger women), panic disorder, phobias, disassociative disorders, borderline personality disorders, and suicide attempts. Males predominate in completed suicide, substance abuse, intermittent explosive disorder, antisocial personalities, early-onset schizophrenia, autism, learning disabilities, and conduct disabilities. A few major categories of mental illness have similar rates in both men and women including obsessive-compulsive disorder, schizophrenia, and bipolar disorder (Blumenthal, 1996; Robins, Locke, & Regier, 1992).

Depression is the most important of the mental illnesses, especially for women. About 7% of women in the United States suffer from major depression during their lifetimes, in contrast to 2.6% of men (Weissman & Klerman, 1992). Depression is discussed in more detail in the next section.

Lifetime prevalence of psychiatric disorders is actually fairly similar for men and women; it is the types of mental health problem that vary between them (NCHS, 1996). Looking at people aged 15 to 54 years of age, 47% of women and 49% of men had experienced a symptom of a psychiatric disorder at some point during their lives. Women who report a symptom, however, are more likely to have received some form of mental health services for it (55% vs. 42%), reflecting the well-established greater propensity of women than men to seek help for problems, especially mental health problems (Gove, 1984; NCHS, 1996).

Many mental disorders are linked with specific stages of life. Eating disorders, for example, have been discussed under problems of young women both because they are the mental health disorder most likely to lead to death and because that mental health problem is so strongly associated with one stage of life. Other problems that are strongly linked with life stage, at least in their onset, are alcoholism and substance abuse. While alcoholism has traditionally been viewed as a problem of men, the rates are increasing among women, although across the lifetime this problem affects about 24% of the male population versus only 5% of women. Drug abuse is also linked with youth and with men, although recent data indicate problems at some point in their lifetime for 41% of men versus 32% of women, a much smaller gender difference than is the case for alcoholism

(Blumenthal, 1996). Alzheimer's is a disease of the old, and one form of schizophrenia typically starts in the early 20s.

Many researchers have pointed out that the gender differences in mental illness seem to parallel differences in gender roles, especially in American society (Gove, 1984; Radloff, 1975). Men display higher rates of disorders linked to violence, such as paranoid schizophrenia and antisocial personality disorders. Some researchers have hypothesized that these disorders may occur when men become oversocialized to their gender role, and see antisocial behavior as a way to display their position in society. This is one reason why men are more successful at accomplishing suicide, even though men and women attempt it at fairly similar rates. One recent medical sociology text notes that the symptoms of antisocial personality disorder parallel expectations within lower class communities for male behavior (Weitz, 1996). Similar role based explanations exist for the gender-based differences in depression and are discussed next.

5.2. Depression and Gender

Some researchers have hypothesized that depression can result from oversocialization to a female role (Gove, 1984; Radloff, 1975). One explanation is learned helplessness theory, which argues that depression develops when individuals learn that they cannot control their lives (Seligman, 1975). Women are socialized differently from men, and perhaps especially so beginning with adolescence and differential social reinforcement at that stage from parents, friends, and other adults. As women mature, they are more likely to believe that their failures and problems in life come from personal deficiencies, resulting in feelings of depression. Moreover, women experience more situations in which they are unable to control their own fates, especially in the past when women were limited in the careers to which they aspired, and this lack of ability to control one's own destiny is also linked to the development of depression.

Gove (1984) argued that adult roles of men are often more structured or fixed than those of women, and that more structured roles lead to better mental health. Also, he argues that women are more often placed in nurturant roles, especially within family systems, and this imposes a strain on them and leads to poorer mental health.

Evidence is also growing that suggests an interaction between biological and psychosocial factors (Blumenthal, 1996). Some gender differences have been observed in brain structure and function and in the physiological reaction to stress. Because sex differences in depression occur after puberty, this may lend credence to an explanation that includes biological as well as social influences. Certain specialized depressions of women (e.g., postpartum depression) are linked to hormonal changes connected with pregnancy. These biological factors do not work alone, but are combined with the greater role stress and nurturing properties expected by women in many different settings.

Women in every racial, ethnic, and socioeconomic group have a higher rate of depression than men in the same group. Despite this, overall rates of depression are lower for African-American and Hispanic women than for white women. Depression is most common among women from 25 to 44, but increasing rates are being reported among young women and the elderly. Rates of depression in elderly women have recently been estimated to be as high as 20% of the population over 60 (Collins et al., 1994; Horton, 1992; Kizialy, 1992). Marital separation or divorce is another major risk factor for depression among women (Anthony & Petronis, 1991).

A last piece of evidence that lends credence to an explanation that intertwines biological and social factors is information on sex differences in rates of depression cross-nationally. One study carefully employed similar sampling and diagnostic criteria to collect information about rates of mental illness in the United States, Canada, Germany, and New Zealand (Weissman, Bland, Joyce, Newman, Wells, & Wittchen, 1993). Rates of major depression were higher in females than in males, whereas rates for bipolar disorders were similar by gender, for all four countries. The mean age at onset by gender also did not vary across the nations. One interesting trend noted is that rates of major depression for males seem to be rising, while rates for females are stabilizing for birth cohorts after 1945. Further research will need to follow trends over time to see if these can help to untangle the complex interaction between social and biological causes.

6. CONCLUDING COMMENTS

What can be concluded about gender and health status from the various topics and articles reviewed in this chapter? Perhaps the most important point, discussed both at the end of the section on life expectancy and mortality and also at the end of the section on mental health, is the complex interplay between gender, biology, and other social factors. One growing area of interest within medical sociology includes an examination of not only gender and its linkages to health status, but also other factors such as ethnicity (Anderson et al., 1991; marital status (Preston, 1995), employment status (Stronks, Van de Mheen, Van den Bos, & MacKenback, 1995), and social class (Koskinen & Martelin, 1994; Krieger & Fee, 1994a; Payne, 1991).

One area of growing research interest that underscores the complex interactions between gender and health in many European countries, as well as in the United States arises from the finding that socioeconomic mortality differentials are more pronounced among men than women (Koskinen & Martelin, 1994). Traditional health studies of socioeconomic mortality differentials have generally focused on men and measured socioeconomic status (SES) in terms of the male head of the household (Haan, Kaplan, & Camacho, 1987; Lahelma & Valkonen, 1990; Navarro, 1990). One recent European study concluded that, after paying attention to how SES is measured, the major explanation for the lower impact of SES on women's mortality combines gender differences in the relative share of causes of death and the influence of marital status (Koskinen & Martelin, 1994). This one study of the complexity of linkages between gender and health, and the need to consider such other social variables as SES and marital status, illustrates a promising direction for future research on gender and health.

In a recent article critiquing the use of sex and race in studies of health in the United States, Krieger and Fee (1994a) pointed out that we need to recognize that many variables we often think about as biological are actually social (e.g., they argue that race is a spurious biological concept) or a mixture of social and biological. Krieger and Fee (1994a, 1994b) argued that to know a person's sex is to know very little about his or her health status or social status. Women, as they note, are a very mixed lot, with gender roles and options shaped by history, culture, and deep divisions across class and color lines. While recognizing, as do all health studies, the importance and biological nature of reproductive differences, their article reminds us of the need to realize that gender as a social reality often transforms and interacts with biology.

REFERENCES

Abercrombie, P. D. (1996). Women living with HIV infection. *Nursing Clinics of North America, 31*, 97–106.

Advisory Panel on Alzheimer's Disease. (1991). *Second report of the Advisory Panel on Alzheimer's Disease, 1990*, Washington, D. C.: U.S. Government Printing Office, DHHS Publication No. (ADM) 91-1791.

Althaus, F. (1991). Special report: An ounce of prevention . . . STDs and women's health. *Family Planning Perspectives, 23*, 173–177.

American Cancer Society. (1992). *Cancer facts and figures*. Atlanta, GA: American Cancer Society.

Anderson, J. M., Blue, C., & Lau, A. (1991). Women's perspectives on chronic illnesses: Ethnicity, ideology and restructuring of life. *Social Science and Medicine, 33*, 101–113.

Anthony, J. C., & Petronis, K. R. (1991). Suspected risk factors for depression among adults 18–44 years of age. *Epidemiology, 2*, 123–132.

Aronson, M. K., Ooi, W. I., & Morganstern, H. (1990). Women, myocardial infarction, and dementia in the very old. *Neurology, 40*, 1102–1106.

Blumenthal, S. J. (1996). Women's mental health: The new national focus. *Annals of the New York Academy of Sciences, 789*, 1–17.

Boston Women's Health Collective. (1973). *Our bodies, ourselves: A book by and for women*. New York: Simon & Schuster.

Brandt, A. (1985). *No magic bullet: A social history of venereal   disease in the United States since 1880*. New York: Oxford University Press.

Brezinka, V., & Kittel, F. (1995). Psychosocial factors of coronary heart disease in women: A review. *Social Science and Medicine, 42*, 1351–1365.

Bush, L. T., Connor, B. E., Cowan, D. L., Criqui, H. M., Wallace, D. R., Suchindran, M. C., Tryoler, A. H., & Rifkand, M. B. (1987). Cardiovascular mortality and noncontraceptive use of estrogen in women: Results from the Lipid Research Clinics Program follow-upstudy. *Circulation, 6*, 1102–1109.

Centers for Disease Control. (1990). Trends in lung cancer incidence and mortality—United States, 1980–1987. *Morbidity and Mortality Weekly Report, 39*, 62–71.

Clancy, C. C., & Massion, C. T. (1992). American women's health care: A patchwork quilt with gaps. *Journal of the American Medical Association, 268*, 1918–1920.

Clark, A. E. (1990). Women's health: Life-cycle issues. In R. D. Apple (Ed.), *Women, health and medicine in America: A historical handbook*. New York: Garland.

Claus, E. B., Risch, N. J., & Thompson, W. D. (1990). Age of onset as an indicator of familial risk of breast cancer. *American Journal of Epidemiology, 131*, 961–972.

Clyne, C. A. (1990). Antithrombotic therapy in the primary and secondary prevention of coronary-related death and infarction: Focus on gender differences. *Cardiology, 77*, (Suppl. 2), 99–109.

Col, N. F., Eckman, M. H., Karas, R. H., Parker, S. G., Goldenberg, R. J., Ross, E., Orr, R., & Wong, J. B. (1997). Patient-specific decisions about hormone replacement therapy in postmenopausal women. *Journal of the American Medical Association, 277*, 1140–1147.

Collins, K. S., Rowland, D., Salganicoff, A., & Chait, E. (1994). *Assessing and Improving Women's Health*. New York: Women's Research and Education Institute, with support from the Commonwealth Fund.

Cooper, R., & David, R. (1986). The biological concept of race and its applications to epidemiology. *Journal of Health Politics, Policy and Law, 11*, 97–116.

Cotton, P. (1992). Women's health initiative leads the way as research begins to fill gender gaps. *Journal of the American Medical Association, 267*, 469–470.

Crane, B. B., & Issacs, S. L. (1995). The Cairo Program of action: A new framework for international cooperation on population and development issues. *Harvard International Law Journal, 36*, 295–306.

Ehrenreich, B., & English, D. (1972). *Witches, midwives, and nurses: A history of women healers*. Old Westbury, NY: Feminist Press.

Ehrenreich, B., & English, D. (1973). *Complaints and disorders: The sexual politics of sickness*. Old Westbury, NY: Feminist Press.

Elliott, S. J. (1995). Psychosocial stress, women and heart health: A critical review. *Social Science and Medicine, 40*, 105–115.

Geary, M. A. S. (1995). An analysis of the women's health movement and its impact on the delivery of health care within the United States, *The Nurse Practitioner, 20*, 24–35.

Gove, W. R. (1984). Gender differences in mental and physical health: The effects of fixed roles and nurturant roles. *Social Science and Medicine, 19*, 77–83.

Gove, W., & Hughes, M. (1979). Possible Causes of the Apparent Sex Differences in Physical Health: An Empirical Investigation. *American Sociological Review, 44*, 126–146.

Grady, D., Rubin, S. M., Petitti, S. B., Fox, C. S., Black, D., Ettinger, B., Estner, V. L., & Cummings, S. R. (1992). Hormone therapy to prevent disease and prolong life In postmenopausal women. *Annals of Internal Medicine, 117*, 1016–1037.

Haan, M., Kaplan, G., & Camacho, T. (1987). Poverty and health: Prospective Eevidence from the Alameda County study. *American Journal of Epidemiology, 125*, 989–998.

Hankinson, U., Vital-Herne, J., & Goldstein, S. (1992). A quantitative assessment of oral contraceptive use and risk of ovarian ancer. *Obstetrics and Gynecology, 80*, 708–714.

Harlow, S. D., & Ephross, S. A. (1995). Epidemiology of menstruation and its relevance to women's health. *Epidemiologic Reviews, 17*, 265–286.

Hendel, R. (1990). Myocardial infarction in women. *Cardiology, 77*(Suppl. 2), 41–57.

Horton, J. (Ed.) (1992). *The woman's health data book: A profile of women's health in the United States*. Washington, D. C.: Jacobs Institute of Women's Health.

Institute of Medicine, Committee to Review the Women's Health Initiative. (1993). *An assessment of the women's health initiative*. Washington, D.C.: National Academy of Sciences.

Jacobs, M. D. (1994). Disordered eating in active and athletic women. *Clinic in Sports Medicine, 13*, 355–369.

Kane, P. (1991). *Women's health: From womb to tomb*. London: Macmillan.

Kelsey, J., & Bernstein, L. (1996). Epidemiology and prevention of breast cancer. *Annual Review of Public Health, 17*, 47–67.

Kendrick, J. S. & Merritt, R. K. (1996). Women and smoking: An update for the 1990s. *American Journal of Obstetrics and Gynecology, 175*, 528–535.

Kiel, D. P., Felson, D. T., Anderson, J. J., Wilson, P. W., & Moskowitz, M. A. (1987). Hip fractures and the use of estrogens in post-menopausal women: The Framingham Study. *New England Journal of Medicine, 317*, 1169–1174.

Kizilay, P. E. (1992). Predictors of depression in women. *Nursing Clinics of North America, 27*, 983–991.

Klass, P. (1987). *A not entirely Benign procedure: Four years as a medical student*. New York: G. P. Putnam's.

Koskinen, S., & Martelin, T. (1994). Why are socioeconomic mortality differences smaller among women than among men? *Social Science and Medicine, 38*, 1385–1396.

Krieger, N. (1990). Racial and gender discrimination: Risk factors for high blood pressure? *Social Science and Medicine, 30*, 1273–1281.

Krieger, N., & Fee, E. (1994a). Man-made medicine and women's health: The biopolitics of sex/gender and race/ethnicity. *International Journal of Health Services, 24*, 265–283.

Krieger, N., & Fee, E. (1994b). Social class: The missing link in US health data. *International Journal of Health Services, 24*, 25–44.

Krieger, N., Rowley, D. L., Herman, A. A., Avery, B., & Phillips, M. T. (1993). Racism, sexism, and social class: Implications for studies of health, disease and well-being. *American Journal of Preventive Medicine, 9*, 82–122.

Lahelma, E., & Valkonen, T. (1990). Health and social inequalities in Finland and elsewhere. *Social Science and Medicine, 31*, 257–268.

Lane, S. D. (1994). From population control to reproductive health: An emerging policy agenda. *Social Science and Medicine, 39*, 1202–1214.

Lappe, J. M. (1993). Bone fragility: Assessment of risk and strategies for prevention. *Journal of Obstetric, Gynecologic, and Neonatal Nursing, 23*, 260–268.

LaRosa, J. H. (1997). Women's health policy and research. In K. M. Allen & J. M. Phillips (Eds.), *Women's Health Across the Lifespan*. Philadelphia, PA: J. B. Lippincott.

Lerner, D. J., & Kannel, W. B. (1986). Patterns of coronary heart disease morbidity and mortality in the sexes: A 26 year follow-up of the Framingham population. *American Heart Journal, 11*, 383–390.

Leonardo, C., & Chrisler, J. C. (1992). Women and sexually transmitted diseases. *Women and Health,. 18*, 1–17.

MacIntyre, S., Hunt, K., & Sweeting, H. (1996). Gender differences in health: Are things really as simple as they seem? *Social Science and Medicine, 42*, 617–624.

Marcus, R., Drinkwater, B., Dalsky, G., Dufek, J., Raab, D., Slemenda, C., & Snow-Harter, C. (1992). Osteoporosis and exercise in women. *Medicine and Science in Sports and Exercise, 24*, s301–s307.

Martin, E. (1987). *The woman in the body: A cultural analysis of reproduction*. Boston: Beacon Press.

Mastroianni, A., Faden, R., & Federman, D. (Eds) (1994). *Women and health research*. Washington, D.C.: National Academy Press.

Mathews, K. A. (1989). Interactive effects of behavior and reproductive hormones on sex differences in risk for coronary heart disease. *Health Psychology, 8*, 373–387.

McBarnette, L. S. (1996). *Race, gender and health*. Thousand Oaks, CA: Sage.

McCrae, F. B. (1983). The politics of menopause: The "discovery" of a deficiency disease. *Social Problems, 31*, 111–123.

McCrae, F. B., & Markle, G. E. (1984). The estrogen replacement controversy in the USA and UK: Different answers to the same question? *Social Studies of Science, 14,* 1–26.

Miller, K., & Rosenfeld, A. (1996). Population and women's reproductive health. *Annual Review of Public Health, 17,* 359–382.

Muecke, M. (1996). The gender analysis imperative: Introduction to the special issue. *Health Care for Women International, 17,* 385–392.

Narragan, D., Zones, J. S., Worcester, N., & Grad, M. J. (1997). Research to improve women's health: An agenda for equity. In S. B. Ruzek, V. L. Olesen, & A. E. Clarke (Eds.), *Women's health: Complexities and differences.* Columbus, OH: Ohio State University Press.

National Center for Health Statistics (NCHS) (1992). *Health, United States, 1991 and prevention profile.* Hyattsville, MD: Public Health Service.

National Center for Health Statistics (NCHS) (1996). *Health, United States, 1995.* Hyattsville, MD: Public Health Service.

Navarro, V. (1990). Race or class versus race and class: Mortality differntials in the United States. *Lancet, 336,* 1238–1240.

Payne, S. (1991). *Women, health and poverty.* New York: Harvester Wheatsheaf.

Pinn, V. W. (1992a). Women's health research: Prescribing change and addressing the issues. *Journal of the American Medical Association, 268,* 1921–1922.

Pinn, V. W. (1992b). Women, research, and the National Institutes of Health. *American Journal of Preventive Medicine, 8,* 324–327.

Phillips, J. M., Sexton, M., & Blackman, J. A. (1997). Demographic overview of women across the lifespan. In K. M. Allen & J. M. Phillips (Eds.), *Women's health across the lifespan.* Philadelphia, PA: J. B. Lippincott.

Preston, D. B. (1995). Marital status, gender roles, stress, and health in the elderly. *Health Care for Women International, 16,* 149–165.

Proceedings of the National Conference on Women's Health. Special Supplement. (1987). *Public Health Reports,* Supplement to the July–August Issue, 1–157.

Radloff, L. (1975). Sex differences in depression: The effects of occupation and marital status. *Sex Roles, 1,* 249–265.

Ray, R. E. (1996). A postmodern perspective on feminist gerontology. *The Gerontologist, 36,* 674–680.

Resnick, N. M., & Greenspan, S. L. (1989). Panel session: Management/education. osteoporosis in the older women: A reappraisal. *Public Health Reports, 104* (Suppl.), 80–83.

Robins, L. N., Locke, B. Z., & Regier, D. A. (1992). An overview of psychiatric disorders in American. In L. B. Robbins & D. A. Regier (Eds.), *Psychiatric disorders in American: The epidemiologic catchment area study* (pp. 328-355). New York: The Free Press,

Rodin, J., & Ickovies, J. R. (1990). Women' health: Review and research agenda as we approach the 21st Century. *American Psychologist, 45,* 1018–1034.

Ruzek, S. (1978). *The woman's health movement: Feminist alternatives to medical control.* New York: Praeger.

Ruzek, C. B., Olesen, V. L., & Clarke, A. E. (Eds.) (1997). *Women's health: Complexities and differences.* Columbus, OH: Ohio State University Press.

Schoenberg, B. S., Anderson, D., & Haerer, A. (1985). Service dementia: Prevalence and clinical features in a biracial U.S. population. *Archives of Neurology, 42,* 740–743.

Schoenberg, B. S., Kokman, E., & Okazaki H. (1987). Alzheimer's disease and other dementing illnesses in a defined United State population incidence rates and clinical features. *Annals of Neurology, 22,* 724–729.

Sechzer, J. A., Griffin, A., & Pfafflin, S. M. (1994). Forging a women's health research agenda: Policy issues for the 1990s. *Annals of the New York Academy of Sciences, 736,* 1–223.

Seligman, M. (1975). *Helplessness: On depression, development and Death.* San Francisco, CA: Freeman.

Stampfer, M. F., & Colditz, G. A. (1991). Estrogen replacement therapy and coronary heart disease: A quantitative assessment of the epidemiological evidence. *Preventive Medicine, 20,* 47–63.

Stapleton, S. (1997). Trying to get more women in clinical trials. *American Medical News. 40,* 1, 9.

Strickland, B. R. (1988). Sex related differences in health and illness. *Psychology of Women Quarterly, 12,* 381–399.

Stronks, K., Van de Mheen, H., Van Den Bos, J., & MackKenback, J. P. (1995). Smaller socioeconomic inequalities in health among women: The role of employment status. *International Journal of Epidemiology, 24,* 559–568.

Taeuber, C. M. (1996). *Statistical handbook on women in America* (2nd ed.). Birmingham: Oryx.

Tinker, L. F. (1994). Diabetes mellitus: A priority health care issue for women. *Journal of the American Dietetic Association, 94,* 976–985.

Turshen. M. (1993). The impact of sexism on women's health and health Ccare. *Journal of Health Policy, 14,* 164–173.

Update: AIDS among women—United States, 1994. (1995). *Journal of the American Medical Association, 273,* 767–768.

Verbrugge, L. M. (1983). Multiple roles and physical health of women and men. *Journal of Health and Social Behavior, 24,* 16–30.

Verbrugge, L. M. (1985). Gender and health: An update on hypotheses and evidence. *Journal of Health and Social Behavior, 26,* 156–182.

Verbrugge, L. M. (1989). The twain meet: Empirical explanations of sex differences in health and mortality. *Journal of Health and Social Behavior, 30,* 282–304.

Weissman, M. M., & Klerman, J. R. (1992). Current understanding and changing trends. *Annual Review of Public Health, 13,* 319–339.

Weissman, M. M., Bland,, R., Joyce, P. R., Newman, S., Wells, J. E., & Wittchen, H.-U. (1993). Sex differences in rates of depression: Cross-national perspectives. *Journal of Affective Disorders, 29,* 77–84.

Weitz, R. (1996). *The sociology of health, illness and health care: A critical approach.* Belmont, CA: Wadsworth.

Wenger, N., Speroff, L., & Packard, B. (1993). Cardiovascular health and disease in women. *New England Journal of Medicine, 329,* 247–256.

Wilkinson, S., & Kitzinger, C. (1994). Feminist perspectives on women and health. In S. Wilkinson & C. Kitzinger (Eds.), *Women and health: Feminist perspectives.* Bristol, PA: Taylor and Francis.

Wingard, D. L. (1982). The sex differential in mortality rates: Demographic and behavioral factors. *American Journal of Epidemiology, 115,* 205–216.

Wingood, G. M., & DiClemente, R. J. (1996). HIV sexual risk reduction interventions for women: A review. *American Journal of Preventive Medicine, 12,* 209–217.

Wooster, R., Neuhausen, S. L., Mangion, J., Quirk, Y., & Ford, D. (1994). Localization of a breast cancer susceptibility gene. *Science, 265,* 2088–2090.

World Health Organization (WHO). (1992). *1991 World Health Statistics Annual.* Geneva, Switzerland: WHO.

CHAPTER 22

Health Care as a Gendered System

MARY K. ZIMMERMAN

SHIRLEY A. HILL

1. INTRODUCTION

Healthcare in society emerges from a system of institutional arrangements and relationships, both formal and informal, that shape and are shaped by socially defined notions about women and men. Our analysis examines healthcare organizations, actors, and issues from a perspective in which gender is posited as a central analytic category and, more generally, as a fundamental means of social differentiation. While we incorporate research on gender differences in health behaviors, we do not intend to present gender as primarily a characteristic of individuals. Rather, we strive to locate gender as a socially constructed element of social relationships and institutions. Explained or justified on the basis of perceived male and female characteristics, gender is an often unequal way of distributing social power. Gender is best seen as an organizing principle of culture and a basic structural element of society.

We conceptualize healthcare organization as gendered in five basic ways following Acker (1990): (1) possessing a division of labor based on gender, (2) incorporating symbols and images to support these divisions, (3) hosting interactions that reinforce male dominance–female submission patterns, (4) producing gendered identities through organizational presentations of self (e.g., language and task orientation), and (5) providing assumptions and an organizational logic for rules and procedures. Rather than focus on these mechanisms sequentially, we weave them throughout our analysis. In healthcare,

MARY K. ZIMMERMAN • Department of Health Policy and Managment, University of Kansas, Lawrence, Kansas 66045

SHIRLEY A. HILL • Department of Sociology, University of Kansas, Lawrence Kansas 66045

Handbook of the Sociology of Gender, edited by Janet Saltzman Chafetz. Kluwer Academic/ Plenum Publishers, New York, 1999.

gender is perhaps most evident through a highly segregated, clinical division of labor, an equally segregated administrative structure, and a formidably complex body of knowledge in which gender-based assumptions, images, and categories are deeply embedded. The technical economy of medical care reflects these highly gendered divisions, contributing to the production of gendered selves and identities, and promoting gender inequalities. Further, the U.S. market economy of healthcare and related state policies reinforce gender divisions. In the following analysis, we also aim to reveal how gender intersects with race and social class inequalities in healthcare. Defining healthcare broadly to include the provision of both formal and informal services, we concentrate on the United States, although where possible we place our discussion in a comparative context. We begin with the rise of the modern era in healthcare in the United States in the latter part of the nineteenth century and end with the more ambiguous, postmodern period that characterizes the present.

2. GENDER AND THE EMERGENCE OF MODERN MEDICINE

Healthcare organizations, practices, and policies in advanced industrial nations have developed in close relationship with the rise of professional medicine (Starr, 1982). American healthcare is a hybrid of medicine and capitalism, both of which have arisen as highly gendered activities. Modern medicine in the United States evolved in the mid to late 1800s, during a period when the industrial economy was rapidly emerging and cultural ideologies were being transformed by technology, science, mass production, and the rise of professional experts. This massive restructuring of the economy triggered the separation of production from the home and radically redefined gender roles. The doctrine of separate spheres, an ideology that defined public economic, political, and professional life as the appropriate arena for men and the private world of home and domestic life as the proper place for women, took hold, creating a powerful public–private dichotomy in social life (Cott, 1977). With a legacy that is still evident, the concept of separate spheres had a profound influence on the healthcare work of men and women as well as on the overall organization of healthcare services.

2.1. Gender and the Provision of Healthcare

The delivery of healthcare is accomplished through a gendered division of labor and stratification system rooted in nineteenth century views of male and female. Physicians, from the time they arrived in America from Europe more than 300 years ago until the past two decades, have been predominantly white and male. They achieved professional dominance within the context of a newly industrialized economy, in which production was separated on the basis of gender and women's activities were confined to the private arena of home, family, and community. Although white men dominated the ranks of those then known as "regular" or allopathic physicians, healthcare in early America was supplied by an array of competing practitioners from all walks of life, including women (Ehrenreich & English, 1973). This variety of healers was integral to frontier survival, where both ideological and structural factors mitigated the dominance of any one group (Starr, 1982). Not only did early American physicians lack scientific medical knowledge, but their potential clients believed strongly in free competition and the self-sufficiency of families in caring for the sick. Moreover, rural isolation and the lack of rapid transporta-

transportation and communication made physician consultations difficult to obtain. Domestic medicine was popular and practical, and women were integrally involved in providing medical therapies and tending to sick family members (Cassady, 1991). Female practitioners prevailed in childbirth where midwives attended deliveries and provided other forms of basic primary care in many communities. By the 1920s, however, most women had been excluded from standard medical practice.

The rise to dominance of allopathic physicians conceals a history of gender struggle (Morantz-Sanchez, 1985; Walsh, 1977). Evidence dating back to the Middle Ages shows that women wanted to study medicine; yet medical education remained primarily a male institution. Early American healthcare providers varied greatly in their training and healing strategies, with allopathic physicians more likely than others to have been trained abroad and to use heroic, interventionist strategies (Starr, 1982). Medical apprenticeship programs began to mushroom in the United States during the middle and late 1700s. As early as the 1830s, there were some American women who apprenticed as physicians and, by 1845, women had applied to enter medical school (Walsh, 1977). Some were admitted, mostly to the women's medical schools that began to proliferate toward the turn of the century, but, for the most part, women were strongly discouraged and systematically denied entry. Those who managed to become doctors were often barred from practice opportunities and otherwise marginalized. Periodically, women mounted campaigns to change this situation; however, it was not until 1945 that the last of the elite U.S. medical schools opened its doors to women, 100 years after the first woman had applied there (Walsh, 1977).

Physician dominance was achieved at a time when there was firmly embedded support for racial segregation in American society. This meant that not only women but also, for the most part, people of color were excluded from becoming physicians (Hulston, 1996). In 1910, publication of the Flexner Report, commissioned by the Carnegie Foundation at the request of the American Medical Association, evaluated the quality of medical education in the United States and recommended the closing of a large number of small, inadequate, and poorly funded medical schools, including most of those educating women and racial minorities (Starr, 1982; Weitz, 1996). Part of a campaign between 1905 and 1920 to reform medical education, this report secured and protected the position of allopathic physicians, guaranteeing that medicine would remain white and male for the next half-century. Disparities in the health status of blacks and whites were documented by medical researchers during the 19th century, and were used to support the notion that blacks were more susceptible to illnesses and thus biologically inferior to whites (Williams, 1998). In addition, by the early 1900s, blacks had been barred from most medical school training and from internships and residencies in hospitals, except for the few with designated "colored wards" (Hart-Brothers, 1994). This situation did not change significantly until well into the second half of the 20th century.

The creation of the first hospital and the first formal medical school accelerated efforts among various groups of doctors to gain control over medical practice. Primarily through the discovery of scientific medicine (i.e., the germ theory of disease) and advances in surgical techniques, the predominantly male allopathic physicians prevailed among a host of competing medical practitioners. During the late nineteenth and early twentieth centuries, allopaths successfully pushed for legal statutes that defined the parameters of medicine and medical licensure in terms of their own interests (Freidson, 1988). By the early 1900s, modern medicine had emerged. As the influence and public trust associated with physicians increased, the prominence of women in the community as informal healers attenuated to informal caregiving and the gendered division of labor in healthcare solidified.

Similar patterns of gender exclusion and segregation in medicine have occurred throughout the world, with women being barred entrance to medical school, especially to elite settings within medicine. There are no examples yet of countries that have achieved gender equity in medicine. In extremely sex-segregated societies, women have been allowed to become physicians solely to treat women and children. There is ample evidence that the gender-based division of labor in healthcare is an international phenomenon (Riska & Wegar, 1993).

2.2. Medical Dominance and Gender

The term "medical dominance" refers to the power and influence of physicians within the healthcare system. It encompasses medicine's attempts to control the conditions of its own work, and also the conditions of supporting and competing occupations (Freidson, 1988; Wolinsky, 1993). While physicians have dominated the medical division of labor, they also have been able to control the power relations and influence the professional activities of other healthcare occupations. Implicit in these arrangements is the fact that medical dominance has also been gender dominance. The divisions and power struggles in healthcare typically are discussed as conflicts over resource and professional turf issues with little, if any, attention to the underlying gender dynamics (Riska & Wegar, 1993). We contend, in contrast, that gender is an essential ingredient of dominance in the medical division of labor.

Gender has been a fault line in healthcare much as it has been throughout society (Doyal, 1995). The dominance of physicians, 80% of whom are male (Barzansky, Jonas, & Etzel, 1997), over nurses, midwives, therapists, and technicians is central to the understanding of healthcare as a gendered institution. Medicine has circumscribed the autonomy and scope of practice of nursing (Donovan, 1983), midwifery (Weitz & Sullivan, 1986), and physical therapy, as well as chiropractic (Coulehan, 1985) and other healthcare occupations (Wardwell, 1994). The American Medical Association's Committee on Allied Health Education and Accreditation oversees accrediting for some 28 allied health occupations, which together are approximately 75% female (Fauser, 1992). Nursing, in particular, has been described in terms of the traditional, patriarchal relationship between husband and wife (Ashley, 1976; Campbell-Heider & Pollock, 1987). The origins of this pattern can be traced back to Florence Nightingale's struggle to get nursing legitimated as a respectable and useful occupation in the nineteenth century. Physician endorsement was essential, but she could obtain it only by promising that nurses would serve and act only on physicians' orders. Nursing thus was defined as a subordinate part of the division of labor surrounding medicine (Freidson, 1988). The growth of non-physician clinicians (such as physician assistants, nurse midwives, chiropractors, acupuncturists, naturopaths, optometrists, podiatrists, nurse anesthetists, and clinical nurse specialists) is likely to alter physician dominance and, as a result, the gendered division of labor in medicine. Non-physician clinician graduates doubled between 1992 and 1997, and growth in their supply into the early 21st century will double compared to that of physicians (Cooper, Laud, & Dietrich, 1998). At the same time, there is evidence that the ability to practice autonomously is increasing for these same practioner groups (Cooper, Henderson, & Dietrich, 1998).

2.3. Male Doctors and Female Patients

Medical dominance also is linked to gender inequality through the historical significance of women as patients and research subjects. In pre-Flexner America, when practitioners were competing for prominence, solving women's health problems helped establish allopathic physicians' therapeutic value. With so many types of healers competing, allopaths needed to impress the public with positive medical outcomes. They required patients with troublesome problems that could be solved effectively enough to enhance medical credibility. To a large extent, women patients served this function. It is ironic that, although elite medical schools at that time barred entrance to most women and persons of color, physicians' scientific and technical expertise expanded in large part because of clinical access to these very populations (Zimmerman, 1987).

Then, as now, sexual and reproductive-related problems yielded eager and potentially enthusiastic patients. Both men and women were targeted as potential patients, sometimes by questionable physicians. Medical advice regarding appropriate sexual functioning abounded, for example, warnings about the presumed dire physical and social consequences of men's masturbation (Barker-Benfield, 1976). Dr. John Brinkley, a Kansas "physician," offered a cure for male impotence in the 1920s through a procedure in which he transplanted goat testicles into hundreds of adult men (Hudson, 1985).

Women, however, provided even greater opportunities for physicians to demonstrate their professional worth. In the late 1880s, Dr. Marion Sims developed a surgical procedure to repair uterine prolapse, offering relief to hundreds of mostly affluent women. A widely respected physician, Sims was able to perfect his procedure by conducting numerous experimental surgeries on slaves and indigent white women (Ehrenreich & English, 1978). Physicians of this period were sought after to treat another common disorder affecting primarily middle- and upper-class women, a complex of chronic fatigue, depression, and anxiety symptoms known as neurasthenia or hysteria (Smith-Rosenberg, 1972). It was thought that when women's delicate reproductive systems were "overly stimulated" by education or sexuality, both physical and mental health would suffer. Physicians treated this disorder with a range of therapies, from total bed rest in semidarkness to surgical removal of the clitoris and/or ovaries to complete hysterectomies. Sigmund Freud, another well-known physician, also relied mostly on women patients in the development of his revolutionary theories of the mind, which served to elevate and legitimate the field of psychiatry. It is interesting that physicians and their theories of female frailty overlooked the contradictory experience of emigrant and working-class women, who were able to labor strenuously as factory, field, or domestic workers during the day and again as wives and mothers in the evening.

Numerous explanations have been offered for the physical and emotional problems that appeared to increasingly afflict women in the newly and rapidly industrializing society. These include the bodily damage produced by tight corseting and other physical restrictions, the effects of drugs and alcohol stemming from unrestricted access to narcotics and patent "medicines," as well as the socioemotional consequences of the upheaval in gender roles (Ehrenreich & English, 1978; Smith-Rosenberg & Rosenberg, 1973). Whatever the cause, women's health problems clearly were medicine's gain. In turn, the new authority of modern medicine served in many ways to reinforce women's dependency and subservient social position.

2.4. Healthcare as a System of Social Control: The Concept of Medicalization

The advice and treatments given to the men and women of the late 1800s and early 1900s can be viewed sociologically as mechanisms of social control, complementing and validating narrowly defined and, for women, repressive social roles. Both medicine as a system of knowledge and medical care as a system of social relationships and institutions have been studied in terms of their coercive effects (Foucault, 1973, 1975; Zola, 1972). These effects include shaping behavior (e.g. sexual practices), identity (e.g. normal or abnormal), and self-worth of individuals (e.g. self-confident versus self-conscious). The notion of medicine as an institution of social control reinforces Acker's (1990) discussion of the impact of gendered organizations on individuals' behavior and life chances. Viewed in this way, medicine is an influential social institution, maintaining and perpetuating gendered assumptions and patterns of gender difference and inequality in social life.

In affluent nations, medical governance over key aspects of individuals' lives is expanding (Freidson, 1988). Growth in the scope of medicine, known as "medicalization," refers not to scientific discoveries, but rather to the process of defining nonmedical or behavioral events as healthcare problems (Conrad, 1992). Women's experiences seem particularly prone to medicalization (Riessman, 1983); however, uniquely male problems, such as impotency and baldness, also have been medicalized in recent years. When social phenomena are redefined as medical, medicine responds as it does to any medical problem, viewing it as pathological (deviant) or potentially pathological. Applying the usual clinical stance, medicine assumes responsibility for eradicating the problem or at least bringing it "under control." While the professional entrepreneurship of physicians (Freidson, 1988) offers one explanation for medicalization, the economic rewards of new treatment markets, in the context of for-profit medicine, provides another.

Feminist theorists have written about the medicalization of women's lives, beginning with the displacement of midwives by physicians (Riessman, 1983). They have pointed out that whereas midwives *assisted* women in the delivery of their child, physicians now *take charge* of labor and delivery. The medicalization of pregnancy and childbirth (Rothman, 1982) has roots, as we have seen, in the professional jurisdictional disputes of the latter 1800s, as does medical authority over menstruation and menopause (Bell, 1987). Another struggle over medicalization was the controversy surrounding the official designation, in 1986, of certain premenstrual symptoms as a mental illness, known since 1994 as premenstrual dysphoric disorder or PMDD (Figert, 1996). Many women's groups fought this decision because it stigmatized a normal characteristic of women. Others welcomed it because it legitimated their symptoms as a "real illness" for which they could claim access to treatment and insurance benefits. During recent years, yet other aspects of women's experience (and in some cases men's) have been medicalized: cosmetic surgery and body shaping (Sullivan, 1993), eating problems and exercise (Hesse-Biber, 1996; Wolf, 1991) and domestic and other forms of violence. As in the life-threatening problems created by the diet medication fenfluramine-phentermine (fen-phen) in the mid-1990s, these seemingly benign procedures may yet prove harmful.

Medicalization solidifies medical authority over events and behavior: physician advice is either required or advised, and physicians are granted authority to determine whether the parameters of the event or behavior are "normal" or "pathological." If pathological, then physician control extends into treatment—through drugs, surgery, or some other form of technological management—so that significant aspects of individuals' lives are brought under the scope of physician authority. To the extent that women have greater portions of their lives under medical supervision than men, they are subject to loss of autonomy over decisions that may have substantial consequences for them. In seeking to improve the quality of their lives, women seeking medical help may end up with lower quality instead (Rothman, 1986, 1989).

It is difficult to avoid interpreting these developments in the United States from an economic perspective. Financial pressures on hospitals and medical practices in an increasingly competitive environment have encouraged newly medicalized areas of healthcare. Services such as surgical or pharmaceutical weight control, cosmetic surgery, and fitness have become lucrative ventures in many Western countries. Americans reportedly spend more than $30 billion in pursuit of weight loss, $43 billion on fitness, and millions more on plastic surgery and infertility (Hesse-Biber, 1996). In these areas, women in particular stand vulnerable to fraud and overtreatment by medicine. In 1990, for example, the Federal Trade Commission settled out-of-court at least four times with infertility clinics that claimed their success rates were substantially higher than they in fact were (*Modern Healthcare*, 1991).

Childbirth in the United States is the prototypical example of medicalization and marketing. Prospective parents with insurance are enticed by hospitals offering sophisticated technology and extra amenities for what is typically a nonmedical event with an increasingly short length of stay. Hospitals want high-volume maternity services to "bond" with their customers, especially women, and establish ties that may bring them future business. In the 1970s, when insurance payments for complicated surgeries were generous and the use of technology unrestrained, medicalization of childbirth was manifest in an escalating Cesarean delivery rate that rose from 5% in 1970 to 25% of all births in the late 1980s (Public Citizen Research Group, 1994). In the 1990s, financial incentives shifted under managed care, and Cesarean rates began to decline. In 1992, state rates varied between 16% (Colorado) and 28% (Arkansas). Moreover, rates within health systems varied to an even greater extent between for-profit systems, on the one hand, and not-for-profit and public systems, on the other. In one study, Cesarean rates ranged from 12.8% in a public system to 28.1% in a for-profit system (Public Citizen Research Group, 1994).

The situation in affluent countries, such as the United States, where childbirth is relatively safe—despite issues of medicalization and loss of women's control—stands in sharp contrast to childbirth experiences in developing, less affluent countries where survival is a key issue (Doyal, 1995). It is important to keep in perspective that the developed world's average maternal mortality rate of 26 deaths per 100,000 live births is only a fraction of the average rate of 420 in developing nations, or 630 in Africa (Lorber, 1997). In the next section, we explore further the implications of capitalism for a gendered healthcare system.

3. HEALTHCARE IN THE CONTEXT OF CAPITALISM AND PATRIARCHY

Healthcare itself is embedded in larger processes, socially shaped by government policies as well as by broader social forces. Healthcare services, and their implications for men and women, differ from country to country; they are defined variably within the apparatus of state governments as part of national and international market economies, and also by the nature of civil society within households and communities. In the United States perhaps more than in any other country, healthcare reflects the combined forces of capitalism and patriarchy.

3.1. Gendered Healthcare and the State

Governments can have a profound impact in organizing gender relations as part of how they adjudicate the delivery of healthcare services. The relationship between individual and state is a fundamental and central issue, specifically the role of the state in providing for the basic welfare of citizens. Welfare, in this sense, refers to healthcare as well as to education and basic sustenance. Esping-Anderson (1990) has suggested comparing nations based on how well individual citizens are able to obtain basic welfare services outside the market—that is, on their "decommodification" or to what extent welfare will be provided if citizens cannot buy the resources they need. His model posits a state–market–family nexus to differentiate types of national systems wherein each of these three social institutions is defined as a potential welfare provider. In the case of healthcare, if the market fails and citizens are unable to purchase healthcare, then the state or family has to take over. If neither the market nor state can provide, then the individual family is left as the sole source of care. A fully decommodified worker presumably would be one for whom the state would provide the full scope of welfare support. This scheme has been criticized for ignoring gender, the gendered nature of care provision, and for building its concept of state–market–family on the experience of male workers rather than on both males and females (Hobson, 1990; Orloff, 1993). In the traditional family configuration of breadwinner husband–homemaker wife, a male workers' ability to purchase welfare services or to be decommodified by the state does not automatically signal that his wife is equally well taken care of. The question of how independent women are outside the market (their decommodification) remains. Feminist social scientists also have pointed out that much standard research on welfare (including healthcare) and the state obscures and undervalues the considerable unpaid work, largely done by women, that exists as a key element in all healthcare systems (Glazer, 1990; Orloff, 1993).

Healthcare services in the United States are commodities, offered either on a fee-for-service or prepaid (capitated) basis. In Canada and Western Europe, the state plays a stronger role than in the United States, which relies primarily on the market and family as the means of access to healthcare (Graig, 1993). Since it is the responsibility of individuals and families to purchase these services, healthcare has become a privilege for those who can afford to pay. Unlike many other market commodities, however, in healthcare those with the least ability to pay—women, children, and disabled persons—are often those who need the goods and services most. The United States stands alone among industrial and postindustrial, democratic nations in having failed to enact a national health insurance plan (Evans, 1997; Steinmo & Watts, 1995). As a result, the existing patchwork system mixes public and private services in a way that leaves more than 17% of the population, 40.3 million individuals, with no way to pay for healthcare except from their own pocket (Fronstin, 1997), and millions more with coverage inadequate to protect them against financial ruin in the event of a major illness (Himmelstein & Woolhandler, 1994). In contrast, most advanced nations consider healthcare as a right of citizenship and provide access for the entire society (Anderson, 1997). Despite being by far the most expensive healthcare system in the world, fragmentation of healthcare services, inefficiency, bureaucratic top-heaviness, as well as inequities in quality and access to care have become the hallmarks of healthcare in the United States (Evans, 1997). The effects of this system are compounded for women both because of their location in the economy and because of the gendered nature of medical care. As we shall see, much of the gendering of medicine, including the ownership and financing of healthcare facilities, access to health insurance, and the use of health services, reflect both the profit-driven economy and the gendered, public–private dichotomy that emerged during the nineteenth century.

3.2. The Contradictions of Public and Private

Healthcare in the United States, for the most part, maintains the ownership and financing structure of the white, patriarchal, capitalist world in which early healthcare organizations and professional relationships developed (Starr, 1982; Stevens, 1989; Steinmo & Watts, 1995). Both hospitals and physician practices originated and have functioned predominantly as privately owned entities, hospitals tending to be not-for-profit and physicians mostly practicing in for-profit arrangements. Accordingly, the healthcare system in the United States reflects the same inequalities in gender relations that exist in other types of private, corporate settings (Spence, 1994; Wiggins, 1994). The board room and highest administrative and clinical positions are occupied overwhelmingly by men, while lower-level occupations, such as nursing assistants, clerks, and cleaning staff, are composed mostly of women (Butter, 1985). Men predominate as physicians and women provide the majority of other types of healthcare, both formal and informal.

The gendering of healthcare systems is organized structurally around two types of public–private dichotomies. On the one hand, there is the economic distinction between public and private, reflecting healthcare ownership and financing accomplished through public taxation as opposed to private capital. Publicly financed and private healthcare are differentially populated by men and women. Women are more likely than men to be employed in the public sector (including publicly funded healthcare), and women are also more plentiful than men among those who seek care from public institutions. Public versus private can also refer to spheres of activity, corresponding in healthcare to the distinction between formal and informal care. In this sense, private means unpaid care delivered usually by family or friends in the personal environment of home or community. From the standpoint of informal caregiving, the gendered nature of healthcare becomes particularly pronounced because of the huge proportion of such services delivered by women (Glazer, 1990; Olesen, 1997).

Public financing of healthcare and related public administrative and regulatory agencies has grown steadily over the last several decades in the United States, mostly owing to the commitment made by the federal government in the 1960s through the Medicare and Medicaid programs, extensions of the Social Security system. Because women live longer and are poorer than men, the major beneficiaries in both programs are women. Sixty percent of U.S. citizens 65 and older are women; 70% of those are 85 and older (U.S. Department of Commerce, 1977). Furthermore, the poorest groups in America are women over 65 living alone, and women raising children alone, together comprising 70% of all people in the United States (Allen & Pifer, 1993). Medicare provides comprehensive health insurance benefits and nearly universal coverage to workers and their spouses over 65. Of the 5% of elderly persons not eligible for Medicare, most are women. Medicaid, on a more limited basis, provides healthcare to those with extremely low incomes, with the vast majority of benefits going to mothers and children as well as to frail, elderly women in long-term care. Twelve and a half percent of the U.S. population received benefits from Medicaid in 1995 (U.S. General Accounting Office, July, 1997). Still, since states determine their own eligibility guidelines, as many as 50% of the poor are not covered by Medicaid (DeLew, Greenberg, & Kinchen, 1992).

There are other public programs as well that are providing healthcare benefits for women, including federal family planning legislation that opened family planning centers throughout the United States in the 1970s and the WIC (Women, Infants and Children) program which stresses proper nutrition during the prenatal period and early childhood. In addition, public sector employment typically provides opportunities for minorities and women (Higginbotham, 1997) with the prospect of greater gender and racial equity than in the private sector. Women are increasingly being covered by public healthcare services; however, in the United States, the proportion of the healthcare system that is public, approximately 43%, is the lowest among major industrialized nations. Comparing the United States to Europe reveals that countries with a higher proportion of public spending for healthcare, in most cases, appear to have better life expectancies for males and females and lower maternal mortality rates (Table 22-1).

3.3. Gender Differences in Public and Private Health Insurance Coverage

Health insurance, whether private or public, must be considered another significantly gendered aspect of the healthcare system in the United States. As we have seen, public health insurance and related health programs focusing on women are generally increasing. For the majority of Americans, however, employment-based health insurance is the primary way of paying for healthcare in the face of rising healthcare costs. During the late 1930s, labor unions successfully negotiated with employers for health benefits and an employment-based health insurance system emerged. Employment-based health insurance was an especially attractive option for business, as state laws were passed making contributions to employee health insurance plans tax deductible for employers (Starr, 1982; Staples, 1989). Because women had limited participation in the labor market until recent decades, their access to formal healthcare services was often possible only through the resources of male family members: 40% of privately insured women were covered as dependents even in 1995 (U.S. General Accounting Office, February 1997). As Meyer &

TABLE 22-1. **Private Health Care Spending and Selected Health Care Outcomes in the United States and 10 Western European Countries**

Country	Private Health Care Spending as a % of Total[a]	Maternal Mortality[b]	Life Exp (F)[b]	Life Exp (M)[b]
Austria	36	1.1	80.3	73.7
Belgium	13	5.6	79.9	73.
Denmark	15	4.3	78.3	72.9
Finland	21	1.6	80.4	72.9
France	28	11.7	82.8	74.4
Germany	20	5.2	79.7	73.1
The Netherlands	22	6.1	80.5	74.7
Sweden	7	5.1	81.0	75.6
Switzerland	35	3.6	82.1	75.3
United Kingdom	10	7.9	79.6	74.2
United States	57	7.2[d]	78.9[c]	72.1[c]

[a] *Source*: Esping-Anderson (1990), p. 70.
[b] *Source*: World Health Organization, Health for All 2000 Data Base, 1997.
[c] *Source*: National Center for Health Statistics.
[d] *Source*: Horton (1995), p. 23.

Pavalko (1996) point out, employment-based health insurance assumes more stability in family life and employment than currently exists in America, especially given the economic restructuring and the growing number of people who are single, divorced, or widowed (Fronstin & Snider, 1996/97). Moreover, healthcare policies are often devised either for women of childrearing age or for the elderly, thus disadvantaging middle-aged women who are more often unemployed or single than their younger counterparts (Doress-Worters, 1996; Keith, 1987; Tallon & Block, 1987). Today, even though more women are employed, labor market inequalities still affect healthcare access for many women, as well as for minorities. Employment-based health insurance provides men and women with differential healthcare access and services, and women's coverage remains inadequate compared to men's.

Recent erosion in employee benefits means that differential placement in the labor market is increasingly important in determining healthcare access for women, as well as for minorities. The percentage of the U.S. population with private health insurance dropped from 80% to 70% between 1980 and 1995 (U.S. General Accounting Office, July, 1997). Escalating healthcare costs in recent decades have caused many employers to reduce the healthcare benefits they offer to workers or to increase premiums and out-of-pocket costs, pricing lower income workers out of coverage even when it is offered (Cooper & Schone, 1997). This is a particular problem in lower level jobs and, therefore, disproportionately affects women and minority workers who tend to be in such jobs. In addition to declining coverage levels and rising out-of-pocket costs, the adequacy of coverage for the dependents of workers has also deteriorated (Fronstin, 1997). Although women's labor force participation has increased, compared to men they tend to work in lower positions, for less hourly pay, in smaller firms with fewer benefits, with less union representation, and more frequently in part-time jobs—all factors that work against favorable insurance coverage (Lindsey, 1997). Even among full-time employees, men are more likely to have employer-paid insurance (68.3% vs. 60.5%). The same discrepancies are found for those working part-time (26% of men and 17% of women) and among discontinuous workers (Miles & Parker, 1997).

Gender differences in insurance coverage are important to explore as yet another part of the gendered healthcare system. On the surface, gender statistics on private health insurance coverage in the United States suggest only small differences. For example, in 1993, 73% of women and 74% of men reportedly were covered by private insurance in the U.S. (Table 22-2). Recent in-depth analyses, however, suggest that aggregate percentages mask significant discrepancies in how healthcare insurance serves the healthcare needs of men and women. Miles & Parker (1997) conclude that in all forms of insurance—in Medicare and Medicaid as well as in private coverage—men are served better than women in relation to their needs. Men and women have different life spans and

TABLE 22-2. **Percentage of Women and Men 18 to 44 Years Old with Health Insurance Coverage in 1993**

Type of Coverage	Women	Men
Private	72.7	73.9
Public	8.4	3.8
Uninsured	19.0	22.2

Source: Women's health care costs and experiences. Washington, D. C.: The Women's Research and Education Institute (1994), p. 5.

illness patterns, making their healthcare needs substantially different and requiring accessibility to different types of healthcare services. For example, a 1998 survey of health insurance plans found that 93% excluded infertility treatment while only 15% excluded impotency or sterilization on services (*Medical Benefits*, 1998). Nine percent of privately insured women have policies that exclude maternity coverage (Braveman, 1988) while 27% and 36% of insurance plans do not cover induced abortion (Horton, 1995). All but 16% of health maintenance organizations cover oral contraceptives, but no more than 31% to 60% of other plans provide such coverage.

Gendered insurance coverage is also important to explore because these biases may lower the quality of healthcare for women (Burstin, Lipsitz, & Brennan, 1992). For example, women are more likely to move in and out of jobs due to childbirth, making them vulnerable to loss of services or higher premiums to cover medical conditions that develop while they are between jobs. Women require preventive screening that is not always provided, such as mammograms and Pap tests, as well as birth control and abortion services. Because women live longer than men, they are more likely to require nursing home services. Associated with living longer, older women have chronic illnesses and disability and are, therefore, more likely than men to require adaptive aids, home health and community-based services, and out-patient prescriptions. Medicare covers most hospital costs, but provides less adequate coverage for nonhospital care, including the very services women need most, such as home healthcare, out-patient medicines, and adaptive aids. Among poor elderly in 1986, Medicaid paid 49% of the healthcare expenses of unmarried men compared to 33% of the expenses of unmarried women (Allen & Pifer, 1993).

Data on the specifics of healthcare coverage are difficult to find; however, it appears that the most generous and unrestrictive healthcare benefits are unevenly distributed by both gender and race. Those with the most abundant insurance coverage and the freedom to choose nearly any provider tend to be white men in upper-level jobs. Women workers, on the other hand, particularly women of color, are likely to be in lower level-jobs that provide poor health coverage or none at all. As indicated previously, coverage varies greatly with the type of employment. In 1996, only 42.7% of workers in jobs paying $7.00 or less per hour were offered health insurance compared to 93.4% of workers making more than $15.00 (Cooper & Schone, 1997). Clearly, gender differences in the quality of insurance coverage is a key aspect of the gendered healthcare system.

4. THE GENDERED PROFESSION OF MEDICINE

The demands of illness have brought men and women together around the delivery of healthcare across both the public and private spheres. This has not, however, accomplished or even in most cases promoted gender equality in medical practice. Despite some significant changes that have occurred in the past two decades, medicine and medical care continue to reproduce aspects of society's gendered and racist past (Abraham, 1993; Morantz-Sanchez, 1985; Walsh, 1977). Medical education has been the site of perhaps the most dramatic gender changes in medicine. In the world of medical practice, both the gender of the physician and the gender of the patient make differences in the dynamics of the doctor–patient relationship. The length of medical education prolongs the time it takes for changes in gender composition to filter through and have noticeable impact among practicing physicians. As the proportion of women physicians increases, however, it is of great interest whether or not their practice styles differ from men's. In the following section, we touch upon these issues.

4.1. Medical Education

For much of last century, medical schools were restricted primarily to white men. As we have discussed, strict standards imposed on U.S. medical schools in the early 1900s forced many women's medical colleges to close and the remaining elite institutions admitted few, if any, women. Admissions of women rarely exceeded 5% until the 1960s. Then, by the 1970s, applications began to increase substantially (see Table 22-3), fueled by federal civil rights legislation and the enthusiasm created by student activism and the women's movement. In 1997, women constituted 43.5% of the entering class of U.S. medical schools (Barzansky, Jonas, & Etzel, 1998). Increasing numbers of women medical students brought a new gender consciousness which resulted in complaints about gender-based discrimination and stereotyping among physicians (Boston Women's Health Book Collective, 1992; Campbell, 1974; Scully & Bart, 1973). Over the same period, medical students became more racially and ethnically diverse. One third of the 1997–1998 entering class of U.S. medical students came from either African-American, Asian, Hispanic/Latino, or Native American backgrounds, with greater numbers of women among the African American students and more men among the Hispanic/Latino and Asian students (see Table 22-4). Data from 1997–1998 also reveal a decrease in underrepresented minority students (African American and Hispanics), a matter of some concern given attacks on affirmative action programs (Barzansky, Jonas, & Etzel, 1998). Similar declines occurred for both men and women.

Gender issues in medical education appear in three major areas: the gender distribution of students and faculty, the treatment of gender in the curriculum, and the gender climate in medical schools and institutions (Zimmerman, 1996). The gender balance of students admitted and graduating has improved in recent years, yet imbalance persists in residency programs and among faculty as they progress through the professorial ranks (Bickel, 1995; Bickel & Ruffin, 1995). About one fourth of U.S. medical school faculties are women, with proportionately more women among junior faculty than senior faculty. Full professors and top administrators are overwhelmingly men. In 1997, only 7 of the 125 accredited U.S. Medical Schools were headed by women (Barzansky, Jonas, & Etzel, 1998).

Medical specialization also is gendered in that women and men are disproportion-

TABLE 22-3. Proportion of Women Students Entering U.S. Medical Schools, 1950–1998

Years	No.	Percentage
1949–50	387	5.5
1959–60	494	6.0
1969–70	929	9.1
1974–75	3263	22.4
1979–80	4575	27.8
1989–90	6404	38.2
1997–98	7325	43.5

Source: Association of American Medical Colleges, Section for Student Services.

TABLE 22.4. Gender and Racial/Ethnic Backgrounds of Students Entering
U.S. Medical Schools, 1991–92, 1996–97, and 1997–98

	% Women			% Men		
	1991–92	1996–97	1997–98	1991–92	1996–97	1997–98
African American (non-Hispanic)	4.2	5.2	4.9	3.3	3.4	3.1
Native American/ Alaskan Native	0.3	0.4	0.4	0.2	0.4	0.4
Hispanic/Latino	2.4	3.2	2.9	3.4	3.9	3.6
Asian/Pacific Islander	6.4	7.4	8.0	9.5	10.2	10.6

Source: Association of American Medical Colleges, Section for Student Services.

ately represented in most fields of medicine. In 1997, for example, 62% of pediatrics residents and 60% of obstetrics–gynecology residents were women, as were 43% of the residents in both family practice and psychiatry. On the other hand, men dominated general surgery (81%), particularly in specific areas such as orthopedic (93%) and thoracic (95%) surgery. Internal medicine had the largest number of residents, approximately one third of whom were women (Barzansky, Jonas, & Etzel, 1998).

An even more fundamental aspect in the differential treatment of women and men in the medical curriculum reflects the way medical specialities are organized. Women's healthcare is partitioned between three different specialties: internal medicine, obstetrics–gynecology, and family medicine (Bartman & Weiss, 1993; Zimmerman, 1996). Internal medicine physicians, the most common provider of healthcare to adults, rarely provide gynecology services themselves. Instead, they typically refer women to an obstetrician–gynecologist for reproductive-related care. Such fragmentation occurs less frequently for men, whose routine care can be provided by a single, primary care specialist.

Medical school curricula have been criticized for focusing on the average white male to the neglect of adequate material covering women and men of color (Harrison, 1990; Lillie-Blanton & Laveist, 1996; Roberts, Kroboth, & Bernier, 1995). In part, this reflects a longstanding gender bias in medical research (Kirschstein, 1991; Rosser, 1994) compounded—at least until recently—by a narrowly defined cultural perspective on gender. Major, federally funded research studies on heart disease, cancer, and other common health problems in the United States routinely excluded women until the 1990s. Although women constituted a majority of the population over age 65, the Baltimore Longitudinal Study of Aging included *no* women (Weisman, 1998), raising questions about the appropriateness of the study report entitled *Normal Human Aging* (Weisman, 1998). In addition to bias in research, medical advice transmits clear gender assumptions. Brochures and other information on caring for sick children may be written to mothers, not to both fathers and mothers. Contraceptive education is often targeted to girls rather than to both boys and girls. Medical attitudes and advice frequently assume the traditional "male breadwinner" family model for the position and roles of men and women, failing to address adequately the circumstances and health needs of dual-earner and single-parent families as well as gay men and lesbians (Doyal, 1995; Zimmerman, 1987). Biases such as these may be particularly difficult to alter because of the nature of medical education, and the way knowledge is transmitted. Much of the clinical teaching in medical schools is conducted on a tutorial basis, meaning that faculty supervise and instruct students as they work. Standards, attitudes, and values are communicated daily, frequently without conscious attention. Faculty awareness and sensitivity to gender and race in these practice settings can have marked impact.

Gender and racial bias in medical education also has been associated with the culture of medical schools and institutions (Grant, 1988), with women and minorities reporting more discrimination and harassment than white males (Lorber, 1984; Baldwin, Daugherty, & Rowley, 1994; Komaromy, Bindman, Haber, & Sande, 1993). Hostler and Gressard (1993) developed a scale to measure gender fairness in the medical school environment that they used to survey all University of Virginia Medical School faculty, residents, and students. They found marked gender differences among both faculty and students: in both groups, women's scores indicated gender inequity and sexism while men's scores did not. In addition, gender climate is also defined by the policies and programs instituted by medical schools, such as maternity and parental leave policies and insurance coverage for reproductive care. A 1995 survey of teaching hospitals affiliated with medical schools found that only 41% offered medical residents paid maternity leave and 23% had no written maternity and parental leave policies at all (Philibert & Bickel, 1995).

4.2. The Doctor–Patient Relationship

Despite dramatic shifts in the gender composition of medical school classes, more than three quarters of practicing physicians in the United States are men. This, in combination with the fact that women make more medical visits than men (Horton, 1995; Marcus & Siegel, 1982; McCaig, 1994), means that the physician–patient relationship remains predominantly a gendered encounter: a male physician and a female or (slightly less often) a male patient. Of central concern is whether this gender skew makes a difference in the nature of the interaction between physician and patient and, ultimately, the quality of medical care. Women have claimed that male physicians strive to dominate medical encounters, failing to listen or to take their complaints seriously (Fisher, 1986; Zimmerman, 1987). Both male and female patients express a preference for physicians of the same sex when discussing issues related to sexuality (Miles, 1991). Difficulties in the doctor–patient relationship are exacerbated for gay men and lesbians, who may delay seeking care as a result. Lesbians frequently do not reveal their sexual orientation to physicians, although this information is considered vital for appropriate healthcare, and often when they do physicians are reported to respond negatively (White & Dull, 1997). A recent study by Stevens (1996) analyzed several hundred healthcare encounters between a racially diverse group of lesbians and their physicians. She found that 77% of the encounters with male physicians were characterized as negative, for example, involved withholding information, sexist comments, etc., compared to 44% of the encounters with female physicians. While the evidence as a whole is complex and difficult to interpret, women primary care physicians appear to be better communicators then men, communicating more emotions, more information, eliciting more patient disclosure, facilitating more patient participation and being better and more empathetic listeners (Weisman, 1998). Women tend to provide more preventive measures and spend more time with patients (Lurie, Slater, McGovern, Estrum, Quam, & Margolis, 1993). Women patients' encounters with women physicians may be particularly beneficial (Weisman, 1998). Franks and Clancy (1993) found the patients with female physicians were less likely than those with male physicians to be deficient in breast examinations, Pap tests, and mammograms. Lorber (1997) has considered the question of whether there are gender differences in "humane" practice style and found mixed results, in part because patients also have gendered expectations. Women medical students were found to have stronger attitudes of responsibility toward disadvantaged patients (Crandall, Volk, & Loemker, 1993); however, how these attitudes might translate into actual practice behavior was not investigated.

There is also evidence that medical encounters are different for women patients than for men. Healthcare researchers have found that men and women who appear to have similar health problems are sometimes treated differently. A number of studies indicate that women are likely to receive less than adequate care in cardiology (Ayanian & Epstein, 1991; McLaughlin, Soumerai, & Wilson, 1996), although it is also possible that some cardiac procedures may be unnessarily high among men. Coronary heart disease is the leading cause of death for both men and women; in fact, since the 1950s the incidence has risen for women while declining for men. Still, it is treated less aggressively among women, who are less likely than men to undergo standard tests or bypass surgery when hospitalized for several different cardiac diagnoses (Ayanian & Epstein, 1991; Maynard, 1997) even when adjusting for age and severity of illness (Iezzoni, Ash, Schwartz, & Mackiernan, 1997). Giacomini (1996) found similar gender inequities for heart-related as well as for other high-technology procedures, and also fewer procedures for blacks, Latinos, and Asians compared to whites. Inadequacy in care may also exist for specifically female health problems. Citing data from the National Health Interview, Woods (1996) found that fewer than half of American women had a Pap smear or professional breast exam within the previous year. Black women have the highest rates of death from breast cancer, yet the use of mammography is lower for black women, regardless of their income, than it is for white women (Avery, 1992; Burack et al., 1983; Burnset et al,, 1996).

Most research on the doctor–patient relationship has focused on communication and decision-making with little attention to gender. Both British and U.S. researchers have looked indepth at the content of doctor–patient communication, documenting a pattern wherein women's complaints are selectively attended to in a context of physician dominance. West (1984) found that women physicians tended to be interrupted more by male patients than the reverse in doctor–patient encounters. Phillips and Schneider (1993) have recently studied sexual harassment of female doctors and found that 77% reported having been sexually harassed at least once in their career. In the majority of these incidents (92%) the perpetrator was male. With women's health activism in the 1970s, more public attention was placed on informed consent and an egalitarian relationship between a woman and her doctor (Zimmerman, 1987). Nelson (1981) studied these new, informed consumers in the context of childbirth experiences. She found that there was little difference between the well-informed, doctor shoppers among expectant mothers and their more traditional counterparts. Both groups had similar birth experiences, including similar rates of Cesarean sections, episiotomies, etc., even though the informed women had attempted to negotiate less intervention with doctors ahead of time.

5. GENDER STRATIFICATION IN HEALTHCARE WORK

Healthcare involves the ongoing application of technology and knowledge. This process is an organized effort among multiple practitioners and caregivers, including highly trained professionals as well as family members and friends. It is important that healthcare work refer to the activities of informal as well as formal caregivers. Across the occupational spectrum, the healthcare division of labor is highly gendered (Riska & Wegar, 1993).

Gender differences abound among healthcare practitioners, including differences in power and autonomy, practice style, and behavior. Some of these differences reflect the different clinical roles men and women occupy (Anspach, 1987), and the organizational environments in which they work (Floge & Merrill, 1986). Other differences have been attributed to ways in which the backgrounds and experiences of men and women differ (Lorber, 1997).

5.1. Gender and Caregiving

Our analysis of the gendered healthcare system has revealed how the state interfaces with market and family in the delivery of healthcare services. The growth of the elderly population, the development of life-extending medical technologies, and rising healthcare expenditures have all contributed to a growing demand for family members to provide unpaid caregiving work for chronically ill relatives. Caregivers for disabled persons over the age of 50 are fairly equally divided by gender, 56% women and 44% men, although women devote significantly more time performing caregiving work, an average of 14.2 hours per week compared to 7.5 for men (*Washington Post*, 1994). Despite the seeming gender equity in providing healthcare to older persons, studies show that, overall, women perform as much as 75% of all caregiving work. Care for sick children, especially those with chronic illnesses, is largely the responsibility of women (Glazer, 1990; Hill, 1994; Hill & Zimmerman, 1995; Zimmerman, 1993). This informal, unpaid work is required by patients and is an essential component of healthcare in all countries. Even so, it is often invisible, rarely acknowledged as "real" productive labor in terms of tax relief and other forms of compensatory benefits. Unlike social welfare states, such as Sweden, where caregivers may receive compensation, the United States recognizes informal caregiving as work only under very limited circumstances. Doress-Worters (1996) places the value of time spent caring for elderly parents alone at $7 billion annually. Noting that women spend about one third of their lives caring for dependents, Hooyman and Gonyea (1995) argue that female caregiving embodies (and perpetuates) the most basic cultural ideologies: that families are natural caregiving institutions and that women are available in the home to provide this work. The same cultural ideologies create barriers for men caregivers.

   Increasingly, there are debates over caregiving and its social implications. Caregiving is a form of caring, an act of love and a family responsibility. Yet, it is also a duty, obligation, and a service to the public. Furthermore, when state support is limited, family caregiving can become a form of social coercion that pulls women (more frequently than men) out of paid labor, limiting their life chances and opportunities for social and economic advancement. Glazer (1993) uses the term "work transfer" to describe the process by which paid medical labor is decommodified and then reassigned to women as unpaid, caregiving work. Women are doubly penalized by this work transfer, as it not only decreases the amount of paid work available to women (e.g., as nurses, nursing aides, etc.) in the healthcare sector, but also increases the amount of unpaid medical work they are expected to perform. The stress and burden associated with caregiving work often undermines the health of caregivers, increasing their own need for medical care, while increasing the dependency status of women (Glazer, 1993; Hooyman & Gonyea, 1995). As more healthcare moves outside institutional boundaries, this raises serious questions about gender equity, especially for women as major providers of these services. As discussed earlier, feminist theorists have argued that welfare state researchers too often avoid or gloss over the issue of gender stratification. When healthcare provision comes primarily from the family, "women/wives/mothers" can replace "family" with little loss in accuracy, and the subordinate status of women is reinforced. On the other hand, when the provision of these services comes from the state, which takes on the "social mothering tasks," women can claim more independence and empowerment.

5.2. Occupational Stratification in Healthcare

Gender and racial equality within the healthcare system can be viewed within a broad, structural context, particularly the advancement opportunities and decision-making authority accorded to women and men of color, and in microbehavioral contexts where the focus is on interpersonal communication, cultural sensitivity, and behavioral inclusiveness (Floge & Merrill, 1986). Structurally, the hierarchy of healthcare occupations reflects the gender and racial stratification systems found in the larger society: those with high-level, prestigious healthcareers are primarily white males, with women and racial minorities "overrepresented" in low-status, low-paying health occupations. Women now constitute 75% of all medical workers and 85% of all hospital workers (Doress-Worters, 1996), yet they continue to be concentrated in low-paying, sex-segregated sectors of the healthcare system. In addition, given the dominance of physicians, female healthcare workers rarely have sufficient autonomy or prestige to be considered professionals.

The most notable example is nursing, the single largest group of healthcare workers. Nursing is highly stratified by both gender and race. More than 90% of practicing nurses are women, with white women most likely to be registered nurses or nurse practitioners and racial minorities most likely to be nursing aides, orderlies, or attendants (Hart-Brothers, 1994). Manley (1995) notes that black women make up only 7% of RNs, but nearly 31% of all nursing assistants. Men are increasingly entering the field of nursing: they now comprise nearly 10% of all nursing students. Interestingly, while women in nursing have struggled for decades to professionalize and upgrade the status of their occupation (Manley, 1995), male nurses have been able to gain status in nursing primarily on the basis on their gender. Williams (1992) points out that, unlike the "glass ceiling" that women encounter in traditionally male occupations, men in nursing often experience a "glass escalator:" they are viewed as more authoritative and capable of administrative and managerial work. Bias in this case works to the advantage of men. Underrepresented in a lower status, female occupation, men are privileged with selective promotion into administrative and other upper-level positions.

The historically gendered and frequently contentious division of labor between physicians and nurses (see, e.g., Donovan, 1983) is closely entwined with the struggle of women for greater gender equality. Women's battle for greater autonomy in marriage and as citizens parallels nursing's efforts to achieve greater professional autonomy. There has been a debate as to whether male dominance reflects men's hold on the powerful positions within organizations or whether it is a consequence of generic masculine characteristics. The "doctor–nurse game" (Stein, 1967) was suggested as a gendered "script" for interaction between (male) doctors and (female) nurses whereby nurses conspired to have decision input while maintaining the illusion of physician dominance. The central norm was for nurses to fulfill a passive role, avoiding open disagreement with physicians at all costs. Nurses' recommendations for care, therefore, had to appear to be ideas initiated by physicians. There is disagreement over the degree to which this interaction pattern has persisted into recent years (Pillitteri & Ackerman, 1993; Stein, Watts, & Howell, 1990). Building on the work of Kanter (1977), Floge and Merrill (1986) studied the interaction and dynamics in hospitals associated with situations of gender reversal, where there was a token female physician or a token male nurse. They found that gender was a more powerful predictor of behavior than occupational status. Hierarchical relations perpetuating racial inequality have also characterized the relations between physicians and lower-level healthcare workers, where there are higher proportions of minorities. The paternalism shown toward minorities in some medical institutions has given way to more bureaucratic policies, with increasing financial competition.

A positive, collaborative relationship between physicians and nurses is critical to successful healthcare outcomes (Aiken, 1995; Mitchell, Shannon, Cain, & Hegyvary, 1996). When these relationships are subject to conflicts produced by gender or racial inequities, quality of care can be seriously compromised.

6. THE USE OF HEALTHCARE SERVICES

Medical sociologists have developed several models to explain the use of healthcare services. The health belief model, developed by Irwin Rosenstock in 1966, attempts to explain why people engage in preventive health behaviors or, once diagnosed with an illness, comply with medical regimens. He saw health behaviors as based on one's belief in susceptibility to a serious illness that could be prevented with medical care, and the lack of barriers to care. A more gender-focused analysis of the model would reveal how social norms and inequities operate to shape perceptions of health and access to care. For example, women are typically socialized to be more attentive to bodily symptoms and more compliant to medical authority, and to embrace social roles (e.g., homemaking) that may facilitate access to physicians. The health belief model, however, has been criticized as oppressive to women and people of color because it focuses on the subjective states of individuals and embodies a patriarchal world view that centers on predicting and controlling behavior (Thomas, 1995). A second widely used model focuses specifically on three variables that predict the utilization of medical services: predisposing, enabling, and need variables (Andersen, 1995; Anderson & Newman, 1973). Here again, each predictive variable clearly includes sociodemographic factors, such as gender, social class, and race, as these factors affect health attitudes and beliefs, access to care, and health status. Research has found that the most salient factor in the use of healthcare services is actual or perceived need for medical care services, but health status and access to care also affect utilization (Rowland, Lyons, Salganicoff, & Long, 1994).

Women have long been thought to use health services more frequently than men (Macintyre, Hunt, & Sweeting, 1996; Verbrugge, 1985). They make approximately one third more physician visits, comprise one fourth more hospital discharges, and spend slightly more time in the hospital than men (Friedman, 1994). Of the 10 most frequently performed surgeries, four are procedures limited to women (C-section delivery, total hysterectomy, repair of obstetric laceration, and low forceps delivery with episiotomy), while only one procedure (transurethral prostatectomy) is limited to men (Healthweek, 1991). Recent research indicates that women are more likely than men to have at least one mental disorder (43% vs. 33%), with the excess of female morbidity concentrated in mood and anxiety disorders (Linzer, Spitzer, Kroenke, Williams, Hahn, Brody, & deGruy, 1996). A closer look reveals that women have higher rates of healthcare seeking than

men only in certain age categories, for specific types of problems, and using certain measures. measured by physician consultations (Tables 22-5 and 22-6). Further, recent data
indicate that when childbirth is excluded, men use more hospital services than women
(see Table 22-7). Men also have higher rates of involuntary admission to state, county,
and veteran psychiatric facilities than women, although the rates of admission to other
mental healthcare settings are about the same for both sexes (Hurst, 1998). As indicated
on Tables 22-5 through 22-7, the gender gap in the use of healthcare services tends to
decline with age. However, because women live an average of 7 years longer than men,
women represent a disproportionate share of the elderly population and of those residing
in nursing homes. According to Woods (1996), women age 65 and older are nearly three
times more likely than their male counterparts to reside in nursing and other personal-
care homes. These institutions in 1985 housed 334,000 men and 983,000 women. In
many ways, the problems of the elderly are the problems of women, and both are reflected
in the use of health services.

6.1. Explaining Gender Differences in the Use of Healthcare Services

Biological factors, socially constructed gender norms, acquired risks, and differential
exposure to environmental stress all shape gender patterns of sickness and utilization of
health services. Medicine's traditionally sexist notions about women's bodies, the
medicalization of normal reproductive functions, and the impact of social factors on physical health all have made the role of biology in health status and the use of health services
a highly contested political issue. Still, biological functions, such as pregnancy, childbirth, menopause, and the longer life spans of women, have traditionally contributed to
the greater use of medical care services by women than men. Males have higher rates of
sickness and healthcare use than females from birth to middle childhood; however, as
Sweeting (1995) has shown, gender reversal occurs around puberty or earlier. Using cross-
national data, Sweeting pointed out that an excess in female morbidity and healthcare use
emerges between the ages of 7 and 15, as girls start to experience and report more physical and mental disorders than boys. This gender reversal in patterns of sickness and
healthcare use, Sweet believes, is the result of children incorporating more gendered
responses to illness during adolescence, a diminution of female self-esteem, and different
social expectations and stresses for males and females. This suggests that by the age of

TABLE 22.5. Percentage of Acute Conditions Medically Attended in the United States,
1995 by Sex, Age, and Type of Condition

Type of Acute Condition	Male		Female	
	18 to 44 Years Old	45 Years and Over	18 to 44 Years Old	45 Years and Over
All acute conditions	59.5	72.0	63.7	71.3
Infective/parasitic diseases	54.9	57.5	57.8	65.8
Respiratory conditions	38.9	53.9	45.0	51.4
Digestive system conditions	70.9	81.6	59.5	87.2
Acute musculoskeletal conditions	95.0	86.3	79.2	88.9
Injuries	91.4	91.7	94.9	88.3

Vital and Health Statistics, Current Estimates from the National Health Interview Survey, 1994. Series 10, No. 199. U.S. Department
of Health and Human Services. October 1998, p. 21.

TABLE 22-6. **Average Number of Physician Contacts per Person per Year: United States, 1995**

Characteristic	All Places	Telephone	Office	Hospital	Other
All persons	5.9	0.8	3.3	0.7	1.1
Males					
Under 18 years	4.4	0.6	2.6	0.6	0.6
18 to 24 years old	3.3	0.4	1.7	0.5	0.7
45 to 64 years old	6.0	0.7	3.2	0.8	1.2
65 years and over	10.4	1.0	5.9	1.1	2.3
All ages	4.9	0.6	2.7	0.7	0.9
Females					
Under 18 years	4.2	0.6	2.4	0.5	0.6
18 to 44 years old	6.4	1.0	3.6	0.7	1.0
45 to 64 years old	8.1	1.0	4.5	1.0	1.4
65 years and over	11.6	1.2	6.0	1.2	3.1
All ages	6.9	0.9	3.8	0.8	1.3

Vital and Health Statistics, Current Estimates from the National Health Interview Survey, 1995. Series 10, No. 199. U.S. Department of Health and Human Services. October 1998, p. 109.

puberty, social factors may start to play as important a role in perceptions of health as biology.

Gendered activities and patriarchal norms and values clearly shape patterns of healthcare utilization, as they help produce specific acquired health risks for men and women. Men acquire more health risks from factors such as substance abuse and hazardous work and leisure activities, while the health of women is often impaired by socially prescribed gender roles and norms (Waldron, 1995). Being a full-time homemaker, for example, has consistently been linked to high rates of physical and mental illness and more doctor visits (Avis & McKinlay, 1990; Verbrugge, 1985). While some have argued that the homemaking role may simply be more compatible with seeking healthcare (Marcus & Siegel, 1982), it is also true that homemakers often experience more distress, isolation,

TABLE 22-7. **Number of Short-Stay Hospital Days During the Year Preceding Interview per Living, for All Causes Excluding Deliveries, United States, 1995**

Characteristic	All Statuses	Number of Episodes		
		1	2	3 or more
Male				
All ages	8.2	5.3	13.8	26.2
Under 18 years	7.3	5.8	9.0	42.3
18 to 44 years	6.0	4.0	12.5	23.3
45 to 64 years	8.0	5.1	11.7	25.2
65 years and over	10.6	6.6	17.1	25.8
Female				
All ages	7.3	4.7	13.0	25.4
Under 18 years	5.8	4.4	10.9	24.7*
18 to 44 years	5.2	3.6	8.4	23.1
45 to 64 years	7.8	4.5	13.5	25.8
65 years and over	9.5	6.1	16.4	26.7

*This figure does not meet standard of reliability or precision.
Vital and Health Statistics, Current Estimates from the National Health Interview Survey, 1995. Series 10, No. 199. U.S. Department of Health and Human Services. October 1998, p. 117.

and devaluation than employed women, and may be overwhelmed by the demands of nurturing and caring for others. Employment, however, does not equalize the health risks of men and women, as employed married women still perform most of the domestic work and frequently hold sex-segregated jobs with low pay and little autonomy, prestige, and career mobility. Gender norms in a state of transition lead women to experience strains as they renegotiate family work and move into new labor market roles. Charlotte Muller's (1986) study of employed men and women found that, overall, occupational quality did not affect the use of medical services, and other gender-related factors did. Women had more doctor visits than men, but women in occupations that were sex typed for men—perhaps because they were under more scrutiny and thus more stress—experienced even higher rates of utilization of medical services. Stress or role overload may also account for her finding that single parents had higher rates of hospitalization than did men and women who were married and/or childless.

Domestic violence, undergirded by norms supporting male dominance and aggression, also leads to a higher utilization of medical services by women (Candib, 1995). Domestic violence is now recognized as one of the most serious public health issues in America, with women of all ages more likely than men to be victimized. More than 4 million women are assaulted by domestic partners each year, resulting in literally thousands of physician visits and hospital days each year (Gerbert, Johnston, Caspters, Bleecker, Woods, & Rosenbaum, 1996). The American Medical Association's Council on Ethical and Judicial Affairs (1992) reported that injury to women from battering and rape (most often committed by a current or former male partner) accounted for as much as 35% of all emergency room visits. Moreover, the rate of physical battering of women increases with pregnancy, thus jeopardizing the health of both the women and that of her unborn child. Medical professionals, however, rarely identify domestic violence as the cause of problems, even when the patient has repeatedly sought medical care for similar injuries (American Medical Association Council on Ethical and Judicial Affairs, 1992; AMA Council on Scientific Affairs, 1992). Thus, battered women, many of whom fear retaliation from their partners if they report their abuse, view physicians as disinterested or unsympathetic toward their needs (Gerbert et al., 1996).

Social factors, especially those linked with gender inequality, contribute significantly to the excess in sickness and use of healthcare services by women. Still, women may not receive healthcare adequate to meet their needs. As noted earlier, preventive healthcare, such as Pap smears and breast exams, are often neglected, and potentially life-threatening illnesses, such as heart disease, may be treated less aggressively in women (Young & Kahana, 1993). Some studies have found that having a regular source of medical care is the most important factor associated with receiving preventive health services (Bindman, Grumbach, Osmond, Vranizan, & Stewart, 1996; Burns et al., 1996). For women, finding a healthcare setting that is both accessible and equipped to offer a full range of services can be difficult. Bartman (1996) found that the majority of women over the age of 44 prefer a family or general practitioner to an obstetrician–gynecologist. Those who did not go to obstetrician–gynecologists received less screening for cervical and breast cancer. Similarly, a study of black women between the ages of 18 and 44 living in Chicago found that they often had to choose between going to a more geographically accessible, office-based physician who offered more limited care, or traveling to a less accessible clinic to receive more comprehensive care and better family planning services (Kelley, Perloff, Morris, & Liu, 1992).

The lack of adequate healthcare and poverty also diminish the quality of healthcare available to women. The lack of adequate insurance significantly diminishes the likelihood of consulting a physician (Hafner-Eaton, 1993). Women with health insurance also experience more gaps in their coverage than do men. As noted in the concept of the feminization of poverty, women are overrepresented among the nearly 39 million Americans who are poor (Beeghley, 1996). Older women, single mothers, and women of color are especially likely to be overrepresented among the poor and near-poor: women represent 58% of the aged, but 71% of the aged poor, while African-American women constitute 5% of the elderly, but 16% of the elderly poor (Doress-Worters, 1996). Studies have consistently found those who are poor have the highest rates of sickness and the greatest need for healthcare services (Abraham, 1993; Dutton, 1986; Krieger & Fee, 1996; Navarro, 1991; Riessman, 1990).

7. CONCEPT OF WOMEN'S HEALTH

We have argued that medicine is an institution of social control, regulating gender as well as other social relations. Medical knowledge both reflects and reproduces gendered cultural and social structures, and thus serves as a primary social control mechanism. Medical research and the clinical treatments and advice given to patients form this body of knowledge, which, although constructed largely from a male standpoint, is applied to both men and women. Women's health and health-related experiences, for the most part, have been understood—whether correctly or not—through this male perspective. The women's health movement was responsible for articulating a critique of these circumstances and stimulating social change to remedy them.

7.1. Women's Health: Social Movement to Market Segment

The concept of women's health as a distinct discipline or subdiscipline within medicine, with the potential to define a unique segment of the healthcare delivery system, has developed recently, roughly since the mid-1980s. The roots of this concept can be traced to the women's health movement of the late 1960s and 1970s, when the gendered nature of medical knowledge, the doctor–patient relationship, and the entire healthcare system came under critical scrutiny in the broader context of political protest and civil rights activism for minorities and women (Ruzek, 1978; Zimmerman, 1987). Weisman (1998) locates apsects of the women's health movement even earlier in the 19th and early 20th centuries. Women's control of their own health and healthcare was the central objective. The movement called into question the increasing medicalization of women's lives; the narrow, treatment-oriented focus of medical care, relying on intervention and technology rather than prevention and self-care; and the hierarchical inequality of medical power relations, including the doctor–patient relationship. The women's health movement was pivotal in drawing attention to what we now refer to as the gendering of healthcare. It created a coherent, consumer-driven critique with specific issues that have since been forged into a new agenda for research, for conceptualizing medical knowledge, and for organizing healthcare services (Rodwin, 1994). In many ways, the original women's critique of mainstream healthcare has been co-opted by the healthcare marketplace. While the social movement politics have been discarded, there is spreading recognition that many health problems of women are unique relative to those of men, and programs are being implemented to increase women's health research and to reform the medical curriculum (Zimmerman, 1996). Out of this critique has come a framework for how women's distinctive healthcare needs can be better met.

Women's health as a concept was adopted by mainstream healthcare organizations in the United States in the 1980s, just at the time competition and market forces were becoming prominent. Hospitals were beginning to more aggressively market their services in an attempt to secure market share, and to begin reclaiming the area of outpatient and ambulatory services that they gave up in the early part of this century. A healthcare consultant, based in Chicago, developed the concept of hospital-based Women's Health Centers in the mid-1980s (Thomas, forthcoming). While presented as improved quality of care for women, the centers frequently provided little more than a repackaging of existing obstetrics–gynecology and diagnostic screening services. The concept of arranging services in this way was sold to hospital boards using the idea that women make healthcare decisions for the entire family. If women preferred a specific hospital or clinic, it was thought that the entire family would become clients. According to estimates, in 1993 some 3,600 women's health centers were in operation, the majority sponsored by hospitals (Weisman, 1998).

The initial Women's Health Center model incorporated movement principles, such as more decision-making control for the patient, more quality time in the doctor–patient relationship, and women physicians. Many centers, however, were unable to move beyond the library and health education programs they featured, and never provided actual medical services. Those that did had to secure established medical practices whose partnership with the hospital did not threaten previously established medical staff relations. The very medical practices that were needed to make the Women's Health Centers successful—those that were financially stable with a sizable patient load—were the most likely to threaten existing physicians and generate conflict. Inevitably, for financial and internal political reasons, the innovative aspects of Women's Centers in many hospitals were phased out, leaving standard services, such as maternity and gynecology, renamed as women's healthcare. By the mid-1990s, the promise of a fundamental shift in the philosophy and organization of private sector healthcare for women had largely disappeared.

7.2. Women's Health as a National Initiative

While the private side of the healthcare system in the United States lost currency in the change-oriented agenda of the women's health movement, the public sector did not. The 1990s saw the longstanding criticisms of the United States' biomedical research establishment and its history of gender bias result in significant social change. After years of pressure, culminating in several task forces and their reports, in 1990 the National Institutes of Health established an Office of Research on Women's Health, and in 1991 a federal Office of Women's Health was established within the U.S. Department of Health and Human Services (Narrigan, Jones, Worcester, & Grad, 1997). In addition, in 1991 the NIH launched a Women's Health Initiative to study three diseases that are leading causes of death in women: cancer, cardiovascular disease, and osteoporosis. During this same period, national medical organizations also mounted significant efforts to reform curricula and develop medical school programs to enhance gender equity (Zimmerman, 1996).

It is too early to evaluate the impact of these developments. Nonetheless, they represent a recognition by the U.S. government of the gender bias and inequities in medical research and practice (Auerbach & Figert, 1995). It also is clear that they represent a federal mandate to address these problems. Women's health as a concept has begun to be integrated into standard practices of medical research and medical education, a process that will result in further changes and eventually alter the gendered nature of healthcare.

8. HEALTHCARE REFORM

Providing health services within the framework of the capitalist economy of the United States has led to escalating medical expenditures and an erosion of healthcare services to all but the most affluent. Dissatisfaction with the inefficiency, inequity, and cost of healthcare paved the way for healthcare reform, beginning with the gradual implementation of cost-cutting strategies in the 1980s. Prior to 1983, hospitals and physicians were reimbursed by insurance for the "reasonable and customary" costs of medical treatment. Owing to escalating costs, the government's Medicare program began to pay hospitals a preestablished sum based on the patient's diagnosis-related group, or DRG. These new arrangements placed more financial risk on healthcare providers, with the goal of eliminating unnecessary treatment and encouraging efficient, cost-effective care. By the late 1990s, a patchwork of regulations had evolved to regulate the excesses of the marketplace, and there was a pronounced social shift toward the notion of individuals being responsible for avoiding sickness through healthy lifestyles. In examining these trends, Clancy and Massion (1992) concluded that the pronounced capitalist and entrepreneurial activity in healthcare in the United States had resulted in significant gender inequities in healthcare quality to the particular disadvantage of women.

8.1. The Gender Implications of Managed Care

Managing healthcare resources efficiently in relation to the processes and outcomes of care has become a prominent idea in American healthcare policy and the focus of health reform. Notoriously difficult to define, managed care refers to a variety of organizational and financial arrangements designed to eliminate unnecessary and inappropriate healthcare, reduce costs, and increase efficiency (Congressional Budget Office, 1992). There is a broad array of managed care initiatives, such as DRG-based reimbursement, mandated second opinions, medical practice guidelines, and health maintenance organizations (HMOs), which themselves vary widely from tightly structured group and staff models to looser, independent practice associations (IPAs). By the end of the 1990s, managed care covered a large segment of Americans, both privately and publicly insured and including Medicare and Medicaid. Women were approximately 53% of all enrollees in 1993 (Weisman, 1998). Publicly funded managed care particularly affected women, since they are disproportionately represented among the poor, disabled, and elderly. In 1997, Medicaid in nearly every state delivered services on a managed care model. Private insurance for middle- and lower-level employees also relies heavily on managed care plans. Most women in the labor market are employed at these levels.

Managed care has significantly different implications for men and women

(Zimmerman & Hill, 1999). Four features of managed care provide insights into how men and women are affected differently. First, managed care, compared to other care arrangements, provides more prevention and early intervention services (Miller & Luft, 1994). A 1993 survey found that women in HMOs received more screening tests for early detection of disease, such as clinical breast examination, mammography, pelvic examinations, and Pap tests, than insured women not in HMOs (Alan Guttmacher Institute, 1994; Louis Harris & Associates, 1993; Makuc, Freid, & Parsons, 1994). Further, HMOs are substantially more likely to cover all types of reversible contraception than other forms of health insurance (Alan Guttmacher Institute, 1994). For example, 81% of HMOs covered diaphragm fittings whereas only 21% of conventional plans did so. The increased access provided to women, combined with the long-established finding that women are more likely to engage in preventive health practices than are men (Miles, 1991), seem to suggest that managed care will enhance preventive care among women. The effects for men are less clear. While research suggests that men are less oriented to prevention, much also depends on the extent to which HMOs and other managed care organizations emphasize screening and encourage prevention practices appropriate for men.

A second feature that may result in differential effects for men and women is that managed care commonly relies on primary care. Primary care typically is more complicated for women than for men because women often have multiple physicians for their regular source of care while men require only one. Women often receive gynecological care from obstetrician–gynecologists and general care from internists or family practitioners (Bartman, 1996). As of 1994, 70% of HMO plans in the United States allowed women to self-refer to an obstetrician–gynecologist other than their primary care provider, but half of these plans limited the visits to one per year (Bernstein, 1996). Managed care organizations that require women to choose a single primary care provider may, in so doing, be putting women at increased risk of inadequate prevention and monitoring for key women's health problems (Johns, 1994). Multiple providers are not consistent with the efficiency concepts of managed care, so over the long term, women's healthcare may need to be reorganized to be efficient.

The third issue in managed care concerns restrictions on services. Available data show that HMO members have lower hospital admission rates, shorter hospital length of stay, and less use of expensive procedures and tests (Bernstein, 1996). This becomes a gender issue because women are disproportionally more likely to use these services owing to childbirth and age. There is particular concern over whether managed care can successfully manage the disabled and chronically ill, groups also disproportionally composed of women. Mental health services and their coverage under managed care, especially depression, may also be a special problem for women.

The fourth feature with implications for gender is the managed care practice of restricting access to physicians and other providers. Consumer choice has become a central issue in American healthcare reform. Moreover, being able to maintain continuity of care with the same physician, or physicians who work closely with each other, promotes positive health outcomes. Being able to choose one's physician or hospital is a particularly prominent concern in managed care plans where choice can be severely limited. Because more women than men receive health coverage in heavily managed plans, having access to the providers one chooses is another gendered issue that disadvantages women. The potential problems related to women's lack of choice are compounded because women need and use healthcare services more frequently than men, and because, as has been discussed, their routine healthcare is divided among multiple providers. Individuals who have a usual source of care also have better healthcare access and a higher likelihood of receiving needed medical services. Between 1987 and 1992, the estimated proportion of adult Americans with no usual source of care rose from 17% to 21% (Moy, Bartman, Clancy, & Cornelius, 1998). This raises additional concerns about the effects of managed care, which significantly expanded during the same time period.

8.2. Individual Responsibility for Sickness and Health

A second force for change in the healthcare system is the focus on personal responsibility for health. Social theorists have analyzed this trend as part of a broader cultural shift from modernism to postmodernism. In healthcare, this transition signifies a move away from the positivism of biomedicine to a more eclectic model of health and illness with greater awareness of the body and personal responsibility for it (see Hall, 1998). Prior to the modern era, disease was feared, but accepted as outside humans' ability to govern or control. During the rise of medicine in the modern era, disease was seen as part of the human struggle against nature, a challenge to be conquered. Science was viewed optimistically as the ultimate weapon in the war against disease. In the last half of the twentieth century, however, social awareness about the limits of scientific medicine and skepticism of the biomedical model of disease, along with the political–economic difficulties of distributing healthcare resources, encouraged yet another shift in cultural thinking about disease. As the role of individuals in the etiology of diseases began to reemerge, people began to be seen as contributing to—even responsible for—their own illness (Hall, 1998). Disease, within this framework, could more easily be viewed as a person's own fault. Lifestyles and behavioral risk factors in chronic diseases received increased attention, with government sponsorship in the 1970s and 1980s emphasizing the effects of diet, exercise, smoking, and stress on heart disease and cancer. The implications of this approach could be viewed alternatively as either heightened accountability or "blaming the victim."

The gender question in this shift to greater personal responsibility is whether its consequences differ for men and women. Miles (1991) argued that women are more easily placed in the sick role than men. As personal accountability increases, this suggests that women also will be more likely to be blamed for illness. The theory of the sick role (Parsons, 1951) holds that sick individuals are exempted from normal social roles and from responsibility for their illness, provided they demonstrate the desire to get well. For Parsons, the sick role allows society to differentiate the "sick" from the "bad," a distinction that is blurred when individuals are seen as causing their own illnesses by either engaging in risky behaviors or failing to engage in healthy ones. Holding individuals responsible for illness contradicts the Parsonian sick role, and opens the possibility that those who are blamed will be subjected to further negative sanctions. Parsons did not offer a gendered perspective on the sick role; however, if the sick role is more readily occupied by women, then they might, in turn, be more readily blamed for their illnesses than men. This is particularly ominous if punishment follows blame—for example, if health benefits were disproportionately denied to women because they are perceived to have contributed to or "caused" their own illness (for additional discussion, see Doyal, 1995; Miles, 1991).

Taking personal responsibility for health can also be viewed from the standpoint of participating in self-care. Men have been found to be more stoic in responding to symptoms and therefore less likely to take corrective actions, while women are thought to pay greater attention to their bodies and to monitoring health signs and symptoms (Mechanic, 1968). To the extent that personal responsibility encourages more self-care, these gender differences may become more significant. Self-care is consistent with the principles of the women's health movement in that it represents individuals taking more control over their bodies and lives. Women, therefore, may be prone to adopt self-care while men would do so less, depending instead on women. Increasing self-care, on the other hand, focuses attention on health as a product of what men and women do as individuals, rather than on what their environment and society does to them sometimes without their knowledge, that is, unsafe conditions and toxic exposures through food, water, air, job and travel safety, etc. Self-care can be a way to deflect attention away from the deficiencies of the healthcare system, including restricted access to care, and can lead to inadequate supervision of both men's and women's healthcare needs.

9. CONCLUSIONS: QUALITY OF HEALTHCARE

Analyzing healthcare as a gendered institution has revealed significant differences in healthcare systems on the basis of gender, and has suggested even more complex differentiation when race, social class, and sexual orientation are taken into account. We have argued that gender is a fundamental way of organizing social life, deeply embedded within the social fabric of society. Consistent with this assertion, we have emphasized gender as a characteristic of organizations rather than solely an individual variable. Healthcare is gendered because men and women occupy different positions within the system, both as patients and providers. Moreover, these differences are such that, often, women are disadvantaged. Women, compared to men, have more illnesses and use more healthcare services, are more likely to have their behaviors medicalized, and are less likely to receive aggressive medical intervention for life-threatening illnesses. As workers, they are more likely to be concentrated in the lower echelons of the healthcare system or, in the case of unpaid workers, to have their labor ignored altogether. We have analyzed gender within the context of macro-level forces such as patriarchy, capitalism, industrialization, and the doctrine of separate spheres for men and women. These forces fostered the ability of white male physicians to achieve medical dominance and construct gender norms that stereotype women and marginalize their roles in medicine. The result has been a gendering of medical knowledge, access to medical education, the organization of healthcare work, and the doctor–patient relationship. Despite some notable gains by women since the 1970s, recent healthcare developments, masked as healthcare reforms, have often served to strengthen and perpetuate the gendering of healthcare. The relegation of unpaid caregiving work to women is a prime example.

Ultimately, healthcare quality is the central issue for both women and men. While the defects and excesses of American healthcare affect both men and women, the consequences are not the same. Women and men occupy different places in social life, and are regarded differently in cultural attitudes and values. Furthermore, in the evolution of healthcare, male dominance has positioned women as "the other," adding to their vulnerability in this type of gendered healthcare system. We have argued that the quality of healthcare available to women has been and still is undermined by patriarchy and capitalism. Women have been primarily patients and (until recently) rarely physicians. The perspective of white men has been the basis for medical education which, until the last few years, has been rife with erroneous and stereotypically gendered information. More recently, this bias has served as a rallying point for consumers and groups within the women's health movement. The quality of healthcare given to women has been shaped by the gendering of the doctor–patient relationship, which has placed women in a subordinate and dependent position. During and following industrialization, women became the primary clientele for physicians and the unwitting victims of allopathic medicine's efforts to prove its efficacy; yet, in the modern era, women are often excluded from systematic medical research.

The medicalization of common female experiences, such as pregnancy, childbirth, and menopause, as well as the more recent emphasis on cosmetic surgery, eating disorders, and fitness, has extended medical control over the lives of women. Yet, while women are often overtreated for problems that are only questionably medical in nature, there is growing evidence that they may be undertreated for serious health problems, such as coronary heart disease. Narrow views of gender roles, such as the well-documented tendency in medicine to think of women's health problems first in relation to the reproductive system, may in part explain these inequities in medical practice. Stereotypes have been cited by minorities, as well as by gays and lesbians, as discouraging their use of medical care with the potential of compromising their health. Limited access to healthcare is also a quality of care issue of special concern to women. Health insurance historically been linked to employment at the same time socially prescribed roles for women precluded employment. Thus, women have been more likely than men to be insured as dependent spouses and, with the recent entry of women into the labor market, to hold positions that lack health insurance. As we have shown, women are overrepresented among the poor and among those likely to receive their healthcare in the public sector of the healthcare system.

Despite continuing gender inequities in healthcare, our analysis has revealed significant challenge to the patriarchal nature of medicine. Women have historically fought for the right to acquire a medical education and to practice medicine, a cause that now has support from both men and women within the medical leadership. In the past 25 years, women have made notable gains in terms of entry into medical schools, challenging the sexism of the medical curricula and sexual harassment in medical schools. The evidence so far suggests that, as physicians, women add desirable and complementary attributes to the doctor–patient relationship. Perhaps most significantly, the women's health movement has provided a patient-oriented critique of healthcare, enhancing the gender consciousness of many women, creating a sense of consumer choice, and empowering both men and women to seek a greater voice in healthcare decisions. If the goal for the future is continued improvement of healthcare, then consumers must continue to be vigilant lest new health reforms repeat and reinforce the inequities of the past.

9.1. Future Research

There are important questions and issues for researchers to explore in each section of this chapter. After years of domination, the biomedical model's hold over medical thinking appears to be weakening and the positivistic notion of medicine's scientific objectivity can now be more easily challenged. There are vast, new opportunities to understand healthcare as a social system where attitudes, values, and ideologies play a role. Gender study in relation to health and medicine has been particularly slow to develop; yet, looking at gender as an organizational phenomenon holds particular promise as a new way to understand healthcare as well as to analyze processes of social inequality.

Three areas are especially important for future research. First, we need to better understand and untangle the way culturally based stereotypes about gender confound medical diagnoses and treatment decisions. This should help to establish the valid healthcare needs of men and women and to clarify issues of overtreatment and undertreatment. Next, more research is needed on the organization of healthcare—the policy arrangements set by insurance schemes (public as well as private) and the ways professional and institutional providers organize services around these policies—in terms of the differential social and health impacts for men and women. This includes studying informal caregiving in relation to broader institutional policies and practices, keeping in mind that both public and private organizational arrangements can structure the lives of men and women differently by influencing the need for family caregiving. Finally, it is essential for researchers to devote greater attention to the social conditions under which variation occurs in gendered healthcare. Male and female are master categories that, despite their analytic significance, dissolve into a multiplicity of subpatterns when additional factors are considered. While the feminist critique of the healthcare system has often focused too narrowly on middle-class white women, studies of racial inequities in healthcare and health status have tended to overlook the issues of gender entirely (see, for example, Williams, 1998). Specifically, future research should systematically consider class and race differences to more fully explore the complexities of healthcare as a gendered system.

REFERENCES

Abraham, L. K. (1993). *Mama might be better off dead: The failure of health care in urban America*. Chicago: University of Chicago Press.
Acker, J. (1990). Hierarchies, jobs, bodies: A theory of gendered organizations. *Gender & Society 4*, 139–158.
Aiken, L. (1995). Transformation of the nursing workforce. *Nursing Outlook, 43*, 201–209.
Alan Guttmacher Institute. (1994). *Uneven and unequal: Insurance coverage and reproductive health services*. New York: Alan Guttmacher Institute.
Allen, J., and Pifer, A. (Eds.) (1993). *Women on the front lines meeting the challenge of an aging America*. Washington, D.C.: Urban Institute Press.
American Medical Association Council on Ethical and Judicial Affairs. (1992). Physicians and domestic violence: Ethical considerations. *Journal of the American Medical Association, 267*, 3190–3193.
American Medical Association Council on Scientific Affairs. (1992). Violence against women: Relevance for medical practitioners. *Journal of the American Medical Association, 267*, 3184–3189.
Andersen, R. M. (1995). Revisiting the behavioral model and access to medical care: Does it matter? *Journal of Health and Social Behavior, 36*, 1–10.
Andersen, R. M., & Newman, J. F. (1973). Societal and individual determinants of medical care utilization in the United States. *Milbank Memorial Fund Quarterly, 51*, 95–124.
Anderson, G. F. (1997). In search of value: An international comparison of cost, access, and outcomes. *Health Affairs, 16*, 163–171.
Anspach, R. R. (1987). Prognostic conflict in life-and-death decisions: The organization as an ecology of knowledge. *Journal of Health and Social Behavior, 28*, 215–231.
Ashley, J. A. (1976). *Hospitals, paternalism, and the role of the nurse*. New York: Teachers College Press.
Auerbach, J. D., & Figert, A. E. (1995). Women's health research: Public policy and sociology. *Journal of Health and Social Behavior, (Suppl.)*, 115–131.
Avery, B. Y. (1992) The health status of black women. In R. L. Braithwaite & S. E. Taylor (Eds.), *Health issues in the black community* (pp. 35–51). San Francisco: Jossey-Bass.
Avis, N. E., & McKinlay, S. M. (1990). Health care utilization among mid-aged women. *Annals New York Academy of Sciences, 592*, 228–238.

Ayanian, J. Z., & Epstein, A. M. (1991). Differences in the use of procedures between women and men hospitalized for coronary artery disease. *New England Journal of Medicine, 325,* 221–225.

Baldwin, D. C., Daugherty, S. R., & Rowley, B. D. (1994). Racial and ethnic discrimination during residency: Results of a national survey. *Academic Medicine, 69,* S19–S21.

Barker-Benfield, G. J. (1976). *The horrors of the half-known life: Male attitudes toward women and sexuality in nineteenth century America.* New York: Harper & Row.

Bartman, B. A. (1996) Women's access to appropriate providers within managed care: Implications for the quality of primary care. *Women's Health Issues, 6,* 45–50.

Bartman, B. A., & Weiss, K. B. (1993). Women's primary care in the United States: A study of practice variation among physician specialties. *Journal of Women's Health, 2,* 261–268.

Barzansky, B., Jonas, H. S., & Etzel, S. I. (1997). Educational programs in U.S. medical schools, 1996–1997. *Journal of the American Medical Association, 278,* 744–784.

Barzansky, B., Jonas, H. S., & Etzel, S. I. (1998). Educational programs in U.S. medical schools, 1997–1998. *Journal of the American Medical Association, 280,* 803–808.

Beeghley, L. (1996) *The structure of social stratification in the United States* (2nd ed.). Needham Heights, MA: Allyn & Bacon.

Bell, S. E. (1987). Changing ideas: The medicalization of menopause. *Social Science and Medicine, 24,* 535–542.

Bernstein, A. B. (1996). Women's health in HMOs: What we know and what we need to find out. *Women's Health Issues, 6,* 51–59.

Bickel, J. (1995). Scenarios for success—enhancing women physicians' professional advancement. *Western Journal of Medicine, 65,* 165–169.

Bickel, J., & Ruffin, A. (1995). Gender-associated differences in matriculating and graduating medical students. *Academic Medicine, 70,* 552–559.

Bindman, A. B., Grumbach, K., Osmond, D., Vranizan, K., & Stewart, A. L. (1996). Primary care and receipt of preventive services. *Journal of General Internal Medicine, 11,* 269–276.

Boston Women's Health Book Collective. (1992). *The new our bodies, ourselves.* New York: Simon & Schuster.

Braveman, P. (1988). Women without health insurance: Links between access, poverty, ethnicity and health. *Western Journal of Medicine,* December: 1.

Burack, R. C., Gimotty, P. A., Stengle, W., Warbasse, L., & Moncrease, A. (1993). Patterns of use of mammography among inner-city Detroit women: Contrasts between a health department, HMO, and private hospital. *Medical Care, 31,* 322–334.

Burns, R. B., McCarthy, E. P., Freund, K. M., Marwill, S. L., Shwartz, M., Ash, A., & Moskowitz, M. A. (1996). Black women receive less mammography even with similar use of primary care. *Annuals of Internal Medicine, 125,* 173–182.

Burstin, H. R., Lipsitz, S. R., & Brennan, T. A. (1992). Socioeconomic status and risk for substandard medical care. *Journal of the American Medical Association, 268,* 2383–2387.

Butter, I. (1985). *Sex and status: Hierarchies in the health workforce.* Washington D.C.: American Public Health Association.

Campbell, M. (1974). *Why would a girl go into medicine?* Old Westbury, NY: Feminist Press.

Campbell-Heider, N., & Pollock, D. (1987). Barriers to physician–nurse collegiality: An anthropological perspective. *Social Science and Medicine, 25,* 421–425.

Candib, L. M. (1995). *Medicine and the family: A feminist perspective.* New York: Basic Books.

Cassady, J. H. (1991). *Medicine in America: A short history.* Baltimore: The John Hopkins University Press.

Clancy, C. M., & Massion, C. T. (1992). American women's health care: A patchwork quilt with gaps. *Journal of the American Medical Association, 268,* 1918–1920.

Congressional Budget Office. (1992) The effects of managed care on use and costs of services [staff memorandum]. Washington, D.C.: U.S. Congress, June.

Conrad, P. (1992). Medicalization and social control. *Annual Review of Sociology, 18,* 137–162.

Cooper, P. F., & Schone, B. S. (1997). More offers, fewer takers for employment-based health insurance: 1987 and 1996. *Health Affairs, 16,* 142–149.

Cooper, R., Henderson, T., & Dietrich, C. (1998). Roles of nonphysician clinicians as autonomous providers of patient care. *Journal of the American Medical Association, 280,* 795–802.

Cooper, R., Laud, P., & Dietrich, C. (1998). Current and projected workforce of nonphysician clinician. *Journal of the American Medical Association, 280,* 788–794.

Cott, N. F. (1977). *The bonds of womanhood: "Women's sphere in New England, 1789–1835.* New Haven, CT: Yale University Press.

Coulehan, J. (1985). Chiropractic and the clinical art. *Social Science and Medicine, 21,* 383–390.

Crandall, S. J., Volk, R. J., & Loemker, V. (1993). Medical students' attitudes toward providing care for the underserved: Are we training socially responsible physician? *Journal of the American Medical Association,* *269,* 2519–2523.

DeLew, N., Greenberg, G., & Kinchen, K. (1992) A layman's guide to the US health care system. *Health Care* *Financing Review, 14,* 151–169.

Donovan, P. (1983). Medical societies vs. nurse practitioners. *Family Planning Perspectives, 15,* 166–171.

Doress-Worters, P. B. (1996). Choices and chances: How a profit-driven health care system discriminates against middle-aged women. In M. B. Lykes, A. Banuazizi, R. Liem, & M. Morris (Eds.), *Myths about the powerless* (pp. 201–218). Philadelphia, PA: Temple University Press.

Doyal, L. (1995). *What makes women sick: Gender and the political economy of health.* New Brunswick, NJ: Rutgers University Press.

Doyal, L. (1996) The politics of women's health: Setting a global agenda. *International Journal of Health Ser-* *vices, 26,* 47–65.

Dutton, D. B. (1986). Social class, health and illness. In L. H. Aiken & D. Mechanic (Eds.), *Applications of social* *science to medical and health policy* (pp. 31–62). New Brunswick, NJ: Rutgers University Press.

Ehrenreich, B., & English, D. (1973). *Witches, midwives, and nurses: A history of women healers.* Old Westbury, CT: Feminist Press.

Ehrenreich, B., & English, D. (1978). *For her own good.* Garden City, NY: Doubleday-Anchor Books.

Esping-Anderson, G. (1990). *The three worlds of capitalism.* Princeton, NJ: Princeton University Press.

Evans, R. G (1997). Going for the gold: The redistributive agenda behind market-based health care reform. *Jour-* *nal of Health Politics, Policy and Law, 22,* 427–465.

Fauser, J. J. (1992) Accreditation of allied health education: Assessing for educational effectiveness. *Journal of the* *American Medical Association, 268,* 1123–1126.

Figert, A. (1996). *Women and the ownership of PMS: The structuring of a psychiatric disorder.* New York: Aldine de Gruyter.

Fisher, S. (1986). *In the patient's best interest: Women and the politics of medical decisions.* New Brunswick, NJ: Rutgers University Press.

Floge, L., & Merrill, D. (1986). Tokenism reconsidered: Male nurses and female physicians in a hospital setting. *Social Forces, 64,* 925–946.

Foucault, M. (1973). *The birth of the clinic: An archaeology of medical perception* (trans. A. M. Sheridan Smith). London: Tavistock.

Foucault, M. (1975). *Discipline and punish.* New York: Vintage Books.

Franks, P., & Clancy, C. M. (1993). Physician gender bias in clinical decisionmaking: Screening for cancer in primary care. *Medical Care, 31,* 213–218.

Freidson, E. (1988). *Profession of medicine: A study of the sociology of applied knowledge* (2nd ed.). Chicago: University of Chicago Press.

Friedman, E. (Ed.) (1994) *An unfinished revolution: Women and health care in America.* New York: United Hospital Fund of New York.

Fronstin, P. (1997). Employee Benefit Research Institute brief no. 185: Trends in health insurance coverage. *Medi-* *cal Benefits, 14,* 2.

Fronstin, P., & Snider, S. C. (1996/97). An examination of the decline in employment-based health insurance be- tween 1988 and 1993. *Inquiry, 33,* 317–325.

Gerbert, B., Johnston, K., Caspters, N., Bleecker, T., Woods, A., & Rosenbaum, A. (1996). Experiences of battered women in health care settings: A qualitative study. *Women & Health, 24,* 1–17.

Giacomini, M. K. (1996). Gender and ethnic differences in hospital-based procedure utilization in California. *Ar-* *chives of Internal Medicine, 156,* 1217–1224.

Glazer, N. Y. (1990). The home as workshop: Women as amateur nurses and medical care providers. *Gender &* *Society, 4,* 479–499.

Glazer, N. Y. (1993). *Women's paid and unpaid labor: The work transfer in health care and retailing.* Philadel- phia, PA: Temple University Press.

Graig, L. A. (1993). *Health of nations: An international perspective on U.S. health care reform* (2nd ed.). Wash- ington, D. C.: Congressional Quarterly.

Grant, L. (1988). The gender climate of medical school: Perspectives of women and men students. *Journal of the* *American Medical Women's Association, 43,* 109–119.

Hafner-Eaton, C. (1993). Physician utilization disparities between the uninusred and insured: Comparisons of the chronically ill, acutely ill, and well nonelderly populations. *Journal of the American Medical Association,* *269,* 787–792.

Hall, L. C. (1998). Illness, identity and survivorship: Modern and postmodem breast cancer narratives. *Illness,* *Crisis, & Loss, 6,* 255–274.

Hanison, M. (1990). The woman as other: The premise of medicine. *Journal of the American Women's Medical Association, 45,* 225–226.

Hart-Brothers, E. (1994). Contributions of women of color to the health care of America. In E. Friedman (Ed.), *An unfinished revolution: Women and health care in America* (pp. 205–222). New York: United Hospital Fund of New York.

Healthweek (1991). Top 25 most frequently performed surgeries, U.S. short-term, general, non-federal hospitals, 1989. February 25, p. 20.

Hesse-Biber, S. (1996). *Am I thin enough yet? The cult of thinness and the commercialization of identity.* New York: Oxford University Press.

Higginbotham, E. (1997). Black professional women: Job ceilings and employment sectors. In D. Dunn (Ed.), *Workplace/women's place* (pp. 234–246). Los Angeles, CA: Roxbury.

Hill, S. (1994). *Managing sickle cell disease in low income families.* Philadelphia, PA: Temple University Press.

Hill, S., & Zimmerman, M. K. (1995) Valiant girls and vulnerable boys: The impact of gender and race on mothers' caregiving for chronically-ill children. *Journal of Marriage and Family, 57,* 43–53.

Himmelstein, D. U., & Woolhandler, S. (1994) T*he national health program book: A source guide for advocates.* Monroe, ME: Common Courage.

Hobson, B. (1990). No exit, no voice: Women's economic dependency and the welfare state. *Acta Sociologica, 33,* 235–250.

Hooyman, N. R., & Gonyea, J. (1995). *Feminist perspectives on family care: Policies for gender justice.* Thousand Oaks, CA: Sage.

Horner, R. D., Lawler, F. H., & Hainer, B. L. (1991). Relationship between patient race and survival following admission to intensive care among patients of primary care physicians. *Health Services Research, 26,* 531–542.

Horton, J. A. (Ed.) (1995). *The women's health data book: A profile of women's health in the United States* (2nd ed.). Washington, D.C.: Jacobs Institute of Women's Health/Elsevier.

Hostler, S. L., & Gressard, R. P. (1993). Perceptions of the gender fairness of the medical education environment. *Journal of the American Medical Women's Association, 48,* 51–54.

Hudson, R. (1985). Immortal quackery. *Medical Heritage,* January/February, 58–67.

Hulston, N. J. (1996). The desegregation of the University of Kansas School of Medicine, 1938. *Kansas History, 19,* 89–97.

Hurst, C. E. (1998). *Social inequality: Forms, causes, and consequences* (3rd ed.). Needham Heights, MA: Allyn & Bacon.

Iezzoni, L. I., Ash, A. S., Schwartz, M., & Mackierman, Y. D. (1997). Differences in procedure use, in-hospital mortality and illness severity by gender for acute myocardial infarction patients. *Medical Care, 35,* 158–171.

Johns, L. (1994) Obstetrics-gynecology as primary care: A market dilemma. *Health Affairs, 13,* 194–200.

Kanter, R. M. (1977). *Men and women of the corporation.* New York: Basic Books.

Keith, P. M. (1987). Postponement of health care by unmarried older women. *Women & Health, 12,* 47–59.

Kelley, M. A., Perloff, J. D., Morris, N. M., & Liu, W. (1992) Primary care arrangements and access to care among African-American women in three Chicago communities. *Women & Health, 18,* 91–106

Kirschstein, R. L. (1991). Research on women's health. *American Journal of Public Health, 81,* 291–293.

Komaromy, M., Bindman, A. B., Haber, R. J., & Sande, M. A. (1993). Sexual harassment in medical training. *New England Journal of Medicine, 328,* 322–326.

Krieger, N., & Fee, E. (1996). Measuring social inequalities in health in the United States: A historical review, 1900–1950. *International Journal of Health Services, 26,* 391–418.

Lillie-Blanton, M., & Laveist, T. (1996). Race/ethnicity, the social environment, and health. *Social Science and Medicine, 43,* 83–91.

Lindsey, L. L. (1997). *Gender roles: A sociological perspective* (3rd ed.). Upper Saddle River, NJ: Prentice-Hall.

Linzer, M., Spitzer, R., Kroenke, K., Williams, J. B., Hahn, S., Brody, D., & deGruy, F. (1996). Gender, quality of life, and mental disorder in primary care: Results from the PRIME-MD 1000 study. *American Journal of Medicine, 101,* 526–533.

Lorber, J. (1984). *Women physicians: Careers, status, and power.* New York and London: Tavistock.

Lorber, J. (1997). *Gender and the social construction of illness.* Thousand Oaks, CA: Sage.

Louis Harris and Associates. (1993). *Commonwealth fund survey of women's health.* New York.

Lurie, N., Slater J., McGovern, P., Ekstrum, J., Quam, L., & Margolis, K. (1993). Preventive care for women: Does the sex of the physician matter? *New England Journal of Medicine, 329,* 478–482.

Macintyre, S., Hunt, K., & Sweeting, H. (1996) Gender differences in health: Are things really as simple as they seem? *Social Science and Medicine, 42,* 617–624.

Makuc, D. V., Freid, M., & Parsons, P. E. (1994) Health insurance and cancer screening among women. Hyattsville, MD: National Center for Health Statistics. Advance Data No. 254, August 3.

Manley, J. E. (1995) Sex-segregated work in the system of professions: The development and stratification of nursing. *Sociological Quarterly, 36,* 297–314.

Marcus, A. C., & Siegel, J. M. (1982) Sex differences in the use of physician services: A preliminary test of the fixed role hypothesis. *Journal of Health and Social Behavior, 23,* 186–197.

Maynard, C., (1997) Association of gender and survival in patients with acute myocardial infarction. *Archives of Internal Medicine, 157,* 1379–1384.

McCaig, L. F. (1994). *National Hospital Ambulatory Medical Care Survey: 1992 Outpatient Department Summary.* Vital and Health Statistics No. 248. Washington, D.C.: Center for Health Statistics.

McLaughlin, T. J., Soumerai, S. B., & Wilson, D. J. (1996). Adherence to national guidelines for drug treatment of suspected acute myocardial infarction. *Archives of Internal Medicine, 156,* 799–805.

Mechanic, D. (1968). *Medical sociology.* Glencoe, IL: The Free Press.

Meyer, M. H., & Pavalko, E. K. (1996). Family, work, and access to health insurance among mature women. *Journal of Health and Social Behavior, 37,* 311–325.

Miles, A. (1991). *Women. health and medicine.* Philadelphia, PA: Open University Press.

Miles, S., & Parker, K. (1997). Men, women, and health insurance. *New England Journal of Medicine, 336,* 218–221.

Miller, R. K., & Luft, H. (1994) Managed care plan performance since 1980. *Journal of the American Medical Association, 271,* 1512–1519.

Mitchell, P. H., Shannon, S. E., Cain, K. C., & Hegyvary, S. T. (1996). Critical care outcomes: Linking structures, processes, and organizational and clinical outcomes. *American Journal of Critical Care, 5,* 353–363.

Modern Healthcare. (1991). Fourth infertility clinic settles on charges of fraudulent claims. November 4, 20.

Morantz-Sanchez, R. M. (1985). *Sympathy & science: Women physicians in American medicine.* New York: Oxford University Press.

Moy, E., Bartman, B. A., Clancy, C. M., & Cornelius, L. J. (1998). Changes in usual sources of medical care between 1987 and 1992. *Journal of Health Care for the Poor and Underserved, 9,* 126–138.

Muller, C. (1988). Health and health care of employed adults: Occupation and gender. *Women & Health, 11,* 27–45.

Narrigan, D., Jones, J. S., Worcester, N., & Grad, M. J. (1997). Research to improve women's health: An agenda for equity. In S. B. Ruzek, V. L. Olesen, & A. E. Clarke (Eds.), *Women's health: Complexities and differences* (pp 551–579). Columbus, OH: Ohio State University Press.

Navarro, V. (1991). Race or class or race and class: Growing mortality differentials in the United States. *International Journal of Health Services, 21,* 229–235.

Nelson, M. K. (1981). Client responses to a discrepancy between the care they want and the care they receive. *Women & Health, 6,* 135–152.

Olesen, V. (1997). Who cares? Women as informal and formal caregivers. In S. B. Ruzek, V. L Olesen, & A. E. Clarke (Eds.), *Women's health: Complexities and differences* (pp. 397–424). Columbus, OH: Ohio State University Press.

Orloff, A. S. (1993). Gender and the social rights of citizenship: The comparative analysis of gender relations and welfare states. *American Sociological Review, 58,* 303–328.

Parsons, T. (1951). *The social system.* Glencoe, IL: The Free Press.

Philibert, I., & Bickel, J. (1995). Maternity and parental leave policies at COTH hospitals: An update. *Academic Medicine, 70,* 1056–1058.

Phillips, S. P., & Schneider, M. S. (1993, December 23). Sexual harassment of female doctors by patients. *New England Journal of Medicine, 329,* 1936–1939.

Pillitteri, A., & Ackerman, M. (1993). The "doctor–nurse" game": A comparison of 100 years—1888–1990. *Nursing Outlook, 41,* 113–116.

Public Citizen Health Research Group. (1994). Unnecessary cesarean sections: Curing a national epidemic. *Medical Benefits,* July 30.

Riessman, C. K. (1983). Women and medicalization: A new perspective. *Social Policy,* Summer, 3–18.

Riessman, C. K. (1990). Improving the health experiences of low income patients. In P. Conrad & R. Kern (Eds.), *Sociology of health and illness: Critical perspectives* (3rd ed.) (pp. 419–432). New York: St. Martin's Press.

Riska E., & Wegar, K. (Eds.) (1993). *Gender, work and medicine: Women and the medical division of labour.* Newbury Park, CA: Sage.

Roberts, M. M., Kroboth, F. J., & Bernier, G. M. (1995). The women's health track: A model for training internal medicine residents. *Journal of Women's Health, 4,* 313–318.

Rodwin, M. A. (1994). Patient accountability and quality of care: Lessons from medical consumerism and the patients' rights, women's health and disability rights movements. *American Journal of Law & Medicine, XX,* 147–167.

Rosser, S. (1994). Gender bias in clinical research: The difference it makes. In A. Dan (Ed.), *Reframing women's health* (pp. 253–265). Thousand Oaks, CA: Sage.

Rothman, B. K. (1982). *In labor: Women and power in the birthplace.* New York: Norton.

Rothman, B. K. (1986). *The tentative pregnancy.* New York: Viking.

Rothman, B. K. (1989). *Recreating motherhood: Ideology and technology in a patriarchal society.* New York: Norton.

Rowland, D., Lyons, B. Salganicoff, A., & Long, P. (1994). A profile of the uninsured in America. *Health Affairs, 13,* 283–287.

Ruzek, S. B. (1978). *The women's health movement: Feminist alternatives to medical control.* New York: Praeger.

Scully, D. &, Bart, P. (1973). A funny thing happened on the way to the orifice: Women in gynecology textbooks. *American Journal of Sociology, 78,* 1045-1-50.

Smith-Rosenberg, C. (1972). The hysterical woman: Sex roles and role conflict in 19th century America. *Social Research, 39,* 652–678.

Smith-Rosenberg, C., & Rosenberg, C. (1973). The female animal: Medical and biological views of women and her role in nineteenth-century America. *Journal of American History, 60,* 332–356.

Spence, R. (1994). Women in health care administration. In E. Friedman (Ed.), *An unfinished revolution: Women and health care in America* (pp. 239–250). New York: United Hospital Fund of New York.

Staples, C. L. (1989). The politics of employment-based insurance in the United States. *International Journal of Health Services, 19,* 415–431.

Starr, P. (1982). *The social transformation of American medicine.* New York: Basic Books.

Stein, L. (1967). The doctor–nurse game. *Archives of General Psychiatry, 16,* 699–703.

Stein, L., Watts, D. T., & Howell, T. (1990). The doctor–nurse game revisited. *Nursing Outlook, 38,* 264–266.

Steinmo, S., & Watts, J. (1995). It's the institutions, stupid! Why comprehensive national health insurance always fails in America. *Journal of Health Politics. Policy. and Law, 20,* 329–372.

Stevens, P. E. (1996). Experiences of solidarity and domination in health care settings. *Gender & Society, 10,* 24–40.

Stevens, R. (1989). *In sickness and in wealth: American hospitals in the twentieth century.* New York: Basic Books.

Sullivan, D. (1993). Cosmetic surgery: Market dynamics and medicalization. *Research in the Sociology of Health Care, 10,* 97–115.

Sweeting, H. (1995). Reversals of fortune? Sex differences in health in childhood and adolescence. *Social Science and Medicine, 40,* 77–90.

Tallon, J. R., & Block, R. (1987). Changing patterns of health insurance coverage: Special concerns for women. *Women & Health, 12,* 119–136.

Thomas, J. E. (forthcoming). Incorporating empowerment into models of care: Strategies from the feminist women's health centers. *Research in the Sociology of Health Care, 17.*

Thomas, L. W. (1995). A critical feminist perspective of the health belief model: Implications for nursing theory, research, practice, and education. *Journal of Professional Nursing, 11,* 246–252.

United States Department of Commerce (1997). *Statistical Abstract of the United States 1997.* Washington, D.C.: Government Printing Office.

United States General Accounting Office. (February, 1997). *Employment-based health insurance.* GAO/HEHS-97-35. Washington, D. C.

United States General Accounting Office. (July, 1997). *Private health insurance.* GAO/HEHS-97–122. Washington, D. C.

Verbrugge, L. M. (1985). Gender and health: An update on hypotheses and evidence. *Journal of Health and Social Behavior, 26,* 156–182.

Waldron, I. (1995). Contributions of changing gender differences in behavior and social roles to changing gender differences in mortality. In D. Sabo & D. F. Gordon (Eds.), *Men's Health and Illness: Gender Power and the Body* (Chapter 2). Thousand Oaks, CA: Sage.

Walsh, M. R. (1977). *Doctors wanted: No women need apply.* New Haven, CT: Yale University Press.

Wardwell, W. I. (1994). Alternative medicine in the United States. *Social Science and Medicine, 38,* 1061–1068.

Washington Post. (1994). Vital statistics: Caring for elders. March 22.

Weisman, C. S. (1998). *Women's health care: Activist traditions and institutional change.*

Weitz, R. (1996). *The sociology of health, illness, and health care: A critical approach.* Belmont, CA: Wadsworth.

Weitz, R., & Sullivan, D. (1986). The politics of childbirth: The re-emergence of midwifery in Arizona. *Social Problems, 33,* 163–175.

West, C. (1984). *Routine complications: Troubles with talk between doctors and patients.* Bloomington, IN: Indiana University Press.

White, J. C., & Dull, V. T. (1997). Health risk factors and health-seeking behavior in lesbians. *Journal of Women's Health, 6,* 103–112.

Wiggins, C. (1994). Differing career patterns and success among female and male health care managers. *AUPHA Exchange,* September/October, 5–6.

Williams, C. (1992). The glass escalator: Hidden advantages for men in the 'female' professions. *Social Problems, 39,* 253–267.

Williams, D. R. (1998). African-American health: The role of the social environment. *Journal of Urban Health: Bulletin of the New York Academy of Medicine, 75*(2), 300–321.

Wolf, N. (1991). *The beauty myth: How images of beauty are used against women.* New York: William Morrow.

Wolinsky, F. (1993) The professional dominance, deprofessionalization, proletarianization an corporatization perspectives: An overview and synthesis. In F. W. Hafferty & J. B. McKinlay (Eds.), *The changing medical profession* (pp. 11–24). New York: Oxford University Press.

Woods, N. F. (1996). Women and their health. In P. Brown (Ed.), *Perspectives in medical sociology* (2nd ed.) (pp. 44–76). Prospect Heights, IL: Waveland Press.

Young, R. F., & Kahana, E. (1993). Gender, recovery from late life heart attack, and medical care. *Women & Health, 20,* 11–29.

Zimmerman, M. (1987). The women's health movement: A critique of medical enterprise and the position of women. In M. M. Ferree & B. Hess (Eds.), *Analyzing gender: A handbook of social science research* (pp. 442–471). Thousand Oaks, CA: Sage.

Zimmerman, M. (1993). Caregiving in the welfare state: Mothers' informal health care work is Finland. *Research in the Sociology of Health Care, 10,* 193–211.

Zimmerman, M. (1996). Status report on women's health in medical education and training. Paper prepared for the Canada-U.S. Forum on Women's Health. U.S. Department of Health and Human Services: Office on Women's Health.

Zimmerman, M., & Hill, S. (1999). Reforming gendered healthcare: An assessment of change. (Unpublished paper). Lawrence, KS: Department of Health Policy and Management, University of Kansas.

Zola, I. K. (1972). Medicine as an institution of social control. *Sociological Review, 20,* 487–503.

CHAPTER 23

Gender and Politics

Elizabeth M. Esterchild

1. INTRODUCTION

The trickle of research on gender and politics that existed prior to the emergence of the contemporary women's movement became a veritable flood in the last few decades. While much of the literature is published in dedicated journals such as *Women's Political Quarterly* or *Journal of Women and Politics* some has made inroads in general political science journals, and pertinent articles occasionally appear in other social science venues as well. The issues and questions addressed cover a large terrain from political socialization in childhood, through gender differences in all types of political behavior and election to political office, to acceptance and behavior of women in public office. Especially in regard to the "gender gap" in political attitudes and behavior, the research mainly addresses differences that stem from differential socialization and from the varied roles that women and men enact. There is little attempt to treat gender as more than a characteristic of individuals; instead it is little more than a demographic characteristic similar to age, education, and income. Rarely are women and men seen as engaged in sets of social relationships that are at least partly structured by differential access to power. In brief the authors do not use a distinction between "'gender as difference' (between men/masculinity and women/femininity) and 'gender-as-power,' which promotes gender-differentiated categories based on power relations" (Peterson, 1995).

The same tendencies are apparent in the myriad studies of election processes and outcomes. Profiles of political candidates show how, historically, women differed appreciably from their male counterparts: they were less often married, less likely to have young children still at home, and less often in the labor force. If they had been working

---

Elizabeth M. Esterchild • Department of Sociology, University of North Texas, Denton, Texas 76203

Handbook of the Sociology of Gender, edited by Janet Saltzman Chafetz. Kluwer Academic/ Plenum Publishers, New York, 1999.

for pay, they were highly likely to be employed in one of the traditional female semiprofessions such as nursing or teaching. Women candidates more often brought a history of involvement in voluntary and nonpolitical organizations to the campaigns while men more often brought a history of involvement in political parties and had more often held a lower level political office. Today, women resemble men candidates much more. Having gained labor force and political experience, more women now run for office and more women win. Again, gender is treated as traits or characteristics of people, not as an analytic category rooted in power relations.

Insightful as this massive literature is, it does not serve to predict future developments very well because it is not strongly grounded in a well-developed theory of either political structure or gender stratification. Nor is there much attempt to theorize the politics of gender differences, that is, little theory is developed in an effort to explain why women and men behave differently in the political arena. Men, and especially white men, are taken-for-granted actors in the political arena. Yet no one has taken on the task of discovering how this fact might affect the everyday behavior of men, or how expectations associated with men's roles in society might condition their behavior as politicians. Instead, men are "normal" in politics; studying gender often means studying women only or studying their differences from men. Finally, little concern is voiced over the representation of minority women in political office. While the Center for the American Woman and Politics (CAWP) faithfully reports the numbers of black women elected to Congress and state legislatures, evidently these are too few to merit much systematic attention. Some research (e.g., Wilcox, 1990) reports attitudes of women and men separately and attitudes of blacks and whites separately and a review (Githens, 1995) of appointments to the federal judiciary shows how women and blacks are viewed differently by members of selection committees. However, this work has not advanced to striving to understand the intersection of race and gender either in the political system or among individuals.

Despite the limitations, there is ample material to fuel the sociologist's interest in understanding the position of women, the relative power of women and men, and other aspects of gender stratification in the political arena. There is so much literature that this chapter covers only a few major topics: (1) the gender gap in political attitudes and voting behavior, (2) patterns of election of women and men to public office, and (3) gender differences in the behavior and acceptance of elected officials. Actual or potential changes in these patterns and behaviors are sketched wherever there is solid evidence.

Some substantive issues potentially interesting to sociologists are deliberately omitted here, in part because there is limited research available on them and in part because they are covered elsewhere in this volume. These include discrimination against women in federal and state bureaucracies (cf., Naff, 1995), issues surrounding women's representation in the military (Segal, 1995, and Chapter 27 of this volume) and the character and progress of women's movements in societies outside the United States (e.g., Margolis, 1993; Patton, 1992; and Chapter 8 in this volume). There is no attempt to portray the gendered political, social, and economic consequences of planned and unplanned changes in developing societies (Acosta-Belen & Bose, 1990; Patton, 1992; and Chapter 5 of this volume). In addition, social scientists (Moghadam, 1995; Molyneux, 1995; Peterson, 1995) have surveyed the massive changes from Communist to Democratic governments in Central and Eastern Europe; in most instances, these changes have been far from beneficial to women. The new regimes seem to be pushing women out of the labor force and into more narrowly defined roles. At the same time, men vent their frustrations by attacking women, and feminists are portrayed as overwhelmingly self-centered. These findings are in sharp contrast to the generally positive changes that political scientists find in Western democracies. Covering these substantive changes in women's political status would require far more space than is allocated here. Indeed, much is omitted from this chapter, most notably dozens of books. Only a few recent, key articles are covered in each topic area; each of these typically refers to quite a few additional research articles in the same topic area. Together, these items suggest the range of questions and answers in contemporary work on gender and politics.

2. THE GENDER GAP IN ATTITUDES AND BEHAVIOR

Women acquired the right to vote in all states with the passage of the Nineteenth Amendment to the U.S. Constitution in 1920. For several decades thereafter, only very small numbers of women became candidates for public office, and women's rates of voting in presidential and Congressional elections were much lower than men's. Over the years, the number of women who voted increased, and by the early 1970s women's voting rates were virtually identical with those of men. Part of the rapprochement in voting rates was due to men's steadily declining rate of voting; women's voter turnout rates did not have to increase very much to equal those of men. In the 1992 presidential election, 62.3% of voting age women, but only 60.2% of voting age men, reported voting. While this difference is not very large, there are more women in the voting age population, so that in 1992, 60.6 million women, compared to only 53.3 million men, participated. This difference in participation rates is consistent across the major race/ethnic groups. The Center for the American Woman and Politics reported that in the three presidential elections of 1984, 1988, and 1992, "the *number* of female voters in recent elections has exceeded the *number* of male voters. . . . (and) the difference in voter turnout rates between the sexes is greatest for Blacks" (CAWP, 1979a, see also Welch & Sigelman, 1992). Women also vote more often in Congressional elections in the "off" (nonpresidential election) years, but the differences are not so marked.

2.1. Styles of Political Participation

The finding that women vote more often than men is partly encouraging, because it suggests that at least some women are beginning to pursue their interests more vigorously and to see themselves as more politically efficacious, and partly puzzling, because it seems to contradict some longstanding differences in styles of participation and voter interest. In the 1980s, for instance, women were significantly less interested in politics than men and the lower interest remained even after controls for age, education, marital status, employment status, and occupation were introduced in the analysis (Bennett & Bennett, 1992, cited in Hayes & Makkai, 1996). In Australian elections, where voters must vote or pay a fine, men paid much more attention than women to televised debates between candidates and used the information gleaned there to decide how to vote. To account for these findings, Hayes and Makkai (1996) review several complementary explanations, summarizing a large array of research on styles of political involvement in the process.

> Women are more likely to engage in local level political activity, such as . . . community and voluntary associations and local rather than national issues are of greater interest to women. . . . Second,

in contrast to their male colleagues, the nature of women's political involvement is highly personalized and intimate. . . . Sources of information are more often ad hoc and of a familial or personalized nature than the abstract party launches and sterile intellectual televised debates of party leaders (p. 65).

Hayes and Makkai also introduce concepts of *disillusionment* with the policies and practices of the major parties and *disinterest*, as when the issue is welfare reform rather than the size of welfare payments, to account for women's lesser involvement in media campaigns. Thus, "politics as usual" appeal much less to women than to men.

2.2. Party and Candidate Preference

For several decades after the passage of the Nineteenth Amendment, women tended to vote for the same candidates that their husbands did. By 1980, however, women had gained more independence, and a gender gap in voting choices emerged. Women were much less likely than men to vote for Republican presidential candidates Reagan and Bush, even though a majority of them did so. After the 1980 election, Susan Carroll (1991, cited in Rosenthal, 1994) found that women who were most *economically* and *psychologically independent* were least likely to favor Reagan, "more than 20 percentage points less than the least autonomous women and men who shared similar demographic characteristics" (Rosenthal, 1994). Throughout the 1980s, women were consistently less likely than men to approve of the way Reagan and Bush handled their job as president. In 1992, women preferred the victorious Democratic presidential candidate Clinton more than men, but the differences were not large: 45% versus 41%. Equal percentages of women and men voted for George Bush, and men voted more often for Ross Perot, the third-party candidate (CAWP, 1997a). Although women's votes and the gender gap have not yet been decisive in determining the outcome of a presidential election, candidates increasingly target the women's vote in their campaigns, and the women's vote has been decisive in some recent statewide elections for governor and for U.S. senator. Throughout the 1980s and 1990s, women claimed membership in the Democratic party more often than men did. In those years, in nearly all of the U.S. Senate and state gubernatorial elections in which an appreciable gender gap in candidate preference was noted, women almost always favored the Democratic candidate more and the Republican candidate less than did men (CAWP, 1997a).

At century's end, it is clear that women register to vote, actually prefer Democratic candidates at all levels of office, and approve of the performance of Democratic presidents in greater numbers than men. Yet it is unclear whether women will recognize their mutual interests and become a much more self conscious voting bloc in the future. In the meantime, other facets of the gender gap and their sources remain to be examined.

2.3. Support for Women Candidates

In addition to differences between women and men in party and candidate preferences already noted, women may be more likely than men to support women candidates. While attitude surveys typically show small differences in willingness to vote for a woman for president, the finding of no substantial gender gap must be weighed against the hypothetical nature of the question and the way in which the question is typically phrased.

Both women and men say they would vote for a woman candidate for president if she represents the respondent's party and is equally qualified as a male candidate. However, women and men candidates are rarely perceived as equally qualified.

For instance, in a survey (Brown, Heighberger, & Shocket, 1993) regarding perceptions of how gender affects candidate ability in carrying out the tasks of city council members, the majority of those surveyed saw no difference between women and men candidates in their ability to handle nearly all of 10 internal or office functions or in their ability to deal with 13 diverse service or policy areas. However, a substantial minority did see differences, and on specific functions and issues, women and men respondents sometimes exhibited sizable differences in their evaluations of candidate gender. Women were seen as better able to handle two internal office functions—working with neighborhoods and citizens—while men were seen as better able to handle six office functions—working with city council members, making decisions, managing the office, solving city problems, dealing with crises, and providing leadership. In the matter of service or policy issues, women candidates were perceived as better able to handle four areas—services and programs for youth, public health, race relations, and recreation—while men were perceived as better able to handle eight areas—economic development, downtown and neighborhood business development, garbage collection, police and fire department services, traffic engineering, and street maintenance. In some, but not all, of these areas women respondents saw men candidates as much more qualified and able than did men respondents.

Traditional stereotypes influenced the respondents' perceptions of candidate quality, as it did in several other studies conducted throughout the 1980s (summarized in Kahn, 1994). The researchers stressed that women are aware of these stereotypes, which serve as one more impediment to women choosing to run for public office; those who do choose to run must provide specific information about themselves to counteract the stereotypes. They conclude that perception of the quality of candidates is enough to sway election outcomes, although women and men are not unified in their perceptions of the quality of women and men candidates.

Information may not effectively counter gendered stereotypes. Kim Kahn (1994) performed a content analysis of newspaper articles on candidates for statewide electoral positions, reasoning that differential coverage and stereotyping may affect voting behavior in these gubernatorial and U.S. Senate races even though previous research suggested that voters did not enact gender stereotyping in lower level contests, such as those for state legislative seats. Controlling for whether the articles concerned incumbents or challengers for the office, she found substantial differences in the press coverage of women and men, with the differences larger in U.S. Senate than in gubernatorial races. For women candidates, the newspapers emphasized the state of the contest, that is, "horserace" or who was likely to win; especially in Senate races, women were described as less viable candidates than men. Meanwhile, the issues stressed by men candidates received a great deal more coverage. Kahn used the actual coverage to produce prototype articles to be used in an experimental design. These prototype articles systematically varied the sex of the candidate and the type of coverage received, as well as whether the candidate was a challenger or an incumbent. Participants in the experiment read these articles and then rated the candidate on a variety of different characteristics.

Ironically, the stereotyping that occurred in the respondents' ratings all applied to women—men appeared not to be stereotyped—and the stereotyping was generally positive for women candidates. Women candidates were seen as better able to deal with health and education issues, as well as more compassionate and honest than men candidates, even when the two hypothetical candidates were described in exactly the same prototypical article. Women consistently rated hypothetical women candidates more positively than did men. Unfortunately, the stereotyping of women would not benefit women in the long run, especially in Senate races, because other issues—such as military deployment—are much more salient in those races. The reasons for the lower level of stereotyping in gubernatorial races may be that issues of health and education are seen as more important there.

2.4. Voting for Women/Voting for Issues

Much of the foregoing research on perceptions of men and women candidates dealt with gender differences in an abstract sense, not with evaluations of specific candidates or with actual political or voting behavior. When we examine the latter, we find a detectable tendency for women to actually vote for women candidates more often than men do. The support for women candidates may stem from a feminist orientation, because women have been known to cross party lines to support a woman candidate. However, in at least one case women's votes were responsible for electing an antifeminist woman (CAWP, 1997a). What is needed, then, is research that not only compares women and men but also examines differences among women and among men.

In one carefully organized survey in Oklahoma City (Rosenthal, 1992), respondents were asked about their preference for "descriptive representation," that is, for having a man or woman represent them in four separate areas. They were asked whether they trusted women or men candidates more, whether they would rather deal with a man or a woman on a problem that required a governmental solution, whether a man or a woman in public office would be more likely to have the same concerns as they do about our country, and the likelihood of voting for a man or woman candidate if they had similar platforms and qualifications. Respondents were given five response categories: would prefer a man much more, would prefer a man somewhat more, would prefer a man or a woman about equally, would prefer a woman somewhat more, and would prefer a woman much more. Men were much more likely to give the equalitarian response (between 10% and 20% more men than women on the various items) while women were more likely to prefer a woman by 8% to 30%. Women and men were about equally likely to prefer a man to represent them. The authors then proceeded to explore the correlates of preferring representation by women, neglecting to highlight the majority who gave at least one gender-neutral response on the four items. All this suggests that men as potential allies for women's and feminists' concerns is an avenue of research that remains untraveled.

2.5. Interpreting Gender Differences

How might we interpret these findings, for instance that women appear less interested in television coverage of candidates but vote more often? Or that women prefer women candidates more often while men more often state that the sex of the candidate makes no difference to them? Sometimes the findings from separate studies differ a good deal, but that is partly because the various research projects concentrate on different levels and types of political activity, and assess the issues for different offices (e.g., city council versus U.S. Senate). Moreover, in a time of rapid social change, behavioral and attitudinal changes in one area or among one group may not correspond with changes in other areas or groups. Thus, for instance, while women in the contemporary U.S. have taken to voting with greater frequency, they may or may not be especially enthusiastic supporters of women candidates. Similarly, while some women may vote for candidates from the Democratic party and for liberal positions on issues, they may not specifically connect their viewpoints with a feminist agenda. Again, in much of the research women and men are treated as individuals who have experienced different socialization content and who play different roles in society. Rarely is there an attempt to go beyond these descriptive differences to distinguish among competing explanations of gendered political behavior.

However, Johnston and Sapiro (1993) noted the strong differences between women and men in support for the military and warfare, and explicitly tested alternative explanations. They reasoned that women's more pacifist orientation could be rooted in sex and gender, in the mothering behavior of women, or in feminism. The sex and gender theme has various strands, some conveying the old-fashioned idea that men are biologically more aggressive (sex) while some suggest that boys and girls are socialized differently (gender). The mothering or maternalist reasoning suggests that not only are women more concerned about the safety and health of their children, but in addition that "many maternal practices incorporate the essential ideals of nonviolent peacemaking: renunciation, resistance, reconciliation, and peacekeeping" (Conover & Sapiro, 1993, p. 1081). In this view, to be effective, women would need to become much more conscious of the possibilities for peacemaking that stem from their mothering behavior. Finally feminist theorists believe it is feminist thinking that motivates people to be peacemakers; because more women than men are feminists, a gender gap in attitudes remains. Measuring general views about militarism and war, as well as specific reactions to the Gulf War, Johnston and Sapiro found little support for the mothering hypothesis, but stress that their measures of mothering are weak and imperfect. They found no support for either the gender or the feminism explanations of general attitudes toward war. Instead, highly militaristic viewpoints were produced by having a strong sense of patriotism, a conservative ideology, and a low educational level. Moreover, there was no gender gap in military ideology to begin with, but women and men apparently take slightly different routes to reach their views. Men are more influenced by identifying with a political party, women are more influenced by educational level (Conover & Sapiro, 1993).

In regard to the Gulf War specifically, there were no gender differences in interest in the war, but other differences did appear.

> . . . because of their heightened sensitivity to the use of violence, feminists might be expected to pay greater attention to the war. And they did. Also as compared to men and nonfeminists, respectively, women and feminists were expected to be less supportive of the war, more opposed to the bombing of civilians, and more emotionally distressed by the war. . . . in every case, these expectations were borne out. (Conover & Sapiro, 1993, p. 1092)

Here, as well as in other contexts, gender differences stem from a number of sources. Women and men are pointed in different directions by variables of age, race, and party identification. The authors conclude that the origins and determinants of attitudes are extremely complex.

A gender gap appears in certain times and places and contexts and disappears in a haze of contradictory influences in others. As with nonpolitical behavior and attitudes, women and men are arguably more similar than different. However, in politics, the marginal differences are often quite enough to affect outcomes. We turn now to a very important outcome: the election of women to political office.

2.6. Women Gaining Political Office

The higher the level of political office, the fewer women who run and the fewer women who are elected. In 1997, women held 21% of state legislative seats but 11% of national congressional seats (CAWP, 1997a, b). Within state legislatures, women had a smaller share of the upper house than the lower house. Winning statewide elective offices has slightly different dimensions. While women held 81 of the 323 of the available positions (25%), they held only two (4%) of the governorships, but 18 (36 %) of the lieutenant governorships. The other 61 women in statewide elective offices were scattered among various state offices, such as treasurer, comptroller, heads of education departments, and so forth (CAWP, 1997b). Whether some states are more likely to elect women to these positions than others is an unanswered question. Overall, women are more likely to win gubernatorial elections than they are to win U.S. Senate seats.

Women have gained national attention in mayoral races; currently 12 of the hundred largest cities in the United States have women mayors. Women hold 21% of the mayoral slots in cities with populations over 30,000. Separate data are not given for smaller cities, but in 1994, in cities with over 10,000 in population, women comprised 21% of the combined mayors and city council members (CAWP, 1997c).

2.7. Women's National Officeholding

Women held only about 2% of the U.S. Congressional seats in 1970 compared to 11% now (CAWP, 1997e). This a fivefold gain, but at this rate of change, it will require 120 years for women to reach parity with men. However, some acceleration of the increase began in the late 1980s, highlighted by the labeling of 1992 as "the year of the woman." Increases have continued since then; in 1970 there were only 11 women in Congress, in 1980 there were 17, in 1990 31, and in 1998 there were 60 (CAWP, 1997e). Over time, 1992 has been more intensively studied than any other Congressional election year. In that year, women's representation jumped from four to seven seats in the Senate and from 28 to 47 Seats in the House. That may have been an unusual year because substantial redistricting had been accomplished, and many incumbents had incentives to retire leaving more seats open in the U.S. House of Representatives than had been available in a long time. Usually, turnover in the U.S. House is extremely slow, allowing few opportunities for newcomers to gain a toehold (Nixon & Darcy, 1996).

Neil Berch (1996) studied the 1992 election, testing six alternative hypotheses concerning the increase. Each of these hypotheses suggest changes that were beneficial to women's candidacy and that may be important for other levels of political offices as well.

1. Women were more willing to seek higher office, in part because they have secured lower level offices and want to proceed further. This reduces the gender gap in ambition, thereby enlarging the pool of women candidates.
2. Women were more likely to have the political experience and background, as well as the occupations that predict being successful candidates.

3. Women were less likely to be "sacrificial lambs," as they competed in more easily winnable election districts.
4. Owing in part to an increase in political action committees devoted to women's interests (National Women's Political Caucus, EMILY's List, etc.), the funding gap between women and men may have decreased.
5. The funds that women spent actually netted more votes per dollar than in previous elections.
6. There was a decrease in voter bias and perhaps in media bias as well.

Comparing 1992 with elections between 1986 and 1990 and with 1994, Berch found that 1992 was a banner year because more women ran for open seats, especially among the Democrats, and because there appeared to be an increase in funding for women and a decrease in the "sacrificial lamb" phenomenon. He concluded that the increase in 1992 was part of a general trend toward more women being elected, and was partly predictable and partly anomalous in terms of the effects of the variables that influence women to run and help them to succeed.

Support for the anomalous character of the 1992 elections comes from Susan Hansen's (1997) research. She focused on proselytizing activities—trying to persuade other people to vote for a given candidate—an area where men have traditionally been more active. She studied this phenomenon in races for the U.S. House, U.S. Senate, and for state governor positions, comparing those that had a woman candidate versus those that did not. She found that

> In 1992, the presence of women candidates was associated with higher levels of political involvement, internal political efficacy, and media use by both sexes, but the effects of candidate gender were stronger for women. In the congressional elections of 1990 and 1994, however, candidate gender had no such impact (Hansen, 1997, p. 73)

Research on congresses and parliaments in countries outside the United States is relatively scanty; comparative cross-national research is rarer still. Clearly, the same kinds of factors that affect women's election to the U.S. Congress often operate in other countries as well. Women are more likely to be elected in progressive Western style democracies in Europe, and less likely to be elected in more traditional and non-Western societies, but the reasons are not completely clear (Oakes & Almquist, 1994). In cross-national studies, it is difficult to disentangle the effects of modernization and women's increasing movement into the labor force from changing attitudes toward women in office and the nature of the party and electoral systems. There is too much overlap (colinearity) among some of these variables while other variables (such as political system) are nonlinear typologies so that multiple regression equations do not capture the significant differences among different societies. As a result, different researchers studying different societies and using different measures and data sources sometimes produce contradictory results.

An especially important issue outside the United States is that of why multimember districts with proportional systems of representation enhance opportunities for women to be elected. In 1993, in Western democracies with party list systems, 20% of the legislators were women, while women comprised only 9% of the legislators in countries with single-member districts (Matland & Studlar, 1996). Studlar and Welch (1991) found that multimember districts aided women candidates in London local elections, but not very much. Multitmember districts with proportional systems and party lists (of candidates) may advantage women because voters are willing to vote for one woman among several candidates rather than cast their *only* vote for a woman. However, Karen Beckwith (1992) argues that cross-national research obscures the real reasons why women may benefit from such systems. Studies of both France and Italy, countries where electoral systems changed repeatedly, revealed that women's chances for success are equally likely to be affected by the behavior of political parties and the degree of party competition *within* the systems, as well as by the development of a political climate that is increasingly favorable to women and by the growth and spread of feminist movements. Similarly, Matland and Studlar (1996), studying Canada and Norway, suggested that the salient effects of multimember districts occurred primarily because of political contagion: smaller leftist parties introduced women candidates first, and larger, more traditional parties then began fielding more women as a way of remaining competitive and appealing to the broadest possible spectrum of voters. Hickman (1997) advocates the use of multimember districts in local, prefectural, and national elections in Japan, because women are so greatly underrepresented at all levels. Regardless of the precise mechanisms involved, Rule (1987) concludes that the use of multimember districts is the single most important factor affecting women's representation in national legislatures.

Other researchers (cf. Studlar & McAllister, 1991) argue that incumbency is the most important factor because it operates as a vicious circle. Incumbents are typically reelected and since women have difficulty being elected in the first place, they cannot become incumbents to be reelected! However, Nixon and Darcy (1996) argue that in the United States, a focus on incumbency as a deterrent to women's election ignores the impact of special elections in increasing the numbers of women in Congress. During the 1980s and 1990s, fully one third of all women elected to Congress won their seats in special elections. Women won a large proportion of the special elections, even when there was a male opponent. Most of these women had already well-established political careers. In this way, vacancies due to death or illness create more opportunities for politically minded women to pursue higher level office.

2.8. State Legislatures in the United States

Both incumbency and multinember districts have been shown to affect women's representation in the United States; incumbency and the subsequent lack of interparty competition diminishes women's success rates across many state legislatures but in the few states that have multimember districts, women have better chances to be elected. Exploring the impact of multimember districts on electoral success, Darcy, Hadley, and Kirksey (1993) found that the underrepresentation of blacks at various levels of government is due almost exclusively to the underrepresentation of black women; black men seem to achieve an equitable share of political offices while black women do not. They suggest *increasing,* rather than decreasing as is currently the case, the number of multimember districts as a way of increasing the numbers of black women elected without in any way undermining the election of black men.

Women's election to public office is most often studied in state legislatures, which is an important location because women represent women's interests more often than even feminist-oriented men do and because the issues addressed there substantially affect women's lives. These include matters such as pay equity/comparable worth, aid to dependent children, domestic violence, the rights of women in marriage and divorce, and the equal rights amendment (Darcy, Welch, & Clark 1987). In addition, state legislative seats serve as springboards for seeking election to higher office.

Grounded in Irene Diamond's (1977) landmark study and fueled by continuing reports from the Center for American Woman and Politics of Rutgers University, this research paints a relatively detailed portrait of the conditions that can predict whether women hold a large, moderate, or small portion of state legislative seats and begins to assess the circumstances that help increase women's representation therein. However, some of these conditions and circumstances, especially those that relate to change in women's involvement in state legislatures, are too blurry to enable one to glean a clear image of future trends.

Diamond (1977) found that for the early 1970s, the size of the legislature relative to the state's population was the most important factor in women's election to office. In states with large legislatures and small populations, women were more successful. This occurred because women could compete for votes more effectively in small election districts. They could more easily reach neighbors and community members in these small districts than they could persuade voters in large anonymous districts that required television advertising to be successful. The small election districts, large legislatures were most prevalent in the Republican-dominated New England states.

Wilma Rule (1990) completed massive research on changes between 1974 and 1984 in factors that improve women's selection for state legislative seats. Among the many structural factors she considered, Republican party dominance of legislatures and moralistic state political culture were continuing favorable factors; small legislatures in high-population states and low average income were no longer unfavorable for women's election; Democratic party dominance, especially in southern states, and traditional political culture continued to impede the election of women. In the meantime, some new conditions emerged as aiding in women's recruitment to legislatures in 1984. These were individualistic political culture, multimember legislative districts, high labor force participation rates among women, and women being strongly represented among professionals. Having more women in Congress and the presence of multiple chapters of the National Organization for Women were also positively correlated with women's share of state legislative seats, but these factors may simply accompany increases in women's share rather than causing such increases. Most of the structural and cultural variables that affect women's success changed very little over the decade between 1974 and 1984, but women were increasingly able to negotiate the structural barriers and increasingly willing to try to surmount the cultural barriers. Rule (1990) was relatively optimistic that increases would continue because women had become increasingly able to amass the resources necessary to compete effectively and were spurred on by commitment to the feminist movement.

Indeed, Rule's predictions were borne out by later elections, but the fact that women's representation continued to increase is not an indicator of uniform success. When the upper and lower houses of the state legislature are considered separately (Dunn & Almquist, 1993), changes are very uneven within states and across the 50 states. Increasing representation of women in the two houses has some similar determinants and some different ones. In both houses, the larger women's share of the total employed persons in the state, the larger the increase in women's share of the legislative seats. However, the more often women with preschool-aged children were employed, the smaller the increase. High levels of interparty competition, which increases turnover and permits women and other underrepresented groups more opportunity to run and win, are also associated with greater increases in women's share of the seats in both houses. Women achieved substantial gains in representation in states where there are a large number of seats in the lower house but not in the upper house. More importantly, in the upper house, women's share of seats in 1980 is *negatively* associated with gains that occurred by 1993, that is, the more state senate seats women held in 1980, the smaller were their gains. This might be interpreted as a glass ceiling effect in state senates, or the possibility that after a few women have been elected to the senate, voters are reluctant to elect still more (Dunn & Almquist, 1993).

Again, the preceding research suggests that structural and cultural changes have been relatively small, but that women have increasingly garnered more political resources and are increasingly willing to take the risks associated with entering state legislative campaigns. Another study of women as state legislators confirms this hunch. Dolan and Ford (1997) developed profiles of all women state legislators serving in 15 states in 1972, 1982, and 1992, and compared them with a sample of men legislators in the same states. Contemporary (1992) women legislators were found to differ significantly from their predecessors: they had more professional occupational experience; they were younger and more often married; they were more likely to belong to business and professional organizations and less likely to come from a background of charity and volunteer work; they were more likely to come to the state legislature from a background of service on city council and less likely to have served in an appointed position in some type of service to the city or community; and finally they were somewhat less likely to be involved in state and national political parties. The researchers asked whether these changes are also characteristic of men legislators so that they do not have special significance for the increased representation of women in these states. They found that men legislators were not appreciably different in 1992 from their predecessors. Men had the same professional occupations and political backgrounds they had exhibited earlier, while their participation in both civic and business or professional groups had declined. Moreover, unlike women, contemporary men were more rather than less likely to be involved in traditional political parties. In summary, women legislators are becoming more like men legislators, who have mostly stayed in the same grooves from which their predecessors operated.

2.9. Campaigning and Campaign Financing

Political elections often pit women directly against men, and it is a truism that women cannot be elected if they do not run. Personal ambition appears to be the only major factor affecting male city council members' decision to run for higher level office, but it is not an important factor for women (Bledsoe & Herring, 1990). Ambition is tempered by perceptions of having won a city council seat by a large or a small margin and by whether the council member was elected at-large or in a single-member district. Women may be socialized to not appear pushy and hence to disavow political ambition; they may require larger margins of victory in city council elections to induce them to pursue higher level offices; they may pursue higher office "out of a sense of service to the community rather than out of a desire to enhance their own careers" (Bledsoe & Herring, 1990, p. 218). Overall, they are more likely to see themselves as amateurs committed to a principle than as professional politicians exercising competitive strategies.

Traditionally in the United States, women with families, especially with young children, have been reluctant to run for political office. While this barrier may be declining in significance in the United States, it remains a major obstacle to women choosing to run in

Australia (Studlar & McAllister, 1991). The presence of families may hamper women's selection for appointive office as well. Panels who select new members of the judiciary have been known to comment "He has a wife and family. She has a husband. He needs this job, and she doesn't" (Githens, 1995). A spouse and children may be regarded as a stabilizing influence on men, but as a potential disruption for women serving in office.

Once women decide to run for office, there is the issue of deciding how to campaign. In recent times, negative ads are increasingly used because negative information carries more weight than positive information, is more memorable, and can sometimes be disassociated from the candidate presenting it. Political challengers are more likely than incumbents to attack with negative ads (Procter, Schenck-Hamlin, & Haase, 1994). While advertising may be especially important for women because they can control the messages that are broadcast, political advisers frequently counsel women to avoid negative ads because an attack on the opponent may backfire and decrease their chances for election. In a study of all statewide elections (governor and U.S. Senate races) that had candidates of both sexes in 1990, women were found to be nearly as likely to use negative advertising as men, and to use substantially similar approaches and content in these ads (Procter, Schenck-Hamlin, & Hasse, 1994). These recent findings imply that women and men campaign similarly and that women no longer stand out as using different approaches to the whole process.

In 1992 races for election to the U.S. House of Representatives, Dabelko and Herrnson (1997) discovered a great deal of convergence in campaign styles. "Women and men (gave) similar reasons for running, assembled comparable campaign resources, and employed similar strategies and communications techniques" (p. 121). However, they campaigned on different issues, with women more likely to campaign on social as well as economic issues. The convergence in campaign styles helped women to win office more often than in earlier years, and the divergence in issues did not significantly damage their chances for success.

Campaign financing is a very important issue for candidates. In Congressional elections in recent years, women candidates acquired as much funding on average as men candidates did. Brian Werner (1997) focused on state legislative campaigns in states where funding data were available, which also happened to be states that had more professional (full-time and research oriented) legislatures with average or higher levels of campaign spending. Women raised as much money as men did across a large number of elections, but their equality in fund raising may not result in net gains in winning elections, because the male opponents of women candidates raised more money than men who did not face women as opponents. Incumbent as well as challenger men exhibited this pattern. ". . . the pattern suggests that women challengers are taken more seriously than the average male challenger" (Werner, 1997, p. 91). This idea that women enter races with a "higher profile" and that they spur men to generate more campaign money is the only clear hint that women and men compete directly for office and for control and power in contested territory.

3. ACTIVITIES AND ACCEPTANCE OF WOMEN IN PUBLIC OFFICE

Over time, women have begun to participate in electoral politics more actively, especially by increasing their rate of voting, supporting liberal Democratic and women candidates, and by choosing to run for office themselves. What do women do once they win office? How are they accepted into the seats of official power? The research evidence is inadequate to provide definitive answers to these questions, but a few studies imply that women are more successful in achieving their political goals now than they were formerly, that they actively pursue women's interests, and that they are gaining acceptance in U.S. state legislatures at least.

In three states—Washington, Minnesota, and Oregon—all states in which women have a larger than average share of state legislative seats (CAWP)—women legislators work actively to support women's interests. Once elected, they give money, help in campaigns, and give advice to newer women candidates; these forms of support are crucial in assisting women to win in some races. Moreover, while women incumbents typically actively support only candidates from their own party, they are also substantially willing to support male candidates who are obviously sympathetic to women's issues (Gierzynski & Budreck, 1995).

Historically, women representatives have been reluctant to push for women's specific interest because they feared being labeled as too "narrow" or as "only" interested in women's issues. Today they are more likely to agree with U.S. Representative Barbara Kelly, who remarked "My business is to get legislation through. My added business is to get legislation through to help women" (cited in Thomas & Welch, 1991). In 12 state legislatures there were no significant differences between women and men in giving speeches in the legislature, meeting with lobbyists, and bargaining to secure votes. The small differences that did exist disappeared when controls for constituency and party variables were introduced. However, in terms of issues, women are "busier" than men. They are more likely to introduce and give priority to bills supporting children, women, and social welfare, while men are more active than women only in regard to bills that reflect business issues (Thomas & Welch, 1991). Committee assignments in these 12 legislatures also revealed that women had gained access to more diverse committees than formerly, but women were less likely than men to serve on business and economics committees and more likely to sit on health and welfare ones. These findings are consistent with their policy priorities.

Women state legislators are also more likely than men to give direct service to their constituencies. Women receive more casework requests, believe that they perform more casework than their male colleagues, and would perform even more services if more staff were available (Richardson & Freeman, 1995). The authors explain these findings by saying that women are more likely than men to be socialized to care about interpersonal relations.

Finally, only one piece of recent research examines the impact of greater numbers of women; this research compares state legislators in Australia and the United States. Considine and Deutchman (1996) distinguish between social structure and culture. They find that sheer numbers of women make little difference in how women legislators are regarded. More women are elected and accepted on various committees than in the past, but this does not necessarily change legislative culture. Men are still regarded as typical politicians; women's differences from men are viewed as both assets (we get another point of view) and liabilities (they have too many things going on to be good legislators); and women and their activities are viewed as conspicuous and subject to different qualities and demands from men's. Thus, while more women are incorporated into the legislature, they are still seen as atypical politicians and have little impact on legislative culture.

4. CONCLUSION AND IMPLICATIONS

The research shows a persistent and possibly increasing gender gap in attitudes and behavior, with women more likely than men to vote and more likely to support women and Democratic liberal candidates. It also reveals that women are increasingly likely to run for office themselves and to win the election contests that they enter. Still, there is persistent evidence that women candidates (either hypothetical or real) suffer from stereotypes about their ability and interests. Even when the stereotypes are positive (e.g., women take more time with their constituents and are more interested in family and education than men), they are viewed as being competent in areas that are of less concern to the typical voter. Women candidates for office are becoming increasingly sophisticated in structuring their campaigns, and are able to garner more resources, often from women, than in the past.

The research reveals a growing effort to map how political opportunity structures exert their deleterious impact on women's issues and women's electability. This is accompanied by a strong tendency to visualize political structure as a "given." Political organization is viewed as being fairly rigid but increasingly permeable so that women can sometimes climb over, around, or through the barriers to their campaigning and being elected. The characteristics of women candidates change, but political structure does not. While women now comprise a sizable minority of officials in some state legislatures and city councils, only a handful of publications ask how women and/or feminists might change the structure and culture of the political system.

Authors in this growing research literature appear to be reluctant to see gender as much more than a shorthand concept for showing that women and men are somewhat different as political participants. There are few, if any, attempts to see gender as power and/or as a relationship. Thus, explanations of why women and men differ in voting and political participation typically refer back to a socialization hypothesis: women and men were treated and raised differently as children; therefore they have learned to be different as adults.

The very limited theorizing about gender and politics means that there is a substantial gap in the research literature, one that sociologists should and could attempt to fill. The findings about political structure and elections could easily be cast within the context of macrostructural theories of gender inequality (Blumberg, 1984; Chafetz, 1984, 1990). These perspectives explain patterns of gender inequality in different arenas, especially in work and family; they have less often been applied to understanding stratification in the political arena. Such an application would extend our understanding of both the gendered world of politics and gender stratification in general.

REFERENCES

Acosta-Belen, E. & Bose, C. E. (1990). From structure subordination to empowerment: Women and development in Third World contexts. *Gender & Society, 4,* 299–319.

Almquist, E., & Dunn, D. (1987). Professions and politics: The status of women in Texas and the other forty-nine states. Paper presented at the University of Texas at Austin.

Beckwith, K. (1992). Comparative research and electoral systems: Lessons from France and Italy. *Women and Politics, 12,* 1–33.

Bendix, J. (1992). Women's suffrage and political culture: A modern Swiss case. *Women and Politics, 12,* 27–56.

Bennett, L., & Bennett, S. (1989). Enduring gender differences in political interest. *American Politics Quarterly, 17*, 105–122.

Berch, N. (1996). The year of the woman in context, a test of six explanations. *American Politics Quarterly, 24*, 169–193.

Bledsoe, T., & Herring, M. (1990). Victims of circumstances: Women in pursuit of political office. *American Political Science Review, 84*, 213–223.

Blumberg, R. (1984). A general theory of gender stratification. In R. Collins (Ed.), *Sociological theory.* San Francisco: Jossey-Bass.

Brown, C., Heighberger, N. R., & Shocket, P. A. (1993). Gender-based differences in perceptions of male and female city council candidates. *Women and Politics, 13*, 1–17.

Bull, A. C. (1997). Class, gender, and voting in Italy. *Western European Politics, 20*, 73–92.

Burrell, B. C. (1994). *A woman's place is in the House, campaigning for Congress in the feminist era.* Ann Arbor, MI: The University of Michigan Press.

Busza, E., & Hahn, J. (1996). Women and politics in Russia: The Yaroslavl' Study. *Women and Politics, 16*, 55–87.

Carroll, S. (1994). *Women as Candidates in American Politics* (2nd ed.) Bloomington, IN: University Press.

Carroll, C. (1995). Gender and politics in contemporary Haiti: The Duvalierist state, transnationalism, and the emergence of a new feminism (1980–1990). *Feminist Studies, 21*, 135–164.

Center for the American Woman and Politics. (1998). Fact sheets. http .//www/rco/ritgers/edi/cawp. a. The gender gap in voting choices, party identification, and presidential performance ratings." b. Women in elective office 1997; c. Women in state legislatures 1997; d. Statewide elective executive women 1997; e. Women in the U.S. Congress 1997.

Chafetz, J. (1984). *Sex and advantage: A comparative macro-structural theory of sex stratification.* Totowa, NJ: Rowman & Allanheld.

Chaftez, J. (1990). *Gender equity: An integrated theory of stability and change.* Newbury, CA: Sage.

Conover, P. J., & Sapiro, V. (1993). Gender, feminist consciousness, and war. *American Journal of Political Science, 37*, 1079–1099.

Considine, M., & Deutchman, I. E. (1996). Instituting gender: State legislators in Australia and the United States. *Women and Politics, 16*, 1–19.

Corrin, C. (1994). Women's politics in Europe in the 1990s. *Women's Studies International Forum, 17*, 289–297.

Costantini, E. (1990). Political women and political ambition: Closing the gender gap. *American Journal of Political Science, 34*, 741–770.

Dabelko, K. la Cour, & Hernson, P. S. (1997). Women's and men's campaigns for the U.S. House of Representatives. *Political Research Quarterly, 50*, 121–135.

Darcy, R. (1999). Women in the state legislature power structure: Committee chairs. *Social Science Quarterly, 77*, 888–898.

Darcy, R., Welch, S., & Clark, J. (1987). *Women, elections and representation.* New York: Longman.

Darcy, R., Hadley, C. D., & Kirksey, J. F. (1993). Election systems and the representation of black women in American state legislatures. *Women and Politics, 13*, 73–89.

Diamond, I. (1977). *Sex Roles in the State House.* New Haven: Yale University Press.

Dolan, K. (1996). Support for women political candidates: An examination of the role of family. *Women and Politics, 16*, 45–60.

Dolan, K., & Ford, L. E. (1997). Change and continuity among women state legislators: Evidence from three decades. *Political Research Quarterly, 50*, 137–151.

Dunn, D. & Almquist, E. (1993). Predicting change in women's representation in state legislatures. Unpublished paper.

Gierzynski, A., & Budreck, P. (1995). Women legislative caucuses and leadership campaign committees. *Women and Politics, 15*, 23–36.

Githens, M. (1995). Getting appointed to the state court: The gender dimension. *Women and Politics, 15*, 1–23.

Hallas, K. (1996). Difficulties with feminism in Estonia. *Women's Studies International Forum, 17*, 299–300.

Hansen, S. B. (1997). Talking about politics: Gender and contextual effects on political proselytizing. *The Journal of Politics, 59*, 73–103.

Hayes, B. C., & Makkai, T. (1996). Politics and the mass media: the differential impact of gender. *Women and Politics, 16*, 45–73.

Herrick, R. (1996). A reappraisal of the quality of women candidates. *Women and Politics, 15*, 25–38.

Herick, R. (1996). Is there a gender gap in the value of campaign resources? *American Politics Quarterly, 24*, 68–80.

Hickman, J. C. (1999). The candidacy and election of women in Japanese SNTV electoral systems. *Women and Politics, 18*, 1–26.

Huddy, L., & Terkildsen, N. (1993). Gender stereotypes and the perception of male and female candidates. *American Journal of Political Science, 37,* 119–147.

Jelen, T. G., & Wilcox, C. (1996). A tale of two senators: Female candidates for the U.S. Senate in Illinois, 1990–1992. *The American Review of Politics, 17,* 299–310.

Kahn, K. F. (1994). Does gender make a difference? An experimental examination of sex stereotypes and press patterns in statewide campaigns. *American Journal of Political Science, 38,* 162–195.

Koch, J. (1997). Candidate gender and women's psychological engagement in politics. *American Politics Quarterly, 13,* 118–133.

Krebs, T. B., & Walsh, M. H. (1996). Nonincumbent female candidate success in the 1992 U.S. House Elections. *Social Science Quarterly, 77,* 697–707.

Luebke, B. F. (1989). Out of focus: Images of women and men in newspaper photographs. *Sex Roles: A Journal of Research, 20,* 121–133.

Malinowska, E. (1995). Socio-political changes in Poland and the problem of sex discrimination. *Women's Studies International Forum, 18,* 35–43.

Margolis, D. R. (1993). Women's movements around the world: Cross-cultural comparisons. *Gender and Society, 7,* 379–399.

Matland, R. E., & Studlar, D. T. (1996). The contagion of women candidates in single-member district and proportional representation electoral systems: Canada and Norway. *The Journal of Politics, 58,* 707–733.

Moghadam, V. M. (1995). Gender and revolutionary transformation: Iran 1979 and East Central Europe 1989. *Gender and Society, 9,* 328–358.

Molyneux, M. (1995). Review essay: Gendered transitions in Eastern Europe. *Feminist Studies, 21,* 637–644.

Naff, K. C. (1995). Subjective vs. objective discrimination in government: Adding to the picture of barriers to the advancement of women. *Political Research Quarterly, 48,* 507–534.

Nechemias, C. (1994). Democratization and women's access to legislative seats: The Soviet case, 1989–1991. *Women and Politics, 14,* 1–18.

Nelson, B. J. (1992). The role of sex and gender in comparative political analysis: Individuals, institutions, and regimes. *American Political Science Review, 86,* 491–495.

Nixon, D. L., & Darcy, R. (1996). Special elections and the growth of women's representation in the U.S. House of representatives. *Women and Politics, 16,* 99–107.

Oakes, A., & Almquist, E., (1993). Women in national legislatures: A cross-national test of macrostructural gender theories. *Population Research and Policy Review, 12,* 71–81.

Patton, C. G. (1992). Making women count: Influencing governments at all levels. *Women and Politics, 12,* 69–72.

Peterson, V. S. (1995). Women and gender in power/politics, nationalism and revolution. *Journal of Politics, 57,* 870–878.

Procter, D. E., Schenck-Hamlin, W. J., & Haase, K. A. (1994). Exploring the role of gender in the development of negative political advertisements. *Women and Politics, 14,* 1–22.

Richardson, L. E., & Freeman, P. K. (1995). Gender differences in constituency service among state legislators. *Political Research Quarterly, 48,* 169–179.

Rosenthal, C. S. (1995). The role of gender in descriptive representation. *Political Research Quaterly, 48,* 599–611.

Rule, W. (1990). Why more women are state legislators: A research note. *Western Political Quarterly, 48,* 437–448.

Segal, M. W. (1995). Women's military roles cross-nationally: Past, present and future. *Gender & Society, 9,* 757–775.

Silverberg, H. (1990). What happened to the feminist revolution in political science. *Western Political Quarterly, 43,* 887–903.

Studlar, D. T., & McAllister, I. (1991). Political recruitment to the Australian legislature: Toward an explanation of women's electoral disadvantages. *Western Political Quarterly, 44,* 466–475.

Studlar, D. T., & Welch, S. (1992). Does district magnitude matter? Women candidates in London local elections. *Western Political Quarterly, 45,* 457–466.

Thomas, S. (1992). The effects of race and gender on constituency service. *Western Political Quarterly, 45,* 169–180.

Thomas, S., & Welch, S. (1991). The impact of gender on activities and priorities of state legislators. *Western Political Quarterly, 44,* 446–455.

Welch, S. & Sigelman, L. (1992). A gender gap among hispanics? A comparison with blacks and anglos. *Western Political Quarterly, 45,* 181–190.

Werner, B. L. (1997). Financing the campaigns of women candidates and their opponents: Evidence from three states, 1982–1990. *Women and Politics, 18,* 81–97.

Wilcox, C. (1990). Race, gender role attitudes and support for feminism. *Western Political Quarterly, 43,* 113–121.

CHAPTER 24

Gender, Crime,
and Criminal Justice

SALLY S. SIMPSON
DENISE C. HERZ

1. INTRODUCTION

A decade ago, the standard opening paragraph of a review chapter such as this would deplore the paucity of criminological research on females and the sexism inherent in theoretical accounts of female crime (and conformity). Owing primarily to the work of feminist criminologists, the field has happily moved beyond such obvious deficiencies. In this chapter, we review the criminological and criminal justice literature that examines the gendered organization of crime and social control. To do so, we briefly discuss the origins of the feminist critique in criminology and review patterns of criminal offending and justice interventions by gender. Specific issues that have arisen within feminist criminology (e.g., the implications of equal treatment for male and female offenders) are used to highlight more recent theoretical and empirical developments in the field.

Relative to other social science disciplines, criminology was a latecomer to feminist concerns. Second wave feminism was well-established when select criminologists noted the absence of females from major theories of criminal offending and/or the sexist treatment of females within theories in which they were not ignored (Harris, 1977; Heidensohn, 1968; Klein, 1973; Leonard, 1982; Rasche, 1974). The work of two female criminologists—Rita Simon (1975) and Freda Adler (1975)—sparked mainstream criminology's

SALLY S. SIMPSON • Department of Criminology and Criminal Justice, University of Maryland, College Park, Maryland 20742
DENISE C. HERZ • Department of Criminal Justice, University of Nebraska at Omaha, Omaha, Nebraska 68182

Handbook of the Sociology of Gender, edited by Janet Saltzman Chafetz. Kluwer Academic/ Plenum Publishers, New York, 1999.

interest in the female offender (along with that of the popular press) by hypothesizing that the women's liberation movement had created a new type of female offender. Simon suggested that as employment opportunities opened up for women, so too had white-collar offending opportunities. Adler predicted that female participation in all crimes (including violence) would converge with male rates as the women's movement changed perceptions of acceptable and unacceptable conduct among females. Criticisms of Simon's and Adler's work provided a springboard from which more explicitly feminist under-standings of crime and justice were launched.

2. PATTERNS OF CRIMINAL OFFENDING BY GENDER

In the mid-1970s, when Simon and Adler were writing, female rates of participation in most kinds of criminal offending—especially serious crime—were low. Their research raised several important questions regarding the gender and crime relationship that fueled somewhat separate research agendas for mainstream and feminist scholars: (1) What can account for such low participation rates in serious crime by women vis a vis men? (2) Are these patterns changing over time (i.e., is a new female offender emerging)? (3) Are the factors that produce crime and conformity in males and females the same? Do the same forces drive changes in male and female rates? (4) How should feminists study crime?

The answers to some of these questions lie in the empirical record. In the Tables 24-1 to 24-3, male and female rates of offending are compared over time using official arrest data (Uniform Crime Reports) and offender self-reports (Monitoring the Future Project).

In Table 24-1, male and female arrest rates per 100,000 are compared across 15-year intervals beginning in 1960 (columns 1 to 6). These statistics demonstrate several important patterns. First, they show that most crimes are committed by males. This pattern is most notable in violent and serious property crime rates, but exists across the board except for prostitution, in which female rates are higher than those for males. For the most part, increases and decreases in male and female rates over time parallel each other, suggesting that the rates of both "are influenced by similar social and legal forces, independent of any condition unique to women or men" (Steffensmeier & Allan, 1996, p. 462).

Looking at the arrest profiles of males and females (i.e., the percentage of total male and female arrests within each crime category for 1960 and 1990) and comparing data from 1960 and 1990 (columns 7 to 10), it is clear that violent crime (excluding simple assault) is a rare offense for both sexes. Females are most apt to be arrested for larceny–theft (20%), alcohol related offenses (i.e., drunkenness and DUI), and, more recently, forgery, frauds, and drug abuse. The greatest proportion of male arrests are for DUI (15% in 1990, up from 5% in 1960) and larceny–theft, followed by public drunkenness (dropping from 36% of all male arrests in 1960 to 8% in 1990).

Overall, females exceed 50% of the total arrests in only one offense area—prostitution (columns 12 to 13). The next highest categories are minor property offenses (including larceny–theft, fraud, forgery, and embezzlement in which female percentages range between 30% and 43% of total arrests). Males, on the other hand, clearly dominate the arrest statistics in more serious crime categories, such as crimes against persons, major property, and malicious mischief (which includes auto theft and arson). They also account for relatively large arrest percentages in some trivial crime categories (e.g., va-

TABLE 24-1. Male and Female Arrest Rates/100,000, Male and Female Arrest Profiles, and Female Percentage of Arrests (uniform crime reports)

Offenses	Male Rates			Female Rates			Offender-Profile Percentage				Female Percentage (of Arrests)		
							Males		Females				
	1960	1975	1990	1960	1975	1990	1960	1990	1960	1990	1960	1975	1990
	(1)	(2)	(3)	(4)	(5)	(6)	(7)	(8)	(9)	(10)	(11)	(12)	(13)
Homicide	9	16	19	2	3	2	.1	.2	.2	.1	17	14	11
Aggravated assault	101	200	317	16	28	50	1	3	2	2	14	13	13
Weapons	69	137	165	4	11	14	1	2	.5	.7	4	8	7
Simple assault	265	354	662	29	54	129	4	6	.4	.5	10	13	15
Robbery	65	131	124	4	10	12	1	1	.5	.5	5	7	8
Burglary	274	477	319	9	27	32	4	3	1	1	3	5	8
Stolen property	21	103	121	2	12	17	.3	1	.2	.5	8	10	11
Larceny-theft	391	749	859	74	321	402	6	10	9	20	17	30	30
Fraud	70	114	157	12	59	133	1	2	2	7	15	34	43
Forgery	44	46	51	8	18	28	.5	.5	1	1	16	28	34
Embezzlement	—	7	8	—	3	5	—	.2	—	.1	—	28	37
Auto theft	121	128	158	5	9	18	2	1	1	1	4	7	9
Vandalism	—	187	224	—	16	28	—	2	—	1	—	8	10
Arson	—	15	13	—	2	2	—	.3	—	.1	—	11	14
Public drunkenness	2573	1201	624	212	87	71	36	8	25	4	8	7	9
DUI	344	971	1193	21	81	176	5	15	3	9	6	5	11
Liquor laws	183	276	428	28	43	102	3	5	4	5	13	14	17
Drug Abuse	49	523	815	8	79	166	1	7	1	6	15	13	14
Prostitution	15	18	30	37	45	62	.2	.4	4	3	73	73	65
Sex offenses	81	55	78	17	5	7	1	1	2	.3	17	8	8
Disorderly conduct	749	597	499	115	116	119	11	5	14	6	13	17	18
Vacrancy	265	45	26	23	7	4	4	.3	3	.2	8	14	12
Suspicion	222	31	13	28	5	3	3	.1	3	.1	11	13	15
Against family	90	57	51	8	7	12	1	.5	1	.5	8	10	16
Gambling	202	60	14	19	6	2	3	.2	2	.2	8	9	15
Other exc. traffic	871	1139	2109	150	197	430	13	23	19	20	15	15	18
Total	7070	7850	9211	831	1383	212					11	15	19

Source: Steffensmeier & Allen (1996), with permission, from the Annual Review of Sociology, Vol. 22, ©1996, by Annual Reviews, Inc.

grancy and gambling). The consistency of most of these figures over time suggests that the new breed of female offender (i.e., becoming more like her male counterpart) is, as described by Steffensmeier (1978) almost 20 years ago, more myth than reality.

In Table 24-2, we present raw arrest statistics for juvenile offenders by sex for the years 1984 and 1994 (*Sourcebook of Criminal Justice Statistics*, 1985; 1995). The figures for juveniles tell a similar but somewhat more complex story. Again, we see that males are arrested much more often than females for almost all types of crimes. For index offenses (murder, rape, robbery, aggravated assault, burglary, larceny–theft, motor vehicle theft, and arson), the ratio of male to female arrests was approximately 3:1 in 1994.

TABLE 24-2. Juvenile Arrests, by Offense Charged and Sex, 1984 and 1994

	Males Under 18		Females Under 18	
Offense charged	1984	1994	1984	1994
Total	1,111,692	1,573,567	316,165	503,382
Murder and nonnegligent manslaughter	836	2,838	96	178
Forcible rape	4,014	4,555	53	93
Robbery	24,135	42,010	1,654	4,258
Aggravated assault	23,773	54,875	4,791	12,523
Burglary	108,313	100,110	8,524	10,568
Larceny-theft	229,973	268,385	84,572	126,949
Motor vehicle theft	27,414	61,299	3,516	9,919
Arson	5,291	7,769	511	1,088
Violent crime	52,758	104,278	6,594	17,052
Property crime	370,991	437,563	97,123	148,524
Total crime index	423,749	541,841	103,717	165,576
Other assaults	47,554	121,580	14,398	43,612
Forgery and counterfeiting	3,982	4,254	1,825	2,436
Fraud	12,945	13,514	3,747	4,751
Embezzlement	274	508	141	282
Stolen property; buying, receiving, possessing	19,110	30,703	2,0971	3,919
Vandalism	73,915	104,738	6,901	12,033
Weapons; carrying possessing	17,776	46,363	1,220	4,062
Prositition and commercialized vice	606	510	1,560	487
Sex offenses (except forcible rape and prostitution)	11,648	12,741	831	1,063
Drug abuse violations	51,805	112,327	9,356	14,898
Gambling	526	1,390	56	73
Offenses against family and children	904	240	497	1,373
Driving under the influence	14,607	8,583	2,361	1,407
Liquor laws	69,818	63,124	24,365	25,421
Drunkenness	18,179	11,746	3,469	2,290
Disorderly conduct	56,223	99,481	12,829	30,274
Vagrancy	1,531	2,913	359	672
All other offenses (except traffic)	192,730	257,226	49,696	72,619
Suspicion (not included in totals)	1,900	1,166	425	297
Curfew and loitering law violations	49,167	72,382	15,163	29,434
Runaways	44,653	65,193	61,577	86,706

Source: Uniform Crime Report Data, taken from the Sourcebook of Criminal Justice Statistics, 1985, 1995.

The arrest ratio was much greater for violent than for property crime (e.g., in 1994, the male-to-female arrest ratio for violence was 6:1; for property, 2.9:1). Within the index, the most common offense for which both females and males are arrested is larceny–theft. Female arrests exceed those for males in two main categories: (1) running away from home and (2) prostitution and vice.

In 1984, the top five offenses for which males were arrested were larceny–theft, all other offenses, burglary, vandalism, and liquor laws, and for females during the same time period, larceny–theft, runaway, all other offenses, liquor laws, and curfew and loitering offenses were the top five arrest categories. There were some changes in arrest patterns by the next decade, although change did not occur at the top of either list. The data in Table 24-2 show that the most common offenses for juveniles are relatively minor. This is particularly true for females where status offenses (such as runaway and curfew and loitering) comprise a significant but declining proportion of female total arrests over time (approximately 24% of all female arrests in 1984 and 23% in 1994).

In Table 24-3, we report findings from a national survey of high school seniors (Bachman, Johnston, & O'Malley, 1988 as reported in the *Sourcebook of Criminal Statistics*, 1995; Johnston, Bachman, and O'Malley, 1983, 1993) in which students report involvement in delinquent activities for the 12-month period prior to their participation in the survey. From these data, we can see that involvement in crime is atypical regardless of gender. As in the arrest statistics, the most common self -reported delinquent activity was theft. In 1983, 34% of the boys and 21% of the girls reported taking something from a store without paying for it on at least one occasion. These numbers increased slightly over the decade. Far fewer reported taking items worth $50.00 or more, offenses that signify involvement in more serious types of theft. Trespassing is the next most commonly reported act for both boys and girls, followed by vandalizing school property and getting into fights—at school or to support friends. Rarely do the latter result in serious injuries—especially when the combatants are female. It is important to note, however, that few of these respondents report frequent involvement in any of these delinquent acts.

3. MAKING SENSE OF THE EMPIRICAL RECORD

Mainstream scholars find little empirical evidence, either in the United States or cross-nationally, to support Adler's or Simon's claims (Mukherjee & Scott, 1981; Steffensmeier, 1978; see Kruttschnitt 1996 and Simpson, 1989, for further discussion of these studies). The empirical record suggested that female crime rates have been remarkably stable over time, particularly in the more serious crime categories. When increases did occur, it was generally in areas in which female crime had been concentrated for decades (e.g., theft). Some increases were noted in nontraditional areas, such as embezzlement, forgery, and fraud (Simon, 1975, 1990), but disentangling occupational crimes from non-white-collar offenses (e.g., accounting from welfare fraud, stock forgeries from writing bad checks) in the statistical record is impossible without much more detailed investigation. Daly's (1989c) research on gender and white-collar crime demonstrated the fallacy of linking changing rates of female arrests for embezzlement, fraud, or forgery to increases in women's labor force participation. The so-called "white-collar" female offenders in Daly's sample were employed in "pink-collar" positions. Unlike most of the male offenders, but similar to conventional female offenders, presentence reports indicated that these women offended not because they were liberated, but because they were economically marginalized. Need, not greed, drove the "white"-collar offending of most women.

Feminist scholars were highly critical of the women's liberation thesis (Leonard, 1982). First, it ran counter to what feminist criminologists had discovered about female criminals, that is, that criminality was concentrated among the economically disadvantaged and minorities. Prejudice and discrimination, unemployment, the economic segregation of women into low-paying, nonunionized, and unstable jobs, and the feminization of poverty were more likely explanations for female offending than liberation (Giordano, Kerbel, & Dudley, 1977; Klein, 1973; Simpson, 1991). Second, the idea that females were becoming more malelike in their offending patterns captured the imagination of the

TABLE 24-3. **Self-Reported Delinquent Involvement by High School Seniors in the Last 12 Months, by Offense and Sex**

Delinquency	Class of 1983		Class of 1988		Class of 1993	
	Male (N = 1,671)	Female (N = 1,641)	Male (N = 1,582)	Female (N = 1,651)	Male (N = 1,294)	Female (N = 1,321)
Taken something from a store without paying for it?						
Not at all	68.4%	79.5%	63.2%	76.2%	62.4%	76.7%
Once	13.9	11.9	13.8	11.9	15.1	11.5
Twice	6.7	3.4	8.5	4.5	6.1	5.1
3 or 4 times	5.6	2.6	6.2	3.5	7.1	3.0
5 or more times	5.3	2.6	8.4	3.9	9.4	3.6
Taken a car that didn't belong to someone in your family without permission of the owner.						
Not at all	92.3	97.0	92.9	96.2	91.2	96.2
Once	3.9	2.3	4.1	2.7	4.3	1.7
Twice	1.6	0.5	1.3	0.5	1.7	1.3
3 or 4 times	1.1	0.1	0.7	0.2	1.4	0.4
5 or more times	1.1	0.1	0.9	0.2	1.4	10.4
Gone into some house or building when you weren't suppose to be there.						
Not at all	69.3	84.2	67.1	78.2	65.9	82.5
Once	13.6	9.1	15.0	10.4	13.9	9.4
Twice	9.5	4.2	8.2	5.4	8.2	5.4
3 or 4 times	4.5	1.6	5.4	2.8	5.2	1.7
5 or more times	3.1	0.9	4.2	3.2	6.8	0.9
Set fire to someone's property on purpose?						
Not at all	97.7	99.9	97.3	99.4	94.1	99.1
Once	1.2	0.1	1.5	0.5	2.4	0.4
Twice	0.4	0.0	0.5	0.1	1.1	0.4
3 or 4 times	0.3	0.0	0.2	(a)	1.0	0.1
5 or more times	0.4	(a)	10.4	(a)	1.3	0.0
Damaged school property on purpose?						
Not at all	78.5	93.3	79.8	91.8	77.7	92.8
Once	9.9	4.2	10.6	5.3	8.6	4.3
Twice	4.8	1.6	4.6	1.6	6.2	1.9
3 or 4 times	4.1	0.5	2.4	0.8	3.3	0.7
5 or more times	2.7	0.5	2.6	0.5	4.2	0.3
Damaged property at work on purpose?						
Not at all	90.1	98.9	89.6	98.4	89.5	98.0
Once	4.3	0.8	5.4	1.1	4.4	1.2
Twice	2.6	0.3	2.6	0.3	2.6	0.4
3 or 4 times	1.8	0.0	0.8	0.1	1.4	0.3
5 or more times	1.2	(a)	1.6	0.1	2.1	0.1

TABLE 24-3. *Continued*

Argued or had a fight with either of your parents?						
Not at all	13.3	8.8	10.8	8.0	15.5	8.0
Once	11.2	10.4	9.6	6.7	11.8	7.3
Twice	10.7	12.5	12.6	9.2	12.2	12.1
3 or 4 times	26.2	22.9	23.8	23.9	18.5	22.1
5 or more times	38.6	45.3	43.2	52.2	42.0	50.5
Hit an instructor or supervisor?						
Not at all	94.9	98.7	95.8	99.0	94.3	98.3
Once	2.9	0.7	2.2	0.6	3.3	1.1
Twice	1.1	0.4	1.0	0.3	1.0	0.1
3 or 4 times	4.1	0.1	0.3	0.1	0.4	0.3
5 or more times	1.4	0.1	0.6	0.0	1.0	0.1
Gotten into a serious fight in school or at work?						
Not at all	75.3	89.6	77.6	86.6	78.4	87.0
Once	14.0	7.2	12.0	9.1	11.2	8.5
Twice	5.1	1.6	5.8	2.5	5.2	2.3
3 or 4 times	4.1	1.3	2.9	1.2	3.1	1.9
5 or more times	1.4	0.4	1.7	0.7	2.1	0.4
Taken part in a fight where a group of your friends were against another group?						
Not at all	78.5	86.1	75.6	85.5	71.0	85.5
Once	11.2	9.0	12.8	9.7	13.8	8.2
Twice	5.3	3.1	12.8	9.7	7.2	4.3
3 or 4 times	3.0	1.3	5.4	3.4	4.1	1.4
5 or more times	2.2	0.5	3.6	1.0	3.9	0.6
Hurt someone badly enough to need bandages or a doctor?						
Not at all	81.4	96.7	82.5	96.6	78.6	95.0
Once	11.9	2.5	10.2	2.2	11.1	3.0
Twice	2.9	0.5	3.0	0.8	4.1	1.4
3 or 4 times	2.5	(a)	2.7	0.3	2.9	0.5
5 or more times	1.5	0.2	1.6	0.1	3.3	0.1
Used a knife or gun or some other thing (like a club) to get something from a person?						
Not at all	95.2	99.0	95.6	99.0	91.9	99.0
Once	2.2	0.7	2.4	0.6	2.6	0.7
Twice	1.0	0.7	0.6	0.3	1.7	0.1
3 or 4 times	0.6	0.0	0.5	(a)	2.2	0.2
5 or more times	1.0	0.1	0.9	0.2	1.6	0.0

Continued

TABLE 24-3. *Continued*

Taken something not belonging to you worth under $50?						
Not at all	61.5	77.2	57.8	74.7	59.9	76.5
Once	16.6	13.3	17.8	12.7	15.8	11.9
Twice	8.8	4.3	9.8	5.0	7.7	6.2
3 or 4 times	6.3	2.9	6.6	3.9	5.7	3.1
5 or more times	6.8	2.3	8.0	3.6	11.0	2.3
Taken something not belonging to you worth over $50?						
Not at all	89.9	97.8	86.9	96.3	82.5	95.6
Once	5.7	1.0	6.3	1.8	7.6	2.3
Twice	2.0	0.5	3.0	1.0	3.4	0.6
3 or 4 times	1.3	0.4	1.3	0.4	2.1	0.7
5 or more times	1.1	0.2	2.4	0.4	4.5	0.9

Source: Adapted from Johnston, Bachman, & O'Malley (1983, 1993); Bachman, Johnston, & O'Malley (1988).

popular press despite the paucity of empirical evidence supporting the claim. The media's emphasis on the dark side of women's liberation created a "moral panic" (Smart, 1976), giving ammunition to a conservative backlash that challenged the legitimacy of second - wave feminist goals (equality between the sexes). Third, within criminology, the gender question was framed within the parameters of the liberation thesis (Howe, 1990), thereby marginalizing more critical challenges of criminological theories, especially those by feminists (Klein, 1973; Leonard, 1982; Smart, 1976).

4. ACCOUNTING FOR CRIMINAL OFFENDING PATTERNS

4.1. Dominant Paradigms

Mainstream explanations for criminal offending are drawn primarily from developmental, social learning, social (and self -) control, social strain, social ecology, and to a lesser extent labeling and rational choice perspectives.[1] Most of these approaches lay claim to general theory status. As such, each should be able to account for the criminality and/or conformity of both males and females. However, close examination reveals a lack of consideration for females and their experiences. Indeed, most theorizing about crime is generated from the experiences of male subjects (whether criminals or conformists) and then generalized to females. Females are treated as "the other," excluded from theories except (perhaps) as a contrast point for males (Naffine, 1986). Few of the dominant explanations for crime explicitly confront the gender-ratio problem or recognize deficiencies in theory generalizability (Chesney-Lind & Daly, 1988, p. 514; Kruttschnitt, 1996).

[1] Many feminist scholars have reviewed and critiqued early criminological writings about female offenders including Freud (1933), Glueck and Glueck (1934), Lombroso and Ferrero (1915), Pollack (1950), and Thomas (1907, 1923). Although it is clear that many current conceptions about female criminality may be traced to these theorists (Chesney-Lind & Shelden, 1992; Klein, 1973; Rasche, 1974; Smart, 1976), most contemporary criminological perspectives tend to ignore females entirely while claiming to be general theories of criminality.

We have too little space to devote much attention to each of these approaches (excellent critiques are supplied by Chesney-Lind & Sheldon, 1992; Leonard, 1982; Messerschmidt, 1993 and Naffine, 1986). However, a cursory review and brief feminist critique is warranted.

The basic premise of strain theories is that there is a disjuncture for some in society between positively valued goals (e.g., financial success, good jobs, social status) and the opportunity structures available to successfully achieve those goals. As stated by Merton (1938), Cohen (1955), and Cloward and Ohlin (1960), criminality is more likely to occur within the lower classes where legitimate opportunities are less available and illegal alternatives (and criminal subcultures) are apt to arise. Theorists either failed to consider how their theory would account for female criminality (e.g., in Merton's theory, females should be more strained and hence have greater involvement in crime than males) or explicitly excluded females from the theoretical framework because they didn't fit. Cohen, for instance, suggested that females are concerned with a narrower set of issues than males, specifically, relations with the opposite sex. When frustrated in their goals, females resort to getting their man in immoral ways (i.e., promiscuity). Their delinquency was not "real delinquency" (i.e., aggressive and violent) but puny and pitiful—sexual and emotional (Naffine, 1986). Similarly, Cloward and Ohlin discounted females from engaging in "real" crime because of their domesticity—it was neither necessary nor important for females to seek either legitimate or illegitimate opportunities. The fact that working class and many minority women worked out of economic necessity, confronted employment bias on a regular basis, and still had crime rates lower than their male counterparts neither illuminated nor challenged these theorists.

Social learning perspectives, including differential association (Akers, 1973; Sutherland, 1934) account for criminality as learned behavior. Criminality is acquired through a process of association and exposure to definitions favorable or unfavorable to the violation of law. Criminal behavior is reinforced or extinguished through the application of rewards or punishments. While somewhat more inclusive of females than other theories (e.g., Sutherland suggests that gender differences in socialization and control account for gender differences in crime and Akers argues that sexual deviance is related to problems with gender identification and sex-role behavior), social learning perspectives are not explicit about how gendered crime develops nor do they recognize that nonsexual kinds of crime, such as white-collar, are also gendered (see Chesney-Lind & Sheldon, 1992, p. 68).

Social control theory assumes that all are capable of crime. Hence, according to control theorists, the more interesting theoretical question to pose and answer is "Why do people conform?" (Hirschi, 1969, p. 10). Different versions of control theory emphasize different factors that produce conformity (i.e., a positive self-concept, high degree of self-control, stakes in conformity, strong social bonds to society); yet, the fact that females are overwhelmingly more conforming than males has *not* produced theories that begin with this empirical truth. Instead, the delinquency of males is the empirical and conceptual starting point for these theories. Hirschi (1969, pp. 35–36) recognizes the duplicity in this approach when he drops girls from his empirical analysis and offers the following disclaimer: "Since girls have been neglected for far too long by students of delinquency, the exclusion of them is difficult to justify. I hope to return to them soon."

More recent control theory developments have a mixed record on the gender issue. Sampson and Laub's (1993) age-graded theory of informal control, for instance, is exclusively based in the experiences of male offenders and a matched male control group of nonoffenders. Gottfredson and Hirschi (1990, p. 148), on the other hand, note the stability of gender differences in rates of delinquency and suggest that such differences emerge early in life, "well before differences in opportunity are possible, and persist into adulthood, where differences in supervision by agents of social control are minimal." Consequently, they theorize that the gender ratio problem is "largely the result of crime differences *and* differences in self-control that are not produced by direct external control" (Gottfredson & Hirschi, 1990, p. 149, emphasis in original). Putatively, these differences are attributable to gender differences in children's susceptibility to socialization and parental initiative to recognize deviance and to discipline and control it. However, the authors suggest that "it is beyond the scope of this work (and beyond the reach of any available set of empirical data) to attempt to identify all of the elements responsible for gender differences in crime" (149).

Developmental theories, such as those advanced by Wilson and Herrnstein (1985), Fishbein (1990), Moffitt (1994), and Patterson, DeBaryshe, & Ramsey (1989), draw upon biological, psychosocial, and social factors to explain initiation and continued participation in criminal offending. Few of these authors focus exclusively on gender (an exception is Caspi, Lynam, Moffitt, & Silva, 1993); yet, different rates of participation in violence between the sexes is an empirical consideration that all confront in some way. Moffitt (1994), for instance, proposed two distinct pathways to delinquency. The pathway for life-course persisters is caused by neuropsychological problems that are exacerbated by parental inabilities to cope with the child's special needs and subsequent problems with social adjustment (a developmental path similar to that proposed by Fishbein, 1990). Life-course persisters become serious chronic offenders, behavior that continues into adulthood. These offenders, Moffitt claims, are almost always male, but she offers little explanation for why this is the case. The other pathway to delinquency emerges in adolescence and is the consequence of a maturity gap between biological maturation and the adolescent desire for, but exclusion from, adult privileges. The delinquency of "adolescent-limited" offenders is minor (e.g., status offenses such as drinking, truancy, smoking; minor property offending, getting into fights). The acts are a statement of defiance of, and "independence" from, adult authority and rules. Adolescent-limited offenders, both males and females, begin offending later than life-course persisters and cease offending in late adolescence as adult opportunities open up to them. Moreover, given the trivial nature of most of their delinquency, there has been no attenuation of the adolescents' bonds to conventional society.

While Moffitt's theory (and other developmental theories) acknowledge gender differences in juvenile crime, there are several noteworthy problems. First, although there are relatively few serious offenders among female adolescents, a recent cohort study (Tracy, Wolfgang, & Figlio, 1990) shows that black female violent crime rates are significantly higher than white female rates. For UCR violent offenses, black female rates are 5.5 times those of white females. Black females are also more apt to be chronic offenders. Therefore, Moffitt's explanation for life-course persistent offenders is not sensitive to potentially important intra-gender differences in crime. Further, although data would support Moffitt's claims that both males and females engage in adolescent limited offenses, it is not clear from her explanation how gender-specific differences would arise. Finally, if Moffitt's arguments are accurate, we would expect few adult females to engage in crime. Although gender differences in crime rates are greater in adulthood than they are during adolescence, adult females do engage in crime. Moffitt's theory offers little in the way of understanding the situation of adult women and the offenses that they commit.

Labeling theory has generated two main arguments in criminology: deviance amplification and status characteristics. In the former, the deviant label is treated as an independent variable such that its application influences future involvement in crime (Lemert, 1951). In brief, the idea behind deviance amplification is that almost all engage in some acts of deviance (primary deviance) but, through the use of neutralizing techniques, manage to maintain a conformist self-image. However, when deviant acts are repetitive and highly visible, they are likely to come to the attention of authorities. This official reaction to deviance results in the application of a deviant label and the increased likelihood that the labeled person will incorporate that label into his or her conception of self and engage in further deviant acts (secondary deviance). From a feminist perspective, one of the key problems with these theoretical arguments rests in the presumption that primary deviance is evenly distributed in society and tends to be nonserious. This prediction is challenged by the empirical reality of crime. Primary participation rates clearly vary by gender (and race) and by crime seriousness.

Moving to the status characteristics argument, the theory predicts who will receive a deviant label (or more specifically, what category of persons are more likely be officially processed and hence officially labeled as a delinquent/criminal). According to Becker (1963), deviance is defined through the creation and application of rules (laws). Those who are more powerful in society create rules to control and manage the behavior of those less powerful. Thus, the lower class and minority members of society are more apt to have their behaviors criminalized and be officially labeled than upper-class and majority group members. Although equivocal, there is some empirical support for these predictions. However, the implications and failures of the theory regarding gender are clear: females are less powerful than males (Becker, 1963) and therefore should be labeled more often than are males. The empirical record fails to support this assertion.

Labeling theory has not been entirely rejected by feminists (see Chesney-Lind & Sheldon, 1992; Leonard, 1982) because, with modification, the ideas may lead to a better understanding of how gender affects the patterning of crime and the juvenile/criminal processing of offenders (e.g., Harris's ideas about typescripting, 1977). Chesney-Lind and Sheldon (1992, p. 70), for instance, note that the theory has given some direction to those "critical of 'status offenses' and other attempts to label women as deviant."

Social ecology theories of crime, such as those of Shaw and McKay (1972), examine the symbiosis between the physical environment of urban areas and its human inhabitants. Building on the work of Burgess (1928), who traces the development of the city from its core outward through a process of invasion, dominance, and succession, Shaw and McKay discovered that official delinquency rates followed similar developmental patterns. They were highest in areas near the core of the city (zones of transition) and successively lower in zones further from the core. Looking at the characteristics of the transition zones and the populations that lived there over time, Shaw and McKay theorized that the physical deterioration of an area and social disorganization of the population that lived there were linked. High rates of delinquency were symptomatic of the social disorganization of the area.

Although Shaw and McKay (1972) did make note of female delinquency rates in several cities and claimed that the female patterns, like those for males, were higher in the center city zones, the male rates were used throughout their works as "delinquency rates" (Chesney-Lind & Shelten, 1992, p. 63). The theory also does not address why male rates in some cities were generally higher and less concentrated than those for females. If the social ecology of a place determines offending levels, the theory has little to say about why rates would be different for boys and girls.

The last dominant paradigm to be discussed, rational choice, has been roundly criticized by feminists in fields other than criminology (see, e.g., England & Kilbourne, 1990). In criminology, rational choice perspectives have emerged from deterrence and economic explanations of crime (see, e.g., Becker, 1968; Paternoster, 1987). The general assumptions of the perspective include the following: (1) the criminal offender is reasoned (rationality is bounded); (2) the decision to engage in crime occurs after the offender has weighed the costs and benefits of his/her action; (3) the offending decision is constrained by situational conditions and individual preferences (Cornish and Clarke, 1986; Nagin & Paternoster, 1993; Piliavin, Thornton, Gartner, & Matsueda, 1986). Some models, but not all (see Piliavin et al., 1986), have incorporated law, norms, and values into the decision mix (Bachman, Paternoster, & Ward, 1993; Grasmick & Bursik, 1990; Paternoster and Simpson, 1993, 1996).

Feminists have criticized rational choice perspectives on two grounds. First, women are generally excluded from consideration in the theory. Second, if included, they generally fail to live up to the predictions of the theory (Friedman & Diem, 1993, p. 92). In criminology, many of the studies that draw from a rational choice perspective either exclude females from the analysis altogether (Bachman et al., 1993) or, treat gender as a control variable (Paternoster, 1989; Nagin & Paternoster, 1993; Paternoster & Simpson, 1996) rather than pondering how the decision process may be gendered (an exception is Tibbetts & Herz, 1996). Even in studies in which gender effects are hypothesized, they are viewed as secondary to "more important hypotheses" (Piliavin et al., 1986, p. 110). The importance of interpersonal comparisons of utility within the theory, that is, situations that occur "when an individual attempts to assess the utilities that other individuals would have derived from alternative social situations and tries to compare these utilities with the utilities that she herself will derive from these alternative social situations" (Friedman & Diem, 1993, p. 112), which arguably are especially relevant for the way that women make decisions (England & Kilbourne, 1990), are not considered in the models.

4.2. Feminist Challenges

From a feminist perspective, the dominant paradigms in criminology have generally failed the gender ratio and generalizability tests (Daly & Chesney-Lind, 1988). Feminists have approached these failures in a number of ways. Some seek to modify the deficiencies of the dominant theories and/or rectify the male-centered research focus (Cernkovich & Giordano, 1987; 1992; Giordano, Cernkovich, & Pugh, 1986; Morash, 1986; Rosenbaum & Lasley, 1990). Others have turned to liberalism and Marxism to confront the gender difference problem (see Messerschmidt, 1986; Moyer, 1992; Simpson & Elis, 1996) or have looked outside of the discipline for answers—particularly to postmodern criticism (Cain, 1990b; Daly, 1997; Morris & Gelsthorpe, 1991; Smart, 1995) and/or ethnomethodology (Brod and Kaufman, 1994; Connell, 1987; Messerschmidt, 1993; Newburn & Stanko, 1994; Simpson & Elis, 1995; West and Fenstermaker, 1995).

Daly and Maher (1998) divide feminist criminology into two phases. In phase one, dominant paradigms were critiqued and more research was conducted on females to fill the knowledge gaps about female offenders and victims. Feminists accomplished a great deal in this first phase by (1) exposing the discipline as androcentric; (2) making female offenders visible; (3) uncovering institutional sexism in the way crime was studied and the ways in which offenders and victims were treated; and (4) problematizing female conformity as natural and self-evident (Gelsthorpe & Morris, 1990, p. 3; Naffine, 1986; Young, 1996). By phase two, feminism had become more self-reflective. Problems with essentialism, the criticism, and in some cases rejection, of both feminist empiricism and standpoint feminism, and the abandonment of grand narratives (structures) shifted the intellectual arena for feminist criminologists.

> ... The major academic activities have been (1) to problematize the term *woman* as a unified category; (2) to acknowledge that *women's experiences* are, in part, constructed by legal and criminological discourses; (3) to revisit the relationship between sex and gender; and (4) to reflect on the strengths and limits of constructing feminist 'truths' and knowledge. (Daly and Maher, emphasis in original, 1998).

Although feminist critiques of criminology and criminal justice have paralleled one another with regard to phase one research, postmodern (or phase two) challenges have been directed primarily toward analyses of the criminal justice sytem (especially law; see Smart, 1989, 1995). Conversely, phase two criminological research has adopted ethnomethodological explanations to account for gender differences in offending. In the next section, phase one and two feminist research in gender and justice is reviewed. We conclude this chapter with a feminist interpretation of how crime is accomplished as a consequence of "doing gender."

5. FEMINIST TRANSITIONS: GENDER AND JUSTICE

Reluctance to include female offenders within discussions of social control has largely been explained by the low representation of female offenders in the criminal justice system. In 1995, for instance, adult female offenders composed only 9.7% of all state and federal prison admissions (Brown, Gilliard, Schnell, Stephan, & Wilson, 1996), and in 1991, only 18% of juvenile offenders in all types of facilities were female (DeComo et al., 1995). However, a closer examination of these statistics reveals at least two patterns. First, female offenders are institutionalized for less serious charges than male offenders (e.g., female status offenders were almost six times as likely as male status offenders to be placed in public facilities and twice as likely as male status offenders to be placed in a private facility in 1991; DeComo et al., 1995; Brenzel, 1983; Carlen, 1983; Dobash, Dobash, & Gutteridge, 1986; Rafter, 1985 for historical and cross-cultural statistics). Second, research on women in prison and juvenile institutions indicates that these offenders are disproportionately nonwhite and poor (Carlen, 1983; Dobash et al., 1986; Rafter, 1985).

In response to these patterns, feminist scholars have focused on several issues with regard to gender and social control, including (1) the relationship between informal and formal controls and gender (Hagan, Simpson, & Gillis, 1979; Schur, 1983; Smart and Smart, 1978); (2) the differential sentencing of male and female offenders (Chesney-Lind, 1973, 1986; Daly & Bordt, 1995); (3) the determinants of institutionalization (Brenzel, 1983; Carlen, 1983; Dobash, et al., 1986; Eaton, 1986; Freedman, 1981; Worrall, 1990); and (4) how the social control of women within the criminal justice system relates to their lives outside of the criminal justice system (Carlen, 1983; Eaton, 1986; Howe,

1994). Research addressing these issues represents both the contributions as well as the limitations of feminist criminology to explain and theorize about gender and social control (Carrington, 1990, 1994; Daly, 1997; Smart, 1995). In the 1970s and early 1980s, feminist criminologists established a place for women in the social control literature by exposing the differential treatment that women received compared to men (Freedman, 1981; Nagel & Hagan, 1983; Rafter, 1985) and by analyzing how the type and amount of social control was determined by prevailing stereotypes or typescripts of femininity (Chesney-Lind, 1973, 1986; Feinman, 1986; Merlo & Pollack, 1995; Moyer, 1992). Feminists in the late 1980s and 1990s, however, argue that these views of gender and social control are overly simplistic and fail to adequately address women as subjects of social control (Carringtom, 1994; Daly, 1997; Gelsthorpe & Morris, 1990; Howe, 1994; Rafter, 1985; Heidensohn, 1995). To fully explore more the research on females and social control, we turn next to a discussion of the prevailing themes found within this literature and the ways in which these themes have been affected by developments in feminist theory.

5.1. Sexualization, Domesticity, and Medicalization

Sexualization, the ideology of domesticity, and medicalization dominate discussions of female offenders and social control and serve as guiding posts to theorizing how the criminal justice system has defined and reacted to female offenders historically as well as currently. Each of these themes is linked to two fundamental elements found in feminist interpretations of social control: patriarchy and the ideology of separate spheres. Since the 1960s, feminists have argued that the subordination of women and the devaluation of femininity is rooted in a culture and social structure dominated by male power. Patriarchy, in turn, creates and perpetuates the ideology of separate spheres, which not only distinguishes the private (i.e., family) from the public sphere (i.e., employment) but also designates women as responsible for the former (e.g., wife and mother) and men for the latter (e.g., breadwinner).

Patriarchy and the ideology of separate spheres specifically lay the foundation for controlling women's sexuality and for viewing women in terms of domesticity by creating images of true womanhood (Feinman, 1986; Freedman, 1981; Moyer, 1992). Prior to the late nineteenth century, women were often regarded as evil and were closely controlled by the church and the community for even the slightest acts of transgression (Dobash et al., 1986; Merlo & Pollack, 1995). Following the rise of capitalism and the ideology of separate spheres, women were redefined in terms of femininity (i.e., true womanhood). Good women, or Madonnas, internalized Victorian standards of sexuality and were expected to be good mothers, submissive wives, and moral guardians of the home, whereas bad women, or whores, blatantly disregarded these roles and were considered evil (Feinman, 1986; Moyer, 1992).

True womanhood became synonymous with the "nature" of women toward the end of the nineteenth century; consequently, explanations for female criminality switched from describing female offenders as "bad" to "mad" (Klein, 1973). Female offenders who, by definition, did not emulate the standards of good wives and mothers, were declared sick and in need of rehabilitation.[2] This pathological view of the female offender

---

[2] Female offenders charged with more traditional, masculine offenses were still considered evil but beyond rehabilitation (Rafter, 1985).

continued throughout the twentieth century, firmly establishing the idea that female offenders need medical (i.e., psychiatric) attention more than their male counterparts
(Chesler, 1972; Dobash et al., 1986; Ehrenreich & English, 1978; Klein, 1973; Phillips
& DeFleur, 1982; Rafter, 1985; Smart, 1976); however, the medicalization of female
criminal behavior was often reserved for middle and upper-class women while their working-class counterparts faced criminalization more often (for a specific example of this
class difference, see Abelson's historical analysis of shoplifting, 1989).

The application of these themes within research on gender and social control depends largely on the theoretical framework and feminist perspective being used in a particular study. A review of both the processing and imprisonment literatures highlights the
different ways in which these themes have contributed to feminist interpretations of gender and social control within the criminal justice system.

5.2. Women and Sentencing

One of the more well-researched areas related to gender and social control is the processing of adult and adolescent female offenders. This research indicates that female offenders receive different treatment than their male counterparts in certain situations, but whether
this treatment is harsher or more lenient seems dependent upon the age of the offender
and the type and quality of the data used (Daly, 1987b). These factors also determine the
extent to which sexualization, domesticity, and medicalization are related to social control decisions. Research on the arrest and processing of female adolescent offenders, for
instance, attributes harsher penalties for female offenders to the control of sexual behavior and a double standard of morality (Campbell, 1981; Chesney-Lind, 1973, 1986; Mann,
1984; Shacklady-Smith, 1976), whereas more lenient sentences for adult female offenders is often explained by an offender's allegiance to the ideology of domesticity and her
parental role (Carlen, 1983; Daly, 1987a; Eaton, 1986; Steffensmeier, Kramer, & Streifel,
1993).

Conclusions regarding the treatment of female offenders often depends on the methodological rigor of these studies. Although early studies on the processing of status offenders found harsh treatment for female offenders (see, e.g., Chesney-Lind, 1973), studies that controlled for relevant legal variables and that were conducted after the Juvenile
Justice Delinquency Prevention Act in 1974 found less support for the differential treatment of offenders by gender (Bishop & Frazier, 1992; Johnson & Scheuble, 1991; Teilmann
& Landry, 1981; for a discussion of subtle/indirect effects, see Bishop & Frazier, 1992;
Zatz, 1987). Conversely, sentencing research consistently indicates that adult female offenders receive lighter sentences than male offenders (for reviews of this literature see
Dale & Bordt, 1995; Nagel & Hagan, 1983; Steffensmeier et al., 1993) despite the changes
in sentencing procedures (Nagel and Johnson, 1994; Steffenmeier et al., 1993) and the
methodological limitations inherent in sentencing research (see Daly & Bordt, 1995;
Hagan & Bumiller, 1983; Steffensmeier et al., 1993).

Several theoretical explanations have been offered to explain these findings. The
chivalry/paternalism hypothesis is arguably the most longstanding explanation for the
differential treatment of women and girls at all stages of the criminal justice process.
Both chivalry and paternalism attribute lenient treatment to the attitudes and perceptions
that male officials hold toward women. These officials view females as incapable of criminality owing to their feminine nature and attempt to shield or protect female offenders

from the harshness of the criminal justice system (Anderson, 1976; Moulds, 1980). Yet, paternalism and the need to protect female offenders can also result in harsher treatment for female offenders (i.e., institutionalization) in an attempt to protect female offenders from themselves (Nagel & Hagan, 1983).

Extensions of the chivalry/paternalism hypothesis include the evil woman hypothesis and typescripting theory (Harris, 1977; Nagel & Hagan, 1983). The evil woman hypothesis attempts to explain harsher treatment for female offenders compared to male offenders by proposing ". . . that women will be more harshly sanctioned because their criminal behavior violates sex stereotypical assumptions about the proper role of women" (p. 115). Typescripting theory expands the evil woman hypothesis by suggesting that females engaging in behavior consistent with stereotypes of female crime (e.g., shoplifting) will receive equal or lesser amounts of formal social control compared to males. On the other hand, females engaging in behavior consistent with stereotypes of male crime (e.g., murder) will receive more social control and will be more likely to be viewed in pathological terms relative to males (Harris, 1977; Harris & Hill, 1986; 1977; Phillips & DeFleur, 1982; Visher, 1983).

Another theoretical framework used to explain the differential treatment of male and female offenders is Black's (1976) assumption that formal social controls vary indirectly with informal controls. Based on this proposition, sentencing decisions depend on the number of individuals on whom an offender is dependent, since these relationships represent the amount and strength of informal controls. Kruttschnitt (1982, 1984) then integrated this proposition with the idea that informal controls play a more significant role in women's lives than on men's to support the contention that informal controls will be more influential in sentencing decisions for female offenders. Although she found support for the influence of informal controls for female offenders in her early research (1982, 1984), additional studies found few consistent patterns over time and no convincing gender effects related to the influence of informal controls (i.e., the influence of informal controls seems to affect both male and female pretrial and sentencing decisions; Kruttschnitt & Green, 1984 and Kruttschnitt & McCarthy, 1985).

Unsatisfied by the explanatory power of paternalism and informal controls, Daly (1987a) interviewed several criminal justice officials in an attempt to learn why gender differences may emerge in the course of 'doing justice' " (p. 267). Daly's interviews revealed that leniency was not necessarily related to the dependency of the offender on others but rather the dependency of others on the offenders (e.g., children and/or a spouse). In other words, defendants who were "familied" were more likely to receive a more lenient sentence than those who were "nonfamilied" (see also Eaton, 1986). Further, officials felt that women in the familied category (as long as they were good mothers) deserved greater leniency than familied men because their responsibilities were consistent with gender role expectations. Thus, Daly replaced paternalism with familial paternalism, arguing that court officials are more concerned with preserving the family (especially from a social cost perspective) than with protecting women from the system (Daly, 1987b, 1989a, 1989b).

Steffensmeier and associates (1993) then extended familial paternalism to the notion of "blameworthiness" to explain disparate sentencing found within the sentencing guideline structure in Pennsylvania. "Blameworthiness" incorporates both the familied position of the female offender and her motivation for the crime. Stealing money to feed her children will result in less blameworthiness than a single woman stealing for greed. Daly (1994) also found that individual cases were scrutinized closely and that "women's biographies were constructed more often than men's with a theme of 'blurred boundaries' between victimization and criminalization" (Daly, 1994, p 163). Such biographies often led to different interpretations of the female offender in relation to her blameworthiness. Less blameworthiness and greater optimism in the potential to reform a woman, in turn, often resulted in less serious sentences for female offenders.

Differences in the treatment of female offenders ultimately leads to a discussion of sentencing disparity as warranted or unwarranted. Different treatment may be appropriate in light of the differences between men and women in offending patterns and in their societal responsibilities. Thus, uncritical acceptance of the equal treatment model is problematic. It assumes that the circumstances and actions that bring men and women to court are comparable, thereby perpetuating the notion that men represent the standard with which to compare women rather than viewing female offenders as subjects in and of themselves (Daly, 1994, 1995). It further assumes that harsher sentences are better for all offenders—a highly debated issue. Finally, the equal treatment model obscures gender interactions with race and class (Daly, 1989a; Gruhl, Welch, & Spohn, 1984; Spohn, Welch, & Gruhl, 1985), the severity of responses over time, jurisdiction variations, and discussion as to whether these sentences are just (see Daly, 1994, p. 163 and Nagel & Johnson, 1994 for more discussion of these issues).

In the same light, gender cannot be discarded from these discussions since seemingly neutral criteria, such as family and offender motivation, can still be gendered (see Daly, 1987a and Steffensmeier et al., 1993). Although family is heavily considered for both male and female defendants, children often have a greater impact on female defendant decisions because (1) females appearing before the court tend to have children more often than do male defendants; (2) being responsible for children is more consistent with role expectations for women than it is for men (i.e., men are traditionally the breadwinners of a family); and (3) such responsibilities signify greater reform potential.

Despite the contributions that this literature has made to understanding the relationship between gender and social control, critics suggest that it is limited in at least two respects. First, this literature has been dominated by quantitative analysis, which, in turn, has discouraged the use of other analytical techniques such as discourse analysis and case study approaches (for critiques and exceptions, see Daly, 1994, 1997; Eaton, 1986; Howe, 1994; Worrall, 1990). Second, its focus on sentencing obscures the inseparable relationship between processing decisions and the institutionalization of female offenders (Carlen, 1983). To address the interrelated nature of sentencing and institutionalization, we turn next to a review of the literature on gender and institutionalization.

5.3. Gender and Institutionalization

Critical studies of gender and institutionalization arguably began in the 1970s when researchers explored the treatment of female adolescent offenders relative to their male counterparts—especially status offenders. These studies consistently found that far more female than male offenders were charged with and institutionalized for these offenses (Brenzel, 1983; Odem, 1991 Rafter, 1985; Schlossman & Wallach, 1978). Each of these studies attributed this differential treatment, in large part, to a double standard of morality for male and female offenders (i.e., the "sexualization thesis"). Carrington (1990), however, questions this longstanding reliance on paternalism and the sexualization thesis to explain such treatment. She points out that these explanations are essentialist, ignoring the influence of race and class on juvenile justice decisions, as well as discussions of wider social welfare issues that justify juvenile justice control over female sexuality (Carrington, 1990, 1994; see also Gelsthorpe, 1986 and Odem, 1991). Further, Carrington argues that the sexualization processes that operate within the juvenile justice system have been invoked primarily by mothers or female social workers rather than by a patriarchal family or male magistrate. Odem (1991), for example, discusses how poor single mothers in Los Angeles accessed the juvenile justice system to control their daughters' immoral and uncontrollable behavior. Gordon (1988) made a similar observation with regard to the regulation of child abuse and neglect in Boston at the turn of the century, and Chesney-Lind (1973, 1986; Chesney-Lind and Sheldon, 1992) noted the relationship between status offense referrals and a mothers' frustration with daughters whom they feel are uncontrollable (e.g., dating a boy of whom the mother does not approve). Thus, the sexualization thesis falls short of providing an accurate reading of the juvenile justice system's control of female delinquency. Such shortcomings require the "de-essentialization" of gender in feminist readings and the interpretation of sexualization within a variety of relevant discourses (Carrington, 1990; Gelsthorpe, 1986; Odem, 1991).

The ideology of domesticity and the sexualization of female offenses has also been used to explain the differential treatment of adult female offenders. In her history of women's imprisonment from 1870 to 1910, Estelle Freedman (1981) proposes that changing roles of women dramatically affected the ways in which female offenders were viewed and treated. Middle-class women became advocates for the redefinition of the female criminal, separate facilities for women offenders, and the rehabilitation of their working-class "sisters" according to the middle-class notions of domesticity and true womanhood. As a result, women's reformatories became a place in which working-class women were trained to perform domestic tasks and to become the moral protectors of the home. Freedman suggests that the development of separate institutions benefitted women prisoners but concedes that the treatment of women inmates, compared to male inmates, perpetuated the sexual inequalities found within a paternalistic society. Differential treatment, such as domestic rather than academic training, rehabilitation based on the internalization of traditional moral standards expected of a woman, incarceration for moral rather than criminal behavior, and indeterminate sentencing serve as the basis for Freedman's call to abolish the double standard of morality and to acquire equal services for women in prison.

In *Partial Justice* (1985), Nicole Rafter expanded upon Freedman's work by presenting a socialist feminist interpretation of the history of women's imprisonment. Specifically, she focused on the relationship between race, gender, and class and social control. Rafter stresses the widening divisions between social classes and the need to control a growing working class throughout the nineteenth and early twentieth centuries as critical factors in the establishment of women's reformatories. The goal of these reformatories for women was to rehabilitate them by controlling their sexuality and providing them with domestic training. By controlling their sexuality, middle-class women reinforced changes in gender roles, maintained the interests of a patriarchal society, and reified their own values and standards of true womanhood. By controlling the vocational training of women inmates, middle-class reformers supplied a cheap work force to a growing class of middle- and upper-class women.

Not all women offenders were placed in reformatories. Rafter identifies the development of a bifurcated system of social control: reformatories for white, minor offenders and traditional, custodial prisons for women who committed more masculine types of crime and African-American women, who were classified as beyond reform. Based on her skin color, an African-American offender was perceived as the "... deceitful Dark Lady who, behind her apparent femininity, hid opposite traits: self-centeredness, the ability to scheme and use cunning, ... and voracious sexuality" (p. 181). According to Rafter, both the differential treatment of female offenders and this bifurcated system of control obscure the issue of equal treatment for female and male offenders.

Dobash et al. (1986) built on Rafter's and Freedman's work by focusing on the development of women's prisons in England and Scotland and by approaching this development from a Foucauldian perspective. They argued that women prisoners were and are controlled, watched, and manipulated more than male prisoners via the therapeutic model and a network of institutions specifically created for female prisoners (e.g., refuges and reformatories). Dobash et al. addressed the widespread influence of the myth that female offenders are mentally ill on both penal ideologies and prison policies. Consequently, this myth creates the assumption that all female prisoners need psychiatric treatment and redefines the prison and prison staff in therapeutic terms. Ironically, however, Dobash et al. argued that despite the rhetoric of therapy contained within penal ideology, principles of discipline and punishment prevailed.

Following their therapeutic experience in prison, female inmates were often encouraged, and sometimes required to spend additional time in a refuge or reformatory (especially prostitutes and idle and neglectful women). Similar to the United States, these institutions were established in an effort to provide paternalistic guidance to prevent a woman from sliding back into a life of sin and crime. A comparable network of social control was not created for male prisoners, who were released upon the completion of their sentence. Thus, medicalizing the deviant behavior of women, defining it in sexualized terms, and strict adherence to the ideology of domesticity seem to encourage the differential treatment of offenders by gender, which often translated into more far-reaching control of women's lives than men's.

These historical accounts of women's imprisonment contribute significantly to our understanding of gender and social control but also serve as examples of the gaps still found in this area of research. Not only do these studies rely on traditional methodologies (e.g., comparative analysis) rather than questioning masculinist approaches and developing feminist methodologies (Howe, 1994), but they also illustrate how the social control of women is influenced by stereotypical images of femininity and traditional role expectations without presenting theoretical ideas that would require a paradigm shift in the way we view the social control of female offenders. Research on the contemporary use of social control responds, to some extent, to these limitations by using different approaches to theorize about gender and social control.

Carlen (1983), for example, takes a standpoint feminist approach to women's imprisonment. She interviewed 20 female inmates and several members of the prison staff at Cornton Vale in Scotland to uncover the relationships between the biographies of women prisoners and the discourses that constitute them, both in the courtroom as well as in prison. Carlen argued that discourses of family are used to evaluate the worthiness of women defendants. Regardless of the offense, good mothers and wives often receive community-based sanctions, whereas women who seemingly reject the ideology of the family receive imprisonment. Court and prison officials view these women as having the appropriate social control mechanisms in their lives but being beyond their control (i.e., "outwith"). Once imprisoned, they are defined in pathological terms and controlled via notions of family and femininity; however, the contradictions inherent in prison discourse and action render these women failures at womanhood. Having been ". . . rejected in penal discourse as 'real prisoners', rejected by hospital alcoholic units as being without motivation; rejected by social workers as being outwith reform and beyond help; and rejected by psychiatrists as being outwith treatment and beyond cured" (p. 155), these offenders represent the women that no one wants.

Worrall (1990) is specifically interested in how court officials and psychiatric experts construct and control women offenders who do not fit into stereotypes by deconstructing the ways in which those in power construct "knowledged" about these offenders. Worrall contended that officials and experts normalize the "female conditions of existence" through discourses of domesticity, sexuality, and pathology. Magistrates interpret atypical female defendants within these discourses, solicitors use these discourses to represent their clients as "normal" women, psychiatrists assess their mental health within these discourses, and probation officers describe and react to them within these discourses. Ironically, female offenders who feel powerless and confined within these discourses reject them by "doing contradictory things and exploiting the contradictions of the gender contract" (p. 161), thereby increasing the extent to which discourses of domesticity, sexuality, and pathology are used to control and ultimately oppress them.

Both Carlen's and Worrall's studies problematize the model of equal treatment even further than the sentencing literature because they expose its contradictory meaning. This model presumes that equality in law and criminal justice treatment rectifies the disparities between male and female offenders; however, the model of equal treatment does not necessarily help women offenders because it neither acknowledges nor addresses gender-based inequality inherent within the larger social structure. Rather, the current state of unequal treatment potentially serves to reinforce traditional roles and expectations of women, especially for poor women, by using ideologies of sexuality, domesticity, and pathology to determine the type and amount of social control a woman will receive and the type and amount of training women offenders will receive when imprisoned.

Taken together, research on gender and sentencing and gender and imprisonment illustrates a slow progression from describing social control in paternalistic terms to a deconstruction of the "knowledge" used to define and assess women offenders. This research does not mark the end of the story, however. As Howe points out, "In sum, feminist analysts of the punishment of women still have a considerable way to go. They may have come to recognize that women's prisons are . . . of theoretical interest. . . . But they have not taken what might be called the project of theorisation very far" (p. 159). Specifically, they have yet to fully address feminist questions about research methodologies, to explain how women's criminal careers are circumscribed by gender, to explore wider issues related to the social control of women, and to explain the ways in which race and socioeconomic status impact the use of social control. Feminists need to expand their analyses to include postmodern interpretations of law, penality, and social control (e.g., Smart, 1995; Worrall, 1991) and also to expand the bounds within which we understand the social control of women. In other words, our challenge as feminists exploring the social control of women is to develop a methodological framework separate from traditional masculinist approaches from which we can deconstruct the social control of women from not only their experiences within the criminal justice system but also from the ". . . the private prisons of docile yet rebellious bodies, drugged and tranquillized bodies, famished self policing bodies in which many women live their lives, 'free' of penal control" (Howe, 1994, p. 207).

6. GENDER, CRIME, AND JUSTICE: FUTURE DEVELOPMENTS

One promising direction for the study of gender, crime, and justice has emerged from work in ethnomethodology (Connell, 1987; West & Fenstermaker, 1995; West & Zimmerman, 1987). Linking social structures (e.g., division of labor, power relations, and sexuality) with individual experience and the situated accomplishment of gender, Messerschmidt (1993, p. 84) described the ways in which crime (which is overwhelmingly enacted by males) is "simply one practice in which and through which power over women can be naturalized." Differently situated males share with other men a construction of masculinity that is unique to their structural position in society. Hence, "different types of masculinity exist in the school, the youth group, the street, the family, and the workplace" (Messerschmidt, 1993, p. 84). The accomplishment of masculinity within these venues will differ according to the types of resources that are available to the males within them. Crime is a means of accomplishing masculinity when other resources to do so are limited.

There are several benefits to theorizing about masculinities and crime: (1) it normalizes the aggressive and violent behavior of men; (2) it situates male behavior in the context of unequal power relations with men; and (3) because gender is viewed as an accomplishment—as "a practice," masculinity and femininity are not essentialized (Newburn & Stanko, 1994, pp. 3, 4). The convention in this body of work is to focus on masculinity; however, as more recent work by Messerschmidt (1995) and Simpson and Elis (1996) demonstrates, the accomplishment of gender and its relationship to crime is not an exclusively masculine process. Doing gender does not require crime and, in fact, "emphasized femininity" (Connell, 1987) may negate the practice of most kinds of crimes for females (Simpson & Elis, 1996). However, accomplishing femininity through crime as, say, a "bad girl" in a gang, also draws on and affirms the ways in which gender relations are accomplished (Messerschmidt, 1995). Thus, the approach helps to untangle the sex-ratio problem while also accounting for female conformity and/or criminality. It can also accommodate race and class differences with the notion of hegemonic and subordinated masculinities.[3]

Other feminists are less enamoured with ethnomethodological approaches. They either find the nonessential argument unconvincing (see, e.g., Collins, et al., 1995) or find the primary focus on masculinity disconcerting and ironic given the past exclusion of women from criminological theorizing (Chesney,Lind, 1995, pp. 85, 86). Others worry that the approach has been inappropriately theorized (i.e., using masculinity to theorize femininity) and quantified (Daly, 1997).

Based on some of these philosophical and epistemological divisions, it is unclear where feminist criminology is heading. Some critics suggest that the only way to transform criminology is to abandon it completely. Howe (1990, p. 7), for instance, argues that criminology is "beyond reclamation." Morris and Gelsthorpe (1991, p. 5) believe that the discipline is impoverished and have "looked elsewhere . . . to where feminists rather than criminologists are working for help in understanding and making sense of our work." Smart (1995, p. 32) casts an even dimmer view by characterizing phase one research as

[3] Doing gender is employed by Martin and Jurik (1996) to account for the accomplishment of gender in the occupation of justice (policing, law, and corrections). Maher and Daly (1996) highlight how notions of masculinity (and ethnicity) permeate the illicit drug economy and contribute to the exclusion of women from lucrative opportunities in drug selling and distribution networks.

"misdirected" and suggesting that "the core enterprise of criminology is problematic." These views emerge primarily from postmodern challenges (Smart, 1995; Young, 1996).

Others, however, are more optimistic about the discipline, in part because they recognize some of the limitations of postmodern analysis (see Schwartz & Friedrichs, 1994 for an excellent review and critique of postmodern thought and criminology) or because their version of postmodernism renders the discipline "limited" and therefore amenable to feminist viewpoints (Young, 1996, p. 49). Carlen (1990), for instance, suggested that deconstruction is a useful analytical tool but that the privileging of feminist discourses over earlier "Truths" is a potential threat. Moreover, she took as given empirical realities that must be confronted by feminist criminologists (see also, Cain, 1990a). [In this, she draws from Harding (1986, p. 301) who argues that the dualisms rejected by postmodernism may be empirically false but "we cannot afford to reject them as irrelevant as long as they structure our lives and our consciousness."] One reality is that women are involuntarily processed and held by the criminal justice system. Feminists need to "suggest principled ways in which the criminal justice and penal systems might become more women-wise" (Carlen, 1990, p. 109). Cain (1990b, p. 6) offers a threefold strategy to "transgress" criminology through reflexivity, deconstruction, and reconstruction. Reflexivity is a strategy in which feminists recognize the real concerns of girls and women *and* the discourses that shape those concerns. Once recognized, it is necessary to deconstruct the internal illogic of the discourse and the manner and sites in which it is deployed. Finally, feminist criminology must help girls and women to move beyond the painful experience of living the dominant discourse (reconstruction). All of this involves female-centered research (so that women will not be compared to men); stepping outside of the discourse of criminology to understand how females live their lives (because criminological discourses have lead nowhere and we need to connect offenders, victims, and the criminal justice system to a broader picture); and ultimately, to "reintroduce men" into the study of crime, law, and criminal justice institutions because gender is a relational concept and the failure to do so repeats the essentialism trap (Cain, 1990b, p. 11).

Our own views are somewhat mixed on the feminist criminological enterprise. As empirical realists (Cain, 1990) and structuralists, we are uncomfortable with the rejection of social scientific knowledge (see also, Daly, 1997) and social structure. While postmodernism has added a compelling set of ideas to the study of crime and justice, we do not see exactly where postmodern interpretations will lead us. At the risk of being labeled equivocators, we argue for a middle ground. The investigation of gender, crime, and justice can only benefit from varied and diverse epistemologies and theoretical frameworks.

REFERENCES

Abelson, E. S. (1989). *When ladies go a-thieving: Middle-class shoplifters in the Victorian department store.* New York: Oxford University Press.

Adler, F. (1975). *Sisters in crime.* New York: McGraw-Hill.

Akers, R. (1973). *Deviant behavior: A social learning approach.* Belmont, CA: Wadsworth.

Anderson, E. A. (1976). The chivalrous treatment of the female offender in the arms of the criminal justice system. *Social Problems, 23,* 349–357.

Bachman, J. G., Johnston, L. D., & O'Malley, P. M. (1988). *Monitoring the future, 1988.* Ann Arbor, MI: University of Michigan Press.

Bachman, R., Paternoster, R., & Ward. S. (1992). The rationality of sexual offending. *Law & Society Review, 26,* 343–372.

Becker, G. S. (1968). Crime and punishment: An economic approach. *Journal of Political Economy, 76,* 169–217.

Becker, H. S. (1963). *Outsiders.* New York: The Free Press.

Bishop, D. & Frazier, C. (1992). Gender bias in juvenile justice processing: Implications of the JJDP act. *Journal of Criminal Law and Criminology, 82,* 1162–1186.

Black, D. (1976). *The behavior of law.* New York: Academic Press.

Brenzel, B. (1983). *Daughters of the state.* Cambridge, MA: MIT Press.

Brod, H. & Kaufman, M. (1994). *Theorizing masculinities.* Thousand Oaks, CA: Sage.

Brown, J., Gilliard, D., Schnell, T., Stephan, J., & Wilson, D. (1996). *Correctional populations in the United States, 1994.* Washington, D.C.: U. S. Department of Justice.

Burgess, E. W. (1928). The growth of the city. In R. E. Park, E. W. Burgess, & R. D. McKenzie (Eds.), *The city.* Chicago: University of Chicago Press.

Cain, M. (1990a). Realist philosophy and standpoint epistemologies or feminist criminology as a successor science. In L. Gelsthorpe & A. Morris (Eds.). *Feminist perspectives in criminology* (pp. 124–140). Milton Keynes: Open University Press.

Cain, M. (1990b). Towards transgression: New directions in feminist criminology. *International Journal of the Sociology of Law, 18,* 1–18.

Carlen, P. (1983). *Women's imprisonment: A study in social control.* London: Routledge.

Carlen, P. (1990). *Alternatives to women's imprisonment.* Milton Keynes: Open University Press.

Carlen, P. (1994). Gender, class, racism, and criminal justice: Against global and gender-centric theories, for poststructuralist perspectives. In G. Bridges & M. Myers (Eds.), *Inequality, crime, and social control.* Boulder, Co: Westview Press.

Caspi, A., Lynam, D., Moffitt, T. E., & Silva, P. A. (1993). Unraveling girls delinquency, biological, dispositional, and contextual contributions to adolescent misbehavior. *Developmental Psychology, 29,* 19,–30.

Campbell, A. (1981). *Girl delinquents.* New York: St. Martin's Press.

Carrington, K. (1990). Feminist readings in female delinquency. *Law in Context, 8,* 5–31.

Carrington, K. (1994). Postmodernism and feminist criminologies: Disconnecting discourses. *International Journal of the Sociology of Law, 22,* 261–277.

Cernkovich, S. A., & Giordano, P. C. (1987). Family relationships and delinquency. *Criminology, 25,* 295–319.

Cernkovich, S. A., & Giordano, P. C. (1992). School bonding, race, and delinquency. *Criminology, 30,* 261–291.

Chesler, P. (1972). *Women and madness.* New York: Avon Books.

Chesney-Lind, M. (1973). Judicial enforcement of the female sex role: The family court and the female delinquent. *Issues in Criminology, 8,* 51–69.

Chesney-Lind, M. (1986). Women and crime: The female offender. *Signs, 12,* 78–96.

Chesney-Lind, M. (1995). Girls, delinquency, and juvenile justice: Toward a feminist theory of young women's crime. In N. Sokoloff & B. Price (Eds.), *The criminal justice system and women* (pp. 71–88). New York: McGraw-Hill.

Chesney-Lind, M., & Sheldon, R. G. (1992). *Girls, delinquency, and juvenile justice.* Pacific Grove, CA: Brooks/Cole.

Cloward, R. A., & Ohlin, L. E. (1960). *Delinquency and opportunity.* Glencoe, IL: The Free Press.

Cohen, A. (1955). *Delinquent boys.* Glencoe, IL: The Free Press.

Collins, P. H., Maldonado, L. A., Takagi, D. Y., Thorne, B., Weber, L., & Winant, H. (1995). Symposium on West and Fenstermaker's "Doing Difference." *Gender & Society, 9,* 491–453.

Connell, R.W. (1987). *Gender and power.* Stanford, CA: Stanford University Press.

Cornish, D. B., & Clarke, R. V. (1987). *The reasoning criminal.* New York: Springer.

Daly, K. (1987a). Structure and practice of familial-based justice in a criminal court. *Law & Society Review, 21,* 267–289.

Daly, K. (1987b). Discrimination in the criminal courts: Family, gender, and the problem of equal treatment. *Social Forces, 66,* 152–175.

Daly, K. (1989a). Neither conflict nor labeling nor paternalism will suffice: Intersections of race, ethnicity, gender and family in criminal court decisions. *Crime and Delinquency, 35,* 136–168.

Daly, K. (1989b). Rethinking judicial paternalism: Gender, work-family relations and sentencing. *Gender & Society, 3,* 9–36.

Daly, K. (1989c). Gender and varieties of white-collar crime. *Criminology, 27,* 769–794.

Daly, K. (1994). *Gender, crime, and punishment.* New Haven, CT: Yale University Press.

Daly, K. (1997). Different ways of conceptualizing sex/gender in feminist theory and their implications for criminology. *Theoretical Criminology, 1,* 25–51.

Daly, K., & Bordt, R. (1995). Sex effects and sentencing: An analysis of the statistical literature. *Justice Quarterly, 12,* 141–175.

Daly, K., & Chesney-Lind, M. (1988). Feminism and Criminology. *Justice Quarterly, 5,* 497–538.

Daly, K., & Maher, L. (1998). *Criminology at the crossroads: Feminist readings in crime and justice.* New York: Oxford University Press.

DeComo, R., Tunis, S., Krisberg, B. Herrara, N., Rudenstine, S., Del Rosario, D., & National Council on Crime and Delinquency. (1995). *Juveniles taken into custody: Fiscal year 1992.* Washington, D.C.: U.S. Department of Justice.

Dobash, R. P., Dobash, R. E., & Gutteridge, S. (1986). *The imprisonment of women.* London: Basil Blackwell.

Eaton, M. (1986). *Justice for women? Family, court, and social control.* Milton Keynes: Open University Press.

Ehrenreich, B., & English, D. 1978. *For her own good: 150 years of the experts' advice to women.* Garden City, NY: Anchor Books.

England, P., & Kilbourne, B. S. (1990). Feminist critique of the separative model of the self: Implications for rational choice theory. *Rationality and Society, 2,* 156–171.

Feinman, C. (1986). *Women in the criminal justice system.* New York: Praeger.

Fishbein, D. H. (1990). Biological perspectives in criminology. *Criminology, 28,* 27–72.

Freedman, E. B. (1981). *Their sisters' keepers.* Ann Arbor, MI: University of Michigan Press.

Freud, S. (1933). *New introductory lectures on psychoanalysis.* New York: W.W. Norton.

Friedman, D., & Diem, C. (1994). Feminism and the pro-(rational-) choice movement: Rational-choice theory, feminist critiques, and gender inequality. In P. England (Ed.), *Theory on gender/feminism on theory* (pp. 91–114). New York: Aldine De Gruyter.

Gelsthorpe, L. (1986). Towards a skeptical look at sexism. *International Journal of the Sociology of Law, 14,* 125–152.

Gelsthorpe, L. & Morris, A. (1990). *Feminist perspectives in criminology.* Milton Keynes: Open University Press.

Giordano, P. C., Kerbel, S., & Dudley, S. (1976). *The economics of female criminality.* Paper presented at the annual meeting of the Society for the Study of Social Problems, San Francisco.

Giordano, P. C., Cernkovich, S. A., & Pugh, M. D. (1986). Friendships and delinquency. *American Journal of Sociology, 91,* 1170–1202.

Glueck, S., & Glueck, E. T. (1934). *Five hundred delinquent women.* New York: Alfred A. Knopf.

Gottfredson, M. R., & Hirschi, T. (1990). *A general theory of crime.* Stanford, CA: Stanford University Press.

Gordon, L. (1988). *Heroes of their own lives: The politics and history of family violence.* New York: Penguin Books.

Grasmick, H. B., & Bursik, R. J., Jr. (1990). Conscience, significant others, and rational choice. *Law & Society Review, 24,* 837–861.

Gruhl, J., Welch, S., & Spohn, C. (1984). Women as criminal defendants: A test for paternalism. *Western Political Quarterly, 37,* 456–467.

Hagan, J., & Bumiller, K. (1983). Making sense of sentencing: A review and critique of sentencing research. In A. Blumstein, J. Cohen, S. E. Martin & M. H. Tonry (Eds.), *Research on sentencing: The search for reform* (pp. 1–54). Washington, D.C.: National Academy Press.

Hagan, J., Simpson, J. H., & Gillis, A. R. (1979). The sexual stratification of social control: A gender-based perspective on crime and delinquency. *British Journal of Sociology, 30,* 25–38.

Harris, A. R. (1977). Sex and theories of deviance. *American Sociological Review, 42,* 3–16.

Harris, A. R., & Hill, G. D. (1986). Bias in status processing decisions. In A. R. Harris (Ed.), *Rationality and social control* (pp. 1–80). Norwood, NJ: Ablex.

Heidensohn, F. (1968). The deviance of women. *British Journal of Sociology, 19,* 160–175.

Hirschi, T. (1969). *Causes of delinquency.* Berkeley, CA: University of California Press.

Howe, A. (1990). Prologue to a history of women's imprisonment: In search of a feminist perspective. *Social Justice, 17,* 5–22.O

Howe, A. (1994). *Punish and critique: Towards a feminist analysis of penality.* New York: Routledge.

Johnson, D., & Scheuble, L. (1991). Gender bias in the disposition of juvenile court referrals: The effects of time and location. *Criminology, 29,* 677–693.

Johnston, L. D., Bachman, J. G., & O'Malley, P. M. (1983, 1993). *Monitoring the future.* Ann Arbor, MI: University of Michigan.

Klein, D. (1973). The etiology of female crime. *Issues in Criminology, 8,* 3–29.

Kruttschnitt, C. (1982). Respectable women and the law. *Sociological Quarterly, 23,* 221–234.

Kruttschnitt, C. (1984). Sex and criminal court dispositions: The unresolved controversy. *Journal of Research in Crime and Delinquency, 21,* 213–232.

Kruttschnitt, C. (1995). Contributions of quantitative methods to the study of gender and crime, or bootstrapping our way into the theoretical thicket. *Journal of Quantitative Criminology, 12,* 135–161.

Kruttschnitt, C., & Green, D. E. (1984). The sex-sanctioning issue: Is it history *American Sociological Review, 49,* 541–551.

Kruttschnitt, C., & McCarthy, D. (1985). Familial social control and pretrial sanctions: Does sex really matter? *Journal of Criminal Law and Criminology, 76,* 151–175.

Lemert, E. M. (1951). *Social pathology.* New York: McGraw-Hill.

Leonard, E. B. (1982). *Women, crime, & society.* New York: Longman.

Lombroso, C., & Ferrero, W. (1915). *The female offender.* New York: D. Appleton .

Maher, L., & Daly, K. (1996). Women in the street-level drug economy: Continuity or change? *Criminology, 24,* 465–491.

Mann, C. R. (1984). *Female crime and delinquency.* . AL: University of Alabama Press.

Martin, S. E., & Jurik, N. C. (1996). *Doing justice, doing gender.* Thousand Oaks, CA: Sage.

Merlo, A. V., & Pollack, J. M. (1995). *Women, law, and social control.* Boston, MA: Allyn and Bacon.

Merton, R. M. (1938). Social structure and anomie. *American Sociological Review, 3,* 672–682.

Messerschmidt, J. W. (1986). *Capitalism, patriarchy, and crime.* Totowa, NJ: Rowman & Littlefield.

Messerschmidt, J. W. (1993). *Masculinities and crime.* Lanham, MD: Rowman & Littlefield.

Messerschmidt, J. W. (1995). From patriarchy to gender: Feminist theory, criminology and the challenge of diversity. In N. H. Rafter & F. Heidensohn (Eds.), *International feminist perspectives in criminology* (pp. 167–188). Buckingham: Open University Press.

Moffitt, T. E. (1994). Natural histories of delinquency. In E. G. M. Witekamp & H. J. Kerner (Eds.), *Cross-national longitudinal research on human development and criminal behavior* (pp. 3–61). Amsterdam, The Netherlands: Kluwer.

Morash, M. (1986). Gender, peer group experiences, and seriousness of delinquency. *Journal of Research in Crime and Delinquency, 23,* 43–67.

Morris, A., & Gelsthorpe, L. (1991). Feminist perspectives in criminology: Transforming and transgressing. *Women & Criminal Justice, 2,* 3–26.

Moulds, E. (1980). Chivalry and paternalism: Disparities of treatment in the criminal justice system. *Western Political Quarterly, 31,* 416–430.

Moyer, I. L. (1992). Crime, conflict theory, and the patriarchal society. In I. L. Moyer (Ed.), *The changing roles of women in the criminal justice system* (pp. 1–24). Prospect Heights, IL: Waveland Press.

Mukherjee, S. K., & Scutt, J. A. (1981). *Women and crime.* Sydney: Australian Institute of Criminology with Allen and Unwin.

Naffine, N. (1986). *Female crime: The construction of women in criminology.* Boston: Allen and Unwin.

Nagel, I. H., & Hagan, J. (1983). Gender and crime: offense patterns and criminal court sanctions. In M. Tonry & N. Morris (Eds.), *Crime and justice: An annual review of research* (pp. 91–144). Chicago: University of Chicago Press.

Nagel, I. H., & Johnson, B. L. (1994). The role of gender in a structured sentencing scheme: Equal treatment, policy choices, and the sentencing of female offenders under the United States Sentencing guidelines. *Journal of Criminal Law and Criminology, 85,* 181–221.

Nagin, D. S., & Paternoster, R. (1993). Enduring individual differences and rational choice theories of crime. *Law & Society Review, 24,* 467–496.

Newburn, T., & Stanko, E. A. (1994). *Just boys doing business? Masculinities and crime.* London: Routledge.

Odem, M. E. (1991). Single mothers, delinquent daughters, and the juvenile court in early 20th century Los Angeles. *Journal of Social History, 25,* 27–44.

Paternoster, R. (1987). The deterrent effect of the perceived certainty and severity of punishment. *Justice Quarterly, 4,* 173–217.

Paternoster, R., & Simpson, S. (1996). Sanction threats and appeals to morality. *Law & Society Review, 30,* 549–583.

Paternoster, R., (1989). Decisions to participate in and desist from four types of common delinquency: Desistance and the rational choice perspective. *Law & Society Review, 23,* 7–40.

Paternoster, R., & Simpson, S. (1993). A rational choice theory of corporate crime. In R. V. Clarke & M. Felson (Eds.), *Routine activity and rational choice: Advances in Criminolgical Theory,* Volume 5. New Brunswick, NJ: Transaction Publishers.

Patterson, G. R., DeBaryshe, B. D., & Ramsey, E. (1989). A developmental perspective on antisocial behavior. *American Psychologist, 44,* 329–335.

Phillips, D. M., & DeFleur, L. B. (1982). Gender ascription and the stereotyping of deviants. *Criminology, 203,* 431–448.

Piliavin, I., Thornton, C., Gartner, R., & Matsueda, R. (1986). Crime, deterrence, and rational choice. *American Sociological Review, 51,* 101–119.

Pollak, O. (1950). *The criminality of women.* Philadelphia, PA: University of Pennsylvania.

Rafter, N. (1985). *Partial justice: Women in state prisons, 1800–1935.* Boston, MA: Northeastern University Press.

Rasche, C. (1974). The female offender as an object of criminological research. *Criminal Justice and Behavior, 1,* 301–320.

Rosenbaum, J. L., & Lasley, J. R. (1990). School, community context, and delinquency: Rethinking the gender gap. *Justice Quarterly, 7,* 493–513.

Sampson, R. J., & Laub, J. H. (1993). *Crime in the making.* Cambridge, MA: Harvard University Press.

Schlossman, S., & Wallach, S. (1978). The crime of precocious sexuality: Female juvenile delinquency in the Progressive era. *Harvard Educational Review, 48,* 65–93.

Schur, E. (1983). *Labeling women deviant.* New York: Random House.

Schwartz, M. D., & Friedrichs, D. O. (1994). Postmodern thought and criminological discontent: New metaphors for understanding violence. *Criminology, 32,* 221–244.

Shacklady-Smith, L. (1978). Sexist assumptions and female delinquency. In C. Smart & B. Smart (Eds.), *Women, sexuality and social control* (pp. 74–86). London: Routledge.

Shaw, C. R., & McKay, H. D. (1972). *Juvenile delinquency and urban areas.* Chicago: University of Chicago Press.

Simon, R. J. (1975). *Women and crime.* Lexington, MA: Lexington Books.

Simon, R. J. (1990). Women and crime revisited. *Criminal Justice Research Bulletin, 5,* 1–11.

Simpson, S. S. (1989). Feminist theory, crime, and justice. *Criminology, 27,* 605–631.

Simpson, S. S. (1991). Caste, class, and violent crime: Explaining diffference in female offending. *Criminology, 29,* 115–135.

Simpson, S. S., & Elis, L. (1995). Doing gender: Sorting out the caste and crime conundrum. *Criminology, 33,* 47–81.

Simpson, S. S., & Elis, L. (1996). Theoretical perspectives on the corporate victimization of women. In E. Szockyj & J. G. Fox (Eds.), *Corporate victimization of women* (pp. 33–58). Boston: Northeastern University Press.

Smart, C. (1976). *Women, crime and criminology.* London: Routledge.

Smart, C. (1989). *Feminism and the power of law.* London: Routledge.

Smart, C. (1995). *Law, crime, and sexuality.* London: Sage.

Smart, C., & Smart, B. (1978). Women and social control: An introduction. In C. Smart & B. Smart (Eds.). *Women's sexuality and social control* (pp. 74–86). London: Routledge.

Sourcebook of Criminal Justice Statistics. (1985, 1995). Bureau of Justice oStatistics, Washington, D.C.

Spohn, C., Welch, S., & Gruhl, J. (1985). Women defendants in court: The interaction between sex and race in convicting and sentencing. *Social Science Quarterly, 66,* 178–185.

Steffensmeier, D. (1978). Crime and the contemporary woman. *Social Forces, 57,* 566–584.

Steffensmeier, D., & Allan, E. (1996). Gender and crime: Toward a gendered theory of female offending. *Annual Review of Sociology* (pp. 459–487).

Steffensmeier, D., Kramer, J., & Streifel, C. (1993). Gender and imprisonment decisions. *Criminology, 31,* 411–446.

Sutherland, E. (1934). *Principles of criminology.* Philadelphia, PA: J. B. Lippincott.

Teilmann, K. S., & Landry, P. H. (1981). Gender bias in juvenile justice. *Journal of Research in Crime and Delinquency, 18,* 47–80.

Tibbetts, S. G., & Herz, D. C. (1996). Gender differences in factors of social control and rational choice. *Deviant Behavior, 17,* 183–208.

Thomas, W. I. (1907). *Sex and Society.* Boston: Little, Brown.

Thomas, W. I. (1923). *The Unadjusted Girl.* New York: Harper & Row.

Tracy, P. E., Wolfgang, M. E., & Figlio, R. M. (1990). *Delinquent careers in two birth cohorts.* New York: Plenum Press.

Visher, C. A. (1983). Gender, police arrest desicions, and notions of chivalry. *Criminology, 211,* 5–28.

West, C., & Fenstermaker, S. (1995). Doing difference. *Gender & Society, 1,* 8–37.

West, C., & Zimmerman, D. (1987). Doing gender. *Gender & Society, 1,* 125–151.

Wilson, J. Q., & Herrnstein, R. (1985). *Crime and human nature.* New York: Simon & Schuster.

Worrall, A. (1990). *Offending women.* New York: Routledge.

Young, A. (1996). *Imagining crime: Textual outlaws and criminal conversations.* London: Sage.

Zatz, M. (1987). The changing forms of racial/ethnic biases in sentencing. *Journal of Research in Crime and Delinquency, 24,* 69–92.

CHAPTER 25

Gender and the Military

Mady Wechsler Segal

1. INTRODUCTION

The military is an important social institution, with effects on other institutions and on people's lives, both directly and indirectly. Despite this, the military is a relatively neglected area of study within sociology. Further, though the military has a gender-defining tradition and gender is endemic in the institution, central works on the sociology of gender usually omit analysis of gender in the military. This neglect of study on armed forces is partly due to anti-military views of many sociologists, especially feminists, and to lack of knowledge of military organization (the latter despite the role of the military in the development of organizational theories, including centrality in the work of Max Weber, 1968). This chapter may help to fill this gap and integrate the study of gender in the military into the larger field.

This chapter describes and analyzes the literature on gender in the military. Of special interest from a macrosociological perspective are historical and current trends in women's participation in the armed forces of the United States and other nations and the factors that affect them. At the micro-level, the emphasis is on the integration of women in armed forces and the social construction of gender in interpersonal interactions. While the literature, and therefore this chapter, focus on women in the military, other related topics are considered. The central role of gender in the military—and the role of the military in defining gender in the larger society—have implications for men's behaviors and for men's and women's views regarding policies on women's military roles and on

Partial support for writing this paper was provided by the U.S. Army Research Institute for the Behavioral and Social Sciences under contract number DASW0195K0005. The views in this paper are the author's and not necessarily those of the U.S. Army Research Institute, the Department of the Army, or the Department of Defense.

MADY WECHSLER SEGAL • Department of Sociology, University of Maryland, College Park, Maryland 20742

Handbook of the Sociology of Gender, edited by Janet Saltzman Chafetz. Kluwer Academic/ Plenum Publishers, New York, 1999.

homosexuality in the armed forces. The construction of gender in military family issues is also discussed. One can study nearly every topic of previous chapters in this volume within the context of the military and in public discourse about the military. One can apply concepts from those areas to the study of gender and the military—as sociologists working on these issues in the military have done.

2. WOMEN IN THE MILITARY AS AN AREA OF STUDY

Until the 1970s, there was almost no scholarly work on women in the military (other than Treadwell, 1954). Research and public policy attention has increased dramatically over the past 20 years. Part of the reason for this increase has been an expansion of women's military roles in the United States and most European nations (as described later).

The literature and the "invisible college" tend to be interdisciplinary, with the major research and/or writing being done by political scientists (such as Enloe, 1983, 1993; Stiehm, 1981, 1989, 1996), historians (including Campbell, 1992, 1993; De Pauw, 1981), anthropologists (such as Rosen of Rosen, Durand, Bliese, Halverson, Rothberg, & Harrison, 1996), psychologists (including Thomas, 1986), journalists (e.g., Rogan, 1981) and military personnel with various backgrounds and generally without social science training who write about their personal experiences (e.g., Barkalow, 1990; Earley, 1989). One of the most comprehensive works on women in the U.S. armed forces that provides a detailed history of policy changes was written by Holm (1992), the first American woman to attain two-star flag rank (as a Major General in the Air Force).

The number of sociologists doing research on women in the military (and on gender in the armed forces more generally) has been increasing, to include Devilbiss (1985) on gender integration and group cohesion, Firestone and Harris (1994) on sexual harassment, Miller (1997) on gender harassment, and Moore (1991, 1996, 1997) on African-American and Japanese-American women in the military. Some of our knowledge comes from sociologists who have written dissertations on the military that they have later published as books. Examples are Rustad's (1982) work on the integration of women into an Army signal unit in the late 1970s and Williams' (1989) book on women marines and male nurses.

There is increasing coverage in our journals and in book chapters of women in the armed forces of other nations (e.g., Cherpak, 1993; Chinchilla, 1990; Cock, 1994; Dandeker & Segal, 1996; Seitz, Lobao, & Treadway, 1993). However, this work tends to cover just one nation at a time and therefore not to be truly comparative. Theory building using a multinational perspective has just begun (Segal, 1995). (Except where indicated, analysis in this chapter refers to the United States.)

3. THE MILITARY AS A GENDER-DEFINING INSTITUTION

Current events have created a media frenzy of coverage and attention to problems of gender integration, such as the recent sexual assault and harassment scandal at Aberdeen Proving Ground or the earlier Tailhook scandal. Such coverage leads to the false impression that the problems revealed (such as sexual harassment) are new or newly known. Despite this impression, these issues have been present in daily interactions of military personnel for some time; they have just now been brought to the public's attention by intense media pressure. This pressure has also created organizational responses that exceed responses to previous indications of widespread sexual harassment (such as revealed by surveys conducted by the Department of Defense in 1988 and 1995).

To understand these dynamics, as well as women's past, current, and future military roles, requires an understanding of the role of gender in the military and of the role of the military in cultural constructions of gender.

Some literature analyzes the military as a gender-defining institution and socializing agent. The older literature in this tradition emphasizes the role of the military in creating or reifying masculinity among men through their processing by the organization. Serving in the military historically has been a rite of passage from boyhood to manhood. The importance of "masculinity" in this transition is especially apparent in the culture of basic training, where new recruits are exhorted to try harder or be labeled "girls" or "sissies" (Arkin & Dobrofsky, 1978; Faris, 1976; Williams, 1989).

This gender-defining function of military service has been undergoing change as the proportion of women in uniform has risen and as more jobs, including many combat and combat support specialties, have been opened to women. But strong resistance to integrating women in the military institution can be seen in public policy discourse and in the everyday interactions of military personnel (as I explore in depth later in this chapter). One source of this resistance is the traditional role of the military in defining masculinity. Recognizing this role is important to analyzing the current situation for gender in armed forces. Recent works on the masculine military culture focus on the problematic nature of this culture for women's integration (e.g., Katzenstein & Reppy, 1999).

Despite institutional resistance and the prototypical male nature of the institution, women have participated in the armed forces of the United States and many other nations through history and their roles have been expanding. I turn now to a cross-national analysis of women's military participation. Then I will look at women's military history and contemporary role in the United States.

4. WOMEN'S MILITARY PARTICIPATION CROSS-NATIONALLY AND THE FACTORS THAT AFFECT IT

The cross-national study of women in the military is in its infancy. There are large gaps in our knowledge. However, there are some generalizations that appear warranted by the available literature, especially about the conditions under which women's military roles expand or contract. Military variables affecting the nature and extent of women's participation include characteristics of the nation's security situation and certain aspects of military organization and activity. Social structural factors include aspects of women's civilian roles and more general civilian social structural variables that affect women's roles. Cultural processes, such as the social construction of gender and family roles, also influence women's participation in armed forces. (For a thorough description of these variables, see Segal, 1995.)

4.1. Military Situation

Of major importance in determining women's military roles in a society is the security situation of the society. When there are shortages of qualified men, especially during times of national emergency, most nations have increased (and will increase) women's military roles. Under some conditions, women have participated in combat; more often, their noncombat military functions increase. Many nations currently conscript men, but few require women to serve in the military; furthermore, where women are drafted, the conditions of their obligation often differ from those of men. Women have been conscripted in the past during wartime—and are likely to be again in the future. Examples of conscription during the World War II era (including actual conscription and laws allowing conscription) can be found in France, Greece, Norway, Germany, and the United Kingdom (Goldman,1982; Stanley & Segal, 1988; Treadwell, 1954). In the United States had the war in Europe not ended, civilian nurses would have been drafted (Holm, 1992; Treadwell, 1954).

Whether or not they conscripted women, nations have greatly increased their participation (in terms of both numbers and roles) during wartime: marked examples of this in many nations were evident during World War II. Although women were still concentrated in a few job classifications, wartime necessity opened other jobs to them (e.g., Binkin & Bach, 1977; Holm, 1992; Treadwell, 1954).

A common pattern is the active involvement of women in revolutionary movements. Women have been in partisan and guerilla operations, including as combatants, in, for example, Algeria, China, El Salvador, Nicaragua, Rhodesia, Russia, Vietnam, Yugoslavia, and the U.S. Revolutionary War; however, after the guerrillas have overthrown the government and formed a new one with a more conventionally organized armed force, women return to more traditional social roles and leave the military—voluntarily or not (Cherpak, 1993; De Pauw, 1981; Enloe, 1980; Goldman, 1982; Isaksson, 1988; Randall, 1981, 1994; Segal, Li, & Segal, 1992; Seitz, Lobao, & Treadway, 1993; Stanley & Segal, 1992).

Similarly, the end of World War II saw a return to limitations on women's military jobs. In the United States, laws passed in 1948 placed restrictions on military women. When women are no longer needed, their military activity is reduced. Women have served as a reserve labor force, both civilian and military (Campbell, 1984; Enloe, 1980; Gluck, 1987).

Women's military roles are socially constructed; public policy, norms, and women's behavior are shaped, at least in part, by public discourse. What has happened in the past in many nations is that when the armed forces need women, their prior military history is recalled to demonstrate that they can perform effectively in various positions. Subsequently, there is a process of cultural amnesia of the contributions women made during emergency situations. In the aftermath of war, women's military activities are reconstructed as minor (or even nonexistent), allowing the culture to maintain the myth "of men in arms and women at home" (Cooke, 1993, p. 178). When a new emergency arises, history is rediscovered.

Women's involvement in armed forces (even as combatants) tends to be high when there is grave threat to the society, regardless of cultural values about gender. There are times when women's military involvement may be seen as an extension of women's roles as mothers protecting their children; such may be the case in partisan activities of women drawn from the ranks of the poor, especially during times of severe oppression (Chinchilla, 1990; Li, 1993, 1995; Montgomery, 1995; Randall, 1981).

In societies with low threats to national security but with cultural values supporting gender equality, women's military participation also increases. Contemporary examples include Canada and Sweden, which allow women to volunteer for combat jobs (Segal &

Segal, 1989; Stanley & Segal, 1992; Törnquist, 1982). In Canada, even ground combat positions are open to women.

The extent of women's participation in combat jobs seems to be minimized when there is a medium threat, that is, when the society is not threatened with imminent extinction or invasion by superior military forces, but there is a moderate to high probability of military action on its soil in the near future. This description has been applicable to Israel, where until recently women were excluded from serving in combat.

The nature of military missions also affects the degree of women's participation. The greater the relative importance of actual war fighting (especially ground combat), the less the participation of women. Women's participation is greater when military forces are engaged in peacekeeping operations or disaster relief activities, as well as in operations that resemble domestic police functions (such as drug interdiction and quelling civil disturbances). The recent rise in frequency of these types of operations may bring increased representation of women in uniform. Women can also be expected to be increasingly involved in military aviation—even in war fighting, as evidenced by the opening of fighter pilot positions to women in several nations (e.g., Canada, the Netherlands, the United Kingdom, and the United States) (Dandeker & Segal, 1996; Dorn, 1994; Segal & Segal, 1989; Stanley & Segal, 1988).

In general, modern nations that have voluntary systems of recruitment of military personnel (notably Canada, the United Kingdom, and the United States) have been increasing women's military roles more rapidly than those with conscription. Demographic patterns also play a role here when combined with voluntary accession. Israel conscripts both men and women, but places strong limitations on women's military positions; contrary to popular mythology, Israeli women have not been allowed to participate in combat (Bloom, 1982; Gal, 1986) until very recently, and then only as the result of a lawsuit.

4.2. Social Structure

4.2.1. DEMOGRAPHIC PATTERNS.
Demographic patterns shape women's roles in various ways. They affect women's use as a reserve source of labor (Campbell, 1984; Gluck, 1987; Kessler-Harris, 1982). When the supply of men does not meet the demand for military labor, women are drawn into service. Thus, when small birth cohorts reach military age, unless there is a concomitant decrease in demand for military personnel, opportunities for women in the armed forces seem to increase. This impact has been evident in most of the NATO nations in the past 20 years, including the United States in the 1970s (Segal & Segal, 1983) and the United Kingdom in the late 1980s and early 1990s (Dandeker & Segal, 1996).

4.2.2. LABOR FORCE CHARACTERISTICS.
Various labor force characteristics affect women's military roles. As the proportion of women employed has increased in many nations, their representation in the armed forces has also increased. This occurs partly because the same factors affect both activities (such as a shortage of male labor) and partly because women's greater involvement in the workplace brings structural and cultural changes in the society that make military service more compatible with women's roles—and makes excluding them from military service less justifiable. Such changes have been evident in, for example, the Scandinavian countries and the United States over the past 20 years (e.g., Stanley & Segal, 1988; United Nations, 1991). Women's labor force participation

in France has also been increasing and so have movements toward increasing their representation in the armed forces (Boulègue, 1991; Hantrais, 1990). The percentage of women in the labor force in the United Kingdom has been relatively lower and their military roles have been limited; both are now increasing (Dandeker & Segal, 1996).

The degree of gender segregation in the civilian occupational structure also affects women's military participation, although the relationship is not linear. When sex segregation is extremely high, the military must rely on women to perform military functions that are dominated by women in the civilian workplace. This is why the United States recruited women civilian telephone operators in World War I (Holm, 1992; Schneider & Schneider, 1991). Nursing is another job that tends to be sex typed as a woman's job, which has led the militaries in many countries to allow women to serve; indeed, nursing has often been the first military job to open to women in substantial numbers. In general, however, sex segregation in the civilian labor market is negatively related to women's military participation. A more gender *integrated* occupational structure is indicative of more gender equality in the culture, which in turn leads to greater acceptance of women in military roles. Further, if women's civilian occupations are similar to men's, then women are more likely to have skills required for military jobs.

4.2.3. ECONOMIC FACTORS.   The state of the civilian economy affects women's civilian and military employment. In periods of economic expansion, women are drawn into employment. In contracting economies, women tend to leave the workforce. High unemployment rates (especially among young men) are associated with a ready supply of men to serve in the armed forces and relatively low opportunities for women in the military. Periods of low male unemployment, especially with volunteer militaries, sometimes lead to expanded military roles for women (and women more motivated to join, especially if they are relatively disadvantaged in the civilian economy). In the United States, major growth in the representation of women in the military occurred in the late 1970s, when unemployment declined. When unemployment rose in the early 1980s, the expansion stalled (Segal & Segal, 1983).

4.2.4 FAMILY ROLES.   Family roles affect women's military participation in two ways. First, there is a strong tendency in most cultures for women's roles generally to be intricately linked to family values and norms. Second, the nature of military activity is socially constructed in many cultures as negatively related to family roles (M. Segal, 1986, 1989).

There are several family structural variables that affect women's military roles. Women's participation in the military is positively associated with later age at first marriage, later age at birth of first child, and fewer children. The average age at onset of family responsibilities is even more important for women's military roles than for civilian employment because of the emphasis on youth for military personnel. In those nations where there has been a delaying of family formation there has also been an increase in women's representation in the military (examples are Canada and the United States in the 1970s and 1980s) (Stanley & Segal, 1988).

4.3. Culture

4.3.1. SOCIAL VALUES ABOUT GENDER.   The meaning of gender is socially constructed. The degree to which people are assigned to social roles on the basis of gender, and the particular roles that are seen as appropriate to each gender, are socially determined—far beyond the impact of biologically based determinants (Lorber, 1993). A division of labor based on sex may have been functional for the society in earlier times, but is clearly less so now (e.g., Marwell, 1975). To the extent that individual traits for which there are large average differences by sex are important for the organization of activities, a sex-based division of labor may be functional. Technology has diminished the importance of two types of physically based traits, namely physical strength and reproduction.

What is important for this chapter is the way in which the culture deals with gender differences. A culture can exaggerate or minimize the importance of sex differences (in physical or psychological traits) and thereby justify or reject a gender-based division of social roles. Thus, I am concerned not with what is "correct" in any objective or evidential sense. Rather, I look at the discourse about gender, the importance attached to gender differences, and the implications for women's roles (including in the armed forces) of the cultural interpretation of gender. Cultures can stress gender equality or differences between the genders and this has strong impacts on women's military roles. The greater the emphasis on ascription by gender (and therefore the less the emphasis on individual differences), the more limited women's military role.

Each society can go through cultural changes in gender roles and such changes are not always linear, but are often cyclical. The causal direction of the link between culture and structure is not always clear. Sometimes cultural change drives structural change. At other times, structural changes (such as women moving into predominantly male jobs) are caused by other factors (such as war) and then the culture changes to justify structural changes (Anderson, 1981; Campbell, 1984; Kessler-Harris, 1982). When the structure changes again, so can the culture (as happens after a war).

Analysis of women's military roles benefits from examination of this process of the social construction of gender—and the analysis of the social construction of women's military roles adds to our knowledge of the social construction of gender in general. For example, one can analyze the public discourse about women's military roles for the underlying constructions of gender and rationales for policy positions (Segal & Hansen, 1992). (Similar analysis can be done on public discourse about the relationship to military service of other characteristics, such as race or sexual orientation.) Chafetz points out in Chapter 1 of this volume that "virtually all macro-level feminist theories agree that cultural or ideological definitions of masculinity/femininity and of gender 'appropriate' behaviors, responsibilities and privileges, are fundamental components of systems of gender inequality." Such cultural definitions can be seen very clearly in policy discourse about gender in the military (as well as in gender interactions in military organizations, as we shall see later in this chapter).

There are some interesting examples from World War II of the social construction of women's military roles, including several of women performing functions that are considered military in other societies but are labeled civilian. Germany conscripted women into what were labeled as civilian jobs; although many women wore uniforms, were under military authority, and performed functions considered military in other nations, they were called civilians (Tuten, 1982). In the United Kingdom, even uniformed women were defined as noncombatants. The definition of the line between combatant and noncombatant involved the firing of weapons. Women performed all tasks associated with the firing of anti-aircraft weapons except the actual firing: they moved ammunition and even loaded the weapons, but, to continue to view them as noncombatants, they were not allowed to fire the weapons they had loaded (they had to get a man to do it!) (Campbell, 1993). In the United States, the WASPs (Women's Airforce Service Pilots) ferried military planes—and 38 were killed in the line of duty—but were treated as civilians. Congress granted them military veterans benefits in 1977 (Holm, 1992), an example of reconstruction of social status.

The cultural contradictions and ideological ambivalence involved in women's military participation can be seen in the reactions of both those who favor maintenance of patriarchal values and radical feminists (Chapkis, 1981; Elshtain, & Tobias, 1990; Enloe, 1980). Those at both ends of the ideological spectrum on gender roles oppose having women serve in armed forces. Having large numbers of military women causes public resistance because it challenges notions of masculinity and femininity (Enloe, 1993).

The more egalitarian the social values about gender, the greater women's representation in the military. On the other side, cultures that support traditional divisions of labor based on gender tend to exclude women from the military or limit their roles substantially. As social values have become more egalitarian in societies, women's military roles have expanded. The citizenship revolution has been expanding to previously disenfranchised social groups. During this century, many nations have enfranchised women in the political system—and cultures increasingly have supported their participation in other social institutions (such as the economy). A driving force toward increasing women's representation in the military has been laws prohibiting discrimination based on gender (which sometimes apply to the military). For example, Canada's Human Rights Law has been directly responsible for breaking down some barriers to women's full participation in the armed forces (Park, 1986; Segal & Segal, 1989; Stanley & Segal, 1988). The European Community is undergoing some similar effects of gender discrimination laws (Dandeker & Segal, 1996).

It is not yet clear how far social values will go toward full gender equality. Given the traditionally masculine nature of the military institution, it is one of the last bastions of male domination and there are forces resistant to gender integration. Substantial segments of many societies' populations remain more traditional. One force for traditional gender roles that limit women's representation in the military may be religious fundamentalism or conservatism, with tenets that place men and women in separate spheres of life (and confine women to the family) (Hawley, 1994).

4.3.2. SOCIAL VALUES ABOUT FAMILY.

The social construction of family also needs to be considered because women's social roles are affected by anything having to do with the family. Women's historically primary societal function has been associated with reproduction and child rearing. The extent to which a culture continues to assign women this primary role affects women's military roles. Cultures often see the mothering role as antithetical to the warrior role; giving life in childbirth is seen as the opposite of taking life in war. In addition, the long dependence of young children on adult caretakers (traditionally mothers) has precluded those caretakers from participating in activities that take them away or require their uninterrupted attention (such as hunting or war).

As conceptions about family and the structures of families have changed, so have cultural expectations about women's devotion to family—and their inclusion in wider social roles increases. Social values about family in many societies have been supportive of family forms that differ from traditional structures. The greater the cultural acceptance of various family structures, the less everyone is expected to fit one pattern, and the less gender determines social roles.

The greater the movement away from certain traditional family forms, especially those based on the nuclear family, the greater the representation of women in the military. This does not mean the demise of family values, but a transformation in the structures that support such values. Indeed, included here can be government-sponsored parental leave and/or community supported child care that enables parents to be involved in their societies without neglecting children. Extended families of various kinds are also more compatible with women serving in the military (and in civilian employment separated from family) than are isolated nuclear families. To the extent that societies support diverse family forms, women are more likely to participate in the military.

4.3.3. INTERSECTIONS OF RACE AND GENDER.

Connections between race or ethnicity and gender play a role in determining social policy with regard to the military in some countries (Enloe, 1980). For example, women gained representation in the white South African Defense Force owing to political aims of the white elite (Cock, 1994). In the United States, comparisons are often made between racial integration of the armed forces and gender integration (D. Segal, 1989); however, there are historical eras in which white women and African-Americans were alternative sources of military labor, such as when civilian nurses were about to be drafted because of a shortage of military nurses, while black nurses were subject to quotas and were prohibited from treating white service members (Hine, 1989).

The current percentage of military women who are African-American is extraordinarily high. While African-American men are overrepresented among enlisted personnel (compared to their percentage in the population), the overrepresentation of African-American women is even higher among enlisted women and among officers is almost double the percentage of male officers who are African-American. The percentage of enlisted women who are black is especially high in the Army: 47% (compared to 27% of enlisted men) (Department of the Army, 1997). This overrepresentation is due primarily to the relative advantages in pay and benefits of military service compared to opportunities in the civilian labor market.

5. WOMEN IN THE ARMED FORCES OF THE UNITED STATES: PAST AND PRESENT

5.1. History

Women's involvement in American wars dates back to the revolution (De Pauw, 1981). In the twentieth century, in response to the demands of World War I, women were employed by military forces in both nursing and non-nursing capacities in unprecedented numbers. The U.S. Navy and Marine Corps established women's units in 1917 and 1918, respectively. The uniformed women were granted military status and were assigned to jobs women normally held in civilian society, such as telephone operator and clerk; some were stationed overseas (Holm, 1992; Schneider & Schneider, 1991). Since these units were established to meet specific personnel needs to free men for combat, the units were temporary and the women were demobilized after the war.

In World War II a major shift occurred in the nature of women's military participation. Not only did they serve in large numbers, but their roles expanded. Large numbers of women were employed in civilian industry essential to the war effort, as well as in uniformed military service (Campbell, 1984; Gluck, 1987; Holm, 1982; Treadwell, 1954).

Women's organizations were formed for all services, with their original designations implying their intended temporary nature (e.g., Women's Army Auxiliary Corps). Although women were mainly assigned to traditional fields, as the war progressed women's activities expanded beyond the usual roles women play (health care, administration, and communications) to include technical and combat support jobs. Small numbers served in almost every specialty, excluding direct combat, including as airplane mechanics, parachute riggers, and weapons instructors.

American women were prohibited from serving as offensive combat personnel, but they were deployed to foreign theaters and were involved in espionage and sabotage activities. They were thus exposed to danger. Nurses stationed in the Philippines and Guam were taken prisoner by the Japanese, and others were captured by the Germans.

Had the war not ended in 1945, civilian nurses in the United States would have been drafted. The bill to conscript nurses had been passed by the House and had cleared the Senate committee (in March 1945). The termination of the war in Europe in May 1945 reversed the shortage of military nurses that had led to the need for conscription.

As in other nations after World War II and other wars, the end of the war saw a return to limitations on women's military roles. Legislation passed in 1947 and 1948 provided for continuing women's armed services but severely limited military women's numbers and activities. As in other areas of social life in the United States following World War II, women were expected to return to more traditional statuses and roles (Campbell, 1984). Despite some modification of these laws in the 1960s and 1970s, American women's military roles were constrained by exclusions prescribed by this legislation for more than 40 years. These laws prohibited women in the Air Force, Navy, and Marine Corps from being assigned to duty on aircraft or combat ships engaged in combat missions. There were exceptions to these exclusions for physicians, nurses, chaplains, and attorneys. The Army had no statutory prohibition against women in combat, but a policy was developed and modified over the years to prevent women from being assigned to units or jobs in which they would routinely be engaged in close combat. These exclusions, however, did not protect women from the risk of exposure to combat. Women in the Air Force were prohibited from flying fighter planes but were permitted to fly tankers, which would be targets in the event of war. Navy women served on support vessels, such as supply ships, which are also likely targets. Women in the Army served in military police, mechanical repair, transportation, intelligence, signal, and other support specialties that would bring them into battle.

Despite the combat restrictions and the lack of wartime necessity, the representation of women in the military increased dramatically in the 1970s. At the start of the All Volunteer Force (AVF) in 1973, there were shortages of qualified men. Congress had passed the Equal Rights Amendment in 1972 and there was anticipation that it would be ratified by the states. The combined effect of these two occurrences was to open job specialties to women from which they had been excluded previously and to increase the number of women recruited into the armed forces. In 1971 there were approximately 43,000 women in uniform (30,000 enlisted and 13,000 officers), constituting only 1.6% of total active-duty military personnel. By the end of 1980, 9 years later, there were about 173,000 women, or about 8.5 % of total active duty forces.

The expansions in women's military roles have led to greater likelihood that women would be involved in military engagements and in roles that are not "traditional" for women. In December 1989, women participated in the U.S. invasion of Panama during "Operation Just Cause." Approximately 800 of the 18,400 soldiers involved in the operation were women (Moskos, 1990). Their roles were varied and included piloting helicopters to ferry troops—some while under enemy fire from the ground.

The missions and experiences of some of the women soldiers involved in the Panamanian operation fueled a renewed debate about women in combat. For example, there was controversy surrounding whether a military police captain was in combat when she led her unit in attempting to capture a military dog kennel believed to be occupied by armed and firing members of the Panamanian Defense Forces.

However, attention to the participation of women in Operation Just Cause pales by comparison with media coverage and potential policy impact of the roles played by women in Operations Desert Shield and Desert Storm. Approximately 41,000 women were deployed to the Persian Gulf between August, 1990 and February, 1991 (Eitelberg, 1991). Women made up about 7% of all military personnel deployed (including all ranks and active duty and reserve personnel combined). The Army accounted for the vast majority of these women.

One of the interesting aspects of women's representation in the Persian Gulf operations was the difference between active duty and reserve forces, especially among officers. While women were 5.6% of active enlisted personnel in the theater of operations, they were 12.2% of reserve enlisted forces. The contrast is even more marked among officers: 7.3% of active duty officers were women, compared to 21.3% of reserve officers.

The experiences of Operations Desert Shield and Desert Storm demonstrate that the policy excluding women from offensive combat roles does not provide complete protection from death or capture: 13 American women were among the 375 U.S. service members who died and two women were prisoners of war (Eitelberg, 1991).

The public attention to women's successful performance in their jobs in the Gulf War increased political pressure to remove barriers to women in combat. It clearly led directly to repeal by Congress (in 1992) of the 1948 law prohibiting women in combat aircraft and contributed to the opening of naval combat ships (in 1993).

5.2. Contemporary Representation

In the 1980s and 1990s, women's representation in the U.S. armed forces continued to rise, although at a slower rate than in the 1970s. Change was not linear: there were periodic reversals of policy, such as opening then closing of certain occupational specialties to women (see Stiehm, 1989 for a discussion of "backlash" in the early 1980s). By 1997, the approximately 196,000 women in the Department of Defense military services (and about 3000 in the Coast Guard, which is part of the Department of Transportation) were about 14% of active duty forces. Their representation was highest in the Air Force (17.8% of enlisted personnel and 16.2% of officers) and lowest in the Marine Corps (5.4% of enlisted personnel and 4.4% of officers) (WREI, 1998, using data from Defense Manpower Data Center).

Differences among the services in the proportion of women are due primarily to the differential occupational distributions in the services. Since women are excluded from some combat positions, the larger the number of such positions there are in a service, the fewer the number of women the service can admit. The absence of medical personnel in the Marines (which gets its medical support from the Navy) contributes to the smaller percentage of women in the Corps than in the other services.

As of 1994, 99.7% of all positions in the Air Force are open to women; those that remain closed are those that collocate with direct ground combat positions that exclude women (Dorn, 1994; WREI, 1996, 1998). In the Navy, 94% of all positions (96% of occupations) are open to women; exclusions include submarines, SEAL (special forces) units, and support positions (such as medical and chaplain) that collocate with Marine Corps units from which women are barred. Women are permitted in 70% of Army positions (91% of occupations); they are barred from serving in the direct ground combat battalions and any support units that collocate with them; positions closed to women include infantry, armor, special forces, field artillery battalions, combat engineer companies, and forward area air defense artillery. Similarly, 62% of the positions in the Marine Corps (93% of occupations) are open to women; women are barred from positions in the infantry regiments and physically collocated support units and positions. (All positions in the Coast Guard are open to women.)

Although women do tend to serve in occupational areas that are traditional for women in the services, substantial numbers serve in other areas. About half of enlisted women serve in the two most traditional areas of support and administration (33.0%) and health care (15.6%); 46.5% of women officers serve in health care positions, while 14.9% are in administrative positions (WREI, 1998).

Examination of women's distribution among military ranks reveals that their representation in the junior and middle pay grades is roughly proportional to their concentration in each service. Women are substantially underrepresented in the senior ranks, especially among officers (WREI, 1996), but their proportion in the senior ranks has been increasing (WREI, 1998).

5.3. Contemporary Process of Gender Integration

As can be seen from all of the information given earlier, we know a great deal at the macro-level about women's participation in armed forces, including laws, policies, the policy development process; the literature on women's military history has been growing, both in the United States and other nations. When we get to the micro-level of interpersonal relations, our knowledge is less systematic. While there are some works that describe women's personal experiences in the military (e.g., Barkalow, 1990; Earley, 1989) and social scientific studies that document problems in gender integration (e.g., Miller, 1997; Rustad, 1982), there has not been as much theory building and testing concerning the conditions under which gender integration is more or less successful. Research does provide the basis for such theory development and one can learn much about gender processes in general from this research.

As women's roles in the U.S. military increased over the past two decades, and as women entered previously all-male jobs and situations, interpersonal processes of fundamental social change were evident in the attitudes and behaviors of the men and in the experiences of the women. Organizational resistance and interpersonal adjustments are still prevalent, although acceptance of women has increased in many military situations and is in some settings more routine and even routinized.

There is substantial documentation of the initial process of gender integration at the service academies: the U.S. Military Academy at West Point, the Naval Academy, the Air Force Academy, and the Coast Guard Academy (e.g., Adams, 1984; DeFleur & Warner, 1987; Durning, 1978; Priest, Vitters, & Prince, 1978; Safilios-Rothschild, 1978; Stiehm, 1981). Women first entered the academies in 1976 (with women first graduating in the class of 1980) as a result (except for the Coast Guard) of Congressional mandate. Male cadets and midshipmen, who tended to hold traditional rather than egalitarian sex role attitudes, were hostile to the admission of women—not unlike their contemporary counterparts at The Citadel and Virginia Military Institute (VMI), which have just begun gender integration following a court battle waged to keep their schools all-male. Research on West Point shows that upperclass cadets exerted a negative socialization influence on the attitudes of men in the first gender-integrated class (as well as in the previous year's class). Researchers at all the academies found that behavior toward the women was well described by Kanter's (1977) work on responses to "token" women. Such behavior is still a common experience for women at the academies, despite more than 20 years of integration and a rise in their representation (recent classes at West Point are approximately 16% women; at the Coast Academy, women are about one-third of recent entering classes). However, acceptance of women has improved and it now no longer makes the news when women hold top leadership positions.

In all military settings there is an active process of "doing gender" (West & Zimmerman, 1987); social construction and role negotiation around gender is common. Indeed, because women in many of these settings violate men's conceptions of gender-appropriate behavior (sometimes even by their mere presence), much attention is paid to gender. Women often constitute a small proportion of their work groups and experience the kind of behavior from the men that Kanter (1977) describes.

Despite the prevalence of reactions to the "token" women, not all research supports Kanter's notions about the effects of group proportions. Dunivin (1988), for example, studying Air Force officers, finds that while women's perceptions of the opportunity structure in their jobs are significantly different from men's, women's attitudes in the most skewed specialties (e.g., pilots and air traffic controllers) actually resembled their male peers' views more than did women in some specialties with relatively higher concentrations of women (e.g., administrators). There are other indications that reactions to women become more seriously negative when their proportions rise, their opportunities within the organization improve, and they constitute more of a threat to men's career advancement—in a manner similar to what Blalock (1967) described for acceptance of minority racial groups as a function of the size of the subgroup within the group.

5.3.1. GENDER HARASSMENT AND SEXUAL HARASSMENT.

Women in the military are particularly vulnerable to sexual harassment owing to the skewed gender ratios, the fact that military personnel often live in close quarters together, and the power involved in the rank hierarchy. While sexual assault is rare (though present) (Morris, 1996), certain kinds of sexual harassment are quite common, especially behaviors such as sexually explicit comments and jokes and suggestive looks and gestures (Department of Defense, 1995; Firestone & Harris, 1994; Martindale, 1990).

Researchers are starting to pay attention to gender harassment and to distinguish it from sexual harassment. Miller (1997) shows that forms of gender harassment in the Army include resisting women's authority, constant scrutiny of women and using any mistakes as evidence of military women's inferiority, gossip and rumors, sabotage of women's work (such as their equipment), and indirect threats. Also quite common are sexist remarks, including statements that women do not belong in the military.

An important component of gender relations in the military has to do with perceptions of inequity. It is not clear whether these perceptions are the cause or the result of sexist attitudes, but the consequences of the perceptions are significant regardless of their cause or even their veracity. One source of such perception of inequity in the Army is the physical fitness test that all soldiers must pass and which has different standards by age and sex. Since a woman can pass the test with a performance for which a man would fail, many male soldiers believe that women are given an unfair advantage. Interestingly, such concerns are rarely voiced with regard to differential standards by age.

Perceptions (by both men and women, military and civilian) that women are inferior to men physically lie at the base of opposition to women being allowed in some military jobs, especially ground combat. This is evident in public and private discourse about the issue (Miller, 1997; Segal & Hansen, 1992). But such opposition is also due to desires to maintain the gender-defining role of military service.

Perceptions of inequity and inequality in physical performance are reinforced by the nature of the physical fitness test and the application of standards by gender. The test was initially designed to measure men's physical fitness efficiently and with limited equipment; it consists of pushups, situps, and a timed run. Physical traits on which women, on average, would outperform men (such as measures of flexibility) are not included in the test. Women are being judged by traits on which average men score higher than average women. Military women sometimes judge themselves by the male standards (just as men judge them) and therefore feel less worthy.

Military women generally do not consider themselves "feminist" even when their beliefs are quite feminist. This is partly because they have been socialized by a male-dominated culture that views "feminism" as antithetical to military, just as "feminine" is antithetical to military. Some military women, especially enlisted women, want to maintain distinctions between men and women. For example, some Army enlisted women oppose opening ground combat roles to women because they want to be different from the men (that is, they do not want to be warriors) and they want to be seen as different from men; that is, they want to maintain their self-definitions as feminine despite being soldiers. Women officers are more likely to favor opening combat roles to women partly because they recognize that continued exclusion serves to maintain systematic gender inequality (Miller, 1995).

It seems that at the very time when the role of the military has been evolving, toward more operations other than war, such as peacekeeping and humanitarian missions, there are increasing pressures to reassert the masculinity of the service member. As the military changes in adaptation to its likely role in the twenty-first century, forces for tradition are resisting changes that they have defined as the "feminization" of the military." The pressures and resistance can be seen not only in interpersonal relations (including gender and sexual harassment), but also in the political arena—as evidenced by attempts in Congress to force basic military training to be gender segregated (Maze, 1997). This reassertion of masculinity may also be seen in policies and public discourse regarding homosexuality.

6. HOMOSEXUALITY IN THE MILITARY

Exclusion of homosexuals is another way to maintain the military as a province of heterosexual males with gender-defining characteristics. There appears to be a relationship between the degree to which a nation's policies allow homosexuals to serve in the military and the extent of gender integration in its armed forces (Segal, Segal, & Booth, 1999). The United States is an outlier in that it has a relatively high degree of gender integration, but excludes open homosexuals from serving. In 1993, newly elected President Clinton attempted to lift the ban. Instead, after much public debate, Congress adopted a "Don't ask, don't tell, don't pursue" policy with regard to homosexuality . Since then, the number of discharges for homosexuality has actually risen and women are disproportionately affected. The policy has been challenged in the courts and some cases are still being heard, which may take the issue to the Supreme Court. (For social scientific analyses of the issues involved, including comparisons with gender and racial integration, see Herek, Jobe, & Carney, 1996; Scott & Stanley, 1994.)

7. GENDER AND MILITARY FAMILY ISSUES IN THE UNITED STATES

Family issues often arise in public debates about women in the military because women are seen as the primary caretakers of children. Most research on military families focusses on male service members and their wives. This is not surprising, given the predominantly male composition of armed forces and the historical exclusion of women with children. Women with children were first allowed to remain in service in the 1970s. It is important for sociologists to examine all the ways that gender plays a role in family issues in the military: for military men, for military women, and for civilian spouses of both genders.

The "greedy" nature of military life creates demands on service members and their families. Civilian wives of military men have traditionally been expected to accommodate their lives to these demands. Changes in gender norms in the wider society have been affecting military families and military family policy. (For a full analysis of these changes, see M. W. Segal, 1986, 1989; Stanley, Segal, & Laughton, 1990.) Social definitions of gender affect marital expectations, interactions, and role negotiations. The rise in military wives' labor force participation has altered military families' adjustments to military lifestyle characteristics, such as frequent moving.

Military family patterns are now more diverse. The number of single parents and dual-service couples has grown in the past two decades and they have received both research and policy attention. There tends to be negative attention in policy debates, such as assumptions that they have more trouble than other personnel in meeting their military and family obligations, an assumption that tends not be supported by research (e.g., Segal & Harris, 1993). Civilian husbands of military women, although increasing in proportion of military spouses, have been neglected both in policy attention and in research. Bourg (1995) shows how their experiences reflect their token status.

8. GENDER AND THE MILITARY: THE FUTURE

There will be continued public debate and social change in the United States and other nations about gender in the military, including women's roles, policy with regard to homosexuality, and family issues. Public policy discourse still reflects pockets of resistance to change and a desire by some to go back to more limited military roles for women. This is evident, for example, in the recent attempt by some members of Congress to require the services to segregate the sexes in basic training. Although the attempt was not immediately successful, study groups were set up to examine the issue and report back.

Women's past military roles have not increased linearly, but rather have gone through cycles of expansion and contraction. Cultural ambivalence exists in the United States and other nations; the issues are likely to continue to be the focus of political conflict. As in the past, women's military roles will be affected both by social definitions of gender and military needs. With the end of the Cold War, the nations of North America and Western and Eastern Europe are making dramatic changes in their military missions and force structures—with implications for gender. Sociologists will find interesting processes at both the macro- and micro-levels to study, which could help to fill the gaps in our knowledge about gender—both in the military and more generally.

REFERENCES

Adams, J. (1984). Women at West Point: A three-year perspective. *Sex Roles, 11*, 525–541.

Anderson, K. (1981). *Wartime women: Sex roles, family relations, and the status of women during World War II.* Westport, CT: Greenwood.

Arkin, W., & Dobrofsky, L. R. (1978). Military socialization and masculinity. *Journal of Social Issues, 34*, 151–168.

Barkalow, C. (1990). *In the men's house.* New York: Poseidon Press.

Binkin, M., & Bach, S. J. (1977). *Women and the military.* Washington, D.C.: The Brookings Institution.

Blalock, H. (1967) *Toward a theory of minority-group relations.* New York: John Wiley & Sons.

Bloom, A. R. (1982). Israel: The longest war. In N. L. Goldman (Ed.), *Female soldiers—combatants or noncombatants? Historical and contemporary perspectives.* Westport, CT: Greenwood.

Boulègue, J. (1991). "Feminization" and the French military: An anthropological approach. *Armed Forces & Society, 17*, 343–362.

Bourg, M. C. (1995). *Male tokens in a masculine environment: Men with military mates.* Paper presented at the American Sociological Association meeting.

Campbell, D'A. (1984). *Women at war with America: Private lives in a patriotic era.* Cambridge, MA: Harvard University Press.

Campbell, D'A. (1992). Combatting the gender gulf. *Minerva, 3–4*: 13–41.

Campbell, D'A. (1993). Women in combat: The World War II experience in the United States, Great Britain, Germany, and the Soviet Union. *The Journal of Military History, 57*, 301–323.

Chapkis, W. (Ed.) (1981). *Loaded questions: Women in the military.* Amsterdam: Transnational Institute.

Cherpak, E. M. (1993). The participation of women in the wars for independence in northern South America: 1810–1824. *Minerva, 6*, 11–36.

Chinchilla, N. S. (1990). Revolutionary popular feminism in Nicaragua: Articulating class, gender, and national sovereignty. *Gender & Society, 4*, 370–397.

Cock, J. (1994). Women and the military: Implications for demilitarization in the 1990s in South Africa. *Gender & Society, 8*, 152–169.

Cooke, M. (1993). Wo-man, retelling the war myth. In M. Cooke & A. Woollacott (Eds.), *Gendering war talk.* Princeton, NJ: Princeton University Press.

Dandeker, C., & Segal, M. W.. (1996). Gender integration in armed forces: Recent policy developments in the United Kingdom. *Armed Forces & Society, 23*, 29–47.

DeFleur, L. B., & Warner, R. L. (1987). Air Force Academy graduates and nongraduates: Attitudes and self-concepts. *Armed Forces & Society, 13*, 517–533.

Department of the Army. (1997). Army demographics: Demographic profile as of 07 Feb. 97. Washington, D.C.: Headquarters, Department of the Army, Office of the Deputy Chief of Staff for Personnel, Human Resources Directorate.

Department of Defense. (1995). *Sexual harassment survey.* Arlington, VA: Defense Manpower Data Center.

De Pauw, L. G. (1981). Women in combat: The Revolutionary War experience. *Armed Forces & Society, 7*, 209–226.

Devilbiss, M. C. (1985). Gender integration and unit deployment: A study of GI Jo. *Armed Forces & Society, 11*, 523–552.

Dorn, E. (1994). Testimony for House Armed Services Committee Subcommittee on Military Forces and Personnel (by Under Secretary of Defense for Personnel and Readiness). Hearing on women in the military, October 6.

Dunivin, K. O. (1988). Gender and perceptions of the job environment in the U.S. Air Force, *Armed Forces & Society, 15*, 71–91.

Durning, K. P. (1978). Women at the Naval Academy: An attitude survey. *Armed Forces & Society, 4,* 569–588.

Earley, C. Adams. (1989). *One woman's Army: A black officer remembers the WAC.* College Station, TX: Texas A & M University Press.

Eitelberg, M. J. (1991). A preliminary assessment of population representation in Operations Desert Shield and Desert Storm. Paper presented at the Biennial Conference of the Inter-University Seminar on Armed Forces and Society, Baltimore, MD.

Elshtain, J. B., & Tobias, S. (Eds.). (1990). *Women, militarism, and war: Essays in history, politics, and social theory.* Savage, MD: Rowman & Littlefield.

Enloe, C. (1980). Women—The reserve army of Army labor. *The Review of Radical Political Economics, 12,* 42–52.

Enloe, C. (1983). *Does khaki become you? The militarization of women's lives.* London: South End Press.

Enloe, C. (1993). *The morning after: Sexual politics at the end of the Cold War.* Berkeley, CA: University of California Press.

Faris, J. H. (1976). The impact of basic combat training: The role of the drill sergeant. In N. L. Goldman & D. R. Segal (Eds.), *The social psychology of military service* (pp. 13-24). Beverly Hills, CA: Sage.

Firestone, J. M. & Harris, R. J. (1994). Sexual harrassment in the U.S. military: Individualized and environmental contexts." *Armed Forces & Society, 21,* 25–43.

Gal, R. (1986). *A portrait of the Israeli soldier.* Westport, CT: Greenwood Press.

Gluck, S. B. (1987). *Rosie the riveter revisited: Women, the war, and social change.* Boston: Twayne Publishers.

Goldman, N. L. (Ed.). (1982). *Female soldiers—combatants or noncombatants? Historical and contemporary perspectives.* Westport, CT: Greenwood.

Hantrais, L. (1990). *Managing professional and family life: A comparative study of British and French women.* Brookfield, Vermont: Dartmouth Publishing.

Hawley, J. S. (Ed.). (1994). *Fundamentalism and gender.* New York: Oxford University Press.

Herek, G. M., Jobe, J. B., & Carney, R. M. (Eds.) (1996). *Out in force: Sexual orientation and the military.* Chicago: University of Chicago Press.

Hine, D. C. (1989). *Black women in white: Racial conflict and cooperation in the nursing profession, 1890–1950.* Bloomington, IN: Indiana University Press.

Holm, J. (1992). *Women in the military: An unfinished revolution* (revised edition). Novato, CA: Presidio Press.

Isaksson, E. (Ed.). (1988). *Women and the military system.* New York: St. Martin's Press.

Kanter, R. M. (1977). Some effects of proportions on group life: Skewed sex ratios and responses to token women. *American Journal of Sociology, 82,* 965–990.

Katzenstein, M., & Reppy, J. (1999). *Beyond zero tolerance: Discrimination in military culture.* Boulder, CO: Rowman & Littlefield.

Kessler-Harris, A. (1982). *Out to work: A history of wage-earning women in the U.S.* New York: Oxford University Press.

Li, X. (1993). Chinese women in the People's Liberation Army: Professionals or quasi-professionals?. *Armed Forces & Society, 20,* 69–83.

Li, X. (1995). Women in the Chinese military. Ph.D. dissertation, Department of Sociology, University of Maryland, College Park.

Lorber, J. (1993). Believing is seeing: Biology as ideology. *Gender & Society 7,* 568–581.

Martindale, M. (1990). *Sexual harassment in the military: 1988.* Arlington, VA: Defense Manpower Data Center.

Marwell, G. (1975). Why ascription? Parts of a more or less formal theory of the functions and dysfunctions of sex roles. *American Sociological Review, 40,* 445–455.

Maze, R. (1997). Battle of the sexes heats up on Capitol Hill. *Army Times,* 2 June, 4.

Miller, L. L. (1995). *Who speaks for women? Feminism and the exclusion of military women from combat.* Paper presented at the American Sociological Association meeting.

Miller, L. L. (1997). Not just weapons of the weak: Gender harassment as a form of protest for Army men. *Social Psychology Quarterly, 60,* 32–51.

Montgomery, T. S. (1995). *Revolution in El Salvador: From civil strife to civil peace,* 2nd ed. Boulder, CO: Westview Press.

Moore, B. L. (1991). "African American women in the U.S. military." *Armed Forces & Society, 17,* 363–384.

Moore, B. L. (1996). *To serve my country, to serve my race: The story of the only African American WACs stationed overseas during World War II.* New York: New York University Press.

Moore, Brenda L. (1997). *Construction of race and gender in America: The case of the Women's Army Corps.* Paper presented at a conference on Military Policy, Military Culture: Issues of Race, Gender, and Sexuality, April 4–6, 1997, College Park, MD.

Morris, M. (1996). By force of arms: Rape, war, and military culture. *Duke Law Journal, 45,* 651–781.

Moskos, C. (1990). Army women. *The Atlantic Monthly* (August), 71–78.

Park, Ry. (1986). *Overview of the social/behavioural science evaluation of the 1979–1985 Canadian Forces trial employment of servicewomen in nontraditional environments and roles.* Research Report 86–2. Willowdale, Ontario: Canadian Forces Applied Research Unit.

Priest, R. F., Vitters, A. G., & Prince, H. T.. (1978). Coeducation at West Point. *Armed Forces & Society, 4,* 589–606.

Randall, M. (1981). *Sandino's daughters: Testimonies of Nicaraguan women in struggle.* Vancouver: New Star Books.

Randall, M. (1994). *Sandino's daughters revisited: Feminism in Nicaragua.* New Brunswick, NJ: Rutgers University Press.

Rogan, H. (1981). *Mixed company: Women in the modern Army.* New York: G.P. Putnam's Sons

Rosen, L. N. Durand, D. B., Bliese, P. D., Halverson, R. R., Rothberg, J. M., & Harrison, N. L. (1996). Cohesion and readiness in gender-integrated combat service support units: The impact of acceptance of women and gender ratio. *Armed Forces & Society, 22,* 537–553.

Rustad, M. L. (1982). *Women in khaki: The American enlisted woman.* New York: Praeger.

Safilios-Rothschild, C. (1978). Young women and men aboard the U.S. Coast Guard barque "Eagle": An observation and interview study. *Youth and Society, 10,* 191–204.

Schneider, D., & Schneider, C. (1991). *Into the breach: American women overseas in World War I.* New York: Viking.

Scott, W. J., & Stanley, S. C. (Eds.). (1994). *Gays and lesbians in the military: Issues, concerns, and contrasts.* New York: Aldine de Gruyter.

Segal, D. R. (1989). *Recruiting for Uncle Sam: Citizenship and military manpower policy.* Lawrence, KS: University Press of Kansas.

Segal, D. R., & Segal, M. W. (1989). Female combatants in Canada: An update. *Defense Analysis, 5,* 372–373.

Segal, D. R., Segal, M. W., & Booth, B. (1990). *Gender and sexual orientation diversity in modern military forces: Cross-national patterns.* In M. Katzenstein & J. Reepy (Eds.), *Beyond zero tolerance: Discrimination in military culture.* Boulder, CO: Rowman & Littlefield.

Segal, M. W. (1986). The military and the family as greedy institutions. *Armed Forces & Society, 13,* 9–38.

Segal, M. W. (1989). The nature of work and family linkages: A theoretical perspective. In G. L. Bowen & D. K. Orthner (Eds.), *The organization family: Work and family linkages in the U.S. military.* New York: Praeger.

Segal, M. W. (1995). Women's military roles cross-nationally: Past, present, and future. *Gender & Society, 9,* 757–775.

Segal, M. W., & Hansen, A. F. (1992). Value rationales in policy debates on women in the military: A content analysis of Congressional testimony, 1941-1985. *Social Science Quarterly, 73,* 296–309.

Segal, M. W., & Segal, D. R. (1983). Social change and the participation of women in the American military. In L. Kriesberg (Ed.), *Research in social movements, conflicts and change.* Greenwich, CT: JAI Press.

Segal, M. W., & Harris, J. J. (1993). *What we know about army families.* Alexandria, VA: U.S. Army Research Institute for the Behavioral and Social Sciences.

Segal, M. W., Li, X., & Segal, D. R.. (1992). The role of women in the Chinese People's Liberation Army. *Minerva, 10,* 48–55.

Seitz, B., Lobao, L., & Treadway, E. (1993). No going back: Women's participation in the Nicaraguan revolution and in postrevolutionary movements. In R. H. Howes & M. R. Stevenson (Eds.), *Women and the use of military force.* Boulder: Lynne Rienner Publishers.

Stanley, J., Segal, M. W., & Laughton, C. J. (1990). Grass roots family action and military policy responses. *Marriage and Family Review, 15,* 207–223.

Stanley, S. C., & Segal, M. W. (1988). Military women in NATO: An update. *Armed Forces & Society, 14,* 559–585.

Stanley, S. C., & Segal, M. W. (1992). Women in the armed forces. *International Military and Defense Encyclopedia.* Washington, D. C.: Pergamon-Brassey's.

Stiehm, J. H. (1981). *Bring me men and women: Mandated change at the U.S. Air Force Academy.* Berkeley, CA: University of California Press.

Stiehm, J. H. (1989). *Arms and the enlisted woman.* Philadelphia, PA: Temple University Press.

Stiehm, J. H. (Ed.). (1996). *It's our military, too!: Women and the U.S. military.* Philadelphia:, PA Temple University Press.

Thomas, P. J. (1986). From Yeomanettes to WAVES to women in the U.S. Navy. In D. R. Segal & H. W. Sinaiko (Eds.), *Life in the rank and file: Enlisted men and women in the armed forces of the United States, Australia, Canada, and the United Kingdom* (pp. 98–115). Washington, D. C.: Pergamon-Brassey's.

Törnquist, K. (1982). Sweden: The neutral nation. In N. L. Goldman (Ed.), *Female soldiers—combatants or noncombatants?: Historical and contemporary perspectives* . Westport, CT: Greenwood.

Treadwell, M. (1954). *The Women's Army Corps*. Washington, D. C.: Office of the Chief of Military History.

Tuten, J. M. (1982). Germany and the World Wars. In N. L. Goldman (Ed.), *Female soldiers—combatants or noncombatants?: Historical and contemporary perspectives*. Westport, CT: Greenwood.

United Nations. (1991). *The world's women: Trends and statistics, 1970–1990*. New York: United Nations Publications.

Williams, C. L. (1989). *Gender differences at work: Women and men in nontraditional occupations*. Berkeley, CA: Universirty of California Press.

Weber, M. (1968). G. Roth & C. Wittich (Eds.). *Economy and society.* New York: Bedminster Press.

West, C., & Zimmerman, D. H. (1987). Doing gender. *Gender & Society, 1*, 125–151.

WREI (Women's Research and Education Institute). (1996). *Women in the military: Statistical update, 1996.* Washington, D. C.: Women's Research and Education Institute.

WREI (Women's Research and Education Institute). (1998). *Women in the military: Where they stand*, 2nd ed. Washington, D. C.: Women and men in nontraditional occupations. Berkeley, CA: University of California Press.

CHAPTER 26

Gender and Sport

MIKAELA J. DUFUR

1. INTRODUCTION

Sport is a useful arena in which to study gender and society. Since ancient times, men have used sport to separate themselves from women by restricting women from participating in games and contests and by using those events to emphasize physical size and strength. In examining the ways men have used sport to exclude women, some scholars conceptualize sport as a mirror of society; sport structures reflect other institutions that benefit men, such as work and political structures (Sabo & Runfola, 1980). Sport can also act as an archetype for masculinity. When sporting events turn into spectacle, as is true for most major competitions today, they transform masculine symbols and behaviors into public ritual.

Despite this masculine orientation toward sport, women and girls have also played recreational and competitive sport for centuries: Women have wrestled in Gambia, Nigeria, and the Congo, boxed in the South Pacific, played ball games in North America, and women ran and threw the javelin in ancient Greece. During the Renaissance, women hunted, golfed, raced, and played in ball games at festivals. Even Victorian women, discouraged from participating in unladylike competition, engaged in light exercise designed to make them more fit for motherhood (Cahn, 1995; Guttman, 1991). During World War II, talented female athletes in the United States played in professional baseball leagues (Weiller & Higgs, 1994). Nevertheless, while it is true that women played sports, they did so under the constraints of gendered domestic roles, ideas of femininity, and the primacy of men's sports. The World War II baseball players, for example, enjoyed enthusiastic

MIKAELA J. DUFUR • Department of Sociology, Ohio State University, Columbus, Ohio 43210

Handbook of the Sociology of Gender, edited by Janet Saltzman Chafetz. Kluwer Academic/ Plenum Publishers, New York, 1999.

support for their athletic endeavors—until the men returned from war, took up their bats again, and expected the women to return to prewar duties and roles.

Although the study of sport and gender encompasses a broad set of topics, the work of most scholars in the field falls into two branches: (1) sport as a means for constructing masculinity and femininity and (2) discrimination against and limited opportunities for women. These subfields tend to echo differences among the major branches of feminism, radical feminism and liberal feminism (Messner & Sabo, 1990, p. 4). This chapter considers the contributions, strengths, and weaknesses of these two approaches. I first explore the ways participants use sport to help define masculinity and femininity. Scholars interested in these issues look at how sport employs and supports a damaging form of aggressive, competitive masculinity, how lower-status men use sport to create new ways of being masculine, and how female athletes struggle with notions of femininity as they compete in a traditionally masculine world. The second branch examines women's access to sports, exploring the growth in women's opportunities to participate, the continued discrimination female athletes face, and legal challenges to sex-based exclusions. Finally, at the end of each section I assess the most prominent issues confronting researchers in each tradition.

2. MASCULINITY AND FEMININITY IN SPORT

Sport scholarship was, from its outset in the late 1950s until the early 1980s, focused on men (Messner & Sabo, 1990, p. v). Even as researchers expanded sport scholarship to examine class and race (see Edwards, 1973 or Hoch, 1972), they largely ignored women. However, as the number of sportswomen increased, interest in a feminist scholarship of sport arose. In addition to empirical research on female athletes, feminist theorists also introduced new ways of understanding men, women, and gender in sport.

According to feminist scholars, sport is an arena in which men reproduce the domination over women that exists in other areas of society. Men construct sport so as to exclude women, suggesting that men enjoy essential physical superiority over women. By valuing sports in which size, strength, and speed are prized, men use the most extreme attributes of their sex to claim inherent biological superiority over women (Brown, 1986; Bryson, 1983; Theberge, 1986; Theberge & Mineau, 1995).

In addition, men use sport to legitimate the segregation of men and women. The gendered division of space in sport—with men competing on the playing field and women allowed to cheer on the sidelines—resembles the gendered division of space in domestic and employment situations and in other spheres. In fact, the roles women play in other arenas limit their sport participation (Thomson, 1990). For example, Australian lawn bowling, a sport played by older men and women, provides an arena in which a woman's place as the second component of a heterosexual couple is highlighted. Playing their roles as wives, these women confirm their husbands' heterosexuality for viewers both on the field of play and on the sidelines. Further, they provide the domestic labor that frees their husbands to bowl; women, although competitive, can bowl only after other needs have been addressed (Boyle & McKay, 1995).

Although American men have long voiced support for women's sport participation, national surveys suggest that they are less supportive when participation changes the balance of domestic roles and responsibilities, requiring men to share more household work (Richardson & Hibbard, 1986). Women and men are separated into different sports, and when in the same sports into different locker rooms and segregated competitions. Even in sports such as riflery or archery, in which physical differences between men and women have little or no impact, athletes are often separated by their sex.

2.1. Effects of Masculinity in Sport

Some scholars who study gender define masculinity as a set of characteristics and behaviors that define who men are and how they should act (Connell, 1990). These scholars note that many of these characteristics are chosen not to create definitions of masculinity for men, but to help men avoid activities sex-typed as feminine (Craib, 1987; Crosset, 1990). Along with aggression, competitiveness, and a lack of visible emotion, a desire for and the power to obtain financial and occupational success are among the characteristics that combine to represent a desired and rewarded form of hegemonic masculinity for adult men. Although sport typically does not address financial and occupational behaviors and symbols, aggression, competitiveness, and impassivity are symbols of hegemonic masculinity that are highly prized in sport (Sabo & Runfola 1980; Laitinen & Tiihonen, 1990). Male athletes and spectators alike use sport to access this type of hegemonic masculinity.

Scholars viewing masculinity in this way suggest that masculinity, as practiced in sport, can be damaging to a wide variety of people. Most observers would expect that sport's brand of hegemonic masculinity can hurt both women and lower-status men, but fewer of those observers consider the ways sport masculinity can damage those who most successfully practice and internalize masculinity. Male athletes damage their own bodies, impair their relationships with others, and commit deviant acts in their pursuit of masculinity. In addition, although it is possible that homosexual men, men of color, and lower-class or -status men use sport to separate themselves from women, these men do not always have the same access to the characteristics, behaviors, and rewards of hegemonic masculinity. Men in these low-status situations may use sport to define an alternative form of masculinity or may shape their sports experiences to conform to their own definitions of masculinity. Below, I review literature that claims that sporting masculinity harms all men; I then examine how lower-status men use sports to create alternative types of masculinity.

By rewarding size, strength, and speed and by requiring men and boys to prove their masculinity by denying pain and competing through injury, sport places masculinity squarely in the realm of the body (Whitson, 1990). Male athletes' bodies become "tools, weapons, and objects of the gaze" (Trujillo, 1995, p. 405). This unusual position for men—objects of the gaze—takes on further significance when we realize that most of the viewers doing the gazing are other men and that both the athletes and the gazers are participating in what they view as very masculine activities. Further, demonstrating masculinity in sport requires athletes to use their bodies in a constant reification of status through victory. This cycle demands aggression of the participants—even the most successful athletes are expected to defend their championships or take on new challengers.

Although accomplished male athletes may successfully defeat challengers to their status, they often experience serious injury; these injuries become symbols of masculinity as well. Sport requires violence to the athlete's own body and often toward other athletes, but rewards only the healthy, a kind of sporting survival of the fittest (McTear, 1994; Young, 1993). Even sports that do not require contact with other athletes, such as running events, take a toll on athletes' bodies. Male teammates and coaches deride a reluctance or inability to play though pain as a marker of weakness (Harvey, 1996). Unfortunately, these injuries often persist after the athletic career has ended (Curry, 1993; Messner, 1994; Young, 1993).

Violence and injury are not the only negative results of sport masculinity; adherence to the masculine ideal also damages relationships with others. Although many athletes describe close relationships with teammates, they do not characterize these relationships as intimate (Messner, 1994). Because masculinity, at least in part, is defined as that which is *not* feminine, male athletes' relationships with women can also be problematic. Men who play sports hold more traditional attitudes toward women than do nonathletes, regardless of the type of sport the men play (Houseworth, Peplow, & Thirer, 1989), and athletes from a variety of competitive levels describe a lack of intimacy with girlfriends and wives (Messner, 1994). Curry's (1991) study of locker room talk demonstrates that stories of sexual conquests, with women framed as sexual objects, are typical locker room discourse. Although this type of disregard for women is not limited to male athletes, the comparatively large number of athletes who are accused of sexual harassment and assault suggests that the hypermasculine ideals of sport encourage sexually aggressive behavior. The few studies available on this subject (e.g., Crossett, Benedict, & MacDonald, 1995), however, are hampered by sample selection bias, poor response rates, and noncomparable populations and hence do not resolve this issue. Critics of these analyses (often coaches, athletic directors, or attorneys for the accused) claim that athletes are not, in fact, responsible for a disproportionate number of sexual crimes, but that athletes' greater notoriety makes their crimes more public (Snyder, 1994). If it is true that male athletes commit a disproportionate number of deviant acts, this may be attributable to risk-taking norms common among male homosocial groups or to the need to impress those higher in the sport hierarchy (Snyder, 1994), but the small and nonrandom samples used to study this connection render any conclusions tenuous.

2.2. Ways of Creating Masculinity in Sport

Although the masculinity described in the previous section is widely embraced in sport, not all men construct masculinity in exactly the same way or have the same opportunities to enjoy high status. In proposing multiple ways of defining masculinity and femininity, Connell (1987) and others have suggested that men of color, lower-class or -status men, and gay men are excluded in many ways from practicing the dominant forms of masculinity; the mechanisms by which these men might achieve high occupational status or acquire wealth are denied them. This exclusion exists in sport as well as in other social institutions, with the result that these men create alternative ways to gain access to the privilege and power associated with masculinity.

Although a large number of successful athletes in a few popular American sports—such as football, basketball, and baseball—are African-American, the vast majority of African-American athletes never reach the professional ranks where they might acquire the financial and occupational trappings of masculinity, and very few successful athletes in high-profile sports such as golf or tennis are from minority backgrounds (Leonard & Reyman, 1988). Further, even the most successful professional African-American athletes face discrimination when attempting to create sports careers after their playing days. Men of color, blocked from the occupational and economic mechanisms of masculinity, have developed as a response "expressive and conspicuous styles of demeanor, speech, gesture, clothing, hairstyle, walk, stance, and handshake" that Richard Majors (1990, p. 111) has termed "cool pose." These athletes import cool poses into amateur and professional sport as touchdown dances, spiked footballs, and improvisational basketball (George, 1992), allowing the athlete of color to "assert his visibility" (Majors, 1990, p. 111). Klein's (1995) excellent ethnography of Latin American baseball players demonstrates that these players, while exhibiting behavior typical of hypermasculine traditions, also display an alternative masculinity that includes physical affection among players and tender public affection for children. An intriguing idea, cool pose behaviors and the motivations behind them remain understudied.

Since complex processes of socialization teach boys and men that homosexuality is a "negation of masculinity," (Connell, 1992, p. 736) gay athletes comprise another group who can find themselves blocked from symbols of hegemonic masculinity, although in this case the symbols are less likely to be occupational or financial. Male athletes use derogatory terms associated with homosexuality in attempts to label opponents—or teammates who do not meet the macho ideal—as less masculine and less powerful than themselves (Dundes & Stein, 1985). As Klein's (1993) in-depth study of bodybuilding demonstrates, the push to distance oneself from homosexuality is so powerful among the sport's practitioners that, although it is common for aspiring professional bodybuilders to act as prostitutes for gay men for supplementary income, these athletes cling to their perception of themselves as straight and claim that they exploit their clients. Gay male athletes may develop an "ironic sensibility" (Pronger, 1990, p. 144) that allows them to move through the homophobic world of masculine sport, working to blend in and appear heterosexual (Pronger, 1990, p. 148) while maintaining an understanding of their own sexualities.

More research is needed to address the ways age and class interact to affect men's perceptions of sport and masculinity. For example, boys are expected to play sports—indeed, sport is a crucial element in boys' peer- and status-systems (Messner, 1990; Thirer & Wright, 1985)—but does the degree and type of sport participation change as boys become men or as men gain financial and occupational success? Do older, upper-class men use golf, yachting, and tennis as masculine symbols in the same ways Majors (1990) might argue that younger men of color might use football or basketball? Some scholars argue that spectatorship becomes the interface through which men access the symbols of sport masculinity (Nelson, 1994), especially if they are not (because of age or lack of ability) proficient athletes themselves. Such spectatorship becomes a masculine behavior in itself, where men identify with teams and players (Nelson, 1994), "bask in the reflected glory" of "their" team's success and identify with "their" player's manly acts, and use the language of sport to define their own masculinity even though they are not doing the masculine acts themselves (Wann & Branscombe, 1990). If sport spectatorship is a way of creating masculinity for a large number of men and boys, a ritual of male culture, more research needs to be done to shed light on what sport spectatorship means to men and what their reactions are to the growing proportion of women who are sports spectators.

2.3. Creating and Defining Femininity in Sport

Since sport symbols are linked so intimately with masculinity, women's display of those symbols does not mesh well with the dominant femininity that defines women as physically attractive, petite, demure, weak, and supportive rather than aggressive. Scholars of sex role theory, such as Myers and Lips (1978) and Matteo (1988), seeking to explain how female athletes fit in a masculine structure such as sport, found that female athletes tend more toward androgyny than other women, especially when the athletes are involved in traditionally masculine team sports such as basketball and volleyball. This approach, however, owes too much of its foundation to theories that limit gender to a few concrete categories, such as masculine, feminine, and androgynous. Further, the findings reflect only the attitudes and behaviors of samples of college students. Other scholars have conceptualized gender as a fluid continuum (Connell, 1987). Further, they have focused on the process of "doing gender" by creating and incorporating the behaviors and symbols associated with particular genders (West & Zimmerman, 1987). This reconceptualization moves the study of female athletes away from sex role categories and toward a more nuanced understanding of the ways these athletes define and practice their own femininity.

Rather than creating an ironic awareness of themselves, as Pronger (1990) argues gay male athletes do, some female athletes counteract the mixed messages they receive about masculinity, femininity, and sport by engaging in impression management and marking themselves with obvious symbols of femininity. Such athletes become, according to Felshin (1974), apologists who behave in especially feminine ways, both on and off the field, to assure onlookers—and themselves—of their status as women. For example, many of the growing number of female boxers in the United States wear pink trunks and trunks with skirts sewn on the back (Halbert, 1997), while some U.S. collegiate athletes wear jewelry, hair ribbons, and makeup during play (Blinde & Taub, 1992). Interviews with both athletes and coaches suggest that coaches propagate this emphasis on heterosexual standards of feminine beauty and encourage female athletes to "dress up," but avoid addressing the subject of sexuality with their athletes (Blinde & Taub, 1992). Publicity campaigns associated with the inauguration of new professional women's basketball leagues in the United States demonstrate that this emphasis on feminine appearance persists.

Perhaps these strategies of "overfeminization" are a reaction to widespread assumptions that all female athletes are lesbians (Lenskyj, 1994). Cahn (1994) argues that such an image grows from the tension between athletic prowess and femininity. Certainly, many lesbians play sports, but, obviously, not all lesbians play sports and not all athletes are lesbians. Still, the negative image of the lesbian athlete persists; in the inaugural issue of *Sports Illustrated*'s spinoff magazine for women, *Women\Sport*, Olympic softball gold medalist Dot Richardson describes the dismay she initially felt when others assumed because of her sports participation that she was a lesbian, telling neighbors, "If you ever have a daughter, don't you ever let her compete in sports, because it's not worth it" (Richardson, 1997, p. 42). According to Blinde and Taub (1992), many female intercollegiate athletes internalize stereotypes concerning lesbians and athletes, leading to the kinds of "apologist" behaviors described previously. Such attitudes are damaging to both lesbian athletes, who are targeted as deviant, and to straight athletes, who find their athletic experiences affected by rumor and innuendo.

Since the form of femininity rewarding physically beauty, small bodies, and passivity that is so dominant in the United States, Canada, and many European countries does not mesh well with masculine sport stereotypes, it is not surprising that sports that sometimes highlight those feminine traits, such as figure skating and gymnastics, are extremely popular among both spectators and young athletes. Television ratings for both sports rival those of traditionally masculine sports such as football (*Simmon's Market Research Bureau of Media and Markets*, 1996). Rules for both of these sports differ for the sexes and emphasize different skills (Feder, 1995); for example, female gymnasts compete on different apparatuses than their male counterparts, and male gymnasts may not use music for their floor exercises. In addition, both sports require different uniforms for men and women; neither female gymnasts nor skaters may wear pants when competing. Unlike football or running, in which objective standards such as crossing a line or finishing before an opponent decide contests, judges determine the winners in both gymnastics and figure skating. Use of judges introduces the subjective component of the scoring, and judges who are displeased with an athlete's choreography, costume, or music may lower that athlete's score. If a female gymnast or skater does not conform to the standards of dominant femininity, such as wearing sequined costumes or heavy makeup, the judges may give her low scores.

Gymnastics and figure skating are also sports that, because of the aerodynamics and the physics involved, reward petite, slender women (or, perhaps more accurately, girls; female Olympic and World Champions in these sports are very often in their teens, while their male counterparts are almost always in their mid-20s). The popularity of these sports reflects the popularity of a particular feminine body type that is prized in the United States and many other parts of the world. As women strive to acquire this body type, a type incompatible with most women's normal maturation, the focus of women's sport often becomes shaping a feminine body, where fitness equals heterosexual attractiveness (Duncan, 1994; Markula, 1995). Women in the United States, Germany, Finland, and Switzerland participate in recreational sport in numbers approaching those of men, but fewer women than men participate in sports that reward bulk, such as weightlifting. Women who participate tend to choose sports that shape traditionally feminine bodies and encourage weight loss, such as aerobic dance, ballet, and body sculpting (Firebaugh, 1989; Gisler, 1995; Lamprecht & Stamm, 1996; Marin, 1988). This emphasis on appearance and the size requirements imposed by sports popular among women and girls may encourage eating disorders among young female athletes (Taub & Blinde, 1992), although scholarly research into this question has so far been limited. Future research in this area should be especially concerned with the intersection of race and class with sports and body images; athletes in the sports that prize this especially "feminine" body type tend to be white and middle- to upper-class. Does this pattern indicate a tighter link between lookism and body image among middle- and upper-class girls? Certainly women and girls of color in team sports wear feminizing accessories such as hair decorations, jewelry, and makeup. Is their exclusion from sports emphasizing feminine body types merely an artifact of the relative class positions of most women of color and the relative expense of such sports? Do girls of color who participate in these sports experience the same body image issues their white counterparts face, and would such patterns increase among girls of color if they entered these sports in large numbers?

To summarize this section, the branch of sports studies that examines the ways masculinity and femininity are played out in sport addresses the fluidity of gender and gender symbolism, extends understandings of the processes involved in creating masculinity and femininity, and increases knowledge about athletes who do not meet traditional norms. It is less proficient, however, in testing theory. The best examples of work in this tradition, such as Klein's studies of bodybuilders (1993) and Latin American baseball players (1995), Connell's interviews with gay surfers and ironmen (1990), and Curry's examination of locker room talk (1993) directly address this issue by outlining new theories of gender creation and relations and then providing detailed and nuanced data to support their theories.

In addition, although there is substantial discussion of how the norms of masculinity and femininity affect male and female athletes, there is little insight into how those norms are generated. Are they imported into sport from other institutions, making sport a mirror of broader society? Or is sport a masculine archetype, creating symbols of a hypermasculinity that go beyond the norms found in other institutions? Finally, the ways women use sport to define their own gender must be further studied. If some female athletes are apologists (Felshin, 1974) who soften their athleticism by conspicuous use feminine symbols such as makeup and jewelry, what are we to make of women who do not use these symbols? This branch of sports studies can illuminate the border between societal expectations of gender norms and individual internalization and use of those norms if more and better data are tied to innovative ideas.

3. OPPORTUNITIES, BENEFITS, AND COSTS FOR WOMEN AND GIRLS IN SPORT

Women have been involved in physical activity throughout history, even in the face of restricted opportunities and constricting notions of femininity; in the past 50 years, however, sport participation by women and girls has increased sharply. More women than ever before are playing sports in Western European countries (Guttman, 1991; Gratton & Tice, 1994), current and former Communist countries (notably Cuba; see Bunck, 1990; Riordan, 1991), Japan (Kanezaki, 1991), and Nigeria (Anyanwu, 1980).

Participation in the United States has increased as well, as Table 26-1 demonstrates. The passage of Title IX of the 1972 Educational Amendment, legislation designed to ensure equal access to education-related resources and opportunities, spurred many of the new opportunities in the United States. Since the passage of Title IX, the number of women playing intercollegiate sports has increased fourfold (Staurowsky, 1996), and the average number of women's sports offered by U.S. colleges increased by 6% between 1992 and 1996 alone (Haworth, 1997). I provide a more extensive discussion of the impact of and challenges to Title IX later.

The growth in women's sport participation does not stem solely from greater female participation in traditionally female sports; instead, women are entering, in increasing

TABLE 26-1. Changes in Athletic Participation

	Men	Women
High school athletes, 1972	3,666,917	300,000
High school athletes, 1997	3,634,052	2,370,000
Intercollegiate athletes, 1972	NA	25,000
Intercollegiate athletes, 1997	222,077	129,376
Number of intercollegiate sports added, 1972–1996	927	2,239
Number of intercollegiate sports eliminated, 1972–1996	853[a, b]	581

Sources: Grant, 1995; Haworth, 1997; 1997 High School Athletic Participation Survey; Intercollegiate Athletics: Status of Efforts to Promote Gender Equity, 1997; Naughton, 1997a and b; Sabo, 1997.
[a]Divisions I-A and I-AA have a net loss of men's teams during the period examined.
[b]Schools disproportionately cut men's "nonrevenue" sports, such as wrestling and gymnastics; more than half of Division I-A men's gymnastics programs have been cut. Grant (1995), however, claims that most cuts in these "nonrevenue" sports came in the early 1980s, when Title IX enforcement was a low priority for schools.

numbers and with increasing publicity, sports that men dominated previously, such as sailing and surfing (Wenner, 1995), boxing (Halbert, 1997), and bodybuilding (Klein, 1993). The marathon, which the Olympic Competition Committee long considered too grueling for female athletes, became a medal sport for women at the 1984 Summer Olympics (Guttman, 1991). Few studies, however, examine the processes by which women enter these sports. Women also enjoy increasing opportunities to make careers as professional athletes; although women have played professional basketball in Europe and Asia for several years, two highly publicized leagues began play in the United States in 1996. In addition, prize moneys for women in some major tennis tournaments are now equal to the men's prizes (Kahn, 1991), and professional tours and competitions are growing rapidly in figure skating and gymnastics, providing career opportunities in sports in which female athletes are very visible and popular.

Numerous studies have documented significant benefits to female participation in sport. In sharp contrast to nineteenth-century beliefs that strenuous exercise would damage a woman's reproductive capacity (Cahn, 1995; Guttman, 1991), modern studies show that heightened physical activity among women leads to greater fitness and health. According to studies medical researchers and physical educators have conducted on large and diverse samples, women who engage in physical activities have higher self-esteem and less depression and anxiety (Hall, Durborow & Progen, 1986; Nelson, 1994, p. 33), osteoporosis is less likely among older women who exercise regularly, and pregnant athletes experience fewer complications than nonathletes (Feyder, 1989). Using nationally representative data, Sabo, Melnick, and Vanfossen (1993) demonstrate that girls who participate in high school sports in the United States have better grades in high school, participate in more extracurricular activities, believe they are more popular than their nonathletic peers, are more likely to go to college, and are less likely to use drugs or get pregnant than are girls who do not play sports. Although some scholars have expressed concern that there are also costs to increased female participation in sports structures administered by men (Grant, 1984; Nelson, 1994), little empirical work has addressed this question; an exploration of whether women suffer in current sports structures would require better data and more detailed studies.

3.1. Continued Sex Discrimination

Although it is true that female participation in sport is growing, sex discrimination in sport continues. Women still make up fewer than half of all professional and interscholastic athletes, receive fewer rewards for their athletic successes, and find access to particular kinds of sports participation, employment, and administrative positions blocked. Table 26-2 outlines some of these outcomes.

Women comprise fewer than half of intercollegiate varsity athletes and receive less than half of the scholarship money schools provide for athletes. The contrast becomes even sharper when looking at particular kinds of expenditures; women receive just over a quarter of recruiting dollars and fewer than one fifth of the dollars spent on personnel. Only 2% of head coaches of men's teams are women, while 45% of head coaches of women's teams are men. Women are similarly underrepresented among administrators, even if we examine only administrators of women's programs.

Continued discrimination against women finds its roots in youth sport, where children are taught competitiveness and gendered behavior early. In her excellent study of

TABLE 26-2. Distribution of Intercollegiate Athletic Participation, Resources,
and Employment by Sex

	Men	Women
Percentage of college students who play intercollegiate sports	7.3	3.9
Percentage of all intercollegiate athletes[a]	61	37
Percentage intercollegiate scholarship money, 1974	99	1
Percentage intercollegiate scholarship money, 1996	62	38
Total expenditures on intercollegiate sports	$354,893,514 (63%)	$142,622,805 (37%)
Recruitment expenditures on intercollegiate sports	$44,581,740 (73%)	$16,322,470 (27%)
Personnel expenditures for intercollegiate sports	$1,900,000	$431,282[b]
Percentage of all head intercollegiate coaches	78	22
Percentage head coaches of men's intercollegiate teams	98	2
Percentage head coaches of women's intercollegiate teams	45	55
Percentage holding administrative jobs in women's athletic programs	64	36
Percentage head administrator over women's athletic programs	81	19

Sources: Grant, 1995; Haworth, 1997; *1997 High School Athletic Participation Survey*; *Intercollegiate Athletics: Status of Efforts to Promote Gender Equity*, 1997; Naughton, 1997a and b; Sabo, 1997.
[a]Two percent of all intercollegiate athletes play co-ed sports.
[b]Personnel expenditures for all women's sports amount to less than half of the personnel expenditures for football ($890,330).

children's gender socialization, Thorne (1993, p. 44) described a distinct geography of gender involved in children's play: boys dominate large spaces used for sports such as baseball, football, soccer, and basketball, relegating girls to smaller spaces closer to the school building. In addition, children ask for gender-typed play equipment that corresponds to these spatial divisions, and playground aides sometimes prevent children from playing in areas "inappropriate" for their gender. As Landers and Fine (1996) observed, coaches of co-ed kindergarten tee ball teams treat prospective female athletes differently from their male counterparts, judging the girls' performance more harshly and transmitting the message that boys have more right to play.

The sexism found in youth sport affects female athletes after they enter their chosen fields of play as well. Female athletes at many events, including the Olympics, must undergo gender verification tests to prove that they are women (Feder, 1995). In the past, these verifications consisted of visual inspection of genitalia; today, women must provide tissue (usually cheek scrapings) for chromosomal testing (Daniels, 1992; Nelson, 1994). Women's athletic teams are often given belittling or demeaning names; more than 50% of 4-year colleges in the United States use sexist names for women's teams, such as adding "Lady" to the mascot name (e.g., Lady Rams or Lady Gamecocks), adding an "ette" suffix to the mascot name (Yellow Jackettes or Thorobrettes), or using a diminutive version of the mascot for women's teams (Kittens or Belles). These naming techniques trivialize women's sport, but students, coaches, journalists, boosters, and a substantial number of faculty react angrily to any suggestion that less sexist mascot names be adopted (Eitzen & Zinn, 1993).

3.2. Title IX

As described previously, Title IX has been influential in increasing the number of opportunities for women and girls in interscholastic sports, but as few as 10% of schools are in full compliance (Naughton, 1997a, b; Sabo, 1997). The Department of Education's definition of and the Office of Civil Rights' clarification of the scope of the law instituted three measures of compliance: "Substantial proportionality," where the percentage of female athletes at a school is within five percentage points of the undergraduate population; "effective accommodation," for schools that can show that they have polled female students on their interest in sport and are providing enough opportunities to fully meet that interest, even if those opportunities fall short of proportionality; and a "history of expanding opportunities," for schools that have made efforts to expand women's opportunities and file plans showing how they intend to progress toward proportionality. The courts view meeting any one of the three prongs as compliance with the law, yet many schools remain out of compliance, resulting in a surge of lawsuits brought by female athletes (Heckman, 1994).

Although courts have tended to rule in favor of female athletes in cases brought against schools (see, e.g., Cohen v. Brown 1997, also known as "Cohen III"), the burden of demanding compliance falls on athletes and coaches to initiate lawsuits. Representatives of men's sports associations, such as the College Football Association and the American Football Coaches Association, have testified at Congressional oversight hearings on the Office of Civil Rights' enforcement of Title IX, alleging that male collegiate athletes are being victimized by aggressive female athletes and lawyers (Staurowsky, 1996). The result is that some members of Congress are discouraging federal oversight of Title IX compliance by proposing legislation that no money designated for the Office of Civil Rights be used to investigate athletic cases (Blum, 1995; Haworth, 1996). While lawmakers debate this particular law, and interested parties debate the intent and interpretation of Title IX, scholarly examination of Title IX and its influence in encouraging female athleticism has gone largely ignored.

3.3. Women in Coaching and Administrative Positions

Women have even more difficulty finding sports opportunities off the field. Abbott and Smith's (1984) study of vacancy chains within the coaching labor market suggests that women have acquired many of the new jobs coaching women, despite the fact that their data predate the more vigorous enforcement of Title IX. Nonetheless, a 25-year study of the coaching labor market shows that women now fill only half of all positions available coaching women and only rarely coach men (Acosta & Carpenter, 1996). In addition, female coaches have lower status, lower salaries, fewer promotion opportunities, and higher exit rates than do their male counterparts (Knoppers, Meyer, Ewing, & Forrest, 1989, 1991). Female coaches' lower pay—coaches of women's U.S. collegiate teams make an average salary that is 44% lower than head coaches of men's teams—results in part from their exclusion from men's sports (Naughton, 1997b; Sabo, 1997). Female coaches in youth leagues more often fill administrative roles, such as record-keeping and transportation, while male coaches more often perform on-field duties (Landers & Fine, 1996), echoing the gendered space and role considerations Thorne (1993) found among children and that occupational scholars have repeatedly demonstrated in the work sphere (Reskin & Padavic, 1994).

Female coaches in the Unietd States, Britain, and Canada also have few opportunities to move into high-level sports administration. Men, who make up the vast majority of athletic directors and organization officials, tend to hire coaches and other staff members who are most like themselves; they also claim that women's family responsibilities dampen female coaches' ambition (Knoppers, 1988; Stangl & Kane, 1991; White & Brackenridge, 1985; Whitson & McIntosh, 1989). Although scholars who examine the trends in coaching opportunities for women have begun to discuss the possible interrelations of human capital factors, structural constraints, and matching processes (Knoppers, 1992), no analysis has yet incorporated all three of these perspectives.

Finally, an interesting opportunity to study women's entrance into another kind of sports authority structure comes as the number of female referees, umpires, judges, and officials grows. The National Basketball Association's October 1997 announcement that two women will be among the referees who officiate men's professional games raises questions about how players, coaches, fans, and sports organizations will respond to women having direct control over the outcomes of both men's and women's events. These questions could also be addressed by examining gymnastics, tennis, and especially figure skating (in which female judges rate men, women, and pairs).

3.4. Female Athletes in the Media

Female athletes also experience discrimination in the sport media. In the United States, Canadian, West German, and Norwegian print media, female athletes are most notable for their invisibility; these women appear in fewer and shorter written articles, fewer photographs, and are described in stereotypically feminine ways (Alexander, 1994; Crossman, Hyslop, & Guthrie, 1994; Fasting & Tangen, 1983; Klein, 1988; Lumpkin & Williams, 1991). In addition, the portrayals of women that appear on television are presented in a highly sex-typed manner. Content analyses demonstrate that television commentators devalue female athletes; commentators more often refer to female than male athletes by their first names, minimize women's accomplishments, discuss female athletes' looks, and describe character flaws that follow gender stereotypes. For example, commentators (who are, for the most part, male) distinguish between basketball and women's basketball, constructing the women's sport as marginal to the men's (Blinde, Greendorfer, & Shanker, 1991); announcers working the Martina Navratilova–Jimmy Connors tennis match referred to Navratilova by her first name but to Connors by his last and praised Connors more frequently (Halbert & Latimer, 1994; see also Messner, Duncan, & Jensen, 1993).

One of the factors driving the gendered representation of women athletes in the media may be the difficulties facing female sportswriters and commentators. Women, while making some gains, still make up a very small proportion of the reporters covering sports. Although the number of female members of the media covering women's events is growing, the majority of these assignments still go to men. Continued growth in the number of female commentators may decrease the sexist coverage of events described previously. Very few women, however, cover men's events. In addition, it is difficult for the female sportswriters who do cover men's sports to gain access to their workplace, possibly because their entrance is seen as an intrusion on the imposed separation between men and women or because "nice" women are expected to avoid masculine bodies and territories. Female reporters continue to be removed from locker rooms and fields while trying to conduct interviews, and most report that they have been the target of sexist gestures and remarks from male athletes (Disch & Kane, 1996; Nelson, 1994)

The strength of arguments concerning discrimination against female athletes—and the perception of sports studies other scholars hold—could be improved by a greater attention to tying findings about sport to broader social trends and theories. The branch of sports studies that looks at discrimination and opportunities would be strengthened by advancing theory or by framing empirical findings in an ongoing theoretical discussion. For example, although there are many descriptions of the kinds of sports into which women athletes and coaches are channeled, scholars have rarely used sex stratification theory, queuing theory, the interactions among political, legal, and economic structures, or weak- and strong-tie social networks to inform the research. Similarly, studies that describe the growth of female participation would benefit from drawing comparisons to the social movements literature.

4. INTERSECTIONS OF RACE, CLASS, GENDER, AND SPORT

Several scholars have called for more critical analyses of sport that consider how race and class work differently among male and female athletes (see, e.g., Birrell, 1989; Wenner, 1994), but few studies have taken this step. Most work that examines both gender and race, while insightful, has focused on whether forms of racism that exist in men's sports are present in women's sports (e.g., Eitzen & Furst, 1989). Scholars who study how men of color create alternative masculinities more fully approach the task of incorporating race and class into their analyses (Majors, 1990; Messner, 1994). Little work has been done on how female athletes of color interpret their sport identities or experiences. Similarly, although there is ample evidence that women of color experience discrimination in the workplace based on both their race and their gender, little research has assessed similar issues among female athletes, coaches, or administrators.

5. CONCLUSION

Sport is an exciting field in which to study gender. Sport as an institution provides an arena in which to examine the dynamics of gender and gender relations, which are highlighted as the sport institution changes. However, the study of sport and gender cannot fulfill its promise until sports scholars address theoretical and methodological shortcomings. One body of scholarship asserts that sport encourages and uses an aggressive, competitive masculinity that damages both the men who practice it and others who consume it as spectators. The dominant form of masculinity has a negative effect on athletes' health and personal relationships and may encourage deviant behavior. In addition, this perspective examines the ways lower-status men, who may have their access to the rewards of hegemonic masculinity blocked, use sport to create alternative types of masculinity, such as incorporating "cool pose" behaviors into sport through celebration dances and improvisational basketball. Finally, this perspective examines the ways female athletes create and internalize ideals of femininity as they compete in a traditionally masculine world, finding that many women use distinct outward symbols of femininity or seek arenas in which they may construct a new definition of sport.

The other body of scholarship, which examines the growth of women's opportunities in sport and continued discrimination toward women, is useful in describing trends, such as the growth of women's participation in sports, the continued exclusion of women from coaching and administrative positions, and the effects of legal strategies such as Title IX on women's access to athletics. Studies drawing on these ideas show that female athletes have made substantial progress in their rates of participation and that these athletes are competing in more sports than ever before. These studies also demonstrate, however, that women and girls still make up fewer than half of all interscholastic and intercollegiate athletes and that the athletes who play at these levels have access to fewer resources than their male counterparts.

The first perspective, while theoretically sophisticated, suffers from a lack of connections between reliable data and analysis and impressive theoretical underpinnings; work in the second tradition more often uses nationally representative and generalizable data, but neglects to place findings into theoretical context. Much work is still to be done in both perspectives. For example, just as scholars have examined how lower-status men create alternative forms of masculinity in sport, it would be fruitful to explore how female athletes create alternative forms of femininity through sport participation. Scholars studying the participation of and opportunities for women in sport might frame the growth in participation rates as a social movement or might integrate human capital, structural, and matching perspectives to examine the relative dearth of female athletes, coaches, and administrators. Integrating the two perspectives' strengths will improve the field's work, and the perception of that work, as scholars generate new studies examining old questions and new ideas about the ways race and class affect gender within sport.

Acknowledgments

I am grateful to Editor Janet Chafetz, Joan Huber, and Barbara Reskin for their comments and suggestions.

REFERENCES

Abbott, A., & Smith, R. D. (1984). Governmental constraints and labor market mobility: Turnover among college athletic personnel. *Work and Occupations, 11,* 29–53.

Acosta, R. V., & Carpenter, L. J. (1996). Women in intercollegiate sport: A longitudinal study—nineteen-year update. Unpublished paper, Department of Physical Education, Brooklyn College.

Alexander, S. (1994). Newspaper coverage of athletes as a function of gender. *Women's Studies International Forum, 17,* 655–662.

Anyanwu, S. U. (1980). Issues in and patterns of women's participation in sport in Nigeria. *International Review of Sport Sociology, 15,* 85–95.

Birrell, S. (1989). Racial relations theories and sport: Suggestions for a more critical analysis. *Sociology of Sport Journal, 6,* 212–227.

Blinde, E. M., & Taub, D. E. (1992). Homophobia and women's sport: The disempowerment of athletes. *Sociological Focus, 25,* 151–166.

Blinde, E. M., Greendorfer, S. L., & Shanker, R. J. (1991). Differential media coverage of men's and women's intercollegiate basketball: Reflection on gender ideology. *Journal of Sport and Social Issues, 15,* 98–114.

Blum, A. (1995). Financial disparity as evidence of discrimination under Title IX. *Villanova Sports and Entertainment Law Forum, 2,* 5–35.

Boyle, M., & McKay, J. (1995). "You leave your troubles at the gate": A case study of the exploitation of older women's labor and "leisure" in sport. *Gender & Society, 9,* 556–575.

Brown, B. A. (1986). Sport science and the myth of women's sport. *Resources for Feminist Research, 15,* 31–33.

Bryson, L. (1983). Sport and the oppression of women. *Australian and New Zealand Journal of Sociology, 19,* 413–426.

Bunck, J. M. (1990). The politics of sport in revolutionary culture. *Cuban Studies, 20,* 111–132.

Cahn, S. K. (1994). From the "muscle moll" to the "butch" ballplayer: Mannishness, lesbianism, and homophobia in US women's sport. *Feminist Studies, 19,* 343–368.

Cahn, S. K. (1995). *Coming on strong: Gender and sexuality in twentieth-century women's sport.* New York: The Free Press.

Connell, R. W. (1987). *Gender and power: Society, the person, and sexual politics.* Stanford, CA: Stanford University Press.

Connell, R. W. (1990). An iron man: The body and some contradictions of hegemonic masculinity. In M. A. Messner & D. F. Sabo (Eds.), *Sport, men and the gender order: Critical feminist perspectives* (pp. 83–96). Champaign, IL: Human Kinetics Books.

Connell, R. W. (1992). A very straight gay: Masculinity, homosexual experience, and the dynamics of gender. *American Sociological Review, 57,* 735–751.

Craib, I. (1987). Masculinity and male dominance. *Sociological Review, 35,* 721–743.

Crosset, T. (1990). Masculinity, sexuality, and the development of early modern sport. In M. A. Messner & D. F. Sabo (Eds.), *Sport, men and the gender order: Critical feminist perspectives* (pp. 45–54). Champaign, IL: Human Kinetics Books.

Crosset, T.W., Benedict, J. R., & McDonald, M. A. (1995). Male student athletes reported for sexual assault: A survey of campus police departments and judicial affairs offices. *Journal of Sport and Social Issues, 19,* 126–140.

Crossman, J., Hyslop, P., & Guthrie, B. (1994). A content analysis of the sports section of Canada's national newspaper with respect to gender and professional/amateur status. *International Review for the Sociology of Sport, 29,* 123–134.

Curry, T. J. (1991). Fraternal bonding in the locker room: A profeminist analysis. *Sociology of Sport Journal, 8,* 119–135.

Curry, T. J. (1993). A little pain never hurt anyone: Athletic career socialization and the normalization of sports injury. *Symbolic Interaction, 16,* 273–290.

Daniels, D. B. (1992). Gender (body) verification (building). *Play and Culture, 5,* 370–377.

Disch, L., & Kane, M. J. (1996). When a looker is really a bitch: Lisa Olson, sport, and the heterosexual matrix. *Signs, 21,* 278–308.

Duncan, M. C. (1994). The politics of women's body images and practices: Foucault, the panopticon, and Shape Magazine. *Journal of Sport and Social Issues, 18,* 48–65.

Dundes, A., & Stein, H. F. (1985). The American game of "Smear the Queer" and the homosexual component of male competitive sport and warfare. *Journal of Psychoanalytic Anthropology, 8,* 115–129.

Edwards, H. (1973). *The sociology of sport.* Homewood, IL: Dorsey.

Eitzen, D. S., & Furst, D. (1989). Racial bias in women's collegiate volleyball. *Journal of Sport and Social Issues, 13,* 46–51.

Eitzen, D. S., & Zinn, M. B. (1993). The sexist naming of college athletic teams and resistance to change. *Journal of Sport and Social Issues 17,* 34–41.

Fasting, K., & Tangen, J. (1983). Gender and sport in Norwegian mass media. *International Review for the Sociology of Sport, 18,* 61–70.

Feder, A. M. (1995). "A radiant smile from the lovely lady": Overdetermined femininity in "ladies'" figure skating. In C. Bauman (Ed.), *Women on ice: Feminist essays on the Tonya Harding/Nancy Kerrigan spectacle.* New York: Routledge.

Felshin, J. (1974). The social view. In E. Gerber (Ed.), *The American woman in sport.* Reading, MA: Wesley.

Firebaugh, G. (1989). Gender differences in exercise and sports. *Sociology and Social Research, 73,* 59–66.

Freyder, S. C. (1989). Exercising while pregnant. *Journal of Orthopaedic and Sports Physical Therapy, 10,* 358–365.

George, N. (1992). *Elevating the game: Black men and basketball.* New York: Harper Collins.

Gisler, P. (1995). Liebliche lieblichkeit: Women, body, and sport. *Schweizerische Zetischrift fur Soziologie, 21,* 651–667.

Grant, C. H. B. (1984). The gender gap in sport: From Olympic to intercollegiate level. *Arena Review, 8,* 31–47.

Grant, C. H. B. (1995). Title IX and gender equity. Presentation at the NACWAA Fall Forum, Cedar Rapids, IA, September 25, 1995.

Gratton, C., & Tice, A. (1994). Trends in sport participation in Britain: 1977–1987. *Leisure Studies, 13,* 49–66.

Guttman, A. (1991). *Women's sports.* New York: Columbia University Press.

Halbert, C. (1997). Tough enough and woman enough: Stereotypes, discussions, and impression management among women professional boxers. *Journal of Sport and Social Issues, 21,* 7–36.

Halbert, C., & Latimer, M. (1994). "Battling" gendered language: An analysis of the language used by sports commentators in a televised coed tennis competition. *Sociology of Sport Journal, 11,* 298–308.

Hall, E. G., Durburow, B., & Progen, J. L. (1986). Self-esteem of female athletes and nonathletes relative to sex role type and sport type. *Sex Roles, 15,* 379–390.

Harvey, S. J. (1996). The construction of masculinity among male collegiate volleyball players. *The Journal of Men's Studies, 5,* 131–151.

Haworth, K. (1996). Report notes progress in gender equity in collegiate sports. *Chronicle of Higher Education,* September 8, 1996, A40.

Haworth, K. (1997). Briefs filed to back Brown U.'s appeal of sports bias case to Supreme Court. *Chronicle of Higher Education,* March 24, 1997, A45.

Heckman, D. (1994). The explosion of title IX legal activity in intercollegiate athletics during 1992-1993: Defining the "equal opportunity" standard. *Detroit College of Law Review, 3,* 953–1023.

Hoch, P. (1972). *Rip off the big game.* New York: Anchor Press.

Houseworth, S., Peplow, K., & Thirer, J. (1989). Influence of sport participation upon sex role orientation of Caucasian males and their attitudes toward women. *Sex Roles, 20,* 317–325.

Intercollegiate Athletics: Status of Efforts to Promote Gender Equity. (1996). Washington, D. C.: General Accounting Office, United States Government, GAO/HEHS-97-10.

Kahn, L. M. (1991). Discrimination in professional sports: A review of the literature. *Industrial and Labor Relatins Review, 4,* 395–418.

Kanezaki, R. (1991). Sociological considerations on sport involvement of Japanese female adults. *International Review for the Sociology of Sport, 26,* 271–287.

Klein, A. M. (1993). *Little big men: Bodybuilding subculture and gender construction.* Albany, NY: SUNY Press.

Klein, A. M. (1995). Tender macho: Masculine contrasts in the Mexican Baseball League. *Sociology of Sport Journal, 12,* 370–388.

Klein, M. L. (1988). Women in the discourse of sports reports. *International Review for the Sociology of Sport, 23,* 139–152.

Knopers, A. (1988). Coaching as a male dominated and sex segregated occupation. *ARENA Review, 12,* 69–80.

Knoppers, A., Meyer, B. B., Ewing, M. E., & Forest, L. (1989). Gender and the salaries of coaches. *Sociology of Sport Journal, 6,* 348–361.

Knoppers, A., Meyer, B. B., Ewing, M. E., & Forest, L. (1991). Opportunity and work behavior in college coaching. *Journal of Sport and Social Issues, 15,* 1–20.

Laitinen, A., & Tiihonen, A. (1990). Narratives of men's experiences in sport. *International Review for the Sociology of Sport, 25,* 185–202.

Lamprecht, M., & Stamm, H. (1996). Age and gender patterns of sport involvement among the Swiss labor force. *Sociology of Sport Journal, 13,* 274–287.

Landers, M. A., & Fine, G. A. (1996). Learning life's lessons in tee ball: The reinforcement of gender and status in kindergarten sport. *Sociology of Sport Journal, 13,* 87–93.

Lenskyj, H. J. (1994). Sexuality and femininity in sport contexts: Issues and alternatives. *Journal of Sport and Social Issues, 18,* 356–376.

Leonard, W. M., & Reyman, J. E. (1988). The odds of attaining professional athlete status: Refining the computations. *Sociology of Sport Journal, 5,* 162–169.

Lumpkin, A., & Williams, L. D. (1991). An analysis of *Sports Illustrated* articles, 1954–1987. *Sociology of Sport Journal, 8,* 16–32.

Majors, R. (1990). Cool pose: Black masculinity and sport. In M. A. Messner and D. F. Sabo (Eds.), *Sport, men and the gender order: Critical feminist perspectives* (pp. 109–114). Champaign, IL: Human Kinetics Books.

Marin, M. (1988). Gender differences in sport and movement in Finland. *International Review for the Sociology of Sport, 23,* 345–359.

Markula, P. (1995). Firm but shapely, fit but sexy, strong but thin: The postmodern aerobicizing bodies. *Sociology of Sport Journal, 12,* 424–453.

Matteo, S. (1988). The effect of gender-schematic processing on decisions about sex-inappropriate sports behavior. *Sex Roles, 18,* 41–58.

McTear, W. (1994). Body talk: Male athletes' reflections on sport, injury, and pain. *Sociology of Sport Journal, 11,* 175–194.

Messner, M. A. (1990). Boyhood, organized sports, and the construction of masculinities. *Journal of Contemporary Ethnography, 18,* 416–444.

Messner, M. (1994). *Power at play: Sports and the problem of masculinity.* Boston: Beacon Press.

Messner, M. A., Duncan, M. C., & Jensen, K. (1993). Separating the men from the girls: The gendered language of televised sports. *Gender & Society, 7,* 121–137.

Messner, M. A., & Sabo, D. F. (1990). *Sport, men, and the gender order: Critical feminist perspectives.* Champaign, IL: Human Kinetics Books.

Myers, A. M., & Lips, H. M. (1978). Participation in competitive amateur sports as a function of psychological androgyny. *Sex Roles, 4,* 571–578.

Naughton, J. (1997a). Confidential report details salaries of athletics officials. *Chronicle of Higher Education,* March 28, 1997, A49.

Naughton, J. (1997a). More colleges cut men's teams to shift money to women's teams. *Chronicle of Higher Education,* February 21, 1997, A39.

Nelson, M. B. (1994). *The stronger women get, the more men love football: Sexism and the American culture of sports*. New York: Harcourt Brace.

1997 High School Athletic Participation Survey. Kansas City, MO: National Federation of State High School Associations.

Pronger, B. (1990). Gay jocks: A phenomenology of gay men in athletics. In M. A. Messner & D. F. Sabo (Eds.), *Sport, men and the gender order: Critical feminist perspectives* (pp. 141–152). Champaign, IL: Human Kinetics Books.

Reskin, B. F., & Padavic, I. (1994). *Women and men at work*. Thousand Oaks, CA: Pine Forge Press.

Richardson, D. (1997). Sex, lies, and softball. *Women\Sport, 1*, 40–45.

Richardson, P. A., & Hibbard, J. E. (1986). Male attitudes toward sport participation by females. *International Review of History and Political Science, 23*, 29–40.

Riordan, J. (1991). *Sport, politics, and communism*. Manchester, NY: Manchester University Press.

Sabo, D. F. (1997). *Gender equity report card*. East Meadow, NY: Women's Sports Foundation.

Sabo, D. F., & Panepinto, J. (1990). Football ritual and the construction of masculinity. In M. A. Messner & D. F. Sabo (Eds.), *Sport, men and the gender order: Critical feminist perspectives* (pp. 115–126). Champaign, IL: Human Kinetics Books.

Sabo, D. F., & Runfola, R. (1980). *Jock: Sports and the male identity*. Englewood Cliffs, NJ: Prentice-Hall Inc.

Sabo, D. F., Melnick, M., & Vanfossen, B. (1993). High school athletic participation and post-secondary educational and occupational mobility. *Sociology of Sport Journal, 10*, 44–56.

Simmons Market Research Bureau. (1996). *Simmons Market Research Bureau Study of Media and Markets, 1996*. New York: Simmons Market Research Bureau.

Snyder, E. F. (1994). Interpretations and explanations of deviance among college athletes: A case study. *Sociology of Sport Journal, 11*, 231–248.

Stangl, M. J., & Kane, M. J. (1991). Structured variables that offer explanatory power for the underrepresentation of women coaches since the Title X: The case of homologous reproduction. *Sociology of Sports Journal, 8*, 46–60.

Staurowsky. E. J. (1996). Blaming the victim: Resistance in the battle over gender equity in intercollegiate athletics. *Journal of Sport and Social Issues, 20*, 194–210.

Taub, D. E., & Blinde, E. M. (1992). Eating disorders among adolescent female athletes: Influence of athletic participation and sport team membership. *Adolescence, 27*, 833–848.

Theberge, N. (1981). A critique of critiques: Radical and feminist writings on sport. *Social Forces, 60*, 341–353.

Theberge, N., & Mineau, S. (1995). Sports, characteristics and sexual differentiation. *Sociologie et Societes, 27*, 105–116.

Thirer, J., & Wright, S. D. (1985). Sport and social status for adolescent males and females. *Sociology of Sport Journal, 2*, 164–171.

Thomson, S. M. (1990). "Thank the ladies for the plates": The incorporation of women into sport. *Leisure Studies, 9*, 135–143.

Thorne, B. (1993). *Gender play: Girls and boys in school*. New Brunswick, NJ: Rutgers University Press.

Trujillo, N. (1995). Machines, missiles, and men: Images of the male body on ABC's Monday Night Football. *Sociology of Sport Journal, 12*, 403–421.

Wann, D. L., & Branscombe, N. R. (1990). Die-hard and fair-weather fans: Effects of identity on BIRGing and CORFing tendencies. *Journal of Sport and Social Issues, 14*, 103–117.

Weiler, K. H., & Higgs, C. T. (1994). The All-American Girls Professional Baseball League, 1943–154: Gender conflict in sport. *Sociology of Sport Journal, 18*, 85–104.

Wenner, L. A. (1994). Behind the green door of intercollegiate athletics. *Journal of Sport and Social Issues, 18*, 107–109.

Wenner, L. A. (1995). Riding waves and sailing seas: Wipeouts, jibes, and gender. *Journal of Sport and Social Issues, 19*, 123-125.

West, C., & Zimmerman, D. H. (1987). Doing gender. *Gender & Society, 1*, 125–151.

White, A., & Brackenridge, C. (1985). Who rules sport? Gender divisions in the power structure of British sports organisations from 1960. *International Review for the Sociology of Sport, 20*, 95–107.

Whitson, D. (1990). Sport in the social construction of masculinity. In M. A. Messner & D. F. Sabo (Eds.), *Sport, men and the gender order: Critical' feminist perspectives* (pp. 19–30). Champaign, IL: Human Kinetics Books.

Whitson, D., & McIntosh, D. (1989). Gender and power: Explanations of gender inequalities in Canadian national sports organization. *International Review for the Sociology of Sport, 24*, 137–150.

Young, K. (1993). Violence, risk, and liability in male sports culture. *Sociology of Sport Journal, 10*, 373–396.

CHAPTER 27

Gender and Religion

ADAIR T. LUMMIS

1. OVERVIEW

The saga of gender and religion, as told in one faith tradition after another, traces a theme of founders' original texts placing equal value on women and men, texts that were later used selectively by male religious leaders to legitimate patriarchy (Holm, 1994). This is not the end of the story, however. External social forces and situational exigencies impinge on any faith community and its members, leading them to change gendered roles temporarily or more permanently (Lindley, 1996; Wessinger, 1996). For such reasons, faith communities across religions, and within one religion in varying regions and times, are likely to exhibit differences in the degree to which women are perceived and treated as the spiritual and mental equals of men. For many decades women's participation in the leadership and development of religions was nearly invisible (Wallace, 1997). However, during the present decade, women and religion has become a major research focus, with many new books and articles in this area appearing annually. Recent publications make it possible to begin answering the question: Under what conditions and circumstances will women gain and retain parity with men in world religions? This chapter summarizes recent answers to this question, based primarily but not exclusively on research focusing on women in twentieth century American religion.

2. RELIGIOUS VALUES AND GENDER PARITY IN RELIGIOUS LEADERSHIP

Scholars generally concur that religious tenets are not the cause of women's lesser standing in the liturgy and leadership of religious or secular communities and institutions.

ADAIR T. LUMMIS • Center for Social and Religious Research, Hartford Seminary, Hartford, Connecticut 06105

Handbook of the Sociology of Gender, edited by Janet Saltzman Chafetz. Kluwer Academic/ Plenum Publishers, New York, 1999.

Rather, religious values are used to justify and "explain" practices arising from more worldly sources for curtailing the leadership role of women (Chafetz, 1989; Holm, 1994; Nason-Clark, 1987; Wessinger, 1996). Although the founders of major faiths may not have gone as far as championing complete parity in men's and women's potential for spiritual growth and fitness for religious leadership, they were unusual for their times in being advocates of greatly increasing the rights of women in society and in their faith communities. For example, Jesus, Muhammad, and Buddha are described in core religious texts as supporting women's assumption of active roles in the new faith communities, and they are cited for promoting more humane treatment of women than existed in their societies during their lifetimes (Holm, 1994). Original texts of major religions contain passages that can be used to support equality between the genders in most, if not all, life arenas, passages that were selectively ignored by later religious patriarchs in favor of passages justifying women's appropriate position in faith and family as clearly under male jurisdiction (Holm, 1994; Wessinger, 1996).

Confluence of emphasis on divine patriarchy and of men's domination of religious and secular leadership has long undergirded women's subordination and limitations in many faith traditions. However, in eras of rapid social change, myths are modified to fit the altered situations into which women and men are thrust. New situations that cause people from different traditions to live and work with one another can disrupt this patriarchal peace. Advocates of new paradigms emphasizing women's divinely sanctioned leadership role in the formation and maintenance of a particular faith are able to gain more legitimacy and acceptance. For a contemporary illustration, women scholars and spiritual feminists of both genders are emphasizing the importance of women in the formation and development of Judaism and Christianity, through retranslations of original texts and new exegesis, and through more thorough examination of women's actual roles in the history of these religions.

Religious and other cultural movements, abetted by industrialization, have brought women together outside their families and communities of faith. Women who gather away from the direct supervision of men, both now and earlier may, through sharing experiences and ideas, begin to question some of the religiously based notions about women's place with which they grew up. Beginning in the latter part of the eighteenth and continuing into the nineteenth centuries, the Second Great Awakening in the United States brought women together in mission activities, inspiring many to take, or attempt to take unprecedentedly active roles in their congregations as well (Lindley, 1996). The industrial and postindustrial revolutions increasingly created jobs for women, and the women's movement led to far greater acceptance of women's salaried employment, even in traditionally male-dominated occupations such as the clergy. These factors not only brought women together outside their religious and family groups, but also increased their motivation for acquiring access to higher education. In turn, increasing education expedited women's refusal to accept the idea that they are not as capable as men of serving as leaders in congregations and in regional and national organizations (Wessinger, 1996).

Immigration or social mobility can also bring women into contact with others who may share some but seldom all of their values. Immigrants with traditional religious faiths who come to the United States may encounter a different set of social values and expectations than those in their country of origin. Younger immigrants, and especially their children, often depart from their familial religious beliefs and modes of gendered participation in worship settings and private life (Lindley, 1996). At least partly as a result of the "export" of American cultural values concerning gender, liberalization of social and religious attitudes pertaining to gender roles among members of traditional religions has also been occurring in other countries. This has resulted from the influence of Americans working abroad as missionaries, business entrepreneurs, and medical personnel; from visiting relatives or touring; and through the export of mass media and translations of English language films and books into the language of the native country (Young, 1994). Such comingling of people who share religious identities but not other social location characteristics (or vice versa) can raise questions about why one's religious leaders, in comparison to those of others one meets, are interpreting texts in a particular way or are less eager to include women in religious organizations (Holm, 1994; Lindley, 1996; Reuther, 1994; Wessinger, 1996).

Migration, imperialism, international travel and communication, and ensuing modernization can contribute to valuing pluralism on a collective level. This pluralism can occasion dissonance for individuals between their core beliefs, changing perceptions of the world around them, and divergent values of others. Some find that such dissonances can be resolved fairly smoothly by altering slightly how they interpret or apply basic beliefs to their new situations; some find it easier to shut out incompatible views by denigrating and avoiding those who express them. However, the more persons interact with those of other faiths and practices, the greater their opportunity to adopt different outlooks.

Congregations, faith communities, denominations, or other divisions within religious traditions that have come to value being seen as "modern" are likely to voice commitment to gender equity in religious participation and leadership (Chaves, 1997; Young, 1994). Changes toward gender equity include: small increments in the number of women in some liturgical roles or supervisory positions; long-term "temporary" measures in which women fill interim positions without doctrinal change or promise of continuation; and more sweeping changes, such as ordaining women to full clergy status. Some apparent changes religious authorities make to better incorporate women are so minor or tentative that they can easily be reversed to the status quo ante, and may well be with a switch in top leadership of the religious body. Some of the changes will be seen as a good by substantial numbers of congregants, legitimated by canon and constitution, and become the new institutional paradigm. Other changes will be accepted by one division or faith community and rejected by others, causing schism and possibly resulting in the formation of new faith communities or larger divisions within the religious body.

The foregoing factors are not unique to any one major religion, but each religion exhibits a different pattern of change toward greater gender equality in religious values and leadership. This is illustrated in the following overview of how these factors combine and interact to affect the inclusion of women in religious leadership in four historic faiths.

3. GENDERED FAITH AND FUNCTION IN FOUR WORLD RELIGIONS

3.1. Judaism

Women heroines, teachers, and prophets appear in the Old Testament but more sparsely than recent scholarship indicates was their influence in biblical times (Elwell, 1996). Jewish law traditionally governed almost all aspects of daily living. The law was considered divinely inspired by most Jews until the nineteenth century and is still by many contemporary Orthodox Jews. Jewish law was the scaffolding of a "separate but equal" theory of gendered authority, in which men were to be the leaders in the external world of synagogue and society, and women were expected to be primarily responsible for seeing that the laws were followed faithfully within their households. In practice, women were clearly subordinate to the men in their homes. In the synagogues, women were expected to sit demurely apart from the men and never lead prayers for a mixed-sex group. Women were revered in the home only (Elwell, 1996; Wright, 1994).

In small, stable communities of preindustrial Europe, women had little choice but to accept their place if they wished to remain Jews. However, during the nineteenth century, in response to the expanding opportunities for Jews to work and socialize with other Europeans in mixed religious and ethnic enclaves, a group of educated younger Jews developed a looser interpretation of Judaic law, more in keeping with the practices of non-Jews near whom they lived and worked. Women in wealthier Jewish families began to obtain education equal or superior to that of most Jewish men. These women and their families were among those who supported the development of Reform Judaism, which does not hold that the law was divinely dictated. Rather, the law could and should be adapted to bring the Jewish faith more in line with the modern world, particularly in equalizing the status of women to that of men in the family and in worship. Women in Reform Judaism were included with men both in prayers and synagogue seating arrangements, but they were still unlikely to hold organizational positions within the synagogue. In keeping with middle-class German and American family life of the nineteenth century, the women's place remained the home and men's the rest of the world. Still, the fact that change was permissible and even desirable in applying religious laws to daily life laid the groundwork for future changes (Davidman, 1991; Lindley, 1996; Umansky, 1985).

Today in the United States, Reform Judaism is second in size to Conservative Judaism. Conservative Judaism is a denomination that came into being in twentieth century America, combining elements of both Reform and Orthodox Judaism. Although it retains more strict adherence to dietary laws and religious observance set forth in Jewish law, Conservative Judaism resembles the Reform movement in its emphasis on the equitable treatment of women (Davidman, 1991). At the end of the twentieth century, women are still not allowed to be rabbis or lead prayer services within Orthodox synagogues in the United States. The Reform tradition, and the small but even more liberal Reconstructionist branch of Judaism, began ordaining women as rabbis in the early 1970s. Under pressure, the Conservative Jewish Seminary followed suit a decade later and in 1984 enrolled women in the program leading to ordination (Schulman, 1996; Umanksy, 1985).

Growing proportions of liberal synagogues not only have women as well as men leading prayers, but they are also using gender-inclusive language to refer to humans and to God in prayers (Elwell, 1996). Some feminist Jewish women want a great deal more change in the treatment of women theologically, including the use of a female image of God in rituals and reinterpreting the Torah to make it less patriarchal in language and application (Carmody, 1994). At the end of the twentieth century, non-Orthodox Jewish women have a far greater role in public worship and synagogue leadership than they did at the beginning of this century. Nonetheless, some Jewish faith communities (e.g., the Hasidim) are almost as restrictive of women's roles as was typical generations earlier (Davidman, 1991; Kaufman, 1991).

3.2. Islam

The Qu'ran is believed by Muslims the world over to be the last revelation of God given only to Muhammad. The Qu'ran was unique for its time in specifically delineating basic rights, as well as duties for women, and in stressing that women are the spiritual equals of men. In addition to the Qu'ran, further interpretation and guidance is given by the *hadith*, or sayings made by or about Muhammad and written down by his followers. The Qu'ran and *hadith* form the basis of Islamic law, guiding all aspects of life. Yet, no set of laws could fit all the changes that were occurring even in the time of Muhammad, not to mention subsequently. Muhammad himself changed practices he instituted but later found unworkable.

Muhammad may well have treated his wives and other women better than many other men of his time. However, toward the end of Muhammad's life, and especially after his death, women's freedom to participate in communal religious life was curtailed for "their protection" (Badawi, 1994; Smith, 1985). In past centuries as in the present, there have been differences among Muslim communities in the extent to which they believe Islamic law should be applied strictly or interpreted to meet the needs of Muslims in their particular social and cultural circumstances. Even "strictly interpreted" Islamic law is not unequivocal. Since the tenth century there have been four classical schools of law: Hanbali, Hanafi, Maliki, and Shafi'i. In Sunni Islam, to which 85% of the world's Muslims belong, it is an accepted tenet that there will be some differences among schools in how to apply religious laws in particular situations (Badawi, 1994). This factor has allowed, if not encouraged, Muslim communities in different areas and of diverse ethnic identities to develop their own variations in applying Islamic law.

Most of the increasing numbers of Muslims in the United States are immigrants or their descendants from Middle Eastern countries, although the number of "indigenous" or Black Muslims is also growing. Muslims of different national origins carried their varying interpretations of Islamic practices to the United States. Serial migration of extended families often resulted in enclaves of Muslims in large cities, each with its own mosque, religious practices, and set of expectations about how Muslim women were to dress and act in the home, in the mosque, and with non-Muslims (Haddad & Lummis, 1987).

Mosques became centers of religious and social life in America to a degree far greater than in their countries of origin. Although women seldom attend mosque prayers in Muslim countries, they are far more likely to do so in the United States, where Islam is not the predominant religion. Also unlike women in Muslim countries, Muslim women in America have taken a major role in developing educational programs for children and youth, and raising funds for missionary outreach in their mosques. One reason Muslim women in the United States are both more active in their mosques and more likely to have their husbands' approval for this involvement than would be true in Muslim countries is because mosques serve as centers of worship, education, and social activities that help families teach their faith and keep their children in an otherwise non-Muslim environment (Haddad & Lummis, 1987; Lindley, 1996) Modern American values that support women's religious and social involvement beyond their front doors also encourage Muslim women's greater involvement in their mosques. Muslim women can see Jewish and Christian women, other "people of the Book," expressing their faith through regular attendance at congregational services and being active in its educational, social, and mission work. Are Muslim women less religious?

Immigrant Muslims in America may have particular difficulty in remaining pious practitioners of Islamic laws if they do not have ongoing involvement with other Muslims in a mosque or Islamic community center. Muslim men and women immigrants who socialize with those of other faiths more readily adopt liberal attitudes toward women's role in the family, society, and religion than those who socialize little, if at all, with non-Muslims. Also, gender egalitarian values in the surrounding culture are transmitted through the mass media and through non-Muslims with whom they work and go to school. The longer immigrant Muslim men and women live in America, the more apt they are to approve of women taking leadership positions in their mosques (Haddad & Lummis, 1987). Even in the most liberal mosques, however, women are still not allowed to be imams.

Women who wear "Islamic dress," or clothing that covers all parts of their bodies and veils that hide their hair, if not their faces as well, are most likely to be those who adhere to a traditional interpretation of women protected and directed by men. Fundamentalist movements in some countries have led to an insistence that, whatever their own inclinations, women wear Islamic dress or be severely punished. There are also, however, well-educated Muslim women, fairly outspoken leaders in this country and in the Muslim world, who wear Islamic dress as a symbol of their commitment to the Islam. They believe that creating needed social reforms to benefit women and children will be easier if by their dress they exemplify dignity and their pride in being Muslim women (Haddad & Lummis, 1987; Lindley, 1996; Smith, 1994).

Smith (1994) predicts that expanding educational and occupational opportunities for Muslim women in more traditional Muslim countries will likely lead to new interpretations of women's appropriate role there as well as in America. However, given the Islamic focus on the family, these interpretations are unlikely to be those that would appeal to most liberal women of other faiths. Further, in the United States as in other countries, some mosques and Islamic movements have taken a conservative, if not reactionary turn, attracting men particularly but also women who prefer traditionally gendered roles in mosque and family. The likelihood is that although the core of Islam will remain stabilized by the Qu'ran, cultural differences in interpretation of Islamic laws will continually maintain Muslim communities that are quite diverse in what they expect and permit women to do in mosque, family, and in the larger society.

3.3. Buddhism

Buddhist central tenets apply equally to women and men. Both genders are capable of and exhorted to attain spiritual enlightenment through disciplined growth in self-knowledge, not through pleasing a Divine Father-Judge. By establishing an order of nuns as well as monks, Buddha demonstrated that he believed that women could rise as high as men in spiritual attainment. However, because Buddhism, like the other major world religions, arose in a patriarchal era, from the outset there was an accompanying cultural expectation that Buddhist women would defer to the authority of men in all settings. Buddha, too, conformed to temporal mores in his lifetime (about 560–480 B.C.) by making the order of nuns subservient to monks, a situation that has not altered in over 2000 years (Gross, 1994).

In the following centuries Buddhism spread from India to other Eastern countries, especially those areas now part of China, Japan, Korea, and Malaysia, changing in various aspects to fit particular local cultures. In medieval Japan, there were eight distinct Buddhist sects and there are even more in contemporary Japan (Martinez, 1994), with varying conceptions of women's spiritual state. Traditional Buddhist sects in Japan held women to be more polluted spiritually than men. Hence, women needed more restrictions placed on their involvement in Buddhist ceremonies, as well as close oversight by men in their families. In newer forms of Buddhism, such as the Reiyukai sect, women are more often seen as spiritual counselors and may come to be regarded as living Buddahs (Barnes, 1994). Yet despite some differences among Buddhist sects, and the prominence of individual women as teachers, counselors, and nuns, Buddhism has remained clearly male dominated in practice throughout the Eastern world (Barnes, 1994; Gross, 1994a).

Buddhist immigrants to America, primarily Asians, brought both their particular versions of this faith and its varying degrees of patriarchal cultural packaging. Although there are Buddhist temples in the United States, most of the worship activities are performed in the home, as they are in other countries. It was not until about the middle of the twentieth century, when Zen Buddhism and other sects began to attract non-Asian Americans, that Buddhism changed in practice. The non-Asian converts were leaders in urging that women's status be improved and that temples more closely resemble American congregations in offering regular prayer services, education, and outreach and other programs. This led to the formation of a new sect, the Buddhist Churches of America, that retain Buddhist core beliefs but also incorporate Western ways of "congregating," even to the extent of allowing some women to lead prayers and a rare few to be ordained (Lindley, 1996). Many traditional Buddhist sects continue to operate in America as they had in their countries of origin, often in cultural enclaves of immigrant and first-generation families residing near one another and maintaining the same gendered division of authority as had their ancestors.

3.4. Christianity

Jesus is portrayed in the New Testament as including women among his friends, followers, and co-workers. Further, it was to women, not men, that Jesus first appeared after death as the resurrected Christ. However, in the ensuing five centuries, men shaped and focused Christian doctrine mainly around those biblical passages that relegated women to positions under men's authority (Drury, 1994; Torjesen, 1993). Change arose in women's perceived theological and actual church status, from colleague to subordinate, as Christianity moved from its radical beginnings to being a well-established religion, a pattern that would be repeated over and over in Christian congregations and sects during the next 2000 years.

In the life cycle of the vast majority of Christian sects and denominations, women who had been spiritual authorities and congregational leaders on a par with men lost their influence and position to men as the congregations grew. However, this trend has not been linear. In some eras, regions, and denominations, women appear to have regained a measure of religious authority, which sometimes they can nourish and expand throughout denominational echelons, and which sometimes they lose again to those who uphold the preeminence of male religious leadership (Barfoot & Sheppard, 1980; Brubaker, 1985; Carroll et al., 1983; Lindley, 1996; Wessinger, 1996).

3.4.1. THE CATHOLIC CHURCH. Roman Catholicism has been the largest and most stably patriarchal Christian denomination since its inception. From the early history of this denomination, both its organizational leadership and spiritual life have been directed by men. Women in the New Testament, and later most women saints, were acknowledged for their gentle piety, caring, and support of men and children. Not all Catholic women accepted this interpretation of women's ideal role in the Christian family and congregation. However, women had no sustained support in their families or social circles to successfully challenge the male hierarchy to reconceptualize women as strong leaders in church, home, and country. One partial escape for such women was to join a convent.

Catholic women's orders of nuns provided opportunities to live independently and fairly comfortably in spiritual community with other women. Not only did Catholic religious orders typically provide some education for nuns, but becoming a nun secured for Catholic women an enhanced social status, if not standard of living, and offered opportunities to become leaders in their orders and other Catholic organizations. Although nuns may have enjoyed more autonomy than other Catholic women in Europe from the close oversight of men, they still deferred to the authority of male clergy in most areas. Nuns who followed Catholics immigrants to nineteenth century America were more successful in gaining independence. They pressed their claim with Rome and their local bishops that for their orders to survive and flourish in America, there had to be an alternative to the European cloistered way of existence. They successfully sought the opportunity to actively serve the educational and material needs of the faithful poor. New duties required new training. By the first decades of the twentieth century, American nuns were better educated than not only most other Catholic women, but also most women of other faiths (Drury, 1994; Lindley, 1996; Neal, 1996).

Vatican II in 1965 instigated many reforms, thereby shaking conceptions of an unchanging church and heightening anticipation for further liberalizing changes. Vatican II reforms appealed to many in the American communities of well-educated nuns. They stretched further, educationally and occupationally, taking positions of authority in schools, hospitals, social service organizations, colleges, and universities. Some of these more modern religious communities supported nuns who pressed the Catholic hierarchy for more operational autonomy and permission to organize across orders to more effectively engage in social justice work. These requests met with resistance from a good number of Catholic bishops, especially those who already disapproved of nuns who now wore secularized dress and were actively involved in community, political, and social justice causes. The bishops' resistance made these nuns more determined to fight for even more extensive changes. They began lobbying the hierarchy to involve women far more in the liturgy and leadership of the Catholic Church (Ebaugh, 1993; Quinonez & Turner, 1992, Weaver, 1985).

The decrease in the number of priests in the United States provided the opportunity for highly educated nuns and other Catholic women, who had earned graduate degrees in Catholic institutions, to become, in effect, "pastors" of priestless parishes in the more liberal dioceses (Wallace, 1993) or to work in parish leadership teams with priests (Finn, 1996). However, in recent years the Pope, who does not look favorably on this practice, has appointed bishops in dioceses across the United States who have terminated the appointment of many women who worked as pastors and pastoral associates in team ministry. The question remains, will the Church be able to continue this practice, given the continuing and worsening shortage of priests?

Nuns are still among the most highly educated women in the United States, but their numbers are decreasing, especially in more socially concerned and actively involved orders. In part, this may be attributable to the fact these orders give their nuns the choice of whether to live in a convent or to reside in the outside community alone, or with one or two others. Because the latter has become the most popular choice, the sharp reduction in the number of convents may be a factor in the diminishing ability of orders to recruit and retain nuns (Wittberg, 1994). However, a recent cross-national study indicates that social structural factors in industrialized countries, which are beyond the control of the Catholic Church, are likely of more importance. Specifically, women in industrialized nations have greater ease in acquiring higher education and gaining employment in managerial and professional occupations outside of the Catholic Church. In developing countries where social mobility for women is blocked, recruiting women to religious orders is still fairly easy (Ebaugh, Lorence, & Chafetz, 1996).

Another possible contributory reason for the decline of nuns is that lay (nonvowed) women are beginning to more closely resemble nuns in taking major roles in the mission and ministry work of parishes and dioceses. Through organizations such as the Grail and the Catholic Worker's Movement in the first part of the twentieth century, Catholic lay women became actively involved in social justice causes (Lindley, 1996). In recent decades, vowed and nonvowed women have joined national organizations (e.g., the Women's Ordination Conference) and local groups that work for a greater role for women in the religious leadership of the Catholic Church (Farrell, 1996; Winter et al., 1994). In the United States, there has been a significant increase in the proportion of Catholic laity, especially women, advocating not only that women be ordained in the Catholic Church, but also that laity have a say in making this decision (D'Antonio, Davidson, Hoge, & Wallace, 1996).

Parishes in the United States and other countries do make some changes in response to parishioners' demands. A recent study found that continual migrations of Catholics from one country to another, with frequent returns to their birth country, actually created reciprocal parishioner- and priest- led changes in procedures and worship practices of parishes in both countries (Leavitt, 1997). The large size and international spread of the Catholic Church gives every reason to assume that continual change will occur, some of it possibly in terms of women's participation, but mostly opening opportunities for women to take leadership roles nationally and internationally.

3.4.2. PROTESTANT CHURCHES.   Unlike the Catholic Church, which is one denomination, Protestantism is composed of diverse denominations, each of which may have as many internal divisions and variations as the Catholic Church. Some of these broad denominational divisions were created within the last half of the twentieth century. Others are several centuries old in identity, basic liturgy, and polity, although these may have subdivided and made some changes in name, worship, and organizational styles. Some of the Protestant faith groups that were strong in the eighteenth and nineteenth centuries did not survive into the twentieth century. In contrast, some currently growing sects and denominations have resulted from schisms and recombinations of groups of congregations and jurisdictions within the last two decades.

In nineteenth century America, the British Empire, and Europe, the degree to which individual Protestant denominations encouraged women's speaking in worship, leading prayers, or taking other active roles in congregational ministries varied widely. These denominational divergences in acceptance of women in leadership roles continued and multiplied during the twentieth century. In changing social times, organized women's groups in denominations rose in influence, fell to the control of men, and sometimes recovered their autonomy. In several denominations, lay women who had led their national women's board to a position of prestige and influence through successful fund-raising efforts saw these boards taken over by men and effectively dismantled (Zikmund, 1993). Theology and church history accounts were variously used by denominations as a means of enhancing the growing chasms between those denominations that ordained women to some but not all positions, those that ordained women to every position open to men, and those that steadfastly refused to ordain women at all. With a few individual exceptions of famous women evangelists who also became organizational leaders of their denominations (such as Evangeline Cory Booth of the Salvation Army; Mary Baker Eddy of the Church of Christ, Scientist; and Aimee Semple McPherson of the Foursquare Gospel Church), women who were allowed to preach, teach, and counsel when their small autonomous congregation or movement began found themselves replaced in these roles by men when the congregation or movement expanded in size, wealth, or joined with a larger congregation or became denominationally affiliated (Brubaker, 1985; Chaves, 1997; Lehman, 1987, 1993, 1994, 1997; Lindley, 1996; Nesbitt, 1995, 1997a, b; Poloma, 1989; Schneider & Schneider, 1997; Zikmund, 1996).

Protestant denominations have waxed and waned in how equitably they incorporate women into congregational, judicatory, and national church leadership. However, certain denominations have more consistently followed a path toward gender equity then others. The denominations that have progressed steadily, with fewer backslides, are the historically liberal Protestant denominations: American Baptist, Episcopal, Disciples of Christ, the Evangelical Lutheran Church in America (merged denomination of the former American Lutheran Church and the Lutheran Church in America), Presbyterian, United Methodist, United Church of Christ, and Unitarian. These are the denominations that ordain the greatest proportion of clergy women to full ministerial standing. It is tempting to attribute the ascendancy of these denominations in promoting women's inclusion in church leadership primarily to their more liberal theology. However, convincing historical analysis by Chaves (1997) shows that it is the extent to which denominations are eager to adapt to the modern world, rather than their theological stance, that is the most important predictor of whether and the extent to which they ordain women. Denominations and sects that maintain an identity of standing firm against cultural winds tend to see women's ordination as symbolic of pressure to conform to the surrounding society. Refusing to ordain women is, therefore, an indicator of how strongly the denomination can be a bulwark of faith against worldly forces (Chaves, 1997).

At the same time, denominations that do not grant full ordination status to women but still wish to flourish in industrialized nations cannot completely ignore the strong secular norms for gender equality. It has not escaped the notice of several scholars that the renewed emphasis placed by conservative denominations on the "separate but equal" argument in maintaining distinct gender roles in congregational and family life is simply a way of rationalizing and legitimating their continuing patriarchal practices (Chaves, 1997; Lindley, 1996; Wessinger, 1996). The culture of the congregation or denomination affects the extent to which its lay and clergy members will accept "separate but equal" arguments and theological justifications for male dominance in formal religious leadership. Congregations most likely to endorse "separate but equal" arguments for preserving gendered spheres of congregational activity are those denominations with an "other worldly" orientation to life. However, these may also be congregations which have pressing realities of life other than sexism with that their membership or immediate community must deal, such as racism, poverty, crime, and substance abuse.

In the conservative Holiness and Spirit-centered denominations, women may be very active as ordained or lay leaders in their churches, but are far less likely to be employed full-time in church work compared to women in the liberal Protestant denominations (Zikmund, Lummis, & Chang, 1998). Studies of evangelical clergywomen in Pentecostal and "Spirit-Centered" denominations (e.g., Assemblies of God, Church of God, Nazarene, Free Methodists, and Wesleyans) indicate that in comparison to men, far fewer women are being ordained and even fewer are receiving full-time paid pastoral positions. Nonetheless, these "Spirited" clergywomen seemed curiously content with this inequitable situation (Kwilecki, 1987; Poloma, 1989; Stanley, 1996; Zikmund et al., 1998). Researchers studying these groups arrived at similar explanations: these clergywomen are primarily focused on heaven, not earth, so earthly leadership is of less importance. Further, among earthly rewards, protecting the traditional nuclear family life is of higher priority than career success. For such reasons, these clergywomen tend to reject feminist values of gender equity in church, family, and occupations.

Women in predominantly African-American/Caribbean congregations (both freestanding and denominationally affiliated) take active roles in the work, worship, and ministry of the churches, but men retain most of the formal leadership roles and "titles," such as chair of church board and pastor (Briggs, 1987; Gilkes, 1986; Lincoln & Mamiya, 1990; Lindley, 1996). For example, in some black Pentecostal churches women are called "teachers" when they preach, and only men hold the title "preacher" (Briggs, 1987). In rural black Baptist churches, women may preach at revival meetings held several times a year, but not on a regular basis as "pastors" of churches (Lincoln & Mamiya, 1990). Like white clergywomen in the evangelical denominations described previously, black clergywomen may also value the nuclear family and heavenly rewards over career success. In addition, black women are also exhorted to support the church leadership of black men who are denied leadership in white society. Not all black churches are equally discouraging of women taking formal leadership positions. In the historic black denominations, African Methodist Episcopal (A.M.E), African Methodist Episcopal Zion (A.M.E. Zion), and the Christian Methodist Episcopal (C.M.E.), where there has been a long history of female ordination, there is also more verbal support for clergywomen as preachers and pastors than in the black Baptist churches (Lincoln & Mamiya, 1990). Like clergywomen in the white evangelical churches, until 1970 A.M.E. clergywomen were either not hired at all or hired for the lowest paying, least pleasant church positions. However, since the mid-1980s, in response to clergy-women's challenge (and probably denominational interest in being seen as modern), A.M.E. clergywomen have been far more likely to serve as church pastors and fill denominational supervisory positions (Dodson, 1996).

Taken as a whole, the trends within Protestant denominations show a very uneven rate of growth in the opportunities for women to take leadership roles. Some denominations continue to refuse to ordain women. Athough from 1977 to 1994 the numbers of clergywomen have stayed about the same or declined in the conservative, evangelical "Spirit-Centered" denominations, in the more liberal Protestant denominations the numbers of ordained women have at least quadrupled during this time period. At the same time, clergywomen are stll being paid $5000 less on the average than clergymen with the same amount of church experience (Zikmund et al., 1998).

3.5. Education, Attitudes, and Orientations Affecting Women's Role in Christian Churches

Clergy and laity in most religions have attitudes and orientations that will impact how well they fit within the leadership expectations of their worship communities. Most of the research to date, however, has been conducted only within Christian or Jewish faith groups. The following discussion is therefore applicable mainly to Christians and Jews, but is likely also applicable to the experiences of women in other religions.

Religious feminists differ in what they see as the major causes of sexism and patriarchy, as well as what solutions they prefer for ending systemic gender discrimination. These solutions vary all the way from including women more equitably with men within the present structures to completely discarding these and rebuilding in a manner more inclusive and less hierarchal (Reuther, 1994; Riley, 1989; Russell, 1993; Schneiders, 1991). There are denominational variations in what feminists stress (Briggs, 1987), although the use of inclusive language, ordination of women, and female preachers and pastors are important to most feminists. Religious feminists have overwhelmingly come from the educated middle class, rather than the working class, and are predominantly Anglo. Women of color and ethnic minority women tend to feel that their major concerns are not heard by Anglo women. Anglo-feminism does not sufficiently take into account the demonics of racism and classism in the opinion of Asian-American women (Southard & Brock, 1987), Latina women (Isasi-Diaz, 1993), and African-American women (Grant, 1989; Williams, 1986). Similarly, women in the middle East and Asia reject much of Western women's individualistic feminism because it is disjunctive with their cultural values (Holm, 1994).

The higher their level of formal education, the more likely American Anglo women are to have a feminist perspective on leadership roles in religious organizations and using inclusive language in worship services, and this is especially true of Catholic women (Winter, Lummis, & Stokes, 1994). One reason clergywomen in the "Spirit-centered" denominations and in the black Baptist and independent congregations do not appear "feminist" is that they have not had their expectations for equality with male clergy raised through seminary education (Wessinger, 1996). For example, Southern Baptist clergywomen, clergywomen in the predominantly white "Spirit-centered" denominations, and in predominantly black denominations who have M.Div. degrees are considerably more likely to protest inequitable treatment of women clergy in their denominations than their sister clergy who have not obtained an M.Div. degree from an accredited seminary (Ammerman, 1990; Blevins, 1996; Carpenter, 1986; Zikmund et al., 1998).

What if the women who are active leaders in denominations with more traditional notions of gendered authority acquire graduate seminary degrees and accompanying convictions that women can be capable clergy, but find their denominations resistant to changing their patriarchal ways? This is the situation with the increasing numbers of Catholic and Southern Baptist women who are earning graduate seminary degrees. Some of these angry Catholic and Southern Baptist women, like women alienated from their churches in other denominations, may join another denomination that they find more compatible, or drop out of Christian churches altogether. They may turn to religious movements such as Wicca or New Age/Neo-Pagan "Goddess groups" which offer them a spiritual antidote to the patriarchy they experienced in their former churches (Griffin, 1995; Neitz, 1991).

Some religions that include goddesses have been just as patriarchal as present denominations with a mother-god (e.g., Church of the Latter Day Saints) and female saints (e.g., the Roman Catholic Church). Nevertheless, strong, wise, independent female images of the Divine are cited by feminist women as essential to their spiritual growth and an important corrective to an exclusively male or subservient female deity (Gross, 1994b; Schneiders, 1991), and a support for their engaging in social justice actions (Lummis & Stokes, 1994). This last statement remains true for feminist women even if they do not envision God only in female forms (Block, 1997; Porterfield, 1987) and even if they remain in traditional churches (Lindley, 1996; Winter et al., 1994).

Sexual orientation is also likely to impact church involvement. Both Catholic and Protestant gay and lesbian persons are painfully aware of the disjunction between most of what their denomination teaches about sexuality and their own lifestyles. Christian gay men may hold either traditional views on women's church involvement, or more activist beliefs stressing gender equality in liturgy and church leadership. Christian lesbians are more likely than gay men to concur that women should have a role in church liturgy and leadership equal to or greater than that of men, and that liturgy should always incorporate female images of the Divine. Like heterosexual men and women disenchanted with organized religion, gays and lesbians may also drop out of church altogether. However, many stay if they can find ways to integrate their personal faith with those church doctrines and practices that reinforce their spirituality, while trying to ignore the hurtful aspects of their church's teachings about or treatment of homosexuals (Kirkman, 1996; Mahaffy, 1996; Yip, 1997; Zikmund et al., 1998). Some denominations are taking a lead in advertising at least certain of their congregations as "open and affirming" of the membership of gays and lesbian members and hiring "out" gays and lesbians as pastors (Wessinger, 1996).

4. ENHANCING WOMEN'S ROLE IN RELIGIONS: OBSTACLES AND SUPPORTS

It has been long observed that women, not men, are the mainstay and most frequent attenders of services offered by communities of faith in almost all religious traditions, almost regardless of where they are located (D'Antonio et al., 1996; Hertel, 1995; Hoge & Roozen, 1979). In Christian churches, moreover, having a female pastor is not a significant predictor of whether the church will grow or decline in membership, or even whether more women will attend services (Lehman, 1985, 1987, 1994; Nesbitt, 1997a; Wallace, 1992, Zikmund et al., 1998.). Such facts do not change the minds of those who direfully predict that the rapidly approaching "feminization" of the ministry produced by an increase in the number of women clergy accompanied by some diminuition in the number of male clergy, will also result in an exodus of men from the pews. This numbers-based fear of "feminization" is a major cause of "backlash" against women clergy in those denominations that ordain women and, in those denominations that do not, is another reason for never starting, when added to theological objections to women's ordination (Nesbitt, 1997a; Wallace, 1992).

"Feminization of ministry" fears are also based on the issue of whether women will "heretically" alter biblical texts, prayers, and reference to God to make them feminine or gender neutral, especially after the 1993 "Re-Imagining" conference in Minneapolis (Schneider & Schneider, 1997; Wessinger, 1996). A recent cross-denominational study found that clergywomen in liberal Protestant denominations are somewhat more likely than clergymen to endorse "inclusive language" in church services, and are much more likely than men to want to use female imagery and names for God in worship. In liberal

Protestant denominations, it is also true that lay leaders of congregations pastored by women are more likely to endorse inclusive language in church services than lay leaders of congregations pastored by men. However, clergywomen in the more evangelical "Spirit-centered" denominations are as ambivalent or opposed to using gender-inclusive language for humans or the Divine as clergymen in these conservative denominations, and their lay leaders are in accord with their clergy (Zikmund et al., 1998).

This suggests that women clergy are more likely than clergymen to be the "avant-garde" in heralding further increases in the "feminization" of liturgy and theology only *in those denominations which are open to modernization,* to extend the argument of Chaves (1997). The very autonomy religious organizations enjoy from state control makes it unlikely that the feminization of clergy or theology will become normative throughout Christian congregations or those of other faiths in the United States. At the same time, industrialization, modernization, pluralism, and relative tolerance for diverse religious beliefs in the Western world have created the conditions under which even the most sacredly masculine organizational structures have been subtly feminized. These developments have greatly expanded the variability among faiths and worship centers in their conceptions of women's place in theology, liturgy, and leadership (Chafetz, 1989; Chaves, 1997; Lindley, 1996; Wessinger, 1996) and have contributed to freedom of religious choice in industrialized democratic countries. In developing countries with autocratic regimes, a new government can curtail any such religious freedom within months, if not overnight (Young, 1994).

Western feminists strongly affirm freedom of religious choice. However, it is dismaying to those who have struggled to ensure gender equality in their faith communities that some young women appear uninterested in using inclusive worship language or taking leadership roles in congregations. Worse, they see some women of their faith among the younger generation remaining in or even joining congregations and sects in which liturgy and leadership are male imaged and controlled (Azria, 1996; Davidman, 1991; Kaufman, 1991; Lindley, 1996; Wessinger, 1996). Among these contemporary women "traditionalists," some may be rejecting gender equality because they want to be taken care of by a man, rather than having to agonize over making choices and taking responsibility for their decisions (Azria, 1996; Davidman, 1991). Other women may value personal autonomy and gender equality in their work and social lives, but attend services in their congregations (churches, synagogues, mosques, and temples) primarily in order to be spiritually uplifted and experience a caring community. As long as they derive this comfort, they do not care who plans liturgies, mission, and ministry programs or who makes financial and personnel decisions (Ozorak, 1996). Some feminist laywomen, nuns, and ordained women leave their congregations and denominations for other faiths or even life completely divorced from organized religion (Carpenter, 1986; Ebaugh, 1993; Lummis, 1996; Schneider & Schneider, 1997; Zikmund et al., 1998). Other women stubbornly stay in their congregation/denomination despite its patriarchy, and try to change it toward more gender inclusion in its liturgy and leadership (Winter et al., 1994). Choices women make in a free society will impact how much equity they and their daughters experience in their religious traditions and in their particular communities of faith.

In the United States during the last two centuries, women in Buddhist, Christian, Jewish, Muslim, and other faiths have moved "two steps forward and one step back," toward gender equity in theology and religious leadership, as Lindley (1996) concludes. The degree to which such change continues to march, however slowly, in a " forward" direction nationally and internationally will depend significantly on the degree to which proponents can convince opponents that more gender equity is inevitable or will produce other outcomes valued by the proponents, such as the expansion of the particular religion (Sered, 1997). This overview of religion and gender indicates that women's full and equal participation in religion will continue to spiral upward, but just to the point where women achieve, not dominance over, but parity with men.

REFERENCES

Ammerman, N. (1990). *Baptist battles: Social change and religious conflict in the Southern Baptist Convention.* New Brunswick, NJ: Rutgers University Press.

Azria, R. (1996), Equality and the gender issue in traditional and modern Judaism. In G. A. Weatherby & S. A. Farrell (Eds.), *The power of gender in religion* (pp. 1–14). New York: McGraw-Hill.

Badawi, L. (1994). Islam. In J. Holm (Ed.) , *Women in religion* (pp. 84–112). London: Pinter.

Barfoot, C. H., & Sheppard, G. T. (1980). Prophetic versus priestly religion: The changing role of women clergy in Pentecostal churches. *Review of Religious Research, 22,* 2–17.

Barnes, N. J. (1994). Women in Buddhism. In A. Sharma (Eds.), *Women in world religions* (pp. 156–169). Albany, NY: SUNY Press.

Blevins, C. D. (1996). Women and the Baptist experience. In C. Wessinger (Ed.), *Religious institutions and women's leadership: New roles inside the mainstream* (pp. 158–179). Columbia, SC: University of South Carolina Press.

Block, J. P. (1997). Countercultural spiritualists' perceptions of the goddess. *Sociology of Religion, 58,* 181–190.

Briggs, S. (1987). Women and religion. In B. B. Hess & M. M. Feree (Eds.), *Analyzing gender: A handbook of social science research (*pp. 408–401). Newbury Park, CA: Sage.

Brubaker, P. (1985). *She hath done what she could.* Elgin, IL: Brethren Press.

Carmody, D. L. (1994). Today's Jewish women. A. Sharma (Ed.),. *Today's woman in world religions* (pp. 245–266) . Albany, NY: SUNY Press.

Carpenter, D. S. (1986). The professionalization of the ministry of women. *Journal of Religious Thought, 43,* 59–75

Carroll, J. W., Hargrove, B., & Lummis, A. T. (1983). *Women of the cloth: A new oppportunity for churches.* New York: Harper & Row.

Chafetz, J. S. (1989). Gender equality: toward a theory of change. In R. A.Wallace (Ed.), *Feminism and sociological theory* (pp. 135–160).. Newbury Park, CA: Sage.

Chaves, M. (1997). *Ordaining women: Culture and conflict in religious organizations.* Cambridge: Harvard University Press.

D'Antonio, W. V., Davidson, J. D., Hoge, D. R., & Wallace, R. A. (1996). *Laity American and Catholic: Transforming the Church.* Kansas City, MO: Sheed and Ward.

Davidman, L. (1991). *Tradition in a rootless world: Women turn to Orthodox Judaism.* Berkeley, CA: University of California Press.

Dodson, J. E. (1996). Women and the African Methodist Episcopal tradition. In C. Wessinger (Ed.), *Religious institutions and women's leadership: New roles inside the mainstream* (pp. 124–138). Columbia, SC: University of South Carolina Press.

Drury, C. (1994). Christianity. In J. Holm (Ed.) *Women in religion* (pp. 30–58). London: Pinter.

Ebaugh, H. R. (1993). *Women in the vanishing cloister: Organizational decline in Catholic religious orders in the United States.* New Brunswick, NJ:Rutgers University Press.

Ebaugh, H. R., Lorence, J., & Chafetz, J. S. (1996). The growth and decline of the population of Catholic nuns cross-nationally, l960–1990: A case of secularization as social structural change. *The Journal for the Scientific Study of Religion, 35,* 171–180.

Elwell, S. L. (1996). Women's voices: The challenge of feminism to Judaism. In C. Wessinger (Ed.), *Religious institutions and women's leadership: New roles inside the mainstream* (pp. 331–343). Columbia, SC: University of South Carolina Press.

Farrell, S. A. (1996). Women-Church and egalitarianism: Revisioning "In Christ there are no more distinctions between male and female." In G. A. Weatherby & S. A. Farrell (Eds.), *The power of gender in religion* (pp. 39–50). New York: McGraw-Hill

Finn, V. S. (1996). Ministerial attitudes and aspirations of Catholic laywomen in the United States. In C. Wessinger (Ed.), *Religious institutions and women's leadership: New roles inside the mainstream* (pp. 244–268). Columbia, SC: University of South Carolina Press.

Gilkes, C. T. (1986). The role of women in the sanctified church. *Journal of Religious Thought, 43*, 24–41.

Grant, J. (1989). *White woman's Christ and black woman's Jesus: Feminist Christology and the womanist response.* American Academy of Religion Series, 64. Atlanta, GA: Scholars Press.

Griffin, W. (1995). The embodied goddess: Feminist witchcraft and female divinity. *Sociology of Religion, 56*, 35–48.

Gross, R. M. (1994a). Buddhism. In J. Holm (Ed.), *Women in religion* (pp. 1–29). London: Pinter.

Gross, R. M. (1994b). Studying women and religion: Conclusions twenty-five years later. In A. Charma (Ed.),. *Today's woman in world religions* (pp. 327–361) . Albany, NY: SUNY Press.

Haddad, Y. Y,. & Lummis, A. T. (1987). *Islamic values in the United States.* New York: Oxford University Press.

Hertel, B. R. (1995). Work, family. and faith: Recent trends. In N. T. Ammerman & W. C. Roof (Eds.), *Work, family and religion in contemporary society* (pp. 81–121). New York: Routledge.

Hoge, D. R., & Roozen, D. A. (1979). *Understanding church growth and decline, 1950–1978.* New York: Pilgrim Press.

Holm, J. (1994). Introduction: Raising the Issues. In J. Holm (Ed.), *Women in religion* (pp. xii–xxi). London: Pinter.

Isasi-Diaz, A. M. (1993). *En la lucha/In the struggle: Elaborating a Mujerista theology.* Minneapolis, MN: Fortress Press.

Kaufman, D. R. (1991). *Rachel's daughters. Newly Orthodox Jewish women.* New Brunswick, NY: Rutgers University Press.

Kirkman, A M. (1996). Ways of being religious: Lesbians and Christianity (Doctoral dissertation). Victoria: University of Wellington.

Kwilecki. S. (1987). Contemporary Pentecostal clergywomen: Female Christian leadership, old style. *Journal of Feminist Studies in Religion, 3*, 57–75.

Levitt, P. (1998). Local-level global religion: The case of U.S.–Dominican migration. *Journal of the Scientific Study of Religion, 37*, 74–89.

Lehman, E. C. (1985). *Women clergy: Breaking through gender barriers.* New Brunswick, NJ: Transaction Books.

Lehman, E. C. (1987). *Women clergy in England: Sexism, modern consciousness, and church viability.* Lewiston, NY: The Edwin Mellen Press.

Lehman, E. C. (l993). *Gender and work: The case of the clergy.* Albany, NY: SUNY Press.

Lehman, E. C. (1994). *Women in ministry: receptivity and resistance.* Melbourne: Joint Board of Christian Education.

Lehman, E. C. (1997). Correlates of lay perceptions of clergy ministry style. *Review of Religious Research, 38*, 211–230.

Lincoln, C. E., & Mamiya, L. H. (1990). *The black church in the African American experience.* Durham, NC: Duke University Press.

Lindley, S. H. (1996). *"You have stept out of your place": A history of women and religion in America.* Louisville, KY: Westminster John Knox Press.

Lummis, A. (1996). Occupational dropout among clergy women and men. In G. A. Weatherby & S. A. Farrell (Eds.), *The power of gender in religion* (pp. 119–138). New York. McGraw-Hill..

Lummis, A., & Stokes, A. (1994). Catholic feminist spirituality and social justice actions. *Research in the Social Scientific Study of Religion, 6*, 103–138.

Mahaffy, K. A. (1996). Cognitive dissonance and its resolution: A study of lesbian Christians. *Journal for the Scientific Study of Religion, 35*, 392–402.

Martinez, D. P. (1994). Japanese religions. In J. Holm (Ed.), *Women in religion* (pp. 168–177). London: Pinter.

Nason-Clark, N. (1987). Ordaining women as priests: Religious versus sexist explanations for clerical attitudes. *Sociological Analysis, 48*, 249–273.

Neal, M. A. (1996). Ministry of American Catholic sisters: the vowed life in church renewal. In Wessinger (Ed.), *Religious institutions and women's leadership: New roles inside the mainstream* (pp. 231–243). Columbia, SC: University of South Carolina Press.

Neitz, M. J. (1991). In Goddess we trust. In T. Robbins & D. Anthony (Eds.), *In goddess we trust: New patterns of religious pluralism in America* (2nd ed.) (pp. 353–372). New Brunswick, NJ: Transaction Books.

Nesbitt, P. D. (1995). First- and second- career clergy: Influences of age and gender on the career-stage paradigm. *Journal for the Scientific Study of Religion, 34*, 153–171.

Nesbitt, P. D. (1997a). *The feminization of the clergy in America: Occupational and organizational perspectives.* New York: Oxford University Press.

Nesbitt, P. D. (1997b). Gender, tokenism, and the construction of elite clergy careers. *Review of Religious Research. 38*, 193–210.

Ozark, E. W. (1996). The power but not the glory: how women empower themselves through religion. *The Journal for the Scientific Study of Religion, 35,* 17–29.

Poloma, M. (1989). *The Assemblies of God at the crossroads: Charisma and institutional dilemmas.* Knoxville, TN: The University of Tennessee Press.

Porterfield, A. (1987). Feminist theology as a revitalization movement. *Sociological Analysis, 48,* 234–244.

Quinonez, L. A., & Turner, M. D. (1992). *The transformation of American Catholic sisters.* Philadelphia, PA: Temple University Press.

Reuther, R. (1994). Christianity and women in the modern world. In A, Charma (Ed.),. *Today's woman in world religions* (pp. 267–302) . Albany, NY: SUNY Press.

Riley, M. (1989). *Transforming feminism.* Kansas City, MO: Sheed and Ward.

Russell, L. M. (1993). *Church in the round: Feminist interpretation of the church.* Louisville: Westminster John Knox Press.

Schneider, C. J., & Schneider, D. (1997). *In their own right: The history of American clergywomen.* New York: Crossroad.

Schneiders, S. M. (1991). *Beyond patching: Faith and feminism in the Catholic Church.* New York: Paulist Press.

Schulman, S. Y. (1996). Faithful daughters and ultimate rebels: The first class of Conservative Jewish women rabbis. In C. Wessinger (Ed.), *Religious institutions and women's leadership: New roles inside the mainstream* (pp. 311–330). Columbia, SC: University of South Carolina Press.

Sered, S. (1997). Women and religious change in Israel: Rebellion or revolution. *Sociology of Religion, 58,* 1–24.

Simon, R. J., & Nadell, P. S. (1995). In the same voice or is it different? Gender and the clergy. *Sociology of Religion, 56,* 63–70.

Smith, J. I. (1985). Women, religion and social change in early Islam. In Y. Y. Haddad & E. B. Findley (Eds.), *Women, religion and social change* (pp. 19–35). Albany, NY: SUNY Press.

Smith, J. I. (1994). Women in Islam. In A. Sharma (Ed.), *Today's woman in world religions* (pp. 303–326) . Albany, NY: SUNY Press.

Southard, N., & Brock, R. N. (1987). The other half of the basket: Asian American women and the search for a theological home. *Journal of Feminist Studies in Religion, 3,* 113–150.

Stanley, S. C. (1996). The promise fulfilled: Women's ministries in the Wesleyan/Holiness movement. In C. Wessinger (Ed.), *Religious institutions and women's leadership: New roles inside the mainstream* (pp. 139–157). Columbia, SC: University of South Carolina Press.

Torjesen, K. J. (1993). *When women were priests: Women's leadership in the early church and the scandal of their subordination in the rise of Christianity.* San Francisco: Harper & Row.

Umansky, E. M. (1985). Feminism and the reevaluation of women's roles within American Jewish life. In Y. Y. Haddad & E. B. Findley (Eds.), *Women, religion and social change* (pp. 477–494). Albany, NY: SUNY Press.

Wallace, R. A. (1992). *They call her pastor: A new role for Catholic women.* Albany, NY: SUNY Press.

Wallace, R. A. (1997). The mosaic of research on religion. *Journal for the Scientific Study of Religion, 36,* 1–12.

Weaver, M. J. (1985). *New Catholic women: A contemporary challenge to traditional religious authority.* San Francisco: Harper & Row.

Wessinger, C. (1996). Women's religious leadership in the United States. In C. Wessinger (Ed.), *Religious institutions and women's leadership: New roles inside the mainstream* (pp. 3–36). Columbia, SC: University of South Carolina Press.

Williams, D. S. (1986). The color of feminism: or speaking the black woman's tongue. *Journal of Religious Thought, 43,* 42–58.

Winter, M. T., Lummis, A., & Stokes, A. (1994). *Defecting in place: Women claiming responsibility for their own spiritual lives.* New York: Crossroad.

Wittberg, P. (1994). *The rise and fall of Catholic religious orders: A social movement perspective.* Albany, NY: SUNY Press.

Wright, A. (1994). Judaism. In J. Holm (Ed.), *Women in religion* (pp. 113–140). London: Pinter.

Yip, A. K. T. (1997). Dare to differ: gay and lesbian Catholics' assessment of official Catholic positions on sexuality. *Sociology of Religion, 58,* 165–180.

Young, K. K. (1994), Introduction. In A. Sharma (Ed.), *Today's woman in world religions* (pp. 1–36) . Albany, NY: SUNY Press.

Zikmund, B. B. (1993). Women's organizations: Denominational loyalty and expressions of Christian unity. In J. Carroll & W. C. Roof (Eds.), *Beyond establishment: Protestant identity in a post-Protestant age* (pp. 116–138). Louisville, KY: Westminster John Knox.

Zikmund, B. B. (1996). Women's ministries within the United Church of Christ. In C. Wessinger (Ed.), *Religious institutions and women's leadership: New roles inside the mainstream* (pp. 58–78). Columbia, SC: University of South Carolina Press.

Zikmund, B. B; Lummis, A. L., & Chang, P. M. I. (1998). *Women clergy: An uphill calling.* Louisville, KY: Westminster John Knox.

Epilogue

Janet Saltzman Chafetz

It is impossible to write a genuine concluding chapter to a handbook comprising 27 chapters that, collectively, examine nearly every social process, structure, and institution of interest to sociologists, through a feminist lens that focuses on the gendered nature of all aspects of social life. Instead, this brief epilogue constitutes my reflections about the state of gender sociology at century's end after 30 years of concentrated scholarship on the topic.

The 30-year-old history of vigorous feminist scholarship overlaps entirely the period of my postdoctoral professional life. I emerged from graduate school in 1968, as a specialist in sociological theory, social stratification, and political sociology, just as feminism awoke from an almost 40-year slumber in the "doldrums" (Rupp & Taylor, 1987). The Women's Movement immediately and permanently altered my career direction, eventually converting my attention specifically to gender theory, gender stratification, and the examination of women's sociopolitical movements. In this conversion process I was very typical of my cohort of female sociologists. Later cohorts could begin to focus on gender during their graduate (even undergraduate) education, but for those of us educated before the early 1970s, our first tasks were to remove our own androcentric blinders, to legitimate this new sociological specialty to our still overwhelmingly male colleagues, and to try to develop new lenses through which to examine social life as a thoroughly gendered phenomenon. The chapter authors in this book represent both the "pioneer" cohort which came of professional age before, or just about the same time as, the flowering of second wave feminism, and younger cohorts who have entered gender sociology after it was established as a (quasi-) legitimate field of inquiry. Indeed, several of the chapters are coauthored by members of different professional cohorts, and some authors are still graduate students, which augers well for the future of feminist scholarship in sociology.

During the last 30 years, sociology as a general discipline has changed remarkably in ways that have influenced and been influenced by feminist/gender sociology. Trained in the heyday of Parsonian hegemony, many of the pioneer cohort began from a sex roles perspective, albeit one revised in ideological flavor from an emphasis on the "functional utility"—even "necessity"—of existing gender arrangements, to a thorough critique of the system. By the late 1960s and early 1970s, radical sociology students (and some faculty) were resurrecting a Marxist analysis of capitalism, a development paralleled by the development of a Marxist–feminist perspective among some gender sociologists (as discussed in Chapter 1). The 1970s also witnessed a resurgence of interest in the broader sociological community, one paralleled by other branches of feminist scholarship, in symbolic interactionism and ethnomethodology, and in the use of qualitative research methods. This, and related theoretical developments in the United States and Europe, developed into an increasing attack on "positivism" by many sociologists, an attack whose feminist variant is represented most clearly by standpoint epistemology (cf. Chapter 2). More recently still, general sociological interest in cultural studies and knowledge production has increased, again paralleled by feminist versions (cf. Chapter 10). The past three decades have also witnessed the burgeoning of new substantive specialty areas, in many of which feminist sociologists have played crucial developmental roles (e.g., the Sociologies of Emotion and of Childhood, Gay and Lesbian Studies, and the Intersection of Race, Class, and Gender). Alongside of these changes, "traditional" theories, topics, and quantitative methodologies continued to flourish in our discipline and among yet other groups of feminist sociologists. It has been, and still is the case that "mainstream" (i.e., male) versions of these various theoretical, topical, and epistemological developments too often ignore their feminist variants (Alway, 1995; Seidman, 1994, p. 304; Stacey & Thorne, 1985; Ward & Grant, 1991), a reality that is beginning to change in recent years, however (Chafetz, 1997, pp. 98–99).

At century's end, with women constituting nearly half of all professional sociologists, and the Sex and Gender Section of the American Sociological Association constituting the single largest specialty section, one cannot understand the state of our discipline without understanding gender sociology, just as one cannot understand the evolution of our specialty without understanding that of our discipline. The days when half of all humans—females—were all but invisible to most sociologists are now gone, but the reverberations of their inclusion are still being assimilated into the discipline's many and varied subspecialties and perspectives. Considerable numbers of feminist sociologists now specialize in virtually every subfield of sociology, challenging traditional theories, research traditions, and interpretations as they create new ones. This handbook demonstrates that fact with regard to a wide array of different topics, although no one volume, including this rather lengthy one, can include all of the myriad ways in which feminist scholarship has contributed to a more robust understanding of social life. Indeed, as I write this, I can easily think of several chapter topics that could (some may say should) have been included. Textbooks for a wide variety of different sociology courses are beginning to reflect gender issues and feminist scholarship. However, they vary widely in the extent to which they do so and, with some exceptions (e.g., many texts in the area of the Sociology of the Family), most still have a long way to go in incorporating both gender as a fundamental component in their analyses (as opposed to the now frequent practice of adding sex as a "control variable") and specifically feminist approaches to understanding the processes, structures, and institutions on which they focus. In short, the ghettoization within sociology of feminist scholarship and the topic of gender is breaking down, but only slowly. Hopefully, this volume can serve to expedite that process.

I see this volume as a celebration of a third of a century of energetic, insightful, and outstanding scholarship by an ever-expanding community of sociologists who share a primary focus on gender and a commitment to feminist values. It is also a celebration of the healthy diversity of methodological, theoretical, and substantive differences among us that contribute to making our field an exciting intellectual enterprise. I have learned an enormous amount from reading these chapters as I edited them. Hopefully, other gender scholars will also broaden their understanding, and their appreciation for the breadth of our field and for the myriad of different ways by which feminist sociologists contribute to our collective enterprise.

REFERENCES

Alway, J. (1995). The trouble with gender: Tales of the still-missing feminist revolution in sociological theory. *Sociological Theory, 13,* 209–228.

Chafetz, J. S. (1997). Feminist theory and sociology: Underutilized contributions for mainstream theory. *Annual Review of Sociology, 1997,* pp. 97–120.

Rupp, L., & Taylor, V. (1987). *Survival in the doldrums: The American women's rights movement, 1945 to the 1960s.* New York: Oxford University Press.

Seidman, S. (1994). *Contested knowledge: Social theory in the postmodern era.* Cambridge, MA: Blackwell.

Stacey, J., & Thorne, B. (1985). The missing revolution in sociology. *Social Problems, 32,* 301–316.

Ward, K., & Grant, L. (1991). On a wavelength of their own? Women and sociological theory. *Contemporary Perspectives in Social Theory, 11,* 117–140.

Index

Tables are indicated by a '*t*' after the page number; Figures are indicated in *italics*.

ISBN 0-306-45978-7

90000